JAMES

JOYCE

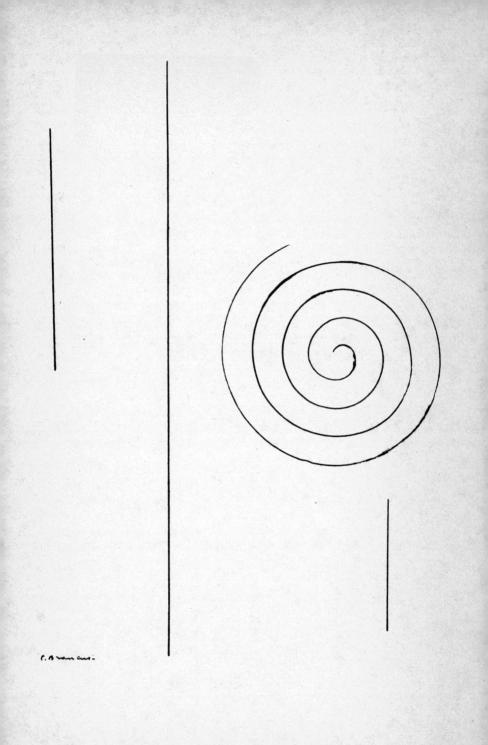

RICHARD ELLMANN

JAMES

JOYCE

OXFORD UNIVERSITY PRESS

NEW YORK   LONDON   TORONTO

OXFORD UNIVERSITY PRESS

Oxford   London   Glasgow

New York   Toronto   Melbourne   Wellington

Kuala Lumpur   Singapore   Jakarta   Hong Kong   Tokyo

Nairobi   Dar es Salaam   Cape Town

Delhi   Bombay   Calcutta   Madras   Karachi

TO *George Yeats*

PREFACE

Twelve years ago in Dublin Mrs. W. B. Yeats showed me an unpublished preface in which Yeats described his first meeting with James Joyce. My book had its origin at that time, although I did not work on it steadily until 1952. When in that year I talked with James F. Spoerri in Evanston and went through his Joyce collection, I felt a new biography could be written. With the encouragement of Frank O'Connor and of Carroll G. Bowen, I went to Europe in 1953 (and then again in 1954 and 1956) to see Joyce's relatives and friends, and to gather records.

Harriet Shaw Weaver, Joyce's literary executor, was constantly generous to me; otherwise I could not have proceeded with the book. I have made use of her published and unpublished correspondence with Joyce and have also benefited from her reading of the manuscript. Mrs. Maria Jolas was one of the first to aid me, and without her help many of Joyce's later experiences would have eluded me. I am grateful to her also for reading the chapters on Joyce in Paris and suggesting improvements. John J. Slocum, Joyce's bibliographer, at once put his collection and knowledge generously at my disposal; and Herbert Cahoon, his fellow-bibliographer, gave me unstinting help from beginning to end, and read the manuscript. Harry Levin, who himself laid the foundation of Joyce scholarship, and John V. Kelleher, who is perhaps the most knowledgeable American on Irish subjects, have gone out of their way to help me throughout my work and, by reading the book before publication, enabled me to make necessary changes. For valuable suggestions I am indebted as in all my work to my brother Erwin B. Ellmann. Ellsworth G. Mason, Librarian of Colorado College, helped to shape my view of *Ulysses* and prompted me to reconsider many aspects of Joyce's life. I have profited, too, from our collaboration in editing *The Critical Writings of James Joyce*.

I had important assistance in Zurich from Dr. Alfred Dutli, and in Dublin from Patrick Henchy, Keeper of Printed Books in the National Library, who gave a good deal of time during seven years to tracing records and interviewing friends of Joyce for me. In recovering Joyce's Dublin background I had the help of T. W. Pugh, with his extraordinary recollection of the details of life sixty years ago, and his minute knowledge of *Ulysses*. For Joyce's residence in Zurich I had the expert help of Ottocaro Weiss, of Riverdale, New York; for Trieste also, his knowledge proved indispensable. He suggested many possibilities, successfully solved many problems of identification, and aided me as well by benevolently reading several chapters more than once and so preserving me from inaccuracies.

Among others to whom I feel special gratitude are Sean and Eileen O'Faolain, Stuart Gilbert (who very kindly gave me much information in the later chapters and then read and made corrections in them), Frank Budgen, the only witness of many important moments in Joyce's life, Samuel Beckett, Myron C. Nutting, Mme Lucie Léon, Alessandro Francini Bruni, J. F. Byrne, Niall Sheridan, and Robert N. Kastor. Mrs. Claire Gorman allowed me to make use of Herbert Gorman's important notes and papers for his biography, now in the Croessmann Collection at Southern Illinois University. Professor Heinrich Straumann of the University of Zurich made it possible for me to meet many friends of Joyce in Zurich, and also generously showed me the important letters from Joyce to Marthe Fleischmann which he had saved from loss. Professor Carlyle King of the University of Saskatchewan was good enough to trace, with immense difficulty, Eileen Vance, Joyce's childhood friend, and to interview her for me.

Several collectors have put important material at my disposal; among them I must mention particularly Dr. H. K. Croessmann, who repeatedly went to trouble and expense to obtain documents that might be of use to me; and Charles E. Feinberg, T. E. Hanley, John H. Thompson, and Edward Naumburg, Jr.

I am greatly indebted to the relatives of James Joyce, who have helped me at every turn: to the late Professor Stanislaus Joyce, who kindly talked with me in 1953 and 1954, and to his widow, Mrs. Nelly Joyce, who gave me information I could not have obtained from anyone else about Joyce's life in Dublin and Trieste; to Joyce's sisters,

Mrs. Eileen Schaurek (and her daughter, Mrs. Boezema Delimata), the late Eva Joyce, and Mrs. May Monaghan, who observed James Joyce shrewdly as well as affectionately, and enabled me to see him as a son and brother. Joyce's sister Margaret, now a nun in a Convent of Mercy in New Zealand, also kindly wrote me about her family. I am happy to thank George Joyce, with his wife Asta, for much information about his father's later years; and Stephen James Joyce, James Joyce's grandson. Mrs. Helen Fleischman Joyce and her son David Fleischman have aided me. Among the relatives of Mrs. James Joyce, I have had great help from Mrs. Kathleen Barnacle Griffin, and have also been assisted by Mrs. Mary Barnacle Blackmore.

In writing this book I have had the indispensable collaboration of my wife, Mary Ellmann, who has improved it everywhere, both in conception and expression.

The names of the many other persons who have helped me are given in the Further Acknowledgments on pp. 819-21 of this book.

I have had a good deal of assistance from libraries. At Yale I must thank particularly Marjorie Wynne for her kindness, and also Donald Gallup; at Cornell I am greatly indebted to Dr. Stephen A. McCarthy, Director of the Library, and to George Harris Healey, Curator of Special Collections, who treated me with the utmost generosity. Professor Arthur Mizener of Cornell has also given me important assistance. At the University of Buffalo Charles D. Abbott, Director of University Libraries, greatly facilitated my work, and I am indebted also to Gene Magner. In the National Library of Ireland, Dr. R. J. Hayes and his staff put me under great obligation. I am indebted to the Houghton Library at Harvard, to the Stanford University Library, the University of Illinois Library, the Pierpont Morgan Library, the Princeton University Library, the New York Public Library, and the British Museum. Jens Nyholm, Librarian of Northwestern University, assisted me with his knowledge of Danish, and his staff has given me continual help.

It is pleasant to acknowledge the very substantial assistance I have received from Northwestern University; I much appreciate the support University officials gave my work from the start. I wish to thank John Crowe Ransom and the *Kenyon Review* for the award of a Kenyon Review Fellowship, and to thank Henry Allen Moe and the John Simon

Guggenheim Foundation for the award of a Guggenheim Fellowship. I am grateful to the American Philosophical Society and to the Modern Language Association for grants-in-aid.

Parts of this book have appeared in different form in the *Kenyon Review, Sewanee Review, Reporter, Yale Review,* and *Commonweal,* in my introduction to Stanislaus Joyce, *My Brother's Keeper,* and in *The Critical Writings of James Joyce.* One section was published as a pamphlet by the Cornell University Library.

For permission to quote material here I am indebted first to Harriet Weaver and Lionel Monro, as administrators of the Estate of James Joyce, and to the Society of Authors. I am also indebted to the following: in the United States, The Viking Press, Inc., for quotations from *The Portable James Joyce,* ed. Harry Levin, including *Dubliners, A Portrait of the Artist as a Young Man, Exiles,* and *Collected Poems,* and for quotations from *Finnegans Wake, The Letters of James Joyce,* ed. Stuart Gilbert, Stanislaus Joyce's *My Brother's Keeper,* and *The Critical Writings of James Joyce;* Random House, Inc., for quotations from *Ulysses;* New Directions for quotations from *Stephen Hero;* Holt, Rinehart and Winston, Inc., for quotations from Herbert Gorman's *James Joyce.* In England I must thank Jonathan Cape for permission to quote from *The Essential James Joyce,* with the same contents as *The Portable James Joyce* above, and from *Stephen Hero;* to Faber & Faber for quotations from *Finnegans Wake, The Critical Writings of James Joyce,* and Stanislaus Joyce's *My Brother's Keeper;* to John Lane The Bodley Head for quotations from *Ulysses.* For permission to quote other material, I must thank the Macmillan Co. (New York) and Rupert Hart-Davis, Ltd. (quotations from *The Letters of W. B. Yeats,* ed. Allan Wade), Ernest Hemingway (an unpublished letter), Oliver D. Gogarty (unpublished letters of his father), Diarmuid Russell (unpublished letters of his father George Russell), Signora Letitia Fonda Savio (quotations from published and unpublished writings of her father [Italo Svevo]), Samuel Beckett (an acrostic), Mrs. Maria Jolas (unpublished letters by her and her husband Eugene Jolas), Mrs. Cynthia Stephens (quotations from James Stephens), Mrs. Nelly Joyce (quotations from Stanislaus Joyce), Mrs. Anne Wyndham Lewis (quotations from Wyndham Lewis), Frank Archer and the British Drama League (letters from William Archer), Mrs. Marjorie Wells (a letter from H. G. Wells), Dr. C. G. Jung (an unpublished letter), Stuart Gilbert (an unpublished letter), Mme Lucie Léon (correspondence from her husband Paul Léon), T. S. Eliot (excerpts from unpublished letters), C. D. Medley (unpublished letters of George Moore), Mrs. W. B. Yeats (unpublished letters of W. B. Yeats), J. F. Byrne (an unpublished letter), and Harcourt, Brace & World, Inc. and Ezra Pound (quotations from *The Letters of Ezra Pound,* ed. by D. D. Paige, copyright 1950 by Harcourt, Brace & World, Inc.).

Quotations from Joyce's works in this book are cited with page numbers from the following editions: for all of his books up to *Ulysses* and *Finnegans Wake, The Portable James Joyce,* ed. Harry Levin (The Viking Press, Inc., 1949), and *The Essential James Joyce,* Jonathan Cape, 1948; for *Ulysses,* Random House, Inc., and Modern Library, 1942, and John Lane The Bodley Head, 1937; for *Finnegans Wake,* The Viking Press, Inc. and Faber & Faber, 1939; for *Stephen Hero,* New Directions, 1955, and Jonathan Cape, 1956; for *The Critical Writings of James Joyce,* ed. Ellsworth Mason and Richard Ellmann, The Viking Press, Inc. and Faber & Faber, 1959; for *The Letters of James Joyce,* ed. Stuart Gilbert, The Viking Press, Inc. and Faber & Faber, 1957. When American and English editions are not identical, reference is made first to the page number in the American edition and then following to the English edition.

R. E.

Evanston, Illinois
March 15, 1959

CONTENTS

Part III: ZURICH

Part IV: PARIS

Part V: RETURN TO ZURICH

ILLUSTRATIONS

'Symbol of Joyce' by Brancusi, 1929.   *frontispiece*

PLATE I
James Joyce with his mother, father, and maternal grandfather.

PLATE II
The long corridor at Clongowes, leading to the rector's office.
The National Library of Ireland.

between pages 48-49

PLATE III
The program of the bazaar Araby in Dublin, May 14-19, 1894.
Freeman's Journal announcement of the concert on August 27, 1904, when Joyce and John McCormack shared the platform.
The Martello Tower at Sandycove, where Joyce and Oliver St. John Gogarty lived in September 1904.

PLATE IV
Joyce, age 20, in graduation robes, October 31, 1902.
Joyce, age 20, in Paris, December 1902.
Nora Barnacle in Galway, about 1904.
Joyce, age 22, in 1904.

between pages 80-81

PLATE V
George Clancy, J. F. Byrne, and Joyce, while at University College.
The Berlitz school in Pola, 1904.

PLATE VI
Stanislaus Joyce in Trieste, about 1905, age about 21.
Alessandro Francini Bruni.

between pages 240-41

PLATE VII
Signora Livia Schmitz (Svevo).
Ettore Schmitz (Italo Svevo).
James Joyce in Trieste, age about 30.

Introduction

As often as I think of that unbloody housewarmer, Shem Skrivenitch, always cutting my brhose to please his phrase, bogorror, I declare I get the jawache! Be me punting his reflection he'd begin his beogrefright in muddyass ribalds.

—*Finnegans Wake* (423)

WE are still learning to be James Joyce's contemporaries, to understand our interpreter. This book enters Joyce's life to reflect his complex, incessant joining of event and composition. The life of an artist, but particularly that of Joyce, differs from the lives of other persons in that its events are becoming artistic sources even as they command his present attention. Instead of allowing each day, pushed back by the next, to lapse into imprecise memory, he shapes again the experiences which have shaped him. He is at once the captive and the liberator. In turn the process of reshaping experience becomes a part of his life, another of its recurrent events like rising or sleeping. The biographer must measure in each moment this participation of the artist in two simultaneous processes.

Individual moments are often undistinguished. But their evidence accumulates along with the evidence of distinguished moments; small particulars begin to define when they had appeared only to multiply, traits become reiterative, a central energy seems to evoke rather than to compile them, and within that energy artist and man rule each other. Respect, which Joyce elicits at once, converges with growing affection.

He was fond of disparaging himself, and those may be pardoned who, missing his irony, have sometimes followed suit. Few writers have achieved acknowledgment as geniuses and yet aroused so much discontent and reproach as Joyce. To his Irish countrymen he is still obscene and very likely mad; they were the last of nations to lift the ban on *Ulysses*. To the English he is eccentric and 'Irish,' an epithet which, considering the variety of the literature produced by Irishmen during the last seventy years, sounds dangerously 'English.' To the Americans, who have received him most kindly (although he could not bear their country), he is a great experimentalist, a great city man, but possibly too hard of heart; while to the French, among whom Joyce lived for twenty years, he lacks the refined rationalism which would prove him incontestably a man of letters. As a result of these reservations, Joyce holds his place of eminence under fire; he is much more assailed than writers who are evidently his inferiors. Though the name of Joyce is as inextricably associated with modern prose as is the name of Eliot with modern verse, or that of Picasso with modern art, it is possible that the current of opinion will swerve, and not-to-like Joyce will become as fashionable tomorrow as not-to-like Picasso is becoming today.

The future of man may appear less sinister to those who hope *Ulysses* and *Finnegans Wake* will be ignored, but they should be cautioned against optimism. In spite of Joyce's reputation of having skirted his age, he is unexpectedly at its center. In his isolation he comments on everything from Adam and Eve to Daddy and Peaches Browning. War and society were not his theme, but they found him out and forced him into attitudes towards them. His work began in the merest lyric and ended in the vastest encyclopedia. He surveys the human landscape from infancy to senility, from birth to death, from the young men knocking at the door to the old men struggling to keep it shut. He is by turns gay, morose, trusting, suspicious, uxorious, and misogynous. Joyce is so various, in fact, that he has been compared promiscuously with great writers of the past. These comparisons are inevitably as unjust as they are just. Joyce is not much like Homer, either in his subject matter or in his preoccupation with autobiography; yet the Homeric myth hovers behind Bloom in *Ulysses,* insistently altering the context of that book. At moments Joyce is as robust as Rabelais, but robustness is not his distinguishing quality, and the more fundamental likeness, as J. M. Cohen suggests,[1] is that he seems to come to things through words, instead of to words through things. Dante was perhaps Joyce's favorite author, and Joyce was as local and as scrupulous in vision; but he put aside Dante's heaven and hell, sin and punishment, preferring like Balzac to keep his comedy human, and he relished secular, disorderly lives which Dante would have punished or ignored.

When Joyce's adherents anxiously compare him with the great, his detractors are apt to call up against him the formidable figure of Tolstoy. A famous critic has remarked that Joyce, unlike Tolstoy, tells us nothing.[2] Certainly in Joyce there is none of the active, external, conclusive life that Tolstoy portrays. Out of all the characters in *War and Peace* only Pierre, and Pierre only so long as he does nothing and remains ineffectual and observant, could have been a Joyce character. Yet if Pierre tells us something, perhaps Joyce tells us something too. Before we assume that he has abdicated the evaluation of human behavior to Tolstoy, the novelist he liked best, and has conceded to Flaubert that the novelist must not judge, we must listen to what, in spite of his cardplayer's face and the ostentatious shuffling of the deck, Joyce is saying to us.

Whether we know it or not, Joyce's court is, like Dante's or Tolstoy's, always in session. The initial and determining act of judgment in his work is the justification of the commonplace. Other writers had labored tediously to portray it, but no one knew what the commonplace really was until Joyce had written. There is nothing like Joyce's commonplace in Tolstoy, where the characters, however humble, live dramatically and instill wisdom or tragedy in each other. Joyce was the first to endow an urban man of no importance with heroic consequence. For a long time his intention was misunderstood: it was assumed he must be writing satire. How else justify so passionate an interest in the lower middle class? Marxist critics leaped to attack him, and Joyce said gently to his friend Eugene Jolas, 'I don't know why they attack me. Nobody in any of my books is worth more than a thousand pounds.' [3] To look into the flotsam of a city was common enough after Zola, but to find Ulysses there was reckless and imprudent. It was an idea quite alien, too, to Irish writers of the time. Yeats was aristocratic and demanded distinctions between men; Joyce was all for removing them. Shaw was willing to accept any man so long as he was eloquent, but Joyce took for his central hero a man not outwardly eloquent, thinking in fits and starts, without Shaw's desire to be emphatic or convincing. Joyce deals in his books with the theme of Tristram and Iseult that his fellow-Dubliners were freshening up, paradoxically, with the more ancient Irish names of Naisi and Deirdre, but the love story interests him hardly at all, his interest is in the commonplace husband. Unimpressive as Bloom may seem in so many ways, unworthy to catch marlin or countesses with Hemingway's characters, or to sop up guilt with Faulkner's, or to sit on committees with C. P. Snow's, Bloom is a humble vessel elected to bear and transmit unimpeached the best qualities of the mind. Joyce's discovery, so humanistic that he would have been embarrassed to disclose it out of context, was that the ordinary is the extraordinary.

To come to this conclusion Joyce had to see joined what others had held separate: the point of view that life is unspeakable and to be exposed, and the point of view that it is ineffable and to be distilled. Nature may be a horrible document, or a secret revelation; all may be resolvable into brute body, or into mind and mental components. Joyce lived between the antipodes and above them: his brutes show a marvellous capacity for brooding, his pure minds find bodies remorselessly stuck to them. To read Joyce is to see reality rendered without the simplifications of conventional divisions.

One of his unexpected fusings takes place between beauty and its opposite. When Livia Svevo heard that Joyce in *Finnegans Wake* was using her flowing hair as a symbol of the lovely river Liffey, she was flattered, but when she heard that in the river were two washerwomen scrubbing dirty linen, she was disgusted.[4] To Joyce the juxtaposition was easy and natural. The river is lovely and filthy; Dublin is dear and dirty; so are the mind and body. In theory we grant these combinations, but in practice seem to hold the units apart. Joyce never does. What other hero in the novel has, like Stephen Dedalus, lice? Yet the lice are Baudelairean lice, clinging to the soul's as well as the body's integument. What other hero defecates or masturbates like Bloom before our eyes? Joyce will not make it easy for us either to contemn or adore. If we go to him thinking he may be the apostle of brotherhood, he shows us brothers in violent quarrel. If we go to him to find a defender of the family, he presents his central hero—the cuckold. If we ask him to be the celebrant of the isolated individual, Joyce shows isolation making him morose and defenseless. If we look for the spokesman of life, he introduces us to the dead. The reconciling factor is the imagination, which, working through wit, brings opposite ends of the mind together, and makes our seeming unlikenesses suddenly gregarious.

Joyce is the porcupine of authors. His heroes are grudged heroes—the impossible young man, the passive adult, the whisky-drinking graybeard. It is hard to like them, harder to admire them. Joyce prefers it so. Unequivocal sympathy would be romancing. He denudes man of what we are accustomed to respect, then summons us to sympathize. For Joyce, as for Socrates, understanding is a struggle, best when humiliating. We can move closer to him by climbing over the obstacles of our pretensions, but as we do so he tasks our prowess again by his difficult language. He requires that we adapt ourselves in form as well as in content to his new point of view. His heroes are not easy liking, his books are not easy reading. He does not wish to conquer us, but have us conquer him. There are, in other words, no invitations, but the door is ajar.

It is not easy, either, to enter into his life with the abandon of comradeship. 'A man of small virtue, inclined to alcoholism,' [5] he described himself to a doctor, and to Louis Gillet, the French Academician who wished to exalt him, he said, 'Don't make a hero out of me. I'm only a simple middle-class man.' He surrounded himself with people who were mostly not known: some were waiters, tailors, fruitsellers, hotel porters, concierges, bank clerks, and this assemblage was as inevitable for Joyce's temperament as marquises and marchionesses were for Proust's. To those who admonished him for wasting his time, he replied, 'I never met a bore,' [6] a remark that from most writers would sound merely sentimental. That he meant it is demonstrated by the thousands of phrases garnered mostly from undistinguished friends with which he filled his books. 'This book,' he said to Eugene Jolas of *Finnegans Wake*, 'is being written by the people I have met or known.' [7] His contemporary John Synge listened to people through a knothole in the floor; Joyce met them face to face, as unassuming in his behavior as he was uncompromising in his aims. People lionized him but he would not roar.

If we ask Joyce to bestride literature like a colossus, he will disappoint us. No generals paid him visits of homage, no one called him the sage of Dublin. As he makes clear enough himself, in the world's eyes he began as a bad boy and ended as an old codger. There is much to rebuke him for, his disregard of money, his regard for alcohol, and other conduct lacking in majesty or decorum. Yet we have to ask with Parsifal the question that Joyce also asked, 'Who is good?' [8] Though Joyce, prophetically enough, called the biographer a 'biografiend,' [9] he also supplied the precedent for seeing his subject in all postures in order to know him. His passion for truth, however unpalatable, is a contagion which he would have his readers and his admirers share.

Yet as the nobility of his heroes gradually overcomes their ingloriousness, so the tenacious craftsman, holding to his idea, gradually surmounts that roving, debt-ridden scene through which Joyce kept his elegant way. Implicit in his work there is a new notion of greatness, greatness not as an effulgence but as a burrowing that occasionally reaches the surface of speech or action. This kind of greatness can be perceived in his life, too, though camouflaged by frailties. To be narrow, peculiar, and irresponsible, and at the same time all-encompassing, relentless, and grand, is Joyce's style of greatness, a style as difficult, but ultimately as rewarding, as that of *Finnegans Wake*.

PART I

DUBLIN

The Family Before Joyce

Wharnow are alle her childer, say? In kingdome gone or power to come or gloria be to them farther? Allalivial, allalluvial! Some here, more no more, more again lost alla stranger.

—*Finnegans Wake* (213)

STEPHEN Dedalus said the family was a net which he would fly past, but James Joyce chose rather to entangle himself and his works in it. His relations appear in his books under thin disguises. In general, those who bear the Joyce name appear to better advantage than those who bear the name of Murray, his mother's family. In this treatment Joyce follows the prejudices of his father,[1] who complained that the name of Murray stank in his nostrils at the same time that he breathed a tipsy perfume from that of Joyce. His immediate ancestors scarcely justified this preference, but, like all Irish Joyces, the family claims descent from the distinguished clan of Galway which has given its name to the Joyce country there. It is impossible to verify this claim—the earliest records show them already in Cork city— but there seems to be no reason to refuse to allow them this innocent distinction.

Joyce's father, John Stanislaus Joyce, owned a framed engraving of the coat of arms of the Galway Joyces, and he used to carry it along, grandly and quixotically, on his frequent enforced *déménagements,* atoning for squandering his family's fortune by parading its putative escutcheon. Joyce represents him in *Ulysses* as crying out, 'Head up! Keep our flag flying! An eagle gules volant in a field argent displayed,'[2] and in *A Portrait of the Artist as a Young Man* Stephen offers to show a doubting classmate the family crest at the Ulster king-at-arms' office in Dublin Castle.[3] The best dreams of noble ancestors occur on straw beds. To the remark, 'We are all kings' sons,' Stephen says, 'Alas,'[4] but James Joyce, like his father or, for that matter, like Shakespeare, took excellent care of the coat of arms. He was careful, too, to add his father's portrait to the group of family portraits by William Roe,[5] which he in turn carried about from flat to flat in later life.*

The name of Joyce is derived by genealogists from the French *joyeux* and Latin *jocax,* and James Joyce, who held that literature should express the 'holy spirit of joy,'[6] accepted his name as an omen. In later life he carried a seventeenth-century picture of a Duc de Joyeux in his wallet, and asked friends if they could not detect a strong resemblance. On the other hand, he enjoyed referring to himself as 'James Joyless,' 'a Joyce in the wilderness,' 'a Joyce of evil,' and considered Freud a namesake, though an undesired one.

The given name James was not new in the family. At the beginning of the nineteenth century George Joyce, a man of property in Cork, named his son James. This James, who was the great-grandfather of the writer, named his only child James Augustine Joyce, and this son in turn intended, according to a boisterous but unreliable family recollection, to name his only child James, but was thwarted by a drunken parish clerk, who wrote down John instead and so broke the line.

The great-grandfather bequeathed a zeal for nationalism, a dislike for the clergy, and an ineptitude for business which survived in the next two generations and are apparent, with due modifications, in the life of the writer. As a young man this Ur-James Joyce joined the 'Whiteboys,' or Catholic agitators against landlords, and was condemned to death, though the sentence was not carried out. Of his anti-clericalism the only remembered example was his remark, 'I'll never let one of them put his two feet under my mahogany.' A little of his history as a businessman may be traced in old deeds. One of 1842 records that he and a Jeremiah Joseph O'Connor obtained a lease of salt and lime works on the lands of Carrigeeny near Cork in 1835; they sold them in 1842 for five hundred pounds. His son, James Augustine, who was born at Rose Cottage, Fermoy, in 1827, became his business partner, but neither seems to have had much skill, for by 1852 there is record that James Joice [sic] and James Joice the younger, who traded under the name of 'James Joice & Son, salt and lime manufacturers and chapmen,' were bankrupt.

James Joyce the younger, grandfather of the writer, had however made an advantageous marriage with a member of a prosperous family of O'Connells. This family came, like Daniel O'Connell the Liberator's, from the Iveragh Peninsula, and claimed to be related to his. The

---

* These now stare from their ponderous frames at the Lockwood Memorial Library of the University of Buffalo, caught, except for Tuohy's roguish picture of John Joyce, in the high-toned banality of a second-class painter.

Liberator was glad to concede the connection, and when he came to Cork twice a year for the Assizes would always pay a visit to his 'cousin' John O'Connell, an alderman, who kept a prosperous draper's and tailor's shop on St. George's Street between St. Augustine's Church and the corner of South Main Street. The tenuous relationship is now impossible to verify, although genealogists have tried to do so. John O'Connell and his wife, born Ellen McCann and from Ulster, had a large family. One son, Charles, became curate of Carrignavar in Cork Harbour and, having private means, declined to accept offerings from his parishioners. He was advised by his bishop that this conduct was unfair to the other clergy, and on his continuing to refuse offerings he was silenced. Another son, William, became a prosperous businessman, but according to *A Portrait of the Artist,* he squandered his fortune; [7] one report says he also attained bankruptcy.[8] He then went to live with John Joyce's family in Dublin, returning to Cork just two days before his death. His grandnephew described William as 'a hale old man with a well tanned skin, rugged features, and white side whiskers,' who was still good for a ten or twelve-mile constitutional, and smoked a pipeful of vile-smelling tobacco every morning in a backyard shack, with his hair carefully greased and his tall hat perched on his head.[9]

Two other children of John O'Connell, Alicia and Ellen, entered the Presentation Convent at Cork as postulants about 1847. Alicia's religious career was unusual. One night she dreamed that she was standing on a hill overlooking the sea, succouring children, and on waking she thought that the place meant was the little village of Crosshaven in Cork Harbour, where her brother William had a seaside house. She collected seven thousand pounds, chiefly from her own family, and planned the Presentation Convent and Boarding School at Crosshaven which flourishes still. Under her convent name of Mother Xavier, she prepared John Joyce for his first communion. In later years John, the father of James Joyce, tried unsuccessfully to persuade her able successor, Mother Teresa, to admit two of his children to the school on reduced fees. Mother Teresa did not like him.[10]

Alicia's sister Ellen was not intended for such piety and enterprise; she was a postulant for about eight months when she decided to leave on the grounds of ill health. Her father was eager to find her a husband, and a priest suggested a match with James Augustine Joyce, then only twenty-one, much younger than Ellen. An older, strong-minded wife would quiet him down, it was thought; he was too dashing for his own good—'the handsomest man in Cork,'[11] his son John called him—and a great hunter. The marriage took place on February 28, 1848, and brought James many advantages, including a portion of a thousand pounds [12] and close connections with men of prominence such as Ellen's first cousins John Daly, later Lord Mayor of Cork, and Peter Paul McSwiney, later Lord Mayor of Dublin.

Their only child, John Stanislaus Joyce, was born July 4, 1849. He was probably named after John O'Connell; his middle name, Stanislaus, came from Saint Stanislaus Kostka (1550-68), one of the three patrons of holy youth, in Ireland somewhat confused with the patron saint of Poland, Stanislaus of Cracow (1030-70), and reflected his parents' sympathy for the struggle of Catholic Poland for liberation. (As Joyce remarked, 'The tenor air in *The Bohemian Girl,* "When the fair land of Poland," always brought down the house.') [13] Neither marriage nor the birth of a son did in fact settle James Augustine Joyce, for after the bankruptcy of 1852 he was soon bankrupt again. But he was, according to Stanislaus Joyce, 'a man of angelic temper'; [14] both families helped him, and he was able to maintain his wife and child in the fashionable Cork suburb, Sunday's Well. No doubt through influence he held down the consequential, and not very demanding, position of Inspector of Hackney Coaches. [15]

With his son John, the only child of an only child, he got on well, treating him as indulgently as he had himself been treated, and training him up to hounds, where John also excelled. When the boy was ten he was sent to St. Colman's College in Fermoy, then only in its second year, perhaps because the Joyces had Fermoy connections. He was the youngest boy in the school, and the favorite of Dr. Croke the rector, later to be Archbishop of Cashel, who always put John Joyce next to him at dinner in the refectory. [16] John did not stay at the school long: he entered on March 17, 1859, and left on February 19, 1860. The college records indicate he had special instruction in piano and in singing, [17] and probably he already showed signs of possessing the tenor voice of which he was later justly proud. But his health was bad: he suffered from rheumatic fever, and then from typhoid fever, and his father decided to withdraw him. The college records disclose that seven pounds of his tuition were never paid, [18] a remissness which John Joyce was to emulate thirty years later when he withdrew his son James from Clongowes.

To build up the boy's health, his father sent John out with the pilot boats to meet the transatlantic ships that stopped at Queenstown, and this therapy worked surprisingly well. It also furnished him, his son Stanislaus suggested, with his remarkable vocabulary of oaths and obscenities. During these years he distinguished himself as a hunter and as a *bon vivant* at the 'jollifications' that followed the hunts. His quick, retentive mind formed the habit of mastering all the local details; he prided himself on knowing the history of every house and householder and, as he boasted later, 'There is not a field in County Cork that I don't know.'[19] His encyclopedia of local trivia was to be transmitted to James Joyce.

John Joyce's life was sobered by the early death of his father, at the age of thirty-nine, on October 28, 1866. The night he lay dying, according to Stanislaus Joyce, he tried to persuade his son to go and hear Mario, who was singing in an opera that night in Cork,[20] and in *Exiles* it is suggested that John actually went and returned to find his father dead.[21] The son entered Queen's College, Cork, the following autumn, and began his studies seriously enough, winning, by his own account, several exhibitions. Fifty-five years later he bemoaned the loss of his prize certificates in a story circumstantial enough to make their existence almost credible: 'I put my portmanteau in pawn one time for ten shillings with a pawnbroker named Cunningham in Marlborough Street,' said John Joyce; 'He was a very decent fellow. There was a set of false teeth in the bag too, but he sold bag, teeth, and certificates which were in it.'[22] Whether he won the exhibitions or not, he successfully passed the first year of the medical course.

The next two years went less well, if more spectacularly. John Joyce became a star performer in sports and in college theatricals. His son Stanislaus records that his father rowed in the college fours, ran cross-country, put the shot, and held the record for the hop, step, and jump.[23] He suffered, in fact, from too much talent. An excellent mimic and singer, he eventually gave all his time to dramatic performances; by March of 1869 he was the leading actor in all the shows. On March 11 he was described by the newspapers as 'exceedingly funny' in singing 'The Groves of Blackpool' and 'Paddy M'Fadden';[24] on April 16 he took the role of a stage Irishman in a play called *The Mummy*, and in May he had the principal part in another play, *The Irish Emigrant*. In June he failed the second year's work and had to take it over again in 1869-70.[25]

His third year also ended in academic failure but it is unlikely that John Joyce cared particularly about that. His father's death had left him heir, on his twenty-first birthday, to properties in Cork that brought him about £315 a year, and on July 4, 1870, his grandfather John O'Connell gave him a thousand pounds on the occasion of his coming of age.[26] The outbreak of the Franco-Prussian War in the same month inspired him to a madcap adventure; he and three friends went off to join the French army. He got as far as London before his indignant mother caught up with him and brought him back. Not at all dashed, he promptly involved himself in some Fenian troubles in Cork. His mother decided that they would go to Dublin in the hope of finding some pacific and lawful outlet for his abilities. She relied upon her family connections to help him find work or something resembling it.

The change from Cork to Dublin, which took place probably in 1874 or 1875, presented no difficulties for John Joyce. He found new friends, and delighted in the character of a Cork man away from home. He did not have to work, and spent a good deal of time sailing around Dalkey, where his mother had taken a house. He had his own boat and a boy to take care of it. Not long after his arrival in Dublin he went to a music teacher who, after listening to him sing for a few minutes, called in her son and said, 'I have found the successor of Campanini.'[27] Probably at the age of twenty-seven, in 1875, he sang in a concert at the Antient Concert Rooms, and Barton McGuckin, the leading tenor of the Carl Rosa Opera Company, happened to be in the audience. As John Joyce told and retold the story later, 'After this concert when McGuckin used to pass me in the street he used watch and look after me. I used wonder why he looked so hard at me and by God I never could make out what it was all about; and it was only after he was dead for some years that I heard the story. John Phelan said to me, "You had the best tenor in Ireland." "Yerra, my God, what put that into your head?" says I, and he said, "I heard it from the very best authority." "Who was that?" says I. "Well," says he, "did you ever hear of a gentleman named Barton McGuckin?" "I did indeed," said I, and John said, "That is my authority." And that accounted for the way he used to look so hard at me.'[28] James Joyce, who knew this story well, remembered it in writing 'The Dead.'

About the year 1877 John Joyce entered into negotiations with Henry Alleyn, a Cork man and a friend of his father's, who was organizing the Dublin and Chapelizod Distilling Company. The company needed money and Joyce offered to buy £500 of shares on condition that he be appointed secretary at £300 a year. The directors agreed, and he was soon working every day in the old building on the Liffey at Chapelizod which, having served as a convent, a soldier's barracks, and a flax factory owned by William Dargan, was now a distillery.* Although Alleyn was a martinet, John Joyce got on with him well enough,[29] and liked Chapelizod. His stories about Broadbent, who had the Mullingar Hotel (now Mullingar House) there, helped his son James to construct *Finnegans Wake* around a hero who is a Chapelizod innkeeper. One day John Joyce discovered that Alleyn was milking

---

* Joyce calls it in *Finnegans Wake* 'the still that was mill' (265). It was later known as the Phoenix Park Distillery.

the firm, and called a meeting of the stockholders. Alleyn departed,* and the stockholders voted their gratitude to Joyce for saving them from a worse loss. He was elected trustee of nothing—the money, including his own, was gone. He liked later to maintain that some of it was still on deposit in his name at the Bank of Ireland, too bound about with legal complications for him to touch. But the Bank, in the cold way of such institutions, reports it has no money in the name of John Joyce.

He drifted next into politics, perhaps through the influence of his relative Peter Paul McSwiney, who was Lord Mayor of Dublin in 1875. The occasion was the general election on April 5, 1880, called by Disraeli's government, which had been in power since 1874. John Joyce was a Home Ruler, but there were no Dublin candidates precisely of his persuasion. He took, nevertheless, the position of secretary of the United Liberal Club in Dublin. The club's sentiment was favorable to Home Rule, but it was co-operating ambiguously with the whole Liberal Party, which, while eager to please Home Rulers and Unionists alike at election time, later tried to suppress the nationalistic Land League. John Joyce does not seem to have investigated deeply the politics of the Liberal Party; he saw an occasion to unseat the last two conservative members for Dublin city, Sir Arthur E. Guinness— a more successful brewer than he himself had been—and James Stirling. The Liberal candidates opposing them were Maurice Brooks and Dr. Robert Dyer Lyons, the latter a Cork man, a point in his favor. Joyce worked indefatigably for Brooks and Lyons during March and until the election of April 5. He later described with gusto the counting of the ballots: 'The count of the votes took place in the Exhibition Palace in a very big room. All the tables were there and I had four men on each table. I didn't at all expect that we would get the two members in—I would have been satisfied if I got Brooks in but I didn't at all expect that Lyons would get in. Towards the end of the count I got the rough figures and I totted them up two or three times and by God what was it but I knew the two were returned.† This was the hell of a thing for me.

'Who should be sitting next to me but Sir Arthur Guinness and his cousin the Hon. David Plunkett, and the two were in evening dress. He lived at the time in Stephen's Green; at the north side of it he had a house, his brother Lord Iveagh has it now. Sir Arthur asked me,

---

* 'Mr Alleyne' is the name of the unpleasant employer in the story 'Counterparts'; James Joyce liked paying off his father's scores.
† The election returns gave Brooks 5763 votes and Lyons 5647 to Guinness's 5446 and Stirling's 5059.[30]

"Have you got the figures?" "I have, Sir Arthur," I replied, and he asked me, "How did it go?" I then had the pleasure of telling Sir Arthur Guinness that he was no longer a member.

'We went out soon after and had a thanksgiving meeting in the Rotunda Bar. I was the cock of the walk that day and I will never forget it; I was complimented by everybody. I got one hundred guineas from each of the members. My God it was three o'clock in the morning and the excitement was great and I was the hero of it all because they said that it was I that won the election. By God Almighty, such drinking of champagne I never saw in my life! We could not wait to draw the corks, we slapped them against the marble-topped counter. The result was we were there drinking for about three hours and when we came out the question was what were we to do with ourselves at that ungodly hour of the morning. The Turkish Baths came into my mind and there I went after having any God's quantity of champagne. Oh dear, dear, God, those were great times.' [31]

The Joyce family continued the celebration into *Finnegans Wake*, where John Joyce's victory is made that of the outs over the ins, of the moneyless over the moneyed: 'since then sterlings and guineas have been replaced by brooks and lions and some progress has been made on stilts . . .' * A leading article in the *Freeman's Journal* of April 7 complimented the United Liberal Club on having exerted a great influence on the results, and a grateful government was asked to reward John Joyce's zeal. The new Lord Lieutenant who succeeded to office on May 5 obligingly assigned him to one of the easy, well-paid positions in the office of the Collector of Rates for Dublin, at that time under the Lord Lieutenant's jurisdiction. The appointment was for life, and carried a salary of £500 a year.

This position enabled John Joyce to get married, as for some time he had intended. A few months before, he had met a young woman, not yet twenty-one, named Mary Jane Murray, who sang on Sundays as he did in the choir of the Church of the Three Patrons in Rathgar. [32] She was the daughter of John Murray, an agent for wines and spirits from Longford, who had made purchases at the distillery. She was good-looking, with fair hair, and had great resources of patience and loyalty, which John Joyce, try as he might, would not exhaust. If he was the principle of chaos, she was the principle of order to which he might cling. He found in her, as his father had found in Ellen O'Connell, a woman who would indulge his boisterousness without

---

* P. 236; compare p. 273, 'The grinning statesmen, Brock and Leon, have shunted the grumbling countedouts, Starlin and Ser Artur Ghinis.' But Parnell was to hunt Lyons out of his constituency in the General Election of 1885.

sharing it, who could live evenly while he frolicked or raged. Neither John Joyce's mother nor Mary Jane Murray's father favored the marriage. John Murray did everything possible to discourage it, rightly foreseeing that John Joyce, already a heavy drinker and known to have broken off two previous engagements in fits of jealousy, would not make his daughter a good husband. One day Murray found his daughter with Joyce on Grafton Street, scolded her and called a cab to take her home. A crowd gathered and a man asked John Joyce what the trouble was. 'Oh, nothing serious,' he replied breezily, 'just the usual story of the beautiful daughter and the irascible parent.' [33] But Mary Jane liked his dash and wit, her mother encouraged the match, and John Joyce apparently precipitated the decision by moving to 15 Clanbrassil Street,[34] only a few doors from the Murrays at No. 7.*
At last Murray consented to the marriage, but John Joyce's mother Ellen remained adamantly opposed to it, regarding the Murrays as beneath her. About the time of the marriage, which took place at the Roman Catholic Church in Rathmines on May 5, 1880,[35] she returned to Cork and died not long after without sending for her only child or forgiving him. Her pride and stubbornness are acknowledged by her grandson in 'The Dead,' where Gabriel's mother stands in 'sullen opposition' to his marriage, and in *Exiles*, where the hard-heartedness of Richard Rowan's mother also never lessens. On the other hand, the month of May, when his parents were married, always seemed a lucky month to James Joyce.

Mary Jane ('May') Murray, born May 15, 1859, was ten years younger than her husband. She came on her mother's side from a family with keen musical interests; her grandfather Flynn, who had the starch mill in Back Lane mentioned in 'The Dead,' arranged for all his daughters to be trained in music. From the age of five to nineteen May Murray had lessons in piano and voice, as well as in dancing and politeness, at the 'Misses Flynn school' at 15 Usher's Island, a street which runs beside the Liffey. The school was operated by two of her mother's sisters, Mrs. Callanan and Mrs. Lyons, with the aid later on of Mrs. Callanan's daughter, Mary Ellen.† It may have been from them that she learned the slightly old-fashioned courtliness of manner which she was to teach to her oldest son.

John Joyce complained a little about the Flynns, but he drew the

---

* In *Ulysses* Bloom's father is said to have lived on Clanbrassil Street, which was a Jewish neighborhood.
† That the school was in good repute is suggested by the fact that Katharine Tynan, the poet and novelist, whose family was comfortably situated, was a fellow-pupil of Mary Jane Murray.
For the use of the Misses Flynn in 'The Dead,' see pp. 254-5.

line at the Murrays. His finest epithets were reserved for the members of this family who had disapproved of him, and the vitriol of Thersites in the *Cyclops* episode of *Ulysses* is modeled in part on his eloquent abuse. 'O weeping God, the things I married into.' * [36] His father-in-law, who had delayed the match, was the 'old fornicator' because he had married a second time.[37] Mary Jane Murray's two brothers, William and John, were 'highly respectable gondoliers.' [38] William Murray was a cost-drawer, or billing clerk, for the well-known firm of solicitors, Collis and Ward, while John, known as 'Red' Murray and so described in *Ulysses*, worked in the accounts department of the *Freeman's Journal*. John Murray, whose marriage was somewhat unhappy (his nephew James once derisively deposited a bag of oysters on his doorstep), and whose temperament was surly and inflexible, provided a good deal of literary material for *Dubliners*, concealed there under other names. John Joyce's favorite story about this brother-in-law told how, as they were walking through an open space in the Phoenix Park, they suddenly saw a company of cavalry galloping toward them. John Murray was about to turn tail and run for the trees, which he could not have made, but John Joyce grabbed him and forced him to stand still while the riders divided into two groups, so as to pass on either side of them. At an order from the officer in charge the soldiers raised their sabers and saluted Joyce.[39] Understandably the incident did not make Murray grateful; he hated John Joyce and once said so to James, who left the house with filial primness.[40]

William Murray appears transparently in *Ulysses* under the name of Richie Goulding. He required his children to call him 'sir,' and when he was drunk treated them savagely enough. But he was a fair singer of operatic arias, and he was married to a woman whom all the Joyce children, including James, depended upon for help and advice. Josephine Giltrap Murray was intelligent, resourceful, and unfailingly generous, attributes that could not be too abundant in those harassed lives. She seemed to her nephew James to be a wise woman, and he brought her his shocking problems without shocking her. She had musical training, too, and sometimes she and John Joyce and May would play trios on the piano.

William and John are the two brothers, Joe and Alphy, sketched in the story 'Clay' in *Dubliners*, who are not on speaking terms with each other. Maria, the little laundress who tries to make peace between

* Mary Jane Murray's uncle, Patrick Murray, was parish priest, from 1878 to 1912, at Carraig and Ballinlough, near Granard in County Cavan. Joyce knew him well enough to remember his accent and detect, long afterwards, a similar one in the speech of Padraic Colum.[41]

them, was also a relative of the Murrays, and one of whom May Joyce was especially fond. On the Flynn side of the family was the priest described in 'The Sisters,' who became harmlessly insane and lost his parish.[42] Bits and pieces of the Murrays appear in the stories; for example, it was William's child who said, as at the end of 'Counterparts,' 'I'll say a *Hail, Mary* for you, pa, if you don't beat me.' [43] But with artistic dispassionateness that transcended family quarrels, Farrington's impudent, frustrated character in that story fuses William Murray's temperament with John Joyce's.

May, the only representative of the Murrays whom he could bear, and John Stanislaus Joyce went off to London for their honeymoon in the late spring of 1880. On their return they settled at 47 Northumberland Avenue, Kingstown (now Dun Laoghaire), and he took up his position in the office of the Collector of Rates. He was collector for Inns Quay and Rotunda wards, later for North Dock ward. His cocksureness and wit quickly became famous in the office. One day the Collector General came downstairs with an elderly clergyman holding a final notice in his hand. The clergyman, known to be a heavy drinker, was named Rhynardt, 'and he complained to the C.G.,' John Joyce wrote much later to his son, 'that I wrongly addressed him as Richard. I apologized for the mistake of my clerk (Bob Cowall) * but said I would be more careful in future in the spelling of his name and would not forget it ended with D.T. The Collector General went upstairs breaking his heart laughing.' [44] On another occasion someone complained that his name had been spelled with two l's instead of one. 'Which *l* would you like to have removed?' asked John Joyce gravely.[45] Paying rates in Dublin must have been an invigorating experience in those days.

Not all John Joyce's jokes were at the expense of others. He liked to tell how, as a civil servant, he was obliged to attend certain functions at Dublin Castle. On one occasion there was a masquerade ball, and for a lark he went dressed as a British officer. The jarvey who drove him in a cab to the castle was expecting a tip befitting his passenger's rank, but John Joyce gave him the minimum. 'Holy Jaysus,' said the jarvey, 'and I thought I had a real officer!' 'And so you have, my man,' said John Joyce, refusing to be intimidated. 'I have,' said the jarvey, looking at the coin in his fist, 'a cotton-ball one.' † [46]

John Joyce applied himself with equal diligence to the begetting

---

* Cowall appears in *Ulysses* under his own name.

† In the *Eumaeus* episode of *Ulysses* (634 [612]), someone says of Captain W. H. O'Shea, the husband of Parnell's mistress, 'Her husband was a captain or an officer.' 'Ay, Skin-the-Goat amusingly added. He was, and a cotton-ball one.'

of children and the contracting of mortgages on his inherited properties. His first child was born in 1881 and did not survive; he lamented, 'My life was buried with him,' [47] but was soon solaced with another. During his wife's second pregnancy, on December 2, 1881, he mortgaged the first of his Cork properties.[48] The second child, James Augusta (as the birth was incorrectly registered), was born on February 2, 1882, by which time the Joyces had moved from Kingstown to 41 Brighton Square West in Rathgar.[49] Three mortgages followed, on March 9, October 18, and November 27, 1883, and then Margaret Alice ('Poppie') was born on January 18, 1884.[50] On August 5, 1884, another property was mortgaged; John Stanislaus ('Stannie') was born on December 17, 1884, and Charles Patrick on July 24, 1886. There were two other mortgages on April 21 and May 6, 1887, and George Alfred was born on his father's birthday, July 4, 1887. Eileen Isabel Mary Xavier Brigit was born on January 22, 1889, Mary Kathleen on January 18, 1890, and Eva Mary on October 26, 1891. Then came Florence Elizabeth on November 8, 1892, who was followed by mortgages on December 24, 1892, and January 13, 1893. Mabel Josephine Anne ('Baby') was born November 27, 1893, and two mortgages, on February 8 and 16, quickly followed her in 1894. The total, not including three misbirths, was four boys and six girls. There were no more babies, and after eleven mortgages, there was no more property. John Joyce filled his house with children and with debts.

This reckless, talented man, convinced that he was the victim of circumstances, never at a loss for a retort, fearfully sentimental and acid by turns, drinking, spending, talking, singing, became identified in his son James's mind with something like the life-force itself. His expressions, 'With the help of God and a few policemen,' 'Like a shot off a shovel,' ' 'Twixt you and me, Caddereesh,' and the like, echo in James's books. He appeared in them more centrally, in fact, than anyone except their author. In the early stories in *Dubliners,* 'The Sisters' and 'Araby,' he is considerably disguised as an uncle; in the later stories, besides contributing to Farrington, he is also in Henchy, Hynes,* Kernan, and Gabriel Conroy. In *A Portrait of the Artist* he is Simon Dedalus, described by his son Stephen as having been 'A medical student, an oarsman, a tenor, an amateur actor, a shouting politician, a small landlord, a small investor, a drinker, a good fellow, a storyteller, somebody's secretary, something in a distillery, a tax-

---

* Hynes's poem about Parnell probably owed a little to a song called 'Erin's Heroes,' composed by John Joyce and sung by him on March 17, 1896, at a meeting of the Bohemians at the Dolphin. The meeting, as Michael J. O'Neill informs me, is reported in the diary of Joseph Holloway.

gatherer, a bankrupt and at present a praiser of his own past.' * [51] In *Ulysses* he is Simon again and also enters into Bloom and the narrator of the *Cyclops* episode; in *Finnegans Wake,* John Joyce is the chief model for Earwicker. Most of his children grew to dislike him intensely, but his eldest son, of whom he was most fond, reciprocated his affection and remembered his jokes. When John Joyce died in 1931, James told Louis Gillet, 'He never said anything about my books, but he couldn't deny me. The humor of *Ulysses* is his; its people are his friends. The book is his spittin' image.' [52] In *A Portrait* Stephen denies that Simon is in any real sense his father, but James himself had no doubt that he was in every way his father's son.

James rendered with equal fidelity John Joyce's defects and merits. In *Finnegans Wake* the artist Shem, seeing his father ambivalently, is 'one moment tarabooming great blunderguns (poh!) about his far-famed fine Poppamore, Mr Humhum, whom history, climate and entertainment made the first of his sept and always up to debt, ... and another moment visanvrerssas cruaching three jeers (pah!) for his rotten little ghost of a Peppybeg, Mr Himmyshimmy, a blighty, a reeky, a lighty, a scrapy, a babbly, a ninny, dirty seventh among thieves and always bottom sawyer.' [53] Out of this Pandoran amplitude all humanity poured. John Joyce was one of the most gifted reprobates in Ireland, and genius was part of his multifarious spawn.

---

* After John Joyce's death Louis Gillet asked James what his father had been, and he replied in the same style, 'He was a bankrupt.' [54] To be insolvent was oddly palatable for both father and son.

1882–1894

I'll close me eyes. So not to see. Or see only a youth in his florizel,
a boy in innocence, peeling a twig, a child beside a weenywhite steed.

—*Finnegans Wake* (621)

JAMES Joyce liked to think about his birthday. In later years, fond
of coincidences, he was pleased to discover that he shared his birth
year, 1882, with Eamon De Valera, Wyndham Lewis, and Frank
Budgen, and his birthday and year with James Stephens. That February 2 was Candlemas and St. Bridget's Day helped to confirm its
importance; that it was Groundhog Day added a comic touch; and
Joyce made it even more his own by contriving, with great difficulty,
to see the first copies of both *Ulysses* and *Finnegans Wake* on that
white day.

He was baptized on February 5 at the Church of St. Joseph, Terenure, by the Reverend John O'Mulloy, C.C.[1] His sponsors were Philip
and Ellen McCann, to whom he was related through his great-grand-
mother, John O'Connell's wife. Philip McCann was a ship's chandler
at 2 Burgh Quay in Dublin; Joyce suggests in *Stephen Hero* that it
was McCann who paid his godson's way through University College
from 1898 to 1902, but McCann died in 1898,[2] and does not seem to
have left money for the purpose. A more genuine connection between
him and Joyce came about through McCann's story, told to John
Joyce, of a hunchbacked Norwegian captain who ordered a suit from
a Dublin tailor, J. H. Kerse of 34 Upper Sackville Street. The finished
suit did not fit him, and the captain berated the tailor for being unable
to sew, whereupon the irate tailor denounced him for being impossible to fit. The subject was not promising, but it became, by the time
John Joyce had retold it, wonderful farce, and it is one of the parables
of native and outlander, humorous but full of acrid repartee, which
found their way into *Finnegans Wake*. If that book ever reached his

father in the afterworld, James Joyce once said, John Joyce's comment
would be, 'Well, he can't tell that story as I used to and that's one
sure five!' [3]

In 1882 the Joyces were living in Rathgar, a south Dublin suburb,
at 41 Brighton Square West. The house, which still stands, was modest
and comfortable. They remained there until 1884 when they moved,
perhaps to have more space, to 23 Castlewood Avenue.[4] But John
Joyce longed to live closer to water and farther from his wife's relatives. At the beginning of May 1887,[5] he took his family down to a
large house in a fashionable neighborhood in Bray. Here, at 1 Martello
Terrace, they were only a few steps from the sea, so close in fact that
the street was occasionally flooded with sea water. John Joyce took
up boating again, and rowed stroke in a four-man boat that won a
race.[6] Bray was easily accessible from Dublin by train, but John
Joyce said—and said again—that the train fare would keep his wife's
family away.

It did not keep away his friends. On Sundays he used to walk to the
station to meet the incoming train and to invite any of them who
were on it to spend the day at his home. They would have lunch,
then take a long walk, return for dinner, and sing and drink all evening in the drawing-room on the second floor. Two frequent guests
were little Alfred Bergan, later assistant to the sub-sheriff of Dublin,
and Tom Devin. Bergan was a good companion with a fund of scato-
logical stories which probably helped James to the opinion he expounded in later life, that most Irish jokes are about excrement. Devin,
a hearty man with a knack for playing the piano, would sing, 'O boys,
keep away from the girls, I say.' May Joyce played and John Joyce
sang songs of Balfe or Moore, or 'My Pretty Jane' (looking at May
Joyce), or '*M'appari*' from Flotow's *Martha*, or any of several hundred
'Come-all-ye's,' ballads, and arias. The art of the house was vocal music
of all kinds, sung indiscriminately as to quality but with surprising
skill. Of these parties James Joyce wrote Bergan in 1934, 'We used to
have merry evenings in our house, used we not?' [7]

It was perhaps the prospect of living in so healthy a resort that
brought John Joyce's uncle, William O'Connell, from Cork to stay with
them. A mild, polite, pompous old man, he got along easily with his
nephew John, who liked nothing better than to discuss old days in Cork
and often said to his daughters with amused modesty, 'Never marry a
Cork man. Your mother did.' [8] William remained with the family for
about six years. Another visitor, much more exciting to the children,
was John Kelly of Tralee, who appears in *A Portrait of the Artist*
under the name of John Casey. Kelly was in prison several times for

Land League agitation, and John Joyce regularly invited him to recu-
perate from imprisonment, at that time very rigorous, at the house in
Bray. In jail three fingers of his left hand had become permanently
cramped from picking oakum,[9] and he would tell the children that
they had become so while he was making a birthday present for Queen
Victoria. Kelly, a 'hillside man,' was frequently in danger of being
rearrested. Once a constable named Joyce, who was friendly with John
Joyce because of their name, came to the house late in the evening
to warn them that he would have to serve a warrant on Kelly in the
morning. Kelly escaped by car that night.[10] Consorting with an enemy
of the crown was probably risky enough for an officeholder, but John
Joyce never equivocated about his nationalism, and his growing and
outspoken devotion to Parnell, which Kelly fully shared, was already
forming the mind of his watchful son.

Soon after the Joyces moved to Bray they were joined by Mrs.
'Dante' Hearn Conway from Cork, who was to act as governess to the
children. A fat, clever woman, she was too embittered by a disastrous
marriage to fit easily into the tolerant, gay household. She had been
on the verge of becoming a nun in America when her brother, who
had made a fortune out of trading with African natives, died and left
her 30,000 pounds. She came back to Ireland to settle her inheritance,
and instead of returning to the United States, gave up the convent and
settled in Dublin to find a husband. She allowed herself to be won
by an overdressed employee of the pillared Bank of Ireland. Soon
after their marriage, to culminate a fine show of considerateness and
good manners, Conway ran off to South America with her money
tucked away in his pockets, and quickly ceased to write her promises
to return.[11] For the rest of her life Dante Conway remained the abandoned bride, and her burning memories of being deserted joined
remorse at having left the convent to make her overzealous, in both
religion and nationalism. She had, as James Joyce wrote, two brushes,
one backed in maroon for Davitt and his Land League, the other in
green for Parnell. Her loyalties clashed bitterly when Parnell was
found to have been an adulterer, but it is not hard to see why she
should have at once abandoned this betrayer of marriage ties and torn
off the green backing from her second brush.

Mrs. Conway was fairly well educated [12] and evidently a competent
teacher. Sitting on a throne-like arrangement of chair and cushions to
soothe her chronically ailing back, wearing a black lace cap, heavy
velvet skirts, and jeweled slippers, she would ring a little bell. James
would then come and sit at her feet for a lesson in reading, writing,
geography, or arithmetic; or he would listen to her recite poetry. Her

piety affected him less than her superstition; she talked a good deal about the end of the world, as if she expected it any moment, and when there was a flash of lightning she taught James to cross himself and say, 'Jesus of Nazareth, King of the Jews, from a sudden and unprovided for death deliver us, O Lord.' [13] The thunderstorm as a vehicle of divine power and wrath moved Joyce's imagination so profoundly that to the end of his life he trembled at the sound. When a friend asked him why he was so affected, he replied, 'You were not brought up in Catholic Ireland.' *

James Joyce was already a well-behaved, slim little boy in adult company, with a pale face and eyes of the palest blue to lend, when he was not laughing, an impenetrable coolness, an odd self-sufficiency, to otherwise regular and predictable features. His nearsightedness was soon to make him wear glasses, though at about the age of twelve he was advised by a foolish doctor to put them aside. His serene disposition made the household call him 'Sunny Jim,' as opposed to his dour brother Stanislaus, who was 'Brother John.' [14] They did not perceive his early discontents, probably because he precociously kept them to himself.

By age and temperament Joyce became the ringleader in the children's games. Across the street, at 4 Martello Terrace (not 7, as *A Portrait of the Artist* says), lived a chemist named James Vance with his family, and although the Vances were Protestant, the families were quickly drawn together. Vance's bass voice boomed against John Joyce's light tenor in 'Come-all-ye's.' The Vances' eldest child, four months younger than James, was a pretty girl named Eileen,† and the two fathers often spoke half-seriously of uniting their first-born.[15] Dante Conway warned James that if he played with Eileen he would certainly go to hell, and he duly informed Eileen of his destination but did not cease to merit it.

Hell and its superintendent had already become useful histrionic counters for him. He loved to arrange little plays, and his brother Stanislaus's earliest memory was of playing Adam to the Eve of his

---

* In *A Portrait of the Artist,* (514 [359]), Stephen Dedalus says that he fears 'dogs, horses, firearms, the sea, thunderstorms, machinery, the country roads at night'; his fear of dogs and thunderstorms is illustrated in *Ulysses,* his fear of thunderstorms gives (with the assistance of Vico) a prominent theme to *Finnegans Wake.*

The fear of dogs originated in childhood too, but without Dante's aid. James and Stanislaus were playing one day on the strand, throwing stones in the water, when a dog bit James, as he said later, on his chin. Stanislaus thought it was on the back of his brother's leg. From then on Joyce took precautions against dogs that would seem more absurd if he had not been bitten again, in 1927, at Scheveningen.

† Another child, Norah, was called 'Boodie,' a name Joyce borrowed for one of Stephen Dedalus's sisters.[16]

sister Margaret ('Poppie'), while James crawled about them in the congenial role of serpent.[17] Satan was useful in another way, as Eileen Vance * remembers. When James wished to punish one of his brothers or sisters for misconduct, he forced the offending child to the ground, placed a red wheelbarrow over him, donned a red stockingcap, and made grisly sounds to indicate that he was burning the malefactor in hellfire.[18] Thirty years later, in Zurich, Joyce was to be dubbed by a landlady 'Herr Satan,' because of his pointed beard and sinewy walk, but by that time he had assured himself, as *A Portrait* makes clear, that the real enemy was Nobodaddy, the spirit of restraint, rather than poor old Nick.

James and Eileen were both sent to a kindergarten kept by a Miss Raynor in Bray, and the two were always paired off together. James had a talent for imagining horrors. One of his tales which impressed Eileen was that when the children were naughty his mother would hold them head downward in the toilet and pull the chain. This same roguery emerged at a party they attended together, where his trick of slipping salt in the children's drinks was much applauded. But the best memory of all for Eileen Vance was the way the Joyce house filled up with music when May Joyce, her hair so fair † that she looked to Eileen like an angel, accompanied John, and the children too sang. Stanislaus had for his specialty 'Finnegan's Wake,' while James's principal offering for a time was 'Houlihan's Cake.' [19] James's voice was good enough for him to join his parents in singing at an amateur concert at the Bray Boat Club on June 26, 1888, when he was a little more than six.

John Joyce was not slow in forming the highest opinion of his oldest son. He grandly determined to give him the best education in Ireland. Having himself been the youngest boy at St. Colman's College, he saw no reason to delay James. Clongowes Wood College, forty miles from Bray at Sallins, County Kildare, was the obvious place to send him; so on September 1, 1888, the father and mother took James there to enter him. The fee of £25 ‡ a year (it went up in 1890) was well within John Joyce's means at the time. James, upon arrival, was asked his age, and replied, 'Half past six,' a phrase that became for some time his school nickname.[20] His tearful mother begged him not to speak to the rough boys; his father reminded him that John O'Connell,

* Eileen Vance, now Mrs. Harris, teaches at an Indian reservation near Saskatoon, Saskatchewan, as Professor Carlyle King discovered.
† It soon turned white.[21]
‡ Reduced, because of Joyce's age, from 45 guineas.[22] I am indebted, as the Notes indicate, to Kevin Sullivan's painstaking book *Joyce among the Jesuits* (1958) for this and several other details of Joyce's education.

his great-grandfather, had presented an address to the Liberator at Clongowes fifty years before.[23] He gave him two five-shilling pieces, and told him never to peach on another boy. Then his parents went off, and James was plunged into the life of Clongowes.

If Joyce retained anything from his education, it was a conviction of the skill of his Jesuit masters, the more remarkable because he rejected their teaching. 'I don't think you will easily find anyone to equal them,' he said long afterwards to the composer Philipp Jarnach,[24] and he corrected his friend Frank Budgen's book on him by remarking, 'You allude to me as a Catholic. Now for the sake of precision and to get the correct contour on me, you ought to allude to me as a Jesuit.'[25] To the sculptor August Suter, who asked him what he retained from his Jesuit education, Joyce replied, 'I have learnt to arrange things in such a way that they become easy to survey and to judge.'[26]

His immediate response to Clongowes is less clear than one would expect; his brother Stanislaus, who had already begun to worship him, remembers him as happy and well there, while *A Portrait* represents him as unhappy and unwell. That a boy of this age, suddenly removed from his family, could have been untroubled is hardly conceivable. The authorities are said to have considerately allowed him to live in the infirmary, instead of a dormitory, so that a nurse, 'Nanny Galvin,' might look after him.* Apparently she could not prevent his feeling homesick and tormented by the other boys' ragging for at least the first few months at Clongowes. The snobbery of small boys was new to him; he countered it, *A Portrait* asserts, by making his father a gentleman, one of his uncles a judge, and another a general in the army.[27] The worst event of the early months was the incident described in *A Portrait* and confirmed by Joyce to Herbert Gorman,[28] when another boy broke 'Stephen's' glasses and 'Father Dolan' pandied the victim on the mistaken premise that he had broken the glasses himself to avoid study. Father Dolan was in real life Father James Daly, the efficient prefect of studies at Clongowes for thirty years, and a martinet. Joyce was to speak of him later to Gorman as 'lowbred.'[29] On this occasion he bravely protested to the rector, Father Conmee, and was sustained by him. Probably at this time the other boys began to respect him; such a development is suggested, a little obscurely, in *A Portrait*, and is borne out by accounts of Joyce's life at the school by contemporaries. Even if, as seems likely, he really was pushed into the square ditch or cesspool by a fellow-pupil and laid up with fever as a result, probably in the spring of 1891, he was generally in good health. His homesickness did not last, as a letter to

* Sullivan, *Joyce among the Jesuits*, p. 31.

Mrs. John Joyce from Rev. T. P. Brown, S.J., Minister and Prefect of Health, indicates:

My dear Mrs Joyce

Jim is getting a formidable letter into shape for you—if he has not already sent it. I attacked him, on getting your letter, for his silence. He met me by saying that he had written but *had not given the letter to be posted.*

He is very well—his face being, as usual, very often well marked with any black thing that comes within reach. He has been taking the codliver oil regularly.

With best wishes and kindest regards to Mr Joyce

Yours very sincerely
T P Brown S J [30]

March 9, 1889

The casualness of the letter suggests that James Joyce was by now serene enough. Father Conmee used to say that James's letters home, which invariably began by announcing he was well and proceeded by listing his current needs, sounded like grocer's lists.[31] To John Joyce they indicated something else; he was to comment on his son, 'If that fellow was dropped in the middle of the Sahara, he'd sit, be God, and make a map of it.' [32] It was this interest in minute detail to which James Joyce also referred when he said to Budgen, 'I have a grocer's assistant's mind.' [33]

After a difficult start, Joyce distinguished himself at Clongowes. He was at the head of his class in his studies, and impressed Father Conmee strongly. Joyce did not forget Conmee's encouragement, and when, long afterwards, his biographer Herbert Gorman described Conmee as 'a very decent sort of chap,' Joyce struck out the words and wrote instead, 'a bland and courtly humanist.' [34] James's memory was not photographic but it was certainly, as Stanislaus Joyce said, 'retentive,' [35] and he could quickly commit prose as well as verse to memory, and even keep whole visual scenes in his head undiminished. Besides being a good student, James was also, as Stanislaus has surprisingly revealed, a good athlete.[36] The physical weakness of Stephen Dedalus and, in *Exiles,* of Richard Rowan, is a fiction based, insofar as it has foundation in fact, upon Joyce's dislike of fights and sports like rugby. He brought home from Clongowes, Stanislaus attests, a variety of cups for his prowess in hurdling and walking, and in spite of being younger and smaller than the other boys, he took a keen interest in cricket. Names of great cricketers continue to bob to the surface of even his last book.

Clongowes Wood, with its elms, large grounds, and storied (if rebuilt) medieval castle, roused its pupils to thoughts of grand action and great suffering. Several of its ancient owners had endured indignity or worse because of their allegiance to Catholicism, especially the Eustaces who saw their castle destroyed in 1641 by the soldiers of General Monk. When Father Peter Kenny bought the grounds from a family named Browne in 1813, he had to circumvent the anti-Catholic laws by pretending to purchase it for individual use rather than for the Jesuit order. But the following year, against the wishes of the government, the school was already inaugurated. Two traditions especially delighted Joyce, who mentioned them both in his writings. One member of the Browne family was a marshal in the Austrian army, and in 1757 took part in the Battle of Prague. His ghost, wearing a bloodstained white uniform, ascended the stairs of the castle to a gallery, then walked along it to a room at the end. His sisters and his servants soon after discovered that the marshal had been killed at Prague at that very moment. The other tradition was that Hamilton Rowan, a patriot and friend of Wolfe Tone, fled to the castle after his conviction in 1794 for sedition. He shut its door just as the soldiers were shooting, so that their bullets entered the door; then he threw his hat on the haha as a decoy, and let himself through a secret door into a tower room. His pursuers were fooled, thinking he had left, and he was able afterwards to make good his escape to France. The name and conduct of Rowan so pleased Joyce that he paid him the compliment of naming after him his autobiographical hero in *Exiles;* at the same time he was careful to make Richard Rowan say he bore no relationship to the famous patriot. Though so scrupulously abjured, there is here some of the longing of both John Joyce and his son for the state of the gentleman.

In the Clongowes that Joyce attended, Father Dolan had revised the curriculum so that it accorded with the requirements of the government. The Jesuits' *Ratio Studiorum* was freely adapted so that the students might do well on the examinations given each year by the state to the older boys. Religious instruction had, of course, a special emphasis,* and James excelled in this too. After making his first communion, he received the honor of being chosen as altar boy. At his confirmation, which also took place at Clongowes, he took for his saint's name Aloysius, the patron of youth and a nobleman who resigned his titles for the sake of his calling. One aspect of Aloysius that im-

---

* So in December 1890, Joyce and his classmates were examined in the first fourteen chapters of the *Maynooth Catechism,* in 150 pages of Bible history (Old Testament), and in 75 pages of Deharbe's *Catechism.* Sullivan, p. 47.

pressed him, for he mentions it later,[37] was that the saint would not allow his mother to embrace him because he feared contact with women. Joyce, less devout than that but devout enough, wrote a hymn to the Virgin Mary which his masters applauded. The refinements of ritual caught his imagination, and he learned precisely the order of the priest's functions, studying the technique of benediction as closely as Stendhal's Bishop of Agde. He took part in a procession to the little altar in the wood, wearing appropriate vestments and bearing the boat of incense. The majesty of the Church excited him and never left him. He was impressed, too, by the portraits of the saints and great men of the Jesuit order that hung along the corridor leading to the rector's room.* Yet questions had begun too, fostered by his father's mocking anticlericalism; for the moment they expressed themselves, Joyce says in *A Portrait*, merely as puzzlement over the fact that his holy teachers could be guilty of rage or injustice.

The records at Clongowes were not well kept at the time, but some glimpses of James Joyce survive in the recollections of schoolmates. Lieutenant-Colonel P. R. Butler, son of a famous British general, attended Clongowes with Joyce, and recalls that each pupil had to make a recitation chosen for its real or fancied appositeness to his own character. Butler's piece was 'The Charge of the Light Brigade,' while Joyce's was 'Little Jim,' which begins

> The cottage was a thatched one,
> Its outside old and mean,
> But everything within that cot
> Was wondrous neat and clean,

and ends with the prayer of the dying Jim's parents,

> In heaven once more to meet
> Their own poor little Jim.

The mawkishness was not lost upon either the scornful listeners or the embarrassed reciter.

But Joyce was very much a part of things. He was in a play at Eastertime, 1891, as an 'imp,' [38] he sang at a Third Line concert about 1890, and took piano lessons beginning before February 1891. About this time, too, he and Thomas Furlong, the second-smallest boy in the school, were caught out of bounds raiding the school orchard, and word went round that 'Furlong and Joyce will not for long rejoice,' a pun that he became fond of in later life. A contemporary at Clon-

---

* See Plate II.

gowes remembers his good-humored way of chaffing his elders. Joyce laughed easily and moved about with the assurance, never quite complete, of the boy in the Third Line who had been there longest; he was, said one classmate, 'the most vivid boy in the Line.' *

His visits home for holidays remained warm in his memory. John Joyce was always delighted to see him, and the whole family made much of him. Eileen Vance still lived across the street, and they were inseparable until one Valentine's Day when her father sent Joyce a Valentine purporting to come from her, on which he had written, paraphrasing a rhyme of Samuel Lover,

> O Jimmie Joyce you are my darling
> You are my looking glass from night till morning
> I'd rather have you without one farthing
> Than Harry Newall and his ass and garden.

Harry Newall was an old and disquieting cripple who drove his cart around Bray, so the compliment was not so extravagant as it first appeared. Mrs. Joyce may have intercepted the Valentine, as Stanislaus Joyce says, but James found out about it. Eileen, hearing of the trick that had been played on her, became shy with her playmate and for years blushed at the sound of his name.[39] He in turn faithfully kept the verse in mind and put it into *Ulysses.*†

When James came home during these Clongowes years, from 1888 to 1891, his father and John Kelly had no subject for talk but Parnell. These were the years during which this unyielding man filled Ireland with his image; Joyce was dazzled by the coldness of Parnell even to his friends. In a famous incident, which Joyce liked to describe,[40] they gave Parnell a check for £38,000, and he said not a word in thanks.[41] Most young men fancy themselves as Hamlets; Joyce, as later hints make clear, fancied himself as a Parnell. Ireland's 'uncrowned king' was now on his way to becoming her tragic hero. There were three final acts to the play. The first was the attempt of the London *Times* to discredit Parnell by printing a letter, alleged to be in his handwriting, that condoned the Phoenix Park murders of 1882.‡ The villain here was Richard Pigott, whose two sons were at Clongowes with James Joyce; in February 1889, before the Special Commission, Pigott was unmasked as a forger by his misspelling of the word

---

* The Third Line included boys under thirteen, the Lower Line boys from thirteen to fifteen, the Higher Line boys from fifteen to eighteen.
† Bloom remembers having sent the Valentine to his daughter Milly. *Ulysses* (62 [55]).
‡ The murderers, intending to assassinate the Viceroy, killed two other men in the Phoenix Park.

'hesitancy.' * He committed suicide, and the Jesuit masters went into each classroom to tell the boys not to reveal the news to the sons. One boy did, however, in a terrible scene.[42]

The vindicated Parnell now reached the height of his reputation, and his country united behind him. But the day before Christmas of that year, 1889, Captain William Henry O'Shea filed a petition for divorce from his wife Kitty on the ground of her adultery with Parnell. He had tolerated the affair for ten years, and in 1886 accepted a seat in Parliament from Galway as a reward for keeping still. The decree was granted without contest on November 17, 1890. At first Parnell showed surprising strength in holding his party together; his lieutenant Tim Healy staunchly declared that the leader should not be abandoned 'within sight of the Promised Land.' † [43] But soon the pressure of Davitt, of Gladstone, of the Catholic bishops, and then of Tim Healy and other close political associates accomplished its purpose and, as Yeats put it, 'dragged this quarry down.' [44] The metaphor of the hunted animal was applied to Parnell in his last phase by his biographer R. Barry O'Brien,[45] and by Yeats in prose as well as in verse; Joyce was to apply it also to himself. Within three weeks of the divorce the party was split in Committee Room 15, and within a year Parnell was dead.

Parnell's defeat was always spoken of by his adherents as his betrayal, with O'Shea, the bishops, and Healy following Pigott as villains, and the word betrayal became a central one in Joyce's view of his countrymen. As he grew up he was to see an increasingly close parallel between his own plight and Parnell's, and in 1912 he compared them directly in 'Gas from a Burner.'

For John Joyce the fall of Parnell, closely synchronized with a fall in his own fortunes, was the dividing line between the stale present and the good old days. He had done everything he could to save 'the Chief,' even to going down to Cork before a by-election to plead with his tenants there (in the days when he still had tenants) to vote for the Parnellite candidate. His anticlericalism acquired a new fierceness, and, while it included all the clergy, he reserved his best effect for Archbishops Walsh and Logue, 'Billy with the lip' and 'the tub of guts up in Armagh.' [46] But his anger against Healy and 'the Bantry gang' was greatest of all, and so uncontrolled that according to one tradition he went up to him at the Theatre Royal to shout in his face, 'You're a traitor!' [47]

---

* Joyce enjoys himself with this mistake in *Finnegans Wake* (35 and elsewhere).
† This Mosaic imagery was commonly applied to Parnell. Joyce continues it in the *Aeolus* episode of *Ulysses*.

Not long after Parnell's death on October 7, 1891, the nine-year-old James Joyce,[48] feeling as angry as his father, wrote a poem denouncing Healy under the title, 'Et Tu, Healy.' John Joyce was so pleased with it that he had it printed and distributed to his friends; * unfortunately no copy survives. Stanislaus Joyce remembered that it ended with the dead Parnell, likened to an eagle, looking down on the grovelling mass of Irish politicians from

> His quaint-perched aerie on the crags of Time
> Where the rude din of this . . . century
> Can trouble him no more.† [49]

Besides seconding John Joyce's attitude, the poem, in equating Healy and Brutus, was Joyce's first use of an antique prototype for a modern instance, Parnell being Caesar here, as in 'Ivy Day in the Committee Room' he would be Christ; and while this equation may be discounted as merely a schoolboy's, it persists in Joyce as Dedalus and Bloom as Ulysses. The final portrait of Parnell as a lofty eagle on the crags is automatic enough, but still seems faintly premonitory of Joyce's description of himself in 'The Holy Office' as a stag on the highest mountain ridges.

In the Joyce household Dante Conway, who stood firmly with the Church in its opposition to Parnell's leadership, must have felt less and less at home. Parnell's death made matters worse by overweighting his tragedy with martyrdom. Joyce has described the Christmas dinner in 1891, when his father and John Kelly raged and wept over Parnell's betrayal and death, and Dante Conway, full of venomous piety, left the table. The argument was so acrimonious that the Vances heard it across the street.[50] Probably the evidence of *Ulysses* can be trusted that Mrs. Conway left the house for good four days later. A more important after-effect was that for the Joyces, father and son, all was bathos now in Ireland; no politician and no politics were worth working for.

---

* 'Remember it?' he said long afterwards to the bookdealer Jacob Schwartz, 'Why shouldn't I remember it? Didn't I pay for the printing of it, and didn't I send a copy to the Pope?' [51]

† John J. Slocum and Herbert Cahoon, in *A Bibliography of James Joyce* (1953), p. 3, give four other lines from the poem:

> My cot alas that dear old shady home
> Where oft in youthful sport I played
> Upon thy verdant grassy fields all day
> Or lingered for a moment in thy bosom shade.

Joyce remarked to Harriet Weaver that he had parodied the lines in *Finnegans Wake* (231).

The family had now to move closer to Dublin. John Joyce, his financial troubles increasing, withdrew his son from Clongowes in June 1891. The Rates office, in the interests of civic efficiency, was to be taken over by the Dublin Corporation at the end of 1892,[52] and preparations were already being made. A few employees were retained, but most of them were pensioned. John Joyce's case looked black. He was known to be inefficient; he had made up some deficiencies in the rates he had collected by selling some Cork properties to the Collector General, perhaps under pressure; his trip to Cork in behalf of Parnell was also held against him. The bravery he had once displayed in defending his collector's pouch against an assailant in the Phoenix Park was forgotten, to be remembered only in *Finnegans Wake*.[53] At first he was given no pension at all, but when Mrs. Joyce made a personal appeal to the authorities[54] (like Molly Bloom to her husband's employer, Joe Cuffe), they agreed to settle the usual pension of £132/2/4 a year on him.[55]

For the rest of his life John Joyce, only forty-two years old when pensioned, was trapped. He was too accustomed to high living to subsist on his low income; in none of the ill-paid jobs that were sometimes available to him could he hope for the erratic hours of the Collector General's office.[56] He blamed his misfortunes on imaginary 'enemies,' and turned on his family, rancorous because their support curtailed his consumption of alcohol, though it did not do so very much. To himself he was never a poor man, always a rich man who had suffered reverses. His family too accepted the state of poverty without ever accepting the word.

The remains of his Cork properties slowed his descent to Dublin's depths. At the beginning of 1892[57] he moved his family to 23 Carysfort Avenue, Blackrock, a house called 'Leoville' because of the stone lion in front of its door.* Some of the children were sent to a convent school, but James was allowed to study by himself; he would interrupt his mother's work every hour to ask her to examine him on lessons he had set himself. He also wrote some florid poems, and began a novel in collaboration with a Protestant boy named Raynold who lived at No. 25. All these have vanished, too.

The Joyces were still in Blackrock in November 1892,[58] but late in this year or at the beginning of 1893 they moved into Dublin. They stayed first in lodgings,[59] then took a big house at 14 Fitzgibbon Street off Mountjoy Square, the last of their good addresses. The children

---

* Stanislaus Joyce places the composition of 'Et Tu, Healy' here, but it is likely that Joyce wrote it sooner, closer to the time of Parnell's death. At any rate he said himself it was written while he was nine, and in 1891.

were not sent to school at once; but eventually John Joyce, with the greatest reluctance, sent them to the Christian Brothers' school on North Richmond Street.[60] James Joyce chose never to remember this interlude with the Christian Brothers in his writings, preferring to have his hero spend the period in two years of reverie, and he did not mention it to Herbert Gorman. It was Joyce's one break with Jesuit education, and he shared his father's view that the Jesuits were the gentlemen of Catholic education, and the Christian Brothers ('Paddy Stink and Micky Mud,' as his father denominated them) its drones.

Just now John Joyce, walking in Mountjoy Square one day, had a fortunate encounter with Father John Conmee, who had left the position of rector of Clongowes to become prefect of studies at Belvedere College. He was not yet Provincial of the Jesuit Order in Ireland; he became so in 1906-9, but he was already influential. Hearing that his former pupil was obliged to attend the Christian Brothers' school, and remembering his ability, Conmee kindly offered to arrange for James, and his brothers too, to attend the fine Jesuit day-school, Belvedere College, without fees. John Stanislaus Joyce returned home pleased with Conmee and himself, and James entered Belvedere on April 6, 1893,[61] in III Grammar, to become its most famous old boy.

Belvedere College, built in 1775 for George Rochfort, second Earl of Belvedere, is one of the best eighteenth-century houses in Dublin. Its principal rooms, decorated by Michael Stapleton, were named after Venus, Diana, and Apollo, divinities superseded but (except for Venus) not painted over when the Jesuits purchased the house in 1841. To it they added in 1884 the adjoining house of Lord Fingall. Joyce found himself again in impressive surroundings, and investigated the history of the Belvedere family to such good effect that a few years later he contemplated writing a small book about it. Where the subversive associations of Clongowes were with rebellion, those of Belvedere were with carnal love. In *Ulysses* Joyce drew upon some of his researches when he had Father Conmee, who mentions the family discreetly in his pamphlet, *Old Times in the Barony*, remember a cloudy moment in the family annals. For Mary Countess of Belvedere, wife of the first earl, was accused of a love affair with her husband's brother in 1743.* The letters which were produced as evidence were probably forged, but Lady Belvedere was induced to say she was guilty so as to be divorced from her debauched husband. The earl, however, instead of divorcing her, cruelly imprisoned her in a house

---

* The story parallels Stephen's theory that Shakespeare was cuckolded by his brothers Edmund and Richard.

in Gaulstown, County Westmeath, where until her death more than thirty years later she continued to declare her innocence.[62]

These were not the things he learned at school. The Jesuit training at Belvedere was close to that at Clongowes, and Joyce had no trouble in adapting himself. His skill in English composition quickly drew attention to him. On routine topics such as 'Make Hay while the Sun Shines,' 'A Walk in the Country,' and 'Perseverance,' he managed to achieve a banality that was superior to his classmates'. The lay teacher of English composition was George Stanislaus Dempsey, a well set-up man who in later years resembled a retired British army officer.[63] He dressed unusually well, wore a moustache, and carried a flower in his buttonhole. His diction and manner were old-fashioned; in characteristic style he soon informed the rector, Father William Henry, that young Joyce was 'a boy with a plethora of ideas in his head.'[64] His pupils irreverently called him 'D'ye see' from his favorite expression; but they respected him, and Joyce treats him well enough under the name of 'Mr Tate' in *A Portrait of the Artist*. In later years he and Dempsey corresponded, and the old teacher rashly suggested that some of Joyce's poems be published in the school magazine.

Among Stanislaus Joyce's papers one of James's weekly themes has survived. The essay begins and ends with the proper formulas, but the signature of 'James A. Joyce,' executed with a mighty flourish, lacks humility, as the rector noticed.

AMDG °

Trust not Appearances

There is nothing so deceptive and for all that so alluring as a good surface. The sea, when beheld in the warm sunlight of a summer's day; the sky, blue in the faint and amber glimmer of an autumn sun, are pleasing to the eye: but, how different the scene, when the wild anger of the elements has waked again the discord of confusion, how different the ocean, choking with froth and foam, to the calm, placid sea, that glanced and rippled merrily in the sun. But the best examples of the fickleness of appearances are:—Man and Fortune. The cringing, servile look; the high and haughty mien alike conceal the worthlessness of the character. Fortune that glittering bauble, whose brilliant shimmer has allured and trifled with both proud and poor, is as wavering as the wind. Still however, there is a "something" that tells us the character of man. It is the eye. The only traitor that even the sternest will of a fiendish villian [sic] cannot overcome. It is the eye that reveals to man the guilt or innocence, the vices or the virtues of the soul. This is the only exception to the proverb "Trust not appearance." In every other case the real worth has to be searched for. The garb of royalty or of democracy are

° *Ad Majorem Dei Gloriam.*

but the shadow that a "man" leaves behind him. "Oh! how unhappy is that poor man that hangs on princes' favours." The fickle tide of ever-changing fortune brings with it—good and evil. How beautiful it seems as the harbinger of good and how cruel as the messenger of ill! The man who waits on the temper of a King is but a tiny craft in that great ocean. Thus we see the hollowness of appearances. The hypocrite is the worst kind of villain yet under the appearance of virtue he conceals the worst of vices. The friend, who is but the fane of fortune, fawns and grovels at the feet of wealth. But, the man, who has no ambition, no wealth no luxury save contentment cannot hide the joy of happiness that flows from a clear conscience and an easy mind.

LDS *
James A. Joyce [65]

The example may give heart to adolescents who are searching their own works for evidence of literary immortality, and not finding much.

While James was bolstering his position at Belvedere, his father's was deteriorating at home. Their house for over a year remained 14 Fitzgibbon Street, for John Joyce gave this address in February 1894, when he disposed of his remaining Cork properties. He took James down to Cork with him, and in *A Portrait of the Artist* Stephen is represented as increasingly alienated from his father, his father's friends, and his father's youth.[66] There were probably many such moments of melancholy, but not undiluted. Stanislaus Joyce remembers that his brother's letters home indicated also that he followed his father about with considerable amusement.[67] In later life he always showed a fellow feeling for Cork men, and would ask them about the Imperial Hotel, where he stayed, about the Mardyke, a fine promenade, and about the special Cork dish, drisheens.[68] Beyond these, he made Stephen remember the word FOETUS inscribed on one of the desks at Queen's College, Cork, the scene of John Joyce's unsuccessful effort to become a doctor. *A Portrait* makes the word concentrate Stephen's sense of puberty,[69] in which sex was reproachful, irresistible. Self-consciously prudish about girls himself, Stephen mulled over his father's reputation as a great flirt, which Cork friends still jollied him about. (Eleven years later James Joyce was still to boast to an Italian friend that his father was a *conquistatore di dame*.)[70] It was now, too, that John took his son to Crosshaven to the Presentation Convent to try, unsuccessfully, to get two of his daughters accepted as free boarders. Unperturbed, they listened to an O'Connell cousin there sing 'The Fisherman's Goodnight,' and both expertly criticized the song as unsuitably low in range for her voice.

The sale of the properties occupied about a week, from February 8 to February 14, 1894. It was made necessary mainly by heavy debts

* *Laus Deo Semper.*

John Joyce had contracted to Reuben J. Dodd, a Dublin solicitor who lent money and who already owned mortgages on the property. The land and buildings had sentimental associations: one piece had come to John Joyce's father, James, at the time of his marriage in 1848; another had been assigned to James by William Pennyfeather and must have been connected with the story, now lost but mentioned in *A Portrait*, of how this earlier James Joyce had broken Pennyfeather's heart.[71] John Joyce's heart was now no doubt broken too, but it mended quickly among his Cork cronies and the rejuvenating atmosphere of public houses. He collected, probably for transfer to Dodd, £1400 that an auction at the end of December 1893 had brought for the ground and buildings to the rear * of the South Terrace, and the coach house and stable adjacent in Stable Lane. He obtained £475 for the ground and buildings at 7 and 8 Anglesea Street, and an unstated consideration for premises in White Street.

John Joyce and his son returned now to Dublin, pockets full of Dodd's money. Their irritation with Dodd for emptying them was a lasting one, fueled for James by the fact that Dodd's son was in his class at Belvedere. He snubbed Reuben, Jr., at school,[72] and in *Ulysses* scored on him again by transferring to 1904 an incident that occurred in 1911.† Of course, if Reuben J. Dodd had not lent him money, John

---

* Joyce always uses the Irish, and particularly the Dublin spelling, *rere*.
† The younger Dodd threw himself into the Liffey to commit suicide for love, but was fished out. The *Irish Worker* of December 2, 1911, carried a leading article about the incident:

Half-a-Crown for Saving a Life

On August the 26th of this year a solicitor named Reuben Jas. Dodd jumped into the Liffey close to the Butt Bridge. Whatever his motive—suicide or otherwise—we care not. After swimming around to cool himself he became exhausted; a life-buoy was thrown him, but he was unable to help himself. A docker who was passing at the time hearing the commotion, asked 'what's up?' 'Man drowning,' was the answer, and without a moment's hesitation he jumped in and brought Dodd, solicitor, to the steps, where another docker and a carter lifted Dodd up the steps on to the quay wall. The inevitable policeman then appeared, and Dodd was taken to Jervis street Hospital, and from there to the house of detention. The father of this Dodd, solicitor, was walking up and down the quay whilst this episode was being enacted, and as a matter of fact had been talking to his son, Dodd, solicitor, previous to him deciding to test the recuperative benefits of Anna Liffey. Now, what of the man who rescued Dodd, eh? He is only a common docker named Moses Goldin, who during the last few years saved some twenty lives. Goldin has a wife and four children to keep. He has been suffering from pulmonary trouble for some time past, brought on by the exposure he submitted himself to in his successful efforts to rescue life. Dodd was taken to hospital on a motor car. Moses Goldin, who saved his life, walked home to his slum. His poor old mother, who minds his children whilst the other heroine—his wife—goes out to earn a few shillings in a sack factory, went out to a publican

Joyce would have borrowed elsewhere, but Dodd was the manifest, if not the basic cause of the poverty which now descended. Besides the £11 a month from his pension, collected punctually each month at David Drimmie and Sons, John Joyce picked up a little money here and there. His calligraphy enabled him to work occasionally for a solicitor on the quays named Aylward; ° he had a random occupation as advertisement canvasser for the *Freeman's Journal;* [73] and at election times he could always depend upon the usual small jobs to make him momentarily affluent and, necessarily, drunk.

The immediate change that the lack of funds brought about was another move, this time to Millbourne Lane in Drumcondra. Stanislaus Joyce describes this house as 'a small semi-detached villa . . . at the foot of a low hill' [74] not far from woods and the river Tolka. Their neighbors, farmhands and navvies, resented the arrival of this family that had known better days. Stanislaus had a fight with one of the local boys, 'Pisser' Duffy, and was amused when his unforgetting brother gave the name of Duffy to the hero of 'A Painful Case,' who in most respects was modeled on Stanislaus. James too had a fight, but not with the local boys. It began at school, according to *A Portrait,* when 'Mr Tate' read out a sentence from 'Stephen's' weekly theme: 'Here. It's about the Creator and the soul. Rrm . . . rrm . . . Ah! *without a possibility of ever approaching nearer.* That's heresy.' Joyce, in using the incident in his book, says Stephen murmured (so that the value of the Church as

---

close by to borrow a shirt so that Goldin might change his clothes. Owing to want of attention Goldin had to go to hospital; whilst lying there his wife lost a day's work and wages amounting to 1s., and went and saw Mr. Dodd, senior. After some delay he condescended to see her, and very kindly told Mrs. Goldin that her husband would have minded his own business. After other fatherly advice he gave Mrs. Goldin 2s.6d. to assist her. Goldin lay in hospital some weeks. He lost his health and wages and got 2s.6d. for saving Dodd, solicitor. It wasn't worth it; was it? Goldin himself did not get thank you. I don't know if the policeman who came up after it was all over got a certificate and recommended promotion or not. We would like to ask what the local hon. sec. to the Royal Humane Society is doing; Goldin also asks. I hope the readers of this paper will ask. Some lives Goldin saved—J. M'Allister and C. Rielly—died after rescue. P. Ryan, W. Hanly, J. Gorman; these persons were all taken to Jervis street and Mercer's Hospital; others rescued taken home; and last, but least, Dodd, solicitor, for which life Goldin's wife got 2s.6d.

Mr. Dodd thinks his son is worth half-a-crown. We wouldn't give that amount for a whole family of Dodds.

Reuben J. Dodd, Jr., who has since died, sued the B.B.C. for libel when Joyce's references to him in the *Hades* episode of *Ulysses* were read on the air; he contended that he had jumped into the Liffey 'after my hat.' [75]

° Aylward's office is probably that described in 'Counterparts,' where his name is changed to Alleyne for reasons explained on pp. 14-15.

intercessor might be preserved), 'I meant *without a possibility of ever reaching.*' [76] In real life, Dempsey was appeased in some such manner, but his fellow-students, who had envied Joyce his success at themes, were not. Several of them took the same route home as he did, and that afternoon, as Stanislaus Joyce helps to establish, they were quick to seize the advantage offered them by Dempsey. They turned the subject to literature, and argued whether Marryat was the greatest writer or not. Then Joyce was asked his opinion. The greatest prose writer, he said, was Newman, a choice that sounded goody-goody but was really stylistic. 'And who is the best poet?' Albrecht Connolly,[77] an excellent student, named Tennyson as he ought, but Joyce named Byron.* 'Byron was a bad man,' said one, and Connolly called out, 'Here, catch hold of this heretic.' They seized him and demanded he admit that Byron was no good, hitting him meanwhile with a stick and bearing him back against a barbed wire fence that tore his clothes. Joyce would no more have judged Byron by his love affairs than he would have Parnell. He did not submit, but, as Stanislaus remembered, went home crying to his mother, who comforted him and mended his clothes. So his sufferings for his art began.†

At school his proficiency was confirmed by the results of the Inter-mediate Examinations held in the spring of 1894. Competing with the boys from all the schools of Ireland in the Preparatory Grade, Joyce won one of the top prizes, an exhibition of £20. The money was paid by the government to John Joyce, who turned it over to his son to spend as he liked, on the grandiose theory that it would teach him the use of money. James had no difficulty, even at the age of twelve, in falling in with his father's ideal of gay improvidence, though as always he made a show of meticulous bookkeeping; while he lent money gen-erously and imprudently to brothers, sisters, and parents, he entered the sums carefully in an account book. He also took his father and mother to theaters and restaurants, including the expensive Jammet's.‡ The family tasted again the luxuries it could no longer afford, and did

---

* Joyce held to these opinions of Newman and Byron in later life.

† Another indignity of this spring is perhaps described much as it happened in a story of *Dubliners*. The bazaar *Araby* came to Dublin on May 14-19, 1894. The boy fixed his mind with accustomed intensity upon the bazaar, and won his uncle's (his father's?) consent to go. But his uncle did not return with money until it was too late, and then said, 'The people are in bed and after their first sleep now.' The boy went anyway, and by the time he arrived, the bazaar was virtually over; the lights were going out, the merriment had ceased.[78] There is perhaps then a particular irony when in *A Portrait* a schoolmate accuses Stephen of not being the sort to go to bazaars. Joyce, like Stephen, seems in some moods to have encouraged other people to regard him as a very virtuous boy.

‡ Probably mistreated in *A Portrait* under the name of 'Underdone's.'

so thereafter every year that James won an exhibition. He thereby attained a sense of his own generosity so pervasive that, when asked to contribute to the family's support a few years later, he replied self-righteously, 'I have done enough.' [79]

He was the only one of the children who got along easily with their father. The two liked to travel together, and that summer of 1894 John Joyce brought James along on a trip to Glasgow. He had made friends with the captain of one of the Duke liners that sail between Dublin and Glasgow, and took up the captain's invitation to make the journey. The visit was spoiled by rain, but it gave John Joyce another sea story; on the return trip he and the captain quarreled violently over Parnell. 'By God, man,' John Joyce would say afterwards, 'if he had been drinking he would have thrown me overboard.' [80]

At home, John Joyce's temper was frayed by the old economic stress. In the late summer or early fall a new son, Freddie, died a few weeks after birth. His wife was scarcely recovered when John Joyce, as Stanislaus remembers, attempted to strangle her. In a drunken fit he grabbed at her throat and roared, 'Now, by God, is the time to finish it.' The children ran screaming between them, but James jumped on his father's back and toppled both father and mother over. Mrs. Joyce snatched up the youngest children from the mêlée and ran to a neighbor's house. For a moment the family squalor became Dostoevskian. A few days later, Stanislaus says,[81] a police sergeant called and had a long conversation with his father and mother. From then on John Joyce contented himself with the threat of violence. Stanislaus detested him, and showed that he did, so that his father would mock him, 'What a loving son!' The other children were abused or, more luckily, ignored, except for James and 'Baby' (Mabel), the youngest, for whom her father retained an affection. Meanwhile bills accumulated, the landlord was upon the family for his rent, and probably late in 1894, the Joyces prepared to move again. The sense of home life as a continual crisis, averted from disaster by pawnbroker, obliging friend, or sudden job, became fixed in James Joyce's mind. He was warily cultivating indifference to such matters, and already, at the age of twelve, was learning to pick his way among the family ruins as nimbly as an archaeologist.

◇◇◇

1894–1898

Cousin Stephen, you will never be a saint. Isle of saints. You were awfully holy, weren't you? You prayed to the Blessed Virgin that you might not have a red nose. You prayed to the devil in Serpentine avenue that the fubsy widow in front might lift her clothes still more from the wet street. *O si, certo!* Sell your soul for that, do, dyed rags pinned round a squaw. More tell me, more still! On the top of the Howth tram alone crying to the rain: *naked women!* What about that, eh?

—Ulysses (41 [37])

HIS Belvedere days supplied Joyce with an arena in which, like inexperienced gladiators, body and mind might clash. He became more actively different from his parents and teachers. At the beginning he read Erckmann-Chatrian's nostalgic novels and at the end of his schooldays he read Ibsen's sardonic plays. As he said in *A Portrait,* his soul threw off the cerements that covered it and spurned the grave of boyhood.[1] His graveclothes included, by one of those curious transvaluations of Christian images that Joyce was to delight in, his allegiance to the Church; and his resurrection, for which Christ's was so useful a descriptive metaphor, was as an artist rather than as a risen god. His sins became serious, and his sense of sin, 'that sense of separation and loss,'[2] brought him to consciousness, from which vantage point he sloughed off all but the vestiges of Christian guilt. He went through a series of violent changes and emerged from them somber and aloof, except with the few friends to whom he exhibited his joy, his candor, his bursting youth; even with these he was a little strange, never wholly companionable because each time he laid bare his soul he importuned greater loyalty, until friendship became for them almost an impossible burden of submission.

When the family had to leave Millbourne Avenue, in late 1894, John Joyce moved them back into town. He found a house for his eleven dependents and himself at 17 North Richmond Street. The short, blind street was well known to his children, for the Christian Brothers' school they had briefly attended was a few doors away. Among the houses through which the Joyce family passed with wraith-like rapidity, this one, solider than most, received more attention from James Joyce than the others. He described it and its musty odor in his story 'Araby,' and mentioned the paperbacked books left by the priest who had recently died there. Behind the house was an untended garden with a central apple tree and a few scraggly bushes; as Stanislaus Joyce says, the children missed the open fields and woods of Millbourne Avenue.

The neighbors on North Richmond Street lent themselves to James Joyce's later fictions. At No. 1 lived the Boardman family, to be oddly memorialized in the *Nausicaa* episode of *Ulysses*, where Gerty Mc-Dowell's friend Edy Boardman is a combination of the names of Eily and Eddie Boardman. When Gerty is said to be jealous because of Edy Boardman's vanity over 'the boy that had the bicycle always riding up and down in front of her window,' Joyce has in mind the fact that Eddie Boardman was famous through all north Dublin because his was the first pneumatic-tired bicycle in the neighborhood; [3] boys came from all over to see it. But when Gerty says of the boy on the bicycle, 'Only now his father kept him in the evening studying hard to get an exhibition in the intermediate that was on and he was going to Trinity College to study for a doctor,' [4] Joyce is thinking of his own assiduity, famed too on North Richmond Street.

Another neighbor, across the street, was Ned Thornton, a tea-taster; he was the father of Eveline for whom the story in *Dubliners* is named,[5] and he is also the hero of 'Grace,' 'Mr. Kernan,' although the fall in the bar in that story occurred not to Thornton but to John Joyce. Thornton's brother, whom Joyce met only once, was the principal model for the character (as John Joyce was f the eloquence) of the *Cyclops* narrator.[6] Joyce says a brother of Eveline worked in the church decorating business; actually he was in Telford's, the organ builder. Eveline did fall in love with a sailor, as in the story, but instead of leaving him at the pier rather than accompanying him to South America, she settled down with him in Dublin and bore him a great many children.[7]

Farther down the street, at No. 7, lived Long John Clancy, sub-sheriff of Dublin, who appears under his own name in *Finnegans Wake* and in a thin disguise in *Ulysses* as Long John Fanning. John Joyce's friend, Alfred Bergan, was Clancy's assistant, and delighted to tell the Joyces how, on one of those rare occasions in Ireland when a criminal had to be hanged, Clancy, having no stomach for the job, betook himself to London, confiding all the preparations to Bergan's equally reluctant hands.[8] Bergan must have advertised for a hangman, for he received a letter from an English barber named Billington, who offered to do the job on his way back from an Irish holiday, and described in detail his skill in fastening and pulling nooses. In *Ulysses* James Joyce remembered the gist of the letter and used it in the *Cyclops* episode, where Bergan himself passes it around, but he changed the name of the barber from Billington to H. Rumbold after Sir Horace Rumbold, British Minister to Switzerland in 1918, against whom he had a grievance.

The Joyce sons were beginning to attain separate individualities. John Stanislaus Joyce, Jr., known as 'Stannie,' was a serious, round-headed boy, heavy-set though athletic, and shorter by several inches than James; he already gave signs of the bluntness and determination that were to characterize his life. The next brother, Charles, was to prove jaunty and capricious, a boy of many careers, with little ability for any of them. The youngest boy was George, who showed signs of his oldest brother's wit and intelligence, but had only a few years to live. Among the girls the personalites were less distinct; Margaret, the oldest, approximated her mother's gentle steadfastness, and played the piano well. Eileen was more excitable and less ordered; Mary ('May') was quiet and pacific; Eva and Florence were withdrawn, Florence especially; while Mabel, the youngest, was unexpectedly gay. Almost all were capable on occasion of those sudden insights that endow their decay as a family with unexpected distinction.

The prevailing tone in the family was male; the girls, 'my twenty-three sisters,' as James Joyce once called them, had a very subordinate place and, frightened of their father's rebukes, did not attempt to assert themselves. Among the boys the emphasis fell strongly on James at the expense of the others;[9] it was James for whom John Joyce, his friends, and most of the relatives freely predicted a great career in some as yet undetermined profession. Stanislaus, almost three years younger but closest to James in age and understanding, trailed him worshipfully. He preferred to study what James studied rather than what Belvedere College prescribed, and so methodically pursued his brother into European literature at the expense of his own grades.

John Joyce, fearsome and jovial by turns, kept the family's life from being either comfortable or tedious. In his better moods he was their comic: at breakfast one morning, for example, he read from the *Freeman's Journal* the obituary notice of a friend, Mrs. Cassidy. May Joyce was shocked and cried out, 'Oh! Don't tell me that Mrs. Cassidy is dead.' 'Well, I don't quite know about that,' replied John Joyce, eyeing his wife solemnly through his monocle, 'but someone has taken the

liberty of burying her.' [10] James burst into laughter, repeated the joke
later to his schoolmates, and still later to the readers of *Ulysses*.[11]

On Sunday mornings John Joyce busied himself hurrying the rest of
the family off to mass, while he stayed home himself. When his two
eldest sons returned he often took them for a walk. His undisguised
preference for James reduced Stanislaus's pleasure in such promenades,
but James was indulgent and fascinated by the little dapper man with
his straw hat. John Joyce spoke to them of Dublin characters, he
pointed out where Swift once lived, where Addison walked, where
Sir William Wilde had his surgery. He knew all the stories, inside and
out; besides what he picked up from other sources, he retained from
his days as a rate collector the most savory details of Dublin's private
life.

James Joyce had his special manner too, though his opportunities for
displaying it were necessarily trivial. On Pancake Night one pancake
was left on the platter, and all four boys—James, Stanislaus, Charles,
and George—dove for it. James made off with the prize and ran up and
down stairs, protesting to his pursuers that he had already eaten it.
At last they were convinced, and he then imperturbably removed the
pancake from the pocket where it lay hidden,[12] and ate it up with the
air of little Jack Horner. Something cold and selfish in his temperament
gave Stanislaus, who was reading *David Copperfield* and liked to find
literary prototypes of people he knew, the notion that James was an
arrogant Steerforth.[13] Philip Sayers thought James had an extraordinarily high opinion of himself.[14] A man named McGinty, who lived
nearby and played on the same street, recalled that 'the great Joyce,'
after observing the boys playing football with a rag doll, decided to
raise the game's level, and persuaded them one day to try the more
dignified and dangerous game of rugby. One or two falls on the hard
pavement made him less eager, and he quickly changed back from a
participant to a supercilious spectator.[15]

Joyce liked taking preposterously long walks. His companion on these
was often little Alfred Bergan, who found Joyce sometimes affable, at
other times utterly silent. Once they walked from Fairview to Dollymount, skirted Lord Ardilaun's demesne, and returned by the Strand
Road to Fairview. Joyce was preoccupied and hardly spoke until they
came to the sea wall at Fairview; then, observing some sea gulls feed-
ing, he remarked to Bergan, 'Seagulls are beautiful birds but greedy.
See how they try to snap food from each other.' [16] On that profound
observation * they parted.

Another time the two walked together to William Murray's house on

* Echoed in *Ulysses* by Bloom (151 [142]).

the south side. One of the children there, a girl of five or six, began to scream and would not stop. Joyce took up a book and pretended to read it. At last Murray came in and took her up in his arms. In a soothing voice he asked, 'Who's been annoying you? They're always annoying you. Daddy's little lump of love. The only bit of sunshine in the house.' At this Joyce looked across at Bergan and sighed.[17] The story got back to John Joyce, who gladly added it to his repertoire of anecdotes about his wife's family, and rephrased it as 'Daddy's little lump of dung.'[18]

Most of the testimony about James Joyce on North Richmond Street suggests his childish gravity, but some indicates a flair for drama. Brendan Gallaher, who knew him at this time, visited the Joyces one day with his mother. James brought him into the kitchen and produced a red cardboard box. With a mysterious air he showed Brendan, who was six or seven, that it had a hinged front and concealed rollers. Finally he judged his audience ready, and cranked before Brendan's stage-struck eyes a lordly sequence of colored pictures of the Port of Southampton, the Pyramids of Egypt, and other splendors. He then handed the box over to Brendan and said grandly, 'It's for you, Brennie. Take it home with you.' There is a pleasant air of contrivance about this display, as if the picture-show was only part of a larger theatrical performance in which James and, unwittingly, Brendan, were taking part.* [19]

---

* The Gallaher family was one Joyce knew well, and it is not surprising to find them well represented in his writings. Brendan's brother, Gerald, is one of the two little boys to whom Father Conmee speaks in the *Wandering Rocks* episode. His mother, Mrs. Joe Gallaher, comes into the *Penelope* episode, where Mrs. Bloom recalls that at the Crosstown races Mrs. Gallaher, driving in a trap with Friery the solicitor, failed to take any notice of her. Here Joyce has slightly altered the facts, for Friery escorted not Mrs. Gallaher but her sister, Mrs. Clinch. Mrs. Clinch is also mentioned, however, for Bloom remembers with embarrassment that he almost accosted her one night under the mistaken impression that she was a prostitute.

Ulysses pursues the family even further: Mrs. Gallaher and Mrs. Clinch were two of four handsome girls whose father was an old soldier named Powell. He called himself Major Powell although he was only a sergeant-major. Major Powell is Joyce's model for Molly Bloom's father, Major Tweedy. He had served many years in the army, took part in the Crimean War and was in the Aldershot Rifles in Australia. On retiring from the service he commuted his pension and bought a farm in Cork. He drank this up, came to Dublin and married a woman with property. She bore him four daughters and a son, then tired of his bullying ways and lived separately from him. Joyce has greatly softened Powell's character. Another Powell, Josie, who is mentioned in *Ulysses*, was actually a Powell by marriage.

The Gallaher who appears most prominently in Joyce's writings is Mrs. Gallaher's brother-in-law Fred. Joyce calls him Ignatius Gallaher, and in the story 'A Little Cloud' and in *Ulysses* gives an accurate account of him. He was a newspaperman in Dublin but because of some scandal was obliged to go to London. There T. P. O'Connor gave him a job, and he worked in Paris, where he eventually died. Joyce

During his first two years at Belvedere Joyce applied himself happily to his studies. He had to choose in his first year a third language to go with Latin and French; his mother urged German, his father Greek, but he decided upon Italian, 'at that time,' as he told Gorman, 'the Cinderella of modern languages.' [20] His lack of Greek he was to bemoan all his life, but in the event Italian proved invaluable to him. His best subject remained English; he contrived sometimes to give hints there of his later self. Assigned the topic 'My Favorite Hero,' for instance, he passed over Hector and Achilles and other burly men to choose the wily Ulysses,[21] of whom he had read in Lamb's *The Adventures of Ulysses*. Lucifer, Parnell, Ulysses—dissimilar as they were, they began to cluster solemnly in his mind. It was not so much that he wanted to become them—he was too proud for that—but he wanted them to become him, or, to put it another way, he wanted an interplay among their images and his own.

The Intermediate Examinations were held each year in June, and Joyce prepared for them with great deliberation. Mathematics was not an easy subject for him, but he successfully worked it up, and the only subject that evaded his zeal was chemistry. At home he had the luxury of a room to himself where he might study, and at examination time his family treated him reverently. One night, when he was reading intently, John Joyce called out to him, 'What do you want if you win the Exhibition, Jim?' and the boy, without raising his head from the page, called back, 'Two chops,' and went on with his reading.[22] The result of his diligence was that he won exhibitions in 1894 and 1895; in the first year he was 103rd of 132 winners, and in the second he luckily scraped through as 164th in a group of 164. The first exhibition was £20 for one year only, but the second was £20 to be paid annually for three years. His grades are preserved in the official records.[23] A quick result of this second victory was that two Dominican priests called on John Joyce and offered to give James free board, room, and tuition at their school near Dublin. John Joyce brought in his son, and left the decision to him. James declared without hesitation, 'I began with the Jesuits and I want to end with them.'

James mitigated his exemplary behavior a little toward the end of this term by persuading Stanislaus to play truant for a day from Belvedere.[24] The two brothers planned an expedition along the strand as far as the Pigeon House—the public power plant which serves Dublin. On the way, as Stanislaus recalls, they ran into the homosexual whose talk and behavior were described later in Joyce's story *An Encounter*. He evoked the dangerous, slightly shameful adult world into which Joyce was about to penetrate.

Joyce was moving closer to that moment which could, as he later held, be pinpointed in a man's psychic as well as physical development, when boyhood changes to adolescence. For some months yet he was still a boy, though with a secret unwillingness to remain so. His conduct was irreproachable enough to earn him admission on December 7, 1895, to the Sodality of the Blessed Virgin Mary, and on September 25, 1896, he was chosen prefect or head.[25] During his fourteenth year (as he told Stanislaus later),[26] and very possibly between these two events, he precociously began his sexual life. *A Portrait* has to represent this 'fall' with dramatic suddenness, but it came about in actuality with at least one incident to herald it. This was a flirtation with a young maid servant. Stanislaus Joyce describes a scene between the two as 'a kind of catch-as-catch-can cum-spanking match,' and prefers, since it came to the notice and disapproval of the Jesuits, to find in it more innocence than perhaps it had.[27] At any rate, it was followed by a more serious episode. On his way home from the theater, where he had seen a performance of *Sweet Briar*, Joyce walked along the canal bank and met a prostitute. Reckless, curious, and valuing any expression of his own temperament, he experimented, and the experiment helped to fix his image of the sexual act as shameful, an image suppressed but never quite abandoned later. Returning to his house, Joyce found Bergan and his father talking gaily about the play, which they also had attended,[28] and kept his feelings to himself.

Yet his demeanor was not so impeccable as he probably wished. Father Henry, the rector of Belvedere, prided himself on his ability to judge character, and Joyce aroused his suspicions. Henry had a convert's harshness, and his students were often perplexed to see him suddenly stop in the middle of a class to pray down some suspect thought. James's manner was too impenetrable for the rector to hope to get anything out of the boy himself, but he cannily called Stanislaus into his office and questioned him first about himself and then, more deviously, about his brother. Stanislaus, intimidated by the rector's reminders of the dangers of telling a lie to the Holy Ghost, mentioned the one thing he knew of—the incident between his brother and the maid. Father Henry pounced on this corroboration of his suspicion, and the next day sent for Mrs. Joyce. Without offering any particulars, and thus alarming her further, he warned her, 'Your son is inclined to

PLATE I

James Joyce with his mother, father, and maternal grandfather (John
Murray), a few hours before Joyce, then 6½, entered Clongowes Wood
College. (p. 26) *Courtesy of Mrs. May Joyce Monaghan*

The long corridor at Clongowes, leading to the rector's office. Joyce, then about 7, walked down it to protest Father Dolan's unjust punishment. (p. 27)

II

The National Library of Ireland. On its steps Joyce talked with Byrne, Cosgrave, and Gogarty.

evil ways.' She returned home very disturbed, and Stanislaus, who by
this time bemoaned his own candor, confessed to both his mother and
brother what he had told the rector. James merely laughed and called
him a fathead, while Mrs. Joyce blamed the servant and discharged
her. To Brendan Gallaher's mother she said that some woman had
tried to seduce her son.[29]

She must have shown enough signs of dismay to arouse the suspicions of John Joyce, who asked his son what the trouble was. 'I am
under a cloud at school,' he replied, as Stanislaus remembered. 'What
about?' asked his father. 'I don't know. You had better ask the rector.'
John Joyce did so, but Father Henry remained vague and monitory.
'That boy will give you trouble,' he warned him, but John Joyce replied
with aplomb, 'No, he won't, because I won't let him.'[30]

Joyce did not heed the rector's warnings, and he was not removed
from his position as prefect of the sodality. The position suited him
very well; he had an adolescent thrill in adoring the Virgin Mary
while his lips still savored 'of a lewd kiss.'[31] His mind longed to adore
and to desecrate. Yet virginity still engrossed him, and he was readier
than he knew for the retreat which began on November 30, 1896. In
charge of the retreat was Father James A. Cullen,* and his sermons,
delivered, as was customary, according to the prescription of St. Ignatius Loyola's *Spiritual Exercises,* elicited a more than customary number of twinges from hell-fire. All Joyce's mounting scruples against his
own conduct found a fierce justification. He saw himself as a beast,
eating like a beast, lusting like a beast, dying like a beast, and dreamed
of a pure love for a virgin heart.†

---

* In identifying Father Cullen as the preacher of the sermons in the retreat, Thomas
Bodkin says: 'Father Cullen's phrasing was characteristic. Where most preachers
would begin their sermons on such occasions by saying "Dear boys," he had a habit
of addressing his congregation as "My dear little brothers in Jesus Christ," which
always struck me as a repellent mode of address. Moreover, he used to wear as few
Jesuits do on such occasions, the heavy cloak over his gown of which Joyce speaks.
Like a good many of the community of Belvedere at that time he had a distinct
trace of sadism in his character, e.g., he found it humorous to offer to shake hands
with young boys and then squeeze their hands until they yelled with pain. Belvedere, during the period when Joyce and I were there as pupils, was not a happy
school. In that it was quite unlike Clongowes which we both also attended. Father
Henry was the rector of Belvedere then, a harsh insensitive man. This, I think, was
ultimately recognised generally by all who had dealings with him and I for one,
who owe a great deal to the Jesuits and regard the order with affection and esteem,
never met among them anyone else of the type.'

† Joyce parodies in *Ulysses* this gamut of sensations, when Bloom cannot bear the
bestial eating in a restaurant, rejects thoughts of death at the cemetery, is depressed
by the brothel. Joyce compares Stephen's soul to a flower, in *A Portrait,* and Bloom's
sexual organ to a flower in *Ulysses.* The change is not merely one of mockery;
rather in *Ulysses* sensations once religious for Joyce have become secularized, matters of preference and fastidiousness rather than of sinfulness.

He did not confess in the college chapel; to abase himself before Father Henry was still too much to bear. He went instead, according to a sister, to the Church Street chapel. A Capuchin there listened to the tale from a boy of a man's sins with sympathy rather than indignation. It was Joyce's first confession since Easter, and it brought about an eager spirituality in his conduct which heightened his reputation, secured until then by hypocrisy, for piety. He prayed interminably, mortified himself and labored to achieve a virtue as extreme as his sinfulness seemed to him before to have been. In *A Portrait of the Artist* Joyce later mocked his own religious revival a little by a commercial metaphor dressed out in purple rhythm: 'His life seemed to have drawn near to eternity; every thought, word and deed, every instance of consciousness could be made to revibrate radiantly in heaven: and at times his sense of such immediate repercussion was so lively that he seemed to feel his soul in devotion pressing like fingers the keyboard of a great cash register and to see the amount of his purchase start forth immediately in heaven, not as a number but as a frail column of incense or as a slender flower.' [32] He was a miser of grace.

The reformation lasted some months, probably well into 1897; his sister Eileen saw him saying his rosary piously on the way to school, [33] and Stanislaus, who was losing his faith with less compunction, watched his brother in perplexity. Then James began to bethink himself once again. It seemed to him now that the sermons during the retreat had played on the weakest part of his nature, and that the confession wrung from him by such methods could only be insincere. What had seemed piety now seemed only the last spasm of religious terror. This point of view, which he gives Stephen in *A Portrait,* was growing in his own mind, as later letters and remarks confirm. It was also true, as he declared flatly some time afterwards to a friend, that sexual continence was impossible for him. He felt he must choose between continual guilt and some heretical exoneration of the senses. By conviction Joyce could not abase himself before Catholic doctrine; by temperament he could not abase himself before other men.

As his faith in Catholicism tottered, a counter-process began: his faith in art, which is written by and about people with faults, grew great. The exterior signs of this change were at first trivial. At Belvedere he took to writing both prose and verse. His brother remembered one story, intended for the magazine *Titbits,* mainly to make money. In it a man who has attended a masked ball dressed as a prominent Russian diplomat is walking by the Russian Embassy on his way home,

thinking about the 'laughing witch,' his fiancée, when a Nihilist tries
to assassinate him. The police arrest him as well as his assailant, but
his fiancée, hearing of the attempt, realizes what has happened and
comes to the police station to explain and release him. Stanislaus Joyce
says that 'the few sentences that described the reverie' about the girl
were 'not without grace.' [34] Three or four years later James rewrote the
story simply as a burlesque—a transformation that he was often to
practice with ideas taken at first with some seriousness—and he refers
to it jocularly in *Ulysses* as 'Matcham's Masterstroke.'

He also began a series of prose sketches to which he gave the title
Silhouettes. They were written in the first person singular, and one
recalled by Stanislaus described a dingy street along which the narrator walks after dark. 'His attention is attracted by two figures in
violent agitation on a lowered window-blind illuminated from within,
the burly figure of a man, staggering and threatening with upraised
fist, and the smaller sharp-faced figure of a nagging woman. A blow is
struck and the light goes out. The narrator waits to see if anything
happens afterwards. Yes, the window-blind is illuminated again dimly,
by a candle no doubt, and the woman's sharp profile appears accompanied by two small heads, just above the window-ledge, of children
wakened by the noise. The woman's finger is pointed in warning. She
is saying, "Don't waken Pa." ' [35] This is avant-garde writing of the
school of General Booth.

Joyce's first collection of poems was called *Moods*, and the title suggests the influence of W. B. Yeats, whose early volumes insisted that
moods were metaphysical realities to be transfixed by the artist. Like
Silhouettes, Moods has not survived. The only example of his verse
of this time is a translation of Horace's ode, '*O fons Bandusiae*.'

> Brighter than glass Bandusian spring
>   For mellow wine and flowers meet,
> The morrow thee a kid shall bring
>   Boding of rivalry and sweet
> Love in his swelling forms. In vain
> He, wanton offspring, deep shall stain
> Thy clear cold streams with crimson rain.
>
> The raging dog star's season thou,
>   Still safe from in the heat of day,
> When oxen weary of the plough
>   Yieldst thankful cool for herds that stray.
> Be of the noble founts! I sing
> The oak tree o'er thine echoing
> Crags, thy waters murmuring.[36]

Crags still echo, streams are still clear, the founts are noble.° The power of language which Joyce was accumulating was still suited better to writing classroom exercises than to vying with Horace.

In 1896 Joyce, being underage,[37] did not take the Intermediate Examinations. In 1897 he made his highest score, and was thirteenth in a group of 49, for which he received an exhibition of £30 a year for two years. He also received the prize of £3 for the best English composition written by anyone in Ireland in his grade. This success made him Belvedere's best scholar; he was captain of the house in the following year, when he was in the Senior Grade, and it was always he whom the other boys deputed to beard the rector about the possibility of a free day.†

After school hours his social life, apart from sporadic visits to Nighttown, seems to have centered chiefly around the home of David Sheehy, M.P., at 2 Belvedere Place. The Sheehys had open house every Sunday night, and encouraged the livelier students to visit them and their six children. James and Stanislaus were there regularly, and at Mrs. Sheehy's invitation James several times stayed overnight. His closest friend in the family was Richard Sheehy, a plump humorous boy who called him James Disgustin' Joyce,‡ and reminded him that the name Sheehy was an Irish variant of the name Joyce,°° but he was on good terms also with Eugene, a year behind him at Belvedere, and with the four Sheehy daughters, Margaret, Hannah, Mary, and Kathleen. For Mary, the youngest and prettiest, Joyce conceived a small, rich passion which, unsuspected by her, lasted for several years. She queened his imagination in a way that, modest and a little abashed before him as she was, she could not have believed. He was more at ease with her brothers; to her his manner, abrupt because of shyness, seemed sometimes rude.[38]

The Sheehys were fond of singing and playing games. Joyce frequently said nothing until the entertainment began. He liked to be asked to sing, and would even get up songs for the purpose. Once he stopped Alfred Bergan on the street to ask him to sing 'McSorley's Twins,' which he committed to memory on the spot and sang that evening at the Sheehys' house. His taste was for sentimental as well as

---

° '. . . that fount Bandusian shall play liquick music and after odours sigh of musk.' *Finnegans Wake* (280).
† Joyce is said to have edited a mimeographed paper informally published at the school, but the report may be inaccurate.[39]
‡ His teacher Dempsey teased him about his middle name by calling him 'Gussie.' [40]
°° Joyce called the name 'Sheehy' later 'epicene,' because 'made up of the feminine and masculine personal pronouns.' Its being cognate to his own jibed with a theory he had later of himself (like Bloom) as a womanly man. See pp. 379-81, 427.

humorous songs, Irish and French and Elizabethan too. Among the Irish songs through which he swaggered or sighed were 'The Man Who Played the Flute at Inniscorthy,' 'Dimetrius O'Flanagan McCarthy,' 'The Croppy Boy,' and 'Blarney Castle.' The English songs included ballads like 'Turpin Hero,' songs of Henry VIII ('Pastime and good company') and later Dowland ('Weep ye no more, sad fountains'), or something more recent such as 'Take a pair of sparkling eyes' from *The Gondoliers*. One of his French songs was the gay '*Viens, poupoule.*' He had a fine bouncy version of 'The Man Who Broke the Bank at Monte Carlo.' Joyce sang all in a sweet but rather weak tenor voice.

While James entertained the company, his brother Stanislaus sat ill at ease, feeling slow-witted in comparison. Mary Sheehy (later Mrs. Kettle) remembered a game in which James's suavity contrasted with his brother's gaucherie. In the game, 'The Queen of Sheba,' the blindfolded victim was permitted to kiss the queen. Stanislaus reluctantly did so, complaining, 'Ohhh, it's like a wet sponge!' while James, on reaching the same point in the game, asked smoothly, 'Is there any alternative?' before administering a perfunctory peck.[41] Yet his boldness in company diminished quickly in tête-à-têtes. When he danced with Mary Sheehy, he held her so limply and loosely that she could scarcely follow him. Once, perceiving her difficulty, Joyce said, 'Hold my thumb.' Thinking he had said 'tongue,' she protested, 'Oh, how can I do that?' Joyce replied, 'My thumb!' 'Oh,' she said, 'I thought you said your tongue.[42] At this Joyce gave a whoop of laughter; verbal slips, especially those that verged unconsciously on indecorum, were already his delight. Then he went on dancing in the same way, as shyly removed as before. Another time a cousin of the Sheehys came up from Limerick for a visit; with a country carelessness she threw her arm around Joyce's shoulder and laughed uproariously whenever he made a witty remark.[43] Joyce, from whom everyone else kept his distance, sat stiff and cold during this demonstration of rural folkways.*

At charades, the favorite game of the household, Joyce could be depended upon to do or say something ingenious. Asked to represent the word *sunset*, he sat in a rounded arm chair with just the top of his head showing over its top.[44] Playing 'Adamant,' in a variation of a charade, he listened expressionless to the reports of catastrophes: his house was on fire, his goods destroyed, his wife and children burned to

* Mary Colum tells a curious incident that happened a year or two later. A girl in a university residence received an anonymous post card requesting a rendezvous, and, assuming it came from Joyce, she wrote a disdainful reply. Joyce answered with greater hauteur that it was ridiculous to suppose he would have sent such an invitation in the first place, that he did not remember having seen her, and in any case never communicated with girl students who were not family friends.[45]

death. Then a look of concern came over his face as he said, 'What happened to my dog?' [46] Once he and a friend were playing the part of lions to whom a Christian was about to be thrown when a sober young solicitor, Charles Murray, who had never visited the house before, came into the room. They sprang upon him, tore at his clothes, and, still more leonine, broke his glasses. Murray, unamused, picked up the pieces and returned no more. [47]

Sometimes there would be burlesques of operas or plays; Joyce was got up in one of Mrs. Sheehy's old gowns as Carmen and, after taking off the stage manners of opera stars, sang beautifully, 'L'amour est l'enfant de Bohème.' Another time he played Hamlet, and, when informed of Ophelia's tragic death, said in the accent of Moore Street (Dublin's market street), 'Ach, the puirr gurrl!' Another game, mentioned by Patricia Hutchins in *James Joyce's World*, was a play on place names: 'What Chapel is it? [Chapelizod]' 'I wasn't Lucan,' or 'Harold's Cross because Terenure [Terry knew her].' [48]

Although he liked this frivolity, Joyce in his intellectual position was drawing further away from his classmates. His period of piety done with, he read a great many books of all kinds at high speed. When he liked an author, as Stanislaus observed, he did not stop until he had read everything by him. There are traces of some of these enthusiasms. One was for George Meredith, whose *The Ordeal of Richard Feverel* and *The Tragic Comedians* he particularly enjoyed.* Another was for Hardy; he went to the nearby Capel Street lending library and borrowed Hardy's *Tess of the D'Urbervilles*. The librarian warned John Joyce his son was reading dangerous books. James reassured his father easily, but perhaps in response, sent Stanislaus to borrow *Jude the Obscure* for him. Stanislaus, confused by what he had heard of Hardy, started out to ask the librarian for *Jude the Obscene*. [49] Joyce liked this slip so well that in later life he told the story as if it had happened to him and not to Stanislaus. [50] In a few years he was bored by Hardy, but he read him with interest now and never lapsed in respect for Hardy's stand against popular taste. [51]

But the principal new pressure upon him was the work of Ibsen, another genius who arose from a small, parochial people. Ibsen was then seventy years old, and his name was of course well known in England, less so in Ireland. He was still the object of both enthusiasm and disdain. The *Athenaeum* continued to frown on his work as immoral, and from another point of view Yeats found it, except in the later symbolical plays, middle-class and passé. Some of the enthusiasts, on the other hand, praised Ibsen for cross-examining conventional

* But see p. 570.

morality; this was the point of view of Bernard Shaw in *The Quintes-sence of Ibsenism* (1891), a book that Joyce read. Joyce's view was different: he caught from Ibsen what he called 'a spirit of wayward boyish beauty' that blew through him 'like a keen wind.' [52] Although he could read him as yet only in translation, drinking him, as Yeats said, through William Archer's hygienic bottle,[53] he perceived that his master's irony went hand in hand with idealism. The notion of artistic honesty carried to the point where it is almost self-defeating encouraged Joyce in his own rigorous self-examination. For him as for Ibsen, truth was then more an unmasking than a revelation. He approved also of the quality of aloofness in Ibsen that led him to leave his country and call himself an exile. Truth as judgment and disclosure, and exile as the artistic condition: these were to be the positive and negative poles of Joyce's own state of mind. The figure of Ibsen, whose temper, he said in *Stephen Hero*, was that of an archangel,[54] occupied for Joyce in art the place that the figure of Parnell had taken on for him in national life.

Through Ibsen, largely, Joyce became convinced of the importance of drama; and, while he did not yet try playwriting, he went to the theater as regularly as he could afford it, and wrote reviews of every play he saw so as to contrast his opinions with those of newspaper reviewers. Stanislaus Joyce reports the curious sequel of one such excursion, to see Sudermann's *Magda*. The next day, discussing the play with his parents, who had gone with him, Joyce said, 'The subject of the play is genius breaking out in the home and against the home. You needn't have gone to see it. It's going to happen in your own house.' * [55]

During this senior year at Belvedere Joyce began to think of himself as a beleaguered citadel constantly refusing the enemy's tempting offers of peace with honor. The first offer, ingenuous but still importunate, was that of physical health. Belvedere was at last opening a gymnasium, with a bald sergeant major named Wright as instructor, and there was a good deal of propaganda for exercise. Joyce did not refuse to par-ticipate; he was in fact elected secretary of the gymnasium, and he performed so tirelessly, raising himself again and again on a horizontal bar, that Wright would tell him at last, 'That's enough, Joyce.' [56] But he was far from converted to being healthy; it smacked too much of other forms of dubious improvement, of the correlative *Spiritual Exer-cises* for example; he mocked it by arriving one day all doubled up and

---

* *Magda's* philosophy of life may well have helped to shape Joyce's. As she says, 'And one thing more, my friend,—sin! We must sin if we wish to grow. To become greater than our sins is worth more than all the purity you preach.' When her father asks her if she is pure, she replies that she has 'remained—true to myself.' Stephen thinks with ecstasy in Chapter IV of *A Portrait* (432 [303]), 'To live, to err, to fall, to triumph, to recreate life out of life!'

saying to Wright, 'I've come to be cured.' [57] The second propaganda he resisted was that of national revival, which had filtered down from various organizations like the Gaelic League into the school. He was not ready to accept all his nation; as a Parnellite he was suspicious of attempts to ignore old wounds, preferring to cherish them, so that he appeared on October 6 at Belvedere with the ivy leaf on his collar to commemorate Parnell's death day. An instructor, Father Tierney, made him take it off inside the school, but granted that he might wear it outside.[58] The last appealing voice was that of the director of studies who suggested to Joyce, in a solemn interview when, according to Stanislaus Joyce,[59] the boy was sixteen, that he consider becoming a priest. By now priesthood meant imprisonment and darkness for the soul, and Joyce was committed to art and to life, whether damnation lay that way or not.

In *A Portrait of the Artist* Stephen Dedalus walks along the north strand, towards the end of his school days, and suddenly sees a handsome girl, skirts drawn up, wading in the water. Her beauty affects him like an illumination of truth, and vindicates his choice of life and art, even if life means also disorder and art suffering. The incident actually occurred to Joyce about that time.[60] No doubt he was looking for a symbol of 'profane perfection of mankind,' [61] and this one remained fixed in his memory as a counter to the shadowy, fleshless face of the beckoning priest. He entered now without scruple 'the fair courts of life.' [62]

Joyce's separation from Catholicism was of course not known; his prestige in the college was established, and in later years he insisted to Gorman that his relations with Father Henry, whom he regarded as quite different from Father Daly at Clongowes, were at the last very good. Other witnesses indicate that Joyce's memory was at fault. As a senior boy he coasted along in his studies, and never arrived on time. Even Dempsey became exasperated, and sent him to report his bad conduct to Father Henry. The rector was teaching a Latin class when Joyce obediently marched in and announced that Mr. Dempsey had instructed him to say he was late for school. Henry delivered a long lecture to him to which he listened, as Eugene Sheehy—who was in the class—remembers, 'in unrepentant silence.' When it was over, he added as if by way of afterthought, in the same bored tone, 'Mr. Dempsey told me to tell you, sir, that I was half an hour late yesterday too.' The rector expostulated at length again. When he had finished, Joyce added, almost with a yawn, 'Mr. Dempsey told me to tell you, sir, that I have not been in time for school any day this month.' [63]

The class depended upon Joyce to ask the rector questions about the

catechism so as to fill up time, and his skill in baiting Henry became
so well known that his friends Albrecht and Vincent Connolly urged
him to take off the rector in the school play, on the grounds that otherwise it would be 'bloody tripe.' [64] The play was F. Anstey's *Vice Versa*,
and was probably given in May 1898. It dealt farcically with the theme
of father against son that Joyce was to use to such good purpose in his
later books. Now, as the schoolteacher, he parodied all the rector's
mannerisms.[*] The audience was amused, and even Henry, who sat in
the first row, professed to enjoy the performance.

Joyce's final dispute with Henry occurred the next month, just before
he left Belvedere. The catechetical examination of the school was held
on June 14, the day before the national Intermediate Examinations.
Joyce, along with Albrecht Connolly and two other boys,[65] failed to
show up for it. The rector was incensed at this public disobedience,
and rejected their plea that they needed the time to study for the other
examinations. He said they had committed an act of rebellion, and
forbade them to take the Intermediates at all. Fortunately, the young
master, MacErlaine, who taught French and considered Joyce his best
pupil, was able to persuade the rector to change his mind. Joyce took
the examinations, consequently, but his extra day of study did not help
him much. Except in English, he did badly, as a comparison of his
results in 1897 and 1898 shows.[66] This time he did not win an exhibition, although he retained the one he had won in 1897; but he did win
the prize of £4 for English composition, and Professor William Magen-
nis of University College, Dublin, who read the papers, remarked that
this young man's was publishable.[67]

Belvedere College had done well for Joyce, by giving him excellent
training in English and three foreign languages. More than that, it had
supplied him with a decorous backdrop for his turbulent uprisings and
downgoings, a standard against which he would set his own standard.
He knew he could disregard its religious teachings, and indifference to
Catholic belief attracted him now, except for sporadic angers, more
than impiety. The image of what he must leave behind was almost
complete.

[*] He was to do so again at the beginning of his story, 'An Encounter.'

1898–1900

You were bred, fed, fostered and fattened from holy childhood up in
this two easter island ... and now, forsooth, a nogger among the
blankards of this dastard century, you have become of twosome twi-
minds forenenst gods, hidden and discovered, nay, condemned fool,
anarch, egoarch, hiresiarch, you have reared your disunited kingdom
on the vacuum of your own most intensely doubtful soul.

—*Finnegans Wake* (188)

UNIVERSITY College, Dublin, when Joyce attended it, was struggling for distinction. The early years of the college,[1] which John
Henry Newman founded as the Catholic University in 1853, were halting and tentative. Newman himself was unable to continue his work
with it; he went back to England in 1857, and resigned the rectorship
a year later. For the next fifteen years the university languished because it had neither private endowment nor governmental support.
It occupied a diminishing part of some magnificent houses on Stephen's
Green, and the faded splendor of Buck Whaley's Mansion at No. 88—
the principal college building—seemed an index of the college's decline.
A new rector devised grandiose plans for building a great university
on the outskirts of Dublin, in the style of Oxford or Cambridge, but
nothing came of them.

The university's chief hope lay in Parliament. After many delays,
and largely because of the proddings of Irish members, a rather inadequate Universities bill was passed in 1879. The government was willing
to provide for higher education in Ireland, and recognized that Trinity
College was too small and Protestant to serve the many Catholic students. But it wished to insure that higher education be as secular as
possible. The bill therefore provided ingeniously for support of University College (a new name for Catholic University), but as a part
of the Royal University, not as an autonomous unit. The Royal Uni-

versity would be the examining body for constituent colleges in Dublin, Cork, Galway, and Belfast. Examinations would be in secular subjects, so that if students were obliged to spend much time on Catholic studies they would suffer in their marks. This procedure set the tone for Joyce's training at the end of the century. Although the Jesuits had taken over the college in 1883, they had not introduced much religious instruction. The president, Father William Delany, was one of the most effective Catholic educators in Ireland, and he disregarded insistence from other Catholic groups that the curriculum be weighted more heavily with religion.[2] He rightly considered that the effect of having at least half the faculty in surplices was profounder than it might seem to those outside.

Students at University College were dimly aware that Trinity College, half a mile away, had a more distinguished faculty. In classics Mahaffy [*] and Tyrrell, lofty and hostile eminences, were beyond their University College counterparts, especially after the death of Gerard Manley Hopkins, who in a state of exalted misery held the U.C.D. classics chair during the 'eighties. In English the professor at Trinity was Edward Dowden, a gifted scholar, while at University College, when Joyce arrived, the professor was Thomas Arnold, less impressive and enfeebled by age.[†] [3] Arnold was Matthew Arnold's brother, and spent much of his life half-drowning in religious crises which his brother neatly forded. He had to be converted to Catholicism not once but twice, the second time at the expense of his candidacy for the chair of Anglo-Saxon at Oxford. Arnold was supple enough in his criticism to approve a paper Joyce wrote for him on the dramatic inadequacies of *Macbeth*.[4]

Joyce studied English for a time also with Father Joseph Darlington, the dean of studies, who like Arnold was a convert and English. Darlington knew of Joyce's wide reading, and in a first lecture in a course he mentioned Stephen Phillips's play, *Paolo and Francesca*, then asked if anyone had read it; there was no response, so he turned to Joyce and said, 'Have you read it, Mr. Joyce?' Joyce answered in a bored voice, 'Yes.' [5] Having demonstrated his omniscience, he thereafter almost never came to class. Darlington was in Joyce's eyes a little sinister, but was generally thought to be harmless and rather pitiable; he seems

[*] J. P. Mahaffy later remarked to Gerald Griffin, 'James Joyce is a living argument in favor of my contention that it was a mistake to establish a separate university for the aborigines of this island—for the corner-boys who spit into the Liffey.' [6]
[†] When Joyce knew him, Arnold had lost the turbulence ascribed to him (under the name of Philip Hewson) in Arthur Hugh Clough's *The Bothie*.

to have suspected Joyce's religious defection, but was too pliant * to
try to take a firm line with him. His mildly disapproving eye followed
Joyce for four years, and Joyce's mildly disapproving eye has followed
Darlington, the dean of studies in *Stephen Hero* and *A Portrait*, into
eternity.

Arnold's successor as professor of English was Father George O'Neill,
a useful man in college activities but an immoderate partisan of the
view that Bacon wrote Shakespeare's plays. The idea held Joyce's
interest long enough for him to guffaw at it during a public discussion
at the college,⁷ and to have Stephen mock and discard it in *Ulysses*.
It was probably O'Neill, according to Judge Eugene Sheehy, who, at
Joyce's oral examination for the Bachelor of Arts degree, asked him,
'How is poetic justice exemplified in the play of *King Lear?*' Joyce
answered 'I don't know.' The examiner prodded him, 'Oh, come, Mr.
Joyce, you are not fair to yourself. I feel sure you have read the play.'
'Oh yes,' replied Joyce in his most obnoxious manner, 'but I don't
understand your question. The phrase "poetic justice" is unmeaning
jargon so far as I am concerned.' ⁸

In Italian and French Joyce had the advantage of studying with
native speakers. In spite of the seeming rigidity of his education, he
was lucky enough to find, at every point in both school and university,
at least one thoroughly sympathetic, liberal teacher. The Italian lecturer was a Jesuit, Father Charles Ghezzi, who had come to Ireland
from a long residence in India. He gave Joyce a good grounding in
Dante and in D'Annunzio, a combination more likely then than it
seems now. He and his student had many passionate discussions of
literature and philosophy, while Eugene Sheehy, the only other member of the class, sat silent. Joyce exalted Dante at the expense of Milton,
whom he fiercely rejected, as Yeats, Pound, and Eliot were to do
also. Ghezzi did not mind,⁹ but all the Irish writers except Yeats, to
whom Joyce later expounded his view, were outraged by it. As to
D'Annunzio, Joyce was convinced that his *Il Fuoco* (*The Flame*) was
the most important achievement in the novel since Flaubert,¹⁰ and
an advance upon Flaubert. He must have arrived at this opinion, an
easier one to come to at that time, because D'Annunzio turned his own
iconoclastic life into fiction, eliminated action, and made the novel a
prolonged lyric in prose. D'Annunzio's taste for the singular adjective,
'white air' for example, also attracted him. Joyce, whose novels read

---

* Father Darlington's manner was so instantly agreeable that, when a student came
to inform him he was going to get married, Darlington replied, according to legend,
'Just the very thing, Mr. Coyne, just the very thing. I was about to do the same
myself.' ¹¹

so differently, yet followed D'Annunzio in these directions. At his last examination in Italian at University College, Joyce was the only male student, the others being eight or nine women. 'A Daniel among the lionesses,' as he described himself later to Louis Gillet, he was ill prepared in the factual material on which he was questioned, but he had studied D'Annunzio so closely that he could imitate his manner, and the examiners, after some disagreement, passed him.[12]

For his courses, and beyond them, Joyce read among Italian poets and storytellers. He talked of Cavalcanti, he grew interested in the conflicts of Guelphs and Ghibellines, and among philosophers he found an unexpected master in Giordano Bruno. Bruno had long been considered a clerical villain, but his vindication had begun. In 1889 a statue to him was erected in Rome in the same Campo dei Fiori where he had been burned at the stake in 1600. Ghezzi piously reminded Joyce that Bruno was a terrible heretic, and Joyce dryly rejoined, 'Yes, and he was terribly burned.'[13] Bruno's theory of an ultimate unity and its terrestrial division into contraries attracted Joyce, perhaps, because he saw his art as a reconciler of those opposites within his own mind which he would later personify as Shem and Shaun. In *Finnegans Wake* he made Bruno of Nola Irish by confusing him with the Dublin booksellers, Browne and Nolan.

Ghezzi had the merit of perceiving his student's interest in esthetics, and of encouraging him to formulate theories about it. Joyce had looked into Thomas Aquinas enough to know Thomas's doctrine that those things are beautiful which, when seen, please us,* and had hit upon the idea of isolating this dictum from Thomas's theory of final causes and using it as the basis for excluding instruction from among the purposes of art. Like Shelley, he spoke of the true and the beautiful, and left out the good; his classmates and most of his professors were scandalized and assumed, quite wrongly, that Joyce was thereby condoning immoral art; in reality he was opposing only a narrow didacticism. Ghezzi was sympathetic to him, and the two men retained an affection for each other. Ghezzi appears in Joyce's books with a benign character and the euphonious name of Almidano Artifoni.†

Joyce's professor of French was Édouard Cadic, a heavily moustached Breton. Cadic was also receptive to his student's talents; he read with delight Joyce's paper on 'Cloches,'[14] in which the style tintinnabulated to suit the subject; and when Joyce invented the term

---

* *Pulchra enim dicuntur ea quae visa placent.' Summa Theologica* I, q. 5, art. 4. See William T. Noon, *Joyce and Aquinas* (1957).
† Joyce took this name from the director of the Berlitz School in Trieste.

idée-mère as a French equivalent for *leitmotif,* he exclaimed happily, 'For that I will give you my daughter.'[15] It is a term that usefully describes the way in which a concept like *river* in Joyce's writing will serve to mother a whole chapter of river names and themes all done in rivery prose.

Joyce found Cadic's class a pleasant setting for flamboyant tom-foolery. He entered the room twenty minutes late one day, and, paying no attention to the professor, went over to one of the large front win-dows, threw it up, and put his head out. Cadic, by way of riposte, went to the other window, opened it, and putting his head out too, stared severely at Joyce. '*Bonjour, monsieur,*' said Joyce gravely, 'I was just counting the carriages in Alderman Kernan's funeral.'[16] Both the impudence and the statistical curiosity were in character.

Joyce and another student, George Clancy, liked to rouse Cadic to flights of miscomprehension. In a favorite little drama, Joyce would snicker offensively at Clancy's efforts to translate a passage into Eng-lish. Clancy pretended to be furious and demanded an apology, which Joyce refused. Then Clancy would challenge Joyce to a duel in the Phoenix Park. The horrified Cadic would rush in to conciliate the fiery Celts, and after much byplay would persuade them to shake hands.[17]

The students at University College were more unusual than their professors. Three of Joyce's close friends, Clancy, Francis Skeffington, and Thomas Kettle, indicated the extent of the earnestness of their youth by losing their lives in battle, each for a different cause. Clancy was to end as a victim of the Black and Tans, murdered while he was mayor of Limerick. His unfortunate death was appropriate in that, even as a young man, Clancy subscribed ardently to every aspect of the national movement. He helped form a branch of the Gaelic League at University College, and persuaded his friends, including even Joyce for a time, to take lessons in Irish. Joyce gave them up because Patrick Pearse, the instructor, found it necessary to exalt Irish by denigrating English, and in particular denounced the word 'Thunder'—a favorite of Joyce's—as an example of verbal inadequacy.[18] Clancy was an enthusiast also for Gaelic sports like hurling, and therefore a great friend of Michael Cusack, the founder of the Gaelic Athletic Associa-tion.* He brought Joyce to meet Cusack a few times, and Joyce liked

---

* Cusack was of middle height but had extremely broad shoulders. He usually wore a broad-brimmed soft hat and instead of trousers wore knee breeches. Carrying a heavy blackthorn, he would come into a pub and shout at the waiter, 'I'm Citizen Cusack from the Parish of Carron in the Barony of Burren in the County of Clare, you Protestant dog!' He was born in 1847, taught at Blackrock College and Clon-gowes Wood College, and later opened a grinding establishment. He founded the Gaelic Athletic Association in 1884, and an article of that time gives some sense of

him little enough to make him model the narrow-minded and rhetorical Cyclops in *Ulysses*. Clancy appears in Joyce's early work as Madden; he is the only friend who calls Stephen by his first name, and Joyce later confirmed that Clancy alone among his classmates did so. Madden (called Davin in *A Portrait*) labors with rustic sincerity to make Stephen more Irish, and Stephen's relations with him are simpler and more relaxed than with his other friends. There is no indication, however, that Joyce ever called Clancy 'George.'

After himself, James Joyce told Stanislaus, the cleverest man at University College was Francis Skeffington. Skeffington, like Clancy, died at the hands of the British, but a few years sooner, during the Easter Rebellion of 1916, when he quixotically tried to dissuade the soldiers from looting.* As a young man Skeffington, four years Joyce's senior, was the college iconoclast. To protest against uniformity in dress he wore plus fours and was known as 'Knickerbockers.' To protest against shaving he grew a beard, then went on to denounce smoking, drinking, and vivisecting. Joyce called him 'Hairy Jaysus.' Skeffington demanded equal rights for women, and supported pacifism and vegetarianism with equal fervor. A great framer and signer of petitions, he sought to persuade Joyce to sign a petition to encourage the Czar in his pursuit of universal peace, but Joyce retorted, according to *A Portrait*, 'If you must have a Jesus, let it be a legitimate Jesus.'

Joyce took pleasure in so puncturing Skeffington's armor, in asking Socratic questions of Socrates. If Skeffington was so rational, how had he managed to preserve his belief in Catholicism? To this Skeffington would reply earnestly, but with some discomfort, that he intended before long to take a year off to study the religious question. He did in fact give up the Church later. If Skeffington believed in feminism, did he think the police force should be composed of women? In *A Portrait* Skeffington appears as McCann, anxious to dispute, very serious, and, with a chocolate bar always in one pocket,[19] a little

---

his style: 'No movement having for its object the social and political advancement of a nation from the tyranny of imported and enforced customs and manners can be regarded as perfect if it has not made adequate provision for the preservation and cultivation of the national pastimes of the people. Voluntary neglect of such pastimes is a sure sign of national decay and approaching dissolution. . . . The corrupting influences which for several years have been devastating the sporting grounds of our cities and towns are fast spreading to our rural population. Foreign and hostile forces and the pernicious influence of the hated and hitherto dominant race drove the Irish people from their trysting places at the crossroads and hurling fields back to their cabins where but a few short years before famine and fever reigned supreme.'

* For this incident see p. 411.

absurd, a less agile debater in fiction than he was in fact. He in turn was always trying to draw Joyce out with some direct question. Once he asked him, according to Stanislaus, 'Have you ever been in love?' Joyce replied with an evasive shift of tense, 'How would I write the most perfect love songs of our time if I were in love? A poet must always write about a past or a future emotion, never about a present one. If it is a regular, right-down, honest-to-God, "till-death-us-two-part" affair, it will get out of hand and spoil his verse. Poetry must have a safety valve properly adjusted. A poet's job is to write tragedies, not to be an actor in one.' [20] This kind of answer, which turned the argument to abstraction, played neatly on Skeffington's own tendency.

In spite of intellectual differences Joyce and Skeffington got on well enough. Joyce devised an amusing test of Skeffington's dogged insistence upon all kinds of rights; he offered to give him a half crown if Skeffington would buy a halfpenny worth of gooseberries at the most expensive fruit shop in Sackville Street and offer a sovereign in payment. Skeffington agreed, and from the doorway Joyce watched the irritated salesgirl and the unintimidated libertarian, and whooped with glee.[21] He met Skeffington chiefly at the Sheehys' house; eventually Skeffington was to marry Hannah Sheehy and, refusing to allow marriage even nominally to compromise the equality of the sexes, he changed his name to Sheehy-Skeffington.

Another gifted friend, whom Joyce alone seems to have rated below Skeffington, was Thomas Kettle, killed while fighting in the British army in 1916.* Kettle followed Skeffington in marrying into the Sheehy family, his wife being Mary, the girl whom Joyce during his university days had not forgotten. Kettle was an intellectual Catholic and nationalist; soon after his graduation he became a Member of Parliament and the spokesman for the younger intellectuals. In the university he was already saying, 'If Ireland is to become a new Ireland she must first become European,' an idea that was Joyce's too, but Kettle's passionate and courageous (or, as Joyce put it, 'too demonstrative') concern with the national question prevented his assuming Joyce's cosmopolitanism. He later disapproved of the unpatriotic candor of *Dubliners*. Kettle does not appear in *A Portrait*, but some of his attitudes, such as the necessity of making Ireland European, are used in *Exiles*. He was the only other student with whom Joyce discussed Thomas Aquinas, and he pleased Joyce with the remark that 'The difficulty about Aquinas is that what he says is so like what the man in the street says.' [22] In Paris later someone was to object to Joyce, who was discussing Aquinas, 'That has nothing to do with us,' and

* For Kettle's death see p. 412.

Joyce replied, perhaps recalling Kettle, 'It has everything to do with us.' [23]

There were three other young men whom Joyce knew well at University College: Curran, Cosgrave, and Byrne. The first two were almost opposites: Constantine P. Curran was goodhearted and controlled; Joyce granted his cleverness as well. *A Portrait* represents him as interested in food (he was inclined to be fat); he was also well-versed in literature and architecture. Afterwards he became Registrar of the Supreme Court. He shared Joyce's taste for trips to the continent, but he was pious, and more pious than continental, as he demonstrated by sympathizing with the mob who jeered in outrage at the first production of Synge's *The Playboy of the Western World.* Joyce respected his critical judgment, however, and in the course of his lifetime was to owe Curran a great many kindnesses.

Vincent Cosgrave had a ruddy Neronic face and careless habits. He had a good mind but did not train it; he appraised Joyce shrewdly and early, and said to Byrne, 'Joyce is the most remarkable man any of us have met.' He was committed to idleness and rancorous unsuccess. As he grew older his character was to deteriorate further, and his death in the Thames, presumably from suicide, was a blunt admission of futility. Cosgrave gratified Joyce by always being ready to walk with him, talk with him, or (if they had money) to accompany him to a Tyrone Street brothel. His talk, whether of religion or women, was coarse and witty; Joyce, who had not yet begun to drink, affected along with abstemiousness a disdain for low talk and public misbehavior that gave him the appearance almost of virtue. He liked the appearance, and enjoyed taking sometimes the anomalous role of chiding schoolmaster with Cosgrave.

But Joyce's closest friendship at the College was with John Francis Byrne, the 'Cranly' of his novels.[24] Though he had known Byrne casually at Belvedere, he did not see much of him until later. 'It was in favor of this young man,' says Joyce in *Stephen Hero,* with deference for his own youthful pomposity, 'that Stephen decided to break his commandment of reticence.' Byrne was handsome, athletic, and clever; he excelled at chess and handball, and disregarded his studies even more cavalierly than Joyce. He had been brought up by two older sisters after the early death of his parents, and during the summer disappeared into Wicklow, where his activities were so unaffectedly rural as to puzzle his city friend. Byrne's distinction was not in his speech; his ideas, said Stanislaus Joyce to his brother, were commonplace, and the best defense James could think of was that they were 'daringly commonplace'; [25] in a world of foppishness, Byrne had the courage to be plain. But it was his manner that attracted: he moved about with the air of a man who knows all the secrets but disinclines to exercise the power he thereby possesses. Standing among other young men on the steps of the National Library or of University College, he listened to their small fallacies and did not deign to correct them. His power over Joyce came from his habit of refraining from comment: Joyce's admissions about his feelings towards family, friends, and church, about his overweening ambitions, struck like waves against Byrne's cryptic taciturnity. Byrne listened to Joyce's confidences without offering any of his own, and, as Joyce noted, without conferring absolution.° 26

Joyce needed no other friend as he did Byrne. He would wait for an hour for Byrne to win a chess game, as he usually did, so that afterwards he might capture that receptive but neutral ear for new disclosures. For his part, Byrne was as fascinated by Joyce's unabashed speech as Joyce was by Byrne's intimidating silences. The friendship was of such importance to Joyce that when it dwindled, as it did later, he felt less at home in Ireland.

When Joyce entered University College's Matriculation (preparatory) course in September 1898, and misspelled his name on the register 'James Agustine Joyce' (a mistake he continued to make until his last year), he was sixteen and a half years old. His strong, brown hair, parted towards the middle when he bothered to comb it, and his stubborn jaw were the strongest features of a face that otherwise looked delicate, with its thin nose, pale blue eyes, and slightly pursed mouth. His face fell less easily into expressions than into an absence of them. His nearsightedness was becoming part of his personality, for rather than stare myopically, or wear glasses, he assumed a look of indifference. He was slender, and his weight to the end of his life remained about the same. A friend met him one day on the Bull, lying in the sun, and Joyce, noticing his gaze, said, 'What do I remind you of?' 'I don't know, what do you remind me of?' 'Hunger,' said Joyce, laughing loudly.27 His strong laugh or whoop was so conspicuous that an old lady, listening to it, asked if there was not something wrong with him. His clothes were generally unpressed and he still rarely washed. In a game at the Sheehys, asked his pet antipathy, Joyce replied, 'Soap and water,' 28 and at a meeting of the Library Com-

° Byrne kept this manner in later life, when he concocted an allegedly unbreakable code without divulging its key; he wrote a memoir, largely about Joyce, in which he made clear he was withholding more information than he was furnishing, added a coded appendix to it, and gave the whole the appropriate title of *Silent Years* (1953). It is one of the most crochety and interesting of the many books by Joyce's friends.

mittee at University College it was probably he who voiced the opinion that there was no advantage in being clean. His sister Eva recalled that he prided himself that lice would not live on his flesh—'That was the one thing they couldn't entertain.'

In his attitudes Joyce mixed unevenly as yet the qualities he would later solidify. He could juggle strong feelings and detachment from them, in a way that was still callow. His love poems were statements of passions that were largely imaginary, as he granted to his brother, and they went along with strict analyses of women as 'soft-skinned animals,' [29] which were only inverted cries of longing. He was beginning to form his position towards the entities of family, church, and state, but was not yet so vehement as he would become. He did not abjure his family, being fond of them, but he did not intend to sacrifice himself either by conforming to their standards or by earning money for their support. His closest companion when he entered the university was his brother Stanislaus, but he gave Stanislaus his company without giving him much affection, and soon began to make him jealous by turning more and more to Byrne and Cosgrave.

As to the church, Joyce probably did not take communion after his burst of piety at Easter in 1897; he allowed himself, however, to be inscribed * in the Sodality at University College and perhaps attended a meeting or two. He also attended, as late as 1901, the inaugural meeting of a Thomas Aquinas Society, though the fact that his name is signed twice and crossed off once, as Kevin Sullivan discovered,[30] suggests his equivocal participation. It was in some such fashion that his religious attitudes expressed themselves; he was still occupied in crossing off his Catholicism. In later life Morris L. Ernst asked Joyce, 'When did you leave the Catholic Church?' and he replied unhelpfully, 'That's for the Church to say.' [31] It was becoming clearer to him that, of the two ways of leaving the Church that were open to him, denial and transmutation, he would choose the second. He would retain faith, but with different objects. He could still reprove others for pretending to be Christian and not being so—this was a position he took in an essay written in September 1899 on the painting 'Ecce Homo' by Munkácsy:

> It is grand, noble, tragic but it makes the founder of Christianity no more than a great social and religious reformer, a personality, of mingled majesty and power, a protagonist of a world-drama. No objections will be lodged against it on that score by the public, whose general attitude when they advert to the subject at all, is that of the painter, only less grand and less interested.

* Kevin Sullivan suggests that Joyce's name was signed by Byrne as a joke.

Munkacsy's conception is as much greater than theirs, as an average artist is greater than an average greengrocer, but it is of the same kind, it is, to pervert Wagner, the attitude of the town. Belief in the divinity of Christ is not a salient feature of secular Christendom. But occasional sympathy with the eternal conflict of truth and error, of right and wrong, as exemplified in the drama at Golgotha is not beyond its approval.[32]

In Trieste later he reproved the Pope for not being Christian enough, his objection being not to impiety but to dilution of feeling. Christianity had subtly evolved in his mind from a religion into a system of metaphors, which as metaphors could claim his fierce allegiance. His brother Stanislaus's outward rebellion, which took the form of rudeness to his masters at Belvedere and defiance at home—his atheism worn like a crusader's cross—did not enlist James's sympathy. He preferred disdain to combat. He was no longer a Christian himself; but he converted the temple to new uses instead of trying to knock it down, regarding it as a superior kind of human folly and one which, interpreted by a secular artist, contained obscured bits of truth. And so he was not inconsistent when, about this time, he urged Stanislaus to moderate his revolt a little in the interests of family harmony.[33]

The demands of his country for national feeling he was prepared to meet, but in his own way. Following Ibsen's example, he detested the grosser forms of nationalism. Yet it would be a mistake to see Joyce as already buying a ticket for Paris; he probably still expected he could live in Ireland. His later depiction of himself makes him more *à cheval* on his principles than he had yet become. For the moment his most basic decision was in favor of art's precedence over every other human activity. The nation might profit or not from his experiment, as it chose. In the creedless church he had found for himself, older than St. Peter's and more immortal, he would be stubborn and daring. It was not long before he found a splendid quarrel in which to display both traits at their best.

The quarrel came about as a result of what seems, in retrospect, to have been the main cultural event of Dublin in the eighteen-nineties, the opening of the Irish theatrical movement in 1899. On May 8 Yeats's *The Countess Cathleen* had its première. Rumors about the play had circulated for several weeks before; Edward Martyn had almost withdrawn his financial backing because Cardinal Logue, without reading the play, called it heretical; but other clerical defenders were hastily mustered to take an opposite view and mollify Martyn. In ten years both Yeats and Moore thought the situation ludicrous, but it did not seem so to them, or to Joyce, at the time. Joyce, with generous condescension, had already marked Yeats out as the principal

living Irish writer; he sat in the gallery at the first performance and
watched Florence Farr as the poet Aileel, and May Whitty as the
countess. A group of young students booed passages in the play which
they considered anti-Irish; and when the curtain fell, as Seumas O'Sullivan has written, 'a storm of booing and hissing broke out around
the seats in which I and a few enthusiasts were attempting to express
our appreciation of the magnificent performance.' Joyce clapped vigor-
ously.³⁴ It was of course apparent to him that the play's Christianity
was symbolic, not doctrinal. He had no objection to representing Irish
peasants as ignorant and superstitious; they were. The theme of a
Faustlike scapegoat for the race appealed to him; the countess's 'sac-
rificial exaltation' ³⁵ was like his Stephen's, who would contract to
suffer like her, or like Lucifer, for his race. Joyce was also moved by
the lyric, 'Who Goes with Fergus?', which Florence Farr sang; its
feverish discontent and promise of carefree exile were to enter his own
thought, and not long afterwards he set the poem to music and praised
it as the best lyric in the world.

His friends took the opposite view. As soon as the performance was
over, Skeffington with others composed a letter of protest to the *Freeman's Journal,* and it was left on a table in the college next morning
so that all who wished might sign it. Joyce was asked and refused.
The signers included Kettle, Skeffington, Byrne, and Richard Sheehy.°
They wanted to claim a role for intellectual Catholics in Dublin's
artistic life, but picked the worst possible occasion. Their letter, published in the *Freeman's Journal* on May 10,³⁶ was intended to be
patriotic but only succeeded in being narrow-minded. It professed
respect for Yeats as a poet, contempt for him as a thinker. His subject
was not Irish, his characters were travesties of the Irish Catholic Celt.
'We feel it our duty,' they wrote, 'in the name and for the honour of
Dublin Catholic students of the Royal University, to protest against
an art, even a dispassionate art, which offers as a type of our people
a loathesome brood of apostates.' The letter must have sounded to
Joyce like something satirized in an Ibsen play. His refusal to sign
was remembered against him by others, and he resented as much their
alacrity to sign. If Ireland was not to be 'an afterthought of Europe' ³⁷—
a phrase he devised for it about this time—it would have to allow the
artist his freedom and would have to muffle the priest.

This was the culminating episode in Joyce's matriculation year, which
came to an end in the following month. He had not spent much time

---

° Father Noon points out that not everyone signed it; but only Joyce made not
signing it a public gesture. See p. 94. 'I was the only student who refused his
signature,' Joyce said proudly later.

on his studies, and only in Latin did he achieve even second class honors on his examinations. Academic distinction had ceased to attract him. His early papers in English are at once perfunctory and pretentious. One ponderous fragment that survives is from an essay on 'Force,' which he wrote on September 27, 1898. He argues that subjugation of men by force is futile, then adds, in a less enlightened manner, that 'Among human families the white man is the predestined conqueror.' The nobler subjections are those achieved by mind against force, as when the sailor outwits the wind: 'When Aeolus has pronounced his *fiat*, there is no direct countermanding his order.' In literature an uncontrolled imagination like Shelley's can only produce vagueness; what is required is self-subjugation, a discipline: 'When however the gift—great and wonderful—of a poetic sense, in sight and speech and feeling, has been subdued by vigilance and care and has been prevented from running to extremes, the true and superior spirit penetrates more watchfully into sublime and noble places, treading them with greater fear and greater wonder and greater reverence, and in humbleness looks up into the dim regions, now full of light, and interprets, without mysticism, for men the great things that are hidden from their eyes, in the leaves of the trees and in the flowers, to console them, to add to their worship, and to elevate their awe.' The writer becomes steadily more oracular: human reason should be '*casta, pacifica et desursum*' * and one day there will be, he predicts, a new subjugation of kindness.[38] Joyce, at the age of sixteen and a half, seeks to impress his professor by his rhythm, not heterodoxy. His stylistic model for this early essay was probably Ruskin, after whose death on January 20, 1900, he wrote a tribute which he entitled, 'A Crown of Wild Olive.' [39] But imitative as it was, the essay on 'Force' expressed a hatred of violence which proved in Joyce to be lifelong.

Since Joyce's entrance in University College his family had sharpened the pace of its removals. In 1898 they were in a two-story, rather pleasant house at 29 Windsor Avenue in Fairview, where they remained at least until May 1899; they then moved in temporarily with a family named Hughes in a house in Convent Avenue; they had part of a larger house at 13 Richmond Avenue, Fairview, in late 1899, and were still there in April 1900; their next move, in May, was to an attached house at 8 Royal Terrace, Fairview. This was the house, separated by a wall from the convent grounds, where they could hear the mad nun's screams; Joyce describes it in *A Portrait*. They remained there until 1901, when they moved to 32 Glengariff Parade off the

* 'Chaste, peaceful, and from above,' as Joyce translates.

North Circular Road.* Even at Belvedere William Fallon, a fellow-student, had asked Joyce how it happened that they moved so often; [40] but Joyce's intellectual scorn was an adequate defense now against more mature snobbery. Circumstances had forced his father to learn how to handle landlords: one dexterous method he used to forestall eviction for non-payment of rent was to offer to leave voluntarily, thereby sparing the landlord legal costs, if the landlord would kindly oblige with a receipt for the rent which had not been paid. Usually the landlord consented, and John Joyce would then exhibit the receipt to another landlord to persuade him to take them in.[41] A second method, used probably when they left the Convent Avenue house which they shared with another tenant, was for the two tenants to exchange simulated receipts, as if they had been each other's landlord; by this stratagem the fact of eviction was concealed, and both were able to find new quarters. When such arrangements had been made, the Joyce family would hire a float, pile as much of their belongings on it as they could, and carry the rest. Stanislaus Joyce remembered that at first two floats were needed, but eventually one was enough.[42] During these moves the family portraits were always carried by hand to prevent damage, but even they could not always escape the universal drift of the furnishings towards Mrs. M'Guinness, the pawnshop operator who walked like a queen. Alfred Bergan saw John Joyce once nodding tragically at the portraits, which some men were carrying out. 'There,' said he, 'goes the whole seed, breed and generation of the Joyce family.' [43] But he managed to scrape together enough shillings to rescue them again.

The food bill was managed with equal address. The family lived on credit from grocers who dwelt in the expectation of being paid at least a little of the debts they had foolishly allowed to accumulate. Once when John Joyce had collected his monthly pension at David Drimmie and Son, his daughter Mabel persuaded him to pay off the grocer, give up drinking, and start afresh. The grocer eagerly accepted the money, then closed the account. John Joyce vowed he would never pay off a bill again,[44] and doubtless he kept his word.

His oldest son surveyed this scene with amusement and spoke of it with disarming candor. He told Eugene Sheehy that when he entered University College and had to put down his father's occupation, he listed it as 'Entering for competitions,' [45] because John Joyce always hoped to triumph in a puzzle contest and so get a windfall. John Joyce, for his part, was not pleased with his son's failure to continue winning scholastic prizes at the university. He would ask him what

* Near the corner was the grocery of Fogarty, who appears in the story 'Grace.'

profession he planned to go into, journalism, the bar, or medicine, and get no answer. He prodded and taunted his son, but got nowhere. Neither of them contemplated doing anything about the family situation; it was irremediable, and they cultivated a disregard for it which the son carried off more easily than his father. There was not much tension between them, however, because James Joyce saw his father principally in the evenings, and sometimes, since they were both out late, John at the pubs and James walking with Stanislaus, Byrne, or Cosgrave, did not see him at all.

The next academic year, 1899-1900, was the crucial one in Joyce's course. On October 9, 1899, he offered to read a paper in January on 'Drama and Life' before the Literary and Historical Society.[46] This society, like the college itself, was one of Newman's creations, and it exists today. There had been a lapse from 1891 to 1897, when Skeffington revived it and served as its first auditor and principal recruiter. He was followed in 1898 by Kettle, who said of it, 'I have a home for my disaffection.'[47] But the college authorities did not tolerate overtly political speeches, and usually the topics were literary or social. Joyce had participated actively in the society during his matriculation year, 1898-99; he was elected to the executive committee of the society on February 18, 1899, and was nominated to be treasurer on March 21, but was defeated by 'the boy orator' L. J. Walsh. On January 14, 1899, Joyce and Kettle took the negative in a debate on the proposition 'That in the last decade of the 19th century English literature has reached a very low ebb.' A month later, on February 11, Hugh Boyle Kennedy, a prissy young man who, John Joyce said, 'had a face like a child's bottom, well-whipped,'[48] and later became Chief Justice of the Irish Free State, read a paper on the incongruous topic, 'The War Machine, A State Necessity'; Joyce rose to attack the paper by ironically translating the eight beatitudes into military terms.[49] The itemizing of 'British Beatitudes' in *Ulysses* as 'Beer, beef, business, bibles, bulldogs, battleships, buggery and bishops,'[50] was probably a reworking of his remarks.

He was particularly roused, however, by a paper of Arthur Clery on February 11. Clery was a rather witty student who afterwards became an ardent nationalist. His talk on this occasion was on the subject, 'The Theatre, Its Educational Value.' It was a mediocre discussion but had the merit of annoying Joyce: Clery spoke of 'the admitted deterioration of the modern stage,' announced that 'The effect of Henrik Ibsen is evil,' celebrated the Greeks and, with *Macbeth* as example, advocated revivals of Shakespeare's plays. 'I consider that in affecting and amusing us the proper end of the theatre should be to produce elevation,' said Clery.[51] All these positions were in conflict with Joyce's. He spoke to the paper and attacked it, and his vigorous support of Ibsen aroused considerable discussion among the students who—Clery perhaps included—had not read any of Ibsen's plays. The repercussions reached Joyce's mother. *Stephen Hero* recounts that she timidly asked her son what sort of writer Ibsen was. He at once brought her some of Ibsen's plays to read, and she stood the test surprisingly well, concluding with her son that Ibsen was not an immoral writer. Even John Joyce, nonplused to see his wife reading for the first time since their marriage, picked up a copy of Ibsen's *League of Youth* and soon laid it down convinced that Ibsen was safely boring.[52]

Joyce put together his thoughts for 'Drama and Life' with great care. Most of his essays at this time were connected with the drama, and he discussed his arguments step by step with Stanislaus, who made useful objections. When he had finished the paper, he gave it to the auditor, Clery, who showed it to the president. Delany refused to allow Joyce to read it. This was Joyce's first encounter with censorship since Dempsey had found the example of heresy in his essay, and he went at once to Father Delany to protest.[53] Delany, who had not expected this onslaught, objected that the paper minimized the ethical content of drama; but Joyce defended himself again with Aquinas's tolerant dictum that beautiful things are those which, when seen, please us. The president decided not to press his objections, but several ortho-dox students were probably coached to attack Joyce.

Perhaps to substantiate his high opinion of his own work, Joyce wrote the editor of the *Fortnightly Review*, W. L. Courtney, to ask brashly if he would like a general article on Ibsen's work. Courtney's reply came the day the paper was to be read; he did not need a general article but would consider a review of Ibsen's new play, *When We Dead Awaken*.[54] With this encouragement Joyce went to the Physics Theatre on January 20, 1900, to read his essay. Professor Magen-nis, who knew his abilities from his Intermediate Examinations, was in the chair. Joyce delivered his paper, as his brother Stanislaus declares, 'without emphasis,' or as he himself puts it rather grandly in *Stephen Hero*, 'He read it quietly and distinctly, involving every hardihood of thought or expression in an envelope of low innocuous melody,' and spoke the final sentences in 'a tone of metallic clearness.'[55]

He was bent upon stating his positions as flatly and unequivocally as possible. He took up Greek drama first; Clery had paid it the usual tributes, but Joyce said it was played out, killed by the greenroom proprieties forced by Attic stage conditions upon it. As for the next great drama, the Shakespearean, that was dead too, mere 'literature in dialogue.' Other dramatists before the modern, Corneille, Metastasio, Calderón, practiced infantile plot-juggling and could not be taken seriously. With Verlaine's pronouncement, *'Et tout le reste est littérature,'* in mind, Joyce argued that drama was not to be confused with literature. Literature dealt with individual quirks in terms of temporary conventions, while drama dealt with the changeless laws of human nature. It was paradoxical but undeniable that only the 'new' dramatists perceived what was ageless and properly concerned themselves with it. We must 'clear our minds of cant,' Joyce said, and mocked the patriots in his audience by urging, 'Let us criticize in the manner of free people, as a free race,' a plea that alluded covertly but deftly to Victoria's impending visit to Dublin. If we do not merely repeat what we have been told, we will know at once 'the respective grades' of *Macbeth* (Clery's example of true greatness) and *The Master Builder*. The artist in drama, said Joyce, foregoes his very self and stands a mediator in awful truth before the veiled face of God. Joyce applied St. Augustine's phrase, *securus iudicat orbis terrarum,** to art; the artist is not concerned to make his work religious, moral, beautiful, or ideal, only to be truthful to fundamental laws, whether these are expressed in myths, as in Wagner's operas, or in realistic fictions.

Joyce's peroration is a strange blending of forthrightness and ornamentation:

... Shall we put life—real life—on the stage? No, says the Philistine chorus, for it will not draw. What a blend of thwarted sight and smug commercialism. Parnassus and the city Bank divide the souls of the peddlers. Life indeed nowadays is often a sad bore. Many feel like the Frenchman that they have been born too late in a world too old, and their wanhope and nerveless unheroism point on ever sternly to a last nothing, a vast futility and meanwhile—a bearing of fardels. Epic savagery is rendered impossible by vigilant policing, chivalry has been killed by the fashion oracles of the boulevardes. There is no clank of mail, no halo about gallantry, no hat-sweeping, no roystering! The traditions of romance are upheld only in Bohemia. Still I think out of the dreary sameness of existence, a measure of dramatic life may be drawn. Even the most commonplace, the deadest among the living, may play a part in a great drama.† It is a sinful foolishness to sigh back for the good old times, to feed the hunger of us with the cold stones they afford. Life we must accept as we see it before our eyes, men and women as we meet them in the real world, not as we apprehend them in the world of faery.

* 'Untroubled, the world judges.' Augustine, *Contra Epistolam Parmeniani*, III, 24. *Securest jubilends albas temoram.' Finnegans Wake* (593). Newman's *Apologia* drew Joyce's attention to the phrase.
† A prophecy of the coming of Bloom.

The great human comedy in which each has share, gives limitless scope to
the true artist, today as yesterday and as in years gone. The forms of things,
as the earth's crust, are changed. The timbers of the ships of Tarshish are
falling asunder or eaten by the wanton sea; time has broken into the fast-
nesses of the mighty; the gardens of Armida are become as treeless wilds.
But the deathless passions, the human verities which so found expression
then, are indeed deathless, in the heroic cycle, or in the scientific age, *Lohen-*
grin, the drama of which unfolds itself in a scene of seclusion, amid half-
lights, is not an Antwerp legend but a world drama. *Ghosts*, the action of
which passes in a common parlour, is of universal import—a deepset branch
on the tree, Igdrasil, whose roots are struck in earth, but through whose
higher leafage the stars of heaven are glowing and astir. It may be that many
have nothing to do with such fables, or think their wonted fare is all that
is of need to them. But as we stand on the mountains today, looking before
and after, pining for what is not, scarcely discerning afar the patches of open
sky; when the spurs threaten, and the track is grown with briars, what does
it avail that into our hands we have given us a clouded cane for an alpen-
stock, or that we have dainty silks to shield us against the eager, upland
wind? The sooner we understand our true position, the better; and the sooner
then will we be up and doing on our way. In the meantime, art, and chiefly
drama, may help us to make our resting places with a greater insight and a
greater foresight, that the stones of them may be bravely builded, and the
windows goodly and fair. '. . . what will you do in our Society, Miss Hessel?'
asked Rörlund—'I will let in fresh air, Pastor.'—answered Lona.[56]

This is Joyce's strongest early statement of method and intention.
His defense of contemporary materials, his interest in Wagnerian myth,
his aversion to conventions, and his insistence that the laws of life
are the same always and everywhere, show him to be ready to fuse
real people with mythical ones, and so find all ages to be one as in
A Portrait, *Ulysses*, and *Finnegans Wake*. The exaltation of drama
above all other forms was to be reformulated later in his esthetic
system and, if he wrote only one play, he kept to his principle by
making all his novels dramatic.* [57]

He ended his paper with the curtain speech of the first act of Ibsen's
Pillars of Society, and had scarcely called for fresh air when his audience sprang to attack him, Clery, Kennedy, and others. Magennis, in
summing up, also disagreed, though more mildly. Their criticisms are
summarized in *Stephen Hero*: one said that Aeschylus 'was an imper-
ishable name' and that 'the drama of the Greeks would outlive many
civilisations.' Another contended that the paper was hostile to religion, and failed to recognize that the Church had fostered the artistic
temper. Ibsen's plays were about drainage; '*Macbeth* would be famous

* See pp. 151, 306, 367-8.

when the unknown authors of whom' Joyce 'was so fond were dead and forgotten.' [58] Finally, in spite of his references to a free Irish people, Joyce was no nationalist; and all his praise was unpatriotically awarded to foreign authors.

Although in *Stephen Hero* Joyce represents Stephen as not deigning to reply to his critics, in fact Joyce rose from his chair at about ten o'clock when the bell was ringing in the landing outside to signal that it was time to wind up the proceedings. As Judge Eugene Sheehy recalls, he spoke without a note for at least thirty minutes, and dealt with each of his critics in turn. His cocksure eloquence won his audience's respect and applause. After the debate one student clapped Joyce on the back and exclaimed, 'Joyce, that was magnificent, but you're raving mad!' [59] His name was soon after proposed by Skeffington for the auditorship of the society for the coming year, but Hugh Kennedy beat him by a vote of 15 to 9.[60]

Joyce made up for this defeat by confounding his classmates with a distinction they could not confer or rival. He obtained a copy of a French translation of Ibsen's *When We Dead Awaken*, and composed the article about the play which Courtney had suggested the *Fortnightly Review* might accept. Joyce wrote with fervor of Ibsen's reticence and refusal to join battle with his enemies—qualities that had impressed him in Parnell also—and confidently offered his own view of Ibsen along with a rather uninspired paraphrase of the play. (The ending of the play, in which there is an awakening to life's possibilities, impressed Joyce so much that he gave Stephen a similar vision at the end of the fourth chapter of *A Portrait*.) It was not a good article, as Joyce later acknowledged, but was good enough to be printed. Courtney wrote to accept it on February 3, 1900, asking only that Joyce cut out a derogatory reference to Pinero and quote from Archer's just published English translation instead of from the French. Joyce made the requested changes.

When the *Fortnightly Review* was published on April 1, 1900, with 'Ibsen's New Drama' by James A. Joyce included in it, his fellow-students were dumbfounded. That he received twelve guineas for it amazed them still more, and encouraged several to try, unsuccessfully, to follow his example. From now on Joyce was the man who had published the article in the *Fortnightly* and this confirmation of his good opinion of himself encouraged him to stand even more aloof. What exalted him, however, was not their admiration, but a compliment from Ibsen himself. The master wrote from Christiania to Archer on April 16: *'Jeg har også laest-eller stavet mig igennem en anmeldelse af Mr. James Joyce i "Fortnightly Review" som er meget velvillig og*

*som jeg vel skulde have lyst til at takke forfatteren for dersom jeg
blot var sproget maegtig.'* [61] Archer relayed this message to Joyce on
April 23: 'I think it will interest you to know that in a letter I had
from Henrik Ibsen a day or two ago he says "I have read or rather
spelt out, a review by Mr. James Joyce in the *Fortnightly Review* which
is very benevolent ('velvillig') and for which I should greatly like to
thank the author if only I had sufficient knowledge of the language." ' [62]

Ibsen's unexpected message arrived at Richmond Avenue while Joyce
was swinging with the girl from across the street, Susie McKernan.[63]
It fell upon him like a benison at the beginning of his career. He had
entered the world of literature under the best auspices in that world.
After meditating his reply for a few days he wrote to Archer:[64]

> 13 Richmond Avenue
> Fairview, Dublin
> April 28, 1900.

Dear Sir

　I wish to thank you for your kindness in writing to me. I am a young
Irishman, eighteen years old, and the words of Ibsen I shall keep in
my heart all my life.

> Faithfully yours,
> Jas A. Joyce.

William Archer Esq.
　Southampton Row,
　　London.

1900–1902

He even ran away with hunself and became a farsoonerite, saying he
would far sooner muddle through the hash of lentils in Europe than
meddle with Irrland's split little pea.

—*Finnegans Wake* (171)

BEFORE Ibsen's letter Joyce was an Irishman; after it he was a
European. He set himself to master languages and literatures, and
read so widely that it is hard to say definitely of any important creative
work published in the late nineteenth century that Joyce had not read
it. His family by now accepted his literary tastes; when a visitor remarked a book of Zola's in the sitting room and remonstrated with
Joyce's parents for allowing him to read it, they replied, 'Jim can read
what he likes.' John Joyce gave him money to buy foreign books
whether or not the family had enough to eat. James's signature and
the dates 1900 or 1901 appear on plays of Hauptmann (*Hanneles Himmelfahrt*) and Ibsen (*The Master Builder* in Dano-Norwegian), and
on Verlaine's *Poètes Maudits*, Huysmans's *Là-bas*, D'Annunzio's *The
Child of Pleasure*, Tolstoy's *The Fruits of Enlightenment*, Italian translations of Sudermann (*The Battle of the Butterflies* and *The Destruction of Sodom*) and Björnson (*Beyond Our Power*). His interest in
Italian brought him to Ferdinando Paolieri, whose 'linguistic purity'
he admired, and in 1902 to Fogazzaro (*Piccolo Mondo Moderno* and
Piccolo Mondo Antico), while it removed him from Rossetti, whom
he denounced as 'an ice-cream Italian.'[1] He continued his study of
Dante, so that it was easy for Oliver Gogarty to dub him a little later
the Dante of Dublin; he read Castiglione's *Courtier*, and became
more polite though, Stanislaus suggested to him, less sincere.[2] He was
interested in Flaubert, less in *Madame Bovary*, according to Curran,
than in 'La Légende de St. Julien l'Hospitalier' and *La Tentation de
Saint Antoine*. After an initial liking for Huysmans he began to com-

plain that Huysmans in his later books was becoming 'more formless and more obviously comedian.' [3] He also joined the rest of intellectual Dublin in taking an interest in occultism; his copy of H. S. Olcott's *A Buddhist Catechism* is dated May 7, 1901. His brother Stanislaus thought James was looking for a substitute religion, but it is probable that he, like Yeats and unlike George Russell, was attracted more by the symbology than by the pious generalizations of Theosophy.

To read Ibsen in the original, Joyce began to study Dano-Norwegian. He quoted Ibsen's lyric from *Brand*, 'Agnes, my lovely butterfly,' to his friends in that language. When they praised Ibsen's better-known works, he dismissed those by saying, 'A postcard written by Ibsen will be regarded as important, and so will *A Doll's House*.' [4] When they evinced an interest in Ibsen's thought, he responded by discoursing instead on the technique, especially of lesser known plays like *Love's Comedy*.[5] Yet the theme of that play, the artist's compulsion to renounce love and marriage for the sake of life on the mountain peaks, must have also been congenial. He came to know the European theater well, and decided that Ibsen's principal disciple was Hauptmann. There being no translations of Hauptmann's recent plays, Joyce paid him the compliment of studying German, a language which until then he had disliked and avoided.

What is notable about his reading is its variety. He was as interested in naturalistic detail, though he thought it a little passé, as in lyrical images. So in 1901 he bought George Moore's *Vain Fortune* and a strange little book that Yeats introduced, Horton's *A Book of Images;* the second put the real world as resolutely behind as *Vain Fortune* attempted to put it before. Hauptmann's *Hanneles Himmelfahrt,* purchased a few months earlier, juxtaposed a naturalistic setting with apparitions of Hannele's father and mother in a way that crudely foreshadows the *Circe* episode of *Ulysses;* Hannele's visionary characters appear with the same authority as the living villagers.

Like everyone else in 1900, Joyce was eager to find a style, and turned for this, perhaps in part as a result of Arthur Symons's *The Symbolist Movement in Literature,* published the year before, to the French. He practiced translating Verlaine,* who had died in 1896,

---

* Verlaine was easier for him to translate than Horace had been, as this version of '*Les Sanglots longs*' suggests:

A voice that sings	My soul is faint	Away! Away!
Like viol strings	At the bell's plaint	I must obey
Through the wane	Ringing deep;	This drear wind,
Of the pale year	I think upon	Like a dead leaf
Lulleth me here	A day bygone	In aimless grief
With its strain.	And I weep.	Drifting blind.[6]

and committed to memory a group of Verlaine's lyrics, which in later life, to the amusement of Wyndham Lewis, he would recite to girls they casually met in Parisian cafés. He also thought of serving as French correspondent to some review, and wrote to the editor of a new one to recommend himself. His plan was perhaps to have the new books sent him by a correspondent in Le Havre.* The editor agreed to his proposal, cautioning him however, 'Light and Bright, please.'⁷ But the review failed to appear.

Not at all dashed, Joyce prepared to make use of the money he had received from the *Fortnightly Review* for his article on Ibsen. He invited his father to go to London with him in May 1900, and, after having magnanimously deposited with Mrs. Joyce £1 from the twelve-guinea fee to pay for household expenses, they departed from Kingstown.⁸ John Joyce livened up the journey by picking quarrels about the Boer War with stolid Englishmen. They found a cheap boarding-house in London; John Joyce dubbed the one-eyed landlady 'Cyclopia,'⁹ an idea that James tucked away for future use. Most of their evenings were spent at theaters and music halls; they saw Eleanora Duse in *La Gioconda* and *La Città Morta,* and Joyce, perhaps aspiring to be D'Annunzio's successor in her affections, wrote her an encomiastic poem which she did not acknowledge; he procured a photograph of her for his desk at home, and continued to admire her.¹⁰ During the days he paid some official calls, one with his father to T. P. O'Connor of *T.P.'s Weekly,* to sound out O'Connor about a journalistic job. Neither was much concerned when O'Connor considered James too young.¹¹ He called also on Courtney, the *Fortnightly Review* editor, and surprised him too by his youth. He wrote Archer for an appointment, and at first had a cold letter asking on what business he had come; then, when Archer was reminded of their correspondence regarding Ibsen, he cordially invited Joyce to lunch with him at the Royal Services Club,¹² where they had wild duck.¹³ Archer was the first important literary man to be obliged to take notice of the determined young man, and for the next two years his support was to be precious.

John Joyce and his son went back to Ireland in good spirits, with twopence left,¹⁴ and James announced oracularly to Stanislaus that 'The music hall, not poetry, is a criticism of life.'¹⁵ Puncturing old solemnities, and making new ones, was a favorite diversion with him, and he was pleased now as always to find value in what he was expected to condemn as commonplace and vulgar.

---

* This was L. Lerouin, a student from Vire, Calvados; Joyce had obtained his name a year or two before from some bureau of cultural interchange, and they had written letters in each other's languages.¹⁶

ADMISSION — ONE SHILLING!

ARABY

IN

DUBLIN

Official Catalogue

GRAND
ORIENTAL
Fête

May 14th to 19th 1894.

Inside

JERVIS St. HOSPITAL

Freeman's Journal announcement of the
concert on August 27, 1904, when Joyce
and John McCormack shared the platform. (p. 173) *Courtesy of Patrick
Henchy*

ANTIENT CONCERT ROOMS.
EXHIBITION OF IRISH
INDUSTRIES
AND
GRAND IRISH CONCERT,
THIS (SATURDAY) EVENING,
At 8 o'clock.

Artistes :—
Miss AGNES TREACY,
Miss OLIVE BARRY,
Madame HALL,
Miss WALKER (Marie Nic Shiubhlaigh).
Mr. J. C. DOYLE,
Mr. JAMES A. JOYCE, and
Mr. J. F. M'CORMACK.
Orchestra conducted by
Miss EILEEN REIDY, A.L.C.M., R.I.A.M.
Prices—3s, 2s, and 1s.

The program of the bazaar Araby in
Dublin, May 14-19, 1894. (p. 40)
Courtesy of Patrick Henchy

III

The Martello Tower at Sandycove, where Joyce and Oliver St. John Gogarty
lived in September 1904. (p. 177) *Courtesy of the* Irish Times

Joyce, age 20, in graduation robes, October 31, 1902. (Croessmann Collection) (p. 109) *Courtesy of the Southern Illinois University Library*

Joyce, age 20, in Paris, December, 1902. (Croessmann Collection) (p. 119) *Courtesy of the Southern Illinois University library*

IV

Nora Barnacle in Galway, *c.* 1904. (p. 162)

Joyce, age 22, in 1904. Asked what he was thinking when C. P. Curran photographed him, Joyce replied, 'I was wondering would he lend me five shillings.' *Courtesy of C. P. Curran*

That summer of 1900 John Joyce was employed to straighten out the
voting lists in Mullingar, and he took James and some of his other
children along.[17] Mullingar, in the center of Ireland, was much more
provincial than Dublin and Cork, the only parts of the country that
James so far knew. Joyce seems to have relished buzzing the local
residents with remarks like, 'My mind is more interesting to me than
the entire country,'[18] and with reproofs for their un-Christian (as he
solemnly considered it) belligerence towards England. He probably
planned later to develop his Mullingar experiences at length; two
epiphanies date from there, and in *Stephen Hero* he described Stephen
at Mullingar; but in *A Portrait* he omitted the episode, preferring to
confine Stephen's debates to his university circle. Some of the places
he noticed, however, such as Phil Shaw's photographic shop, stayed
with him, and he put Milly Bloom to work there in *Ulysses*.

While in Mullingar Joyce had nothing to do, so he fulfilled a swelling
ambition to write a play of his own. He called it *A Brilliant Career*, and
with due sense of its importance and his own, inscribed on the dedica-
tory page:

> To
> My own Soul I
> dedicate the first
> true work of my
> life.[19]

It was the only work he was ever to dedicate to anyone. He wrote the
play out easily, with few corrections, and when he had finished it
brought it in to his father, who was sitting up in bed. John Joyce turned
from the title page to the dedication and exclaimed, 'Holy Paul!'[20]

In late August John Joyce brought his entourage back to 8 Royal
Terrace in Dublin, and from here James sent *A Brilliant Career* to
William Archer on August 30 with a letter saying, 'I am most anxious
to hear your judgment upon it.'[21] What the play was like can be discovered from Stanislaus Joyce's account of it and from Archer's letter
of criticism.[22] The hero was, like Stockmann in *An Enemy of the
People*, a young doctor; Joyce was himself toying with the idea of a
medical career, and continued to toy with it for three years more. The
doctor exhibits a ruthlessness in pursuing success in art; but for the
doctor it is a poor sort of success. He betrays his love for a woman
named Angela by finding himself a wife better able to further his
career. This move enables him to become mayor of the town. A plague,
as symbolical as Dr. Stockmann's sewage problem, breaks out, and the
mayor has to combat it. He is greatly aided by an unknown woman who

organizes assistance for the sick. In the third act the plague is defeated, and there is public merrymaking.* A demonstration of gratitude to the mayor takes place, and in the course of it he is confronted with his unknown coadjutor only to discover it is Angela, now married to a jealous husband. The last act, the fourth, is devoted to a private discussion of past and future by Angela and the mayor. The doctor sees his brilliant career now turned lusterless; Angela bitterly departs; and a servant comes in to announce dinner. It is hard not to exclaim, with *Finnegans Wake*, 'Ibscenest nansense!' [23]

William Archer read the play impatiently but carefully, and wrote Joyce a long, helpful letter:

> 2, Vernon Chambers,
> Southampton Row, W.C.
> 15 Sept. 1900

Dear Mr. Joyce,

I have at last found time to read your play. It has interested me and puzzled me a good deal—indeed, I scarcely know what to say of it. You seem to me to have talent—possibly more than talent—and yet I cannot say that I think this play a success. For the stage, of course—the commercial stage at any rate—it is wildly impossible. No doubt you realize that. But taking it simply as a dramatic poem, I cannot help finding the canvas too large for the subject. It narrows in the last act into a sort of love tragedy—almost a duologue—but in order to reach that point you construct a huge fable of politics and pestilence, in which the reader—one reader at any rate—entirely loses sight of what I presume you intend for the central interest of the drama. I have been trying to read some elaborate symbolism into the second and third acts to account for their gigantic breadth of treatment, but if you had a symbolic purpose, I own it escapes me. It may be very good symbolism for all that—I own I am no great hand at reading hieroglyphics.

On the other hand, you have certainly a gift of easy, natural and yet effective dialogue, and a certain amount of scenic picturesqueness. The scene between Paul and Angela is curiously strong and telling, if only it were led up to, or, in its turn, led to anything definite. On the whole, however, you seem to me to be deficient as yet in the power of projecting characters so as to seize upon the reader's attention and kindle his imagination. It is true that you unduly handicap yourself in this respect by crowding your stage with such a multitude of figures that Shake-

---

* The only fragment of the play that survives is four lines from a gipsy song, sung during the merrymaking:

> We will leave the village behind,
> Merrily, you and I,
> Tramp it smart and sing to the wind,
> With the Romany Rye.[24]

speare himself could scarcely individualize them. At the end of the first act I didn't begin to know one of your characters from another, and as for guessing that the interest of the play was to centre in the 'dépit amoureux' of Paul and Angela, I had no such divination. You may say that I clearly didn't read with sufficient attention. Perhaps not—but then it was your business to arouse my attention. Indeed it was only in the third act that the characters began to stand out for me at all. I tell you frankly what I felt—no doubt other people might be more keenly perceptive, but it is always something to know the effect you have produced upon one entirely well-disposed reader.

I don't know whether you want really to write for the stage. If you do, I have no hesitation at all in advising you, by way of practice, to choose a narrower canvas and try to work out a drama with half a dozen clearly designed and vividly projected characters. If you could show me such a play, I should at least be able to form a fair judgment of your real talent. At present I am interested and a good deal impressed, but also, I must confess, a good deal bewildered.

If you do not think me too much of a wet blanket, I shall be very glad to read anything else in the dramatic way that you care to send me.

Yours very truly,
William Archer

I will return the MS on Monday.

No doubt Archer was right about the play's impossibility; yet some of its defects were capable of one day becoming virtues. To accumulate a large, turbulent scene only to focus at the end on the isolated relations of a man and a woman is the technique of *The Dead, Ulysses,* and *Finnegans Wake;* to conclude by reinstating the dreary disorder of life which has been temporarily heightened in the direction of tragedy is the technique of *Dubliners.* Perhaps in these ways the play did exhibit, as Archer conceded, 'possibly more than talent.'

Joyce responded to Archer's letter by thanking him for his criticism, adding in his most obnoxious vein, that he himself disliked the play, though for other reasons. These he did not, of course, trouble to specify, and Stanislaus thought Archer would be exasperated. Fortunately, he did not take offense. James kept the play for a while, but in 1902 he destroyed it.[25]

He was now at work on several schemes. Besides the prose play, he wrote one in verse entitled *Dream Stuff,* of which only one stanza from a song was accidentally preserved:

> In the soft nightfall
> Hear thy lover call,
> Hearken the guitar!

> Lady, lady fair
> Snatch a cloak in haste,
> Let thy lover taste
> The sweetness of thy hair ...

He wrote also a group of poems some of which lamented sins and others invoked joys, under the title of *Shine and Dark*. Most of the fragments that his brother preserved [26] belong to dark rather than to shine. There is Byronic posturing:

> And I have sat amid the turbulent crowd,
> And have assisted at their boisterous play;
> I have unbent myself and shouted loud
> And been as blatant and as coarse as they.
>
> I have consorted with vulgarity
> And am indelibly marked with its fell kiss,
> Meanly I lived upon casual charity
> Eagerly drinking of the dregs of bliss.

The beauty of his mistress and the transiency of flesh, so anyone can see, drive him mad:

> Yea, for this love of mine
> I have given all I had;
> For she was passing fair,
> And I was passing mad.
>
> All flesh, it is said,
> Shall wither as the grass;
> The fuel for the oven
> Shall be consumed, alas!

He sententiously predicts death and destruction for the chief of sinners, apparently himself:

> Of thy dark life, without a love, without a friend,
> Here is, indeed, an end.
>
> There are no lips to kiss this foul remains of thee,
> O, dead Unchastity!
> The curse of loneliness broods silent on thee still,
> Doing its utmost will,
> And men shall cast thee justly to thy narrow tomb,
> A sad and bitter doom.

but musters up sympathy for a dead enemy:

> 'Requiem eternam dona ei, Domine';
> Silently, sorrowfully I bent down my head,
> For I had hated him—a poor creature of clay:

And all my envious, bitter cruel thoughts that came
Out of the past and stood by the bier whereon he lay
Pointed their long, lean fingers through the gloom . . .
                              O Name,
Ineffable, proud Name to whom the cries ascend
From lost, angelical orders, seraph flame to flame
For this end have I hated him—for this poor end?

The last lines suggest how carefully he had read Yeats's book, *The Countess Cathleen and Various Legends and Lyrics*, where the description of God and the angelic hosts is couched in the same language:

And of the embattled flaming multitude
Who rise, wing above wing, flame above flame,
And, like a storm, cry the Ineffable Name. . . .[27]

A witches' sabbath in another poem suggests the orgiastic dance in Yeats's story, *The Tables of the Law*, whole pages of which Joyce knew by heart: [28]

I intone the high anthem,
Partaking in their festival.
Swing out, swing in, the night is dark,
Magical hair, alive with glee,
Winnowing spark after spark,
Star after star, rapturously.
Toss and toss, amazing arms;
Witches, weave upon the floor
Your subtle-woven web of charms . . .

Some are comely and some are sour,
Some are dark as wintry mould,
Some are fair as a golden shower.
To music liquid as a stream
They move with dazzling symmetry;
Their flashing limbs blend in a gleam
Of luminous-swift harmony.
They wear gold crescents on their heads,
Hornèd and brilliant as the moon . . .

Another poem, while equally silly,

Wind thine arms round me, woman of sorcery,
While the lascivious music murmurs afar:
I will close mine eyes, and dream as I dance with thee,
And pass away from the world where my sorrows are.

Faster and faster! strike the harps in the hall!
Woman, I fear that this dance is the dance of death!
Faster!—ah, I am faint . . . and, ah, I fall.
The distant music mournfully murmureth . . .

shares the same frame of mind as the 'Villanelle of the Temptress,' used in *A Portrait* at a later stage of Joyce's development, but dating, according to Stanislaus Joyce,[29] from this period. The 'Villanelle' and 'A Prayer,' in *Pomes Penyeach*, ambiguously entertain the idea of a supplication addressed to a woman who is both temptation and doom. Joyce, in many ways so controlled, relished the notion of being overcome.

As if to remind us that the other poems had not expressed his whole character, Joyce left one example of a *shine* poem:

Let us fling to the winds all moping and madness,
Play us a jig in the spirit of gladness
On the creaky old squeaky strings of the fiddle.

The why of the world is an answerless riddle
Puzzlesome, tiresome, hard to unriddle.
To the seventeen devils with sapient sadness:
Tra la, tra la.

These examples seem more fitful because they survived capriciously as fragments on the backs of sheets which James Joyce or his brother Stanislaus wished to preserve for what was written on the front.[30] If they do not present more than a juvenile talent for poetry, their relegation suggests some critical sense.

In the late summer of 1901 Joyce put together a collection of his poems. They had such titles as 'Wanhope,' 'The Final Peace,' 'Commonplace,' 'The Passionate Poet,' 'Tenebrae,' and 'Valkyrie.'[31] Since Archer was editing a book of modern poets, Joyce sent them to him as a year before he had sent *A Brilliant Career*. He also recommended to Archer a little book of poems by another Irishman, Paul Gregan, in whose lyrics he found an affinity.* Archer's book was already compiled, but, as before, he offered Joyce some criticism.[32] The lyrics were deficient in content; although Yeats and Arthur Symons were composing and defending at this time a poetry of moods, Archer did not care for verse conceived on so insubstantial a foundation. He advised Joyce

---

* Gregan's book, *Sunset Town*, had just been published by Standish O'Grady at Kilkenny and by the Hermetic Society in Dublin. It bore the strong influence of Yeats and Russell. Some phrases in the final poem, 'Recreant,' may have helped Joyce in writing the final poem of *Chamber Music*, 'I hear an army charging upon the land.'

that there was 'as yet more temperament than anything else in your
work.'

Such comments must have been a little dispiriting, though Joyce did
not overvalue Archer as a critic, but quite independently he was uncertain about his verse. The principal source of uncertainty, as he acknowledged candidly to Stanislaus and to himself, was that he could not
rival his countryman Yeats, whose volume of lyrics, *The Wind among
the Reeds,* had awakened his intense admiration when it appeared in
1899. About his prose, however, he had no such modesty, and he was
already beginning to feel he might outdo George Moore, Hardy, and
Turgenev, if not Tolstoy. In prose he thought he might achieve more
subtlety than in meter. Accordingly he began in 1900, and continued
until 1903, to write a series of what, because he was following no one,
he declined to call *prose poems* as others would have done. For these
he evolved a new and more startling descriptive term, 'epiphanies.' The
epiphany did not mean for Joyce the manifestation of godhead, the
showing forth of Christ to the Magi, although that is a useful metaphor
for what he had in mind. The epiphany was the sudden 'revelation of
the whatness of a thing,' the moment in which 'the soul of the com-
monest object . . . seems to us radiant.' The artist, he felt, was charged
with such revelations, and must look for them not among gods but
among men, in casual, unostentatious, even unpleasant moments. He
might find 'a sudden spiritual manifestation' either 'in the vulgarity of
speech or of gesture or in a memorable phase of the mind itself.'
Sometimes the epiphanies are 'eucharistic,' * another term arrogantly
borrowed by Joyce from Christianity and invested with secular meaning.[33] These are moments of fullness or of passion. Sometimes the
epiphanies are rewarding for another reason, that they convey precisely
the flavor of unpalatable experiences. The spirit, as Joyce characteristically held, manifested itself on both levels. They vary also in style:
sometimes they read like messages in an unfamiliar tongue; their brilliance lies in their peculiar baldness, their uncompromising refusal of
all devices which would render them immediately clear. At other times
they are deliberately unenciphered, and lyrically biased.

The unpalatable epiphanies often include things to be got rid of,
examples of fatuity or imperceptiveness, caught deftly in a conversa-
tional exchange of two or three sentences. Joyce presents without ceremony, for example, this scene, presumably in his great-aunts' house on
Usher's Island after Mrs. Callanan's death:

---

* 'I must wait for the Eucharist to come to me,' says Stephen Dedalus, and then
set about 'translating the word into common sense.' *Stephen Hero* (30 [36]).

High up in the old, dark-windowed house: firelight in the narrow room; dusk outside. An old woman bustles about, making tea; she tells of the changes, her odd ways, and what the priest and the doctor said. . . . I hear her words in the distance. I wander among the coals, among the ways of adventure . . . Christ! What is in the doorway? . . . A skull—a monkey; a creature drawn hither to the fire, to the voices: a silly creature.
—Is that Mary Ellen?—
—No, Eliza, it's Jim.—
—O . . . O, goodnight, Jim—
—D'ye want anything, Eliza?—
—I thought it was Mary Ellen . . . I thought you were Mary Ellen, Jim— [34]

As in 'The Sisters' in *Dubliners,* Joyce never insists, and lets the effect seem to trail off. He cradles here the technique which has now become a commonplace of modern fiction. Arrogant yet humble too, it claims importance by claiming nothing; it seeks a presentation so sharp that comment by the author would be an interference. It leaves off the veneer of gracious intimacy with the reader, of concern that he should be taken into the author's confidence, and instead makes the reader feel uneasy and culpable if he misses the intended but always unstated meaning, as if he were being arraigned rather than entertained. The artist abandons himself and his reader to the material.

The more eloquent epiphanies are sometimes splenetic, but often portray the accession of a sudden joy. An early one describes, unlike the others, a religious experience. By itself it is not good, though if put into a context it might become so:

It is time to go away now—breakfast is ready. I'll say another prayer . . . I am hungry, yet I would like to stay here in this quiet chapel where the mass has come and gone so quietly . . . Hail, holy Queen, Mother of Mercy, our life, our sweetness and our hope! Tomorrow and every day after I hope I shall bring you some virtue as an offering for I know you will be pleased with me if I do. Now, goodbye for the present . . . O, the beautiful sunlight in the avenue and O, the sunlight in my heart!

It was probably a reminiscence rather than a resurgence of religious feeling, if it was in fact Joyce's own experience. It is transitional to the finished type, a secular moment such as he put almost without change at the end of *A Portrait of the Artist;* this one is a call to the soul too, but not a call from Mary:

The spell of arms and voices—the white arms of roads, their promise of close embraces, and the black arms of tall ships that stand against the moon, their tale of distant nations. They are held out to say: We are alone—come. And the voices say with them, 'We are your people.' And the air is thick with their company as they call to me their kinsman, making ready to go, shaking the wings of their exultant and terrible youth.

This kind of epiphany, which suggests the secret life of the spirit, connects with a group of dreams. There was much talk of dreams in Dublin at this time; both Yeats and AE were writing theirs down, and Joyce's source of inspiration was probably the poets rather than the psychologists.* The strangest of his dream epiphanies is one that he interpreted to be about Ibsen:

Yes—they are the two sisters. She who is churning with stout arms (their butter is famous) looks dark and unhappy; the other is happy because she had her way. Her name is R . . . Rina. I know the verb 'to be' in their language.
 —Are you Rina?—
I knew she was.
But here he is himself in a coat with tails and an old-fashioned high hat. He ignores them: he walks along with tiny steps, jutting out the tails of his coat. . . . My goodness! how small he is! He must be very old and vain—maybe he isn't what I. . . . It's funny that two big women fell out over this little man . . . But then he's the greatest man on earth.

He neatly contrasts commonplace remarks with a strange, dreamlike indefiniteness of person and place, so that the total effect is peculiar, almost uncanny.

The subtlety of these sketches was not lost upon Joyce or upon the few people to whom he showed them. Although the epiphanies were clearly preparatory, Joyce played for a time with the thought of forming them into a small book, and it was only later, in 1904, that he saw he could insert them instead in *Stephen Hero* to aid in the exposures and illuminations of that novel. Well before this rescue, they gave him assurance of his artistic mission, which he expressed directly in a letter he wrote to Ibsen in Dano-Norwegian in March 1901:

8 Royal Terrace
Fairview, Dublin.
March 1901

Honoured Sir,

 I write to you to give you greeting on your seventy-third birthday and to join my voice to those of your well-wishers in all lands. You may remember that shortly after the publication of your latest play, 'When We Dead Awaken,' an appreciation of it appeared in one of the English reviews—The Fortnightly Review—over my name. I know that you have

---

* Freud's *Traumdeutung* appeared late in 1899, but Joyce's interest in dreams is pre-Freudian in that it looks for revelation, not scientific explanation.

seen it because some short time afterwards Mr. William Archer wrote to me and told me that in a letter he had from you some days before, you had written, 'I have read or rather spelt out a review in the 'Fortnightly Review' by Mr. James Joyce which is very benevolent and for which I should greatly like to thank the author if only I had sufficient knowledge of the language.' (My own knowledge of your language is not, as you see, great but I trust you will be able to decipher my meaning.) I can hardly tell you how moved I was by your message. I am a young, a very young man, and perhaps the telling of such tricks of the nerves will make you smile. But I am sure if you go back along your own life to the time when you were an undergraduate at the University as I am, and if you think what it would have meant to you to have earned a word from one who held as high a place in your esteem as you hold in mine, you will understand my feeling. One thing only I regret, namely, that an immature and hasty article should have met your eye, rather than something better and worthier of your praise. There may not have been any wilful stupidity in it, but truly I can say no more. It may annoy you to have your work at the mercy of striplings but I am sure you would prefer even hotheadedness to nerveless and 'cultured' paradoxes.

What shall I say more? I have sounded your name defiantly through a college where it was either unknown or known faintly and darkly. I have claimed for you your rightful place in the history of the drama. I have shown what, as it seemed to me, was your highest excellence—your lofty impersonal power. Your minor claims—your satire, your technique and orchestral harmony—these, too I advanced.* Do not think me a hero-worshipper. I am not so. And when I spoke of you, in debating-societies, and so forth, I enforced attention by no futile ranting.

But we always keep the dearest things to ourselves. I did not tell *them* what bound me closest to you. I did not say how what I could discern dimly of your life was my pride to see, how your battles inspired me—not the obvious material battles but those that were fought and won behind your forehead—how your wilful resolution to wrest the secret from life gave me heart, and how in your absolute indifference to public canons of art, friends and shibboleths you walked in the light of your inward heroism. And this is what I write to you of now. Your work on earth draws to a close and you are near the silence. It is growing dark for you.† Many write of such things,‡ but they do not know. You have only opened the way—though you have gone as far as you could upon it—to the end of 'John Gabriel Borkman' and its spiritual

* Joyce originally wrote: 'The minor claims—your strength, your vision, your technique, your sense of form—these too I advanced. And let me say that as far as one man's efforts avail, I have done my part.'
† Joyce added this sentence after finishing the draft.
‡ Joyce originally wrote, 'Many write of such things sentimentally ...'

truth—for your last play stands, I take it, apart. But I am sure that higher and holier enlightenment lies—onward.

As one of the young generation for whom you have spoken I give you greeting—not humbly, because I am obscure and you in the glare, not sadly because you are an old man and I a young man, not presumptuously, nor sentimentally—but joyfully, with hope and with love, I give you greeting.

Faithfully yours,
James A. Joyce.

Mr. Henrik Ibsen,
Arbens Gade, 2,
Kristiania

This is the sort of letter that the recipient discards hastily and the writer files away; Joyce did in fact keep the English draft of it.[35] With whom does 'higher and holier enlightenment' lie? Presumably with the young correspondent, but Joyce also had in mind Gerhart Hauptmann. During the summer of 1901, which he spent with his father in Mullingar, he translated two of Hauptmann's plays. The first, *Vor Sonnenaufgang (Before Sunrise)*,[36] was the play which had made Hauptmann famous a dozen years before, while *Michael Kramer* was Hauptmann's most recent work (1900). Joyce wanted to study how Hauptmann had begun and where he was now going, and he could still feel himself a discoverer of these plays because neither of them had as yet been included in the Heinemann edition of Hauptmann's works. *Vor Sonnenaufgang* described the problem of an idealistic socialist who falls in love with the sister-in-law of a treacherous friend; he discovers however that her heredity is bad and idealistically throws her over. The theme seems wooden enough today, but interested Joyce because it dealt with the problem of Ibsen's *Ghosts* in another regional (Silesian) setting. Then too, his own hatred of force was leading him to conceive of socialism as a possible antidote to it, and so the dramatic use of a political theme might prove relevant to his purposes. He found the Silesian dialect too much for his inadequate German; the simpler passages he rendered in an Irish country dialect, but the difficult ones he could not translate at all, and simply marked his text with asterisks to indicate omissions. Of the two plays, *Michael Kramer* was much more to his taste: he could sympathize both with the father who wanted his son to yield all to art, and with the gifted son who is maddened and destroyed by his love for a waitress. Joyce, perhaps more than most young men, felt a similar threat of ruin in his own sensuality, and the image of a foolhardy, unavoidable surrender held his mind for years. Besides wishing to know Hauptmann better and to improve his German, Joyce had another motive for translating the plays; he hoped to persuade the Irish Literary Theatre to present them. He had followed with close attention the first performances of this theater in May 1899. In addition to *The Countess Cathleen,* the actors gave Martyn's *The Heather Field,* a play about an idealistic Irish hero which suggested that the theater might follow Ibsen. In February 1900, Joyce had attended the new play of Moore and Martyn, *The Bending of the Bough,* and his own *A Brilliant Career,* which he wrote later, owed something to its municipal theme. Yeats had said that the Irish Literary Theatre would perform plays by Continental as well as Irish dramatists, and Joyce was very likely preparing his translation of Hauptmann, complete with asterisks, for submission when, in October 1901, he learned with dismay that the next plays would be offensively Irish. They were Douglas Hyde's Irish language play, *Casadh-an-tSugáin,* and a play taken by Yeats and George Moore from Irish heroic legend, or as Joyce put it, from 'the broken lights of Irish myth,' [37] *Diarmuid and Grania.* On the morning of October 14, 1901, Joyce indignantly wrote an article condemning the theater for its parochialism.

He brought his essay to his *bête noire* Hugh Kennedy, the editor of a new college magazine, *St. Stephen's.* The editor consulted the adviser, Father Henry Browne,[38] who rejected Joyce's work. When Joyce heard this news, he furiously went again to beard President Delany, but Delany, while disavowing any responsibility for what had happened, refused to intervene. Meanwhile Joyce's friend Skeffington had met the same rebuff for an essay advocating equal status for women at the University. Joyce proposed they publish the essays together at their own expense. Since neither agreed with the other's position, while both resented censorship, they added a preface saying: 'These two Essays were commissioned by the Editor of St. Stephen's for that paper, but were subsequently refused insertion by the Censor.* The writers are now publishing them in their original form, and each writer is responsible only for what appears under his own name. F.J.C.S. J.A.J.' They went into Gerrard Brothers,[39] a stationery shop, across Stephen's Green from the College, which took on small printing jobs, and had 85 copies printed, probably in November 1901. The two authors distributed them with the assistance of Stanislaus Joyce, who had the duty of handing one in to George Moore's maidservant.

Joyce's article was entitled, 'The Day of the Rabblement.' [40] It began

---

* The word 'Censor' was chosen with some sarcasm, since Father Browne was merely the adviser. It is likely that Kennedy 'commissioned' the two papers only in the sense that he suggested Joyce and Skeffington write something for the magazine.

with a surly quotation; 'No man, said the Nolan, can be a lover of the true or the good unless he abhors the multitude; and the artist, though he may employ the crowd, is very careful to isolate himself.' By ignoring the Nolan, the Irish Literary Theatre had succumbed to 'the trolls' instead of warring with them as Ibsen had instructed.* The Irish rabblement, 'the most belated race in Europe,' must be countered, not appeased. No dramatist of European stature had emerged from the theater. The artists were not giants but giantlings. Yeats, while he might have had genius, was too much the esthete and had too floating a will; Moore had once deserved the place of honor among novelists in English, but had failed to keep up with the tide of the novel which had now swept from Flaubert's naturalism through Jacobsen to D'Annunzio's lyricism. 'But truth deals largely with us. Elsewhere there are men who are worthy to carry on the tradition of the old master who is dying in Christiania. He has already found his successor in the writer of *Michael Kramer*, and the third minister will not be wanting when his hour comes. Even now that hour may be standing by the door.'

The publication of *Two Essays* roused a good deal of talk. No one knew who the Nolan was. As Joyce told Herbert Gorman later, 'University College was much intrigued by this personage whom it supposed to be an ancient Irish chieftain like the MacDermott or the O'Rahilly.'[41] Some students thought it was Joyce himself, later identified in the columns of *St. Stephen's* as 'the dreamy one of Nola'; others thought it was the porter at the St. Cecilia medical school, whose name was Nolan.[42] 'Said the Nolan' became a catch phrase.[43] Stanislaus had urged him to clarify this reference to Giordano Bruno of Nola, but James replied, 'Laymen should be encouraged to think,' and fancied that when the students discovered who the Nolan was, they might go on to read some of his work. 'The writer of *Michael Kramer*' was probably also a baffling phrase to most of his readers, though more easily illuminated. The implications of Joyce's final sentence about the successor to Ibsen, which he had adapted from the curtain speech in the first act of *The Master Builder*, were not lost; he was twitted for them at the Sheehys', where speaking of some Dublin event, Hannah Sheehy said, 'O, there are sure to be great crowds.' Skeffington chimed in, 'In fact it'll be, as our friend Jocax would say, the day of the rabblement.' And Maggie Sheehy declaimed, 'Even now the rabblement may be standing by the door!'[44] Joyce wrote the dialogue down in an epiphany, perhaps to suggest how in Ireland all things are cheapened.

In *St. Stephen's* the essay was handled both lightly and heavily.

---

* Ibsen wrote in '*Et Vers*,' 'To live is to war with the trolls,' and used the word frequently to depict the enemies of art.

Arthur Clery, writing as 'Chanel,' pretending to quote a State Paper, *Aet. Eliz.*, said that Joyce was 'corrupted, as we do verily believe, by the learning of Italie or othere foreigne parts, hath no care for Holye Religion, but is fain to mislead our players.' [45] A leading article, perhaps by Kennedy, took issue with Joyce more sharply. The multitude that he so detested was Catholic, it pointed out, and this multitude was willing to forego art if art interfered with the spirit. Only Joyce had refused to join in the protest against *The Countess Cathleen*, the writer reminded him, and smugly concluded: 'If Mr. Joyce thinks that the artist must stand apart from the multitude, and means he must also sever himself from the moral and religious teachings which have, under Divine guidance, moulded its spiritual character, we join issue with him, and we prophesy but ill-success for any school which offers the Irish public art based upon such a principle.' Joyce had succeeded in flouting both the Irish Literary Theatre and the students who disliked its plays for the wrong reasons. He had found his private mountain top.

Although he was profoundly disaffected, Joyce was not like Skeffington a rebel day in and day out. He accepted the enemies he had sought, but did not much bother himself about them. Most of the rabblement liked him better than he desired. Clery's subsequent columns in *St. Stephen's* treat him with respect tinged with amusement; he is not the pariah but the Mad Hatter, as in this version of a Literary and Historical Society debate:

> 'I call upon the Hatter to open the debate,' said the Red Queen.
> The Hatter as usual was dreaming beautiful dreams; but a sharp prod of a needle awoke him. He stood, and commenced.
> Alice, the only human, could not understand, but supposed it all right, although there was much mention of Ibsen, Hauptmann, Bjornson, and Giacosa.
> Everyone said that it was divine, but no one seemed quite to know what it meant.

Another article, reporting a speech by the patriotic barrister John F. Taylor, said that Taylor's style compared with that 'of our own Joyce at his best,' and had a 'broadness of sympathy that the latter has yet to acquire.' During Taylor's address, it went on, 'Dreamy Jimmy and J. F. Byrne, standing on a window-sill, looked as if they could say things unutterable.' [46]

This praise must have pleased Joyce, for Taylor was an orator whom he respected. Among his activities outside the college, he appears to have attended the meeting of the Law Students' Debating Society on

October 24, 1901, where Taylor made the superb defense of the study of the Irish language which Joyce improved in *Ulysses.**

Probably in pursuit of rhetoric again, Joyce, in October 1899, attended the trial of Samuel Childs, who was defended against the charge of having killed his brother by Seymour Bushe, one of the most eloquent Irish barristers, as well as by Tim Healy. Bushe spoke of Michelangelo's Moses in words [47] that Joyce refurbished in *Ulysses:* 'that stony effigy in frozen music, horned and terrible, of the human form divine, that eternal symbol of wisdom and prophecy which, if aught that the imagination or the hand of man has wrought in marble of soultransfigured and of soultransfiguring deserves to live, deserves to live.' † But Joyce was equally pleased by the testimony of a witness who claimed to have recognized the accused man entering the house

---

* The newspaper account of Taylor's speech was pallid:

> Now as regards the language [said Taylor], suppose a great message was to be given to the human race, in what language was it likely to be given? What was the greatest message ever given to man? Christian and non-Christian alike were agreed upon that matter. Was that message given in the language of Imperial Rome or the language of intellectual Greece? No, it was given in the rustic dialect of the far-off land 'out of which no good could come.' Had that fact any meaning for them there and now?
>
> He could very well understand an intellectual Egyptian speaking to Moses, 'Why bother about these people of yours in Egypt? I know possibly we have not treated them very well, but all that is over now, and you may be chosen to rule over Egypt, and every public position is open to your people. I have no patience with you talking about your history and literature. Why, I asked one of the learned professors of your literature the other day what it was like, and he told me it was made up of superstitions and indecency (prolonged applause and laughter).'
>
> If Moses had listened to the counsels of that learned Professor he would never have come down from the mountain, his face glowing as a star, and bearing the Tables of the Law (applause).[48]

Joyce changed the peroration to read in *Ulysses* (141 [133]):

> But, ladies and gentlemen, had the youthful Moses listened to and accepted that view of life, had he bowed his head and bowed his will and bowed his spirit before that arrogant admonition he would never have brought the chosen people out of their house of bondage nor followed the pillar of the cloud by day. He would never have spoken with the Eternal amid lightnings on Sinai's mountaintop nor ever have come down with the light of inspiration shining in his countenance and bearing in his arms the tables of the law, graven in the language of the outlaw.[49]

He evidently had access to a pamphlet, 'The Language of the Outlaw,' published in Dublin about 1903, which gave as Taylor's concluding words, 'And if Moses had listened to these arguments, what would have been the end? Would he ever have come down from the Mount, with the light of God shining on his face and carrying in his hands the Tables of the law written in the language of the outlaw?' [48]

† In a notebook Joyce noted down what perhaps were more precisely Bushe's words: 'which, if anything that the hand of man has wrought of noble and inspiring and beautiful deserves to live deserves to live.'

on a dark night, though he saw only the man's back. When pressed by Bushe he explained that he identified him by his walk: 'He walked *like a tailor*'[50] (with legs half crossed). The Childs murder case served Joyce in *Ulysses* as a parallel to the betrayal of Shakespeare, as Stephen alleges, by his two brothers.

For more casual diversion Joyce continued to frequent the Sheehys' house. He took a special liking to the younger son, Eugene, who haplessly lost his voice in making a maiden speech at the Literary and Historical Society in the fall of 1899. Joyce seized his arm leaving the hall and said, 'Eugene, you have gone up a lot in my estimation,'[51] sensitive inarticulateness being preferable to the usual bombast. Such acts of kindness were infrequent with Joyce, but they occurred throughout his life to surprise those who thought he was incapable of affection. He displayed his good will more comically one day when he and Eugene were walking in Parnell Street. A beggar came up to them and asked, 'Could you spare us a copper?' Joyce was hard up, but asked, 'And why would you want a copper?' 'To tell the honest truth,' said the man, 'I was dyin' for a drink.' Joyce gave him his last penny and commented to Sheehy, 'If he'd said he wanted it for a cup of tea, I'd have hit him!'[52]

To the Sheehys his humor seemed often impish. He met Richard and Eugene on Phibsborough Road and displayed to them a curtain blind which he asserted to be a Sanskrit manuscript written on ribbed grass; he was going to sell it to the professor of Oriental languages in Trinity College. Just then a nursemaid wheeled a large and empty perambulator close to him, and Joyce allowed himself to tumble into it. Sitting there with his manuscript still unrolled, he drawled, 'Are you going far, miss?'[53] He liked to tell the Sheehys stories of his sisters' conversations, such as one about the Mater (Misericordiae) Hospital. 'Why is it called that?' asked one sister, and another gravely replied, 'Because you go there when something is the matter with you.'[54] Or he would suggest new inscriptions for Dublin statues: for Tom Moore in College Green, who stands with right forefinger raised, the legend: 'Oh! I know,' and for Bishop Plunket in Kildare Street, who is posed with finger placed thoughtfully on his brow, 'Now, where on earth did I put that stud?'[55] *

Joyce's name appears as one of the witnesses on a mock agreement signed by the Sheehy sons and daughters on September 30, 1900, promising to attend the Paris Exposition in 1910, or, if that did not

---

* In *Exiles* (557 [390]), Robert says: 'Once I made a little epigram about statues. All statues are of two kinds. *He folds his arms across his chest.* The statue which says: "How shall I get down?" and the other kind (*he unfolds his arms and extends his right arm, averting his head*) the statue which says: "In my time the dunghill was so high." '

take place, the Passion Play at Oberammergau.[56] He also participated in the mock election of a new pope to replace Leo XIII (who died in 1903). The most likely candidate at the time was Cardinal Rampolla. Joyce first played the part of an election official, and as the cardinals filed in advised them, 'If youse can't write, will ye make your mark?' Having tallied the vote, he announced, 'Rampolla, nothing,' a phrase that his friends recalled for years afterwards.[57] Joyce bribed the cardinals to vote for him, and won the election; asked for his blessing, he apologized, saying he had left it in his suitcase. Such incidents suggest that taste for callow foolery which Joyce chose never to renounce.

These frolics inspired Margaret Sheehy to write a play, *Cupid's Confidante*, which was staged first at the rear of the X.L. Café on Grafton Street on March 21, 1900, then at the Antient Concert Rooms on January 8, 1901.[58] Joyce took the role of the suave villain, Geoffrey Fortescue. One of his best effects was to *ad lib*, at a time when Sinn Fein urged Irishmen to buy Irish only, as his match failed to ignite, 'Damn these Irish matches!'[59] He did so well in the part that J. B. Hall, the drama critic for the *Evening Telegraph*, described his work as 'a revelation of amateur acting.' and with less ambiguity went on, 'But for the fact that he was too young to copy, plagiarise, or otherwise hamper himself by such a thing, one might say that he followed with extraordinary skill the combined methods of Charles Matthews and Robertson of "Hawtree" fame.'[60] This clipping remained in Joyce's wallet for a long time thereafter.

The success of *Cupid's Confidante* led the Sheehys one Christmas to produce Robertson's *Caste*, perhaps to afford Joyce the opportunity of playing Captain Hawtree. Years later Eugene Sheehy could still recall the aplomb with which Joyce arranged his tie in the mirror and said, 'I don't pretend to be a particularly good sort of fellow, nor a particularly bad sort of fellow. I suppose I'm about the average standard sort of thing.'[61] *

The calm of Joyce's last months at University College was rudely checked early in 1902 by the illness of his brother George, who had contracted typhoid fever. George was not yet fifteen years old; the rest

---

* Joyce, for his part, remembered how Polly describes in Act II the mimicking, at Astley's Amphitheatre in London, of Napoleon on horseback before the battle of Waterloo. He used it in the *Anna Livia Plurabelle* section of *Finnegans Wake* (214):

> Is that the great Finnleader himself in his joakimono on his statue riding the high horse there forehengist? . . . You're thinking of Astley's Amphitheayter where the bobby restrained you making sugarstuck pouts to the ghostwhite horse of the Peppers.

of the family were fond of him, and especially Stanislaus, who saw in him a more openhearted companion than James could be. As he lay in bed, wasted by disease, even John Joyce was touched and read to him in the evenings.[62] George asked James to sing to him, and took comfort in his brother's melancholy chant of Yeats's poem, 'Who Goes with Fergus?'. The doctor thought the boy had recovered, and instructed Mrs. Joyce to feed him anything she liked; but he was not ready for the solid food she gave him, and, perhaps as a result of it, suddenly relapsed. There then occurred the horrible scene described in one of Joyce's epiphanies and later inserted in *Stephen Hero*:

> Mrs. Joyce—(*crimson, trembling, appears at the parlour door*) . . . Jim!
> Joyce—(*at the piano*) . . . Yes?
> Mrs. Joyce—Do you know anything about the body? . . . What ought I do?
> . . . There's some matter coming away from the hole in Georgie's stomach . . .
> Did you ever hear of that happening?
> Joyce—(*surprised*) . . . I don't know. . . .
> Mrs. Joyce—Ought I send for the doctor, do you think?
> Joyce—I don't know. . . . What hole?
> Mrs. Joyce—(*impatient*) . . . The hole we all have . . . here. (*points*)* [63]

James ran to the sickroom and tried helplessly to revive his brother.[64] George died of peritonitis on March 9, 1902, as James himself was to die. The bond between the two is suggested by another epiphany:

> They are all asleep. I will go up now. . . . He lies on my bed where I lay last night! they have covered him with a sheet and closed his eyes with pennies . . . Poor little fellow! We have often laughed together. He bore his body very lightly . . . I am very sorry he died. I cannot pray for him as the others do. Poor little fellow! Everything else is so uncertain!

Three years later he decided upon George as the name for his first child.

Joyce was to leave the University in June. He had done well enough to pass, but had not bothered to excel.[65] His principal effort during his last year was devoted to a paper he was to read to the Literary and Historical Society on February 1, 1902. His subject this time was not a European, but the Irish poet James Clarence Mangan (1803-49), two of whose poems he had set to music. By choosing Mangan, Joyce implied that, however widely he might range in European literature, he was altogether ready to discover merit in his countrymen when it existed. The burden of his talk was that Mangan, though a nationalist poet, had been neglected and maligned by the nationalists. It was left to an Irishman with European standards to recover him.

---

* Joyce turned George into Stephen's sister Isabel in *Stephen Hero*.

Where his 'Drama and Life' paper two years before had been aggressive and declaratory, this one was meant to be seductive and lyrical.[66]
Joyce's air of discovering Mangan was a little pretentious, for Yeats
(who had proclaimed in verse that Mangan along with Davis and
Ferguson was his literary ancestor) and Lionel Johnson had both preceded him in admiring Mangan's work, and several editions of Mangan
had appeared during the ten years before Joyce spoke. But Mangan
was still unknown among the students, and Joyce insisted that he take
his place among the literary saints. Five years later he was to make a
more quixotic effort to bring Mangan to the notice of the Italians, and
in later life he urged on the reputations of other obscure or forgotten
writers like Svevo and Dujardin with the same zeal.

To set forth Mangan's merits, Joyce chose to use a highly adorned,
rhythmical style. With it he tries to outdo Pater, summoning up 'Vittoria
Colonna and Laura and Beatrice—even she upon whose face many
lives have cast that shadowy delicacy, as of one who broods upon
distant terrors and riotous dreams, and that strange stillness before
which love is silent, Mona Lisa.' The argument is not easy to follow,
partly because the style is often involved, and partly because Joyce
wishes to develop a theory of the artistic needs of Ireland at the same
time that he describes and defends Mangan's unhappy career. He
strongly rejects as irrelevant the criticism of Mangan as opium and
alcohol addict. Mangan's life, lived in poverty and abuse, and ended
in neglect, was the kind of life an artist might be expected to lead. His
intense broodings upon Ireland's woe and his own were splendid.
They were, however, too unrelieved by the perception of 'the holy
spirit of joy.' The literature to come must be a fusing of Mangan's
intense romantic imagination with a classical strength and serenity.
Joyce's *o altitudo* peroration was obscure but overwhelming:

As often as human fear and cruelty, that wicked monster begotten by
luxury, are in league to make life ignoble and sullen and to speak evil of
death the time is come wherein a man of timid courage seizes the keys of
hell and of death, and flings them far out into the abyss, proclaiming the
praise of life, which the abiding splendour of truth may sanctify, and of
death, the most beautiful form of life. In those vast courses which enfold us
and in that great memory which is greater and more generous than our
memory, no life, no moment of exaltation is ever lost; and all those who have
written nobly have not written in vain, though the desperate and weary have
never heard the silver laughter of wisdom. Nay, shall not such as these
have part, because of that high original purpose which remembering painfully or by way of prophecy they would make clear, in the continual affirmation of the spirit?

This talk was more insinuating than that on 'Drama and Life.' A phrase like 'that great memory' was deliberately ambiguous; no Christian could legitimately oppose it, since the memory might be God's, but it had a peculiar sound and was in fact borrowed from Yeats, who had it from Henry More and the occultists. That death was the most beautiful form of life * was another conception which, while compatible with Christian belief, jarred Joyce's listeners as much as the paradox 'timid courage' and an earlier reference to the footsteps of the gods leaving the world. They mocked it later in *St. Stephen's* by suggesting that absence was the highest form of presence, a quip Joyce preserved and used again in a letter to his daughter thirty-three years later. But unknown to his audience he had been quoting the eloquent final speech of the father in *Michael Kramer* as he looks down upon the body of his son who has drowned himself:

There are people who take fright. But I am of the opinion, Lachmann, that one should know no fear in this world . . . Love, it is said, is strong as death. But you may confidently reverse the saying: Death is as gentle as love, Lachmann. I tell you that death has been maligned. That is the worst imposture in the world. Death is the mildest form of life: the masterpiece of the eternal Love . . . [*His eye falls upon the death-mask of Beethoven. He takes it down and, contemplating it, continues:*] Where shall we land? Whither are we driven? Why do we cry our cries of joy into the immense incertitude—we mites abandoned in the infinite? As though we knew whither we are tending! This you cried too! And did you know—even you? There is nothing in it of mortal feasts! Nor is it the heaven of the parsons! It is not this and it is not that. What . . . [he stretches out his hands to heaven] . . . what will it be in the end?

The members of the Literary and Historical Society were generally dazzled, but one speaker leaped up to attack the paper. This was Louis J. Walsh, who had won the society's gold medal for oratory over Joyce two years before.† [67] (Joyce satirizes his fustian in *Stephen Hero*.) According to the report of the meeting in *St. Stephen's*, 'the Hatter's paper proved highly interesting,' but 'the rabblement, whom the mention of Giacosa and Paracelsus customarily appalls, rallied with timid courage' to Walsh's side.[68] One member of the audience thought he recalled the young man's arising briefly to brag, like Disraeli, that the time would come when his audience would hear him.[69] If he did, there was no need, for the *Freeman's Journal* reported next day, 'Mr. James Joyce read an extremely able paper on "Mangan," and was deservedly

---

* 'Death is the highest form of life. Bah!' *Ulysses* (493 [479]).
† His defeat of Joyce for treasurer of the Society's executive committee occurred the year before that.

applauded at the conclusion for what was generally agreed to have
been the best paper ever read before the society.' ⁷⁰ The paper was
published, this time without argument, in *St. Stephen's* in May 1902,
and helped to make clearer that Joyce was quarreling with bad art and
petrified morality, not with his nation except insofar as it condoned
these. And he stated once and for all his lifelong conviction that literature was the affirmation of the human spirit.

How the human spirit might subsist while engaged in its affirmations
was his next problem. His father, remembering his own experience in
a distillery, and looking forward eagerly to being supported by his
gifted son, urged him to seek a clerkship in Guinness's brewery. James
declined this gambit, and followed instead another of his father's many
precedents in registering, along with his friend Byrne, for the Cecilia
Street Medical School in April 1902. The writer, who had Ireland for
patient, to anatomize and purge, might plausibly be physician too. Such
a conjunction helped lure Joyce on to what did not prove 'a brilliant
career' in medicine.

1902

> . . . If one has the stomach to add the breakages, upheavals, distortions,
> inversions of all this chambermade music one stands, given a grain of
> goodwill, a fair chance of actually seeing the whirling dervish, Tumult,
> son of Thunder, self exiled in upon his ego. . . .
>
> —*Finnegans Wake* (184)

IN 1902 literary life in Dublin was ambitious and intense. Joyce could
be as distrustful as he liked of the directions that Yeats and Moore
were taking, but in English there was no one writing verse or fiction
whom he admired more. Synge had begun to write his plays; Lady
Gregory at the age of fifty had revealed an unexpected skill at peasant
comedy; George Russell, talented himself, was hospitably encouraging
a *cénacle* that included Padraic Colum, 'Seumas O'Sullivan,' and other
writers who, if they were minor, were young and lively. The Irish
literary movement, fostered by Standish O'Grady, John O'Leary, Yeats,
Douglas Hyde, and others, had made Dublin an intellectual center,
and in spite of his careful dissociation of himself from many shibboleths
of the new literature, Joyce profited from its momentum.

During the summer of 1902 he decided to make himself known in
Dublin literary circles. He presented himself first to George Russell,
who was approachable and indulgent, and who, unlike Yeats, was
always in Dublin. Russell, then thirty-five, was the youngest of the
senior figures of the revival, Yeats being thirty-seven and Moore the
same age as Lady Gregory. Russell's mysticism, and his bearded pro-
lixity, led skeptics to suppose he was foolish, but in fact he was clever.
His own verse was not first-rate, but neither was it untalented; and he
had a sharp eye for ability in others and an unexpected power of
criticism. Joyce chose, perhaps on impulse, to call upon Russell at ten
o'clock one night early in August. When his knock was not answered,
he walked up and down the street until Russell returned. It was then
midnight, but, unwilling to give up his idea, Joyce knocked at the door
anyway and asked if it was too late to speak to him. 'It's never too late,'
Russell courageously replied and brought him in. They sat down and

Russell looked at Joyce inquiringly. Since Joyce seemed to experience some difficulty in explaining why he had come, Russell talked for a bit and then asked, 'Has it emerged yet?' It had not. Russell's life was divided, he told Joyce, into the three parts: economics, literature, and mysticism. Was it the economics that interested Joyce? No, it was not that. Joyce finally said shyly what he had prepared as part of his bold offensive in advance, that he thought it possible an avatar might be born in Ireland.* He may have been referring to himself, but his implication, as Russell understood it, was that the sight of his host comfortably smoking his pipe in an armchair, had made Joyce think that the avatar was not in front of him. He remained nevertheless for hours, talking. He allowed that Russell had written a lyric or two, but complained that Yeats had gone over to the rabblement. He spoke slightingly of everyone else, too. When pressed by Russell, he read his own poems, but not without first making clear that he didn't care what Russell's opinion of them might be.¹ Russell thought they had merit but urged him to get away from traditional and classical forms, concluding (as he afterwards remembered with great amusement), 'You have not enough chaos in you to make a world.'²

They took up Theosophical subjects as well, although Joyce was skeptical of Theosophy as being a recourse for disaffected Protestants. He had remarked to his brother that the Dublin mystics had left the churches only to become latter-day saints. 'As such they do not compare either for consistence, holiness, or charity with a fifth-rate saint of the Catholic Church.'³ Nevertheless he was genuinely interested in such Theosophical themes as cycles, reincarnation, the succession of gods, and the eternal mother-faith that underlies all transitory religions. *Finnegans Wake* gathers all these up into a half-'secret doctrine.' Russell conceived what Joyce called 'the quaint misconception' that he had a new recruit for the Hermetic Society, and afterwards, if the evidence of *Ulysses* can be trusted, told 'some Yankee interviewer' that Joyce. 'came to him in the small hours of the morning to ask him about planes of consciousness.'⁴ But if Russell misconceived the motive of Joyce's visit, so did Joyce's friends, who thought the young man was merely pulling the older man's leg. Russell, on several planes of consciousness, was integral in Joyce's plans. He was full of useful information about Eastern philosophy, and he was a means of access to other writers.

When they at last broke off their conversation, it was arranged that Joyce should come again a few nights later. He had succeeded in making Russell feel uncomfortable, as Russell admitted in a letter to Sarah

---

* In *Finnegans Wake* (42), Earwicker is 'the vilest bogeyer but most attractionable avatar the world has ever had to explain for.'

Purser of August 15: 'I expect to see my young genius on Monday and will find out more about him. I wouldn't be his Messiah for a thousand million pounds. He would be always criticising the bad taste of his deity.' [5] To Thomas Mosher he wrote, 'There is a young boy named Joyce who may do something. He is proud as Lucifer and writes verses perfect in their technique and sometimes beautiful in quality.' [6] Russell spoke to Moore about Joyce, and Moore, it seemed, had read 'The Day of the Rabblement' and said it was 'preposterously clever.' Then tirelessly, Russell wrote to Lady Gregory and finally signaled Joyce's advent to Yeats: 'I want you very much to meet a young fellow named Joyce whom I wrote to Lady Gregory about half-jestingly. He is an extremely clever boy who belongs to your clan more than to mine and still more to himself. But he has all the intellectual equipment—culture and education, which all our other friends here lack, and I think writes amazingly well in prose, though I believe he also writes verse and is engaged in writing a comedy which he expects will occupy him five years or thereabouts as he writes slowly . . . I think you would find this youth of twenty-one with his assurance and self-confidence rather interesting.' [7] So in a few weeks Russell, as Joyce hoped, had sounded the alarm.

In early October 1902, Yeats came to Dublin, and Russell, who had told him a year before that a new generation would arise to find them both obvious, announced, 'The first spectre of the new generation has appeared. His name is Joyce. I have suffered from him and I would like you to suffer.' [8] Yeats submitted, and Russell wrote Joyce to go to see the poet at the Antient Concert Rooms where he was helping to rehearse *Cathleen ni Houlihan* and some other plays.[9] But Joyce preferred to meet Yeats more privately and haphazardly on the street, near the National Library. They went from there to a café.

Their meeting has a symbolic significance in modern literature, like the meeting of Heine and Goethe. The defected Protestant confronted the defected Catholic, the landless landlord met the shiftless tenant. Yeats, fresh from London, made one in a cluster of writers whom Joyce would never know, while Joyce knew the limbs and bowels of a city of which Yeats knew well only the head. The world of the petty bourgeois, which is the world of *Ulysses* and the world in which Joyce grew up, was for Yeats something to be abjured. Joyce had the same contempt for both the ignorant peasantry and the snobbish aristocracy that Yeats idealized. The two were divided by upbringing and predilection.

At the age of thirty-seven, Yeats had not yet begun to display the deliberate savagery or the worldly beauty of his later poetry, but he

had reached a point in his early work from which he knew he must
veer sharply. *The Wind among the Reeds* (1899) and *The Shadowy
Waters* (1900) had been too concerned with beauty, and Yeats needed
now to find roughness and spontaneity. For this purpose he had violently turned to writing peasant plays in peasant dialect. To Joyce
this interest in the Irish folk on the part of an Anglo-Irishman was
patronizing, and on the part of an elaborate artist was self-defeating.
Not understanding the complicated dialectic by which Yeats flung
himself from unpopular to popular art, he saw only volatility; he had
spoken in 'The Day of the Rabblement' of Yeats's 'floating will,' and in
Finnegans Wake would call him 'Will-of-the-wisp.' [10] He did not conceal his uncomplimentary, and misguided, views now, but spoke to
Yeats 'with a gentle and engaging smile and presently apologized by
saying, "I am not, as you see, treating you with any deference, for
after all both you and I will be forgotten."' Modest as Yeats was, such
an apology could only ruffle him. He is said to have remarked to his
friends, 'Never have I seen so much pretension with so little to show
for it.' Probably he did make the remark in momentary pique—Dubliners usually make the remarks which are attributed to them—but he
was nonetheless impressed by Joyce. The young man was so certain.
When Yeats imprudently mentioned the names of Balzac * and of
Swinburne, Joyce burst out laughing so that everyone in the café
turned round to look at him. [11] 'Who reads Balzac today?' he exclaimed.
Joyce read Yeats some epiphanies on 'Love and Death and the Soul,'
which Yeats said were 'very beautiful but immature,' but Yeats also
compared Joyce's 'joyous vitality' to that of William Morris, at which
Joyce commented, 'I don't have his physique.' [12]

Yeats wrote an account of the interview which suggests how pleased
he was with this young man who talked back to him. He intended to
use it as a preface to his book of essays, *Ideas of Good and Evil*, but
changed his mind and put it away among his papers: †

* In a review of Ibsen's *Catilina*, published on March 21, 1903, Joyce seems to be
referring to this conversation again: 'But meanwhile a young generation which has
cast away belief and thrown precision after it, for which Balzac is a great intellect
and every sampler who chooses to wander amid his own shapeless hells and heavens
a Dante without the unfortunate prejudices of Dante will be troubled by this preoccupation [of Ibsen], and out of very conscience will denounce a mood so calm,
so ironical.' The 'young generation' here appears to be Yeats, with a dash of George
Russell.
† The reliability of Yeats's account has been questioned. In later life it is true that
both he and Joyce denied that Joyce had said, 'You are too old for me to help
you.' But Joyce, in looking over the proofs of Gorman's biography, had this to say:
'The story as constantly retailed in the press is another story of Dublin public
house gossip. J.J. at this time had an immense admiration for Yeats as a poet and
though he did say the words or something to the effect attributed to him they were

I had been looking over the proof sheets of this book one day in Dublin lately and thinking whether I should send it to the Dublin papers for review or not. I thought that I would not, for they would find nothing in it but a wicked theology, which I had probably never intended, and it may be found all the review on a single sentence. I was wondering how long I should be thought a preacher of reckless opinions and a disturber who carries in his hand the irresponsible torch of vain youth. I went out into the street and there a young man came up to me and introduced himself. He told me he had written a book of prose essays or poems, and spoke to me of a common friend.

Yes, I recollected his name, for he had been to my friend who leads an even more reckless rebellion than I do, and had kept him up to the grey hours of the morning discussing philosophy. I asked him to come with me to the smoking room of a restaurant in O'Connell Street, and read me a beautiful though immature and eccentric harmony of little prose descriptions and meditations. He had thrown over metrical form, he said, that he might get a form so fluent that it would respond to the motions of the spirit. I praised his work but he said, 'I really don't care whether you like what I am doing or not. It won't make the least difference to me. Indeed I don't know why I am reading to you.'

Then, putting down his book, he began to explain all his objections to everything I had ever done. Why had I concerned myself with politics, with folklore, with the historical setting of events, and so on? Above all why had I written about ideas, why had I condescended to make generalizations? These things were all the sign of the cooling of the iron, of the fading out of inspiration. I had been puzzled, but now I was confident again. He is from the Royal University, I thought, and he thinks that everything has been settled by Thomas Aquinas, so we need not trouble about it. I have met so many like him. He would probably review my book in the newspapers if I sent it there. But the next moment he spoke of a friend of mine [Oscar Wilde] who after a wild life had turned Catholic on his deathbed. He said that he

---

never said in the tone of contempt which is implied in the story.' [13] Yeats said much the same thing to L. A. G. Strong. He also wrote down in his *Autobiographies* another remark made by Joyce at their first meeting: 'A young poet, who wrote excellently but had the worst manners, was to say a few years later, "You do not talk like a poet, you talk like a man of letters..."' In an unpublished manuscript entitled 'Some Characters of the Irish Literary Movement,' George Russell gives an account from memory of the meeting of Joyce and Yeats:

'When Yeats returned to Dublin the famous poet and the unknown youth met. Yeats asked Joyce to read him some of his poems. "I do so since you ask me," said Joyce, "but I attach no more importance to your opinion than to anybody one meets in the street." Yeats made him some compliments on the verses, which were charming. But Joyce waived aside the praise. "It is likely both you and I will soon be forgotten." He then questioned Yeats about some of his later poetry. Yeats began an elaborate and subtle explanation the essence of which was that in youth he thought everything should be perfectly beautiful but now he thought one might do many things by way of experiment. "Ah," said the boy, "that shows how rapidly you are deteriorating." He parted from Yeats with a last shaft, "We have met too late. You are too old for me to have any effect on you."' [14]

hoped his conversion was not sincere. He did not like to think that he had
been untrue to himself at the end. No, I had not understood him yet.

I had been doing some little plays for our Irish theatre, and had founded
them all on emotions or stories that I had got out of folklore. He objected
to these particularly and told me that I was deteriorating. I had told him
that I had written these plays quite easily and he said that made it quite
certain; his own little book owed nothing to anything but his own mind
which was much nearer to God than folklore.

I took up the book and pointing to a thought said, 'You got that from
somebody else who got it from the folk.' I felt exasperated and puzzled and
walked up and down explaining the dependence of all good art on popular
tradition. I said, 'The artist, when he has lived for a long time in his own
mind with the example of other artists as deliberate as himself, gets into
a world of ideas pure and simple. He becomes very highly individualized
and at last by sheer pursuit of perfection becomes sterile. Folk imagination
on the other hand creates endless images of which there are no ideas. Its
stories ignore the moral law and every other law, they are successions of
pictures like those seen by children in the fire. You find a type of these two
kinds of invention, the invention of artists and the invention of the folk, in
the civilization that comes from town and in the forms of life that one finds
in the country. In the towns, especially in big towns like London, you don't
find what old writers used to call the people; you find instead a few highly
cultivated, highly perfected individual lives, and great multitudes who imitate them and cheapen them. You find, too, great capacity for doing all
kinds of things, but an impulse towards creation which grows gradually
weaker and weaker. In the country, on the other hand, I mean in Ireland
and in places where the towns have not been able to call the tune, you find
people who are hardly individualized to any great extent. They live through
the same round of duty and they think about life and death as their fathers
have told them, but in speech, in the telling of tales, in all that has to do
with the play of imagery, they have an endless abundance. I have collected
hundreds of stories and have had hundreds of stories collected for me, and
if one leaves out certain set forms of tale not one story is like another. Everything seems possible to them, and because they can never be surprised, they
imagine the most surprising things. The folk life, the country life, is nature
with her abundance, but the art life, the town life, is the spirit which is
sterile when it is not married to nature. The whole ugliness of the modern
world has come from the spread of the towns and their ways of thought,
and to bring back beauty we must marry the spirit and nature again. When
the idea which comes from individual life marries the image that is born
from the people, one gets great art, the art of Homer,* and of Shakespeare,
and of Chartres Cathedral.'

* At this time Joyce had no interest in Homer. He told Padraic Colum that the
Greek epics were before Europe, and outside the tradition of European culture.
The *Divine Comedy* was Europe's epic, he said.[15] He distrusted Plato, as Herbert
Gorman says, and described Hellenism in an early notebook as 'European appendi-
citis.' [16]

I looked at my young man. I thought, 'I have conquered him now,' but I was quite wrong. He merely said, 'Generalizations aren't made by poets; they are made by men of letters. They are no use.'

Presently he got up to go, and, as he was going out, he said, 'I am twenty. How old are you?' I told him, but I am afraid I said I was a year younger than I am. He said with a sigh, 'I thought as much. I have met you too late. You are too old.'

And now I am still undecided as to whether I shall send this book to the Irish papers for review. The younger generation is knocking at my door as well as theirs.[17]

That Yeats took Joyce's remarks in good part is borne out by the fact that he invited the young man to write a play for the new theater; Joyce promised to do so in five years. Yeats kept the poems and epiphanies to read more closely, and then wrote Joyce a long and complimentary letter which, like Archer's about *A Brilliant Career*, suggests how strong and immediate an impression Joyce's work and character generated. A part of Yeats's letter has survived:

> but I cannot say more than this. Remember what Dr. Johnson said about somebody 'let us wait until we find out whether he is a fountain or a cistern.' The work which you have actually done is very remarkable for a man of your age who has lived away from the vital intellectual centres. Your technique in verse is much better than the technique of any young Dublin man I have met during my time. It might have been the work of a young man who had lived in an Oxford literary set. However men have started with as good promise as yours and have failed and men have started with less and have succeeded. The qualities that make a man succeed do not show in his verse, often, for quite a long time. They are much less qualities of talent than qualities of character—faith (of this you have probably enough), patience, adaptability (without this one learns nothing), and a gift for growing by experience and this is perhaps rarest of all.
>
> I will do anything for you I can but I am afraid that it will not be a great deal. The chief use I can be, though probably you will not believe this, will be by introducing you to some other writers who are starting like yourself, one always learns one's business from one's fellow-workers, especially from those who are near enough one's own age to understand one's difficulties.
>
> Yours sincerely
W B Yeats [18]

Through Yeats and Russell, Joyce went on next to Lady Gregory, who was fascinated by his way of reading his poems, and largely overlooked his bad manners. She invited him, with Yeats and Yeats's father, to dine with her at the Nassau Hotel on November 4.[19] The members of the Irish literary movement were doing their best for Joyce, but all were to discover that he was not a man to be helped with impunity.

In October Joyce began the medical course for which he had registered the previous spring.[20] His father was eager that James might succeed where he himself had failed, but James was to prove himself by the same history his father's son. He attended a few lectures in biology, chemistry, and physics, but his faculty of application to disagreeable subjects, which had sustained him at Belvedere, had diminished during his truant years at University College. He probably suspected that he would not be able to complete the course, although he admitted the suspicion to no one. His state of mind during this month is suggested by his indifferent and flamboyant behavior when, on October 31, he went to receive his Bachelor of Arts degree from the Royal University. He and his fellow-students were as obstreperous as possible, especially during the playing of 'God Save the King.' Leaving the hall, a group clustered around Joyce, who was about to address them when the police forced him and some friends, as St. *Stephen's* reported, 'to take refuge on an outside car.' When the crowd collected at another place, Joyce 'addressed a "large and excited gathering," ' not to argue against the singing of the anthem, but to plead the students' right to 'make as much noise as they liked.' [21]

While at the medical school Joyce encountered another old difficulty; his father was even more strapped for money than before. John Joyce had decided, now that his children were, as he assumed, growing toward independence, that he would commute his pension and buy a house. By cutting his pension in half, he was able to realize enough money to purchase, on October 24, a house at 7 St. Peter's Terrace, Phibsborough (Cabra).* As a result he had now only £5/10/1½ a

---

* He celebrated the purchase by getting drunk. Alfred Bergan liked to remember the occasion: 'I was standing with a friend of mine near Nelson's Pillar; we were waiting for the last tram home, when my friend espied John Stanislaus trying to make his way home. It was apparent that he had been enjoying himself not wisely but too well. Fearing that he might not reach home in safety we said that we would see him into a tram. My friend said, "Where does he live?" I said, "I don't know but I believe in Dollymount." He changed his address so often that it was impossible to know the correct one. My friend said, "That will be all right. Leave him to me. I know every conductor on that line and they will do anything I wish."

'Poor Joyce was seen into the tram and my friend gave the conductor strict instructions not to allow him out until Dollymount was reached. The tram moved out and we were quite happy at having done a good turn. All went well and the tram had covered nearly the distance when Joyce woke up and tried to get out, but no use; the conductor, obeying instructions, was determined that he would not let him out and brought the unfortunate man to Dollymount. It appeared that within two or three days of our meeting him, he had changed his address to 7 St. Peter's Terrace, Cabra, a very considerable distance from Dollymount.

'I met him two or three days afterwards and he was limping. On my asking what

month to spend. The move was ill-advised in every way. It plunged John Joyce into such financial discomfort that he took an immediate mortgage of £100 on the house, then on December 18 another of £50, on April 24, 1903, another of £50, and on November of that year the last of £65. The family remained at St. Peter's Terrace until May 26, 1905, when they sold what remained of their interest in the house and moved once more.

James Joyce was therefore badly in need of money to pay his expenses at medical school. He wished to do the same grinding (tutoring) that Byrne was doing, but the authorities said they had no work of this kind for him. On this tenuous basis, and with his usual impetuous quickness to discover enemies, Joyce now concluded that the authorities were leagued against him. His irritation over what he considered mistreatment joined with his dislike of his science courses and propelled him towards a violent change.

Having decided that medical school in Dublin did not suit him, Joyce rather illogically resolved to try medical school in Paris. Of course he wanted to go to Paris anyway, but he always presented his caprices as reasoned plans. Whether a Paris degree would be of any use to him in Ireland he did not investigate, and he did not bother his head over other questions he might have asked himself, such as how he could hope to pass chemistry in French when he could not do so in English. Migration to Paris was flamboyant; other Irish writers, Shaw, Wilde, and Yeats, had gone to London, and he would do something else. Paris would separate him further than London from familiar things,

---

was the matter, he said, "A night or two ago some blackguards put me into the wrong tram and sent me off to Dollymount. I had taken a drop too much and did not realize where I was until the tram was approaching Dollymount. I jumped up, told the conductor I was in the wrong tram and to let me out. The conductor shook his head, smiled, and said that the two gentlemen who put me into the tram knew better than I did where I was to be let out. All my arguments were unavailing, and there was nothing further I could do but remain until the end of the journey. I did not know then that I was on the last tram from Dublin and no tram returning.

' "When I realized my position I could do nothing but go over and sit on the sea wall and cry. I thought of my wife and family and how anxious they would be at my non-arrival home. After resting on the wall for some time, there was nothing for it but to walk home." He then gave a description of the long walk home, the distances being slightly exaggerated, and continued, "The walk from Dollymount to Fairview appeared to me seven miles long, and when I arrived at Clonliffe Road and looked up it appeared to me about five miles long. However, after resting two or three times, I got as far as Whitworth Road, and it appeared to be at least four miles in length. After struggling along for hours, I eventually arrived at St. Peter's Terrace about 5 o'clock in the morning. I was so exhausted I barely had energy enough to reach up and use the knocker. The door was opened by my wife and I fell into her arms and believe I fainted. I was in bed all next day and could not walk as I had a blister on my heel as big as a pigeon's egg.' 22

and he would advance upon Europe with the missionary zeal (though not the piety) of his fellow Celts, 'fiery Columbanus,'[23] the subtle doctor John Scotus, and Fiacre, eponymous saint of the cab drivers.

Joyce wrote the Faculté de Médecine on November 18, 1902, to request admission, and was told that each case was decided on its own merits by the Ministre de l'Instruction Publique.[24] The term had already begun, but all such details he thought he might safely disregard. Having made his decision, he proceeded by writing everyone he could for help. His letter to Lady Gregory is a mixture of dependence and posturing independence, and shows that he was already attaching emblematic importance to his flight from Dublin:

> 7 St Peter's Terrace
> Cabra, Dublin.
>
> Dear Lady Gregory,
>
> I have broken off my medical studies here and am going to trouble you with a history. I have a degree of B.A. from the Royal University, and I had made plans to study medicine here. But the college authorities are determined I shall not do so, wishing I dare say to prevent me from securing any position of ease from which I might speak out my heart. To be quite frank I am without means to pay my medical fees and they refuse to get me any grinding or tuitions or examining—alleging inability—although they have done and are doing so for men who were stuck in the exams I passed. I want to get a degree in medicine, for then I can build up my work securely. I want to achieve myself—little or great as I may be—for I know that there is no heresy or no philosophy which is so abhorrent to my church as a human being, and accordingly I am going to Paris. I intend to study medicine at the University of Paris supporting myself there by teaching English. I am going alone and friendless *—I know of a man who used to live somewhere near Montmartre but I have never met him †—into another country, and I am writing to you to know can you help me in any way. I do not know what will happen to me in Paris but my case can hardly be worse than it is here. I am leaving Dublin by the night boat on Monday 1st December and my train leaves Victoria Station for Newhaven the same night. I am not despondent however for I know that even if I fail to make my way such failure proves very little. I shall try myself against the powers of the world. All things are inconstant except the faith in the soul, which changes all things and fills their inconstancy with light. And though I seem to have been driven out of my country here as a misbeliever I have found no man yet with a faith like mine.
>
> Faithfully yours
> James Joyce

* That Joyce liked this phrase is suggested by his referring to himself in 'The Holy Office' two years later as 'Unfellowed, friendless and alone.'
† Probably Joseph Casey. See pp. 129-30.

Lady Gregory invited him to Coole to talk over his plans, and prudently suggested he consider attending the Trinity College medical school, an idea which did not suit Joyce at all. Since his resolution was inflexible, she urged him in motherly fashion to take warm clothing to Paris, and wrote some letters for him.° Joyce did not go to Coole, but he did follow another of her suggestions in going to see E. V. Longworth, the editor of the *Daily Express,* to whom she had written. Longworth talked with Joyce three days before his departure, and agreed to send books for review to help him support himself. Lady Gregory also wrote a doctor friend in London asking him to recommend Joyce to Paris friends, and the doctor obligingly wrote a French doctor, Joseph Rivière, to look out for his young friend Joyce.

A third letter from Lady Gregory to Yeats produced unexpectedly good results. Yeats replied at once from London,

My dear Joyce,

I have just heard from Lady Gregory about your plan of going to Paris to study. It seems that you leave Dublin Monday night, and cross to Paris Tuesday night. If I am right I hope you will breakfast with me on Tuesday morning. I shall set my alarm clock and be ready for you as soon as the train gets in. You can lie down on my sofa afterwards to sleep off the fatigue of the journey. You can dine with me and catch your Paris train afterwards. I hope you will come to me as I should like a good talk. I think you should let me give you one or two literary introductions here in London as you will find it much easier to get on in Paris (where perhaps a great many people do not want to learn English) if you do some writing, book reviews, poems etc. for the papers here. This kind of work never did anybody any harm. Your poems will bring you something at once, I should think.

                                        Yours sincerely
                                        W B Yeats

PS I could get 'The Speaker' I have little doubt to take verses from you and to give you a chance of doing some reviewing. I brought them a young man a while back, whom they look upon as one of their best writers and I have no doubt they will be quite ready to expect as good from you. But we can talk over these things.

° Lady Gregory did everything except furnish him with what is referred to in *Ulysses* as 'some of the ready,' and now or later Joyce sadly memorialized her in a limerick:

> There was a kind lady called Gregory,
> Said 'Come to me, poets in beggary,'
> But found her imprudence
> When thousands of students
> Cried, 'All, we are in that category.' [25]

Thus encouraged, Joyce completed his preparations. He secured a letter from his father's friend, Timothy Harrington, the Lord Mayor of Dublin, which vouched for his good character.[26] He wrote of his plans to William Archer, and Archer did his best to dissuade him from trying to teach English in Paris, arguing that the field was already overcrowded. 'It is hard enough by giving lessons all day to keep body and soul together in Paris; and how you can expect to do that, and at the same time qualify as a doctor, passes my comprehension. Forgive my frankness. It is, of course, no business of mine; but I am sure you are making a mistake.'[27] But Joyce had gone too far to be influenced by sage counsels. He intrusted his manuscripts to George Russell, in part, as he implied later to his brother, to flatter him for future use;[28] and that bewildered mystic wrote to Yeats, 'Of all the wild youths I have ever met he is the wildest. I wonder why I meet them. I am sane even to dullness in my soul.'[29] Joyce informed Stanislaus that, in case of his untimely death, copies of both his verses and epiphanies should be sent to all the great libraries of the world, the Vatican not excepted.[*][30] His sense of his departure as a *beau geste* had deepened when he left from Kingstown pier—that disappointed bridge, he later called it—on the evening of December 1, 1902.

This was the departure which he was to fuse, in *A Portrait of the Artist*, with his 1904 departure. He was not yet using the word 'exile,' but there are hints of it in his letter to Lady Gregory. Joyce needed exile as a reproach to others and a justification of himself. His feeling of ostracism from Dublin lacked, as he was well aware, the moral decisiveness of his hero Dante's exile from Florence, in that he kept the keys to the gate. He was neither bidden to leave nor forbidden to return, and after this first departure he was in fact to go back five times. But, like other revolutionaries, he fattened on opposition and grew thin and pale when treated with indulgence. Whenever his relations with his native land were in danger of improving, he was to find a new incident to solidify his intransigence and to reaffirm the rightness of his voluntary absence. In later life he even showed some grand resentment at the possibility of Irish independence on the grounds that it would change the relationship he had so carefully established be-

---

[*] He satirized this histrionic gesture in *Ulysses* (41 [37]) when Stephen says to himself: 'Remember your epiphanies on green oval leaves, deeply deep, copies to be sent if you died to all the great libraries of the world, including Alexandria? Someone was to read them there after a few thousand years, a mahamanvantara. Pico della Mirandola like. Ay, very like a whale.'

Joyce probably remembered that at the Childs murder trial, it was brought out that the murdered brother left instructions in his will that if at his death his six volumes of verse were unpublished, they should be published by his estate and a copy deposited in the library of Trinity College.

tween himself and his country. 'Tell me,' he said to a friend, 'why you think I ought to change the conditions that gave Ireland and me a shape and a destiny.' [31] That Joyce could not have written his books in Ireland is likely enough, but he felt the need for maintaining his intimacy with his country by continually renewing the quarrel with her which was now prompting him to leave for the first time.

Joyce's books were to describe various kinds of separation, and he was busy gathering material for them. His heroes were to seek freedom, which is also exile, by will and by compulsion. To some extent they were society's victims, but Joyce was not so masochistic as to identify himself completely with the helpless quarry; at the very moment that he attacked society most bitterly as his oppressor, he did not completely deny the authorship of his own despair.* Like the boy in the ballad of the Jew's daughter, he was immolated, *consenting*.[32] On the other hand he was not so possessed with self as to adopt utterly the part of the anarchic individual. Those of his heroes who triumphed in their self-righteousness were unhappy, as if they had gone too far.

Joyce, as he dimly recognized already, throve on the incursions he could make upon conventions, and upon the resistance he could stimulate. Departure from his country was a strategy of combat. Another strategy, which was closely connected with it, was writing. In later life Joyce told his friend Claud Sykes that, so long as he could write, he could live anywhere, in a tub, like Diogenes.[33] Writing was itself a form of exile for him, a source of detachment. When a young man came up to him in Zurich and said, 'May I kiss the hand that wrote *Ulysses*?' Joyce replied, somewhat like King Lear, 'No, it did lots of other things too.'[34] Only in writing, which is also departing, is it possible to achieve the purification which comes from a continual rebaptism of the mind.

Joyce was too candid with himself not to recognize that his motives for leaving Dublin transcended any irritations he had with the Jesuits and any desire he had for medical education. The experiment in living which he had told Stanislaus he would conduct [35] required that he experiment with living elsewhere. To measure himself and his country he needed to take the measure of a more alien world.

---

* Stephen finds the same paradoxes in God and in Shakespeare. God begets himself, sends himself between himself and others, is put upon by his own fiends. *Ulysses* (195 [186]). As to Shakespeare, 'His unremitting intellect is the hornmad Iago ceaselessly willing that the moor in him shall suffer.' Ibid. (210 [201]).

1902–1903

Paris rawly waking, crude sunlight on her lemon streets. Moist piths of farls of bread, the froggreen wormwood, her matin incense, court the air. Belluomo rises from the bed of his wife's lover's wife, the kerchiefed housewife is astir, a saucer of acetic acid in her hands. In Rodot's Yvonne and Madeleine newmake their tumbled beauties, shattering with gold teeth *chaussons* of pastry, their mouths yellowed with the *pus* of *flan breton.* Faces of Paris men go by, their wellpleased pleasers, curled conquistadores.

—*Ulysses* (43 [39])

PARIS was Dublin's antithesis. The daydream of himself as Dr. Joyce, poet, epiphanist, and physician, surrounded by fair women, was not at all dampened by the small amount of money beyond his fare that his father could give him, or by the difficulties which he knew he must soon face. His reception in London kept up his exhilarated spirits. Yeats, informed beforehand of his arrival time, came to Euston Station at six in the morning to meet him. Joyce was grateful and, Yeats thought, 'unexpectedly amiable'; he 'did not knock at the gate with his old Ibsenite fury.'[1] The older poet spent the whole day with Joyce, wasting, as he ruefully reported to Lady Gregory, a good deal of time, but obviously anxious to help the young man. He bought him breakfast, lunch, and dinner, paid for cabs, and took him to the people he thought would be most useful. Yeats thought Joyce could best make his way by writing articles about French literature, reviews of books, and occasional poems, so he brought him to the offices of the *Academy* and the *Speaker,* and in the evening to the flat of Arthur Symons, who for about ten years had been the principal middleman between Paris and London.

Symons was to play as central a part in the publication of Joyce's early work as Ezra Pound was to play later. A Cornishman born in Wales, who prided himself on not being English, he had himself come to London while still young, and had soon persuaded the Londoners that they, rather than he, were the provincials. He sought out sensations, so that he might become their connoisseur, even taking hashish once or twice so as to taste his way towards new thresholds. All the arts attracted him; in music he was a Wagnerian, and he played for Joyce the Good Friday music from *Parsifal*, remarking in a manner that seemed to Joyce 'ninetyish, 'When I play Wagner, I am in another world.' ² Symons found Joyce at this first meeting 'a curious mixture of sinister genius and uncertain talent,' ³ while Joyce, after sampling this remarkable sampler of artistic sensations, enjoyed the remark Yeats made to him when they were alone again. 'Symons has always had a longing to commit great sin, but he has never been able to get beyond ballet girls.' ⁴ But Symons's enthusiasms were genuine, and his promise to help Joyce get his poems printed was not idle.

Joyce took a train to Newhaven that night, a boat to Dieppe, and then the train for Paris. He went directly to the Hotel Corneille in the Latin Quarter, the favorite stopping-place for British tourists without money. He wasted no time in presenting his letter of introduction, obtained through Lady Gregory, from Dr. MacLagan of London to Dr. Joseph Rivière ⁵ of Paris, who proved to be a specialist in physical therapy. Rivière invited him to luncheon the next day, and served a magnificent meal of seven courses which made Joyce write happily home, 'So much saved!' ⁶ The doctor pressed him for details about MacLagan, which Joyce, never having met his recommender, had to dodge as best he could.⁷ Joyce also called to see Maud Gonne, to whom Yeats had written on his behalf, but her niece was ill and she was quarantined; she wrote him a kind letter inviting him to call later,⁸ a suggestion over which he agonized for several weeks.

On December 4 Joyce wrote his first reviews for the *Daily Express*,⁹ one on the patriotic poems of William Rooney and another on a book on Meredith by Douglas Jerrold. These were unsigned and probably written straight off. In the first he chided Rooney for spoiling his art by patriotism, and spoke of 'those big words which make us so unhappy,' a sentence that annoyed the *United Irishman*, which had published the poems, so much that they derisively used it to advertise the book.° On December 5 Joyce went to find out about the medical course. He would need, it seemed, a French *baccalauréat*, or failing that, a dispensation from the Minister of Public Instruction, not ordinarily

° The advertisement, published on December 20, 1902, quoted much of the hostile review, and added, as the only comment, a single bracketed word to Joyce's sentence: 'And yet he might have written well if he had not suffered from one of those big words [Patriotism] which make us so unhappy.' ¹⁰ For a similar twitting of Gabriel Conroy in 'The Dead,' see p. 256.

granted after December 1. The Minister's office thought he might nevertheless receive one in a few days; in the meantime he prevailed upon Dr. Paul Brouardel, dean of the faculty at the École de Médecine, to grant him a provisional card of admission to the course for the certificate in physics, chemistry, and biology. He could take his first examination in July of 1903.[11]

During these first few days his letters home were full of energy and of sedulous detail. He wished to impress his family with his rigid economies:

I have bought an alarm clock (4 francs) to waken me in time in the mornings, as the school is some distance away. I had a bath just now (7½): warm. I can get breakfast for 3d, dejeuner (soup, meat, dessert, coffee) for 8d or 9d and dinner (soup, fish, meat and vegetables, dessert, coffee) for 1ˢ/-. But I am obliged to take coffee constantly through the day. Coffee is taken here during the day without milk but with sugar. This I find to my taste as the weather here is very severe, sometimes going down to 7 or 9 degrees below zero. The wind too is very keen but there is neither fog nor rain.[12]

Yet his economy was a spendthrift's mask. In the same letter of December 6, 1902, he tells them blandly: 'There is magnificent Norman furniture in a shop here—heavy wooden presses with parallel doors—5£ for one about twice as big as your wardrobe and though I cannot buy these yet for my room I shall certainly get them as soon as I can when I have definitely settled myself in Paris for my medical course.' He pleased his mother, however, by extravagantly promising to devote his first earnings to buying her a new set of teeth.[13]

Joyce probably attended his first classes on December 7. He told Gorman later that he stopped at once because he found he would have to pay his fees immediately;[14] but it seems likely, too, that he was discouraged to find his French inadequate for the highly technical lectures. His next letters developed the themes of the cold weather and of a sudden, mysterious access of ill health. The change of water and diet may have been responsible for his malaise, but he offered no such easy explanation, and his mother replied quickly in alarm. His next letter of December 15, in which he confessed to a 'curious weariness,'[15] which had made him sleep till eleven and want to sleep again at two in the afternoon, did little to calm her.

Notwithstanding his meticulously reported illness, he had by this time investigated the possibility of teaching English. A full-time position was available at the École Berlitz, at 150 francs or £7/10/0 a month. He was uncertain whether he should take it; to stop going to classes was one thing, but to abandon his medical career completely and formally was another. In the meantime he contracted to give private lessons in English to a champagne dealer named Joseph Douce, a young socialist with a full, blond beard, for about a pound a month.[16] He also wrote to Yeats, who replied on December 18:

My dear Joyce,

The last time I went to the 'Speaker,' and I think I have been twice since I wrote, I succeeded in finding somebody in. But when I spoke of my business, the man asked me to see the Editor, as he alone could act in such a matter and told me that the Editor would not be in town till after Xmas. I am sorry, but for the present you can send some prose to the 'Academy' if you feel an impulse to write. You had better mention my name so as to remind the Editor of what I told him. I won't give him your little poem, for I gather from his conversation that he does not like publishing verse, unless it has an obvious look of importance. He told me, for instance, that he would prefer two columns of verse if it were good, to a little lyric. If I had had all your MS I might have picked a little bundle of lyrics, but I think you had really better keep such things for the 'Speaker,' which makes rather a practice of publishing quite short scraps of verse. I think the poem that you have sent me has a charming rhythm in the second stanza, but I think it is not one of the best of your lyrics as a whole. I think that the thought is a little thin. Perhaps I will make you angry when I say that it is the poetry of a young man, of a young man who is practicing his instrument, taking pleasure in the mere handling of the stops. It went very nicely in its place with the others, getting a certain richness from the general impression of all taken together, and from your own beautiful reading. Taken apart by itself it would please a reader who had got to know your work, but it would not in itself draw attention to that work.[17] ...

To be 'alone and friendless' was tolerable; to have his poem rejected was less so. 'I am afraid,' Joyce wrote his mother, 'I shall not easily settle down.' 'I should not like to live in Paris but I should like to divide my existence,' [18] presumably between Paris and Dublin. And finally, compounding these hints with a child's helplessness, he said, 'Write again if you like, and say if I should go home for Christmas.' A fortnight of exile would do well enough for a start.

Mrs. Joyce talked the matter over with her husband, who agreed that their son must come home, and took his second mortgage on the house on December 18 to make it possible. To James she wrote: 'I only wish I was near you to look after and comfort you, but we will be united very soon again. Thank God for *home you must come* if only for a week.' [19] He had complained of one of her letters, and her apology is touching:

My dear Jim if you are disappointed in my letter and if as usual I fail to understand what you would wish to explain, believe me it is not from any want of a longing desire to do so and speak the words you want but as you so often said I am stupid and cannot grasp the great thoughts which are yours much as I desire to do so. Do not wear your soul out with tears but be as usually brave and look hopefully to the future. Let me have a letter *by return* and for God's sake take care of your health and if you get the little stove be very careful with it.[20]

Joyce was relieved, but continued to complain of bad health; he was not sure, he wrote, that he could stand up to the Dieppe route, he thought it better his parents should buy him a slightly more expensive ticket for the shorter Calais-Dover crossing.[21] The prospect of going home, even if he was seasick on the way, was delightful.

As a last gesture he seems to have gone to a theater and a brothel, and had himself photographed wearing a heavy, ill-fitting coat and a long-suffering look.* He sent off three copies of a photo-postcard, one to his family, mentioning his shortage of funds, the second to Cosgrave, discussing the *scorta* (prostitutes) of Paris in dog-Latin, and the third—to give play to yet another aspect of his mind—to Byrne, with a new poem on it, headed, 'For the beginning of the second part —the journey of the soul.' [22] The title and content indicated his firm decision to continue his travels:

> All day I hear the noise of waters
>   Making moan,
> Sad as the sea-bird is, when going
>   Forth alone,
> He hears the winds cry to the waters'
>   Monotone.
>
> The grey winds, the cold winds are blowing
>   Where I go.
> I hear the noise of many waters
>   Far below.
> All day, all night, I hear them flowing
>   To and fro.

As if to prove that he had more still to say about Paris, he wrote someone, probably Stanislaus, the same day:

Paris amuses me very much but I quite understand why there is no poetry in French literature . . .

> Es war ein König in Thule
> Gar treu bis an das Grab

* See Plate IV.

The whole menagerie, beginning with round little M. Loubet [president of the Republic], couldn't produce that because the Kingdom of God cometh not with observation.[23]

And so Joyce recovered his urbanity on the eve of departure. Money arrived from Dublin, and he left on Monday night, December 22, called on Yeats in London between trains, and reached Dublin the night of December 23.

In Dublin he discovered he had lost a friend. The photo-postcard which he had sent to Byrne, with the poem written in the space for a message, had pleased Byrne very much. He showed it to Cosgrave and said proudly that no man in Dublin knew more about Joyce than he did. Cosgrave, making the retort irresistible, slyly took a similar photograph from his pocket and showed it to Byrne saying, 'Perhaps that's something you didn't know.' Byrne read Joyce's description in dog-Latin of Paris whoredom with consternation; he had explicitly warned Joyce not to confide in Cosgrave, and the details were evidently shocking to him. He handed both post cards to Cosgrave saying, 'You can have this one, too.' [24]

Cosgrave told Stanislaus Joyce in great amusement what had happened, and gave him Byrne's card, saying he didn't need two. Joyce heard the story on his return, and experienced some snub from Byrne, for he said rather pompously to Stanislaus, 'I think I have been mistaken in Byrne.' [25] Stanislaus, who had been jealous of Byrne's preeminence in his brother's intimacy, took off his hat and solemnly began to intone the *Te Deum*. James began to refer to Byrne as 'His Intensity' and 'the Sea-Green Incorruptible.' [26]

What made the collapse of his principal friendship more serious was that Joyce had no relationships with women that were not coarse or distant. In his writing more is at stake in the friendship of Stephen and Cranly (Byrne) than in the relationship of Stephen and Emma Clery. Friendship becomes, in fact, a focal point, for if friendship exists, it impugns the quality of exile and of lonely heroism. If the world is not altogether hostile, we may forgive it for having mistreated us, and so be forced into the false position of warriors without adversaries. Joyce allows his hero to savor friendship before discovering its flaws, and then with the theme of broken friendship represents Stephen's broken ties with Ireland and the world.°

In actual life Joyce searched in vain for any foundation for his feeling that Byrne's change in attitude toward him was a betrayal, but

---

° 'Away then; it is time to go. . . . His friendship was coming to an end. Yes; he would go. He could not strive against another. He knew his part.' *A Portrait of the Artist* (516 [360-61]).

in his books he propounded various theories to explain it. The first, suggested by Stephen's brother Maurice, is that 'Cranly wants to become more and more necessary to you until he can have you in his power.' [27] Stephen repudiates this analysis, which he contends is based upon a 'novel' conception of friendship. The second reason appears on the surface to be an esthetic disagreement, Cranly's cool reception of Stephen's paper on 'Drama and Life.' Stephen now detects 'in Cranly's attitude toward him a certain hostility, arising out of a thwarted desire to imitate.' [28] The third is Cranly's growing interest in Emma Clery.*

These three reasons, the desire to dominate, to emulate, and to steal away his friend's girl, have in common the fact that it is Cranly who takes the first steps towards enmity, and that all explanations of his behavior are essentially proof of his dependence upon Stephen. In *A Portrait* Joyce goes further to evolve the fiction that Cranly's motivation is homosexual.† To Stanislaus, James Joyce owned himself baffled by Byrne's behavior, though he said, too, that Byrne must accept him whole, in the words of *Ulysses:* 'As I am. All or not at all.' [29] The incident of the post card kept the friends at odds, so that they did not meet any more during Joyce's Dublin holiday.

To fill the void left by Byrne's defection Joyce discovered, about this time, a new and more spectacular comrade. One night at the National Library, where he spent a good deal of time, he fell into talk with a young man who was also waiting at the counter for a book. They spoke of Yeats, both in decisive fashion. The young man was handsome, lithe, prosperous, and gay. He introduced himself as Oliver Gogarty, and said he was taking a degree at Oxford. Gogarty was as

---

* In *Stephen Hero* (215 [220]) Emma Clery walks by the two men, and when they bow to her she disregards Stephen to bow only to Cranly. To Cranly's question, 'Why did she do that?' Stephen replies with a laugh, 'Perhaps she meant it as an invitation.' What in *Stephen Hero* is only a suspicion becomes in *A Portrait of the Artist* (501 [350]) a virtual certainty. Stephen asks Cranly to come and talk with him, but Cranly delays. During the delay Emma Clery passes by, and again bows across Stephen in response to Cranly's greeting. Stephen is affronted and pounces upon this deliberate misdirection of her favor. 'Was there not a slight flush on Cranly's cheek?' he asks himself. 'Did that explain his friend's listless silence, his harsh comments, the sudden intrusions of rude speech with which he had shattered so often Stephen's ardent wayward confessions?' In the last pages of the book he writes in his journal of Cranly's growing intimacy with Emma, 'Is he the shining light now? Well, I discovered him. I protest I did. Shining quietly behind a bushel of Wicklow bran.' (522 [365])

† Cranly reminds Stephen that if he leaves his country he will be alone. 'And you know what that word means? Not only to be separated from all others but to have not even one friend . . . And now to have any one person . . . who would be more than a friend, more even than the noblest and truest friend a man ever had.' Stephen looks at him and wonders if he has spoken of himself. 'Of whom are you speaking?' he asks at last, and receives no answer. (519 [362-3])

addicted to obscenity and blasphemy as Cosgrave, and was also talented and remarkably witty. The clerk from Oxford and the clerk from Paris, who was four years younger, began to consort together. Gogarty admired Joyce's poems, and proffered his own, which Joyce admired less. Joyce however liked Gogarty's bawdy songs, and used three of them ('Landlord, landlord, bring us some wine, saboo, saboo,' 'Medical Dick and Medical Davy,' and 'Shimbad the Sailor and Rosalie the Coal Quay Whore') in *Ulysses*. From the start the two young men felt as much rivalry as friendship for each other; both were interested in medicine as a career, both were ambitious as writers. Gogarty spoke of Hellenizing Ireland, Joyce (who knew no Greek) of Europeanizing it. Joyce saw Gogarty as Ireland's 'gay betrayer,' [30] devoid of the deep feeling that makes loyalty possible; while Gogarty saw Joyce as an inverted Jesuit whom he must rouse from Firbolg melancholy to Attic joy.

Joyce's holiday was distinguished chiefly by its length; he stayed almost a whole month. Stanislaus Joyce remembered his brother's throwing a loaf of bread in at their front door at midnight on New Year's Eve, a rite that did not produce the hoped for abundance. James visited the Sheehys, playing the role of the Paris student. ('Just say in the most natural tone: when I was in Paris, *boul' Mich'*, I used to.' [*]) Called upon to sing French songs, he amused himself maliciously by censoring perfectly innocent lines so as to see the guests smile knowingly at what they assumed to be a salacious passage.[31] It was a good game for an expatriate.

He also came to know the members of the staff of the National Library in Kildare Street: Lyster, the director, he was already acquainted with, for Lyster had congratulated him, when the Ibsen article appeared in the *Fortnightly Review*, on becoming 'a man of letters.' [32] But he now visited Richard I. Best, destined to be Lyster's successor, and W. K. Magee, who had written essays in a graceful style modelled on Matthew Arnold's, under the more euphonious name of 'John Eglinton.' Best and Magee were well-read, intelligent men. Best had spent much time in Paris, and had just translated H. d'Arbois de Jubainville's book *Le Cycle mythologique Irlandais;* he spoke with a prissiness that Joyce mocked in *Ulysses*. Magee was strictly celibate, drank not at all, and was down on the imagination, which he fancied interfered with the exercise of reason and was bad for a Celt. (A Celt was Matthew Arnold's version of an Irishman.) Magee became a favorite butt of Joyce and Gogarty; Gogarty mocked his plain face and abstemious habits by speaking of 'the never-moistened muzzle of Magee,' and Joyce came up with a limerick:

* *Ulysses* (42 [38]).

There once was a Celtic librarian
Whose essays were voted Spencerian,
   His name is Magee
   But it seems that to me
He's a flavour that's more Presbyterian.[33]

But for the moment he was not indifferent to Magee's good opinion; employing what was by now a favorite device, he accosted him on the street one night, gave his name, and immediately launched into a strange, sententious discussion of intellectual questions. Among other things, he spoke of the disciplined indifference of the artist, and to illustrate pointed to a lamppost and stated emphatically, 'If I knew I were to drop dead before I reached that lamppost, it would mean no more to me than it will mean to walk past it.' * [34] Magee was half impressed, half put off by this odd young man; he could not keep from acknowledging some weeks afterwards to Gogarty, 'There is something sublime in Joyce's standing alone.' [35] Joyce offered no such encomium.

Before he left Dublin, on January 17, 1903,[36] Joyce heard from his father that a man named O'Hara, on the *Irish Times,* might be able to arrange for a French correspondent to the newspaper. Joyce imaginatively transformed such remote possibilities into certainties, and departed with the conviction that the *Irish Times* would soon be providing him with a regular income. Arrived in London, he nevertheless pursued some suggestions of Yeats. He went to C. Lewis Hind, the editor of the *Academy,* and was given a book to review to see if he would suit. He wrote an unfavorable notice, which he brought to Hind.

'This will not do, Mr. Joyce,' said Hind.

'Sorry,' said Joyce and started to leave the room, characteristically not condescending to argue the point.

'Oh, come, Mr. Joyce,' said Hind, 'I am only anxious to help you. Why don't you meet my wishes?'

'I thought,' replied Joyce, 'that I was to convey to your readers what I considered to be the esthetic value of the book you gave me.'

'Precisely. That is what I want.'

'Well!' Joyce went on. 'I don't think it has any value whatsoever, esthetic or otherwise, and I have tried to convey that to your readers.'

Hind was annoyed and said, 'Oh well, Mr. Joyce, if that is your attitude, I can't help you. I have only to lift the window and put my head out, and I can get a hundred critics to review it.'

'Review what, your head?' asked Joyce, ending the interview.[37] (Yeats scolded him for this callow behavior later, and Joyce took his

---

* To someone else's question, 'What do you think about life?' Joyce replied, 'I don't think about it.' [38]

rebuke 'unexpectedly well,' probably feeling he had acted foolishly.)
He would perhaps have been less bold if he had not felt fortified by
his *Irish Times* expectations, and also by the chance of another position
with a new magazine called *Men and Women*, which was to begin
in March. Yeats introduced him to the prospective editor, D. N. Dunlop,
who asked him for an immediate contribution and promised to pay
him two guineas per thousand words if all went well. But payment
could not begin until March.[39] Joyce went to see Courtney of the
Fortnightly Review, called on William Archer at the Liberal Club, and
also met Lady Gregory who was visiting in London.[40] Another Irishman, John Synge, was in London too, for the same reason as Joyce;
they did not meet, but both knew of the other's presence, and Synge
wrote his mother on January 21, 'I have several more editors to see on
the papers I have written for already, but I could not go to them last
week as I was uncertain about my address. This week Joyce—on his
way back to Paris—is going to them all so I will not go round for a
few days as it is better not to have too many Irishmen turning up at
once.'[41] Synge's delicacy was wasted—he was to have as little luck as
Joyce.

Joyce reached Paris on January 23, 1903, full of good resolutions to
budget his expenses, to spend his time reading and writing, and to
continue the 'experiment' of his life. His card of admission to the
Bibliothèque Nationale is dated January 24;[42] he spent his days there,
and his nights at the Bibliothèque Sainte-Geneviève. His reading
showed the same desire for formalism: Shakespeare having proved too
lax, he took up Ben Jonson, studying both plays and poems to improve
his own technique; and after a day reading Jonson he would go on to
Cousin's translation of Aristotle's *De Anima, Metaphysics*, and of course
Poetics, reading 'sheltered from the sin of Paris, night by night.'[43]
He wrote his own apothegms down in a notebook and signed his
name and the date after each as if to guarantee its importance as well
as to identify its author. The manner as well as the topics of Aristotle
attracted him; unleashing 'dagger definitions,'[44] Joyce enlarged the
Poetics by making pat the difference between tragedy and comedy.

He argued that comedy is superior to tragedy in that it makes for
joy while tragedy makes for sorrow, the sense of possession in the one
being superior to the sense of deprivation in the other. Then he expertly
redefined pity and terror:

Desire is the feeling which urges us to go to something and loathing is the
feeling which urges us to go from something: and that art is improper which
aims at exciting these feelings in us whether by comedy or by tragedy. Of
comedy later. But tragedy aims at exciting in us feelings of pity and terror.

Now terror is the feeling which arrests us before whatever is grave in human
fortunes and unites us with its secret cause and pity is the feeling which
arrests us before whatever is grave in human fortunes and unites us with the
human sufferer.[45]

In the arrest of these emotions by tragedy, and of the emotion of joy
by comedy, he finds the stasis proper to art. He then distinguishes
among the lyrical, epical, and dramatic modes, covertly granting the
highest award to drama because it is the most impersonal and most
genuinely creative. Finally, he insists that art moves toward an esthetic,
not a moral or otherwise useful end. This conclusion was not new, but
it was expressed with succinct finality.

While engaging in these studious formulations Joyce also wrote two
poems, one of them the best of his early verse, 'I hear an army
charging upon the land,' the other, 'When the shy star goes forth in
heaven,' the first based upon Yeats and Gregan,° the second on lyrics
of Ben Jonson. In a letter to Stanislaus of February 8, enclosing the
two poems, he announced he had written also fifteen epiphanies,
twelve to be inserted among those already completed, and two to be
added at the end, the destination of the fifteenth undisclosed. George
Russell would not care for them, he said, but no matter: 'And so help
me devil I will write only the things that approve themselves to me
and I will write them the best way I can. It is the same way with
boots. O, I have revelled in ties, coats, boots, hats, since I came here—
all imaginary! So damn Russell, damn Yeats, damn Skeffington, damn
Darlington, damn editors, damn free-thinkers, damn vegetable verse †
and double damn vegetable philosophy!'[46] He was also at work on a
comedy, and on March 20, challenged his mother, 'My book of songs
will be published in the spring of 1907. My first comedy about five
years later. My "Esthetic" about five years later again. (This *must* interest you!)'[47]

His own contentment with this future was checked by reverses elsewhere. The magazine *Men and Women,* for which he had written an
article, never appeared. The *Irish Times* did not take him on as a
correspondent. The *Speaker* asked him to review a French translation
of Ibsen's early play, *Catilina,* but offered nothing else. Joyce wrote
a review of Sarah Bernhardt for the *Daily Express,* and an account
of a carnival in Paris for the *Irish Times;* neither was accepted. To
demonstrate that his critical judgment was not to be swayed by a kind
word, he wrote an uncomplimentary review of Lady Gregory's *Poets*

° See p. 86.
† Many Theosophists were vegetarians and wrote verse.

and Dreamers for the *Daily Express;* Longworth delayed printing it, then finally broke precedent by using it over Joyce's initials, and asked him to review the next batch of books favorably.

For two crowded weeks life in Paris went easily enough. Joyce was back at the Hotel Corneille, and still had some of the money he had brought with him. He expected some money on his birthday, but got instead only 'a budget of cards' from his family, a cigarette case from Aunt Josephine, and a letter in shifting modes from his father:

31st Jany 03
12.30

My dear Jim

May *I* be permitted to offer you my best wishes for your future, which I, at one time, fancied may have been more rosey [sic] on your attaining your majority—but circumstances alter cases and all my cases are circumcised. I must ask you to forgive me, Jim, for the 'might have been.' However I hope you will believe me that I am only now, under I must tell you, *very trying* times, endeavouring to do my *little* best, but Jim you are my eldest Son. I have always looked up to your being a fitting representative of *our* family one that my father would be proud of. I now only hope that you may carry out *his* ideas through your life and if you do, you may be sure you will not do anything unbecoming a gentleman. But that I am pressed for time I should write you more fully but tomorrow, Jim, I will write to you again.

Your fond father.[48]

Joyce kept the letter.

By the third week in February hunger had become Joyce's principal theme in his letters home. Scarcity was succeeded by famine, famine, after a brief splurge, by scarcity and famine again, diminuendos of stomach twinges followed by crescendos of starvation. His mother, whose own health was beginning to deteriorate, was beside herself for her son; every letter from Paris sent her into tears [49] and provoked a new sacrifice to the pawnbroker of some household necessity, miraculously preserved up to now. With the proceeds she would send him a money order of three or four shillings. He pursued her relentlessly with the glazed, unseeing eye of the very hungry man, his pity reserved for himself:

Grand Hotel Corneille
Paris, 21 February 1903

Dear Mother

Your order for 3s/4d of Tuesday last was very welcome as I had been without food for 42 hours (forty-two). Today I am twenty hours without food. But these spells of fasting are common with me now and when I get money I am so damnably hungry that I eat a fortune ($1^s/$-) before you could say knife. I hope this new system of living won't injure my digestion. I have no news from 'Speaker' or 'Express.' If I had money I could buy a little oil stove (I have a lamp) and cook macaroni for myself with bread when I am hard beat. I hope you are doing what I said about Stannie—but I daresay you are not. I hope the carpet that was sold is not one of the new purchases that you are selling to feed me. If this is so sell no more or I'll send the money back to you by return of post. I think I am doing the best I can for myself but it's pulling the devil by the tail the greater part of the time. I expect to be served with my bill (£ 1-6-0 with oil) any day and then my happiness is complete. My condition is so exciting that I cannot go to sleep at night often till four in the morning and when I wake I look at once under the door to see if there is a letter from my editors and I assure you when I see the wooden floor only morning and morning I sigh and turn back to sleep off part of my hunger. I have not gone to Miss Gonne nor do I intend to go. With the utmost stretching your last order will keep me Monday midday (postage half a franc probably)—then, I suppose, I must do another fast. I regret this as Monday and Tuesday are carnival days and I shall probably be the only one starving in Paris.

Jim

But on the back of the letter, as if to qualify its abject blackness, he wrote a few bars of a song called 'Upa-Upa' by Pierre Loti, and added a note: 'This is an air played on a lute by a single player, followed by a chorus of women. It is played before the queen of some Indian island on occasions of state and her women sing the chorus.'

This letter elicited a mighty effort from John Joyce, who gathered together a pound or two and sent it to his son. It arrived the evening of the carnival, and James reported that with it he bought 'a cigar, confetti to throw, and a supper. I bought a stove, a saucepan, a plate, a cup, a saucer, a knife, a fork, a small spoon, a big spoon, a bowl, salt, sugar, figs, macaroni, cocoa &c. and got my linen from the laundry. I now try to do my own cooking.' [50] His mother wrote him on March 2 one of those maternal and heartening letters for which he was always importuning her, not because he intended to follow her advice but because he needed to feel that she was altogether enmeshed in his plight:

I think your future life in Paris will chiefly depend on the new paper [*Men and Women*] as without some certainty to live on it would be misery to keep struggling in such a way and your health would suffer. Do not despair though for I still feel full of hope for you and this month will tell a great deal. *Keep all your friends* and in a suitable time call on Mrs MacBride who received

you well and whose marriage and love making naturally kept her from looking after more serious business and you will make a big mistake by not
keeping as yr Pappie says 'in touch with her' *You cannot get on in your line
without friends.* Stannie works steady and fumes because he has no money
to send you. . . .

His mother was full of anxious and, as it proved, unnecessary fear that
her son would not be practical enough.

He did not go to see Maud Gonne, preferring to be offended with
her rather than to have her see his threadbare clothes, worn boots, and
the dirty shirt which, to avoid the cost of laundering, he covered with
a great flowing tie. He formed, however, a number of acquaintances
of a less demanding kind. At a café in the Carrefour de l'Odéon he
joined in excited discussions with other expatriates, Riciotto Canudo
from Italy, Teodor Däubler, a German born in Trieste, Villona, a
Frenchman, and Eugene Routh,[51] of origin unknown. They argued
about literature in French, and when their knowledge of that language failed, in Latin. Däubler, a mystic in temperament, found Joyce
outrageous, and threatened to challenge him to a duel. When Stanislaus
asked him later what he would have done if the challenge had actually
been given, Joyce replied without hesitation, 'Taken the next train for
Dublin.' * [52]

His main literary association in Paris was not with these but with
his fellow-Irishman, John Synge, who arrived at the Hotel Corneille
on March 6, 1903, and stayed for a week to sell out, having failed to
get on in Paris. Synge had dealt, desperately too, with editors, and
over a longer period, and he warned Joyce not to fast too long; his
own protracted spells of hunger had obliged him, he said, to undergo
a £30 operation.[53] Joyce soon found that Synge was not the silent
man Yeats had described to him; evidently his silence was with the
eloquent Yeats alone. He seemed to Joyce a great lump of a man who
could not be argued with,[54] but since Joyce was equally doctrinaire
they in fact argued a great deal. Sometimes the dispute was over
nothing, as when Joyce tried to persuade Synge to come with him to
St. Cloud for the carnival; but Synge was annoyed and said, 'You
want to behave just like a bourgeois going out and sitting in a park
on holiday.' [55]

Synge had by this time begun to prove himself as a dramatist. At
Yeats's suggestion he had given up his notion of becoming, like Arthur
Symons, a critic of French literature, and had gone to the Aran
Islands in 1898. Then, and during the summers from 1899 to 1902, he

* He remained interested enough in Däubler, however, to ask Philipp Jarnach in
1919 to lend him one of his books.[56]

listened to the nuances of Aran speech, and found the material for
four plays, including *Riders to the Sea*. He had shown this play to
Yeats late in 1902, and Yeats, when he saw Joyce in January, had
aroused his jealousy by praising Synge's play as quite Greek. During
his short stay in Paris, Synge lent Joyce the manuscript of *Riders to
the Sea*. No manuscript was ever read with less sympathy. 'I am glad
to say,' Joyce wrote to Stanislaus, 'that ever since I read it, I have been
riddling it mentally till it has [not] a sound spot. It is tragic about all
the men that are drowned in the islands: but thanks be to God, Synge
isn't an Aristotelian.'[57] This corner Joyce had for himself, and he
proceeded to point out to Synge the play's Aristotelian defects. In particular he objected to its catastrophe, because it was brought about
by an animal (a pony) rather than by the sea, and to its brevity.
It was, he said, a tragic poem, not a drama. He told Synge to make
a lasting argument or make none. Synge protested, 'It's a good play,
as good as any one-act play can be.' Joyce rejoined that Ireland needed
less small talk and more irrefutable art; 'No one-act play, no dwarf-
drama,' he asserted, 'can be a knockdown argument.'[*][58]

Did he really like the play so little? It does not seem so, for already
he knew the final speeches of Maurya by heart, and a few years later
in Trieste he took the trouble to translate the play. But he gave Synge
no quarter and went on to expound his esthetic theories; Synge listened and said to him ungrudgingly, 'You have a mind like Spinoza's,'[59]
a remark Joyce relayed to his mother with an explanation of who
Spinoza was. Thus encouraged, Joyce showed Synge a notebook containing *Memorabilia*, which turned out to be merely solecisms by
contemporaries:

> And more I may not write for them that cleave
> The waters of sleep can make a chattering tongue
> Heavy as stone, their wisdom being half silence.
> —W. B. Yeats

> Hereafter her rank will be considerably higher
> than now.   —Herbert Spencer

> Everybody is thinking about themselves.
> —Walter Sichel

Synge was annoyed, pushed the notebook aside, and said, 'What of it?
It is not important at all.'[60] He found Joyce obsessed by rules. They
parted amicably on March 13, respecting and disdaining each other.[61]
Another Irish friend was Joseph Casey, whom Michael Davitt de-

---

[*] In 1909, Joyce continued in the same vein by complaining to Joseph Holloway
that the last act of *The Playboy* was taken from *The Master Builder*.

scribed as a man 'with a leaning toward dynamite and a decided taste
for absinthe,' [62] and whom Joyce was to characterize as 'a gray ember.' [63]
Once a leading Fenian, Casey was now a typesetter for the *New
York Herald* of Paris; he and Joyce used to meet for lunch in the
little Restaurant des Deux-Écus close to the *Herald* building on the
rue du Louvre. There Casey, with 'raw facebones,' rolled his 'gun-
powder cigarettes,' lighting them with matches that burned like fuses,
and drank absinthe without water while he talked about the blows
that had been struck for Ireland. He told how his cousin James
Stephens, after escaping from prison, got away disguised as a bride;
but his favorite story was of the Manchester rescue in 1867, of his own
imprisonment with Colonel Ricard Burke in Clerkenwell prison because of their suspected part in the rescue, and of the attempt by
some Fenian dynamitards to enable them to escape.* Casey made his
way later to Paris where, Joyce said, he was 'unsought by any save
by me.' [64] He lived in rue de la Goutte-d'Or, and his wife lived in a
street with an equally fine name, rue Gît-le-Cœur, across the river.
They had been separated long before, and their son, Patrice, now a
soldier in the French army, sided with his mother and did not meet
his father. Joyce was sorry for the old man, who eagerly fancied Joyce
was as Fenian as he. In *Ulysses*, where Casey is called Kevin Egan
(a name borrowed from another Fenian), Stephen remembers with
pity their lunches together: 'Weak wasting hand on mine. They have
forgotten Kevin Egan, not he them. Remembering thee, O Sion.' [65] He
contrasts him with Casey's bunny-faced soldier son, who returned to
Paris on furlough: to Patrice socialism, atheism, and the French sweep-
stakes were of equal consequence; his father, however, was an aged
nuisance.

Besides meeting his friends, always a more important part of his
life than he cared to admit, Joyce entered into some of the pleasures
of Paris, which he called 'that lamp for lovers hung in the wood of
the world.' [66] He wrote his family he could not afford to go to the
theater, but he managed to attend one of the first performances of
Debussy's *Pelléas et Mélisande* at the Opéra Comique; he saw Bernhardt and Réjane; he saw Signoret act in Heijermans's *La Bonne
Espérance* at the Théâtre Antoine. At the high cost of 7 francs 50 centimes he bought a gallery seat to hear Jean de Reszke sing *Pagliacci*,

---

* The attempt did not succeed, but Casey was acquitted at his trial. In *Ulysses*
Joyce heightens the facts: 'Lover, for her [Ireland's] love he prowled with colonel
Richard Burke, tanist of his sept, under the walls of Clerkenwell and, crouching,
saw a flame of vengeance hurl them upward in the fog. Shattered glass and toppling
masonry. In gay Paree he hides, Egan of Paris. . . .' (44 [40])

and marvelled to discover that his father's voice had the same quality. (He was delighted later when an Italian musician in Dublin, Michele Esposito, said that James Joyce's own voice was like de Reszke's.)[67] He considered taking singing lessons again, found a teacher, but gave up the idea when payment was demanded in advance. He enjoyed some of the sexual pleasures of Paris, and he also attended vespers at Notre-Dame and St. Germaine l'Auxerrois.

He was able to take two trips away from the city. One was to Nogent, where he watched the confluence of the Seine and the Marne, as in Zurich later he would go often to see the confluence of the Sihl and the Limmat; he walked back through the woods to Sèvres and took a river steamer to the city. The second trip, to Tours, was to have an unexpected influence in helping him put English literature out of countenance. Joyce made friends with a Siamese who was also reading at the Bibliothèque Sainte-Geneviève, and arranged with him to go to Tours to hear a remarkable tenor sing there at the cathedral. On the way he picked up at a railway kiosk a book by Édouard Dujardin,[68] whom he knew to be a friend of George Moore. It was *Les Lauriers sont coupés,* and in later life, no matter how diligently the critics worked to demonstrate that he had borrowed the interior monologue from Freud, Joyce always made it a point of honor that he had it from Dujardin.* The Siamese was also to make an appearance afterwards, for on learning of Joyce's success he paid him the compliment of changing his name to René-Ulysse;[69] with comparable deference Joyce used to emphasize, in telling the story, that René-Ulysse had royal blood.

These activities freshened his financial anxieties. Joe Casey lent him small sums, and Patrice too; a man named Chown lent him a few shillings; Gogarty, appealed to, sent him a pound. He learned to cadge meals from his acquaintances by calling upon them at lunchtime, a dodge that worked, he reported,[70] with Frenchmen and failed with Englishmen and Americans. A new pupil, A. Auvergniat, met him at Douce's flat and paid for some lessons in advance. Occasional dribbles came in from perfunctory reviews for the *Daily Express;* the *Speaker* paid for his review of *Catilina,* but very slowly and very little. His landlady, whom he nicknamed 'Baa-baa black sheep' because of the black looks she gave him, was impatient for her money.[71] He complained again to his mother of 'a most villainous hunger,' and said that his 'lenten regulations,' which had dictated two meals in sixty hours, 'have made me somewhat weak.'[72] His clothes were wearing out, he stopped shaving and let his beard grow. He could not attend

*See pp. 534, 647.

the Irish ball on St. Patrick's Day because he had no dress clothes, a deprivation that seems ludicrous for a man without food to complain of.[73] His mother decided to have at least some new street clothes made for him. He formed a new idea of interviewing Henri Fournier, the leading French contender for the James Gordon Bennett automobile race, to be held the following summer in Dublin; and he succeeded through Matthew O'Hara in persuading the *Irish Times* to buy his bored and indifferent article as 'fresh news from Paris.' *

By such expedients Joyce contrived to assure himself, on his second trip to Paris, that he could somehow manage to live abroad and so continue the 'journey of the soul,' which his book of songs was to log. What he was now writing he wrote with full conviction, and no longer felt tempted to destroy. His purposes were becoming more certain. The batch of fifteen new epiphanies made him see more clearly that he had been right, shortly before he left Dublin, in forming these isolated spasms of insight into a linked chain of moments in which, as Stephen confides to Davin, 'the soul is born.' His research in style led him back to Ben Jonson's precision and fastidiousness, a useful check upon his own penchant for lyricism. His consideration of artistic possibilities brought him to form the basis of an esthetic system which justified his favorite genre, drama, and his favorite disposition, comedy. What he did not yet know was that his esthetics could have no independent publication, that it must justify itself by helping to shape his work and by becoming an event in his fictional autobiography. Similarly, his epiphanies would have to give up their disembodied existence to become parts of a narrative, which in its turn would be affected by the prior existence of these 'spots of time.' Instead of being the author of short works, he must pour them into his long ones, without waste.

Joyce would probably have remained in France for some months more, scrambling and making his parents scramble for money to subsist on, had it not been for his mother's ill health. She had been failing for some time and blaming her weakness first on her teeth, then on her eyes. Then came a hint of something more serious. Joyce was staggered and wrote her on Good Friday, April 10, 1903:

Dear Mother

    Please write to me at once if you can and tell me what is wrong.

                       Jim

* Joyce's opinion of auto racing was, he said, like the opinion of horse racing of the late Shah of Persia. When the Shah was invited by King Edward to go to the races he replied, 'I know that one horse runs quicker than another but which particular horse it is doesn't interest me.'

He attended mass that day at Notre-Dame, standing in the rear of the church to compare, with the aid of a missal from Ireland, the French style of *Tenebrae*. Then he took a long walk through the streets of Paris, and did not return to his little room at the hotel until late that night. A telegram was waiting for him, and he opened it with foreboding. It read, 'MOTHER DYING COME HOME FATHER.' [74]

He had of course no money for a trip, and after some thought decided that the best chance of getting a loan lay with his pupil Douce. He managed to rouse Douce at midnight and showed him the telegram.[75] Douce obligingly provided 375 francs and Joyce left Paris the next morning, Saturday, April 11. He crossed from Dieppe to Newhaven and spoke broken English on the pier to avoid tipping a porter to carry his bag.[76]

1903–1904

Fabulous artificer, the hawklike man. You flew. Whereto? Newhaven-Dieppe, steerage passenger. Paris and back. Lapwing. Icarus. *Pater, ait.* Seabedabbled, fallen, weltering. Lapwing you are.

—*Ulysses* (208 [199])

LEAVING Montparnasse for Cabra was filial but anticlimactic. May Joyce was very low when her son arrived, but to his relief seemed to improve a little. Her doctors had diagnosed her disease as cirrhosis of the liver—a malady more appropriate to her husband than to her —and it was not until she was near her death that it became apparent even to them that she was suffering from cancer. Her fear of death put her in mind of her son's impiety, and on the days following Easter she tried to persuade him to make his confession and take communion. Joyce, however, was inflexible; he feared, as he had Stephen Dedalus say later, 'the chemical action' which would be set up in his soul 'by a false homage to a symbol behind which are massed twenty centuries of authority and veneration.'[1] His mother wept, and vomited green bile into a basin, but he did not yield. His aunt Josephine Murray argued with him, and Joyce said, 'I believe in a Supreme Being,'[2] but made no other concessions. On the street one day in April Joyce met Yeats, told him it was uncertain whether his mother would live or not, and added the artistic flourish, 'But these things really don't matter.'[3]

They did matter, however, and to him. He had never felt so close to his mother, or so much in need of her approbation, as during the months in Paris, when his letters continually prodded her for sympathy, not merely to obtain money, but to sustain his ambitions. His father had pointed him away from home towards irreverence and footless gaiety, but had none of the indomitable, and at its best, selfless patience which could vindicate a break for freedom. This quality Joyce had to derive, paradoxically, from his conventional, loving mother. So his letters home exhorted her to admire his earnestness. Having put himself several hundred miles away from her, he depended upon her more heavily than before. His mother was part of the stable world he was engaged in renouncing; yet he did not want her to renounce him. If she died he could neither hurt nor please her; death was abandonment of response to him. There was nothing to do, as she lay helpless in her room, but to feel desolate and anticipate a deeper separation.

John Joyce, too, was subdued by his wife's illness. He curbed his drinking and tried in his erratic way to show himself a devoted husband. To meet the heavy medical costs he took out, on April 24, 1903, a penultimate £50 mortgage on his house, and grandly sent £3 of it to repay Douce in Paris, accompanying the money with one of those letters which, after having enforced utter quiet upon the whole household, he would indite in an ornate hand.

Away from home his son played the Parisian, with long hair, a small beard, a wide bow tie, and a Latin Quarter hat (not a tam), but was uneasy. He felt more keenly the loss of Byrne as a confidant, and sought him out to try to repair their friendship. Byrne was still offended over the incident of the post card, however. He granted that the cause of the quarrel was trivial, but argued convincingly that it was symptomatic. So long, he said, as Joyce retained his present character, Byrne could not possibly be friendly with him; if Joyce should change his character, then Byrne would not consider him worth knowing. There was no pleasing this fastidious taste. Byrne summed up his conviction that Joyce took human beings, and especially women, too lightly, by saying, 'You are too mineral'; Joyce replied, 'You are too plebeian.' Byrne asked him to analyze his feelings, and Joyce replied, 'I feel so absurdly pleased to be sitting on the wall beside you and listening to the sounds of your voice that I can't analyze them.' [4] They at last solemnly agreed to remain friends but not to meet. The next day, however, Joyce sent his friend a letter:

Dear Byrne:

Would you care to meet me tomorrow (Sunday) in Prince's St. at one o'clock? Perhaps you will not get this tomorrow morning as the post is upset.

J A J

7 S Peter's Terrace, Cabra
Saturday night [5]

Byrne of course turned up at the appointed time, and they spent the afternoon and evening walking around Dublin, resuming a little of their old intimacy. Joyce confided his recent quarrels with his mother, and Byrne disapproved. 'Would you not try to save her from suffering?' he asked; 'Whatever else is unsure in this stinking dunghill of a world a mother's love is not.' But Joyce replied ironically that he must follow the examples of Pascal and his patron saint Aloysius Gonzaga, and of Christ himself, in ignoring his mother's entreaties.[6]

Byrne's persistence in refusing to endorse this conduct led Joyce to seek support elsewhere. Gogarty, Cosgrave, and another medical student, John Elwood, had less difficulty than Byrne in indulging his sense of artistic mission. Elwood (Temple in *A Portrait of the Artist*) and Cosgrave, both neglectful of their studies, were Joyce's hangers-on, while Gogarty met him on more equal terms, and was afterwards to call him 'a medical students' pal.' Gogarty took it upon himself to make Joyce over, shaving off his Parisian beard on the pretext of making him look more like Dante, seeing to his medical care, lending him his best clothes and giving him his worst, and bestowing on him the nickname of 'Kinch' in imitation of the cutting-sound of a knife.[7] Joyce repaid this ironic compliment by gravely asking Gogarty to lend him his .22 rifle for some fearsome, unspecified purpose and then pawning it. To make up, he suggested a final line for Gogarty's poem on 'The Death of Shelley,' submitted for the Vice-Chancellor's Prize at Trinity College; Joyce's line was, 'Shines on thee, soldier of song, Leonidas,' and Professor Dowden, in awarding the prize, did not delight Gogarty by singling out this line for special commendation.[8]

There were many points of friction between Gogarty and Joyce. Joyce did not conceal his conviction of his own superiority, and all Gogarty's good cheer and wit could not impair it. 'To think that a genius like me should have to borrow from the likes of you,' he said, or more probably, implied. There was, however, one weak point in Joyce, his decision not to become a drinker, probably a reaction against his father's intemperance. The wines of Paris had already shaken this resolution. Gogarty said to Elwood, in a sudden burst of malice, that he would 'make Joyce drink to break his spirit,'[9] and when Elwood told Joyce and his brother, they both accepted it as evidence of Gogarty's permanent ill intentions, whereas it may have indicated only ill humor. In any case, Gogarty did propagandize for the delights of alcohol, and when he heard Joyce quote one day from Autolycus's song, 'And a quart of ale is a dish for a king,' he cried out, 'A quart of ale! A quart of milk is more in your line.' Stanislaus Joyce, who was present, heard his brother defend rather lamely his right to appreciate the song; Gogarty brushed the defense aside and said, 'Oh, I know all about that sort of thing, Aquinas and the rest of them.'[10]

Under Gogarty's able tutelage, which he decided not to refuse, Joyce began to drink heavily. At first, to assert a fancied resemblance between himself and the buoyant Elizabethans, he called for sack. The news of his 'fall' got round, and the day after his first night of utter drunkenness, he was teased by some young men on the street. 'Who are these people?' he said haughtily and walked on. Gradually he shifted from sack to Guinness's unpretentious and less expensive stout, 'the wine of the country.' [11] His capacity for alcohol was small, and he was prone to drunken collapses. All releases from excessive consciousness attracted him; he wrote in one of his epiphanies of the pleasure of another kind of release, 'What moves upon me from the darkness subtle and murmurous as a flood, passionate and fierce with an indecent movement of the loins? What leaps, crying in answer, out of me, as an eagle to eagle in mid air, crying to overcome, crying for an iniquitous abandoment?' [12] His soul, fed on pride, and declining attachments, longed to give way, to swoon, to be mutilated, and he brought this happy consummation about with the help of porter.*

Once, emerging from a drinking session with his Paris hat which resembled that of a Protestant cleric, Joyce heard some street gamins call out, 'Jay, look at the drunken minister!' † [13] Such exploits would end in his being trundled home by some friend. His brother Stanislaus would look on in disgust as one by one his brother James, his father (whose temporary abstinence had been relaxed), and another brother Charles—who had given up studying for the priesthood in order to become secretary to a wine merchant—tottered into 7 St. Peter's Terrace, their respective frustrations for the time being reveled away. He thought his brother was destroying himself, but James met his expostulations with sardonic balderdash. 'What's the matter with you,' he said to Stanislaus, 'is that you're afraid to live. You and people like you. This city is suffering from hemiplegia of the will. I'm not afraid to live.' Stanislaus expostulated, 'Then you don't want to be a writer?' 'I don't care if I never write another line. I want to live. I should be supported at the expense of the state because I am capable of enjoying life. As for writing, I may perhaps employ my sober moments in correcting the grammatical errors of the more illiterate among the rugged geniuses.' When Stanislaus asked him what he could find to say to 'those drunken yahoos of medical students,' Joyce replied, 'At least, they don't bore me as you do.' [14]

---

* 'Swooning' was a word, and an act, of which Joyce was fond. Stephen at the end of Chapter II of *A Portrait* experiences the 'swoon of sin'; Gabriel's soul, at the end of *The Dead*, 'swooned softly.' See also p. 86.
† Used in the boozing scene of *Ulysses* (417 [405]).

Stanislaus was now started on the long course of humiliation from which his brother rarely allowed him to play truant. He had formed a desire to become a writer like James, and tried his hand at a philosophical essay, which, however, he destroyed because his conclusions were not exciting enough. His main effort was expended in keeping a diary, but James read it and said that it was dull except when it dealt with him, and that Stanislaus would never write prose. Stanislaus burned it, but then doggedly began again. Besides analyses of his character and his brother's, he liked to jot down aphorisms such as, 'Every bond is a bond to sorrow,' and 'Love between man and man is impossible because there must not be sexual intercourse and friendship between man and woman is impossible because there must be sexual intercourse.' James read them, labeled them 'Bile Beans,' and remembered them mockingly when, a year or two later, he came to write 'A Painful Case.' * Another entry in the diary quoted John Joyce's stipulation, when going on a retreat with his friends Matthew Kane, Charles Chance, and Boyd,† 'I bar the candles.' This remark made its way later into the story 'Grace.' ‡ Stanislaus used the diary for literary experiments as well; when he read Tolstoy's *Sebastopol Sketches*, the description of Praskukhin's random thoughts on the verge of death stirred him to try to write down the random thoughts of someone on the verge of sleep. Joyce read the effort and contemptuously threw it aside as the work 'of a young Maupassant,' but may have drawn from it, as from Dujardin, a hint for the interior monologue. He was content to use Stanislaus as what he called a 'whetstone,' [15] and kept in his mind Stanislaus's sarcastic account, sent him a few months before in a letter to Paris, of serving with their father on an election committee. This gave James the core of 'Ivy Day in the Committee Room.'

Such usefulness did not deter Stanislaus from being almost always irritating. His face was so serious, his expression so attentive, that James, in the middle of telling him something, would say, 'Please turn your face away. It bores me,' or, 'I wouldn't like to be a woman and wake up to find your phiz on the pillow beside me in the morning.' [16]

* Stanislaus also told in his diary of a meeting with a married woman at a concert, which Joyce took over for his story.
† Matthew Kane was the original of Martin Cunningham, a character in both *Dubliners* and *Ulysses*. He had a long beard and was fond of oraculating, usually on the basis of misinformation, as in the story 'Grace.' Charles Chance's wife was one of the models for Molly Bloom; see pp. 385-6.
‡ In 'Grace,' Mr. Kernan is mainly the Joyces' old neighbor, Ned Thornton (p. 43). Father Purdon in the story is based upon Father Bernard Vaughan, and as Stanislaus Joyce notes, the name was given him sarcastically because Purdon Street was in the brothel area.

The younger brother's mind was polemical, the older brother's was playful. Stanislaus had a way of taking some idea of James's, of worrying it, chewing it, and then of exhibiting it proudly to his brother, who no longer deigned to recognize it. He would develop anti-Christian notions, to suggest that Jesus was unchaste, or that the mass was cannibalistic, and bring them to James, who would either dismiss them jocularly by saying, 'And are these the thoughts ye do be thinkin' as ye walk around Dublin's fair city?' or would reply tangentially that the mass was a fine drama.[17] At his warmest he treated Stanislaus with chaffing affection, at his coldest with impatient scorn.

Stanislaus experienced somewhat similar treatment from others. He followed James in taking an interest in their cousin Katsy, William Murray's daughter, but she boasted to him of having received James's attentions and was indifferent to his own. John Joyce referred to Stanislaus commonly as 'this fellow's [James's] jackal,' and made clear a dislike for him which Stanislaus wholeheartedly returned. Gogarty nicknamed Stanislaus 'Thug'; Cosgrave considered him James's ape. Sometimes the abuse was patently unfair: Stanislaus describes how one day, passing a photographer's studio with his brother and noting the *embonpoint* of the ladies pictured in the window, he remarked, 'It's like the briskets hanging in a butcher's shop.' James made the same remark to Cosgrave the next day as if it were his own.[18] Stanislaus said nothing, but cherished his wounds. He spent his days as a clerk in Apothecaries' Hall, receiving little pay, and champed at wasting the ability which he still hoped he possessed. At night he would write with half-conscious pathos some account of his attempt to see his relations with James in perspective. His diary for September 1903 poses the problem most distinctly:

My life has been modelled on Jim's example, yet when I am accused by my unprepossessing Uncle John or by Gogarty of imitating Jim, I can truthfully deny the charge. It was not mere aping as they imply, I trust I am too clever and my mind too old for that. It was more an appreciation in Jim of what I myself really admire and wish for most. But it is terrible to have a cleverer older brother. I get small credit for originality. I follow Jim in nearly all matters of opinion, but not all. Jim, I think, has even taken a few opinions from me. In some things, however, I have never followed him. In drinking, for instance, in whoring, in speaking broadly, in being frank without reserve with others, in attempting to write verse or prose or fiction, in manner, in ambition, and not always in friendships. I perceive that he regards me as quite commonplace and uninteresting—he makes no attempt at disguise—and though I follow him fully in this matter of opinion I cannot be expected to like it. It is a matter beyond the power of either of us to help.

As May Joyce's condition became worse, James moved aimlessly about the city, waiting for her to die. He did no reviewing and little writing, and made no attempt to further his career. Occasionally he saw George Russell, who continued to praise the 'perfect art' of his poems, finding them 'as delicate and dainty as Watteau pictures.' [19] Russell was beginning to feel, however, that a more assured future awaited another of his young men, Padraic Colum, and freely predicted, 'Colum will be our principal literary figure in ten years.' Rumors of this new luminary reached Joyce, who allowed Colum to catch up with him one night as both were leaving the National Library. He brought up the Irish revival, in which Colum was an eager participant, and remarked contemptuously, 'I distrust all enthusiasms.' They spoke of poetry, and Joyce informed Colum, who was interested in content, 'A lyric is a simple liberation of a rhythm.' When Colum amiably mentioned that his name had a variant spelling of Columb, Joyce allowed himself to ask, 'And which do you use when your singing robes are about you?' Ibsen was the next subject, and Joyce dismissed, again contemptuously, *A Doll's House,** which an amateur company had recently produced in Dublin, and contrasted it with Ibsen's 'great plays' *Hedda Gabler* and *The Wild Duck.* He asked to see a play that Colum had just written and took it home with him. A few days later he came up to Colum in the street and handed back the manuscript with the words, 'Rotten from the foundation up!' Waving his ashplant at his fellow-author, he said, 'I do not know from which of them you derive the most misunderstanding—Ibsen or Maeterlinck.' But later, under less pressure to assert his pre-eminence, he admitted that Colum was not without ability, and in 1909 praised his poem, 'Across the Door,' with the only slightly ambiguous comment, 'I couldn't have written that.' [20]

He saw little of other writers. Lady Gregory was annoyed with his review, though she seems to have forgiven him before long out of sympathy with his mother's condition. She did, however, hold a literary party to which she invited most of the young men with literary pretensions, and did not include Joyce. He came anyway, as John Eglinton recalls, 'with his air of half-timid effrontery, advancing towards his unwilling hostess and turning away from her to watch the crowd.' [21] Eglinton thought he detected 'the mute appeal' in Joyce's eyes. He was slighted also by George Moore, who never invited him to his evenings at home, though Gogarty was a constant guest. Moore had seen Joyce's poems—Russell showed him some—and handed them back with the derisive but acute comment, 'Symons!' Hearing of Joyce's small borrow-

---

* Yet it affects his story, 'The Dead,' where Gabriel also discovers his doll has a mind and heart distinct from his own.

ings, Moore exclaimed impatiently, 'Why, he's nothing but a—but a *beggar!*'[22] Such remarks found their way back to Joyce, who of course affected unconcern.

Resentful and inert, angry and indifferent, Joyce watched the marionettes outside his house, and inside saw his mother slowly die. She had not been out of bed since early April, and Josephine Murray nursed her with boundless devotion, neglecting her own family so she might help her sister-in-law. Mrs. Joyce had tried to be lighthearted; she nicknamed the dapper doctor 'Sir Peter Teazle,'[23] but sickness frayed her temper, and in the summer her vomiting grew worse. James sang to her, as he had sung to his brother George, Yeats's lyric, 'Who Goes with Fergus?', accompanying himself on the piano. His father became increasingly difficult to handle as his drinking caught up with the pace of May Joyce's decay. One hopeless night he reeled home and in his wife's room blurted out, 'I'm finished. I can't do any more. If you can't get well, die. Die and be damned to you!' Stanislaus screamed at him, 'You swine!' and went for him murderously, but stopped when he saw his mother struggling frantically to get out of bed to intercept him. James led his father out and managed to lock him in another room.[24] Shortly after, tragedy yielding to absurdity, John Joyce was seen disappearing around a corner, having contrived to escape out a second-floor window.[25]

May Joyce died on August 13, 1903, at the early age of forty-four.[26] In her last hours she lay in coma, and the family knelt about her bed, praying and lamenting. Her brother John Murray, observing that neither Stanislaus nor James was kneeling, peremptorily ordered them to do so. Neither obeyed.[27] Mrs. Joyce's body was taken to Glasnevin to be buried, and John Joyce wept inconsolably for his wife and himself. 'I'll soon be stretched beside her,' he said, 'Let Him take me whenever he likes.'[28] His feelings were genuine enough, and when Stanislaus, goaded to fury by what he regarded as his father's hypocritical whinings, denounced him for all his misdeeds, John Joyce listened quietly and merely said, 'You don't understand, boy.'[29] The whole family was dismayed and sad, but especially Mabel, the youngest, not yet ten years old. James sat beside her on the stairs, his arm around her, saying, 'You must not cry like that because there is no reason to cry. Mother is in heaven. She is far happier now than she has ever been on earth, but if she sees you crying it will spoil her happiness. You must remember that when you feel like crying. You can pray for her if you wish, Mother would like that. But don't cry any more.'[30]

A few days later he found a packet of love letters from his father to his mother, and read them in the garden. 'Well?' asked Stanislaus.

'Nothing,' James replied. He had changed from son to literary critic. Stanislaus, incapable of such rapid transformations, burnt them unread.[31] Joyce was not demonstrative, but he wrote in *Ulysses* of 'Her secrets: old feather fans, tasseled dancecards, powdered with musk, a gaud of amber beads in her locked drawer,'[32] and he summed up his feelings in the poem, 'Tilly,' * which he did not publish until 1927:

> He travels after a winter sun,
> Urging the cattle along a cold red road,
> Calling to them, a voice they know,
> He drives his beasts above Cabra.
>
> The voice tells them home is warm.
> They moo and make brute music with their hoofs.
> He drives them with a flowering branch before him,
> Smoke pluming their foreheads.
>
> Boor, bond of the herd,
> Tonight stretch full by the fire!
> I bleed by the black stream
> For my torn bough!

The month after May Joyce's death Stanislaus wrote in his diary a portrait of James, censorious but spellbound. It is another desperate effort to fix and so to master his protean brother:

Jim is a genius of character. When I say 'genius' I say just the least little bit in the world more than I believe; yet remembering his youth and that I sleep with him, I say it. Scientists have been called great scientists because they have measured the distances of the unseen stars and yet scientists who have watched the movements in matter scarcely perceptible to the mechanically aided senses have been esteemed as great, and Jim is, perhaps, a genius though his mind is minutely analytic. He has, above all, a proud wilful vicious selfishness out of which by times now he writes a poem or an epiphany, now commits the meanness of whim and appetite, which was at first protestant egoism, and had perhaps, some desperateness in it, but which is now well-rooted—or developed?—in his nature, a very Yggdrasil.

He has extraordinary moral courage—courage so great that I have hoped that he will one day become the Rousseau of Ireland. Rousseau, indeed, might be accused of cherishing the secret hope of turning away the anger of disapproving readers by confessing unto them, but Jim cannot be suspected of this. His great passion is a fierce scorn of what he calls the 'rabblement'— a tiger-like, insatiable hatred. He has a distinguished appearance and bearing and many graces: a musical singing and especially speaking voice (a tenor), a good undeveloped talent in music, and witty conversation. He has a dis-

---

* The word 'tilly' means the thirteenth in a baker's dozen; Joyce had thirteen (instead of twelve) poems in *Pomes Penyeach,* which sold for a shilling.

tressing habit of saying quietly to those with whom he is familiar the most
shocking things about himself and others, and, moreover, of selecting the
most shocking times for saying them, not because they are shocking merely,
but because they are true. They are such things that, even knowing him as
well as I do, I do not believe it is beyond his power to shock me or Gogarty
with all his obscene rhymes. His manner however is generally very engaging
and courteous with strangers, but, though he dislikes greatly to be rude, I
think there is little courtesy in his nature. As he sits on the hearthrug, his
arms embracing his knees, his head thrown a little back, his hair brushed up
straight off his forehead, his long face red as an Indian's in the reflexion of
the fire, there is a look of cruelty in his face. Not that he is not gentle at
times, for he can be kind and one is not surprised to find gentleness in him.
(He is always simple and open with those that are so with him.) But few
people will love him, I think, in spite of his graces and his genius and whoso-
ever exchanges kindnesses with him is likely to get the worst of the bargain.[33]

Joyce read what Stanislaus had written and commented only that 'moral
courage' did not describe him. 'When the Bard writes,' he said, looking
for more esthetic language to describe his detached severity, 'he intel-
lectualizes himself.'[34]

The Bard had now no money and no immediate goal, and at the same
time, with his mother dead, no reason for doing nothing. He dressed
in black, a Hamlet without a wicked uncle, and as Mallarmé had written (in a line Joyce liked), '*Il se promène, pas plus, lisant au livre de
lui-même.*' * He experienced sporadic bursts of energy, and in one of
them, roused by the plight of some French sailors in North Africa,
wrote a letter to the editor of, presumably, the *Irish Times,* to protest
their mistreatment.† The plight of individuals trapped in the great

---

* This aspect of himself appears in the Stephen Dedalus of the beginning of
Ulysses, who is filled with ill-will and grief.
† Joyce's letter, which was not published at the time but is included in *The Critical
Writings of James Joyce,* said in part:

> Empire building does not appear to be as successful in Northern, as it has
> been in Southern Africa. While his cousins are astonishing the Parisian public
> by excursions in the air M Jacques Lebaudy, the new Emperor of the Sahara,
> is preparing to venture into the heavier and more hazardous atmosphere of
> the Palais. He has been summoned to appear before M André at the suit of
> two sailors, Jean Marie Bourdiec and Joseph Cambrai, formerly of the
> *Frosquetta.* They claim 100,000 francs damages on account of the hardships
> and diseases which they have contracted owing to M Lebaudy's conduct.
> The new emperor, it would seem, is not over-careful of the bodily welfare
> of his subjects. He leaves them unprovided for in a desert, bidding them wait
> until he returns. They are made captive by a party of natives and suffer the
> agonies of hunger and thirst during their captivity. They remain prisoners
> for nearly two months and are finally rescued by a French man-o'-war under
> the command of M Jaurès. One of them is subsequently an inmate of a
> hospital at the Havre and after a month's treatment there is still only con-
> valescent. Their appeals for redress have been all disregarded and now they

schemes of others always aroused his sympathy, and he liked to show
how thoroughly he understood the French situation by ironies addressed to a small circle of the equally informed.

At the end of August 1903, Joyce went back to Longworth for more
books, and from September 3 to November 19 fourteen reviews by him
appeared unsigned in the *Daily Express*. When Padraic Colum praised
one of them, Joyce said merely, 'I received for it thirty shillings which
I immediately consecrated to Venus Pandemos.' The reviews exhibit
a pervasive confidence characteristic of Joyce's criticism; only occasional comments or preferences, however, otherwise bear his stamp.
In general he depreciates melodrama and speaks well of Crabbe's realism, of Zola's naturalism, and of the 'splendour' of Dutch realistic
painting. He remarked to Gogarty at this time, to keep him abreast of
new literary exigencies, 'Tell the truth; don't exaggerate,' and 'Describe
what they do.' [35] He insists also in his reviews that the tragic poet must
avoid seeing his characters through a moral screen; instead he must
treat even pathological behavior with 'indifferent sympathy.' [36] Occasionally he chooses a passage to praise for style, and is sometimes singularly indulgent to lush clichés; he praises, for example, a passage which
includes the sentence, 'Nothing lived under the vault of heaven but the
man and woman intoxicated by their kiss.' [37] He was still a little spellbound by gaudiness.

Two books seem to have affected him more deeply than the others.
One was J. Lewis McIntyre's *Giordano Bruno*, which revived his old
admiration for the philosopher who, disregarding tradition, marched
heretically 'from heroic enthusiasm to enthusiasm' towards God. The
other was Marcelle Tinayre's *The House of Sin*, the story of a young
man named Augustine who, after a strict Jansenist upbringing, is
swayed slowly away from the spirit to the flesh. He has by inheritance
what Joyce calls a 'double temperament.' 'Little by little,' Joyce writes,
'the defences of the spiritual life are weakened, and he is made aware
of human love as a subtle, insinuating fire.' Though Augustine comes
at last to a tragic end, the author's sympathies are not with 'the horrible
image of the Jansenist Christ' that looms over him, but with 'the fair

---

are having recourse to law. . . . The hearing of a case, in which such singular
issues are involved, will doubtless divide the attention of the Parisians with
such comparatively minor topics as Réjane and *les petits oiseaux*.

> (James A. Joyce
> 7 S. Peter's Terrace
> Cabra, Dublin) [38]

In the *Cyclops* episode of *Ulysses* (323 [313]), there is similar sympathy for British
sailors.

shows of the world.' Joyce must have seen the parallel to his own rearing by the 'mirthless' Jesuits, and his escape from them to 'life.' He
admired also the way Tinayre's prose seemed to fall in with the pathol-
ogy of the hero: a lessening of the young man's vitality was subtly
suggested by pauses, and in the end the prose seemed to expire along
with Augustine's soul.[39] *The House of Sin* was one of the many odd
spots where Joyce found a useful idea.

His reviewing came to an end with a quarrel; Longworth, in a rage,
threatened to kick Joyce downstairs if he ever turned up there again.[40]
Probably Joyce had been insolent about a book that the editor wished
him to treat indulgently. While Joyce regretted the loss of income, he
did not like reviewing and never did it again, though he had opportunities. He had meanwhile considered other ways of attaining solvency.
The first was to call on Professor Edward Dowden at Trinity College,
to ask his support for a position in the National Library. Dowden found
him 'extraordinary' and 'quite unsuitable.'[41] Then on September 29,
1903, Skeffington, who had become registrar of University College,
sent him a note saying he might teach some evening classes in French
at the college.[42] Joyce chose to interpret this as a plot on the part of
the college authorities to put him in their debt, and went to see the
dean, Father Darlington, to decline the offer with thanks, on the ground
that he did not feel his French was good enough. Darlington tried to
reassure him, but without success. 'What career do you intend to take
up, Mr. Joyce?' he asked. 'The career of letters.' The dean persisted,
'Isn't there some danger of perishing of inanition in the meantime?'
And Joyce, as his brother recorded, said this was one of the perils, but
there were prizes too. The dean urged him to consider the precedent
of a prominent barrister who had worked his way through the university by doing journalism on the side. 'As it was generally rumoured in
Dublin,' writes Stanislaus Joyce, 'that the young law student had given
early proof of his cleverness by writing leading articles contemporane-
ously for two newspapers of opposite politics, my brother said dryly:
"I may not have that gentleman's talents." ' 'You never know till you try,'
said Darlington encouragingly.[43]

In spite of his scorn for Darlington Joyce did attend a few classes in
law, then stopped. He also drifted back toward the Cecilia Street
Medical School, but, put off again by the chemistry course,[44] drifted
away, and accepted a suggestion, made this time by Kettle, that he wait
until the following autumn and start at the Trinity College Medical
School, where presumably chemistry was quite different. From his three
exposures to this discipline (for he never tried the fourth), he kept
only a taste for the medical vocabulary, and liked to explain coolly to

Stanislaus that his power to live so intensely came from his 'highly specialized nervous system.' [45] He also elaborated upon his theory that Dublin suffered from 'hemiplegia of the will,' by the corollary that all Europe suffered from an incurable contagion which he called 'syphilitic' [46] and would some day make public knowledge.

Another plan was conceived a little later, and was more ambitious. The trouble with Dublin, it now appeared, was that its newspapers were corrupt. Joyce concerted with Francis Skeffington, his old collaborator, to begin a new weekly newspaper of the continental type. It would be primarily literary rather than political, although he conceded to Skeffington that general issues such as the emancipation of women, pacifism, and socialism might be given some space. Its name would be *The Goblin*, [47] a merrily sinister contrast to the *Freeman's Journal, Irish Times,* and *Daily Express.* They prepared to register the name at once, and Joyce carefully calculated the amount of capital necessary for the venture at £2000. They settled upon a man named Gillies, editor of the *Irish Bee-Keeper,* to be business manager.

For a time they were unsure where to obtain the capital, but then Joyce heard that an American millionaire, Thomas F. Kelly, living near Dublin, had made an agreement with Padraic Colum to pay him more during three years than Colum was now making at his business, on condition that Colum live among country people and write. In return Kelly expected to own the American copyright of all books produced by Colum during this period. Colum had let it be known that he would take with him into the country only Shakespeare, Walt Whitman, and the Bible. [48]

The scheme filled Joyce with envy. He walked the fourteen miles to Kelly's home at Celbridge * on December 10, 1903, only to be refused admittance by the porter and have to trudge fourteen miles home again. He wrote Kelly an indignant letter, and Kelly, who had not intended the slight, apologized in two telegrams but added in a letter that he was not at present able to put up the £2000. [49] To salvage something Joyce went to Gillies and offered to translate Maeterlinck's *La Vie des abeilles* for the *Irish Bee-Keeper,* but Gillies looked the book over and declined with the comment, 'I don't think Maeterlinck ever kept a bee in his life.' [50] He obligingly appointed Joyce sub-editor, however, and Joyce, as he afterwards said, retained the position 'for about twenty-four hours.' [51]

He had almost as much trouble finding a shilling as finding £2000, and employed the same abortive ingenuity. One of his stratagems he confided to Padraic Colum. A medical student had given Joyce a pawn

* Swift once courted Hester Vanhomrigh there.

ticket for some books, supposedly expensive technical volumes like
Gray's *Anatomy*. Joyce proposed to Colum that they pay seven shillings
to the pawnbroker, Terence Kelly, in Fleet Street, and sell the books at
a big profit to George Webb, the bookseller on Crampton quay. Colum
put up the seven shillings. But after removing the books from pawn
they found them to be only Scott's *Waverley Novels,* with one volume
missing. They took the books to Webb anyway, and Joyce loftily
broached their mission. 'Some of your Italian books, Mr. Joyce?' asked
Webb hopefully. 'No, Webb, these are special.' When Webb found
them to be only Scott's novels, and heard how they had come by them,
he said, 'There's only one thing for you to do about it, boys. Take the
books back to Terence Kelly; maybe you can get him to let you have
six shillings on them again.' The transaction closed with the loss of
only one shilling.[52]

These contretemps did not seriously shake Joyce's optimism, but they
were a reserve upon which he could draw for proof, when he needed it,
that he was the prey of fools, niggards, and circumstances. They encouraged him in his feeling that socialism should come, for how else
should he be fed? He needed a redistribution of wealth if he was to be
a spendthrift, and attended occasional meetings of a socialist group
in Henry Street, where milder prophets of the new day than Marx were
discussed. The anarchist theories of the American Benjamin Tucker
also attracted him for a time. Finally, he came to know the writings of
Nietzsche, 'that strong enchanter'[53] whom Yeats and other Dubliners
were also discovering, and it was probably upon Nietzsche that Joyce
drew when he expounded to his friends a neo-paganism that glorified
selfishness, licentiousness, and pitilessness, and denounced gratitude
and other 'domestic virtues.'[54] At heart Joyce can scarcely have been
a Nietzschean any more than he was a socialist; his interest was in the
ordinary even more than in the extraordinary; but for the moment, in
the year's doldrums, his expectations everywhere checked, it was emol-
lient to think of himself as a superman, and he meditated a descent
from the mountain to bring his gospel of churchless freedom to the
unreceptive rabblement. To his Aunt Josephine Murray he confided,
'I want to be famous while I am alive.'[55]

1904

Pillowed on my coat she had her hair, earwigs in the heather scrub my hand under her nape, you'll toss me all. O wonder! Coolsoft with oint-ments her hand touched me, caressed: her eyes upon me did not turn away. Ravished over her I lay, full lips full open, kissed her mouth.

—*Ulysses* (173)

To keep one's equilibrium in 7 St. Peter's Terrace required all possible dexterity. The disarray that had marked the Joyce house-hold since their move from Blackrock to Dublin a dozen years before, changed to near-chaos after May Joyce's death. The house was in dis-repair, the banister broken, the furniture mostly pawned or sold; a few scrawny chickens scrabbled at the back for food. John Joyce took out another mortgage for £65 on November 3, 1903, and knew that this would be the last, and that nothing was left of the nine hundred pounds he had obtained a year before by commuting his pension. The house was to drop away from him in 1905. When the new mortgage money moved from his hands to those of the Dublin publicans, he sold the piano,[1] a desperate act for a musical man and one which roused James to fury when he came home to discover it.

Since May Joyce's death in August, Margaret ('Poppie'), now twenty years old, had taken charge of the house; Aunt Josephine hovered near to mother and advise her and her sisters and brothers, including James. Margaret became fairly adept at wheedling shillings from her father to support the family, which still included the three sons James, Stanis-laus, and Charles, and five daughters besides herself: May, Florence, Eileen, Eva, and Mabel. But sometimes there was nothing to eat. Gogarty met Joyce one day and asked, 'Where have you been for two days? Were you ill?' 'Yes.' 'What were you suffering from?' 'Inanition,' Joyce answered without hesitation.[2] His hunger fed his pride.

John Joyce, still mourning his wife and dislocated by her death, was exasperated by both sons and daughters. James's idleness he might condone, but Charles was volatile, and drank so heavily that he became known at the police station, and Stanislaus was ostentatiously sober and surly. To make matters worse, Stanislaus quit his clerkship at Apothecaries' Hall on January 30, 1904,[3] and joined James in sensitive inactivity, trying to decide what to do next. John Joyce felt put upon. After drinking heavily at the Ormonde bar he would return home, tonguelash his sons and perhaps whip any small daughter who happened to be within reach. 'An insolent pack of little bitches since your poor mother died,' he would say, and rebuke them for fancied ingratitude, 'Wouldn't care if I was stretched out stiff.' He anticipated their response to his death, 'He's dead. The man upstairs is dead.' He threatened to go back to Cork, 'I'll leave you all where Jesus left the jews.' * [4] This family life weighed so heavily on Margaret that it gave her a distaste for life in the world, and impelled her, a few years later, to become a nun.

James Joyce withdrew too, but in his own way. The very incongruity of ambition in such a setting helped to sustain it in him. In the gloomy, rancorous house, he prepared to become great. At the beginning of 1904 he learned that Eglinton and another writer he knew, Fred Ryan, were preparing to edit a new intellectual journal named *Dana* after the Irish earth-goddess. On January 7 he wrote off in one day, and with scarcely any hesitation, an autobiographical story that mixed admiration for himself with irony. At the suggestion of Stanislaus, he called it 'A Portrait of the Artist,' and sent it to the editors. This was the extraordinary beginning of Joyce's mature work. It was to be re-molded into *Stephen Hero,* a very long work, and then shortened to a middle length to form *A Portrait of the Artist as a Young Man.* But this process took ten years.

In 'A Portrait of the Artist,' for the first time since writing *A Brilliant Career,* Joyce was willing to attempt an extended work, to give up the purity of lyrics and epiphanies. He was resolved to gather the stages of his spiritual experience together in a connected pattern. It is difficult to say whether what he wrote was essay or story, for it has elements of both, the essay strained by apostrophe and dramatic exhortation, the narrative presented for the most part discursively. At the age of twenty-one Joyce had found he could become an artist by writing about the process of becoming an artist, his life legitimizing his portrait by sup-plying the sitter, while the portrait vindicated the sitter by its evident admiration for him. That admiration was already a little complicated by the attitude which, in the later book *A Portrait of the Artist as a Young Man,* has led some readers to suppose that Joyce could not bear

---

* His daughters confirm the evidence of *Ulysses* that John Joyce made these remarks.

his own hero. But in both portraits, as well as in the intermediate *Stephen Hero,* there is no lack of sympathy on the author's part; he recognizes, however, that earlier stages of the hero's life were necessarily callow, and makes the callowness clear in order to establish the progression towards the mature man.

The tone of this first draft is belligerent. Joyce begins by insisting on the psychological theory that 'the features of infancy' belong to a portrait as much as the features of adolescence. The past has no 'iron memorial aspect,' but implies 'a fluid succession of presents.' What we are to look for is not a fixed character but an 'individuating rhythm' not 'an identificative paper but rather the curve of an emotion.' This conception of personality as river rather than statue is premonitory of Joyce's later view of consciousness.

The development of the unnamed hero is already stylized, though the stages are less clearly marked than in the final *Portrait* they became. The hero first enters upon a period of religious zeal: 'He ran through his measure like a spendthrift saint, astonishing many by ejaculatory fervors, offending many by airs of the cloister. One day in a wood near Malahide a labourer had marvelled to see a boy of fifteen praying in an ecstasy of oriental posture.' This zeal steadily diminishes and ends after he enters the university. It is followed by his creation of 'the enigma of a manner' to protect from intrusion 'that ineradicable egoism which he was afterwards to call redeemer.' While the writing exhibits both candor and presumption, presumption has the better of it:

Is the mind of boyhood medieval that it is so divining of intrigue? . . . For this fantastic idealist, eluding the grunting booted apparition with a bound, the mimic hunt was no less ludicrous than unequal in a ground chosen to his disadvantage. But behind the rapidly indurating shield the sensitive answered. Let the pack of enmities come tumbling and sniffing to the highlands after their game. There was his ground and he flung them disdain from flashing antlers.

What is astonishing about this passage, however, is something else: the prose has been infected by the hero's mind. With symbolist reticence hunter and deer ° are not named, but their attendant metaphors, 'the grunting booted apparition' and 'flashing antlers,' are weighted with the hero's attitude toward them. The resultant bias colors phrases which might otherwise seem derogatory, 'this fantastic idealist' and 'the sensitive.' The prose works through emotional image rather than

° The image of himself as a deer remained Joyce's favorite self-portrayal. It appears more pretentiously in 'The Holy Office' a few months later, and in the *Proteus* episode of *Ulysses,* Stephen says, 'I just simply stood pale, silent, bayed about.' (46 [42]) See also p. 452.

through idea, and, without admitting sympathy for the hero, implies it by allowing him, as it were, to describe himself. Though the technique is not impeccable—the facile heroics of 'flashing antlers,' for example— Joyce's discovery of it made possible *A Portrait of the Artist as a Young Man*. In *Ulysses* and *Finnegans Wake* he carried the discovery further; there the language reflects not only the main characters, as when the river is described in words which sound like rivers or when the style tumesces with Gerty MacDowell's sexual excitement, but also the time of day or night, as when, late in the evening at 7 Eccles Street, the English language is as worn-out as the day and can produce only clichés, or when, early in the morning at the end of Earwicker's dream, the style dies away with the night. Joyce even learned to make language reflect aspects of the setting, as when, in a butcher shop, Bloom's mind unconsciously borrows metaphors from meat even when he is thinking of quite other things. This magnetization of style and vocabulary by the context of person, place, and time, has its humble origin in the few pages Joyce wrote for *Dana*.

Joyce's hero chooses his ground 'to his disadvantage' because he wishes to be hunted so as to defy his pursuers; he seeks not loyalty but betrayal. He is sharply differentiated from silly fellow-students and from worldly Jesuit masters; against both groups Joyce poses the artist's holy office, which the young man accepts in two stages. In the first he searches for 'an arduous good,' and his mind, like that of Yeats's alchemical heroes, is 'ever trembling towards its ecstasy.' Over his soul 'the image of beauty had fallen as a mantle,' and he leaves the church through the gates of Assisi to find in art an unworldly bliss.

Searching for sanctions he studies not St. Francis but the heresiarchs Joachim Abbas, Bruno, and Michael Sendivogius. He seeks with their help to 'reunite the children of the spirit, jealous and long-divided, to reunite them against fraud and principality. A thousand eternities were to be reaffirmed, divine knowledge was to be reestablished.' The plan has Yeats, the Theosophists, and Blake behind it, but Joyce plunges away: 'Alas for fatuity! as easily might he have summoned a regiment of the winds.' The treasons of the heretics were too 'venial.' The disconsolate young man meditates on the strand like Stephen Dedalus after him, and gradually loses interest in 'an absolute satisfaction' to become instead 'conscious of the beauty of mortal conditions.'

This is the second stage, and in it he develops a great interest in sexual freedom and a concomitant spiritual freedom. There follows a lyrical apostrophe of an unidentified female figure, his secular correlative of the Virgin Mary. It is she, presumably the girl that Joyce had seen at the sea's edge in 1898, who has led his soul to exfoliation. Like

Sudermann's Magda, she has taught him that he must sin if he wishes to grow, and enabled him through sin to discover his self. 'Thou wert sacramental,' he tells her, 'imprinting thine indelible work of very visible grace. A litany must honour thee. Lady of Apple Trees, Kind Wisdom, Sweet Flower of Dusk.' In imagined intercourse with her, in actual intercourse with prostitutes, he establishes that he must go forward 'to the measurable world and the broad expanse of activity.' He bursts with new life and endeavor. He will change the world, not by violence, but by subtlety, by 'urbanity.' His audience will not be those already born; they, like Yeats, are too old for him to help; it will be those 'surely engenderable.' In a stirring peroration compounded of Zarathustra, a dash of Marx, and Joyce, he calls to these: 'Man and woman, out of you comes the nation that is to come, the lightening of your masses in travail. The competitive order is employed against itself, the aristocracies are supplanted; and amid the general paralysis of an insane society, the confederate will issues in action.' [5]

The essay narrative was duly submitted to Eglinton and Ryan, and by them duly rejected. Eglinton told Joyce, 'I can't print what I can't understand,' [6] and objected to the hero's sexual exploits, whether with the dream lady of his litany or with the real prostitutes. Joyce took this rejection as a challenge to make the fictional history of his own life the call to arms of a new age. Stanislaus, in his diary for February 2, 1904, shows James's response most intimately:

2nd February: 1904: Tuesday. Jim's birthday. He is twenty-two [to] day. He was up late and did not stir out all day, having a bad cold. He has decided to turn his paper into a novel, and having come to that decision is just as glad, he says, that it was rejected. The paper . . . was rejected by the editors, Fred Ryan and W. Magee ('John Eglinton') because of the sexual experiences narrated in it. Jim thinks that they rejected it because it is all about himself, though they professed great admiration for the style of the paper. They always admire his style. Magee has an antipathy for Jim's character, I think. Magee is a dwarfish, brown-clad fellow, with red-brown eyes like a ferret, who walks with his hands in his jacket pockets and as stiffly as if his knees were roped up with sugauns.° He is sub-librarian in Kildare Street, and I think his mission in Ireland is to prove to his Protestant grand-aunts that unbelievers can be very moral and admire the Bible. He is interested in great thoughts and philosophy, whenever he can understand it. Jim is beginning his novel, as he usually begins things, half in anger, to show that in writing about himself he has a subject of more interest than their aimless discussion. I suggested the title of the paper 'A Portrait of the Artist', and this evening, sitting in the kitchen, Jim told me his idea for the novel. It is to be almost autobiographical, and naturally as it comes from Jim,

° Hay ropes (Irish).

satirical. He is putting a large number of his acquaintances into it, and those Jesuits whom he has known. I don't think they will like themselves in it. He has not decided on a title, and again I made most of the suggestions. Finally a title of mine was accepted: 'Stephen Hero,' from Jim's own name in the book 'Stephen Dedalus.' The title, like the book, is satirical. Between us we rechristened the characters, calling them by names which seemed to suit their tempers or which suggested the part of the country from which they come. Afterwards I parodied many of the names: Jim, 'Stuck-up Stephen'; Pappie, 'Sighing Simon'; myself, 'Morose Maurice'; the sister, 'Imbecile Isobel'; Aunt Josephine (Aunt Bridget), 'Blundering Biddy'; Uncle Willie, 'Jealous Jim.'

Pappie came in very drunk, and—an unusual thing for him—went straight up to bed. Today we have had a grand dinner and tea. It rained heavily after dark. We spent the evening playing cards—in honour of the occasion—Jim and Charlie smoking. Jim wanted to ask Pappie to come down but it was thought better to let him sleep.

Abruptly within a month, for Joyce always moved very quickly when the matter was crucial, he recognized his theme, the portrait of the renegade Catholic artist as hero. He could draw upon two types of books he had read: the defecter from religion and the insurgent artist.* He joined the two together. His own conflict with the Church, his plunge into callow sexuality, his proud recalcitrance in the name of individuality and then of art, his admiration for Parnell, for Byron, for Ibsen and Flaubert, his Parisian exile, all began to merge as parts of this central conception in which the young man gives up everything for art. But Stephen's esthetic notions are not renunciant; he becomes an artist because art opens to him 'the fair courts of life' which priest and king were trying to keep locked.

Joyce finished the first chapter of his book by February 10, 1904, and by midsummer he had written already a large volume. The earliest chapters, now lost, were lyrical, according to C. P. Curran, the tone becoming more bitter and realistic as Joyce proceeded. But there was a limitation upon even his candor; as Stanislaus said shrewdly in his diary, 'Jim is thought to be very frank about himself but his style is such that it might be contended that he confesses in a foreign language —an easier confession than in the vulgar tongue.'[7] To suggest the Christian and pagan elements in his mind, even to the point of absurdity, Joyce called himself Stephen Daedalus (then, to make it a little less improbable, Stephen Dedalus) after Christianity's first martyr and paganism's greatest inventor. Stephen would be a saint of literature,

---

* The first type he knew from Samuel Butler, Shaw, Gosse, Moore, and Tinayre; the second from Moore's *Vain Fortune*, Ibsen's *Love's Comedy*, Hauptmann's *Michael Kramer*, Sudermann's *Magda*, Flaubert's *Letters*.

and like Dedalus would invent wings to soar beyond his compatriots, and a labyrinth, a mysterious art based on great cunning. The choice of the hero's name determined the bird imagery of the book, though Joyce did not fully develop that in the chapters we have of *Stephen Hero;* it became more thematic in *A Portrait of the Artist as a Young Man,* where he was willing to parade his symbols with greater audacity. He had not yet decided that the book would end with his departure for the continent in 1902, and before long had carried it beyond that date. But the convergence of its plot upon alienation probably encouraged him, as he adjusted his life to art's exigencies, to consider leaving Dublin again and for good.

In later life Joyce, in trying to explain to his friend Louis Gillet the special difficulties of the autobiographical novelist, said, 'When your work and life make one, when they are interwoven in the same fabric...'[8] and then hesitated as if overcome by the hardship of his 'sedentary trade.'[9] The fact that he was turning his life to fiction at the same time that he was living it encouraged him to feel a certain detachment from what happened to him, for he knew he could reconsider and re-order it for the purposes of his book. At the same time, since he felt dependent for material upon actual events, he had an interest in bringing simmering pots to a strong boil, in making the events through which he lived take on as extreme a form as possible. The sense that they were characters in his drama annoyed some of his friends, especially Gogarty, who did not much care for the role of culprit in a court where Joyce was both judge and prosecuting attorney. Joyce did not keep his book to himself; he showed the manuscript to chosen friends, and, without perhaps saying so directly, threatened some of them with the punishments he would mete out for slights suffered at their hands. They became, as Gogarty said, 'accessories before the fact.' His art became a weapon which had an immediate effect upon his circle of acquaintances, and so altered the life it depicted. At first he allowed Stephen to have one loyal adherent, his brother Maurice, modeled on Stanislaus, but later he virtually obliterated him too, feeling that his hero must be entirely alone. He waited in trepidation for Cosgrave, Gogarty, and others to betray him as he imagined Byrne had done, and so to earn their places in the circles of his hell. He himself was a blend of celebrated victims (Christ and Parnell), light-bringing malefactors (Lucifer and Giordano Bruno), and exiles (Dante and Daedalus), while they were Intensities and Bullockships.[10]

The writing of *Stephen Hero* enabled Joyce, like the little boy in 'Araby,' to carry his chalice among a crowd of foes. He returned also to writing verse. 'I wrote *Chamber Music,*' he confessed later to Her-

bert Gorman, 'as a protest against myself.' [11] On the straggling, dis-
colored thread of his jobless days and dissipated nights he strung his
verses. He finished a poem on April 8, probably 'Silently she's combing,'
which Arthur Symons, to whom he appealed for help, placed for him
the following month in the *Saturday Review*. Two other lyrics that date
from about this time were written after an excursion with Mary Sheehy,
Francis Skeffington, and others into the Dublin hills. Joyce, swaggering
a little in his yachting cap and canvas shoes and sporting an ashplant,
spent most of his time watching Mary. He admired her beauty, and
interpreted her silence in company as a contempt like his for the
people around her. He did not give himself away now or at any other
time, but they exchanged a few words on the way back from the hills.
Mary, gazing at the moon, thought it looked tearful, while Joyce, with
mild daring, contended that it was 'like the chubby hooded face of
some jolly fat Capuchin.' 'I think you are very wicked,' said Mary, and
he replied, 'No, but I do my best.' [12] After they had separated he tore
open a cigarette box and wrote, 'What counsel has the hooded moon,'
the point of which, though somewhat murkily expressed, was that
earthly love with her would be joyful and not sad. He spoke again for
love and laughter in 'Lightly come or lightly go,' which also rose from
the conversation. He would revive the gaiety, as he had revived the
song, of the Elizabethans; this is the purport also of another poem
written about now but never published:

> Come out to where the youth is met
> Under the moon, beside the sea,
> And leave your weapon and your net,
> Your loom and your embroidery.
>
> Bring back the pleasantness of days
> And crystal moonlight on the shore.
> Your feet have woven many a maze
> In old times on the ivory floor.
>
> The weapons and the looms are mute
> And feet are hurrying by the sea.
> I hear the viol and the flute,
> The sackbut and the psaltery.[13]

Between his sudden rushes of creative activity Joyce played his part
in the family annals, recorded devotedly by Stanislaus, of drunkenness,
sloth, and bickering. He did not measure up to his father's record,
which Stanislaus noted, for the month of May, as an average of 3.97
days drunk out of every week. But he lived altogether irregularly, his
laxity justified in his mind by the rigorous discipline he practiced in his

art. On February 22, for example, he and Stanislaus slept until about four in the afternoon, and so enraged John Joyce by their indolence that he threatened and bullied them until James went out, 'avowedly for the police'; on the other hand, he spent the whole day of March 4 writing, and told Stanislaus he hoped to get his hand into such training that style would be as easy to him as singing. On March 13, he was out all night, and not long after he had to write Gogarty, who was away at Oxford, to give him the name of a physician who would cure a minor ailment contracted during a visit to Nighttown.

He had never pursued, but at the same time never abandoned, the possibility of a singing career, and suddenly now, in the middle of his rich book and poor circumstances, he reconsidered it. His voice was sweet and mellifluous. Curiously enough, it had never broken; his aunt, Mrs. Callanan, told him that even as a child his voice was not a treble but a weak tenor.[14] Since he was twenty Joyce had never been able to sing higher than G or at most A flat, although at the age of thirteen or fourteen he had been able to reach B natural. Perhaps his voice could be trained into the strength it lacked. There was the example of John McCormack to indicate where skill might lead. McCormack's reputation was then only two years old. After having sung at local concerts he had entered the tenor competition at the Feis Ceoil (Festival of Music, or, as it was familiarly known, fish coil) in 1903, and as a result of his victory had won a scholarship for a year's vocal study in Italy. He was back in Dublin now, and in March Joyce spent several evenings with him and with Richard Best, who took a keen interest in the Feis. They encouraged him to enter the contest himself, and he pawned some books to pay the entrance fee just in time to become the twenty-second candidate in a list of twenty-two.

The best voice teacher in Dublin was Benedetto Palmieri. Joyce borrowed from Byrne and from Gogarty (who returned from Oxford on March 24) to pay for a few lessons at seven shillings each. These proved helpful, and were not without their comic aspect. Joyce turned up for one lesson with a black eye, and explained that he had fallen into a manhole on a poorly lit street. Palmieri accepted the story in all innocence. What had happened was that Joyce had been walking through Stephen's Green with Cosgrave, when he had somehow become embroiled in a fight. Cosgrave stood by, 'hands in pockets,' [15] as Joyce bitterly recalled, while his friend was knocked about.* Joyce some months later determined upon the fictional name of 'Lynch' for

---

* 'For one role at least I seem unfit—that of man of honour,' Joyce wrote Curran ruefully. He claimed to have a sprained wrist and ankle, cut chin and cut hand, as well as the black eye.[16]

Cosgrave, because Lynch as mayor of Galway had hanged his own son, and in *Ulysses* he shows Lynch leaving Stephen in the lurch. Cosgrave did not like the name.

While the lessons were proceeding, Joyce needed a piano to practice with, and there was none at home now. He seized upon this pretext for taking a room in town. Having borrowed more money (Gogarty suggested to him in verse that since he had touched all his friends, he should now touch his lute), he found a very large room that spanned the first floor of a house at 60 Shelbourne Road, where a family named McKernan lived.* The next move was to secure a piano. He could have accepted the invitation of Gretta Cousins, the wife of the Theosophical poetaster James Cousins, to come and use her piano in the mornings, but he preferred to hire one. He paid something down at Piggott's and had a grand piano delivered at a time when he was out, so as to avoid tipping the haulers.[17] Eventually Piggott's took it back, but by that time the Feis was over. The McKernans liked Joyce well enough, and allowed him to get behind in his rent, though for a few days in June it was politic for him to sleep elsewhere until he had scraped together enough to make a show of paying.[18] He stayed with the McKernans until the end of August.

When he ran out of money to pay Palmieri, Joyce took a few lessons from Vincent O'Brien, a less expensive teacher who had helped McCormack. He sang, miserably according to his brother, at a concert given by the St. Brigid's Panoramic Choir and Fingall Ladies' Orchestra on the occasion of the Countess Fingall's visit, on Saturday night, May 14. The Feis Ceoil took place two days later. Joyce sang charmingly the two set pieces, 'No Chastening' from Sullivan's *The Prodigal Son*, and 'A Long Farewell,' an Irish air arranged by A. Moffat. He must have been aware that he would be required to sing an easy piece at sight, but when the piece was put in front of him, he waved it aside and strode from the platform. Neither then nor later could he read at sight, and he sought comfort now with John Elwood and Vincent Cosgrave, who were equally indignant that an artist should be asked to sing something he had not prepared.[19] The startled judge had intended to give Joyce the gold medal. He was Professor Luigi Denza of the London Academy of Music, composer of 'Funiculi-Funicula' and other pieces. The rules prevented his awarding Joyce anything but honorable mention, but when the second place winner was disqualified Joyce received the bronze medal. He could not pawn it, and according to

---

* To this room Joyce invited his sisters to tea, in what Eva Joyce jokingly described as 'one of Jim's spasms of brotherly love.'

Gogarty, threw it into the Liffey. But he treasured the newspaper clippings.* [20]

Denza in his report urged that Joyce study seriously, and spoke of him with so much admiration to Palmieri that the latter, who had made the mistake of refusing to help McCormack, offered to train Joyce for three years for nothing in return for a share of his concert earnings for ten years. But Joyce's ardor for a singing career had already begun to lapse; the tedious discipline did not suit him, and to be a second McCormack was not so attractive as to be a first Joyce.

His next venture was as a schoolteacher. There was a temporary vacancy for a gentleman usher at the Clifton School, Dalkey, a private school founded a few years before at Summerfield Lodge, once the residence of the minor poet Denis Florence McCarthy whose name keeps coming up in *Finnegans Wake*. The founder and headmaster was an Ulster Scot, very pro-British, named Francis Irwin, a Trinity College graduate. Joyce devotes the second chapter of *Ulysses* to describing Stephen's activities at a school clearly modeled on Irwin's.

As usual, his account is tenacious of remembered facts. The students whom Stephen teaches are based in part at least on actual ones: Armstrong, for example, is described as living on Vico Road, with a brother in the Navy, and eating figrolls; and Joyce appears to be blending Cecil Wright, the figroll-eater, with Clifford Ferguson,[21] who suits the rest of the description. Irwin is presented under the name of Deasy, oddly inappropriate for an Ulster Scot, and his personality is merged with

* He probably anticipated that they might be useful to him as publicity material should he revert to a singing career, so he asked 'Seumas O'Sullivan' (the pen-name of James S. Starkey) to type copies of them for him. He parodied O'Sullivan's poem, 'Praise,' which begins:

> Dear, they are praising your beauty,
>   The grass and the sky:
> The sky in a silence of wonder,
>   The grass in a sigh.

Joyce's version ran:

> Dear, I am asking a favour
>   Little enough
> This, that thou shouldst entype me
>   This powdery puff

> I had no heart for your troubling
>   Dearest, did I
> Only possess a typewriter or
>   Money to buy

> Thine image, dear, rosily bitten
>   Ever shall be
> Thereafter that thou hast typewritten
>   These things for me—

> J.A.J.[22]

that of an Ulsterman Joyce knew in Trieste, Henry Blackwood Price, who had Deasy's preoccupation with a distinguished Ulster ancestry and shared his interest in the hoof-and-mouth disease. Joyce represents Deasy as a grass widower, although Price was happily married and Irwin was a bachelor who lived with a sister, but in other respects treats him indulgently, sparing, for example, any mention of his red nose, or of the shutting-down of the school soon after because of Irwin's alcoholism. Joyce can have taught there only a few weeks.

Late in April he received the first of a series of invitations from Gogarty to pay him a visit at Oxford.[23] If Joyce could raise three pounds for the fare, Gogarty would cover the rest of his expenses. He wisely declined to send money ahead for fear Joyce would not turn up. Joyce would have liked to see Oxford, and perhaps did not mind the prospect of being exhibited there by ringmaster Gogarty as a rare specimen of undomesticated Hibernian man. But he could not raise three pounds. The invitations continued, and read—as did Joyce's replies—rather like messages exchanged in a secret society. Gogarty covered the margins with notes that went in every direction; he addressed Joyce as 'Wandering Aengus'* and as 'Scorner of Mediocrity and Scourge of the Rabblement.' In a letter of May 3 he informed him he had won only second prize in the Newdigate, subjoined that he had two new suits, one for Joyce to wear, and urged him again to come. Joyce replied by asking for a loan, representing his condition as desperate. Gogarty countered by sending him a budget to detail the reasons for his being unable to oblige. Joyce returned the budget, and shifted adroitly to ask for something else:

> 60 Shelbourne Road,
> Dublin.
>
> Dear Gogarty
>
> I sent you back the budget. I am still alive. Here is a more reasonable request. I am singing at a garden-fête on Friday and if you have a decent suit to spare or a cricket shirt send it or them. I am trying to get an engagement in the Kingstown Pavilion. Do you know anyone there? My idea for July and August is this—to get Dolmetsch to make me a lute and to coast the south of England from Falmouth to Margate, singing old English songs. When are you leaving Oxford? I wish I could see it. I don't understand your allusion. 'Chamber Music' is the title for the suite. I suppose Jenny is leaving in a day or so. I shall call to say farewell and adieu.† Her letter did not annoy me. The others did.‡

* Mulligan says in *Ulysses* (245 [235]), 'Wandering Aengus I call him.'
† Joyce liked to sing the old song, 'Farewell and adieu to you, Spanish ladies,/ Farewell and adieu to you, ladies of Spain.'
‡ The letters were presumably to console him for his failure to win the Feis Ceoil competition.

I enclose one lest you should plume yourself. Ellwood is nearly cured.°
I have a rendezvous with Annie Langton—but you forget her? I have
no news to report. Their Intensities and Their Bullockships continue to
flourish.† His Particular Intensity walks now unencumbered.‡ Mac-
Auliffe is going for Greenwood Pim's job in CPI °°—desires to be
remembered to you. You will not have me faithfully. Adieu then,
Inconsequent.

Stephen Daedalus.[24]

3 June 1904

The remark about *Chamber Music* refers to an episode, much distorted in after accounts, which occurred about a month before. Gogarty,
who was then in Dublin, had brought Joyce to visit Jenny, an easy-
going widow, and while they all drank porter Joyce read out his poems,
which he carried with him in a large packet, each written in his best
hand in the middle of a large piece of parchment. The widow was
pleased enough by this entertainment, but had to interrupt to withdraw
behind a screen to a chamber pot. As the two young men listened,
Gogarty cried out, 'There's a critic for you!' Joyce had already accepted
the title of *Chamber Music* which Stanislaus had suggested; and when
Stanislaus heard the story from him, he remarked, 'You can take it as
a favorable omen.' †† [25]

The plan for the lute mentioned in the letter was one that Joyce
followed up. He said to Padraic Colum that the tour would be 'personally conducted, like the Emperor Nero's tour in Greece.' He remarked soberly to Joseph Holloway, the annalist of the Dublin theater,
that he expected the English not to rise above Negro minstrels. 'My tour
will not be a success,' he predicted, 'but it will prove the inadequacy
of the English.' [26] On June 16 he wrote to the London Academy of
Music for the address of Arnold Dolmetsch; [27] he was of course aware
that Dolmetsch had made a psaltery—a lute-like instrument—for Yeats,
to aid him in illustrating his theories of the speaking of verse. Yeats
lectured and the actress Florence Farr performed on the psaltery and

---

° Of an ailment presumably contracted in Nighttown.
† Stuart Gilbert notes: 'Their Intensities: earnest Sinn Feiners. Their Bullockships:
countrified louts . . .'
‡ 'His Particular Intensity' was J. F. Byrne, who 'walks now unencumbered'
because he has broken with Cosgrave, his usual companion.
°° Pim was, as Gilbert points out, secretary to the committee of management of
Conjoint (Medical) Examinations Office, Royal College of Physicians, Ireland
(CPI).
†† In *Ulysses* (278 [268]), Bloom thinks: 'Chamber music. Could make a kind of
pun on that. It is a kind of music I often thought when she. Acoustics that is.
Tinkling. Empty vessels make most noise. Because the acoustics, the resonance
changes according as the weight of the water is equal to the law of falling water.'

chanted poems. Joyce recklessly supposed that Dolmetsch would do as much for him, but the musician replied without enthusiasm on July 17:

Dear Sir,

Lutes are extremely rare. I have not heard of any for sale for years. You should read my articles on this subject in 'The Connoisseur' for April and May. I have made one lute, some years ago, but it is doubtful whether I shall make any others. It would certainly be very expensive, and I could hardly say when it would be finished. The lute is moreover extremely difficult to play, and very troublesome to keep in order.

A spinet or some simple kind of Harpsichord, or even a very early piano would be far more practicable.

I could get you one of these fairly easily. £30 to £60 would get one.

Yours faithfully,
Arnold Dolmetsch [28]

Joyce dropped the plan at once, but in *Ulysses* he mentions it and also parodies it with Bloom's notion of accompanying Molly on a concert tour of the English watering-places.[29]

Several aspects of Joyce's life converge upon June 16, 1904,* the day he afterwards chose for the action of *Ulysses*. It was on that day, or at least during the month of June,[30] that he began to work out his theory that Shakespeare was not prince Hamlet but Hamlet's father, betrayed by his queen with his brother as Shakespeare was—Joyce thought—betrayed by Anne Hathaway with his brother. Joyce was at his search for distinguished victims—Parnell, Christ, himself. Instead of making the artist Shakespeare an avenging hero, he preferred to think of him as a cuckold. Joyce developed the theory with excitement and told it to Eglinton, Best, and Gogarty.

He was not yet living at the famous Martello tower at Sandycove, as *Ulysses* would suggest. On June 15 the McKernans, with whom he had his room, encouraged him to leave until he could pay his rent, and he went to his friends James and Gretta Cousins and asked them to take him in.[31] They hospitably turned over the spare room in their tiny house on the sea's edge at Ballsbridge.[32] After dinner on June 15 the Espositos came to call. Michele Esposito was an accomplished teacher of music who had brought his family, including his two attractive daughters Vera and Bianca, to Ireland several years before. Vera noted in her diary later that Joyce was very quiet and scarcely opened his mouth except to sing, to his own piano accompaniment, Henry VIII's 'Pastime with good companee, I love, and shall until I dee,' and the

---

* June 16, 1904, was a fine, breezy day, with four hours of sunshine, and a clear night.

ballad of 'Turpin Hero.' The Esposito girls also sang. They and their
father were impressed by Joyce and suggested he call on them. But
for two reasons this visit never took place.[33] One was that he offended
the Esposito sisters, the other that he fell in love.

It was falling in love that gave June 16 its talismanic importance for
Joyce. The experience of love was almost new to him in fact, though he
had often considered it in imagination. A transitory interest in his
cousin Katsy Murray had been followed by the stronger, but unex-
pressed and unrequited, interest in Mary Sheehy. He shocked Stanislaus
a little by quoting with approval a remark of a Dublin wit, 'Woman is
an animal that micturates once a day, defecates once a week, men-
struates once a month and parturates once a year.'[34] Yet tenderness
was as natural to him as coarseness, and secretly he dreamed of falling
in love with someone he did not know, a gentle lady, the flower of
many generations, to whom he should speak in the ceremonious accents
of *Chamber Music*.[35]

Instead on June 10, 1904, Joyce was walking down Nassau Street in
Dublin when he caught sight of a tall young woman, auburn-haired,
walking with a proud stride. When he spoke to her she answered pertly
enough to allow the conversation to continue. She took him, with his
yachting cap, for a sailor, and from his blue eyes thought for a moment
he might be Swedish.[36] Joyce found she was employed at Finn's Hotel,
a slightly exalted rooming house, and her lilting speech confessed that
she was from Galway. Her name was a little comic, Nora Barnacle, but
this too might be an omen of felicitous adhesion. (As Joyce's father
was to say when he heard much later her last name was Barnacle,
'She'll never leave him.')[37] After some talk it was agreed they should
meet in front of Sir William Wilde's house at the turning of Merrion
Square on June 14. But Nora Barnacle failed to appear, and Joyce sent
her a note in some dejection:

60 Shelbourne Road

I may be blind. I looked for a long time at a head of reddish brown
hair and decided it was not yours. I went home quite dejected. I would
like to make an appointment but it might not suit you. I hope you will
be kind enough to make one with me—if you have not forgotten me!

James A Joyce [38]

15 June 1904

The appointment was made, and for the evening of June 16, when
they went walking at Ringsend, and thereafter began to meet regularly.
To set *Ulysses* on this date was Joyce's most eloquent if indirect tribute
to Nora, a recognition of the determining effect upon his life of his

attachment to her. On June 16 he entered into relation with the world around him and left behind him the loneliness he had felt since his mother's death. He would tell her later, 'You made me a man.' June 16 was the sacred day that divided Stephen Dedalus, the insurgent youth, from Leopold Bloom, the complaisant husband.

To any other writer of the time, Nora Barnacle would have seemed ordinary; Joyce, with his need to seek the remarkable in the commonplace, decided she was nothing of the sort. She had only a grammar school education; she had no understanding of literature, and no power or interest in introspection. But she had considerable wit and spirit, a capacity for terse utterance as good in its kind as Stephen Dedalus's. Along with a strain of coquetry she wore an air of insulated innocence, and, if her allegiance would always be a little mocking, it would be nevertheless thoroughgoing. She could not be an intellectual companion, but Joyce was not inclined to care. Though his compatriots Yeats and Lady Gregory might prate of symbolic marriages of the artist and the peasantry, here was a living union. Purer than he, she could receive his litanies, and better still, his confidences.

Nora Barnacle's simplicity seemed something that could develop only in a place more provincial than Dublin. She had come from Galway City some six months before. Her father was a baker, and being also a heavy drinker, kept his large family poor. When Nora was five, her mother, surrounded by small children and pregnant once more, sent her to stay with a grandmother on Nun's Island.[39] She was to return after the birth, but when the grandmother offered to keep her, the arrangement continued. Her mother eventually separated from her father, so her maternal uncles assumed some responsibility for her care and discipline. Until she was almost thirteen Nora attended the convent school of the Sisters of Mercy, and then went to work as a portress at the Presentation Convent, also in Galway City.[40] Her closest friend in Galway was Mary O'Holleran, who dictated an account of Nora's early life: *

We were pals for years we were then only 16 years old my name was Mary O. Holleran then we were always together until she went to Dublin she was working in the presentation convent then she was the straightest pal I ever had. When we used to get a penny for sweets which was very seldom in those days we would go to a Mrs Francis she was nearly blind and had a sweet shop in Prospect Hill. While she would be looking for the half-penny weight we would have the pound weight on the scales and Nora would hold up her

___

* This was taken down by Mrs. John Griffin, née Kathleen Barnacle (Nora's sister), from Mrs. Mary O'Holleran Morris's dictation, because Mrs. Morris is not good at writing.

pinafore for the sweets and we would be away like hell with roars of laughter
and our pinafores full of sweets we would go into another old woman and
ask for a pennyworth of cough lozenges and pinch as much more out of the
jar while her back was turned and again have a great laugh. There was a
young man Jim Connell, he used to come into our house he was always waiting for his passage for America. This night Nora and I bought a card of Jelly
babys they were sweet babys niggers what we call nigger babys they were
black sweets we got the largest envelope we could get and sent the card of
nigger babys by post to Jim as Jim could not read he ran across to our house
thinking he had his passage for America and when the packet was open he
had 12 nigger babies we had to run and could not be seen for a week he left
it on his sweetheart a girl by the name of Sarah Kavanagh from the country
and he never spoke to her after that.

We had a party one Holly eve night My father used to make games for us
such as cross sticks hanging from the ceiling there would be an apple on one
stick soap on the other and a lighted candle on the other stick our eyes would
be covered so we could not see and my father would spin the sticks around
and we would bite at the apple my father would put the soap in Noras mouth
the house would be in roars of laughter while Nora would be getting the soap
out of her mouth we would fill our mouths with wheat and then go round the
house listening at the doors to hear if a boys name mentioned as he would
be our supposed future husband and we would burst out laughing and run
like the dickens for fear of the boys would catch us but they could never
catch us we would then go to another house and buy a pennyworth of pins
we would stick 9 pins into the red part of the apple and throw the 10th pin
away we would put the apple with the pins in, in our left foot stocking and
tie it with our right foot garter and put it under our head when we would
go to bed to dream of our future husband we would steal a head of cabbage
out of a garden we never stood in before on a moonlight night on Hallow
eve and have a mirror we would go into a field and stand on a dunghill and
eat the head of cabbage and looking through the mirror to see if we could
see the face of our future husband. Those were the old fashioned charms we
used to play on Hallow eve.

Nora knew another boy whom she was very fond of his name was Michael
(Sonny) Bodkin he was going to the Universarty College here he was a very
handsome young man with a beautiful head of black wavy hair he was a
great admirer of Nora but she was too young and afraid to be seen with the
boys. We used to go to his father's shop for a pennyworth of conversation
lozenges the flat sweets with rhymes on them (such as I love you and will
meet you tonight). Sonny Bodkin died very young.

Some time after this Nora met Willie Mulvey she just met him on the
bridge he asked her would she meet him and Nora said to me Mary what
will I do. I told her to go out with him she then asked me what I would do.
I said I would wait for her I would have to sit in the Abbey Church wait for
her as I supposed to be out with her and we had to be home before 10 o.c.
at night or she would get a beating. She was afraid of her uncle Tommy

Healy as he would be on the town watching Nora with his walking stick [41] and always whistling a tune (My Mountain Maid Arise). He was a beautiful whistler and singer Nora was terribly afraid of him As I dare not be seen till she would back I would have to stay in the Abbey Church till she would come she would have a large box of chocolates and would scatter them all on the table in my house and share them with us all.* Nora would meet me after she leave Willie Mulvey at the Abbey Church and we would be home together and a box of sweets to enjoy.

Then one night poor Nora was caught with her Uncle Tommy he followed her down till she went in home and he gave her a bad beating. The following week she left for Dublin she wrote to me once when she was in Dublin saying, My old Pal here I am up in Dublin and my uncle Tommy won't follow me any more. She was six months in Dublin when she came home to pay one visit. She went away and never wrote home for seven years.

I was married in November 1906 and became Mrs. Morris and am the mother of 6 children 3 boys and 3 girls one of my sons is a school teacher here in Galway and I now have 13 grandchildren, I live opposite Kathleen [Barnacle Griffin] with my sister Annie and when I'm alone in the evening the tears come into my eyes as I often think of the nights when Nora and I used to dress up in men's clothes. We would ramble round the square and our hair stuck up under our caps. We were never caught at this we met her Uncle Tommy one night and Nora says to me here's my uncle and I says to Nora come on, don't shirk it, I said good night to him as I could imitate a mans voice he never knew and Im still here but my Nora is gone.†

This then was the young woman from Galway, handsome, jaunty, daring, and untutored, who in a short time was joined to one of the most rarefied minds of the century. She remarked in later life to Maria Jolas, 'You can't imagine what it was like for me to be thrown into the life of this man.' [42] Her immediate response to him, however, was not befuddled but self-possessed, and afterwards Joyce liked to think of her as 'sauntering' into his life, a careless acceptance of him which came to seem an essential part of the female temperament. (In *Finnegans Wake* both Anna Livia and her daughter go sauntering.) Soon she was writing him as 'My Precious Darling' and in a letter of July 8 he addressed her as 'Little Pouting Nora' and as 'dear little brown head.' Yet he was embarrassed to sign himself 'Jim,' and for some time the couple must have addressed each other as 'Nora' and 'Mr. Joyce.' The

---

* Bodkin, who gave her a bracelet, seems to fuse with Mulvey, who gave her cream sweets, in a note Joyce wrote about the character of Bertha in *Exiles:* 'She weeps over Rahoon too, over him whom her love has killed, the dark boy whom, as the earth, she embraces in death and disintegration. He is her buried life, her past. His attendant images are the trinkets and toys of girlhood (bracelet, cream sweets, palegreen lily of the valley, the convent garden).' [43] See also p. 327.
† The transvestism in the *Circe* episode of *Ulysses* owes something to this masquerading of Nora's girlhood.

letter of July 8 is only initialed 'J.A.J.' Having borne off one of her gloves as a token after an early meeting, like Leopold Bloom, he sent her on July 21 a new pair and signed himself 'Aujey,' a partial anagram of his initials which suggests the mind that conceived of Henry Flower as Bloom's clandestine *nom de plume.* An August 2 he wrote out for her a copy of 'The Salley Gardens,' which he had evidently sung for her, and signed it only, 'W. B. Yeats.' On August 15 he wrote her a letter in which he again failed to sign his name:

> 60 Shelbourne Road
>
> My dear Nora,
>
> It has just struck me. I came in at half past eleven. Since then I have been sitting in an easy chair like a fool. I could do nothing. I hear nothing but your voice. I am like a fool hearing you call me 'Dear.' I offended two men today by leaving them coolly. I wanted to hear your voice, not theirs.
>
> When I am with you I leave aside my contemptuous, suspicious nature. I wish I felt your head on my shoulder. I think I will go to bed.
>
> I have been a half-hour writing this thing. Will you write something to me? I hope you will. How am I to sign myself? I won't sign anything at all, because I don't know what to sign myself.
>
> 15 August 1904.

The constraint over his nickname was connected with a constraint over saying he was in love. With his customary candor, he analyzed his symptoms minutely for the benefit of his friends who came incredulously to inspect them. His brother Stanislaus did not care for James in the role of lover or quasi-lover, jealous a little of Miss Barnacle's dominion, but also disconcerted to find his brother, usually so unpredictable, acting much like other people. That such an ill-assorted match could prosper did not strike him as likely, but James did not ask his advice. Joyce's most intimate friend, Vincent Cosgrave, reacted differently. He did his best to take Nora away from Joyce, telling her Joyce's love wouldn't last and that in any case the man was mad. (In *Exiles* Bertha wonders aloud if her husband is not a little mad.) [44] But Nora paid scant attention, and Cosgrave felt humiliated by his role of unsuccessful rival. 'Poor Cosgrave!' said Nora to James, not altogether displeased by this second conquest. Joyce's affection flowered on this flattery, and he felt confirmed in his belief that she had an extraordinary soul.

Not, however, that his habits were immediately altered or his character regenerated. He did not stop drinking. His most public exhibition of drunkenness occurred, in fact, on June 20, four days after his memorable first evening with Nora. On this night he turned up at a rehearsal

of the National Theatre Society, which was then meeting in a make-
shift theater, really a large storehouse behind a grocery shop in Camden
Street. After closing time, this backroom, later to be dignified as the
Camden Hall, could only be reached through a long narrow passage
dimly lit by a gas jet. Joyce's visits were usually tolerated by the actors
because he would entertain them by singing in the breaks during
rehearsal, and Holloway records that Joyce had been present ten days
before when Synge announced to the society that he had a new play
ready for them, *The Well of the Saints.*[45] Synge's productivity probably encouraged Joyce to demonstrate splenetically his continued contempt for the Irish theater, for he arrived so drunk on June 20 that he
collapsed in the passageway. Just then Vera Esposito, who was one of
the actresses, came out with her mother; walking through the passage
she stumbled over something and heard with astonishment its maudlin
grunts. Hastily retreating she informed Frank and William Fay, the
company's directors, of the presence of the obstacle. They crowded in
with candles and identified the prostrate form. After a slight scuffle
Joyce was evicted and the door slammed and bolted behind him. From
outside came the sound of his heavy ashplant banging on the door and
his voice shouting, 'Open the door at once, Fay. You can't keep us out
of your bawdy house. We know you.' The diminutive Fays, reinforced
by George Roberts and Seumas O'Sullivan, opened the door and quietly
informed Joyce that it was the refined Miss Esposito who had stumbled
into him. Joyce was put down a little, and Roberts, with the help of
another actor, Dossie Wright, took him home.[46] But as soon as he
recovered his wits he revenged himself by a poem:

> O, there are two brothers, the Fays,
> Who are excellent players of plays,
>   And, needless to mention, all
>   Most unconventional,
> Filling the world with amaze.

> But I angered those brothers, the Fays,
> Whose ways are conventional ways,
>   For I lay in my urine
>   While ladies so pure in
> White petticoats ravished my gaze.

> J.A.J.* [47]

* The incident is recalled in *Ulysses* (214 [205]), where Joyce makes it occur
before June 16. Buck Mulligan chaffs Stephen, 'O, the night in the Camden Hall
when the daughters of Erin had to lift their skirts to step over you as you lay in
your mulberrycoloured, multicoloured, multitudinous vomit!' Stephen replies, 'The
most innocent son of Erin for whom they ever lifted them.'
He was reconciled later to the Fays, and in 1926 W. G. Fay produced *Exiles.*

After this episode Joyce settled down for a time. He returned to Shelbourne Road from the Cousins's vegetarian house, complaining of stomach trouble induced by a 'typhoid turnip,' [48] and applied himself to his novel. He finished a 102-page chapter of *Stephen Hero* and sent it to George Russell, and on June 23 sent all he had written to Constantine Curran 'by my 23rd sister.' [49] Curran praised the manuscript and spoke of George Meredith as one of its models, a remark which made Joyce's eyes assume a look of 'indignant wonder.' He was more pleased by Curran's perception of his 'desperate hunger for truth.' [50]

Joyce's letters of this time mix a little posturing with a great deal of importunity. A note to Curran of July 3, promises to call at his office, and concludes, 'Suis dans un trou sanguinaire.' [51] Curran made him several small loans with uncomplaining generosity. Richard Best was asked but, cued by John Eglinton, he gave an excuse. [52] A card to George Roberts of July 13 asks for a pound and is signed 'James Overman,' [53] an ironic allusion to Nietzsche on the order of Mulligan's 'Toothless Kinch the Superman' in *Ulysses*. A 'bog-Latin' letter in mid-August to Byrne, who was spending the summer at Rathdrum in Wicklow, asked him 'in the name of the crucified Jesus' for a loan, but Byrne replied in the same idiom that he was helpless to oblige:

> Carrigmore,
> Rathdrum
> Co. Wicklow.
> August 19th, 1904

Non possum tibi dare libram, quia maxima in impecuniosa conditione sum. Miro cur habes satirizatum amicos vestros, num pecunia eorum defuit? aut habent illi tecum pugnatum quando in periculis fuistis, et tibi datum nigrum oculum aut nasum fractum. Fleo quod non habeo pecuniam, sed impossibile est ex petro trahere lactam, aut ab ille qui summis in locis terrae nudus vivet, arripere quod non habet super crures eius.

> Sum, sicut dicunt populi,
> vester S. S. Joannes * [54]

As proud as he was needy, Joyce conferred his debts like favors; his friends were permitted to recognize their duties.

* 'I can't give you a pound, because I'm in an extremely impecunious condition. I wonder why you have satirized your friends; was it because they had no money? Or did they fight with you when you were in difficulties and give you a black eye or a broken nose? I weep that I have no money, but it's impossible to draw milk from a stone, or to snatch from him who lives naked on the highest places of the earth [the Wicklow hills] what he doesn't have on his shanks.

> I am, as the populace says,
> Your Saint John'

One person who sympathized with his need was George Russell, carefully kept by Joyce in cultivation. Russell, who had read and admired *Stephen Hero* as it was being written, asked Joyce in July if he could write a short story suitable for the *Irish Homestead,* something 'simple, rural, live-making, pathos [pathetic],' which would not shock his readers. The payment would be a pound. 'It is easy earned money if you can write fluently and don't mind playing to the common under- standing and liking once in a way. You can sign any name you like as a pseudonym.' [55] Russell's suggestion was the beginning of *Dubliners;* Joyce wrote at once his first story, 'The Sisters,' based on the death of the old, paralyzed, and demented priest to whom he was related on his mother's side. He mystified Curran by informing him, 'I am writing a series of epicleti—ten—for a paper. I have written one. I call the series *Dubliners* to betray the soul of that hemiplegia or paralysis which many consider a city.' [56] The word epicleti, an error for *epicleses* (Latin) or *epicleseis* (Greek), referred to an invocation still found in the mass of the Eastern Church, but dropped from the Roman ritual, in which the Holy Ghost is besought to transform the host into the body and blood of Christ. What Joyce meant by this term, adapted like *epiphany* and *eucharistic moment* from ritual, he suggested to his brother Stanis- laus: 'Don't you think there is a certain resemblance between the mystery of the Mass and what I am trying to do? I mean that I am trying . . . to give people some kind of intellectual pleasure or spiritual enjoyment by converting the bread of everyday life into something that has a permanent artistic life of its own . . . for their mental, moral, and spiritual uplift.' [57] In another attempt to explain his method, he said to his brother: 'Do you see that man who has just skipped out of the way of the tram? Consider, if he had been run over, how significant every act of his would at once become. I don't mean for the police inspector. I mean for anybody who knew him. And his thoughts, for anybody that could know them. It is my idea of the significance of trivial things that I want to give the two or three unfortunate wretches who may eventually read me.' [58]

'The Sisters' was totally uncompromising in its method. Just as the lyrical epiphanies had led Joyce towards *A Portrait of the Artist,* so the bald, underplayed epiphanies led him toward the first story in *Dubliners.* Although he never allows himself to say so in the story, he makes the priest's actual paralysis a symptom of the 'general paraly- sis of the insane' with which Ireland was afflicted. Irishmen did not move from point to point; they stuck fast and deteriorated. Joyce allowed the priest's character to form itself through the testimony of different witnesses—the narrator recovering this troubled memory of his childhood, the suspicious family friend and the uncle, and finally the two sisters with whom the priest has lived. Each of these furnishes the reader with another hint of the priest's failure, of his sense of his own ruin, of his attempt in ambiguous little ways to transmit corruption to the susceptible boy; yet this unhealthiness remains an intimation, to be contrasted with the invulnerability of the two well-informed sisters and their mixture of malapropism and acuteness. The words are plain, but the sentences are subtly cadenced, and Joyce demonstrates his power to capture the inflections of speech.

As the child, Joyce made use of himself in print for the first time, and as the uncle he made use of his father. The story, surprisingly, was accepted. H. F. Norman, the editor of the *Irish Homestead*, sent Joyce a sovereign on July 23 and said, probably in response to Joyce's demand, that he would change nothing but the name of the parish.[59] It was published on August 13—the first anniversary of May Joyce's death—over the pseudonym of Stephen Daedalus. James forebore to sign his own name, Stanislaus says, because he was ashamed of publishing in 'the pigs' paper.'[60]

On the basis of this success, Joyce went to a literary friend named T. G. Keller and offered to sign over his expected payment of £6 for his next six stories if Keller would give him £5 at once. Keller did not have the money. Then Joyce offered to various friends (probably on the basis of Colum's arrangement with the millionaire Kelly) to turn himself into a joint-stock company and sell shares, which would increase spectacularly in value as his books began to appear. But this idea, like the first, failed to arouse enthusiasm. Joyce had to accept payment in the normal way for his next two stories in the *Irish Homestead*: 'Eveline' (published September 10, 1904), and 'After the Race' (published December 17). Both these stories challenged the work of Joyce's compatriots. Yeats's *The Countess Cathleen* had extolled the virtue of self-sacrifice; 'Eveline' evokes the counter virtue of self-realization. When Joyce's character is held by Ireland, she reduces herself to a 'helpless animal,' as if surrendering the very qualities that had made her human. In 'After the Race' Joyce may have been thinking of Yeats's story of card-playing, 'Red Hanrahan,' which appeared the year before. At any rate, there are in both illusion and disenchantment. But Joyce, instead of using a half-legendary hero, writes of Jimmy Doyle, who hungers for a foreign sophistication which he thinks he finds in some racing-car drivers. The closing words, 'Daybreak, gentlemen!', bring him back to the Dublin world of I.O.U.'s, which he is obviously not equipped to leave. Yeats's story is Celtic, Joyce's Irish. Yeats is melancholy and warm, Joyce is meticulous. Norman accepted this third story but asked Joyce then not to submit any more because there were too many letters of complaint from readers in both the country and the city.

A few other small opportunities came his way. He sold three poems, all probably inspired by Nora Barnacle. So complicated in his thought and in his prose, Joyce longed to sing; a dream of his youth was to be a bird, both in its song and in its flight; and his unassuming lyrics, which he was to disparage and to cherish, were spurts of this lost, bird-like aspiration. Two of the poems, 'O sweetheart, hear you,' and 'I would in that sweet bosom be,' were published in the *Speaker* in July and September 1904; the other, 'My love is in a light attire,' was accepted by John Eglinton for the August issue of *Dana,* and Joyce even persuaded Eglinton to pay him (unlike all the other contributors), chortling as he pocketed a guinea.⁶¹ Then John Baillie, the editor of a new book-magazine, *The Venture,* to whom Symons had spoken of Joyce, asked for a poem; Joyce sent Baillie two poems he had written earlier, 'What counsel has the hooded moon' and 'Thou leanest to the shell of night.' The poems were accepted but Joyce did not succeed in getting paid before their publication in November.⁶² Constantine Curran, who was now editing *St. Stephen's,* the University College magazine, asked Joyce to send him something he could not market elsewhere, but was staggered when Joyce disingenuously submitted a new and scabrous broadside, 'The Holy Office.' Curran returned the 'unholy thing' with a humorous letter to Joyce on August 8, but mollified him with a little money.⁶³

'The Holy Office' was Joyce's first overt, angry declaration that he would pursue candor while his contemporaries pursued beauty. His short stories, with their grim exactitude and submerged lyricism, had broken away from the Irish literary movement in which, though he denied the fact, his poems fitted pretty well.° As the author of these stories, he was free to attack his literary compatriots for dealing in milk and water which tasted no better for being called Irish and spiritual. For the moment the whole literary movement seemed to him as much a fraud as the Irish virtues, among which cruelty masqueraded as high-minded moralism, and timid onanism masqueraded as purity. One could meet these writers of the 'revival' and read their works without suspecting that the writers were made of flesh and bone. Joyce's 'holy office,' he says, yoking Christian ritual to Aristotle, is 'Katharsis,' the revelation of what the hypocritical and self-deceived mummers hide:

° The closest parallels to Joyce's stories are Chekhov's, but Joyce said he had not read Chekhov when he wrote them.⁶⁴

Myself unto myself will give
This name, Katharsis-Purgative.
I, who dishevelled ways forsook
To hold the poets' grammar-book,
Bringing to tavern and to brothel
The mind of witty Aristotle,
Lest bards in the attempt should err
Must here be my interpreter.

With quick thrusts he disposes, more or less thoroughly, of his contemporaries. Yeats has allowed himself to be led by women; Synge writes of drinking but never drinks; Gogarty is a snob, Colum a chameleon, Roberts an idolater of Russell, Starkey a mouse, Russell a mystical ass.

But all these men of whom I speak
Make me the sewer of their clique.
That they may dream their dreamy dreams
I carry off their filthy streams
For I can do those things for them
Through which I lost my diadem.

His time-serving contemporaries are lumped together as Mammon's minions, and only he is on the side of Leviathan, to them the devil of base impulses, to him the high spirit of freedom and strength:

But Mammon places under ban
The uses of Leviathan
And that high spirit ever wars
On Mammon's countless servitors,
Nor can they ever be exempt
From his taxation of contempt.
So distantly I turn to view
The shamblings of that motley crew,
Those souls that hate the strength that mine has
Steeled in the school of old Aquinas.
Where they have crouched and crawled and prayed
I stand, the self-doomed, unafraid,
Unfellowed, friendless and alone,
Indifferent as the herring-bone,
Firm as the mountain ridges where
I flash my antlers on the air.
Let them continue as is meet
To adequate the balance-sheet.
Though they may labour to the grave
My spirit shall they never have

> Nor make my soul with theirs as one
> Till the Mahamanvantara be done:
> And though they spurn me from their door
> My soul shall spurn them evermore.*

This pronouncement was too important for Joyce to allow it to remain unpublished; he decided to print it at his own expense, but when the printer, in late August,[65] asked him to pay for the broadsheets and collect them, he could not find the money. Eventually, after he had left Dublin, he had it printed again.[66]

Fortified by his conviction of Nora Barnacle's love for him, Joyce could afford to be severe with the world. He was as astonished as his friends were by the tenderness of his feelings for her. In this emergency he drew closer to his old friend J. F. Byrne than he had been since his return from Paris two years before. He discussed with Byrne a sudden flight of rhetoric in a letter Nora had written him on August 16, which said, 'It seems to me that I am always in your company under every possible variety of circumstances talking to you walking with you meeting you suddenly in different places until I am beginning to wonder if my spirit takes leave of my body in sleep and goes to see you, and what is more finds you or perhaps this is nothing but a fantasy.'[67] Byrne said (though he disclaims it now), 'It sounds as if it came from a letter-writing book.'[68] Joyce, as much composition teacher as lover, made Nora confess that the words were not her own, and she agreed to shift to a simpler vocabulary and a more natural syntax. But the notion of her pathetically adopting so much artifice in the face of his own attempt at total sincerity gave Joyce a hint for the amorality of woman, to be invoked later in force.

In August he was pleased to be able to show her how well he could sing. The first time, on August 22, was at an afternoon concert, where he sang, 'My love she was born in the north countree,' and 'The Coulin.' Then he was invited to share the platform at the Antient Concert Rooms with John McCormack and J. C. Doyle on August 27, the last night of Horse Show week.† It was the high point of his musical career.

---

* Joyce probably borrowed this image in part from Ibsen, who is fond of representing the artist on the heights, both in plays and poems. In 'On the Vidda,' for example, Ibsen writes (in M. C. Bradbrook's translation):

> Now I am steel-set: I follow the call
> To the height's clear radiance and glow.
> My lowland life is lived out: and high
> On the vidda are God and Liberty—
> Whilst wretches live fumbling below.

† Bloom brags in *Ulysses* (92 [85]) that his wife is to go on tour with 'all topnobbers. J. C. Doyle and John MacCormack I hope and. The best in fact.'

He rehearsed one morning at the home of Eileen Reidy, the accompanist. There his manner was swaggering; when her mother asked him what he would like for refreshment, expecting him to say tea or coffee, he replied memorably, 'A whisky.' [69] But when the night came he was nervous, as he had warned Nora in advance he would be. He recovered his aplomb, however, according to Joseph Holloway's account of the evening:

> The attendance was good but the management of the entertainment could not have been worse. The Irish Revivalists are sadly in need of a capable manager. At present they invariably begin considerably after the time advertised and make the audience impatient; thus they handicap the performers unwarrantably. Tonight was no exception to the rule; and after the first item, the delay was so long that the audience became quite noisy and irritable . . . The substitute appointed as accompanist in place of Miss Eileen Reidy, who left early in the evening, was so incompetent that one of the vocalists, Mr. James A. Joyce, had to sit down at the piano and accompany himself in the song 'In Her Simplicity,' after she had made several unsuccessful attempts to strum out 'The Croppy Boy,' the item programmed over the singer's name. . . . Mr. Joyce possesses a light tenor voice, which he is inclined to force on the high notes but sings with artistic emotionalism. One of his selections, 'Down by the Sally Gardens,' suited his method best; and, as an encore, he tenderly gave 'My Love Was Born in the North Countree,' a short and sweet piece.[70]

Miss Reidy's abrupt departure must have been embarrassing at the time, but, as M. J. O'Neill points out, it gave Joyce a hint for his short story, 'A Mother.' The *Freeman's Journal* praised his singing,* and Nora Barnacle was delighted with him. She formed the abiding impression, to the consternation of his friends in later years, that 'Jim should have stuck to music instead of bothering with writing.' They were drawn even closer together, but Joyce was as always anxious to question contentment.

As he became increasingly bound to Nora Barnacle, Joyce began to feel compunction, fearing that she did not know him as he was. One

---

* The item, entitled 'Saturday Night's Concert,' said in part:

A concert was given in the large hall of the Antient Concert Rooms on Saturday night, and attracted a full house. The programme was a first-rate one. The Exhibition Spring Band played selections of Irish melodies and of operatic music of Irish composers. Mr. J. C. Doyle sang a number of songs in first-rate style. . . . Mr. James A. Joyce, the possessor of a sweet tenor voice, sang charmingly 'The Salley Gardens,' and gave a pathetic rendering of 'The Croppy Boy.' . . . Mr. J. F. M'Cormack was the hero of the evening. It was announced as his last public appearance in Ireland, and the evident feeling of the audience at the parting seemed to unnerve him a good deal.[71] . . .

night he described to her his sexual life before their meeting, and Nora was predictably shocked and disturbed, like Bertha in *Exiles.* Her reaction made him feel more misgivings, for no one believed more strongly than Joyce in his essential innocence. He wished to wound her image of him by swaggering as a desperado, and also wanted her to break through this second image and detect the vulnerable boy. She was not allowed to ignore his crimes; she must absolve them out of love, out of mercy, out of awareness that his real nature was not in them. He fed, as he was to say in *Exiles,* the flame of her innocence with his guilt; * ⁷² but this was not quite enough: his guilt was a kind of innocence too. Though he knew Nora to be a churchgoer, he told her unhesitatingly, in a letter of August 29, of his defection from religion and all its concomitants:

60 Shelbourne Road

My dear Nora

I have just finished my midnight dinner for which I had no appetite. When I was half way through it I discovered I was eating it out of my fingers. I felt sick just as I did last night. I am much distressed. Excuse this dreadful pen and this awful paper.

I may have pained you tonight by what I said but surely it is well that you should know my mind on most things? My mind rejects the whole present social order and Christianity—home, the recognised virtues, classes of life, and religious doctrines. How could I like the idea of home? My home was simply a middle-class affair ruined by spend-thrift habits which I have inherited. My mother was slowly killed, I think, by my father's ill-treatment, by years of trouble, and by my cynical frankness of conduct. When I looked on her face as she lay in her coffin—a face grey and wasted with cancer—I understood that I was looking on the face of a victim and I cursed the system which had made her a victim. We were seventeen in family. My brothers and sisters are nothing to me. One brother alone is capable of understanding me.

Six years ago I left the Catholic Church, hating it most fervently. I found it impossible for me to remain in it on account of the impulses of my nature. I made secret war upon it when I was a student and declined to accept the positions it offered me. By doing this I made myself a beggar but I retained my pride. Now I make open war upon it by what I write and say and do. I cannot enter the social order except as a vagabond. I started to study medicine three times, law once, music once. A week ago I was arranging to go away as a travel-ling actor. I could put no energy into the plan because you kept pulling

---

* He wrote in a notebook, with more objectivity, a slightly different point, that she spoke as often of her innocence as he of his guilt.

me by the elbow. The actual difficulties of my life are incredible but
I despise them.

When you went in tonight I wandered along towards Grafton St
where I stood for a long time leaning against a lamp-post, smoking.
The street was full of a life which I have poured a stream of my youth
upon. While I stood there I thought of a few sentences I wrote some
years ago when I lived in Paris—these sentences which follow—'They
pass in twos and threes, amid the life of the boulevard, walking like
people who have leisure in a place lit up for them. They are in the
pastry cook's, chattering, crushing little fabrics of pastry, or seated
silently at tables by the café door, or descending from carriages with
a busy stir of garments soft as the voice of the adulterer. They pass in
an air of perfumes. Under the perfumes their bodies have a warm
humid smell'—°

While I was repeating this to myself I knew that that life was still
waiting for me if I chose to enter it. It could not give me perhaps the
intoxication it had once given but it was still there and now that I am
wiser but more controllable it was safe. It would ask no questions,
expect nothing from me but a few moments of my life, leaving the rest
free, and would promise me pleasure in return. I thought of all this
and without regret I rejected it. It was useless for me; it would not
give me what I wanted.

You have misunderstood, I think, some passages in a letter I wrote
you and I have noticed a certain shyness in your manner as if the
recollection of that night troubled you. I however consider it a kind
of sacrament and the recollection of it fills me with amazed joy. You
will perhaps not understand at once why it is that I honour you
so much on account of it as you do not know much of my mind. But
at the same time it was a sacrament which left in me a final sense of
sorrow and degradation—sorrow because I saw in you an extraordinary,
melancholy tenderness which had chosen that sacrament as a compromise, and degradation because I understood that in your eyes I was
inferior to a convention of our present society.

I spoke to you satirically tonight but I was speaking of the world
not of you. I am an enemy of the ignobleness and slavishness of people
but not of you. Can you not see the simplicity which is at the back of
all my disguises? We all wear masks. Certain people who know that
we are much together often insult me about you. I listen to them
calmly, disdaining to answer them but their least word tumbles my
heart about like a bird in a storm.

It is not pleasant to me that I have to go to bed now remembering
the last look of your eyes—a look of tired indifference—remembering the
torture of your voice the other night. No human being has ever stood
so close to my soul as you stand, it seems, and yet you can treat my
words with painful rudeness ('I know what is talking now' you said).

° Adapted in *Ulysses* (43 [39]).

When I was younger I had a friend [Byrne] to whom I gave myself freely—in a way more than I give to you and in a way less. He was Irish, that is to say, he was false to me.

I have not said a quarter of what I want to say but it is great labour writing with this cursed pen. I don't know what you will think of this letter. Please write to me, won't you? Believe me, my dear Nora, I honour you very much but I want more than your caresses. You have left me again in an anguish of doubt.

JAJ

29 August 1904.

Nora resisted his extremism by trying to bring him within the range of people she had known or could imagine, and he, half-pleased and half-resentful at being considered human, confessed more crimes to appall her and test her. Then he would tell her penitently, as in a letter of September 9, 'There is something also a little devilish in me that makes me delight in breaking down people's ideas of me and proving to them that I am really selfish, proud, cunning and regardless of others.' Nora felt what he was about; she refused to believe he was evil; she cut through his posturings so ruthlessly that sometimes, when they happened not to be posturings or were especially dear posturings, he was discomfited. Their relationship was becoming as complex as any young novelist could have wished.

His mind was playing with departure, but he was not yet sure in what company. He could still unbind this tie with Nora which might prove an encumbrance, and he gave up slowly another notion, of going off with an acting troupe.[73] While he was trying to decide what to do, he was obliged to change his quarters. The McKernans went off on holiday and closed their house. Joyce did not want to return to 7 St. Peter's Terrace, where his family lived. At James Cousins's earnest entreaty he stayed two nights with Cousins and his wife on Strand Road, Sandymount, but disliked their do-good household. Then, more a vagabond than ever before, he stayed a few nights at his Aunt Josephine Murray's, but his Uncle William became annoyed, perhaps because of his unseemly hours, and locked him out. He stayed one night with a medical student named O'Callaghan, and at last, on September 9, ended up with Oliver St. John Gogarty in the strangest residence he was ever to have, the Martello tower at Sandycove.* [74]

This tower had been built a hundred years before as a defense

---

* The tower was probably so named from Cape Mortella in Corsica, itself named after a kind of wild myrtle that grew around it. In 1794 the British managed to seize a tower on this cape only with the utmost difficulty and after lengthy bombardment, so they copied it to protect their own coasts.

against Napoleonic invasion, but with its eight-foot-thick walls it had
the look of a medieval bastion. The entrance was about ten feet from
the ground, and since at that time there was no staircase to the door,
a ropeladder was used. The enormous key, made of copper so as not to
give off sparks, opened a ponderous door and gave admission to the
tower's living quarters, a round room with a fireplace, dimly illuminated
by light from two slanted apertures. An interior staircase led down to
the storage room and up to the tower roof, enclosed by a stone deck,
with a gunrest in the center. The tower commanded one of the finest
views on the Irish coast: there was a chaotic heap of rocks, with a
diving pool (the Forty Foot) among them, and a group of islands,
including Dalkey and the Muglins. Gogarty has said it was Joyce who
rented the tower from the Secretary of State for War, but the records
show it was Gogarty who did so and paid the £8 annual rent.

Life in the tower was free and easy and not very wild. But it was
pleasant to think of it as a haven of unrespectability in 'priestridden
God-forsaken' Ireland; [75] Gogarty liked to call it the *omphalos* both
because it resembled a navel and because it might prove a temple of
neo-paganism as important to the world as the navel-stone at Delphi.
Rumors of a new cult were allowed to circulate, not entirely in self-
mockery. Nietzsche was the principal prophet. There were many visitors, among them Arthur Griffith, whose Sinn Féin ('We Ourselves')
movement was just gathering momentum, and young writers such as
Joseph Hone and Seumas O'Sullivan. On festive occasions someone
would bring a cooper of stout up the ladder, then pull up the ladder
behind him, cutting off all undesired access.

Besides Joyce there was one other guest in the tower, Samuel Chene-
vix Trench, a member of an old Anglo-Irish family. Trench, whom
Gogarty knew from Oxford, had embraced the Irish revival so passionately, and to Joyce so offensively, that he called himself Diarmuid
Trench.* He was just back from a canoeing trip through the country,
and felt that he now knew what Ireland was really like. Gogarty introduced Joyce to him with a rising tone of wonder, 'This is the man who
intends to write a novel in fifteen years.' † [76]

---

* A Dublin wag thereupon cried out in the Old Testament manner, 'Samuel,
Samuel, where art thou, Samuel?' [77]
† A picture of the three men living in the Martello tower is given in a travel book
by William Bulfin, who happened to visit them at this time:

> As we were leaving the suburbs behind us my comrade ... said casually
> that there were two men living in a tower down somewhere to the left who
> were creating a sensation in the neighbourhood ... We turned off to the left
> at the next crossroads, and were soon climbing a steep ladder which led to
> the door of the tower. We entered, and found some men of Ireland in

Trench was insufferable, and Joyce felt less at home than a few months before with Gogarty's blend of savage wit and ambition. There were bursts of camaraderie, however. One day they saw Yeats's father, John Butler Yeats, walking on the strand, and Gogarty, prodded by Joyce, said to him, 'Good morning, Mr. Yeats, would you be so good as to lend us two shillings?' The old man looked from one to the other and retorted, 'Certainly not. In the first place I have no money, and if I had it and lent it to you, you and your friend would spend it on drink.' Joyce came forward and said gravely, as Gogarty afterwards recalled, 'We cannot speak about that which is not.' Yeats had already moved on, so Joyce had to make his point only to Gogarty, 'You see, the razor of Occam forbids the introduction of superfluous arguments. When he said he had no money that was enough. He had no right to discuss the possible use of the non-existent.' [78] Another curious episode probably occurred also during Joyce's early days at the tower. He and Gogarty made an investigatory raid upon the rooms of the Hermetic Society, a group of middle-class mystics, led by George Russell, who met in Dawson chambers. The members had not yet arrived for their meeting, so the two men surveyed the 'yogibogeybox,' with its occult reference books such as Madame Blavatsky's *Isis Unveiled*, and the bench where Russell throned, 'filled with his god,' 'the faithful hermetists . . . ringroundabout him.' [79] In a corner was a suitcase belonging to George Roberts, who combined wandering in the astral envelope with traveling for ladies' underwear. Gogarty took a pair of women's drawers from the suitcase, strung them up, placed a broomstick in the middle, and attached a note signed John Eglinton, at that time an ostentatious celibate, with the rubric, 'I never did it.' Then he and Joyce

---

possession. . . . One of them [Trench] had lately returned from a canoeing trip of hundreds of miles through the lakes, rivers, and canals of Ireland, another [Gogarty] was reading for a Trinity College degree, and assiduously wooing the muses, and another [Joyce] was a singer of songs which spring from the deepest currents of life. The returned marine of the canoe was an Oxford student, whose buttonhole was adorned by the badge of the Gaelic League—a most strenuous Nationalist he was, with a patriotism, stronger than circumstances, which moved him to pour forth fluent Irish upon every Gael he encountered, in accents blent from the characteristic speech of his *alma mater* and the rolling *blas* of Connacht. The poet [Gogarty] was a wayward kind of genius, who talked in a captivating manner, with a keen, grim humour, which cut and pierced through a topic in bright, strong flashes worthy of the rapier of Swift. The other poet listened in silence, and when we went on the roof he disposed himself restfully to drink in the glory of the morning. [80]

It is hardly necessary to add that Joyce did not like Bulfin any better than he liked Trench.

departed. Russell assumed that Joyce alone was responsible for this 'obscene image,' [81] but soon tolerantly overcame his annoyance.°

Aside from these co-operative expeditions, Joyce and Gogarty did not get on without tension. Stanislaus noted in his diary about James:

At present he is staying on sufferance with Gogarty in the Tower at Sandycove. Gogarty wants to put Jim out, but he is afraid that if Jim made a name some day, it would be remembered against him (Gogarty) that though he pretended to be a Bohemian friend of Jim's he put him out. Besides Gogarty does not wish to forfeit the chance of shining with a reflected light. Jim is scarcely any expense to Gogarty. He costs him, perhaps, a few shillings in the week, and a room, and Gogarty has money. Jim is determined that if Gogarty puts him out it will be done publicly.[82]

Gogarty evidently feared that Joyce might turn into a permanent and rather hostile dependent. Joyce was too concerned with Nora to treat Gogarty with any ceremony. Two poems written at this time suggest the break with him:

> He who hath glory lost, nor hath
>   Found any soul to fellow his,
> Among his foes in scorn and wrath
>   Holding to ancient nobleness,
> That high unconsortable one—
> His love is his companion.

Cosgrave, seeing this, took to calling Nora Barnacle Joyce's 'companion.' The other poem alludes to Gogarty more specifically:

> Because your voice was at my side
>   I gave him pain,
> Because within my hand I held
>   Your hand again.
>
> There is no word nor any sign
>   Can make amend—
> He is a stranger to me now
>   Who was my friend.

It was not a good poem but Joyce retained it in *Chamber Music*, probably to help suggest the changed mood of the later poems in that collection.

In cold prose Joyce regarded himself as put out of the tower. What happened was that Trench began to scream one night in a nightmare

---

° He did not, however, include Joyce in a book of young Dublin poets that he edited this year. Whether or not he intended this as an affront, Joyce took it as one in *Ulysses* (190 [180]).

involving a black panther; he woke up sufficiently to snatch a revolver and fired some shots at the fireplace. Then he fell back to sleep and Gogarty removed the gun. Joyce was understandably frightened. When Trench began to scream about the panther again, Gogarty called out, 'Leave him to me.' He then shot at some pans on the shelf above Joyce's cot.[83] The terrified Joyce considered this fusillade his dismissal; he dressed and left in the rain without a word on September 15.[84] His revenge, he told Cosgrave, would come later in the pages of *Stephen Hero*.

He went back to the Murrays, smoothing down his Uncle William, then after a few days returned to his family's house. His father, who had seen little of him during the summer, was cordial and had long talks with him. Joyce did not mention Nora Barnacle, knowing that his father would consider a liaison with a Galway girl of no family foolhardy and, what was worse, ungentlemanly. But he delineated his difficulties in Ireland, and told of the debacle at the tower; his father felt it confirmed his low opinion of Gogarty, whom he called 'the counterjumper's son.' * [85] James felt that he must quit Ireland, and John Joyce, to his relief, agreed with him.[86]

Joyce felt himself justified in leaving the 'trolls,' as he continued to call the forces that threatened his integrity. He did have a holy office, and had revealed it in his first stories and in the opening chapters of *Stephen Hero*. He had in mind more stories and more chapters, none of them flattering. There was little hope that the trolls would suffer his indictment gladly, or that, laboring against the grain, he could continue his work in his own country. He wished to be a writer, not a scapegoat, and foresaw a less irritated life on the continent. The question, however, was whether Nora Barnacle would come with him. He asked J. F. Byrne if it was right for him, without money or prospects, to go away with her, and whether, if he asked her, she would accept. Byrne, never averse to the role of oracle, asked, 'Are you very fond of Nora?' 'Yes, I am,' said Joyce. 'Do you love Nora?' Byrne persisted, and Joyce replied that he could not feel the same way about any other girl. Byrne then pronounced, 'Don't wait and don't hesitate. Ask Nora, and if she agrees to go away with you, take her.' [87] Thus encouraged, Joyce perhaps had what he described later as 'the luminous certitude' that his was 'the brain in contact with which she must think and understand,' that his was 'the body in contact with which her body must feel.' He went to her, told her his plans, and asked, 'Is there one who understands me?' † [88] Correctly interpreting this egotistical appeal as a pro-

---

* Ulick O'Connor denies that Gogarty's father had once clerked in a department store.

† See p. 725.

posal, Nora replied, 'Yes.' Then they must go away together at once.
He wrote her a letter on September 16 in oddly formal diction that
suggested his recognition of the perhaps irrevocable decision they had
just made: 'It seemed to me that I was fighting a battle with every
religious and social force in Ireland for you and that I had nothing to
rely on but myself. There is no life here—no naturalness or honesty.
People live together in the same houses all their lives and at the end
they are as far apart as ever . . . The fact that you can choose to stand
beside me in this way in my hazardous life fills me with great pride and
joy. . . . Allow me, dearest Nora, to tell you how much I desire that
you should share any happiness that may be mine and to assure you
of my great respect for that love of yours which it is my wish to deserve
and to answer.' Her love seems independent, his a reply to it.

Joyce marshalled all his forces to prepare the continent for his
coming. He wrote the Berlitz school in London asking for a European
post, and he answered an advertisement by an Englishwoman named
E. Gilford,[89] who claimed that her foreign agency could find teaching
jobs for applicants. Miss Gilford replied promptly, on September 17,
that she was reserving a position for him in a Berlitz school in
Europe and, on payment of two guineas, would tell him which it was.
Joyce had the good sense to be cautious, and consulted both the
Berlitz school in London and the police in Miss Gilford's town. Neither
knew anything of the particular project, but the police said she had a
good character, and Joyce paid her the two guineas and waited to find
out where he was to live.

There were last-minute difficulties, stratagems to be adopted if Nora's
Galway relatives found out what she was doing, plans for raising
money. There were fresh tensions between them, too, as his letter of
September 19 discloses:

Carissima,

   It was only when I had left you some time that the connection
between my question 'Are your people wealthy?' and your uneasiness
afterwards struck me. My object, however, was to find out whether
with me you would be deprived of comforts which you have been
accustomed to at home. . . . You ask me why I don't love you, but
surely you must believe I am very fond of you and if to desire a person
wholly, to admire and honour that person deeply, and to seek to secure
that person's happiness in every way is to 'love' then perhaps my
affection for you is a kind of love. I will tell you this that your soul
seems to me to be the most beautiful and simple soul in the world and
it may be because I am so conscious of this when I look at you that
my love or affection for you loses much of its violence. . . .

Joyce believed in his own selfhood too exclusively to find the word 'love' an easy one to employ; in *Exiles* a character declares, 'There is one word which I have never dared to say to you,' and when challenged, can say only, 'That I have a deep liking for you.' [90] Nora had no use for such delicate discriminations between love and Joyce's composite of affection, lust, and benevolence. One can imagine her saying, like Molly Bloom, 'Oh rocks. Tell us in plain words.' [91] But what he told her was evidently good enough.*

On September 29 there were new possibilities, of a job in Amsterdam for him, of a job in London for her. Perhaps they would stop in London for a time and get money to proceed to Paris, where Joyce really wanted to go. 'Sometimes,' he wrote her, 'this adventure of ours strikes me as almost amusing. It amuses me to think of the effect the news of it will cause in my circle. However, when we are once safely settled in the Latin quarter they can talk as much as they like.' On the other hand, he found Nora's insouciance about their departure vexatious. She was too much like a girl going off to summer camp, and he tried to make clear to her how reckless and drastic a step they were taking. He was anxious she should relish and explore the unpleasant aspects of what he proposed she should do. But what he suspected of being naiveté was not so; Nora had made up her mind about him, and any recklessness that ensued was acceptable to her. Even for him there were not many doubts left, and he wrote her: 'Why should I not call you what in my heart I continually call you? What is it that prevents me unless it is that no word is tender enough to be your name?' † But his anxieties expressed themselves in a series of 'ill-omened' dreams.

Joyce now sought help from his literary friends. He asked Arthur Symons where to submit *Chamber Music*, and at Symons's suggestion sent it in September to Grant Richards. Joyce wrote to Yeats to ask him to return his translations of Hauptmann's *Before Dawn* and *Michael Kramer*, if the Abbey Theatre could not use them, and also requested financial help. Yeats replied at once:

> Coole Park, Gort, Co. Galway
> October 2
>
> My dear Joyce,
>
> I cannot send you your plays today, as it is Sunday, and the post won't take parcels. I shall send them tomorrow, but have not quite finished them. I gave them to a friend who is a German scholar to read

* On September 26 she wrote him, 'I feel so lonely tonight,' a remark Bloom was to echo in his letter to Martha Clifford, 'I feel so sad today, so lonely.' *Ulysses* (275 [266]).

† See p. 255.

some time ago, and she saw, what indeed you know yourself, that you are not a very good German scholar. I have been meaning however myself to go over them, and have just got into them. I think however it is very unlikely that we can make any use of them for the theatre. I have already a translation of a Sudermann play made by a friend who seems anxious to do anything of that kind. You see at present we have absolutely no fund out of which we can pay for work of any kind. We are given a theatre but we shall have to make out of our performances every penny of our working capital. Later on of course we hope to be able to pay. Nor do I think it very likely we could attempt German work at present. We must get the ear of our public with Irish work. I am very sorry I cannot help you with money. I did my best to get you work as you know, but that is all I can do for you.

Yrs scy
W B Yeats [92]

In spite of this rebuff, and others, Joyce began to feel more joyful about his prospects. He wrote to Nora in early October, 'What a lovely morning! That skull, I am glad to say, didn't come to torment me last night. How I hate God and death! How I like Nora! Of course you are shocked at these words, pious creature that you are.'

He made a final levy. Lady Gregory, asked to contribute £5 to his start on the continent, replied that she would if he could give her evidence of a concrete plan. A telegram from Miss Gilford arrived on October 4, instructing him to proceed at the end of the week to Switzerland. Joyce sent it to Lady Gregory and wrote her, 'Now I will make my own legend and stick to it.' [93] She immediately telegraphed £5 'with all good wishes.' Joyce borrowed relentlessly for the trip. 'I'm not like Jesus Christ,' he told Padraic Colum, 'I can't walk on the water.' He wrote to George Russell, who probably sent £1.* He asked Cousins for £5, but did not get them. He demanded £1 of George Roberts and Fred Ryan with the curious reasoning, 'That is not exorbitant, I think, as it is my last.' [94] He appealed to Skeffington, who thought the plan of going off with Nora was unfair to her, and resented Joyce's failure to repay previous 'loans': 'You have my best wishes for your welfare,' he wrote Joyce on October 6, 'and for that of your companion, which is probably much more doubtful than your own.' [95] Joyce was deeply annoyed. Finally he wrote Seumas O'Sullivan: 'I am going tonight. I shall call here in twenty minutes. As you cannot give me money will you do this for me: Make up a parcel of—

---

* Stephen Dedalus in *Ulysses* (187 [178]) perhaps remembers this debt to Russell (AE), when he says 'A.E.I.O.U.'

1 toothbrush and powder
1 nail brush
1 pair of black boots and any coat and vest you have to spare

These will be very useful. If you are not here meet me outside Davy Byrne's with the parcel at 10 past 7. I have absolutely no boots.

J. A. J.' [96]

At last he had enough money together to take Nora Barnacle and himself as far as Paris, but no farther. He would think of something when he got there. His Aunt Josephine tried to dissuade him from going, and so did his sister Margaret, but his decision was unalterable. Margaret helped Nora buy a few necessaries for the trip, and she, along with Aunt Josephine and Stanislaus, came down to see them off. John Joyce came too, but it was thought better not to let him know that his son was going off with a woman, so the two voyagers kept apart. Joyce went on the boat first, and the possibility that Nora might change her mind at the last moment, like the girl of his story 'Eveline,' must have been in his thoughts, but Nora did not hesitate. Once aboard, they thought they were safely concealed, but Tom Devin, John Joyce's friend, saw them together [97] and guessed what was happening, so that it was not long before John Joyce learned he had been taken in.

The couple went on to London. As yet neither wholly trusted the other. When they arrived in the city, Joyce left Nora for two hours in a park while he went to see Arthur Symons. She thought he would not return. [98] But he did, and he was to surprise his friends, and perhaps himself too, by his future constancy. As for Nora, she was steadfast for the rest of her life.

PART II

POLA, ROME, TRIESTE

1904–1905

He was grey at three, like sygnus the swan, when he made his boo to
the public and barnacled up to the eyes when he repented after seven.
. . . He was down with the whooping laugh at the age of the loss of
reason the whopping first time he prediseased me. He's weird, I tell
you, and middayevil down to his vegetable soul. Never mind his falls
feet and his tanbark complexion. That's why he was forbidden tomate
and was warmed off the ricecourse of marrimoney, under the Helpless
Corpses Enactment. . . . Then he caught the europicolas and went into
the society of jewses. With Bro Cahlls and Fran Czeschs and Bruda
Pszths and Brat Slavos.

—*Finnegans Wake* (423-4)

POETS,' Henri Michaux has written, 'love trips.' Joyce was a traveler
by nature as well as necessity. When he had sufficiently complicated
his life in one place, he preferred, instead of unraveling it, to move on
to another, so that he piled involvement upon involvement. One of the
several reasons for his high spirits on leaving Dublin was that he felt
he had been forced into doing what he liked.

There were enough brambles to make him sure he had chosen the
right path.* In London Arthur Symons was not at home when Joyce
called, so there was no chance to discuss publishers for *Chamber Music*
or to float a small loan. Thwarted in London, Joyce and Nora went on
to Paris the same night, October 9. Their money was almost gone; they
had little more than the fare for the open carriage that brought them,
their trunk, and their single suitcase, from the Gare St. Lazare to the
Gare de l'Est.[1] But after consigning Nora to the inevitable park, Joyce
went undismayed to ask his Paris friends for help. His old pupil Douce,
who had assisted him in his travels before, was away in Spain on

---

* 'Why did you leave your father's house?' Bloom asks Stephen, and is answered,
'To seek misfortune.' *Ulysses* (603-4)

holiday; but his next application, to Dr. Joseph Rivière, who had given him his first good meal in Paris two years before, was successful. The doctor generously lent him sixty francs to continue his journey, and invited him to return later to meet the director of the largest bank in Zurich.[2] But Nora was lonely in the park, her new shoes hurt, and he had to decline. During the day he managed to meet Curran and another former classmate, James Murnaghan, who were visiting Paris,[3] but he concealed Nora from their quizzical eyes. That night he and Nora took a train which brought them to Zurich on the morning of October 11.

An eloquent hotel porter persuaded them to go to the Gasthaus Hoffnung at 16 Reitergasse. The name, which means hope, seemed a good augury, and became a better one in 1915 when they returned there and found it had been changed to Gasthaus *Dœblin*. Here for the first time since their elopement they were by themselves, and Joyce retained a special feeling for the dingy hotel where he and Nora first consummated their love.[4]

Confident that their difficulties would soon be over, Joyce went round late in the morning to the Berlitz School to announce his arrival. The teaching, he supposed, would be dull but easy, and would afford him time to complete his book of ten stories and his sixty-three chapter novel. Buoyed up by such thoughts, he called on Herr Malacrida, the director of the school, and was shocked to hear that Malacrida did not know of his coming and had no vacancy for him to fill.[5] Joyce's suspicions of Miss Gilford returned; she had tricked him, he decided, in spite of his care in checking her credentials. He wrote her an angry letter, to which she replied by enclosing one that purported to come from the director of the Vienna Berlitz school, which was the European headquarters, promising a position in Zurich. Joyce wrote to Vienna, where the director denied all knowledge of the affair. It is impossible now to discover how Miss Gilford had been deceived, but Joyce's situation, so full of hope on October 11, was suddenly desperate.

In this emergency Malacrida was sympathetic and obliging. He offered to try to find Joyce a position in another Berlitz school in Switzerland or Italy. During the anxious week that followed, Joyce was capable of detaching himself sufficiently to write the eleventh chapter of *Stephen Hero* about his days at Belvedere.[6] Then at last Malacrida got wind of a vacancy in Trieste, so off went Joyce and Nora with their suitcase, their trunk stored temporarily with a friend they had somehow made in Zurich. They arrived in Trieste on October 20,[7] and Joyce needed only an hour or two to cap his honeymoon by putting himself in jail. He fell into casual talk in the handsome Piazza Grande with three drunken English sailors, and when a policeman arrested the sailors for drunken behavior, he tried to intercede in their behalf. The policeman listened to his expostulations and then cagily suggested that Joyce accompany them to the police station and interpret for them. Once there, Joyce was clapped in jail with the rest. He urgently demanded to see the British consul, who came reluctant to interfere. Had not Joyce jumped ship? he asked. Joyce angrily protested that he was a Bachelor of Arts of the Royal University of Ireland and had come to teach in the Berlitz school. The consul was not taken in by this unlikely story. Had Joyce not committed some crime in England? At last he effected Joyce's release, but with the worst grace. His coldness helped to intrench Joyce's loathing and contempt for English officialdom, which he corroborated afterwards by many instances.

The same bad luck followed him to the Berlitz school. The man in charge, Bertelli, did not need him after all. Joyce spent several days looking for private lessons or a position as English correspondent for a Triestine business firm. He found a pupil or two,[8] but could not live on what they gave him; he borrowed meanwhile, as he wrote Stanislaus, 'right left and centre,'[9] tasking even his ingenuity in a city where he knew no one. Like oysters to the walrus, Triestines flocked to become his creditors. In the best family tradition, he changed his address almost daily. With a lofty disregard for such details, he wrote a twelfth chapter of his novel and began a story, 'Christmas Eve,'[10] about his Uncle William Murray. It is possible that he would have landed on his feet without help even in this impossible situation; in later life he always did. But fortunately help came, in the person of Bertelli's superior at the Berlitz school, Almidano Artifoni.

Artifoni, a courteous man whose euphonious name Joyce wove into *Ulysses*, had come from Vienna not long before with instructions from the Berlitz headquarters to run the Trieste school and to set up a new school at Pola, 150 miles south of Trieste on the Istrian peninsula. He had just made arrangements there and returned to Trieste. Joyce went at once to see him. Artifoni proved to be a socialist too; he liked Joyce's politics and manner. It was true that he had already appointed one English teacher, a man named Eyers, for the Pola school, but he decided he could use another. Of course, unmarried men were preferred, he said questioningly. Joyce announced he was unmarried but was traveling with a young woman; Artifoni paternally advised him, as one socialist to another, to avoid trouble by signing all papers as man and wife.[11] He obligingly went down to Pola to smooth their way, and arranged an announcement in the *Giornaletto di Pola* on October 31 that Mr. James Joyce, Bachelor of Arts, was on his way there. A sub-

sequent announcement exalted him further as 'Dottore in filosofia,'
Joyce having discovered that this was the Italian equivalent of his
degree. Next Artifoni went to the wharf to meet the boat on which they
were coming, and smiled to see them, ragged from travel, Joyce proud
and impervious, Nora confused and curious in a strange-looking hat,
descending the gangplank with their one old suitcase out of which
bulged indifferently bits of dirty clothing and miscellaneous neces-
saries.¹²

Pola * was like Trieste, a mixture of provincial town and international
center, but smaller. It was founded, according to legend, by the
Colchians who were pursuing two other ill-assorted lovers, Jason and
Medea, after the theft of the Golden Fleece. Under the Romans the
city took on considerable importance, and a fine amphitheater and two
small temples remain from this period as a contrast to the rest of the
architecture, which except for the Duomo is almost all late nineteenth-
century. The excellent harbor of Pola led the Austrians to build there,
in 1863, their principal naval arsenal and dockyard, so that men-of-war
and torpedo boats lay along the quays, and naval officers and sailors
crowded the town. The three languages, Italian, German, and Serbian,
could be heard on any street corner. Artifoni's new Berlitz school was
intended to meet the needs of the naval officers.¹³ The most famous
pupil in Pola then was Admiral Horthy, at that time a lieutenant-
commander, later to make one among Europe's small dictators.

Although the city was decked out with flags a day or two after their
arrival, to celebrate the unveiling of a monument to the empress Elizabeth,† Joyce and Nora soon found that the festive atmosphere was
transitory. To Nora, Pola was 'a queer old place,' and she urged Joyce
to finish his book and get rich so they could live in Paris; she even
began to study French to prepare herself for that pleasure. To Joyce,
Pola was 'a back-of-God-speed place,' in fact, 'a naval Siberia.' ¹⁴ The
whole Istrian peninsula he dismissed as 'a long boring place wedged
into the Adriatic, peopled by ignorant Slavs who wear little red caps
and colossal breeches.' Austria was no better: 'I hate this Catholic
country with its·hundred races and thousand languages, governed by
a parliament which can transact no business and sits for a week at the
most and by the most physically corrupt royal house in Europe.' But
his teaching situation was good enough. The Berlitz school could not

---

* Pola, now called Pulj, is in Yugoslavia. The Yugoslavs have taken more interest
in Joyce's work than the Russians, and a translation of *Ulysses* has been published
there.
† Elizabeth, born in 1837, wife of Francis Joseph, was stabbed in the back and
killed by the anarchist Luigi Luccheni on September 10, 1898.

have been more dramatically located: * it stood next to a handsome Roman arch built by the Sergii, a family that had been dominant in the city both in Roman and medieval times. Joyce learned that for sixteen hours of teaching English to naval officers he would receive £2 a week, terms which for the moment seemed good. He and Nora found a furnished room and kitchen on the third floor of a house at Via Giulia 2, only a few doors from the school, and settled down there 'among pots, pans and kettles,'[15] to be bitten by the mosquitoes which the still summery weather enabled to survive.

Artifoni's deputy in the Pola school was a friendly little man named Alessandro Francini, who, to distinguish himself from the multitude of other Francinis, had added his wife's name Bruni to his own. Francini had a gift for fantastic, ironic verbal caricature, which attracted Joyce to him at once. Rather like Joyce, who was four years younger, Francini had left his family and his native Florence to elope. His wife was a young woman with a fine soprano voice, whose singing career Francini had not allowed her to continue after marriage. They had stayed in Trieste for a time and had a child, then had come to Pola two or three weeks before Joyce.[16] Francini and his wife were to be the closest friends of Joyce and Nora Barnacle for several years. The two women docilely exchanged visits without, at first, understanding each other's language.

To Francini, as he wrote later, Joyce was 'inconceivable and absurd, a composite of incompatibilities with the unchanging laws of the elements, which, however, by a miracle of molecular aggregation, formed a whole.'[17] He was 'constitutionally fragile and hysterical, suspended by natural gravitation between the mud in which he wallows and a refined intellectualism that touches the limits of asceticism. He accepts unquestioningly the existence of the rabbit and the eagle, sun and mudheap.'[18] Francini and Joyce discovered they had in common a Catholic education with a humanistic bias, the one from the Padri Scalopi, the other from the Jesuits. Francini was not an apostate, but he did not mind Joyce's irreverence, and they often talked about church institutions and rituals. He was equally indulgent towards the fact that his friends were not married, and kept it to himself although Joyce had not enjoined him to secrecy.[19]

At first Francini was greatly amused by Joyce's brand of Italian, which used, for example, the old word for sister, *sirocchia,* instead of the modern *sorella.* When Francini corrected him, Joyce replied with spirit, 'I learned my Italian from Dante and Dino [Compagni].'[20] He spoke, in fact, as Francini said, 'a dead language that had come alive

* See Plate V.

to join the babel of living tongues' that were spoken in this hole-in-the-corner of Pola. Joyce soon understood that Francini had an exceptional command of the best Italian, the Tuscan, both in its formal aspects and in its character of a local dialect with special words and meanings. He offered to exchange lessons in Dublin English for lessons in Tuscan Italian. Francini agreed, and kept his part of the bargain so well that Joyce became almost faultless; when, however, it was Joyce's turn to teach Francini, he was apt to find some excuse.[21] In December they formed a plan together to translate Moore's *Celibates* into Italian for a publisher Francini knew in Florence, but did not proceed beyond the opening chapters.[22]

The teachers in the Scuola Berlitz at Pola were thrown much together. Francini's assistant in managing the school was Fräulein Amalija Globocnik*; she liked the Joyces and visited them often in their tiny room, where Joyce would usually be sitting on the bed writing when she came in. The poverty of the young couple distressed her: Joyce never changed his suit, and Nora never changed her dress, and once they even had to borrow paraffin from her for their lamp. The room had no stove and by December it became chilly and then cold. Nora was nonetheless hospitable, and if there was money she would make, at Joyce's request, English puddings which their friends would be invited to share.[23] Fräulein Globocnik found Joyce affable but impenetrable; he showed emotion chiefly in the scorn with which he would speak of priests or discuss Ireland as '*L'isola di santi e savi.*' †

The other English instructor at the school, Eyers, was distant at first but soon, as Joyce wrote with some vanity to his brother, showed signs of coming 'under the Daedalean spell.'[24] Eyers played the piano well; so there were evenings of playing and singing as in Dublin. He nursed a great many grievances about the school, and aired them to Joyce who could not take them seriously and often received them with howls of laughter. Eyers quarreled with Fräulein Globocnik and eventually left Pola to go to Spain.[25] There were two French teachers, Joseph Guye, amiable but always drunk, and Soldat, and a German teacher named Marckwardt, whose methodical pedagogy Joyce mocked with a rhyme that amused Francini:

> Wer ist hier? Herr Professor.
> Wer ist dort? Herr Collessor.
> Herr Professor. Herr Collessor.[26]

---

* Fräulein Globocnik is still living in Zagreb, and Stanislav Šimič, who translated *A Portrait* into Serbo-Croatian, has kindly interviewed her for me.
† 'The isle of saints and sages.'

But he soon began to exchange lessons with Marckwardt in the same way as with Francini, surmising that a knowledge of German might prove useful to him some day.[27]

Nora Barnacle had more trouble in adapting herself. She felt isolated from her family, to whom she had dared to write only a noncommittal post card from Paris. She longed to know what the people at Finn's Hotel were saying of her, and Joyce sent Stanislaus to ask for her, but Stanislaus was informed only that 'Miss Barnacle has gone away.' She had no great hankering to return home, but did not know what to do with herself in Pola. Joyce's writing baffled her: the thought that sentences could be framed with varying degrees of skill was new to her and on the whole unacceptable. Joyce read her a chapter of his novel, but noted impatiently in a letter of December 3 to Stanislaus, 'She cares nothing for my art.' When he copied his epiphanies from a notebook into his new chapter, she asked frugally, 'Will all that paper be wasted?' He set her to read 'Mildred Lawson,' the first story in Moore's *Celibates*, which ends with a woman ruminating in bed, almost as inconclusively as *Ulysses* or a story in *Dubliners*, and she complained, 'That man doesn't know how to finish a story.'[28]

Eight years later Joyce said of William Blake that he was not attracted to cultured and refined women, and suggested as a possible reason that, 'in his unlimited egoism, he wanted the soul of his beloved to be entirely a slow and painful creation of his own, freeing and purifying daily under his very eyes, the demon (as he says) hidden in the cloud.'[29] 'She is yours, your work.... You have made her all that she is,' Richard Rowan is told in *Exiles*.[30] But this was not altogether true of Joyce and Nora, though not false either. There remained ways in which Nora, in spite of Joyce's encircling influence, remained quite invulnerable to him. That he was extraordinary in his wit or brilliance does not seem to have occurred to her until much later. He, for his part, was passionately concerned with everything about her. Sometimes her ignorance was a little troublesome, but usually the spontaneity of her remarks pleased him. One night at a bioscope, watching a lover toss his betrayed mistress into the river, she cried out, 'O policeman, catch him!' She told him he had a beautiful character and a saint's face, while he was confident his face was a debauchee's, and was not at all sure that he wanted his character to be defined as beautiful. When they were reconciled after a quarrel, she told him he was childish and called him 'Simple-minded Jim.'[31] He was content to find her stronger and in her way more self-assured than he was. The great fact remained that she was his confederate, and on New Year's Eve, 1904, he swept any doubts aside in writing his aunt Mrs. Murray a decisive tribute:

'I have nothing to relate about myself except that though I am often quickly disillusioned I have not been able to discover any falsehood in this nature which had the courage to trust me. It was this night three months that we left the North Wall. Strange to say I have not yet left her on the street, as many wise men said I would. In conclusion I spit upon the image of the tenth Pius.' [32] It was as if his bond with her somehow confirmed his repudiation of the Church.

By this time Nora was pregnant. Joyce asked Stanislaus to read, or have Cosgrave read, some books on midwifery and embryology and to send him the results,[33] instructions which must have been baffling to the young gentlemen. But the process of gestation went forward without them. By the end of December Nora could no longer stand their unheated room, so Francini kindly offered them a place on the second floor of his relatively new house at via Medolino 7 (now No. 1), where they had a stove and even a writing desk. They moved by January 13, 1905, and remained with the Francinis the rest of the time they were in Pola.

Joyce had had trouble with his novel; it had bogged down in November, and he began to feel it was not as good as it should be. 'And yet,' he wrote Stanislaus, 'how is Stephen's nature to be expressed otherwise. Eh?' [34] He turned back for the moment to his story, 'Christmas Eve,' and suddenly saw the possibility of reshaping it as 'Hallow Eve' [35] (the final title being 'Clay'); he shifted the emphasis from his Uncle William Murray to his distant relative Maria who worked in the 'Dublin by Lamplight' Laundry.* The tone of the story accordingly slanted away from irony to guarded sympathy. He did not finish the story until January 19, when he sent it to Stanislaus and asked him to try to sell it to the *Irish Homestead.* Stanislaus tried and failed, and Joyce was most annoyed with George Russell, whom he blamed for the rejection.†

In November, Joyce wrote a second series of *dicta* for his esthetic philosophy. He had dealt in Paris with the distinctions between tragedy and comedy, and between lyric, epic, and drama; now he inquired into the role of morality in the creation of beauty. He took from Thomas Aquinas the sentence, 'The good is that towards the possession of which

---

* The implication of the name was that the laundresses were kept off the streets.
† Stanislaus had kept his brother informed of Russell's reactions to the flight to Pola. When Russell first heard that Joyce had eloped with Nora, he said to Stanislaus, 'Your brother is a perfect little cad,' and 'A touch of starvation will do him good.' When Stanislaus heard James had a job at the Berlitz school in Pola, he went to see Russell well past midnight, hoping to disturb his sleep; Russell, however, was still up. 'My brother has wired to me that he has obtained a position in a school.' 'I am very glad to hear it,' said Russell. 'I am sure you are, that's why I came to tell you. I knew you'd be delighted but I'm afraid that touch of starvation must wait a little while longer.' [36]

an appetite tends,' [37] and argued that since the good is what is desirable, and since the true and the beautiful are most persistently desired, then the true and the beautiful must be good. This is his only concession to the ethical aspect of art. Art is not immoral and not amoral, but its purposes so far transcend conventional morality that it is better to regard the good as a by-product of the pursuit of the true and the beautiful.

Returning to his favorite sentence from Aquinas, which he translated, 'Those things are beautiful the apprehension of which pleases,' he insists that beauty may often include what is commonly termed ugly. He finds three stages in the apprehension of a beautiful work: it must be perceived, then recognized, then it must confer satisfaction on its beholder. This theory anticipates the one he develops in *A Portrait*, where these phases of apprehension are made to correspond to the three aspects of beauty laid down by Thomas Aquinas, *integritas, consonantia*, and *claritas*.

Having played esthetics long enough to refresh himself, Joyce returned to his novel early in December. He had finished Chapters XII and XIII by December 12,[38] and most of the two following chapters by the end of the year. On January 13, 1905, he sent Stanislaus all the completed chapters with instructions to lend them only to Cosgrave and Curran, and to read them aloud to Aunt Josephine. He was most anxious to know their opinions, which Stanislaus duly garnered and sent on. Curran praised the new work but made some careful criticisms, suggesting that the tone changed too abruptly from the nostalgic opening chapters to the satiric university descriptions. Joyce had intended this effect and did not change it. Stanislaus wrote a long letter, extremely detailed in its comments, glowing with admiration for his brother's work, which he compared favorably to that of acknowledged masters. Joyce was not displeased but not immodest either; he took occasion to reply at length on February 7, 1905:

> 7 Via Medolino,
> Pola, Austria.
>
> Dear Stannie,
>
> Your card announcing your receipt of my story relieves me greatly. I expect a dilated reference thereto. I have also received birthday honours from you, Charlie and Aunt J—thanks. On the 2nd Nora, Eyers, Fräulein Globocnik and I went by a little steamer to the Island of Brioni (famous for cheese). Every tiny feast is a holiday in this country. It seems a long two years since I was in Paris.
>
> Your criticism of my novel is always interesting. The sentence 'to sustain in person &c.' is not legitimate if the phrase, 'and to protect

thereby' is between commas but is legitimate if the phrase is in brackets. I shall change the verb however. Mrs Riordan who has left the
house in Bray returns you have forgotten to the Xmas dinner-table in
Dublin. The immateriality of Isabel is intended. The effect of the prose
piece 'The spell of arms' * is to mark the precise point between boyhood (pueritia) and adolescence (adulescentia)—17 years. Is it possible you remark no change? Again, no old toothless Irishman would
say 'Divil an elephant,' he would say 'Divil elephant.' † Nora says
'Divil up I'll get till you come back.' Naif sequence! Your criticism of
the two aposopeiae is quite just but I think full dress is not always
necessary, Stephen's change of mind is not effected by that sight as
you seem to think but it is that small event so regarded which expresses the change. His first skin falls. Fulham is not old Sheehy—he
comes in later. Are my documents on the road?

The elaborate intentions of your antepenultimate and penultimate
frigidities are a compliment. But you are not careful or just. Curran, in
my opinion, behaved to me in a generous fashion: Cosgrave, whom
you must recognise as a torpid animal once for all, was, so far as I can
remember, guilty of no duplicity towards me. Do you think I am saying
what is true? You are harsh with Nora because she has an untrained
mind. She is learning French at present—very slowly. Her disposition,
as I see it, is much nobler than my own, her love also is greater than
mine for her. I admire her and I love her and I trust her—I cannot tell
how much. I trust her. So enough.

You might amplify the allusion you make to Finn's Hotel as she
wants to know what went on there. I sent a song 'Bid adieu' to Harper's but it was returned. I wrote to Baillie of the Venture twice but
no answer. I wrote to Grant Richards (who, Symons wrote to me, was
bankrupt) and he answers:—I must apologise for not having sooner
answered your letter with reference to the MS of your verses. I regret
to say that it is not at present possible for me to make any arrangements
for the publication of the book; but I may say that I admire the work
exceedingly and if you would leave the matter open for a few weeks
it is possible that I might then be able to make you some offer. The
MS, I regret to say, has by some mistake been packed up with some
furniture of mine that has been warehoused and it is not easy for me
at the moment to get at it, so that in any case I shall be glad if you
can leave the whole question over for a short time—You might find out
[whether] he is really in business still and also get me the address of
the English Ill. Magazine.

Is Skeffington still registrar? Is Maggie Sheehy married? I wrote a
postcard once to May—why did she never answer me? Are the girls

---

* See *Stephen Hero* (237) and *A Portrait of the Artist* (525 [367]).
† 'He seen the pictures on the walls and began pesterin' his mother for fourpence
to see th' elephants. But sure when he got in an' all divil elephant was in it.'
Stephen Hero (242).

'snotty' about Nora? Look through the reviews to see if 'La Figlia di Iorio' * has been reviewed. I want to write an article to get money. There is an anxiety at the back of my mind for which I want to be ready materially. † I wish some damn fool would print my verse. I intend to dedicate 'Dubliners' to you—do you mind—because you seem to find the stories to your taste. Do you think they are good? or are they only as good as the stories in French daily papers. You must know that I can't answer such questions in my worse than solitude of the intellect. It is fine spring weather here. I wish I might get to Italy by summer. An Austrian officer and his mistress live in the next room. She is pretty and cheerful: they laugh at night and chase each other about the room. I am 'working in' Hairy Jaysus ‡ at present. Do you not think the search for heroics damn vulgar—and yet how are we to describe Ibsen? I have written some fine critical sentences lately. They have discovered a novel of Disraeli's.

I find your letters dull only when you write about Nora or Henry James but no doubt both of these subjects bore you as you have no special affinity for either of them. No damn nonsense about writing short letters in future. I write short letters because I have a lot to do. I have English to teach, German to learn (I have learnt a good deal) a novel to translate, a novel to write besides letters and stories, marketing to do—Jaysus. I think I'm a hell of an industrious chap lately. And then Nora! So no more bile beans, brother John, and please smile your citron smile.

I have finished Chap XV and Chap XVI and am now at Chap XVII. I was examined by the doctor of the Naval Hospital here last week and I now wear pince-nez glasses on a string for reading. This [prescription?] is very strong—could you find out what is Pappie's. As soon as I get money I shall have my teeth set right by a very good dentist here. I shall then feel better able for my adventures. I am anxious to know if you think my writing has suffered any change. My life is far less even than formerly in spite of its regularity. I reach prostrating depths of impersonality (multiply 9 by 17—the no of weeks) but on the other hand I reach levels of great satisfaction. I am sure however that the whole structure of heroism is, and always was, a damned lie and that there cannot be any substitute for the individual passion as the motive power of everything—art and philosophy included. For this reason Hairy Jaysus seems to me the bloodiest impostor of all I have met. Tell him if you meet him, that I am about to produce a baboon baby by sitting for six hours on a jug full of soda water and ask him will he be godfather.

Jim.

7 February 1905

* By D'Annunzio.
† Presumably the birth of a child.
‡ Skeffington ('MacCann' in Joyce's work).

Stanislaus was gratified by his brother's respect for his opinion, but answered that James must surely not care whether his readers liked his work or not. James replied practically: 'I am not likely to die of bashfulness but neither am I prepared to be crucified to attest the perfection of my art. I dislike to hear of any stray heroics on the prowl for me.' [39]

During February 1905, in a better mood about his book, he got on to Chapters XVII and XVIII, in which he depicted Stephen, as a student at the university, conversing with his brother and various friends.[*] Its length, he insisted, was essential: 'It would be easy for me to do short novels if I chose but what I want to wear away in this novel cannot be worn away except by constant dropping.' [40] He thought of changing the title from *Stephen Hero* back to *A Portrait of the Artist* or *Chapters in the Life of a Young Man*, apparently because he felt the first title might imply a more sardonic view of his hero than he intended.

He read meanwhile whatever he could find in Pola or could persuade Stanislaus to send him. To reinforce his socialism he read pamphlets of Lassalle, but admitted to little understanding of political science.[41] The life of Christ continued to fascinate him: he read Renan's *Souvenirs* and disliked Renan's attitude of regret that he could no longer be a Christian,[42] but was surprised to find the temper of the *Vie de Jésus* ingratiating.[43] He also read Strauss's *Life of Jesus*, foreseeing that Jesus would serve almost as well as Lucifer for one of Stephen's mythical prototypes. 'That nice old Henry James' [44] continued to interest him; he found his story, 'The Madonna of the Future,' [45] very pleasant writing, and James's review of Baudelaire 'damn funny.' [46] He read pell-mell Tolstoy, Conan Doyle, Marie Corelli's *Sorrows of Satan*, Elinor Glyn, and Jacobsen. His special irritations were reserved for Irish writers, for Moore, because a character in *The Untilled Field* looks up the train schedule from Bray to Dublin, though of course these trains run regularly,[47] and for *The Celtic Christmas*, a dismal publication influenced by George Russell, which made Yeats write, 'Damn all Celtic Christmases now and forever,' [48] and made Joyce say, 'What is wrong with all these Irish writers—what the blazes are they always snivelling about?' [49]

Dublin was not allowed to become remote. Joyce kept up a steady correspondence, chiefly with Stanislaus. He wrote occasionally to his father, carefully omitting all reference to Nora on the theory that John Joyce was still imperfectly aware of her existence. As early as November 1904, he broached the idea that Dublin might come to Trieste or at least to Europe in the person of Stanislaus. The younger brother, at

[*] The surviving pages of *Stephen Hero* begin shortly before this point, in the middle of Chapter XV.

loose ends in Dublin, was interested but hesitant. James advised him to grow a moustache, pretend to know everything, and dress magnificently, thus assuring himself of a fine future on the continent. Finally, he announced to Stanislaus on February 28 that he interpreted his own condition as that of an exile: 'I have come to accept my present situation as a voluntary exile—is it not so? This seems to me important both because I am likely to generate out of it a sufficiently personal future to satisfy Curran's heart * and also because it supplies me with the note on which I propose to bring my novel to a close.'⁵⁰ His departure from Dublin with Nora would give the book its conclusion.

Joyce did not like Pola, but he was not badly off there. He put on weight, grew a moustache, and with Nora's help in curling began to wear his hair *en brosse*. He felt the first stirrings of dandyism. He went to the dentist as planned, and had some teeth fixed; † then he bought a new suit.⁵¹ He rented a piano and sang his songs. But this cultivated life was not to last. The Austrians suddenly discovered an espionage ring in Pola, in which an Italian was prominently involved; in reprisal, they decided to expel all aliens from the city. Francini through influence was able to stay on for two weeks to settle his affairs, but Joyce had to leave at once.⁵² Fortunately, Artifoni asked him to join the Trieste branch of the Berlitz school, so, on a Sunday morning at the beginning of March, Joyce and Nora Barnacle left for the city that was to be their home during most of the next ten years, and the birthplace of their children.

* Curran had feared he would run out of autobiographical material and have no subject for a second book.

† In Paris his teeth had been so bad that, when he occasionally yielded to his fondness for onion soup, the hot soup striking his teeth made him writhe in pain.

◇◇◇

1905

And trieste, ah trieste ate I my liver!

—*Finnegans Wake* (301)

JOYCE had now an opportunity of appraising Trieste. The city slopes back in terraces from the gulf toward the Carso hills. The old section, the Città Vecchia, with its crooked, narrow ways, is dominated by the Cathedral of San Giusto (whose saint's day, November 2, Joyce never forgot), which dates back to the sixth century and earlier, and by the seventeenth-century castle which shares the crest of the hill. The new section, where Joyce lived and worked, was developed by Joseph II late in the eighteenth century; land was reclaimed from the gulf for large squares and wide streets. At the time that Joyce arrived, the Austrians were carrying out their ambitious plans for developing the city further. Ships crowded into the harbor, some at port, some waiting impatiently to put in. The sailing vessels had prows elaborately carved with saints' figures, a medieval touch that interested Joyce. He was curious also about the eastern influence that showed in the Greek, Turkish, and Albanian costumes in the streets; he often went to the Greek Orthodox Church to compare its ritual, which he considered amateurish, with the Roman.[1]

Though today Trieste's significance for western Europe consists mostly in being its terminus, in Joyce's day it was a leading port of southern Europe, with a distinguished past. There is a legend that Dante paid a visit to the nearby castle of Duino, the ruins of which still stand; and the *Duino Elegien* are the product of Rilke's prolonged sojourn, part of it contemporary with Joyce's residence nearby, in the modern castle which adjoins the ancient ruins. Closer than Duino is another castle, Miramare, built in the Norman style by the Archduke Maximilian in 1854-56. It was from the dock in front of this preposterous but fetching building, where two sphinxes still stare dubiously, that Maximilian departed in 1864 on his journey to Mexico. Joyce came to share the sentimental feeling of native Triestines who see the white marble castle as their train brings them home along the coast. His master Ibsen, too, recalled in old age the moment when, after passing through dark Alpine tunnels, he suddenly encountered at Miramare 'the beauty of the South, a wonderful soft brightness,' which, he said, 'was destined to set its stamp on all my later production, even if that production was not all beauty.'[2] The south had a similar effect upon Joyce; slowly, in spite of many flare-ups, his anger cooled, his political ideas, at first assertive, almost vanished, his literary aim shifted imperceptibly from exposure to revelation of his countrymen; he applied himself to creating a subtle and elaborate art, less incriminating, more indulgent than the chapters of *Stephen Hero* or the early stories of *Dubliners.* So he brought, in the person of Ulysses, the bright though unsentimentalized Mediterranean world to somber Dublin.

Joyce did not suspect he would change in this way in Trieste. Although for the moment he did not like the city much, he saw in it certain resemblances to Dublin and felt he understood it. Like Dublin, Trieste had a large population but remained a small town. Everyone looked familiar; the same people went to the same cafés, to the opera and to the theater. Joyce was particularly taken with the dialect; if Dublin speech is distinctive, Triestine speech is much more so, having its own spellings and verb forms and an infusion of Slovene and other words.* Not only was *Triestino* a special dialect, but the residents of Trieste, who had congregated there from Greece, Austria, Hungary, and Italy, all spoke the dialect with special pronunciations. The puns and international jokes that resulted delighted Joyce.

Trieste resembled Dublin, too, in its Irredentist movement; the similarity here was so striking that Joyce found he could interest his Italian friends in Irish political parallels, though no doubt he would have compelled them to listen in any case. While three-fourths of the city's population was Italian, and its language an Italian dialect, it was still under the control of the Austrians who had held it almost continuously from 1382. The efficient Austrian administration practiced tolerance towards the Irredentists, and attempted to persuade the people that they enjoyed under the empire benefits they could not possibly keep under the Italian monarchy. Irredentist feeling ran very high nonetheless, and was especially strong in the merchant class. The Jewish merchants in particular, largely because there was anti-Semitism in Austria and none in Italy, were Irredentist almost to a man. One of the movement's leaders was Teodoro Mayer, the publisher of the evening newspaper, *Il Piccolo della Sera.* Mayer was the son of a Hungarian-Jewish postcard-

---

* Oddly enough, *Triestino* had once been close to the language spoken nearby called *Friulano,* which is of Celtic origin.

peddler who had settled in Trieste. He founded the *Piccolo* in 1881 as a one-page journal (hence the name); but by the time Joyce arrived in Trieste it was the principal newspaper. Mayer was later to be rewarded for his work by being made an Italian senator, but the irony of a Hungarian Jew leading the Italian nationalists in Austrian Trieste was not lost on Joyce, who used Mayer's face and ancestry as part of the character of Leopold Bloom, also a newspaperman and also reputed to have done his bit for nationalism.° It was not feasible for Mayer to edit as well as publish the *Piccolo,* and so he hired as editor Roberto Prezioso, an intelligent, dapper Venetian who became almost at once a pupil of Joyce.

Joyce's own politics were not Irredentist but socialist, and Trieste had a great many socialists too. He found friends among the workers in the cafés of the Città Vecchia, with whom before long he often spent an evening drinking.³ Just over three years before, in February 1902, the socialists in Trieste had fomented a general strike which was not far short of an insurrection; the revolutionary uprising in Russia in 1905 helped to keep them stirred up. Joyce's socialism was compounded of his own simples: his arguments for it now, in his letters to Stanislaus, kept shifting. Mainly he wanted socialism to prevent the Church from dominating politics:

> You have often shown opposition to my socialistic tendencies. But can you not see plainly that a deferment of the emancipation of the proletariat, a reaction to clericalism or aristocracy or bourgeoisism would mean a revulsion to tyrannies of all kinds. Gogarty would jump into the Liffey to save a man's life but he seems to have little hesitation in condemning generations to servitude. Perhaps it is a case which the piping poets should solemnise. For my part I believe that to establish the Church in full power again in Europe would mean a renewal of the Inquisition—though, of course, the Jesuits tell us that the Dominicans never broke men on the wheel or tortured them on the rack.⁴

He thought, too, that a political conscience would give his work distinction, as he thought it had given distinction to the work of Ibsen and Hauptmann. More immediately, the triumph of socialism might make for some sort of state subsidy of artists like himself, who could thereby achieve the freedom which financial uncertainty made almost impossible under capitalism. Stanislaus ignored these subtleties to

° '—And after all, says John Wise, why can't a jew love his country like the next fellow?

—Why not? says J.J., when he's quite sure which country it is.' *Ulysses* (331 [321])

In the manuscript of this episode, which is at the University of Buffalo, Stephen Dedalus makes this remark.

charge that his brother, who had once pooh-poohed love as a matter for clerks, had become a universal lover. Joyce in his reply labored to make socialism an integral part of his personality:

It is a mistake for you to imagine that my political opinions are those of a universal lover: but they are those of a socialistic artist. I cannot tell you how strange I feel sometimes in my attempt to lead a more civilized life than my contemporaries. But why should I have brought Nora to a priest or a lawyer to make her swear away her life to me? And why should I superimpose on my child the very troublesome burden of belief which my father and mother superimposed on me. Some people would answer that while professing to be a socialist I am trying to make money: but this is not quite true at least as they mean it. If I made a fortune it is by no means certain that I would keep it. What I wish to do is secure a competence on which I can rely, and why I expect to have this is because I cannot believe that any State requires my energy for the work I am at present engaged in.

If you look back on my relations with friends and relatives you will see that it was a youthfully exaggerated feeling of this maldisposition of affairs which urged me to pounce upon the falsehood in their attitude towards me as an excuse for escape.[5]

Socialism has rarely been defended so tortuously.

Neither clerical nor imperial tyranny was so immediately discommoding for Joyce in Trieste as the petty tyranny of Almidano Artifoni and his subdirector Bertelli at the Scuola Berlitz. The salary paid to Joyce, and usually (against the officious advice of Bertelli's wife)[6] paid in advance, was forty-five crowns, a sum which had seemed munificent when he first arrived in Pola and was, in fact, more than he had been able to wrest or wheedle from editors and friends while living in Dublin. But now Joyce was firmly committed to living in debt, and he frequently found himself returning a small loan in the morning only to borrow it back again in the afternoon. Both Artifoni and Bertelli were married, but neither had children, and the sight of pregnant Nora caused them great consternation, for the Scuola Berlitz required of its employees a gentlemanly appearance, and made no allowance for the begetting of small and unproductive Joyces. Joyce's new suit from Pola did not look respectable in Trieste. The other English teacher [*] came up to him one day and said in his Cockney accent, 'I often notice that eccentric people have very little taste; they wear anything. I give you a tip. If you have no taste go in for grey. Stick to grey. Doesn't matter what kind—always looks gentlemanly.' Joyce said nothing for

---

[*] This man's comments on his landlady and her daughter roused Joyce, according to Stanislaus, to write 'The Boarding House.' In it the name 'Polly Mooney' was that of a childhood friend of Nora's.[7]

the moment but felt irritated at being patronized by a nonentity. 'Some day,' he threatened mildly, 'I shall clout my pupils about the head, I fear, and stalk out.' [8] But it was a year before this horrendous resolution could be realized.

What favor Joyce enjoyed in the school came from his success as a teacher with wealthy pupils, and particularly with Count Francesco Sordina, a wealthy merchant of Greek origin and, as Joyce liked to mention in later life, the first swordsman in Trieste. Sordina encouraged his friends to take lessons from this clever young man, and Almidano Artifoni was so gratified by this tribute to the school from the nobility that he began to worry that Joyce might not stay. He therefore called him in to warn him that at the first sign that he planned to set up a rival establishment, he would be discharged; with some rascality he informed him also that the school's copy of Joyce's contract was legally stamped, but that Joyce's copy was not. Joyce wrote to Stanislaus on July 12 to complain of this 'reign of terror.' But Joyce was by nature a disgruntled employee. Artifoni was not always harsh; he gave loans readily and let Joyce have some of his furniture.

Joyce did not leave his enrichment entirely to the Scuola Berlitz. In Trieste he began the series of madcap schemes which he was to continue sporadically for many years. He was determined to make the world compensate him for thinking badly of it by disgorging some of its treasures to him. There were four such schemes in 1905, all waged with great and short-lived enthusiasm. The first was based upon Nora's vague notion that her grandmother had left money for her in her will which had never been paid. Nothing came of this. The next was to obtain a concession to sell Irish Foxford tweeds in Trieste; Joyce let this idea slide but revived it later and attached great importance to it. The third was to take more singing lessons and become a professional tenor; [9] Joyce went in May to a composer and singing-teacher, Giuseppe Sinico,* the composer of the opera *Marinella*, in which one aria, 'Inno di San Giusto,' is famous in Trieste. Sinico was convinced he could make Joyce a professional, but after a time the lessons lapsed, presumably because the fees were not paid. Even more remarkable was a scheme with which his father would have sympathized, the winning of a puzzle contest. He came across the puzzle in the London magazine *Ideas,* and at the end of May wrote Stanislaus that he had solved forty-two of forty-eight parts and was waiting for the last six. Anticipating treachery, he promised to send Stanislaus a sealed, registered letter containing his answers, which could be produced in court if for any reason the magazine failed to award him the £250 prize.[10] But distance

---

* He gave the name of Mrs. Sinico to the woman in 'A Painful Case.'

made Joyce's entry a day late, and a good deal of work went for nothing.

His letters home reveal that while he seemed to immerse himself in activity, he was struggling for a hold on the meaning of his exile. The letters were already set in the three modes that he held to throughout his life: the assertive, the plaintive, and the self-exculpatory. He was caught between his conception of himself as the fire-eating hero of a Byronic romance and another conception—more inchoate—of himself as the put-upon husband and, soon, the devoted father. His life was to be thought of as a 'martyrdom,' he wrote Stanislaus irascibly on May 27. His friends had played him false in order to remain true to conventions, which were his real enemies. Joyce imagined himself, in a letter of July 19, as a prisoner at the bar answering the charges against him by asserting the immemorial right of the soul to live without fetters:

> The struggle against conventions in which I am at present involved was not entered into by me so much as a protest against these conventions as with the intention of living in conformity with my moral nature. There are some people in Ireland who would call my moral nature oblique, people who think that the whole duty of man consists in paying one's debts; but in this case Irish opinion is certainly only the caricature of the opinion of any European tribunal. To be judged properly I should not be judged by 12 burghers taken at haphazard, judging at the dictation of a hidebound bureaucrat in accordance with the evidence of [a] policeman but by some jury composed partly of those of my own class and of my own age presided over by a judge who had solemnly forsworn all English legal methods. But why insist on this point? I do so only because my present lamentable circumstances seem to constitute a certain reproach against me.

In other words, he would be acquitted by a jury composed of people who thought exactly as he did. Ludicrous as this scene appears, it derives perhaps from Ibsen's tenet (in the poem '*At Digte*') that the artist must perpetually hold doomsday over himself. (Both Ibsen and Joyce interpreted this rather circuitously to mean that *they* should not be doomed.) For the moment Joyce was not averse to a little special pleading before this tribunal, but he mocked himself and his court by the time he came to write *Ulysses*, where Bloom confesses to an imaginary judge all sorts of committed and uncommitted crimes, and *Finnegans Wake*, where Earwicker clears himself of one crime only to admit a dozen others. The image of himself making a public self-defense with the eloquence of Seymour Bushe and John F. Taylor never quite left Joyce.

He haled his betrayers also before the bar. In June 1905, he obtained from a printer in Trieste fifty copies of 'The Holy Office,' and sent them to Stanislaus with orders to distribute them to Byrne, Curran, Roberts, Ryan, Russell, Gogarty, Magee, Best, Cousins, Starkey, Keller, George Moore, O'Leary Curtis,° G. A. McGinty,† Elwood, and Cosgrave. He had enough discretion not to send copies to Yeats, Lady Gregory, or Annie Horniman, though all were involved in it. To take so much trouble to print the broadside almost a year after writing it did not strike Joyce as strange; his quarrels had lost nothing from distance. This splendid attack, in which the scatology only enhances the pride, was a foretaste of vengeance; the main attack would come in his novel and stories, as he announced to Stanislaus in early autumn with a burst of humorous ferocity:

By the Lord Christ I must get rid of some of these Jewish bowels I have in me yet. I went out yesterday for a walk in a big wood outside Trieste. The damned monotonous summer was over and the rain and soft air made me think of the beautiful (I am serious) climate of Ireland. I hate a damn silly sun that makes men into butter. I sat down miles away from everybody on a bench surrounded by tall trees. The Bora (the Trieste Wind) was ro-aring through the tops of the trees. I sniffed up all the fragrance of the earth and offered up the following prayer (not identical with that which Renan offered upon the Acropolis).
'O Vague Something behind Everything!

For the love of the Lord Christ change my curse-o'-God state of affairs. Give me for Christ' sake a pen and an ink-bottle and some peace of mind and then, by the crucified Jaysus, if I don't sharpen that little pen and dip it into fermented ink and write tiny little sentences about the people who betrayed me send me to hell. After all, there are many ways of betraying people. It wasn't only the Galilean suffered that. Whoever the hell you are, I inform you that this [is] a poor comedy you expect me to play and I'm damned to hell if I'll play it for you. What do you mean by urging me to be forbearing? For your sake I refrained from taking a little black fellow from Bristol by the nape of the neck and hurling him into the street when he spat some of his hatched venom at me. But my heroic nature urged me to do this because he was smaller than I. For your sake I allowed a cyclist to use towards me his ignoble and cowardly manners, pretending to see nothing, pretending that he was my equal. I sorrowfully confess to you, old chap, that I was a damn fool. But if you will only grant that thing I ask you for I will go to Paris where, I believe, there is a person by the name of Anatole France much admired by a Celtic philologist by the name of Goodbetterbest and I'll say to him, "Respected master, is this pen pointed enough?" Amen.' 11

While he kept green his memory of old injuries, it was as well that Joyce did not wait for peace of mind. He never possessed it. Instead

° Curtis was a newspaperman; see p. 347.
† It was McGinty of Irish Industries who had invited Joyce to sing at the concert of August 27, 1904, at the Antient Concert Rooms.12

he moved from crisis to crisis, from exacerbation to exacerbation. For the moment the chief cause of concern was Nora Barnacle. A few days after their arrival in early March of 1905 they moved into a room on the fourth floor at Piazza Ponterosso 3, and remained there a month until the landlady predictably notified them that she did not want a baby on the premises. Since Joyce then found that this phobia affected all Triestine landladies, he was pleased to discover one woman, Signora Moise Canarutto, next door to the Scuola Berlitz, on the third floor of 31 via San Nicolò, who was more impressed by his respectable teaching position than put off by Nora's condition.

They moved into a room in her flat early in April. Whatever Joyce may have learned by this time of ontogeny from Stanislaus and Cosgrave, he was totally ignorant of the malaise of pregnancy. Gravely he accepted and relayed Nora's belief that her ill health was caused by Trieste.[13] The cold had bothered her in Pola; now as summer came the hundred-degree heat of Trieste, which the *bora* made more penetrating, caused her to lie listlessly in bed all day. She did not like to cook in the landlady's kitchen, so they went out to both lunch and supper. But the restaurant dishes did not agree with her, and the expense was staggering. 'I am continually borrowing money,'[14] even Joyce worried. Going out was a trial too; Nora had learned only about thirty words of Triestino by summer, so she could do little by herself, and the Triestine women looked down their noses, Joyce said, at her poor dress and swollen body. In her misery she cried a good deal, and sometimes did not speak a word all evening. When she did speak, her remarks bore a Galway stamp. She looked at an article in *T. P.'s Weekly* and said, 'Is this the Ibsen you know?' or came in from the hall to announce, 'The landlady has her hen laying out there. O, he's after laying a lovely egg.'[15] Joyce was amused, but less amused than distressed. 'I do not know what strange morose creature she will bring forth after all her tears,' he wrote Stanislaus, 'and I am even beginning to reconsider the appositeness of the names I had chosen ("George" and "Lucy").'[16]

There was more to her unhappiness than he admitted. He had taken to drinking heavily in the evening, and Nora was never sure at what hour he would turn up again. One evening she appealed to Francini Bruni to go look for him, and Francini found him lying in a gutter in the Città Vecchia. Joyce said nothing of this change in his manner of living to Stanislaus, but it was probably in his mind when, on July 8,[17] not long before the baby was born, he asked Stanislaus to try to come for a week to Trieste for a serious conversation. Since, on reflection, he saw that Stanislaus could hardly be expected to make so long a trip,

he made a new proposition by letter. For the sake of Nora and the yet
unborn child, he was willing to give up the pleasure of eating exile's
salt bread:

I think it is best for people to be happy and honestly I can see no prospect
of her being happy if she continues to live this life here. You know, of course,
what a high esteem I have for her and you know how quietly she gave our
friends the lie on the night when she came with us to the North Wall. I think
that her health and happiness would be much improved if she were to live a
life more suited to her temperament and I don't think it right that even I
should complain if the untoward phenomenon of 'Love' should cause dis-
turbance even in so egoistically regulated a life as mine. The child is an
unforgettable part of the problem. I suppose you know that Nora is incapable
of any of the deceits which pass for current morality and the fact she is
unhappy here is explained when you consider that she is really very helpless
and unable to cope with any kind of difficulties. I do not know exactly the
attitude of your mind towards her or towards the child which will be hers
and mine but I think that in most essential things you share my opinions.
As a matter of fact I know very little about women and you, probably, know
less and I think you ought to submit this part of the case to Aunt Josephine
who knows more than either of us. One of the English teachers said that she
was not worthy of me and I am sure that this would be many people's verdict
but it requires such a hell of a lot of self-stultification to enter into the mood
which produces such a verdict that I am afraid I am not equal to the task.
After all, it is only Skeffington, and fellows like him, who think that woman
is man's equal. Cosgrave, too, said I would never make anything of her but
it seems to me that in many points in which Cosgrave and I are deficient
she does not require any making at all. I have certainly submitted myself
more to her than I have ever done to anybody and I do not believe I would
have begun this letter but that she encouraged me. Her effect on me so far
has been to destroy (or rather to weaken) a great part of my natural cheer-
fulness and irresponsibility but I don't think this effect would be lasting in
other circumstances. With one entire side of my nature she has no sympathy
and will never have any and yet once, when we were both passing through
an evening of horrible melancholy, she quoted (or rather misquoted) a poem
of mine which begins 'O, sweetheart, hear you your lover's tale.' That made
me think for the first time in nine months that I was a genuine poet. Sometimes she is very happy and cheerful and I, who grow less and less romantic
do not desire any such ending for our love-affair as a douche in the Serpentine. At the same time I want to avoid as far as is humanly possibly any such
apparition in our lives as that abominable spectre which Aunt Josephine
calls 'mutual tolerance.' In fact now I am well on in my letter I feel full of
hope again and, it seems to me, that if we can both allow for each other's
temperaments, we may live happily. But this present absurd life is no longer
possible for either of us.... I often think to myself that, in spite of the
seeming acuteness of my writing, I may fail in life through being too ingenu-

ous and certainly I made a mistake in thinking that, with an Irish friendship [Byrne] aiding me, I could carry through my general indictment or survey of the island successfully. The very degrading and unsatisfactory nature of my exile angers me and I do not see why I should continue to drag it out with a view to returning 'some day' with money in my pocket and convincing the men of letters that, after all, I was a person of talent.[18]

What he had to propose was as usual meticulously detailed and ludicrously impractical: the following April, he, Nora, the expected child, and Stanislaus would take a small cottage in the Dublin suburbs.* In August of this year he would begin sending Stanislaus a part of his salary, and Stanislaus would put aside part of his. During their communal life, which they could try out for a year, James would keep up his share of the expenses by selling stories and poems. He could not anticipate Stanislaus's reaction, he said, but assumed that the atmosphere of the 'supposititious cottage' [19] could be no more unpleasant for him than that of their father's house. The scheme expressed his dissatisfaction with his life in Trieste, if it did nothing else. He admitted also to a longing for a slice of boiled leg of mutton with turnips and carrots, and said that Nora wanted to see a kettle on the hob.[20] Stanislaus pointed out the obvious difficulties of the proposal; but in any event it was put out of James's mind by the birth of his first child.

On July 27 he was considering a trip to a bathing beach in the afternoon, but fortunately returned home from a café instead to find Nora in pain. Since the pain continued for a long time Joyce summoned his landlady; she perceptively diagnosed the complaint as not indigestion, as Nora and Joyce both thought, but parturition. A midwife, hastily summoned, confirmed this view, and Joyce hurried to bring one of his pupils, Dr. Sinigaglia, to deliver the child. The landlady helpfully persuaded Joyce to take dinner with her family, and came in about nine o'clock 'smiling and nodding'; she announced '*Xe un bel maschio, Signore.*' The baby was not premature, Dr. Sinigaglia assured him; Joyce had simply miscalculated by a month.[21] Joyce took the baby and hummed to him, astonished to find him happy.[22] Then he went out to cable Stanislaus, 'Son born Jim.' [23] The news spread quickly among his family and friends in Dublin, and Cosgrave lengthened the cablegram by announcing it had concluded, 'Mother and bastard doing well,' a poor joke which, besides being altogether out of Joyce's character, was beyond the reach of his pocketbook. It remained current, however, in

---

* 'A roseschelle cottage by the sea for nothing for ever.' *Finnegans Wake* (179). Bloom also wishes 'to purchase by probate treaty in fee simple a thatched bungalowshaped 2 storey dwellinghouse of southerly aspect, surmounted by vane and lightning conductor. . . .' *Ulysses* (697 [673])

Dublin mythology about him, and Joyce made his hero in *Exiles* refer bitterly to the scandal aroused in Dublin by his 'godless nameless child.'²⁴

Joyce wrote the details of the birth to Stanislaus and asked him to borrow a pound from Curran to help pay expenses.²⁵ The child would be named Giorgio. There would be no baptism; 'Thanks be to the Lord Jaysus,' he remarked a few weeks later, 'no gospeller has put his dirty face within the bawl of an ass of him yet.' ²⁶ On July 29 he noted with pleased amusement, 'The child appears to have inherited his grand-father's and father's voices.' There was a resemblance to early pictures of himself. As if to preserve himself against conventional responses, he declared at the end of September, 'I think a child should be allowed to take his father's or mother's name at will on coming of age. Paternity is a legal fiction.' ²⁷ This is the voice of Stephen Dedalus, but Joyce also remarked, 'I hope to Christ he won't have to make allowances for me when he begins to think.' The event staggered and delighted him; a few years later he said to his sister Eva, 'The most important thing that can happen to a man is the birth of a child.' ° ²⁸ And in composing a three-page history of English literature for use by the Berlitz school, he justified his awarding first rank to Wordsworth (along with Shake-speare and Shelley)²⁹ by citing the lyric, 'Where art thou, my beloved son?' ³⁰

Joyce's friends in Dublin had no idea of this keen interest in father-hood, but the news made Gogarty hope for a reconciliation. A rare and amusing letter from Cosgrave soon brought Joyce this news:

Dear Joyce,

Nora has just reminded me of my rudeness in leaving your last card unanswered; but you know my indolence. I had half a letter written after receipt of your novel but was unable to continue so I consigned it to domestic uses. News is plethoric so expect a short letter. Rumour engages Byrne to a Miss Heyden—Mrs Skeffington's anteroposterior diameter is unaltered. I regret not having been the first to communicate the joyful intelligence of Nora's delivery to Skeffington. Meanwhile accept congratulations and give them to Nora for me. Hope the B. is doing well. I am unable to say anything about your novel as I have lost the continuity. Please send some more soon to Charlie and I will

° 'He said that to take care for the future is to destroy hope and love in the world.' (*Exiles* (548 [384])) In his Paris Notebook Joyce quoted prominently a sentence of Aristotle, 'The most natural act for living beings which are complete is to produce other beings like themselves and thereby to participate as far as they may in the eternal and divine.' Many years later Joyce said to Louis Gillet, 'I can't understand households without children. I see some with dogs, gimcracks. Why are they alive? To leave nothing behind, not to survive yourself—how sad!'

do my best to help you with criticism. Meanwhile why in the name of J.—Lynch? Anything but that. Gogarty has his M.B. at last and is now up for the Fellowship of the Surgeons. His sailor is going further still. Last time I met him he had almost reached the North Pole, but he complained of the weather,

The Sailor feels   Oh whales that swim and snort and blow!
The climatic rigor   O Walruses whose front-teeth show!
                    Oh Seals that still select a floe
                         To cool desire!
                    I don't know how the Hell you go
                         Without a fire.

The judgment of Providence overtook the crew captain for so ruthlessly chucking Sinbad overboard. They were driving on Death but before the final disaster

The Sailors hear   Where weighed Atlantic's lift and power
The Syren Voices   And thunder down on Labrador
                    They heard beyond a din and roar
                         Like Thor's great mallet
                    The calling of the Coal-Quay Whore
                         Which has no palate.

At Christmas 'a stranger to you now' [Gogarty] gave me the following 'little carol' explaining that Christtime was limited to a few moments at Christmas and as he couldn't combat the misrepresentation of centuries he had to grin and bear it. He also added a long harangue about the virtues of the Cross—providing the protagonist with a backbone and being the sign in which he conquered. He takes a great deal of credit to himself about the success of the ménage à Trieste the town of the Man of Sorrows.

     The Song of the Cheerful (but slightly sarcastic) Jesus

    I'm the queerest young fellow that ever was heard
    My mother's a Jew; my father's a Bird
    With Joseph the Joiner I cannot agree
    So 'Here's to Disciples and Calvary.'

    If any one thinks that I amn't divine,
    He gets no free drinks when I'm making the wine
    But have to drink water and wish it were plain
    That I make when the wine becomes water again.

    My methods are new and are causing surprise:
    To make the blind see I throw dust in their eyes
    To signify merely there must be a cod
    If the Commons will enter the Kingdom of God

Now you know I don't swim and you know I don't skate
I came down to the ferry one day and was late.
So I walked on the water and all cried, in faith!
For a Jewman it's better than having to bathe.

Whenever I enter in triumph and pass
You will find that my triumph is due to an ass
(And public support is a grand sinecure
When you once get the public to pity the poor.)

Then give up your cabin and ask them for bread
And they'll give you a stone habitation instead
With fine grounds to walk in and raincoat to wear
And the Sheep will be naked before you'll go bare.

The more men are wretched the more you will rule
But thunder out 'Sinner' to each bloody fool;
For the Kingdom of God (that's within you) begins
When you once make a fellow acknowledge he sins.

Rebellion anticipate timely by 'Hope,'
And stories of Judas and Peter the Pope
And you'll find that you'll never be left in the lurch
By children of Sorrows and Mother the Church

Goodbye, now, goodbye, you are sure to be fed
You will come on My Grave when I rise from the Dead
What's bred in the bone cannot fail me to fly
And Olivet's breezy—Goodbye now Goodbye.

The appended Song of J. is of course Gogarty's. He bids me send it. He desires you back in Dublin.

. . . I write to Nora tomorrow. Is that a tinted photograph of her on the card. If so compliment her for me. She looks much healthier than in Brown Dublin. It seems that Gogarty desires reconciliation so that if you write to me be unequivocal. Meanwhile I rot and am athirst. So goodbye

> Yours
> Vincent Cosgrave [31]

Gogarty could not guess how thoroughly committed Joyce was to keeping on bad terms with him. For Gogarty conduct was a series of larks. He was quite willing to turn past mistreatment into a perhaps unfortunate joke. But to Joyce the episode at the tower had become symbolic, and he first intended to have Stephen leave Ireland because of it. He had made this known to Stanislaus and to Cosgrave, who remarked in the course of a conversation with Stanislaus at the end of

July, 'I wouldn't like to be Gogarty when your brother comes to the Tower episode. Thanks be to God I never kicked his arse or anything.'[32] Joyce waged literature like a battle; while Stanislaus was reading some new chapters of *Stephen Hero* Joyce wrote to tell him of an odd coincidence between his book and Lermontoff's:

> The only book I know like it is Lermontoff's 'Hero of Our Days.' Of course, mine is much longer and Lermontoff's hero is an aristocrat and a tired man and a brave animal. But there is a likeness in the aim and title and at times in the acid treatment. Lermontoff describes at the end of the book a duel between the hero and G-, in which G- is shot and falls over a precipice in the Caucasus. The original of G-, stung by the satire of the writer, challenged Lermontoff to a duel. The duel was fought on the verge of a precipice in the Caucasus as described in the book. Lermontoff was shot dead and rolled over the precipice. You can imagine the thought that came into my mind.* [33]

Gogarty and Joyce never dueled on top of the Sugarloaf Mountain, but they took part in a lifelong battle in which Gogarty was severely worsted.

There was still much to write before the tower episode, however. Joyce was only now reaching the end of Stephen Dedalus's university career. By March 15 he had finished 18 chapters, 20 by April 4, 21 by May, 24 by June 7. The last of these chapters represented Stephen's proposal that Emma Clery go to bed with him for one night; Joyce was justly proud of his skill in this scene. He sent the chapters off to Stanislaus with instructions to show them only to Cosgrave and Curran. Curran lent them to Kettle, but when Stanislaus told his brother, Joyce ordered him peremptorily to recover the manuscript. He did not distrust Kettle, he said, but Kettle's friends.[34] He enjoyed conspiring against conspirators.

While he still had 39 chapters to write in *Stephen Hero*, he was able to bring *Dubliners* towards completion much more rapidly. He rewrote 'A Painful Case' by May 8, wrote 'The Boarding House' by July 13 and 'Counterparts' by July 16, 'Ivy Day in the Committee Room' by September 1, 'An Encounter' by September 18, 'A Mother' by the end of September, 'Araby' and 'Grace' during October. In July, anticipating that he would finish the book soon, he announced he would follow it with a second book, *Provincials*.[35] Early in the autumn he settled on a plan for *Dubliners*. In the essay 'A Portrait of the Artist' and in *Stephen Hero* he had emphasized the necessity of representing the self

---

* Joyce added, 'The book impressed me very much. It is much more interesting than any of Tourgenieff's.' Lermontoff offered, in his own words, 'bitter remedies, acid truths' instead of 'sweetmeats,'[36] and his merciless irony, though turned on different targets, resembled Joyce's.

in its childish beginnings as well as in its completion. In *Dubliners* he saw the city itself as a person, with four stages of life to be represented, the first by its children, the last by its settled figures:

The order of the stories is as follows. *The Sisters, An Encounter* and another story [*Araby*] which are stories of my childhood: *The Boarding House, After the Race* and *Eveline,* which are stories of adolescence: *The Clay, Counterparts* and *A Painful Case,* which are stories of mature life: *Ivy Day in the Committee Room, A Mother* and the last story of the book [*Grace*] which are stories of public life in Dublin. When you remember that Dublin has been a capital for thousands of years, that it is the 'second' city of the British Empire, that it is nearly three times as big as Venice, it seems strange that no artist has given it to the world.*

An ambiguity of motive creeps into his discussion of his book and city. 'Is it not possible,' he asks Stanislaus on September 1, 1905, 'for a few persons of character and culture to make Dublin a capital such as Christiania has become?' His old intention of excoriating the city was mixed now with a new one of creating a helpful guide to its improvement. Two of the most savage of the stories, 'The Boarding House' and 'Counterparts,' left him 'uncommonly well pleased' [37] at first, but a week later, on July 19, he blamed their mercilessness on the Triestine heat: 'Many of the frigidities of *The Boarding House* and *Counterparts* were written while the sweat streamed down my face on to the handkerchief which protected my collar.' The reading of Goldsmith made him uneasy, too, about his portrait of modern society:

The preface of *The Vicar of Wakefield* which I read yesterday [he wrote Stanislaus on July 19] gave me a moment of doubt as to the excellence of my literary manners. It seems so improbable that Hardy, for example, will be spoken of in two hundred years. And yet when I arrived at page two of the narrative I saw the extreme putridity of the social system out of which Goldsmith had reared his flower.† Is it possible that, after all, men of letters are no more than entertainers? These discouraging reflections arise perhaps from my surroundings. The stories in *Dubliners* seem to be indisputably well done but, after all, perhaps many people could do them as well. I am not rewarded by any feeling of having overcome difficulties. Maupassant writes very well,

---

* In a letter of October 15, 1905, to Grant Richards, he emphasized the same intention: 'I do not think that any writer has yet presented Dublin to the world. It has been a capital of Europe for thousands of years, it is supposed to be the second city of the British Empire and it is nearly three times as big as Venice. Moreover, on account of many circumstances which I cannot detail here, the expression Dubliner seems to me to bear some meaning and I doubt whether the same can be said for such words as 'Londoner' and 'Parisian,' both of which have been used by writers as titles.'
† A reference to the arrangement of marriages with a sharp eye to the fortunes of bride and groom.

of course, but I am afraid that his moral sense is rather obtuse. The Dublin papers will object to my stories as to a caricature of Dublin life. Do you think there is any truth in this? At times the spirit directing my pen seems to me so plainly mischievous that I am almost prepared to let the Dublin critics have their way. All these pros and cons I must for the nonce lock up in my bosom. Of course do not think that I consider contemporary Irish writing anything but ill-written, morally obtuse, formless caricature.

Stanislaus wrote Joyce a meticulous criticism of the stories, concluding with the highest praise. His brother was pleased, as he had been with Stanislaus's praise of his novel, but argumentative too in his reply of August 18, 1905:

I am much obliged for your careful criticism of my stories. Your comparison of them with certain others is somewhat dazzling. The authors you mention have such immense reputations that I am afraid you may be wrong. Lermontoff says, apropos of the Confessions of Rousseau, that they were vitiated by the fact that Rousseau read them to his friends. I hardly think, arguing from the conditions in which they are written, that these stories can be superlatively good. I wish I could talk to you fully on this as on many other subjects. Your remark that *Counterparts* shows a Russian ability in taking the reader for an intercranial journey set me thinking what on earth people mean when they talk of 'Russian.' You probably mean a certain scrupulous brute force in writing, and, from the few Russians I have read, this does not seem to be eminently Russian. The chief thing I find in nearly all Russians is a scrupulous instinct for caste. Of course I don't agree with you about Turgenieff. He does not seem to me to be very much superior to Korolenko (have you read any of his?) or Lermontoff. He is a little dull (not clever) and at times theatrical. I think many admire him because he is 'gentlemanly' just as they admire Gorky because he is 'ungentlemanly.' Talking of Gorky what do you think of him? He has a great name with Italians. As for Tolstoy, I disagree with you altogether. Tolstoy is a magnificent writer. He is never dull, never stupid, never tired, never pedantic, never theatrical. He is head and shoulders over the others. I don't take him very seriously as a Christian saint. I think he has a very genuine spiritual nature, but I suspect that he speaks the very best Russian with a St Petersburg accent and remembers the Christian name of his great-great-grandfather (this, I find, is at the bottom of the essentially feudal art of Russia). I see that he wrote a 13 column letter to *The Times* of London attacking governments. Even the English 'liberal' papers are indignant. Not merely does he attack armament, he even alludes to the Tsar as a 'weak-minded Hussar officer, standing below the intellectual level of most of his subjects, grossly superstitious and of coarse tastes.' The English liberals are shocked. They would call him vulgar but that they know he is a prince. A writer in the *Illustrated London News* sneers at Tolstoy for not understanding *WAR*. 'Poor dear man!' he says, Now, damn it, I'm rather good tempered but this is a little bit too much. Did you ever hear such impudence? Do you think the author of the *Resurrection* and

Anna Karénin is a fool? Does this impudent, dishonourable journalist think
he is the equal of Tolstoy, physically, intellectually, artistically or morally?
The thing is absurd. But when you think of it, it's cursedly annoying also.
Perhaps that journalist will undertake to revise Tolstoy more fully—novels,
stories, plays and all. I agree with you, however, about Maupassant. He is
an excellent writer. His tales are sometimes a little slipshod but that was
hardly to be avoided, given the circumstances of his life.

He was doubtful whether his own stories would ever find a publisher,
and remained doubtful for nine years more. 'I cannot write without
offending people,' [38] he decided. Yet it was the naturalism of the stories
to which he clung as their special talent. Before sending them to Grant
Richards for consideration on December 3, he conscientiously had all
their details verified. Stanislaus was required to make sure that a priest
can be buried in a habit, like Father Flynn in 'The Sisters'; that Aungier
and Wicklow Streets are in the Royal Exchange Ward, and that a
municipal election can take place in October (for 'Ivy Day in the Committee Room'); that the police at Sydney Parade are of the *D.* division,
that the city ambulance would be called out to Sydney Parade for an
accident, that a person injured there would be taken for treatment to
Vincent's Hospital (for 'A Painful Case'); and that the police (for
'After the Race') are supplied with provisions by government rather
than private contract.[39] He had written the book, he informed Grant
Richards, 'with the conviction that he is a very bold man who dares to
alter in the presentment, still more to deform, whatever he has seen
and heard.' [40] There was no point in suggesting to the publisher his fear
that the stories might be caricatures.*

He emphasized to Grant Richards also that the book was written,
'for the most part, in a style of scrupulous meanness,' and spoke of 'the
special odour of corruption which, I hope, floats over my stories.' [41]
These qualities are present in *Dubliners*, but they do little to describe
the pathos which is involved, even when not dominant, in all the stories,
or the humor which is in most of them. The writer's mature attitude
is that of the boy in 'Araby,' a mixture of 'anguish and anger,' mitigated
by his obvious pleasure in Dublin talk. Like Mr. Duffy in 'A Painful
Case,' the Dubliners are 'outcast from life's feast'; with a pity which he
rarely condescends to make explicit, Joyce portrays their famine.

He had now completed *Chamber Music* and *Dubliners*, though he
was later to add three stories † to the second book. He had written

* He justified this quality in 1907 in a lecture on 'Ireland, Island of Saints and
Sages,' which he delivered in Trieste, by saying that Ireland itself was 'a country
destined to be the everlasting caricature of the serious world.' [42]
† 'Two Gallants,' 'A Little Cloud,' and 'The Dead.'

five hundred pages of *Stephen Hero*, learned a good deal of German
and Danish, 'besides discharging' (as he wrote Stanislaus) 'the intolerable (to me) duties of my position and swindling two tailors.'[43] As the
responsibilities of fatherhood pressed down on him, he longed for
irresponsibility. In a notebook he spoke of the change in himself,
'Before he [Giorgio] was born I had no fear of fortune.'[44] The thought
of being the sole support of a woman and child drove him to new
bouts of drinking; yet inwardly he reacted from his dissipation to seek
some point of equilibrium. The steadiest influence available was his
brother. Stanislaus might be tedious but he was a rock. He could listen
and understand, as his criticism had demonstrated. Joyce had suggested
in 1904 that Stanislaus come to the continent; in the summer of 1905
he had proposed living in Dublin with him; now in the autumn he
returned to his original idea. Stanislaus must come, and to Trieste.
There was a vacancy at the Scuola Berlitz because the other English
teacher had left. Artifoni needed a replacement now that the cold
weather was drawing more pupils in to get warm, and readily agreed
to accept Stanislaus. Joyce wrote his brother that a post was ready for
him and he must write immediately if he would come or not.[45]

For Stanislaus, not yet twenty-one, the decision was not easy. He
loathed Dublin, but was not quite sure how much. His future there was
black; a clerkship at fifteen shillings a week was all he could hope for,
and he would share that with his sisters. But he did not wish to abandon them either. What would happen to him in Trieste had, however,
the virtue of being at least unknown. Teaching English could scarcely
be as humiliating as clerking. He understood, but at a cool distance,
that his brother would cling to his money and patronize his talents.
Yet where his brother was was culture for him. John Joyce might
furnish arguments against his departure,[46] but he was himself an argument in favor of it. Probably too, Stanislaus, who fancied himself in
love with his young cousin Katsy Murray, thought to impress her by
acting with some of his brother's flamboyance. Though in later years
he was inclined to view his departure as animated principally by a
desire to help James, he could not have done otherwise once the possibility of a career elsewhere had been opened to him. With some
trepidation, he allowed himself to rescue and be rescued.

As soon as Stanislaus gave his consent, James was a demon of
efficiency, planning his itinerary, instructing him to cable his time of
arrival in as few words as possible, advising him to dress well and to
avoid being fleeced along the way, and sending money with great
precision to points *en route*. Succumbing to this barrage, Stanislaus
left Dublin on October 20, 1905.

1905–1906

Enchainted, dear sweet Stainusless, young confessor, dearer dearest, we herehear, aboutobloss, O coelicola, thee salutamt.

—*Finnegans Wake* (237)

STANISLAUS Joyce, invoked like a recalcitrant spirit by his brother, arrived in Trieste after several days of travel across the continent. The journey, marked by seasickness on the Channel and monastic economies on third- and fourth-class trains through Germany and Austria, had not been agreeable. Rightly anticipating that the larder in Trieste would be bare, Stanislaus allowed himself only two dinners, two coffees, two eggs, and a beer en route. Joyce greeted him warmly at the Trieste station and commented, in a phrase that Stanislaus afterwards chose to interpret as ambiguous, 'You are so changed I would have passed you in the street.' [1] James had thought of his brother as still a boy, but in his new sedate clothing—worn at James's prescription —Stanislaus looked a mature man. He was twenty but acted forty-five. His sober mien and his firm, shortish, broad-shouldered body gave him an air of substance that his tall and angular brother lacked. As *Finnegans Wake* puts it, 'Lefty takes the cherubcake while Rights [James] cloves his hoof.' [2] In later life, when Stanislaus's blunt speech brought him into difficulties first with the imperial, then with the fascist regimes, his friends were to compare him to Cato; and already he was falling into the role of policeman which served as foil to his brother's François Villon. Yet underneath he remained a boy, troubled like other boys, brazening out his awkwardness as brusqueness, and yearning for sympathy and intellectual recognition which his brother could not supply.

Stanislaus had scarcely been installed in a room next to his brother's at Signora Moise Canarutto's when James apprised him that he and Nora had one centesimo between them, and asked whether any money was left from his trip. Five years later Stanislaus was to write his father

—in a harsh letter which he decided not to send—that James had 'asked me very few other questions of importance concerning myself since I came here.' Next day he took up the position at the Scuola Berlitz, for which he received forty crowns ($8, or 33/4) * a week. He agreed that James should use his salary to pay household expenses, and for some weeks turned over his pay as soon as they reached the school door. Eventually, to simplify matters, Joyce began to sign the paybook for Stanislaus and to take the money directly. With the 42 crowns that James earned, their combined pay was $17 (£3/8/4), a sum ample enough at the time if managed sensibly, which it never was. Such 'necessities' as dining out every night, even at a cheap socialist restaurant, kept them in the vestibule of poverty, for which James at least had a certain predilection. James borrowed a pair of Stanislaus's trousers and kept them, and trivial exploitations of this kind, to which Stanislaus consented at first cordially, later more slowly, and finally with the utmost reluctance, marked their relationship from the start. James saw no reason to limit his brother's sacrifices to genius, especially when genius had a family to support. Stanislaus was bound to James by affection and respect, but also by indignity and pain.

Living, eating, and working together, they quickly got on each other's nerves. Joyce's drinking was the main source of tension. Nora, and Francini Bruni too, were both relieved when Stanislaus appeared, for he resolutely applied himself to dragging his brother away from the workers' cafés in the Città Vecchia.[3] James offered no physical resistance, but his thoughts turned once more to escape.† The pinch of responsibility was painful enough, Stanislaus's reproachful looks made it worse. His brother's arrival had wrought no miracles and Joyce felt himself being shouldered relentlessly into something dangerously like stability. It seemed that he had flown by the net of his father's family only to catch himself in one of his own. He recalled a rumor that Henrik Ibsen, dying now in Christiana, had ended his marriage by leaving his wife,[4] and the precedent seemed at times inviting enough.[5]

Stanislaus was disturbed by his view of the Joyces at home. He confided in a letter card to his cousin Katsy that he longed to hear the mournful foghorn of the Pigeon House again.[6] More important, he wrote several letters in November to Aunt Josephine, the wise woman of Drumcondra, complaining of the behavior of James and Nora towards each other and towards him. He was especially disconcerted by James's growing habit of silence with him. Then James wrote to Aunt Josephine too, ostensibly to inform her that he was planning to leave Nora, but

---

* The Austrian crown was worth about 20 cents, the British shilling about 25 cents.
† Stendhal had felt the same boredom when he was in Trieste in 1831.

probably with the half-conscious motive of having Mrs. Murray dissuade him. Then his constancy would be nobler. Having sent off *Dubliners* to Grant Richards on December 3, he tried the next day to settle his personal as he had his literary affairs:

Via S. Nicolò, 30,^{II}
Trieste, Austria

Dear Aunt Josephine

I have been a very long time answering your letters but I have been very busy. Yesterday I sent my book *Dubliners* to a publisher. It contains twelve stories, all of which you have read except the third story *Araby* and the last one *Grace*. I have also been deterred from writing by the knowledge that voluminous correspondence was taking place between Stannie and some person or persons unknown and I was waiting until I was [sure] I would find disengaged ears. Moreover I have very little news to send you. I imagine you must be tired hearing my explicit or implicit complaints about my present life and therefore I shall not trouble you with many in this letter. You are not to argue from this that I am in the least resigned. In fact I am simply waiting for a little financial change which will enable me to change my life. At the latest it will come at the end of two years but even if it does not come I shall do the best I can. I have hesitated before telling you that I imagine the present relations between Nora and myself are about to suffer some alteration. I do so now only because I have reflected that you [are] a person who is not likely to discuss the matter with others. It is possible that I am partly to blame if such a change as I think I foresee takes place but it will hardly take place through my fault alone. I daresay I am a difficult person for any woman to put up with but on the other hand I have no intention of changing. Nora does not seem to make much difference between me and the rest of the men she has known and I can hardly believe that she is justified in this. I am not a very domestic animal—after all, I suppose I am an artist—and sometimes when I think of the free and happy life which I have (or had) every talent to live I am in a fit of despair. At the same time I do not wish to rival the atrocities of the average husband and I shall wait till I see my way more clearly. I suppose you will shake your head now over my coldness of heart which is probably only an unjust name for a certain perspicacity of temper or mind. I am not sure that the thousands of households which are with difficulty held together by memories of dead sentiments have much right to reproach me with inhumanity. To tell the truth in spite of my apparent selfishness I am a little weary of making allowances for people.

Perhaps you can send me a *critique* from a Dublin paper on Moore's novel [*The Lake*] in which Father O. Gogarty appears. I hope you are in good health.

4 December 1905   Jim

Joyce's intention began to fade as he articulated it; yet this was the first of two major crises in his conjugal life. His bill of complaint against Nora now added the charge of indifference to the earlier imputation of ignorance. Instead of being man's faithful, passionate slave, woman, as he now began to see and, in a different mood, would later write to Frank Budgen, was 'perfectly sane full amoral fertilisable untrustworthy engaging shrewd limited prudent indifferent *Weib. Ich bin das Fleisch das stets bejaht.*' [7] The adjective 'indifferent' was the hardest for him to accept. He needed time also to accept the fact that freedom and love might take the less exhilarating form of home and family. Stanislaus was able to help his brother and Nora over this crisis, not so much, as he supposed, by the force of his admonitions, as by supplying them with a common target of complaint—himself.

In January 1906, Francini Bruni suggested that they all take a flat together and share expenses. The possibility of saving a little money, of perhaps buying some furniture, and of living closely again with the Francinis as before in Pola, was agreeable. On February 24, the Joyces and Francinis moved into a house at 1 via Giovanni Boccaccio on the outskirts of the city. The arrangement worked out well enough. The Joyces continued to dine out a good deal, usually at the Restaurant Bonavia, and sometimes prevailed on the Francinis to come along, which they could not well afford to do. On other evenings Joyce would sometimes shake off his brother and get drunk; then Stanislaus would hunt him down in disgust, and make him come home. Francini would hear Joyce singing boisterously the Bolognese song, '*Viva Noé, il gran Patriarca,*' or the Triestine drinking song,

> No go le ciave del porton
> pe' ndar a casa. . . .
> Ancora un litro di quel bon. . . .*

Sometimes Stanislaus, in a fury over his brother's resolute efforts to cause his own ruin, would pummel James when he got him home, and Francini, hearing blows and cries, would go up, against the advice of his wife, to tell Stanislaus, 'It's no use.' [8]

Such nightmarish moments became less frequent as Stanislaus grew more vigilant. In some ways time passed agreeably enough. Joyce continued to perfect his Tuscan in Francini's company, and learned from him all kinds of Florentine expressions which he would then use at the wrong moment to the amusement of his hearers. His speech in Italian

---

* 'I don't have my front-door keys / To go home.... / Another liter of your best....' Front-door keys had a special interest for the author of *Ulysses*, in which both Bloom and Stephen lack them.

was freer than his speech in English, and gradually became more so.
At first Francini could still shock him when, for instance, he said of the
dog which, to Joyce's dismay, skulked about the Scuola Berlitz, *'Il cane
ha pisciato nell' anticamera e ha lasciato uno stronzolo davanti alla tua
aula.'* [9] Joyce laughed and blushed like a girl. But soon Nora said to
him, 'Since you've come to know Francini, I can't recognize you any
more.' She herself learned a good deal of more ladylike Italian from
Francini's wife, having resolved, as she told her friend, to speak Italian
as well as James. Stanislaus also learned the language quickly, although
his accent was never quite so impeccable as his brother's.

Meanwhile the two young men taught steadily at the school. Stanislaus's method was systematic and punctilious, while James's was
flamboyant. Francini has preserved a number of Joyce's pedagogical
gambits.† Some were thrown out like interjections in the midst of his
lessons:

'Berlitz, Berlitz, what have I done to deserve this from you?
'Signor Berlitz and Signor Joyce, fool and beggar.
'A husband is usually an ox with horns. His wife is brainless. Together
they make a four-legged animal.
'A stuffed bun—the Virgin with the infant Jesus.
'The woman who commits adultery makes her husband a sorehead.
'What is a pachyderm? See that man there with a trumpet for a nose and
that sizable belly—there's a pachyderm.'

These were maxims for beginners; gradually Joyce would bring them
into profounder discussions:

'Signor Berlitz is an insatiable sponge. His teachers have had their
brains sopped up. And their flesh? We've been crucified on the pole
till we're skin and bones. I present myself to my pupils as an example
of the giraffe species in order to teach zoology objectively according
to the gospel of my master, Signor Berlitz.

'That woman has a nice small breast, but her conscience is as wide
as a sewer. Her husband is happy because her boyfriends are helping
to develop her good points. I am developing myself too. Go you and
do likewise. Sop up fourteen shots of absinthe on an empty stomach
and you'll see. If this cure doesn't develop you, why, you're hopeless.
You may as well give up trying to learn English according to this
method.

'My wife has learned Italian—enough to enable her to run up debts
comfortably. I won't pay them. Will Berlitz pay them? It's not my

* 'The dog pissed in the outer office and left a turd in front of your classroom.'
† In his lecture, published as a pamphlet, *Joyce Intimo Spogliato in Piazza* (Trieste,
1922).

business. My creditors tell me they'll bring me to court for a judgment. But I've *no* judgment. If it were a matter of collecting money, that would be something else again . . . but as for paying? Not on your life. And so I tear up their bills.

'The tax collector's an imbecile who's always bothering me. He's littered my table with handbills on which "Warning, Warning, Warning," is written. I've told him if he doesn't stop I'll send him to his purse-snatching boss to be bugg . . . ywhipped. The purse-snatcher is the government of Vienna, and maybe tomorrow will be the government of Rome; but Vienna, Rome, or London, for me all governments are the same—pirates.

'As far as those little scraps of paper are concerned, I've told him he can send me as many as he likes. They'll be good for doodling on. Unless they finally serve my wife for those little chores all mothers perform for their children.

'Ireland is a great country. It is called the Emerald Isle. The metropolitan government, after centuries of strangling it, has laid it waste. It's now an untilled field.* The government sowed hunger, syphilis, superstition, and alcoholism there; puritans, Jesuits, and bigots have sprung up.

'Proverbially and by nature our peasants walk in their sleep, closely resembling fakirs in their froglike and renunciatory sterility. I think they are the one people who, when they are hungry, eat symbolically. Do you not know what it means to eat symbolically? I'll clear it up for you in no time: the peasant family, a big roomful of them, sit round a rustic table as if it were an altar. In the middle of the table, suspended on a string from the ceiling, is a herring which could feed the lot of them. The headman arms himself with a potato. Then with it he makes the sign of the cross (my Tuscan friends say, "He makes the big cross") high up on the back of the fish instead of just rubbing it as any hypocrite would do. This is the signal, and after him, hieratically, each member of the family performs the same trick so that at the end the members, that is to say the diners, find themselves left contemplating a potato in their hands, and the herring, if it doesn't get eaten by the cat, or rot, is destined to be mummified for posterity. This dish is called the indicated herring. The peasants are gluttons for it, and stuff their bellies full.

'Dubliners, strictly speaking, are my fellow-countrymen, but I don't care to speak of our "dear, dirty Dublin" as they do. Dubliners are the most hopeless, useless, and inconsistent race of charlatans I have ever come across, on the island or the continent. This is why the

* The title of a book of Irish stories by George Moore.

English Parliament is full of the greatest windbags in the world. The Dubliner passes his time gabbing and making the rounds in bars or taverns or cathouses, without ever getting 'fed up' with the double doses of whisky and Home Rule, and at night, when he can hold no more and is swollen up with poison like a toad, he staggers from the side-door and, guided by an instinctive desire for stability along the straight line of the houses, he goes slithering his backside against all walls and corners. He goes "arsing along" as we say in English. There's the Dubliner for you.

'And in spite of everything, Ireland remains the brain of the United Kingdom. The English, judiciously practical and ponderous, furnish the over-stuffed stomach of humanity with a perfect gadget—the water closet. The Irish, condemned to express themselves in a language not their own, have stamped on it the mark of their own genius and compete for glory with the civilised nations. This is then called English literature....

'This morning—strange to say, for it never happens to me—I hadn't a cent. I went to the director and told him how things were. I asked him for an advance on my pay. This time the keys of the safe weren't rusted (as they usually are), but the director refused, calling me a bottomless well. I told him to go and drown himself in it, and took myself off. Now what am I to do? Wretch that I am. My wife is no good at anything except producing babies and blowing bubbles. Fine then, we'll never die of hunger; the Italian proverb says, "Children constitute wealth." That's all very well, but Giorgio's feet are bursting through his shoes, and my wife goes on blowing bubbles. If I'm not careful, she'll follow up George the First by unloading a second male successor for the dynasty. No, no, Nora, this game doesn't suit me. So long as there are bistros in Trieste, I'm afraid your man will have to pass his nights away from home, flapping around like a rag in the breeze.

'Italian literature begins with Dante and finishes with Dante. That's more than a little. In Dante dwells the whole spirit of the Renaissance. I love Dante almost as much as the Bible. He is my spiritual food, the rest is ballast. I don't like Italian literature because the mentality of the degenerate Italian writers is dominated entirely by these four elementary themes: beggared orphans and hungry people (will these Italians never stop being hungry?), battlefields, cattle, and patriotism. Italians have a strange way of going through the gymnastics of patriotic ambition. They want to impose, by their fists, the recognition of their intellectual superiority to other peoples. Humanism, Lorenzo the Magnificent, Leonardo, Titian, Michelangelo, Galileo: Quite so, all very fine

people. But I've yet to find an Italian who was able to silence *me* by
saying, "Shut up, you fool! The one immortal work for which the Italians are responsible is the foundation of the Roman church." Why, even
I declare that the Roman church is manifold in its bigness—big as a
church and as . . . shall we say . . . a whore. You could say no less of a
hussy who offers herself among perfumes, songs, flowers, and music,
sadly mourning in silken robes on a throne.' [10]

Here, in Chaplinesque caricature, are most of Joyce's central preoccupations: his financial need, his family, his country, his irreligion,
his love of literature. Wives make cuckolds; Italy is, except for the
church, a fraud, and the church is an old whore; Ireland is horrible but
unforgettable. His remarks are bitter, but they are also funny. It is easy
to forget, in the midst of his descriptions of his troubles in letters, how
repugnant to his personality 'Celtic' melancholy remained. There were
long evenings at home with the Francinis when Francini—a small man
—would hoist himself into Giorgio's baby carriage and, with shrill cries,
be wheeled wildly around the house by an equally tipsy Joyce while
their consorts and Stanislaus looked on with patience and some amusement.[11] Or Joyce would make off to a tavern kept by a Sicilian, who had
a way of standing with neck twisted and one foot up which made Joyce
nickname him 'Il Cicogno,' the Stork. They found each other comical,
and the barkeeper would say, 'Joyce, Cicogno's a character, all right,
but you're an odd-ball yourself.' [12] Joyce delighted in pouring out all
sorts of fanciful tales of Ireland to the Stork's unsuspicious ear. Trieste,
as the familiar pun had it, was *triste*, but Joyce, spurred by only a little
alcohol, could relax in banter.

Besides tension with Nora, Joyce's main frustrations had to do with
his books. *Chamber Music* suffered a series of reverses first; Grant
Richards managed to lose the manuscript, then asked Joyce for a
second copy only to turn it down in May 1905, unless Joyce could help
pay for the printing (which he could not),[13] while John Lane followed
suit in June, Heinemann in July, and Constable in October. *Dubliners*
offered a different problem; the market for stories was a little better
than that for poems, and Joyce hopefully sent the manuscript off to
Grant Richards on December 3, 1905. Grant Richards, somewhat
startled at receiving from Trieste a book called *Dubliners*, liked it
himself and, when his reader Filson Young agreed, he accepted it on
February 17, 1906, and signed a contract for it in March. For a month
all seemed well. Richards affably inquired into Joyce's circumstances,
and Joyce allowed his impatience with his present life to show through
in his reply:

I am an English teacher here in a Berlitz School. I have been here for sixteen months during which time I have achieved the delicate task of living and supporting two other trusting souls on a salary of £80 a year. I am employed to teach young men of this city the English language as quickly as possible with no delays for elegance and receive in return tenpence for every sixty minutes so spent. I must not omit to mention that I teach also a baroness.

My prospects are the chance of getting money enough from my book or books to enable me to resume my interrupted life. I hope these details will not bore you as much as they bore me. In any case, I give them to you only because you have asked for them.[14]

At the same time on February 22, he sent Richards an additional story, 'Two Gallants,' * which was destined to precipitate disaster. Richards, without bothering to read the story, sent it on to the printer, and the printer objected to it and went on to mark passages in other stories. Joyce meanwhile unsuspectingly wrote 'A Little Cloud' † and was preparing to send it to Richards too when, on April 23,[15] Richards informed him that some changes would have to be introduced to meet the printer's objections.

Joyce made a point of not understanding the English law, that the printer of objectionable material is as guilty of breaking the law as the publisher, and equally subject to criminal prosecution. 'In no other civilised country in Europe,' he wrote Richards, 'is a printer allowed to open his mouth.'[16] But Richards could scarcely afford trouble. He had just been through bankruptcy, and had returned to publishing by setting up his firm in his wife's name. He stood his ground, and Joyce, who had threatened to withdraw the book, tried a different tack of persuasion. As for 'Two Gallants,' he asked on May 5, 1906, what the printer objected to:

---

* Stanislaus Joyce says, and a letter of James seems to confirm,[17] that the story was inspired by a reference in Guglielmo Ferrero's *Europa Giovane* to the relations between Porthos and the wife of a tradesman in *The Three Musketeers*. The prototypes of Lenehan and Corley were Irish, however; Lenehan was based mostly on Michael Hart (see pp. 376-7) and Corley was in fact as well as in fiction a policeman's son. When on a visit to Dublin Joyce ran into Corley and said he was in a story, Corley was delighted!
† Ignatius Gallaher in 'A Little Cloud' was Fred Gallaher, as explained above, p. 46. But Joyce also associated Gallaher with Gogarty, and wrote to Stanislaus on the occasion of Gogarty's marriage, 'Long health to Ignatius Gallaher!' Now as later, Joyce was much occupied with the personality of loud-mouthed burly men, among whom Corley, Gogarty, and Fred Gallaher were the three he knew best. There is no reason to assume, as some have done, that Joyce identified himself with either Little Chandler or Lenehan simply because he was not burly himself.

Is it the small gold coin in the former story or the code of honour which the two gallants live by which shocks him? I see nothing which should shock him in either of these things. His idea of gallantry has grown up in him (probably) during the reading of the novels of the elder Dumas and during the performance of romantic plays which presented to him cavaliers and ladies in full dress.

He took up the three marked passages in 'Counterparts,' which referred to 1) 'a man with two establishments to keep up,' 2) 'having' a girl, and 3) a woman's changing the position of her legs often, and brushing against a man's chair.

His marking of the first passage makes me think that there is priestly blood in him: the scent for immoral allusions is certainly very keen here. To me this passage seems as childlike as the reports of divorce cases in *The Standard*. . . .

It is easier to understand why he has marked the second passage, and evident why he has marked the third. But I would refer him again to that respectable organ the reporters of which are allowed to speak of such intimate things as even I, a poor artist, have but dared to suggest. O one-eyed printer! Why has he descended with his blue pencil, full of the Holy Ghost, upon these passages and allowed his companions to set up in type reports of divorce cases and ragging scenes and cases of criminal assault—reports, moreover, which are to be read by an 'inconveniently large section of the general public'? [18]

Then, shifting to higher ground, he urged Richards to pioneer in changing English taste: 'I know very little of the state of English literature at present nor do I know whether it deserves or not the eminence which it occupies as the laughing-stock of Europe. But I suspect that it will follow the other countries of Europe as it did in Chaucer's time.' After all, George Moore or Thomas Hardy or even Pinero, in such a work as *The Second Mrs. Tanqueray*, would have been rejected in the middle Victorian period. 'And if a change is to take place I do not see why it should not begin now.' [19]

Richards did not yield; instead he emphasized his objection to the use of the word 'bloody' in 'Grace.' Joyce in reply imprudently pointed out that the word appeared in other stories as well:

And one night, man, she brought me two bloody fine cigars, etc.
'Two Gallants'

Here's this fellow come to the throne after his bloody owld mother keeping him out of it till the man was grey, etc.
'Ivy Day in the Committee Room'

... if any fellow tried that sort of a game on with his sister he'd bloody
well put his teeth down his throat, so he would ...

'The Boarding House'

Joyce wrote on May 13:

The first passage I could alter. The second passage (with infinite regret)
I could alter by omitting the word simply. But the third passage I absolutely
could not alter. The word, the exact expression I have used, is in my opinion
the one expression in the English language which can create on the reader
the effect which I wish to create. Surely you can see this for yourself? And
if the word appears once in the book it may as well appear three times. Is it
not ridiculous that my book cannot be published because it contains this
one word which is neither indecent nor blasphemous? [20]

He asked why Richards had not objected to 'An Encounter,' and of
course Richards promptly did, and asked him to remove it. Joyce was
beside himself with outraged logic. For him these were not mere
'details,' as Richards suggested; in short stories they were crucial;
effacing them would leave *Dubliners* 'like an egg without salt.'

The points on which I have not yielded are the points which rivet the
book together. If I eliminate them what becomes of the chapter of the moral
history of my country? I fight to retain them because I believe that in composing my chapter of moral history in exactly the way I have composed it
I have taken the first step towards the spiritual liberation of my country.
Reflect for a moment on the history of the literature of Ireland as it stands
at present written in the English language before you condemn this genial
illusion of mine which, after all, has at least served me in the office of a
candlestick during the writing of the book. [21]

The more Joyce conceded the more was asked of him; Richards now
declared that 'Two Gallants' would have to be omitted. Joyce could
not, the publisher suggested, afford to be so heroic about his art:
'If I had written your stories I should certainly wish to be able to afford
your attitude.' Joyce denied that his attitude was heroic; it was merely
logical; but he would not prostitute whatever talent he might have.
'I have written my book with considerable care, in spite of a hundred
difficulties and in accordance with what I understand to be the classical
tradition of my art.' Richards's correspondence with him had stiffened
Joyce's sense of his mission and obliterated his fear, expressed the
previous year to Stanislaus, that his impulsion in the stories was 'mischievous.' He declared ironically to Richards on June 23: 'It is not my
fault that the odour of ashpits and old weeds and offal hangs round
my stories. I seriously believe that you will retard the course of civilisation in Ireland by preventing the Irish people from having one good
look at themselves in my nicely polished looking-glass.' [22]

During June Richards agreed to countenance the inclusion of 'Two Gallants' if Joyce would make other concessions, and on July 9 Joyce sent him back the whole manuscript in a slightly altered form. He had rewritten 'The Sisters' and inserted 'A Little Cloud'; he had expunged six uses of the word 'bloody' and retained one; * he had rewritten an incident in 'Counterparts.' 'I will not conceal from you,' he said, 'that I think I have injured these stories by these deletions but I sincerely trust you will recognize that I have tried to meet your wishes and scruples fairly.' [23] He expected to hear from Richards at once about the manuscript, but the matter was not to be settled so quickly.

In the uncertainty over *Dubliners* Joyce was unable to do any more work on *Stephen Hero,* which had bogged down after Chapter XXV. The sense of being at check in Trieste deepened and made that city intolerable. Joyce was not sorry when he was forced to another change. The Scuola Berlitz was suddenly in an uproar; Bertelli had, it seemed, decamped with some of the school's funds, and Artifoni, as the lean summer approached, warned the two Joyce brothers that the school could not support two English teachers over the summer months. Joyce had no desire to remain. He scanned the advertisements in the *Tribuna* of Rome, and came upon one for a correspondence clerk, fluent in Italian and English, to work in a bank. He at once wrote, early in May, to the bank, Nast-Kolb and Schumacher, and offered his services. He referred to some experience he had had as a translator for a business-man in Trieste named Greenham, and he obtained an eloquent recommendation from his pupil Prezioso, the editor of *Il Piccolo della Sera.* He also sent off the letter Timothy Harrington, Lord Mayor of Dublin, had given him in 1902. After a month's negotiations,[24] it was agreed by mid-June that he should be given a two-month trial, beginning August 1, at $62.50 (£ 12/10/0) a month.

There were a few debts to pay, and some to leave unpaid, including rent to Francini and a salary advance of thirty crowns to the Scuola, but Stanislaus agreed to take care of them. There was furniture bought on the installment plan and now abandoned, at a loss of 120 crowns. It was repossessed so quickly by the alert seller that Stanislaus spent some time sleeping on the floor before he could buy another bed. But these were trivia. With a feeling of relief, and a conviction that Rome would yield him money and fame as it had previously done for Attila and other less civilized invaders, Joyce and Nora packed up their few belongings and, with the unbaptized Giorgio in arms, started for the Eternal City.

* In 'The Boarding House.'

1906–1907

O! the lowness of him was beneath all up to that sunk to! No likedby-
like firewater or firstserved firstshot or gulletburn gin or honest brew-
barrett beer either. O dear no! Instead the tragic jester sobbed himself
wheywhingingly sick of life on some sort of a rhubarbarous maundarin
yellagreen funkleblue windigut diodying applejack squeezed from sour
grapefruice. . . .

—*Finnegans Wake* (171)

IN an entry in his diary in 1903 Stanislaus Joyce remarked that his
brother lived 'on the excitement of events.' No one was in fact
quicker to find life tedious, or more eager to shun equilibrium, whether
by drinking or moving. Joyce throve on flurry, and wrote his best when
he had least time. He did not bother to consider whether his position
as a bank clerk in Rome would satisfy him for long; it was a change,
and he was interested to see what Rome and he might make of each
other. He probably did not expect Rome to please him, but to be dissatisfied by Rome is a grander destiny than to be dissatisfied by Trieste.
Forty-two years before, Ibsen had whiled away a period of exile in
Rome thinking about Norway, and Ibsen's example was still one to
which Joyce attended. But Ibsen, secure with his small pension, could
afford to debate with friends whether it was better to become an office
clerk or to swallow the latch key and die of starvation.[1] Joyce, like
T. S. Eliot after him, chose to be a clerk.

Father, mother, and son traveled by train from Trieste to Fiume,
where they took a night boat to Ancona, sleeping on deck. Fiume they
found clean and energetic, but Ancona, where Joyce managed to be
cheated three times in an hour, was 'a filthy hole like rotten cabbage,'[2]
with 'something Irish in its bleak, gaunt, beggarly ugliness.'[3] They
drove three miles from the pier to the Ancona railroad station, and
reached Rome by train July 31. Joyce took a temporary lodging on the
third floor of a house belonging to a Signora Dufour at 52 via Frattina.

He reacted to Rome violently. Mocking a favorite construction of his friend Yeats, he wrote later in *Finnegans Wake*, 'One has thoughts of that eternal Rome.'[4] Though he was moved a little on his first night by the sight of the house where Shelley wrote *The Cenci*, Roman grandeur, in its twentieth-century setting, quickly ceased to fill him with awe; he felt quite other emotions, none of them suitable for travel brochures. 'The Tiber frightens me,'[5] he wrote; he was accustomed to narrower rivers. The modern city and its government he thought insipid, while the ancient city, as he remarked a few months later to Francini, was like a cemetery. That 'exquisite panorama' is made up of 'flowers of death, ruins, piles of bones, and skeletons.' A week after his arrival, he wrote Stanislaus on August 7, 1906, that the neighborhood of the Colosseum was 'like an old cemetery with broken columns of temples and slabs.' The ghoulish presence of English tourists did nothing to mitigate the effect. While Joyce, Nora, and Giorgio were in the Colosseum, 'looking at it all round gravely from a sense of duty,' Joyce told his brother:

> I heard a voice from London on one of the lowest galleries say:
> —The Colisseum—
> Almost at once two young men in serge suits and straw hats appeared in an embrasure. They leaned on the parapet and then a second voice from the same city clove the calm evening, saying:
> —Whowail stands the Colisseum Rawhm shall stand
> When falls the Colisseum Rawhm sh'll fall
> And when Rawhm falls the world sh'll fall—
> but adding cheerfully:
> —Kemlong, 'ere's the way aht—[6]

He was willing to grant that in the time of Caesar Rome had been a fine city, but papal Rome he thought to be like the Coombe in Dublin or like old Trieste, 'and the new Ludovisi quarter is like any secondary quarter of a fine metropolis. Not as fine as Pembroke township, for example. I wish I knew something of Latin or Roman History. But it's not worth while beginning now. So let the ruins rot.'[7] He was indignant with Henry James for what he called 'tea-slop' about Rome, which ignored its funerary reality. Even his dreams were affected. He complained on August 19 of a series of 'horrible and terrifying dreams: death, corpses, assassinations, in which I take an unpleasantly prominent part.'[8] On September 25, after a sightseeing expedition to the Forum, he summed up, 'Rome reminds me of a man who lives by exhibiting to travellers his grandmother's corpse.'

On August 1, Joyce went round for his momentous interview at the bank, which stood at the corner of the Via S. Claudio near Piazza

Colonna. Schumacher, who proved to be consul for Austria-Hungary as well as banker, received him kindly enough. He looked 'like Ben Jonson with a big belly,' [9] and walked sideways, wearing a cap on his head. He asked Joyce about his age, his father, and his family's friendship with the Lord Mayor of Dublin to which Harrington's letter had borne witness.[10] Satisfied with Joyce's answers, he paid him 65 lire for his traveling expenses and conceded an advance of 100 lire of his first month's salary of 250 lire.

Joyce found himself in a thriving establishment which employed fifty to sixty people. There were four owners, Schumacher and his little white-haired brother, who always had a pen behind his ear, and two Nast-Kolbs, the father 'very old and bandy-legged, with thick white eyebrows. Every morning he patters in here, stops, looks about him, says Good-morning and patters out again.' The son was brisk and, Joyce said, 'like Curran in manner and complexion.' [11] As for his fellow-clerks, they annoyed him from the start. They were forever having something wrong with their testicles ('broken, swollen, etc') [12] or their anuses, he wrote Stanislaus, and they insisted upon describing their ailments in detail. Even an Irish naturalist could not bear them. He found their names offensive: 'A clerk here is named (he is round, bald, fat, voiceless) Bartoluzzi. You pronounce by inflating both cheeks and prolonging the u. Every time I pass him I repeat his name to myself and translate "Good day, little bits of Barto." Another is named Simonetti: They are all little bits of something or other, I think. This is my first experience of clerks: but do they all talk for 5 minutes about the position &c of a penwiper?' [13] Then too, he could not endure their politics. He sat in an office with three other clerks, and about two weeks after Joyce's arrival, one of them, a German, ridiculed Lombrosianism and antimilitarism. 'When children cry they should be caned,' [14] he announced, and decreed in favor of corporal punishment in schools, conscription, religion. Joyce, who never spanked Giorgio, burst out with a socialist argument.

For a month and a half Joyce remained in the correspondence department. It was dull, busy work. He had to write between two hundred and two hundred and fifty letters a day, beginning at 8:30 in the morning and ending at 7:30 at night and often later, with two hours off for lunch. The effect was to wear out his trousers. He had two large patches on them, and to conceal these he had to keep on his tailcoat even during the August heat. He complained to Stanislaus, from whom he had lifted the trousers, that they had been made too thin for steady desk work. In September his ability received a slight nod when he was transferred, probably because of his tailcoat, to the reception desk,[15] where the work was easier and more responsible. But here, where Joyce had to cash cheques for important visitors, he was obliged to buy new trousers.

In handling its unusual employee the bank made the great error of paying him a salary each month instead of each week or even each day as the Scuola Berlitz had done. Joyce was incapable of keeping money about him, and inevitably began to ask Stanislaus again for help. By August 16 he had used up the money advanced him by the bank. Not only were his trousers giving way,[16] but the Roman air—which with Roman water were the two things he approved of—gave him an enormous appetite. He patronized the famous Caffè Greco, 'frequented by Amiel, Thackeray, Byron, Ibsen and Co.' where the bill of fare was in English and he could read the English newspapers. But though the cost was not high, he had no money. 'Remember that keen questioner, Mr M. D. Berlitz, who asks somewhere abruptly "How long can we resist the desire for food?"'[17] Stanislaus was indignant. He was still paying off some of his brother's debts in Trieste and being dunned for others. James gave careful instructions for handling such creditors: the two tailors, whom he had swindled, should be told that his present address was Edinburgh or Glasgow; the doctors should receive his Roman address and his compliments; Stanislaus should wait until Francini asked for his brother's rent, then refuse to pay it on the grounds that he had no responsibility for his brother's debts; Artifoni's thirty crowns must be repaid; Stanislaus should try to get Signora Canarutto's brother to refund a little of the money deposited on the furniture and forfeited when that was repossessed.[18]

For two weeks Stanislaus sent no money. James's importunities increased in skill; he pictured his starving wife and child with considerable effect, for Stanislaus was fond of the boy and could not bear to have him go hungry. James offered intricate budgets of his expenditures to justify his being allowed to continue them with Stanislaus's help. Stanislaus did not give in without a struggle. When James said his trousers were torn, he countered that Artifoni, at the school, had commented on his own shabby dress, suggested he was sending money to his brother, and told him he must keep up appearances if people were not to suppose he had secret vices. He absolutely must have a suit. James offered to send him some money. Soon, however, he informed Stanislaus that he and his family were all eating enormous meals, even sending a list of what they had consumed at one.[19] Stanislaus replied that he was forced to live on bread and cooked ham which he took home to his room. But he yielded at last and sent his available money. Next Joyce urged him to obtain a week's pay in advance from Artifoni.

Artifoni, however, suspected who was behind this request, which Stanislaus had never made before, and refused. Stanislaus, unable to withstand the barrage of alternately wheedling and hortatory letters from Rome, grew increasingly disheartened. Early in October he wrote that he was thinking of returning to Dublin. James in his reply urged that he give up this folly and try Artifoni again for an advance.

When Stanislaus failed a second time, Joyce asked for a loan from a pompous Anglo-Irish friend named Wyndham, to no avail, and then went to the English consul in Rome and demonstrated his remarkable powers of persuasion by eliciting a loan of 50 lire there. He had somehow to increase his income. He noticed an advertisement in the *Tribuna* for an English teacher, and began to give lessons to a man named Terzini after leaving the bank. Nora would go to a cinematograph with Giorgio and wait for him there until ten o'clock, when they would at last go to dinner. In November Joyce answered another advertisement in the same newspaper, which he now considered lucky for him, and as a result began teaching in a second-rate equivalent of the Berlitz school, the École des Langues, on November 20.[20] The additional income made no difference; he continued to implore Stanislaus for help, promising that each month would see the end of his desperation, but finding a new cause for being desperate as each month went by. He would soon be able to bring Stanislaus to Rome to join them, he said. Stanislaus coldly surmised that his brother was drinking, but James denied it, saying he had too much to do [21] and 'Wurruk is more dissipating than dissipation'; [22] but of course drinking was the principal levy upon his income.

It was probably his drinking and unstable behavior that caused Signora Dufour to raise his rent for the room on the via Frattina in November. She hoped he would leave voluntarily, and when he did not, she gave him notice on November 12 that he would have to leave at the beginning of December. To Joyce's surprise she kept her word, and on Friday, December 3, he found himself without a place to live. To Stanislaus's question he replied that he did not know why she did it.[23] Since he had made no preparation, he had to hire a car at 11:30 at night to transport his family in the rain first to one hotel, which proved to be full, and then to a second one. There they remained for four days. Joyce spent the weekend 'traipsing about, accompanied by a plaintive woman with infant (also plaintive), running up stairs, ringing a bell, "Chi c'è?" "Camera" "Chi c'è?" "Camera!" No go: room too small or too dear: won't have children, single man only, no kitchen. "Arrivederla!" Down again.' [24] Finally on December 7 he found two small rooms on the fifth floor of 51, via Monte Brianzo, and on December 8 moved in.

He and Nora were accustomed to occupying separate beds, but now they had only one. Their resolution of the problem was conveyed to Stanislaus: 'We sleep "lying opposed in opposite directions," the head of one towards the tail of the other.' [25] So in *Ulysses* Bloom and Molly were also oriented.

Joyce wrote an epiphany to depict his domestic situation: '[Scene: draughty little stone-flagged room, chest of drawers to left, on which are the remains of lunch, in the centre, a small table on which are *writing materials* (He never forgot them) and a saltcellar: in the background small-sized bed. A young man with snivelling nose sits at the little table: on the bed sit a madonna and plaintive infant. It is a January day.] Title of above: *The Anarchist*.' [26]

He naturally vented some of his irritation on the Italians. Every letter reported some new cause of fury. In August he determined that Rome, unlike Trieste, had not one decent café. In September an official refused to cash a telegraphic money order from Stanislaus because Joyce did not have his passport with him. Joyce cried in rage, 'By Jesus, Rossini was right when he took off his hat to the Spaniard, saying "You save me from the shame of being the last in Europe."' [27] The quotation did not win the official over. Once Joyce had a more legitimate tantrum: a cab-driver who was whipping his horse accidentally caught Giorgio just under the eye with the end of his lash, and raised a welt which did not disappear for some days. But most of Joyce's anger was born of impatience, as when on December 3 he declared the 'chief pastime and joke' of Henry James's 'subtle Romans' to be 'the breaking of wind rereward. . . . However, it is an expletive which I am reserving for the day when I leave the eternal city as my farewell and adieu to it.' * [28] This was his first hint that he would not stay in Rome, and his attacks on the city became quickly more and more virulent. Four days later he remarked, 'I am damnably sick of Italy, Italian and Italians; outrageously, illogically sick.' He went on grudgingly, 'I hate to think that Italians ever did anything in the way of art. But I suppose they did.' Then, as if he had conceded too much, he wrote in the margin, 'What did they do but illustrate a page or two of the New Testament!' [29] He was weary of their '*bello*' and "*bellezza*,' † [30] and carried on his irritation to *Ulysses*, where Bloom, on hearing some cabmen talk Italian, com-

---

* In fact, he reserved it for the end of the *Sirens* episode, where the rhetorical, patriotic last words of Emmet's speech at the dock have a carminative effect upon Bloom.

† Yet once, hearing for the first time the famous Neapolitan song, '*Guard'u mare com'é bello*,' played by a man on a barrel organ, Joyce followed him for hours through the Roman streets. [31]

ments on their 'beautiful language' and *'Bella Poetria,'* * [32] only to be
assured by Stephen that they were haggling obscenely over money.
When Stanislaus took James to task for his blanket repudiation of Italy,
he retorted, 'Do you imagine that you are corresponding with the indif-
ferential calculus that you object to my vituperation on Italy and
Rome? What the hell else would I do?' [33]

Joyce blamed Rome not only for his material insecurity but for his
failure to write anything. He did, however, revise the two stories in
Dubliners which he considered weakest, 'A Painful Case' and 'After the
Race,' near the beginning of his Roman sojourn, in August, and in
November he went to the Biblioteca Vittorio Emanuele to check the
details of the Vatican Council of 1870 which he had used in 'Grace.'
He sent Stanislaus this version of what he had found out: 'Before the
final proclamation many of the clerics left Rome as a protest. At the
proclamation when the dogma [of papal infallibility] was read out the
Pope said "Is that all right, gents?" All the gents said "Placet" but two
said "Non placet." But the Pope "You be damned! Kissmearse! I'm
infallible!" ' [34] The story 'Grace' employed the tripartite division of the
Divine Comedy, beginning with the Inferno of a Dublin bar, proceeding to the Purgatorio of a drunkard's convalescence, and ending in the
Paradiso of a highly secularized Dublin church. [35] He proceeded from
that to conceive of another story with a mock-heroic, mythic background, 'The Last Supper,' to deal with Joe McKernan, the son of his
old landlady in Dublin. Four other stories, planned but never written,
had the titles: 'The Street,' 'Vengeance,' 'At Bay,' and 'Catharsis.' [36]
Joyce said he was too cold to write them, for one thing, and, unlike
Ibsen, not enough of an egoarch, [37] an impediment he had not pleaded
before. It was probably an allusion to his selflessness in continuing to
live with his wife and son.

Two other plans for stories were of much greater consequence. The
first, which he mentioned to Stanislaus on September 30, was to be
called 'Ulysses' and to portray, evidently with irony similar to that of
'Grace' and 'The Last Supper,' a dark-complexioned Dublin Jew named
Hunter who was rumored to be a cuckold. [38] Joyce's interest in the Jews
was growing as he recognized his own place in Europe to be as ambiguous as theirs. He was interested in a Jewish divorce case in Dublin,† [39]

---

* A humorous corruption of *'poesia'* (poetry), perhaps by blending with *'porcheria'*
(filth).
† This was a suit heard in Dublin November 5-8, 1906. Kathleen Hynes Harris
petitioned for divorce from her husband, Morris Harris, on grounds of cruelty and
misconduct. Harris was a bearded sacerdotal 85, his wife was much younger. They
had been married by a priest, Archbishop Walsh having granted dispensation
because of a 'very serious circumstance,' not specified. Later they had been married

in the fact that Georg Brandes was a Jew, and in Ferrero's theories of anti-Semitism.[40] His new story filled his mind, but on November 13 he had still not begun it. He asked Stanislaus what he thought of the title, then on December 3 asked him to write what he remembered of Hunter. (Joyce had only met him twice.) On February 6, 1907, he said regretfully, '"Ulysses" never got any forrarder than its title.' The figure of the cuckolded Jew did not leave him, however.

To write the second story, 'The Dead,' Joyce had to come to a more indulgent view of Ireland, and there are signs of this in his letters.* In one letter he suddenly and surprisingly announced that the Irish, because they are the least bureaucratic, are the most civilized people in Europe. And on September 25 he questioned the implications of the other stories of *Dubliners:*

I have often confessed to you surprise that there should be anything exceptional in my writing and it is only at moments when I leave down somebody else's book that it seems to me not so unlikely after all. Sometimes thinking of Ireland it seems to me that I have been unnecessarily harsh. I have reproduced (in *Dubliners* at least) none of the attraction of the city for I have never felt at my ease in any city since I left it, except in Paris. I have not reproduced its ingenuous insularity and its hospitality. The latter 'virtue' so far as I can see does not exist elsewhere in Europe. I have not been just to its beauty: for it is more beautiful naturally in my opinion than what I have seen of England, Switzerland, France, Austria or Italy. And yet I know how useless these reflections are, For were I to rewrite the book as G. R. † suggests 'in another sense' (where the hell does he get the meaningless phrases he uses) I am sure I should find again what you call the Holy Ghost sitting in the ink-bottle and the perverse devil of my literary conscience sitting on the hump of my pen. And after all *Two Gallants*—with the Sunday crowds and the harp in Kildare Street and Lenehan—is an Irish landscape.[41]

With such mixed blame and praise for his stories, he waited irritably during August and September for Grant Richards's final decision about them. At the end of September Richards wrote that he could not now

---

also by a rabbi. Mrs. Harris alleged that her husband was having an affair with his housekeeper, Sarah White, who was 80 years old, that he had committed indecent acts (not particularized) in the dining room; that he had once put excrement into her nightgown; that he had had relations with little girls. He had been accused, in fact, of almost as many crimes as are alleged in *Ulysses* against Bloom and in *Finnegans Wake* against Earwicker. The judge said the case was 'perfectly nauseous'; the jury found Harris guilty of cruelty but disagreed on adultery, and a verdict was granted of divorce *a mensa et thoro*, with costs. Joyce was acquainted with Harris's grandchildren (by a previous marriage), and had this additional motive for following the case as closely as he could.

* See p. 254.
† Grant Richards.

publish *Dubliners,* but would like to publish Joyce's autobiographical
novel and then do the stories later.[42] Joyce went to the British consul
and secured from him the name of an international lawyer, St. Lo Malet,
whom he next consulted about Richards's breach of contract.[43] St. Lo
Malet advised him to try Richards again by letter, but Richards, on
October 19, reaffirmed his decision over Joyce's protests. Even though
Joyce, in his desperation, was now ready to suppress 'Two Gallants'
and 'A Little Cloud' and to modify two passages in 'Counterparts' and
'Grace,' Richards did not want the book. St. Lo Malet wrote the Society
of Authors on October 22, asking if they would help an unnamed
young man. The Society, after requiring a guinea for membership,
found it could do nothing. For another pound St. Lo Malet helped
Joyce to compose some legalistic letters to Richards, but again advised
him against going to law. Joyce ended by offering the book, on November 20, to John Long. When his brother tried to encourage him to keep
writing, he replied angrily on September 18, 'I have written quite
enough, and before I do any more in that line I must see some reason
why. I am not a literary Jesus Christ.'

In this mood of dissatisfaction, he not only felt *Dubliners* was too
harsh, but thought *Chamber Music* too soft. Yet this book was to find
a publisher first. When Richards failed him, Joyce wrote to Arthur
Symons, to whom he owed his first introduction to Richards. He had
not been in touch with Symons since sending him a copy of 'The Holy
Office,' and was half-surprised to receive one of Symons's prompt and
generous replies. As for *Dubliners,* all that Symons could suggest was
to accede as far as possible to Richards's demands. But he thought he
could place Joyce's poems with Elkin Mathews for publication in his
shilling Garland series. When Joyce gratefully agreed, Symons wrote
to Mathews on October 9, asking if he would care to have 'for your
Vigo Cabinet a book of verse which is of the most genuine lyric quality
of any new work I have read for many years? It is called "A Book of
Thirty Songs for Lovers," and the lyrics are almost Elizabethan in their
freshness but quite personal. They are by a young Irishman named
J. A. Joyce. He is not in the Celtic Movement, and though Yeats admits
his ability, he is rather against him, because Joyce has attacked the
movement.' [44]

Mathews was very willing to consider the poems, and Joyce got them
ready to send.[45] He exaggerated his own indifference to their fate, and,
remembering that Stanislaus had some time before proposed a new
arrangement of the poems, asked what it was, agreeing to accept it
'perfunctorily.' He professed little confidence or interest in them, but
said he supposed they had some merit. The poem called 'Tilly' should

George Clancy, J. F. Byrne, and Joyce, while at University College. (Croessmann Collection) (pp. 62, 65)
Courtesy of the Southern Illinois University Library

The Berlitz school in Pola, 1904 (at right of the Roman arch of Sergius). (p. 192)

V

Stanislaus Joyce in Trieste, about 1905, age about 21.
(p. 220) *Courtesy of Mrs. Nelly Joyce*

VI

Alessandro Francini Bruni, a close
friend in Pola and Trieste. *Courtesy
of Alessandro Francini Bruni*

be excluded because its somber tone was out of keeping with the rest and belonged to that period when 'my dancing days are over.' Stanislaus wished to revert to the original title, *Chamber Music*, but Joyce argued that it was 'too complacent.' 'I should prefer a title which to a certain extent repudiated the book, without altogether disparaging it.'[46] But he allowed Stanislaus to have his way, and only commented in the same tone, on October 18, 'A page of *A Little Cloud* gives me more pleasure than all my verses.'

Mathews was slow to make up his mind, but on January 17 sent a contract. It was not likely that Joyce would earn any royalties by it and before accepting the terms he went again to St. Lo Malet, who with his usual good sense advised him to accept them. The proofs accordingly arrived in February. There was 'an open pianner' on the frontispiece, Joyce informed his brother, then added:

> I don't like the book but wish it were published and be damned to it. However, it is a young man's book. I felt like that. It is not a book of love verses at all, I perceive. But some of them are pretty enough to be put to music. I hope someone will do so, someone who knows old English music such as I like. Besides they are not pretentious and have a certain grace. I will keep a copy myself and (so far as I can remember) at the top of each page I will put an address or a street so that when I open the book I can revisit the places where I wrote the different songs.[47]

The realization that *Chamber Music* was a part of him softened his tone towards it a little. The book's final justification was as a memorial of his youth, just as he could sometimes charitably excuse the existence of Dublin because it was there he had lived.

Although Joyce did little writing in Rome, he got into the habit of leaving the house early and sitting down in a café with a book until it was time to go to the bank. He read eagerly and widely. In his letters to Stanislaus at this time he wrote his sharpest criticism, chiefly, it is apparent, to find his own bearings in the literature of the world. He weighed whatever he read meticulously for its naturalistic accuracy, honesty of purpose, and style. On August 16, 1906, he picked up Wilde's *The Picture of Dorian Gray* in an Italian translation, and complained that Wilde had veiled the homosexual implications. He commented to his brother, 'Wilde seems to have had some good intentions in writing it—some wish to put himself before the world—but the book is rather crowded with lies and epigrams. If he had had the courage to develop the allusions in the book, it might have been better. I suspect he has done this in some privately-printed books.'[48] Wilde, like most of the authors he now read, was not toughminded enough.

Thomas Hardy, George Gissing, and George Moore might have been expected to please him better, but he rejected them all. At the beginning of December, having read Hardy's *Life's Little Ironies,* he complained of the absurdity of situation and dialogue:

One story is about a lawyer on the circuit who seduces a servant, then receives letters from her so beautifully written that he decides to marry her. The letters are written by the servant's mistress who is in love with the lawyer. After the marriage (servant is accompanied to London by mistress) husband says fondly 'Now, dear J. K.-S- &c, will you write a little note to my dear sister, A B X. etc & send her a piece of the wedding-cake. One of those nice little letters you know so well how to write, love.' Exit of servant wife. She goes out and sits at a table somewhere and, I suppose, writes something like this 'Dear Mrs X— I enclose a piece of wedding-cake.' Enter husband, lawyer, genial. Genially he says 'Well, love, how have you written' and then the whole discovery is found out. Servant-wife blows her nose in the letter and lawyer confronts the mistress. She confesses. Then they talk a page or so of copybook talk (as distinguished from servants' ditto). She weeps but he is stern. Is this as near as T. H. can get to life, I wonder? O my poor fledglings, poor Corley, poor Ignatius Gallaher! . . . What is wrong with these English writers is that they always keep beating about the bush.[49]

It is clear that the whole idiom of twentieth-century fiction was established in Joyce's mind by 1906.

Gissing's *Demos: A Story of English Socialism* (an ancestor of the proletarian novel) was worse. 'Why are English novels so terribly boring?' he asked, and derided the conventional melodrama of having a worker inherit a fortune, marry a lady, become a big employer, and then take to drink. 'There is a clergyman in it with searching eyes and a deep voice who makes all the socialists wince under his firm gaze.'[50] A second book of Gissing's, *The Crown of Life,* was written outrageously; Joyce gave two instances: ' "'Arry, in fact, to use a coarse but expressive phase, was a hopeless blackguard," ' and ' "When he left, which he did later in the day (to catch a train), the conversation resumed its usual course &c." '[51] Gissing's books reminded him of *pasta e fasoi* (noodles and beans), a Triestine soup.[52]

George Moore's *The Lake* he found amusing, mainly because a leading character had the name of Father Oliver Gogarty. 'I think that may either have been laughingly suggested by O St Jesus for his greater glory,' Joyce wrote Stanislaus on September 18, 'or hawk-eyedly intended by Moore to put O St. Jesus in an *embarras.*' He mocked its symbolism on August 31:

You know the plot. She writes long letters to Father Oliver Gogarty about Wagner and the Ring and Bayreuth (memories of my youth!) and about

Italy where everyone is so happy (!!!!!!!!!!!!!!) and where they drink nice wine and not that horrid black porter (O poor Lady Ardilaun over whose lily-like hand he lingered some years back) and then she goes (in all senses of the word) with a literary man named Ellis—one of Moore's literary men, you can imagine what, silent second cousin of that terribly knowing fellow, Harding—and Father Oliver Gogarty goes out to the lake to plunge in by moonlight, before which the moon shines opportunely 'on a firm erect frame and grey buttocks'; and on the steamer he reflects that every man has a lake in his heart and must ungird his loins for the crossing. Preface written in French to a French friend who cannot read or write English (intelligent artist, however, no doubt) * and George Moore, out of George Henry Moore and a Ballyglass lady, explains that he only does it 'because, *cher ami* (dear friend), you cannot read me in my own language.' Eh?

When Stanislaus, to whom he had sent the book, contended that the last part was well done, Joyce asked, 'Yerra, what's good in the end of *The Lake?* I see nothing.' [53] But this rejection did not keep him from making use of the book later. He remembered the ending when he came to write the visionary scene at the end of the fourth chapter of *A Portrait of the Artist as a Young Man;* there Stephen, like Father Gogarty, undergoes a rite of secular baptism, and Joyce's water and bird imagery, while he has made it altogether his own, seems to owe something to Moore's symbolism of lake, stagnant pool, and fluttering curlew. Joyce winnowed Moore of the preposterous; he found him a good man to improve upon.

Whenever Joyce read a review in the English newspapers that suggested that a writer was doing the same sort of thing he was, he ordered the book. So he sent for Arthur Morrison's *Tales of Mean Streets,* but soon put it indifferently aside. Having heard that a classmate of his at the University, Seamus O'Kelly, had just published a group of stories called *By the Stream of Killmeen,* he obtained the book through his Aunt Josephine but quickly commented:

The stories I have read were about beautiful, pure faithful Connacht girls and lithe, broad-shouldered open-faced young Connacht men, and I read them without blinking, patiently trying to see whether the writer was trying to express something he had understood. I always conclude by saying to myself without anger something like this 'Well there's no doubt they are very romantic young people; at first they come as a relief, then they tire. Maybe, begod, people like that are to be found by the stream of Killmeen only none of them has ever come under my observation, as the deceased gent in Norway remarked.' [54]

* Joyce remembered this preface when he presented Moore later with a copy of *Ulysses,* but in French translation; see p. 631.

On the other hand, Kipling's *Plain Tales from the Hills* stirred his admiration for at least its factual accuracy: 'If I knew Ireland as well as R. K. seems to know India,' he wrote Stanislaus in January 1907, 'I fancy I could write something good. But it is becoming a mist in my brain rapidly.'

He refused to share his brother's admiration for Turgenev after read-ing *Smoke* and *A Sportsman's Notebook* in a French translation. He wrote indulgently, however, of Octave Mirbeau's *Sebastian Roch*, ad-miring both its grim account of life in a Jesuit college and its style: 'It must be difficult to succeed in France,' he remarked on December 7, 'where nearly everyone writes well.' Some praise, rather grudging, he meted out to Anatole France: 'Crainquebele ['L'Affaire Crainquebille'], of course, is very fine and parts or rather phrases, of his other books.' [55]

Perhaps because of Ibsen's death he picked up a copy of *Hedda Gabler* in Gosse's translation, but said Gosse had done it very badly.[56] He was confirmed in this view by a man named Pedersen, from whom he was now taking Danish lessons—a luxury which Joyce reported to Stanislaus without bothering to justify. He also bought a play of Hauptmann, another old admiration, and told Stanislaus on October 9:

> I finished Hauptmann's *Rosa Bernd* on Sunday. I wonder if he acts well. His plays, when read, leave an unsatisfying impression on the reader. Yet he must have the sense of the stage well developed in him by now. He never, in his later plays at least, tried for a curtain so that the ends of his acts seem ruptures of a scene. His characters appear to be more highly vivified by their creator than Ibsen's but they also are less under control. He has a difficulty in subordinating them to the action of his drama. He deals with life quite differently, more frankly in certain points (This play opens with Rosa and her lover emerging one after the other from opposite sides of a bush, looking at each other first and then laughing) but also so broadly that my personal conscience is seldom touched. His way of treating such types as Arnold Kramer and Rosa Bernd is, however, altogether to my taste. His temperament has a little of Rimbaud in it. Like him, too, I suppose somebody else will be his future.* But, after all, he has written two or three master-pieces—'a little immortal thing' like *The Weavers*, for example. I have found nothing of the charlatan in him yet.

This final praise was Joyce's highest.

Meanwhile he kept plaguing Aunt Josephine, his only regular Dublin correspondent, for copies of everything to do with Ireland, particularly newspapers but also magazines and books. Irish history continued to

---

* Joyce was evidently alluding here to the famous and misleading final sentence in Arthur Symons's essay on Rimbaud in *The Symbolist Movement in Literature* (1899): 'Even in literature he had his future; but his future was Verlaine.'

fascinate him, and he reminded Stanislaus of his old project of writing about Lady Belvedere and her lover as his contribution to the subject.* [57] He wished he had a map of Dublin and Gilbert's † history and some photographs of the country. He was astonished to find in the Irish press how prominent Sheehy-Skeffington, Kettle, and even Gogarty had become. Gogarty continued to make overtures to Joyce, and Joyce to repel them. Early in 1906 Charles Joyce reported from Dublin that Gogarty had questioned him with great concern about James's life and attitude towards him, and had then gone on to ask what all the other members of the family thought of him.[58] After this conversation Gogarty had written Joyce asking him to forget the past, 'a thing beyond my power,'[59] as Joyce said in return. Now Gogarty, who had recently been married, wrote to Joyce in Rome, and Joyce again fended him off, this time with a formal suggestion that they might meet in Italy. The reply came from New York, where Gogarty and his bride had gone on their wedding trip; he hoped to be able to accept Joyce's 'kind invitation,' and added, 'I suppose I will be gladder to see you than you to see me, but I miss the touch of a vanished hand and the sound of a voice that is still.'[60] Stanislaus, informed of this high-flown correspondence, said his brother should have terminated it earlier, but Joyce wanted the wound kept open.

Joyce felt more kindly towards Thomas Kettle, who had become a Member of Parliament. When he heard Kettle had published a book, *Dialogues of the Day*, he sent for it, but disliked its 'alert,' reasonable plea for a parliamentary solution of the national question.[61] Stanislaus advised him to be friends with Kettle, but Joyce was not amenable; it was not, he explained, that he disliked Kettle, but that he felt his relationships with other men, except for Stanislaus, had been unrewarding:

> . . . it seems to me my influence on male friends is provocative. They find it hard to understand me and difficult to get on with me, even when they seem well-equipped for these tasks. On the other hand two ill-equipped women, to wit, Aunt Josephine and Nora, seem to be able to get at my point of view, and, if they do not get on with me as well as they might they certainly manage to preserve a certain loyalty which is very commendable and pleasing. Of course I am not speaking of you. On all subjects—except socialism (for which you care nothing) and painting (of which I know nothing)—we have the same or like opinions.[62]

---

* See pp. 35-6.
† J. T. Gilbert, *Historic and Municipal Documents of Ireland* (London, 1870). As John V. Kelleher has written, Joyce studied intensively the 'Dublin Annals' at the back of Thom's Directory of Dublin, and in later life read up on Irish history.

Stanislaus urged that at any rate Kettle had the right political theory, but James surprised him by rejecting parliamentarianism and supporting Arthur Griffith and Sinn Fein. In this stand he was not inconsistent; Parnell had gone as far with Parliament as was possible, and Kettle could scarcely accomplish what Parnell had failed in. Griffith's newspaper, the *United Irishman,* was the only one of any merit in Ireland, he asserted.[63] The Sinn Fein policy would benefit Ireland very much. On September 25, 1906, Joyce wrote of Griffith:

... as far as my knowledge of Irish affairs goes, he was the first person in Ireland to revive the separatist idea on modern lines nine years ago. He wants the creation of an Irish consular service abroad and of an Irish bank at home. What I don't understand is that while apparently he does the talking and the thinking two or three fatheads like Martyn and Sweetman don't begin either of the schemes. He said in one of his articles that it cost a Danish merchant less to send butter to Christiania and then by sea to London than it costs an Irish merchant to send his from Mullingar to Dublin. A great deal of his programme perhaps is absurd but at least it tries to inaugurate some commercial life for Ireland. . . . What I object to most of all in his paper is that it is educating the people of Ireland on the old pap of racial hatred whereas anyone can see that, if the Irish question exists, it exists for the Irish proletariat chiefly.

He favored the Sinn Fein policy even if its effect would be at first only to substitute Irish for English capital. He had absorbed enough Marxist thought to argue that capitalism was a necessary transition to socialism. 'The Irish proletariat has yet to be created. A feudal peasantry exists, scraping the soil, but this would with a national revival or with a definite preponderance of England surely disappear.'[64] Stanislaus contended that Griffith feared the Church too much to do anything important; his brother replied, on November 6:

I quite agree with you that Griffith is afraid of the priests—and he has every reason to be so. But, possibly, they are also a little afraid of him too. After all, he is holding out some secular liberty to the people and the Church doesn't approve of that. I quite see, of course, that the Church is still, as it was in the time of Adrian IV, the enemy of Ireland: but I think her time is almost up. For either *Sinn Fein* or Imperialism will conquer the present Ireland. If the Irish programme did not insist on the Irish language I suppose I could call myself a nationalist. As it is, I am content to recognise myself an exile: and, prophetically, a repudiated one. You complain of Griffith's using Gogarty & Co. How do you expect him to fill his paper: he can't write it all himself. The part he does write, at least, has some intelligence and directness about it. As for O.G. I am waiting for the *S.F.* policy to make headway in the hope that he will join it for no doubt whatever exists in my mind but that, if he gets the chance and the moment comes, he will play the part of MacNally & Reynolds.* I do not say this out of spleen. It is my final view of his character, a very native Irish growth, and if I begin to write my novel again it is in this way I shall treat them. If it is not far-fetched to say that my action, and that of men like Ibsen &c, is a virtual intellectual strike I would call such people as Gogarty and Yeats and Colm the blacklegs of literature. Because they have tried to substitute us, to serve the old idols at a lower rate when we refused to do so for a higher.

He burst out again when he read Gogarty on 'venereal excess' in *Sinn Fein;* the correct term, he suggested, was 'venereal ill luck.'

Anyway, my opinion is that if I put down a bucket into my own soul's well, sexual department, I draw up Griffith's and Ibsen's and Skeffington's and Bernard Vaughan's and St. Aloysius' and Shelley's and Renan's water along with my own. And I am going to do that in my novel (inter alia) and plank the bucket down before the shades and substances above mentioned to see how they like it: and if they don't like it I can't help them. I am nauseated by their lying drivel about pure men and pure women and spiritual love and love for ever: blatant lying in the face of the truth. . . . I presume there are very few mortals in Europe who are not in danger of waking some morning and finding themselves syphilitic. The Irish consider England a sink: but, if cleanliness is important in this matter, what of Ireland? Perhaps my view of life is too cynical but it seems to me that a lot of this talk about love is nonsense. A woman's love is always material and egoistic. A man, on the contrary, side by side with his extraordinary cerebral sexualism and bodily fervour (from which women are normally free) possesses a fund of genuine affection for the 'beloved' or 'once beloved' object. I am no friend of tyranny, as you know, but if many husbands are brutal, the atmosphere in which they live (vide Counterparts) is brutal, and few wives and homes can satisfy the desire for happiness. In fact, it is useless to talk about this any further. I am going to lunch.[65]

In spite of this outburst against Griffith's newspaper, Joyce continued to support its political position. The policy of Sinn Fein, if rigorously followed, would achieve economic and political independence at home, just as he would achieve abroad artistic independence. Underneath his sympathy for Griffith lay a continuing sympathy for socialism, which the socialist congress, held in Rome during his stay, kept warm. He compared Griffith with the Italian Labriola, whom he admired, in his opposition to parliamentary process, and cited Labriola's view that parliaments can never change the social order.[66] When Stanislaus called Labriola an intellectualized socialist, James replied that, on the con-

---

* Leonard MacNally (1752-1820) and Thomas Reynolds (1771-1832) were informers, notorious for having betrayed the United Irishmen. MacNally also betrayed Robert Emmet. In *Ulysses* (15 [12]), Stephen refers to Mulligan, modelled mostly on Gogarty, as Ireland's 'gay betrayer.'

trary, he sought an immediate emergence of the proletariat, a proletariat as politically and religiously inclusive as possible.[67] (Such a
proletariat might include even an unnamed indigent foreign writer.)
Stanislaus insisted that his brother's socialism was thin, and James
agreed at once, 'It is so and unsteady and ill-formed.' [68] But he continued to argue the matter with great energy.

His liking for Griffith, and his reservations about all Irish writers but
himself, had soon an opportunity to combine. At the beginning of
February 1907, the riot at the Abbey Theatre over Synge's *The Playboy
of the Western World* occurred. The phrase that caused it was, 'If all
the girls in Mayo were standing before me in their shifts.' Joyce commented, dryly, 'Wonderful vision.' [69] But he was particularly interested
in Padraic Colum,* who, haled to police court for disorderly conduct,
announced 'that nothing would deter him from protesting against such
a slander on Ireland.' [70] He was fined 40 shillings or fourteen days.
Joyce recounted the proceedings—which he found in the *Daily Mail*—
with gusto, but to Stanislaus's surprise sided with the nationalists
against the literary men. 'I believe Colum and the Irish Theatre will
beat Y. and L. G. and Miss H., which will please me greatly, as Yeats
cannot well hawk his theatre over to London. . . . Synge will probably
be condemned from the pulpit, as a heretic: which would be dreadful:
so that Stiffbreeches [Eglinton] and Ryan really *ought* to start another
paper in defense of free thought, just for a week or so.' [71] Like the Irish
goddess, the Morrigu, Joyce fed on conflict.

For Yeats he had no sympathy at all. He was 'a tiresome idiot' and
'quite out of touch with the Irish people, to whom he appeals as the
author of "Countess Cathleen." ' [72] Joyce had been misinformed; Yeats
had angrily and rather successfully confronted the Abbey Theatre mob
with the words, 'The author of *Kathleen ni Houlihan* [an entirely different play] addresses you.' [73] Synge repelled Joyce a little less, for he
at least could 'set them by the ears.' [74] But this was one Irish row Joyce
hated to miss. 'This whole affair has upset me,' he wrote Stanislaus on
February 11, 1907. 'I feel like a man in a house who hears a row in the
street and voices he knows shouting but can't get up to see what the
hell is going on. It has put me off the story I was "going to write"—
to wit: *The Dead.*' [75] Stanislaus, who had no patience with Colum's
attitude, could not stomach his brother's either, and noted in his diary
that he was utterly baffled by it; but James's position was mostly an
airing of resentments. He refused to take this theatrical dispute seriously and preferred to consider it a Donnybrook fair of contending
pettinesses, in which he wanted to see the established writers beaten

---

* Not the writer, but the writer's father, as it turned out.

and so would not acknowledge that in the battle with censorship he had common cause with them. He was much less indulgent towards his own censors than towards Synge's.

The dispute exhilarated him so much that it reminded him by contrast of his apathy in Rome. The quarrels of the socialist congress had seemed exciting at the time, but now they were tame when he compared them with the Abbey Theatre riot. A memorial procession in honor of his old favorite, Giordano Bruno, failed to stir him, and he had no patience, either, with a performance of Wagner's *Götterdämmerung*.[76] He was resolved to find nothing to admire. The only pleasure in his life came, he said, from Giorgio, whose chatter delighted him.

Much of this depression was due to his drinking more and more heavily. Another cause was the family's living quarters, which made Nora, too, anxious for some change. She needled him to move. Early in February they gave their landlady notice for February 15 and placed a deposit on a room on the Corso. Joyce added to the disorder by giving up his teaching at the École des Langues on the vague promise of securing a second private pupil, who changed his mind. To make matters worse, Joyce spent the salary he received on February 1 lavishly. 'I have new hat and boots and vests and socks and a Danish book and Georgie has a new coat and hat and I gave a dinner. Now when you get this you will have to send me 10 crowns,' he wrote Stanislaus on February 11. The same month he suddenly assessed his present and future, and decided that both his bank job and Rome were insufferable:

I have come to the conclusion that it is about time I made up my mind whether I am to become a writer or a patient Cousins. I foresee that I shall have to do other work as well but to continue as I am at present would certainly mean my mental extinction. It is months since I have written a line and even reading tires me. The interest I took in socialism and the rest has left me. I have gradually slid down until I have ceased to take any interest in any subject. I look at God and his theatre through the eyes of my fellow-clerks so that nothing surprises, moves, excites or disgusts me. Nothing of my former mind seems to have remained except a heightened sensitiveness which satisfies itself in the sixty-miles-an-hour pathos of some cinematograph or before some crude Italian gazette-picture. Yet I have certain ideas I would like to give form to: not as a doctrine but as the continuation of the expression of myself which I now see I began in *Chamber Music*. These ideas or instincts or intuitions or impulses may be purely personal. I have no wish to codify myself as anarchist or socialist or reactionary. The spectacle of the procession in honour of the Nolan left me quite cold. I understand that anti-clerical history probably contains a large percentage of lies but this is not enough to drive me back howling to my gods. This state of indifference ought to indicate artistic inclination, but it doesn't.[77]

With his accustomed abandon in crises, Joyce told the bank that he would leave at the end of February. (He actually stayed until March 5.) He next informed Stanislaus of his decision, and wrote letters to various agencies in Italy and France to see what he could turn up. He wanted a city that was not, like Rome, a tourist center, and first hit on Marseilles as a place to live. The virtue for which he praised it, that it was a port like Trieste,[78] suggests that his real bent was towards his old city. Bank work was detestable, but he thought of trying a shipping office. No one, however, needed his services.

On February 15 Joyce told his landlady he would stay a little longer, and next day he wrote Stanislaus that he had decided after all to return to Trieste and the Scuola Berlitz. Stanislaus was dismayed; he had already gone to Artifoni to see whether the director was willing to keep his promise, made in all innocence to Joyce before the latter's departure for Rome, to give him his position back if he should ever want it. Artifoni absolutely refused. Nor was Stanislaus himself enthusiastic at his brother's throwing over another reliable job. He urged him to stay in Rome; in Trieste he would find no work and would be worse off. But Joyce was determined to cash no more checks for other people. He replied that if the school was really full, he could at least return and give private lessons. There were none to be had, said Stanislaus. Joyce refused to give up his idea. His trip to Rome had been a *'coglioneria,'* he admitted.[79] But in Trieste he could be sure of finding one congenial person, and besides, the city was full of associations for him with the writing of *Dubliners*.[80]

Afflicted with a dripping nose by the Roman winter, disheartened by John Long's rejection of *Dubliners* (on February 21), rendered frantic by Nora's insistence that their life become more tolerable, Joyce made a last effort to find a position in Marseilles but failed. 'My mouth is full of decayed teeth and my soul of decayed ambitions,'[81] he lamented. Nora, to cap it all, was pregnant again. In November he had bravely written that he had surpassed his friends' expectations by his success in Rome: 'Eglinton was sure I would come back begging to Dublin and J. F. B. [Byrne] that I would become a drunkard and Cosgrave that I would become a nymphomaniac.* Alas, gentlemen, I have become a bank clerk—and now that I think of it, bad as it is, it's more than either of my three prophets could do.'[82] But now, four months later, he tacitly admitted to Stanislaus that he had been drinking: 'A little more of this life and J. F. B.'s prophecy would be fulfilled.'[83] After a few final hesitations Joyce brought his Roman visit to an orgiastic close. One night he got drunk with two mailmen and went

* He meant *satyr*.

with them to dance on the Pincio, and the night before he left, having just received his month's pay from the bank, he drank heavily in a cafe and indiscreetly allowed two hangers-on with whom he was talking to see the contents of his wallet. They followed him out, knocked him down, and made off with his 200 crowns.* [84] In the resulting hubbub he would have been arrested, as when he first arrived in Trieste in 1904, if some people in the crowd had not recognized him and taken him home, a good deed which he reproduced at the end of the *Circe* episode in *Ulysses*. A few crowns had fortunately been left in the house. Joyce wired his brother to herald his return. Then he packed Nora and Giorgio into a train and fled from Rome.

* In *Exiles* (561 [393]), the boy Archie asks his father, 'Are there robbers here like in Rome?'

The Backgrounds of 'The Dead'

The silent cock shall crow at last. The west shall shake the east awake.
Walk while ye have the night for morn, lightbreakfastbringer. . . .

—*Finnegans Wake* (473)

T HE stay in Rome had seemed purposeless, but during it Joyce
became aware of the change in his attitude toward Ireland and
so toward the world. He embodied his new perceptions in 'The Dead.'
The story, which was the culmination of a long waiting history, began
to take shape in Rome, but was not set down until he left the city. The
pressure of hints, sudden insights, and old memories rose in his mind
until, like King Midas's barber, he was compelled to speech.

Although the story dealt mainly with three generations of his family
in Dublin, it drew also upon an incident in Galway in 1903. There
Michael ('Sonny') Bodkin courted Nora Barnacle; but he contracted
tuberculosis and had to be confined to bed. Shortly afterwards Nora
resolved to go to Dublin, and Bodkin stole out of his sickroom, in spite
of the rainy weather, to sing to her under an apple tree and bid her
goodbye. In Dublin Nora soon learned that Bodkin was dead, and
when she met Joyce she was first attracted to him, as she told a sister,
because he resembled Sonny Bodkin.[1]

Joyce's habit of ferreting out details had made him conduct minute
interrogations of Nora even before their departure from Dublin. He
was disconcerted by the fact that young men before him had interested
her. He did not much like to know that her heart was still moved, even
in pity, by the recollection of the boy who had loved her. The notion
of being in some sense in rivalry with a dead man buried in the little
cemetery at Oughterard was one that came easily, and gallingly, to a
man of Joyce's jealous disposition. It was one source of his complaint
to his Aunt Josephine Murray that Nora persisted in regarding him as
quite similar to other men she had known.[2]

A few months after expressing this annoyance, while Joyce and Nora

Barnacle were living in Trieste in 1905, Joyce received another impulsion toward 'The Dead.' In a letter Stanislaus happened to mention attending a concert of Plunket Greene, the Irish baritone, which included one of Thomas Moore's *Irish Melodies* called 'O, Ye Dead!' [3] The song, a dialogue of living and dead, was eerie enough, but what impressed Stanislaus was that Greene rendered the second stanza, in which the dead answer the living, as if they were whimpering for the bodied existence they could no longer enjoy:

> It is true, it is true, we are shadows cold and wan;
> And the fair and the brave whom we loved on earth are gone;
> But still thus ev'n in death,
> So sweet the living breath
> Of the fields and the flow'rs in our youth we wandered o'er,
> That ere, condemn'd, we go
> To freeze, 'mid Hecla's snow,
> We would taste it awhile, and think we live once more!

James was interested and asked Stanislaus to send the words, which he learned to sing himself. His feelings about his wife's dead lover found a dramatic counterpart in the jealousy of the dead for the living in Moore's song: it would seem that the living and the dead are jealous of each other. Another aspect of the rivalry is suggested in *Ulysses*, where Stephen cries out to his mother's ghost, whose 'glazing eyes, staring out of death, to shake and bend my soul, . . . to strike me down,' he cannot put out of mind: 'No, mother. Let me be and let me live.' [4] That the dead do not stay buried is, in fact, a theme of Joyce from the beginning to the end of his work; Finnegan is not the only corpse to be resurrected.

In Rome the obtrusiveness of the dead affected what he thought of Dublin, the equally Catholic city he had abandoned, a city as prehensile of its ruins, visible and invisible. His head was filled with a sense of the too successful encroachment of the dead upon the living city; there was a disrupting parallel in the way that Dublin, buried behind him, was haunting his thoughts. In *Ulysses* the theme was to be reconstituted, in more horrid form, in the mind of Stephen, who sees corpses rising from their graves like vampires to deprive the living of joy. The bridebed, the childbed, and the bed of death are bound together, and death 'comes, pale vampire, through storm his eyes, his bat sails bloodying the sea, mouth to her mouth's kiss.' [5] We can be at the same time in death as well as in life. [*]

---

[*] The converse of this theme appears in *Ulysses* (113 [107]), when Bloom, walking in Glasnevin, thinks, 'They are not going to get me this innings. Warm beds: warm fullblooded life.'

By February 11, 1907, after six months in Rome, Joyce knew in general what story he must write. Some of his difficulty in beginning it was due, as he said himself,° to the riot in Dublin over *The Playboy of the Western World.* Synge had followed the advice of Yeats that Joyce had rejected, to find his inspiration in the Irish folk, and had gone to the Aran Islands. This old issue finds small echoes in the story. The nationalistic Miss Ivors tries to persuade Gabriel to go to Aran (where Synge's *Riders to the Sea* is set), and when he refuses twits him for his lack of patriotic feeling. Though Gabriel thinks of defending the autonomy of art and its indifference to politics, he knows such a defense would be pretentious, and only musters up the remark that he is sick of his own country. But the issue is far from settled for him.

'The Dead' begins with a party and ends with a corpse, so entwining 'funferal' and 'funeral' as in the wake of Finnegan. That he began with a party was due, at least in part, to Joyce's feeling that the rest of the stories in *Dubliners* had not completed his picture of the city. In a letter of September 25, 1906,† he had written his brother from Rome to say that some elements of Dublin had been left out of his stories: 'I have not reproduced its ingenuous insularity and its hospitality, the latter "virtue" so far as I can see does not exist elsewhere in Europe.' He allowed a little of this warmth to enter 'The Dead.' In his speech at the Christmas party Gabriel Conroy explicitly commends Ireland for this very virtue of hospitality, though his expression of the idea is distinctly after-dinner: 'I feel more strongly with every recurring year that our country has no tradition which does it so much honour and which it should guard so jealously as that of its hospitality. It is a tradition that is unique as far as my experience goes (and I have visited not a few places abroad) among the modern nations.' This was Joyce's oblique way, in language that mocked his own, of beginning the task of making amends.

The selection of details for 'The Dead' shows Joyce making those choices which, while masterly, suggest the preoccupations that mastered him. Once he had determined to represent an Irish party, the choice of the Misses Morkans' as its location was easy enough. He had already reserved for *Stephen Hero* a Christmas party at his own house, a party which was also to be clouded by a discussion of a dead man. The other festive occasions of his childhood were associated with his hospitable great-aunts Mrs. Callanan and Mrs. Lyons, and Mrs. Callanan's daughter Mary Ellen, at their house at 15 Usher's Island, which was also known as the 'Misses Flynn school.' [6] There every year the

° See p. 248.
† See p. 239.

Joyces who were old enough would go, and John Joyce carved the goose and made the speech. Stanislaus Joyce says that the speech of Gabriel Conroy in 'The Dead' is a good imitation of his father's oratorical style.*

In Joyce's story Mrs. Callanan and Mrs. Lyons, the Misses Flynn, become the spinster ladies, the Misses Morkan, and Mary Ellen Callanan becomes Mary Jane. Most of the other party guests were also reconstituted from Joyce's recollections. Mrs. Lyons had a son Freddy, who kept a Christmas card shop in Grafton Street.[7] Joyce introduces him as Freddy Malins, and situates his shop in the less fashionable Henry Street, perhaps to make him need that sovereign Gabriel lent him. Another relative of Joyce's mother, a first cousin, married a Protestant named Mervyn Archdale Browne, who combined the profession of music teacher with that of agent for a burglary insurance company. Joyce keeps him in 'The Dead' under his own name. Bartell d'Arcy, the hoarse singer in the story, was based upon Barton M'Guckin, the leading tenor in the Carl Rosa Opera Company. There were other tenors, such as John McCormack, whom Joyce might have used, but he needed one who was unsuccessful and uneasy about himself; and his father's often-told anecdote about M'Guckin's lack of confidence † furnished him with just such a singer as he intended Bartell d'Arcy to be.

The making of his hero, Gabriel Conroy, was more complicated. The root situation, of jealousy for his wife's dead lover, was of course Joyce's. The man who is murdered, D. H. Lawrence has one of his characters say, desires to be murdered; [8] some temperaments demand the feeling that their friends and sweethearts will deceive them. Joyce's conversation often returned to the word 'betrayal,' [9] and the entangled innocents whom he uses for his heroes are all aspects of his conception of himself. Though Gabriel is less impressive than Joyce's other heroes, Stephen, Bloom, Richard Rowan, or Earwicker, he belongs to their distinguished, put-upon company.

There are several specific points at which Joyce attributes his own experiences to Gabriel. The letter which Gabriel remembers having written to Gretta Conroy early in their courtship is one of these; from it Gabriel quotes to himself the sentiment, 'Why is it that words like these seem to me so dull and cold? Is it because there is no word tender enough to be your name?' These sentences are taken almost directly from a letter Joyce wrote to Nora in 1904.[10] It was also Joyce, of course, who wrote book reviews, just as Gabriel Conroy does, for the *Daily*

---

* He excepts the quotation from Browning, but even this was quite within the scope of the man who could quote Vergil when lending money to his son.[11]

† See p. 14.

Express. Since the *Daily Express* was pro-English, he had probably been teased for writing for it during his frequent visits to the house of David Sheehy, M. P. One of the Sheehy daughters, Kathleen, may well have been the model for Miss Ivors, for she wore that austere bodice and sported the same patriotic pin.[12] In Gretta's old sweetheart, in Gabriel's letter, in the book reviews and the discussion of them, as well as in the physical image of Gabriel with hair parted in the middle and rimmed glasses, Joyce drew directly upon his own life.

His father was also deeply involved in the story. Stanislaus Joyce recalls that when the Joyce children were too young to bring along to the Misses Flynns' party, their father and mother sometimes left them with a governess and stayed at a Dublin hotel overnight instead of returning to their house in Bray.'[13] Gabriel and Gretta do this too. Gabriel's quarrels with his mother also suggest John Joyce's quarrels with his mother, who never accepted her son's marriage to a woman of lower station.[14] But John Joyce's personality was not like Gabriel's; he had no doubts of himself, in the midst of many failures he was full of self-esteem. He had the same unshakable confidence as his son James. For Gabriel's personality there is among Joyce's friends another model.[15] This was Constantine Curran, sometimes nicknamed 'Cautious Con.' He is a more distinguished man than Joyce allows, but Joyce was building upon, and no doubt distorting, his memories of Curran as a very young man. That he has Curran partly in mind is suggested by the fact that he calls Gabriel's brother by Curran's first name Constantine, and makes Gabriel's brother, like Curran's, a priest.[16] Curran has the same high color and nervous, disquieted manner * as Gabriel, and like Gabriel he has traveled to the continent and has cultivated cosmopolitan interests. Curran, like Conroy, married a woman who was not a Dubliner, though she came from only as far west as Limerick. In other respects he is quite different. Gabriel was made mostly out of Curran, Joyce's father, and Joyce himself. Probably Joyce knew there was a publican on Howth named Gabriel Conroy; or, as Gerhard Friedrich has proposed,[17] he may have borrowed the name from the title of a Bret Harte novel. But the character, if not the name, was of his own compounding.†

Joyce now had his people, his party, and something of its development. In the festive setting, upon which the snow keeps offering a

---

* See Joyce's letter, p. 234.
† The name of Conroy's wife Gretta was borrowed from another friend, Gretta (actually Margaret) Cousins, the wife of James H. Cousins. Since Joyce mentioned in a letter at the same time that he was meditating 'The Dead,' the danger of becoming 'a patient Cousins,'[18] this family was evidently on his mind.

different perspective until, as W. Y. Tindall suggests,[19] the snow itself
changes, he develops Gabriel's private tremors, his sense of inadequacy,
his uncomfortable insistence on his small pretensions. From the beginning he is vulnerable; his well-meant and even generous overtures are
regularly checked. The servant girl punctures his blithe assumption that
everyone is happily in love and on the way to the altar. He is not sure
enough of himself to put out of his head the slurs he has received long
ago; so in spite of his uxorious attitude towards Gretta he is a little
ashamed of her having come from the west of Ireland. He cannot bear
to think of his dead mother's remark that Gretta was 'country cute,'
and when Miss Ivors says of Gretta, 'She's from Connacht, isn't she?'
Gabriel answers shortly, 'Her people are.' He has rescued her from that
bog. Miss Ivors's suggestion, a true Gaelic Leaguer's, that he spend his
holiday in the Irish-speaking Aran Islands (in the west) upsets him;
it is the element in his wife's past that he wishes to forget. During most
of the story, the west of Ireland is connected in Gabriel's mind with a
dark and rather painful primitivism, an aspect of his country which
he has steadily abjured by going off to the continent. The west is
savagery; to the east and south lie people who drink wine and wear
galoshes.

Gabriel has been made uneasy about this attitude, but he clings to it
defiantly until the ending. Unknown to him, it is being challenged by
the song, 'The Lass of Aughrim.' Aughrim is a little village in the west
not far from Galway. The song has a special relevance; in it a woman
who has been seduced and abandoned by Lord Gregory comes with
her baby in the rain to beg for admission to his house. It brings
together the peasant mother and the civilized seducer, but Gabriel does
not listen to the words; he only watches his wife listening. Joyce had
heard this ballad from Nora; perhaps he considered also using Tom
Moore's 'O, Ye Dead' in the story, but if so he must have seen that 'The
Lass of Aughrim' would connect more subtly with the west and with
Michael Furey's visit in the rain to Gretta. But the notion of using
a song at all may well have come to him as the result of the excitement
generated in him by Moore's song.

And now Gabriel and Gretta go to the Hotel Gresham, Gabriel fired
by his living wife and Gretta drained by the memory of her dead lover.
He learns for the first time of the young man in Galway, whose name
Joyce has deftly altered from Sonny or Michael Bodkin to Michael
Furey. The new name implies, like the contrast of the militant Michael
and the amiable Gabriel, that violent passion is in her Galway past,
not in her Dublin present. Gabriel tries to cut Michael Furey down.
'What was he?' he asks, confident that his own profession of language

teacher (which of course he shared with Joyce) is superior; but she replies, 'He was in the gasworks,' as if this profession was as good as any other. Then Gabriel tries again, 'And what did he die of so young, Gretta? Consumption, was it?' He hopes to register the usual expressions of pity, but Gretta silences and terrifies him by her answer, 'I think he died for me.' * Since Joyce has already made clear that Michael Furey was tubercular, this answer of Gretta has a fine ambiguity. It asserts the egoism of passion, and unconsciously defies Gabriel's reasonable question.

Now Gabriel begins to succumb to his wife's dead lover, and becomes a pilgrim to emotional intensities outside of his own experience. From a biographical point of view, these final pages compose one of Joyce's several tributes to his wife's artless integrity. Nora Barnacle, in spite of her defects of education, was independent, unself-conscious, instinctively right. Gabriel acknowledges the same coherence in his own wife, and he recognizes in the west of Ireland, in Michael Furey, a passion he has himself always lacked. 'Better pass boldly into that other world, in the full glory of some passion, than fade and wither dismally with age,' Joyce makes Gabriel think. Then comes that strange sentence in the final paragraph: 'The time had come for him to set out on his journey westward.' The cliché runs that journeys westward are towards death, but the west has taken on a special meaning in the story. Gretta Conroy's west is the place where life had been lived simply and passionately. The context and phrasing of the sentence suggest that Gabriel is on the edge of sleep, and half-consciously accepts what he has hitherto scorned, the possibility of an actual trip to Connaught. What the sentence affirms, at last, on the level of feeling, is the west, the primitive, untutored, impulsive country from which Gabriel had felt himself alienated before; in the story, the west is paradoxically linked also with the past and the dead. It is like Aunt Julia Morkan who, though ignorant, old, grey-skinned, and stupefied, seizes in her song at the party 'the excitement of swift and secure flight.'

The tone of the sentence, 'The time had come for him to set out on his journey westward,' is somewhat resigned. It suggests a concession, a relinquishment, and Gabriel is conceding and relinquishing a good deal—his sense of the importance of civilized thinking, of continental tastes, of all those tepid but nice distinctions on which he has prided himself. The bubble of his self-possession is pricked; he no longer

* Adaline Glasheen has discovered here an echo of Yeats's nationalistic play, *Cathleen ni Houlihan* (1902), where the old woman who symbolizes Ireland sings a song of 'yellow-haired Donough that was hanged in Galway.' When she is asked, 'What was it brought him to his death?' she replies, 'He died for love of me; many a man has died for love of me.' [20]

possesses himself, and not to possess oneself is in a way a kind of death. It is a self-abandonment not unlike Furey's, and through Gabriel's mind runs the imagery of Calvary. He imagines the snow on the cemetery at Oughterard, lying 'thickly drifted on the crooked crosses and head-stones, on the spears of the little gate, on the barren thorns.' He thinks of Michael Furey who, Gretta has said, died for her, and envies him his sacrifice for another kind of love than Christ's. To some extent Gabriel too is dying for her, in giving up what he has most valued in himself, all that holds him apart from the simpler people at the party. He feels close to Gretta through sympathy if not through love; now they are both past youth, beauty, and passion; he feels close also to her dead lover, another lamb burnt on her altar, though she too is burnt now; he feels no resentment, only pity. In his own sacrifice of himself he is conscious of a melancholy unity between the living and the dead.

Gabriel, who has been sick of his own country, finds himself drawn inevitably into a silent tribute to it of much more consequence than his spoken tribute to the party. He has had illusions of the rightness of a way of life that should be outside of Ireland; but through this experi-ence with his wife he grants a kind of bondage, of acceptance, even of admiration to a part of the country and a way of life that are most Irish. Ireland is shown to be stronger, more intense than he. At the end of *A Portrait of the Artist,* too, Stephen Dedalus, who has been so reso-lutely opposed to nationalism, makes a similar concession when he interprets his departure from Ireland as an attempt to forge a conscience for his race.

Joyce did not invent the incidents that conclude his story, the second honeymoon of Gabriel and Gretta which ends so badly. His method of composition was very like T. S. Eliot's, the imaginative absorption of stray material. The method did not please Joyce very much because he considered it not imaginative enough, but it was the only way he could work. He borrowed the ending for 'The Dead' from another book. In that book a bridal couple receive, on their wedding night, a message that a young woman whom the husband jilted has just committed suicide. The news holds them apart, she asks him not to kiss her, and both are tormented by remorse. The wife, her marriage unconsum-mated, falls off at last to sleep, and her husband goes to the window and looks out at 'the melancholy greyness of the dawn.' For the first time he recognizes, with the force of a revelation, that his life is a failure, and that his wife lacks the passion of the girl who has killed herself. He resolves that, since he is not worthy of any more momentous career, he will try at least to make her happy. Here surely is the situa-tion that Joyce so adroitly recomposed. The dead lover who comes between the lovers, the sense of the husband's failure, the acceptance of mediocrity, the resolve to be at all events sympathetic, all come from the other book. But Joyce transforms them. For example, he allows Gretta to kiss her husband, but without desire, and rarefies the situation by having it arise not from a suicide but from a memory of young love. The book Joyce was borrowing from was one that nobody reads any more, George Moore's *Vain Fortune*; but Joyce read it,* and in his youthful essay, 'The Day of the Rabblement,' overpraised it as 'fine, original work.' 21

Moore said nothing about snow, however. No one can know how Joyce conceived the joining of Gabriel's final experience with the snow. But his fondness for a background of this kind is also illustrated by his use of the fireplace in 'Ivy Day,' of the streetlamps in 'Two Gallants,' and of the river in *Finnegans Wake*. It does not seem that the snow can be death, as so many have said, for it falls on living and dead alike, and for death to fall on the dead is a simple redundancy of which Joyce would not have been guilty. For snow to be 'general all over Ireland' is of course unusual in that country. The fine description: 'It was falling on every part of the dark central plain, on the treeless hills, falling softly upon the Bog of Allen and, farther westward, softly falling into the dark mutinous Shannon waves,' is probably borrowed by Joyce from a famous simile in the twelfth book of the Iliad, which Thoreau translates: 22 'The snowflakes fall thick and fast on a winter's day. The winds are lulled, and the snow falls incessant, covering the tops of the mountains, and the hills, and the plains where the lotus-tree grows, and the cultivated fields, and they are falling by the inlets and shores of the foaming sea, but are silently dissolved by the waves.' But Homer was simply describing the thickness of the arrows in the battle of the Greeks and Trojans; and while Joyce seems to copy his topographical details, he uses the image here chiefly for a similar sense of crowding and quiet pressure. Where Homer speaks of the waves silently dissolving the snow, Joyce adds the final detail of 'the mutinous Shannon waves' which suggests the 'Furey' quality of the west. The snow that falls upon Gabriel, Gretta, and Michael Furey, upon the Misses Morkan, upon the dead singers and the living, is mutuality, a sense of their connection with each other, a sense that none has his being alone. The partygoers prefer dead singers to living ones, the wife prefers a dead lover to a live lover.

The snow does not stand alone in the story. It is part of the complex imagery that includes heat and cold air, fire, and rain, as well as snow.

---

* He evidently refreshed his memory of it when writing 'The Dead,' for his copy of *Vain Fortune*, now at Yale, bears the date 'March 1907.'

The relations of these are not simple. During the party the living people, their festivities, and all human society seem contrasted with the cold outside, as in the warmth of Gabriel's hand on the cold pane. But this warmth is felt by Gabriel as stuffy and confining, and the cold outside is repeatedly connected with what is fragrant and fresh. The cold, in this sense of piercing intensity, culminates in the picture of Michael Furey in the rain and darkness of the Galway night.

Another warmth is involved in 'The Dead.' In Gabriel's memory of his own love for Gretta, he recalls incidents in his love's history as stars, burning with pure and distant intensity, and recalls moments of his passion for her as having the fire of stars. The irony of this image is that the sharp and beautiful experience was, though he has not known it until this night, incomplete. There is a telling metaphor: he remembers a moment of happiness, standing with Gretta in the cold, looking in through a window at a man making bottles in a roaring furnace, and suddenly calling out to the man, 'Is the fire hot?' The question sums up his naïve deprivation; if the man at the furnace had heard the question, his answer, thinks Gabriel, might have been rude; so the revelation on this night is rude to Gabriel's whole being. On this night he acknowledges that love must be a feeling which he has never fully had.

Gabriel is not utterly deprived. Throughout the story there is affection for this man who, without the sharpest, most passionate perceptions, is yet generous and considerate. The intense and the moderate can meet; intensity bursts out and declines, and the moderated can admire and pity it, and share the fate that moves both types of mankind towards age and death. The furthest point of love of which Gabriel is capable is past. Furey's passion is past because of his sudden death. Gretta is perhaps the most pitiful, in that knowing Furey's passion, and being of his kind, she does not die but lives to wane in Gabriel's way; on this night she too is fatigued, not beautiful, her clothes lie crumpled beside her. The snow seems to share in this decline; viewed from inside at the party, it is desirable, unattainable, just as at his first knowledge of Michael Furey, Gabriel envies him. At the end as the partygoers walk to the cab the snow is slushy and in patches, and then, seen from the window of the hotel room, it belongs to all men, it is general, mutual. Under its canopy, all human beings, whatever their degrees of intensity, fall into union. The mutuality is that all men feel and lose feeling, all interact, all warrant the sympathy that Gabriel now extends to Furey, to Gretta, to himself, even to old Aunt Julia.

In its lyrical, melancholy acceptance of all that life and death offer, 'The Dead' is a linchpin in Joyce's work. There is that basic situation of cuckoldry, real or putative, which is to be found throughout. There is the special Joycean collation of specific detail raised to rhythmical intensity. The final purport of the story, the mutual dependency of living and dead, is something that he meditated a good deal from his early youth. He had expressed it first in his essay on Mangan in 1902, when he spoke already of the union in the great memory of death along with life; [23] even then he had begun to learn like Gabriel that we are all Romes, our new edifices reared beside, and even joined with, ancient monuments. In *Dubliners* he developed this idea. The interrelationship of dead and living is the theme of the first story in *Dubliners* as well as of the last; it is also the theme of 'A Painful Case,' but an even closer parallel to 'The Dead' is the story, 'Ivy Day in the Committee Room.' This was in one sense an answer to his university friends who mocked his remark that death is the most beautiful form of life by saying that absence is the highest form of presence. Joyce did not think either idea absurd. What binds 'Ivy Day' to 'The Dead' is that in both stories the central agitation derives from a character who never appears, who is dead, absent. Joyce wrote Stanislaus that Anatole France had given him the idea for both stories.[24] There may be other sources in France's works, but a possible one is 'The Procurator of Judaea.' In it Pontius Pilate reminisces with a friend about the days when he was procurator in Judaea, and describes the events of his time with Roman reason, calm, and elegance. Never once does he, or his friend, mention the person we expect him to discuss, the founder of Christianity, until at the end the friend asks if Pontius Pilate happens to remember someone of the name of Jesus, from Nazareth, and the veteran administrator replies, 'Jesus? Jesus of Nazareth? I cannot call him to mind.' The story is overshadowed by the person whom Pilate does not recall; without him the story would not exist. Joyce uses a similar method in 'Ivy Day' with Parnell and in 'The Dead' with Michael Furey.

In *Ulysses* the climactic episode, *Circe,* whirls to a sepulchral close in the same juxtaposition of living and dead, the ghost of his mother confronting Stephen, and the ghost of his son confronting Bloom. But Joyce's greatest triumph in asserting the intimacy of living and dead was to be the close of *Finnegans Wake.* Here Anna Livia Plurabelle, the river of life, flows toward the sea, which is death; the fresh water passes into the salt, a bitter ending. Yet it is also a return to her father, the sea, that produces the cloud which makes the river, and her father is also her husband, to whom she gives herself as a bride to her groom. Anna Livia is going back to her father, as Gabriel journeys westward in feeling to the roots of his fatherland; like him, she is sad and weary. To him the Shannon waves are dark and mutinous, and to her the sea is cold and mad. In *Finnegans Wake* Anna Livia's union is not only with love but with death; like Gabriel she seems to swoon away.*

That Joyce at the age of twenty-five and -six should have written this story ought not to seem odd. Young writers reach their greatest eloquence in dwelling upon the horrors of middle age and what follows it. But beyond this proclivity which he shared with others, Joyce had a special reason for writing the story of 'The Dead' in 1906 and 1907. In his own mind he had thoroughly justified his flight from Ireland, but he had not decided the question of where he would fly *to*. In Trieste and Rome he had learned what he had unlearned in Dublin, to be a Dubliner. As he had written his brother from Rome with some astonishment, he felt humiliated when anyone attacked his 'impoverished country.' [25] 'The Dead' is his first song of exile.

* See also pp. 724-6.

1907–1909

Perhaps you feel that some new thing is gathering in my brain. . . .

—*Exiles* (533 [373])

DURING Joyce's early years on the continent he demonstrated a remarkable capacity to fall from every slight foothold, to teeter over every available precipice. Stanislaus, like Joyce's friends in Dublin, may be pardoned for supposing that each debacle was the beginning of the end. No artist ever inspired gloomier predictions from his associates than Joyce did. The wonder was that each time he contrived, with little effort, to fall on his feet.*

His trip back to Trieste could scarcely have been less auspicious. There was no job awaiting him in Trieste as the year before there had been one in Rome; his brother had made clear that Joyce was neither needed nor wanted in the Scuola Berlitz, that Artifoni would not help him, that he himself was about to explode with rage over the constant demands for money. Joyce does not seem to have given these difficulties a thought. He no doubt knew he could get round both Artifoni and Stanislaus. But also, his life was charmed; he did not really believe in the poverty in which he dwelt. He could be as gloomy about his prospects as Stanislaus, then suddenly stretch out a weak hand and recover irresistibly ground he had never surely held.

One of these homely miracles took place in Trieste. On March 7 Stanislaus, alerted by two last-minute telegrams [1] that his brother was returning to Trieste by the evening train instead of going to Marseilles or some other improbable port, went to the station to meet him.[2] The sober Stanislaus looked over the returning pilgrims; James, not so sober, had 1 lira (20 cents or 10 pence) in his pocket; a year and a half before,

---

* The predominant characteristic of Stephen Dedalus, as Bloom notes, is 'Confidence in himself, and equal and opposite power of abandonment and recuperation.' *Ulysses* (657 [634]).

when Stanislaus arrived in Trieste, James had 1 centesimo. Like Shem Joyce could say, 'We're spluched. Do something. Fireless.'[3] 'What do you mean to do?' Stanislaus asked. His brother replied, 'To give lessons.' Stanislaus repeated the arguments he had put forward in his letters, and added that with summer coming no one would want lessons. Joyce laughed and replied, 'Well, then, I have you.'[4] Yet if there had been no Stanislaus, Joyce would doubtless have invented one.

Almost at once Joyce began to show that his brother had too little faith in his dexterity. It was true that he owed Francini money, but Francini kindly took him into his house for a few days notwithstanding. It was true that Artifoni had no need for a second English teacher; on the other hand, he did not want Joyce entering into competition with him, and he was particularly reluctant to lose such prominent pupils as Count Sordina, Baron Ralli, and Roberto Prezioso, who were devoted to Joyce. He therefore thought the matter over again, and offered Joyce fifteen crowns (12/6) a week for six hours' teaching.[5] Joyce agreed at once; the work was more palatable than that at the bank, the schedule was easy, Artifoni could never resist an importunate borrower. That the job was badly paid and precarious did not ruffle him.

All Joyce's old pupils were pleased to see him again, and Prezioso was especially friendly. He had hired Francini as a reporter for *Il Piccolo della Sera* the previous June,[6] and it occurred to him now to commission Joyce to do a series of articles on the evils of empire as found in Ireland. The *Piccolo's* readers could be depended upon to see the parallel with the evils of empire as found in Trieste. 'I will pay you at a higher rate than other contributors,' he told Joyce, 'for two reasons, first, because you are writing in a foreign language, and second, because you need money.'[7] Joyce at once set to work, happy to be able to demonstrate the elegance of his Italian. He wrote the first article on March 22, the second on May 19, and the third on September 16. Prezioso asked the novelist Silvio Benco to go over the articles for possible errors; Benco found Joyce's language a bit hard and cautious, but still expressive and precise. He made a few corrections but when Joyce contradicted him on one point, and proved to be right, Benco withdrew.[8]

Joyce was himself well content with the result, and remarked to Stanislaus, 'I may not be the Jesus Christ I once fondly imagined myself, but I think I must have a talent for journalism.'[9] The text of these curious articles[10] might be Stephen's assertion at the beginning of *Ulysses* that as an Irishman he serves two masters, an English and an Italian.[11] Their force as Irish propaganda is, however, considerably diminished by Joyce's reservations about his own people. The first two articles have as much to say against them as against the British empire and the Vatican; only the third treats them sympathetically, as if Joyce had succumbed to his nation at last.

Joyce focused the first article, '*Il Fenianismo*,' on the death in Dublin on St. Patrick's Day of John O'Leary. Like Yeats, Joyce sees the old man's death as the end of an era of heroic though abortive violence:

> Romantic Ireland's dead and gone;
> It's with O'Leary in the grave.[12]

But his main theme is not that the Fenians were heroic but that they were always betraying each other. Surveying the history of the Fenian movement, he notes approvingly that James Stephens had organized it into small cells, a plan 'eminently fitted to the Irish character because it reduces to a minimum the possibility of betrayal.'[13] 'In Ireland, at the proper moment, an informer always appears.'[14] Joyce predicted that O'Leary's funeral would be marked with great pomp, 'because the Irish, even though they break the hearts of those who sacrifice their lives for their native land, never fail to show great respect for the dead.'[15] This final sentence of the first article is echoed by that of the second, where Joyce, after attacking the Irish Parliamentarians for seeking their own fortunes rather than their country's, concludes: 'They have given proof of their altruism only in 1891, when they sold their leader, Parnell, to the pharisaical conscience of the English Non-conformists without exacting the thirty pieces of silver.'[16]

Economic or intellectual despair has caused a mass emigration. The thought of this enables Joyce to make his sharpest thrusts against the Church. His Roman sojourn had made him more bitter than ever towards the Vatican, and, as Francini Bruni reports, he shocked his pupils by saying: 'I like Papal Rome because it makes me think of that pig of a pope, Alexander VI, in the arms of his mistress and daughter Lucrezia Borgia, and of Julius II, who built his tomb during his lifetime, and of Leo X and Clement VI, two popes who besides being great rakes were great friends of Martin Luther. I can easily understand why Ibsen felt uncomfortable in that city.'[17] The wealth of the Church in Rome offended him, but that of the Church in Ireland offended him more:

And almost as if to set in relief this depopulation there is a long parade of churches, cathedrals, convents, monasteries, and seminaries to tend to the spiritual needs of those who have been unable to find courage or money enough to undertake the voyage from Queenstown to New York. Ireland, weighed down by multiple duties, has fulfilled what has hitherto been considered an impossible task—serving both God and Mammon, letting herself be milked by England and yet increasing Peter's pence. . . .[18]

The real sovereign of Ireland, Joyce declared in his third article, is the Pope; and he takes pleasure in pointing out that another pope, Adrian IV, gave Ireland ('in a burst of generosity') [19] to Henry II of England, and that the modern papacy is as deaf to the Irish cries for help as the medieval papacy was:

> Already weakened by their long journey, the cries are nearly spent when they arrive at the bronze door. The messengers of the people who never in the past have renounced the Holy See, the only Catholic people to whom faith also means the exercise of faith, are rejected in favor of messengers of a monarch, descended from apostates, who solemnly apostatized himself on the day of his coronation, declaring in the presence of his nobles and commons that the rites of the Roman Catholic Church are 'superstition and idolatry.' [20]

Although Joyce had himself left the Church, he continued to denounce all his life the deviousness of Papal policy, which incongruously preferred to conciliate Edward VII rather than to take care of a people of proven Catholic loyalty.

In his second article, 'Home Rule Comes of Age,' Joyce gave a surprisingly detailed history of home rule legislation and of the emasculated bill then being considered by the House of Lords. He regarded Gladstone as a hypocrite who pretended an interest in the problem only because he knew that the Lords would reject the Commons' bill. Neither the Liberal Party nor the English Catholics could be trusted; they were as unreliable as the Irish Parliamentarians. As he had said earlier to Stanislaus but now declared publicly, the real hope lay in Griffith's Sinn Fein movement, with its policy of economic resistance and passive disloyalty to British rule. The boycott was the one weapon of which Joyce thoroughly approved, especially since it was of Irish manufacture.

The third article, 'Ireland at the Bar,' Joyce wrote four months after he had written his previous article, and its tone is quite different.* Never more Irish than when he attacked his country for attacking itself, he could not help now invoking its special pathos in the face of English oppression. The new article was inspired by the English newspapers' denunciations of some recent acts of agrarian terrorism in Ireland. Joyce illustrated the inarticulate struggle of his people by recounting the murder trial 'some years ago' (actually in 1882, the year of his birth) of Myles Joyce. This old man spoke nothing but Irish, and tried desperately to defend his innocence in that language before an uncom-

---

* He had just written 'The Dead' in the same mood of tenderness. See p. 263 and p. 274.

prehending judge and jury, and with an interpreter who made no attempt to render his story fairly. 'The figure of this dumbfounded old man, a remnant of a civilisation not ours, deaf and dumb before his judge, is a symbol of the Irish nation at the bar of public opinion.' [21] The rare agrarian crimes must be understood as acts of desperation; Ireland, whatever the British journalists might say, was not a country of louts and savages. To find brutality one should look not to Irish terrorism but to British mistreatment of Irishmen and (an odd charge in this context) of English cattle. On this last point, Joyce rather irrelevantly offered a number of instances worthy of Mr. Bloom, that animal lover, or of Stephen Dedalus, 'bullockbefriending bard.' [22] The articles demonstrate that the Citizen in *Ulysses*, who windily discusses the plight of cattle in terms of Irish glories and English injustices, is an aspect of Joyce's mind as well as the butt of his satire. Joyce held tenaciously to the character of the exile, punishing himself and his country, full of distrust and nostalgia for her.

His articles brought him a certain réclame in Trieste. Shortly before the first one appeared, his pupil Dr. Attilio Tamaro, later the author of a nationalistic history of Trieste, gave him another opportunity. Would Joyce be willing to present a series of three public lectures on Ireland at the Università del Popolo? Joyce agreed at once, and prepared his lectures carefully.[23] The first, on April 27, 1907, was 'Ireland, Island of Saints and Sages.' Francini, who also lectured at the evening university, advised him to speak extempore, but Joyce, not wanting to risk mistakes, wrote everything out.[24]

In this first lecture Joyce was less ironic than might be expected. Its point was that Ireland had once deserved the name of Island of Saints and Sages—and a good deal of evidence, only occasionally inaccurate, is marshalled as proof—but had deteriorated monstrously under British rule. At moments his eloquence becomes bombastic:

The economic and intellectual conditions that prevail . . . do not permit the development of individuality. The soul of the country is weakened by centuries of useless struggle and broken treaties, and individual initiative is paralyzed by the influence and admonitions of the church, while its body is manacled by the police, the tax office, and the garrison. No one who has any self-respect stays in Ireland, but flees afar as though from a country that has undergone the visitation of an angered Jove.[25]

The priest and the king would have to be shaken off, but Joyce was not sanguine. As for the first, he commented sardonically, 'In time, perhaps there will be a gradual reawakening of the Irish conscience, and perhaps four or five centuries after the Diet of Worms, we shall see an

Irish monk throw away his frock, run off with some nun, and proclaim in a loud voice the end of the coherent absurdity that was Catholicism and the beginning of the incoherent absurdity that is Protestantism.' * [26] He had no immediate hopes for supplanting the king either: 'Ireland has already had enough equivocations and misunderstandings. If she wants to put on the play that we have waited for so long, this time let it be whole, and complete, and definitive. But our advice to the Irish producers is the same as that our fathers gave them not so long ago—hurry up! I am sure that I, at least, will never see that curtain go up, because I will have already gone home on the last train.' These sentences ended his first lecture on a note of skepticism rather than of nationalism. By Italian standards Joyce's delivery was rather cool and wanting in vivacity, but the cultivated audience, composed largely of his pupils and Stanislaus's, received the lecture with applause. Artifoni was delighted because of the credit it brought the school.

The second lecture, given a week or two later, was 'James Clarence Mangan,' and the third, which has not survived, 'The Irish Literary Renaissance.' The Mangan lecture was based, economically enough, upon Joyce's University College lecture of five years before, but wrestled with Mangan's limitations which five years before had been glossed over. Joyce now conceded that Mangan had not sufficiently freed himself from 'the idols without and within.' [27] Mangan no longer seemed to him a great poet, but a great symbolic figure rather, who enshrined in his verse the limitations, as well as the griefs and aspirations, of his people. Mangan belonged, however, to Ireland's past, not its present, and Joyce clearly dissociated his own personality from Mangan's fainting rhythms.

The articulation, in lectures and articles, of his disconsolateness about Ireland helped Joyce to maintain his ties there. One breach he was happy to begin mending was that with his father. John Joyce was still displeased by the elopement, but in a forgiving mood, he had written his son in Rome to ask him for a pound at Christmas time. James had no pounds, but got Stanislaus to send one to Rome so he might remail it to Dublin as his own gift.[28] He followed this gesture with a letter of February 9 to his father, written in his character of bank clerk: 'I have a great horror lest you should think, that now that I have gained some kind of a position for myself, I wish to hear no more of you. . . . On the contrary I assure you, if you will show me what I can do or get others to do I shall do my best to give the ball another kick.' [29] John

* Stephen Dedalus says in *A Portrait* (514 [359]), 'What kind of liberation would that be to forsake an absurdity which is logical and coherent and to embrace one which is illogical and incoherent?'

Joyce was silent for a time (during which his son lost 'some kind of a position'), but on April 24 wrote him for the first time about the dejection which Joyce's elopement had caused in him: 'I need not tell *you* how much your incredible mistake affected my already well crushed feelings, but then maturer thought took more the form of pity than anger, when I saw a life of promise crossed and a future that might have been brilliant blasted in one breath.'[30] The rest of the letter was predictably financial, and Joyce scraped together an occasional pound to confirm his filial piety. Smoothing down his father was exceedingly important to him. He even tried to arrange a visit home by offering to report the Dublin Exposition for the *Corriere della Sera* of Milan, but was turned down.[31]

Meanwhile Joyce at last published a book, though with considerable misgivings. Elkin Mathews sent him the page proofs of *Chamber Music* to Rome, and they were forwarded to Trieste at the end of March. Joyce corrected and returned them, then became suddenly queasy about the poems. At the beginning of April he informed his brother one evening that he was on his way to the post office to cable Mathews not to publish the book. Stanislaus, who liked it, pleaded with him to reconsider, and when James was adamant, walked with him to the Piazza delle Poste, arguing against such folly. James said, 'All that kind of thing is false.' He was no love 'pote'; he had never known any love except the love of God. He did not wish to stand behind his own insincerity and fakery. It was true that some of the 'pomes' had introduced an ironic note into the 'feudal terminology' so as to make them modern, but this was not keen or sustained enough; essentially the poems were for lovers, and he was no lover. Stanislaus walked about the square with him until early morning, expostulating,[32] until at last he persuaded him to publish *Chamber Music* with all its dishonesty so that he might publish his other books with all their honesty. As so often, Stanislaus was sensible and practical, but James had cause to feel that *Chamber Music* was pale beside his other work.

True to his word, Arthur Symons wrote the first review when the book was published in early May. He said in the *Nation* that it was a book of pure poetry, free of schools, each poem an 'instant of "made eternity."' The poems were delicate and musical and had, too, an occasional 'sharp prose touch, as in Rochester, which gives a kind of malice to sentiment.'[33] He cited as an example:

> For elegant and antique phrase,
>   Dearest, my lips wax all too wise;
> Nor have I known a love whose praise
>   Our piping poets solemnize,

> Neither a love where may not be
> Ever so little falsity.

Symons was faithful to the precepts of the Rhymers' Club, but Joyce, while grateful, was more interested in what his fellow-Dubliners might say of the book. Almost none of them except Thomas Kettle, Arthur Clery, and someone who signed himself 'Mananan' said anything.[34] Kettle reviewed it in the *Freeman's Journal*, Clery much later in the *Leader* (under his old pseudonym of 'Chanel').[35] Though Joyce wrote letter to Kettle and Clery to thank them, he forgot two of the reviews when he said to Herbert Gorman that Kettle's article was for more than twenty years the first and last mention of him in any Dublin newspaper.[36]

Kettle's review was laudatory, though it had a slight edge to it that Joyce noticed at once. The book was pretty enough, but it denied much of the life Joyce had known in Ireland:

> Those who remember University College life of five years back will have many memories of Mr. Joyce. Wilful, fastidious, a lover of elfin paradoxes, he was for the men of his time the very embodiment of the literary spirit. . . . The inspiration of the book is almost entirely literary. There is no trace of the folklore, folk dialect, or even the national feeling that have coloured the work of practically every writer in contemporary Ireland. Neither is there any sense of that modern point of view which consumes all life in the language of problems. It is clear, delicate, distinguished playing, of the same kindred with harps, with wood birds, with Paul Verlaine.[37]

Kettle approved but with reservations; he was not entirely on the side of wood birds, nor, certainly, unconcerned with problems. Joyce kept this review in mind, and found its attitude suited his purposes perfectly seven years later when he was writing *Exiles*. There Robert Hand writes a leader for an Irish newspaper about the return of Richard Rowan to Ireland. Hand takes up the distinction Joyce made in his Italian writings between those who left Ireland for economic and those who left it for intellectual reasons. But some of the wording and all the ambiguity of this position were suggested by Kettle's review:

> Not the least vital of the problems which confront our country is the problem of her attitude towards those of her children who, having left her in her hour of need, have been called back to her now on the eve of her long awaited victory, to her whom in loneliness and exile they have at last learned to love. In exile, we have said, but here we must distinguish. There is an economic and there is a spiritual exile. There are those who left her to seek the bread by which men live and there are others, nay, her most favoured children, who left her to seek in other lands that food of the spirit

by which a nation of human beings is sustained in life. Those who recall the intellectual life of Dublin of a decade since will have many memories of Mr. Rowan. Something of that fierce indignation which lacerated the heart. . . .[38]

Joyce adapted the review to suit the author of *Dubliners* and *A Portrait of the Artist* instead of the author of *Chamber Music*, emphasizing Swift's indignation instead of Verlaine's delicacy and music. Yet in both authors invoked by Kettle and Hand he might have recognized the poles of his own character.

The publication of *Chamber Music* brought no financial change. Royalties were not to be paid until three hundred copies were sold, and by July 24, 1908, only 127 out of 507 were gone; by 1913 the number was still less than 200.[39] But the Irish musician G. Molyneux Palmer wrote Joyce in July to ask permission to set some of the lyrics to music, and Joyce slowly came to think better of them again. He liked Palmer's first settings and urged him to continue, adding a rare note of explanation: 'The central song is XIV after which the movement is all downwards until XXXIV which is vitally the end of the book. XXXV and XXXVI are tailpieces just as I and II are preludes.' [40]

He was nevertheless discontented again with his life in Trieste. Having failed to persuade the *Corriere della Sera* to send him to Dublin, he took an even less plausible notion into his head, and early in July wrote to the South Africa Colonisation Society for a position.[41] They had no vacancy. He would probably have moved somewhere, whether to Afghanistan or Timbuctoo, if all movement had not suddenly become impossible. The new disaster was rheumatic fever, which afflicted him in mid-July, possibly, he suspected, as an aftermath of his carefree nights in Roman and Triestine gutters.[42] He had to be put in the city hospital, and remained there into August. He was not fully recovered until well into September. Long afterwards he said that Nora had taken in washing to make ends meet, but Stanislaus reported, probably more accurately, that the burden of support shifted entirely to him and made the summer 'a hell' for him.[43] Artifoni came to offer his solicitude, and promised Joyce the Scuola Berlitz would pay the expenses of his illness. On the strength of this commitment Stanislaus borrowed heavily from the school, expecting the debt to be cancelled, but it was not.[44]

Some days after Joyce was hospitalized Nora's labor began, and she too went to the hospital. The baby was born on July 26 in the pauper ward, 'almost born on the street,' as she admitted later.[45] It was St. Anne's day, and so, since Anne was also the name of Nora's mother,[46] they added Anna to the first name of Lucia, the patron saint of eyesight, which Joyce had decided on earlier. When Nora left the

Ettore Schmitz (Italo Svevo) holding the manuscript of his novel
Senilità. (p. 280) *Courtesy of the
late Signora Livia Schmitz*

Signora Livia Schmitz (Svevo),
whom Joyce associated with Anna
Livia Plurabelle. (p. 572) *Courtesy
of the late Signora Livia Schmitz*

VII

James Joyce in Trieste, age
about 30. (Croessmann Collection) *Courtesy of the Southern
Illinois University Library*

Giorgio and Lucia Joyce in Trieste, about 1914.

Frantisek Schaurek and Eileen Joyce at their wedding in Trieste, April 12, 1915. (p. 396) *Courtesy of Cornell University Library*

VIII

Eva Joyce with Lucia, 1909, in Trieste. *Courtesy of Cornell University Library*

hospital she was given twenty crowns in charity.[47] This child was to affect Joyce's life much more deeply than he would have believed possible. But the immediate disruption was serious enough: the household was in turmoil, Joyce sick, Stanislaus surly, Nora weak and nursing, Lucia crying, Giorgio rambunctious.

By the time Joyce had recovered, Artifoni had leased the Scuola Berlitz to two of its employees, a French and a German teacher, and had also made over Stanislaus's debt to them, much to his indignation. Joyce decided at once that the new management would not suit him, and left the school without notice.[48] For several years he had meditated giving private lessons, and he now offered them at ten crowns a lesson ($2.00, 8/-). This was seven crowns more than Artifoni would have turned back to him. Stanislaus was strictly enjoined by the school from helping him in any way. One woman came to ask his brother's address, but Stanislaus replied that as a Berlitz employee he could not give it. She said, 'Very well, I'll get it anyway.' That night Stanislaus came home to find her taking a lesson from his brother. She said, 'You see, I told you I'd find him,' and Stanislaus replied, 'I'm glad you did.' [49] But during late September and October Joyce had only two or three lessons a week, so the family continued to incur new expenses while Stanislaus frantically tried to pay off the old debt.

Then Joyce had a new prospect, this time thanks to Oliver Gogarty. Gogarty had heard, on his return from New York to Dublin, that Joyce had rheumatic fever, and had sent him a pound, which however seems to have been intercepted by some Dublin member of that consistently needy family, perhaps Charles.[50] In the early autumn of 1907, Gogarty came to Vienna to complete his medical studies, and wrote Joyce that he had left the Dubliners 'at their priest-like task / Of self-pollution still.' On receiving a pleasant reply, he invited Joyce on December 1 to go to Athens and Venice with him, then invited him to visit him for a week in Vienna, and next proposed that Joyce settle in Vienna. There were three pupils awaiting him.[51] Joyce pondered this invitation more seriously than it deserved, but at last yielded to Stanislaus's objections and declined.[52] He agreed, however, to help Gogarty publish some of his unpublishable poems, which Gogarty alternately called *Ditties of No Tone* and *Cockcrows*. The correspondence came to an end early in January 1908 with an unsigned note from Gogarty:

> Spitalgasse.1.
> Vienna. IX.

Is there any reason why your Ashplant shall not be made the centre of the Collection in the 'National Joyce Museum, Cabra'?

I am going to Dresden; when I come back I will arrange with you
about the publication of my 'Cockcrows.'
Thanks for promising to see it through.[53]

Actually, Gogarty never published any of his pornographic verse, and
resented suggestions, whether they came from Joyce or others, that his
bawdry was more important than his lyric verse. Joyce disobliged him
nevertheless by publishing two stanzas of 'The Ballad of Joking Jesus'
in *Ulysses*.

As his strength returned at the beginning of September, Joyce returned eagerly to his own work. The period of his illness, which to
Stanislaus had seemed so abject, had actually been for James a time
to concentrate on what he wanted to do. During his illness and the
three months that followed, he plotted his literary life for the next
seven years. On September 6 he had almost completed 'The Dead' *; his
rheumatic fever probably helped him to see more clearly the ending
of the story in an atmosphere of fatigue, of weariness, of swooning.
On September 8 he informed Stanislaus that as soon as he had completed the story he would rewrite *Stephen Hero* completely. 'He told
me,' Stanislaus noted in his diary, 'he would omit all the first chapters
and begin with Stephen, whom he will call Daly, going to school and
that he would write the book in five chapters—long chapters.' The use
of the name Dedalus must have seemed for the moment too strange,
but it is hard to conceive of Joyce's hero with the name Daly. In the
plan for five chapters, however, Joyce had evidently hit upon the book's
final structure.†

By November 29 Joyce had finished revising his first chapter. He
continued to work at his novel until April 7, 1908, by which time he
had finished the third chapter. The book had an intensity and concentration it had not possessed before. Then he bogged down abruptly.
In any case, he confided to Stanislaus, it would never be published.
'What I write with the most lugubrious intentions would probably be
prosecuted in England as pornographical.' [54] He had only to generalize
to become sad, sighing on March 12, 'In my opinion the general comment on Renan's statement, "I thank God for this life, which I never
asked for," would be, "And if it were offered me again, I shouldn't
accept it." ' [55]

During the autumn of 1907 his old conception of Ulysses stirred
Joyce's mind again. On November 10 Stanislaus noted in his diary:
'Jim told me that he is going to expand his story "Ulysses" into a short

---

* He dictated the ending to Stanislaus a few days later.
† For an explanation of this, see pp. 306-9.

book and make a Dublin "Peer Gynt" of it. I think that some suggestions of mine put him in the way of making it important. As it happens
in one day, I suggested that he should make a comedy of it, but he
won't. It should be good. Jim says that he writes well because when
he writes his mind is as nearly normal as possible, that what he says
is worth listening to because he has an uncommon amount of good
sense at times. I think I have written this before. He repeats it very
often and appears pleased with this explanation of himself.' It is clear
that Joyce continued to feel that writing disengaged him from obsession. In what sense *Ulysses* was to be a *Peer Gynt* is not altogether
clear, except that the hero was to sample all aspects of Dublin life.
How he could be at once the clear-eyed Ulysses and the self-deceived
Peer Gynt is also unexplained. It is easier to understand another remark to Stanislaus that the book would depict an Irish Faust, heroic
and full of presumption. Probably Joyce already intended it to be in
part autobiographical, for some time later, on February 21, 1908, he
condemned Bourget's attempt at psychology in vehement language:
'Psychologist! What can a man know but what passes inside his own
head?' Stanislaus replied, 'Then the psychological novel is an absurdity,
you think? and the only novel is the egomaniac's? D'Annunzio's?' Joyce
replied, 'I said as much in my pamphlet' ['The Day of the Rabblement'].

Much of Joyce's conversation dwelt on drama rather than on fiction.
With the help of Francini, who could get free tickets because he wrote
for the *Piccolo della Sera,* he went to the theater as often as he could.
'The Italians have an immense genius for the theatre,' he remarked.
'On *life*'s stage they are the greatest actors in existence.' [56] He saw
Eleanora Duse at the end of February 1908, and compared this performance with her performance in *La Città Morta* in London in 1900,
full of admiration for both.[57] He went to see Ermete Zacconi play
Oswald in Ibsen's *Ghosts,* and when Oswald began to go mad, Joyce
writhed in pain in his seat and made wild gestures.[58] Afterwards he
said to Francini, 'Zacconi has drawn even more from Ibsen's drama
than is actually contained in it. It would be interesting to know what
Ibsen himself would think.' [59] When Zacconi played, in his '*verismo*'
style, the count in Turgenev's *Il Pane Altrui,* Joyce cried out in the
theater, after the scene of the old count in misery, '*Di questi artisti
nessuno se ne sogna da noi.*' * [60] By this time the Triestines were accustomed to his outbursts.

To Stanislaus he continued to disparage Shakespeare at Ibsen's expense. As he had objected to *Macbeth* at University College for its

* 'Nobody back home has any idea there are artists like these.'

improbabilities, now he took *Hamlet* to task. He had just seen Salvini play the part in Trieste when, on February 6, 1908, he complained of the play's gross dramatic blunders. 'He said,' wrote Stanislaus, 'that Ophelia's madness took all the force out of Hamlet's simulation, and that her love for her father, whom the audience have seen to be a paltry old imbecile, is a caricature of Hamlet's passion; and the evil in the King's character that accounts for Hamlet's hatred must be supposed for it is not dramatically explained.' Ibsen was much better, although perhaps lacking in variety; Joyce remarked on March 2, 1908, 'Ibsen has persisted in writing what was essentially the same drama over and over again. I suspect that Ibsen met the four or five characters whom he uses throughout his plays before he was twenty-five.' Like other great artists, Joyce tended to find in the works of other writers anticipations of his own spiritual history. So he remarked to Stanislaus on February 25, 1908, that Rosmer was more interesting than Rebecca.

The riot at the Abbey over Synge continued to confront his mind. After his initial pleasure at the embarrassment of Yeats and the others, he confided that he thought highly now of Synge and even said, with unwonted modesty, on May 5, 1907, that Synge's art 'is more original than my own.' On March 6 of the following year he reread *Riders to the Sea*, and got his friend and pupil, the lawyer Nicolò Vidacovich, to help him translate it into Italian.° ⁶¹ He wrote to the talented actor-manager, Alfredo Sainati, of the Italian Grand Guignol company, to interest him in it, and when Sainati replied favorably, got in touch with the Synge estate soon after Synge died in 1909. But the Synge heirs refused consent.

Other literary negotiations fared just as badly. The publication of *Chamber Music* did not help with *Dubliners;* Elkin Mathews rejected the second manuscript in November 1907, but said that he had mentioned it to Joseph Hone of Maunsel & Co., the Dublin publishers, and that Hone wished to read it. Though Joyce knew that his old acquaintance and creditor George Roberts was the managing director of this firm, and though Roberts had early in 1905 expressed interest in publishing Joyce, there seemed to be hope of a wider, less provincial audience if some English publisher would take the book. Joyce offered it to Hutchinson & Co., who told him not to bother sending it; Alston Rivers rejected it in February 1908, and Edward Arnold in July. In February 1908, Hone, who was giving Maunsel some of its financial

---

° In 1911 Joyce and Vidacovich translated Yeats's *The Countess Cathleen,* but had to give up their plans for production or publication because Yeats did not like the unrevised version of the play they had used. Joyce tried unsuccessfully to bring him around.

backing,* wrote asking formally to see the manuscript,[62] but Joyce still held it back. He did not send the manuscript to Maunsel until the following year.

For over a year now the Joyces had also had the domestic problem of finding a flat. They had stayed only a few days with Francini in 1907, then took some adjoining rooms, rather than a flat, at 1 via Santa Catarina, where Stanislaus, to save money, joined them. As usual, the living arrangements were a little squalid; to reach their own room James and Nora had to go through Stanislaus's. James found this arrangement particularly troublesome because it meant that, when he returned drunk, Stanislaus woke up to give him a tongue-lashing or even a beating. 'Do you want to go blind?' he would say. 'Do you want to go about with a little dog?'[63] Nora in the next room received him with the same disfavor. On February 6, when James started to go to a café, she cried out, 'Yes, go now and get drunk. That's all you're good for. Cosgrave told me you were mad. Faith I tell you I'll have the children baptized tomorrow.'[64] It was a singular but effective threat. His brother's vigilance, his wife's contemptuous abuse, and his own awareness that alcohol seemed to exacerbate the eye trouble which had begun to bother him after his rheumatic fever, made him on February 12, 1908, grandly renounce drinking.[65] This resolution was kept imperfectly: on one notable occasion, when the British fleet was in the harbor, Joyce was invited aboard a battleship and got magnificently unconscious.[66] But at the end of May he had an attack of iritis (inflammation of the iris) so bad that leeches were applied,[67] and this time he was terrified enough to stop drinking for some months.

In June he resolved to find a 'quarter,' a permanent flat, and one on the second floor at 8 via Scussa looked adequate. The first difficulty was to raise a guarantee of 600 crowns ($120, £25). One pupil, Ettore Schmitz, was willing to put up 200, but no more, and Nicolas Santos, a Greek fruit merchant with a buxom wife,† also would have helped. But Stanislaus had a rich pupil who had often volunteered to assist him, and now James prevailed upon his brother to borrow 400 crowns from this eligible source. They were ready to move when the landlady on the via S. Catarina refused to let them go until they paid their back rent, and threatened to confiscate their furniture. If they paid the back rent, they could not take the quarter. If they lost their furniture, they would have to buy more and could not afford to do that either.[68]

---

* It was said in Dublin of the distinguished biographer of Yeats and Moore, 'At first Hone had the money and Roberts the experience; a few years later their roles were reversed.'

† See p. 386.

While this intricate little disaster was in preparation, Nora, who was about three months pregnant, suffered a miscarriage on August 4. She did not much mind losing the third child, but Joyce carefully examined the foetus, 'whose truncated existence,' he said to Stanislaus, 'I am probably the only one to regret.' [69] This miscarriage helped to make Bloom's chief sorrow, in *Ulysses,* the death just after birth of his son Rudy.

The slack summer season, when almost no one wished to take English lessons, set Joyce to pondering more satisfactory methods of survival than teaching. As before these fancies came so thick and fast that Stanislaus complained his brother had 'too many futures.' [70] On June 28, 1908, Joyce announced a new plan to become a commission agent for Irish tweeds, and wrote two letters at once. On July 5 he considered training his voice again. On July 14 he thought of entering for a civil service appointment, and then four days later approved Stanislaus's suggestion that he try for the three-year scholarship in modern literature at the Royal University. On August 25 he announced that the following April he would try for a teaching job in Florence.[71] Meanwhile Stanislaus grimly noted in his diary for September 12 that he had saved his brother and Nora six times from starvation. On October 5 James's pace slowed a little, and Stanislaus found him stretched on the sofa, comfortably proclaiming 'that he had retired from public life.' 'For the present,' he said, 'I am going to devote my attention to getting rid of my rheumatism, having my voice trained, and fattening myself.' [72] He did in fact take some lessons from a second Triestine maestro, Romeo Bartoli, who was an expert in old music. But these lessons, like those with Sinico three years before, came to an end the next year, not however before he had sung at a concert in the quintet from *Die Meistersinger,* an opera he regarded as 'pretentious stuff.' [73]

There was one plan which came to something. Joyce decided to placate his father by sending Giorgio and Stanislaus back to Dublin during the summer of 1909. He began on December 8, 1908, with a letter to his sister Margaret (Poppie), who was still running the house at 44 Fontenoy Street:

Via S. Caterina 1, I°p°
Trieste (Austria)

Dear Poppie,

Thanks for sending on the music. I have seen your letter to Stannie and his reply which is enclosed with this. I have an idea which you will tell me if you like. I will send Georgie among you for six weeks or so next summer in charge of Stannie if you think such a proposal would have the effect desired. Neither he nor Stannie would be any expense as (if we can manage the thing at all) we shall pay all expenses of travelling and board with you. Perhaps he might be a good influence in your household and I fancy all of you would be glad to make his acquaintance. He could go about the end of July and come back to Trieste about the end of August or first of September. If you like the idea and think it likely to do good I shall write to Pappie myself.

I suppose you will think this a hare-brained idea like all the others I have had hitherto but if you walk round it for a quarter of an hour and look at it from all sides it will begin to look right enough.

I will send him gladly if that will make yiz all happy and loving. I told him I was going to, and he has been canvassing all the people in the house for a valise to put his clothes in and go to 'Dubirino.'

Thank you, I feel a little better of the rheumatism and am now more like a capital S than a capital Z. Hoping this will find you as it leaves me at present, thank God, I am, dear sister,

Your
Most Affectionate Brother
Jim [74]

8.12.08

Stanislaus, when James broached the idea to him, listened sympathetically, but rightly suspected that it would be Georgie's father, not his uncle, who would eventually accompany the little boy to Dublin.

In the autumn of 1908 the projected move to 8 via Vincenzo Scussa, failed at first to come off. Caught between two landladies, the old and the new, the Joyces stayed put at 1 via S. Catarina, but not before they had a nasty quarrel with Stanislaus. Joyce wanted his brother to delay repaying the 400 crowns he had borrowed from his pupil, but Stanislaus absolutely refused to violate his creditor's confidence in him by making any excuses. To James this was simply pigheadedness. He changed from cajoleries to jeers, at last suggested his brother leave. Stanislaus left in a rage and took a room at 27 via Nuova, on the fourth floor. Then James, quickly cooling off and aware he had gone too far, sought him out to say that he and Nora had made a mistake; [75] they were reconciled but remained in separate quarters. In March 1909, the move to via Scussa took place at last. Soon after, Stanislaus was distracted from family troubles when Artifoni asked him to serve as acting director of the Scuola Berlitz, the previous director having failed badly. The work load proved, however, very heavy, and the pay, while now up to four pounds a week, was not really compensatory. Stanislaus had sought apostasy, but believed he had found martyrdom. He itemized his grievances, yet he liked Trieste.

Since April 1908, Joyce had been unable to bring himself to do any writing. The first three chapters of the *Portrait* were written; they brought him as far as his burst of piety in his fifteenth year. The years that followed were more complicated, and he did not see his way clear to going on. In this discouraged state, early in 1909, one of his pupils gave him decisive support. This was Ettore Schmitz, the middle-aged manager of a company that made an anti-corrosive paint for ships' hulls. The formula was so successful that the paint was used all over Europe, and the company had factories in Trieste, Burano (Venice), Riga, and Deptford (London). To facilitate his dealings with the Deptford factory, Schmitz had decided in 1907 to improve his English by having Joyce, whom he called '*il mercante di gerundi*' [76] (gerund-purveyor), give him lessons.° These took place three times a week at the factory at Servola on the outskirts of Trieste, and Signora Schmitz began to learn English too. Late in 1907 Joyce brought along his story, 'The Dead,' which he had just completed, and read it to his pupils. Signora Schmitz was so moved by it that she went into the garden of their villa, which was near the factory, and gathered a bunch of flowers to present to Joyce.[77]

Prodded by Joyce's interest in literature, Schmitz diffidently confessed one day that he too had tried his hand at writing, and had even gone so far as to publish two novels. No one had noticed them; 'There is no unanimity so perfect as the unanimity of silence,' [78] he confided sadly. 'I could come to only one conclusion, that I was not a writer.' [79] The novels had been published ten years before under the *noms de plume* first of *Ettore Samigli,* then of *Italo Svevo,* the latter chosen to suggest Schmitz's Swabian and Italian origin and, as he said, 'out of pity for the one vowel surrounded by six consonants in the name Schmitz.' [80] Joyce glanced at the titles, *Una Vita* and *Senilità,* and brought them home with him. He remarked to Stanislaus that evening, 'Schmitz has given me these two novels of his to read. I wonder what kind of thing it is.' [81]

To his surprise he discovered that Schmitz had considerable ability. The gentle irony of his writing was not what he sought for himself, but it had its own unassuming power. The Triestine color of the books—the proper names and occasional dialect phrases—attracted him as much as they repelled purist Italian critics. He brought them back to Schmitz at the next lesson, and remarked with his usual assurance, 'Do you know that you are a neglected writer? There are passages in *Senilità* that even Anatole France could not have improved.' [82] He then quoted some of them to the amazed Schmitz, who forgot his lunch and accompanied Joyce half way back to the center of Trieste, talking excitedly

---

° It is not clear that these were always useful. Stanislaus Joyce says that when Schmitz asked Joyce the meaning of the line, 'And brass eternal slave to mortal rage,' Joyce replied, 'I don't know what it means, but I suppose Shakespeare was thinking of German bands.' [83]

of his literary aims.[84] As a result he began to write again more seriously than he had for some years.

Schmitz, who was nineteen years older than Joyce, had concealed his talent under amiability. His manner, simple and cordial, was the same with his workers as it was with his friends. At parties he was quickly surrounded, and turned his rather wistful cleverness against himself to the entertainment of the company. He said once, for example, 'There are three things I always forget: names, faces, and—the third I can't remember.'[85] He was married to Livia Veneziani, a charming, wealthy woman. Signora Schmitz was not Jewish; Schmitz was, although he had long since lost his interest in Judaism as a religion. In a few years he became, with humorous reluctance,[86] one of Joyce's chief sources for the Jewish lore of *Ulysses*.

A record has survived of Schmitz's impressions of his young teacher because Joyce asked him to write a description of him as one of his assignments. Schmitz did so with great skill if imperfect English:

Mr. James Joyce described by his faithful pupil Ettore Schmitz.

When I see him walking on the streets I always think that he is enjoying a leisure a full leisure. Nobody is awaiting him and he does not want to reach an aim or to meet anybody. No! He walks in order to be left to himself. He does also not walk for health. He walks because he is not stopped by anything. I imagine that if he would find his way barred by a high and big wall he would not be shocked at the least. He would change direction and if the new direction would also prove not to be clear he would change it again and walk on his hands shaken only by the natural movement of the whole body, his legs working without any effort to lengthen or to fasten [quicken] his steps. No! His step is really his and of nobody else and cannot be lengthened or made faster. His whole body in quiet is that of a sportsman. If moved [that is, in movement] that of a child weakened by the great love of his parents. I know that life has not been a parent of that kind for him. It could have been worst and all the same Mr. James Joyce would have kept his appearance of a man who considers things as points breaking the light for his amusement. He wears glasses and really he uses them without interruption from the early (?) morning until late in the night when he wakes up. Perhaps he may see less than it is to suppose from his appearance but he looks like a being who moves in order to see. Surely he cannot fight and does not want to. He is going through life hoping not to meet bad men. I wish him heartily not to meet them.* [87]

---

* 'He went without saying that the cull disliked anything anyway approaching a plain straightforward standup or knockdown row and, as often as he was called in to umpire any octagonal argument among slangwhangers, the accomplished washout always used to rub shoulder with the last speaker and clasp shakers ... and agree to every word as soon as half uttered. ...' *Finnegans Wake* (174). Here Joyce mocks his own pacifism.

It was inevitable that, since Joyce had read Schmitz's work, Schmitz should have to read his. The three chapters of *A Portrait of the Artist* were duly produced, and Schmitz had to write a criticism of them. The letter he sent Joyce on February 8, 1909, roused his teacher from inertia:

Dear Mr. Joyce,

Really I do not believe of being authorised to tell you the author a resolute opinion about the novel which I could know only partially. I do not only allude to my want of competence but especially to the fact that when you stopped writing you were facing a very important development of Stephen's mind. I have had already a sample of what may be a change of this mind described by your pen. Indeed the development of Stephen's childish religion to a strong religion felt strongly and vigorously or better lived in all its particulars (after his sin) was so important that none other can be more so. I like very much your second and third chapters and I think you made a great mistake doubting whether you would find a reader who could take pleasure at the sermons of the third chapter. I have read them with a very strong feeling and I know in my little town a lot of people who would be certainly struck by the same feeling. Every word of these sermons acquires its artistic significance by the fact of their effect on poor Stephen's mind. At last the reader has a full knowledge of the education got by Stephen, it could not be fuller even if the two previous chapters had dealt especially with it. I object against the first chapter. I did so when I had read only it but I do so still more decidedly after having known the two others. I think that I have at last also discovered the reason why these two chapters are for me so beautiful while the first one which surely is of the same construction by the same writer who has surely not changed his ways, written evidently with the same artistic aims, fails to impress me as deeply. I think it deals with events deprived of importance and your rigid method of observation and description does not allow you to enrich a fact which is not rich of itself. You are obliged to write only about strong things. In your skilled hands they may become still stronger. I do not believe you can give the appearance of strength to things which are in themselves feeble, not important. I must say that if you had to write a whole novel with the only aim of description of everyday life without a problem which could affect strongly your own mind (you would not choose such a novel) you would be obliged to leave your method and find artificial colours to lend to the things the life they wanted in themselves.

Excuse me, dear Mr. Joyce, these remarks which prove perhaps only my conceitedness and believe me yours very truly,

Ettore Schmitz [88]

There was much in the letter that was wrong, and Joyce made no changes in Chapter I. On the other hand, Schmitz's approval of the daring introduction of the three sermons, and of Stephen's development in general, was a tribute to his powers that he valued. He announced to Stanislaus he was now going to continue his novel and would also send off *Dubliners*, flung aside for a year, to Maunsel & Co. in Dublin. He sent the book in April. With the same energy, he wrote to his father to make sure the trees at Clongowes were beeches.[89] Perhaps now he decided to cut out Gogarty (whom he had given the name of Goggins in *Stephen Hero*). The effect was to put on Stephen's frail shoulders the whole burden of heresy in the book, rather than, as he had intended earlier, to contrast the sensitive heretic with the insensitive one.[90] This latter effect he reserved now for *Ulysses*, the material for which was beginning to agglomerate.

The increased sharpness of his image of himself is reflected in an article on Oscar Wilde which Joyce wrote for the *Piccolo della Sera* on March 24, 1909. The first performance in Trieste of Strauss's *Salomé*, based on Wilde's play, with Bellincioni in the leading role, was the immediate occasion for the article.[91] But Joyce had been interested in Wilde for a long time, and even wrote to Robert Ross asking permission to translate *The Soul of Man under Socialism*.* [92] He took the occasion of his article to see in Wilde something of what he was coming to regard as his own personality, the miserable man who sings of joy. Behind the façade of Heliogabalus, the Roman emperor who proclaimed a Syrian divinity to be greater than the gods of the Romans, and who treated his crown as a plaything, was the man who was poor enough to pawn his medals. Only when he became 'court jester' to the English did Wilde acquire the wealth which he then gaily squandered. His fall was 'greeted by a howl of puritanical joy,' the more reprehensible because homosexuality † is fostered by the English educational system. Abandoned by his friends, hunted out by his enemies, Wilde became 'a dishonored exile' and the type of the 'betrayed artist,'[93] in fact, a Christlike figure. The artist pretends to be Lucifer but is really Jesus.

It was time for Joyce to go to Jerusalem, which for him was Dublin. What had happened to his own betrayers? What new crisis could be brought about by his return to the scene of their betrayals? These thoughts were in his mind all spring. He had, of course, forgotten his

---

* The permission was accorded on June 19, 1909, but events of the summer put it out of Joyce's head.

† Joyce avoids using this word in his article. Compare 'Wilde's love that dare not speak its name' in *Ulysses* (50 [46]).

earlier plan to send Stanislaus with Georgie; he must go in his own person. But then Stanislaus could not be asked to pay. In July Joyce suddenly secured payment in advance for a year's lessons from one of his pupils, and he and Georgie left at the end of the month. The next six weeks were to provide him with material central to two books, though he did not anticipate that the acquisition would be so painful. He plunged deeper than ever before into the black pool of Dublin.

<><><><><><><><><><><><><><><><><><><><><><><><><><><><><><><><><><><><>

1909

With what antagonistic sentiments were his subsequent reflections affected? Envy, jealousy, abnegation, equanimity.

—Ulysses (716-17 [692])

JOYCE, like Gabriel Conroy, was now making the journey westward, and thereby tacitly granting the hold over him of the past. He promised Nora to take Giorgio to visit her family in Galway, and in Dublin he anticipated encounters with all those whose lives had crossed his own, mutual testings in which he did not intend to come off the worse. He had also two practical objectives, to come to terms if possible with Maunsel & Co. over *Dubliners,* and to look into the possibility of a professorship at his old university, which was in the process of being reconstituted as the National, rather than the Royal, University. He was excited but not optimistic; he had mixed feelings about everything to do with Ireland except the necessity of his return to it.

The mailboat which carried him and Giorgio across the Irish Sea from Holyhead arrived at Kingstown pier on July 29. By coincidence Oliver Gogarty, now a surgeon, was waiting to meet someone on the same boat. Joyce avoided his eye, but noticed Gogarty had got fat.[1] He and Giorgio went to 44 Fontenoy Street, the Joyces' dingy house, and were greeted warmly and with some surprise. 'Where is Stannie?' they all asked.[2] John Joyce was delighted with his grandson, and full of advice to James to leave Trieste for some place less remote. Everyone thought him melancholy. Aunt Josephine told him he had 'lost all boyishness,' while his sister Eileen commented, with more flattery, that he was 'very foreign-looking.' All agreed on one point, that he was very thin.[3]

The sight of his son and grandson made John Joyce reconsider his old objections to his son's elopement. He took James for a walk into the country, and stopped with him at a village inn for a drink. There was a piano in the corner; John Joyce sat down at it and without comment began to sing. 'Did you recognize that?' he asked James, who

285

replied, 'Yes, of course, it's the aria sung by Alfredo's father in *Traviata*.' * John Joyce said nothing more, but his son knew that peace had been made.[4]

Joyce was not long in seeking out Vincent Cosgrave, who thought him (as Joyce reported to Stanislaus) 'in splendid health.' [5] Cosgrave quickly notified Gogarty that Joyce was in town, and on July 29 Gogarty sent him a note inviting him to lunch in an almost supplicatory fashion: 'Do come if you can or will. I am looking forward to see you with pleasure. There are many things I would like to discuss and a plan or two to divert you. You have not yet plumbed all the deeps of poetry. There is Broderick the Bard! Of whom more anon.' [6] He sent the note round with his man and his motor, and asked Joyce to come at once for a talk. Joyce was either out or made excuses, for his first meeting with Gogarty took place accidentally in Merrion Square. He remained convinced of Gogarty's basic cruelty and hostility, manifested, he felt, long ago by his threat to break Joyce's spirit by making him drink, and by his expulsion of Joyce from the tower. So in spite of the letters they had exchanged during the intervening years, he now passed Gogarty without speaking.[7]

Gogarty ran after him, took him by the arm, and made a speech which Joyce described to Stanislaus as long and confused. He looked Joyce over with a medical eye and said, 'Jaysus, man, you're in phthisis.' He insisted that Joyce come to his impressive house in Ely Place. 'He made me go in,' Joyce wrote his brother, 'and rambled on.' [8] Joyce walked to the bay window and looked out at the handsome garden. 'Is this your revenge?' he inquired. 'Revenge on what?' asked Gogarty, puzzled. 'The public, of course.' [9] The implication was that Gogarty had pretended to embrace conventions he had once scornfully combated.†
But Gogarty continued to try to win Joyce over. 'He invited me to go down to Enniskerry in his motor and lunch with him and his wife. I declined. I was very quiet and sober.' The sobriety was no doubt intended to remind Gogarty that Joyce's spirit was unbroken. 'He offered me grog, wine, coffee, tea, but I took nothing.' Joyce was unconcessive: 'To everything I said, "You have your life, leave me to mine." ' [10]

One source of Gogarty's goodwill was his anxiety over what Joyce intended to write about him. 'He fears the lancet of my art as I fear

---

* This aria is sung by Germont to his son when he discovers his son's beloved, Violetta, is dying: 'Don't torture me more . . . My soul is too eaten by remorse. Her words strike me like lightning. Ah, foolish old man! Only now I see the harm I did.'

† In *Exiles* (555 [389]) Richard recalls that he and Robert had once planned to make their house 'the hearth of a new life.'

that of his,' Joyce wrote in a notebook later,[11] and used the phrase in *Ulysses*. The Irish *fili* used to strike terror by threatening to write satirical verses about those who offended them, and Joyce's coolly announced intention of describing the tower episode put Gogarty in some trepidation. In the end Gogarty said, 'blushing'(as Joyce noticed), 'Well, do you really want me to go to hell and be damned?' Joyce replied, 'I bear you no ill will. I believe you have some points of good nature. You and I of six years ago are both dead. But I must write as I have felt.' Gogarty answered, 'I don't care a damn what you say of me so long as it is literature.' 'Do you mean that?' Joyce asked. He said, 'I do. Honest to Jaysus. Now will you shake hands with me at least?' Joyce replied, 'I will on that understanding,' and left. From the detailed account of this meeting that Joyce sent to Stanislaus it is clear that he relished it as the fulfillment of a daydream, in which he, the lofty, cool, untouchable hero, discomfited his suppliant enemy.

To walk in Dublin was to meet friends and enemies 'ineluctably.' * [12] So Joyce ran into Francis and Hannah Sheehy-Skeffington. Skeffington wanted to be friends, and seemed to have forgotten, as Joyce had not, his refusal to be friendly in October 1904. He pronounced Joyce 'somewhat blasé,' [13] but Hannah said he was not a bit changed. Joyce treated them coolly, as befitted an old debtor with an old creditor, and subsequently refused an invitation to dine with them. With the same casualness he encountered George Russell and W. K. Magee (Eglinton), who were 'very friendly.' Russell told him he looked like a 'man of business,' while Eglinton detected an 'ecclesiastical' air. Joyce called on Curran, but said he found him disposed to be unfriendly.[14] Byrne was away in Wicklow, but returned to Dublin when he received Joyce's note; they spent a pleasant afternoon together, Joyce proudly exhibiting Giorgio, in Byrne's house at 7 Eccles Street,[15] which becomes in *Ulysses* the Blooms' house. One friend Joyce did not at first succeed in meeting; this was Thomas Kettle, who was out of town, but promised to come back to see him. Joyce was fascinated to learn that Kettle was to marry Mary Sheehy on September 8, in a fitting conjunction of his principal Irish reviewer and his secret adolescent love.

He also opened negotiations with George Roberts, of Maunsel & Co., by standing him a drink while he himself, in a burst of abstinence, took lithia water. Roberts was annoyed that Joyce, who knew him well, should have approached the firm through Hone, whom he did not know at all, but gradually his manner thawed a little.[16] It was agreed

* In *Ulysses* Bloom struggles to avoid meeting Boylan, but keeps running into him all day long.

that he and Hone should meet with Joyce the following week and come
to a decision about *Dubliners*.

In such meetings Joyce passed the first week of his stay pleasantly
enough. Occasionally people cut him because of his rumored immorality, but he looked at them with hard contempt and passed on. He was
frequently with Cosgrave, for Cosgrave's life was consecrated to idleness, and he was free whenever Joyce was. Clever as always, he had
sunk deeper into a purposeless existence. Joyce, who had only one small
grudge against Cosgrave, of being abandoned by him during a scuffle
in Stephen's Green in 1904, did not realize that Cosgrave bore several
grudges against him. After all, Joyce had succeeded with Nora when
Cosgrave had failed with her, Joyce had put him into his book with
the unsavory name of Lynch in spite of his remonstrances, Joyce had
somehow made a go of things—or so it appeared—in Trieste, with
mistress, son, and job, while Cosgrave had got nowhere. Joyce's manner, more formal now than of old, and perhaps a little complacent,
probably irritated him also, and made him long to puncture it. On the
afternoon of August 6 he did so.[17]

Their conversation lit on Nora. Cosgrave reminded Joyce that Nora
used to go out only every other night because, she said, her duties at
the hotel kept her busy on the alternate evenings. Joyce had believed
her. But really, as Cosgrave felt free now to inform him, she had not
stayed in the hotel on those evenings, but had gone for walks in the
darkness along the river bank with another escort—himself.[18] Joyce
was struck with consternation. The inherent improbability of the tale,
his knowledge of Nora's innocence and fidelity, weighed nothing for
the moment beside the horrible possibility that she had betrayed him.
Cosgrave had struck deeper than he knew into Joyce's pride. The
Dublin visit had sharpened Joyce's feelings of ancient treachery, and
predisposed him to find it all-pervasive. He was to have his hero
Richard in *Exiles* say to the man who is supposedly his best friend,
'In the very core of my ignoble heart I longed to be betrayed by
you and by her . . . I longed for that passionately and ignobly, to be
dishonoured for ever in love and in lust, to be for ever a shameful
creature and to build up my soul again out of the ruins of its shame.'[19]
It must be said, however, that while Joyce shared something of Richard's
secret longing, he was mightily upset at the possibility of Nora's having
been faithless.

Within an hour he wrote Nora a letter heavy with accusation and
sorrow. All was over for him, he would not go to Galway, he would
leave Dublin at once without having completed anything he had
come for.

I have heard this only an hour ago from his lips. My eyes are full of tears, tears of sorrow and mortification. My heart is full of bitterness and despair. I can see nothing but your face as it was then raised to meet another's. O, Nora, pity me for what I suffer now. I shall cry for days. My faith in that face I loved is broken. O, Nora, Nora, have pity for my poor wretched love. I cannot call you any dear name because tonight I have learnt that the only being I believed in was not loyal to me.

O Nora is all to be over between us?

Write to me, Nora, for the sake of my dead love. I am tortured by memories.

Write to me, Nora, I loved you only: and you have broken my faith in you.

O, Nora, I am unhappy. I am crying for my poor unhappy love.

Write to me, Nora.

Jim

6 August 1909

That night he scarcely slept, and at dawn of the next day wrote her again in the same despair.

O Nora! Nora! Nora! I am speaking now to the girl I loved, who had red-brown hair and sauntered over to me and took me so easily into her arms and made me a man.*

I will leave for Trieste as soon as Stannie sends me the money, and then we can arrange what is best to do.

O, Nora, is there any hope yet of my happiness? Or is my life to be broken? They say here that I am in consumption.† If I could forget my books and my children and forget that the girl I loved was false to me and remember her only as I saw her with the eyes of my boyish love I would go out of life content.

How old and miserable I feel!

All that day he walked around Dublin in horror, and on the morning of August 8 he wrote Stanislaus without explanation that his business in Dublin was ended; he would leave, he said with less dignity, as soon as the money arrived for his fare. But he could no longer keep his secret to himself. That afternoon he went again to 7 Eccles Street to call on Byrne, a friend in whose good will and discretion he had once trusted completely. Byrne had never violated his confidence, and to him Joyce now bared his distress. Joyce 'wept and groaned and gesticulated in futile impotence' as he related Cosgrave's story. Byrne wrote later that he had never 'seen a human being more shattered.' [20] When Joyce had

---

* Bertha says of her husband in *Exiles* (614 [430]), 'I made him a man.'
† A tribulation based upon Gogarty's raillery.

finished, Byrne, a great discoverer too of conspiracies, rendered an un-
hesitating verdict. Cosgrave's brag was 'a blasted lie.' [21] It was probably
the second stage in a joint plot of Cosgrave and Gogarty to wreck
Joyce's life, he said; Gogarty having failed in his attempt at cajolery,
the pair had decided to try slander. Byrne's explanation could not have
been more fortunate: as long as there was treachery somewhere, and
especially if Gogarty was somehow involved in it, Joyce could be
persuaded of Nora's innocence. He began to feel ashamed of himself
and grateful to Byrne, whose trust in Nora and distrust of Cosgrave
were so much more appropriate than his own hysterical self-pity.

It was time to repent. Joyce's letters to Nora had made her feel
wretched and helpless. For several days she wrote nothing, then at last
she sent her husband a pathetic yet strangely dignified letter; [*] he had
already been too kind to the ignorant girl he had taken up with and
ought to separate himself from her. At the same time, in her distraction,
she showed Stanislaus the letters she had received, and found unexpected comfort and support from him. In 1904 he had seen Cosgrave
one night in a public house looking morose, and had asked him what
the trouble was. Cosgrave swore him to secrecy, then said he had been
trying to 'get inside' Joyce with Nora, and had just been rebuffed. Over
several years Stanislaus had darkly hinted to James that Cosgrave made
one among his betrayers, but kept his word and never said anything
explicit. Now he felt free to write him the truth, and he did so in his
downright, unimpeachable way. [22] The news of Cosgrave's humiliating
defeat at Nora's hands helped James to reassert his self-esteem. [†]

But even before these letters arrived, Byrne's advice had been decisive. Joyce continued with his business in Dublin. He informed
Stanislaus on August 17 that his meeting with Hone and Roberts had
been successful; they had agreed to publish *Dubliners* on better terms
than those Grant Richards had offered and then recalled. On August 19
he signed the contract. [23] His other piece of business was the application
for a professorship in Italian at National University. For this he needed
letters from the *Piccolo della Sera* and the Università Popolare to confirm his proficiency in Italian, and as early as August 10, while the
question of Nora's fidelity was supposedly still unresolved, he wrote
Stanislaus to obtain these for him. His friend Kettle promised to use

[*] It is lost, but can be partly reconstructed from a letter of his that refers to it. [24]
[†] Not long afterwards he was able, in a notebook, to dispose of Cosgrave's character with a description more hostile than effective: 'The long slender flattened skull
under his cap brought up the image of a hooded reptile: the eyes, too, were
reptilian in glint and gaze but with one human point, a tiny window of a shrivelled
soul, poignant and embittered.' [25]

his influence as a Member of Parliament to help, but on investigation
the position proved to be only a lectureship in commercial Italian at
£100 a year, with evening classes, and Joyce decided to apply instead
for an examinership in Italian,[26] the duties of which he could perform
in Trieste. He also energetically pursued his efforts to secure acting
rights for the translation of *Riders to the Sea* into Italian, but made no
headway with the Synge estate.

Confronted with Nora's silence and a keen sense of his own misbehavior towards her, his affection for her redoubled. On August 19
he wrote to her:

44 Fontenoy Street
Dublin

My darling

I am terribly upset that you haven't written. Are you ill?

I have spoken of this affair to an old friend of mine, Byrne, and he
took your part splendidly and says it is all a 'blasted lie.'

What a worthless fellow I am! But after this I will be worthy of you,
dearest.

I sent you three enormous bags of shell cocoa today. Tell me if you
get them right.

My sister Poppie goes away tomorrow.

Today I signed a contract for publication of *Dubliners*.

Excuse me to Stannie for not writing to him.

My sweet noble Nora, I ask you to forgive me for my contemptible
conduct but they maddened me, darling between them. We will defeat
their cowardly plot, love. Forgive me, sweetheart, won't you?

Just say a word to me, dearest, a word of denial and O I shall be
so transported with happiness!

Are you well, my darling? You are not fretting, are you? Don't read
over those horrible letters I wrote. I was out of my mind with rage at
the time.

I must be down now all the way to the G.P.O. to post this as the
post has gone here: it is after one at night.

Good night 'my precious.'

No man, I believe, can ever be worthy of a woman's love.

My darling, forgive me. I love you and this is why I was so maddened only to think of you and that common dishonourable wretch.

Nora darling, I apologise to you humbly. Take me again to your
arms. Make me worthy of you.

I will conquer yet and then you will be at my side.

Good night 'my dearest' 'my precious.' A whole life is opening for
us now. It has been a bitter experience and our love will now be
sweeter.

Give me your lips, my love.
   'My kiss will give peace now
   And quiet to your heart.
   Sleep on in peace now,
   O you unquiet heart'

                                      Jim
19.viii.09

Two days later, still struggling to express the change that had come
over him as a result of his great trial, he said:

Do you know what a pearl is and what an opal is? My soul when you
came sauntering to me first through those sweet summer evenings was
beautiful but with the pale passionless beauty of a pearl. Your love
has passed through me and now I feel my mind something like an opal,
that is, full of strange uncertain hues and colours, of warm lights and
quick shadows and of broken music. . . . I wrote today to your mother
but really I don't want to go. They will speak of you and of things
unknown to me. I dread to be shown even a postcard of you as a girl
for I shall think 'I did not know her then nor she me. When she
sauntered to mass in the morning she gave her long glances sometimes
to some boy along the road. To others but not to me.'

I will ask you, my darling, to be patient with me. I am absurdly
jealous of the past.

To his great delight Nora wrote him that she was reading *Chamber
Music.* He replied joyfully:

My dear little Nora

I *think* you are in love with me, are you not? I like to think of your
reading my verses (though it took you five years to find them out).
When I wrote them I was a strange lonely boy, walking about by myself at night and thinking that some day a girl would love me. But I
never could speak to the girls I used to meet at houses. Their false
manners checked me at once. Then you came to me. You were not in a
sense the girl for whom I had dreamed and written the verses you find
now so enchanting. She was perhaps (as I saw her in my imagination)
a girl fashioned into a curious grave beauty by the culture of generations before her the woman for whom I wrote poems like 'Gentle lady'
or 'Thou leanest to the shell of night.' But then I saw that the beauty
of your soul outshone that of my verses. There was something in you
higher than anything I had put into them. And so for this reason the
book of verses is for you. It holds the desire of my youth and you,
darling, were the fulfillment of that desire.

His suspicions allayed, his spirits lifted at last, the letters to Nora,
which had gone so quickly from the extreme of rage to that of peni-
tence, now became full of desire. On August 22 he wrote:

What can come between us now? We have suffered and been tried. Every veil of shame or diffidence seems to have fallen from us. Will we not see in each other's eyes the hours and hours of happiness that are waiting for us?

Adorn your body for me, dearest. Be beautiful and happy and loving and provoking, full of memories, full of cravings, when we meet. Do you remember the three adjectives I have used in *The Dead* in speaking of your body. They are these: 'musical and strange and perfumed.'

My jealousy is still mouldering in my heart. Your love for me must be fierce and violent to make me forget *utterly*.

At last he could feel, because of the outrageous trial to which they had been put, that Nora also regarded their relationship as something special and set apart, and with this conviction his injury healed.

Of course his ruminations soon became more complex. He began to think about the subject of constancy as he had once considered the subject of love, and applied a method of analysis which was, in his own term, jesuitical. As soon as he was reassured of her loyalty, he took pleasure in proving it, trying it, questioning it, allowing himself to have doubts of it. So he has Richard say at the end of *Exiles:* 'I have wounded my soul for you—a deep wound of doubt which can never be healed. I can never know, never in this world. I do not wish to know or to believe. I do not care. It is not in the darkness of belief that I desire you. But in restless living wounding doubt. To hold you by no bonds, even of love, to be united with you in body and soul in utter nakedness.' [27] Here Joyce seems to be returning to his old difficulty of deciding what to be in love is, but now he resolves it, for Richard at any rate, by urging that his emotion for Bertha, instead of being as he once feared less than love, was more than love, a naked union of body and soul.

Apart from his own troubles, Joyce shared briefly those of his family in Dublin. His sister Margaret, after six years of running the house, was about to leave 44 Fontenoy Street to become a Sister of Mercy in a New Zealand convent, and her departure took place during her brother's visit.[28] Charles had left the house the year before to make an unhappy marriage. Still with John Joyce were the five sisters May, Eileen, Eva, Florence, and Mabel. Joyce felt a burst of pity for them and resolved to do something. It was clear he could not do much, but he arranged to have Eileen, whose voice was fine but undeveloped, take singing lessons [29]—to be paid for jointly by him and Stanislaus; and he decided to bring one sister back to Trieste with him. At first it was to be Mabel, but Margaret quietly decided it should be Eva, who was more religious and might have a beneficial influence on her brother's impiety.[30] Stanislaus, informed of the new plan, made his usual reasonable objections, but James pushed them aside. They would need help in the house, and Eva would save them that expense. Before they left he would have her tonsils removed, because they had affected her speech.[31] Stanislaus reluctantly submitted to his brother's generous impulse, and made further efforts to raise the considerable sum needed to bring the lot of them home. To do so he had to be paid off by Artifoni, but Artifoni was in no hurry to oblige him because Stanislaus had given notice that he, too, was leaving the school to teach privately.

Delayed by Artifoni's pretexts, Joyce busied himself in Dublin with his usual energy. Caruso was in town for a concert, and Joyce offered to interview the singer in Italian; but all three Dublin newspapers were disinclined. A better idea was to write an article for the *Piccolo della Sera* on the première of Shaw's *The Shewing-Up of Blanco Posnet* at the Abbey Theatre. The play had been banned in England, but Yeats and Lady Gregory had taken advantage of the technicality that the Lord Chamberlain's authority over theaters did not extend to Ireland. They successfully challenged the viceroy's attempt to prevent the performance. Joyce got Stanislaus to arrange with Prezioso for an article in the *Piccolo*, and armed with Prezioso's consent he tackled the Abbey manager for a press pass and got it. Pleased with his success, he next had visiting cards printed with his name and 'Piccolo della Sera, Trieste,' and with them prevailed upon the manager of the Midland Railway to give him a press pass to Galway on the understanding that he would write about Galway in a projected series of articles on Ireland for the Italian press.* [32]

The première of *Blanco Posnet* took place on August 25, the last night of Horse Show week. Joyce approved of defying British censorship, but did not care for the play. In his article for the *Piccolo* he branded Shaw 'a born preacher' who was incapable of 'the noble and bare style appropriate to modern playwriting.' The play 'shewed up' Shaw himself as a refugee from atheism, he suggested.[33] But he liked the acting and enjoyed the experience of being a reporter. During the interval he saw Eugene Sheehy, tapped him on the shoulder with his walking stick, and greeted him casually.† He soon told Sheehy mysteriously, 'There will be interesting news about me in a few weeks.' [34] After the play he met a number of other journalists, to whom he

---

* In *Ulysses* (78 [72]), Bloom plans with similar ingenuity to 'work a pass' to Mullingar.
† He remarked to Sheehy on this occasion that he greatly admired *The Tragic Comedians* of George Meredith.[35]

represented himself as having been sent to Dublin by the *Piccolo* for
the purpose of attending Shaw's play. He then hastily wrote his article
and sent it the same night to Stanislaus, asking him to check it before
giving it to Prezioso.

The next day he took a train with Giorgio to Galway. Not sure of
his welcome, he sent Giorgio into the house ahead of him; [36] but the
Barnacles were very glad to see both. Nora's uncle, Michael Healy,
a Galway port official, put them up in his house on Dominick Street.
The well-mannered son-in-law with the thin moustache had no difficulty in pleasing them, and Giorgio entertained his relatives by his
persistence in running after the ducks on the road.[37] Joyce went to the
house in Augustine Street where Nora had lived with her grandmother,
and, so that he might see the room she had slept in, pretended to consider buying the property. He took care also to see Lynch's Memorial,
which commemorated not only the mayor who hanged his own son,
but, in Joyce's mind, Cosgrave, now more 'Lynch' than ever. Sometimes
he walked on the strand with Nora's sister Kathleen, 'taking lessons
from the sea,' as she said.[38]

Most of the weekend, however, he sat in the kitchen at 4 Bowling
Green with Mrs. Barnacle and talked of Nora. He got her to sing 'The
Lass of Aughrim,' including some of the verses that Nora did not
remember. The last stanzas, in which Lord Gregory asks the lass to
prove her identity, Mrs. Barnacle, affected by the tragedy, was reluctant
to sing:

> If you'll be the lass of Aughrim
> As I am taking you mean to be
> Tell me the first token
> That passed between you and me.
>
> O don't you remember
> That night on yon lean hill
> When we both met together
> Which I am sorry now to tell.
>
> The rain falls on my yellow locks
> And the dew it wets my skin;
> My babe lies cold within my arms;
> Lord Gregory, let me in.*

Joyce found his mother-in-law very like Nora, and wrote Nora to say
that perhaps next year they might return to Galway together: 'You will
take me from place to place and the image of your girlhood will purify

---

* Lord Gregory refuses and the lass drowns herself.

again my life.'[39] He felt so lonesome for Nora that he gave vent to frequent sighs, and Mrs. Barnacle, not without admiration, warned him he 'would break his heart at it.'[40] His letters veered between blunt sexual excitation and extreme spirituality, and on September 2 he spoke of the oscillation himself:

> Tonight I have an idea madder than usual. I feel I would like to be flogged by you. I would like to see your eyes blazing with anger.
>
> I wonder is there some madness in me. Or is love madness? One moment I see you like a virgin or madonna the next moment I see you shameless, insolent, half-naked and obscene. What do you think of me at all? Are you disgusted with me? . . . Are you too, then, like me, one moment high as the stars, the next lower than the lowest wretches?
>
> I have enormous belief in the power of a simple honourable soul. You are that, are you not, Nora?
>
> I want you to say to yourself: Jim, the poor fellow I love, is coming back. He is a poor weak impulsive man and he prayed to me to defend him and make him strong.
>
> I gave others my pride and joy. To you I give my sin, my folly, my weakness and sadness.
>
> Jim.

His sense of his weakness and her strength persisted and grew in his mind. (It is parodied in *Circe* where Bloom turns into a woman and is flogged by Bella-Bello.) On September 5, back in Dublin, he attended a reception at the Gresham Hotel, probably in honor of Kettle's marriage, and was introduced to everyone as the future great writer of his country. 'I thought I heard my country calling towards me,' he wrote Nora, 'or her eyes being turned toward me expectantly. But, O my love, there was something else I thought of. I thought of one who held me in her hand like a pebble, from whose love and in whose company I have still to learn the secrets of life.'[*][41] Nora, with her country strength, stood for Ireland for him, much as Maud Gonne, the single-minded aristocrat, stood for Ireland for Yeats. His love for her was like a patriot's for his native land; it was like the devotee's love for his god; it was more than that, even:

> Guide me, my saint, my angel. Lead me forward. *Everything* that is noble and exalted and deep and true and moving in what I write comes, I believe, from you. Take me into your soul of souls and then I will become indeed the poet of my race. I feel this, Nora, as I write it. My body soon will penetrate into yours, O that my soul could too! O that I could nestle in your womb

---

[*] Richard says to Bertha in *Exiles* (589 [413]), 'There is something wiser than wisdom in your heart.'

like a child born of your flesh and blood, be fed by your blood, sleep in the warm secret gloom of your body!

My holy love, my darling Nora. O can it be that we are now about to enter the heaven of our life? [42]

Before entering heaven, it is necessary first to leave purgatory. Joyce waited impatiently for money from Trieste, but Stanislaus could not wrest it from Artifoni until the beginning of September, when he instantly wired £7/5/0. It was not quite enough, for Joyce had just spent a good deal of money on a present for Nora, which consisted of a chain ° hung with five ivory dice over a hundred years old, and a little tablet on which was engraved, in fourteenth-century letters, the line from one of his poems, 'Love is unhappy when love is away.' Joyce explained it to her lugubriously, in a letter of September 3, 'The five dice mean the five years of trial and misunderstanding and the tablet which unites the chain tells of the strange sadness we felt and our suffering when we were divided.' She was his confederate in grief if not in guilt. 'Save me, my *true* love!' he added, 'Save me from the badness of the world and of my own heart!' When the chain was ready he tried to find Cosgrave to show him what he thought of the treacherous story, but Cosgrave made himself scarce.

During these last days in Dublin Joyce visited several times the offices of the *Evening Telegraph*,[43] where the editor, Patrick J. Mead, introduced him to the staff. The *Evening Telegraph*, closely associated with the *Freeman's Journal*, was one of Dublin's old newspapers, dating back to 1763. It was to survive a fire in 1916 and to last until 1926. The offices which the two papers shared were also old, and very big and rambling; they extended from Prince's Street to Middle Abbey Street. The editorial staff used the Abbey Street exit, and Joyce, who remembered these visits in the *Aeolus* episode of *Ulysses*, has the newspaper boys using the same exit, when in fact the despatch room was on the Prince's Street side. This transposition may have been inadvertent, but was more probably a deliberate decision to add to the Aeolian atmosphere of haste and confusion. The publisher of the *Freeman's Journal* was Thomas Sexton, a Parnellite who was feuding with Archbishop Walsh; consequently his paper minimized whatever the Archbishop did and enlarged upon everything that Cardinal Logue did. Walsh evidently made frequent protests, which Joyce referred to without explanation in the sentence in *Ulysses*, 'His grace phoned down twice this morning.'

° Joyce wished to have it made of Claddagh gold from Galway, but none was obtainable.[44] In *Ulysses* (747 [722]), Molly remembers being given a 'clumsy Claddagh ring for luck.'

The evolution of the character of Aeolus, god of the winds, blended memory and art. Joyce calls him in *Ulysses* Myles Crawford, and the name suggests that of the editor of the Evening Telegraph in 1904, Morris Cosgrave. The personality of Crawford is not that of Cosgrave, however, but of Mead, in 1904 only sub-editor, but now editor. Pat Mead, like most of the staff in 1909, was about fifty years old. A big, stout man, with red hair and a red face, he dressed like a dandy, and was invariably clean shaven with a flower in his buttonhole, although he had usually spent most of the previous night drinking.* He was a widower with a daughter and two sons. Mead had a terrible temper, but was basically kind and probably an 'easy touch'; in *Ulysses,* however, the barrister O'Molloy fails to 'raise the wind' with him. While the description in *Ulysses* of Mead as Crawford is mostly literal, Joyce has inflated him somewhat as god of the winds of news. Mead was never guilty of either profanity or obscenity, but Joyce heightens his irascible temper in *Ulysses* with frequent oaths, and makes him say, 'Kiss my royal Irish arse.' Mead never said this, but Joyce did not invent it either. It was said by John Wyse Power, who was famous at the *Evening Telegraph* offices for the expression.

Joyce paid close attention to what he saw in the *Evening Telegraph* offices.† The cashier of the newspaper was a man named Ruttledge, who had a high, squeaky voice. On payday Ruttledge carried a money box around with him, paying out from office to office of the old building; and his coming was announced by the phrase, 'The ghost walks,' spoken in *Ulysses* by Professor MacHugh. MacHugh himself was, as his name suggests, Hugh MacNeill, a scholar of the classical modern languages, clever and lazy. Ordinarily careless in dress, he had for a time a position as teacher of romance languages at Maynooth, and so was obliged to wear hat and tailcoat; he usually left them unbrushed. Gogarty, speculating upon this garb, evidently made the remark, 'In mourning for Sallust,' which passes through Stephen's mind. MacNeill used to arrive early in the morning at the *Evening Telegraph* offices, read the paper, and remain all day. As the members of the staff arrived, he reprimanded them for being late. The title of professor was accorded him out of slightly ironic politeness, for in fact he never attained that eminence.

In spending time with the journalists Joyce was probably not con-

---

* Following the pattern of life set by their editor, the other staff members were generally also good drinkers; drinking capacity was reputed to be a primary consideration in hiring them.

† Joyce was friendly with Piaras Béaslai, a reporter for the paper and later a well-known Irish writer.

sciously gathering material. He thought it pleasant, as well as politic, to have good relations with them. As a result of his associations, the *Evening Telegraph* ran an article about his *Piccolo* review of Shaw's play on September 8. Joyce was anxious to make the most of this. He sent copies of the review to various Dublin friends * in connection with the examinership at National University, and Roberts, probably at Joyce's instigation, sent a copy to Shaw himself with a request that he do what he could to help promote the fortunes of the same author's coming book, *Dubliners.* Joyce sent copies of the *Evening Telegraph* article to Stanislaus with instructions to show them to Prezioso, Vidacovich, and Schmitz.

September 8 was also the day of Kettle's wedding; Joyce did not attend it, but sent the bride and groom a copy of *Chamber Music* on that day, and invited them to visit Trieste on their honeymoon. He informed Nora of what he had done, pointed out that Kettle was his best friend in Dublin, and implored her to clean up the house before the newlyweds' arrival.[45] By now he had collected some money; Stanislaus, already overstrained, refused to send more, but Roberts unprotestingly advanced three pounds on the royalties of *Dubliners.* Joyce was then affluent enough to pay for Eva's tonsillectomy. He also went round to Byrne's house to thank his friend again for his help in the crisis Cosgrave had precipitated. He stayed for supper and afterwards they went walking to revisit familiar places in Dublin. Trivial episodes in the walk, which lasted until three in the morning, took on importance in *Ulysses.* They stopped at a penny scale and weighed themselves, then went back to 7 Eccles Street, where Byrne discovered he had forgotten his key. Undismayed, he agilely let himself down to the front area and entered the house by the unlocked side door; then he went round to

---

* Joseph Holloway noted in his journal (*A Dublin Playgoer's Impressions*) for September, 1909, a conversation he had had with Joyce and W. A. Henderson, also a devotee of the theater:

> James Joyce was then announced (O'Donoghue told me he had returned to Italy on Tuesday last) and came in with an Italian paper with his critique of *The Shewing-up of Blanco Posnet* in it. He hoped to make the Italians interested in the Irish Theatrical movement. He did not give Henderson the copy of the paper but said he would send him one on. He leaves Dublin tomorrow, every day he stays here means a loss of money to him. He had translated Synge's play *Riders to the Sea* for the love of the thing and handed his MS over to the manager about to produce it; therefore, he told H. to communicate direct with the manager as he did not want to be personally troubled about it further. I asked him how he liked the acting of the company and he said 'Well.' He got a few postcards of scenes in *Riders to the Sea*, and leaving his address left himself also. He told us he chiefly remained in Dublin so long in connection with a book of short stories he intended bringing out through Maunsel & Son.[46]

the front and admitted his companion.[47] In *Ulysses* Bloom, returning to the same address at about the same hour with Stephen Dedalus, finds himself in a similar predicament and solves it in the same way. Bloom's height, five feet nine and a half inches, is Byrne's height, and his weight, eleven stone and four pounds, was the very weight which Byrne had registered on the scale.

Almost five years after his first departure from the North Wall, Joyce, on the evening of September 9, departed from Dublin with Eva and Giorgio. With his usual bravado he managed to secure a first-class ticket to London on the strength of his press pass.[48] The three went from London to Paris, where Joyce had to leave his sister and son in a park to search a lavatory for a ring given him by Nora which he had lost. With the assistance of an attendant he found it at last at the bottom of a drain.[49] Eva felt the same fear of abandonment that Nora had felt in the parks of London and Paris five years before. At last Joyce rejoined her, and they went on to Milan. From there Joyce wired Stanislaus in rare Italian he would arrive next morning: 'Domattina otto. Pennilesse.' Stanislaus, bent as fanatically on making ends meet as James was on keeping them apart, telegraphed some money care of the Milan station master; but James, adept at snatching rescues, had already persuaded that obliging official to let him have a ticket on the strength of his baggage, which he left as a deposit. Stanislaus, the family's official greeter, met them without enthusiasm at the Trieste station.

The trip to Dublin had been at once turbulent and pointed. Moving through the events of Joyce's brief stay there are, in phantasmagoria, the outlines of *Exiles* and *Ulysses*. In *Ulysses* Gogarty fades into Boylan as well as Mulligan, Cosgrave into Lynch, Nora into Molly, Joyce into Bloom. There were other contributions,* but the main ones are from the trip to Dublin. In *Exiles* Robert Hand, Richard Rowan's best friend, cordially tries to help him secure a post as professor of Italian at the University, writes about him in the newspaper, and at the same time tries to cuckold him. The cordiality is Gogarty's, the attempt to help him with a teaching position and an article in the newspaper is Kettle's, the attempt to cuckold him is Cosgrave's. Long afterwards Ettore Schmitz, having just seen a performance of *Exiles* in London, said to Joyce, 'Exiled? People who return to their home country!' 'But don't you remember,' said Joyce, 'how the prodigal son was received by his brother in his father's house? It is dangerous to leave one's country, but still more dangerous to go back to it, for then your fellow-countrymen, if they can, will drive a knife into your heart.'[50]

* See pp. 326-8, 340.

In the end Joyce throve on the plots and counterparts, tensions and countertensions, which he was able to find or often to read into his native city. The intrigue was as complicated as that of some medieval principality of the fourteenth century, and well suited to the mind of Dedalus, maker of labyrinths.

◇◆◇

The Growth of Imagination

> . . . the childman weary, the manchild in the womb.
>
> —*Ulysses* (722 [697])

THE agitation of Joyce's feelings during his visit to Dublin in 1909 laid bare for a moment topics of that conversation with himself which, like Yeats, he never ceased to conduct. One was his bond to Dublin, which his books indicate he thoroughly understood. Although Stephen Dedalus in both *Stephen Hero* and *A Portrait* assumes his isolation, he surrounds himself with friends and family to whom he can confide it. When he rebels he hastens to let them know of his rebellion so that he can measure their response to it. He searches for disciples who must share his motives vicariously. As he demands increasing allegiance from them, step by step, he brings them to the point where they will go no further, and their refusal, half-anticipated, enables him to feel forsaken and to forsake them. He buys his own ticket for Holyhead, but claims to have been deported. Yet his mother prepares his clothing for the journey; she at any rate does not break with him. Of this young man it may be safely predicted that he will write letters home.

Joyce's life wears a similar aspect. Having stomped angrily out of the house, he circled back to peer in the window. He could not exist without close ties, no matter in what part of Europe he resided; and if he came to terms with absence, it was by bringing Ireland with him, in his memories, and in the persons of his wife, his brother, his sister. So in later life, when asked if he would go back to Ireland, he could reply, 'Have I ever left it?' In memory his closest ties to the past were with the scenes of his early childhood. This childhood was dominated rhetorically by his father, but emotionally by his mother with her practicality, her unquenchable indulgence, her tenacity, even her inveterate pregnancy. As a small boy he had gone to her to ask that she examine him in his school work; as a young man, the letters from Paris in 1902 and 1903 confirm, he asked her support for his ambitions and ideas. His confidences went to his mother, not to his father, a man (as his sister May remembered) impossible to confide in.

His attitude toward his mother is clarified by his attitude toward Nora Barnacle. In the letters he sent to Nora in that discomposed summer of 1909, there are many testimonies that Joyce longed to reconstitute, in his relation with her, the filial bond which his mother's death had broken. Explicitly he longs to make their relationship that of child and mother, as if the relationship of lovers was too remote. He covets an even more intimate dependence: 'O that I could nestle in your womb like a child born of your flesh and blood, be fed by your blood, sleep in the warm secret gloom of your body!' *

Joyce seems to have thought with equal affection of the roles of mother and child. He said once to Stanislaus about the bond between the two, 'There are only two forms of love in the world, the love of a mother for her child and the love of a man for lies.' In later life, as Maria Jolas remarked, 'Joyce talked of fatherhood as if it were motherhood.' [1] He seems to have longed to establish in himself all aspects of the bond of mother and child. He was attracted, particularly, by the image of himself as a weak child cherished by a strong woman, which seems closely connected with the images of himself as victim, whether as a deer pursued by hunters, as a passive man surrounded by burly extroverts, as a Parnell or a Jesus among traitors. His favorite characters are those who in one way or another retreat before masculinity, yet are loved regardless by motherly women.

The sense of his family life as warm and tranquil, which was established in Joyce's mind during his earliest years, was disturbed for him by his father's irresponsibility. To some extent John Joyce served his son as model, for he continually tried his wife's steadfastness, which however proved equal to every challenge, including the drunken attempt on her life. James, contesting for his mother's love, learned to use the same weapons with a difference. A merely good boy would have been submerged, unable to compete with his father in the inordinate demands upon a mother's affection, but a prodigal son had a better chance. His mother must be encouraged to love him more than his father because he was just as errant and much more gifted, so more pitiable and lovable. For his irresponsibility was the turbulence of genius, motivated —unlike his father's—by courage rather than by failure.† At first it took

* See Joyce's letter of September 2, 1909, pp. 296-7.
† Joyce writes of Mr Dedalus in *Stephen Hero* (110 [115]), 'He had his son's distaste for responsibility without his son's courage.'

the form of arousing his mother to question his conduct. His answers proved surprisingly sweeping and persuasive. Then he tried her further: John Joyce had been anticlerical, James exceeded him by becoming irreligious.

This change, which was not easy for him to undergo, presented an added complication. For one thing, in the figure of the Virgin he had found a mother image which he cherished. He had gone to prostitutes and then prayed to the Virgin as later he would drum up old sins with which to demand Nora's forgiveness; the Virgin's love, like his mother's and later his wife's, was of a sort especially suited to great sinners. But there was an aspect of Irish Catholicism which he was glad to abandon. It was not a mother church but a father church, harsh, repressive, masculine. To give it up was both consciously and unconsciously to offer his mother's love its supreme test, for his mother was deeply religious. She was disconcerted but did not abandon him. Yet her death not long after one of his open defiances of her belief seemed a punishment; he felt as if he had killed her by trying her too far. This thought he confided to Nora, who called him reproachfully, 'Woman-killer.' [2]

When Joyce met Nora Barnacle in 1904, it was not enough for her to be his mistress; she must be his queen and even his goddess; he must be able to pray to her. But to gain all her love, and so increase her perfection, he must make sure she will accept even the worst in him. He must test her by making her his wife without calling her that, by denying legal sanction to the bond between them, just as in dealing with his mother he had wanted her to acknowledge him as her son even though in so many ways he was not filial. Nora Barnacle passed this test easily, no doubt aware that their attachment was indispensable to him. Then he tried her further, not by flouting her religion, which she did not care deeply about, but by doubting her fidelity. That the accusation might be false did not deter him; in a way, it encouraged him, for if he was accusing her falsely he could be, when reassured of her innocence, more humble and so more childlike than before. When this test too was surmounted, Joyce made a final trial of her: she must recognize all his impulses, even the strangest, and match his candor by confiding in him every thought she has found in herself, especially the most embarrassing. She must allow him to know her inmost life, to learn with odd exactitude what it is to be a woman. This test, the last, Nora passed successfully later in 1909. In so doing she accepted complicity, she indulged his reduction of her motherly purity just as she had indulged his insistence upon that purity. Joyce's letters during his two subsequent absences from her in Trieste were full of thoughts about 'adoration' and 'desecration' of her image, extravagant terms that he himself applied.

What was unusual about his attitude was not that he saw his wife as his mother or that he demanded inordinate fulfillment of either role. The novelty lay in his declining to confuse the two images and instead holding them remorsefully apart, opposing them to each other so that they became the poles of his mind. He was thereby enabled to feel that with Nora, as with his mother, he was a prodigal son, full of love and misbehavior; he was pleased that she 'saw through him,' as he said, and detected the boy in the man. This view of himself he encouraged. In *Ulysses* and *Finnegans Wake* he apportioned womanhood in its sexual aspect to Molly Bloom, and in its maternal aspect to Anna Livia Plurabelle. But he understood and marveled that Nora had no sense of the dichotomy that bothered him. He represented her attitude, which he took to be feminine in general, when Molly, though primarily the sensualist, thinks of Stephen Dedalus as child and as lover, without incompatibility, and Anna Livia, though primarily the mother, recollects her once passionate attachment to her husband.

Joyce studied his mental landscape and made use of it in his books. *Dubliners* is written on the assumption that Ireland is an inadequate mother, 'an old sow who eats her farrow,' and he associates himself with the masticated children. As he wrote to Georg Goyert, the book did not describe the way 'they' are in Dublin, but the way 'we' are.[3] We are foolish, comic, motionless, corrupted; yet we are worthy of sympathy too, a sympathy which, if Ireland denies us, the international reader may give. But the reader must be tested like a loving mother by an errant child, must be forced to see the ugly, undecorated reality before he is allowed to extend his pity, a pity compounded of outraged affection, amusement, and understanding.

Joyce's own preoccupations emerge through the impersonal façade of *Dubliners*. Two stories, 'A Mother' and 'The Boarding House,' portray mothers who fail in their role by browbeating, a type Joyce could never endure. 'The Dead' represents in Gretta a woman with genuine maternal sympathy, which she extends both to the dead boy who loved her and to her inadequate husband. She overwhelms Gabriel's sexual passion by letting her thoughts dwell upon the boy, with whom Gabriel at the last associates himself. Other stories, especially 'Araby' and 'Ivy Day in the Committee Room,' play on the theme of the loss of warmth in the past: the bazaar closed, the radiant image of Parnell chilled by small feelings. Throughout the book the women usually hold together when the men do not, 'The Sisters' in that they survive so solidly their brother the priest, Chandler's wife in 'A Little Cloud' in her relegation of her husband in favor of her child. Yet there is pity for them too, especially for those who, like Corley's girl in 'Two Gallants,' like 'Eveline,' like Maria in 'Clay,' cannot achieve full maternal being, and for Gretta in 'The Dead' because of her inevitably lost girlhood. In the book women act (or fail to act) the mother, men drink, children suffer.

To write *A Portrait of the Artist as a Young Man* Joyce plunged back into his own past, mainly to justify, but also to expose it. The book's pattern, as he explained to Stanislaus, is that we are what we were; our maturity is an extension of our childhood, and the courageous boy is father of the arrogant young man. But in searching for a way to convert the episodic *Stephen Hero* into *A Portrait of the Artist,* Joyce hit upon a principle of structure which reflected his habits of mind as extremely as he could wish. The work of art, like a mother's love, must be achieved over the greatest obstacles, and Joyce, who had been dissatisfied with his earlier work as too easily done, now found the obstacles in the form of a most complicated pattern.

This is hinted at in his image of the creative process. As far back as his paper on Mangan, Joyce said that the poet takes into the vital center of his life 'the life that surrounds it, flinging it abroad again amid planetary music.' He repeated this image in *Stephen Hero*, then in *A Portrait of the Artist* developed it more fully. Stephen refers to the making of literature as 'the phenomenon of artistic conception, artistic gestation and artistic reproduction,' and then describes the progression from lyrical to epical and to dramatic art:

The simplest epical form is seen emerging out of lyrical literature when the artist prolongs and broods upon himself as the centre of an epical event and this form progresses till the centre of emotional gravity is equidistant from the artist himself and from others. The narrative is no longer purely personal. The personality of the artist passes into the narration itself, flowing round and round the persons and the action like a vital sea. . . . The dramatic form is reached when the vitality which has flowed and eddied round each person fills every person with such vital force that he or she assumes a proper and intangible esthetic life. . . . The mystery of esthetic like that of material creation is accomplished.[4]

This creator is not male but female; Joyce goes on to borrow an image of Flaubert by calling him a 'god,' [*] but he is really a goddess. Within this womb creatures come to life. No male intercession is necessary

---

[*] Stephen says the artist is 'like the God of the creation,' remaining 'within or behind or beyond or above his handiwork, invisible, refined out of existence, paring his fingernails.' But Lynch sardonically qualifies this statement by saying, 'Trying to refine them [the fingernails] also out of existence.' Stephen makes no reply. *A Portrait* (481-2 [336-7]).

even; as Stephen says, 'In the virgin womb of the imagination the word was made flesh.'

Joyce did not take up such métaphors lightly. His brother records that in the first draft of *A Portrait,* Joyce thought of a man's character as developing 'from an embryo' with constant traits. Joyce acted upon this theory with his characteristic thoroughness, and his subsequent interest in the process of gestation, as conveyed to Stanislaus during Nora's first pregnancy, expressed a concern that was literary as well as anatomical. His decision to rewrite *Stephen Hero* as *A Portrait* in five chapters occurred appropriately just after Lucia's birth. For *A Portrait of the Artist as a Young Man* is in fact the gestation of a soul, and in the metaphor Joyce found his new principle of order. The book begins with Stephen's father and, just before the ending, it depicts the hero's severance from his mother. From the start the soul is surrounded by liquids, urine, slime, seawater, amniotic tides, 'drops of water' (as Joyce says at the end of the first chapter) 'falling softly in the brimming bowl.' The atmosphere of biological struggle is necessarily dark and melancholy until the light of life is glimpsed. In the first chapter the foetal soul is for a few pages only slightly individualized, the organism responds only to the most primitive sensory impressions, then the heart forms and musters its affections, the being struggles toward some unspecified, uncomprehended culmination, it is flooded in ways it cannot understand or control, it gropes wordlessly toward sexual differentiation. In the third chapter shame floods Stephen's whole body as conscience develops; the lower bestial nature is put by. Then at the end of the fourth chapter the soul discovers the goal towards which it has been mysteriously proceeding—the goal of life. It must swim no more but emerge into air, the new metaphor being flight. The final chapter shows the soul, already fully developed, fattening itself for its journey until at last it is ready to leave. In the last few pages of the book, Stephen's diary, the soul is released from its confinement, its individuality is complete, and the style shifts with savage abruptness.

The sense of the soul's development as like that of an embryo not only helped Joyce to the book's imagery, but also encouraged him to work and rework the original elements in the process of gestation. Stephen's growth proceeds in waves, in accretions of flesh, in particularization of needs and desires, around and around but always ultimately forward. The episodic framework of *Stephen Hero* was renounced in favor of a group of scenes radiating backwards and forwards.* In the

---

* It is a technique which William Faulkner was to carry even further in the opening section of *The Sound and the Fury,* where the extreme disconnection finds its justification, not, as in Joyce, in the haze of childhood memory, but in the blur of

new first chapter Joyce had three clusters of sensations: his earliest memories of infancy, his sickness at Clongowes (probably indebted like the ending of 'The Dead' to rheumatic fever in Trieste), and his pandying at Father Daly's hands. Under these he subsumed chains of related moments, with the effect of three fleshings in time rather than of a linear succession of events. The sequence became primarily one of layers rather than of years.

In this process other human beings are not allowed much existence except as influences upon the soul's development or features of it. The same figures appear and reappear, the schoolboy Heron for example, each time in an altered way to suggest growth in the soul's view of them. E——— C———, a partner in childhood games, becomes the object of Stephen's adolescent love poems; the master at Clongowes reappears as the preacher of the sermons at Belvedere.* The same words, 'Apologise,' 'admit,' 'maroon,' 'green,' 'cold,' 'warm,' 'wet,' and the like, keep recurring with new implications. The book moves from rudimentary meanings to more complex ones, as in the conceptions of the call and the fall. Stephen, in the first chapter fascinated by un-formed images, is next summoned by the flesh and then by the church, the second chapter ending with a prostitute's lingual kiss, the third with his reception of the Host upon his tongue. The soul that has been enraptured by body in the second chapter and by spirit in the third (both depicted in sensory images) then hears the call of art and life, which encompass both without bowing before either, in the fourth chapter; the process is virtually complete. Similarly the fall into sin, at first a terror, gradually becomes an essential part of the discovery of self and life.

Now Stephen, his character still recomposing the same elements, leaves the Catholic priesthood behind him to become 'a priest of eternal imagination, transmuting the daily bread of experience into the

---

an idiot's mind. Faulkner, when he wrote his book, had read *Dubliners* and *A Portrait;* he did not read *Ulysses* until a year later, in 1930, but knew about it from excerpts and from the conversation of friends. He has said that he considered himself the heir of Joyce in his methods in *The Sound and the Fury*.[5]

* In both these instances Joyce changed the actual events. His freedom of recompo-sition is displayed also in the scene in the physics classroom in *A Portrait* (453 [319]), where he telescopes two lectures, one on electricity and one on mechanics, which as Professor Felix Hackett remembers, took place months apart. Moynihan's whispered remark, inspired by the lecturer's discussion of ellipsoidal balls, 'Chase me, ladies, I'm in the cavalry!', was in fact made by a young man named Kinahan on one of these occasions. In the same way, as J. F. Byrne points out in *Silent Years*,[6] the long scene with the dean of studies in *A Portrait* (446-51 [313-17]) happened not to Joyce but to him; he told it to Joyce and was later displeased to discover how his innocent description of Father Darlington lighting a fire had been converted into a reflection of Stephen's strained relations with the Church.

radiant body of everlasting life.' Having listened to sermons on ugliness
in the third chapter, he makes his own sermons on beauty in the last.
The Virgin is transformed into the girl wading on the strand, symboliz-
ing a more tangible reality. In the last two chapters, to suit his new
structure, Joyce minimizes Stephen's physical life to show the dominance
of his mind, which has accepted but subordinated physical things. The
soul is ready now, it throws off its sense of imprisonment, its melancholy, its no longer tolerable conditions of lower existence, to be born.

Joyce was obviously well-pleased with the paradox into which his
method had put him, that he was, as the artist framing his own development in a constructed matrix, his own mother. The complications of
this state are implied in Stephen's thought of himself as not his parents'
true son, but a foster-son.[7] In *Ulysses* Joyce was to carry the method
much further; he makes that book the epic of the whole human body,
the womb being the organ only of the *Oxen of the Sun* episode. In that
episode, as Joyce said later,[*] Stephen is again the embryo. But, in a
parody of the method of *A Portrait*, Stephen emerges not to life but
to Burke's pub. The theme of *Ulysses*, Joyce intimates, is reconciliation
with the father. Of course, the father whom Joyce depicts in Bloom is
in almost every way the opposite of his own father, and is much closer
to himself.[†] Insofar as the movement of the book is to bring Stephen,
the young Joyce, into *rapport* with Bloom, the mature Joyce, the author
becomes, it may be said, his own father. Stephen is aware enough of
the potential ironies of this process to ponder all the paradoxes of the
father as his own son in the Trinity, and of Shakespeare as both King
Hamlet and Prince Hamlet. Yet the book is not without its strong
woman; Bloom is appropriately under the influence of his wife, whom
he dissatisfies (to some extent intentionally), and wishes to bring
Stephen under her influence too.

In both these books Joyce seems to reconstitute his family relationships, to disengage himself from the contradictions of his view of himself as a child and so to exploit them, to overcome his mother's conven-
tionality and his father's rancor, to mother and father himself, to
become, by the superhuman effort of the creative process, no one but
James Joyce.

[*] See his letter to Frank Budgen, pp. 489-90, and the discussion of *Finnegans
Wake*, p. 729.
[†] Pp. 384-5.

1909–1911

Every evening at lighting up o'clock sharp and until further notice in Feenichts Playhouse. (Bar and conveniences always open, Diddlem Club douncestears.) Entrancings: gads, a scarb; the quality, one large shilling. Newly billed for each wickeday perfumance. Somndoze massinees. By arraignment, childream's hours, expercatered.

—*Finnegans Wake* (219)

To the secret disgust of Stanislaus, Nora and Joyce encountered each other like bride and bridegroom. James gave her the 'little gift' of the necklace, and when Stanislaus read the inscription on the pendant, 'Love is unhappy when love is away,' he drily commented, 'So is love's brother.'¹ But Joyce had no attention to spare for his brother's mutterings. All that Stanislaus could elicit from him about Dublin was an account of the reception, as of a visiting dignitary, which he had been accorded there. 'Did nobody ask about me?' Stanislaus at last timidly inquired. 'Oh yes, everybody,' said his brother, 'I got a whole lot of messages for you but I've forgotten them.'² Stanislaus had borne the expenses of supporting Nora and Lucia at home and James and Giorgio in Dublin, he had paid for the trip back, he had helped to prevent an ugly rift between James and Nora. He was not amused.

There would probably have been a violent quarrel between the two brothers if Joyce had not got away again. The new departure came about by accident: Eva Joyce, small and timid but observant too, found herself homesick for Dublin and at once spoke of returning. She liked, however, one aspect of Trieste, its cinemas, and remarked one morning how odd it was that Dublin, a larger city, had not even one.³ This casual word set James off like a fuse. He must find a syndicate to back him. In Trieste, as it happened, there was a group of four small businessmen who had been remarkably successful not only with two theaters

in the city (the Edison and the Americano), but with a third, the
Cinematograph Volta, in Bucharest. The dominating member of the
group was Antonio Machnich, an upholsterer who had invented a new
type of sofabed; the others were the leather merchant Giovanni Rebez,
the draper Giuseppe Caris, and the proprietor of a bicycle shop, Francesco Novak, the technical expert among the four. Joyce knew better
than to approach them directly; he got his friend Nicolò Vidacovich,
who was acquainted with them, to arrange a meeting.

Joyce seems to have managed the venturesome but careful businessmen very well. He began by saying, 'I know a city of 500,000 inhabitants where there is not a single cinema.' 'Where is it?' they wanted to
know. He would not say at first, the secret was too valuable to be
thrown away. At last he told them it was in Ireland. They got out a map
and he pointed to Dublin first, then to Belfast and Cork; there were no
cinemas in any one of them.⁴ By moving quickly they could capture the
whole country. They warmed to the project, but how could it be
arranged? Joyce was graciously willing to put aside his work in Trieste
to act as their advance agent in Dublin; he would see about hiring a
hall and other preliminary arrangements. The initial cost would be
infinitesimal: a few pounds to send him to Dublin, and a per diem
allowance of ten crowns ($2 or 8/-) to keep him there. If all went well
they could come over and start up the business. If he ran into unexpected complications, they had lost virtually nothing.

The partners were persuaded. The next question was Joyce's share
in the profits. Since he had no capital to risk he could scarcely expect
an equal share. On the other hand, for initiating the scheme, and for
giving up his work in Trieste to open the cinema, he seemed entitled
to ten per cent of the profits. The agreement, drawn up probably by
Vidacovich who was a lawyer, was signed by all five partners, and
Joyce was off.

He entrained for Dublin on October 18, just over a month after
leaving it. He made the journey in high spirits, stopped briefly in Paris
and wished he could stay for the operas, but dutifully proceeded to
London. There, by exploiting his *Piccolo della Sera* visiting card, he
persuaded the manager of the L.N.W. railroad to give him another
first-class ticket.⁵ He arrived in Dublin on October 21, and threw himself at once into the search for possible premises. By October 28 he
had located a building at 45 Mary Street,⁶ off Dublin's principal thor-
oughfare, Sackville Street, and had made sure by consulting the theater
inspector that it would be eligible for a license. He sent word to
Machnich to come over at once, and meanwhile obtained an estimate
for the installation of electricity in the building.⁷ Machnich was slow

to arrive, and the Mary Street landlord threatened to rent the premises to someone else if they did not put up earnest money. The partners sent Joyce fifty pounds to hold the building.[8] At last, on November 19, Machnich and Rebez reached Dublin,[9] and Joyce, attentive as usual to small ironies, installed them in Finn's Hotel where Nora had once been employed.

The sight of these two foreigners with their lanky Irish friend amused the Joyce household, and John Joyce labelled Rebez 'the hairy mechanic with the liontamer's coat.'[10] They went over Joyce's plans methodically, then decided to see what Belfast was like. On November 27 they canvassed that city unsuccessfully,[11] and Joyce took the occasion to admire Belfast's factories (he liked factories)[12] and linen sheets, and to call on W. B. Reynolds, the music critic of the *Belfast Telegraph*, who had set some of his poems to music. Machnich and Rebez now summoned their partner Novak to Dublin, to manage the theater, and an Italian to operate the projector. These cohorts arrived on December 2, and the theater was to open a week later. But an unexpected delay developed because the Recorder, who was the only official empowered to issue a license, was not then sitting. There was a postponement during which the partners obtained a provisional permit, and meanwhile went down to Cork on December 12 to survey the possibilities there. This expedition was carried out with great speed and made Joyce feel sorry for himself. He wrote Stanislaus on December 15 that he had been up until 4:30 in the morning sending express letters and telegrams for the group to Trieste, London, and Bucharest, then was awakened 'by a cannon' at 7:00. 'I drove in the pelting rain and fog to Kingsbridge [station]. We left for Cork at 8 A.M. and arrived at 1 P.M. For five rainy dreary hours we were mooning about Cork. At 6 P.M. we left for Dublin, and arrived at 11.30 P.M. I was home at midnight, dined and sat down to write with the result that I got to my ricketty, naked bed at 3 A.M. Since this work began I have never been in bed before 3 or 3.30.'

He was busy 'night, noon, and morning,'[13] he complained. He bought wooden benches and, for the élite, kitchen chairs.[14] The Irish electrician quit abruptly, and the partners blamed Joyce for hiring him. He had to hire a second, and this one too left them at the last moment. A third was found. Joyce himself designed the posters for the opening, and sent copies to Stanislaus for use in staving off creditors by proving the success of the Volta project. He advertised for staff hands, received 200 replies, and interviewed about 50 people before choosing those he needed.[15]

On Monday, December 20, the theater opened at last. The *Evening Telegraph* received the venture cordially with an article entitled 'Volta':

Yesterday at 45 Mary Street a most interesting cinematograph exhibition was opened before a large number of invited visitors. The hall in which the display takes place is most admirably equipped for the purpose, and has been admirably laid out. Indeed, no expense would appear to have been spared in making the entertainment one deserving of the patronage of the public. Perhaps its special feature is that it is of Italian origin, and is in that respect somewhat out of the ordinary and more conventional forms of such displays.* For an initial experiment it was remarkably good, remembering how difficult it is to produce with absolute completeness a series of pictures at the first stage of their location in new surroundings the occasion may be described as having been particularly successful. The chief pictures shown were 'The First Paris Orphanage,' 'La Pourponniere,' and 'The Tragic Story of Beatrice Cenci.' The latter, although very excellent, was hardly as exhilarating a subject as one would desire on the eve of the festive season. But it was very much appreciated and applauded. An excellent little string orchestra played charmingly during the afternoon. Mr. James Joyce, who is in charge of the exhibition, has worked apparently indefatigably in its production and deserves to be congratulated on the success of the inaugural exhibition.[16]

Copies were sent to Stanislaus with instructions to show them to Prezioso and get a 'par' [paragraph] in the *Piccolo*: 'I nostri Triestini in Irlanda—or like that. A little allusion to *me* and a little to the enterprise of the proprietors of the Edison and Americano (*without* giving their names) in opening here.'[17] The petty scale of these efforts to advertise himself should not conceal their skill.

Although the notices were all favorable, bad weather gave the theater a slow start. But the partners were satisfied that it would catch on, and prepared to leave. Machnich and Rebez left on Christmas day for Bucharest, and Joyce stayed on only to appear before the Recorder for a permanent license on December 29. When this was granted he left the management of the theater in the hands of Novak, for he did not want to remain in Dublin.

Two other pieces of business occupied a little of his time. Someone had suggested that he import skyrockets into Trieste, but he found this trade would be too dangerous.[18] He also pursued his old plan of becoming agent for Irish tweeds, and made arrangements with the Dublin Woollen Company to act for them in Trieste. As he told Gorman, he did eventually clothe several of his Triestine male pupils in Irish homespuns.[19]

* While Dublin had no regular cinema, films were shown from time to time in hired halls.

He did not see many of his friends on this trip, but there were a few encounters. He ran into Richard Best at Bewley's cafe on Grafton Street, and, as if to suggest that Best need not fear he would borrow money from him, ostentatiously fingered a roll of pound notes. (He did not explain that this was Volta money.) He spoke of his literary ambitions, and said he hoped to write something as important as D'Annunzio.[20] A pleasanter glimpse of him is afforded by Charles Duff, then still a boy.* Duff was interested in German and Italian, and Joyce, meeting him by chance, invited him to see the films at the Volta free, and when they were over, treated him to a bun and cup of tea.[21] Joyce also saw George Roberts from time to time, and Roberts hoped to have galley proofs of *Dubliners* ready for him during his stay. These were, however, delayed.

Set quite apart from his business with the Volta was another of Joyce's intense little dramas, conducted mostly with Nora. The second absence from her was more tumultuous than their reconciliation after the first would have indicated. During his first few days away from her in October Joyce was still annoyed at her for having called him an imbecile when he returned home late one night, and punished her by sending only a chilly post card. Then on October 27, he wrote her a letter full of hatred for the Irish and full, too, of his own loneliness: 'I see nothing on every side of me but the image of the adulterous priest and his servants and of sly deceitful women. It is not good for me to come here or to be here. Perhaps if you were with me I would not suffer so much.' Yet he could not forbear mentioning three recent incidents in which she too had failed him:

A few days before I left Trieste I was walking with you in the Via Stadion (it was the day we bought the glass jar for the conserva). A priest passed us and I said to you 'Do you not find a kind of repulsion or disgust at the sight of one of those men?' You answered a little shortly and drily 'No, I don't.' You see, I remember all these small things. Your reply hurt me and silenced me. It and other similar things you have said to me linger a long time in my mind. Are you with me, Nora, or are you secretly against me?

I am a jealous, lonely, dissatisfied, proud man. Why are you not more patient with me and kinder with me? The night we went to *Madame Butterfly* together you treated me most rudely. I simply wanted to hear that beautiful delicate music in your company. I wanted to feel your soul swaying with languor and longing as mine did when she sings the romance of her hope in the second act *Un bel dì:* 'One day, one day, we shall see a spire of smoke rising on the furthest verge of the sea: and then the ship appears.' I am a

---

* He was later to write *James Joyce and the Plain Reader* (London, 1932).

little disappointed in you. Then another night I came home to your bed from the cafe and I began to tell you of all I hoped to do, and to write, in the future and of those boundless ambitions which are really the leading forces in my life. You would not listen to me. It was very late I know and of course you were tired out after the day. But a man whose brain is on fire with hope and trust in himself *must* tell someone of what he feels. Whom should I tell but you?

She must feel exactly as he feels; otherwise she is an enemy. But his mood changes. 'My love for you,' he wrote her at the same time, 'is really a kind of adoration.' Nora could not understand these abrupt shifts in tone; she wrote him that she was miserable and feared he was tired of her. He consoled and reassured her; she must not doubt him, 'I know and feel that if I am to write anything fine or noble in the future I shall do so only by listening at the doors of your heart.'²² He announced he was looking for a set of sables, including cap, stole, and muff, for her.²³ Probably he had not yet sampled prices, for a day or two later, on November 1, sable had degenerated to squirrel: 'A gray squirrel cap with violets at the side and a long broad flat stole of gray squirrel and a beige granny muff of the same on a steel chain, both lined with violet satin.' He could not make this pleasant purchase yet, but if the Volta succeeded he would certainly do so. Meanwhile, as a love token he sent off several pairs of gloves and twelve yards of Donegal tweed, obtained in the course of becoming Triestine agent for Irish tweeds. He also told her of a more special present, which would take him some time to prepare; this was a manuscript of *Chamber Music*, copied out in India ink on specially cut sheets of parchments, with her initials and his entwined on the cover. With these testimonies of affection Joyce tried to make Nora more blithe: 'You are a sad little person and I am a devilishly melancholy fellow myself so that ours is a rather mournful love I fancy. Do not cry about that tiresome young gentleman in the photograph [Joyce himself]. He is not worth it, dear.'²⁴

Nora might have been consoled had it not been for the difficulty of keeping the household in Trieste without Joyce there to beguile the creditors. Their landlord, a man named Scholz, proved singularly lacking in the indulgence necessary to house Joyces without fuss. In mid-November he had a court writ served upon Stanislaus to compel him to pay the rent for October and November, a sum of two pounds, on pain of immediate eviction. Stanislaus, who had looked with a cold eye on his brother's second trip to Dublin and had not written him, now suddenly cabled for money.

Joyce wished to meet his brother's unprecedented request but as usual had let most of his *dieta* flutter away. For one thing, news of his affluence had spread about the Dublin circle, and he was a target for borrowers if not for old creditors. 'Devin has borrowed money from me twice and wants me to ask M and R [Machnich and Rebez] to go security for him for a loan!! MacDonnell, the medical student, also borrows from me every time I see him, so does "Corley" whom I ran into a tram to avoid.* I don't refuse them, because I am thinking of my book.' [25] Few authors have done as much to attract readers. He had also a new plan: 'I have bought clothes for Eileen to help her get away from here with me and train her voice.' [26] Then there were the gloves and the tweeds. Worst of all, John Joyce had suffered an attack of conjunctivitis and was in Jervis Street Hospital, so that the unsteady support of the house at 44 Fontenoy Street had also fallen on James. As if to vie with Scholz in Trieste, the landlord threatened to evict the Dublin branch on December 1. 'We'll be on the streets by Christmas,' Joyce warned Stanislaus, at the same time offering him a third of the putative profits of the Volta. He gathered together a few shillings and wired them to Trieste; on Christmas eve John Joyce produced a few more to wire to Nora, quoting Vergil almost accurately, *'Non ignara malorum miseris succurrere disco.'* † James also sent precise instructions for staving Scholz off with one month's rent in lieu of two, and for slowing down other creditors by showing them the Volta posters.

These instructions worked well enough, but Nora's temper was understandably frayed. She wrote Joyce that she could not bear this state of separation and near eviction any longer. Joyce replied with sentimental obsequiousness, which his absence and non-support undercut, 'You write like a queen. As long as I live I shall always remember the quiet dignity of that letter, its sadness and scorn, and the utter humiliation it caused me.' Lacerating himself, he urged her to leave him, for he deserved as much: 'If you leave me I shall live for ever with your memory, holier than God to me. I shall pray to your name.' [27]

Nora made his prayers unnecessary. She had already repented of her fit of temper, and crossed his letter with two affectionate ones. Joyce replied on November 19 in a distraught, romantic style, describing her in the third person as if she were still too aloof and majestic for him to venture more direct address. He related how he had gone to Finn's Hotel to arrange lodgings for his Triestine partners:

The place is very Irish. I have lived so long abroad and in so many countries that I can feel at once the voice of Ireland in anything. The dis-

---

* The prototype in name and physique of one of the 'Two Gallants.'
† 'Having suffered myself, I know how to help those in trouble.' In the *Aeneid* Dido says *mali,* not *malorum.* Joyce improves Vergil's phrase further in *Ulysses* (601 [579]): *'Haud ignarus malorum. . . .'*

order of the table was Irish, the wonder on the faces also, the curious-looking eyes of the woman herself and her waitress. A strange land this is to me though I was born in it and bear one of its old names. . . . My God, my eyes are full of tears! Why do I cry? I cry because it is so sad to think of her moving about that room, eating little, simply dressed, simple-mannered and watchful, and carrying always with her in her secret heart the little flame which burns up the souls and bodies of men. . . . I have loved in her the image of the beauty of the world, the mystery and beauty of life itself, the beauty and doom of the race of whom I am a child, the images of spiritual purity and pity which I believed in as a boy.

Her soul! Her name! Her eyes! They seem to me like strange beautiful wild-flowers growing in some tangled rain-drenched hedge. And I have felt her soul tremble beside mine, and have spoken her name softly to the night, and have wept to see the beauty of the world passing like a dream behind her eyes.

The letter shows Joyce reaching for the lyrical imagery of passages in the last two chapters of *A Portrait* such as this: 'Its rays burned up the world, consumed the hearts of men and angels: the rays from the rose that was her wilful heart.'[28] There too a girl becomes an image of the beauty of the world. By an odd transposition, Joyce uses another phrase from the letter in *Exiles*, attributing it there not to himself as Richard but to his adversary Robert Hand, who says to Bertha: 'Your face is a flower too—but more beautiful. A wild flower blowing in a hedge.'[29] In *Ulysses* Bloom names Molly, 'a flower of the mountain,'[30] with equal success.

Happy to be reconciled once more, Joyce alternated, as during his previous visit, between detailed testimony of his desire for Nora's body and pious adoration of her spiritual image. Again he owned his role as a wayward child to be loved and, yes, to be chastised. The style is Verlaine's, but the voice is Masoch's.* Then, like Richard in *Exiles*, he begged to be informed of the minute details of her promenades with young men before she met him. Half-disgusted with himself, but a little complacent as well as penitent, he asked, '*How on God's earth* can you possibly love a thing like me?'[31] He and Nora exchanged letters much more open than Bloom's and Martha Clifford's.

A new burst of affection was set off on December 10, when Joyce paid the landlady at Finn's Hotel for the Triestines' rooms, they having decided to save money by moving above the theater on Mary Street. He took the occasion to get the waitress to show him Nora's room. 'You can imagine my excited appearance and manner,' he wrote her.[32] He seized upon Christian imagery to express his devotion:

* Joyce parodies this aspect of himself in the *Circe* episode of *Ulysses*.

Tonight I will not write to you as I have done before. All men are brutes, dearest, but at least in me there is also something higher at times. Yes, I too have felt at moments the burning in my soul of that pure and sacred fire which burns for ever on the altar of my love's heart. I could have knelt by that little bed and abandoned myself to a flood of tears. The tears were besieging my eyes as I stood looking at it. I could have knelt and prayed there as the three kings from the East knelt and prayed before the manger in which Jesus lay. They had travelled over deserts and seas and brought their gifts and wisdom and royal trains to kneel before a little new-born child and I had brought my errors and follies and sins and wondering and longing to lay them at the little bed in which a young girl had dreamed of me.[33]

For Christmas he sent her the parchment manuscript of his poems 'in return for your faithful love,' and added, in the lofty style of his twenties, with only a slight repetition of image at the end:

Perhaps this book I send you now will outlive both you and me. Perhaps the fingers of some young man or young girl (our children's children) may turn over its parchment leaves reverently when the two lovers whose initials are interlaced on the cover have long vanished from the earth. Nothing will remain then, dearest, of our poor human passion-driven bodies and who can say where the looks that looked on each other through their eyes will then be. I would pray that my soul be scattered in the wind if God would but let me blow softly for ever about one strange lonely dark-blue rain-drenched flower in a wild hedge at Aughrim or Oranmore.[34]

Joyce's two and a half months in Dublin were marked by some trouble with sciatica first and then with iritis, which returned, as his sisters suggested, because Dublin disagreed with him.[35] 'I am going back to civilization,' he told John Eglinton. As soon as he had received the license for the Volta from the Recorder [36] he got ready to leave with Eileen. Stanislaus objected that one sister was enough, but Joyce insisted upon bringing her. The 'dreadful house' at 44 Fontenoy Street was no place for her, and they must try to manage.[37] He got her some gloves and a warm coat [38] and on January 2 they left for Trieste.

This time his iritis was worse, and the Adriatic climate did not help it. Joyce had to rest his eyes for a month, while Stanislaus kept the house going. James could not bestir himself until February, and even then his approach to active living did not suit his brother. Since leaving the Scuola Berlitz Joyce had grown accustomed to a gentlemanly morning, an industrious afternoon (when, he said later to Budgen, 'the mind is at its best'),[39] and a chaotic evening. He woke about 10 o'clock, an hour or more after Stanislaus had breakfasted and left the house. Nora gave him coffee and rolls in bed, and he lay there, as Eileen described him, 'smothered in his own thoughts'[40] until about 11 o'clock. Sometimes his Polish tailor called, and would sit discoursing on the edge of the bed while Joyce listened and nodded. About eleven he rose, shaved, and sat down at the piano (which he was buying slowly and perilously on the installment plan). As often as not his singing and playing were interrupted by the arrival of a bill collector. Joyce was notified and asked what was to be done. 'Let them all come in,'[41] he would say resignedly, as if an army were at the door. The collector would come in, dun him with small success, then be skillfully steered off into a discussion of music or politics. That visit over, Joyce returned to the piano, until Nora interrupted, 'Do you know there's a lesson?' or 'You've put on a filthy shirt again,' to which he would calmly reply, 'I'll not take it off.'[42] There was lunch at 1 o'clock, cooked by Nora with some skill now.

After lunch the lessons went on fairly regularly from 2 to 7, 8, or 9 o'clock in the evening. Joyce usually gave them at home, but sometimes at the Scuola Municipale, and sometimes at his pupils' houses. He told Herbert Gorman of his laborious excursions to teach one of his pupils, a Captain Dehan, who commanded a boat that used to come every fortnight to Trieste from Bari. 'On these days,' Gorman says, 'Joyce would leave his house, walk across the Piazza Giambattista Vico, walk through the tunnel of Montuzza, take an electric tram to the gate of the Free Port, enter and take a horse tram to the Punto Franco, make signals to the ship until a small boat was sent out for him, board the boat and be taken to the ship, climb aboard and have a sailor search for the Captain, look for a quiet spot to give the lesson, give it (the Captain was intensely stupid), then look for a sailor to take him back to the Punto Franco, enter the horse tram and ride to the gate of the Free Port, board the electric tram which would take him to the mouth of the Montuzza tunnel, walk back through it, cross the Piazza Giambattista Vico and so reach his house. For this extraordinary exertion he received payment amounting to thirty pence [62¢].'[43]

At the lessons he smoked the long cheroots, Virginias, which are an Austrian specialty, and between lessons he drank black coffee. Sometimes he had tea during the afternoon. In the evening he could either continue with the lessons or, if he and Nora had decided, as they did perhaps twice a week, to go to the opera or play, he stood outside the door and sent his pupils away. Eva and Eileen often took the children to a cinema so that the whole entourage might not return until about 11 o'clock. When the children had been fed, Joyce played with Giorgio and rocked Lucia to sleep with a lullaby, affectionate rather than artistic, that ran:

C'era una volta, una bella bambina
Che si chiamava Lucia
Dormiva durante il giorno
Dormiva durante la notte
Perché non sapeva camminare
Perché non sapeva camminare
Dormiva durante il giorno
Dormiva durante la notte.[44]

On Sundays Eva and Eileen went regularly to church while the Joyces stayed at home. Nora often asked Eva to offer up a prayer for her, but made no move to offer up one of her own.[45] Eva was shocked to learn that James and Nora were not married, and tried to persuade them to have a ceremony performed. Nora was willing enough, but Joyce would not hear of it; so the matter was dropped.[46] Joyce occasionally went, however, to the Greek Orthodox Church, as he had sometimes done since his arrival in Trieste. He liked the way the priest was visible only a few times during the mass, the rest of the time being hidden behind gates, and he was amused at the end when 'a boy comes running down the side of the chapel with a large tray full of little lumps of bread. The priest comes after him and distributes the lumps to scrambling unbelievers. Damn droll!' [47] During Holy Week he behaved in a way that seemed odd to his sisters. Too fond of the liturgy and music to forego them, but determined to make clear his indifference, he avoided going with Eileen and Eva or sitting with them. Instead he came by himself and stood in a corner; and when the mass was over left quietly without waiting. He did not attempt to dissuade his sisters from going, but made clear that his own motive was esthetic, not pious.°

His distance from Dublin helped to put his two enterprises there, *Dubliners* and the Volta, out of his control, and both went badly. In Dublin George Roberts's promise to send proofs had still not been fulfilled. Roberts had begun to feel that the book might do him harm: after all, he was now a settled publisher, and there was a likelihood that he would soon become a solid married man. As word of the book's contents leaked out, the subtle pressures that exist in Dublin to this day were slowly brought to bear. Roberts's anxieties became localized

---

° Of the two sisters, Eileen was more confident and adaptable. She stayed on, but Eva, though inured to disorder from her experiences with the Dublin Joyces, found the disorder in Trieste too much for her, and left for home on July 9, 1911. Shortly after her return, another sister, Mabel ('Baby'), died of typhoid in Dublin. James wrote his father a letter which has not survived but in which, as other correspondence reveals, his regret for the dead girl was combined with bitterness over the conditions in which she had been forced by Ireland to live.[48]

in a strong passage in 'Ivy Day in the Committee Room,' which was a
little stronger now than when the book was sent to Grant Richards:

—But look here, John,—said Mr. O'Connor.—Why should we welcome the
king of England? Didn't Parnell himself . . .—

—Parnell,—said Mr. Henchy,—is dead. Now, here's the way I look at it.
Here's this chap come to the throne after his old mother keeping him out
of it till the man was grey. He's a jolly fine decent fellow, if you ask me,
and no damn nonsense about him. He just says to himself:—The old one
never went to see these wild Irish. By Christ, I'll go myself and see what
they're like.—And are we going to insult the man when he comes over here
on a friendly visit? Eh? Isn't that right, Crofton?—

Mr. Crofton nodded his head.

—But after all now,—said Mr. Lyons, argumentatively,—King Edward's
life, you know, is not very . . .—

—Let bygones be bygones,—said Mr. Henchy.—I admire the man personally. He's just an ordinary knockabout like you and me. He's fond of his
glass of grog and he's a bit of a rake, perhaps, and he's a good sportsman.
Damn it, can't we Irish play fair?—

Joyce agreed to make certain alterations, and on March 23, 1910,
Roberts wrote him the firm hoped to send proofs to him in early April
and publish in May. He did not, however, return the manuscript of
'Ivy Day' for changes until later; on June 10 he complained that Joyce's
substitution of 'old mother' for 'bloody old bitch of a mother' was not
'effective,' and asked him to rewrite the whole passage. Joyce declined
to do so, pointing out that Grant Richards raised no objection to the
passage when Edward VII was alive, and therefore an Irish publisher
had no reason to object when Edward VII was dead. Roberts did not
reply, and on July 10 Joyce wrote angrily to say, 'If no reply is sent me
to this letter I shall consider that you have no intention of publishing
the book and shall communicate the whole matter of the dispute in a
circular letter to the Irish press and at the same time take legal action
against you through my solicitor in Dublin for breach of contract.' No
reply did come, so Joyce wrote to Hone asking his intercession. Hone
was traveling on the continent when the letter, after many delays,
reached him; he was not in a position to change Roberts's mind. At any
rate, the publication, while not finally given over, was delayed from
month to month.

While *Dubliners* was blocked, the Volta stumbled and fell. Under
Novak's management the theater failed to break even. Stanislaus suspected, perhaps rightly, that his brother's neglect of the enterprise had
doomed it. Certainly James would have been able to sense the quirky

turns of the Dublin public better than a Triestine bicycle shop proprietor. The heavy emphasis on Italian films probably did not help
much. The partners decided they must cut the theater adrift so as to
avoid losing more than the 1600 pounds they had already invested, of
which Novak had himself contributed the larger share. Joyce asked his
father to offer the Volta to the Provincial Theatre Company, an English
firm; but before John Joyce bestirred himself, Novak negotiated the
sale to them for a thousand pounds, a loss of almost 40 per cent.[49]
Joyce labored briefly under the impression that he would receive forty
pounds as his share, but his partners, pointing to their losses, undeceived
him. He got nothing or almost nothing, and complained bitterly to
Schmitz that he had been cheated, a charge that was hardly justified.
Schmitz sent him a consolatory letter: 'You were so excited over the
cinematograph-affair that during the whole travel [that is, a trip Schmitz
took] I remembered your face so startled by such wickedness. And I
must add to the remarks I already have done that your surprise at being
cheated proves that you are a pure literary man. To be cheated proves
not yet enough. But to be cheated and to present a great surprise over
that and not to consider it as a matter of course is really literary.' [50]

In July, during the days immediately preceding the Volta's final sale,
Stanislaus and James became more deeply embroiled than ever before.
A series of petty quarrels had arisen to prepare for a more serious break.
One was over a library card which James wished to borrow; Stanislaus
thundered, 'You never return anything I lend you,' and made as if to
leave. James put his foot in the door to prevent its being closed, and
argued until Stanislaus at last turned over the card.[51] The aggregation
of Joyce sisters around James and Nora did nothing to alleviate Stanislaus's resentment; Eileen and Eva seemed to have joined the con-
spiracy to keep his pockets empty. Once Eileen asked him for money
for a new blouse, which he gave only to discover that her request had
been a trick of James to get money for household expenses. His stomach
was often empty, too; to his demands for dinner (he paid for his
board), his sisters sometimes snappishly replied, 'We didn't come to
Trieste to stay in and cook for you.' [52] On occasion he came punctually
for dinner at 9:30 o'clock to find the house dark, the whole family
having dispersed to opera and cinema; he continually tried to enforce
a schedule which was as continually broken. He felt some jealousy too,
at his brother's hold over Nora, whom he also found very attractive,
and he was sensitive to her indifference to him.

Many of these thoughts Stanislaus religiously put down in his diary.
James asked to read it but Stanislaus refused; James undoubtedly knew
the kind of thing that was in it whether or not he read the diary clan-

destinely as he had done in the past. But while the tensions in the mind of Stanislaus made him miserable, they made James comfortable, like a man who, having nourished a few doubts about the roundness of the earth, gets some excellent confirmation. Relations between men, he felt, must inevitably have this coloration of uncertainty, jealousy, hostility, and affection; the usual name for this hodgepodge was friendship. Fraternal relations could scarcely be exempt from the general law. And in Stanislaus, anger only proved dependence.

Stanislaus was too intelligent not to grasp this situation, but he lacked the will and the confidence in his own powers to extricate himself from it. His brother could create, while he could only criticize. One day, nonetheless, he made a more spirited protest than usual at having to eat by himself; he threatened to dine at a restaurant henceforth. For a day or two meals were served punctually, then on one pretext or another Joyce and Nora began to delay again. One Sunday night in July 1910, they entered the room just as Stanislaus was standing up to go away. In a fit of anger, the younger brother swore he would never come near the house again. James characteristically started to dispute the lateness of the hour, but Nora said bluntly, 'Ah, let him go out of that.'[53] The next day they hoped to receive the forty pounds from the sale of the Volta, so she was not in the mood for surrender.

The money was not forthcoming, however, and after three days Eva wrote Stanislaus a note saying, 'Jim says you'll have to leave him some money,' and James sent one, 'If you don't give us some money we must starve.' Even Giorgio, meeting Stanislaus in the street, said to him in Italian, 'We had no dinner today. Keep that in your head.' The pressure upon the young man was very great, but he won support from the Francinis who told him, after hearing the lamentable developments, that they had always felt he was mistreated in the house.[54]

If Stanislaus was unhappy, his brother's household was hungry. Eileen recalled a typical emergency of this period: James was paid for a lesson and with the money, all there was in the house, was sent to buy food. He returned instead with a handpainted silk scarf for Nora, whose appetite at the moment was not for finery.[55] This was one of the occasions when she threatened to go home to Galway and even went so far as to write her mother to that effect. Joyce looked over her shoulder and commented, 'If you're going home at least write 'I' with a capital letter.' 'What difference does it make?'[56] said Nora. But an hour or two later her anger subsided to the level of her orthography, and she tore up this letter as she had similar ones.

After a few more days of short rations Nora was as ready as the others to capitulate to Stanislaus, and James went round to his brother's room at 7 via Nuova, to bring him back. They had made a mistake, he said, and wanted Stanislaus to eat with them as in the past. Stanislaus, who could not bear the rift any better than they, allowed himself to be cajoled, and, as he confided in an unmailed letter to his father, 'The mistake began again.'[57] His own clothes grew threadbare as he paid under protest for new dresses or other furbelows for Nora. But he could not stop the flood by whipping it. In later life he reminded James that, though 1910 and 1911 had been difficult years for them, they had even then earned about £200 apiece, an amount which would have been adequate if James had not continually 'done things.'[58] Stanislaus, by nature and conviction a man with money in the bank, had to share in the folly of the rest of the family, without James's excuse of flaunting disdain for mere comfort and prudence. In August he was persuaded to help them take a flat at 32 via Barriera Vecchia, where they remained for a year and a half. He kept his own room on the via Nuova. The tension between the two brothers continued into the following year, when on January 12, James wrote coldly to announce, 'I take the opportunity of letting you know (as you have no doubt heard) that I am about to leave Trieste.' There had been some dispute involving their pupils, in which Stanislaus was apparently to blame, and Joyce went on: 'I intend to do what Parnell was advised to do in a similar occasion: clear out, the conflict being beneath my dignity, and leave you and the *cattolicissime* [Eva and Eileen] to make what you can of the city discovered by my courage (and Nora's) seven years ago, whither you and they came in obedience to my summons, from your ignorant and famine-ridden and treacherous country. My irregularities can easily be made the excuse of your conduct. A final attempt at regularity will be made by me in the sale of my effects, half of which will be paid in by me to your account in a Trieste bank where it can be drawn on or left to rot according to the dictates of your conscience. I hope that . . . when I have left the field, you and your sisters will be able, with the meagre means at your disposal, to carry on the tradition I leave behind me in honour of my name and my country.' But again there was a rapprochement.

The Volta's fall made *Dubliners* the center of Joyce's extra-familial attention. It was impossible to bring Roberts to the point; yet he never let *Dubliners* drop. In December 1910, he wrote Joyce he was sending the proofs of 'Ivy Day in the Committee Room,' which had been delayed because of the changes, and said he expected to publish on January 20.[59] The proofs did not arrive, however, though Roberts, tender of his author and the holiday season, sent two books to Joyce and Giorgio. When Joyce thanked him and warily asked whether January 20 was really the publication day,[60] Roberts brusquely informed him that there had been another postponement. Joyce wrote on January 22, 1911, to Stanislaus, with whom he was temporarily not on speaking terms, 'I know the name and tradition of my country too well to be surprised at receiving three scrawled lines in return for five years of constant service to my art and constant waiting and indifference and disloyalty in return for the 150,000 francs of continental money which I have deflected into the pockets of hungry Irishmen and women since they drove me out of their hospitable bog six years ago.' (The reference was to his agency for Irish tweeds.) Then Roberts wrote on February 9, 1911, that he was still worried about 'Ivy Day,' and wanted Joyce to remove all references to the king. At this point Joyce consulted a Dublin solicitor, probably his father's friend George Lidwell. The solicitor said that he should accede to Roberts's wishes, since, not being officially domiciled in the United Kingdom, he would have to deposit £100 in order to sue Maunsel & Co. for breach of contract, and would probably get no satisfaction from a Dublin jury if the passage 'could be taken as offensive in any way to the late King.'[61]

His helplessness made Joyce bitter, and his bitterness got on Nora's nerves. One day, after a particularly unpleasant exchange about writing and eating, Joyce took the manuscript of the unfinished *Portrait of the Artist* and threw it into the fire. Fortunately Eileen came in just at the moment, saw what he had done, and rescued the papers from the flames, slightly burning her fingers as she did so. The next morning her brother came back from a store and presented her with three bars of different-colored soap and a new pair of mittens, saying gratefully, 'There are pages here I could never have re-written.'[62] But so long as *Dubliners* was unpublished he could not finish the *Portrait*, and the smudged, invaluable pages were put aside, tied up in an old sheet.[63]

On August 1 Joyce had the notion of writing to George V for help in the dispute with Roberts. Eccentric as the plan was, it was consonant with his feeling, as Herbert Gorman points out, that appeals should always be made to the 'top dog.'[64] At Clongowes he had appealed to the rector, at University College to the president. Now he addressed himself earnestly to His Majesty. He enclosed a printed proof of the story 'Ivy Day' with the doubtful passage marked, and begged him 'to inform me whether in his view the passage (certain allusions made by a person of the story in the idiom of his social class) should be withheld from publication as offensive to the memory of his father.' It is not surprising that George V replied only through his secretary on August 11 that 'it is inconsistent with rule for His Majesty to express his opinion in such cases.' To receive any reply at all was a help, and

Joyce, on August 19, wrote up the whole history of *Dubliners,* beginning with Grant Richards, and sent it as an open letter to the Irish
press; * its publication, he said, would throw 'some light on the present
conditions of authorship in England and Ireland.'

After presenting a rather slanted account of negotiations, Joyce gave
the passage in dispute, cleverly calculating that if any editor should
venture to publish the letter with the passage in it the fact would serve
as evidence that there was really no danger. The letter concluded with
a paragraph that seemed to surrender to Roberts, but in such a way
as to make victory too shameful for Roberts to accept:

> I wrote this book seven years ago and hold two contracts for its
> publication. I am not even allowed to explain my case in a prefatory
> note: wherefore, as I cannot see in any quarter a chance that my rights
> will be protected, I hereby give Messrs Maunsel publicly permission
> to publish this story with what changes or deletions they may please
> to make and shall hope that what they may publish may resemble
> that to the writing of which I gave thought and time. Their attitude
> as an Irish publishing firm may be judged by Irish public opinion. I, as
> a writer, protest against the systems (legal, social and ceremonious)
> which have brought me to this pass.
>
>   Thanking you for your courtesy
>
>   I am, Sir,
>   Your obedient servant.
>   JAMES JOYCE
>
> 18 August 1911

This letter, one of Joyce's most outlandish moves in the dispute, was
published in full by *Sinn Fein* on September 2, and, with the contro-
versial passage omitted, by the *Northern Whig* of Belfast on August 26,
but it had no effect on Roberts, whom it did not even impel to break
off negotiations.

There now began a new episode in the relations of Nora and James.
Secure in the knowledge of her fidelity, he had for some time taken a
certain pleasure in observing her attraction for other men as well as
himself. Nora was handsomer with time; she had become fuller in body,
even on their diet, and had something of the queenly aspect that Joyce
uxoriously claimed for her. With old friends Joyce sometimes boasted
of the interest of other men in his wife, as he would make Bloom do
later. But attentions were one thing and advances another. There is a
curious entry in Joyce's preliminary notes for *Exiles,* dated November

---

* Copies went also to Roberts and Richards; the latter replied on August 28, 1911,
to thank Joyce for sending him the copy, and adding, 'I don't think you quite
realise a publisher's difficulties. But still. . . .' 65

12, 1913. It consists of a series of associations with 'N.(B.),' that is, with Nora Barnacle: 'Garter: precious, Prezioso, Bodkin, music, palegreen, bracelet, cream sweets, lily of the valley, convent garden (Galway), sea.' Bodkin was Nora's young Galway suitor who brought her boxes of cream sweets. In this series the new item is Prezioso, the jaunty, dapper Venetian who had been one of Joyce's best friends in Trieste. He had furnished Joyce with references for various positions, and had paid him well for his articles in the *Piccolo della Sera.* There is, however, no article by Joyce there between December 22, 1910, when he published a rather dull piece on British parliamentary betrayal of home rule policy, and September 5, 1912; it was probably during this period that the rift with Prezioso occurred.

Prezioso was a journalist of some intellectual distinction. He was married to a woman of a good and well-to-do family, and like Joyce he had two children. He dressed with great elegance and had the reputation of success with women.[66] For several months he had been in the habit of dropping in to see Nora in the afternoon, and often stayed for dinner.[67] Joyce did not object to these visits, but rather encouraged them. Nora enjoyed Prezioso's admiration, and went so far as to have her hair done. The new attention to her appearance gave her more charm, and prompted the Triestine painter Tullio Silvestri, who was to paint her in 1914, to say she was the most beautiful woman he had ever seen.[68]

Prezioso's admiration for Nora was combined with an admiration for Joyce, whose musical and literary knowledge he tried to absorb. It was probably this peculiar relationship with Prezioso that Joyce drew upon in the later chapters of *A Portrait,* where, with homosexual implications, Stephen's friend is as interested in Stephen as in Stephen's girl. At first Joyce followed Prezioso's activities, of which Nora kept him informed, with detachment, and studied them for secrets of the human spirit. But at some time in 1911 or 1912 Prezioso endeavored to become Nora's lover rather than her admirer. He said to her, '*Il sole s'é levato per Lei.*'[69] Nora checked him, and told Joyce, who later had Bloom say to Molly on Howth Head, 'The sun shines for you,'*[70] but who now was much disturbed.

Unlike Bloom, he did not submit tamely to the possibility of adultery. Instead he sought Prezioso out and expostulated with him in the name of friendship and broken confidence. The painter Silvestri happened to pass by the two men as they stood engaged in this crucial talk in the Piazza Dante, and saw tears running down Prezioso's humiliated face.[71]

---

* In *Exiles* (603 [423]), the maid says to Bertha, 'Sure he thinks the sun shines out of your face, ma'am.'

Joyce too retained the image of Prezioso weeping, and several years later found himself dreaming about it.

With this spectacle he had helped produce, Joyce (quick to be cool again) had the rest of the plot for *Exiles* where Prezioso's overtures form a considerable part of the action. Prezioso, for his pain, was honored by having his first name, Roberto, given to Richard's dishonorable friend in the play, Robert Hand. Joyce was half-responsible for Prezioso's conduct, in an experiment at being author of his own life as well as of his work. No doubt he was taking too much upon himself, but he did not do so for pleasure, except perhaps the pleasure of self-laceration.

1912

You let me tell you, with the utmost politeness, were very ordinarily
designed, your birthwrong was, to . . . do a certain office . . . in a certain
holy office . . . during certain agonising office hours . . . and do your
little thruppenny bit and thus earn from the nation true thanks, . . .
but, slackly shirking both your bullet and your billet, you beat it backwards like Boulanger from Galway . . . to sing us a song of alibi, . . .
nomad, mooner by lamplight, antinos, shemming amid everyone's repressed laughter to conceal your scatchophily by mating . . . masculine
monosyllables of the same numerical mus, an Irish emigrant the wrong
way out, sitting on your crooked sixpenny stile, an unfrillfrocked quack-
friar, you (will you for the laugh of Scheekspair just help mine with
the epithet?) semisemitic serendipidist, you (thanks, I think that describes you) Europasianised Afferyank!

—Finnegans Wake (190-91)

J OYCE was to turn thirty without any change in his misfortunes, and
the year 1912, in which exacerbations multiplied, was the most dis-
heartening of his life. On February 2 he celebrated his birthday by
being unable to pay the rent, and after the middle of the month his
new landlord, Picciola, gave notice. When Joyce scraped together
enough money to pay for three months' rent, Picciola allowed him to
remain without, however, relinquishing his legal right to evict him at
any moment in view of the previous default.[1]

In early March Joyce made a little money by delivering a second
series, of two lectures this time, at the Università Popolare. Four years
before he had spoken there on Irish subjects, but this time he announced
he would deal with 'Verismo ed idealismo nella letteratura inglese
(*Daniele De Foe—William Blake*).' This combination is less odd than
may at first appear. While he took pride in grounding his art like Defoe
in fact, he insisted also with Blake on the mind's supremacy over all
it surveyed. His lectures suggest two specific affinities as well. In their
different ways Defoe and Blake, like Joyce, conceived of an archetypal

man. England is not truly represented by John Bull, Joyce told his audience.* The English mind finds its epitome in Robinson Crusoe— 'the manly independence, the unconscious cruelty, the persistence, the slow but effective intelligence, the sexual apathy, the practical and well-balanced religiosity, the calculating silence.' So Crusoe, 'shipwrecked on a lonely island with a knife and a pipe in his pocket,' 'became architect, carpenter, knife-sharpener, baker, astronomer, shipbuilder, potter, farmer, saddle-maker, tailor, umbrella-maker, and clergyman.'[2] It was fitting that Crusoe should have been evolved by Defoe, who, Joyce told his audience, was the first English writer to throw off the Italian influence under which English literature had until then labored.[3]

In Blake the archetypal human figure is Albion, a vaster conception than Crusoe (or Bloom, who compares with him), but like Humphrey Chimpden Earwicker, father of humanity and symbol of everybody in *Finnegans Wake*. Blake came to this symbol through Swedenborg; as Joyce says, 'Eternity, which seemed to the favorite disciple [John] and to St. Augustine a celestial city and to Alighieri a celestial rose, appears to the mystical Swede under the semblance of a celestial man, animated in all his members by a fluid angelic life, eternally issuing and reissuing, systole and diastole of love and wisdom.'[4]

In his life as well as in his archetype of humanity Blake bore a curious resemblance to the Dubliner living in Trieste. Most writers on Blake in the nineteenth century saw him in their own image; to Rossetti he was an early Pre-Raphaelite, to Yeats he was in all probability an Irishman and a member of an occult society to which Yeats belonged. Joyce chose to emphasize Blake's marriage to an uneducated woman, paralleled by his own quasi-marriage, Blake's sympathy for the poor, similar to his own socialism, Blake's feeling for children, an important claim of his own, and Blake's understanding, in 'The Crystal Cabinet,' of gestation, a process so important in both *A Portrait* and *Ulysses*.[5] Joyce acquits Blake peremptorily of the charges of insanity and vague mysticism: For the first, 'To say that a great genius is mad, while at the same time recognizing his artistic merit, is no better than to say he is rheumatic or diabetic.'[6] For the second, he was a mystic only insofar as he could be one and remain an artist; his mysticism was no swooning ecstasy like that of St. John of the Cross, but a western mysticism filled with an 'innate sense of form and the coordinating power of the intellect.'[7]

A newspaper article added a third to this triad with which Joyce was

---

* He had written his brother from Rome that, compared to the English, all other peoples are puppets.

concerned. In the *Piccolo della Sera* of May 16, 1912, he wrote an article on '*L'Ombra di Parnell.*' It seemed, now that the House of Commons had twice passed a bill granting Ireland home rule, that the fight had been won. (Actually the House of Lords rejected it.) Joyce declared that, among the perfidies of the English and the self-betrayals of the Irish, one ghost would haunt the new state.* It was Parnell who had started the country towards parliamentary victory only to receive obloquy for his pains. Joyce admires Parnell's Joycean qualities, his utter coldness in the face of adulation or hostility, 'his sovereign bearing, mild and proud, silent and disconsolate.' † After his fall, Parnell 'went from county to county, from city to city, "like a hunted deer." ' ⁸ 'The citizens of Castlecomer threw quicklime in his eyes,' Joyce says, and a few months later called up this detail again in 'Gas from a Burner.' But the closest connection between himself and Parnell was Parnell's profound conviction that, in his hour of need, one of the disciples who dipped his hand in the same bowl with him would betray him.... That he fought to the very end with this desolate certainty in mind is his greatest claim to nobility.' ‡ ⁹ Richard Rowan, in *Exiles*, announces to Robert, 'There is a faith still stranger than the faith of the disciple in his master.... The faith of a master in the disciple who will betray him.' In Defoe's mastery of fact, in Blake's mastery of imagination, and in Parnell's mastery of his betrayers, Joyce adumbrated his view of his own powers.

From these lofty comparisons he descended to make a new effort to gain a livelihood. Late in 1911 the idea of teaching in an Italian public school had come to him. He learned from inquiries that he would have to pass examinations offered by the Italian government at the University of Padua. Some preliminary correspondence with officials there in November, 1911, persuaded him that the scheme might work, and that his British citizenship and Austrian residence would not prevent his receiving a teaching assignment in Italy. So encouraged, he travelled to Padua, managed to find a room in the crowded city at the Albergo Toretta, and took a series of written examinations there from April 24 to 26, 1912. On April 25 he wrote Stanislaus, 'Today I had to write my English theme—*Dickens* and saw my English examiner, an old, ugly spinster from the tight little island—a most dreadful *fRump*

---

* Yeats's poem, 'To a Shade,' written a year and a half later, uses Parnell in the same role of disapproving revenant.
† He emphasizes Parnell's speech impediment, attributed later to Earwicker in *Finnegans Wake*.
‡ In the early 1920's Joyce estimated Parnell more closely, and said to Djuna Barnes, 'The Irish have produced one skeleton—Parnell—never a man.' ¹⁰

(reformed spelling).' The University's records indicate the following results on the first three days:

I. Italian composition—30 out of 50 points
II. English composition—50 out of 50 points
III. Dictation in English—50 out of 50 points
IV. Translation into English of a passage from an Italian author—50 out of 50 points.

The low mark in Italian composition was offensive to Joyce's vanity. He went back to Trieste and then returned on April 30 for an oral and an additional written examination. This time his results were:

I. Translation into Italian of a passage from an English author—46 out of 50 points
II. Translation into English of an Italian passage, with grammatical commentary—50 out of 50 points
III. Answers to questions in English and other problems in grammar—50 out of 50 points
IV. Answers in Italian to questions about the history of English literature—45 out of 50 points

The final written examination required a discussion of 'The Rise of the Drama' and 'The Good Parson of Chaucer,' on which Joyce scored 50 out of 50 points. Since he had obtained 421 points out of a possible 450, the judging committee ruled he had passed,[11] an achievement not altogether astonishing for the major prose stylist of his century.

Then the complications began. The Minister of Education in Florence informed him in May that the validity of his Dublin degree would have to be established before he could teach. Then the University of Padua, instructed by the officials at Rome, informed him that his degree did not conform with requirements. Joyce wrote to the Board of Education in London to find out if there was reciprocity between the two countries in the recognition of degrees, but the Board replied that no reciprocity had been established so that the decision was entirely in the hands of the Italian officials.[12] He next appealed to influential friends, including Senator Guido Mazzoni and Carlo Galli, but neither of them could help him.

The mistreatment of Joyce by the Italian bureaucrats became known in Trieste, and spurred several other of his friends, including Schmitz, Veneziani, and Vidacovich, to try to arrange a place for him at the Scuola Revoltella Superiore di Commercio, a commercial high school.*

---

* This had been founded many years before by Pasquale Revoltella. This millionaire, somewhat like Blazes Boylan's father in *Ulysses* (314 [304]), had sold meat twice over to make a fortune, but then erased the bad reputation of his money by generosity in spending it.

An elderly man now taught English at the school, and was soon to be pensioned off. Stanislaus wrote James urging him to apply at once, but James said he must delay until his predecessor had left, and meanwhile asked for the loan of a florin.[13]

He continued to cast about for some way of persuading Roberts to publish *Dubliners.* Since Nora, after eight years of absence from home, had begun to correspond with her family and was eager to see them, he decided to send her and Lucia to Ireland. To keep the trip from taking too simple a form, they would stop in Dublin so that Nora could intercede for him with Roberts.* She would then proceed to Galway, and there try to extract money from her Uncle Michael Healy so that Joyce could join her there. Nora was delighted, but foresaw embarrassment over her ringless finger, and asked Joyce if she might not wear a ring while with her family. This he resolutely forbade,[14] but Nora seems to have evolved some stratagem to prevent her mother's guessing the truth; though Joyce wished her to be straightforward, it must be remembered that he had not brought up the subject himself with Mrs. Barnacle during his 1909 visit.

Joyce saw Nora and Lucia off at the station and went round to Ettore Schmitz to tell him and Signora Schmitz what a relief it was to have only men in the house.[15] But his temper changed rapidly when Nora failed to write him at once on her arrival in Dublin. Within a week he was back at Schmitz's house, this time to ask for payment for twelve lessons in advance so that he and Giorgio might go to Ireland too. He also left with them for safekeeping a small, oddly misshapen dog whose name, he said, was Fido. The dog was not housebroken and one day, being let out, disappeared. Schmitz sent out his servant to hunt for him, for Joyce, he remarked, would be greatly distressed if the dog were not there on his return. After an hour the servant returned to announce that 'he' had pupped with a litter of twelve. Joyce had never properly ascertained Fido's sex.[16] On the other hand, he had shrewdly calculated Schmitz's forbearance.

Before leaving for Dublin, Joyce dispatched a furious letter to Nora:

Via della Barriera Vecchia 32[III],
Trieste (Austria)

Dear Nora

    Having left me five days without a word of news you scribble your signature with a number of others on a postcard. Not one word of the places in Dublin where I met you and which have so many memories

---

* So Molly Bloom in *Ulysses* (737 [712]) was to intercede for her husband with Joe Cuffe.

for us both! Since you left I have been in a state of dull anger. I consider the whole affair wrong and unjust.

I can neither sleep nor think. I have still the pain in my side.* Last night I was afraid to lie down. I thought I would die in sleep. I wakened Georgie three times for fear of being alone.

It is a monstrous thing to say that you seem to forget me in five days and to forget the beautiful days of our love.

I leave Trieste tonight as I am afraid to stay here—afraid of myself. I shall arrive in Dublin on Monday. If you have forgotten I have not. I shall go *alone* to meet and walk with the images of her whom I remember.

You can write a wire to me in Dublin to my sister's address.

What are Dublin and Galway compared with our memories?

Jim

His letter disconcerted Nora, but perhaps flattered her a little too. She had meanwhile arrived at Westland Row Station on Monday, July 8, where John Joyce, Charles, Eva, and Florence greeted her. John Joyce wept copiously every time he looked at little Lucia.[17] He brought Nora to Finn's Hotel, where, in contrast to her husband's lachrymose visits to the shrine, she experienced a small triumph at being guest instead of chambermaid. She went to see Roberts, but unfortunately took John and Charles Joyce with her, so that Roberts, after listening briefly to their trio of expostulation, adopted his official tone and asked them to call again since he was busy.[18] Next day he avoided them, so Nora went on to Galway, leaving the matter in Charles's ineffectual hands. From Galway she wrote Joyce affectionately: 'My darling Jim, Since I left Trieste I am continually thinking about you how are you getting on without me or do you miss me at all. I am dreadfully lonely for you. I am quite tired of Ireland already. . . .'[19] But he had left in her pursuit.

Joyce and Giorgio arrived in London on July 14 or 15. They called on Yeats, and Joyce wrote Stanislaus, 'For a wonder he was polite. Gave me tea and Georgie fruit. He has rewritten *Countess Cathleen* and sends the new version of it to Vidacovich through you.'[20] He also saw Joseph Hone at the London office of Maunsel & Co., and said grandiloquently, 'I have crossed Europe to see you.'[21] But Hone could only refer him to Roberts. Joyce went on to Dublin, where his family was surprised to see his 'apology for a moustache,' as Charles Joyce called it.[22] He decided to try to find a job for Charles, but devoted himself to the main business of calling on Roberts. The publisher told him, 'The Giant's Causeway is soft putty compared with you.'[23] He offered Joyce

---

* Joyce had peculiar pains all his life, and regularly referred to them when upbraiding Nora.

alternative proposals, the first to make all requested deletions with an explanatory preface, the second to bring out the book under his own name. Since Stanislaus had often urged his brother to publish *Dubliners* himself and promised to find the money somewhere, Joyce wrote to ask him which course he should follow.[24] Then he rushed on to Galway and Nora.

Aside from the uneasiness over Roberts's intentions the next three weeks were bucolic enough. Nora enjoyed showing Joyce off to the friends of her childhood, and wrote a little boastfully to Eileen on August 14, 'well what have you to say to Jim now after all our little squabbles he could not live without me for a month.' Joyce took up rural sports; he rowed and one Sunday bicycled forty miles. The pain in his side did not trouble him. He and Nora went together to Galway Races and, more lugubriously, he paid a visit by bicycle to the grave-yard at Oughterard where Michael Bodkin, Nora's early sweetheart, lay buried.[25] Joyce related the scene a year later to that of Shelley's grave in Rome, and wrote in the notes to *Exiles* under his wife's initials:

Moon: Shelley's grave in Rome. He is rising from it: blond she weeps for him. He has fought in vain for an ideal and died killed by the world. Yet he rises. Graveyard at Rahoon by moonlight where Bodkin's grave is. He lies in the grave. She sees his tomb (family vault) and weeps. The name is homely. Shelley's is strange and wild. He is dark, unrisen, killed by love and life, young. The earth holds him.
Bodkin died. Kearns died. In the convent they called her the man-killer: (woman-killer was one of her names for me). I live in soul and body.
She is the earth, dark, formless, mother, made beautiful by the moonlit night, darkly conscious of her instincts. . . . Rome is the strange world and strange life to which Richard brings her. Rahoon her people. She weeps over Rahoon too, over him whom her love has killed, the dark boy whom, as the earth, she embraces in death and disintegration. He is her buried life, her past. . . . His symbols are music and the sea, liquid formless earth, in which are buried the drowned soul and body. There are tears of commiseration. She is Magdalen who weeps remembering the loves she could not return.[26]

Still trying to penetrate her soul, he wrote a poem to express what he felt to be her thoughts about her dead lover and her living one. He shifted Bodkin's grave from Oughterard, seventeen miles from Galway, to the Galway cemetery at Rahoon with its more sonorous name:

She Weeps over Rahoon

Rain on Rahoon falls softly, softly falling,
Where my dark lover lies.
Sad is his voice that calls me, sadly calling,
At grey moonrise.

Love, hear thou
How soft, how sad his voice is ever calling,
Ever unanswered and the dark rain falling,
Then as now.

Dark too our hearts, O love, shall lie and cold
As his sad heart has lain
Under the moongrey nettles, the black mould
And muttering rain.

The dead sweetheart was brought into a mortuary triangle with the two living lovers.

With a sense of sacred coincidence Joyce found a headstone at Oughterard with the name of J. Joyce on it,[27] an occult verification of the journey westward of Gabriel in 'The Dead.' He also went with Nora to the Aran Islands, and wrote two articles for the *Piccolo della Sera* about them. The articles display none of the contempt for Irish rural life and folklore which he had evinced in 1902 and 1903 in talking with Yeats and Lady Gregory; as he predicted in 'The Dead,' Joyce came round to sharing Ireland's primitivism. He depicted Aran with the affection of a tourist who has read Synge, noted the peculiarities in the islanders' dialect, and described curious local customs and history. He was interested in the fact that each year a Dominican friar blesses the sea at the start of the herring season, and patriotically proclaimed that 'Christopher Columbus . . . was the last to discover America,'[28] the real discoverer having been the Irish St. Brendan, who made the voyage from Aran centuries earlier.

Another episode of these days in Galway suggests the same pastoral solicitude. Before he left Trieste, Joyce's friend Henry N. Blackwood Price, an Ulsterman who was Assistant Manager of the Eastern Telegraph Company there, asked him to obtain the address of William Field, M.P., the Blackrock butcher who was president of the Irish Cattle Traders' Society. Price had heard, in Austria, of a cure for the hoof and mouth disease which was then so prevalent in Ireland that the English had declared an embargo on Irish cattle. He kept importuning Joyce from Trieste: 'Be energetic. Drop your lethargy. Forget Leinster for Ulster. Remember that Sir John Blackwood died in the act of putting on his topboots in order to go to Dublin to vote against the Union. You will get your name up if you write this up.'[29] Joyce forwarded to Field a letter from Price,* which Field had published in the

---

* Price's letter to Field, since Joyce parodied it, is worth quoting in part:

　　Dear Sir—I have this morning received from my friend, Professor Joyce, a letter in which he gives me your address. I therefore lose no time in giving you all the particulars with which I am acquainted, as to the treatment of foot-and-mouth

Evening Telegraph; [30] and then early in September Joyce surprised himself by writing a sub-editorial about the disease for the *Freeman's Journal.*[31] But privately Joyce wrote to his brother, 'I think Price ought to look for a cure for the foot and mouth disease of Anna Blackwood Price.' [32]

---

disease in this Province of Austria. I must premise that I am an Irishman without politics, except a sincere desire to serve my country with any means in my power, and as far as I can in a practical manner. Many years ago I was in County Meath when there was a severe outbreak of foot-and-mouth disease. Then, as now, all affected beasts were destroyed. I was surprised last autumn to learn that a case of this disease was cured in eight or nine days, not half a mile from my house. When therefore I learned that the outbreaks in the British Isles had assumed so vast a proportion I determined to do the best I could to bring the method of cure, adopted in Styria, to the knowledge of my countrymen. I will not waste time in enumerating all the railway journeys I have taken, or the letters I have written on the subject, but will as briefly as is consistent with clearness, put you in possession of all I know with reference to the method of treatment here. The methods adopted in Austria are by a serum of inoculation, which is brought here from Berlin. There are varying opinions among the Veterinary Authorities here as to the efficacy of this remedy. In any case it deserves a trial in Ireland. The case in the Alpine village where I live was treated, I believe, exclusively with Pyoktanin as a disinfectant followed by tannic acid. . . . I sent on the 9th inst. a registered letter to the County Veterinary Surgeon for the County Down (where I was born) giving him full particulars. . . . I did the same to Mr. Runciman, Minister of Agriculture, on the 7th instant. . . . On the 10th instant I wrote to the Department of Agriculture in Dublin at their request, in answer to an offer on my part to give them information as to the Styrian mode of treatment of foot-and-mouth disease. Sufficient time has not yet elapsed to allow of my having any reply or acknowledgment.

. . . I hope you will not regard me as an enthusiast who imagines that he has found a specific for this disease. I do not go so far as that, but I say that in the hands of experienced veterinary surgeons Pyoktanin is, in an enormous percentage of cases, absolutely successful and, therefore, saves a great deal of money to the cattle owners. . . . There are two points in this question which should not be lost sight of. First, the cure may be quite successful in the case of the Murzthaler or the Murthaler breeds, the two breeds which are here best known, and yet with shorthorns and higher bred cattle less successful. Anyway, it should have a trial in Ireland. . . . Second, a great deal depends upon experienced veterinary treatment. I am in almost daily communication with three gentlemen who have had great success. . . . They are all three quite ready to go to the British Isles without pay. . . . Herr E. Boehme . . . is now looking after some cases of foot-and-mouth disease near the Emperor's shooting lodge at Murzsteg. . . .

I have absolutely no interest of a personal nature in this matter. My friend, Mr. Jas Joyce, will tell you I am not that sort. . . .

                  —I am, sir, yours faithfully,
                     Henry N. Blackwood Price, M.I.E.E.

Joyce wrote in the *Nestor* episode of *Ulysses* (33-34 [30]):

—I have put the matter into a nutshell, Mr. Deasy said. It's about the foot and mouth disease. . . .

May I trespass on your valuable space. That doctrine of *laissez faire* which so often in our history. Our cattle trade. The way of all our old industries. Liverpool

Even in this garden of the west Joyce managed to be plagued by Triestine creditors. On August 15 his landlord informed Eileen, who had been left behind in the flat, that the Joyces would have to leave at the end of the quarter, nine days later. She rushed to Stanislaus, who wrote to James to ask how this new mess had come about. Joyce replied with immense self-righteousness:

The story about the flat is this. I received on the 24 Feb notice. That was unpleasant but valid. I then with Nora went about looking for a flat and visited thirty. The house-agent *himself* stopped me in Via Bellini and asked me had I found a flat. I said no. He said the matter would be smoothed over, to leave it to him, that he did not want me to leave as he did not know what kind of people might come into the flat, that Picciola [the landlord] was very fond of me and intended to take English lessons from me during the winter, and that if any repairs were necessary he even believed that Picciola would pay for them!!! Similar conversations took place 4 times. I told the porter and everyone who visited the flat that I was remaining. When I paid the last quarter I asked had he spoken to Picciola. He said he would see in a few days and repeated the story about English lessons. I consider (and will contest by force and by law) that this is a verbal revocation of the notice. On the strength of it I left Trieste. I have written the whole story to Picciola himself and say, if he will not have me in the house, I shall vacate the flat for the 24 Feb or 24 November. For the 24 Aug. *no*. . . . If in spite

---

ring which jockeyed the Galway harbour scheme. European conflagration. Grain supplies through the narrow waters of the channel. The pluterperfect imperturbability of the department of agriculture. Pardoned a classical allusion. Cassandra. By a woman who was no better than she should be. To come to the point at issue.
—I don't mince words, do I? Mr. Deasy asked as Stephen read on.
Foot and mouth disease. Known as Koch's preparation. Serum and virus. Percentage of salted horses. Rinderpest. Emperor's horses at Mürzsteg, lower Austria. Veterinary surgeons. Mr Henry Blackwood Price. Courteous offer a fair trial. Dictates of common sense. Allimportant question. In every sense of the word take the bull by the horns. Thanking you for the hospitality of your columns.
—I want that to be printed and read, Mr. Deasy said. You will see at the next outbreak they will put an embargo on Irish cattle. And it can be cured. It is cured. My cousin, Blackwood Price, writes to me it is regularly treated and cured in Austria by cattledoctors there. They offer to come over here. I am trying to work up influence with the department. Now I'm going to try publicity. I'm surrounded by difficulties, by . . . intrigues, by . . . backstairs influence, by . . .
. . . —I wrote last night to Mr. Field, M.P.

Joyce is parodying not only Blackwood Price but himself. He described the Galway harbour scheme in 'The Mirage of the Fisherman of Aran,' the second of his two articles in the *Piccolo* in 1912. The word 'pluterperfect' he borrowed from his earlier essay, 'L'Ombra di Parnell,' where the Italian equivalent is '*sopraperfetto*.' The phrase, 'Grain supplies through the narrow waters of the channel,' echoes a sentence in the Aran article: 'From Canada, the granary and warehouse of the United Kingdom, great cargoes of grain would enter the Irish port, thus avoiding the dangers of navigation in St. George's Channel, and the enemy fleets.' [33]

of that Picciola insists on putting me and my family on the street I promise
you you will see some fun in the house. If he does so he is an inhuman
person and I will treat him as such. I am however almost sure that he will
agree to my proposal. . . . Take possession of the house till I return. Don't
let my debts trouble you. Tell them I am away and will return in the month
of September. They would get the same answer at Economo's door and
would salute and go away.[34]

Belligerence was easy in Galway, but Stanislaus, confronted by an
adamant landlord, knew better than to follow James's directions about
legal action. 'My brother,' he wrote Herbert Gorman later, 'has still
illusions about the law.' [35] He was not impressed, either, by James's comparison of himself to Baron Economo, one of the wealthiest men in
Trieste. He therefore rented a smaller, newer, and cleaner flat at 4 via
Donato Bramante, close to the Duomo of San Giusto, into which he
moved James's and Nora's belongings on October 1.[36] Here his brother
was to live the rest of his time in Trieste.*

While Joyce's furniture in Trieste was on the move again, *Dubliners*
remained inert in the offices of Maunsel & Co. He wrote from Galway
to Joseph Hone, asking his intercession again, but the letter was
answered coldly by Roberts. He pretended to have slowly come to
realize the book's implications were anti-Irish and therefore out of
keeping with his aims as an Irish publisher. He was not afraid of the
charge of immorality, he said, for he had published Synge's *The Playboy of the Western World,* 'shift' and all. But he must take account, in
a country notoriously addicted to libel actions, of the possible loss
of money and goodwill in court suits.[37] He may also have had a private
reason: one Dublin rumor of the time said he had promised his fiancée,
out of regard for her honor, that he would not publish a questionable
book. Joseph Hone suggested later, though Roberts denied it, that the
Vigilance Committee, in which one of Maunsel's chief customers,† the
Lord Lieutenant's wife, Lady Aberdeen, was active, had exerted pressure on the firm.[38] Roberts must have borne resentment against Joyce
for his letter to *Sinn Fein* and the *Northern Whig* the year before, complaining publicly of Roberts's treatment. The publisher was quite capable of responding with subtle and lingering malice. Then he was by nature incapable of being altogether straightforward in dealing with any of
his writers. He specialized in adding new conditions after the first had
been accepted. As George Russell wrote a friend on May 12, 1913, after
bringing up grievances of his own against Roberts, 'The list of Irish

---

* It was a fortunate location in that a near neighbor was the blind Triestine composer, Antonio Smareglia, with whom Joyce soon became friends.
† Lady Aberdeen had Roberts publish tracts in her campaign against tuberculosis.

writers with whom he has quarreled includes Yeats, Lady Gregory, Stephens, Alice Milligan, Seumas O'Sullivan, Joyce, and I believe there are others.' * A remark Roberts later made of Liam O'Flaherty, 'I don't know why O'Flaherty cuts me; after all, I never published him,' [39] seems to summarize his publishing history.

Roberts's proposal in his letter to Joyce was that he persuade Grant Richards to take over the sheets. Since Richards's previous difficulty had been to find a printer willing to set the stories in type, he could in this way circumvent the 'English moral printer.' This letter brought Joyce quickly back to Dublin in mid-August, Nora and the children remaining behind in Galway to save expenses. He retained as solicitor his father's friend George Lidwell, a poor choice since Lidwell's practice was largely confined to police court work. On August 18 he had a two-hour discussion with Roberts, which grew so excited that twice Roberts left the room in a fury. Roberts's stipulations became steadily more rigorous: he now demanded the omission of 'An Encounter,' further deletions from the passage about King Edward VII in 'Ivy Day,' and the substitution of fictitious names for the public houses in 'Counterparts' and four other places. At this point Padraic Colum, who accompanied Joyce to help out, glanced at the proofs and asked with mock-innocence whether the book was all about public houses. [40] He was less co-operative with 'An Encounter,' which he read on the spot and pronounced 'a terrible story.' [41] Joyce now agreed to the changes proposed on condition that the book be published before October 1912, but Roberts said he would have to see what his solicitor said before finally confirming the arrangement. [42]

In this crisis Joyce called upon two old friends to help. Thomas Kettle was unresponsive; he thought the book would do harm to Ireland. 'I'll slate that book,' [43] he declared. Joyce pointed out that he had actually taken part in the events described in such a story as 'An Encounter,' and Kettle granted, with reference to the homosexual in that story, 'Yes, we have all met him.' [44] But he considered 'An Encounter' 'beyond anything in its outspokenness he had ever read,' [45] and would not help. He warned that Maunsel might incur libel suits. Joyce next tried C. P. Curran, of whose support he felt uncertain, and was delighted when Curran proved friendly and willing to speak to Roberts on his behalf. On August 19 he felt optimistic again. He asked his own solicitor,

* The letter, to be included in Alan Denson's edition of Russell's correspondence, to be published by Abelard-Schuman, gives an account of Roberts's dealings with Katharine Tynan which sound extremely like his dealings with Joyce. Although Joyce knew Roberts's reputation for roguery, he was understandably not disposed to make this an extenuating factor.

George Lidwell, for a statement that the book was not libelous. But Lidwell's letter, collected from him next day, slanted the matter quite differently:

I have read . . . 'Ivy Day in the Committee Room' and I think that beyond the questionable taste of the language (which is a matter entirely for the author) in referring to the memory of the last two reigning Sovereigns of these Realms, the vulgar expressions put into the mouths of the characters in the dialogue are not likely to be taken very serious notice of by the Advisers of the Crown.

As to the last paragraphs in the Chapter under the head of 'An Encounter' the matter is different. . . . I might quote Gibbon's 'Decline and Fall' to show how much the subject is loathed: 'I touch with reluctance and dispatch with impatience this most odious vice of which modesty rejects the name and nature abominates the idea.'

It would be well to remember that although these paragraphs in your book might possibly escape notice that there is at present in existence in this city a Vigilance Committee whose object is to seek out and suppress all writings of immoral tendencies and I am of opinion that if the attention of the Authorities be drawn to these paragraphs it is likely they would yield to the pressure of this body and prosecute. Whether a conviction could be obtained is another matter altogether. But I would advise you to take no risks and under the circumstances either delete or entirely alter the paragraphs in question.

Curran read this letter and said it was thoroughly bad for Joyce's case. Joyce went to see Lidwell at the Ormonde bar,* but had no chance to talk to him privately until the next day. After an hour's argument he persuaded Lidwell to write an apter letter, 'Referring to our correspondence concerning the stories "Ivy Day in the Committee Room" and "An Encounter." As the passages you have shown me are not likely to be taken serious note of by the Advisers of the Crown, they would not interfere with the publication, nor do I consider a conviction could be easily obtained.'⁴⁶ This statement, which had its equivocations too, Joyce bore to Roberts at once, but Roberts said slyly that to carry any weight it should be addressed not to Joyce but to him. Joyce dutifully trudged back to Lidwell and asked him to write the same letter to Roberts, but Lidwell—braver in bars than offices—refused on the ground that Roberts was not his client. Joyce returned to Roberts and told him this. Roberts now demanded that Lidwell write him a letter saying what Joyce was prepared to do by way of indemnifying his firm in the event of prosecution. Joyce offered to sign an agreement to pay him the cost of the whole first edition, which, by the way, was only sixty pounds, if the book were seized. Roberts demanded instead two securi-

* Where he keeps him in *Ulysses*.

ties for a thousand pounds each. 'No one admires me so much as that,' [47] said Joyce, and insisted that such a loss was beyond possibility. Roberts now flatly announced that he would not publish the book.

Joyce went into the back room of the office to ponder what to do. There, as he wrote Nora, 'sitting at the table, thinking of the book I have written, the child which I have carried for years and years in the womb of the imagination as you carried in your womb the children you love, and of how I had fed it day after day out of my brain and memory, [I] wrote him the enclosed letter.' [48] This letter agreed very unwillingly to omit 'An Encounter' from the book on four conditions:

1) That the following note be placed by me before the first story:
    This book in this form is incomplete. The scheme of the book as framed by me includes a story entitled An Encounter which stands between the first and second story in this edition.   J.J.

2) That no further changes be asked of me.

3) That I reserve the right to publish the said story elsewhere before or after the publication of the book by your firm.

4) That the book be published by you not later than the 6th of October, 1912.

Roberts noncommittally agreed to forward this letter to his London solicitor. Again Joyce's hopes soared, though his father, when informed of these concessions, warned him Roberts would find another reason for not publishing.

John Joyce was right. Roberts received a letter from his solicitors— Charles Weekes, once a poet in George Russell's school, in London, and Collins in Dublin—informing him that the proposed omission was entirely insufficient. Roberts wrote Joyce on August 23, that he had been advised that actions in libel would lie in practically every case where any going concern, public house, railway company or whatever was mentioned by actual name. Joyce, said the solicitors, must put up two sureties of £500 each. They even advised Roberts that Joyce had broken his contract by submitting for publication a book he knew to be libelous, and offered to bring suit to recover Roberts's expenses. Roberts brusquely requested that Joyce 'make a substantial offer towards covering our loss.'

Joyce received the letter at Roberts's office, where it had been left for him. 'I read it,' he wrote Nora, 'and walked down the street feeling the whole future of my life slipping out of my grasp.' [49] He had no money, hope, or youth left. He sat for an hour on a sofa in Lidwell's office, and considered buying a revolver to 'put some daylight into my publisher.' [50] Lidwell, appealed to once more, was now on Roberts's side. John Joyce, who told Charles privately that *Dubliners* was 'a black-guard production,' urged James to buck up and find another publisher. But after pawning his watch and chain so he could stay a little longer, Joyce went back to Roberts for a last try. At his most dogged, ironic, and practical, he took up one by one the points made by Roberts's solicitor:

1) A railway company is mentioned once and then exonerated from all blame by two witnesses, jury and coroner.

2) Public houses are mentioned in four stories out of fifteen. In three of these stories the names are fiction. In the fourth the names are real because the persons walked from place to place ('Counterparts').

3) Nothing happens in the public houses: people drink.

4) I offered to take a car and go with Roberts, proofs in hand, to the three or four publicans really named and to the Secretary of the railway company. He refused.

5) I said the publicans would be glad of the advertisement.

6) I said that I would put fictitious names for the few real ones but added that by so doing the selling value in Dublin of the book would go down.

7) I said that even if they took action for libel against Maunsel that the jury would be a long time before awarding damages on such a plea.

8) I said that his legal adviser was a fool to advise him to sue me. If he sued me (even if I lived in Dublin) a jury would say he had the MS. for ten months and I was not liable for his error of judgement. But if he sued me in Trieste I would hold the whip and would laugh him out of court.

9) I suggested that his lawyer encouraged correspondence and litigation for his own profit.[51]

Roberts, to be rid of these importunities, promised (in defiance of Joyce's point 9) to consult his solicitors again.

From Trieste Stanislaus, pinching to support his absent brother, cabled him on August 25, 'Come without delay.' Joyce paid no attention. In Dublin he observed a change of tone. A solicitor named Dixon, with whom he discussed his affairs, remarked, 'It's a pity you don't use your undoubted talents for some other purpose than writing a book like *Dubliners*. Why don't you use them for the betterment of your country and your people?' Joyce gave an odd reply: 'I am probably the only Irishman who is writing leading articles for the Italian press,' he said, 'and all my articles in the *Piccolo della Sera* have been about Ireland and the Irish people.' Then he added his by now well-worn casuistry, 'I was the first person to introduce Irish tweeds in Austria although that business is not the least in my own line.'[52] A loftier answer to the imputation of treachery against his country is contained in a letter to Nora in Galway, asking her to join him in Dublin during Horse Show week: 'The Abbey Theatre will be open and they will give plays of Yeats and Synge. You have a right to be there because you are my bride: and I am one of the writers of this generation who are perhaps creating at last a conscience in the soul of this wretched race.' And in the same letter he vowed, 'If only my book is published then I will plunge into my novel and finish it.' [53] Goaded by the slurs of Kettle and Dixon, he felt firmly in command now of the ending of his novel, in which he used some of the same phrasing: 'I go to encounter for the millionth time the reality of experience and to forge in the smithy of my soul the uncreated conscience of my race.' *[54] Even if Dublin rejected *Dubliners,* he would still be able to conquer Ireland, in the artist's traditional way, by setting up the criteria by which it must judge and be judged.

James Stephens, whom he described to his brother as 'my rival, the latest Irish genius,' and met for the first time on Dawson Street during the negotiations, received some of his irritation. They were introduced abruptly by a friend of Joyce who at once left them together. As Stephens recalled the scene, 'Joyce looked at me without a word in his mouth and I looked at him with nothing in my mouth except vocabulary. We halted upon each other. We were very different-looking people. Joyce was tall, which I wasn't; he was thin, which I wasn't; he wore specs, which I didn't; he looked down at me, which I couldn't; he rubbed his chin at me, which I wouldn't. Suddenly I remembered a very cultivated remark which I had once heard a gentleman in a tall hat make to another in a straw hat whom he didn't know what to do with, and I repeated it to Joyce: "Come and have a drink," said I. He turned, and we walked towards Grafton Street, and I regaled him with the gayest remarks that I could think of about what is known as the weather and this and that: "An American," said I, "holds that it never rains in Ireland except between the showers." "Ah," said Joyce. "But a French lady," I continued, "told me that it rains in Ireland whether there are showers or not." "Ah," said Joyce. "This is Pat Kinsella's," I continued as we halted outside the first tavern that we came to. "Ah," said Joyce; and we went in. The barman brought the refreshment that I ordered. It was called a "tailor of malt." It was larger than a single, and it only escaped being a double by the breadth of a tram-ticket, and it cost me threepence. When Joyce had silently dispatched one-third of a tailor into his system he became more human. He looked at me through the spectacles that made his blue eyes look

---

* He may have remembered Montaigne's statement, 'I must forge as well as furnish the mind.'

nearly as big as the eyes of a cow—very magnifying they were. "It takes," said I brightly, "seven tailors to make a man, but two of these tailors make twins. Seven of them," I went on, "make a clan." Here Joyce woke up: he exploded moderately into conversation. He turned his chin and his specs at me, and away down at me, and confided the secret to me that he had read my two books, that, grammatically, I did not know the difference between a semi-colon and a colon, that my knowledge of Irish life was non-Catholic and so, non-existent, and that I should give up writing and take to a good job like shoe-shining as a more promising profession. I confided back to him that I had never read a word of his, and that, if Heaven preserved to me my protective wits, I never would read a word of his unless I was asked to review it destructively.

'We stalked out of Pat Kinsella's; that is, he stalked, I trotted. Joyce lifted his hat to me in a very foreign manner and I remarked: "You should engrave on your banner and on your notebook the slogan "Rejoyce and be exceedingly bad." "Ah," said Joyce, and we went our separate ways...." * [55]

* It was on this occasion that Joyce first sang for Stephens 'The Yellow Ale,' a song of which he was particularly fond. He had first come across it, Roger McHugh suggests,[56] in the Christmas number of the *Irish Homestead* for 1901, but the version there, a prose translation by Lady Gregory from the Irish original, is not exactly the one Joyce sang. Joyce's version was as follows:

> As I was going the road one fine day,
> (O the brown and the yellow ale!)
> I met with a man that was no right man.
> (O love of my heart!)
>
> He asked was the woman with me my daughter
> (O the brown etc.)
> And I said that she was my married wife
> (O, love etc.)
>
> He asked would I lend her for an hour and a day
> And I said I would do anything that was fair.
>
> So let you take the upper road and I'll take the lower
> And we'll meet again at the ford of the river.
>
> I was walking that way one hour and three quarters
> When she came to me without shame.
>
> When I heard her news I lay down and I died
> And they sent two men to the wood for timber.
>
> A board of holly and a board of alder
> And two great yards of sack about me.
>
> And but that my own little mother was a woman
> I could tell you another pretty story about women.[57]

When in 1928 Joyce taught Ada (Mrs. Archibald) MacLeish to sing this song for a concert, it was apparent that it meant a great deal to him.[58] It was, of course, another evocation of the theme of the cuckold.

Roberts had two final moves to make in his game with Joyce. On August 30 he demanded that Joyce change the first paragraph in 'Grace,' three paragraphs in 'Ivy Day,' part of 'The Boarding House,' and every proper name.[59] Joyce refused to change anything but the proper names, and consulted Arthur Griffith, who told him what he knew already, that this was the way Roberts had played for years. On September 5 Roberts proposed Joyce take over the sheets for *Dubliners* for thirty pounds, and Joyce agreed, saying he would give him a bill at ten days' date and would pay it in Trieste. He would publish, he said, under the imprint of the 'Jervis Press.' Roberts objected that Maunsel & Co. had works in Jervis Lane, so Joyce changed it to the 'Liffey Press.' By a ruse he managed to get a complete set of the proofs from Roberts, and was barely in time, for now the printer, John Falconer, suddenly interposed. Having heard of Roberts's difficulties with Joyce, he announced he would neither turn over the unpatriotic sheets nor take any fee for the printing.[60] Joyce went to plead with him, but uselessly. He walked about the streets and came back to Mrs. Murray's house, where he and Nora were staying, utterly disconsolate. His aunt had prepared a special supper, but he went directly upstairs and sang a love song, accompanying himself on the piano. Nora, embarrassed by this behavior, stayed below until Mrs. Murray cried, 'Ah! do go up to him! Can't you see, all that is for you!'[61] It was for her, and for *Dubliners,* too.

On September 11 the sheets were destroyed;[62] Joyce said by fire, Roberts, stickling for accuracy in his later accounts, insisted they were destroyed by guillotining and pulping.[63] Burnt or dismembered in effigy, Joyce had no further business in Dublin, and he left with Nora and the children that same night.

He stepped in London long enough to offer his book to the *English Review* and to Colum's publisher, Mills & Boon, without success, then crossed to Flushing, Holland. As he waited for the train at the station, he was provoked to write a new broadside, 'Gas from a Burner,' ostensibly spoken by Roberts himself, but blended with Falconer, and he finished it in the train on the way to Munich. Unlike 'The Holy Office,' it was wholly personal invective:

Gas from a Burner

Ladies and gents, you are here assembled
To hear why earth and heaven trembled
Because of the black and sinister arts
Of an Irish writer in foreign parts.
He sent me a book ten years ago;
I read it a hundred times or so,

Backwards and forwards, down and up,
Through both ends of a telescope.
I printed it all to the very last word
But by the mercy of the Lord
The darkness of my mind was rent
And I saw the writer's foul intent.
But I owe a duty to Ireland:
I hold her honour in my hand,
This lovely land that always sent
Her writers and artists to banishment
And in a spirit of Irish fun
Betrayed her own leaders, one by one.
'Twas Irish humor, wet and dry,
Flung quicklime into Parnell's eye. . . .

He mocked Roberts's defense of his courage as a publisher:

To show you for strictures I don't care a button
I printed the poems of Mountainy Mutton [Joseph Campbell]
And a play he wrote (you've read it, I'm sure)
Where they talk of 'bastard,' 'bugger' and 'whore,'
And a play on the Word and Holy Paul
And some woman's legs that I can't recall,
Written by [George] Moore, a genuine gent
That lives on his property's ten per cent:
I printed mystical books in dozens:
I printed the table-book of [James] Cousins
Though (asking your pardon) as for the verse
'Twould give you a heartburn on your arse:
I printed folklore from North and South
By [Lady] Gregory of the Golden Mouth:
I printed poets, sad silly and solemn:
I printed Patrick What-do-you-Colm:
I printed the great John Milicent Synge
Who soars above on an angel's wing
In the playboy shift that he pinched as swag
From Maunsel's manager's travelling-bag.*
But I draw the line at that bloody fellow
That was over here dressed in Austrian yellow,
Spouting Italian by the hour
To O'Leary Curtis and John Wyse Power
And writing of Dublin, dirty and dear,
In a manner no blackamoor printer could bear.
Shite and onions! Do you think I'll print

---

* A reference both to Roberts's claim to intrepidity for having published Synge, and to his former profession of traveler for ladies' underwear.

The name of the Wellington Monument,
Sydney Parade and Sandymount tram,
Downes's cakeshop and Williams's jam?
I'm damned if I do—I'm damned to blazes!
Talk about *Irish Names of Places!* °
It's a wonder to me, upon my soul,
He forgot to mention Curly's Hole.
No, ladies, my press shall have no share in
So gross a libel on Stepmother Erin,†
I pity the poor—that's why I took
A red-headed Scotchman to keep my book.‡
Poor sister Scotland! Her doom is fell;
She cannot find any more Stuarts to sell.
My conscience is fine as Chinese silk:
My heart is as soft as buttermilk.° °
Colm can tell you I made a rebate
Of one hundred pounds on the estimate
I gave him for his *Irish Review.*
I love my country—by herrings I do!

．　．　．

Who was it said: Resist not evil?
I'll burn that book, so help me devil.
I'll sing a psalm as I watch it burn
And the ashes I'll keep in a one-handled urn.
I'll penance do with farts and groans
Kneeling upon my marrowbones.
This very next lent I will unbare
My penitent buttocks to the air
And sobbing beside my printing press
My awful sin I will confess.
My Irish foreman from Bannockburn
Shall dip his right hand in the urn
And sign crisscross with reverent thumb
Memento homo upon my bum.

Joyce had this broadside printed in Trieste, where he arrived on
September 15, and sent it to his brother Charles to distribute in Dublin.
Charles hesitated over it, especially since, as he wrote James, 'Pappie
kicked up blue hell' when he read it and said, 'He's an out and out
ruffian without the spark of a gentleman about him.' [64] John Joyce clung

° By P. W. Joyce, no relation to James.
† Roberts was an Ulster Scot.
‡ Roberts was his own bookkeeper.
° ° An allusion to his remark to Joyce that the Giant's Causeway was soft putty
compared to him.

to his conception of himself as a gentleman as to a last fig leaf. But Joyce insisted that Charles deliver the sheets, and at length he did.

This was to be Joyce's last visit to Ireland. Of his experience there he was soon to write, 'I find it difficult to come to any other conclusion but this—that the intention was to weary me out and if possible strangle me once and for all. But in this they did not succeed.' [65] The indignities he had suffered from Cosgrave in 1909 combined with the mistreatment he had received from Roberts in 1912, the latent hostility he thought he saw in Gogarty and even in Kettle, as well as in Dixon and Falconer, brought him to fear irrationally that his next appearance would bring on physical abuse to match the mental abuse to which he had been subjected. Old friends like Curran regarded his attitude as paranoiac, but, like Blake, he saw his private quarrels writ large on a symbolic screen. He was angry and unforgiving and he thought as badly as he could of his tormentors. In 1939 Joyce added a note to the proofs of Herbert Gorman's biography to summarize his attitude:

He was invited to Ireland twice by the late William Butler Yeats in connection with the Tailteann Games and then in connection with the foundation of the Irish Academy of Letters.* These invitations (the first was personal) and this membership were declined by him. He has not even sought refuge there during the present calamitous events in Europe. Having a vivid memory of the incident at Castlecomer when quicklime was flung into the eyes of their dying leader, Parnell, by a chivalrous Irish mob, he did not wish a similar unfortunate occurrence to interfere with the composition of the book he was trying to write.[66]

The first stage of Joyce's exile, the most bitter, had ended in Rome, when he succumbed to a mood of tenderness in planning 'The Dead.' It had been followed by three visits home. Now Ireland was visitable only in imagination. Joyce did not return, but he sent his characters back, and shared vicariously their presence in the Dublin scene as well as their partial estrangement from it. To Ettore Schmitz he made the curious comment, on his return to Trieste from Dublin, 'What is certain is that I am more virtuous than all that lot—I, who am a real monogamist and have never loved but once in my life.' [67]

* See p. 672.

1 9 1 3 – 1 9 1 4

The veripatetic image of the impossible Gracehoper on his odderkop
in the myre, after his thrice ephemeral journeeys, sans mantis ne shoo-
shooe, featherweighed animule, actually and presumptuably sinctifying
chronic's despair, was sufficiently and probably coocoo much for his
chorous of gravitates.

—*Finnegans Wake* (418)

SHEM'S artistic miracle in *Finnegans Wake* is to make the dead
speak; in Trieste Joyce had to achieve not only this resuscitation
by art, but also the homelier feat, with his creditors, of making the
vociferous be dumb. Some debts he paid with the help of Stanislaus,
who complained again in a letter to Charles Joyce that no matter how
much he helped he was 'not appreciated.'[1] Other debts were dex-
terously juggled and so Joyce rode out the storm or rather, rode in it,
as another man might sail in fair weather. He contrived to pay not
only for necessaries but also for the luxury of first restoring and then
shipping the Joyce family portraits from Dublin to Trieste. John Joyce
was anxious to entrust them to the care of his eldest son, rightly supposing that he best understood their value. In the spring of 1913 these
arrived and were prominently displayed to pupils and visitors in the
flat at 5 via Donato Bramante. Their stolid respectability lent piquancy
to their new owner's caprices.

Joyce's daily life became less confused as a result of his being given
the position at the Scuola Superiore di Commercio Revoltella, of which
he had heard a few months earlier. This time the complications of
foreign citizenship were surmounted.* He taught there in the mornings,
and then in the afternoons continued with private pupils. His official
position at the school made him even more sought after as a teacher
than before, and his unpunctuality and eccentric methods were coun-

---

* On the employment form, in response to the question, 'Religion?', Joyce wrote
curtly, '*Senza*' ('Without').

tenanced by indulgent pupils. Among these was Paolo Cuzzi, now an eminent Triestine lawyer, who heard about Joyce from Ettore Schmitz, and took lessons from 1911 to 1913. Joyce was impatient with the early stages of learning; he brought Cuzzi quickly through the elementary Berlitz texts, then moved on to Boswell's *Life of Johnson.* But the principal part of the lesson was devoted to conversation. Master and pupil sat in a room in Joyce's flat which was furnished, oddly enough, only with chairs. The chairs were exact replicas of some antique Danish chairs Joyce had seen in a photograph; perhaps in a burst of post-Ibsenite feeling, he had commissioned a Triestine carpenter to duplicate them. Joyce stretched his back on one chair, his legs on another, and puffed at the Virginia in his yellowed fingers. Soon he and Cuzzi were off on a discussion which, as Cuzzi said, might end anywhere. A favorite subject was Thomistic morality, about which Joyce theorized with precision and ingenuity. But often their subjects were less predictable, as when Cuzzi, who was studying Vico in school, discovered that Joyce was also passionately interested in this Neapolitan philosopher.* Freud too became a subject of conversation. Cuzzi was reading Freud's *Five Lectures on Psychoanalysis,* and he talked with Joyce about slips of the tongue and their significance. Joyce listened attentively, but remarked that Freud had been anticipated by Vico.[2]

Cuzzi's sister Emma, and two of her friends, also became Joyce's pupils.[3] Their lessons were held in the Cuzzis' house. The three fourteen-year-old girls liked their master, who usually appeared wearing the hunting waistcoat which his father had given him in 1912. Almost anything could serve as the text of the girls' lesson: a Shakespearean song, or, one day, a fortune which Joyce had purchased from a beggar. The fortune, which was intended for a woman, predicted that its recipient would suffer the loss of something precious to her but would recover it. The master was credulous, the pupils skeptical. When Emma accompanied Joyce to the front door at the lesson's end, he suddenly asked her if in fact she had not lost something dear to her. Then, to demonstrate the truth of the fortune, he pulled out of an inside pocket a glass engagement-book which he had often eyed ironically on her desk. 'This will teach you not to mock at superstitions,' he told her.

---

* Joyce also knew Croce's *Estetica,* with its chapter on Vico.[4] Croce's restatement of Vico, 'Man creates the human world, creates it by transforming himself into the facts of society: by thinking it he re-creates his own creations, traverses over again the paths he has already traversed, reconstructs the whole ideally, and thus knows it with full and true knowledge,' is echoed in Stephen's remark in *Ulysses* (494 [479]), 'What went forth to the ends of the world to traverse not itself. God, the sun, Shakespeare, a commercial traveller, having itself traversed in reality itself, becomes that self. . . . Self which it itself was ineluctably preconditioned to become. *Ecco!*'

One of his favorite among many superstitions was a ring, composed of different kinds of metals, which he wore on his finger as a preventative against blindness. It resembled a wedding-ring, but he denounced wedding-rings as symbols of slavery to which no free man could submit. 'Then why are you willing to wear this ring?' asked his pupils. 'Because I am already the slave of my eye trouble,' Joyce replied.

On the spur of the moment he concocted stories ostensibly to illustrate points of grammar. Emma one day accented the word 'generally' on the wrong syllable; Joyce told her she must pronounce the word as if it were the name of the famous Chinese General Li; then he quickly sketched out the career of this general which ended by his being hanged from a tree, a scene which Joyce illustrated by a drawing in Emma's notebook. During another lesson he offered to paint a word picture of each of his pupils. One he described floridly as an enchanted garden, full of flowers and rare and many-colored birds; but when you drew close to this beauty, the better to admire it, you saw suddenly that it was—only a heap of coal. The second, he said, was like a large, wide street; but watch out! There was something on it to make you slip! As for Emma, she was like a neat, well-arranged scene in which all the objects stood docilely at their posts and every one of them had its boring label. This sharp raillery was often followed by his sitting at the piano and singing 'Mr. Dooley,' while they sang the chorus. Or they might have a match to see who could duplicate the kick of the prima ballerina at Covent Garden, and Joyce, with his thin, loose-jointed frame, always won.

Joyce's disregard of discipline won the girls' affection, and they often told him secrets kept from their parents. Emma one day confided that, since she was forbidden to buy cigarettes, she had tried drying rose-leaves from the garden, and making these into cigarettes which she smoked in secret. Joyce, who feared that tobacco might be a contributing cause of his eye trouble, eagerly asked to try one. After a few puffs he began to say by way of compliment that the cigarette was redolent of the farm, for he could taste in it the aromas of hay, of farm animals, of flowers, and—of dung.*

The lessons often ended with Joyce sliding down the balustrade, his pupils close behind him. But one day Signora Cuzzi happened to observe this exercise, and the English lessons came to an abrupt stop.

Another of Joyce's pupils was a young man of twenty named Boris Furlan,[5] later to be prominent in Yugoslavian politics. Furlan was in a phase of enthusiasm for Schopenhauer and Nietzsche, which Joyce

---

* There is an echo in *Ulysses* (70 [63]): 'Tell him if he smokes he won't grow. O let him! His life isn't such a bed of roses!'

tried to choke by urging that Thomas Aquinas was the greatest philosopher because his reasoning was 'like a sharp sword.' He read him, he said to Furlan, in Latin, a page a day. Joyce took pleasure in demonstrating to his young pupil that morality was not confined to heroic decisions. 'Have you,' he asked him one day, remembering the incident with Skeffington ten years before, 'the moral courage to go round to the corner shop and ask for five centesimi worth of rock drips?' Furlan enjoyed this kind of discussion, but was less pleased when he was asked to describe an oil lamp. He fumbled helplessly for the technical language, and Joyce then took over and spent half an hour, in what seemed to Furlan 'a descriptive lust,' explaining the lamp's obvious and minute details.

So easy and intimate was the relationship of this teacher to his pupils that it is no wonder that with one of his girl students Joyce dreamed of a closer intimacy. This was Amalia Popper, the daughter of a Jewish businessman whose first name was Leopoldo. She was to serve as one of the models for the character and Southern European looks of Molly Bloom. But Joyce also wrote an account of the affair in his best calligraphy under the ironic title of *Giacomo Joyce*.* ⁶ Joyce conveys the overwhelming desire and ironic amusement involved in all the incongruities of the affair. He envisions her as a Jewess come out of the dark East to hold his western blood in thrall.

The notebook opens abruptly, 'Who?' and answers, 'A pale face surrounded by heavy odorous furs. Her movements are shy and nervous. She uses quizzing-glasses. *Yes:* † a brief syllable. A brief laugh. A brief beat of the eyelids.' He hymns and mocks his desire:

Cobweb handwriting, traced long and fine with quiet disdain and resignation: a young person of quality.

I launch forth on an easy wave of tepid speech; Swedenborg, the pseudo-Areopagite, Miguel de Molinos, Joachim Abbas. The wave is spent. Her classmate, retwisting her twisted body, purrs in boneless Viennese Italian: *Che coltura!* The long eyelids beat and lift: a burning needleprick stings and quivers in the velvet iris.

High heels clack hollow on the resonant stone stairs. Wintry air in the castle, gibbeted coats of mail, rude iron sconces over the windings of the winding turret stairs. Tapping-clacking heels, a high and hollow noise. There is one below would speak with your ladyship.

She never blows her nose. A form of speech: the lesser for the greater.

---

* Giacomo (from 'Giacomo' [Jacques] Casanova) is a familiar epithet in Italy for a great lover.
† A hint of the ending of *Ulysses*.

Rounded and ripened: rounded by the lathe of intermarriage and ripened in the forcing-house of the seclusion of her race.

A ricefield near Vercelli, under creamy summer haze. The wings of her drooping hat shadow her false smile. Shadows streak her falsely smiling face, smitten by the hot creamy light, grey whey-hued shadows under the jawbones, streaks of eggyolk yellow on the moistened brow, rancid yellow humour lurking within the softened pulp of the eyes.

. . .

Twilight. Crossing the *piazza*. Grey eve lowering on wide, sagegreen pasture-lands, shedding silently dusk and dew. She follows her mother with ungainly grace, the mare leading her filly foal. Grey twilight moulds softly the slim and shapely haunches, the meek supple tendonous neck, the fine-boned skull. Eve, peace, the dusk of wonder. . . . . . Hillo! Ostler! Hilloho!

Papa and the girls sliding downhill, astride of a toboggan: the Grand Turk and his harem. Tightly capped and jacketted, boots laced in deft crisscross over the flesh-warmed tongue, the short skirt taut from the round knobs of the knees. A white flash: a flake, a snowflake.

> *And when she next doth ride abroad*
> *May I be there to see!*

I rush out of the tobacco-shop and call her name. She turns and halts to hear my jumbled words of lessons, hours, lessons, hours: and slowly her pale cheeks are flushed with a kindling opal light. Nay, nay, be not afraid!

. . .

Moving mists on the hill as I look upward from night and mud. Hanging mists over the damp trees. A light in the upper room. She is dressing to go to the play. There are ghosts in the mirror. . . . . Candles! Candles!

A gentle creature. At midnight, after music, all the way up the via San Michele, these words were spoken softly. Easy now, Jamesy! Did you never walk the streets of Dublin at night sobbing another name?

. . .

There follows a dream picture of her:

She raises her arms in an effort to hook at the nape of her neck a gown of black veiling. She cannot: no, she cannot. She moves backwards towards me mutely. I raise my arms to help her: her arms fall. I hold the websoft edges of her gown and drawing them out to hook them I see through the opening of the black veil her little body sheathed in an orange shift. It slips into ribbons of moorings at her shoulders and falls slowly: a little smooth naked body shimmering with silvery scales. It slips slowly over the slender buttocks

of smooth polished silver and over their furrow, a tarnished silver shadow.
. . . Fingers, cold and calm and moving. . . . A touch, a touch.

Small witless helpless and thin breath. But bend and hear: a voice. A sparrow
under the wheels of Juggernaut, shaking shakes of the earth. Please, mister
God, big mister God! Goodbye, big world! . . . . *Aber das ist eine Schweinerei!*

Great bows on her slim bronze shoes: spurs of a pampered fowl.

The lady goes apace, apace, apace . . . pure air on the upland road. Trieste is
waking rawly: raw sunlight over its huddled browntiled roofs, testudoform; a
multitude of prostrate bugs await a national deliverance. Belluomo rises from
the bed of his wife's lover's wife: the busy housewife is astir, sloe-eyed, a
saucer of acetic acid in her hand * . . . . Pure air and silence on the upland
road: and hoofs. A girl on horseback. Hedda! Hedda Gabler!

She walks before me along the corridor and as she walks a dark coil of her
hair slowly uncoils and falls. Slowly uncoiling, falling hair! She does not
know and walks before me, simple and proud. So did she walk by Dante in
simple pride and so, stainless of blood and violation, the daughter of Cenci,
Beatrice, to her death:

> . . . *Tie*
> *My girdle for me and bind up this hair*
> *In any simple knot.*

This lover is too observant not to find out her quirks: one of them
is her Irredentism. 'She thinks the Italian gentlemen were right to haul
Ettore Albini, the critic of the *Secolo,* from the stalls because he did
not stand up when the band played the Royal March. She heard that
at supper. Ay. They love their country when they are quite sure which
country it is.' † Other persons move briefly through this muted, sardonic,
prose poem to his desire. One is her father, who remarked to Joyce one
day after her lesson as they walked down the hill from the house on
via San Michele, '*Mia figlia ha una grandissima ammirazione per il suo
maestro inglese.*' ‡ Joyce comments: 'O! Perfectly said: courtesy, benevolence, curiosity, trust, suspicion, naturalness, helplessness of age, confidence, frankness, urbanity, sincerity, warning, pathos, compassion:
a perfect blend.' Yet while he respected the old man with his handsome
features and white whiskers, he also half-humorously resented the
father-daughter relationship. On November 11, 1912, he delivered the
first of a series of twelve lectures on *Hamlet* at the Università del
Popolo, and he had Signorina Popper, who was present, in mind when
he spoke one passage: 'I expound Shakespeare to docile Trieste: Hamlet,

* Used in *Ulysses* to describe Paris.
† *Ulysses* (331 [321]).
‡ 'My daughter has the greatest admiration for her English teacher.'

quoth I, who is most courteous to gentle and simple is rude only to Polonius. Perhaps, an embittered idealist, he can see in the parents of his beloved only grotesque attempts on the part of nature to produce her image. . . . Marked you that?'

In his daily activities a daydream of her persecuted his mind. One day he went with a man named Meissel—'Pimply Meissel,' he calls him —to the Jewish cemetery, to visit the grave of Meissel's wife who died by suicide.° The experience reminded him of Signorina Popper's mortality, and he noted in *Giacomo Joyce:* 'The tomb of her people and hers: black stone, silence without hope: and all is ready. Do not die!'

One day he called to give her a lesson only to be informed by the maid that his beloved had been removed to the hospital for an operation. He walked away, as he said, feeling he was about to cry. 'Operated. The surgeon's knife has probed in her entrails and withdrawn, leaving the raw jagged gash of its passage on her belly. I see her full dark suffering eyes, beautiful as the eyes of an antelope. O cruel wound! Libidinous God!' In *Ulysses* Stephen Dedalus attacks God with similar vehemence for his mother's death as 'Eater of carrion.' But Signorina Popper survived the removal of her appendix and soon was taking English lessons again.

Once more in her chair by the window, happy words on her tongue, happy laughter. A bird twittering after storm, happy that its little foolish life has fluttered out of reach of the clutching fingers of an epileptic lord and giver of life, twittering happily, twittering and chirping happily.

The poems which Joyce composed between 1912 and 1916 reflect his relationship with Signorina Popper. It was she who gave Lucia a flower, as he noted in the *Giacomo Joyce* notebook: 'A flower given by her to my daughter. Frail gift, frail giver, frail blue-veined child.' In verse this became:

> ### A Flower Given to My Daughter
>
> Frail the white rose and frail are
> Her hands that gave
> Whose soul is sere and paler
> Than time's wan wave.
>
> Rosefrail and fair—yet frailest
> A wonder wild
> In gentle eyes thou veilest
> My blueveined child.

° Bloom considers a visit to the grave of his father, also a suicide, in Ennis.[7]

Joyce could still succumb in verse to the Swinburnian allurements of sere, pale souls and the wan waves of time, and the poem's archaic phrasing—except in the astonishing last line—strangely conjoined his romantic longing and his paternal affection. In 'Nightpiece' (dated 1915) he reworks, with a similar loss of precision, this dream image of her standing next to him at Notre-Dame in Paris:

In the raw veiled spring morning faint odours float of morning Paris: aniseed, damp sawdust, hot dough of bread: and as I cross the Pont Saint Michel the steelblue waking waters chill my heart. They creep and lap about the island whereon men have lived since the stone age. . . . Tawny gloom in the vast gargoyled church. It is cold as on that morning: *quia frigus erat.* Upon the steps of the far high altar, naked as the body of the Lord, the ministers lie prostrate in weak prayer. The voice of an unseen reader rises, informing the lesson from Hosea. *Haec dicit Dominus: in tribulatione sua mane consurgent ad me. Venite et revertamur ad Dominum.* . . . She stands beside me, pale and chill, clothed with the shadows of the sindark nave, her thin elbow at my arm. Her flesh recalls the thrill of that raw mist-veiled morning, hurrying torches, cruel eyes. Her soul is sorrowful, trembles and would weep. Weep not for me, O daughter of Jerusalem! [8]

The images of Signorina Popper and of Paris faded, and left only worshippers praying to nothingness:

Nightpiece

Gaunt in gloom,
The pale stars their torches,
Enshrouded, wave.
Ghostfires from heaven's far verges faint illume,
Arches on soaring arches,
Night's sindark nave.

Seraphim,
The lost hosts awaken
To service till
In moonless gloom each lapses muted, dim,
Raised when she has and shaken
Her thurible.

And long and loud,
To night's nave upsoaring
A starknell tolls
As the bleak incense surges, cloud on cloud,
Voidward from the adoring
Waste of souls.

Another poem from this sequence,* written on September 7, 1913, mourns the lost intensity of youth. This poem was conceived as he watched Stanislaus, who preferred to take part in sports, in a race of needleboats (racing shells) at San Sabba, near Trieste.⁹ As the scullers pulled towards shore, they began to sing an aria from Puccini's *La Fanciulla del West*. Joyce's poem played lugubriously on the last line, '*e non ritornero piu*':

> ### Watching the Needleboats at San Sabba
>
> I heard their young hearts crying
> Loveward above the glancing oar
> And heard the prairie grasses sighing:
> *No more, return no more!*
>
> O hearts, O sighing grasses,
> Vainly your loveblown bannerets mourn!
> No more will the wild wind that passes
> Return, no more return.†

This is the melancholy of the lover who anticipates his own failure. Joyce continued his silent, secret wooing of Signorina Popper, always in the presence of another person, into 1914. He gave her some of *A Portrait of the Artist as a Young Man* to read, and she remarked to him that, if the book had 'been frank only for frankness' sake, she would have asked why I had given it to her to read.' He noted ironically, 'O you would, would you? A lady of letters.' ‡ This affair, of eyes rather

---

* The poem 'Tutto è Sciolto' ('All is unloosed'), which he dated July 13, 1914, is probably another prettified memorial to this failure:

> A birdless heaven, seadusk, one lone star
> Piercing the west,
> As thou, fond heart, love's time, so faint, so far,
> Rememberest.
>
> The clear young eyes' soft look, the candid brow,
> The fragrant hair,
> Falling as through the silence falleth now
> Dusk of the air.
>
> Why then, remembering those shy
> Sweet lures, repine
> When the dear love she yielded with a sigh
> Was all but thine?

† He sent it to Stanislaus 'with the rheumatic chamber poet's (or pot's) compliments,' and a line from Horace, '*Quid si prisca redit Venus?*' ¹⁰ ('What if the old love should return?')

‡ *Ulysses* (49 [45]).

than of bodies, drew towards an end in the summer of 1914. The *Giacomo Joyce* notebook indicates the closing phases:

My voice, dying in the echoes of its words, dies like the wisdom-wearied voice of the Eternal calling on Abraham through echoing hills. She leans back against the pillowed wall: odalisque-featured in the luxurious obscurity. Her eyes have drunk my thoughts: and into the moist warm yielding welcoming darkness of her womanhood my soul, itself dissolving, has streamed and poured and flooded a liquid and abundant seed. . . . Take her now who will! . . .

Now, when he meets her outside Ralli's house, she averts her eyes, and the next time greets him 'wintrily.'

Jan Pieters Sweelink. The quaint name of the old Dutch musician makes all beauty seem quaint and far. I hear his variations for the clavichord on an old air: *Youth has an end*. In the vague mist of old sounds a faint point of light appears: the speech of the soul is about to be heard. Youth has an end: the end is here. It will never be. You know that well. What then? Write it, damn you, write it! What else are you good for?

The next entry recounts her rebuff of his attentions:

'Why?'
'Because otherwise I could not see you.' °
Sliding—space—ages—foliage of stars—and waning heaven—stillness—and stillness deeper—stillness of annihilation—and her voice.

Non hunc sed Barabbam!

Like her ancestors before Pilate, she prefers Barabbas to Christ. On his next visit to her she is impregnable:

Unreadiness. A bare apartment. Torpid daylight. A long black piano: coffin of music. Poised on its edge a woman's hat, red-flowered, an umbrella, furled. Her arms: a casque, gules, and blunt spears on a field, sable.

Envoy: Love me, love my umbrella.

And so Signorina Popper, with shy needle-thrusts from her velvet iris, carried her umbrella slowly out of his life. She was to marry and live in Florence.†

In spite of the irony of the *Giacomo Joyce* notebook, the affair interested Joyce exceedingly. He knew its absurdity and his own, but he had not been so stirred for several years. It was part of a resurgence of his whole being that took place after his return from Dublin. His failure

---

° 'Otherwise I could not see you.' *Exiles* (533 [373]).
† In 1933 Signorina Popper, now Signora Risolo, asked and received permission to translate *Dubliners*;[11] this was the only favor she conferred on Joyce.

with Signorina Popper made him write verse again, as perhaps he dimly anticipated in a letter of 1909 to G. Molyneux Palmer, 'There is no likelihood of my writing any more verse unless something unforeseen happens to my brain.' [12] His failure with George Roberts made him seek other publishers with great vigor. In December 1912, he sent off *Dubliners* to Martin Secker, and asked Yeats, with whom he had begun to correspond again about translating *The Countess Cathleen*,* to intercede in his behalf: 'You would do me a great service . . . and, I hope, some service also to the literature of our country.' [13] Secker rejected the book, but Joyce, not put down, sent it off to Elkin Mathews and offered to defray the printing costs himself, promising with his old blitheness payment 'in advance, if necessary.' [14] Mathews also turned it down in April 1913. Joyce, too preoccupied perhaps with Signorina Popper and with his gathering ideas for *Exiles* and *Ulysses* to search out a new rejector, did not send it out again; but he did succeed in publishing his poem about the needleboats in the *Saturday Review;* and in a letter informing G. Molyneux Palmer, the composer who had set some of his poems to music, about the new lyric, he remarked that he continued to have hopes for *Dubliners.*[15]

In November and December 1913 the temper of Joyce's life changed. Two letters arrived in Trieste, neither of them in the least expected. The first, dated November 25, was from Grant Richards,[16] to whom Joyce had written despairingly. Richards, his conscience troubled about Joyce,[17] wished to see *Dubliners* again. The second, dated December 15, was from Ezra Pound, who, it seemed, was an American friend of Yeats. After all the mealy-mouthed letters from publishers, this one, while promising nothing, had an air of what Pound later called 'the factive personality' about it. Pound said that he had heard about Joyce from Yeats, and was writing for the first time to someone outside his own circle to find out if Joyce had any work on hand. He was connected, he said, with two impecunious English reviews, the *Egoist* and the *Cerebralist*, and with two fairly affluent American magazines, H. L. Mencken's *Smart Set* and Harriet Monroe's *Poetry*. He did not know what Joyce was writing now, so could only offer to read whatever Joyce chose to send him. He was *bonae voluntatis,* he said, and did not in the least know if he could be of any use to Joyce or Joyce to him. He supposed they shared at least a hate or two, but recognized this as a very problematical bond.

Before Joyce replied Pound wrote again, this time to say that Yeats

---

* See p. 334. Vidacovich did not want to translate Yeats's later version of the play, and, since Yeats was adamantly opposed to an Italian translation of the earlier version, the project had to be abandoned.

had just turned up the poem, 'I Hear an Army.' They were both much impressed by it, and Pound wanted to use it in his anthology, *Des Imagistes,* and would pay for it. Thus encouraged, Joyce made final revisions on the first chapter of *A Portrait of the Artist as a Young Man,* and sent it, along with *Dubliners,* to Pound in mid-January. Pound wrote him immediately, on January 19, 1914, that while he was not supposed to know anything about prose, he thought Joyce's novel was fine stuff, readable as no recent English prose but James's, Hudson's, and some of Conrad's was readable. He was sending it off at once to the *Egoist.* There might be some caviling about Joyce's language, but Pound thought he would be able to persuade the editor. He added a few days later, about *Dubliners,* that he thought the stories good. He did not know if Mencken would take any of them for the *Smart Set,* but would send 'An Encounter,' 'The Boarding House,' and 'A Little Cloud' to him anyway. Had Joyce any more verses, especially of the sort that stood up objective like 'I Hear an Army'? If so, Pound could send them to *Poetry,* which would pay well. In Ezra Pound, as avid to discover as Joyce was to be discovered, the writings of Joyce found their missionary.

Pound was then the most active man in London. Full of contempt for the world of contemporary writing, he had made himself its strident reformer. In the American *Smart Set* and *Poetry,* H. L. Mencken and Harriet Monroe followed many of his instructions. In England Ford Madox Ford of the *English Review* and most of the staff of the *Egoist* were his friends; and in Paris he had connections with Henry Davray and others on the *Mercure de France.* He had come to London in 1908, having just printed in Venice a little book of romantic verse, and rather fancying himself as a troubadour in the school of Bertrand de Born. He was convinced then that the best poet writing in English was Yeats, and had soon delighted the older man by his vivacity and shrewdness. Their closest period of friendship was during the summers of 1913 and 1914, when they shared a cottage in Sussex and tried to remake each other. Pound had been deep in the Imagist movement, under the influence of T. E. Hulme, but was about ready to leave it for Vorticism, a tougher objectivism in which Gaudier-Brzeska, the sculptor, and Wyndham Lewis accompanied him. Pound had read widely in six or seven languages, and had tried translating even from Japanese and Chinese, languages which he did not know. Much of his time went into finding what was new and valuable in any of the arts, he bought new paintings and sculptures or persuaded richer friends to buy them, and he was always educating his friends in what to look at as well as what to read and what to think. In 1913 he discovered, before anyone else of prominence, the talent of Robert Frost, and in a burst of enthusiasm would have refashioned both the man and his verse had not Frost rebelled and fled London.[18] Now at the beginning of 1914 he found out Joyce, in April he married, and in late September he discovered T. S. Eliot, an American studying philosophy at Merton College, Oxford, whose verse revealed he had 'modernized himself *on his own*,' [19] a feat Pound particularly admired because he had needed so many abettors in his own modernization. In his theory of literature Pound was caught somewhere between an instinctive romanticism, of which under the pressure of Hulme and Lewis he had begun to feel a bit ashamed, and a belief in the objectivity of works of art. He was ripe for reading *A Portrait of the Artist as a Young Man,* which participates in both theories, the author sporadically withdrawing a little from his hero only to join him firmly once more. Many of the difficulties of Pound's own attempt at self-portraiture in *Hugh Selwyn Mauberley* a few years later come from his desire to achieve Joyce's variety of tone; but his irony, like Eliot's, is much harsher than Joyce's. Mauberley is ridiculous where Stephen Dedalus is only young.

Pound saw at once that the place to publish Joyce was in the *Egoist.* The editor of this review was Dora Marsden, a small, handsome, grimly intellectual woman. Like Annie Besant, Miss Marsden began as a feminist and gradually shifted toward Theosophy. After her graduation from Manchester University she became a teacher and then, as a member of the Women's Social and Political Union, founded the *Freewoman* in 1911. Out of this she begot the *New Freewoman,** founded in June 1913, with herself as editor and Rebecca West as assistant editor. The articles quickly became less concerned with feminism, and more with the liberation of the human spirit of whichever sex. Rebecca West gave up her position after two issues on account of a dispute. At this point Ezra Pound, whom she had brought into the editing circle, took charge of the review's literary department. But the name of the review justly bothered him, and in December he, along with Allen Upward, Huntley Carter, Reginald W. Kauffman, and Richard Aldington, wrote a letter to the editor asking her to change the title to some other which would 'mark the character of your paper as an organ of individualists of both sexes, and of the individualist principle in every department of life.' [20] Miss Marsden obligingly decided to call it the *Egoist,* by which she implied a Berkeleyan subjectivism. She continued to write the leading articles, which gradually and impenetrably fulfilled her intention 'to probe to the depths of human nature,' [21] with a philosophy in which

* 'I'm so keen on that New Free Woman with novel inside.' *Finnegans Wake* (145). The novel inside was *A Portrait.*

space was mother and time father, the problem of gender being thus distributed to the universe. The business of editing gradually fell into the hands of others. Richard Aldington replaced Rebecca West as assistant editor in January 1914; later Hilda Doolittle and then T. S. Eliot became assistant editors. Pound continued to play an influential part, but the main responsibility fell, in June 1914, on Harriet Weaver, until that time business manager. Miss Marsden decided to devote herself to writing and, accepting the title of contributing editor, gave up the principal editorship to Miss Weaver.[22]

Harriet Shaw Weaver was to complete what Pound began for Joyce. She came, as she told Joyce later, from an overgrown village called Frodsham in Cheshire. Her father was the doctor of the district and she lived there until she was fifteen, when she moved to Hampstead. When Joyce inquired hopefully if she had not a little Irish blood, she responded sadly, 'I am afraid I am hopelessly English.' [23] Miss Weaver was now, in 1913, thirty-seven years old. She had been reared strictly and piously, and retained some external marks of her training in an old-fashioned propriety of manner and dress which Virginia Woolf was to find incongruous with her *avant-garde* convictions. Without giving up her personal devotion to her family, she had broken away from their ideas, first by becoming a feminist. Shy, intelligent, and understanding, unsparing of her time, she took on all the burdens of detail and then all the public responsibilities that go with editing a review; and if no one could have expected her to assume this role, no one could complain that she did not do it well.

The *New Freewoman* had unconsciously heralded *A Portrait of the Artist* in an editorial of the December 1913 issue, which called for a minute examination of personality: 'If we could get into the habit of describing a man as he feels himself instead of in the terms of the physical image under which he presents himself to sight, we should break through this deadening concept of unity.' [24] Miss Marsden at once agreed, when the first chapter of *A Portrait* was shown to her by Pound, to publish it in serial form, beginning with the issue of February 2, which, as Joyce recognized with satisfaction, was his birthday.[25] In the meantime, to stir up interest, Pound published in the January 15 issue an article entitled, 'A Curious History,' which embodied the material about the rejection of *Dubliners* that Joyce had circulated to the Irish press in August of 1911.°

The *Egoist's* interest in him made Joyce feel his position with Grant Richards was strengthened, and he wrote him therefore on January 19,

---

° Joyce had brought the material up to date for use as a preface to *Dubliners,* but Grant Richards discouraged this idea.

1914, asking for an immediate reply to his letter of a week before which had requested a decision about *Dubliners*. On January 29, in this *annus mirabilis*, Richards agreed to publish. The contract was not advantageous, for Joyce was to receive no royalties on the first 500 copies, and had to engage to take 120 copies himself, but he did not quibble over terms. He was eager to preserve one typographical feature of the manuscript, the use of dashes instead of quotation marks, on the grounds that the latter 'are most unsightly and give an impression of unreality,' in short, are 'an eyesore,' but compliantly offered on March 4, 1914, to give way if Richards insisted.

The first proofs, with quotation marks retained, reached him at the end of April, and he returned them quickly along with press notices of *Chamber Music* to be used as advertising, a maneuver to which he was to resort constantly during the next eight years. Richards hoped for an introduction by Filson Young, but could not get it. On May 16 Joyce urged that the book be published in that month 'as May is a lucky month for me,' but it did not appear until June 15, 1914, in an edition of 1250 copies.

Considering all the trepidation that *Dubliners* had aroused in the timid heart of George Roberts, its publication was marked by a surprising lack of trouble. The reviews were good enough; most of them found the stories cynical or pointless or both, but Ezra Pound in the *Egoist* (July 15, 1914) insisted that they marked a return of style into English prose and the introduction of a new subject-matter into Irish literature.[26] Gerald Gould, in the *New Statesman*,[27] found in the stories evidence of the emergence of a man of genius, but perhaps of a sterile order. Joyce regularly dispatched notes of thanks to the reviewers so as to impress his name even more deeply upon their memories, and watched over them all like a mother over naughty children. Richards was satisfied that the book had 'made a sensation in a small way.' [*][28]

The necessity of meeting deadlines for the *Egoist* installments of *A Portrait* spurred Joyce to try to finish that book. He sent the manuscript along chapter by chapter to Ezra Pound, who transmitted it to the *Egoist;* it was published there in installments of about fifteen pages each. Pound continued to be enthusiastic, and said Joyce was obtaining at least a *'gloire de cénacle'* from Wyndham Lewis, Ford Madox Ford, and others. Lewis had not cared for *Dubliners*, but called the novel 'good stuff.' (He changed his mind later.) Pound busied himself daily in Joyce's cause, now enlisting Frank Harris's help against possible

---

[*] By May 1, 1915, Richards had sold only 379 copies, including the 120 bought by Joyce. When Joyce complained that the situation was 'disastrous,' Richards assured him that few books were selling well in wartime.

charges of obscenity, now talking him up to '*les jeunes*.' Of the third chapter, which reached him on July 21, he wrote, 'I think you have bundled up the hell fire preaching very finely. The intonation of cant etc.' [29]

After the publication of the third chapter a hiatus occurred. This was officially attributed to the outbreak of war, but there is some reason to guess that Joyce, in spite of his good resolutions of 1909, had not yet written the fourth and fifth chapters. Since he wished to appear more strictly faithful to his old promise of writing a novel in ten years, so that he might put at the end,

> Dublin, 1904.
> Trieste, 1914

he did not admit later that the composition may, in fact, have overlapped into 1915. In bringing the book together he found unexpected help in Balzac, who made Lucien de Rubempré say in *Splendeurs et misères des courtisanes*, '*J'ai mis en pratique un axiome avec lequel on est sûr de vivre tranquille: Fuge . . . Late . . . Tace*.' [30] These Stephen translates as his own watchwords, 'Silence, exile, and cunning.' Joyce also emphasized, partly as a result of his experiences in 1912, the patriotism of Stephen's effort to hit the conscience of his race and cast his shadow over its imagination. And finally, he allowed the Stephen of twenty to display a sense of humor which until this stage of the novel had been almost undisclosed. He remains a *young* man, and Joyce was to emphasize later that his title said so, but it is the youth of genius.

By November 1914, Joyce was sending further installments of *A Portrait* to the *Egoist*, using as an intermediary address (since postal service between England and Austria had been cut off) the paint factory of Schmitz's father-in-law, Bruno Veneziani, in Murano. The last few pages did not reach Pound until July or August of 1915, when he wrote at once to Joyce that he had just read the 'splendid' ending, and was tempted to use 'insane hyperboles.' The book, he said, was hard, perfect, permanent, and comparable to Hardy and James, the only other recent writers of value. [31]

To know that he was being read was more important to Joyce than he would have admitted. It was not that he demanded praise alone; he enjoyed dispraise too, and in fact all attention. He needed to feel that he was stirring an international as well as a Triestine pot, that the flurried life he created about him had somehow extended itself to the English-speaking world, so that everyone, friend or foe, was worried about him. He wanted to be commended, rebuked, comforted, but above all, attended to. Discovered and coddled by Pound, mothered by Miss Weaver, he managed not only to finish *A Portrait of the Artist* but also to begin to write *Exiles* and *Ulysses*.

His notes for *Exiles* are dated November 1913, and show the conception of the play to be already formed. The themes, of return, friendship, and cuckoldry, are close to those of *Ulysses*. Joyce focuses attention in both books on husband rather than on lover; in the notes he attributes to the newly published pages of *Madame Bovary* (discarded by Flaubert) the current movement in thought which takes more interest in the husband's dilemma than the lover's glamor.[32] But principally the husband-hero was a figure through whom he could keep his own matured *persona* as the center. As antagonist for the projection of himself in *Exiles*, Richard Rowan, he made Robert Hand out of Gogarty, Cosgrave, Kettle, and Prezioso.* From his experiences with them Joyce drew the picture of friendship which appears in the play: a friend is someone who wants to possess your mind (since the possession of your body is forbidden by society) † and your wife's body, and longs to prove himself your disciple by betraying you.

The hero's motivation is ambiguous. Richard mainly desires that his wife share in his own freedom; he would like, but cannot require, that her freedom should result in fidelity. But secretly he wishes also to feel the thrill and horror of being cuckolded. Her infidelity and Robert's will confirm his view of the impossibility of a genuine tie between people; yet in his partial wish for this confirmation, he is an accomplice in the infidelity. He is caught in his two conceptions of himself: as a searcher for freedom he cannot try to control another, as a necessary victim he cannot resist for himself. There is also another element, his love for his wife, to keep him from acting. But to his wife, love is not what it is to Richard; rather than the bestowal of freedom, it is the insistence upon bonds. She waits for the sign which he will not give, and encourages Robert less for himself than in the hope of bestirring her husband to express his love. Richard has begotten the situation from which he proceeds to suffer.

Richard and Robert watch each other in what Joyce called 'three cat-and-mouse acts.'[33] The winner is not named, but there can be no doubt that Robert feels he has lost, and that Richard retains his moral ascendancy. His mind dominates the actions of Robert and Bertha, whatever their actions may be. Richard is a metaphysical exile, and a metaphysical victor.

---

* See pp. 328, 349.
† In *Ulysses* (199 [190]), Stephen holds that Shakespeare was betrayed with the dark lady of the sonnets by his 'dearmylove,' that is, by Mr. W. H.

The Backgrounds of Ulysses

Then, pious Eneas, conformant to the fulminant firman which enjoins
on the tremylose terrain that, when the call comes, he shall produce
nichthemerically from his unheavenly body a no uncertain quantity
of obscene matter not protected by copriright in the United Stars of
Ourania or bedeed and bedood and bedang and bedung to him, with
this double dye, brought to blood heat, gallic acid on iron ore, through
the bowels of his misery, flashly, faithly, nastily, appropriately, this
Esuan Menschavik and the first till last alshemist wrote over every
square inch of the only foolscap available, his own body, till by its
corrosive sublimation one continuous present tense integument slowly
unfolded all marryvoising moodmoulded cyclewheeling history (thereby,
he said, reflecting from his own individual person life unlivable, trans-
accidentated through the slow fires of consciousness into a dividual
chaos, perilous, potent, common to allflesh, human only, mortal) but
with each word that would not pass away the squidself which he had
squirtcreened from the crystalline world waned chagreenold and
doriangrayer in its dudhud. This exists that isits after having been said
we know.

—Finnegans Wake (185-6)

J OYCE had been preparing himself to write *Ulysses* since 1907. It
grew steadily more ambitious in scope and method, and represented
a sudden outflinging of all he had learned as a writer up to 1914. Its use
of many styles was an extension of the method of *A Portrait of the Artist*,
where the style, at first naive, became romantic and then dramatic to
suit Stephen's ontogeny. Now Joyce hit upon the more radical device
of the undependable narrator with a style adjusted to him. He used
this in several episodes of *Ulysses*, for example in *Cyclops*, where the
narrator is so obviously hostile to Bloom as to stir up sympathy for him,
in *Nausicaa*, where the narrator's gushiness is interrupted and counter-
acted by Bloom's matter-of-fact reporting, and in *Eumaeus*, where the

narrator writes in a style that is constabular. The variety of these devices made T. S. Eliot speak of the 'anti-style' of *Ulysses,* but Joyce does not seem to oppose style so much as withdraw it to a deeper level. His ebullient hand shows through its concealments.

The most famous of the devices of *Ulysses,* the interior monologue,° was also the result of earlier experiments. Joyce had been moving rapidly towards a conception of personality new to the novel. Unlike Henry James, who worked by analysis of great trends in moral life, he had begun to evolve in *Dubliners* and *A Portrait* a synthetic method, the construction of character by odds and ends, by minutiae. He did not allow his characters the sudden, tense climaxes towards which James ushered the people of his books, and preferred instead to subdue their dramas. His protagonists moved in the world and reacted to it, but their basic anxieties and exaltations seemed to move with slight reference to their environment. They were so islanded, in fact, that Joyce's development of the interior monologue to enable his readers to enter the mind of a character without the chaperonage of the author, seems a discovery he might have been expected to make.†

He had observed approaches to the interior monologue in Dujardin, George Moore, Tolstoy, even his brother's journal. He had toyed with Freud's theories of verbal association; his notes to *Exiles* first list a group of words: 'Blister-amber-silver-oranges-apples-sugarstick-hair-spongecake-ivy-roses-ribbon,' and then proceed to gloss them: 'The blister reminds her of the burning of her hand as a girl. She sees her own amber hair and her mother's silver hair. . . .' [1] The notion of dispensing with the gloss and slightly elaborating the key words, as if a multitude of small bells were ringing in the mind, was close at hand. Joyce's first interior monologue was inserted at the end of *A Portrait of the Artist,* where however he makes it seem less extraordinary by having Stephen write it in a journal. It had a dramatic justification there in that Stephen could no longer communicate with anyone in Ireland but himself. But it was also a way of relaxing by sentence fragments and seemingly casual connections among thoughts the more formal style of most of the narrative:

March 21, morning. Thought this in bed last night but was too lazy and free to add it. Free, yes. The exhausted loins are those of Elizabeth and Zacchary. Then he is the precursor. Item: he eats chiefly belly bacon and dried figs. Read locusts and wild honey. Also, when thinking of him, saw always a stern

---

° Stuart Gilbert argues persuasively that 'silent monologue' would be a more accurate translation of *monologue intérieur.*[2]

† Other writers, like Dorothy Richardson, achieved a different kind of monologue for different reasons.

severed head or death mask as if outlined on a grey curtain or veronica. Decollation they call it in the fold. Puzzled for the moment by saint John at the Latin gate. What do I see? A decollated precursor trying to pick the lock. . . .

March 22. In company with Lynch, followed a sizable hospital nurse. Lynch's idea. Dislike it. Two lean hungry greyhounds walking after a heifer.

March 23. Have not seen her since that night. Unwell? Sits at the fire perhaps with mamma's shawl on her shoulders. But not peevish. A nice bowl of gruel? Won't you now?

Having gone so far, Joyce in *Ulysses* boldly eliminated the journal, and let thoughts hop, step, jump, and glide without the self-consciousness of a journal to account for their agitation.

Another formative element in *Ulysses,* the counterpoint of myth and fact, was begun when Joyce first evolved the name and character of Stephen Dedalus, when he allowed the imagery of Calvary to play over the last scene in 'The Dead,' when he parodied Dante's division into three parts in 'Grace.' In his notes to *Exiles* Joyce constantly compares his characters to Biblical ones: Robert Hand is the elder brother in the parable of the Prodigal Son; Bertha's state at one point is 'like that of Jesus in the garden of olives,' and she is also like Isolde, her 'sister-in-love.' [3] And Richard and Robert are Sacher-Masoch and Sade.[4] In *Ulysses* Joyce uses not only the Homeric and post-Homeric legend, but a variety of other identifications: Stephen is not only Daedalus but Icarus, Hamlet, Shakespeare, Lucifer. But the principal task in the book was to find a pagan hero whom he could set loose in a Catholic city, to make Ulysses a Dubliner. Stephen Dedalus could not take this role, for he was Joyce's immature *persona;* as a mature *persona* Joyce chose Leopold Bloom. Stephen and Bloom came from opposite ends of his mind and life, but there were necessarily many resemblances, which Joyce emphasized and justified by making the older man like a father to Stephen.

This counterpoint, which Joyce from the first intended, enabled him to secure the same repetition with variations that he had obtained in *A Portrait.* In the earlier book he had conceived of the whole work as a matrix in which elements of Stephen's being might form and reform; in *Ulysses* he plays Stephen's youthful point of view against Bloom's mature point of view, often confronting them with the same places and ideas. So the two traverse at different times the same parts of Dublin, or think of like things at the same moment. They repeat each other, and then the events are recapitulated on a deeper level in the *Circe* episode, and again, in wider contexts, in the last two episodes, *Ithaca* and

*Penelope.** The enclosing framework in *Ulysses* is in part the body, which supplies an organ to preside over each episode, but it is also the day, which interacts with the minds of the characters, certain hours encouraging certain moods. In the end the whole day seems to terminate in Molly Bloom's nocturnal mind; life returns to its source.

Joyce did not have his book all in mind at the beginning. He urged a friend later not to plan everything ahead, for, he said, 'In the writing the good things will come.' [5] He knew his modern Ulysses must go through Dublin in a series of episodes like those of the Odyssey. The narrative coalesced excitingly: the Cyclops as a nationalist, Circe as madam of a brothel, were principal connections with Homer, and soon there were more subtle relationships as well. The Trojan horse, for example, is scarcely mentioned in Homer, but Joyce remembered that Dante made it the reason for Ulysses' being in hell. He turned this Odyssean adventure into Bloom's misadventure in volunteering an unconscious tip about the prospects of a dark horse in the races. Joyce's high spirits made him see many parallels of this kind: in the *Cyclops* episode, as Stuart Gilbert notices, the cigar Bloom keeps brandishing in front of the citizen is like the spear Ulysses uses to blind the Cyclops; the post-Homeric legend tells how Ulysses stole the statue of Pallas Athena, and in Joyce's book Bloom takes an erotic, profane look at the goddesses in the National Museum. The many light-hearted cross-references of this kind have lent support to the idea that *Ulysses* is a great joke on Homer, but jokes are not necessarily so simple, and these have a double aim. The first aim is the mock-heroic, the mighty spear juxtaposed with the two-penny cigar. The second, a more subtle one, is what might be called the ennoblement of the mock-heroic. This demonstrates that the world of cigars is devoid of heroism only to those who don't understand that Ulysses' spear was merely a sharpened stick, as homely an instrument in its way, and that Bloom can demonstrate the qualities of man by word of mouth as effectively as Ulysses by thrust of spear.

Joyce's version of the epic story is a pacifist version. He developed an aspect of the Greek epic which Homer had emphasized less exclusively, namely, that Ulysses was the only good *mind* among the Greek warriors. The brawny men, Achilles and Ajax and the rest, relied on

---

* There is also a repetition of incidents from *A Portrait,* often with parodic changes. Stephen's vision of the girl at the seashore, with its stages of excitement carefully delineated, is parodied in *Nausicaa* by Bloom's orgasmic but equally detached contemplation of Gerty MacDowell. In the same way, Stephen's announcement, while walking with Cranly in *A Portrait,* that he is leaving the Church in favor of art, is parodied by Bloom's announcement to his friends Mastiansky and Citron that he is giving up religion for Darwinism. See also note, p. 49.

their physical strength, while Ulysses was brighter, a man never at a loss. But of course Homer represents Ulysses as a good warrior, too. Joyce makes his modern Ulysses a man who is not physically a fighter, but whose mind is unsubduable. The victories of Bloom are mental, in spite of the pervasive physicality of Joyce's book. This kind of victory is not Homeric, though Homer gestures toward it; it is compatible with Christianity, but it is not Christian either, for Bloom is a member of a secular world. Homer's Ulysses has been made less athletic, but he retains the primary qualities of prudence, intelligence, sensitivity, and good will. Consequently Joyce, as might be expected, found the murder of the suitors at the end of the book to be too bloody as well as too grand, so he has Bloom defeat his rival, Blazes Boylan, in Molly Bloom's mind by being the first and the last in her thoughts as she falls off to sleep. In the same way Joyce enabled Richard Rowan in *Exiles* to defeat Robert Hand in Bertha's mind.

Another aspect of his hero Joyce borrowed as much from Dante as from Homer. In Dante Ulysses makes a voyage which Homer does not mention, a voyage which expresses his splendid lust for knowledge. In Canto XXVI of the *Inferno*, Ulysses says: 'Neither fondness for my son, nor reverence for my aged father, nor the due love that should have cheered Penelope, could conquer in me the ardor that I had to gain experience of the world, and of human vice and worth.' This longing for experience, for the whole of life, is related to that of Stephen crying at the end of *A Portrait*, 'Welcome, O life,' but Bloom is able, with the persistent, ruminative curiosity which is his middle class correlative for Ulysses' lust, to cover even more of life and the world in his thoughts than Stephen is. He does so, too, without the element of ruthlessness that Dante, modifying Homer's picture of a less hasty hero, criticizes in Ulysses, and which is also prominent in the Stephen of *A Portrait*.

The relationship of Bloom and Ulysses has sometimes been thought to be more tenuous than this: Ezra Pound, for example, insists that the purpose of using the Odyssey is merely structural, to give solidity to a relatively plotless work. But for Joyce the counterpoint was important because it revealed something about Bloom, about Homer, and about existence. For Bloom *is* Ulysses in an important sense. He is by no means a Babbitt. Our contemporary notion of the average man, *l'homme moyen sensuel,* is a notion conditioned by Sinclair Lewis and not by Joyce. It is not a notion which is congenial in Ireland. Irishmen are gifted with more eccentricities than Americans and Englishmen. To be average in Ireland is to be eccentric. Joyce knew this, and moreover he believed that every human soul was unique. Bloom is unusual in his

tastes in food, in his sexual conduct, in most of his interests. A critic
has complained that Bloom has no normal tastes, but Joyce would
undoubtedly reply that no one has. The range of Bloom's peculiarities
is not greater than that of other men.

At the same time, Bloom maintains his rare individuality. His responses to experience are like other people's, but they are wider and
cleverer. Like Ulysses, though without his acknowledged fame, he is a
worthy man. Joyce does not exalt him, but he makes him special. Aldous
Huxley says that Joyce used to insist upon a 'thirteenth-century' etymology for the Greek form of Ulysses' name, Odysseus; he said it was a
combination of *Outis*—nobody, and *Zeus*—god.⁶ The etymology is
merely fanciful, but it is a controlled fancy which helps to reinforce
Joyce's picture of the modern Ulysses. For Bloom is a nobody—an
advertisement canvasser who, apart from his family, has virtually no
effect upon the life around him—yet there is god in him. By god Joyce
does not intend Christianity; although Bloom has been generously
baptized into both the Protestant Church and the Catholic Church, he
is obviously not a Christian. Nor is he concerned with the conception
of a personal god. The divine part of Bloom is simply his humanity—
his assumption of a bond between himself and other created beings.
What Gabriel Conroy has to learn so painfully at the end of 'The Dead,'
that we all—dead and living—belong to the same community, is accepted
by Bloom from the start, and painlessly. The very name Bloom is chosen
to support this view of Bloom's double nature. Bloom is, like Wallace
Stevens's Rosenbloom, an ordinary Jewish name, but the name also
means flower, and Bloom is as integral as a flower. Lenehan in the
book comments about him, 'He's not one of your common or garden
... he's a cultured allround man, Bloom is.'⁷ He achieves this distinction in part by not belonging in a narrow sense, by ignoring the
limits of national life; he is not so much an Irishman as a man.

The desire Joyce has that Bloom be respected encourages him to give
Bloom the power that he has himself, to infuse common things with
uncommonness.° Bloom's monologue is a continuous poetry, full of
phrases of extraordinary intensity. In the first chapter in which he
appears, his mind wanders to thoughts of the East; he imagines himself

° Bloom's rather fatuous conversation in the *Eumaeus* episode must be understood
in terms of the time of day and his physical exhaustion. As Stuart Gilbert writes,
'The *Eumaeus* episode—I remember Joyce's insisting on this point—was meant to
represent the intercourse and mental state of two fagged-out men. Stephen is suffering from a mild hangover and inclined to be snappish, while Bloom, half asleep,
rambles on—perhaps even intending his talk to have a mildly sedative effect on his
young protégé. Bloom can talk and think intelligently when he makes an effort, but
he's too tired to make an effort. Personally I find him rather endearing in this
episode, and so I think did Joyce.' ⁸

walking by mosques and bazaars, and says to himself, 'A mother watches from her doorway. She calls her children home in their dark language.' [9] Passing Larry O'Rourke's public house, he says, 'There he is, sure enough, my bold Larry, leaning against the sugarbin in his shirtsleeves watching the aproned curate swab up with mop and bucket.' [10] Or, when he considers the cattlemarket where he once worked, he says to himself, 'Those mornings in the cattlemarket the beasts lowing in their pens, branded sheep, flop and fall of dung, the breeders in hobnailed boots trudging through the litter, slapping a palm on a ripemeated hindquarter, there's a prime one, unpeeled switches in their hands.' [11] Or when he thinks of modern Palestine: 'A barren land, bare waste. Volcanic lake, the dead sea: no fish, weedless, sunk deep in the earth. No wind could lift those waves, grey metal, poisonous foggy water. Brimstone they called it raining down: the cities of the plain: Sodom, Gomorrah, Edom. All dead names. A dead sea in a dead land, grey and old. Old now. It bore the oldest, the first race. A bent hag crossed from Cassidy's clutching a naggin bottle by the neck. The oldest people. Wandered far away over all the earth, captivity to captivity, multiplying, dying, being born everywhere.' [12]

It might be supposed that this is Joyce talking for Bloom, and not Bloom's way of thinking at all, that just as the scullions in Shakespeare speak like poets, so does everyone in Joyce. But this is not so. Stephen and Molly, it is true, have their own particular forms of eloquence, although Molly's is limited in scope and Stephen's is hyperconscious; Bloom's surpasses theirs. But there are other examples of interior monologue in *Ulysses* which show none of this disparity between conversation and inward thought. In the *Wandering Rocks* episode, Father Conmee is on his way to the Artane orphanage to arrange to have one of Dignam's children admitted there, and Joyce writes: 'The Superior, the Very Reverend John Conmee S.J. reset his smooth watch in his interior pocket as he came down the presbytery steps. Five to three. Just nice time to walk to Artane. What was that boy's name? Dignam, yes. *Vere dignum et iustum est.* Brother Swan was the person to see. Mr. Cunningham's letter. Yes. Oblige him, if possible. Good practical catholic: useful at mission time.' [13]

And here is another example, of the Dignam boy himself: 'Master Dignam walked along Nassau street, shifted the porksteaks to his other hand. His collar sprang up again and he tugged it down. The blooming stud was too small for the buttonhole of the shirt, blooming end to it. He met schoolboys with satchels. I'm not going tomorrow either, stay away till Monday. He met other schoolboys. Do they notice I'm in mourning? Uncle Barney said he'd get it into the paper tonight. Then they'll all see it in the paper and read my name printed and pa's name.' [14] Bloom differs from lesser Dubliners in that his internal poetry is continual, even in the most unpromising situations. It is one of the primary indications of the value Joyce attaches to him.

The verisimilitude in *Ulysses* is so compelling that Joyce has been derided as more mimic than creator, which charge, being untrue, is the greatest praise of all. After his death, when the British Broadcasting Corporation was preparing a long program about him, its representatives went to Dublin and approached Dr. Richard Best to ask him to participate in a radio interview. 'What makes you come to me?' he asked truculently. 'What makes you think *I* have any connection with this man Joyce?' 'But you can't deny your connection,' said the men of the B.B.C., 'After all, you're a character in *Ulysses*.' Best drew himself up and retorted, 'I am not a character in fiction. I am a living being.' [15] The incident is a useful warning. Even with a *roman à clef*, which *Ulysses* largely is, no key quite fits. Art lavishes on one man another's hair, or voice, or bearing, with shocking disrespect for individual identity. Like Stephen in the *Circe* episode, art *shatters* light through the world, destroying and creating at once. So, when Dubliners asked each other in trepidation after the book appeared, 'Are you in it?' or 'Am I in it?' the answer was hard to give. A voice sounded familiar for an instant, a name seemed to belong to a friend, then both receded into a new being. For instance, the name of Mrs. Purefoy, whose labor pains end in the *Oxen of the Sun* episode with the birth of a boy, comes appropriately enough from Dr. R. Damon Purefoy, in 1904 Dublin's leading obstetrician. As *Finnegans Wake* insists, 'The traits featuring the chiaroscuro coalesce, their contrarieties eliminated, in one stable somebody.' [16] Even the personages who retain their actual names, like Dr. Best himself, are often altered; so Best is depicted as saying ceaselessly, 'Don't you know?' not because this was one of his expressions, which it was not, but because it seemed to Joyce the sort of expression that the fictional Best should use.

Still Joyce made Stephen Dedalus emphasize in *Ulysses* that the artist and his life are not distinct. Stephen fabricates Shakespeare's personal development from the evidence of his work. *Venus and Adonis* demonstrates for him that Shakespeare was seduced by Anne Hathaway, like Venus, an older woman; the gloomy *Richard III* and *King Lear* testify that Anne betrayed her husband with his two brothers-in-law Richard and Edmund, whose names Shakespeare accordingly attributes to the villains of those plays; the late plays show by their lightened feelings that the birth of a granddaughter had reconciled Shakespeare to his lot.

This theory, which according to friends Joyce took more seriously than Stephen,* suggests that *Ulysses* divulges more than an impersonal and detached picture of Dublin life; it hints at what is, in fact, true: that nothing has been admitted into the book which is not in some way personal and attached. In *Finnegans Wake* Joyce goes so far as to say of Shem the Penman that, like a spider, he produced 'from his unheavenly body a no uncertain quantity of obscene matter' and 'with this double dye . . . wrote over every square inch of the only foolscap available, his own body. . . .' [17] Instead of being creation's god, the artist, Joyce now says, is its squid. Of course Joyce was both.

The daughters of memory, whom William Blake chased from his door, received regular employment from Joyce, although he speaks of them disrespectfully. His work is 'history fabled,' [18] not only in *A Portrait* but in *Ulysses* as well. He was never a creator *ex nihilo;* he recomposed what he remembered, and he remembered most of what he had seen or had heard other people remember. The latter category was, in a city given over to anecdote, a large one. For the main body of his work Joyce relied chiefly upon his early life in Dublin and the later visits he had made there.† Certain comic material was ready at hand, and, in thinking back upon his native city, he prepared his great convocation of the city's eccentrics. There was Professor Maginni, the dark, middle-aged dancing master of North Great George's Street. Everyone knew his costume of tailcoat and dark grey trousers, silk hat, immaculate high collar with wings, gardenia in buttonhole, spats on mincing feet, and a silver-mounted, silk umbrella in hand. There were also Mrs. M'Guinness the queenly pawnbroker, and the five Hely's sandwichmen, each bearing a letter of the name; there was 'Endymion' Farrell, who carried two swords, a fishing rod, and an umbrella, who wore a red rose in his buttonhole, and had upon his head a small bowler hat with large holes for ventilation; from a brewer's family in Dundalk, he was said to have fallen into a vat and never recovered. Then there was the one-legged beggar known as 'The Blackbird,' who used to sing and to curse under his breath if he got nothing for it.

Less known than these, but familiar to Joyce or his family, was a cluster of other characters. [19] When Molly Bloom objects to the singing of Kathleen Kearney, the name is a modification of that of Olive Kennedy, who appeared on a concert program with Joyce in 1902. Other

---

* Stephen says he does not believe his own theory, but means perhaps only that he believes in nothing. The theory nevertheless suits him.
† An amusing use of later information is Bloom's advocacy of the Poulaphouca reservoir scheme, which, as Joyce knew, was later adopted, and his prediction that Nannetti would be Lord Mayor of Dublin before long, as indeed he became in 1906.

names brought up by Molly had a similar basis in fact; Tom Devin's two sons were friends of the Joyces, and Connie Connolly was the sister of his Belvedere classmates Albrecht and Vincent Connolly. Even the dog Garryowen was not made up of stray barks and bites, but belonged to the father of Joyce's Aunt Josephine Murray, whom Gerty McDowell accurately identifies as 'Grandpapa Giltrap.' To find some of his characters Joyce went among the dead, the best example being Pisser Duff, whose name he delicately altered to Pisser Burke. Duff looked harmless, but was a violent man who hung around the markets, brushing down horses while their owners drank at pubs. He was beaten to death by the police in Gardiner Street about 1892, but Joyce evoked him to be a friend of the equally vicious narrator of the *Cyclops* episode. One of the most curious composites is Lenehan, the parasite who speaks French. The name is borrowed from Matt Lenehan, a reporter on the *Irish Times*, but the personality Joyce took from a friend of his father named Michael Hart, who was dead by about 1900. Mick Hart, because of his habit of speaking French, was called Monsart (that is, Monsieur Hart). He worked, as Joyce implies, for a racing paper called *Sport,* and always attended the races in flashy attire. 'Lenehan' makes his first appearance in Joyce's work in 'Two Gallants,' when he is depicted accurately as longing to marry a rich girl. For this purpose Hart paid court for a time to the daughter of Joseph Nagle, one of the three brothers who kept a big public house in Earl Street; but nothing came of it. He knew a great deal about racing and was fond of writing doggerel; his greatest day was that, still recalled by Dubliners, when he 'tipped the double' in verse; that is, he predicted the winners of both the Lincolnshire Handicap and the Grand National Steeplechase.

Not long after this triumph he went downhill, and spent his later days in 'knocking around on the hard.' He continued to write verse; Joyce gives one of his less successful productions, a limerick, in the *Aeolus* episode.* Yet, as if to belie his reincarnation in *Ulysses,* Joyce includes Michael Hart in a list of Bloom's friends who are now dead.

* Most of Hart's poems had to do with attempts to get money and credit; one was entitled, 'On Looking for the Loan of a Tanner [sixpence]'; another dealt with his effort to obtain a pint of stout at Darden's Public House:

> One day I asked a pint on tick
> From Mr. Darden, who
> In lordly accents told me
> 'Twas a thing he didn't do.
>
> In Fanning's I owed threepence,
> In Bergin's one and four,
> In McGuire's only sixpence
> For they wouldn't give me more.

Joyce's surface naturalism in *Ulysses* has many intricate supports, and one of the most interesting is the blurred margin. He introduces much material which he does not intend to explain, so that his book, like life, gives the impression of having many threads that one cannot follow. For example, on the way to the funeral, the mourners catch sight of Reuben J. Dodd, and Mr. Dedalus says, 'The devil break the hasp of his back.' This reaction seems a little excessive unless we know that Dodd had lent money to Joyce's father, and that the subsequent exactions were the efficient cause of Mr. Dedalus's irritation. In the *Circe* episode Mulligan says, 'Mulligan meets the afflicted mother,' a remark based upon a story current in Dublin that Gogarty, returning home late one night during his medical course, staggered up the steps of his home on Rutland Square, reciting a station of the Cross at each step until, as he reached the top of the stairs and his worried mother opened the door, he concluded, 'Gogarty meets the afflicted mother.' Stephen's allusions to 'The Tinahely twelve' and 'Cranly's eleven true Wicklowmen to free their sireland' refer to a remark that J. F. Byrne had made to George Clancy; they agreed that twelve men with resolution could save Ireland, and Byrne said that he thought he could find twelve such men in Wicklow. With numerous truncated references of this sort Joyce edged his book.

The *Circe* episode offers an extended instance of Joyce's merging observations and reading into a new form. There was, to begin with, the necessity of finding an adequate setting. Following a long series of Homeric commentators who have moralized Circe's den as a place of temptation where the bestial aspects of men emerge, Joyce decided on the red-light district of Dublin for his scene. The word 'Nighttown' he had picked up from Dublin journalists, who always spoke of the late shift as 'Nighttown.' Joyce used it instead of the customary word for the brothel area, 'Monto,' so called from Montgomery Street. Monto was labeled about 1885 by the Encyclopaedia Britannica as the worst slum in Europe. It was concentrated chiefly in Mecklenburg Street, which became Tyrone Street and is now a dreary Railway Street, the name having been changed twice as part of an effort, vain until recently, to change its character. The street is made up of eighteenth-century houses; while some of these had by 1900 decayed into tenements,

---

> When makes ° is gone and nothing's left
> To shove into the pawn,
> I ramble up to Stephen's Green
> And gaze on Ardilaun.†

(° *Makes* are halfpence. † *Ardilaun* is the statue of a member of the Guinness family, who made porter.)

others, the 'flash houses,' were kept up beautifully by women who appeared in full evening dress before their select clientele.

Horse Show week in August was especially grand in Monto. The British officers arrived in numbers for the event, and the Monto ladies sent their cards at once to the officers' mess. The ladies drove to the races in pony traps, and afterwards a procession of innumerable cabs followed them back to Monto. The Boer War also proved a great boon to their business. In 1902 the Irish Battalion of Yeomanry returned from South Africa, and a dull-witted society paper published an anonymous poem sentimentally celebrating the heroes' return, in which however the first letter of each line formed the acrostic sentence, 'Whores will be busy.' This poem, which was quickly comprehended, killed the paper. It was usually attributed to Gogarty, then a medical student.

Joyce's knowledge of Monto was of course as complete as his knowledge of the *Evening Telegraph,* which he used in the *Aeolus* episode. He does not have Bloom and Stephen patronize the lower numbers of Mecklenburg Street, near Mabbot Lane, since these were usually patronized by English 'tommies'; these houses were full of religious pictures, behind which the ladies kept 'coshes,' pieces of lead pipe, to prevent trouble. Joyce asked one of his visitors in the 'thirties to secure a complete list of the names and addresses on Mecklenburg Street, and seems to have retained his interest in them. A lady appropriately named Mrs. Lawless lived at No. 4; her neighbour, at No. 5, was Mrs. Hayes, a grandmotherly type. But at the upper end of the street were the principal houses. Bloom, searching for Stephen at Mrs. Cohen's (No. 82), knocks first by mistake at No. 85, but is told that this is Mrs. Mack's house. Actually Mrs. Mack kept two houses, No. 85 and No. 90, and was so well known that the whole area was sometimes called 'Macktown.' *

As for Mrs. Cohen, she was older than Mrs. Mack, and by 1904 had either retired or died, but Joyce restored her in business because her name suited the Jewish themes in the book. Her girls were probably modelled on contemporary prostitutes. Florry Talbot, for instance, was probably Fleury Crawford.† The description of another girl, Kitty

---

* The medical students had a bawdy song that began:

> O there goes Mrs. Mack;
> She keeps a house of imprudence,
> She keeps an old back parlor
> For us poxy medical students.

† This young woman's father had a political job as scrivener in the Education Board. A priest came to see him to ask that he do something about his daughter; but Mr. 'Crawford' twirled his villainous moustaches and replied, 'Well, the girl appears to be enjoying herself, and besides, she's a source of income to me.'

Ricketts, suggests Becky Cooper, probably the best known among Dublin prostitutes from the beginning of the century until the 'twenties.*
Joyce was probably familiar also with Lady Betty and May Oblong (Mrs. Roberts); he reserved the latter's name for *Finnegans Wake,* where all Dublin is *d'Oblong.*[20]

Yet the deeper problem of *Circe* was to relate Bloom and Stephen on the unconscious level, to justify the father-son theme that Joyce had made central in his book. He does so chiefly in terms of one trait which the two men share, their essentially inactive roles. Joyce is quite earnest about this. He has shown Bloom throughout as the decent man who, in his pacific way, combats narrowmindedness, the product of fear and cruelty, which Stephen combatted in *A Portrait* and still combats. Once it is understood that Joyce sympathizes with Bloom and Stephen in their resistance in terms of mind rather than body, an aspect of the library episode becomes less baffling. Stephen Dedalus asserts there that Shakespeare was not Hamlet but Hamlet's father. Since Stephen in so many ways resembles Hamlet, and since he obviously thinks of himself as like Shakespeare, this identification may seem capricious. But it fits Joyce's notion both of the artistic temperament and of the desirable man. Joyce, Stephen, and Bloom share the philosophy of passivity in act, energy in thought, and tenacity in conviction. Hamlet, on the other hand, is the hero of a revenge-play; however unwittingly and fumblingly, he sheds a great deal of blood. Joyce does not encourage this view of the artist, and so he relates Shakespeare to the suffering father, the victim, rather than to the avenging son. The artist endures evil—he doesn't inflict it. 'I detest action,' says Stephen to the soldiers.[21] Because he takes this position, he belongs, in the extended metaphor which underlies all *Ulysses,* to the family of Bloom,† who tells the Citizen, 'It's no use. . . . Force, hatred, history, all that. That's not life for men and women, insult and hatred.'[22] They are son and father mentally, if not physically, and both of them argue that what is physical is incidental.

The kinship of Stephen and Bloom, on the surface so unlikely, is

---

* Becky Cooper was noted for the prodigality of her charities as well as for her favors; young men who took her fancy were the surprised and sometimes embarrassed recipients of gifts of money and new clothes. A familiar song about her celebrated not her generosity, however, but her accessibility:

> Italy's maids are fair to see
> And France's maids are willing
> But less expensive 'tis to me:
> Becky's for a shilling.

† This method of reinforcing his theme by multiplying instances of similar behavior becomes even more prominent in *Finnegans Wake.*

established with great adroitness. Joyce makes use of two sources to aid him, both literary; the first is Leopold von Sacher-Masoch, the second is William Blake. In the worst light Bloom's passivity in the face of Boylan's advances to Molly, and his rejection of force in the *Cyclops* episode, seem part of a willing submission comparable to that of Sacher-Masoch. In the best light they are Blake's rejection of the corporeal.

While writing the *Circe* episode Joyce drew heavily upon Sacher-Masoch's book, *Venus im Pelz.** Much of the material about flagellation is derived from it. *Venus in Furs* tells of a young man named Severin who so abases himself before his mistress, a wealthy woman named Wanda, and so encourages her cruelty toward him, that she becomes increasingly tyrannical, makes him a servile go-between, and then, in a rapturous finale, turns him over to her most recent lover for a whipping. There are many similarities to *Circe*. The society ladies who appear to Bloom, Mrs. Yelverton Barry (a name modified from that of a suspected transvestist) and Mrs. Bellingham (an actual name) are as fond of wearing furs as Wanda. Mrs. Bellingham recounts accusingly of Bloom, 'He addressed me in several handwritings † with fulsome compliments as a Venus in furs and alleged profound pity for my frost-bound coachman Balmer while in the same breath he expressed himself as envious of his earflaps and fleecy sheepskins and of his fortunate proximity to my person, when standing behind my chair wearing my livery and the armorial bearings of the Bellingham escutcheon garnished sable, a buck's head couped or.' [23] The hero of *Venus in Furs* wears his lady's livery, has to follow her at ten paces, and suffers luscious indignities comparable to those of Balmer.

Like Severin too, Bloom is depicted as welcoming his being birched, as even requesting this privilige. Wanda, reluctant at first to yield to her lover's strange importunities, is gradually attracted by them: 'You have corrupted my imagination and inflamed my blood,' she tells him; 'Dangerous potentialities were slumbering in me, but you were the first to awaken them.' Mrs. Mervyn Talboys puts it more ludicrously in *Ulysses,* 'You have lashed the dormant tigress in my nature into fury.' [24] Severin asks to be allowed to put on his mistress's shoes, and is kicked for performing the task too slowly. Bloom is similarly set to lacing the shoes of Bella Cohen, and fears she will kick him for his ineptitude. The more fearful and hateful Bella is, the more Bloom admires her; so Bella, like Wanda, puts her foot on Bloom's neck. The willing slavery of Severin to Wanda, which is sealed by an agreement she makes him

---

* W. Y. Tindall first pointed out an allusion to this book. Joyce had several of Sacher-Masoch's books in his library.

† See p. 463 for Joyce's use of a special handwriting.

sign, is echoed in Bloom's promise never to disobey Bella, and in her announcement to him, 'What you longed for has come to pass. Henceforth you are unmanned and mine in earnest, a thing under the yoke.' [25]

The degradation of Bloom continues. Like Severin he is forced to usher in Bella's new lover, Blazes Boylan. A scene in *Venus in Furs,* in which Severin attends Wanda at her bath, is reflected in an equivalent scene in *Ulysses.* And the climax of Sacher-Masoch's book, when Wanda, pretending affection, coyly persuades Severin to let her bind him against a pillar, and then turns him over to her new lover for a merciless flogging, is echoed in Bella's pretense of affection which facilitates her pulling Bloom's hair. Even the references to the marble statuette that Bloom takes home in the rain, and to the nymph, 'beautiful immortal,' whose 'classic curves' are pictured above his bed,[26] are paralleled in the 'stonecold and pure' plaster cast of Venus to which Severin prays in *Venus in Furs.*

Closely as he followed his source, Joyce made two major modifications. First, his version of Sacher-Masoch is a vaudeville version; and second, Bloom's masochistic fantasies occur in his unconscious mind; he berates himself, and makes himself worse than he is, because he is *conscious* of having allowed too much in reality. Then masochism is modified by Blakeism. Several references are made to Blake in the *Circe* episode, the most important at its end. There Stephen falls out with two soldiers, who accuse him of attacking the king because of his declaration, 'But in here it is I must kill the priest and the king.' [27] Joyce has in mind here an incident that occurred during Blake's stay at Felpham, when he put two soldiers out of his garden in spite of their protests that as soldiers of the king they should not be handled so. He replied to them, or was alleged to have replied, 'Damn the king,' was therefore haled up for treason, and barely got off. (In *Finnegans Wake* the two soldiers become three, and have an equally unpleasant role to play.) Stephen does not put the soldiers to flight; rather, to parody Blake as well, they knock *him* down, but not before he has stated his contention that the authorities, religious and secular, must be defeated in spiritual rather than corporeal warfare. This is Blake's central conception of the conquest of tyranny by imagination.*

Having displayed the body's defeat and the spirit's victory in both their ridiculous and noble aspects, Joyce brings about the mental purgation of Bloom and Stephen at the end of the episode. They are purged in a surprising way, for so reserved a book, that is, by love. The theme of family love, the love of parent for child and of child for parent, runs covertly throughout *Ulysses.* Molly Bloom's thoughts return to the

* Joyce said to Stanislaus as early as October 1, 1901, 'Cruelty is weakness.'

lambswool sweater she knitted for her son Rudy, who died when he was only eleven days old. The hyperborean Stephen, who claims to have denied his family, almost yields to affection when he comes upon his sister reading Chardenal's French primer, and remorse over his treatment of his mother accounts for his vision of her at the end of *Circe*. But Bloom emerges even more decisively from the Circean sty with his vision of Rudy as he might be now:

Against the dark wall a figure appears slowly, a fairy boy of eleven, a changeling, kidnapped, dressed in an Eton suit with glass shoes and a little bronze helmet, holding a book in his hand. He reads from right to left inaudibly, smiling, kissing the page.

BLOOM

(Wonderstruck, calls inaudibly.) Rudy!

RUDY

(Gazes unseeing into Bloom's eyes and goes on reading, kissing, smiling. He has a delicate mauve face. On his suit he has diamond and ruby buttons. In his free left hand he holds a slim ivory cane with a violet bowknot. A white lambkin peeps out of his waistcoat pocket.) [28]

Tenderness is not contrary to Joyce's temperament. This is the vision of a fond father, colored as such visions are; and the sentimental coloring is offset by the bizarre attire and the detachment of the child, both of which establish a sense of distance and estrangement from Bloom. The relation of Bloom and Rudy, as of Molly and Rudy, is profoundly moving; so is the relation of Bloom to his own father, who committed suicide by taking aconite poison.* Joyce deliberately says nothing about its emotional quality, but he has Bloom at one point recall a few snatches from the letter found at his father's bedside: 'To my dear son Leopold. Tomorrow will be a week that I received . . . it is no use Leopold to be . . . with your dear mother . . . That is not more to stand . . . to her . . . all for me is out . . . be kind to Athos, Leopold . . . my dear son . . . always . . . of me . . . das Herz . . . Gott . . . dein. . . .' [29] Paternity is a more powerful motif in the book than sexual love.

The phrase, 'Be kind to Athos,' refers to Bloom's father's dog—and kindness to animals, who are so much like children, and can repay affection only with affection, is another of those quite ordinary and undistinguished aspects of human nature that Joyce underlines. Even the Citizen, like Homer's Cyclops, is good to Garryowen. The kindness of Bloom on June 16, 1904, begins with animals and ends with human beings. So he feeds his cat in the morning, then some sea gulls, and in the *Circe* episode a dog. He remembers his dead son and dead father,

* His death is made to take place at the Queen's Hotel in Ennis because Joyce remembered a suicide that occurred there early in the century.

he is also concerned about his living daughter, and he never forgets his wife for a moment. He helps a blind man cross a street. He contributes very generously—beyond his means—to the fund for the children of his friend Dignam who has just died; and, when he begins to see Stephen as a sort of son, he follows him, tries to stop his drinking, prevents his being robbed, risks arrest to defend him from the police, feeds him too, and takes him home in what Joyce calls, half-humorously, 'orthodox Samaritan fashion.' [30] Stephen will not stay the night with Bloom—the barrier between man and man breaks down only occasionally and usually only a little, and the barrier quickly reforms—but in the temporary union of the two Joyce affirms his perception of community.

The relation of Bloom and Stephen confirms Joyce's point of view in another way: Bloom's common sense joins Stephen's acute intelligence; Stephen Dedalus, the Greek-Christian-Irishman, joins Bloom Ulysses, the Greek-Jewish-Irishman; the cultures seem to unite against horsepower and brutality in favor of brainpower and decency. The two men are contrasted in the book with those who are strong: Stephen can't swim while Mulligan swims beautifully; Bloom is only a walker, while the Citizen is the holder of the shotput record for all Ireland; and Bloom is a cuckold while Blazes Boylan is the loud-mouthed adulterer; but we spend most of the book inside Bloom's consciousness, and never enter Boylan's, as if coarseness had no consciousness. It is true that Mulligan is clever as well as strong, but it is a cleverness that goes with brutality. Stephen and Bloom, the mental men, are ranged against Mulligan and Boylan, the burly men, and Joyce's partisanship is clear.

The scheme of value of *Ulysses* comes closer to explicit expression in the *Circe* episode than it does anywhere else. It is buttressed by another passage in the *Ithaca* episode. When Bloom and Stephen are walking home to 7 Eccles Street from the cabman's shelter, they discuss a great many things, and Joyce notes, with some understatement, that their views were on certain points-divergent. 'Stephen,' he writes, 'dissented openly from Bloom's view on the importance of dietary and civic selfhelp while Bloom dissented tacitly from Stephen's views on the eternal affirmation of the spirit of man in literature.' [31] While the loftiness of Stephen's statement is mocked, that literature embodies the eternal affirmation of the spirit of man is not a crotchet of Stephen but a principle of Joyce, maintained by all his books. It is no accident that the whole of *Ulysses* should end with a mighty 'yes.' *

In making his hero Leopold Bloom, Joyce recognized implicitly what he often spoke of directly, his affinity for the Jews as a wandering,

* For Joyce's use of this final word, see p. 353 and pp. 531, 536.

persecuted people. 'I sometimes think,' he said later to Frank Budgen, 'that it was a heroic sacrifice on their part when they refused to accept the Christian revelation. Look at them. They are better husbands than we are, better fathers and better sons.' * [32] No doubt the incongruity of making his good Dubliner a Jew, and one so indifferent to all religious forms as to have sampled (without accepting) both Protestantism and Catholicism, attracted him with its satirical possibilities. But he must have been affected also by the Dreyfus uproar in Paris, which continued from 1892 to 1906; it had reached one of its crises in September 1902, just before Joyce's arrival in Paris, when Anatole France, a writer he respected, delivered his eloquent oration at the funeral of Zola, whose *J'accuse* was still stirring up Europe. A connection between the Jew and his artist-defender may have been fixed in Joyce's mind by the connection between Zola, France, and Dreyfus. When he returned to Dublin in 1903, he was in time for one of the rare manifestations of anti-Semitism in Ireland, a boycott of Jewish merchants in Limerick that was accompanied by some violence. [33]

Joyce was not a propagandist for better treatment of minorities. The conception of the likable Jew attracted without overwhelming him. He decided to make Bloom amiable and even noble in a humdrum sort of way, but to save him from sentimentality by making him also somewhat absurd as a convert, a drifter, a cuckold. His remarks make clear that the two characteristics of the Jews which especially interested him were their chosen isolation, and the close family ties which were perhaps the result of it.

These characteristics he saw in himself as well, and they gave him a sense of affinity. A great deal of his own experience became Bloom's. He not only took over the theme of adultery and the address of 7 Eccles Street from his 1909 trip to Dublin; he surrounded his hero with a Joycean atmosphere. For example, the Joyce family in Dublin employed for a time a charwoman, Mrs. Fleming; [34] in *Ulysses* she works in a similar capacity for the Blooms. The name of the Joyces' midwife was Mrs. Thornton; it is she who is credited with having delivered both the Blooms' children. Joyce was born at Brighton Square, and the Blooms lived there shortly after their marriage. While at Belvedere, Joyce took part in a dramatized version of Anstey's *Vice Versa;* Bloom acted in this as a boy also, though not in the same role. Both Joyce and Bloom took out books from the Capel Street Library. They shared an admiration for the poetry of Byron, and Bloom gave Molly a copy of his works during their courtship. Not all these details were unique, but

---

* He was interested too, in the way that, as he said, 'A Jew is both king and priest in his own family.' [35]

their accumulation is important. Sometimes Joyce mocks himself, as in the *Nausicaa* episode, where Bloom's contemplation of Gerty Mac-Dowell parodies the stages of Stephen's (and Joyce's own) vision of the girl at the seashore in *A Portrait*. Stephen's revulsion against his body during the retreat in *A Portrait* is paralleled in *Ulysses* by many examples of Bloom's fastidiousness. Molly's proposed concert tour of English watering places parodies Joyce's plans to buy a lute and sing Dowland's songs in the same area. This technique of self-depreciation is used especially in the swelling and ridiculing of the *Cyclops*, *Nausicaa*, and *Oxen of the Sun* episodes, but it operates less conspicuously throughout the book. Like Shem in *Finnegans Wake*, Joyce is 'for ever cracking quips on himself.' [36]

But Bloom is more (and less) than Joyce. He had at least one Triestine prototype, for, when Dr. Daniel Brody asked Joyce later, 'Mr. Joyce, I can understand why the counterpart of your Stephen Dedalus should be a Jew, but why is he the son of a Hungarian?' Joyce, taking off his glasses and looking at him casually yet with an air of pronouncement, replied, 'Because he was.' [37] One model may have been Teodoro Mayer, the publisher of the *Piccolo della Sera*, whose father like Bloom's was a Hungarian peddler, but most of the principal details came from Ettore Schmitz, whose grandfather was a peddler in Hungary. Schmitz said once to Stanislaus, 'Tell me some secrets about Irishmen. You know your brother has been asking me so many questions about Jews that I want to get even with him.' [38] The difference in age between Schmitz and Joyce was, as Harry Levin points out, roughly the same as that between Bloom and Stephen, and Stanislaus Joyce thought there was a resemblance, although Signora Schmitz always denied it.[39] Schmitz was in many ways quite different from Bloom; but he had married a Gentile, he had changed his name (though only for literary purposes), he knew something of Jewish customs, and he shared Bloom's amiably ironic view of life. Joyce could not abide the inner organs of animals and fowl, while Schmitz, like Bloom, loved them.° Some of these are small similarities, but Joyce had a spider's eye.

Several Dubliners helped Joyce to complete his hero. The first was the man named Hunter, about whom he had asked Stanislaus and, later, his Aunt Josephine Murray to send him all the details they could remember. But in making Bloom an advertisement canvasser Joyce had someone else in mind. This man is first mentioned in the story 'Grace' under the name of C. P. M'Coy,[40] and is identified there as having been a clerk in the Midland Railway, a canvasser for advertisements for the *Irish Times* and *Freeman's Journal*, a town traveler for a coal firm on

° So did John Joyce.

commission, a private inquiry agent, a clerk in the office of the sub-sheriff, and secretary to the City Coroner. His wife had been a soprano and still taught young children to play the piano at low terms. These facts all point to M'Coy's actual prototype, Charles Chance, whose wife sang soprano at concerts in the 'nineties under the name of Madame Marie Tallon. In the variety of his jobs, in the profession of his wife, Chance fitted the description of Bloom; and that Joyce intended to combine him with Hunter is suggested by the juxtaposition of 'Charley Chance' with 'Mr. Hunker' in *Finnegans Wake*.[41]

'Leopold Bloom' was named with due deliberation. Leopold was the first name of Signorina Popper's father in Trieste; Bloom was the name of two or three families who lived in Dublin when Joyce was young. One Bloom, who was a dentist, had been converted to Catholicism in order to marry a Catholic woman; they had five children, including a son, Joseph, who also became a dentist and practiced like his father on Clare Street in 1903 and 1904. The son was renowned for his wit.[42] Joyce deliberately confuses Joseph Bloom the dentist with Leopold in one chapter, and in another he lists as one of Leopold's old addresses 38 Lombard Street, which was actually Joseph Bloom's address.[43] Joyce no doubt also knew of another Bloom, who was committed in Wexford early in the century for the murder of a girl who worked with him in a photographer's shop. He had planned a double suicide; after having killed her and, as he thought, himself, he scrawled the word LOVE (but misspelt it as LIOVE) with his blood on the wall behind him. He was let off on mental grounds and, after some time in an institution, left the country. This incident presumably gave Joyce the plan of establishing Bloom's daughter Milly as an apprentice in a photographer's shop. He put the shop in Mullingar because he remembered that there was such a shop there when he visited the town with his father in 1900 and 1901.[44]

The concert name of Mrs. Charles Chance, 'Madame Marie Tallon,'[45] bears a deliberate resemblance to Madame Marion Tweedy, Mrs. Bloom's concert name. In using the Chances Joyce neatly concealed their identity, however; he prevented anyone's supposing they were the Blooms by introducing them into his book as the M'Coys, and by inventing a professional rivalry between Mrs. M'Coy and Mrs. Bloom. The character which he attributes to Mrs. Bloom is also unlike that of Mrs. Chance, whom he probably did not know; it is closer to that of the buxom wife of a fruit store owner named Nicolas Santos, with whom he was acquainted in Trieste and in Zurich. Signora Santos stayed indoors all day to preserve her complexion, for which she mixed her own creams. That Mrs. Santos had a share in Mrs. Bloom was an open secret in the Joyce family later.[46] But the seductiveness of Molly came, of course, from Signorina Popper. For the Spanish quality in her Joyce drew upon one of the many daughters of Matt Dillon, an old friend of his family who is mentioned in *Ulysses* too. This daughter had been in Spain, smoked cigarettes, and was considered a Spanish type.[47]

If bits and pieces of Mrs. Chance, Signora Santos, Signorina Popper, and Matt Dillon's daughter helped Joyce to design the outer Molly Bloom, he had a model at home for Molly's mind. Nora Joyce had a similar gift for concentrated, pungent expression, and Joyce delighted in it as much as Bloom did. Like Molly she was anti-intellectual; and like Molly she was attached to her husband without being awestruck. The rarity of capital letters and the run-on sentences in Molly's monologue are of course related to Joyce's theory of her mind (and of the female mind in general) as a flow, in contrast to the series of short jumps made by Bloom, and of somewhat longer ones by Stephen. But he had in mind as well Nora's carelessness in such matters.

Joyce also returns to the subject that had so bothered him in his early years of living with Nora, her refusal to recognize a difference between him and the other young men she had known. Bloom recognizes this characteristic in Molly, but Molly manifests it independently as well. Throughout her monologue Joyce lets her refer to various men she has known chiefly as 'he,' with only occasional indication of a change of the person involved. Her husband and her past lovers, among whom Mulvey of Galway makes an unexpected appearance, are speedily interchanged in her mind. At the end of her monologue she remembers the supreme moment in Bloom's courtship of her, when

he asked me to say yes and I wouldnt answer first only looked out over the sea and the sky I was thinking of so many things he didnt know of Mulvey and Mr Stanhope and Hester and father and old captain Groves . . . and Gibraltar as a girl where I was a Flower of the mountain yes when I put the rose in my hair like the Andalusian girls used or shall I wear a red yes and how he kissed me under the Moorish wall and I thought well as well him as another and then I asked him with my eyes to ask again. . . .

The 'he' who kissed her under the Moorish wall was not Bloom but Mulvey; but it is Bloom of whom she says, 'I thought well as well him as another.' Molly, like Nora, fails to differentiate, though she is paradoxically aware that Bloom is rather special.* Joyce attributes to his heroine the character of woman as Nora had shown it to him, not the character, so often presumed by novelists, of an irresponsible, passion-

---

* So Nora Joyce acknowledged in later life to Carola Giedion-Welcker, 'I don't know whether my husband is a genius, but I'm sure of one thing, there is nobody like him.' [48]

ate, romantic creature. As he told Frank Budgen, Molly was intended to represent 'perfectly sane full amoral fertilisable untrustworthy engaging shrewd limited prudent indifferent *Weib*.' [49] The last adjective is, appropriately, *indifferent*. If Joyce was wrong in this analysis, the error was not for lack of observation.

Apart from her prototypes, Molly is a woman who has been much misunderstood. The celebrated monologue in which 'flesh becomes word' [50] does not deserve its reputation as the summit of promiscuity, nor does it fit its description, by some writers, as the summit of cruel, unfair, and anti-feminine dissection. If Molly were really promiscuous in her conduct, Joyce would not have used her for heroine, for he needed an everyday woman to counterpoise Bloom's oddities. It is true that Bloom, and critics after him, lists no less than twenty-five lovers of Molly. But on examination the list contains some extraordinary names: there are two priests, a lord mayor, an alderman, a gynecologist, a bootblack, a professor. In the book it is clear that she has confessed to the priests, consulted the gynecologist, and coquetted with the rest. But only the most rigorous interpretation of infidelity—a burlesque of Richard Rowan's interpretation in *Exiles*—could include these episodes.

The two lovers Molly has had since her marriage are Bartell D'Arcy and Boylan. While adultery is not excused by its infrequence, her behavior is not unpredictable in view of the fact that for eleven years, since she was twenty-two, her husband has not had adequate sexual relations with her. Most of her internal monologue is devoted to her reminiscences of love-making before her marriage, but even these are on examination less glamorous, and much less numerous, than usually recognized. It is suggested that she was a demi-vierge when she was married. The impression of voluptuousness remains, but is based more on her longings or potentialities than on her activities. Joyce delights in heightening her into someone beyond herself, and then in pulling her back to 7 Eccles Street.

There is no reason to exalt her, because she is earthy, into an earth goddess. She has had two children, a boy and a girl, but the boy died shortly after birth. Her motherhood was only an aspect of that femininity which Joyce was trying to report. It may be objected that if she has not engendered everything, at least she accepts everything. Actually she does not. She is dissatisfied with the coarseness of Blazes Boylan, and beyond that, seems dissatisfied with the male body and with the consummation of physical love. She remains a wife more than a goddess of acquiescence; married to Bloom, she will remain married, even if dissatisfied with him too. For Molly also acknowledges, though with considerable reluctance and appropriate feminine indirection, the importance of mind as opposed to body, the importance of decency, and the bonds of the family. The virile Boylan is nothing but a shell, while the much less virile Bloom is, with all his shortcomings, a man of both intellect and body.

In forming the character of Boylan, Joyce made his villain the negative reproduction of his hero. Joyce's notes for *Exiles* show that he regarded the relation of protagonist and antagonist as complicated by admiration as well as repugnance for each other. The mindless swagger of Boylan has an air about it. While Joyce's clear preference is for the mental men, the Shems, he may have had a sneaking regard for those burly men, the Shauns, with whom Boylan belongs.

The models for Boylan had to be opposite to Bloom in their manner of dress and speech, in their conduct of life. *Ulysses* supplies a few particulars, that Boylan's father was a horse dealer off Island Bridge who sold horses to the British during the Boer War, that Boylan is a flashy dresser, especially notable for his straw hat, and that he has just managed a prize fighter. The horse dealer who had his premises off Island Bridge was James Daly, who does not fit the other details except that, like all other horse dealers in Dublin, he sold horses to the British during the Boer War. There was, however, a horse dealer during the 'nineties who bore the name Boylan, and had Blazes or Blazer for a nickname. Joyce took his name, and perhaps borrowed the occupation and appearance of the character from another man named Ted Keogh. Keogh ran a junk shop under Merchant's Arch in almost exactly the same location as the hawker's car where Bloom buys *The Sweets of Sin* for Molly. He did not know Joyce personally; his only connection with the family, he declared,[51] was that as a boy he shot a peashooter at John Joyce's top hat and hit it. Keogh in 1909 was, like his father, a horse dealer; he dressed expensively, and habitually wore a straw hat; and when Joyce visited Dublin Keogh was managing a well known prize fighter. Keogh's character was not, however, what Joyce needed for Boylan's. Some of Boylan's flashiness and breeziness may have come from Prezioso.

Boylan's first name is not Blazes, as he is always called, but Hugh; and the provenance of this name is diverting. It is likely that Joyce had in mind his classmate at University College, Dublin, the prim and proper Hugh Boyle Kennedy. Kennedy was later to become Chief Justice of the High Court, and Joyce must have keenly enjoyed his little private joke.

Joyce had fixed upon June 16, 1904, as the date of *Ulysses* because it was the anniversary of his first walk with Nora Barnacle. He was able to obtain, perhaps on his last visit to Dublin, copies of the newspapers of that day. In his book, Bloom's fondest memory is of a moment of affection plighted among the rhododendrons on Howth, and so is Mrs. Bloom's; it is with her recollection of it that the book ends. In this sense *Ulysses* is an epithalamium; love is its cause of motion. The spirit is liberated from its bonds through a eucharistic occasion, an occasion characterized by the joy that, even as a young man, Joyce had praised as the emotion in comedy which makes it a higher form than tragedy. Though such occasions are as rare as miracles, they are permanently sustaining; and unlike miracles, they require no divine intercession. They arise in quintessential purity from the mottled life of everyday.

The theme of *Ulysses* is simple, and Joyce achieves it through the characters of Bloom, Molly, and Stephen. Casual kindness overcomes unconscionable power. Stephen's charge against Mulligan is that Mulligan is brutal and cruel; * Molly's complaint against Boylan is again on the score of brutality, of animal sensuality without feeling. Bloom is allowed to formulate this theme of the book, though in comic circumstances, when he defends love to the Cyclops, and defines it meekly but deftly as 'the opposite of hatred.' [52] It is opposite also to chauvinism and force. So in the *Penelope* episode, Molly, faithful in spite of herself, ends the day by yielding once more to her husband and dismissing Boylan as inconsequential. In Joyce's work the soul—a word which he never renounced—carries off the victory.

Whatever else about the book was unclear to Joyce in 1914, as he set himself for what he knew would be a long period of work, this point of view was firm. All the trivia of Dublin and many of Trieste must be conscripted to express it. In his art Joyce went beyond the misfortune and frustration he had grown accustomed to regard as the dominant notes of his life, and expressed his only piety, a rejection, in humanity's name and comedy's method, of fear and hatred.

---

* Joyce completed in this character his analysis of Gogarty. He had written it long before for *A Portrait,* but had put it aside. The earlier version was much more essaylike:

'Doherty's gibes flashed to and fro through the torpor of his mind and he thought without mirth of his friend's face, equine and pallid, and of his pallid hair, grained and hued like oak. He had tried to receive coldly these memories of his friend's boisterous humour, feeling that his coarseness of speech was not a blasphemy of the spirit but a coward's mask, but in the end the troop of swinish images broke down his reserve and went trampling through his memory, followed by his laughter . . .' [53]

1914-1915

What clashes here of wills gen wonts, oystrygods gaggin fishygods! Brékkek Kékkek Kékkek Kékkek! Kóax Kóax Kóax! Ualu Ualu! Quaouauh! . . . Killykillkilly: a toll, a toll.

— *Finnegans Wake* (4)

WAR broke out, without decent regard for exiled writers, just when Joyce was intent upon finishing *A Portrait of the Artist* and upon beginning *Exiles* and *Ulysses*. When Austria declared war upon Serbia, on July 28, 1914, he hastened to the British consulate with Giorgio, but was assured that there was no reason for concern on the part of British subjects. He called next upon Boris Furlan, who lived close to the Italian consulate, to ask what seemed likely to happen. Furlan was very pessimistic, anticipating that the war would spread; but Joyce reported what he had heard at the consulate and was calming himself when suddenly a mob surrounded the Italian consulate and tried to remove the Italian flag. Within a few moments a detachment of soldiers enfiladed in front of the building. Joyce was frightened, seized Giorgio's hand, and rushed away from Furlan's house.[1]

It was, however, not he but Stanislaus who got into trouble. For some years Stanislaus had been an outspoken Irredentist, basking in the anticlerical liberalism which Garibaldi had left behind him in Italy. He expressed himself with reckless candor against the Holy Roman Empire and the Vatican 'empire.' When war began he did not become circumspect, and his forthright remarks drew the attention of the authorities to him. Stanislaus paid no attention, and even went on a tour of the fortifications at Trieste with a friend of his named Petz.[2] As a result he was arrested on January 9, 1915, and sent to Austrian detention centers for the rest of the war. The ant was interned, but the grasshopper continued his dance.

Not that James Joyce's life sounded much like dancing. He was permitted to go on teaching at the Scuola di Commercio, and he also kept a part-time job, which he had held since January 1914, as English correspondent for Gioachino Veneziani's paint factory, at 100 crowns a month. Stanislaus's pupils came over to him, too, among them a young man named Oscar Schwarz, as cynical about the conflict as Joyce himself. Schwarz went for his first lesson to Joyce's flat on the Via Donato Bramante, and like Paolo Cuzzi before him found the surroundings odd. There was the long room with the many chairs, furnished now also with an upright piano, and perfumed by a burning cone of incense. On a reading desk, ecclesiastical in style, lay throned the vellum-covered, missal-like volume of *Chamber Music* which Joyce had copied on parchment pages and sent to Nora from Dublin. To enhance the atmosphere of ritual, three photographs of sculptures by Meštrović took the place of icons. Schwarz recognized them as among the sculptures exhibited at the Expositione Biennale in Venice the previous year. Joyce had cut them from a catalogue, sent them to be framed, and then inscribed his own titles below them. One represented a peasant woman, belly swollen, face contorted with labor pain, her sparse hair half covered by a wretched wig. Joyce's title for this was 'Dura Mater.' The second was a mother and child, the bony infant hanging from a withered breast, and under this he had written 'Pia Mater.' The third photograph was of an ugly old woman naked, and under it Joyce had had engraved the lines from Canto V of the Inferno:

> *Elena vidi, per cui tanto reo*
> *Tempo si volse. . . .**

Schwarz asked indignantly, 'Why Helen?' For answer Joyce made a rapid calculation of the number of years Helen lived with Menelaus before she met Paris, of the time she spent at Troy, and of the time she had been back in Sparta when Telemachus met her; he then calculated the age she must have been when Dante saw her in the Inferno. Schwarz chided him, 'But Helen remains for ever the beautiful woman admired by the old men at the gate! You have killed Helen!' Joyce's reaction was extraordinary; he laughed and repeated several times, as though approvingly, 'Killed Helen!' [3] He would afterward be accused of killing Ulysses and Penelope.

Joyce was amused to learn from Schwarz that the textbook which Stanislaus had given him to study was *Dubliners*. He at once shifted his pupil to *Hamlet*. This was not the only difference in pedagogical technique that Schwarz noted. Stanislaus had enjoyed the impiety of asking his pupils, 'Who inhabited the British Isles in the first centuries

---

* Helen see, for whom so long
a time of ill revolved. . . .

after the birth of Mr. Berlitz's savior (not mine)?' James never indulged in such crudities, but he made clear his skepticism.[4]

Joyce's assertive conversation ranged over many subjects, both during Schwarz's lessons and on other occasions when they drank white wine together at the Antica Trattoria Bonavia. Joyce had no patience with the current adulation of Wagner, objecting that '*Wagner puzza di sesso*' (stinks of sex); Bellini, he said, was far better. He differed also with the usual conception of Italian as the ideal language for lyric verse; it was too heavy, he said, because it used its seven vowel sounds (including two e's and two o's) so constantly. English, with its multitude of vowel sounds, was a far subtler poetic medium, he maintained, 'the most wonderful language in the world.' One day he brought in a new poem, 'Simples,' addressed to Lucia, and began to explain its meaning to Schwarz; but his young pupil, deeply imbued with Croce's expressionism, told him the explanation was all wrong, that the poem was pure music. Joyce listened attentively and then surprisingly yielded, saying, 'You *do* understand my poem.' (In later years he defended *Finnegans Wake* as music.) He was not so tractable when Schwarz brought up the subject of psychoanalysis; Joyce brushed it aside as absurd, saying its symbolism was mechanical, a house being a womb, a fire a phallus.

The question of national traits interested him very much. At the Trattoria Bonavia one day, Joyce allocated the seven deadly sins among the European nations. Gluttony, he said, was English, Pride French, Wrath Spanish, Lust German, Sloth Slavic. 'What is the Italian sin? Avarice,' he concluded, recalling how often he had been cheated by shopkeepers and how wickedly he had been robbed in Rome. As for his own people, the Irish, their deadly sin was Envy, and he quoted the song of Brangäne in *Tristan und Isolde* as a perfect expression of Celtic envy. Schwarz asked, 'Then what is the deadly sin of the Jews?' Joyce pondered, excluded one after the other, then said, 'None, except of course the one mortal sin. . . .' 'Which?' 'To have crucified Jesus.' [5]

Another companion of Joyce's during this time was the painter Tullio Silvestri, a Venetian-born artist who had his studio in the Città Vecchia. In 1913 he painted his portrait of Nora and the next year he painted Joyce. Silvestri was lively, gay, and invariably poor. He painted impressionistically; disdaining preliminaries, he lunged at the canvas with his brush, sometimes with fine results. Silvestri and Joyce used to sing and drink together. Joyce was astounded by Silvestri's ability, which even surpassed his own, to squeak through the most trying financial crises, and several times helped out his friend, as Silvestri has recorded,[6] by emptying his own pocket. Silvestri's technique for selling his pictures was curious: he went to see Ettore Schmitz, carrying a mysterious package; then he said, 'This package contains a coat and shoes for my daughter. I will show you.' Opening the package, he disclosed his latest canvas, which Schmitz had to buy for the sake of the daughter.[7] Joyce accompanied Silvestri once on a similar errand to the shipping magnate, Count Diodato Tripcovich, who was deliberating whether or not to buy a picture Silvestri had left with him. It was the time when the Irredentist sentiment was expressing itself in the song, '*Tripoli sarà Italiana, sarà Italiana al rombo del cannon.*' The optimistic Silvestri, as he waited with Joyce outside, suddenly burst into a parody of Tripcovich's Slavic name by chanting, '*Tripcovich sarà Italianska, sarà Italianska. . . .*'[8] The count bought the picture. Joyce, always fascinated by local jokes, remembered the incident afterwards with great amusement.* In August 1914, Silvestri needed money badly to enable him to convey himself and his family to Italy; Joyce raised 100 crowns for him.[9]

The entry of Italy into the war in May 1915 did not impress Joyce. He remarked skeptically to Schwartz, 'If the Italians think it will be a cakewalk to Vienna . . .' Recalling the size of Victor Emmanuel and the Kaiser's loss of voice, he said, 'It's a duel between a man who can't be seen at twenty paces and another who can't be heard at the same distance.'[10] He remarked to Francini, 'My political faith can be expressed in a word: Monarchies, constitutional or unconstitutional, disgust me. Kings are mountebanks. Republics are slippers for everyone's feet. Temporal power is gone and good riddance. What else is left? Can we hope for monarchy by divine right? Do you believe in the Sun of the Future?'[11] † He was supremely indifferent to the result and, so long as gunfire could not be heard, to the conflict itself. It was becoming apparent, however, that he could not long remain where he was; after the conscription of most of the teachers the Scuola Superiore di Commercio had to close down, and his private pupils entered the army or escaped to Italy. Joyce put the matter more comically to Silvio Benco: 'Now that everyone in Trieste knows English,' he said, 'I will have to move on.'[12]

He did not, however, make any immediate effort to leave, but kept on with *Exiles*, which he had in nearly final form by April of 1915, and with *Ulysses*, which he had brought as far as the first pages of the third episode by June.[13] In London the ferment which Pound and the *Egoist*

---

* He liked also the Triestine alteration of the Italian battle cry from '*Avanti, Savoia,*' to '*Avanti, cagoia* [snails],' and the change of the Austrian anthem from '*Salvi Dio l'austriaco regno*' to '*Salvi Dio la panza per i fighi,*' which means in Triestine dialect, 'God save his belly for the figs.'[14]

† That is, do you believe in socialism? The Sun of the Future is a phrase from the Italian Socialist anthem.

had created for him persisted in spite of the war; and even though
Grant Richards decided on May 18 not to publish *A Portrait,** Joyce
had no reason to feel discouraged. On February 10, 1915, he received
an unexpected letter from J. B. Pinker, the London literary agent, offering at the suggestion of H. G. Wells to act for Joyce.[15] Wells himself
wrote in April that he had 'an unstinted admiration' [16] for Joyce's work,
which he had read in the *Egoist*. As he later explained, he thought
Joyce had succeeded in preserving an example of the products of
Catholic education for the 'amazement of posterity.' [17] Joyce followed
Wells's advice by signing an agreement with Pinker in April. It did not
work out very well, for the agent was to have little luck in marketing
such peculiar merchandise; he did, however, serve Joyce as the amiable
recipient of the innumerable letters about small matters which Joyce
soon began painstakingly to send him.

In America, B. W. Huebsch read *Dubliners* and recognized the merit
of the stories. He would have liked to publish them at once, but at the
moment could not afford to do so, as he informed Joyce. His acuteness
led to an association which endured until Joyce's death. Huebsch combined a sense of English style with the frankness and honesty which in
Roberts had been so lacking. For the moment, he contented himself
with urging H. L. Mencken, as Pound had already done, to publish
some of the stories in the *Smart Set*, and Mencken bravely obliged by
using 'The Boarding House' and 'A Little Cloud' in the May issue.

Another change took place now in Joyce's household. His sister Eileen
was engaged in 1914 to a Czech bank cashier in Trieste, Frantisek
Schaurek. She had written at the time to John Joyce, and the news
brought on a sudden letter from Dublin:

> Beaumont,
> Upper Drumcondra,
> 5.5.14.

Dear Jim,

As you see by above, I am located here. I have been two months in
hospital and am trying to get well in this convalescent home and am
feeling somewhat better. I note all you say about yourself, and as soon
as I am able to write you I will do so more fully. I am most anxious
to know the full particulars concerning Eileen, namely, who and what
this gentleman is. I am satisfied both you and your brother will look to
her future and see that she does not take any step that may mar her
future. I am and always was very fond of Eileen. She is the only one
of my daughters (now alive) who never gave me insolence or showed

---

* He had sent it to a reader in April with the remark that the book seemed to him
'quite hopeless.' [18]

contempt for me, so that I look to you to take my part and see after her interests. I had a letter from her telling me that she is very fond of this young gentleman, and of course that counts for a good deal, but at the same time is not everything. As you know, I had experience in that respect. I am enclosing you a letter to her as she requested.

As regards my portrait (which I am very glad to see you appear so anxious to have), as soon as I get some flesh, etc., I certainly will get it done for you, and as you again ask me to go over, perhaps, as things have turned out here and the cruel treatment I have received from my daughters here, I may go over to you on a visit for a month. Of course, only on the understanding that I would not be any inconvenience to you or Nora and that I should pay my way, as I have to do here.

Not having heard from Stannie for some years, I take it my memory is entirely obliterated from his filial mind. I dare say. 'Tempora mutantur, etc.'? I will be here for at least a fortnight, so that you can write me to this address, as my future one is, to say the least of it, doubtful. Let me know exactly when you mean I should go, as I will require time to make some preparations. I need not say it would afford me great pleasure to see you before I die, also to again look upon the portraits of those who did love me and whom I so loved.

Good bye now Jim, or perhaps better say Au Revoir. Write me now fully concerning Eileen. Dont forget. With fond love to all.

> Believe me to be
> What is left of
> Your Father

James suggested to Eileen that she postpone her marriage until the war ended, but she decided not to wait. The ceremony was arranged for April 12, 1915, with James as best man. He borrowed a dress suit, much too big for him, from Marckwardt, the German teacher at the Scuola Berlitz.[19] At the wedding he tendered his sister only one piece of advice, the information that she was not really changing her name at all, because Schaurek in Irish meant Joyce.[20] (It doesn't.) * He announced also that Yoyce—as the Triestines usually mispronounced the name—meant 'eggs' in Czech,[21] a point that diverted him beyond measure, and augured fertility. Eileen and her husband soon left for Prague, where they spent the war years. They later named their first child Beatrice Bertha, after the two women in *Exiles*.

The large Italian population of Trieste made the city a potential trouble-center after Italy had entered the war, and the military authorities ordered a partial evacuation. Joyce had no choice but to make arrangements at once. The first step he was forced to take proved disagreeable: he applied to the United States consul in Trieste, who

* He was thinking of Seoghach, one of several Irish forms of the name Joyce.[22]

was in charge of British interests, for a passport. Joyce's bored replies made the irritated consul raise his voice to declare, 'I am proud to feel that I am acting for the British consul, the representative of the King of England.' Joyce answered coldly, 'The British consul is not the representative of the King of England. He is an official paid by my father for the protection of my person.' [23] (The notion of John Joyce paying taxes for any reason must have secretly entertained him.) * The consul granted the visa notwithstanding, but there remained the difficulty of securing permission to depart from the Austrian authorities, who might prefer to intern him. Joyce sought help from two of his most influential pupils, Baron Ambrogio Ralli and Count Francesco Sordina. The Austrian authorities were promised, safely enough, that he would not take part in any belligerent activity against the emperor, and so raised no objection to the exit permit Ralli and Sordina requested. In later years Joyce wrote a footnote for Herbert Gorman's biography:

Sordina was one of the greatest swordsmen in Europe and during the brief transition period of Triestine severance from Austria was the first and last Chief Magistrate of the once Immediate City. Both Ralli and Sordina are now dead but till the times of their deaths, which took place in the last few years, they regularly received (and replied) at Christmas and the New Year messages of grateful remembrance from the writer whose life they had possibly saved.[24]

Joyce left his furniture and his books [25] in his flat, and in late June started with his family for Switzerland. The trip was a much easier one than expected, because of a series of beneficent coincidences. The first person he met in the train was a Greek pupil, Mario Megavis,[26] and this encounter seemed an omen that all would go well. As it happened, the first control officer was another pupil, who took Joyce's word for the contents of his baggage, and so on towards the Swiss border. At Innsbruck the train was detained, to the family's trepidation, but only to allow the emperor's train to go by. Switzerland, where they arrived a few hours later, was more than a refuge; it was a symbol of artistic detachment, *au-dessus de la mêlée*, and it was fitting that Joyce should not only write the bulk of his greatest book there, but also return there in the end to die.

---

* Joyce himself paid no income tax during most of his stay in Trieste because the tax collector was an admirer of his. Then a new collector demanded he pay. Joyce was so annoyed he stopped smoking until he had deprived the government of an equal amount of money in tobacco tax.[27]

PART III

ZURICH

◇◇

1915–1916

Now it is notoriously known how on that surprisingly bludgeony Unity Sunday when the grand germogall allstar bout was harrily the rage between our weltingtoms extraordinary and our pettythicks the marshalaisy and Irish eyes of welcome were smiling daggers down their backs, when the roth, vice and blause met the noyr blank and rogues and the grim white and cold bet the black fighting tans, categorically unimperatived by the maxims, a rank funk getting the better of him, the scut in a bad fit of pajamas flad like a leveret for his bare lives, to Talviland . . . and, without having struck one blow, . . . kuskykorked himself up tight in his inkbattle house, badly the worse for boosegas. . . .

—Finnegans Wake (176)

W HEN Joyce arrived in Zurich at the end of June 1915, he was twice an expatriate. Trieste—'my second country'[1]—had gradually won his difficult affection, and the affection of his family. He had lived there almost eleven years, half as long as he had lived in Dublin. During this time he had published *Chamber Music*, finished *Dubliners*, revised *Stephen Hero* into *A Portrait of the Artist as a Young Man*, written *Exiles*, and begun *Ulysses*. Afterwards he was to dismiss all talk of democratic Utopias with the remark that he had never been happier than under the lax rule of the Austro-Hungarian emperor in Trieste. 'They called it a ramshackle empire,' he said later to Mary Colum, 'I wish to God there were more such empires.'[2] In Switzerland he and his family retained their loyalty to Trieste by speaking its language *en famille* and associating for some time chiefly with Triestines or friends of Triestines. In Paris too they continued nostalgically to speak Italian, Joyce insisting it was the easiest language on the voice.[3]

The Joyces might have gone to Prague and joined Eileen Schaurek and her husband; this move was suggested by the Austrian authorities. Joyce preferred, however, to go to Zurich, which had been his destination eleven years before when he left Dublin with Nora Barnacle. At first he was not sure he would stay. 'I stopped here,' he wrote Miss Weaver on June 30, 'as it is the first big city after the frontier. I do not know where I shall live in Switzerland. Possibly here.' [4] The surrounding mountains—'those great lumps of sugar,' [5] as he called them—bored him when they did not give him claustrophobia, and Nora was not happy at the prospect of having to learn another language; but they were amazed by the city's cleanliness, so different from Trieste's complacent disorder. Early in their stay Nora was forced by a policeman to pick up a piece of paper she had dropped in a hallway. The first thing Joyce said to his friends from Trieste, the Bliznakoffs, when he met them at the station in Zurich in August, was, 'Zurich is so clean that if you spilled minestra on the Bahnhofstrasse you could eat it right up without a spoon.' [6]

Joyce had no money, yet money, in uncomfortably small quantities at first, began to drift his way. So did fame. Shortly after his arrival in Zurich he received an entry form for *Who's Who* (1916), and listed himself modestly as 'teacher of the Scuola Superiore di Commercio, Trieste, and writer.' In London Ezra Pound, supported by Wells, Miss Weaver, and *'les jeunes,'* continued to make Joyce's fame his business, forcing the *Egoist* installments into indifferent hands, and eliciting interest from unlikely sources. Joyce's long exile in Trieste began to lend him a romantic air in London, and gave added interest to the celebration, in *A Portrait of the Artist,* of a voluntary expatriation peculiarly like his own. His difficulties in making a living in Zurich were also romantic at a distance.

Nora's uncle, Michael Healy, who was not romantic, sent Joyce and Nora fifteen pounds on June 29; this gift rescued them on their arrival in Zurich. He continued to send them similar sums throughout their stay. Then came a loftier gift. Pound roused Yeats, already strongly disposed to help Joyce, to try to obtain a grant for him from the Royal Literary Fund, a private endowment which had been helping writers for a hundred years. They decided that the approach had better be made by Edmund Gosse, as an official of the Fund and an Englishman, rather than by an Irishman or American, and Yeats wrote to Gosse: 'I have just heard that James Joyce, an Irish poet and novelist of whose fine talent I can easily satisfy you, is in probably great penury through the war. He was at Trieste teaching English and has now arrived at Zurich. He has children and a wife. If things are as I believe, would it be possible for him to be given a grant from the Royal Literary Fund?' [7] After learning more of the situation from Joyce himself, Yeats sent Gosse further details on July 8 and 24, and said firmly, 'I believe him to be a man of genius.' Gosse obligingly wrote to the secretary of the

Royal Literary Fund to confirm that Joyce's works measured up to the
Fund's standards; at the same time he objected to Yeats that neither
Yeats nor Joyce had given any statement of loyalty to the Allies in the
war. Yeats mollified him by replying: 'I certainly wish them victory,
and as I have never known Joyce to agree with his neighbours I [a line
missing] in Austria has probably made his sympathy as frank as you
could wish. I never asked him about it in any of the few notes I have
sent him. He had never anything to do with Irish politics, extreme or
otherwise, and I think disliked politics. He always seemed to me to
have only literary and philosophic sympathies. To such men the Irish
atmosphere brings isolation, not anti-English feeling. He is probably
trying at this moment to become absorbed in some piece of work till
the evil hour is passed. I again thank you for what you have done for
this man of genius.' [8]

Yeats wrote also to the secretary of the Fund saying,

> I think that Mr. Joyce has a most beautiful gift. There is a poem on the
> last page of his *Chamber Music* which will, I believe, live. It is a
> technical and emotional masterpiece. I think that his book of short
> stories *Dubliners* has the promise of a great novelist and a great novel-
> ist of a new kind. There is not enough foreground, it is all atmosphere
> perhaps, but I look upon that as a sign of an original study of life.
> I have read in a paper called *The Egoist* certain chapters of a new
> novel, a disguised autobiography, which increases my conviction that
> he is the most remarkable new talent in Ireland today.

The secretary asked Joyce to send an account of his situation, and
Joyce replied:

> Dear Sir
>
>   . . . At the outbreak of war I was in Trieste where I have lived for
> the last eleven years. My income there was derived from two sources:
> i) my position in the Higher School of Commerce ii) private lessons.
> After the outbreak of war I was confirmed in my position by the
> Austrian Ministry of Public Instruction, Vienna, from whom I held and
> hold it. The school however closed in spring, nearly all the professors
> having been called up as officers of the reserve. My second source of
> income in normal times, viz., private lessons, produced very little in
> the first months and nothing at all in the next months owing to the
> critical conditions of the city. In these circumstances I lived with great
> difficulty and was obliged to recur to the assistance of friends, as stated
> above.
>   When, one month after the Italian declaration of war, the military
> authorities decided on the partial evacuation of the city I asked for,
> and obtained at once, a safe conduct for myself, my wife and children

to the Swiss frontier. I have been here one month now. I received from a relative of my wife's a small sum of money, £15, of which some remains. In order to leave Trieste I effected a loan on my furniture and this sum went for trainfare (owing to the fact that the railways of Austria and South Tyrol were in our war zone we were obliged to come by a circuitous route) and clothing.

I receive nothing in the way of royalties. My contributions to reviews etc. were made twelve years ago. From my first publisher and from my second I did not receive any money for royalties, the sale in both cases being below the required number. In the case of my second publisher I bought and paid for at trade price 120 copies of my book as a condition of publication. For my contributions to reviews in the current year, *The Smart Set* and *The Egoist,* I received no payment.

I enclose a medical certificate which attests my state of health and shall be much obliged if you will kindly return it to me under registered cover when it has been examined. In present circumstances in this country where I may have to remain for some time it seems very difficult to obtain any work of the kind which I do. My literary work during the last eleven years has produced nothing. On the contrary my second book *Dubliners* cost me a considerable sum of money owing to the eight years of litigation which preceded its publication. I have tried to obtain an engagement with several schools here but have not succeeded.

I trust that I have given you a clear statement of the facts of the case. I am writing to my friends W. B. Yeats and Mr Ezra Pound who, I am sure, will corroborate me in my statements.

I am, dear Sir,
Sincerely yours,
James Joyce

Debts contracted in the course of the war.

  i) to Baron Ambrogio Ralli, Palazzo Ralli, Trieste, Austria

Crowns/Austrian/300.-

 ii) to Gioachino Veneziani Esq., Murano, Venice, Italy,

Crowns/Austrian/250.-
C.A, 550.-

30 July 1915 [9]

The most outspoken letter was from Ezra Pound, who began contentiously by announcing that he did not suppose his opinion could carry any weight with the committee. Still he derived some satisfaction from saying that Joyce was a good poet and the best of the younger prose writers. He thought *Dubliners* uneven, but considered *A Portrait* to be of indubitable value. Joyce had managed to remain totally uncorrupted by commercial demands and standards; his work had the hard clarity of a Stendhal or a Flaubert, and the richness that comes from erudition.

Pound anticipated that the committee would jib at such lofty claims, but insisted that he was convinced Joyce deserved them.[10]

The joint result of the sedate and the flamboyant interventions of his friends was that the Royal Literary Fund awarded Joyce a grant of seventy-five pounds, payable in installments over nine months. Its importance to him was enhanced by the sense of quasi-official recognition of his work. It opened up, as well, a vista of future patronage. His sense of becoming somewhat established helped to poise the more relaxed tone of the Bloom episodes in *Ulysses*, to which he now bent his mind. In the tempestuous days at Trieste, complicated by a new wife and children, by old and new scores with Stanislaus, by financial pressure, he had had an appropriate setting in which to write of his youth, with Dedalus for the symbol of his presumptuous flight. The vision which now attracted him was not so insurrectionary. Instead of Prometheus, Lucifer, and Faust, those bachelors, disobedient sons, and brilliant failures, he conjured up Ulysses, Dante, Shakespeare, men of substance and family whether they were voyagers, exiles, or homekeepers. The city of Zurich, its *bürgerlich* quality challenged by the influx of refugees and war profiteers, was a good place to write of Ulysses, a haven noisier but as safe as the one Ulysses himself found in the realm of Calypso. Joyce's age, almost thirty-four, was roughly that of Dante when he began the *Divine Comedy* in mid-journey 'in a dark wood,' and of Shakespeare when he had his grim contest with the Dark Lady of the Sonnets. These resemblances would be merely grandiloquent if Joyce had not asserted them both in conversation and correspondence, and if his subsequent experience in Zurich had not confirmed them.

In Switzerland Joyce quickly attracted a number of friends, at first Italians and Austrians, then Greeks. Oscar Schwarz, his pupil in Trieste, had given him a letter of introduction to a young man named Ottocaro Weiss, and the notion of someone named 'Black' (Schwarz) introducing him to someone named 'White' (Weiss) amused Joyce and eventually found its way into *Ulysses*.[11] Ottocaro Weiss had come from Trieste to study political economy at the University of Zurich, then the foremost Swiss university. A tall, handsome, warm-hearted young man, he could discuss music expertly, and had a good knowledge of literature. One of his brothers was Dr. Edoardo Weiss, who was among the earliest disciples of Freud and the first psychoanalyst in Italy; from his brother, and from Dr. C. G. Jung, with whom he was also acquainted, Ottocaro Weiss had a knowledge of psychoanalysis which Joyce disparaged but found useful.

Weiss and Joyce, who lived fairly close to each other, began to attend operas and concerts together, and Weiss was able to get Joyce into the

Tonhalle with a student ticket. At home Joyce impressed Weiss with
his fine, pleasant voice, but scandalized him by a totally unacceptable
accompaniment, played at that time on a guitar, and later on an old
upright piano badly out of tune. His favorite operatic composer was
Verdi, and he could intoxicate himself on a single phrase from him, such
as 'Addio! del passato bei sogni ridenti,' from *La Traviata,* which he
sang again and again. He would call on his son Giorgio to sing it in
his clear boy's voice, then he would repeat lovingly the one word
'ri-i-i-ide-e-enti.' Sometimes he recited the litany of the Blessed Virgin—
a cherished prayer of Stephen Dedalus in *A Portrait*—'Rosa mystica, ora
pro nobis; Turris Davidica, ora pro nobis; Turris eburnea, ora pro
nobis . . . ,' with a half-mocking expression. Or he might sing a favorite
song from Massenet's *Werther,* 'Pourquoi me réveiller, O souffle du
printemps.' As though to add dignity to it, he said more than once to
Weiss, 'You know, the words are taken from Ossian.'

Their talk often turned to political science and literature. Weiss told
Joyce of Montesquieu's theory that political institutions were inevitably
the special product of local conditions. Joyce was uniformly skeptical
and ironical about all such theories, although some of them made an
appearance in *Ulysses* and *Finnegans Wake.* Weiss made an unsuccessful effort to interest Joyce in the writings of Gottfried Keller, assuring
him they would make him look at Zurichers as less stolid. Joyce did
not respond, perhaps because he found Keller technically conventional;
but when a reviewer compared Keller's *Der Grüne Heinrich* to *A Portrait of the Artist,* he evinced more attention, and later he translated
some of Keller's poems into English. For the moment, however, literature in German did not attract him, and he scoffed even at Goethe as
'un noioso funzionario' (a boring civil servant).

In the course of their conversations Weiss was able to persuade Joyce,
who was physically lazy and said that every room should have a bed
in it, to take long walks up the Uitliberg and Zurichberg, or along the
lake to Küsnacht. Once they were coming down the Uitliberg when
they caught up with two youngsters who were trying to push a heavy
cart. Weiss helped them and Joyce, not to be outdone, said, 'I will help
you too.' He took his thin walking stick, placed it on the cart, and
walked with an air of great co-operation beside them.*

* Joyce soon epitomized his attitude towards long hikes in a limerick about another
friend:

> There is a keen climber called Sykes
> Who goes scrambling o'er ditches and dikes,
>   But to skate on his scalp
>   Down the side of an Alp
> Is the kind of enjoyment he likes.

Sometimes during their walks a storm broke out, and at such moments Joyce's panic was comic. When a friend asked him, 'I suppose thunder affects your nervous system, Mr. Joyce?' he replied, 'No, I'm frightened.' Weiss, to reassure and divert him, told him funny stories about thunderstorms. But Joyce was not amused; thunder was not to be joked about. Every house, he solemnly lectured his friends, should be equipped with lightning protectors. The subject roused him to eloquence.

He got along easily with Weiss's student friends, for he comported himself as youthfully as they did. No one could laugh more wholeheartedly or more infectiously. On one occasion he came to tea in Weiss's rooms and was introduced to two of his fellow-students. The animated conversation was in French, and in the course of it Joyce told them how two diplomats in Brussels had tried to discomfit the cultured Archbishop Pecci, then papal nuncio to Belgium and later Pope Leo XIII. They approached him with a tabatière of ebony on which a nude woman was inlaid in ivory, and one said, '*Vous aimez les objets d'art, monseigneur. Regardez cela!*' Pecci looked it over, then handed it back calmly and replied, '*O, c'est très beau. C'est Madame, sans doute?*'

Weiss and his guests began to trade stories of repartee. Joyce's preference was for examples of self-possession in difficult situations, the quality with which he endowed Stephen Dedalus, especially in *Ulysses*. He told a second anecdote about Léopold II of Belgium, whose mistress was the famous dancer Cléo de Merode. Léopold's connection with her was so notorious that he was called Cléopold. One day the Archbishop of Brussels came to remonstrate with the king about this liaison. The king listened to him and said, '*Votre Éminence, on m'a raconté la même chose de vous, mais moi, je ne l'ai pas crue.*' Joyce had another incident that displayed the Prince of Wales at his most dignified. It was understood among Edward's friends that, although he might be treated without special ceremony, the prince's rank must be kept always in mind. But in the course of a drinking bout at Karlsbad, a young man forgot himself and called out, 'Ring that bell for me, Eddie, will you?' The prince rang the bell, and when the maître d'hôtel came in response and bowed low before him, he said simply, '*La voiture pour monsieur.*'

The afternoon drew to a close, and Joyce, obviously delighted by his company, said merrily to Weiss as he rose to go, '*Merci de votre bonté, et de votre bon thé.*'

Now that Joyce was free to devote himself to *Ulysses*, he often discussed topics related to the book. One such subject was the similarity of the Jews and the Irish, on which Joyce insisted. They were alike, he declared, in being impulsive, given to fantasy, addicted to associative

thinking, wanting in rational discipline.* He held, perhaps with Arnold's
'Hebraism and Hellenism' in mind, that there were two basically different ways of thinking, the Greek and the Jewish, and that the Greek
was logical and rational. One day he and Weiss were walking and met
a Greek, with whom they talked for a long time. Afterwards Joyce
remarked, 'It's strange—you spoke like a Greek and he spoke like a Jew.'
He had perhaps already conceived the brothel scene in *Ulysses*, when
Bloom and Stephen come together and Joyce writes, 'Extremes meet.
Jewgreek meets greekjew,' following which Bloom becomes utterly
rational and self-contained, and Stephen is impulsive. Joyce recognized
his own affinities to both groups. He had a little book on the Jews by
a man named Fisher, which had pictures of Chinese Jews with pigtails,
Mongolian Jews with Mongolian features, and the like. Such curiosities
about the race were what especially interested Joyce. He knew little of
Zionism, which was already taking hold among European Jews; but
when one day Weiss commented on the possibility of a Jewish state,
Joyce wryly remarked, 'That's all very well, but believe me, a warship
with a captain named Kanalgitter and his aide named Captain After-
duft would be the funniest thing the old Mediterranean has ever seen.' †

Through Weiss Joyce met Rudolf Goldschmidt, a grain merchant,
and Goldschmidt introduced him to the circle of his friends. These men
were well-to-do and they agreed readily to take lessons in English from
Joyce, in some instances not because they wanted to learn the language
but because they wanted to help him discreetly.[12] (He would have
been quite open to *indiscreet* help.) By November 1915, Joyce inscribed
a copy of *Dubliners* to Goldschmidt 'with gratitude,'[13] and he had good
reason. For his sympathetic pupils often paid for lessons they never
took, and Claud W. Sykes later remarked that Joyce was sometimes
humorously indignant if a pupil insisted upon having the lessons he
had paid for. The relationship of teacher and pupil frequently turned
into friendship, as with Victor Sax, Edmund Brauchbar, and Georges
Borach. With all three, Joyce's lessons went far afield. Once with Sax
he proposed that they write limericks for their lesson that day, and
after overseeing the productions of Sax in this form he turned out two
of his own:

> There is a young gallant named Sax
> Who is prone to hayfever attacks
>   For the prime of the year
>   To Cupid so dear
> Stretches maidens—and men!—on their backs.

---

* These are made qualities of Bloom's mind.
† About Zionism Bloom says, 'Nothing doing. Still an idea behind it.' *Ulysses*
(60 [53]).

The second was a parody of the Austro-Hungarian dual monarchy:

> There's a monarch who knows no repose
> For he's dressed in a dual trunk hose
>   And ever there itches
>   Some part of his breeches;
> How he stands it the Lord only knows.[14]

He continued to be friendly with these men for the rest of his life, and it was Brauchbar who, twenty-five years later, put up half the surety so that Joyce and his family might return to Zurich from occupied France during the second World War.

Two other pupils of Joyce were the Bliznakoff sisters, Olga and Vela, who came to Zurich from Trieste shortly after he did. Their father, Marco Bliznakoff, had been Bulgarian consul in Trieste, and could not remain in the Austrian zone. His wife was sister to Signora Schmitz, so Joyce had often seen them before. He remembered one example of the consul's behavior which he told Weiss with much amusement: Marco took his ten-year-old son Boris to a country place near Trieste, and there gave him so much beer that he was sick. He then brought the boy home and proudly informed his outraged family that by this object-lesson he had saved him forever from becoming a drunkard. His mother-in-law, Signora Veneziani, the real head of the family, berated him with choice Triestine epithets.[15] In *Ulysses* this episode is attributed to Bloom: 'And one time he led him the rounds of Dublin and, by the holy farmer, he never cried crack till he brought him home as drunk as a boiled owl and he said he did it to teach him the evils of alcohol and by herrings if the three women didn't near roast him. . . .'[16]

Vela and Olga Bliznakoff, both handsome young women, were entertained by their new teacher. His body was loose-limbed, floppy, and his handshake almost boneless. Ordinarily he came to his lessons neatly, if not elegantly, dressed. He never wore a complete suit, always the jacket of one and the trousers of another. When he was ill, Nora Joyce found it impossible to persuade him to wash or shave, so one day when Vela Bliznakoff came to call on them, Nora asked her to speak to him about it, thinking her pretty face might have an influence. She did so, Joyce humorously gave her his word to shave and wash as early as the very next day; and afterwards she fancied she detected some improvement.[17]

At lessons with the Bliznakoff sisters, Joyce talked about English and Italian literature, then got on to politics, especially Irish politics. He told them Ireland eats her own young. Sometimes he brought along the manuscript of *Ulysses* and read them a few pages from it, but he omitted sentences or whole paragraphs, on the grounds that these were not for girls. It may be said of the long history of censorship of that book that Joyce himself began it. He sometimes used *Ulysses* to demonstrate that even English, that best of languages, was inadequate. 'Aren't there enough words for you in English?' they asked him. 'Yes,' he replied, 'there are enough, but they aren't the right ones.' He had to make neologisms. 'For example, take the word *battlefield*. A battlefield is a field where the battle is raging. When the battle is over and the field is covered with blood, it is no longer a *battlefield*, but a *bloodfield*.' [18] This idea, premonitory of *Finnegans Wake*,* was much on his mind, and he remarked a little later to another friend, 'I'd like a language which is above all languages, a language to which all will do service. I cannot express myself in English without enclosing myself in a tradition.' [19] At a time when others were questioning the liberties he took with English, Joyce was conscious only of its restraints upon him.

Joyce's income from teaching was still meager, and he kept looking out for other jobs. He applied to teach at the Château de Lancy, but the director wrote that the position was filled. At the end of 1915 he obtained some work from a bearded messianic professor from Vienna, Siegmund Feilbogen. Feilbogen was concerned with humanity, *Menschlichkeit*, and had come to neutral Zurich to publish, with American funds, his *International Review*. The review appeared in both English and German, and was devoted chiefly to proving that the atrocity stories on both sides were groundless. Feilbogen employed Joyce as a translator, and remarking his skill, engaged him in conversation. For a few minutes he felt disappointed with this thin, sharp man with sharp words, and not very many of them, so listless and self-enclosed. But they began to talk of Ibsen, and Joyce proved Ibsen's superiority to Shakespeare so eloquently that he won Feilbogen over. His work for the review continued for a few months, and was faultless except for absent-minded omissions of an occasional sentence or paragraph. But the review was short-lived: while the Germans allowed it to circulate freely, the English and American authorities considered it enemy propaganda and refused to admit it, so that it failed early in 1916 after less than a year of publication. Joyce's British citizenship made his work a little awkward, though he does not appear to have cared about that. He continued to see a good deal of Feilbogen, whom he liked, and of another editor, the poet Felix Beran. [20]

In Switzerland Joyce stayed out of politics and said little about the war, feeling perhaps with Yeats, 'I think it better that in times like these / A poet keep his mouth shut.' [21] His favorite war story was sheer

* In *Finnegans Wake* (10), he goes further by making it *bluddle filth*.

burlesque. One evening when Ottocaro Weiss had been discussing Freud's theory that humor was the mind's way of securing relief, through a short cut, for some repressed feeling, Joyce replied gaily, 'Well, that isn't true in this case.' He then told his father's story of Buckley and the Russian General, which was to be mentioned in *Ulysses* and to wind in and out of *Finnegans Wake*. Buckley, he explained, was an Irish soldier in the Crimean War who drew a bead on a Russian general, but when he observed his splendid epaulettes and decorations, he could not bring himself to shoot. After a moment, alive to his duty, he raised his rifle again, but just then the general let down his pants to defecate. The sight of his enemy in so helpless and human a plight was too much for Buckley, who again lowered his gun. But when the general prepared to finish the operation with a piece of grassy turf, Buckley lost all respect for him and fired. Weiss replied, 'Well, that isn't funny.' Joyce told the story to other friends, convinced that it was in some way archetypal.*

Yet he could not remain altogether apart from the World War. At the end of 1915 his friend Weiss was called up by the army; he did not see Joyce again until after the Armistice. Two other events, deaths of old friends, came to intrude upon Joyce's neutrality. On Easter, 1916, there occurred the Rising in Dublin. Among the executed leaders was Patrick Pearse, for whom Joyce had no liking, either as a man or as his first teacher of Irish; but at the same time came the wholly unnecessary death in April of Francis Sheehy-Skeffington, with whom he had published 'The Day of the Rabblement' in 1902. Skeffington, recklessly faithful to his pacifist views, was arrested for urging the soldiers to stop looting. A British officer, later judged guilty of murder but insane, had him shot without trial.† Joyce followed the events with pity; although he evaluated the rising as useless, he felt also out of things. His attitude towards Ireland became even more complex, so that he told

---

* Joyce had some difficulty working the story into *Finnegans Wake*, and in Paris said to Samuel Beckett, 'If somebody could tell me what to do, I would do it.' He then narrated the story of Buckley; when he came to the piece of turf, Beckett remarked, 'Another insult to Ireland.' This was the hint Joyce needed; it enabled him to nationalize the story fully, and in *Finnegans Wake* (353) he uses Beckett's words: 'For when meseemim, and tolfoklokken rolland allover ourloud's lande, beheaving up that sob of tunf for to claimhis, for to wolpimsolff, puddywhuck. Ay, and untuoning his culothone in an exitous erseroyal *Deo Jupto*. At that instullt to Igorladns! Prronto! I gave one dobblenotch and I ups with my crozzier. Mirrdo! With my how on armer and hits leg an arrow cockshock rockrogn. Sparro!' As early as 1920 Joyce saw Buckley in his own role of the ordinary Irishman in combat with imperial authority.

† The British offered his widow indemnity, which she refused. Bernard Shaw, who knew her, wrote to urge her to be practical and take the money, but she kept to her decision.

friends, when the British had to give up their plans to conscript troops
in Ireland, *'Erin go bragh!'* and predicted that some day he and Giorgio
would go back to wear the shamrock in an independent Ireland; but
when this temporary fervor waned, he replied to someone who asked
if he did not look forward to the emergence of an independent country,
'So that I might declare myself its first enemy?' [22] Would he not die for
Ireland? 'I say,' he said, 'let Ireland die for me.' Balanced between bitterness and nostalgia, he declined an invitation from a woman on the
Journal de Genève, Fanny Guillermet, to write an analysis of the Irish
events, replying with some inaccuracy: *'Je n'écris jamais d'articles.'* [23]

The Sheehy family suffered another violent loss in September 1916,
when Thomas Kettle, Mary Sheehy's husband, was killed in action
while fighting in the British army in France. (Kettle had volunteered
with the idealistic notion that England would reward Irish help in the
war by granting independence.) Joyce at once wrote Mrs. Kettle a
letter earnest in its sympathy but oddly formal in view of their long
acquaintance:

> Seefeldstrasse 54
> Zurich   Switzerland

Dear Mrs. Kettle

> I have read this morning, with deep regret in the 'Times' that my
> old school fellow and fellow student Lieutenant Kettle has been killed
> in action. I hope you will not deem it a stranger's intrusion on your
> grief to accept from me a word of sincere condolence. I remember very
> gratefully his benevolent and courteous friendliness to me when I was
> in Ireland seven years ago. May I ask you also to convey to your
> sisters (whose addresses I do not know) my sympathy with them in
> the losses they have suffered. I am grieved to learn that so many mis-
> fortunes have fallen on your family in these evil days.
> Believe me to be, dear Mrs. Kettle

> Very sincerely yrs
> James Joyce [24]

Sept. 25th '16

Meanwhile Joyce's business correspondence fastened with tenacity
upon three problems. The first was an effort to push *Dubliners*: during
1914 Richards sold 499 copies, one short of the number after which
Joyce was to receive royalties. Joyce had high hopes of augmenting his
income from this book, and prodded Pinker to obtain a statement of
sales. When it arrived, it was disappointing. In the first six months of
1915 only 26 copies were sold, in the next six months, less, in the six
months after that, only 7. Joyce had to content himself for the moment
with a *succès d'estime.*

His second purpose was to follow up the serial publication of *A Portrait of the Artist* by its publication in book form. The final installment appeared in the September 1915 issue of the *Egoist,* but there had already been signs of coming difficulties. In July Joyce received the January 1915 issue, which had been delayed by wartime postal complications, and was irked to find that the printer had carelessly omitted whole sentences. Miss Weaver corrected him, however: the cause was not carelessness but squeamishness. When the printer began to revise the August installment in the same way, she sought out a new printer. Joyce was grateful for this and other services, and on August 28 he wrote to her, 'As this will be the last installment of my novel I feel that I owe you my sincere thanks for the interest you have taken in my writing and for the trouble you have taken to protect my text. I am very grateful to your paper and to your staff and hope you will have a more prosperous career when these bad days are past.' [25]

The serial publication of *A Portrait* should have facilitated its publication in a book, but it did nothing of the sort. Grant Richards rejected it on May 18, 1915, on the grounds that it was not possible to get hold of an intelligent audience in wartime. Pinker, beset by Joyce, offered the book in July to Martin Secker, stipulating that the original text, not the slightly expurgated one used in the *Egoist,* be printed. When Secker turned it down, Pinker offered it to Duckworth, who held the manuscript for several months. It became clear that English publishers were not enthusiastic, and Joyce proposed to Pinker to try a publisher in Paris, as years later he would do with *Ulysses.* In November, nothing being decided, he wrote for help to Arthur Symons, who this time could do nothing. Then Miss Weaver, with her customary generosity, made an unexpected proposal. She offered on November 30, 1915, if her editorial board could be persuaded to do something without precedent in the *Egoist's* history, and if no regular publisher could be found, to have the *Egoist* publish *A Portrait* in book form. This proposal comforted Joyce: he wrote thanking her on December 6, and remarked with some bitterness: 'I have never received any money from either of my two publishers, and I dislike the prospect of waiting another nine years for the same result. I am writing a book *Ulysses,* and want the other published and out of the way once and for all because correspondence about publishing is too tiresome for my (very lazy) temperament.' [26] (Actually his correspondence about such matters was indefatigable.) But they decided to wait for Duckworth's decision, and, if that proved to be negative, to try T. Werner Laurie, whom Violet Hunt had interested in the novel, and John Lane, similarly goaded by Pound. At the end of 1915 the matter was still unresolved, but Miss Weaver sent Joyce, on January 14, 1916, £50 to pay for the use of 'your wonderful book' in the *Egoist* during the previous two years.

Joyce devoted himself with the same application and almost the same futility to arrangements for the publication and production of *Exiles*. He brought the completed manuscript with him to Zurich, and wrote Pinker on July 17 that he had just had it typed and would send it to him in three installments, an act at a time, for fear of its being lost in the mail.[27] In England Pound read it and thought it 'exciting,' but 'not nearly so intense as Portrait.' He did not think it would do for the stage, but at the beginning of October [28] obligingly wrote an article on the play for the Chicago review, *Drama*, which accepted the criticism for its February 1916 issue, but rejected the play itself a few months later. Pound also approached the manager of an American theater, Cecil Dorrian, who admired *Exiles* but decided it was not suitable for production. Then Pound urged Joyce to try theaters abroad. Joyce wrote offering it to Yeats and the Abbey Theatre, but Yeats, though predisposed in its favor,* decided against it for the time, considered it again later and again rejected it:

> I do not recommend your play to the Irish Theatre because it is a type of work we have never played well. It is too far from the folk drama; and just at present we do not even play the folk drama very well. . . . It is some time since I read your play and my memory is not very clear—I thought it sincere and interesting but I cannot give you the only criticism worth anything, detailed criticism of construction. I could at the time I read it, I have no doubt. I do not think it at all so good as 'A Portrait of the Artist' which I read with great excitement and recommended to many people. I think 'A Portrait' very new and very powerful. Ezra tells me that you have some new work of the kind on hand and that book I await with impatience.[29]

In early November 1915, Joyce asked William Archer for help, but Archer was leaving London and would have to read it on his return. A later letter said, à propos of *A Portrait*, that he did not much care for Joyce's form of realism. During the autumn of 1915 Joyce wrote a gloomy letter to Michael Healy, who at once sent him £9 and encouragement. Joyce wrote to thank him on November 2:

* He wrote Pound on February 11, 1917:

> My dear Ezra
>   I have almost finished 'A Portrait of the Artist' I think it a very great book—I am absorbed in it.
>   If you have the play bring it tomorrow night. If it is at all possible the Abbey should face a riot for it.
>
> Yrs s
W B Yeats

Kreuzstrasse 19^{III}

Zurich VIII

(Switzerland)

My dear Mr. Healy:

I received the day before yesterday your kind letter and this morning your Money Order (£ 9) for which I thank you most sincerely. It is most welcome and useful. Nora has bought a lot of flannels and other clothes which the children need in this climate, and a hat which she finally selected from the few hundred which were shown to her. We are now fairly well fortified against the cold. As for myself I am to be seen in a shell cocoa-coloured overcoat which an absent-minded German left behind him and I bought for eleven francs. Of his moral character I know nothing. But I am sure that he has (or had) uncommonly short arms. I presume the overcoat is mine now since I paid for it to his late landlady but I feel, as Mr. R. G. Knowles used to sing,

> 'I'm only airing it for him:
> It doesn't belong to me.'

I was introduced to the millionaire I wrote you of some days ago. He told me that his daughter is rather ill and asked me to give him my address, as he says he wishes to speak with me about my play of which he has heard. I was also introduced to the president of the Russian Club here who talks of translating it into Russian and producing it. Besides I have written to Geneva to see if it can go on there in a French version. I also met the chief actor here who presented me to the director of the Zurich Stadttheater and, through another friend, I got an introduction to a solicitor here whose father is director of the Stadttheater in Bern. My poor shoes are nearly worn out after it all, as you can imagine, but I hope something will come out of it all. Immediately I have good news I shall let you know. I hope you managed to get that copy of *The New Age*. I hear now that there is a long article about me and the play, the name of which by the way is *Exiles,* in a Chicago review called *Drama* but I have not seen it yet.

I thank you for your inquiries about my brother. He sent me his photograph last week. He has a long full beard and looks like the late Duke of Devonshire. He tells me that he sprained his wrist, playing tennis, but is now better. If you send him a postcard with greetings from Galway I am sure he will answer you. His address is:

Stanislaus Joyce

(internierter britischer Staatsangehöriger)

Schloss Grossau bei Raabs

Nieder Österreich

My sister was when I last heard from her well and still in Prague. I believe her husband has been exonerated from military service much to her (and I fancy his) relief. I forget whether I thanked you for having verified the quotation about our excellent friend Bombados. If I did not I do so now. I shall correct it on the proof—if I ever see one. I am sorry to hear you have so much to do. However, as you say, it is a good thing to be alive in such times. I had letters from Trieste on Saturday. So far as my flat is concerned it seems to be as I left it but life is certainly pleasanter here just at present. Today is the feast of S. Justin Martyr, patron of Trieste, and I shall perhaps eat a cheap small pudding somewhere in his honour for the many years I lived in his city. As for the future it is useless to speculate. If I could find out in the meantime who is the patron of men of letters I should try to remind him that I exist: but I understand that the last saint who held that position resigned in despair and no other will take the portfolio.

In conclusion I thank you very sincerely for your great kindness and also for your kind and encouraging message to me. You may be sure that I do and will continue to do all that I can. Nora Giorgio and Lucia send you all their warm regards with which I include mine also.

> With renewed thanks to you
> Sincerely yours,
> James Joyce [30]

The year 1915 ended nowhere, but 1916 was an improvement. The correspondence with Pinker, Miss Weaver, and Pound went on regularly, and at first disappointments came regularly too, which inspired Pound to write a limerick about a young writer named Joyce, whose friends' woes were caused by the fact that his prose never filled anyone's purse. *A Portrait* was rejected by Duckworth's reader, who, as it later turned out, was Edward Garnett; and the firm, on being asked the reason by Pinker, sent him Garnett's report:

James Joyce's 'Portrait of the Artist as a Young Man' wants going through carefully from start to finish. There are many 'longueurs.' Passages which, though the publisher's reader may find them entertaining, will be tedious to the ordinary man among the reading public. That public will call the book, as it stands at present, realistic, unprepossessing, unattractive. We call it ably written. The picture is 'curious,' it arouses interest and attention. But the author must revise it and let us see it again. It is too discursive, formless, unrestrained, and ugly things, ugly words, are too prominent; indeed at times they seem to be shoved in one's face, on purpose, unnecessarily. The point of view will be voted 'a little sordid.' The picture of life is good; the period well brought to the reader's eye, and the types and characters are well drawn, but it is too 'unconventional.' This would stand against it in normal times. At the present time, though the old conventions are in the background, we can only see a chance for it if it is pulled into shape and made more definite.

In the earlier portion of the MS. as submitted to us, a good deal of pruning can be done. Unless the author will use restraint and proportion he will not gain readers. His pen and his thoughts seem to have run away with him sometimes.

And at the end of the book there is a complete falling to bits; the pieces of writing and the thoughts are all in pieces and they fall like damp, ineffective rockets.

The author shows us he has art, strength and originality, but this MS. wants time and trouble spent on it, to make it a more finished piece of work, to shape it more carefully as the product of the craftsmanship, mind and imagination of an artist.[31]

Pinker sent the report to Pound, and received an apoplectic letter in return.[32] He now submitted the manuscript to T. Werner Laurie; on Laurie's determined refusal to publish it without changes, Pinker submitted it to Duckworth, whom Jonathan Cape had urged to reconsider it, instead of turning it over to the *Egoist.* Joyce had meanwhile received an advance of £25 from Miss Weaver, and instructed Pinker to turn the book over to her and accept unconditionally her terms, whatever they might be. But, while Duckworth surrendered the manuscript promptly, there was a new snag. By March 25, 1916, a succession of seven printers, alarmed by the recent prosecution of Lawrence's *The Rainbow,* had refused to print the text as it stood. Pound came up with the desperate suggestion, 'If all printers refuse . . . I suggest that largish blank spaces be left where passages are cut out. Then the excisions can be manifolded (not carbon copies, but another process) by typewriter on good paper, and if necessary I will paste them in myself. The public can be invited to buy with or without restorations and the copyright can be secured [on] the book as *printed.* That is to say, the restorations will be privately printed and the book-without-them "published." And damn the censors.'[33] Joyce agreed to this well-meant, unlikely scheme,[34] but Miss Weaver kept hoping that the next printer she tried would agree to print the book entire. None did.

Pound's next plan was to have the book published in New York. A new publisher there, John Marshall, who had published Alfred Kreymborg, was about to bring out a book of Pound's called *This Generation.* Pound advised him to bring out Joyce's book, if necessary at the expense of his own. Miss Weaver could then import copies from America to England. Marshall responded at first with fervor,[35] but in the end published neither Joyce's book nor Pound's. On July 1, 1916, Joyce wrote to Miss Weaver that *Exiles* had made as little headway as *A Portrait:* 'I hear that there is some hope that the play (*Exiles*) will be put on by the Stage Society in London. The typescript is in New York—or in Chicago and there is an Italian version in Rome or in Turin. I offered it here and in Bern, but they say it is too daring (gewagt). My manuscripts are dispersed like little Bo Peep's sheep, but I hope they will come home as safely as hers did.' [36] At last, on July 19, Miss Weaver was able to inform the anxious shepherd that the book would be published, but not by Marshall. B. W. Huebsch, encouraged by Miss Weaver's promise to take 750 copies for English publication, had agreed to bring it out in New York. [37] It was a memorable decision. The papers were signed at the end of October.

Another form of assistance for Joyce was also forthcoming. Pound, who knew that Yeats had a Civil List pension, asked him whether one might not be obtained for Joyce. Yeats replied that to confer a pension a parliamentary grant was required, but that the Prime Minister had the right to award a Civil List grant simply at his own discretion. Pound went round to Lady Cunard, [38] and got her to lend Joyce's books to Asquith's secretary, Edward Marsh. Marsh was favorably impressed, and wrote to Yeats and George Moore to ask their opinion. Yeats, doggedly patient in writing letters for Joyce, and even managing to vary the form of his encomiums, responded that Joyce's work 'has a curious brooding intensity' and that Joyce was 'just such a man as it is well to help.' George Moore replied with an anti-Irish tirade in which Joyce was almost forgotten:

> The only book of Joyce's that I have read is a collection of stories called 'Dubliners,' some of them are trivial and disagreeable, but all are written by a clever man, and the book contains one story, the longest story in the book and the last story which seemed to me perfection whilst I read it! I regretted that I was not the author of it.[*] But this story, which I am sure you would appreciate as much as I did, does not prove that Joyce will go on writing and will end by writing something like a masterpiece. A talent, musical, literary or pictorial, is a pale fluttering thing that a breath will extinguish. I will get 'Dubliners' from Heinemann to whom I lent the book and you will see for yourself. Of the novel I know nothing. Joyce left a disagreeable reputation behind him in Dublin, but he came back after some years a different man and everything I heard of him is to his credit. Of his political views I know nothing. He was not in Ireland during the sowing of the Sinn Fein seed and I hope he is not even a home ruler. Democratic principles are unsuited to Ireland. Already the people are beginning to regret their landlords and to hate the congested District Board. The Irish like priests and believe in the power of priests to forgive them their sins and to change God into a biscuit. They are only happy in convents and monasteries. The only reason that the Irish would tolerate home rule would be if they were given permission to persecute someone, that is

---

[*] It was fitting that Moore should wish to have written 'The Dead,' for in a sense he *had* written it, or at least had given Joyce an idea for its ending. See pp. 259-60.

the Roman Catholic idea of liberty. It always has been and always will be.

I am an admirer of Mr. Asquith and regret that he cannot bring himself to believe that there can be no settlement, and that all attempts at settlement will fail. The Irish like discipline, and if Mr. Asquith would treat the Irish as the Pope does he would be the most popular man in Ireland.

Yours sincerely,
George Moore

P.S. I am sure that from a literary point of view Joyce is deserving of help.[39]

In August the Prime Minister granted Joyce £100 from the Civil List. Joyce wrote to thank Yeats and the 'wonder worker,' Pound, and said to the former, 'I hope that now at last matters may begin to go a little more smoothly for me, for, to tell the truth, it is very tiresome to wait and hope for so many years.'[40] He came to feel that the 'royal bounty,' while unconditional, implied an obligation to England, which he paid off later in his own way. He also received small sums from other quarters, £25 sent anonymously through Pound in June and July, and £2 a week for thirteen weeks from the Society of Authors, also at Pound's instigation. The Society later extended the subsidy for three additional months.

Although there were further contretemps in his publishing enterprises, and Joyce suffered in late October a kind of nervous collapse,[41] probably a fit of depression, at the end of the year his pertinacity, which made Pound address him in one letter as 'Dear Job,' was rewarded. Huebsch brought out in December an American edition of *Dubliners*,[42] using sheets imported from Grant Richards, and then on December 29, *A Portrait of the Artist as a Young Man* in its first edition anywhere.* Joyce's difficulties were not over; his temperament, as much as his circumstances, prevented their ever being so. But for several years to come they were largely of his own making.

---

* Joyce had decided that 1916 was a lucky year for him, and insisted the book should be published before the end of it or dated 1916 anyway. Huebsch obliged him.

1916–1918

Look, look, the dusk is growing. My branches lofty are taking root. And my cold cher's gone ashley. Fieluhr? Filou! What age is at? It saon is late. 'Tis endless now senne eye or erewone last saw Waterhouse's clogh. They took it asunder, I hurd them sigh. When will they reassemble it? O, my back, my back, my bach! I'd want to go to Aches-les-Pains. Pingpong! There's the Belle for Sexaloitez! And Concepta de Send-us-pray! Pang! Wring out the clothes! Wring in the dew!

—*Finnegans Wake* (213)

THE Joyce family moved about Zurich with more than Odyssean rapidity. On their arrival in June 1915, they stopped briefly and nostalgically at the Gasthaus Hoffnung, where Joyce and Nora had stayed in 1904 after their elopement from Dublin. Then in a week or two they found a two-room, scantily furnished flat at 7 Reinhardstrasse. Since they intended to return to Trieste after the war, and still had furniture there, they depended in Zurich on furnished flats. The next one was a third-floor flat at 10 Kreuzstrasse, where they moved on October 15, 1915. In March 1916, they moved again, this time to 54 Seefeldstrasse, where they had a kitchen, living room, and two bedrooms, one of them very tiny, for about 40 Swiss francs a month. They remained there, not liking it, until early in 1917.

His time being his own, Joyce lived as irregularly as he could wish. He stayed late at cafés and restaurants, and rose late in the mornings. During the day he gave occasional lessons and worked on *Ulysses*. Through his efforts to have *Exiles* produced, and through his long convivial evenings, he soon came to know great numbers of people in Zurich, just as he had known almost everyone in Trieste. One of his favorite meeting places was the Restaurant zum Roten Kreuz, a short way up the Seefeldstrasse. There a group calling themselves the Club des Étrangers used to assemble once a week. Joyce became friendly with the members, especially with Paul Phokas, who satisfied his need for a Greek friend with whom he could discuss his work.* There were also a Pole named Czernovic who kept a cigarette shop, a wine merchant Paul Wiederkehr, and a German, Marquis, who sang in a choir. Through the Club des Étrangers Joyce occasionally turned up a pupil, and one of these, Paul Ruggiero, became a close friend. Ruggiero, who was employed in a bank, was a simple, modest man, and found Joyce simple and modest too. They spoke Italian together and sometimes Greek, for Joyce had picked up a smattering of the language in Trieste, and Ruggiero knew it because he had spent several years in Greece.[1] Joyce felt keenly his ignorance of classical Greek; later in his Zurich stay he said to Frank Budgen, who also lamented his ignorance of the language, 'But just think, isn't that a world *I* am peculiarly fitted to enter?' [2] His imperfect acquaintance with the language served the useful purpose, however, of making him wild and daring in etymological speculation, a favorite subject when with Ruggiero and Phokas. He came to know, at about this time, the contention Victor Bérard first formulated about the beginning of the century, that the Odyssey had Semitic roots, and that all its place names were actual places, often detectable by finding a Hebrew word that closely resembled the Greek.† This theory suited his own conception of Bloom as Ulysses.

The Club des Étrangers came to know Joyce well. Sometimes he gloomily recounted his publishing difficulties to Ruggiero, who would reply, 'Courage!' But he was more likely to be gay, and at the Restaurant zum Weisses Kreuz or the Café Terrasse he was a superb drinking companion. His laugh, still uninhibitedly executed with the head back and the mouth wide, resounded through the room. He would occasionally burst into 'I'm going to New York city, / But I will come back to you,' or if no women were present, he had a rather bawdy French chanson:

> Connaissez-vous l'histoire
> D'un vieux curé de Paris,
> D'un vieux cu—, d'un vieux cu—
> D'un vieux curé de Paris?
>
> Il aimait la botanique,
> Il en cultivait les fleurs,
> Il en cul—, il en cul—,
> Il en cultivait les fleurs. . . .[3]

In January 1917, Joyce complained to Ruggiero that he was tired of his flat at 54 Seefeldstrasse. It was too stuffy and small. Ruggiero said,

---

* Phokas translated Joyce's poem, 'Sleep Now,' into modern Greek on March 14, 1917.
† He frequently consulted in 1918 and 1919 Dr. Isaiah Sonne now at the Hebrew Union College in Cincinnati, for Greek-Hebrew cognates.

'All right, take my father's old place.' [4] His father had just moved out of a large third-floor flat at 73 Seefeldstrasse; so Joyce moved in even though his rent went up to 120 francs, three times what he had paid before. Here, with two large rooms facing the street, the family was less uncomfortable. There was one defect, however. The two rooms were part of a five-room flat with a single entrance, and the other three rooms were to be occupied by another tenant. This was Philipp Jarnach, secretary and assistant Kapellmeister to Ferruccio Busoni, the celebrated composer, pianist, and conductor.

Jarnach, accustomed to write music during the mornings, was appalled to hear, soon after Joyce moved in, a tenor voice, not always correctly pitched, singing all morning long a few feet away. With the harsh judgment of a captive listener, he found Joyce's voice 'extraordinarily powerful but rough' (all other witnesses agree it was pleasant and weak), and also disliked the accompaniment on an untuned piano. He bore the uproar as long as he could, then in desperation knocked at the neighbor's door and introduced himself. Would the gentleman consider an agreement fixing the hours when he might sing? Joyce was eminently reasonable, and invited Jarnach in. [5] Their conversation so mollified the young composer that he wrote Joyce a note after it, [6] apologizing for the circumstances of their meeting, and testifying to his admiration for the qualities of mind he had perceived in Joyce. He hoped they would become friends, and they did, their intimacy increasing after they moved to separate flats the following year. Jarnach liked Joyce's witty skepticism, though it puzzled him a little too. In music their tastes were quite different; Joyce theoretically was interested in modern music, but Donizetti and Bellini—for Jarnach, out of date—were the composers he wished to discuss. Joyce went to Busoni's concerts, but poked fun again and again at what he called '*Orchesterbetriebe*' (orchestral goings-on). [7] One day Jarnach brought Busoni and Joyce together in the Kronenhalle at the Bellevue-Platz, but the two did not take to each other. Joyce used his old gambit of depicting Shakespeare as no dramatist, but a fine poet. Busoni replied indignantly, 'You deny him the main thing and grant him the lesser.' [8] *

Although Joyce and Nora disliked the muggy Zurich climate, they could scarcely help finding Zurich interesting. It was crowded with refugees, some of them speculators in currency or goods, others political exiles, others artists. The atmosphere of literary experimentation braced Joyce for *Ulysses.* In 1915 at the Café Voltaire in the old city, the surrealist movement was fomented by Tristan Tzara, Hans Arp, and

---

* His considered opinion of Joyce, however, as expressed to Jarnach later, was that he was 'a great personality.' [9]

others, and this group, with which Joyce was sometimes mistakenly identified, was to move on like him to Paris after the war. There was political excitement, too. In the Café Odéon, where Joyce frequently went, Lenin was a constant customer, and on one occasion, it is said, they met.[10] In March the Russenzug, which was to carry Lenin back to Moscow in a sealed car, departed from the Zurich station, and later people were to remember how no one paid any attention to it at the time. In April Joyce saw for the first time the fertility rite, *Sächselüte* (the ringing of six o'clock), a Zurich ceremony which celebrates the burial of winter. After *Sächselüte* the church bells sound the angelus at six o'clock instead of seven. For two hours great equestrian processions wound through the city, the guilds trying to outdo each other in the splendor of their regalia. By exactly six o'clock in the evening they had congregated at the Bellevue-Platz, in the middle of which was the *Bögg* or winter-demon. This was a huge man, about sixty feet high, all in white cotton with a great white hat and a white pipe, set on a wooden pyre with firecrackers on all his limbs. The fire was lighted promptly, and the *Bögg* exploded piece by piece, each firecracker carrying off one limb or another. Joyce often timed his arrival in Zurich in later years so that he might see this ceremony, and in *Finnegans Wake,* also a fertility rite, and probably also taking place in April, the washerwomen hear the bells announcing the Bögg's death.

During this spring of 1917 Joyce received a visit from a small, dark-haired young man named Jules Martin, as he then called himself. Though insignificant in appearance, Martin had grandiose ideas. He was trying to set up a music hall in the Holbeinstrasse, and was also full of a plan to move into film making, which had advanced as far as some stationery headed 'New York Film Studio.'[11] Joyce, immediately ready to garner some of the film profits which the Volta in Dublin had failed to yield, listened with interest to Martin's proposals. Martin had a scenario with the not unpredictable title of *Wine, Women, and Song;* Joyce had only to retouch it here and there, and then Martin would secure a cast.

Joyce looked at the scenario closely enough to perceive that Martin intended to use him, with some deviousness, as a front man. The real plan came out slowly. 'We'll get wealthy women into it,' Martin said excitedly, 'women in fur pelts. We'll teach them how to walk and then charge them a fee for being in the film.'[12] * The studio was to have a

---

* Joyce mocks the plan as one of Shem's in *Finnegans Wake* (179-80): 'an entire operahouse (there was to be stamping room only in the prompter's box and ever-themore his queque kept swelling) of enthusiastic noblewomen flinging every coronetcrimsoned stitch they had off at his probscenium, one after the others, in-amagoaded into ajustiloosing themselves, in their gaiety pantheomime....'

Kino Schule as an adjunct. But for that matter, as he darkly hinted, there need be no film, really. His method of financing was more blunt. He went to Ruggiero and asked him how to arrange for a bank loan. Ruggiero replied, 'First you must establish credit.' 'I don't care about credit,' replied Martin, 'I simply need a little cash.' Ruggiero asked Joyce if he thought anything should be done for Martin; Joyce, old master of loanship, answered at once, 'Don't lend him anything.' [13]

Martin pushed his scheme far enough to advertise in the newspapers for a cast, and among those who applied was a professional actor, Claud W. Sykes. Sykes was supporting himself by teaching English but longed to return to the stage. He was not taken in by the screen test which Martin pretended to give him, or by the congratulations on his passing it successfully. When he pressed Martin for details of the film, he was told that the script was not quite ready for shooting; it was being given some finishing touches by a writer named Joyce, who was brilliant but dilatory. Martin suggested Sykes call on Joyce and urge him on.

Sykes had often seen Joyce reading English newspapers at the *Museumgesellschaft,* and had heard him described as a very clever man. He went to see him and was affably received. Joyce showed him the scenario, which was an impossible melodrama; they agreed that nothing could be done about it. But their acquaintance continued, and Joyce was pleased to discover that Mrs. Sykes, whose stage name was Daisy Race, had written a play in which one character, a woman, bore the name Joyce [14]—a sure sign to him that their friendship was booked in advance. Nora Joyce was especially delighted to be able to talk English again with somebody, and Daisy Race, a tiny woman, was pleasantly pert and animated.

Joyce and Sykes met often to discuss subjects connected with Joyce's work. When Joyce discovered that Sykes had acted for a time with Mrs. Bandman Palmer's company, he spent a whole afternoon quizzing him about the possibility of her having played *Leah* in Dublin in 1904. Sykes had joined the company several years after that, and had no idea of its earlier repertoire, but Joyce questioned him relentlessly, intending to refer to the play, as well as to Mrs. Bandman Palmer's other roles, in *Ulysses.* He repeated to Sykes his theory that the Odyssey was of Semitic rather than Greek origin; he had, he said, found a man named Butler at Ascona who agreed with him. [15] Sykes had his own theory of origins, not of the Odyssey but of Shakespeare's plays. He subscribed wholeheartedly to the idea, which he had first read in a book by Karl Bleibtreu, published in 1908, that the Earl of Rutland, not 'the Stratford clown,' was the real author of the plays. To interest Joyce in the notion he lent him Bleibtreu's book. Joyce, however, returned it a few days later without a word. But through Sykes he struck up an acquaintance with Bleibtreu, also living in Zurich, and mentioned him in *Ulysses*.[16] Looking for sacred coincidences, he asked whether Bleibtreu had formed his theory before June 1904—the time when his own theory of *Hamlet* began to take shape; he also wanted to know what Bleibtreu thought of Dowden, and was interested to learn that Sidney Lee's name had been changed from Simon Lazarus.[17]

In 1917 Zurich, by the ironic fortune of war, was the most important theatrical center in the world. All the well-known theaters sent companies there in a quixotic rivalry for cultural preëminence.[*] So Max Reinhardt's theater came to present *A Midsummer Night's Dream*, Aeschylus' *Agamemnon*, Büchner's *Dantons Tod*, Strindberg's *Totentanz* and *Gespenster Sonata*.[†] At that time it was generally held that Strindberg was as good as Ibsen. Joyce did not think so; he said, 'The gilt is wearing off the gingerbread,'[18] and 'No drama behind the hysterical raving,'[19] but he went to see all Strindberg's plays.[20] He met René Schickele, the Alsatian writer, who asked him to translate his play *Hans im Schnakenloch*. Joyce refused. He was much interested in Frank Wedekind, and attended performances of *Francesca* and other plays which the dramatist himself produced in Zurich. The two writers met without becoming intimate. Joyce's attitude towards dramaturgy remained surprisingly casual for a student of Ibsen. 'When things get dull,' he remarked, 'bring a woman on the stage.'[21] Occasionally, however, he seemed to discover something he needed; so one night at *Troilus and Cressida* at the Pfauen Theatre, he pointed out to Claud Sykes that all the Greek heroes but one in the play were comic butts, the exception being Ulysses, who kept his dignity throughout.

Joyce longed to have *Exiles* produced, but could obtain no support, except from Martin, who offered to play Richard himself and to persuade Mrs. Harold McCormick, who lived in the Hotel Baur au Lac and was reputed to be the wealthiest woman in Zurich, to play the part of Bertha. Her *embonpoint*, dresses, furs, and diamonds, all of which drew Martin's attention, would make her perfect for the role. Joyce was willing enough but Martin had no luck. Claud and Daisy Sykes, as eager to act as Joyce was to have his play acted, sympathized with his frustration. As the next best thing they went

---

[*] Joyce heard that Édouard Dujardin was in Geneva to produce one of his own plays and wrote to ask if he was the author of *Les Lauriers sont coupés*. Unfortunately the letter was never delivered.

[†] Joyce had read Strindberg's *The Son of a Servant* in Trieste.

regularly to the theater together, very much to the irritation of the Joyce children. Giorgio and Lucia protested vehemently against their parents' departure by shouting after them in Italian, 'And now we're going to be shut up again like pigs in a sty.' [22]

During 1917 Joyce's eye troubles, which had begun in Trieste, became acute. His history as an 'international eyesore,' as he later called himself,[23] began shortly after his move to the new apartment at 73 Seefeldstrasse, when he suffered an attack of glaucoma * and synecchia, diseases of the retina which, if untreated, lead to blindness. The first attack lasted for four weeks, into March; in April he was still under a doctor's care, and felt depressed that the attack, 'possibly on account of the infamous weather,' [24] was lasting longer than any he had ever had before. At the end of April the glaucoma again became painful; his doctor talked of operating, but Joyce understandably resisted the prospect of having bits of the iris removed at intervals. In June 1917, he wrote Miss Weaver that he was 'better but still in cure. I can also read and write more easily and yesterday could go out without black glasses. I have been to see a specialist who confirms the opinion of my doctor but agrees to postpone the operation. He says, however, that I must not go to the country as I must always have a doctor at hand, glaucoma being very dangerous and my eye very "launisch" [peevish]—like its owner. In these circumstances I have not been able to do very much with my book *Ulysses;* but I have done what I could.' [25] The next month he was laid up with tonsillitis, and his doctors advised him to winter in Italian Switzerland where the climate was milder.

Joyce was cheered during these illnesses by admiration and help from abroad. One day during his eye trouble he was sitting in a darkened room talking with the poet Felix Beran, when the mailman rang the doorbell to deliver a registered letter. Joyce asked Beran to open and read it.[26] The letter proved to be from a firm of solicitors, who wrote:

22 February 1917

Dear Sir,

We are instructed to write to you on behalf of an admirer of your writing, who desires to be anonymous, to say that we are to forward you a cheque for £50 on the 1st May, August, November and February next, making a total of £200, which we hope you will accept without any enquiry as to the source of the gift.

---

* He explained the glaucousness of glaucoma to Sylvia Beach later by a high-flown classical parallel, 'You know, the grey eyes of Athena.' [27]

We trust that this letter will reach you, the address having been taken by our client from 'Who's Who' for 1917.

Yours faithfully,
Slack Monro Saw & Co.

Joyce was of course intensely curious about the identity of his bene-factor, but could not guess who it might be. He sent copies of his books to the solicitors, and wrote a letter of gratitude. In return he had another letter saying that the arrangement would continue while the war lasted and until he was able to settle down again. When he asked what his patron liked in his work, the solicitors replied (on June 24, 1918), 'Briefly, the qualities in your writing that most interest her are your searching piercing spirit, your scorching truth, the power and startling penetration of your "intense instants of imagination."' He knew now it was a patroness.

Another good word came from John Quinn, the New York lawyer and patron of the arts, whom Ezra Pound had deflected toward Joyce's work. Quinn sent him some money in March 1917, in return for the manuscript of *Exiles*,* and wrote a laudatory review of *A Portrait* in *Vanity Fair* for May 1917. Pound wrote that Yeats thought the book 'very great,' † that Lady Gregory pronounced it 'a model autobiog-raphy,' that Eliot 'approved' of it. Harriet Weaver had meanwhile imported sheets of *A Portrait* from B. W. Huebsch in New York, and brought out an English edition of 750 copies on February 12, 1917. She asked H. G. Wells to review it; at first he protested that he hadn't time, but, spurred by Rebecca West, he thought better of his decision, and wrote a highly appreciative notice in the *Nation* for February 24. Stephen Dedalus he thought real, but not modern, a pathetic re-minder of the 'limitations of a great mass of Irishmen.' He declared that Sterne himself could not have done the Christmas dinner better, and praised 'this most memorable novel' for 'its quintessential and unfailing reality.' He had a few minor objections; to his statement that Joyce, like Swift, had 'a cloacal obsession,' Joyce replied to Frank Budgen later, 'Why, it's Wells's countrymen who build water-

---

* Joyce found Quinn faint-hearted about *Exiles*, as he suggests in a limerick sent some months later to Claud Sykes:

> There's a donor of lavish largesse
> Who once bought a play in MS.
>   He found out what it all meant
>   By the final installment
> But poor Scriptor was left in a mess.

† See p. 414.

closets wherever they go.' * [28] A few days later Arthur Clutton-Brock, also approached by Miss Weaver, wrote in an unsigned review in the *Times Literary Supplement,* 'It is wild youth, as wild as Hamlet's, and full of wild music.' [29] He wished, however, that Joyce had used a subject-matter of more distinction, which Joyce understood to mean that he should have used people of more obvious importance. 'He is stating the English preference for tawdry grandeurs,' Joyce commented; 'Even the best Englishmen seem to love a lord in literature.' [30] Dora Marsden reviewed the book in the March 1917 issue of the *Egoist,* with details about its publishing history which Miss Weaver supplied to her. The 750 copies were sold out by early summer. Joyce was moved by the enthusiastic response to a little self-mockery, and, still in a limerick-writing phase, versified his book for Ezra Pound:

> There once was a lounger named Stephen
> Whose youth was most odd and uneven
>   He throve on the smell
>   Of a horrible hell
> That a Hottentot wouldn't believe in. [31]

He continued, in spite of the encouraging sales and the help of his new, still unidentified patroness, to regard his economic plight as deplorable. When Pound asked him for magazine contributions, he said he would be glad to write some simple translation or review. He warned, however, that he was a bad critic, adducing as evidence that someone had recently given him a two-volume novel called *Joseph Vance,* which he had read for some days before observing that he had started with the second volume. [32]

His correspondence about *Exiles* continued to vex him. Grant Richards, to whom Pinker was compelled by the terms of the *Dubliners* contract to submit *Exiles* for consideration, considered it interminably. After five months Richards agreed late in August to publish it. [33] When Pinker remonstrated with Joyce for having committed his future work to Richards by the *Dubliners* contract of 1914, Joyce replied on July 8, 1917, with some exasperation:

You have written to me several times of what you call the 'disastrous' and 'dreadful' character of my contract with Mr. Richards and ask why I signed it. I signed it in 1915 after a struggle of 9 years for the publication of my

---

* Wells complained that the hero, while intolerant of sounds, was singularly indulgent of smells. Joyce wrote a limerick of which only three lines have survived:

> There once was an author named Wells
> Who wrote about science, not smells. . . .
> The result is a series of cells. [34]

book—written in 1905. You will find the story set forth by Mr Pound in *The Egoist* (14 January 1914). My New York publisher has recently published a pamphlet about it. The book cost me in litigation and train fare and postal expense about 3000 francs: it cost me also nine years of my life. I was in correspondence with seven solicitors, one hundred and twenty newspapers, and several men of letters about it—all of whom, except Mr Ezra Pound, refused to aid me. The type of the abortive first English edition (1906) was broken up. The second edition (Dublin 1910) was burnt entire almost in my presence. The third edition (London, 1914) is the text as I wrote it and as I obliged my publisher to publish it after 9 years. Possibly the terms of *his* contract are unfair. I neither know nor care anything about that matter—so long as he does with the help of his printer the work he undertakes to do for me. *Dubliners* was refused by *forty* publishers in the intervals of the events recorded above. My novel *A Portrait of the Artist as a Young Man* was refused by every publisher to whom you offered it and, when the *Egoist* decided to publish it, about twenty printers in England and Scotland refused to print it. As you know, I suppose, it was printed in America and published in New York in December 1916 and in London in February 1917. *The Egoist* intends to bring out a second edition in September and as recent regulations seem to stand in the way of importing printed sheets from New York Miss Weaver has found a printer who will print it now after it has been reviewed. At least so she writes me.

The Stage Society took an even longer time to think about *Exiles*. Pinker sent the play to the society on January 27, 1916, and they rejected it on July 11, then asked to have it again on April 1, 1917, and had not yet decided about it when Joyce ordered Pinker to withdraw it on July 2.[35] Among the members, Sturge Moore was active in Joyce's behalf, but the opposition was equally determined to resist 'Filth and Disease,' as one member called it.[*] Yeats was not able to help, and William Archer, to whom Joyce again appealed, does not seem to have done anything. Joyce continued to agitate in behalf of the play; Moore took it back for reconsideration in November 1917; but it was some time before these efforts met with any success.

While Joyce's correspondence might suggest that he was altogether given over to thoughts of his old books, his conversation at the time indicates that he was really preoccupied with his new one. His language pupil Georges Borach kept a journal, and in it noted on August 1, 1917, what Joyce had said to him the previous evening at the Pfauen Café.

---

[*] Joyce wrote Carlo Linati on September 19, 1919, that *Exiles* was placed on the program of the Stage Society, along with *The Way of the World* and *La Città Morta*, but was removed following the protest of Bernard Shaw who found it obscene.

J. J. thinks:

'The most beautiful, all-embracing theme is that of the Odyssey. It is greater, more human, than that of *Hamlet, Don Quixote,* Dante, *Faust.* The rejuvenation of old Faust has an unpleasant effect upon me. Dante tires one quickly; it is like looking at the sun. The most beautiful, most human traits are contained in the Odyssey. I was twelve years old when we took up the Trojan War at school; only the Odyssey stuck in my memory. I want to be frank: at twelve I liked the supernaturalism in Ulysses. When I was writing *Dubliners,* I intended at first to choose the title *Ulysses in Dublin,* but gave up the idea. In Rome, when I had finished about half the *Portrait,* I realized that the Odyssey had to be the sequel, and I began to write *Ulysses.*

'Why was I always returning to this theme? Now *in mezzo del cammin* I find the subject of Ulysses the most human in world literature. Ulysses didn't want to go off to Troy; he knew that the official reason for the war, the dissemination of the culture of Hellas, was only a pretext for the Greek merchants, who were seeking new markets. When the recruiting officers arrived, he happened to be plowing. He pretended to be mad. Thereupon they placed his little two-year-old son in the furrow. Observe the beauty of the motifs: the only man in Hellas who is against the war, and the father. Before Troy the heroes shed their lifeblood in vain. They want to raise the siege. Ulysses opposes the idea. [He thinks up] the stratagem of the wooden horse. After Troy there is no further talk of Achilles, Menelaus, Agamemnon. Only one man is not done with; his heroic career has hardly begun: Ulysses.

'Then the motif of wandering. Scylla and Charybdis—what a splendid parable. Ulysses is also a great musician; he wishes to and must listen; he has himself tied to the mast. The motif of the artist, who will lay down his life rather than renounce his interest. Then the delicious humor of Polyphemus. "Outis is my name." On Naxos, the oldster of fifty, perhaps baldheaded, with Nausicaa, a girl who is barely seventeen. What a fine theme! And the return, how profoundly human! Don't forget the trait of generosity at the interview with Ajax in the nether world, and many other beautiful touches. I am almost afraid to treat such a theme; it's overwhelming.' [36]

Although the exclamations do not convey the 'halting, meditative manner' which Joyce used, as his brother Stanislaus noted, in working out something in his mind, the substance of Borach's note rings true. It is not surprising that Joyce's description of Ulysses as pacifist, father, wanderer, musician, and artist, ties the hero's life closely to his own.

During this same month of August 1917, Joyce decided to follow his doctors' advice and winter in Locarno, partly on his own account and partly on Nora's, for she too found the Zurich climate very unhealthy. She went down first with the children, and when he telegraphed her to ask if she felt better, she replied cheerfully, '*Benissimo.*' [37] He sent her a book by Sacher-Masoch, for whose works they

shared a jocular affection. But during her absence, his eyes suddenly
failed. On the evening of August 18, the birthday of Franz Josef, as
he afterwards insisted, when he was walking down the Bahnhofstrasse,
he suffered an attack of glaucoma so severe that for twenty minutes
he was almost insensible with pain. His ophthalmologist, Professor
Ernst Sidler, decided there was no choice but to operate; six days later
he performed an iridectomy on Joyce's right eye at the Augenklinik.
The operation was well done but so unnerved Joyce that he collapsed,
and for three days even Nora, who had come back from Locarno to
join him, was not allowed to see him.[38] As often happens, the exuda-
tion from the eye flowed over into the incision and reduced the vision
permanently.

Joyce was able to carry out his project of going to Locarno. B. W.
Huebsch gave him £54, a generous advance on future royalties, and
he also had the August payment of £50 from his anonymous donor
in London. On October 12 he and his family went to the station,
accompanied by Paul Ruggiero, who was amused to see them all,
characteristically, running to catch the train just as it began to pull
out.[39]

For a few days all went well in Locarno except that the cat was in
a catfight. The milder climate was a pleasant change, and Joyce had
thoughts of settling in Locarno permanently. Then the city began
to pall. Joyce had assumed, as he told Sykes, that he could live anywhere so long as he had a place to write. But he was a more gregarious
man than he supposed, and Locarno proved to be a backwater. He
stayed at the Pension Villa Rossa on his arrival, then moved in mid-
November to the Pension Daheim. Soon he was making occasional
hurried trips to Zurich, one on an errand of mercy. Jules Martin had
the temperament of a swindler but not the talent; through some luckless scheme he had landed himself in jail in Lausanne. Joyce had
obligingly posted letters from him to his family on appointed dates,
so they would not guess their son's whereabouts, and Martin blithely
told him that he was gathering excellent material for a comedy from
his prison experiences. Near the end of 1917 Joyce went to the Dutch
consul in Zurich on Martin's behalf, and helped to arrange for the
young man's release from prison to a hospital. Soon after he received
a letter of gratitude from an Amsterdam gynecologist, de Vries, who
revealed that Jules Martin was really his son Juda, 'the black sheep
of my family.'[40] Martin presented Joyce with a gift he had made for
him in prison, a wooden box shaped like a family Bible with 'My
First Success. By James Joyce,' printed on the spine. 'When you make

money,' said Martin, 'you can conceal it in the box. Everybody will
think it's a book.' [41]

During the first weeks at Locarno Joyce completed the three initial
episodes of *Ulysses,* the *Telemachiad.* He mailed them episode by
episode to Claud Sykes, who had agreed to type them if Joyce could
find him a typewriter. Joyce sent him to Rudolf Goldschmidt, who,
besides being a grain merchant, was an official in an organization
which assisted Austro-Hungarian subjects resident in Switzerland.
Sykes found Goldschmidt in this office with nothing to do; on learning that he was an emissary from Joyce, Goldschmidt received him
benevolently and lent the typewriter at once. Herbert Gorman prints
a verse composed by Joyce when he heard of the incident from Sykes;
it was to the tune of the 'Amorous Goldfish' in Sidney Jones's *The
Geisha,* and seems rather hard on the man who lent the typewriter:

> A Goldschmidt swam in a Kriegsverein
> As wise little Goldschmidts do,
> And he loved every scion of the Habsburg line,
> Each Archduke proud, the whole jimbang crowd.
> And he felt that they loved him, too.
> Herr Rosenbaum and Rosenfeld
> And every other Feld except Schlachtfeld;
> All worked like niggers, totting rows of crazy figures,
> To save Kaiser Karl and Goldschmidt, too.
>
> Chorus:
> For he said it is bet—bet—better
> To stick stamps on some God-damned letter
> Than be shot in a trench
> Amid shells and stench,
> Jesus Gott—Donner wet-wet-wetter.* [42]

Sykes received the first episode about November 20, the second
about December 20, and the third shortly afterwards. As usual with
Joyce, there were last-minute corrections and additions. 'Please change
the word "captive,"' he wrote Sykes on November 24, 'in phrase "Mr
Deasy held his nose captive for a few moments" etc to "tweaked."
The reason I trouble you so often is that I make notes on stray bits
of paper which I then forget in the most unlikely places, in books,
under ornaments and in my pockets and on the back of advertisements.' [43] Occasional postcards bore limericks:

---

* Goldschmidt was actually a Swiss citizen, so was not evading military service by
this sinecure.

James Joyce in Zurich, 1915. Photograph by Ottocaro Weiss.
Courtesy of Ottocaro Weiss

ἄνδρά μοι ἔννεπε μοῦσα πολύτροπον ὡς μάλα πολλὰ

Joyce's caricature of Leopold Bloom (drawn in Myron C. Nutting's studio in the 1920's). The Greek line is the beginning of the Odyssey, 'Tell me, Muse, of the man of many devices, who over many ways . . .' *Courtesy of Myron C. Nutting and the Northwestern University Library*

X

The Joyce family at a Zurich restaurant in 1915. Photographed by Ottocaro Weiss. *Courtesy of Ottocaro Weiss*

> There's a George of the Georges named David
> With whose words we are now night and day fed.
>   He cries: I'll give small rations
>   To all the small nations.
> Bully God made this world—but I'll save it.[44]

A running joke was Nora Joyce's failure to write letters; in October her husband tells Sykes, 'My wife says every morning: I must write to Mrs. Sykes. So she will—before Christmas.'[45] In December he announces, 'My wife is mobilizing with the purpose of writing a letter to Mrs. Sykes.'[46] The same month he becomes more serious: 'Please convey my wife's excuses for her taciturnity both to Mrs. Sykes and Mrs. Bleibtreu from whom she had a card today. She has been constantly ill and has even had very bad nervous breakdowns here so that I really do not know what to do—whether to go to Zurich on the offchance of finding a flat or leaving this pension and looking for a flat here. Instead of doing her good the stay here has made her much worse. But for the dreadful weather you have we would perhaps go back but on the other hand my health has to be thought of.'[47] The winter in Locarno did not become mild; Joyce grew increasingly morose. His letters mention a snowstorm and then an earthquake, and the latter seems to have decided him. 'An earthquake here the other night,' he writes Sykes on December 12. 'We return to Zurich after New Year.'[48]

He brought his family back to Zurich early in January 1918, after only three months away. They all went at once to pay a visit to Claud and Daisy Sykes, and Nora confided that she was never so pleased to talk with anyone before. 'Jim never spoke a word to me at the Pension Daheim,' she declared, 'and the rest of the family were tubercular.'[49] Like her husband's allusion to her 'nervous breakdowns,' the word 'tubercular' was hyperbolic. The family now took a flat at 38 Universitätstrasse, and Joyce plunged back into work on *Ulysses*.

The early chapters had been brought to the point where they could be published. He entered into correspondence with Miss Weaver and Pound about the possibility of printing the book first in serial form, as he had done with the *Portrait*. Miss Weaver was more than willing, and offered £50 for the rights. In December and January Joyce sent the three opening chapters to Pound, who was delighted with them. After reading the first, he complimented Joyce on December 18 with the dreary humor of his pseudo-American lingo, 'Wall, Mr Joice, I recon your a damn fine writer, that's what I recon'. An' I recon' this here work o' yourn is some concarn'd literature. You can take it from me, an' I'm a jedge.'[50] Pound was then in the course of shifting his primary American allegiance from Harriet Monroe's *Poetry* to the *Little Review* of Margaret Anderson and Jane Heap, which was more avant-garde in its interests and which intended to print chiefly prose. The two women were interested in Joyce but were not allowed to communicate directly with him; Pound, acting as intermediary, discouraged such an approach and, as they later complained, treated Joyce like a private possession.[51] They were none the less delighted when Pound sent them the *Telemachiad* in February. No sooner did Margaret Anderson read the opening words of the *Proteus* episode, 'Ineluctable modality of the visible; at least that if no more, thought through my eyes. Signatures of all things I am here to read, seaspawn and seawrack, the nearing tide....' than she cried, 'This is the most beautiful thing we'll ever have. We'll print it if it's the last effort of our lives.'[52]

They did in fact start the book in the March 1918 issue of the *Little Review,* and nobly piloted the magazine towards the reef of censorship on which it temporarily foundered. John Quinn was taken a little aback by the language of the first episode, and Pound had to write him on April 3 a vigorous defense: 'I can't agree with you about Joyce's first chapter. I don't think the passages about his mother's death and the sea would come with such force if they weren't imbedded in squalor and disgust. I may say that I rec'd the fourth chapter some days ago, and deleted about twenty lines before sending it off to N.Y.; and also wrote Joyce my reasons for thinking the said lines excessive. He does not disgust me as Wells does.'[53] Joyce paid no attention to the controversy beyond resolving that there would be no such high-handed deletions when *Ulysses* was published in book form. He moved ahead quickly, the knowledge that chapters were being published stimulating him to prepare the next installments. He was eager to hear what people thought of it, whether Daisy Sykes, for example, liked it or not.[54] He read passages to Nora, but she found the language distasteful and offered no encouragement.

His work was pleasantly interrupted late in February by a visit from Charlotte Sauermann, a soprano at the Zurich opera house. Fräulein Sauermann had followed Jarnach as tenant in the Seefeldstrasse flat the previous year, and had knocked and introduced herself one evening when Joyce was singing, not because she was, like Jarnach, annoyed by his voice, but because she liked it. They had sung together occasionally, and she had offered to try to find Joyce work at the opera house, but he replied at once, 'No, I don't want to sing professionally. I tried it once and didn't care for it.' She came in now with an air of mystery and said, 'Oh, Mr. Joyce, do you own a black suit?' 'No,' said he, 'why?' She replied guardedly, 'Maybe you'll need one some day soon.' 'Well,' said Joyce, uncertain what she meant, 'if I do, I will borrow one from somebody.' A day or two later, on February 27, 1918, he received a letter from the managing director of the Eidgenössische Bank of Zurich, asking him to call in connection with some money. Joyce borrowed the black suit that was essential for calls upon Zurich bankers, and went. The director received him cordially and said, 'A client of the bank who is much interested in your work knows that you are in bad straits financially, and wishes to give you a kind of fellowship. We have 12,000 francs deposited to your credit. You will receive a thousand francs a month beginning March 1.' Joyce was dazzled and perplexed by this gift which, added to his previous anonymous benefaction, brought his monthly income up to 1500 francs.*

He importuned the manager to tell him who his patron was, but the manager was under instructions to keep the identity secret. On leaving the bank, Joyce recalled Charlotte Sauermann's odd question and realized she must have known. He went and asked her; at first she refused to say, but Joyce insisted that it was essential for him to know. At last she revealed that it was Mrs. Harold McCormick,[55] who had been living in Zurich since 1913 and, besides heavily endowing the psychologist Jung, had patronized a great many writers and musicians. Joyce paid her a visit and thanked her. She replied graciously, 'I know you are a great artist.'[56]

He did not conceal his good fortune from his friends. Ruggiero said, 'I told you so.' Professor Feilbogen of the now extinct *International Review* was delighted, and said to Cecil Palmer, who had supervised the work of English translation for the review, 'Just see what a good thing has happened: Joyce has been given a thousand francs a month by a rich lady.' Shortly afterwards Palmer ran into Joyce and congratulated him effusively, but Joyce, who by this time had recovered his reserve, merely remarked, 'It's high time.'[57] He dropped some of his lessons, as he usually did when money came in, and was seen more and more often at the Pfauen Café.

Claud Sykes, having heard of Joyce's good fortune, came to him with a new plan for doubling it; he suggested they form a troupe to produce plays in English. The consul-general had encouraged him to expect at least semi-official support for such a venture, since Zurich had plays in every language but English. Joyce had much to do, but he was always ready to be diverted, knowing that no diversions could seriously affect his secret discipline. So he agreeably said, 'Why not?'

* $300 or £60.

They formed a partnership, Sykes to be producer and director, Joyce, as ex-banker, ex-movie-magnate, and ex-agent for Irish tweeds, to be business manager of the new company, which at his suggestion was named the English Players.[58] The enterprise had from the start a patriotic air; Joyce had received letters from the consulate in 1916 and 1917, asking him if he would be willing to serve and ordering him in any event to report for a physical examination, and he had also received Edmund Gosse's hint that his Treasury grant implied an obligation. This he expected now to discharge. He had other motives too which were perhaps more prominent: he wished to secure the production of *Exiles*, which was accordingly listed as one of the plays in the company's repertoire. Another object, which Sykes unpretentiously shared, was to make some money in an exciting way. If the notion of creating pro-British propaganda in Switzerland was ever a strong one—and it was not really—it was quickly dissipated. He eventually stirred up anti-British propaganda instead.

Sykes proposed that the first play should be Wilde's *The Importance of Being Earnest*, and Joyce seconded the plan of beginning with a play by an Irishman. 'To me,' he told Sykes, 'an Irish safety pin is more important than an English epic.'[59] He threw himself into this project with the same fervor that he had displayed in 1909 for the Volta Theatre, and would display in 1930 for John Sullivan's operatic career. He persuaded several professional actors to accept small fees with the understanding that these would be increased if the theater gained a foothold. He persuaded his pupils and their friends to buy tickets, whether or not they had succeeded in learning English from him. In the course of making these arrangements he visited A. Percy Bennett, the consul-general. Bennett was annoyed with Joyce for not having reported to the consulate officially to offer his services in wartime, and was perhaps aware of Joyce's work for the neutralist *International Review* of Feilbogen and of his open indifference to the war's outcome. He may even have heard of Joyce's version of 'Mr. Dooley,' written about this time:

Dooleysprudence

Who is the man when all the gallant nations run to war
Goes home to have his dinner by the very first cablecar
And as he eats his cantelope contorts himself in mirth
To read the blatant bulletins of the rulers of the earth?
    It's Mr Dooley,
    Mr Dooley,
    The coolest chap our country ever knew

'They are out to collar
The dime and dollar'
Says Mr Dooley-ooley-ooley-oo.

Who is the funny fellow who declines to go to church
Since pope and priest and parson left the poor man in the lurch
And taught their flocks the only way to save all human souls
Was piercing human bodies through with dumdum bulletholes?
　　　It's Mr Dooley,
　　　Mr Dooley,
　　　The mildest man our country ever knew
　　　'Who will release us
　　　From Jingo Jesus'
　　　Prays Mr Dooley-ooley-ooley-oo.

Who is the meek philosopher who doesn't care a damn
About the yellow peril or problem of Siam
And disbelieves that British Tar is water from life's fount
And will not gulp the gospel of the German on the Mount?
　　　It's Mr Dooley,
　　　Mr Dooley,
　　　The broadest brain our country ever knew
　　　'The curse of Moses
　　　On both your houses'
　　　Cries Mr Dooley-ooley-ooley-oo.

Who is the cheerful imbecile who lights his long chibouk
With pages of the pandect, penal code and Doomsday Book
And wonders why bald justices are bound by law to wear
A toga and a wig made out of someone else's hair?
　　　It's Mr Dooley,
　　　Mr Dooley,
　　　The finest fool our country ever knew
　　　'They took that toilette
　　　From Pontius Pilate'
　　　Thinks Mr Dooley-ooley-ooley-oo.

Who is the man who says he'll go the whole and perfect hog
Before he pays the income tax or license for a dog
And when he licks a postage stamp regards with smiling scorn
The face of king or emperor or snout of unicorn?
　　　It's Mr Dooley,
　　　Mr Dooley,
　　　The wildest wag our country ever knew
　　　'O my poor tummy
　　　His backside gummy!'
　　　Moans Mr Dooley-ooley-ooley-oo.

Who is the tranquil gentleman who won't salute the State
Or serve Nebuchadnezzar or proletariat
But thinks that every son of man has quite enough to do
To paddle down the stream of life his personal canoe?
        It's Mr Dooley,
        Mr Dooley,
        The wisest wight our country ever knew
        'Poor Europe ambles
        Like sheep to shambles'
        Sighs Mr Dooley-ooley-ooley-oo.[60]

If Mr Dooley's anarchism was peculiar to Joyce, his indifference to the war's outcome was common enough among Irishmen, some of whom were conducting their own war against the British. But it was hardly calculated to make him popular among English officials. Consequently Bennett, Joyce reported, treated him in an offhand and superior way until Joyce needled him with some remark, after which he lapsed into silence and pretended to be looking for something thrown by mistake into his wastepaper basket. Joyce began the process of immortalizing Bennett, which he would complete in *Ulysses*, by enshrining him and the basket in a limerick:

> There's an anthropoid consul called Bennett,
> With the jowl of a jackass or jennet,
>   He must muzzle or mask it
>   In the waste paper basket,
> When he rises to bray in the Senate.

He wrested from Bennett, however, official approval for the Players.[61]

Meanwhile Sykes was piecing together a cast. There were not many professional English actors in Zurich, but he turned up Evelyn Cotton and one or two others. An important find was Tristan Rawson, a handsome man who had sung baritone roles for four years in the Cologne Opera House but had never acted in a play. After much coaxing, Rawson agreed to take on the role of John Worthing in *The Importance of Being Earnest*. He became the company's principal actor. Sykes recruited Cecil Palmer as the butler, and found a woman named Ethel Turner to play Miss Prism. Mrs. Turner had been married three times, and Joyce composed a rhyme about her that began,

> This is the Turner that turned about
> And turned six husbands inside out.[62]

As yet, however, there was no one to take the leading role of Algernon Moncrieff. In an unlucky moment, Joyce nominated a tall,

good-looking young man named Henry Carr, whom he had seen in
the consulate. Carr, invalided from the service, had a small job there.
Sykes learned that he had acted in some amateur plays in Canada,
and decided to risk him.

The rehearsals began in April and continued for two weeks. Jules
Martin, now unmasked as de Vries, was encouraged by Joyce to turn
up at one of them and offer himself as prompter, but Sykes sensibly
sent him away. Joyce followed the progress of the Players, and got
along well with all the members of the cast except Carr, who evidently
accepted the official view that Joyce's conduct in Zurich was not quite
cricket. With Rawson in particular Joyce became friendly. One night
when Rawson had accompanied him home, Joyce steered the conversation round to the Odyssey, remarking, 'Do you know the Rider Haggard theory about the Odyssey?' Rawson did not. 'He thinks that two
books of the Odyssey have been lost, and that they fulfilled two
prophecies by Tiresias—one about Ulysses wanting another son, the
other about a country without salt. Haggard thinks these are not fulfilled. But I don't agree at all. I maintain that the two prophecies are
fulfilled; but that the Odyssey has been mistranslated. One of these days
I am going to trump up a Joyce theory.' [63] His mind was playing with
Bloom's desire for another son, and perhaps with the idea that the salt-
less country would be Ireland in his own book.

The preparations for the play went on. Joyce booked the Theater zu
den Kaufleuten on Pelikanstrasse for the night of April 29, and made
other business arrangements, such as inducing his friend Ruggiero to
usher. Professional actors were to receive thirty francs, while ama-
teurs were not to receive anything; but Sykes suggested to Joyce that
they be given ten francs to reimburse them for tram fares to rehearsals,
and this amount was settled upon. Carr threw himself enthusiastically
into his part, and even bought a pair of trousers, a new hat, and a
pair of gloves. He played the role well, and the performance as a
whole was a small triumph. During the intermission Bennett congratulated Joyce, and in the applause at the end Joyce called out to
Borach in the audience, 'Hurrah for Ireland! Poor Wilde was Irish
and so am I.' Largely because of Joyce's efforts the house was full,
and the partners made a profit.

A quarrel began immediately after the play. Joyce handed each
member of the cast an envelope containing 10 or 30 francs * depend-
ing upon amateur or professional status. When Carr saw that his
envelope contained only 10 francs, he was piqued; although he had
agreed to the amount, he understandably expected a bonus for his
* $2 or $6, 8/- or 1/4/0.

skillful performance. He made an excuse for not attending the dinner for the cast, and next day went to Sykes with his complaints. Joyce, he said, had handed him the envelope as if it were a tip. Moreover, Carr claimed to be entitled to reimbursement for the cost of his new clothing, 150 francs. Sykes calmed him, but Joyce, when he heard about Carr's conduct, went into a fury of his own. Sykes pointed out that the company was billed for a tour of French Switzerland, and persuaded Joyce to let matters ride for a few days.

But Joyce's annoyance with Carr swelled again overnight; he forgot his promise of patience, and at 11:30 the next morning, May 1, went to the consulate. He found Carr with two other employees named Smith and Gann, and with measured tactlessness he asked Carr for some money owing on tickets. Carr had been given twenty tickets to sell for the performance, and as yet had handed in money for only twelve. His temper mounting before Joyce's manner, Carr gave Joyce 15 francs and said he had not yet been paid for the others. He then demanded 150 francs from Joyce for his costume. Joyce replied that Carr had surely not had the suit made only for this performance, and that his participation in the play had been a matter of honor for a British subject. This retort was too much for Carr, who shouted at Joyce, 'You're a cad. You've cheated me and pocketed the proceeds. You're a swindler. If you don't get out, I'll throw you down stairs. Next time I catch you outside I'll wring your neck.' Joyce was left momentarily speechless by 'these monstrous injuries inflicted on his honor,' as his lawyer later called them, but recovered himself sufficiently to say limply, 'I don't think this is fit language to be used in a Government office.' [64]

When he encountered Cecil Palmer soon afterwards, he was still trembling with indignation. He had just composed two letters, which he exhibited to Palmer: one was to Bennett, the consul-general, and one was to the Zurich police. The first asked that Carr be dismissed from the consular service and the second that the police protect him against Carr's threats. Palmer was not sympathetic.[*] [65] Joyce then went to Sykes, who was flabbergasted. He asked Rawson to try to patch up the matter with Carr, but Rawson found Carr seething with anger at what he in turn considered Joyce's offensive behavior. Consul-General Bennett, 'that public servant' as Joyce ironically called him, took the part of Carr, and made clear to Sykes that if he continued

---

[*] Joyce was not often kind to Palmer either. Palmer was a little bald on the front part of his head, and Joyce said that when Palmer spoke to anyone, his eyes seemed to be asking mutely, 'What have you done with my front hair?' When Palmer did a sketch of Mrs. Sykes, Joyce remarked, 'It's a very good likeness of Mr. Palmer.' It did seem to raise her forehead.

to be associated with Joyce, he would withdraw official support for the Players. Sykes, caught in the middle, elected to stay with Joyce. Joyce, for his part, went to Goldschmidt's lawyer, Konrad Bloch, and had him institute two suits against Carr on May 3. The first was for 25 francs owing for five tickets; against this Carr counterclaimed 450 francs as his share in the company's net profits, which he alleged to be 2600 to 3000 francs,* or, if this claim were disallowed, 300 francs as a fee for his acting and his expenses for costume. Joyce's second suit was for libel, based upon Carr's insulting words in the consulate.

Joyce had always been litigious and saw the incident as another example of his war with authority, represented on this occasion by a British consular official. There were moments when he recognized that the episode was absurd, but nevertheless he inexorably pushed both suits to a final conclusion. The affair colored the rest of his stay in Zurich.

* $520 to $600, £ 104 to £ 120.

1918

Still we know how Day the Dyer works, in dims and deeps and dusks
and darks.

—*Finnegans Wake* (226)

JOYCE might have been more cast down by his quarrel with British
imperial power as concentrated in Henry Carr if it had not been
for a new friend. This was Frank Budgen, with whom he became
more intimate than with any friend in his life except Byrne. Joyce
and Budgen met at a dinner party given by Horace Taylor, an English
friend of Budgen who had brought a show of English paintings to
Zurich and had several times encountered Joyce. The party went badly
at first; Joyce was reserved and distant because he suspected that
Budgen, who worked for the Ministry of Information in a building
near the consulate, had been sent by the consul-general to spy on
him. Half-way through the meal, however, he suddenly relaxed and
became amiable, because, as he revealed to Budgen later in their acquaintance, he suddenly noticed how much Budgen resembled the
noted cricketer Arthur Shrewsbury.[1]

Budgen's manner was disarming and so was his background. He
had had little schooling in England before he went to sea, but there
he had educated himself, reading widely in literature and philosophy.
His mind was sensitive and receptive, and curiously without precon-
ceptions about literature, so that he had no difficulty in sympathizing
with Joyce's innovations. After giving up the sea he had spent some
time in Paris learning to paint and supporting himself by modeling
for the sculptor August Suter. When war began Suter, who was a
Swiss, persuaded Budgen to come on to Zurich with him and to try
his luck there.[2] The luck had been good enough: he had found his
small job at the Ministry and was enabled to continue his painting.
His closest friend was the sculptor's younger brother Paul, and Joyce
quickly admitted both of them to his fellowship.

His conduct with them was delightfully unpredictable. When the
mood came over him, he might suddenly interrupt a Saturday after-

noon walk in the fashionable Bahnhofstrasse by flinging his loose
limbs about in a kind of spider dance,° the effect accentuated by his
tight trouser-legs and wide cloak, diminutive hat, and thin cane. Or
passing a crowd of people on the street, he might suddenly stop to
gaze at them through half-closed eyes while he hummed Palestrina's
mass for Pope Marcellus, which, he said, had saved music for the
Church. Or he might launch into a protest against a Bach oratorio
based on Matthew, on the ground that the gospels had been mixed:
'It's like lumping together Shakespeare and Dostoevski.'[3]

He made no pretense of sharing his friends' interest in other arts,
such as painting, although once he asked Budgen if the *Cyclops*
episode did not strike him as futuristic.†[4] Bewildered by an art
which used neither words nor sounds, he asked the painter Rudolf
Maglin, a friend of the Suters, what he was driving at in his paintings.
Maglin replied, 'I want to express my experience.' *'Dann werden Sie
den Kopf verlieren'* ('Then you'll lose your head'), said Joyce at once.[5]
Another day he joined his contempt for painting with his disrespect
for women, by asking Paul Suter, 'Do you know how to tell whether
a woman is any good or not?' 'No,' said Suter. 'Well, take her to a
picture gallery, and explain the pictures to her. If she breaks wind,
she's all right.'[6] In sculpture he entertained his friends by his predilec-
tions; he repeatedly brought them to look at a small wooden statue
of the Trinity in an antique shop; both God and Jesus looked young
and had slight beards, resembling Joyce. 'They look like brothers,'
Joyce would point out, in some wonder at the conception.[7] He purchased a statuette of bronzed plaster, in execrable taste,‡ representing
a woman reclining in an armchair with a cat nestling along her neck
and shoulders. Notwithstanding protests he kept this on his desk,
underneath a huge photograph of a Triestine (presumably Ettore
Schmitz), whom he would not identify except as the model for Bloom.
On his wall also was a photograph of a Greek statue of Penelope,
seated and looking at her raised forefinger. 'What is she thinking
about?' Joyce asked. 'She is weighing up her wooers,' Budgen suggested, 'trying to decide which one of them will make the most man-
ageable husband.' 'To me,' said Paul, 'she seems to be saying: "I'll
give him just one week more."' 'My own idea,' said Joyce, 'is that
she is trying to recollect what Ulysses looks like. You see, he has been

° As his daughter-in-law, Helen Joyce, was to put it, 'Liquor went to his feet, not
head.'
† He probably attended the important exhibition of futurism which was held in
Trieste about 1908.
‡ A friend in Paris, Madame Yasushi Tanaka, said of him, 'He had not taste, only
genius.'

away many years, and they had no photographs in those days.' [8]
But his favorite statue in Zurich was one for which Budgen had served
Suter as model, a huge figure on the Uraniabrücke; and often late
at night he would say to a group that included Budgen, 'Let's go and
see Budgen,' and would conduct them to the statue which depicted
his not too industrious friend in the nude with a hammer and a long
beard as an allegory of labor. Sometimes he would honor this idol with
his spider dance.

The association with Budgen restored Joyce's old conviviality. He
brought Budgen and Paul Suter to the Zimmerleuten, a well-known
restaurant on the right bank of the river, to celebrate the receipt of
one of his monthly installments from Mrs. McCormick. When closing-
time came they did not want to leave, but the upstairs room was
already occupied by a private party. Joyce asked permission of the
proprietress to have a party on the landing; she agreed on condition
that they drink champagne, and collected at once for each bottle
that was brought them. Budgen at last protested against this treatment, and Joyce said the best solution would be for her to join them.
So she did, and before long waiters, cooks, and chambermaids had
sat down too, and they all drank together until dawn.

An especially gay party took place within an office of the hated
consulate. The restaurants having closed, Budgen invited Joyce and
Suter to come to the rooms of the commercial department, where
they sat round on the carpet. Joyce recited Verlaine's '*La lune blanchit
sur les toits*,' and '*Il pleut dans mon cœur*,' in which he said one
could hear the very sound of the rain. Paul Suter, also an enthusiast,
recited,

> Les roses étaient toutes rouges
> Et les lierres étaient tout noirs.
>
> Chère, pour peu que tu te bouges,
> Renaissent tous mes désespoirs.

'That is perfection,' said Joyce. 'No more beautiful poem has ever
been made. And yet I wonder at what hour, A.M. or P.M., are roses
quite red and ivy perfectly black?' [9] He did not much care for German
verse, but said that the one poem that interested him, and the only
good war poem that he knew, was by Felix Beran:

> ### Des Weibes Klage
>
> Und nun ist kommen der Krieg der Krieg
> Und nun ist kommen der Krieg der Krieg
> Und nun ist kommen der Krieg
>   Krieg

Nun sind sie alle Soldaten
Nun sind sie alle Soldaten
Nun sind sie alle Soldaten
    Soldaten

Soldaten müssen sterben
Soldaten müssen sterben
Soldaten müssen sterben
    Sterben müssen sie

Wer wird nun küssen
Wer wird nun küssen
Wer wird nun küssen
    Meinen weissen Leib

The word 'Leib,' as Budgen has written, 'moved him to enthusiasm. It was a sound that created the image of a body in one unbroken mass.... He spoke of the plastic monosyllable as a sculptor speaks about a stone.' * 10

Joyce took pleasure in undercutting romanticism, so when Budgen happened to speak of the 'heart,' Joyce commented, 'The seat of the affections is lower down, I think.' As the party grew more festive Budgen, who knew a great many sea chanties from his sailor days, delighted Joyce by singing 'The Raughty Tinker,' which begins:

There was a raughty tinker
Who in London town did dwell
And when he had no work to do
His meat ax he did sell.

* Joyce translated the poem, giving it the title, 'Lament for the Yeomen':

And now is come the war, the war:
And now is come the war, the war:
And now is come the war, the war!
War! War!

For soldiers are they gone now,
For soldiers all!
Soldiers and soldiers!
All! All!

Soldiers must die, must die!
Soldiers all must die!
Soldiers and Soldiers and Soldiers
Must die!

What man is there to kiss now,
To kiss, to kiss,
O white soft body this
Thy soft sweet whiteness? 11

With me solderin' iron and taraway
Hammer legs and saw
Brave old Donald we are off to Castlepool.

Came up a gay old lady,
Her age was one hundred and three.
She said, 'You raughty tinker,
Will you have a rasp at me?'
With me solderin' iron and taraway
Hammer legs and saw.
Brave old Donald we are off to Castlepool.

It seemed to Suter that Joyce savored the obscene words like candy, though his more detached comment was that such songs constituted a kind of primitive sex education.[12] At the party's height Budgen stood on top of the money-safe and performed an Indian belly-dance, while Joyce performed his spider-dance on the carpet below. None of them remembered how or when they got home. In the morning Budgen expected to be reprimanded for the mess, but when he came to work, not a trace of the party could be seen. The house-porter had heard them and quietly cleaned up the room after their departure. Only a number of pairs of big scissors, used for cutting articles from newspapers, were missing. Joyce had stuffed his pockets full of them with no explanation and taken them away. Doubtless he was tipsily preparing himself for the avalanche of reviews he hoped soon to have to clip. But the consulate had no sooner got under way than Giorgio arrived to return the missing items.[13]

Joyce's roistering with Budgen and Suter became so frequent that, as he told them one day, he quarreled with Nora about them. She said they were leading him into overdrinking. Budgen, who admired her very much, went at once to Joyce's flat to ask her to join them and discuss the question. Looking like Queen Victoria, she entered the café where they were sitting and rebuked them. While they were defending themselves, a prostitute entered the café, to Nora's intense annoyance. She wanted to leave at once but was coaxed into remaining. After this conference she was much pleasanter to Budgen and Suter and considered them friends.[14] Her signature appears among those at the bottom of a poem that Joyce indited to the absent Budgen one night:

To Budgen, Raughty Tinker

Oh! Budgen, boozer, bard, and canvas dauber,
If to thine eyes these lines should some time come
Bethink thee that the fleshpots of old Egypt

> Nothing avail if beauty's heart would beat;
> Wherefore forswear butter besmeared Ravioli
> Which do the mainsprings of thy talent clog
> On Roggenbrot, and Joghurt, and cold water
> Paint and be damned. We wait. Begin, and end.

> James Joyce
> Ethel Turner
> Nora Joyce
> W. H. Kerridge [15]

But if she indulged her husband's friends, Nora did not indulge him. One day in desperation at his drinking she suddenly informed him she had torn up his manuscript. Joyce became instantly sober, and remained so until he found the manuscript was intact.

Generally, as Budgen and Suter observed, Nora handled Joyce as if he were still half a child, and his book as if it were child's play of a rather disgusting kind. Once when they came to call she greeted them with the words, 'My husband is writing a book; I tell you [this for the benefit of Suter, whose English, like her German, was poor] *das Buch ist ein Schwein.*' [16] Joyce, on hearing this, smiled tolerantly and said, reaching for an issue of *Perl-Romane,* a sentimental periodical available at railway kiosks, 'And this is what my wife reads.' He said to Budgen on another occasion, 'Some people were up at our flat last night and we were talking about Irish wit and humor. And this morning my wife said to me, "What is all this about Irish wit and humor? Have we any book in the house with any of it in? I'd like to read a page or two." ' [17] He was always bewildered by her supreme indifference, and even aversion, to his writing. He summarized her special quality to Budgen, 'You know, you can see I am some sort of personality. I have an effect of some kind on people who come near me and know me and who are my friends. But my wife's personality is absolutely proof against any influence of mine.' [18]

Perhaps for this very reason Nora suited Joyce. She endured her husband's erratic life as graciously as possible, and endeavored only to moderate his frailties. Joyce was profoundly attached to her and to his children. He was especially fond of Lucia, whom he tended to spoil. Nora attempted to rear her more severely, and did not hesitate to spank Lucia or Giorgio when necessary; but Joyce, mindful of Father Daly's pandying which he had endured at Clongowes, never punished either child at all, and said, 'Children must be educated by love, not punishment.' [19]

Giorgio was becoming a tall and good-looking youngster. He was a champion swimmer at the two-mile distance. He had already shown a proficiency in singing as well, and Joyce, when he invited people to come to his flat, would say, 'Come early so you can hear Giorgio sing.' [20] Echoing his father's taste for Verdi, Giorgio sang airs from *Il Trovatore* and *Rigoletto*. He did not share his father's literary interests. One day Joyce said to Sykes, 'What was my son doing when you came in?' 'Reading,' said Sykes. 'My son with a book!' Joyce remarked in astonishment. Giorgio assured his father that he would never write anything so good as Wild West stories.

His schoolmates got on well with Giorgio. A couple of them (of whom one was Walter Ackermann,[21] later a famous flier), used to call him 'the Englishman,' but Giorgio would flare up at the name, asserting that he was no Englishman but an Irishman. He told them his father was a writer, and they asked what books he wrote. Giorgio answered that his father had been working on a book for five years and that it would take him another ten years or so to finish it. Then they wanted to know how his father earned his money. Giorgio replied that when there was no more money his father wrote to England and got a couple of hundred pounds from a lord.

One day he invited Ackermann and another boy to his home. They were eager to know what the habitation of a real writer looked like, but were disappointed, for it looked exactly like their own flats, and had neither rifles nor swords on the wall. It even smelled of cooking as their own homes did. Nora Joyce welcomed them kindly, and Giorgio played on the piano and sang to them. When they were going out they met what seemed to them 'an entirely black man' in the hall. He wore a black jacket, had a black goat's beard and black, bristly hair on his head. He shook hands with them and looked at them with his dark eyes from behind very thick glasses. Unable to bear this concentrated gaze, they left as quickly as they decently could, agreeing as they went down the stairs that Giorgio's father looked exactly like the devil. While the details of the picture were not accurate, the impression must have been genuine enough, for a landlady of the Joyces referred to him as 'Herr Satan.'

Although Joyce talked with Budgen and Suter about many things, he always came back to the book he was writing. Nora chided him at first for boring them, but seeing that they were not bored, she came to feel that perhaps there was something in this work after all. Budgen became Joyce's particular confidant; Joyce took full advantage of his friend's attentive mind. At their second meeting, as Budgen has told, Joyce announced to him that he was writing a book based on the Odyssey, but dealing with eighteen hours in the life of a contemporary man. He was at pains to point out to Budgen, as he had to Borach, the many-sided nature of his hero. 'You seem to have read a lot, Mr. Budgen,' he said. 'Do you know of any complete all-round character presented by any writer?' To Budgen's nomination of Christ Joyce objected, 'He was a bachelor, and never lived with a woman. Surely living with a woman is one of the most difficult things a man has to do, and he never did it.'

'What about Faust,' Budgen asked, 'or Hamlet?'

'Faust!' said Joyce. 'Far from being a complete man, he isn't a man at all. Is he an old man or a young man? Where are his home and family? We don't know. And he can't be complete because he's never alone. Mephistopheles is always hanging round him at his side or heels. We see a lot of him, that's all.'

'Your complete man in literature is, I suppose, Ulysses?'

'Yes,' said Joyce. 'No-age Faust isn't a man. But you mentioned Hamlet. Hamlet is a human being, but he is a son only. Ulysses is son to Laertes, but he is father to Telemachus, husband to Penelope, lover of Calypso, companion in arms of the Greek warriors around Troy, and King of Ithaca. He was subjected to many trials, but with wisdom and courage came through them all. Don't forget that he was a war dodger who tried to evade military service by simulating madness. He might never have taken up arms and gone to Troy, but the Greek recruiting sergeant was too clever for him and while he was ploughing the sands, placed young Telemachus in front of his plough. But once at the war the conscientious objector became a jusqu'au-boutist. When the others wanted to abandon the siege he insisted on staying till Troy should fall.' Then he went on, 'Another thing, the history of Ulysses did not come to an end when the Trojan war was over. It began just when the other Greek heroes went back to live the rest of their lives in peace. And then—' Joyce laughed—'he was the first gentleman in Europe. When he advanced, naked, to meet the young princess he hid from her maidenly eyes the parts that mattered of his brine-soaked, barnacle-encrusted body. He was an inventor too. The tank is his creation. Wooden horse or iron box— it doesn't matter. They are both shells containing armed warriors.'

'What do you mean,' said Budgen, 'by a complete man? For ex- ample, if a sculptor makes a figure of a man then that man is all-round, three-dimensional, but not necessarily complete in the sense of being ideal. All human bodies are imperfect, limited in some way, human beings too. Now your Ulysses....'

'He is both,' said Joyce. 'I see him from all sides, and therefore he is all-round in the sense of your sculptor's figure. But he is a com- plete man as well—a good man.' [22]

In subsequent conversations he emphasized to Suter and Budgen that Ulysses was not a god, for he had all the defects of the ordinary man, but was kindly. For Suter's benefit he would distinguish in German: 'Ulysses was not "gut" but "gutmütig" [decent]. Bloom is the same. If he does something mean or ignoble, he knows it and says, "I have been a perfect pig." ' [23]

Having denominated the type of his hero, Joyce proceeded to instruct Budgen in the book's rationale and technique. Writing a novel, he said, was like composing music, with the same elements involved. But how can chords or motifs be incorporated in writing? Joyce answered his own question, 'A man might eat kidneys in one chapter, suffer from a kidney disease in another, and one of his friends could be kicked in the kidney in another chapter.' [24] As a matter of fact, he announced, his book was to be among other things the epic of the human body. One organ or another would dominate each episode. To override the dichotomy of body and soul, to reveal their fundamental unity, he was displaying the mind's imagery under the influence of particular physical functions. For example, he cited Bloom's thought on his way to lunch, 'Molly's legs are out of plumb.' 'At another time of day,' he said, Bloom 'might have expressed the same thought without any underthought of food.' [25] Joyce was close to the new psychoanalysis at so many points that he always disavowed any interest in it. 'Why all this fuss and bother about the mystery of the unconscious?' he asked Budgen at the Pfauen one evening. 'What about the mystery of the conscious? What do they know about that?' [26] But he partly belied himself by the keen interest he took in the notebook Budgen kept to record his dreams; Joyce's interpretations showed the influence of Freud. He did not tell Budgen of a dream book he had kept in 1916, in which he had noted down Nora's dreams with his own interpretations:

1)   At a performance in the theatre
       A newly discovered play by Shakespeare
       Shakespeare is present
       There are two ghosts in the play.
       Fear that Lucia may be frightened.

Interpretation: I am perhaps behind this dream. The 'new discovery' is related to my theory of the ghost in Hamlet and the public sensation is related to a possible publication of that theory or of my own play. The figure of Shakespeare present in Elizabethan dress is a suggestion of fame, his certainly (it is the tercentenary of his death) mine not so certainly. The fear for Lucia (herself in little) is fear that either subsequent honours or the future

development of my mind or art or its extravagant excursions into forbidden
territory may bring unrest into her life.

2)   Lying alone on a hill
     A herd of silver cows
     A cow speaks, making love
     A mountain torrent
     Eileen appears
     The cow has died of its love

Interpretation: That silver seems to her a fine metal (and not a cheaper form
of gold) shows a freedom from conventional ideas, a freedom more strongly
shown by the fact that she feels no repulsion at being made love to by a
female beast. The cow is warm-bodied, soft-skinned and shining for she
expects elements of preciousness (Prezioso?) in her women. The suggestion
of the Italian word *vacca* with its connotations of easy morals is in the
neighbourhood and possibly, but much more remote, the old poetic name of
Ireland 'Silk of the Kine.' Here there is no fear either of goring or of pregnancy. An experience more in life and therefore not to be avoided. Eileen
appears as a messenger of those secret tidings which only women bear to
women and the silver mountain torrent, a precious and wild element, accompanies the secrecy of her messages with the magic of romance. That it has
died of love is an old story. Her lovers are all posting to death, death of the
flesh, death of youth, death of distance, of banishment or of a despair lit
only by her memory.

3)   Prezioso weeping
     I have passed him in the street
     My book 'Dubliners' in his hand

Interpretation: The motive of *Tutto è sciolto* played back to the front. The
point with which he tried to wound has been turned against him—by her: the
motive from which I liberated myself in art he is unable to liberate himself
from in life. Again a suffering and aging wooer. His complaint that I pass
him (it is to be read the other way round) is a secret disappointment that
for her so far it is impossible to unite the friendship of two men through the
gift of herself differently to both for that which seemed possible in the first
case is almost impossible in the second case.

4)   Fully dressed, shitting in her grandmother's garden
     Mary, her sister, bids the lover wait
     The lover has a puce face
     His hair in curling papers
     He is bald
     He sits outside a strange house.
     A woman no longer young is also there
     The woman puts her leg up
     Her cunt is hairless

Georgie passes smoking a cigarette
Anger
She follows him home
A quarrel about smoking with Eileen and Stannie
She screeches with anger
Her lover expects her to dinner *

Everything Joyce did or thought seemed to move in some way toward his book. The sculptor August Suter was rather irritated to see how Joyce seemed to stage-manage conversations as if to use his friends as subjects for experiment. Budgen and Paul Suter did not notice this or if they did, did not mind it. Sometimes Joyce entertained them by producing a miniature pair of drawers (he never accepted the word 'panties'), which appeared to exert the same fascination upon him that they do upon Bloom.† He scandalized a homosexual poet, to his friends' entertainment, by placing two fingers inside the drawers and walking them towards the unhappy poet. Once he said to Daniel Hummel, another friend, 'Human beings sometimes appear to me to take the shape of animals. Budgen, for example, is a beaver.' 'What am I?' asked Hummel. 'I've always thought of you as a calf,' Joyce answered without mercy. 'Thank you very much. And do you have an animal in mind for yourself?' 'Yes,' Joyce replied, 'a deer.' [27] He was thinking of his old image of himself as the hunted quarry, which appears comically in the pursuit of Bloom at the end of the *Cyclops* episode.

Almost every day he had a problem or solution to talk about. Once he announced to Suter that he had found an analogy for the Argonautic pigeon which flies safely between the Clashing Rocks: it was the throwaway which is cast by Bloom into the Liffey to float successfully between the North and South walls. The finny tails of the sirens he found equivalent to the dirty skirts and shoes worn by barmaids because these articles of clothing didn't show above the counter. He asked Budgen what he might use as correspondences in the other senses to the sense of absolute pitch in music. Budgen suggested the sense of value in painting, but Joyce dismissed this as creative rather than passive. Then Budgen suggested tea-tasting, an idea which pleased Joyce, who said, 'I shall probably use that.' [28] But in the *Sirens* epi-

---

* Joyce offers no interpretation of this dream, but it suggests the transvestism, coprophilia, and cuckoldry which pursue at moments the thoughts of Bloom and of his creator.
† When Budgen was writing his book on *James Joyce and the Making of Ulysses,* Joyce urged him to treat 'Le Manteau de Tanit,' that is, female drawers, 'with IMMENSE seriousness, respect, circumspection, historical sense, critical acumen, documentary accuracy, citational erudition and sweet reasonableness.' [29]

sode, as Budgen points out, he uses instead Molly Bloom's comprehension of the hurdy-gurdy boy without understanding a word of his language. 'Gift of nature,' Bloom comments on it. For the *Sirens* episode Joyce quizzed Philipp Jarnach one day about sirens, from those who inhabit Mediterranean rocks to those that are found in factories.[30] He hoped, as a rule, not so much to obtain the right answer from a friend as to stimulate his own imagination. As he said to Budgen, 'Have you ever noticed, when you get an idea, how much *I* can make of it?'[31] Since the material of *Ulysses* was all human life, every man he met was an authority, and Joyce carried dozens of small slips of paper in his wallet and loose in his pockets to make small notes. When he had filled up the front and back of these, he continued to write on them diagonally. At home he would decipher his notes with a magnifying glass, a hint of what he had written being usually enough.

One preoccupation that never ceased to be fundamental to him was fidelity to fact. He had a pointed illustration one day for Budgen [*] and Suter, telling them: 'A German lady called to see me today. She is a writer and wanted me to give an opinion on her work, but she told me she had already shown it to the porter of the hotel where she stays. So I said to her, "What did your hotel porter think of your work?" She said, "He objected to a scene in my novel where my hero goes out into the forest, finds a locket of the girl he loves, picks it up and kisses it passionately." "But," I said, "that seems to me to be a very pleasing and touching incident. What did your hotel porter find wrong with it?" And then she tells me he said, "It's all right for the hero to find the locket and to pick it up and kiss it, but before he kissed it you should have made him wipe the dirt off it with his coat sleeve." '

'And what did you tell her?' his friends asked.

'I told her,' said Joyce, 'and I meant it too, to go back to that hotel porter and always to take his advice. "That man," I said, "is a critical genius. There is nothing I can tell you that he can't tell you." '[32]

While Joyce worked indefatigably every day on his book, regardless of hangovers, he also kept the fortunes of the English Players in mind. Their continued existence was a matter of great concern to him, especially as the consulate's hostility became more open. In May Sykes prepared to follow up their first success with a production of Chesterton's *Magic*. He found two new actors, one English and one

---

[*] Budgen tells the story in his extremely interesting book, *James Joyce and the Making of Ulysses* (London and New York, 1934; reprinted Bloomington, Indiana, 1960).

American; but after rehearsals had started both suddenly withdrew. The consulate had evidently represented the enterprise as obnoxious to English and American interests. Sykes refused to yield, and got together a triple bill for which the smaller company would be sufficient. The plays were to be Barrie's *The Twelve Pound Look,* Synge's *Riders to the Sea,* and Shaw's *The Dark Lady of the Sonnets.* Joyce had no interest in Barrie, and considered Shaw a mountebank.[33] As for Synge's play, Joyce's objection to the nature of the tragedy, which he had made to Synge in Paris sixteen years before, remained in the still guarded program note which he composed for the performance: 'Whether a brief tragedy be possible or not (a point on which Aristotle had some doubts) the ear and the heart mislead one gravely if this brief scene from "poor Aran" be not the work of a tragic poet.' He took special interest in Synge's play because he persuaded Nora to play a minor role. She had never acted before and was timid at first, but her rich contralto voice, with its strong Galway accent, gradually acquired confidence. Joyce trained the other actors to imitate her speech and the Aran speech rhythms. He also charged himself with the publicity, and wrote to Borach, among others, to come, saying: *'Je vous envoie un autre programme, que j'ai arrangé. J'ai un peu d'énergie n'est-ce pas? Malheureusement la caisse est basse comme les valeurs des empires (pardon!) républiques centrales. TOUT POUR L'ART!* * [34]

While plans for the triple bill were maturing, Joyce's iritis began again, this time in both eyes, and he was almost incapacitated. The operation of the previous year for glaucoma had not succeeded in preventing this recurrence. It was an especially unfortunate time to become ill, for his pain reduced the pleasure he would otherwise have taken in the publication of *Exiles* on May 25, 1918, by Richards in England and by Huebsch in the United States. It also exacerbated his irritation over the Carr affair, which came up for a preliminary hearing on June 8. Carr's attorney, Dr. Georg Wettstein, who was Norwegian Vice-Consul in Zurich, was known to Joyce, for Joyce had done some translating for him in February 1918. Wettstein implied that his client was willing to drop his suit if Joyce would compensate him for his clothing. Carr denied that he had called Joyce either 'cad' or 'swindler.' But Joyce refused to give way, and insisted on continuing the suit. In a minor harassing action, Bennett, the consul-general, wrote Sykes on June 11 and June 22 to ask if he was prepared to enlist. On June 14 Joyce's lawyer Konrad Bloch sent the court a list of the witnesses who would

---

* 'I send you another programme that I've set up. I do have a bit of energy, don't I? Unfortunately the cash box is low like the bonds of central European empires (excuse me!) republics. ALL FOR ART!'

be called to testify; it contained the names of Bennett, Smith, and Gann. The next move was the consulate's: a letter was sent Joyce, asking him in the most peremptory manner, with more than a hint of blacklisting him if he refused, to volunteer for military duty. Joyce sent the letter back with the curt notation: 'James Joyce presents his compliments to the B. M. Consul General and returns a document addressed to him in error.'[35] As he described this gesture later, 'In July 1918 when I lay dangerously ill and in danger of blindness Mr. Consul Bennett wrote me a registered letter inviting me to compound a felony with him * and threatening to penalise me if I refused to do so. Of this document I declined in courteous terms to take service.'[36] His fury against the British became unbounded; he praised the German offensive, changed his daily newspaper from the pro-Allied *Neue Zürcher Zeitung* to the pro-German *Zürcher Post*, and often expressed his pleasure at the difficulties the British were having in Ireland.[37]

So matters rested when the triple bill was presented on June 17 at the Pfauen Theatre,[38] with Nora performing brilliantly and the players scoring another hit. The consulate officials had boycotted the production, but unsuccessfully; they now made themselves felt again. Bennett informed the court through Wettstein on July 1 that Joyce had included his name among the witnesses only from spite, since he had not been present at the conversation. The allegation was no doubt true. Four days later Bennett, Smith, and Gann refused to appear before the court, claiming that consular officials were exempt from interrogation, not because the consulate was extraterritorial (which it was not), but because the sale of tickets was for patronage and propaganda and therefore a consular preserve. The argument was shaky but the court withheld decision, sending the matter to the ministry at Bern for consideration. It was eventually decided against Bennett. Meanwhile the trial of the first suit, for money owed by Carr for tickets, was set for July 8, but Joyce had to ask for a postponement because of a violent attack of iritis, the genuineness of which his doctor attested. The attack receded quickly enough, however, for him to go a week later as far as Lausanne with the English Players who, with a new Algernon named Charles Pusey, were touring Lausanne, Geneva, Montreux, and Interlaken. His eye trouble ended temporarily on July 29, but recurred in late October and November.

Whenever the pains of iritis let up, Joyce went on with *Ulysses*, struggling to keep up with the *Little Review* installments. The regularity he was able to maintain can be seen in the following table:

---

* A reference to the necessity of breaking his promise to the Austrian officials in Trieste that he would remain neutral for the duration of the war.

Episode		Date of Completion	Date of Publication
I	Telemachus	To Sykes in November 1917	March 1918
II	Nestor	To Sykes in December 1917	April 1918
III	Proteus	To Sykes in December 1917 *	May 1918
IV	Calypso	To Pound in March 1918	June 1918
V	Lotus-Eaters	April (?) 1918	July 1918
VI	Hades	To Pound in May 1918	September 1918
VII	Aeolus	To Pound in August 1918	October 1918
VIII	Lestry-gonians	To Pound October 25, 1918	Jan.-Feb.-Mar. 1919
IX	Scylla and Charybdis	October 1918–February 1919 †	April-May 1919
X	Wandering Rocks	To Pound February 1919	June-July 1919
XI	Sirens	June 1919	Aug.-Sept. 1919
XII	Cyclops		November 1919-March 1920
XIII	Nausicaa	Begun Zurich in fall, 1919 to Budgen in February or March 1920	April-August 1920
XIV	Oxen of the Sun	To Pound in October 1919; rewritten May 18, 1920	September-December 1920
XV	Circe	To Pound in April 1921; written June 1920–December 1920	
XVI	Eumaeus	February 1921	
XVII	Ithaca	February-October 1921	
XVIII	Penelope	January or February-October 1921 (before Ithaca) ‡	

The *Little Review* continued to publish *Ulysses,* although the threat of post office prosecution drew steadily closer. The book was making an impression, and occasionally it was mentioned in the reviews. T. S. Eliot, writing in the *Athenaeum* for July 4, 1919, about a new book of Yeats, remarked, 'Crudity and egoism' are 'justified by exploitation to the point of greatness, in the later work of Mr. James Joyce.' Ezra Pound, also sensing crudity, tried to persuade Joyce to abolish Bloom's flatulence and other questionable elements in the book. In a letter dated Good Friday, 1918, he said some accommodation must be made to legal

---

* Herbert Gorman says Joyce had gone as far as the phrase 'kidneys of wheat,' *Ulysses* (41 [37]), before leaving Trieste.[39]
† Joyce's manuscript which he sold to John Quinn has a note at the end of *Scylla and Charybdis:* 'End of first part of *Ulysses,* New Year's Eve, 1918.'
‡ This table is mainly the work of Walton Litz, who has kindly authorized its use here.

authorities, but added hopefully, 'Perhaps an unexpurgated text of you can be printed in a greek or bulgarian translation later.' He was worried about Joyce's 'arsthetic' obsession, as he called it, yet otherwise Bloom roused him to enthusiasm. So on November 22, 1918, he wrote, 'Bloom is a great man, and you have almightily answered the critics who asked me whether having made Stephen, more or less autobiography, you could ever go on and create a second character. . . .'

In London Miss Weaver continued to look for a printer willing to set the episodes for serial publication in the *Egoist*, but she had no luck until early in 1919, when one printer was prevailed upon to do a few episodes (II, III, VI, and X) only. She informed Joyce through Pinker, in March 1918, that she wished to publish *Ulysses* in book form, and Joyce replied on March 20 that he would be pleased, 'though I am sure it is in more senses than one a Greek gift.' The possibility of having it published in a more regular way came up again in June 1918, when Roger Fry suggested Miss Weaver call on Leonard and Virginia Woolf to induce them to publish the book at their new Hogarth Press. Virginia Woolf noted in her diary the incongruous appearance of Miss Weaver as the 'buttoned-up' and wool-gloved missionary for a book that 'reeled with indecency.' The Woolfs told her they could not print it because it would take two years on their handpress, though they said they were very much interested in the first four episodes which they read. Actually they seem to have regarded it as 'underbred,' though Katherine Mansfield, who looked at the manuscript one day while paying them a visit, began by ridiculing it and then suddenly said, 'But there's something in this: a scene that should figure I suppose in the history of literature.' [40]

Joyce continued to hope for the production of *Exiles*, which was receiving a good press. Arthur Clutton-Brock reviewed it in a long, laudatory article in the *Times Literary Supplement* of July 25, 1918, suggesting the Stage Society produce it, but they still could not agree to do so. Joyce afterwards blamed Bernard Shaw for preventing acceptance,[41] but apparently without direct evidence. Desmond McCarthy spoke well of the play in the *New Statesman* on September 21, and Joyce's friend Silvio Benco wrote a favorable article in the Trieste journal *Umana*, on July 6. A new adherent was Stefan Zweig, who showed great interest in *Exiles*,* and may have been instrumental in securing

---

* Zweig wrote to Joyce:

Rüschlikon bei Zürich   12 September 1918
Hotel Belvoir

Dear Sir, Your book arrived in a good moment. I had just finished in these days a new work of mine, my mind was quite free for new impressions and your piece (which I read in two following nights) was for me a great artistic

a German translator, Hannah von Mettal, for it, and later in having it produced in Munich. A troupe in Dublin seemed about to present the play at the end of 1918, but the plan came to nothing. As for the English Players, they had no one to play Richard Rowan; Joyce suggested Sykes, but Sykes said he could not play the lead and direct as well. In turn Sykes proposed that Joyce take the role, but Joyce refused; [42] he seems to have identified himself too closely with the hero to wish to appear before the public in the part. He asked Paul Suter one day whether he thought Bertha in the play was unfaithful or not, and Suter, perceiving that Joyce was uneasy about his answer, avoided giving one.[43]

The Players started the fall season boldly by presenting their second Shaw play, *Mrs. Warren's Profession*, which was still banned in England. This performance, on September 30, was followed by the first trial

revelation. Excuse me, if I give you not in detail the extract of my gratitude: I am nearly in the same situation in belong to English language like you to German, I read it perfectly, have even a fairly developed sense for the refinements of the language, but quite out of exercise since several years, I am a little ashamed to explain my sentiments and ideas in a scolars way, who just learned the language without to possess her. So I would be very glad to make your personal acquaintance and if possible, become known also with your other books: unfortunately I cannot render the service for the moment, car [for] the only two books of mine, which are translated in English (my book on Verhaeren at Constable & Comp, London 1914, and my book on Verlaine, New York 1912) are not in my possession now and I do not even know, if there is any possibility to get them here during the war.

I have the intention to stay here at Rüschlikon the whole winter, but Tuesday I make a fortnights trip to the lake of Geneve and before my time is very scarce, I would be delighted to see you as soon as possible, but do you not mean it would be better to meet each other not in the hurry of a departure? I have a very strong impression of your work and all what I can do for it on the German stage shall be done: I am sure, that after the war a translation could be placed *immediately* on a first theatre. We will talk after my journey from all that: today I render you (not willingly, but with much regret) your copy and hope soon to have the good chance to meet you. If you prefer I come to Zurich or you to my more distant and quiet place. Many thanks and good greetings from

                                        yours sincere
                                        Stefan Zweig

In his autobiography, *The World of Yesterday* (New York, 1943), p. 276, Zweig wrote sensitively of Joyce: 'He was inclined to be testy, and I believe that just that irritation produced the power for his inner turmoil and productivity. His resentment against Dublin, against England, against particular persons became converted into dynamic energy and actually found release only in literary creation. But he seemed fond of his own asperity; I never saw him laugh or show high spirits. He always made the impression of a compact, somber force and when I saw him on the street, his thin lips pressed tightly together, always walking rapidly as if heading for a definite objective, I sensed the defensive, the inner isolation of his being even more positively than in our talks. It failed to astonish me when I later learned that just this man had written the most solitary, the least affined work—meteor-like in its introduction to the world of our time.'

in Joyce's legal battle against Carr, won handily on October 15. The court declared his claim for 25 francs due on tickets was valid; it rejected Carr's counterclaims for salary and expenses, on the ground that he had agreed to act for nothing, and that his clothes were not stage costumes but ordinary wearing apparel capable of further use. Carr had to pay court costs of over 39 francs, and to pay Joyce 60 francs for his trouble and expenses.[44] Joyce celebrated this victory by a song to the tune of 'Tipperary':

The C.G.* Is Not Literary

Up to rheumy Zurich came an Irishman one day,
And as the town was rather dull he thought he'd give a play,
So that the German propagandists might be rightly riled,
But the bully British Philistine once more drove Oscar Wilde.

CHORUS: Oh, the C.G. is not literary,
          And his handymen are rogues.
          The C.G.'s about as literary
          As an Irish kish of brogues.
          We have paid up all expenses
          As the good Swiss Public knows,
          But we'll be damned well damned before we pay for
          Private † Carr's swank hose.

When the play was over Carr with rage began to dance,
Saying I want twenty quid for them there dandy pants,
So fork us out the tin or Comrade Bennett here and me,
We're going to wring your bloody necks, we're out for liberty.

CHORUS: As before.

They found a Norse solicitor to prove that white was black,
That one can boss in Switzerland beneath the Union Jack;
They went off to the Gerichtshof, but came back like Jack and Jill
For the pants came tumbling after, and the judge is laughing still.

CHORUS: Oh, the C.G. is not literary,
          And his handymen are rogues.
          The C.G.'s about as literary
          As an Irish kish of brogues
          So farewell, bruiser Bennett,
          And goodbye, Chummy Carr,
          If you put a beggar up on horseback,
          Why 'e dunno where 'e are.

---

* Consul-General.

† The special slur here was that Carr had let it be thought he was an army officer when in reality he was a soldier.

Joyce made a more serious statement of his position to Georges Borach six days after the first trial. He told him on October 21, 1918, 'As an artist, I attach no importance to political conformity. Consider: Renaissance Italy gave us the greatest artists. The Talmud says at one point, "We Jews are like the olive: we give our best when we are being crushed, when we are collapsing under the burden of our foliage." Material victory is the death of spiritual preëminence. Today we see in the Greeks of antiquity the most cultured nation. Had the Greek state not perished, what would have become of the Greeks? Colonizers and merchants.' He went on to explain, 'As an artist I am against every state. Of course I must recognize it, since indeed in all my dealings I come into contact with its institutions. The state is concentric, man is eccentric. Thence arises an eternal struggle. The monk, the bachelor, and the anarchist are in the same category. Naturally I can't approve of the act of the revolutionary who tosses a bomb in a theatre to destroy the king and his children. On the other hand, have those states behaved any better which have drowned the world in a blood-bath?'[45]

On a more trivial level the English Players, heartened by the decision against Carr, and amused by Joyce's song of victory, next began rehearsals on a play of Sykes's choosing, which Joyce thought mere commercialism, *Hindle Wakes* by Stanley Houghton. But the war intruded upon even Zurich's dramatic life. Before the Armistice was signed on November 11, the German revolution spread to Switzerland and caused a general strike. The cantonal government divided Zurich into sections and filled it with mountain troops who disliked the Zurichers and could be depended upon to enforce order. Each night the English Players, who generally rehearsed at the flat of Mrs. Turner, had to make their way on foot past wary sentinels. The city's disruption, and the influenza epidemic which took the life of one member of the cast, delayed production of the play until December 3, and it lost money. Joyce then thought of a new way of attracting a polyglot audience instead of just an English-speaking one; he proposed they give three short plays, in Italian, French, and English. Accordingly he coached some amateur Italian actors in Felice Cavallotti's *Il Cantico dei Cantici;* two actors from the Théâtre-Français of Zurich gave Banville's *Le Baiser;* and the English Players presented Browning's *In a Balcony*. The performance took place on December 11, 1918. Joyce sang Giovanni Stefani's song, '*Amante Tradito,*' behind the scenes just after the curtain rose on Browning's play, and his friend Ruggiero accompanied him on a guitar which Joyce lent and afterwards gave him.[46]

Meanwhile Joyce wrote to the Prime Minister, Lloyd George, to ask his help in the dispute with Consul-General Bennett. The secretary to the Prime Minister replied politely but vaguely on October 10, 1918, to wish the Players every success. Then Joyce wrote on November 30 to Sir Horace Rumbold, British Minister to Bern, to complain that the Players had been boycotted by Bennett since May 1. He asked grandly for 'that protection and redress from the insult of violence which are the right and the privilege of the least of His Majesty's subjects,' [47] but neither was forthcoming. The second case against Carr began to go badly; Carr had left Switzerland, and Joyce's evidence was unsupported. On December 6 Joyce's lawyer asked that the preliminary hearing, scheduled for the following day, be postponed to make possible a settlement out of court; Wettstein however insisted that it proceed. Smith testified that he had not heard Carr utter any of the words alleged; Sykes testified to Joyce's version of the quarrel, but had to admit he was not himself present at it. Rawson testified that Carr had told him of ordering Joyce out of the consulate, but had not specified what epithets he used. Joyce's case sounded very thin at this hearing [48] and his lawyer despaired of it and wanted to drop it. Joyce refused.

He did, however, acknowledge that his jousting with the consulate was detrimental to the English Players, and he withdrew from them so that they might reconcile themselves with the consulate. But their luck had turned. The new business manager mismanaged; the reconciliation with the consulate never took place; and the financial difficulties of the Players increased. It was perhaps as well that just at this moment Joyce's interests shifted in a remarkable way.

◇◆◇

1918–1919

MARTHA

(Thickveiled, a crimson halter round her neck, a copy of the *Irish
Times* in her hand, in tone of reproach, pointing.) Henry! Leopold!
Leopold! Lionel, thou lost one! Clear my name. . . . (Sobbing behind
her veil.) Breach of promise. My real name is Peggy Griffin. He wrote
to me that he was miserable. I'll tell my brother, the Bective rugger
fullback, on you, heartless flirt.

—*Ulysses* (448)

EARLY in December, 1918, Joyce was going home to his flat at 29
Universitätstrasse ° when he observed a young woman walking
ahead of him. She moved with a slight limp, her head held high. As
she turned to enter a house he saw her face, and his own was lit up—
as she discreetly noted—'*mit grösstem Erstaunen.*' † ¹ For it seemed to
Joyce that he was seeing again the girl he had seen in 1898 by the
strand, wading in the Irish Sea with her skirts tucked up. That girl had
appeared to him like a vision of secular beauty, a pagan Mary beckoning him to the life of art which knows no distinction of spirit and body.
The sight of this woman who looked so much like her—for she was not
of course the same—struck Joyce as of equal talismanic significance.
His passion for coincidence impelled him towards a passion for her.

He spent his time watching for her—she lived at 6 Culmannstrasse,
around the corner from the Universitätstrasse. She was aware of his
presence but pretended to ignore it. Then he wrote her a passionate
letter in French (his French being better than his German), asking her
to cease to disregard him, confessing he did not even know her name
but found her astonishingly like the girl he had seen in Ireland sixteen
years before. She will not mind, he hopes, if he suggests that perhaps
she is Jewish, though she may not be, for after all Jesus lay in the womb

---

° He had moved there in October 1918.
† 'With great amazement.'

462

of a Jewish mother. As for himself, he is a writer, and at a pivotal moment in his life: his age is the same as Dante's when he began the *Divine Comedy,* and as Shakespeare's when he fell in love with the Dark Lady of the Sonnets. He is very unhappy; he must see her.[2] So began an episode in Joyce's life which is almost as moving as it is comic.

The young woman whom he saw was a Swiss named Marthe Fleischmann, the first of two Fleischmanns to be prominent in his life. On her mother's side Marthe was descended from the Bernese gentry, and prided herself on her aristocratic bearing. Her father was from an ordinary middle-class family, and she had only to remember this undercutting of her noble origins to grow distressed. A few years before Joyce met her she had become, by a romantic series of events, the mistress of an engineer, Rudolf Hiltpold. The affair began on a *Sächselüte* day. She was watching the pageantry in the Bahnhofstrasse when Hiltpold, whom she did not know, came riding by at the head of the fashionable *Kämbelzunft* (Camel Guild). He carried a bouquet of red roses, and when he caught sight of Marthe, instead of following the usual custom of tossing a rose or two at a handsome girl, he paid her the pretty compliment of flinging his whole bouquet at her feet. She did not see him again until the next year at the same festival. Standing then on a balcony, she saw him riding past again, this time alone, on his way to join his guild. He caught sight of her, dismounted, and talked with her; they exchanged letters and before long she had broken off an engagement with another man and was occupying a flat next to Hiltpold's. Later on she moved into the same flat.[3]

Marthe did not work; she spent her days smoking, reading romantic novels, and primping. She was vain and wished to be snobbish. When she realized that Joyce was in some way distinguished, she wrote to him, and they began a correspondence that was kept from both Nora's eyes and Hiltpold's. Joyce's attitude toward her was full of his old romanticism with one curious exception: he signed his letters to her with Greek *e*'s instead of Roman *e*'s in the name James Joyce. It seems unlikely that he could have supposed that this slight graphic change would be of any use in a court test of handwriting; it could have meant to him little more than a sign that he was reserving part of himself in the correspondence, amusing himself with his own folly. In *Ulysses* Marthe Fleischmann is one of the prototypes of the limping Gerty MacDowell, whom Bloom ogles from a distance, and in part the prototype of Bloom's penpal Martha Clifford, to whom, as Joyce emphasizes, Bloom is always careful to write with Greek *e*'s. Joyce evidently felt himself a little absurd in yielding to his rhapsodical inclination; but he yielded to it nonetheless.

His mood in the affair—if the word can be applied to so uncommitted a relationship—was probably like that in the poem, 'Bahnhofstrasse,' written in Zurich in 1918. It was on this street that Joyce had his glaucoma attack in 1917, and the poem embodies his recognition of the ageing process—his eyes its symptom, and of the impossibility of recovering youth and young love:

> *Bahnhofstrasse*
>
> The eyes that mock me sign the way
> Whereto I pass at eve of day.
>
> Grey way whose violet signals are
> The trysting and the twining star.
>
> Ah star of evil! star of pain!
> Highhearted youth comes not again
>
> Nor old heart's wisdom yet to know
> The signs that mock me as I go.

He saw Marthe as often as he could. Like Bloom peeping on the strand, he eyed her from the street as she moved about her sitting room. A second letter begged her to see him, and eventually, with suitable archness, she did. That sexual intercourse took place between them is problematic; Marthe liked to be looked at, not embraced, so that Hiltpold kept other mistresses at the same time that he maintained her in his flat, and in later life she always sugared over her intrigue with Joyce as '*eine Platonische Liebe.*' [4] The parallel relationship of Bloom and Martha Clifford also suggests that this Nausicaa wished to arouse but not requite desire. The affair could hardly have got far: Hiltpold was vigilant, Marthe extremely coy, Joyce shy and ailing. His association with Marthe occupied his mind from December 9, 1918, to March 28, 1919 (the date when he gave her the German translation of *Exiles*),[5] but he was more onlooker than lover, and a looker with pathetically blurred vision to boot. Yet it was a final burgeoning of his desire for dark, unknown, passionate, preferably Semitic women who would envelop him in their arms. Marthe Fleischmann took for these months the place that Amalia Popper had occupied.

On February 2, 1919, his birthday, Joyce prepared a strange ritual to celebrate Candlemas, which also falls on that day. He wrote a letter to Marthe Fleischmann, dating it *Marias Lichtmesse*. A day or two before he had sent her a copy of *Chamber Music*, and from his vantage point on the street had watched her self-consciously take it from the letter box and sit down to read it. He hoped this evidence of his dis-

Joyce in Zurich, about 1917. (Croessmann Collection) *Courtesy of Southern Illinois University Library*

Nora Joyce in Zurich. *Courtesy of University of Buffalo Library*

Joyce's friend Frank Budgen in Zurich. (p. 442) *Courtesy of Frank Budgen*

XI

Marthe Fleischmann and her 'guardian' Rudolf Hiltpold in Zurich, about
1918. (p. 462) *Courtesy of Frau Walter Bollmann*

XII

tinction would win her favor, and it did. She gave some indication that she would be willing to see him on the evening of February 2, and early that day Joyce went to Rudolf Goldschmidt and asked for the loan of a handsome ceremonial candlestick, lighted during the Jewish festival of Chanukah, and so appropriate to his first impression of Marthe. That evening he called for her and brought her over to Frank Budgen's studio; on the pretext that the light there was poor he lit the candlestick so she might be seen at once more clearly and more ceremoniously. He told Budgen that he had explored the coldest and hottest parts of a woman's body. A day or two later a friend, who had heard from Goldschmidt of the curious loan, asked Joyce what he had borrowed it for; Joyce replied a little shamefacedly, '*Per una serata nera*' ('For a black mass').[6] After this evening of Marthe's illumination, they did not meet again for a long time. They did, however, exchange letters.

These reached a comic stop a few months later. Joyce received a sudden communication from Marthe Fleischmann's lover, or as she preferred to call him, her guardian (*Vormund*), Rudolf Hiltpold. Marthe, who suffered from nervous attacks, had been away in a sanitarium; on her return she informed Hiltpold of her clandestine correspondence, and hysterically blamed Joyce for her state of mind. Joyce sent Budgen, who was away on a holiday, an account of the latest developments on June 19:

> Private. This morning a threatening violent letter from Mr Vormund. The sister has been dying. M— in a madhouse or Nervenanstalt but now back again threatening suicide. Gave him all my correspondence. Violent gestures towards me. I did not know she was back nor have I seen her since the feast of candles. Well, I got up and went to the Lion's Den. Long interview wherein I displayed all that suave human diplomacy, that goodness of heart, that understanding of others, that timidity which yet is courage, those shining qualities of heart and head which have so often . . .* Result; stasis: Waffenstillstand. Mem. No allusion to this in your reply which I expect confidently twenty years after.
>   J. J.

In spite of this man-of-the-world tone Joyce was not one to forget any woman for whom he had felt strong emotion, and Marthe swam vaporously again into his life later on. Her haughty, naughty beguilements also helped him in composing the episode *Nausicaa*.

Shortly after his thirty-seventh birthday, Joyce took part in another dramatic episode, this time as litigant rather than as lover. His second suit against Carr, for libel, came to trial on February 11, 1919. Dr. Bloch,

---

* Joyce's ellipsis.

Private

Letter about Marthe Fleischmann from Joyce to Budgen, June 19, 1919.

Joyce's lawyer, had urged him to withdraw it, since with no witness but himself he could not hope for a favorable verdict. At first Joyce stubbornly persisted, but at last agreed to let Bloch withdraw the suit. In giving his version of the events afterwards he implied that Bloch had been influenced by the sinister hand of British authority, but this notion was unfounded. Bloch asked the court to cancel the indemnification ordinarily payable to the defendant in such a case, on the grounds that Carr had caused the quarrel and had needlessly prolonged the proceedings by his appeal to extra-territorial privileges. Carr's attorney, Wettstein, insisted on damages, and the judge ruled that Joyce should bear the court costs of 59 francs and damages of 120 francs.[7] Joyce avoided paying them then, and refused to pay them afterwards, so that the case was not yet quite over.

It was an appropriate coincidence that in February, with Marthe luring from one direction and Carr glowering from the other, he should have been working on the *Scylla and Charybdis* episode. For this he drew upon his lecture on *Hamlet* in Trieste, supplemented by a good deal of further reading. He then decided to add an episode not in Homer, the *Wandering Rocks*, based upon the voyage of the Argonauts; his purpose was to bring the city of Dublin even more fully into the book by focusing upon it rather than upon Bloom or Stephen. From there he went on to the *Sirens* episode. He wrote Miss Weaver on February 25, 1919, of his literary progress and its impedimenta:

Dear Miss Weaver:

I ought to apologise for my impossible health which so often obliges me to appear discourteous. I enclose some press notices of my play *Exiles* of which you were so good as to write favorably. I appreciate very much your friendly words about the Scylla-Charybdis episode of my book *Ulysses* but am sorry that it deprived you of sleep. On most other readers I daresay it will have the contrary effect. I sent some days ago the Wandering Rocks episode to Mr. Pound who is ill also. If he has not sent it to you could you write to him. As soon as I am able to work again I shall finish the Sirens and send it. I am much better this evening but my eyes are so capricious that I may be ill tomorrow. This time the attack was in my 'good?' eye so that the decisive symptoms of iritis never really set in. It has been light but intermittent so that for five weeks I could do little or nothing except lie constantly near a stove like a chimpanzee whom in many things I resemble. I received a copy of *The Egoist* with the second episode. I hope I shall be able to finish the book this year or early next year. It is as difficult for me to write it as for my readers to read it. I asked Mr. Chalas * to convey my thanks

---

* A Zurich friend.

to Mr [Richard] Aldington and would ask you to convey my excuses to Mr [Wyndham] Lewis. Two notices of his book *Tarr* were promised me but neither has appeared. As soon as I begin to go about I shall try to push the matter. One was sent to a Dutch review eighteen months ago and published last week! Mr [Carlo] Linati wrote to me during my illness and I shall write to him if the Italo-Swiss frontier is open now. I must not omit to thank you for your prompt remittance of royalties in December. It was very useful to me. I hope that wretched book some day will repay you even in part for all the trouble it has caused you.

> With renewed thanks and kind regards
> Sincerely yours
> James Joyce

25.ii.919

The eye trouble continued, but did not greatly impede his bustling about with several new projects. He persuaded the authorities of the Municipal Theatre to stage Purcell's opera, *Dido and Aeneas,* but the plan collapsed because the Consulate would have nothing to do with a project with which Joyce was associated. Resilient, Joyce next advised Sykes to present as the new offering of the English Players *The Heather Field* by Edward Martyn. This play, which Joyce remembered from its first performance in Dublin in 1899, was a precursor of *Exiles,* and Joyce wrote in the program note: 'Edward Martyn . . . is an accomplished musician and man of letters. As a dramatist he follows the school of Ibsen and therefore occupies a unique position in Ireland, as the dramatists writing for the National Theatre have chiefly devoted their energies to peasant drama. . . .' But, with the impartiality which had led him to lecture on both Defoe and Blake in Trieste, he urged Sykes also to stage a play in another tradition, Yeats's *The Land of Heart's Desire;* Sykes could not find a proper cast for it. In April the Players put on *The Mollusc* of Hubert Henry Davies, which Joyce disapproved of as vulgar.[8] During the boring second act, he made off with Budgen to the men's lavatory where he successfully perpetrated his old dodge of having drinks sent up without Nora's knowing.[9]

He was sensitive enough to her complaints, however, to decide to give up absinthe, which he liked very much, in favor of wine. He did not care for red wine, which he said was 'beefsteak,' and greatly preferred white, which was 'electricity.'[*] Several evenings were spent in tasting various *crus,* until one night drinking with Ottocaro Weiss, who had returned from the army in January 1919, he sampled a white Swiss

---

[*] Carola Giedion-Welcker told him once that she liked Burgundy; he replied by asking, 'Do you drink beefsteak?'

wine called Fendant de Sion. This seemed to be the object of his quest, and after drinking it with satisfaction, he lifted the half-emptied glass, held it against the window like a test tube, and asked Weiss, 'What does this remind you of?' Weiss looked at Joyce and at the pale golden liquid and replied, '*Orina*.' '*Si*,' said Joyce laughing, '*ma di un'arciduchessa*' ('Yes, but an archduchess's'). From now on the wine was known as the Archduchess, and is so celebrated in *Finnegans Wake*.* Joyce never became the connoisseur of wines that he fancied himself, but he delighted in them and said, 'I'd like to have seven tongues and put them all in my cheek at once.' [10]

In April Joyce learned that, since he refused to pay costs and damages in the Carr case, the court would have to proceed against him by distraint. This news capped his dubious conviction that the incident was a symbol of the hounding of art by authority. He resolved to make his plight known to the world, and in late April and early May dispatched to James Pinker and the British Foreign Office in London, to Curran in Dublin, to the two chief delegates of the Irish-American mission in Paris (who might make it a political issue), and to B. W. Huebsch and Padraic Colum in New York, copies of a lengthy statement about the affair. Without directly asking for financial help he made clear that this was necessary, saying that 10,000 francs were at stake. The large sum, several times what was actually involved, lent the circumstances a gravity which they would otherwise have lacked. Pinker refused to circulate the bill of complaint,[11] but Colum and his wife began at once to try to raise money.

While he was waiting to hear from his friends, and perhaps in anticipation of the bailiff's call, Joyce went off with Frank Budgen to Locarno for a few days, from May 8 to May 14. The visit did no more than postpone his judicial difficulties, but it gave him some excellent material for the *Sirens* episode, on which he was working, and even more for the *Circe* episode. He had heard of a Baroness St. Leger who lived and made dolls on the Isola da Brissago in the Lago Maggiore. She was rumored to have 'tearlessly buried' seven husbands there, and admitted to three. Because of this high mortality rate, and because of her wild parties and her uncertain origin, she was known variously as the Siren

---

* 'Instead the tragic jester sobbed himself wheywhingingly sick of life on some sort of a rhubarbarous maundarin yellagreen funkleblue windigut diodying applejack squeezed from sour grapefruice and, to hear him twixt his sedimental cupslips when he had gulfed down mmmmuch too mmmmany gourds of it ... it came straight from the noble white fat, jo, openwide sat, jo, jo, her why hide that, jo jo jo, the winevat, of the most serene magyansty az archdiochesse, if she is a duck, she's a douches, and when she has a feherbour snot her fault, now is it? artstouchups, funny you're grinning at, fancy you're in her yet, Fanny Urinia.' *Finnegans Wake* (171)

or as Circe. As if to confirm the identification, her walls were decorated with painted rolls on which were successive scenes from the Odyssey, and she also had a tapestry woven with the motto in Greek, 'Good friend and good foe.' Joyce wrote and asked her if he might see the Homeric pictures since he was writing of Ulysses, and in reply the baroness came herself across the lake, standing up in a little boat, a great hat of straw on her head, her dog beside her. When she was within hailing distance she called out that she was sure he was no Englishman. 'No, Irish!' Joyce called back, much pleased. She invited Joyce and Budgen to her island home. While Budgen painted a grove of eucalyptus trees, Joyce went with her to look at the pictures. These proved to be disappointingly unconvincing: 'The sirens,' Joyce said later, 'had never been in a wind at all, for their hair was as set as a German wig, and the sea was just as appropriately watered.' The only one of the lot he admired had a slight naturalistic detail: in it the artist had conceived of Ulysses as tired and so sitting down to draw his bow. Bloom, in the comparable episode, is also exhausted.

The baroness, an old woman now, brought Joyce into a room which contained a trunk full of books on erotic perversions and a packet of obscene letters. 'These I want you to have,' she said to him, and went on in her middle European accent a little histrionically: 'They were collected through many years of a roving dissatisfied life, the life of a lover of mine, a Greek.' The photograph of this Ulysses was at the foot of her bed, and showed a fine fellow, with a black clipped beard and, as Joyce said, 'a wild look under the skin of his face.' Although he took the books and letters gladly, and listened to her adventures with much interest, he found the tale too extraordinary for his use. 'A writer,' he remarked to Djuna Barnes in retelling the incident, 'should never write about the extraordinary. That is for the journalist.' [12]

Joyce and Budgen returned to Locarno, and the next day Budgen arose late to find a brief note from Joyce saying only that he had returned to Zurich. Budgen packed his bag in some irritation and followed him; but when he caught up with his friend, he learned the reason for the abrupt departure. Joyce had been awakened that morning, May 14, by a telegram which read: 'Hope you are well letter from Monro client wishes to settle 5000 pounds 5% war loan upon you hearty congratulations letter following Nora Joyce.' At last Joyce saw himself as a wealthy man, independent of the monthly stipends the 'Monro client' had given him before. He bent all his thoughts to trying to decide who his benefactress was. After a time he wrote to the solicitors in London, saying that he now knew her identity, and asked whether he need respect her anonymity any longer. The solicitors replied that he need not. It was not clear that Joyce had guessed right, however, and to prevent embarrassment Harriet Weaver wrote him on July 6, 1919, 'Perhaps I had better add that it was I who sent the message through Messrs Monro, Saw & Co. and that I am sorry I sent it in the way and in the form I did. It is rather paralysing to communicate through solicitors. I fear you will have to withdraw all words about delicacy and self effacement. I can only beg you to forgive my lack of them.' So this extraordinary woman made known her extraordinary gift, half apologizing for it. Her generosity continued for the rest of Joyce's life.* She made no demands upon him, and gave up projects of her own so that he might get on with his, resolved to give his genius the reward which the world had so far withheld. Her benefaction did not make Joyce rich; no amount of money could have done that; but it made it possible for him to be poor only through determined extravagance.

With this support Joyce was no longer alarmed by the prospect of the distraint proceedings in the Carr case. Those proceedings proved to be lenient enough. An officer of the court looked over the Joyces' flat and noted that the furnishings were all rented. He proposed taking the books, but Joyce successfully objected that these were necessary to his profession as writer. The bailiff then claimed the typewriter, but Joyce asserted that his eye trouble made this utterly essential. 'Then I am afraid, Herr Doktor,' said the officer politely, 'I must ask you to show me what money you have on you.' Joyce had a hundred francs in his wallet, and the official took fifty and closed the proceedings.[13] A few days later Joyce learned from Padraic and Mary Colum, in a letter dated May 30, 1919, that their millionaire friend, Scofield Thayer, who was financing the *Dial,* had heard from them of Joyce's plight and had cabled him seven hundred dollars.† On June 12, J. S. Watson, Jr., a friend of Thayer's, sent three hundred more. Joyce paid two hundred to the English Players to alleviate their immediate difficulties, and in July offered to finance them. 'After prolonged deliberations,' he wrote to Budgen, who was away on a holiday, 'they very kindly and most considerately consented to accept 10,000 francs of my dirty money in consideration of my former good behaviour and unstained character.'[14]

Although the affair, from a financial point of view, ended success-fully, it left Joyce with his horror of officialdom confirmed. He also chose to believe that his stiffnecked refusal to kowtow to authority had had an effect on the Foreign Office. Bennett was in fact transferred to

---

* It continued even afterwards, for she paid the costs of his funeral.

† It was perhaps on this occasion that Nora rushed to inform Joyce, who was with the English Players, of the good news. While he was receiving their congratulations, the wife of one of the actors turned to Nora to say acidly, 'And so, Mrs. Joyce, you open your husband's mail!'[15]

Panama at a higher rank, though not because of Joyce, and a little
later, as Budgen was duly notified, 'Sir Whorearse Rumhole has been
"gently removed" from Bern.'[16] Rumbold became ambassador to Poland soon afterwards, and Joyce sent Sykes a poem 'for your next
production of Pippa Passes,' that ran:

The Right Man in the Wrong Place

> The pig's in the barley,
> The fat's in the fire:
> Old Europe can hardly
> Find twopence to buy her.
> Jack Spratt's in his office,
> Puffed, powdered and curled:
> Rumbold's in Warsaw—
> All's right with the world.[17]

Many years later Joyce was invited by a student group to lecture at
Oxford, and was amused to see that the name signed to the invitation
was that of Richard Rumbold, presumably a son of Sir Horace. He did
not accept.

Joyce reserved his full retribution for *Ulysses*, where he allotted
punishments as scrupulously and inexorably as Dante. There Sir Horace
Rumbold, British Minister to Switzerland, offers his services as a hangman to the sheriff of Dublin:

> Honoured sir i beg to offer myservicesintheabovementioned painful
> case i hanged Joe Gann in Bootle jail on the 12 of February 1900 and
> i . . . was assistant when Billington executed the awful murderer Toad
> Smith . . . i have a special nack of putting the noose once in he can't
> get out hoped to be favoured i remain, honoured sir, my terms is five
> ginnese.
>
>   H. Rumbold,
>   Master Barber.

'Joe Gann' and 'Toad Smith,' the two dreadful malefactors, are the two
consular employees in Zurich who would not testify in Joyce's behalf.
(Joyce always referred to Smith, who was squat and unprepossessing, as
'the toad.') Originally Joyce intended to make Consul-General Bennett
and Henry Carr the two drunken, blasphemous, and obscene soldiers
who knock Stephen Dedalus down in the *Circe* episode; but he eventually decided that Bennett should be the sergeant-major, with authority over Private Carr, who however refers to him with utter disrespect.
The other private Joyce decided should be Compton, the man who, he
believed, had bungled the affairs of the English Players.

In the *Cyclops* episode, too, on which he was now at work, Joyce found opportunities to vent his tireless indignation. As he wrote to Frank Budgen, 'The chapter of the Cyclops is being lovingly moulded in the way you know. The Fenian ... unburdens his soul about the Saxo-angles in the best fenian style and with cloacal vituperativeness alluding to their standard industry.* The epic proceeds "explanatorily." "He spoke of the English, a noble race, rulers of the waves, who sit on thrones of alabaster, silent as the deathless gods." ' [18]

In London his friends had received an earlier episode, the *Sirens*, with some disquiet. Joyce was elated when he finished it, but on June 18 he received a letter from Pound, 'disapproving of the Sirens [as Joyce informed Budgen], then modifying his disapproval and protesting against the close and against "obsession" and wanting to know whether Bloom (prolonged cheers from all parts of the house) could not be relegated to the background and Stephen Telemachus brought forward.' [19] The letter made Joyce comment to Budgen, 'Stephen no longer interests me. He has a shape that can't be changed.' [20] Pound complained also that 'a new style per chapter not required,' but Joyce had no intention of lowering any of his sails. On June 18 he walked with George Borach around the Zürichsee, justifying himself: 'I finished the Sirens chapter during the last few days. A big job. I wrote this chapter with the technical resources of music. It is a fugue with all musical notations: *piano, forte, rallentando,* and so on. A quintet occurs in it, too, as in *Die Meistersinger,* my favorite Wagnerian opera. . . . Since exploring the resources and artifices of music and employing them in this chapter, I haven't cared for music any more. I, the great friend of music, can no longer listen to it. I see through all the tricks and can't enjoy it any more.' [21]

The subject continued to occupy his thoughts. He read some of the *Sirens* episode to Ottocaro Weiss shortly before they went off together to a performance of Wagner's *Die Walküre.* In the first act, when Siegmund sings the famous love song, '*Winterstürme wichen dem Wonnemond*,' Joyce complained that the song's melodiousness was in bad taste and said to Weiss, 'Can you imagine this old German hero offering his girl a box of chocolates?' During the intermission Weiss lauded the music with the fervor of a young Wagnerian. Joyce listened gravely and then said, 'Don't you find the musical effects of my *Sirens* better than Wagner's?' 'No,' said Weiss. Joyce turned on his heel and did not show up for the rest of the opera, as if he could not bear not being preferred. [22]

---

* The Citizen says, 'You wouldn't see a trace of them or their language anywhere in Europe except in a cabinet d'aisance.' *Ulysses* (319 [309]) This is, of course, the allusion in 'thrones of alabaster.'

The irreverence with which, in the *Circe* episode, Joyce treats *Die Walküre*, may have been affected by this irritating moment. Joyce half-copies, half-parodies the incident in the opera when Siegmund tears the sword out of the ashtree into which Wotan has plunged it, and victoriously lifts the sword on high. Joyce has Stephen Dedalus in the brothel lift his ashplant with comparable magniloquence, to knock down only the brothel lampshade. Similarly, Joyce mocks the pathetic scene in which Siegmund, explaining to Sieglinde why he chose the name of Wehwald, addresses her as 'Fragende Frau.' Joyce edits this text to read:

> Hangende Hunger,
> Fragende Frau,
> Macht uns alle Kaput.[23]

Some days later Joyce had another opportunity to display his temporary dislike of music. He and Weiss went together to a concert of the Tonhalle Orchestra, which was playing the *Indianisches Tagebuch* of Ferruccio Busoni, with Busoni himself in the audience. To mock Weiss's interest in Busoni's music, Joyce applied himself to describing the obscene implications of each musical instrument in turn. Weiss could not contain his laughter and was embarrassed because Busoni stared at them.[24] *

Among Joyce's friends only Budgen responded to the *Sirens* with the admiration he expected and hoped for. Even Miss Weaver was lukewarm, writing on July 6, 'Mr. Pound sent me the Sirens episode a little time ago. I think I can see that your writing has been affected to some extent by your worries; I mean that the episode seems to me not quite to reach your usual pitch of intensity.' Joyce replied in July with a letter which was at once disappointedly resigned, and stubborn:

Dear Miss Weaver:

. . . You write that the last episode sent [the *Sirens*] seems to you to show a weakening or diffusion of some sort. Since the receipt of your letter I have read this chapter again several times. It took me five months to write it and always when I have finished an episode my mind lapses into a state of blank apathy, out of which it seems that neither I nor the wretched book will ever more emerge. Mr Pound wrote me rather hastily in disapproval, but I think that his disapproval is based on grounds which are not legitimate and is due chiefly to the varied interests of his admirable and energetic artistic life. Mr Brock

---

* Joyce's belittlement of music did not prevent his busying himself in July with a new project. The leading baritone of the Municipal Theatre was Augustus Milner, an Irishman by birth, and Joyce arranged for him to give a concert of Irish music in the Tonhalle.[25] But he left Zurich before it took place.

also wrote to me begging me to explain to him the method (or methods) of the madness. But these methods are so manifold, varying as they do from one hour to the other, from one organ of the body to another, from episode to episode, that, much as I appreciate his critical patience, I could not attempt to reply. . . .

If the Sirens have been found so unsatisfactory, I have little hope that the Cyclops or later the Circe episode will be approved of, and moreover it is impossible for me to write these episodes quickly. The elements needed will only fuse after a prolonged existence together. I confess that it is an extremely tiresome book but it is the only book which I am able to write at present. . . . The word scorching has a peculiar significance for my superstitious mind—not so much because of any quality or merit in the writing itself as for the fact that the progress of the book is in fact like the progress of some sandblast. As soon as I mention or include any person in it, I hear of his death or departure or misfortune, and each successive episode dealing with some province of artistic culture (rhetoric or music or dialectic), leaves behind it a burnt up field. Since I wrote the Sirens, I find it impossible to listen to music of any kind.

As you are the person who introduced my book, A *Portrait of the Artist as a Young Man,* to the 'notice' of the public, I shall feel very thankful to you if you will accept from me the MS of that book. It is in Trieste and, as soon as circumstances there are more favorable, I shall get and forward it to you.[26]

He did not suffer errant disciples gladly, and two weeks later, on August 6, returned to the subject with the same firmness:

Perhaps I ought not to say any more on the subject of the Sirens, but the passages you alluded to were not intended by me as recitative. There is in the episode only one example of recitative on page 12 in preface to the song. They are all the eight regular parts of a *fuga per canonem:* and I did not know in what other way to describe the seductions of music beyond which Ulysses travels. I understand that you may begin to regard the various styles of the episodes with dismay and prefer the initial style, much as the wanderer did who longed for the rock of Ithaca. But in the compass of one day to compress all these wanderings and clothe them in the form of this day is for me only possible by such variation which, I beg you to believe, is not capricious.

In confirmation of what I said in my last letter, I enclose a cutting from a Dublin paper just received announcing the death of one of the figures in the episode [J. G. Lidwell].[27]

In August a theatrical ambition was realized, though with unfortunate results. Probably through Stefan Zweig's influence, *Exiles* was presented on the stage in Munich on August 7 with an important German actress in the role of Bertha. Mrs. McCormick, whom Joyce duly notified of the première, offered to pay his expenses, but he was unable to obtain a visa, and instead spent the evening at the home of Arnold Korff, then a guest star at the Pfauen Theater. Korff and his wife, Joyce and Nora, and Ottocaro Weiss waited expectantly for a telephone call from Munich. They talked a little about the play, and Weiss asked Joyce why he had made Bertha moisten her handkerchief with saliva before wiping her son's face clean. Joyce replied, 'Did you ever see a mother cat cleaning her kitten?' The relationship of mother and son seemed to him equally animal and natural. As no word came from Munich the atmosphere grew tense. Then at last a telegram arrived announcing that the play had not been successful. Joyce commented, 'A fiasco!' [28]

The next day he received the *Münchner Neueste Nachrichten* which rudely ended its article on the play with the question, '*So viel Lärm um ein Irisch Stew?*' * The *München-Augsburger Abendzeitung* was more respectful, pointing to the play's dialectical subtleties and original psychological observation, but it suggested that the play was not for the general public. Joyce repeated all this to Budgen, and when an acquaintance passed them and asked how *Exiles* had gone, he replied at once, 'A flop!' and explained to Budgen that it was better to anticipate such epithets by making them oneself. But at the end of the month he wrote Miss Weaver in a way that indicated his renewed confidence in the play: 'As regards *Verbannte* I cannot find out what has happened. It seems to have been a stormy evening. The play was at once withdrawn. The management of the theatre wrote, saying that it was "a great success" and that "they were very glad to have been the first to produce it." The *Berliner Tageblatt, Vossische Zeitung*, and *Neue Freie Presse* had articles about the performance—one contradicting the other. Now I hear it was withdrawn because the chief actor fell ill—perhaps as a result of my lines—and that it is to go into the autumn bill. I wrote to Mr Linati about an Italian translation.' [29] He said to Schmitz later of the German audience, 'Did they want a steeplechase?'

Joyce had far too much sense of his own powers to be more than temporarily cast down by any criticism. He continued his work on the *Cyclops* episode. His friend Weiss was one of those who unknowingly assisted him with it. They often discussed political theory, and Joyce liked to reduce Weiss's arguments *ad absurdum*. One day, talking of the nature of the state, Weiss quoted some eminent authority to the effect that three elements are necessary to constitute a state: a people, a territory, and sovereignty. Joyce kept bringing up examples of smaller and smaller states, until he got Weiss to agree that a state could be only

* 'All that noise for an Irish stew?'

one person. He stepped on a chair, which he said was his territory, and declared, 'Then I'm a state.' * Joyce reworked this conversation in the *Cyclops* chapter:

—But do you know what a nation means? says John Wyse.
—Yes, says Bloom.
—What is it? says John Wyse.
—A nation? says Bloom. A nation is the same people living in the same place.
—By God, then, says Ned, laughing, if that's so I'm a nation for I'm living in the same place for the past five years.
So of course everyone had a laugh at Bloom and says he, trying to muck out of it:
—Or also living in different places.
—That covers my case, says Joe.[30]

His old curiosity about the Jewish nature, which he had exercised in Trieste with Schmitz, he now returned to with Weiss. Some of the information about alleged ritual murders by Jews in the *Eumaeus* episode came from a protest meeting about a false accusation of ritual murder which the two men attended together in 1919. A pet theory, borrowed from Otto Weininger's *Sex and Character*, was that Jews are by nature womanly men—a phrase which, incidentally, is applied to Bloom in *Ulysses*.[31] Weininger held that woman (like womanly man) is negation, is nothing, is non-existent, illogical, passive. 'Her instability and untruthfulness are only negative deductions from the premise of non-existence.' 'She is the sin of man,' he insisted. Joyce largely agreed with this view, and was always laboring to isolate female characteristics, from an incapacity for philosophy to a dislike for soup.[32] He supplemented Weininger with a contention of his own, that putting books in the bookcase upside down was a feminine trait; when he found some of his own books inverted, he would ask Nora and Lucia which of them had done it, smiling triumphantly if either confessed. He used to twit Weiss when he found a book upside down in Weiss's rooms, asserting that Weininger's contention about Jews as womanly men was thereby proved. In *Ulysses* Joyce attributes the same trait to Bloom, several of whose books are upside down.[33]

Carrying out the same idea he decided to give Bloom the middle name of a woman, Paula; and this probably came about indirectly through an excursion that Weiss, his sister Paula, and Joyce and Nora

---

* Bertrand Russell says in *Portraits from Memory* (1956), p. 188, 'In Petrograd, as it then was, during the time of Kerensky, a certain single house proclaimed itself a nation rightly struggling to be free, and appealed to President Wilson to give it a separate Parliament. This, however, was felt to be going too far.'

made to the waterfalls of the Rhine at Schaffhausen during the summer of 1919. They sat at a little table in a restaurant and admired the scene. Weiss asked the innkeeper if it was possible to cross the Rhine there in a boat, and he was told that two expert rowers would take him just underneath the deep rock which divides the falls into two parts. Weiss at once accepted, and Paula and Nora volunteered to go with him. Joyce refused and stayed at the table. The two oarsmen took them across in a flat-bottomed boat, standing all the time to overcome the strong currents which several times spun the boat round. The women clung in terror to Weiss. Joyce sat where they had left him, a long Brissago in his mouth, observing them. As they rowed away they lost sight of him, and when they returned, the women relieved to be safe, Joyce was still sitting there; but instead of smoking he was eating tomatoes bought from a peddler. When they told him of their thrilling ride he said, 'I enjoyed it too, watching you. Your boat looked like Charon's in the *Divina Commedia*, which ferried the souls of the dead to the other world.'

While the connection with *Circe* is slight, echoes of the incident appear there. The waterfall is evoked, the yews several times repeat the word 'sister,' and Leopold Paula Bloom is looking down at the water. Elsewhere in the book Bloom is shown to have a slightly awkward gait, comparable perhaps to that of Paula Weiss.*

---

* Bits of the conversations of Joyce and Weiss crop up unexpectedly in Joyce's books. Once Weiss told him of the grief of a young mother of his acquaintance over the death of her child; she was concerned that the pillow on which his head rested in the casket might not be soft enough. Joyce at once made a note in his notebook and said, 'I'll use that.' He did, but in greatly altered form, in the lambswool sweater that Molly Bloom remembers having knit for her dead son. At another time, drinking with Weiss, Joyce remarked that he liked women to have breasts like a she-goat's. In *Ulysses* (63 [56]), Bloom looks at his wife's 'large soft bubs, sloping within her nightdress like a shegoat's udder,' and later remembers how in their first embraces on Ben Howth a nanny-goat walked by them. In *Finnegans Wake* (215), the sentence, 'He had buckgoat paps on him, soft ones, for orphans,' is part of the same context.

Joyce learned from Weiss two stories which appear close together in the *Anna Livia Plurabelle* section of *Finnegans Wake*. Weiss told him that the students at the University of Vienna who came from Trieste, Istria, and Trento held a party every year for the freshmen. At one of these 'Feste delle Matricole' a boy dressed himself up as a priest and delivered a sermon in which he imitated a Slovene priest preaching in Italian. Instead of saying, in correct Italian,

Il Signore disse: Si faccia l'uomo! e l'uomo fu. Il Signore disse: Si faccia Adamo! e Adamo fu (God said: Let there be man, and man was. God said: Let there be Adam, and Adam was.),

or in good Triestine,

El Signor ga dito: Se fazi l'omo! e l'omo se ga fato. El Signor ga dito: Se fazi Adamo! e Adamo se ga fato,

On September 3, 1919, Joyce finished the *Cyclops* episode and sent it off to Pound. During the summer he had come to the conclusion that he would return to Trieste as he had planned when he left that city. Zurich was becoming dull as the war refugees departed; the climate was bad for his eyes; living costs were high, and four years was a long time for Joyce to spend in one place. He began to pack up his belongings. As he stamped each of his books with *J.J.* and put them into suitcases, Giorgio suddenly protested, 'Don't do that. I'm going to have your books when you die, and your initials will be on them.'[34] Joyce was faintly distressed and amused.

There were, however, unforeseen complications before he left. G. Herbert Thring, the secretary of the Society of Authors, wrote to the English Players to protest their production of a play without the dramatist's consent and without payment of royalties. Joyce returned a protest of innocence on September 21:

> Dear Sir: My attention has been drawn to a letter recently written by your society to Mr Curti, solicitor, of Zurich. As a partner of Mr Sykes, I should like to bring a few facts to your notice.
>
> Mr Sykes and I founded the English Players Co. in Zurich in April 1918, for the production of plays in the English language. The company produced plays in English in spite of difficulty, boycott, and financial loss, it was the only enterprise of the kind in Switzerland during the war. It was impossible for Mr Sykes to obtain in some cases the consent of the dramatist, owing to the postal delays, censorship, and frequent and prolonged closure of frontiers, although every effort was made to avoid what might have seemed an infringement of literary courtesy. Mr Sykes was in direct communication with Mr Edward Martyn, who gave him permission to produce The Heather Field; with Mr Meyer, agent of the late Stanley Houghton, who gave him permission to produce Hindle Wakes, and with Mr Robert Ross (deceased) and Mr Samuel French with regard to the production of Wilde's The Importance of Being Earnest. He has asked Mr Curti, therefore, to let

---

he intoned in a heavy Slovene accent, and with a syntax which after the Slavic fashion omitted the definite article and in other ways sounded barbarous:

Senior ga dito: Faciasi Omo! E omo fu fò. Senior ga dito: Faciasi Hidamo! Hidamo se ga facessà.

These words are given verbatim in *Finnegans Wake* (212). The same mixture of languages is to be found in another anecdote by J. P. Hebel, which Weiss told Joyce and which appears half a page farther on in *Anna Livia Plurabelle* (213). A Frenchman shouted across the Rhine at a German, 'Filou! Filou!' ('Scoundrel!') The German understood him to say, 'Wieviel Uhr? Wieviel Uhr?' He looked at his watch and shouted back obligingly, 'Halber sechse.' Both stories were apposite for the two washerwomen attempting to communicate with each other by shouting across the Liffey.

him know the names of the authors who are claiming fees. The question of production on the Continent of Europe of plays in the English language seems, moreover, to be an exceptional case, not foreseen in the clauses of the Berne Convention. Mr Sykes was legally advised on this subject at the outset that such productions were free.

The aims and achievements of the company are such, I believe, as will be approved of by the members of your society. And, owing to Mr Sykes' energy and persistence, the prospects financially and artistically, are now much brighter.

My name as a writer will perhaps not be unknown to you, and I am indebted to your society for generous and timely aid in the past. I trust that the proposal which Mr Curti is forwarding you on our behalf will meet with your approval and put an end to any misunderstanding which may have arisen.

> I am, dear sir, sincerely yours,
> James Joyce [35]

21.ix.19

The dramatist whose rights were alleged to have been violated turned out to be Bernard Shaw. The Players had given *Mrs. Warren's Profession*, and Joyce suggested to Thring in the ensuing correspondence that no rights could exist for a play the production of which was in England an indictable offense. Thring consulted Shaw, who informed him that the Lord Chamberlain had licensed a modified version of the play, and that it had been performed in London and could be performed in Ireland and other parts of the British Empire where the Lord Chamberlain had no control. Thring relayed this information to Joyce with some heat.

This correspondence was not likely to detain Joyce in Zurich. He wound up his affairs, and counted on living easily in Trieste, what with the combined bounty of Mrs. McCormick and Miss Weaver. But Mrs. McCormick was known to be capricious, and she had lately become annoyed with Joyce when he vehemently refused to submit—at her suggestion and at her expense—to analysis by Jung. 'It was unthinkable,' he said to Sykes.* Nora found the episode, and in fact the whole relationship of her husband and Mrs. McCormick, merely funny, and some-

---

* In *Finnegans Wake* (522), Joyce refers to the incident in Zurich in this passage:

—You're a nice third degree witness, faith! But this is no laughing matter. Do you think we are tonedeafs in our noses to boot? Can you not distinguish the sense, prain, from the sound, bray? You have homosexual catheis of empathy between narcissism of the expert and steatopygic invertedness. Get yourself psychoanolised!

—O, begor, I want no expert nursus symaphy from yours broons quadroons and I can psoakoonaloose myself any time I want (the fog follow you all!) without your interferences or any other pigeonstealer.

times speculated aloud on what kind of expensive underwear the rich American woman wore.[36] Joyce said nothing, merely looked at her over his glasses. But the contract of patron and artist had a somber end, and with it the friendship of Joyce and Ottocaro Weiss.

The two men had been dining together frequently as Joyce prepared for his departure, and when Joyce proposed they share a final bottle of Fendant de Sion after a meal, Weiss sometimes had to decline because he could not afford it. Joyce offered to pay for the extra bottle and keep a record of what he spent, so that Weiss could repay him. Weiss agreed, and on several occasions they shared a bottle with this understanding. One morning, following such an evening together, Weiss was awakened by an express post card from Joyce, saying he was in urgent need of the sum he had lent, which amounted to about 50 francs; would Weiss be so good as to send it to him at once? Since on the previous evening Joyce had not mentioned this dire need, Weiss was irked at the suddenness of the demand. But he dressed and went to the pawnshop of the Züricher Kantonalbank—Swiss pawnshops are under state control—and pawned his gold watch. He brought the money to Joyce's flat, and left without many words.

After staying away from Joyce for a few days, he decided to make up with him. He went to the Pfauen Café and found Joyce, Nora, Budgen, and an Italian named Mario Lenassi sitting around a table. He greeted Joyce, who hardly answered him; the others were silent and embarrassed. When Weiss sat down they did not offer him a drink; he asked, 'What's the matter?' but got no reply. He ordered a glass of his own, and when the silence continued he paid for his drink and left. As he went out Lenassi rose and said, 'I'll come with you.' When they were outside he asked Weiss, 'What do you have against Joyce?' 'Why, nothing,' said Weiss. 'A little coolness over some money, but nothing of any consequence. What does he have against me?' Lenassi offered no explanation and they parted.

This singular reception, as well as the demand that Weiss repay his debt, grew out of Joyce's call at the bank on October 1 for his monthly stipend from Mrs.McCormick. The banker informed him curtly, '*Der Kredit ist erschöpft.*'[37] * Flinging about for someone to blame, Joyce remembered that Weiss knew Jung, Mrs. McCormick's analyst, and was slightly acquainted with Mrs. McCormick herself. He quickly concluded that Weiss had persuaded her to cut off the subsidy. Nora did not agree with him, Weiss protested his innocence, but Joyce did not swerve from his conviction. There had been treachery somewhere, and he was accustomed to look for it among his close friends. In 1939

---

* 'Your credit is cut off.'

he wrote a footnote for Herbert Gorman's biographical discussion of the incident, to summarize his liability to betrayal:

Several times in Joyce's career this brusque and unexplained [change of] attitude of certain admirers of his has taken place. There were at least two instances of it in Dublin—one before he left [Gogarty] and one during his last visit there [Cosgrave], another in Trieste after he had become famous (his friend Francini delivered a lecture about him as already explained to you and to be embodied in your book elsewhere), and it has happened in Paris also. There is no single explanation so far as these different admirers are concerned that will fit all these cases, but the fact remains that all through his life he seems to have had admiration both in its spiritual and its material form spontaneously and suddenly offered him and subsequently just as suddenly transformed into passive or open hostility.[38]

He did not yield easily to the supposed treachery: he wrote asking to see Mrs. McCormick, informing her he was about to leave for Trieste and had found at last an English publisher (presumably the *Egoist*) for his book. She replied politely on October 10 that she was not free at the suggested time and would therefore say goodbye in her letter.[39] As a last gesture, with the faint hope of winning her over still, Joyce sent her part of the manuscript of *Ulysses*. This drew a final note from her dated October 13:

Dear Mr. Joyce:—

Thank you for the fine manuscript—which I am glad to keep for you with the understanding that when for any reason, you want it, you have only to write for it. As the Bank told you, I am not able to help you any longer financially, but now that the difficult years of the war are past, you will find publishers and will come forward yourself, I know.

Wishing you a good journey,

Sincerely,
Edith McCormick.[40]

In later years Joyce became less certain where to place the blame. Ettore Schmitz persuaded Joyce to meet Weiss in the early nineteen-twenties, but the old friendship was not renewable. Joyce shifted most of his suspicion to Jung, upon whom Mrs. McCormick leaned heavily for advice. Jung had not met Joyce in 1919, but had heard reports of *Ulysses* which did not impress him; he was probably aware of Joyce's heavy drinking, and skeptical of his ability to write well. He may have been piqued by Joyce's refusal to be analyzed by him. Jung had just effected a cure, as he thought, of Ermanno Wolf-Ferrari, another recipient of Mrs. McCormick's patronage, by urging her to withdraw her subsidy; Wolf-Ferrari had pulled himself out of dissipation and inertia and had begun to compose music again. It is possible, though Jung does not remember for sure, that he gave Mrs. McCormick similar advise about Joyce.[41] He did not know Joyce well enough to see that he was not debauched. But while Jung may have had a share in Mrs. McCormick's decision, his intervention is not essential to explain it. Her caprices were well known and needed no special instigation; she withdrew a subsidy from Philipp Jarnach with the same suddenness. In later life Mrs. McCormick managed to spend away her enormous fortune with a similar instability.

It is unlikely that Joyce would allow her to escape scot-free from artistic punishment; and in the *Circe* episode of *Ulysses*, Mrs. Mervyn Talboys, the society woman with a riding crop and a sadistic bent, may owe something to Edith Rockefeller McCormick, a noted horsewoman. But when Joyce heard of her death in 1932, he wrote a more considered tribute: 'I am sorry to learn of the death of Mrs McCormick. She was very kind to me at a difficult moment and was a woman of considerable distinction. I do not know what happened afterwards though I suspect but this does not obliterate her act prompted by humanity and generosity.' [42] She had, in fact, helped to give him a year of comparative ease during which he wrote an important part of *Ulysses*.

It was with this unpleasant sense of a breach with his patron that Joyce, his means greatly reduced, took his family to Trieste in mid-October of 1919.

◇◇

1919–1920

Everything's going on the same or so it appeals to all of us, in the old holmsted here. Coughings all over the sanctuary, bad scrant to me aunt Florenza.

—*Finnegans Wake* (26)

A POINT about Ulysses (Bloom),' Joyce wrote to Budgen in 1920; 'He romances about Ithaca (Oi want teh gow back teh the Mawl Enn Road, s'elp me!) and when he gets back it gives him the pip.' [1] Trieste, the scene of several happy returns in the past, had changed, and no doubt Joyce had changed too. Under Austria the city had been full of ships, now its harbor was almost deserted. Old residents straggled back, wounded by the war in body or mind, seeking vainly to find Trieste in Trieste. As for Joyce, there was no possibility of recovering his old flat on the via Donato Bramante; it had been requisitioned the previous year because of the housing shortage.[2] Fortunately his furniture, books, and papers were in storage. His brother-in-law and sister, Frantisek and Eileen Schaurek, had returned to Trieste at the end of 1918 with their two small children. They took an unusually large fourth floor flat at 2 Via Sanità in 1919. Soon Stanislaus was released from internment at Katzenau (near Linz) and joined them there. Schaurek resumed his old position as Prokurist (holder of joint signature, a semi-managerial position) at the Zivnostenska Banka, while Stanislaus quickly found English pupils again.

When James informed them from Zurich of his impending arrival, Stanislaus was not pleased and threatened to leave the flat if James came into it. He felt that his independence was to receive a new challenge. During the war he and James had exchanged letters occasionally, and Stanislaus had written in one that, though internment was inconvenient, he hoped when the war was over to take better care of himself.[3] This he was now proceeding to do. The old grievances too had furnished him with bitter thoughts during four confined years.

Besides the ingratitude for his financial help, he remembered the un-
kept promise to dedicate *Dubliners* to him; there was also the transformation of *Stephen Hero* into *A Portrait of the Artist,* which had
relegated Maurice—Stephen's brother—into obscurity. The change was
made for good artistic reasons, but probably was not more palatable
to Stanislaus because of them.

Schaurek also anticipated uneasily his brother-in-law's return, but
Eileen became James's advocate, and after some controversy won her
point. Stanislaus gave up his study and took a smaller room. James
got his furniture from storage and distributed it about the flat; Giorgio
and Lucia had to sleep on hard sofas, but otherwise the situation was
tolerable. Joyce made no comment upon the state of his finances,
though he had been forced to pawn his silver watch before leaving
Zurich, but Nora, as soon as she was alone with Eileen, said to her,
'Thanks, Eileen. We didn't have a penny left.' [4] Eileen counseled her,
'Don't tell Stannie or Frank for a while.' This time their poverty was
easily abolished; Joyce wrote urgently to Pinker to request an advance
from Huebsch, and with this, which was quickly forthcoming, the
immediate stress was over and he could wait less impatiently for the
next installment of Miss Weaver's gift. He also wrote a long letter
to Mrs. McCormick asking a renewal of her patronage, but this was
fruitless. The flat was overcrowded, but so was the city; it was impossible to find another place to live. Prices were high, and as Joyce
wrote Budgen lachrymosely on November 7, 'No wine here like the
archduchess. . . . As for *Ulysses*—it is like me—on the rocks.' [5]

To re-establish connections did not prove easy—one cannot swim
twice in the same river. Stanislaus treated his brother coolly, listened
to him less attentively, and allowed himself to be a little bored by
the intricacies of *Ulysses,* particularly the technical complications. [6] He
could not bear his brother's intemperance, which seemed to him worse
than ever, but James retorted that he was 'the foolish author of a
wise book.' [7] It was patent from the beginning that James, with money
of his own, would not accept his younger brother's surveillance, which
had been one of their strongest, if most chafing, bonds in the past;
and Stanislaus, for his part, pursued a life of his own with a group
of friends who liked and admired him apart from his brother.

Old friends also felt that Joyce was altered. To Francini he seemed
more stylized, and Signora Francini commented, *'Joyce non è piu
quello'* [8] ('Joyce is somebody else now'). Only on rare occasions could
the conviviality of the old days be recovered, as when Joyce, Argio
Orell (the Triestine poet), Silvio Benco (editor now of the *Piccolo
della Sera*), and Francini foregathered with their wives at Francini's

flat for wine and talk. Joyce's conversation often began with a flat dismissal of subjects that interested his friends. So he said to Francini, 'Ideas, classifications, political terminologies leave me indifferent; they are things one has passed beyond. Intellectual anarchy, materialism, rationalism—as if they could get a spider out of his web!' [9] His spirits, however, gradually rose; he and Francini shifted from Italian to Latin, and he recited passages from the liturgy interspersed with comic irrelevancies in Triestino, French, German, Greek, and even Russian, in which he was now taking an interest. Or he sang them a mocking song he had made up about Vittorio Emmanuele III, Italy's diminutive king, which concluded with the words, '*El xe picio ma 'l xe talian*' [10] ('He's little, but at least he's Italian'). Then perhaps the next day Joyce would call on Benco at the *Piccolo* office and invite him for a drink, but Benco, a conscientious editor, always refused to leave his post. He did, however, oblige Joyce by inserting a paragraph or two about his work in the newspaper. Occasionally Joyce met another old friend, Ettore Schmitz, and once shocked him a little by dismissing Schmitz's interest in psychoanalysis with the comment, 'Well, if we need it, let us keep to confession.' * [11]

Joyce spent a good deal of time with Oscar Schwarz, his old language pupil, and with Silvestri the painter. When Schwarz first encountered him on the street, Joyce was wearing his usual costume, a loose-fitting overcoat that was too short for him, pulled together by a military belt. Schwarz asked him, 'And how have you spent the war years, professor?' Joyce replied with utter nonchalance, 'Oh yes, I was told that there was a war going on in Europe.' [12] To Silvestri he confided one night at the Restaurant Dreher in the Piazza della Borsa, where they had met after dinner, 'Silvestri, I'm rich now.' 'Then let me paint your portrait,' said Silvestri eagerly. It was arranged, but Joyce proved incapable of sitting still. Then Silvestri had the ingenious idea of arranging a mirror so that Joyce could watch the lunges and darts of the brush. With this help he sat as if hypnotized. [13] The portrait was delivered but Joyce, in spite of his 'wealth,' did not succeed in paying for it until about a year later.

He did not wish to give private lessons any more, but he reclaimed his position at the Scuola Superiore di Commercio Revoltella, which was in process of becoming the Università di Trieste, or as Joyce called it, 'the revolver university.' [14] The work was only an hour a day, [15] six days a week, but Joyce had little stomach for it. His pupils found him preoccupied; one, Lojce Berce, recalled that Joyce would smile abstractedly for almost a minute in the middle of a class. Often he stared

* He derides psychoanalysis similarly in *Finnegans Wake* (115 and elsewhere).

at them blankly or made gestures that were trancelike. His teaching was as usual unsystematic; he found drills too tedious, so he spent an inordinate amount of time in giving his students the names of foods, insisting, 'These words are very important.' He attempted a disquisition upon Gladstone to explain the Gladstone bag, but was thwarted, to his great irritation, by their not knowing who Gladstone was. To a student who timidly inquired how long one must study a language to master it, Joyce replied pessimistically, 'I have been studying Italian for fifteen years and am at last beginning to know it.' He complained at the university's paying his salary for the first time in March, after he had already taught for two months; and, not in the mood for indulgence, at the end of the academic year he gave (without troubling to examine them) all except one or two of his students the minimum grade of 18 (18 to 30 being the range of passing grades).[16]

In November, anxious to finish *Ulysses* during the year 1920, he brought himself to begin work on *Nausicaa*. He felt keenly the 'privation' of being unable to discuss it with Frank Budgen, to whom however he wrote of it in great detail. By November 9 he had fixed upon the 'general plan of the specially new fizzing style (Patent No 7728SP. ZP.BP.LP.),' which on January 3 he described more particularly to Budgen as 'a namby-pamby jammy marmalady drawersy (alto là!) style with effects of incense, mariolatry, masturbation, stewed cockles, painter's palette, chitchat, circumlocutions, etc etc.).' [17] To help with the Gerty MacDowell style, he wrote to his Aunt Josephine Murray for novelettes and a penny hymnbook. Wishing to oppose to Gerty's floridly imaginative consciousness the realistic observation of Bloom, he asked his aunt to check 'whether there are trees (and of what kind) behind the Star of the Sea Church in Sandymount visible from the shore and also whether there are steps leading down at the side of it from Leahy's Terrace.' [18] During his work Budgen's absence distressed him more and more, and he kept urging his friend to consider a trip to Trieste, depicting his own plight with the ironic pathos which he reserved for this subject, as in a letter of January 3, 1920:

> via Sanità, 2, III
> Trieste (Italia)

Dear Budgen: I hope you are alive, well, and sold something in Basel. Your pictures came all right and are up, machine [typewriter] arrived broken, books safe: total cost about 400 frs! The situation here is highly unpleasant. No flat or sign of one. I have refused lessons up to the present but am appointed to the school again—it is now a commercial university. One hour a day. For six weeks after my arrival I never read nor wrote nor spoke. But as it cannot go on so I started Nausicaa and have written less than half. Perhaps I can finish it for February 2. No reply from Mrs M[cCormick]. It seems that gentility cannot be acquired in a single generation. Quinn replied after a month offering 700 frs down on account of *Ulysses* MS. I did not answer. He now offers 1500 frs down without naming the ultimate sum. I shall write to Mrs M to know if she wants it. Miss Weaver sent me her photo with a melancholy letter about her age—43. I heard nothing more from Sykes—thank God—or the English foulplayers but people tell me they still perform. Lenassi was here twice smelling around—God knows for what. Weiss I met on New Year's Day in the street. He approached smiling (I suppose at my disreputable get-up) and saluted. I replied. We now cook for ourselves in this household. Till yesterday I was paying about 35 lire a day to my brother-in-law. Now I pay him half rent, gas, coal and we pig for ourselves. Jolly! Apart from this is the damnable boredom. Not a soul to talk to about Bloom. Lent two chapters to one or two people but they know as much about it as the Parliamentary side of my arse. My brother [knows] something but he thinks it a joke, besides he was 4 years in [Katzenau?], has a devil of a lot to do and likes a gay, elegant life in his own set. O shite and onions! When is this bloody state of affairs going to end. Have you the copies of *Verbannte*.* If so sell them if anyone will take 'em, and keep the cash for yourself. I suppose P.S. [Paul Suter] is now married. Give him my best wishes. Are you staying on in Zurich? Is there any God's chance of your coming here for a week. I doubt if I can raise the whole lot. I could put you up however for that length of time and feed but there is the bloody fare. I might be able to go halves in it. Perhaps next month? *Nausikaa* will be finished, I hope. To abandon the book now would be madness. First half of *Cyclops* appeared in November with excision of the erection allusion.† Do you ever see Siegfried Lang. I wish he would send me back *registered* my novel. The copy is not mine but dedicated. On receipt of this approach an inkbottle with intention. I know it is a bore but I should like to hear your views and plans. By the way do you or did you know any Weavers in St. Ives. I ask because Miss W. sent me a snapshot taken there. *Verbannte* appears to have gone under in Germany. Writing Ulysses is a tough job enough without all this trouble. The prospect of starting lessons next month is damn pleasant. Winter here is mild enough and will soon be over. Plenty of good opera but I never go. Can't because 'somebody' either sold or pawned my dress suit and it costs about 600 lire to buy one. Perhaps if I had my own flat it might not be so bad (I may remark that the greater part of the furniture here is mine). Doing any kind of business upsets me. Schlie (Mrs Piazza's man) is here. A decent kind of fellow—not a psychoanalyst. Had a card from Ruggiero. Thank him if you see him. I wish you a

* *Exiles* in German translation.
† *Ulysses* (299 [289]).

happy New Year and hope to see you soon. As for travelling, being exbritish consul you should find no difficulties, I suppose—but I daresay I am selfish as usual suggesting such a troublesome and (to you) unprofitable move. In any case please write by return. . . .

Arrivederci *ben presto*
James Joyce [19]

3.1.1920.

Budgen could not afford to go to Trieste, even if Joyce paid half fare as he offered to do, but he cheerily caught up a sentence from Joyce's letter to reply on January 13, 1920, 'What's this about abandoning Ulysses? As if that were possible! The Zurich skies might just as easily quit raining. Perhaps the gods or fates or who or whatever decides these matters will yet make it decently humanly possible for me to hear the story of that magical evening where wan weary Ulysses' heart responds to maidenly ejaculations recounted by yourself. Speriamo.'

Joyce succeeded in completing *Nausicaa* by his birthday, and sent it off to Ezra Pound, who turned it over to Miss Weaver. About this episode she had no complaints, and wrote to Joyce, 'You are very good for the soul, I think, medicinal, you are so unflattering to our human nature: so, though you are neither priest nor doctor of medicine, I think you have something of both—the Reverend James Joyce S.J., M.D.' [20] Joyce was pleased and jocular in his reply: 'I was interested to read what you told me in your last letter, as I myself started to study medicine three times, in Dublin, Paris, and again in Dublin. I would have been even more disastrous to society at large than I am in my present state had I continued.' [21]

He had already gone on quickly to the *Oxen of the Sun* episode, which he described to her as 'the most difficult episode in an odyssey, I think, both to interpret and to execute.' [22] During the writing he kept before him a diagram showing the ontogeny of the foetus during nine months,[23] and also studied Saintsbury's *A History of English Prose Rhythm*.[24] His elaborate plans for the episode were delineated in a letter to Budgen on March 22:

Am working hard at *Oxen of the Sun*, the idea being the crime committed against fecundity by sterilizing the act of coition. Scene, lying-in hospital. Technique: a nineparted episode without divisions introduced by a Sallustian-Tacitean prelude (the unfertilized ovum), then by way of earliest English alliterative and monosyllabic and Anglo-Saxon ('Before born the babe had bliss. Within the womb he won worship.' 'Bloom dull dreamy heard: in held hat stony staring') then by way of Mandeville ('there came forth a scholar of medicine that men clepen,

&c') then Malory's *Morte d'Arthur* ('but that franklin Lenehan was prompt ever to pour them so that at the least way mirth should not lack') then the Elizabethan 'chronicle style' ('about that present time young Stephen filled all cups'), then a passage solemn, as of Milton, Taylor and Hooker, followed by a choppy Latin-gossipy bit, style of Burton-Browne, then a passage Bunyanesque ('the reason was that in the way he fell in with a certain whore whose name she said is Bird-in-the-hand'). After a diarystyle bit Pepys-Evelyn ('Bloom sitting snug with a party of wags, among them Dixon jun, Ja. Lynch, Doc. Madden and Stephen D. for a languor he had before and was now better he having dreamed tonight a strange fancy and Mistress Purefoy there to be delivered, poor body, two days past her time and the midwives hard put to it, God send her quick issue') and so on through Defoe-Swift and Steele-Addison-Sterne and Landor-Pater-Newman until it ends in a frightful jumble of Pidgin English, Nigger English, Cockney, Irish, Bowery slang and broken doggerel. This procession is also linked back at each part subtly with some foregoing episode of the day and, besides this, with the natural stages of development in the embryo and the periods of faunal evolution in general. The double-thudding Anglo-Saxon motive recurs from time to time ('Loth to move from Horne's house') to give the sense of the hoofs of oxen. Bloom is the spermato-zoon, the hospital the womb, the nurse the ovum, Stephen the embryo.
    How's that for high? [25]

The intricacy of this scheme should not conceal a fact about all Joyce's writing which he had mentioned to Budgen, that his complexity was only in his means. 'With me,' he said, 'the thought is always simple.' [26] T. S. Eliot read the episode as a revelation of 'the futility of all the English styles,' [27] but it is likely that Joyce intended the desecration of style to suit the mood of desecration which pervades the episode and is implicitly condemned in it. He worked 1,000 hours by his own calculation on the episode; his mind was so possessed by his theme that he felt as though he were himself eating the oxen, as though they were everywhere. It was hard to sit down to a meal without having his stomach turn. He was relieved to be able to write to Budgen on May 18, 'The Oxen of the bloody bleeding Sun are finished.' [28] Miss Weaver's comment on it was, 'I think this episode might also have been called Hades for the reading of it is like being taken the rounds of hell.' [29] Joyce had not intended anything so infernal, but was inter-ested and asked her, 'Do you mean that the Oxen of the Sun episode resembles Hades because the nine circles of development (enclosed between the headpiece and tailpiece of opposite chaos) seem to you to be peopled by extinct beings?' [30] No, Miss Weaver replied, that was not what she meant. 'I must ask you once more not to pay the slightest attention to any foolish remark I may make—which really I must give up making—if I can.' [31]

Joyce continued to importune Budgen. He offered him Silvestri's studio, a room in his own flat, and English pupils at 6 or 7 (later raised to 10) lire an hour. Among the inducements, he wrote on March 15, 'You will see ME. You will hear (till you get sick) the bloody Oxen of the bloody Sun.' 'BE ENERGETIC,' he coaxed in large capitals.[32] But Budgen, though tempted, foresaw that Trieste would be a backwater for his painting career, and preferred to go to London or, perhaps, Cornwall, where he had been brought up. This news made Joyce consider again the possibility of taking a holiday in England, Wales, Ireland, or even Cornwall as soon as the university term was finished.[33] He would have liked to see his father again, and John Joyce had a friend inform James in Trieste that his father was 'still of opinion that you alone care for him and believe in him, and his whole thoughts are centered on your coming over so that he may see you before he dies.' [34] But the gunfighting in Ireland between patriots and Black and Tans discouraged this prospect. Just the same, Joyce did not wish to summer in Trieste. It was at this moment that Ezra Pound exercised for the second time a decisive influence upon his career.

Pound was in Venice early in May, and wrote to Joyce suggesting a meeting there or in Trieste. Joyce was willing, but a sudden illness of Mrs. Pound forced her husband to take her away at once to the pleasanter climate of the Lago di Garda. Pound suggested Joyce come there, and after further correspondence Joyce agreed to come on June 1 to Sirmione. A train accident forestalled his departure, and at first he thought he would present his problems by letter instead of in person:

via Sanità 2,[III]
Trieste
1 June 1920

Dear Pound: I went to the station this morning to start at 7:30. On my arrival there I was told that a passenger train which had left some hours before had collided with another, result as per enclosed cutting. Luckily I was not on it. I was also told that the 7:30 express Trieste Paris is now off owing to strike. There are two trains between T[rieste] and Desenzano, viz: one at 11:30 A.M. reaching there about the witching hour of midnight. The other at 5, travelling (or crawling) all night and reaching there about 6 next morning. This train is impossible for me.

Now it is my intention to travel over that line en route for England

and Ireland as soon as possible but I think it is unprofitable to go now.
I suppose after 12 June you will go to London. In that case we shall
meet then, I hope. My only reason for accepting your kind invitation to
Sirmione was to meet you. But still it would be a big expense for you.
And also for me if I travelled second class. You may judge of the state
of the railway here by second cutting.

My reasons for travelling north are these. I am in need of a long
holiday (by this I don't mean abandonment of *Ulysses* but quiet in
which to finish it) away from here. Without saying anything about this
city (*De mortuis nil nisi bonum*) my own position for the past seven
months has been very unpleasant. I live in a flat with eleven other
people * and have had great difficulty in securing time and peace
enough to write those two chapters. The second reason is: clothes.
I have none and can't buy any. The other members of the family are
still provided with decent clothes bought in Switzerland. I wear my
son's boots (which are two sizes too large), and his castoff suit which
is too narrow in the shoulders, other articles belong or belonged to my
brother and to my brother-in-law. I shall not be able to buy anything
here. A suit of clothes, they tell me, costs 600-800 francs. A shirt costs
35 francs. I can just live with what I have but no more. Since I came
here I suppose I have not exchanged 100 words with anybody. I spend
the greater part of my time sprawled across two beds surrounded by
mountains of notes. I leave the house at 12:22 and walk the same
distance along the same streets buy the Daily Mail which my brother
and wife read and return. Idem in the evening. I was once inveigled
into a theatre. I was once invited to a public dinner, as professor of the
Scuola Superiore here, and next day received from there a request to
subscribe 20,000 or 10,000 or even 5000 lire of Italian war loan. I must
buy clothes so I think I ought to go to Dublin to buy them.

Thirdly, my two children have not slept in a bed since we came.
They repose on hard sofas and the climate here is very trying in July-
September.

Fourthly, the rate of exchange is readjusting itself. While the pound
(I mean the other pound, the English not the American one) stood at
100 or 90 I could fight the prices here because my money was in English currency. Today the pound is at 62 and my brother-in-law (who is
cashier of a bank here) says it is gravitating towards a lower price
owing to certain trade manoeuvres or nobody could buy at such high
figures. If it reaches 50 I cannot swim any more but disappear under
the surface. If I went to Switzerland I could not keep myself or family
there: besides I dislike returning to places. Prices here are from 8 to
10 times what they were in 1914.

I could give lessons here (most people expected it of me) but I will
not. I have a position in that school which the government has now

* What felt like eleven was probably only eight: his wife and children, four
Schaureks, and his brother.

raised to the rank of a university. My pay is about 3/- an hour for 6 hours a week. This I shall resign as it wastes my time and my nerves.

I cannot find a flat here. To find one you must hold in the right hand a check for 20,000 or 30,000 lire as keymoney.

So I propose to pass three months in Ireland in order to write *Circe* and the close of the book. I should return here with my family in October (if anyone finds a flat for us in the meantime) or, if not, without them in order to write the end of it.

Financially my position is that I shall receive on 25 June (£ 62-10-0) and if my New York publisher advances (£ 25). I presume that by the time this £ 87 is finished I shall [be] within measurable distance of 25 September when I get another £ 62-10-0. My wife and children could stay in Galway. I too there or in Dublin. The disturbed state of Ireland is of course a reason for not going. There may be other reasons. But I could not go to an English seaside town as it would be too dear. If I manage to do this and if you are in London at the end of June there are, I suppose, several things I could do such as seeing my agent. What do you think of this plan? I must finish my book in quiet even if I sell off the furniture I have here.

I hope you received safely *The Oxen of the Sun* and have sent it off to London and New York. I was bringing down another copy this morning. The worst of it is I fear that Linati may come down on you. I wrote him yesterday express that I should be in Sirmione tonight and mentioned your suggestion of our meeting!

Have you seen *Poesia* or shall I send it?

I hope Mrs. Pound is still well. It is a pity that I cannot see my way to go now but perhaps it is better so if I can manage the other and in that case we can meet more comfortably.

Let me know as soon as possible about the safe arrival of chapter.

With many regrets and regards

Sincerely yours
James Joyce

Like many of Joyce's presentations of his chronically hopeless situation, this one has its absurdities. He cannot abide Trieste, it appears, yet he meditates leaving it for only three months. The notion of taking an expensive trip to England and Ireland with his whole family in order to buy clothing there at a low price exemplifies his power to read into his own inclinations the imperatives of cruel necessity. By the end of the letter he was detached enough from it to add the embarrassed postscript:

This is a very poetical epistle. Do not imagine that it is a subtly worded request for secondhand clothing. It should be read in the evening when the lakewater is lapping and very rhythmically.[35]

Pound read the letter with his accustomed sympathy. He wrote from Sirmione that they had waited until eight o'clock before sitting down to dinner, and that he had prepared an elaborate opening speech to offer Joyce either food or an invitation to the comely laundress up the road. There had been a storm so furious that night that he had hoped it might yet portend the arrival of Vulcan-Dedalus.[36] A second letter written the same day suggested Joyce try living in Sirmione, and buy clothes in Verona, where they could be had more cheaply than in London. Ordinarily the information about storms would have prevented Joyce from stopping even temporarily at Sirmione, but he abruptly recognized that the meeting with Pound was essential. 'In spite of my dread of thunderstorms and detestation of travelling,' he wrote Miss Weaver, 'I went there bringing my son with me to act as a lightning conductor.'[37]

Pound greeted him warmly, and, when he arrived on June 8,[38] asked him almost at once about the identity of his mysterious patron. 'Was it John Quinn, then?'[39] Joyce quickly undeceived him, with the more emphasis since he did not consider Quinn especially generous. They discussed Joyce's situation at length, and agreed that Joyce should stop for a few days at least in Paris to survey that city and make arrangements if possible, for the French translation of *A Portrait of the Artist,* and perhaps of *Dubliners* as well. Pound would go before and prepare the way for him. There was also a transfer of clothing, which Joyce memorialized in a limerick:

> A bard once in lakelapped Sirmione
> Lived in peace, eating locusts and honey
>   Till a son of a bitch
>   Left him dry on the beach
> Without clothes, boots, time, quiet or money.[40]

(The clothes and boots were too small, but Joyce wore the suit in Paris anyway.) Pound summarized the occasion, too, in a letter to John Quinn:

> Joyce—pleasing; after the first shell of cantankerous Irishman, I got the impression that the real man is the author of *Chamber Music,* the sensitive. The rest is the genius; the registration of realities on the temperament, the delicate temperament of the early poems. A concentration and absorption passing Yeats'—Yeats has never taken on anything requiring the condensation of *Ulysses.*
>
> Also great exhaustion, but more constitution than I had expected, and apparently good recovery from eye operation.

He is coming up here later; long reasons, but justified in taking a rest from Trieste.

He is, of course, as stubborn as a mule or an Irishman, but I failed to find him at all *unreasonable.** Thank God, he has been stubborn enough to know his job and stick to it.

Re his personal arrangements, etc., all seems clear in light of conversation.

He is also dead right in refusing to interrupt his stuff by writing stray articles for cash. Better in the end, even from practical point of view. Also justified in sticking it out in Trieste, at least for the present. Both climate and other considerations.

In the stories of his early eccentricities in Dublin, I have always thought people neglected the poignant features, i.e., that his 'outrageous' remarks were usually *so*.[41]

Joyce returned to Trieste with his mind resolved on departure. He still planned, or said he did in a note to Mrs. Murray, to go to London after staying in Paris for a week or two.[42] With considerable fuss and bother the family packed up again.† Joyce had recovered his manuscript from Mrs. McCormick, and had reached an understanding with John Quinn about its sale. He resigned his position at the Università di Trieste, and asked that it be given to his brother Stanislaus. The authorities tried someone else for a year, then acceded to his suggestion. There were goodbyes exchanged with Schmitz, Benco, Silvestri, and Francini; Joyce remained in touch with all of them, although Francini annoyed him two years later by a lecture in Trieste, '*Joyce Intimo Spogliato in Piazza*' ('Joyce Stripped in Public'), which treated him in a high-spirited way that appeared to Joyce debunking, and ended with a reverent prayer that Joyce's soul might yet be saved.‡ He concluded this way mostly for the sake of a final flourish, at which Joyce, egged on by Stanislaus, chose to take offense. The Schaureks came to the station to see the Joyces off, but Stanislaus, after commissioning his brother to buy him a Burberry coat, refused in a pet to join them. He wrote later to apologize for not being 'in a very sociable mood during your stay here,'[44] and Joyce replied fraternally enough, 'I regretted to observe the barometric depression to which you allude. The perusal of my innocent pages is the only dispeller of illusions which repays the money invested.'[45] The brothers

---

* Pound said however in the first number of *New Review,* 1931, 'I respect Mr. Joyce's integrity as an author in that he has not taken the easy part. I never had any respect for his common sense or for his intelligence, apart from his gifts as a writer.'

† Part of Joyce's inventory of his books has survived. See note 43, pp. 793-5.

‡ P. 482.

were never close again.* It is easy to see that James was a difficult older brother, yet Stanislaus was a difficult younger one. If James was casual and capricious, Stanislaus was punctilious and overbearing. James knew his laxity of behavior to be an appearance he could, in sudden tautness, brush aside; Stanislaus knew his own self-discipline to be largely a revolt against his brother's faults. The artist and his reformer made poor house-mates. Stanislaus remembered with many instances that he had been abused in Trieste. Yet he had also been lifted away from ignominy in Dublin and given a career and an intellectual life. The debts were due and had been paid on both sides.

The travelers stopped in Venice for two days, and stopped again in Milan to see Carlo Linati, who was translating *Exiles,* then went through Switzerland to Dijon, where they stopped another night,[46] so that they did not reach Paris until July 8. Ezra Pound was immediately and entirely at their disposal. He was living at the Hôtel Elysée, 9 rue de Beaune, and found temporary lodgings for them close by at 9 rue de l'Université in a private hotel, which pleased Joyce by reminding him of Dublin.[47] He came to Paris to stay a week and remained for twenty years.

* James wrote a footnote for Gorman's biography saying of this departure, 'The relations between the two brothers practically end here.' (He was annoyed by Stanislaus's persistent criticism of his later work.) Actually they continued to correspond, and met three more times. See also p. 753.

PART IV

PARIS

1 9 2 0

Parysis, *tu sais,* crucycrooks, belongs to him who parises himself.

—*Finnegans Wake* (155)

SIGNOR Yoyce' now became 'Monsieur Joyce.' With the arrival in Paris Joyce's private life was suddenly a public concern; his gambols in Trieste and Zurich over, he adopted a somber, restrained manner more expressly than ever before. While other writers practiced their *mots,* he measured his silences. The new move, like the previous wanderings, was not easy for his children; almost the only continuity in their lives, besides their parents, was the habit they kept up in Paris of speaking Italian together. Giorgio, over six feet tall, was now fifteen, and had completed his schooling; it was uncertain what he would do next. When a friend asked Joyce if he were not concerned about his son's situation, he replied, 'I'm so preoccupied with my own that I have no time to think about his.' [1] Actually he did think about Giorgio, but by fits and starts, and in Paris managed later to obtain for him a position in a bank; then, remembering his own dismal experience, he sympathized with Giorgio's dislike of it. Lucia was thirteen, with a beautiful oval face marred slightly by crossed eyes, over which she already felt undue concern. She had suffered most from the family's frequent displacements, but as yet she did not show any special oddity of behavior. Both children were heavily influenced by their father, but both spoke up boldly to him. Lucia, because of his practice of using mild exclamations, teased him by calling him *'L'Esclamadore,'* [2] while Giorgio liked to display in argument an obstinacy of the same weave as his father's, informing him for example that the greatest novelist was Dostoevski, the greatest novel *Crime and Punishment.* His father said only that it was a queer title for a book which contained neither crime nor punishment. [3]

In Paris Joyce felt, as he had that first day at Clongowes, that he

499

was caught up in the whirl of a scrimmage.* In a few days he had met dozens of people, in a few weeks he had received visitors, reverent or merely curious, from New York, London, and Dublin, made new friends and enemies, and played the starveling and then the seigneur, both rather convincingly. Money came in and he spent it. Fame appeared, in Rilke's sense of the quintessence of all the misunderstandings that collect around a new name; and he was sometimes diverted by it. More to the point, Joyce, the artist, now thirty-eight, completed *Circe* and then the final three episodes of *Ulysses.*

Pound, whom Giorgio and Lucia called 'Signor Sterlina,' had already done a good deal of work as advance agent. Among those conscripted was Jenny Serruys, a literary agent.[4] Pound had met her in the hospitable salon of Natalie Clifford Barney (the friend of Remy de Gourmont and Paul Valéry), and persuaded her to translate *A Portrait of the Artist* into French. When she decided after a few days that she could not find time for so large a task, Pound took the book to Madame Ludmila Bloch-Savitsky, the mother-in-law of the English poet John Rodker. Madame Bloch-Savitsky was about to translate something else but Pound masterfully removed the other book, placed *A Portrait* in her hands, and said, 'You must translate Joyce's book, and right away. There's nothing in the literature of the world today, and not much in the literature of the past, that is up to it.'[5] She had to consent. The plan at first was to publish it serially in *L'Action,* which proved impossible, and then the *Mercure de France* was approached, but unsuccessfully. At length a contract was signed with Éditions de la Sirène on August 11, 1921, but the book was not published until March, 1924. Madame Bloch-Savitsky worked at the book with great care, and refused to hurry when Joyce became impatient. She offered to abandon the work in someone else's favor if he liked,[6] but at this point Joyce wisely decided to let her proceed at her own pace. Occasionally he offered her advice; she should change the given names of the characters to their French equivalents: Étienne Dedalus, Jean Lawton. '*Et Jacques Joyce, alors?*' '*Mais bien sûr, pourquoi pas?*' he said, but insisted no more. It was she who determined, with Joyce's consent, to call the French version *Dedalus,* more flamboyant than *Portrait de l'Artiste Jeune.*[7]

Copies of *A Portrait* were placed by Pound in other strategic hands, as well, and Joyce followed them with folders of press notices of his

---

* As in Rome 14 years earlier, he had no patience with monuments. Valery Larbaud said to him as they drove in a taxi past the Arc de Triomphe with its eternal fire, 'How long do you think that will burn?' Joyce answered, 'Until the Unknown Soldier gets up in disgust and blows it out.'[8]

books, so that the effect of the double barrage was to convince Paris that an established writer was now established there. This schedule—while highly effective—put Joyce into a bad humor, and he was frequently, out of irritation as well as shyness, stiff and unbending with the people he met. They were impressed enough to help him nonetheless.

The first to give Joyce material assistance was Madame Bloch-Savitsky. She and her husband offered him in mid-July a flat, rent-free, at 5 rue de l'Assomption, in Passy, close to the Bois de Boulogne.[9] It was a small three-room flat, with two bedrooms facing the street, a storage room, and a tiny kitchen. In this 'matchbox,' as Joyce called it, the family stayed from July 15 to November 1. A bed was lacking for Giorgio, and Joyce therefore paid a visit to Jenny Serruys, whom Pound had indoctrinated with the idea, 'You must help Joyce.'[10] He came into her office and gazed myopically at her. He needed a bed; she promised to find him one, then forgot; Joyce reminded Pound, Pound reminded her, and she sent over a portable bed.[11] A formal letter in what Wyndham Lewis called 'staid, copybook French' arrived to thank her: *'Je vous remercie de votre intérêt bienveillant et vous prie d'agréer l'assurance de ma parfaite considération.'*[12] Perfect consideration is more often accorded to a notary than to a patron.

Joyce and Mlle Serruys had a number of such encounters. He waited patiently to see her if she happened to be busy, then adopted the stratagem of arriving at the inconvenient hour of 1 o'clock. 'I'm afraid I'm inconveniencing you,' he would begin. 'Not at all,' she would reply efficiently, 'I'm just going. Let me give you a lift in a taxi.' During the short ride to the Palais-Royal, where he always got out, he sadly disclosed his affairs. His extreme dignity made borrowing a complicated and grave matter. A table to write on was needed; she had one sent over. (When he moved to a furnished flat, he punctiliously returned it.) Where could he obtain sheets and blankets? How could he recover a package of books sent from Trieste, and inexplicably delayed? Or could she lend him money for some noble triviality? He was later to thank her by saying, 'You never attached any importance to small matters—a quality unusual in a woman.'[13]

When her fiancé William Aspenwall Bradley * was present, Joyce, who took a quick liking to him, was more expansive. He was preoccupied with the writing of *Circe*, and explained the episode, more to himself, as it seemed, than to them. He kept prodding them for hints and suggestions. Bradley happened to remark that General Grant's

---

* Bradley had written some books and had also translated Remy de Gourmont; he was Paris agent for Harcourt, Brace and Co.

first name was Ulysses, and Joyce wrote the fact down on his cuff.° Bradley added, 'He smoked big cigars,' an item duly registered in the same place. Joyce lent Bradley his manuscript of the final episode and was eager to know his opinion. Sometimes, but rarely, they discussed other writers. André Gide was one of the few whom Joyce did not dismiss; he said of *La Symphonie Pastorale*, which he had read in Zurich, that it was not a perfect artistic work but a piece of fine artistic touches.[14] He allowed that Gide wrote a pure French. The name of Proust came up and Joyce, having read a few pages, commented, 'I cannot see any special talent but I am a bad critic.'[15] Jenny Serruys lent him T. S. Eliot's second book of verse, *Ara Vus Prec*, but he made no comment. When the weather grew chilly, Bradley gave Joyce his old army overcoat, and Joyce announced with winning simplicity, 'I never had a better coat.'[16]

Jenny Serruys now offered to translate *Exiles*. Joyce wanted desperately to have it produced in Paris: 'A comedy unperformed is just a dead exile,' he said.[17] He was glad to accept her offer to persuade Lugné-Poë to produce it at the Théâtre de l'Œuvre, where his skill with experimental plays was already well known. If that approach failed, there was a possibility of interesting Jacques Copeau of the Vieux Colombier. Joyce spurred other acquaintances also to put in a word with Lugné-Poë and Copeau. With this aim he came to a soirée of Natalie Clifford Barney, attended by Paul Valéry and other French writers. He was ill at ease, averse as always to discoursing at large, but he made some effort to converse with them about French literature, and had got as far as saying he couldn't bear Racine and Corneille when Miss Barney, embarrassed by this opinion, interrupted rudely, 'Don't you think that sort of remark shows something about the person who says it?'[18] Joyce was silent, and spent the rest of the evening draped around a column in the drawing room. He found occasion, however, to ask before he left for her help with his play. Incidents of this kind helped to develop in him a kind of peasant scorn of Parisian sophistication; his literary life he lived at home, his outings he had to devote to borrowing beds, books, money, or influence.

Only one of his many encounters with literary people was of great importance. Ludmila Bloch-Savitsky wrote her friend André Spire, the poet, to announce that Ezra Pound's group of Joyces had arrived. On what day would he receive them? Would he want one Joyce, two Joyces, three Joyces, four Joyces, or no Joyces at all? Spire settled for two Joyces, and on a Sunday afternoon, on July 11, Madame Bloch-

---

° Molly Bloom remembers 'when General Ulysses Grant whoever he was or did supposed to be some great fellow landed off the ship . . .' *Ulysses* (742 [716]).

Savitsky and her husband, the poet André Fontanas and his wife, and the two Joyces drove out to Neuilly. Spire had also invited Pound and Adrienne Monnier, the bookseller whose shop, La Maison des Amis des Livres ('the Monnier chapel,' as some called it) at 7 rue de l'Odéon, was already frequented by the makers as well as the readers of modern French literature. Adrienne, plump and dressed in a peasant gown which she had made herself, seemed, as William Carlos Williams said, 'to stand up to her very knees in heavy loam.' [19] She had brought along her American friend, Sylvia Beach, the daughter of a Presbyterian minister in Princeton and in refuge from all that implied. Sylvia Beach had in November 1919 opened a shop under the name of Shakespeare and Company at 8 rue Dupuytren, later at 12 rue de l'Odéon, across the street from Adrienne Monnier's shop. The afternoon passed amiably enough. Joyce declined to drink until evening, and so, after refusing various wines offered by his host, turned his glass down. Ezra Pound jocularly collected all the wine bottles and ranged them in front of the teetotaler, to the diversion of the rest of the company, and to Joyce's embarrassment.

Most of the company gathered around another guest, Julien Benda, who was denouncing to Adrienne Monnier her friends Valéry, Claudel, and Gide, while she defended them with equal vigor. Joyce withdrew to another room and was looking at a book when Sylvia Beach, half-diffident, half-daring, approached to ask, 'Is this the great James Joyce?' 'James Joyce,' he responded, holding out his hand to be shaken. She expressed her admiration for his books, and he asked her what she did in Paris. When he heard the name of her bookstore, he smiled gently and wrote it down in a little notebook which he nearsightedly held close to his eyes. He promised to come to see her, and in fact arrived at her shop the next day. He wore, she noticed, a dark blue serge suit, a black felt hat on the back of his head, and rather dirty tennis shoes, with a twirling cane contributing an incongruously dapper element to this costume. He explained his situation in Paris, and asked her help in finding a flat, which she gladly promised. He was short of money, he said, and thought he had better give English lessons; would she let him know of anyone who wanted them? She would. Before he left he borrowed *Riders to the Sea* from her lending library.[20] Sylvia Beach was delighted with her visitor, and Joyce liked her intelligent sympathy and her willingness to help him with all her energy. She and Adrienne Monnier were to be his main sources of information about French literature of the nineteen-twenties; 'He listened to all they told him,' said Jean Paulhan, 'and never said a word.' [21] Sylvia Beach bustled endlessly about to help the tall, thin, myopic, languid man burdened with so many cares, whom she and Adrienne referred to in private by two names he had given himself, 'Melancholy Jesus' and 'Crooked Jesus.' [22] He became the chief luminary (not only in Paris but the world) about whom the American and English customers of Shakespeare and Company had to be kept posted.

Joyce waited impatiently for money from Pinker, who was supposed to obtain it from Huebsch, and from Quinn, who was paying for *Ulysses* in installments. Pound had a plan 'to get the Duchess of Marlborough to apply for the position vacated by Mrs M.[cCormick],' Joyce wrote Stanislaus, with whom he corresponded occasionally, but it 'fell through' because 'her bloody old father W. K. Vanderbilt died here in the next street to us the day before yesterday, very inconsiderately I think.' [23] Pound generously put whatever spare money he had into Joyce's capacious pocket, and in one way or another the Joyces escaped famine. In spite of financial anxiety and his accustomed plaintiveness, Joyce was not entirely displeased with Paris. For one thing, it was a new and heady feeling to discover he was a leader in a movement. As he wrote to Stanislaus on July 25, 1920, 'Odyssey very much in the air here. Anatole France is writing *Le Cyclope*, G. Fauré, the musician, an opera *Pénélope*. Giraudoux has written *Elpénor* (Paddy Dignam). Guillaume Apollinaire *Les Mamelles de Tirésias*. . . . Madame Circe advances regally towards her completion after which I hope to join a tennis club.' * [24]

The day after writing this letter, Joyce went at the suggestion of Pound to call on Fritz Vanderpyl, the jovial, bearded Belgian art critic of *Le Petit Parisien*, whose novel, *Marsden Stanton à Paris*, had been one of the more interesting recent experiments in fiction. Vanderpyl received with his usual lusty amiability the gentleman who, except for his startling tennis shoes, looked like a professor. After an hour's talk they went for a walk in the Jardin du Luxembourg, a few yards away from Vanderpyl's flat in the rue Gay-Lussac. There they met a friend of Vanderpyl with whom they conversed for a time about literature. Then Joyce abruptly pulled Vanderpyl to one side and asked, 'Does your friend know English?' 'No.' 'Well, can you lend me a hundred francs? Tomorrow is my son's birthday and I want to give him something.' At that time a hundred francs ($20, £4) was a not inconsiderable sum, but Vanderpyl, who had no money with him, obligingly borrowed it from his friend and then lent it to Joyce. [25]

By afternoon of the following day the money was spent, and Joyce was sitting gloomily in his flat contemplating his penury when John Rodker and his wife rang the bell. Rodker was a regular contributor

* A reference to his shoes.

to the *Egoist* and had begun to publish books on a small hand press. Mrs. Rodker came in wearing a red cloak which reminded Joyce of the Irish claddagh or shawl and would therefore, he predicted, be lucky for him. And so it proved. Rodker rescued the family from hunger by inviting them all to dinner,[26] and during dinner made tentative arrangements to print *Ulysses* in France, with the financial backing of the *Egoist*, and then to publish it in England under his imprint. This business over, Joyce turned the conversation to other subjects. He quizzed Rodker earnestly on which horse had won the derby in 1904 (when Rodker was ten); he spoke about books; he commented that the name Joyce meant the same thing in English as Freud in German, a remark he usually left to his friends; and he overpowered both Rodkers with the one subject he never mentioned, his sense of his mission in art.[27]

Pinker sent £10 at last, but Joyce nevertheless wrote to Pound on July 31 suggesting a series of press notices to proclaim, 'Joyce Gets Large Haul. Prompt Pinker Saves Desperate Dedalus. Glut of Greenbacks for Poet in Poverty.'[28] His financial difficulties, several times alleviated but promptly renewed by spending, were more effectively countered by a new benefaction from Miss Weaver, intended as she said to free his 'best and most powerful and productive years'[29] from material worries. Joyce proudly informed Stanislaus of this new evidence of the esteem in which he was held, but forgot to send him the Burberry waterproof.

Joyce's associations in Paris grew more numerous and complex, and, as he tried to accustom himself to them, he was sometimes genial but often prickly. Mrs. Yasushi Tanaka (Louise Gebhart Cann), the American wife of a Japanese painter, heard from Pound that Joyce was more worthwhile than anyone in Paris, and asked him to call. Joyce came round and staggered her a little by the ready violence of his opinions. Painting, he announced, did not interest him, except for portraiture—a hard blow for Tanaka. She referred with great respect to Yeats, and Joyce, not in the mood for other admirations, sneered at him as Lady Gregory's lover, saying she financed him. (To another woman who asked him at this time, 'Whom do you consider the greatest writers in English today?' he replied, 'Aside from myself, I don't know.'[30]) He invited the Tanakas to join him frequently at restaurants and bistros, but he had a way of also inviting people with no artistic interests. Madame Tanaka was amused to see him sit utterly immobile as the wife of a businessman flattered him and squeezed his arm invitingly. Nora was along, obviously wishing she weren't, and she laughingly agreed when Madame Tanaka said to her, 'You are a martyr to a man of genius.' Joyce encouraged the composition by Madame Tanaka of an article about him for an American newspaper, but the Tanakas themselves he had to give up because they disliked late hours.[31]

Many pilgrims came to the new shrine. The poet Ivan Goll, whom Joyce had known slightly in Zurich, came in July, on behalf of the Rhein-Verlag (Zurich), to talk about publishing *A Portrait* in a German translation. Philippe Soupault, who was translating Blake, discussed *Jerusalem* with him.[32] Clive Bell met Joyce, and did not like him.[33] Joyce wrote Miss Weaver on August 16, 'Mr Pound introduced me to a number of people here on whom I created anything but a good impression.' He remarked in a letter to Budgen, 'I observe a furtive attempt to run a certain Marcel Proust of here against the signatory of this letter. . . . I think a fall of mine would not altogether disappoint some admirers. It seems to me I have made a bad impression here. I am too preoccupied (Bloomesque word) to rectify it.'[34] And to Pound, who had gone back meanwhile to what he called 'this brass-bound clay-hummock' Joyce commented on his failure to play the social game spryly, 'I heard and saw no more of the many lucky mortals who made my acquaintance here. I suspect that the pleasure my exhilarating company gave them will last for the rest of their natural existences. Except Vanderpyl.'[35]

It was impossible not to find Vanderpyl companionable. Joyce liked his joviality and explosiveness, while Vanderpyl was a little awed by this writer who seemed to know too much and carried himself like a bishop who was still a seminarist at heart. Joyce was not above playing the pedagogue; one day he dined with Vanderpyl and another writer, Edmond Jaloux, at a restaurant in the rue St. Honoré. As they drank champagne and Fendant de Sion, Jaloux, who happened to be carrying a copy of Flaubert's *Trois Contes*, began to praise the faultlessness of its style and language. Joyce, in spite of his own admiration for Flaubert, bristled, '*Pas si bien que ça. Il commence avec une faute.*' And taking the book he showed them that in the first sentence of '*Un Cœur simple,*' '*Pendant un demi-siècle, les bourgeoises de Pont-l'Évêque envièrent à Mme Aubain sa servante Félicité,*' *envièrent* should be *enviaient*, since the action is continued rather than completed. Then he thumbed through the book, evidently with a number of mistakes in mind, and came to the last sentence of the final story, 'Hérodias,' '*Comme elle était très lourde, ils la portaient alternativement.*' '*Alternativement* is wrong,' he announced, 'since there are *three* bearers.'[36]

In mid-August Joyce received his first direct communication from

T. S. Eliot, whose shape Ezra Pound had been limning for seven years. Eliot wrote from London that Pound had entrusted to his keeping a package for Joyce, which he would bring with him on August 15 to the Hôtel de l'Élysée. 'I hope you can dine with me that evening. Please,' he said graciously, and added, 'You won't have time to answer. But please come.'[37] Actually Eliot was not traveling alone, but with Wyndham Lewis, whose book *Tarr*, published like *A Portrait* by the Egoist Press, Joyce had read in Zurich, and whose story *Cantleman's Spring Mate* had earned the *Little Review* its only suppression that was not caused by Joyce's *Ulysses*. Lewis's work had impressed Joyce, but he was still dubious of Eliot's verse.

Eliot and Lewis duly arrived at their hotel, Eliot having lugged Pound's clumsy parcel on train, boat, and train again. Joyce, accompanied by Giorgio, came over to see them, and the presence of Lewis startled and pleased him. Lewis's admirable description reveals that Joyce had at last shed his tennis shoes: 'I found an oddity, in patent-leather shoes, large powerful spectacles, and a small gingerbread beard; speaking half in voluble Italian to a scowling schoolboy; playing the Irishman a little overmuch perhaps, but in amusingly mannered technique.'[38] For the moment Joyce seemed more manner than man. The meeting proceeded with a dignity befitting an encounter of Titans, but undercut by Pound's gift. As Lewis recounts,

We all then sat down. But only for a moment.

Joyce lay back in the stiff chair he had taken from behind him, crossed his leg, the lifted leg laid out horizontally upon the one in support like an artificial limb, an arm flung back over the summit of the sumptuous chair. He dangled negligently his straw hat, a regulation 'boater.' We were on either side of the table, the visitors and ourselves, upon which stood the enigmatical parcel.

Eliot now rose to his feet. He approached the table, and with one eyebrow drawn up, and a finger pointing, announced to James Joyce that *this* was that parcel, to which he had referred in his wire, and which had been given into his care, and he formally delivered it, thus acquitting himself of his commission.

'Ah! Is this the parcel you mentioned in your note?' enquired Joyce, overcoming the elegant reluctance of a certain undisguised fatigue in his person. And Eliot admitted that it was, and resumed his seat. . . .

James Joyce was by now attempting to untie the crafty housewifely knots of the cunning old Ezra. After a little he asked his son crossly in Italian for a penknife. Still more crossly his son informed him that he had no penknife. But Eliot got up, saying 'You want a knife? I have not got a knife, I think!' We were able, ultimately, to provide a pair of nail scissors.

At last the strings were cut. A little gingerly Joyce unrolled the slovenly swaddlings of damp British brown paper in which the good-hearted American had packed up what he had put inside. Thereupon, along with some nondescript garments for the trunk—there were no trousers I believe—a fairly presentable pair of *old brown shoes* stood revealed, in the centre of the bourgeois French table. . . .

James Joyce, exclaiming very faintly 'Oh!' looked up, and we all gazed at the old shoes for a moment. 'Oh!' I echoed and laughed, and Joyce left the shoes where they were, disclosed as the matrix of the disturbed leaves of the parcel. He turned away and sat down again, placing his left ankle upon his right knee, and squeezing, and then releasing, the horizontal limb.

With a smile even slower in materializing than his still-trailing Bostonian voice (a handsome young United States President, to give you an idea—adding a Gioconda smile to the other charms of this office) Eliot asked our visitor if he would have dinner with us. Joyce turned to his son, and speaking very rapidly in Italian, the language always employed by him, so it seemed, in his family circle, he told him to go home: he would inform his mother that his father would not be home to dinner after all. Yes, his father had accepted an invitation to dinner, and would not be back after all, for the evening meal! Did he understand? To tell his mother that his father—. But the son very hotly answered his father back, at th's, after but a moment's hesitation on account of the company: evidently he did not by any means relish being entrusted with messages. It was, however, with greater hotness, in yet more resonant Italian, that the son expressed his rebellious sensations when the imperturbable Jimmie handed him the parcel of disreputable footwear. That was the last straw—this revolting, this unbecoming packet. Having exchanged a good number of stormy words, in a series of passionate asides—in a good imitation of an altercation between a couple of neapolitan touts, of the better order—Joyce, père et fils, separated, the latter rushing away with the shoes beneath his arm, his face crimson and his eyes blazing with a truly southern ferocity—first having mastered himself for a moment sufficiently to bow to me from the hips, and to shake hands with heroic punctilio. This scene took place as we were about to leave the small hotel.[39]

Joyce proposed to Lewis and Eliot that they dine at a restaurant he knew nearby, and from that moment he became their host. When they sat down at the table he had selected for them, he remarked, 'It appears that I have the melancholy advantage of being the eldest of the band.'[40] He then ordered an excellent dinner and wines, and paid for it afterwards, tipping munificently. His hospitality continued during the rest of their visit. As Lewis says, 'If we were in a taxicab with James Joyce, out he would spring in front of us. And before even we reached the pavement the fare was settled and the cabman was pocketing a disproportionately massive tip: whereas in a café no beer or coffee, whoever had ordered it, was ever paid for by anyone but the eminent recipient of the parcel of old shoes.'[41]

Towards Eliot Joyce acted with 'a punctilious reserve.' * [42] In conversation with Lewis he referred to him as 'Your friend Mr. Eliot,'
and Eliot remarked to Lewis with some amusement, 'He does not take
much notice of me.' [43] Joyce's 'grand talk' pleased Eliot, but awoke
reservations, too. Alone together, Lewis said,

'I find our friend . . . very affable and easy don't you, if a shade stilted?' But
Eliot found him definitely burdensome, and *arrogant*. . . . 'I do not think he
is *arrogant*,' I said. . . . 'He may not seem so!' Eliot answered, in his grim
Bostonian growl. 'He may not seem arrogant, no.'
 'You think he is as proud as Lucifer?'
 'I would not say Lucifer!' Eliot was on his guard at once, at this loose use
of the surname of the Evil Principle.
 'You would not say Lucifer? Well, I daresay he may be under the impres-
sion that he is being "as proud as Lucifer," or some bogtrotting humbug of
that order. What provincials they are, bless their beastly brogues!'
 'Provincials—yes!' Eliot agreed with contemptuous unction. 'Provincials.'
 'However he is most polite.'
 'He is polite.'
 'I have never succeeded in getting out of the door *behind* him, have you?
He is very *You First*. He is very *After you!*'
 'Oh yes. He is polite, he is polite enough. But he is exceedingly arrogant.
Underneath. That is why he is so polite. I should be better pleased if he
were less polite.' [44]

To be Irish was to be too Irish for Lewis's taste. But Eliot was making
in 1920 the same criticism of Joyce's politeness that Stanislaus Joyce
had made in 1903, when he accused him of insincerity. Politeness had
become one of Joyce's principal social defenses, and one he resorted
to constantly in Paris. Nevertheless, the three men became, after their
fashion, friends. Eliot had to continue in a somewhat inferior role
because Joyce gave almost no indication of having read a line of his
verse. Only once did he allow himself to say, 'I was at the Jardin des
Plantes today and paid my respects to your friend the hippopotamus.' [45]
But after reading *The Waste Land*, he remarked to a friend, 'I had
never realized that Eliot was a poet.' She replied, 'I liked it too but
I couldn't understand it,' and Joyce retorted with the question that
Eliot might himself have asked, 'Do you have to understand it?' [46]
He objected to the notes to the poem for the same reason.† Later he

---

* 'I can see him sitting on the kitchen table, swinging his legs and spinning out
of him yards of talk about you and him and Ireland and all kinds of devilment—
to an ignorant old woman like me. But that was always his way. But if he had to
meet a grand highup person he'd be twice as grand himself.' *Exiles* (604 [423])
† When Max Eastman asked why he did not supply help to the reader, Joyce
replied, 'You know people never value anything unless they have to steal it. Even

parodied *The Waste Land* in a letter * and then in *Finnegans Wake*,†
and in a notebook he wrote, 'T. S. Eliot ends idea of poetry for ladies,' [47]
a sentence which suggests that he perceived more affinity than he
acknowledged. As for Lewis, he was on cordial terms with Joyce until
late in the 'twenties, and for several years he, like Eliot, always looked
up Joyce in Paris.

In between paying and receiving visits, Joyce kept at *Circe*. The
Homeric story delighted him, especially the Circean transformation.
'Think of that,' he said, 'swine and yet with men's memories.' There
were considerable difficulties to be resolved in portraying the suppressed
desires of Bloom and Stephen in vaudeville form, psychoanalysis turned
into a vehicle of comedy. Joyce longed again to discuss his work with
Budgen. But Budgen still dallied and delayed, and Joyce mocked him
in a letter of late July:

> When travelling you get into those waggons called railway coaches,
> which are behind the locomotive. This is done by opening a door and
> gently projecting into the compartment yourself and your valise. A man
> in an office will give you a piece of cardboard in exchange for some
> money. By looking at it attentively you will see the word *Paris* printed
> on it which is the name of this stop. There are seats for you to sit on
> in the carriage but you must not get out of it while it is moving as you
> might in that case be left behind. Now, may the Almighty God bless
> you and enable you to carry out all these instructions of mine to you
> this afternoon. Saying which I hereby take you by the hand and remain,
> dear sir,
>
> most expectantly yours,
> J.J.[48]

When Budgen still did not come, Joyce wrote on September 5 to ask
him for ideas. 'A catch word is enough to set me off,' [49] he reminded his
friend when Budgen said his ideas were not worth sending. For the
moment the particular crux was the magic flower, *Moly*, which Hermes
gave to Ulysses to preserve him from Circe's wiles. 'Think of that symbolism,' Joyce commented, 'a white flower with a black root. Other
flowers are tinctured all through with their color, but this alone of all

---

an alley cat would rather snake an old bone out of the garbage than come up and
eat a nicely prepared chop from your saucer.' [50]
* Pp. 583-4.
† 'Their orison arises miquewhite as Osman glory, ebbing *wasteward,* leaves to
the *soul of light its fading silence* (*allahlah lahlah lah!*). . . .
  '*Xanthos! Xanthos! Xanthos!* . . . becoming a *bank* midland mansioner . . . at La
*Rose*raie. . . . *Fyat-Fyat shall be our number* . . . [A Cooking Egg]. . . . T [Tristram]
will be waiting for uns as *I sold* U. . . . wealthy gentrymen wib*frufrocksfull* of
fun!' (235-6) . . . 'washes his fleet in annacrwatter; whou missed a porter. . . .' (135)

flowers has a black root with a white flower.' [51] To William Bradley, whom he consulted as well as Budgen, Joyce pointed out that if Circe's palace was a brothel, then Moly must be something to confer immunity from syphilis. Syphilis, he fancied, derived from *syn phileis*, 'together with loving, connected with it,' but Bradley took the view that it derived from *su philos*, 'swine love.' [52] Joyce (unlike the etymologists) was persuaded, but still had to find a naturalistic equivalent for Moly. He consulted by mail his old friend the Baroness St. Leger, and she suggested that Moly was *allium niger—garlic*,[53] an interpretation homely enough to interest him.* In his notebook Joyce jotted down as possible interpretations of the flower 'absinthe [which he described elsewhere as 'the cerebral impotentising (!!) drink or chastity'], mercury; chastity, chance (narrow shoes); inexperience; beauty; laughter, satire; conscience; escape from poison; Met-salt.' † [54] In late September the problem was solved, and he announced to Budgen:

My latest is this. Moly is the gift of Hermes, god of public ways, and is the inaudible influence (prayer, chance, agility, *presence of mind*, power of recuperation) which saves in case of accident. This would cover immunity from syphilis. . . . Hermes is the god of signposts—i.e. he is especially for a traveller like Ulysses the point at which roads parallel merge and roads contrary also. He is an accident of providence. In this special case his plant may be said to have many leaves, indifference due to masturbation, pessimism congenital, a sense of the ridiculous, sudden fastidiousness in some detail, experience.[55]

He hoped to finish *Circe* before Christmas, and at last, on December 20, after having rewritten the episode from start to finish six or seven or eight or nine times (the count varied), he pronounced it done.[56] In a rare moment of appraisal he commented to Francini Bruni, 'I think it is the best thing I have ever written.' [57]

It would have been agreeable to know who would publish *Ulysses*, but for the moment no plan was firm. On August 25 Miss Weaver had to give up her last hope for an English edition printed in England, when

---

* Victor Bérard also found a homely equivalent; he wrote in *Did Homer Live?* (New York, 1931) p. 120:

> *Moly* . . . is not a Greek word; it is found nowhere else in ancient literature: it does not even belong to men's language, but to the language of the gods. The Scriptures give the name of m. l. ou. h. to a sand-plant which the poor sometimes made into a dish—a *salad*, as we should say: the Hebraic root m. l. h. in fact means salt. The exact equivalent in Greek is *halimos* and the plant indicated is our *atriplex halimus* commonly called *sea purslane*, which is eaten as a salad, or pickled in vinegar. It is a shrub, and only the leaves and young shoots are edible. The flower is a milky yellow—'milk-white,' the Poet calls it.

† 'Met-salt' is probably, as Walton Litz suggests, 'metamorphosis of salt.' [58]

the last of a series of printers decided not to risk it. Rodker's notion of printing in Paris was still possible, but an American edition was by far the most promising plan. B. W. Huebsch had published *A Portrait* and *Dubliners* in 1916, *Exiles* and *Chamber Music* in 1918, and had expressed his interest in *Ulysses*. There was, however, the fact to reckon with that the United States Post Office had confiscated and burned four issues of the *Little Review* because of the episodes from *Ulysses* contained in them. It seemed likely that the government would prosecute the publisher for obscenity. John Quinn suggested in December that the edition be privately printed and limited to 1500 copies, of which half would be sold in Europe. The price would be $12.50, and Joyce would receive a thousand pounds, or so he wrote Ettore Schmitz on January 5, 1921. (The actual amount suggested by Quinn was $2000-$3000.) The publisher would be Huebsch or perhaps Boni and Liveright, whose Paris agent, Leon Fleischman, had come to know Joyce recently and evinced an interest in securing the rights for *Ulysses*.[59] Since this firm had published Huneker's *Painted Veils*, they might be willing to risk prosecution again. But the first decision was up to Huebsch, and he was hard put to it to make up his mind: whether to risk a jail sentence and fine, or to lose the book to another publisher. Joyce was annoyed by what seemed to him a want of alacrity, but in the atmosphere of censorship in 1921 Huebsch's hesitation was understandable. In an unguarded moment Joyce remarked jocularly to Ezra Pound, 'No country outside of Africa will print it.' For the moment he was right.

The production of *Exiles* was also blocked for the time being. Lugné-Poë vacillated about the play during August, then in October informed Joyce he and Suzanne Desprès would produce it during December or January. There was no money in it, but he would do it anyway. Joyce must agree in advance to *'une révision scénique du texte,'*[60] and Joyce, eager to see *Exiles*, acceded to this vague stipulation. Jacques Natanson accordingly adapted it, but his version discouraged the producer; then Lugné-Poë's success with Crommelynck's *Le Cocu Magnifique* forced a postponement of *Exiles* until spring; and, since the first treated the same theme of cuckoldry but in farcical terms, it made a production of Joyce's play less likely to succeed.[61] In June 1921, Lugné-Poë abruptly informed Joyce that he had no intention of losing 15,000 francs on *Exiles*.[62]

Joyce had meanwhile changed his living quarters twice over. He spent October 1920 in hunting a flat, sometimes with acquaintances like André Suarès, whom he flattered in a letter by calling him 'my colleague in art, whose literary works I admire'[63] and whose help in finding a place to live he therefore required. He found nothing, so moved from

the Bloch-Savitsky flat back to 9 rue de l'Université, 'the twentieth
address,' [64] he notified John Quinn, at which he had written *Ulysses*.
Then he heard of an expensive flat at 5 Boulevard Raspail; with help
from various sources, he took the flat, for 2000 lire a month or £300
a year, at the beginning of December, and marveled to Budgen on the
tenth of the month, 'By the way is it not extraordinary the way I enter
a city barefoot and end up in a luxurious flat.' [65] His luck did not hold
for his eyes, however; in November and early December he suffered an
eye attack which was painful though it did not affect the iris. 'I think
Circe must be revenging herself for the unpleasant things I have written
about her legend,' [66] he wrote Miss Weaver on December 9, and on
December 30, 1920, he requested the devil to take the old year away
as quickly as he liked.[67]

1921—1922

It would have diverted, if ever seen, the shuddersome spectacle of this
semidemented zany amid the inspissated grime of his glaucous den
making believe to read his usylessly unreadable Blue Book of Eccles,
édition de ténèbres (even yet sighs the Most Different, Dr. Poindejenk,
authorised bowdler and censor, it can't be repeated!) turning over
three sheets at a wind. . . .

—*Finnegans Wake* (179)

VALERY Larbaud, among the principal French writers of the
1920s, had the distinction of being the most receptive to the
achievements of others. The excellence of his own work in poetry and
the novel lent authority to his generous recognition of fellow talents.
Besides his creative understanding of the literature in his own language, he was well versed in Italian and English literature. He was
to make available to a French audience such writers as Coleridge and
Landor. Most recently he had translated Samuel Butler. Though a man
of subtlety and refinement, he had a most winning simplicity and
directness.

Sylvia Beach turned naturally to Larbaud° as a writer whom Joyce
would value and who would value Joyce in turn. She arranged the first
meeting between them for the afternoon before Christmas, 1920, so
that geniality might be fostered by the festive season. Larbaud and
Joyce got on well, and Larbaud expressed more than a polite interest
in *Ulysses*, about which Joyce talked to him. The next move was made
slowly. In mid-February Sylvia Beach lent Larbaud the numbers of the
Little Review. There followed a week of silence, and then suddenly,
on February 22, 1921, Sylvia Beach received a letter from Larbaud
which began, 'I am raving mad over *Ulysses*.'[1] The book, he said, is as
'great and comprehensive and human as Rabelais.'[2] Mr. Bloom is 'as
immortal as Falstaff.' † Since reading it he had been unable to write

° He had called himself 'godfather' of Sylvia Beach's bookshop.[3]
† In relaying this phrase to Budgen, Joyce added in brackets after it: '[except that
he has some few more years to live—Editor].'[4]

514

or sleep; and he now proposed to translate some pages to go with an article on Joyce in the *Nouvelle Revue Française*, the best and most fashionable of the reviews dedicated to contemporary letters. Would the author send him a photograph? Shakespeare and Company went into an ecstasy; Joyce, careful not to be effusive, wrote to thank Larbaud for his *'paroles encourageantes et amicales'* but quickly informed Miss Weaver, Budgen, Francini, and other friends of his new and eminent recruit. He also sent Larbaud the typescript of the *Oxen of the Sun* episode. Mlle Monnier was too enamored of Larbaud's own work to encourage greatly his enthusiasm for another writer; but he swept her and Sylvia Beach along with his plan to bring Joyce to public notice in France. Before publishing his article he would give a *conférence* on Joyce at Mlle Monnier's bookshop. He had done this with great success for Samuel Butler, and was fortified to do it for an author who might interrupt.

But before the *conférence* on *Ulysses* could take place it was incumbent upon the author to finish his book. Joyce kept expecting to complete it by April or May of 1921, and worked as quickly as he could, groaning with melancholy as he evolved the high comedy of the final episodes. *Eumaeus* went quickly; he amused himself by borrowing a bit (a very small bit) of Frank Budgen for the wily sailor in the episode, and a bit of Daniel Hummel, his Zurich friend who was now living in Paris, for one of the jarveys. He sent the last of *Eumaeus* to the typist in the middle of February, then hurried on to *Ithaca*, which he described to Miss Weaver as my 'last (and stormiest) cape,' [5] and to *Penelope*, which came easier for him. There were notes for these two episodes left in Trieste, and Joyce, after having waited four months for his books to arrive from there, decided he could not trust the mails. He therefore sent a letter—mostly in Triestine dialect—to Ettore Schmitz, who frequently traveled to Paris and London:

> There is in Trieste, in my brother-in-law's quarter, an apartment house bearing the street and building number 2 via Sanità; situated precisely on the fourth floor of this building in the bedroom now occupied by my brother, towards the back of the building in question and over-looking the house of public insecurity [police station], there is an oil-cloth brief-case fastened with a rubber band having the colour of a nun's belly ° and of the approximate dimensions of .95 by .70 centi-metres. In this brief-case I placed the written symbols of the languid lights which occasionally flashed across my soul. The total weight is estimated to be Kg. 4.78. Having urgent need of these notes in order to complete my literary work entitled *Ulysses* or your bitch of a mother ° I address myself courteously to you, honoured colleague, begging you to inform me if any member of your family intends to

° Triestine expressions.

come to Paris in the near future; in the event that someone should come, I would be most grateful if such a person would have the kindness to bring me the sheaf of papers indicated on the back of this letter.

Thus, dear Signor Schmitz, if there is someone of your family who is travelling this way, he would do me a great favour by bringing me the bundle which is not heavy even for a man since, as you will understand, it is full of papers of which I have made fair copies in ink and occasionally even in 'bleistiff' when I had no pen. But be careful not to break the rubber band because then the papers will fall into disorder. The best plan would be to take a suitcase which can be locked so that no one can open it. There are many articles of this kind on sale at 'Greinitz Neffen's' just opposite the 'Piccolo' which my brother, the 'Berlitz-Cul' Professor, passes by.[6]

Schmitz delivered the packet himself in March, and Joyce put together the old notes with new ones. He intended *Ithaca* and *Penelope* to be counterparts, the first to exhibit what he called to Robert McAlmon 'a tranquilising spectrality.'[7] In May he reported to Claud Sykes that he was 'struggling with the acidities of Ithaca—a mathematico-astronomico-physico-mechanico-geometrico-chemico sublimation of Bloom and Stephen (devil take 'em both) to prepare for the final amplitudinously curvilinear episode *Penelope*.'[8] He set forth this purpose more fully in a letter to Budgen:

> I am writing *Ithaca* in the form of a mathematical catechism. All events are resolved into their cosmic physical, psychical, &c equivalents, e.g., Bloom jumping down the area, drawing water from the tap, the micturition in the garden, the cone of incense, lighted candle and statue so that not only will the reader know everything and know it in the baldest coldest way but Bloom and Stephen thereby become heavenly bodies, wanderers like the stars at which they gaze.
>
> The last word (human, all too human) is left to Penelope. This is the indispensable countersign to Bloom's passport to eternity.[9]

By August 16 the *Penelope* episode was fully planned. As usual in writing of it to friends, Joyce advertised its technical structure and complications; he liked to give a bald account, close to being ironic yet also proud. He launched *Penelope* with scientific precision; as he told Budgen,

> Penelope is the clou of the book. The first sentence contains 2500 words. There are eight sentences in the episode. It begins and ends with the female word *yes*. It turns like the huge earth ball slowly surely and evenly, round and round spinning, its 4 cardinal points being the female breasts, arse, womb and cunt expressed by the words *because*, *bottom* (in all uses bottom button, bottom of the class, bottom of the sea, bottom of his heart), *woman*, *yes*. Though probably more obscene

than any preceding episode it seems to me to be perfectly sane full amoral fertilisable untrustworthy engaging shrewd limited prudent indifferent *Weib. Ich bin das Fleisch das stets bejaht.*[10]

The writing of these two episodes was accompanied by a series of small crises. In February the *Little Review* was brought to book for its courageous impropriety. Over several years Margaret Anderson and Jane Heap had defended their magazine against sporadic assaults by authority. They were helped by a Serbian printer who did not mind obscene words in English or even in Serbo-Croatian,[11] and who continued imperturbably to print the review even after the Post Office began to harry it. There had been no difficulty from April 1918, when the serializing of *Ulysses* began, and it looked as if John Quinn's fears of prosecution were groundless. Then in 1919, the January number, containing *Lestrygonians,* and the May number, containing *Scylla and Charybdis,* were confiscated, Quinn's protests to the Solicitor of the Post Office being disregarded. In 1920 the January number, containing the *Cyclops* episode, was confiscated. Confiscation meant burning, and the method afforded Joyce some sardonic amusement. As he wrote to Miss Weaver on February 25, 1920, 'This is the second time I have had the pleasure of being burned while on earth so that I hope I shall pass through the fires of purgatory as quickly as my patron S. Aloysius.'[12] With his penchant for litigation he dreamed of a trial of *Ulysses* as successful as that of *Madame Bovary.* Eventually this came about, but the trial of the *Little Review* was not so splendidly notorious.

The disputed issue was that of July-August 1920, which contained part of the *Nausicaa* episode. It came to the attention of John S. Sumner, the mild-mannered secretary of the New York Society for the Prevention of Vice, who lodged an official complaint in September 1920. Pound and John Quinn had warned Joyce for several months that legal trouble was in store, and had urged him to withdraw the book from the *Little Review.*[13] They felt that the defense of the book was the whole book, and that isolated passages would certainly be found obscene. But when Margaret Anderson and Jane Heap were summoned to court, Quinn agreed, although they had flouted his advice, to serve without fee as their attorney. Still, he did not like the *Little Review;* he said he wished it was back in the Chicago stockyards where it came from. He did not much like Margaret Anderson or Jane Heap, nor did they care much for him, facts which all three were at pains to make perfectly clear. Ezra Pound had to keep writing letters from remote European cities to reconcile the lawyer and his clients.[14]

At a preliminary hearing in police court on 22 October, the magistrate bound the defendants over for trial in the Court of Special Sessions. Quinn tried unsuccessfully to have the case shifted to another court, in the hope that a year's delay might enable Joyce to publish the book before the issue was decided. But after several postponements the trial began on February 14, 1921. Quinn elicited a promise from his clients to keep still and leave the argument to him, though he warned them that conviction was certain. The case was heard before three judges; several hundred Greenwich Villagers filled the courtroom. Quinn began by challenging the competence of the tribunal to decide a case of this sort; when this gambit failed he called his witnesses. These were Scofield Thayer, the editor of the *Dial*, Philip Moeller of the Theatre Guild, and John Cowper Powys. Powys declared unequivocally that *Ulysses* was 'a beautiful piece of work in no way capable of corrupting the minds of young girls.' Moeller attempted tortuously to justify it in terms of Freud, a name as new to the judges, and therefore as suspect, as that of Joyce. Thayer praised the book but conceded that he would probably not have published the *Nausicaa* episode in the *Dial*.

It was now time to read the obscene passages, carefully culled by Sumner. One judge urged that they not be read in the presence of Miss Anderson. 'But she is the publisher,' said John Quinn with a smile. 'I am sure she didn't know the significance of what she was publishing,' the judge gallantly replied.[15] When the passages were read two of the judges found them incomprehensible. Quinn was glad to agree, since if they could not be understood they could not corrupt; but rather lamely attributed the difficulty to the lack of punctuation, which, lamely again, he attributed to the failure of Joyce's eyesight. It was decided to adjourn the trial for a week to give the judges time to read the whole *Nausicaa* installment.

On February 21, when trial was resumed, Quinn made a final argument, drawing an analogy between Joyce's work and cubist painting, and then, to suit more closely what he regarded as the judges' mentality, emphasizing that the episode was disgusting rather than indecent. As for Gerty MacDowell's exhibition of her drawers, the mannikins of Fifth Avenue were much more revealing. The prosecuting attorney rejected these arguments loudly and apoplectically, and Quinn took advantage of his opponent's choler to point to his face and say, 'There is my best exhibit. There is proof that *Ulysses* does not corrupt or fill people full of lascivious thoughts. Look at him! He is mad all over. He wants to hit somebody. He doesn't want to love anybody.... That's what *Ulysses* does. It makes people angry.... But it doesn't tend to drive them to the arms of some siren.' The judges laughed and Quinn thought he had won.[16] But they recovered sobriety and convicted the two editors of publishing obscenity, sentencing them both to pay $50 fines. It was understood that the publication of *Ulysses* would be discontinued, and Quinn had to certify that the *Nausicaa* episode was the worst in the book to save his clients from being sent to prison. When they had left the courtroom Quinn said, 'And now for God's sake don't publish any more obscene literature.' 'How am I to know when it's obscene?' asked Margaret Anderson. He replied, 'I'm sure I don't know, but don't do it.'[17]

Not to receive a jail sentence was a small disappointment, both for the editors and their friends.[18] There was some feeling, too, that Quinn's defense had been equivocal and had prevented the issue from being fully joined. Quinn wrote to Joyce to explain that a loftier defense would have been of no use with these judges.[19] The trial served the useful purpose of stirring both the *New York Times* and the *New York Tribune* to editorial comment.*

Another effect of the *Little Review* decision was, as Quinn had warned, to make the publication of *Ulysses* as a book even less feasible. B. W. Huebsch wrote Quinn reluctantly on March 24 that he could not publish *Ulysses* without some alterations in the text. Quinn, on Joyce's behalf, refused all changes, and on April 5 Huebsch formally declined the manuscript. Joyce cabled huffily at once to withdraw it. Quinn tried Boni and Liveright, but their interest had also abated. This news filled Joyce with misgivings close to despair. He went round to Shakespeare and Company to tell Sylvia Beach of this new unhappy development, 'My book will never come out now.' A thought struck her. 'Would you let Shakespeare and Company have the honor of bringing out your *Ulysses*?' she asked. Joyce was as startled to hear this proposal as she was to make it; he warned her mournfully that no one would buy the book,[20] but at the same time he unhesitatingly accepted.[21]

They arranged to meet next day to talk over the terms, and Sylvia Beach consulted Adrienne Monnier, who encouraged her and suggested that she employ Maurice Darantière, an intellectual printer in Dijon who had just published for her the *Cahiers des Amis des Livres*. About April 10, Sylvia Beach proposed an edition of 1,000 copies, to be subscribed as far as possible in advance. A hundred copies on Holland

---

* The *New York Times* thought the book incomprehensible and dull but not immoral, though the use of certain 'realistic' words was deplorable and deserved punishment. The *New York Tribune*, under the heading of 'Mr. Sumner's Glorious Victory,' more tolerantly agreed with Quinn that the book was disgusting rather than indecent, and pointed out that the sentences objected to were not nearly so broad as the Porter's speech in *Macbeth*, then being produced on Broadway.[22] This argument, with some flattering allusions to his earlier work, pleased Joyce, and he copied it.

paper would be signed by the author and sell for 350 francs; 150 copies
on *vergé d'arches* would sell for 250 francs; and the other 750, on
slightly less costly linen paper, would sell for 150 francs. Joyce was to
receive the astonishing royalty of 66% of the net profits. These plans
agreed to, it was decided to go to the Bal Bullier, a dance hall, to celebrate. On leaving his flat Joyce pointed to the concierge's son who was
playing on the steps and remarked to Miss Beach, 'One day that boy
will be a reader of *Ulysses*.' [23]

The festive occasion gave him an opportunity to be avuncular, a
luxury he rarely permitted himself during these busy days. A young
Irishman named Arthur Power was brought to his table, and Joyce
asked if he were 'a man of letters.' Power, embarrassed at the label,
said he was interested. 'What do you want to write?' Joyce asked.
'Something on the model of the French satirists.' 'You will never do it,'
Joyce said decisively, 'you are an Irishman and you must write in your
own tradition. Borrowed styles are no good. You must write what is in
your blood and not what is in your brain.' Power objected, as Joyce
himself might once have done, that he was tired of nationality and
wanted to be international, like all the great writers. 'They were national
first,' Joyce contended, 'and it was the intensity of their own nationalism
which made them international in the end, as in the case of Turgenev.
You remember his *Sportsman's Notebook*, how local it was—and yet out
of that germ he became a great international writer. For myself, I always
write about Dublin, because if I can get to the heart of Dublin I can
get to the heart of all the cities of the world.* In the particular is contained the universal.' [24] 'But how do you feel about being Irish?' asked
Power. Joyce responded, 'I regret it for the temperament it has given
me.' [25]

Later they left the dance hall and went to the Closerie des Lilas, and
Joyce developed a theme that was frequently in his mind during these
days, the power of words and particularly of English words. When
Power protested in favor of French, Joyce supported his argument for
the superior depth and sonority of English by quoting passages from the
Bible in two languages. He contrasted the weakness of '*Jeune homme,
je te dis, lève-toi,*' with the strength of 'Young man, I say unto thee,
arise.' [26] It was clear that in *Ulysses* he was confident that he had joined

---

* Desmond Harmsworth writes of Joyce's efforts some years later to associate him
too with Ireland. 'Do you not feel that Dublin is your town—your, shall I say,
spiritual home?' Joyce inquired. 'Well, no,' said Harmsworth, 'I'm a Cockney, even
if most of my antecedents were in Ireland.' 'Yes, but don't you think that you feel
that Dublin . . . ?' Nora Joyce interrupted, 'Ah, let him alone, Jim. Can't you see
he doesn't think he's a Dubliner?' But Joyce persisted all evening.[27]

the best possible words (English) to the best possible subject matter (Irish).

Sylvia Beach would have been more staggered by her own intrepidity if she had not been so busy with preparations for the book. She received immediate support from Harriet Weaver, who on April 13, 1921, promised to send her all the names of persons and shops in England who had inquired about *Ulysses*.[28] Miss Weaver also sent Joyce £200 as an advance on royalties of the English edition, which she would publish with the French sheets under the imprint of the Egoist Press after the limited French edition was sold out.* Her royalty terms outdid even Miss Beach's. Besides Miss Weaver's list of subscribers, Sylvia Beach collected names of interested Frenchmen from Léon-Paul Fargue, Larbaud, and Adrienne Monnier, of Americans from Ezra Pound and Robert McAlmon. André Gide brought in his subscription in person, Pound brought in the subscription of Yeats, Hemingway sent in his own enthusiastically.[29] A four-page prospectus, containing among others Larbaud's encomium, 'With *Ulysses* Ireland makes a sensational return

---

* Of the history of this edition Miss Weaver wrote John Slocum: 'When Miss Sylvia Beach's first edition of *Ulysses* was exhausted in the summer of 1922, the Egoist Press bought from her the plates that had been made by the French printers and fixed up a somewhat curious edition. Printed in Dijon by those printers [Darantière] it was, as announced on the title page, "Published for the Egoist Press, London, by John Rodker, Paris," the edition, a private one like Miss Beach's, comprising 2,000 copies. John Rodker hired a room in Paris to act as office. Copies from the printers were delivered to him there and he dispatched by post to all the people who had given us direct orders for the book, including persons in the U.S.A. and elsewhere abroad. I think he also posted some copies direct to shops in London who had ordered them from us. He also dispatched to London through a mailing agency a number of packing cases full of the books and these remained in store with the agency till wanted. I had a certain number of them at our small Egoist office and also stored some at my private address, for we never knew when there might be an official raid. There never was at our own office. Shops used to send for the book discreetly to supply customer's orders and often I delivered copies myself to shops which ordered them. Usually they were put away out of sight under the counter with some haste! A good number of copies sent by ordinary book post to the U.S.A. got through to their various destinations, but some time between October 1922 (when the Egoist edition was published) and December 1922 the U.S.A. censorship authorities evidently became suspicious; copies were held up and accumulated at the U.S.A. post offices until finally 400-500 copies were confiscated and burnt. In January 1923 an edition of 500 copies was printed to replace them. One of these was posted to London, the remaining 499, as you will doubtless know, were seized by the English Customs authorities at Folkestone and made away with—or preserved privately for their own delectation! We never heard what actually happened to them beyond the seizure. After that the book was banned in England.'

John Rodker's recollection was that he sold 150 copies to Galignani in Paris, and 800 to an English bookseller named Jackson, who cut them into pieces and sent them over to America wrapped in newspaper for rebinding there. The first mate on an American merchant line took home hundreds of copies and got them through. He thought that only 400 copies had been seized in 1923 at Folkestone.[30]

into the best European literature,' was mailed to several hundred people. Among those who replied were the son or nephew of Bela Kun, an Anglican bishop, a chief of the Irish revolutionary movement, and Winston Churchill. In Trieste only Baron Ralli subscribed, and Joyce complained to Francini, 'If you find a Triestine who will pay 300 lire for a book of Zois, light a candle to St. Antonio Thaumaturgo.' [31] The most amusing refusal came from Bernard Shaw, who wrote Miss Beach on June 11 that he had read parts of *Ulysses* and found in them a repulsive but accurate picture of Ireland. He would like to force every male Irishman to read it, to see if any of them could bear looking at himself in this mirror. As for Shaw, he had fled Dublin when he was twenty, but now, at sixty, he had to learn that nothing had changed and that the city was as full as ever of 'slackjawed blackguardism.' * At least someone had possessed the courage to write it down so as to rub Irish noses in it. If Miss Beach, whose literary enthusiasms Shaw glanced at jocularly, fancied that an Irishman, especially of Shaw's age, would pay the price she asked for the book, she had little acquaintance with Shaw's nation. Joyce saw the letter some time afterwards, and was immensely pleased with it, especially since he thereby won a bet for a box of Voltigeurs from Sylvia Beach. He wrote Miss Weaver he was sure Shaw would subscribe anonymously,[32] but Shaw, though he was willing enough to forget the English Players' reluctance to pay him royalties, did not enjoy Joyce's work any better than William Archer and lesser members of an older generation. He was not allowed to rest easy in his refusal, however, for Pound wrote him several stern letters of rebuke; Shaw contested their arguments, and terminated his side of the correspondence with a final quip, 'I take care of the pence and let the Pounds take care of themselves.' † [33]

Sylvia Beach found Joyce a series of typists to finish the *Circe* episode, but for one reason or another they dropped out in quick succession. One had to stop because her father suffered a seizure, and Joyce noted that coincidentally this was an incident in the chapter.[34] At last he found a Mrs. Harrison, whose husband had a post at the British

---

* In the same summer of 1921, Shaw wrote in his preface to *Immaturity:* 'In 1876 I had had enough of Dublin. James Joyce in his *Ulysses* has described, with a fidelity so ruthless that the book is hardly bearable, the life that Dublin offers to its young men, or, if you prefer to put it in the other way, that its young men offer to Dublin. No doubt it is much like the life of young men everywhere in modern urban civilisation. A certain flippant futile derision and belittlement that confuses the noble and serious with the base and ludicrous seems to me peculiar to Dublin, . . .'

† Pound gave Shaw another thump in his Paris letter to the *Dial* in June 1922, when he said that Joyce's picture of Dublin was 'so veridic that a ninth rate coward like Shaw (Geo. B.) dare not even look it in the face.'

Embassy. She made good progress until on April 8 her husband glanced at the manuscript, and, scandalized, threw it into the fire. She rushed to tell Joyce that she had hidden most of it,[35] and surreptitiously managed to convey it to him a few days later. The missing pages had to be rewritten with the aid of a photostat of an earlier draft which Quinn sent from New York. Another typist was then found and the episode completed. Joyce made sure that Miss Weaver, Pound, Larbaud, Eliot, and Budgen saw the new episodes as they became available in readable form. Eliot and Richard Aldington agreed to review the book from opposite points of view, and Aldington's article appeared in the *English Review* for April 1921. It was somewhat fault-finding but Joyce shrewdly saw the advantage of any mention of the book. Pound, whose enthusiasm for *Ulysses* had seemed to Joyce, in spite of the controversy with Shaw, to wane with some of the middle chapters, exhibited his old fervor when he read *Circe*. 'Magnificent, a new Inferno in full sail,'[36] he wrote his father.

Joyce was now more at home in Paris, which, he told Wyndham Lewis, was 'the last of the human cities,'[37] guarding its intimacy in spite of its size. In May 1921,[38] Sydney Schiff ('Stephen Hudson'), the English novelist whom Joyce had met a few times, invited him to a supper party for Stravinsky and Diaghilev following the first performance of one of their ballets. Joyce appeared late and apologized for not having dressed; at this time he had no formal clothes. He was drinking heavily to cover his embarrassment when the door opened and Marcel Proust in a fur coat appeared, as Joyce said later, 'like the hero of *The Sorrows of Satan.*'[39] Schiff had mentioned the party to Proust but had not ventured to invite him because of Proust's known unwillingness to emerge from his flat. Joyce followed Schiff and Mrs. Schiff to the door, was introduced to Proust, and remained seated beside him. The conversation has been variously reported. According to one account, which William Carlos Williams heard and set down,[40] Joyce said, 'I've headaches every day. My eyes are terrible.' Proust replied, 'My poor stomach. What am I going to do? It's killing me. In fact, I must leave at once.' 'I'm in the same situation,' replied Joyce, 'if I can find someone to take me by the arm. Goodbye.' '*Charmé*,' said Proust, 'oh, my stomach.'* Margaret Anderson writes that Proust said, 'I regret that I don't know Mr. Joyce's work,' and Joyce countered, 'I have never read Mr. Proust,' the conversation ending there.[41] Joyce told Arthur Power that Proust asked him if he liked truffles, and Joyce answered, 'Yes, I do.' He com-

---

* Mrs. Schiff denies that the conversation took this turn, and it sounds like later embroidery.

mented, 'Here are the two greatest literary figures of our time meeting and they ask each other if they like truffles.'[42] To Budgen he gave a slightly more extended version: 'Our talk consisted solely of the word "No." Proust asked me if I knew the duc de so-and-so. I said, "No." Our hostess asked Proust if he had read such and such a piece of *Ulysses*. Proust said, "No." And so on. Of course the situation was impossible. Proust's day was just beginning. Mine was at an end.'[43]

The party, as Mrs. Schiff remembers, broke up when Proust suggested that the Schiffs accompany him to his flat in a taxi. Joyce drifted into the taxi with them. Unfortunately his first gesture was to open the window with a bang. Proust being sensitive to fresh air, Schiff immediately closed it. When they arrived, Proust pressed Joyce to let the taxi take him home. Joyce still lingered, a little tipsy and anxious to have a chat; Proust, fearful of exposure, hurried in, leaving Schiff to persuade Joyce to leave.[44] 'If we had been allowed to meet and have a talk somewhere—,'[45] Joyce said later, a little wistfully. But it was difficult for either man to see the grounds on which they might have met. Joyce insisted that Proust's work bore no resemblance to his own, though critics claimed to detect some. Proust's style did not impress Joyce; when a friend asked whether he thought it good, he replied, 'The French do, and after all, they have their standards, they have Chateaubriand and Rousseau. But the French are used to short choppy sentences, they are not used to that way of writing.'[46] He expressed himself in a notebook more directly: 'Proust, analytic still life. Reader ends sentence before him.'[47] What he envied Proust were his material circumstances: 'Proust can write; he has a comfortable place at the Étoile, floored with cork and with cork on the walls to keep it quiet. And, I, writing in this place, people coming in and out. I wonder how I can finish *Ulysses*.'[48] Proust died on November 18, 1922, and Joyce attended his funeral.[49]

The meeting with Proust quickly became legend; Joyce was, in fact, the center suddenly of many legends. In *Finnegans Wake* he was to take pleasure in showing the same process overtaking Earwicker, bloating and distorting his past, and in *Ulysses* Bloom's peccadilloes are magnified out of all recognition in the *Circe* episode. Already in September 1920, Joyce wrote to Stanislaus of reports that he had been a spy in Dublin for the Austrians, in Zurich for the British or for the Sinn Feiners, that his *Ulysses* was a pre-arranged German code, that he was a cocaine addict, the founder of dadaism, a bolshevik propagandist, and 'the cavalier servente of the Duch—— of M——, Mme M— R— M—, la princ— de X——, Mrs T-n-t A— and the Dowager Empress of Ch-na.'[50] A few months later, evidently caught by the theme, he wrote to Miss Weaver on June 24, 1921:

71 rue du Cardinal Lemoine
Paris V

Dear Miss Weaver:

. . . A nice collection could be made of legends about me. Here are some. My family in Dublin believe that I enriched myself in Switzerland during the war by espionage work for one or both combatants.[*] Triestines, seeing me emerge from my relatives' house occupied by my furniture for about twenty minutes every day and walk to the same point, the G.P.O., and back (I was writing *Nausicaa* and *The Oxen of the Sun* in a dreadful atmosphere) circulated the rumour, now firmly believed, that I am a cocaine victim. The general rumour in Dublin was (till the prospectus of *Ulysses* stopped it) that I could write no more, had broken down and was dying in New York. A man from Liverpool told me he had heard that I was the owner of several cinema theatres all over Switzerland. In America there appear to be or have been two versions: one that I was an austere mixture of the Dalai Lama and sir Rabindranath Tagore. Mr Pound described me as a dour Aberdeen minister. Mr Lewis told me he was told that I was a crazy fellow who always carried four watches and rarely spoke except to ask my neighbour what o'clock it was. Mr Yeats seemed to have described me to Mr Pound as a kind of Dick Swiveller. What the numerous (and useless) people to whom I have been introduced here think I don't know. My habit of addressing people I have just met for the first time as 'Monsieur' earned for me the reputation of a *tout petit bourgeois* while others consider what I intend for politeness as most offensive. . . . One woman here originated the rumour that I am extremely lazy and will never do or finish anything. (I calculate that I must have spent nearly 20,000 hours in writing *Ulysses*.) A batch of people in Zurich persuaded themselves that I was gradually going mad and actually endeavoured to induce me to enter a sanatorium where a certain Doctor Jung (the Swiss Tweedledum who is not to be confused with the Viennese Tweedledee, Dr Freud) amuses himself at the expense (in every sense of the word) of ladies and gentlemen who are troubled with bees in their bonnets.

I mention all these views not to speak about myself but to show you how conflicting they all are. The truth probably is that I am a quite commonplace person undeserving of so much imaginative painting. There is a further opinion that I am a crafty simulating and dissimulating *Ulysses*-like type, a 'jejune Jesuit,' selfish and cynical. There is some truth in this, I suppose; but it is by no means all of me (nor was it of *Ulysses*) and it has been my habit to apply this alleged quality to safeguard my poor creations. . . .

[*] The origin of this story was that Joyce courteously served in Zurich as mailing intermediary for his Triestine friend Mario Tripcovich and the latter's fiancée, who were separated by the war. Ezra Pound also heard that for a time British censorship suspected *Ulysses* of being a code.

This letter begins to remind me of a preface by Mr George Bernard Shaw. It does not seem to be a reply to your letter after all. . . . You have already one proof of my intense stupidity. Here now is an example of my emptiness. I have not read a work of literature for several years. My head is full of pebbles and rubbish and broken matches and lots of glass picked up 'most everywhere.' The task I set myself technically in writing a book from eighteen different points of view and in as many styles, all apparently unknown or undiscovered by my fellow trades-men, that and the nature of the legend chosen would be enough to upset anyone's mental balance. I want to finish the book and try to settle on my entangled material affairs definitely one way or the other (somebody here said of me: 'They call him a poet. He appears to be interested chiefly in mattresses.'). And, in fact, I was. After that I want a good long rest in which to forget *Ulysses* completely.

I forgot to tell you another thing. I don't even know Greek though I am spoken of as erudite. My father wanted me to take Greek as third language, my mother German and my friends Irish. Result, I took Italian. I spoke or used to speak modern Greek not too badly (I speak four or five languages fluently enough) and have spent a great deal of time with Greeks of all kinds from noblemen down to onionsellers, chiefly the latter. I am superstitious about them. They bring me luck.

I now end this long rambling shambling speech, having said nothing of the darker aspects of my detestable character. I suppose the law should now take its course with me because it must now seem to you a waste of rope to accomplish the dissolution of a person who has now dissolved visibly and possesses scarcely as much 'pendibility' as an uninhabited dressinggown.[51]

The stories about him grew more extraordinary as his life became outwardly more domestic. Journalists indulged their fancy freely, and mentioned his daily swim in the Seine, the mirrors with which he sur-rounded himself while he worked, the black gloves he wore when he went to bed. These rumors he at once resented and enjoyed.

Late in May he suffered a mild attack of iritis, but shook it off with-out much discomfort. His lease was about to expire, however, and he was beginning to feel anguished about that again when Valery Larbaud, who was going to Italy, offered him rent-free his small but handsome flat at 71 rue du Cardinal Lemoine, a ten-minute walk from the Jardin du Luxembourg. This was a most unusual favor for Larbaud, who lived reticently and never received at home.[52] The Joyces moved in on June 3, and were delighted with the new surroundings.[53] He wrote to Francini on June 7, 'Is it possible that I am worth something? Who'd have thought so after my last experience in Trieste?' He quoted to Francini the compliment of Larbaud, 'The *Circe* episode alone would make the reputation of a French writer for life,' listed some prominent subscribers, and concluded dryly, 'I've become a monument of *vespasian*° eminence.' [54]

He was encouraged to make great progress with *Ithaca* and *Penelope*. At the new flat, on June 10, he received from Darantière the first galley proofs, and by September 7 he had read them through *Scylla and Charybdis*. With Joyce the reading of proof was a creative act; he insisted on five sets, and made innumerable changes, almost always additions, in the text, complicating the interior monologue with more and more interconnecting details. The book grew by one third in proof. Darantière's characteristic gesture, throwing up his hands in despair, became almost constant when the type had to be recast time after time, and Sylvia Beach was much tried; but Joyce won his point.

During 1921 he had time for many visitors and for some new friends, chiefly Irish and American. Most of them perceived, at least dimly, that he was a genius. Among the first of the Irishmen to see him was A. J. Leventhal, a young graduate of Trinity College and now a lecturer there. They spoke of the various Jewish families whose names were mentioned in *Ulysses*, of one with the incongruous name of Higgins, whom Joyce had related to Bloom; of Citron, Abramovitz, and of Morris Solomons, who was an oculist and Austro-Hungarian vice-consul. Joyce asked particularly about the Blooms, and was relieved to hear from Leventhal that they had all left the city. He showed Leventhal some of the Hebrew words in *Ulysses*, but refused to credit his suggestion that there was some confusion between the Spanish and German transliterations—an error that persists in the published text. Before his visitor left Joyce sat down at the piano and played and sang the Hebrew song, the *Hatikvah*.[55] Leventhal returned to Dublin to write under the pseudonym of 'L. K. Emery' one of the first and most appreciative reviews of *Ulysses*.

Joyce's closest Irish connection during these months was with Arthur Power. They met frequently and Joyce inevitably asked him to read some of *Ulysses*. Power labored at the *Nausicaa* episode, but, being unaccustomed to the technique, misunderstood parts of it as actual events. Joyce was irritated: 'That didn't take place at all,' he said, 'only in Bloom's imagination.' [56] Power smoothed him down by assuring him it would bring about a literary revolution. Joyce was glad of his company and did not mind his partial lack of understanding, but when Power asked why Joyce treated him so kindly, Joyce put him off by saying, 'I'm always friends with a person for a purpose.' [57] He thought he knew too much about friendship to avow it again. The chastened

° French colloquial for 'urinal.'

Power tried to hit back by remarking, 'You are a man without feelings.' Joyce said in surprise, 'My God—I, a man without feelings!' [58] Power often spent Sundays with Joyce and Nora at Robinson or Saint-Germain, which they reached by hired car. If a storm broke out on the way, Joyce at once ordered the driver to turn about and take them home. 'Why are you so afraid of thunder?' asked Power, and Joyce replied gravely, 'You were not brought up as I was. Take my children, for instance; they are afraid of nothing.' [59] Joyce's fears were part of his identity, and he had no wish, even if he had had the power, to slough any of them off.

Another close friend throughout 1921 was Robert McAlmon, the American poet and short story writer. McAlmon was married to Winifred Ellerman ('Bryher'), whose father, Sir John, was one of the richest men in England; and McAlmon was glad to spend his father-in-law's money. He generously advanced Joyce about $150 a month during 1921 to tide him over until *Ulysses* appeared, and he did not care whether repayment occurred or not. Some of Joyce's punctilious notes of hand survive among McAlmon's papers as evidence of Joyce's almost equal indifference to the subject. [60] Joyce may have had at first a notion that McAlmon, a small, handsome, pugnacious, independent man, might fill a place in his life like that of Budgen in Zurich; and he regularly asked McAlmon's opinion of his latest pages. But McAlmon had his own books to write and did not give Joyce unqualified adherence; he also took less interest in subtleties of Catholic thought and Irish politics than Joyce wished. They were much together anyway; Joyce would say to him importunately at the end of an evening, 'You'll be round tomorrow, McAlmon?' [61] He treated McAlmon as a colleague, and was pleased to find some resemblance between their short stories. To another friend he said indulgently, 'Maybe McAlmon has a *disorderly* sort of talent,' [62] and, tongue in cheek, he suggested the title which McAlmon put on his book of stories, *A Hasty Bunch*. [63] Joyce made no pretense of being indulgent towards other writers, and quizzed McAlmon dreamily, 'Do you think Eliot or Pound has any real importance?' McAlmon replied, 'Now, Joyce, is that a question for you to ask, who can doubt anything, even yourself?' Joyce laughed but looked disgruntled. [64]

When no typist was available for *Penelope*, McAlmon offered to help, and so won a small place, by accident, in the book's authorship. For the manuscript was so complicated and Joyce's insertions so numerous that occasionally McAlmon got some of Molly's thoughts out of place; he told himself it didn't much matter in what order her unsystematic mind took them up. Later he observed that Joyce had retained the changes, and asked whether he had noticed them or not. Joyce answered,

'I did, but I agreed with you.' [65] He cannot have retained many, however, for a letter to Miss Weaver of June 13, 1925, *à propos* of printer's changes in *Finnegans Wake*, mocks McAlmon's cavalier attitude to *Penelope:*

> Did Faucett change those words? They was two. Doesn't matter. 'Gromwelling' I said and what? O, ah! Bisexcycle. That was the bunch. Hope he does, anyhow. O rats! It's just a fool thing, style. I just shoot it off like: If he aint done it, where's the use? Guess I'm through with that bunch.
>   (With apologies to Mr Robert McAlmon)
> (Re-enter Hamlet) * [66]

During the spring of 1921 Valery Larbaud was an occasional drinking companion. Ernest Hemingway appeared, bearing a letter of introduction from Sherwood Anderson, who had met Joyce once or twice the previous year; Samuel Roth, the future pirate of *Ulysses*, wrote to announce his honest admiration. Sisley Huddleston was often about, but complained to McAlmon that Joyce's conversation was dull and his jokes were damp.[67] On a few occasions, however, even the blasé Huddleston was pleased: one night at his house, a cantatrice was singing when a moth flew straight for her open mouth; she stopped suddenly, and Joyce broke the embarrassed silence by murmuring, 'The desire of the moth for the star!' [68]

Wyndham Lewis was much in Paris and would often join Joyce at the Gipsy Bar near the Panthéon or at a small café. Alcohol helped to make them companionable, though they often disagreed. So, when Lewis objected to the cathedral at Rouen because of its heavily encumbered façade, which he described as 'a fussy multiplication of accents, demonstrating a belief in the virtue of *quantity*,' and argued against Gothic for ' "its scholasticism in stone": the dissolving of the solid shell,' Joyce remarked that he liked this multiplication of detail and added, 'As a matter of fact, I do something of that sort in words.' [69] Or they would get on inevitably to national traits, Joyce insisting that the Irish and the Jewish destinies were much alike. Lewis countered that the Irish were pugnacious. 'Would you say they were pugnacious?' asked Joyce in sudden perplexity, 'of course, I know very little about them.' Lewis, unabashed, said, 'Yes.' 'That's not been my experience—,' Joyce said slowly and thoughtfully, 'a very gentle race.' [70]

As they sat at the café, Lewis invariably invited the same two local prostitutes to sit with them. The women were given plenty to drink, but otherwise received little attention. Once, when Lewis broke precedent

---

* That is, Joyce himself.

by a lapse of decorum with one of them, Joyce solemnly called him to order, 'Remember you are the author of *The Ideal Giant*.' [71] The conductor of the little café orchestra interested Joyce, and he asked the older prostitute to tell him something about the man. She said curtly, '*Il a quarante ans. Il est vieux.*' Joyce, nearing forty himself, said, '*Est-ce que quarante ans est vieux?*' Then he pedantically pointed out that for the Romans one was *junior* until fifty. [72] As he became drunker he would quote Verlaine or Dante and the girls listened to him with big eyes. '*Qu'est-ce qu'il dit, le poète?*' they asked Lewis. One night Lewis and Joyce knocked at the bar door after closing time and were asked to identify themselves. Joyce did so by quoting Verlaine, upon which the door was immediately thrown open for *le poète*. [73]

In the spring and summer of 1921 Joyce added some new American friends. The first, and strangest, was Dr. Joseph Collins, later to write *The Doctor Looks at Literature*. Collins admired *A Portrait* and wrote to two Americans in Paris, who had worked under him in the Red Cross during the war, that he understood Joyce was living blind and poor in Paris. He asked them to look him up, relieve any immediate need, and arrange a meeting between him and Collins. So Richard Wallace, a book illustrator, and Myron Nutting, a painter, came into Joyce's life. Soon they all had lunch together and Joyce lent Collins the *Little Review* installments of *Ulysses*. Collins groaned to Nutting next day, 'I have in my files writing by the insane just as good as this,' and gave a medical explanation of the deterioration of the artist's brain. [74] Later on, however, he began to think better of the book. Joyce had Molly Bloom memorialize Collins's manner in *Ulysses*: 'Floey made me go to that dry old stick Dr Collins for womens diseases on Pembroke road your vagina he called it I suppose thats how he got all the gilt mirrors and carpets getting round those rich ones off Stephens green....' At the same time he hoped Molly's comments would not offend Collins, and pointed out that they concluded with a compliment: 'I wouldn't trust him too far to give me chloroform or God knows what else still I liked him when he sat down to write the thing out frowning so severe his nose intelligent....' [75]

The two younger Americans and their wives were better suited by temperament than Collins to understand Joyce's work. Joyce used to tease them by saying that Molly Bloom was sitting at another table in the restaurant, and they would try to guess which woman she was, always without success. This game he continued for years. Another was to ask them, 'Who was the man in the mackintosh?' in *Ulysses*. [76] * It was through the Wallaces that Joyce got an important hint for *Ulysses*.

---

* Stuart Gilbert says it was Wetherup, a disreputable friend of John Joyce.

One day in July he visited them at their small country house at Châtillon, and happened to overhear a conversation between Mrs. Wallace and a young painter. The conversation went on and on, Mrs. Wallace repeating the word 'yes' over and over in different tones of voice. Joyce suddenly realized he had found the word he needed to begin and end the last episode of *Ulysses, Penelope,* as many years later he would discover with the same excitement that the final word of *Finnegans Wake* should be *the*. He wrote at once to Larbaud, '*Vous m'avez demandé une fois quelle serait la dernière parole d'Ulysse. La voilà:* yes.' [77] *

The summer did not pass altogether smoothly. Early in July Joyce was with McAlmon at the Brasserie Lutétia. The approaching publication of his book had made him especially alive to omens; if the heavens were ever to strike him, surely it must be now. The printing house might burn up; a toothache meant a spell cast on him. The year 1921 added up to 13,[78] a number he considered lucky for him, though, since it was also the day of his mother's death, he was never quite sure. (It was eventually to be his own.) † One hopeful sign was that Penelope was a weaver, like his English benefactress. Now, after ordering *vin mousseux*—his favorite and not fashionable French substitute for Fendant de Sion, which was hard to get in Paris—he superstitiously worried over the way the knife and fork were placed on the table; and when the wine arrived, he was troubled by the way McAlmon poured it. They had drunk one glass when McAlmon remarked a rat running down the stairs from the floor above, and, the naturalist *pur sang*, pointed it out as a curiosity to Joyce. He said, 'Where? Where? That's bad luck,' and a minute later lost consciousness. McAlmon got him into a taxi and with the aid of the driver carried him to his flat. Nora was about to scold him but became tender when she saw he was suffering from fright rather than alcohol.[79]

The next night the Joyces were having coffee and liqueur with McAlmon at the Café d'Harcourt when Nora suddenly called a taxi. Joyce's face was contorted with pain. He had suffered another attack of iritis, and was to spend five weeks recuperating with the aid of repeated doses of cocaine to relieve the pain.[80] During the day Arthur Power called frequently to cheer him up in his darkened room as he lay on the bed stuping his eye, and sometimes accompanied him in the evening to the ophthalmologist.[81] Joyce tested his eyes on the way by counting the total number of lights in the Place de la Concorde, a number which he knew. By early August he was much improved, and wrote to Miss Weaver on August 7:

---

* 'You asked me one time what the last word of *Ulysses* would be. Here it is: *yes*.'
† Joyce knew the superstitions of most of Europe, and adopted them all.

71 rue du Cardinal Lemoine, Paris V

Dear Miss Weaver:

I have had five weeks of delightful vacation with my eyes—the strangest but not at all the worst attack because instead of coming to a head in three weeks it did so in three hours. The people who persisted in regarding me as a foot-in-the-grave young man would have [been] edified to see me rolling over the carpet. The good point was that the attack was shorter in the recovery stage. I am now advised to go to Aix-les-Bains but am in Ithaca instead. I write and revise and correct with one or two eyes about twelve hours a day I should say, stopping for intervals of five minutes or so when I can't see any more. My brain reels after it but that is nothing compared with the reeling of my readers' brains. I have not yet quite recovered and I am doing the worst thing possible but can't help it. It is folly also because the book will probably not repay a tithe of such labour. The subscriptions have been rather slow and poor and now seem to have come or be coming to an end. . . . I am trying to make up for lost time. Not a single subscription came from Trieste except one from baron Ralli a Greek to whom I owe my liberation from Austria in 1915.

About three months ago I received a note of four lines from Mr Pinker to which I replied by a note of no lines at all—which is shorter still. I think it would be well if *Ulysses* makes my name to unify my publishers. . . .

I was going to take a forty-eight hour holiday somewhere but decided not to do so. If I lay down in some remote part of the country I am so tired that I should never have the energy to get up.

I have the greater part of *Ithaca* but it has to be completed, revised and rearranged above all on account of its scheme. I have also written the first sentence of *Penelope* but as this contains about 2500 words the deed is more than it seems to be. The episode consists of eight or nine sentences equally sesquipedalian and ends with a monosyllable. Bloom and all the Blooms will soon be dead, thank God. Everyone says he ought to have died long ago. . . .[82]

These exertions, combined with the sight of another rat on August 23 as he was seeing McAlmon off to London,[83] prepared him for another dead faint on August 26. This time he was at the Alhambra music hall with Giorgio, and collapsed in the middle of the program with what he called a syncope fit.[84] A policeman helped him out of the theater and into a taxi, and Giorgio took him to a night pharmacy where ether was administered to revive him. The attack lasted about an hour, leaving him short of breath, pale and weak. He began to take long walks along the Champs-Élysées to the Étoile, and exercise too became a kind of punishment. As he wrote Miss Weaver on August 30, 1921, 'I have been training for a Marathon race by walking 12 or 14 kilometres every day and looking carefully in the Seine to see if there is any place where I can throw Bloom in with a 50 lb weight tied to his feet.'[85]

The impending return of Larbaud at the beginning of October made it necessary to hunt another place to live. Late in September Joyce invited Wyndham Lewis to come up and see Larbaud's flat before they left it. The visit proved farcical: after they passed through the empty dining room they came to Giorgio's room. Giorgio had his feet on the stove, and Lewis felt embarrassed. Then they went into the next room where Nora, who was supposed to be looking for a flat, had her feet on the table. On the balcony they came upon Lucia, reading a book, her feet on the railing.[86] This policy of genial recumbency brought no new flats to light, so the Joyces had to move back again to 9 rue de l'Université, 'this damned brothel.' There they slept three in one room, one in the other. In the larger room Joyce kept a series of potted phoenix palms: as one died it was replaced by another. He said the plant reminded him of the Phoenix Park, and he attached great importance to it. A French friend visiting him there spoke of the strange effect of Joyce '*éclatant dans la banalité totale.*'[87]

Joyce went on working. By October 7 *Penelope* was with the printers; he had recast *Aeolus,* amplified *Hades* and the *Lotus-Eaters,* and retouched the other episodes except for the *Telemachia,* which he left almost alone. He looked forward to the 'expiration of my seven years' sentence.'[88] But he kept thinking of other emendations, and on October 12, wishing to add a few details to *Penelope,* he wrote to Mrs. Josephine Murray to ask about old Major Powell (the model for Molly Bloom's father) and his daughters, and about Matt Dillon and his daughters. 'Get an ordinary sheet of foolscap and scribble any God damn drivel you may remember about these people.'[89] She complied, and he wrote again on November 21 to ask, 'Is it possible for an ordinary person to climb over the area railings of no 7 Eccles Street, either from the path or the steps, lower himself from the lowest part of the railings till his feet are within 2 feet or 3 of the ground and drop unhurt. I saw it done myself but by a man of rather athletic build [J. F. Byrne]. I require this information in detail in order to determine the wording of a paragraph.'[90] Myron Nutting came up to him at the theater and said, 'How is your corporosity sagatiating?' Joyce rewarded him with a rare grin, and next day put the phrase into the *Oxen of the Sun* episode.[91] So the composing of *Ulysses* went on almost until publication day.

The date of Larbaud's lecture was now set for December 7, and the knowledge of this deadline made Joyce continue to work at the headlong pace which was more congenial to him than he admitted. On

October 20 he was able to send the virtually completed *Penelope* to Larbaud,[92] and on October 29 he finished *Ithaca* and announced to McAlmon that the book was complete.[93] He had left to revise only the last four episodes. Early in November Joyce lent Larbaud, as the previous year he had lent Linati, the intricate scheme for *Ulysses* which showed its Odyssean parallels and its special techniques. He also discussed with Larbaud the method of what Larbaud, borrowing a term from Paul Bourget's *Cosmopolis* (1893), called the '*monologue intérieur.*' Joyce remarked that the form had been employed, and in a sustained way, by Édouard Dujardin in *Les Lauriers sont coupés;* 'in that book,' he said, 'the reader finds himself established, from the first lines, in the thought of the principal personage, and the uninterrupted unrolling ('*déroulement ininterrompu*') of that thought, replacing the usual form of narrative, conveys to us what this personage is doing or what is happening to him.'[94] Larbaud paid no attention to this disclosure of source,* and late in 1921, dedicated his *Amants, heureux amants,* where he used the method, to Joyce. But Joyce was determined

---

* André Gide, in his lectures on Dostoevsky in February and March 1922, insisted that the new method was not Joyce's but a joint development of Poe, Browning, and Dostoevsky. Dujardin's role was challenged later, too, but is now generally accepted. Larbaud, like Joyce, took some pleasure in the revival of Dujardin; he dedicated one of his own books to the old man in 1923 with the words: 'A Édouard Dujardin, auteur de *Les Lauriers sont coupés* a quo . . .' and then in 1924 wrote a preface to the new edition of *Les Lauriers* which the fanfare had evoked. William Carlos Williams had also said in 1923, in *The Great American Novel,* that Dujardin was the originator of the method that he and Joyce used. In 1931 Dujardin published a book on *Le Monologue intérieur* to establish its history.

Dujardin and Joyce exchanged a series of elaborate compliments. Dujardin inscribed a copy of his book: 'A James Joyce, maître glorieux, au créateur illustre, et aussi à celui qui a dit au mort et enseveli: Relève-toi Lazare.'[95] Joyce responded by inscribing a copy of *Ulysses* with the words: 'A Édouard Dujardin, annonciateur de la parole intérieure, / Le larron impénitent, / J.J.'[96] He encouraged and helped Stuart Gilbert to translate *Les Lauriers sont coupés.* Dujardin had originally dedicated the book to Racine, but wrote a new dedication for a later edition:

Dédicace

Ma jeunesse qui cherchait un signe dans le passé
a dedié son espérance à Racine
un grand nombre d'années ont traversé l'horizon
et j'ai vu le signe apparaître aux portes de l'avenir
mon espérance je la dédie aujourd'hui
à JAMES JOYCE
au glorieux nouveau-venu
au suprème romancier d'âmes
E.D.
1930

Joyce reciprocated by addressing Dujardin in letters as 'Maître' and by referring to his *Lauriers* as 'evergreen.'[97] Secretly he believed he was giving Dujardin 'cake for bread.'[98] The method of the *monologue intérieur* was of consequence only because Joyce saw what could be done with it.

to have Dujardin's work recognized: 'Read it, you will see what it is.' [99]
In August of 1923 Larbaud obtained a copy of the scarce book. He was
convinced and soon began to persuade his incredulous countrymen
that Dujardin, whom they considered merely a relic of the symbolist
movement, was in fact the inaugurator of the latest literature.

Sylvia Beach and Adrienne Monnier decided Larbaud's séance
should be for Joyce's financial benefit. They persuaded everyone to
come except Ezra Pound, who was rather annoyed to have his discovery
rediscovered. Larbaud proposed to them that parts of *Ulysses* be translated and read aloud, but had no time to do this additional work himself. In October Adrienne Monnier enlisted for the purpose Jacques
Benoît-Méchin, only twenty years old but clever and already one of
Joyce's firm admirers.* [100] He applied himself enthusiastically to the
work, pleased that it kept him in touch with Joyce. In later years he
remarked that, though he had met several geniuses in his lifetime,
Joyce always seemed to him to give the strongest impression of human
genius he had ever encountered.[101] He could talk of nothing and still
seem a genius. There was something extreme and excessive in him,
besides an extraordinary dignity. He looked to Benoît-Méchin like a
Shakespearean prince, a Prospero.

To translate *Penelope* exactly, Benoît-Méchin wished to see the
scheme for the book. Joyce gave him only bits of it, and protested
humorously, 'If I gave it all up immediately, I'd lose my immortality.
I've put in so many enigmas and puzzles that it will keep the professors
busy for centuries arguing over what I meant, and that's the only way
of insuring one's immortality.' [102] But after repeated beseechings by the
young man, Joyce gave him the whole scheme. Sylvia Beach asked to
see it, Benoît-Méchin could not refuse her, and the invaluable page
began to circulate a little in typescript under the most solemn injunc-
tions of secrecy until 1931, when Stuart Gilbert published most of it
in his book, *James Joyce's Ulysses*.†

* At that time Benoît-Méchin wished to become a composer; he played some of
Samuel Butler's musical compositions at Larbaud's séance the year before. Joyce
had him write out some musical notations in *Ulysses* (675 [652]), and his work
was photographed for subsequent editions.
† Until then most critics had S. Foster Damon's experience of asking for the plan
in vain. But Joyce had sent it to Carlo Linati as early as 1920, for his personal use
only. In his letter of September 21 enclosing it, he said: 'I have given only catch-
words in my scheme but I think you will understand it all the same. It is an epic
of two races (Israelite—Irish) and at the same time the cycle of the human body
as well as a little story of a day (life). The character of Ulysses always fascinated
me—even when a boy. Imagine, fifteen years ago I started writing it as a short
story for *Dubliners*! For seven years I have been working at this book—blast it!
It is also a sort of encyclopedia. My intention is to transpose the myth *sub specie
temporis nostri*. Each adventure (that is, every hour, every organ, every art being

In the version of *Penelope* that was given to Benoîst-Méchin, Joyce inscrutably omitted the final *yes*, so that the episode ended,

and first I put my arms around him yes and drew him down to me so he could feel my breasts all perfume yes and his heart was going like mad and yes I said yes I will.

Benoîst-Méchin found the final 'I will' difficult to render in French, since in that language the woman says, *'je veux bien,'* which sounds weaker than *'je veux.'* He therefore tacked on a final *'oui.'* Joyce had apparently been testing out the last words, and was surprised to see Benoîst-Méchin's alteration. 'But I didn't write that—,' he said. 'It sounds better that way,' said Benoîst-Méchin. 'But this is a big question,' Joyce replied, 'the last word of a book is very important.' They talked for several hours about it, Benoîst-Méchin insisting that the acknowledgment of the universe should end optimistically with 'yes' rather than authoritatively with 'I will.' Eventually Joyce pretended to be persuaded of what he had already decided, that 'I will' was too Luciferian, and 'yes' a submission to a world beyond himself, and he concluded: 'Yes, you're right. The book must end with yes. It must end with the most positive word in the human language.' [103]

Benoîst-Méchin's translations were reviewed by Léon-Paul Fargue, who was also becoming a member of the Joyce group (though Joyce was always shocked by the stories Fargue told in the presence of women). Fargue, whose own work was filled with brilliant wordplay, had so many possible variants to suggest that the translation was not completed until December 5. Another coadjutor was the American actor Jimmy Light, who was to read part of the *Sirens* episode in English to convey its musicality. Even the night before the séance Sylvia Beach heard the young man repeating with Joyce, 'Bald Pat was a waiter hard of hearing...', as he labored to attain the proper rhythm.[104] Then Larbaud, who finished writing his talk on December 6, decided the translation needed further revision, so there was little sleep that night.

The bookstore had two hundred and fifty people overcrowding it on Wednesday, December 7. Larbaud, on his way to the speaker's table, told Joyce he was omitting a few lines from *Penelope*. Although Joyce did not object, he remarked later that they would not have disturbed the solar system.[105] Larbaud's talk was necessarily introductory. He began by referring to Joyce's notoriety, to the fact that literary

---

interconnected and interrelated in the structural scheme of the whole) should not only condition but even create its own technique. Each adventure is so to say one person although it is composed of persons—as Aquinas relates of the angelic hosts.' [106]

people were as accustomed to hearing his name as scientific people the names of Freud or Einstein. He sketched briefly Joyce's life in Ireland and on the continent, and made, as Joyce complained mildly to Miss Weaver later, some errors.* ('Nobody,' said Joyce, 'seems to be inclined to present me in my unadorned prosaicness.') [107] Then Larbaud took up each of Joyce's books in turn, and showed that each had supplied an element for *Ulysses* to combine. *Chamber Music* had supplied lyricism, *Dubliners* the unmistakable atmosphere of a particular city, *A Portrait* clusters of images, analogies, and symbols. In *Ulysses*, he explained, the principal personages move like giants through a seemingly miscellaneous day. The key to the book was the Odyssey, the hero being like Ulysses and his adventures paralleling those described by Homer. Joyce remarked to Miss Weaver that Larbaud, in one of his allusions at this point, had welded two episodes together.† ('Seemingly,' he wrote her, 'such an attitude is compatible with much understanding of the book and friendliness towards its writer.') [108] Larbaud hinted at the extraordinary organization of each episode in terms of hour, organ, and the like, but understandably did not dwell upon it. The book had the complexity of a mosaic, he said, and referred to Joyce's workbooks in which abbreviated phrases were underlined in different-colored pencils to indicate in which episode they should be inserted. In concluding he anticipated two misconceptions: Joyce's modern Ulysses was not made Jewish for anti-Semitic reasons; and the distastefulness of the lower functions of man could not justify their exclusion from a book dedicated to the whole man.

Adrienne Monnier now introduced Jimmy Light, with a reminder that some of the passages to be read might seem 'audacious.' [109] (During the reading of the *Cyclops* episode, Joyce informed Miss Weaver, 'the light went out very much as it did for the Cyclops himself, but the audience was very patient.') [110] Joyce himself was hidden behind a screen, but was obliged, much against his will, to come forward afterwards in response to enthusiastic applause. Larbaud fervently embraced him, and Joyce blushed with confusion.[111] On the whole he felt that the séance had gone well.[112] Subscriptions flowed into Shakespeare and Company.

The day of publication was becoming, in Joyce's superstitious mind, talismanic. He wrote Miss Weaver on November 1,

A coincidence is that of birthdays in connection with my books, *A Portrait of the Artist* which first appeared serially in your paper on

---

* Larbaud said Joyce attended the University of Dublin.
† He referred to Elpenor in the *Aeolus* (instead of the *Hades*) episode.

2 February [his birthday] finished on 1 September [her birthday].
Ulysses began on 1 March (birthday of a friend of mine, a Cornish
painter [Budgen, who was half Cornish]) and was finished on Mr
Pound's birthday [October 30], he tells me. I wonder on whose it will
be published.[113]

Chance was too important for Joyce to allow it complete freedom;
he resolved to have the book appear on his own fortieth birthday,
February 2, and from December through January he kept sending
letters and telegrams, and making telephone calls, to Miss Beach and
Darantière, embodying his latest corrections and additions. Djuna
Barnes, who met him during this period fairly often, said he looked
'both sad and tired, but it is a sadness of a man who has procured
some medieval permission to sorrow out of time and in no place,'
and 'a weariness of one self-subjected to the creation of an over-
abundance in the limited.'[114] At Les Deux Magots he said slowly,
'The pity is the public will demand and find a moral in my book, or
worse they may take it in some serious way, and on the honor of a
gentleman, there is not one single serious line in it.' He had put the
great talkers into his book, he went on. 'They are all there, the great
talkers, they and the things they forgot. In *Ulysses* I have recorded,
simultaneously, what a man says, sees, thinks, and what such seeing,
thinking, saying does, to what you Freudians call the subconscious—
but as for psychoanalysis,' he broke off, consistent in his prejudice,
'it's neither more nor less than blackmail.'[115] Just before *Ulysses* was
to appear Joyce and Nora were walking with Miss Barnes in the
Bois de Boulogne when a man brushed by and mumbled something
she did not catch. Joyce trembled and went white. To Miss Barnes's
question he said, 'That man, whom I have never seen before, said
to me as he passed, in Latin, "You are an abominable writer!" That is a
dreadful omen the day before the publication of my novel.'[116]

In Dijon, Darantière rose to the occasion and on February 1 sent
Sylvia Beach a letter promising that three copies would definitely
go off by mail on that day and would surely arrive by noon of the
next day. Miss Beach, prodded by Joyce, who described himself as
'in a state of energetic prostration,'[117] telephoned that this method
was too uncertain. Darantière then thought of dispatching them by
the conductor of the Dijon-Paris express, which would reach Paris at 7
in the morning. Miss Beach met the train promptly, found the conductor and was handed a package which proved to be two copies. In
less than ten minutes her taxi brought her to Joyce's door; she turned
over one copy to him and kept the other to exhibit in her shop. Every-

one crowded in from nine o'clock until closing time to see it.[118]

Joyce's friends shared his pleasure. Helen Nutting, the painter's wife, sent him bluets and white carnations that morning as a *Ulysses mazzo dei fiori*.[119] That night the Nuttings, Wallaces, and Helen Kieffer (daughter of Quinn's law partner) dined with the Joyces at the Italian restaurant Ferrari's. Joyce sat at the head of the table, sideways, his legs crossed with the toe of one crossed again under the calf of the other. He wore a new ring, a reward he had promised himself years before. He seemed already melancholy, sighing now and then as he ordered dinner and ate nothing. He had brought with him a package containing his copy of *Ulysses,* and placed it under his chair. Nora remarked that he had thought about the book for sixteen years, and spent seven years writing it. Everyone asked to see it opened, but he seemed to shrink from producing it. After the dessert he at last untied the parcel and laid the book on the table. It was bound in the Greek colors—white letters on a blue field—that he considered lucky for him, and suggested the myth of Greece and of Homer, the white island rising from the sea.* There was a toast to the book and its author which left Joyce deeply moved. The two Italian waiters came up to ask if he had written this 'poem,' and obtained his permission to exhibit it to the padrone. At the Café Weber, where they went next, Joyce showed Helen Nutting that her name was in the book along with Lillian Wallace's and Dorothy Pound's.† He also pointed out a coincidence, as he was to do more and more often for the rest of his life, this time the fact that he had mentioned the name of the Duke of Tetuan ‡ and that the present Duke was at that moment in Paris at the Irish convention.[120] His feeling of the book's prophetic and magical nature seized upon every corroboration.

When the café closed Joyce longed to spend the night out, but Nora emphatically shepherded him toward a cab. Joyce said to Wallace, 'I must be saved from these scenes.' Helen Nutting, taking leave of Joyce on the wet sidewalk of the rue Royale, thanked him for letting her share in the double-birthday of author and book; he took her hand as if to kiss it, then thought better of it.[121]

A slight mistake about the cover of *Ulysses* caused Darantière to delay sending more copies, and Joyce became very impatient. A week after publication less than fifty copies had arrived, and on March 17

---

* Nutting had mixed the exact shade of blue for him, since the binders could not get it right and needed something to copy.

† 'Dorothy Canebrake,' 'Mrs Helen Vinegadding,' 'the Misses Lilian and Viola Lilac,' *Ulysses* (321 [311]).

‡ *Ulysses* (324 [314]).

Miss Beach went to Dijon to straighten out the difficulties.[122] Joyce had promised to send Miss Weaver the No. 1 copy of the de luxe edition. The first copy of the book, which Sylvia Beach had brought to him, he inscribed to his wife and presented to her in Arthur Power's presence. Here, in Ithaca, was Penelope. Nora at once offered to sell it to Power.[123] Joyce smiled but was not pleased. He kept urging her to read the book, yet she would not. Several months later, the writer Gilbert Seldes * invited Joyce and his wife to come to the ballet to celebrate June 16; Joyce informed Nora of the invitation, emphasizing the date. 'Why on that particular day?', she asked. 'Because,' Joyce replied, with a rage born of many such affronts, 'that is the day on which that book is supposed to have taken place.' [124] After some time Nora must have begun to give way a little; for, when a new edition appeared with an errata sheet, he left a note for her which confirms that her indifference to his book hurt him more than he allowed to be known:

> Dear Nora: The edition you have is full of printers' errors. Please read it in this. I cut the pages. There is a list of mistakes at the end.
>
> Jim.[125]

Shortly thereafter Joyce went to visit his friend August Suter, who was carving a statue of Karl Spitteler, using as his model the Prometheus in Spitteler's poem, 'Prometheus und Epimetheus.' Joyce observed him for a time, then asked, 'What sort of a monument would you make for me?' 'I suppose—Mr. Bloom,' said the sculptor. Joyce became grave at once. '*Mais non! Mais non!*' [126]

---

* Seldes had reviewed *Ulysses* in the *Nation*, and received a note from Sylvia Beach saying that Joyce thanked him particularly for his praise of the *Oxen of the Sun* episode, which so many critics had disliked. When he came to Paris some time afterwards, he went with John Peale Bishop to call on Joyce. After an exchange of civilities, and a few comments on the comic strip 'Gasoline Alley' which was on Joyce's mantelpiece, there was a total silence. In desperation Seldes remembered that three months before an Irishman, who said he had been a classmate of Joyce, came to the offices of the *Dial* to offer a copy of 'The Holy Office' for sale. On hearing this Joyce shot off a volley of questions: what was the man's name? what did he look like? how was he dressed? Seldes answered as best he could. The next day he had a telegram from Joyce asking him to come back. This time Joyce was ill at ease and walked up and down with suppressed excitement. Finally he stopped and said, 'Mr. Seldes, I know that the *Dial* is not an eleemosynary institution—' Then he smiled delightfully, 'Oh dear, this is rather like a sentence by Henry James, isn't it? Let's start again.' What he wanted was for Seldes to hunt down the man and buy the broadside at Joyce's expense. Seldes did not succeed in finding him, but after this incident Joyce and he always met on easy terms.[127]

1922–1923

...fame would come to you twixt a sleep * and a wake † ...

—*Finnegans Wake* (192)

T HE ironic quality of Joyce's fame was that it remained a *gloire de cénacle,* even when the *cénacle* had swelled to vast numbers of people. To have read *Ulysses,* or parts of it, became the mark of the knowledgeable expatriate. The saturnine *A Portrait of the Artist* led critics to suppose that Joyce was castigating modern society in *Ulysses* with Swiftian rigor; Bloom became a slightly depraved non-entity, his wife a wholly depraved whore. Joyce's emphasis in conversation on his literary means led to an unwarranted belief in the book's anti-humanist indifference. Another view had it that Joyce's criticism of society was fundamentally Catholic and that the Hound of Heaven was harrying him back into the fold. The fact which Larbaud had clarified in comparing Joyce to Rabelais, that *Ulysses* was a *comédie humaine,* was less often pursued.

Like other modern writers, such as Yeats and Eliot, Joyce made a point of not challenging any interpretation; the more controversy the book aroused, the better pleased he was, though he noted wistfully that no critic pursued Larbaud's insistence upon the relation of *Ulysses* to the Odyssey,[1] and through Miss Weaver urged Eliot to take it up. Even Pound, in the several excellent notices he wrote of the book, minimized the Odyssean parallels; but Eliot perceived, and wrote in the *Dial,* that 'manipulating a continuous parallel between contemporaneity and antiquity' had 'the importance of a scientific discovery.'[2] Joyce was gratified and in his note of thanks urged Eliot to coin some short phrase such as one Eliot had devised in conversation, 'two-plane.'[3] Larbaud's phrase, 'interior monologue,' was worn out after six months,

* Molly Bloom's.
† Finnegans.

Joyce said (underestimating critical habit), and the reading public
had need of a new one.

Eliot had more to say of the book than he wrote down. It undoubtedly impressed him deeply ('I wish, for my own sake, that I
had not read it,' he wrote Joyce on May 21, 1921) and encouraged
him in his own innovations in *The Waste Land*, which he had composed late in 1921. After *Ulysses* was published he came to tea with
Virginia Woolf at Hogarth House, and in discussing *Ulysses* was for
the first time in her experience 'rapt, enthusiastic.' 'How could anyone
write again after achieving the immense prodigy of the last chapter?' [4]
he asked. To her it was 'underbred,' [5] 'the book of a self taught working man,' of 'a queasy undergraduate scratching his pimples,' * [6] but
Eliot insisted that Joyce had killed the nineteenth century, exposed
the futility of all styles, and destroyed his own future. There was nothing left for him to write another book about. Yet the book gave no
new insight into human nature such as *War and Peace* did, Eliot
granted, and added, 'Bloom tells one nothing. Indeed, this new method
of giving the psychology proves to my mind that it doesn't work. It
doesn't tell as much as some casual glance from outside often tells.' [7]
Joyce himself came later to regard the interior monologue as a styliza-
tion, rather than a total exposition, of consciousness. As he said to
Stuart Gilbert, 'From my point of view, it hardly matters whether

---

* In short, of a Tansley in *To the Lighthouse*. A more violently hostile view than
Virginia Woolf's was taken by Edmund Gosse, who now regretted the help he had
given Joyce during the war. Gosse wrote Louis Gillet on June 7, 1924:

My dear Mr. Gillet,
   I should very much regret your paying Mr. J. Joyce the compliment of an
article in the 'Revue des Deux-Mondes.' You could only expose the worthlessness and impudence of his writings, and surely it would be a mistake to
give him this prominence. I have a difficulty in describing to you, *in writing*,
the character of Mr. Joyce's notoriety. . . . It is partly political; it is partly
a perfectly cynical appeal to sheer indecency. He is of course not entirely
without talent, but he is a literary charlatan of the extremest order. His
principal book, 'Ulysses,' has no parallel that I know of in French. It is an
anarchical production, infamous in taste, in style, in everything.
   Mr. Joyce is unable to publish or sell his books in England, on account of
their obscenity. He therefore issues a 'private' edition in Paris, and charges
a huge price for each copy. He is a sort of Marquis de Sade, but does not
write so well. He is the perfect type of the Irish *fumiste*, a hater of England,
more than suspected of partiality for Germany, where he lived before the
war (and at Zurich during the war).
   There are no English critics of weight or judgment who consider Mr. Joyce
an author of any importance. If, as you tell me, 'on fait grand bruit du
nommé J. J. . . . à Paris,' it must be among persons whose knowledge of English literature and language is scanty. He is not, as I say, without talent, but
he has prostituted it to the most vulgar uses.

Yours very sincerely,
Edmund Gosse

the technique is "veracious" or not; it has served me as a bridge over which to march my eighteen episodes, and, once I have got my troops across, the opposing forces can, for all I care, blow the bridge sky-high.' [8]

On the rue de Fleurus a few blocks from Shakespeare and Company, Gertrude Stein was irritated to have her position as arch-experimentalist challenged. 'Joyce,' she admitted, 'is good. He is a good writer. People like him because he is incomprehensible and anybody can understand him. But who came first, Gertrude Stein or James Joyce? Do not forget that my first great book, *Three Lives*, was published in 1908. That was long before *Ulysses*. But Joyce *has* done *something*. His influence, however, is local. Like Synge, another Irish writer, he has had his day.' [9] She brooded over the fact that Joyce never took advantage of the opportunity of seeing her.* But, as he pointedly told Mary Colum later, 'I hate intellectual women.' He kept his friendship with Gertrude Stein's protégé, Ernest Hemingway, who praised *Ulysses* without compunction and wrote to Sherwood Anderson on March 9, 1922:

> Joyce has a most goddamn wonderful book. It'll probably reach you in time. Meantime the report is that he and all his family are starving but you can find the whole celtic crew of them every night in Michaud's where Binney and I can only afford to go about once a week.
>
> Gertrude Stein says Joyce reminds her of an old woman out in San Francisco. The woman's son struck it rich as hell in the Klondyke and the old woman went around wringing her hands and saying, 'Oh my poor Joey! My poor Joey! He's got so much money!' The damned Irish, they have to moan about something or other, but you never heard of an Irishman starving.[10]

At the Restaurant Voltaire on April 25, George Moore regarded his younger compatriot's work with distaste. 'Take this Irishman Joyce,' he said to Barrett Clark, 'a sort of Zola gone to seed. Someone recently sent me a copy of *Ulysses*. I was told I must read it, but how can one plow through such stuff? I read a little here and there, but, oh my God, how bored I got! Probably Joyce thinks that because he prints all the dirty little words he is a great novelist. You know, of course, he got his ideas from Dujardin? What do you think of *Ulysses*?' Before Clark could answer, he went on, 'Joyce, Joyce, why he's nobody—from the Dublin docks: no family, no breeding. Someone else once sent me his *Portrait of the Artist as a Young Man*, a book entirely

---

* They did meet once, at a party at Eugene Jolas's, and Joyce said, 'How strange that we share the same quartier and have never met.' Gertrude Stein said doubtfully, 'Yes.' [11]

without style or distinction; why, I did the same thing, but much better, in *The Confessions of a Young Man*. Why attempt the same thing unless you can turn out a better book?' He allowed there was merit in 'The Dead,' 'But *Ulysses* is hopeless; it is absurd to imagine that any good end can be served by trying to record every single thought and sensation of any human being. That's not art, it's like trying to copy the London Directory. Do you know Joyce? He lives here in Paris, I understand. How does he manage to make a living? His books don't sell. Maybe he has money? You don't know? I'm curious. Ask someone that question.' [12]

Several French writers were quick to dissociate themselves from Joyce. Paul Claudel returned an inscribed copy of *Ulysses* 'as devilish,' and André Gide referred to the book privately as 'a sham masterpiece.' [13] Gide was uneasy, however, and in 1931, in answer to some small request from Joyce, began his reply * with the orotund sentence, '*Quelle émotion de recevoir une lettre du grand Joyce.*' [14] But at the same time, when Jean Paulhan proposed that the French *Ulysse* be included in the *Éditions de la Pléiade,* Gide would have none of it.[15] After Joyce's death Gide spoke of him more handsomely.†

Off in Dublin copies reached Mrs. Murray and John Stanislaus Joyce. Neither of them liked the book. Mrs. Murray was scandalized and put it away in a press—then lent it so it would not be in the house; John Joyce, after staring at parts of the book through his monocle, observed without rancor to his daughter Eva, 'He's a nice sort of blackguard.' Joyce waited in vain for their commendation. A tremor went through quite a few of his countrymen, who feared the part he might have assigned them. 'Are you in it?' or 'Am I in it?' they

---

* He wrote Adrienne Monnier on April 24, 1931, '*Oui, Joyce vient de m'écrire— une lettre exquise. Ma considération pour lui est si grande que j'ose à peine lui répondre.*'

† His 'Interview Imaginaire' in *Le Figaro* for May 30-31, 1942, is still quite reserved; [16] but a tribute he wrote for the Catalogue of the exhibition of Joyce's works at La Hune in 1949 is less so:

> *Il n'est pas malaisé d'être hardi quand on est jeune. L'audace la plus belle est celle de la fin de la vie. Je l'admire dans Joyce comme je l'admirais dans Mallarmé, dans Beethoven et dans quelques très rares artistes, dont l'œuvre s'achève en falaise et qui présentent au futur la plus abrupte face de leur génie, sans plus laisser connaître l'insensible pente par où ils ont atteint patiemment cette déconcertante altitude.* 27 juillet 1949.

> ('It is not difficult to be bold when one is young. The finest audacity is that of the end of life. I admire it in Joyce as I have admired it in Mallarmé, in Beethoven, and in some very rare artists, whose work terminates in a cliff and who present to the future the steepest face of their genius, never allowing the imperceptible slope, by which they have patiently reached that disconcerting height, to be known.')

asked the few people known to have copies.[17] Joyce's old friend Yeats had read a chapter or two in the *Little Review,* and his first thought was, 'A mad book!' But a little later he said to L. A. G. Strong, 'I have made a terrible mistake. It is a work perhaps of genius. I now perceive its coherence.'[18] And his first written comment was, 'It is an entirely new thing—neither what the eye sees nor the ear hears, but what the rambling mind thinks and imagines from moment to moment. He has certainly surpassed in intensity any novelist of our time.'[19] Yeats and his wife, the Pounds, and the Joyces met for dinner in Paris late in 1922, with Yeats doing most of the talking. Joyce seemed to Yeats to have still 'that touch of pugnacity of manner' that he had had as a very young man.[20] Yeats took up the book in earnest on his return to Ireland, and read the Martello tower episode, on which he commented, 'It has our Irish cruelty and also our kind of strength and the Martello Tower pages are full of beauty. A cruel playful mind like a great soft tiger cat.'[21] His sense that the art was alien to his own, implied in the remark about the 'rambling mind,' grew upon him, and he began to play truant by reading Trollope and *Ulysses* alternately, finally confessing in June 1923 that he had not been able to finish the book.[22] But he began to praise it publicly, and in the same month asked Joyce to come to Ireland for a visit. Joyce pleaded the excuse of his eyes.[23]

In Trieste Stanislaus read the book with qualified admiration. 'Dublin is spread out before the reader,' he wrote James, but added that parts of it were merely technical monstrosities, and that the whole of it lacked serenity and warmth. He disliked the *Circe* episode and was bored and repelled by *Penelope.*[24] He also insistently laid claim to some of the ideas in the book, but got no confirmation from his brother.

The reviews came in much too slowly for Joyce's taste. He helped Sylvia Beach to package copies for mailing, fondled the subscription lists, and cursed his friends in Trieste for not being on them, and in other ways made himself useful and plaintive. When reviews did not appear at once, he attributed the delay at first to the book's length, then was quick to assume that a boycott existed.[25] Sisley Huddleston's review in the *Observer* for March 5, which acknowledged Joyce's genius amid much criticism of the book's vulgarity and materiality, was the first, and brought in 136 orders in a day. Joyce began to prod other friends to review the book, usually, as with McAlmon, sending a copy, asking his opinion, then proposing he write a review, then suggesting phrases, and finally indicating where the review should be sent.[26] McAlmon brashly turned out a review without bothering to finish the book, and informed Joyce he was planning to throw *Ulysses* out the window. Joyce responded mildly, 'Don't throw *Ulysses* out the window as you threaten. Pyrrhus was killed in Argos like that. Also Socrates might be passing in the street. . . . Write again when recovered from Bloomitis.'[27] Joyce was flattered when Desmond Fitzgerald, a minister in the new Irish Free State government, paid him a visit and said he was about to propose that Ireland nominate Joyce for the Nobel Prize; such a move, Joyce wrote Stanislaus, would not gain him the prize and would lose Fitzgerald his portfolio.[28] He importuned Miss Weaver to find out whether or not the British Museum had obtained a copy.[29] Then Middleton Murry, in an impassioned mood, reviewed the book in the *Nation* as 'an immense, a prodigious self-laceration, the tearing away from himself, by a half-demented man of genius, of inhibitions and limitations,'[30] while Arnold Bennett, who had been bored by *A Portrait,* said in the *Outlook* that the best portions of *Ulysses,* chiefly *Circe* and *Penelope* in his view, were superb, magical even.[31] Each duly received a letter of thanks from the half-demented man of genius.[32] Joyce asked Miss Weaver to suggest to Eliot that he review the book in the *Times Literary Supplement,* but Eliot sadly told her no hope lay in that quarter.[33] To Miss Weaver, Joyce proposed more and more elaborate advertising plans, then half apologized with the words, 'I am sure all of this will seem very disingenuous to you but alas you must speak Helvetian to a Swiss is the experience of this *voyageur malgré lui.'*[34]

The notion of taking a trip was not so uncongenial now. He would have gone somewhere in March if there had not been new difficulties with Darantière, and new possibilities, unfortunately not realized, of finding a flat. To McAlmon, who urged him to come down to the Riviera where he was staying, Joyce had to say no, but asked if McAlmon could spare him a necktie * for consolation.[35] McAlmon made a special trip to Cannes, bought several ties and a ring, and mailed them to Joyce, who replied in pleased embarrassment,

I didn't mean you to go to Cannes to buy ties for me! God forbid. I thought you always travelled with a trunk full of them and threw out a few dozens a week, but evidently I was misled by rumour:

> The press and the public misled me
> So brand it as slander and lies
> That I am the bloke with the watches †
> And that you are the chap with the ties.

The ring is very nice and episcopal.[36]

---

* Joyce formed a large collection of ties in Paris, and came to pay almost dandiacal attention to his clothes.[37]
† See p. 525.

In March Joyce received another gift from Miss Weaver, this time of £1500; now, he wrote Stanislaus, he had received from her £8500 in all. There being no financial impediment, Nora suggested they go back to Ireland so the children could see their grandparents. Joyce had no sympathy with the idea, Ireland and he being still out of phase.

The recent events in his country had not pleased him, even though they represented the triumph of the Sinn Fein principles which in Rome and Trieste he had vigorously espoused. During the last two years of the Irish fight for independence, the only incident that had stirred his imagination was the hunger strike of the Lord Mayor of Cork, Terence MacSwiney—possibly a distant relation—in October 1920. For a moment at least he had associated MacSwiney's battle with his own against English officialdom in Zurich, and sent Stanislaus a bitter poem to that effect:

The Right Heart in the Wrong Place

> Of spinach and gammon
> Bull's full to the crupper
> White lice and black famine
> Are the Mayor of Cork's supper;
> But the pride of old Ireland
> Must be damnably humbled
> If a Joyce is found cleaning
> The boots of a Rumbold.

As the prospect of Irish independence improved, however, Joyce was like his father and other old Parnellites, in that the reality of freedom did not requite the desire for it. 'Ireland sober is Ireland free,' Father Matthew's legend for Ireland, Joyce was soon to alter to, 'Ireland sober is Ireland stiff.' [38] The earnestness of the new nation was part of its unpleasantness, and for the moment there was the additional problem of civil war, brought on by De Valera's refusal to accept the treaty ratified by the Dail on January 7, 1922. Besides the trepidation that even sporadic fighting roused in a physically unaggressive man, Joyce still felt the fear that he would return to Ireland, after publishing his three prose books, with the same notoriety as Parnell after Captain O'Shea's divorce action, and might suffer the same horror of having quicklime thrown in his eyes—a danger particularly close to a man with eye trouble. So when Desmond Fitzgerald, Irish Minister of Information, asked him cheerily if he would return to Ireland now that the government was changed, Joyce replied with the ironic understatement, 'Not for the present.' [39]

He tried to dissuade Nora from the trip, but her mind was fixed on it. There was a serious quarrel, in which Joyce's resentment of her indifference to *Ulysses* boiled up with other irritations. It ended in her departure with the children on April 1, and a final threat not to return, which Joyce seems to have met with a counterthreat of equal vehemence. They had hardly gone before he thought better of it, and tried to hold them up again in London by warning telegrams and mollifying letters. But after ten days' delay there, Nora stubbornly proceeded to Dublin. Michael Healy met the travelers and they spent an evening with him and with John Joyce. The next day they went on to Galway, where at first all was quiet. Nora brought the children to the Presentation Convent, where she had worked as a girl, and showed them off to the Mother Superior. In Paris Joyce became gloomier and gloomier. 'And do you think they're safe, really?' he asked McAlmon repeatedly. 'You don't understand how this is affecting me. I am worried all of the day and it does my eye no good.' [40] He wrote Nora to say, 'I am like a man looking into a dark pool,' [41] and begged her to return. A businesslike letter from her brought a desperate answer:

8:30 a.m.
Thursday

My darling, my love, my queen: I jump out of bed to send you this. Your wire is postmarked 18 hours later than your letter which I have just received. A cheque for your fur will follow in a few hours, and also money for yourself. If you wish to live there (as you ask me to send two pounds a week) I will send that amount (£ 8 and £ 4) rent on the first of every month. But you also ask me if I would go to London with you. I would go anywhere in the world if I could be sure that I could be alone with your dear self without family * and without friends. Either this must occur or we must part forever, though it will break my heart. Evidently it is impossible to describe to you the despair I have been in since you left. Yesterday I got a fainting fit in Miss Beach's shop and she had to run and get me some kind of a drug. Your image is always in my heart. How glad I am to hear you are looking younger! O my dearest, if you would only turn to me even now and read that terrible book which has now broken the heart in my breast and take me to yourself alone to do with me what you will! I have only 10 minutes to write this so forgive me. Will write again before noon and also wire. These few words for the moment and my undying unhappy love.

Jim

---

* Probably a reference to relatives in Ireland and London.

Just then fighting broke out in Galway between the Free State troops and the Irish Republican Army. Nora was terrified to see soldiers tramping in to use their bedroom as a firing position, and decided to leave at once. Her irritation with her husband was quickly dispelled by the new emergency; when Joyce heard from her he brilliantly arranged to have a plane go to Galway for his family, but she did not wait for it. She and the children boarded the train for Dublin with relief only to have the troops of both factions begin to fire at it. Nora and Lucia dove to the floor, while Giorgio, prouder but less reasonable, steadfastly kept his seat. So did an old Irishman who sucked his pipe, looked at the boy, and said, 'Aren't you going to get down?' 'No.' 'You're right,' said the old man, 'they never shoot straight. They're probably shooting blanks anyhow.' [42] No one was hurt, and Michael Healy, when told in Dublin of their adventure, thought it merely funny.[43] But he obligingly put them on the boat for Holyhead that same night, and they went back to Paris at once, Nora's dissatisfaction with her life there cancelled out. Joyce was delighted to see them. He did not laugh about the attack; [*] instead he interpreted it as really aimed at himself, and old Dublin friends like C. P. Curran, who visited him in Paris, found him preposterous on the subject. But a belief in the malevolence of certain people in Dublin remained essential to Joyce's understanding of his own situation. He reacted to the affair as strenuously as William Blake to Hayley's seemingly innocent overtures.

He made up his mind to travel nonetheless, and in May 1922 planned to go to London. But during the month his iritis recurred, and became so painful that he consulted a well-known French ophthalmologist, Dr. Victor Morax,[44] on May 23. In his notes the doctor wrote that Joyce blamed the origin of his ailment upon a night's drinking at Pirano in 1910, after which he had spent the early hours of the morning on the ground. This had started arthritic pains in his right shoulder and left the deltoid muscle in his right arm atrophied. Siedler's operation on the right eye in 1917 had been fairly successful, though the vision was impaired; but the iritis had now spread to the left eye. With Morax's treatment it improved a little, but there was always blood in the interior of the eye, and glaucoma was incipient. At the end of May Joyce had a burst of new pain, and telephoned Morax, who, unable to come himself, sent his student, Dr. Pierre Mérigot de Treigny, to bring him some relief. When the door of the room at 9 rue de l'Université was opened to the young doctor, he was aston-

---

[*] The only incident that amused him in the Irish Civil War was Gogarty's escape from I.R.A. troops by plunging into the Liffey and swimming to safety.

ished by the disorder: trunks half empty, clothes hanging everywhere, toilet accessories spread on chairs, tables, and mantelpiece. Wrapped in a blanket and squatting on the floor was a man with dark glasses who proved to be Joyce, and facing him in the same posture was Nora. Between them stood a stewpan with a chicken carcass, and beside it a half empty bottle of wine. Such were the felicities of a furnished room. There being no free chair, Mérigot de Treigny squatted down himself to examine the patient's eyes. He administered a local remedy which alleviated the pain for a few days, but on a second emergency visit warned Joyce he would need an operation. This advice was so objectionable to the patient, who had learned in 1917 how disturbing a violation of the body an eye operation is, that he asked Morax not to send Mérigot de Treigny again. 'A strange fellow,' Morax commented to his pupil, 'but a *big boss* * just the same.' [45]

In July, at Ezra Pound's instigation, Dr. Louis Berman, a New York endocrinologist then visiting Paris, gave Joyce an examination. For the arthritic back he proposed endocrine treatment, and after one look at Joyce's teeth insisted upon their being X-rayed at once.[46] They proved to be in such bad condition that he advised complete extraction. Joyce accepted the endocrine treatment, but postponed having anything done to his teeth while he hopefully consulted another prominent ophthalmologist, Dr. Louis Borsch. Borsch thought it would be safe to make a trip to London before anything was done to eyes or teeth, and Joyce accordingly went in August.

He and his wife stayed at the Euston Hotel, which, because it is patronized by people taking the morning boat-train from Euston Station to Holyhead, calls itself 'The Gateway to Ireland.' 'I feel that I am near Number Thirteen platform—the Irish Mail (*absit omen!*),' Joyce told a friend.[47] By special permission of the management he was allowed to remain in this hotel,† which is intended for transients, indefinitely. He quickly got in touch with Miss Weaver, whom he met now for the first time, admiring and liking her integrity and

---

* He used the American phrase.

† Its advantages he later described to Miss Weaver as '732 rooms, 2 wings, liveried porters, chatty meteorologist in the lift, whispering lounge, English breakfast, *videlicet,* Danish bacon, Irish eggs, American sugar, French milk, Canadian marmalade, Scotch porridge, New Zealand butter, Dutch toast. Mr E. H. Knight, manager. I met him every morning and wished him good kday, Mr Knight. He is a very knice kman.' [48] Or, as he put it in *Finnegans Wake* (245), 'here's dapplebellied mugs and troublebedded rooms and sawdust strown in expectoration and for ratification by specification of your information, Mr Knight, tuntapster, buttles; his alefru's up to his hip.'

He liked the night porter at the Euston Hotel, and in 1930 had Herbert Gorman present him with a signed copy of *Ulysses*.

selflessness. He had apparently decided how he would act towards her, and proudly made no concessions in his behavior. So, when the choice lay between a taxi and a bus, Joyce unhesitatingly sprang for the taxi and tipped the driver lavishly with Miss Weaver's former money. Miss Weaver recognized that the inner promptings of his nature were as extravagant as her own were frugal, and, if she winced at times, she never thought of admonishing him. He got rid of over £200 in a few weeks. Miss Weaver asked him what he would write next and he said, 'I think I will write a history of the world.' [49]

Another pleasant encounter was with his Aunt Josephine Murray's daughter Kathleen, then working in a London hospital, whom, with her sister Alice, Joyce invited to dinner. As Patricia Hutchins writes,[50] Joyce began the evening by announcing as they drove to Soho in a taxi that he very much wanted a fresh pair of socks. The taxi driver said he had a friend who could oblige, and soon after called Joyce out of the restaurant. Joyce returned looking pleased and wearing the new pair. The only discordant note in the gay, well-hosed evening was Joyce's question about their mother's response to *Ulysses*. Kathleen was embarrassed but said, 'Well, Jim, Mother said it was not fit to read.' 'If *Ulysses* isn't fit to read,' Joyce replied, 'life isn't fit to live.' [51]

His eyes, instead of being benefited by the trip, suddenly became worse. Joyce had to consult two London ophthalmologists, Doctors Henry and James, whose names, he noted with fine indifference to a fellow-author, were also the name of a clothing store in Dublin.[52] They warned him that the fluid in the left eye had begun to 'organize' and become immovable, a presage of glaucoma, and advised an immediate operation. This advice was enough to drive Joyce back across the Channel.[53] He fled to Paris in mid-September to consult Dr. Borsch, hoping the French and English diagnoses would contradict each other. Borsch being away on holiday, and 9 rue de l'Université depressing beyond belief, Joyce secured a furnished flat at 26 avenue Charles Floquet, his tenancy to begin sooner than he wished, on November 1. He had hoped, if Borsch would permit, to go before that to Nice so as to avoid the Paris winter. His eyes, meanwhile, looked perpetually red; too many lights, or too many people, seemed to make them worse. 'I always have the impression that it is evening,' [54] he confided to Philippe Soupault. Yet his sense of hearing seemed to sharpen, and he professed to be able to judge men by their voices.

Borsch returned from his holiday at the beginning of October, and advised Joyce to have his teeth extracted while at Nice so that a milder eye operation (not an iridectomy but a sphincterectomy, the sphincter being the oval muscle surrounding the eyelid) could take place on his return. He thought the English doctors had exaggerated the danger of glaucoma, since the nebula or film over the eye had split at the top and was thinning slightly in the center. At any rate, he saw no danger of glaucoma *foudroyant,* the disease which Dr. Berman had suggested was probably the cause of Homer's blindness.[55] On October 13 the Joyces were at Marseilles and by October 17 they were installed at the Hôtel Suisse in Nice. But Joyce's attempt to winter on the Côte d'Azur in 1922 was no more satisfactory than his attempt to winter in Locarno in 1917-18. The weather suddenly turned inclement, and the rain and windstorms had a deleterious effect upon his eye. He had to consult Dr. Louis Colin, who applied five leeches to drain the blood from the eye,[56] and then, to dissolve the nebula, dosed it with a strong and painful dionine solution (salicylate of soda). Under this treatment part of the nebula disappeared and the condition became less acute. Dr. Colin advised Joyce to drink red wine rather than white, but this sacrifice was more than his patient could bear.

The holiday, however, was a failure. Some of Joyce's resultant bad temper emerged in a letter to his aunt, Mrs. Murray, written near the end of October 1922:

> Hotel Suisse
> Quai des États-Unis
> Nice
> (France)

Dear Aunt Josephine: A few days before I left Paris I got a letter from you which seemed very wrathful. The facts are these. *Ulysses* was published on 2 February. When the edition was sold out Nora said she wanted to go to Ireland to her mother. I did all I could to dissuade her but her friends here and in Ireland told her it was as simple as anything. Finally as my father also wished to see the children I let them go but made them promise to stay a week or so in London and watch. I managed to hold them up in London for ten days by means of express letters and telegrams. Then they suddenly left for Ireland. They stopped a night in Dublin and Lucia kindly suggested that they should visit my father whose address she remembered. This they did and went on to Galway. In Galway my son was dogged about the streets and as he told me since he could not sleep at night with the thought that the Zulus, as he calls them, would take him out of bed and shoot him. A drunken officer swaggered up to him blocking the path and asked him 'How does it feel to be a jintleman's son?' Meanwhile in Paris utterly exhausted as I was after eight years ceaseless labour I was on the verge of lunacy. Needless to say what I had foreseen took place and the next thing was that I got a telegram from London to say that they wanted to come back to Paris. The warehouse opposite their lodgings in Galway was seized by rebels, free state troops invaded their bedrooms and planted machine guns in the windows. They ran through the town to the station and escaped in a train lying flat on their bellies (the two females that is) amid a fusillade which continued for an hour from right and left between troops on the train and ambushes along the line. They fled through Dublin in the dark and so came back to Paris. I then sent Lucia to a summer camp on the coast of Normandy for four months and Giorgio to the Austrian Tyrol. After which I collapsed with a furious eye attack lasting until a few weeks ago—but apparently that does not interest. I am here at present in the hope of regaining my sight and my health.

The second cause of your wrath seems to be my book. I am as innocent in this case as in the former. I presented it to you seven months ago but I never heard anything more about it beyond a few words acknowledging receipt and an allusion in your last letter. The market price of the book now in London is £ 40 and copies signed are worth more. I mention this because Alice told me you had lent it (or given?) and people in Dublin have a way of not returning books. In a few years copies of the first edition will probably be worth £ 100 each,* so book experts say, and hence my remark. This of course has nothing to do with the contents of the book which it seems you have not read. I sent it however as I sent all my other books and at your request in a letter of a year or so ago. There is a difference between a present of a pound of chops and a present of a book like *Ulysses*. You can acknowledge receipt of the present of a pound of chops by simply nodding gratefully, supposing, that is, that you have your mouth full of as much of the chops as it will conveniently hold, but you cannot do so with a large book on account of the difficulty of fitting it into the mouth.

The third point of wrath is the fact that no reply was made to Mabel † when she announced her marriage by sending a piece of wedding cake till I dictated a letter from London. That succulent morsel arrived when I was lying in a darkened room in continual pain and danger of loss of sight and continually threatened with an operation. I gave instructions that the letter be answered and our congratulations sent. This was not done. A violent and dangerous illness for months in a hotel in the centre of Paris in the middle of the intense excitement (letters, telegrams, articles) caused by the publication of *Ulysses* explains why there was some slight confusion, I suppose.

I ought not to have been obliged to write this long letter but it is better to write it than not as the letter Nora is going to write will probably not reach you before the early spring of 1931 A.D. In the meantime if you have any remarks or information to transmit to me about whatever you think I take an interest in well and good but

---

* The price of Middleton Murry's copy at Sotheby's on November 26, 1957, was £ 140.

† A daughter of Mrs. Murray.

wrathful epistles should be addressed preferably to Nora or her advisers there and here or to the president of your free fight or the
leader of the irregulars or to the parish priest at Fairview or to the
Sacred Heart to whom Ireland is dedicated and not to me. No doubt
you will see Nora some other time when she goes to revisit her native
dunghill though it is doubtful if Giorgio or Lucia will go. The air in
Galway is very good but dear at the present price. The only enliven-
ing feature of their journey appears to have been their interview with
my father, who amused them vastly by the virulence, variety and in-
candescence of curses which he bestowed on his native country and
all in it—a litany to which his eldest son says *Amen* from the bottom,
that is to say, the nethermost or lowest part of his heart.

Nora and Lucia are here with me and Giorgio who is in Paris will
probably come down too as I think I shall take a place here for the
winter. All are well as we hope you all are too.

A second edition of *Ulysses* was published on the 12 October. The
entire edition of 2000 copies at £2-2-0 a copy was sold out in four
days.

Kind regards and remembrances from us all.

Jim

23/x/922

P.S. That reminds me that in your letter you seem to assume that Nora
and the children (the 'child' Giorgio is taller than his father and Lucia
after her camp work could go on a circus trapeze) went to Ireland for
the purpose of visiting Mr Devan and the second Mrs Devan. This
had not struck me till you mentioned it but you might be right for all
that. They have gone out to have tea and ladies' music at a café on
the esplanade but I will ask them when they come back. I expect they
will both deny it but who knows whether they will be telling the truth
or not? That's the point.

J.[57]

When Mrs. Murray replied with distress at the hardening of his heart,
he wrote a pleasanter letter on November 10, suggesting they might
meet in London in the spring. Two days later, on November 12, 1922,
the Joyces packed up and returned to their Paris flat on the avenue
Charles Floquet.

Shortly after his return Joyce had serious quarrels first with Sylvia
Beach and then with Frank Budgen. That with Miss Beach was the
result of his daily importunities during the last year, though the imme-
diate cause was his suggestion that she arrange a third edition of
Ulysses and also check with a group of critics (Pound, Eliot, Colum,
Kate Buss, Hemingway, Linati, Benco, Jaloux, George Slocombe, J. C.
Squire, S. P. B. Mais, Aldington, Ford Madox Ford, Charles du Bos,

and Muriel Ciolkowska) to see if they had as yet reviewed the book anywhere. She replied impatiently by letter, according to Joyce, that she was not interested in 'hustling to boom the book,' [58] and, with less conviction, that she had been warned that the second edition imitated the first so closely that it might subject her to court action for publishing a bogus first edition. 'She ended by saying about my suggestion of an article that the rumours that were current in Paris about *Ulysses* and its author were such that it was more advisable that nothing concerning me or the other be printed in any paper here for some time to come.' [59] After perusing Miss Beach's angry letter, 'I gazed at the buttons of the Swiss concierge,' Joyce wrote Miss Weaver, catching, as he often managed to do for her, the comic possibilities of his misadventures, 'until I had discovered the answers of the various questions and then with a deep sigh stood up among my multicoloured multitudinous valises and fare[d] forth once more over the widewayed earth.' [60] He pointed out that the second edition was properly identified in two places, and showed Sylvia Beach a letter from Darantière assuring him that no law had been violated. Miss Beach was calmed, but the ground was prepared for later quarrels. Joyce wrote to Miss Weaver, 'Possibly the fault is partly mine. I, my eye, my needs and my troublesome book are always there. There is no feast or celebration or meeting of shareholders but at the fatal hour I appear at the door in dubious habiliments, with impedimenta of baggage, a mute expectant family, a patch over one eye howling dismally for aid.' [61]

The quarrel with Budgen was brought on by Joyce himself. During the last two years in Paris, Budgen had occasionally visited him, and, though he felt a little out of place with Joyce's new friends, he was glad to find that Joyce clung tightly to their friendship. Joyce continued to write to him with his old frankness, and in one of his letters spoke out so directly and compromisingly that, in a burst of gratuitous mistrust, he decided he must get the letter back. He therefore asked Budgen to bring it along because he wished to see what he had said. Budgen did so, and Joyce entertained him that night in a grand drinking-bout, ordering and reordering the glasses with such rapidity that Budgen was several times inclined to protest. At the end of the evening Budgen was quite drunk, and, deposited by Joyce at a bus stop, got back to his hotel with some difficulty. In the morning he was awakened by a special messenger bringing his wallet and a note from Joyce saying that, in view of Budgen's condition, he had thought it prudent to safeguard his friend's property for him. Budgen looked into the wallet: his money was there and so, to his embarrassment, were some bills, but the compromising letter had been lifted. The game was finely played, too finely for Budgen's taste; he was deeply hurt and for three years was estranged from Joyce.[62] But Joyce, thinking of Cosgrave and others, had too little faith to allow even Budgen to possess a compromising letter.[*]

The dental operations scheduled for January 1923 filled Joyce with uneasiness, and he was not sorry to have to postpone them with Dr. Borsch's consent. An attack of conjunctivitis in March abated after about a week, and on April 4 six or seven decayed teeth were extracted, the rest a few days later.[63] Joyce stayed in a *maison de santé* for two weeks recovering. The loss of the teeth did not greatly bother him; he remarked to his son, 'They were no good anyway.'[64] But the extractions were painful. Then in stages, on April 3, 15, and 28, with this source of infection removed, Borsch performed the sphincterectomy. A month later Joyce felt none of the improvement Borsch had predicted, but by June 10 he was able to read a little, and Borsch assured him that his eye would recover its health fully in a few months. Meanwhile the dentist had finished his new plates, and when these had been inserted on June 10,[65] Joyce and his family left for a holiday in England. In spite of the rigors of the last few months he was feeling better, and had no serious eye trouble for the rest of the year.

The materials for a new book had been forming slowly in his mind. The structure of it was still obscure to him, so that when the sculptor August Suter asked what he was writing, he could answer truthfully, 'It's hard to say.' 'Then what is the title of it?' asked Suter. This time Joyce was less candid: 'I don't know. It is like a mountain that I tunnel into from every direction, but I don't know what I will find.'[66] Actually he did know the title at least, and had told it to Nora in strictest secrecy. It was to be *Finnegans Wake*, the apostrophe omitted because it meant both the death of Finnegan and the resurgence of all Finnegans. The title came from the ballad about the hod-carrier who falls from a ladder to what is assumed to be his death, but is revived by the smell of the whisky at his wake.[†] But behind this

---

[*] Joyce repaired the friendship by asking Budgen, who he had heard was in Paris, to call. After a pleasant evening Joyce said just before they parted, 'I hope you'll always believe that I'm a good friend, Budgen.'

[†]   *Finnegan's Wake*

Tim Finnegan lived in Walkin Street,
   A gentleman Irish mighty odd.
He had a tongue both rich and sweet,
   An' to rise in the world he carried a hod.
Now Tim had a sort of a tipplin' way,
   With the love of the liquor he was born,
An' to help him on with his work each day,
   He'd a drop of the craythur every morn.

Irish master builder was a more ancient Irish prototype, the legendary hero and wise man Finn MacCumhal. As Joyce informed a friend later, he conceived of his book as the dream of old Finn, lying in death beside the river Liffey and watching the history of Ireland and the world—past and future—flow through his mind like flotsam on the river of life. This was the 'universal history' of which Joyce had spoken to Miss Weaver; it would mix history and fable in a comic leveling. The characters would be the dreamlike shapes of the eternal, unholy

---

Chorus

Whack folthe dah, dance to your partner,
   Welt the flure, yer trotters shake,
Wasn't it the truth I told you,
   Lots of fun at Finnegan's Wake.

One morning Tim was rather full,
   His head felt heavy which made him shake,
He fell from the ladder and broke his skull,
   So they carried him home his corpse to wake,
They rolled him up in a nice clean sheet,
   And laid him out upon the bed,
With a gallon of whiskey at his feet,
   And a barrel of porter at his head.

His friends assembled at the wake,
   And Mrs. Finnegan called for lunch,
First they brought in tay and cake,
   Then pipes, tobacco, and whiskey punch.
Miss Biddy O'Brien began to cry,
   'Such a neat clean corpse, did you ever see,
Arrah, Tim avourneen, why did you die?'
   'Ah, hould your gab,' said Paddy McGee.

Then Biddy O'Connor took up the job,
   'Biddy,' says she, 'you're wrong, I'm sure,'
But Biddy gave her a belt in the gob,
   And left her sprawling on the floor;
Oh, then the war did soon enrage;
   'Twas woman to woman and man to man,
Shillelagh law did all engage,
   And a row and a ruction soon began.

Then Micky Maloney raised his head,
   When a noggin of whiskey flew at him,
It missed and falling on the bed,
   The liquor scattered over Tim;
Bedad he revives, see how he rises,
   And Timothy rising from the bed,
Says, 'Whirl your liquor round like blazes,
   Thanam o'n dhoul, do ye think I'm dead?'

The Irish phrase in the last line means, 'Your souls from the devil!'

family, Everyman, his wife, their children, and their followers, bobbing up and down on the river. In the twentieth century Everyman's avatar was to be Humphrey Chimpden Earwicker, keeper of a public house in Chapelizod, whose wife was Anna Livia, whose children were the twins Shem and Shaun and their sister with the split personality, Isabel. Behind and within Earwicker, that compound of bounce and bluster, were all men of enterprise, strong or weak; his twin sons were every possible pair of brothers or opponents, his wife was all homekeepers, his daughter every heart's desire from Iseult of Ireland to Swift's Vanessa. Beyond these manifestations, Earwicker was a primordial giant, a mountain, a god, with a double aspect suggested by the sons, and Anna a river, a principle of nature, her daughter a cloud. It was a wholly new book based upon the premise that there is nothing new under the sun.

In many ways the book was to be a sequel to *Ulysses;* for example, the last page of *Ulysses* showed Molly and Leopold eating the same seedcake like Eve and Adam eating the 'seedfruit' (as Joyce called it) [67] when man fell, and *Finnegans Wake* also began with the fall of man. It is possible, too, that a plan Joyce discarded in 1920,[68] of beginning *Ulysses* with a *matutine*, ending it with a *nocturne*, and inserting an *entr'acte* in the middle, had envisaged a theme of riverlike flow. *Finnegans Wake*, which begins and ends with the river and centers in the *Anna Livia Plurabelle* section, was perhaps the legatee of this unused idea. Some long mulled-over stories, such as the meeting of his father with a thief in the Phoenix Park, the story of the Norwegian captain and the tailor (alluded to in *Ulysses*), and the story of Buckley and the Russian general, were rehabilitated for new uses. Myron Nutting was surprised to see Joyce sorting out old notes for *Ulysses* in February 1923, especially when Joyce announced proudly that the unused notes weighed twelve kilos.[69]

In his correspondence there are occasional hints of the new book. Joyce sent Miss Weaver Sir Edward O'Sullivan's *The Book of Kells* (a facsimile of some pages, with commentary) in December 1922 as a Christmas present, and this book was not only to be mentioned prominently in *Finnegans Wake,* but also stood as a kind of model for him.* When Arthur Power confessed to Joyce he would like to write but did not know how to proceed, Joyce urged him to study *The Book of Kells,* saying, 'In all the places I have been to, Rome, Zurich, Trieste, I have taken it about with me, and have pored over its workmanship for hours. It is the most purely Irish thing we have, and some of the big initial letters which swing right across a page

---

* In *Finnegans Wake* (122), Joyce makes the *Book of Kells* derive from the *Wake.*

have the essential quality of a chapter of *Ulysses*. Indeed, you can compare much of my work to the intricate illuminations. I would like it to be possible to pick up any page of my book and know at once what book it is.' [70] There are casual allusions in his letters to Miss Weaver to Tristram and Napoleon, two heroes with whom Earwicker and his sons are associated, but, as if to insure that Everyman should not be too cosmopolitan, he wrote also to Mrs. Murray in Dublin on December 21, 1922, asking her to set down in a notebook all she remembered of some 'curious types' he had known as a child.[71]

That *Finnegans Wake* should be a night book as *Ulysses* was a day book was also already decided. The night required and justified a special language. '*Je suis au bout de l'anglais.*' * [72] Joyce said to August Suter, and he remarked to another friend, 'I have put the language to sleep.' [73] As he explained to Max Eastman in a later effort, valiant but unsuccessful, to win a convert to his method, 'In writing of the night, I really could not, I felt I could not, use words in their ordinary connections. Used that way they do not express how things are in the night, in the different stages—conscious, then semi-conscious, then unconscious. I found that it could not be done with words in their ordinary relations and connections. When morning comes of course everything will be clear again. . . . I'll give them back their English language. I'm not destroying it for good.' [74] Joyce set out upon this radical technique, of making many of the words in his book multilingual puns, with his usual conviction. He called it 'working in layers.' After all, he said to Frank Budgen, 'The Holy Roman Catholic Apostolic Church was built on a pun. It ought to be good enough for me.' To the objection of triviality, he replied, 'Yes. Some of the means I use are trivial—and some are quadrivial.' † [75]

Joyce wished also to invade the world of dreams. From his youth in Dublin, in spite of his distaste for Freud, he had taken a great interest in dreams, his own and other people's, and in their interpretation. In Zurich he often talked about dreams with Budgen, and in Paris with other friends. He said to Edmond Jaloux that his novel would be written 'to suit the esthetic of the dream, where the forms prolong and multiply themselves, where the visions pass from the trivial to the apocalyptic, where the brain uses the roots of vocables to make others from them which will be capable of naming its phantasms, its allegories, its allusions.' [76] He astonished his friends by the

* 'I'm at the end of English.'
† He said more defiantly to John Eglinton at a later meeting, 'I write in that way simply because it comes naturally to me to do so, and I don't care if the whole thing crumbles when I have done with it.' [77]

minuteness of his interest in dream phenomena. 'Tell me, Bird,' he said to William Bird, a frequent companion in these days, 'do you ever dream you are reading?' 'Very often,' said Bird. 'Ah. Now at what speed do you read in your dreams?' Bird said that he seemed to read slowly and with difficulty, because of bad light or poor print. Joyce leaped at this. 'Do you know that when we dream we are reading, I think it's really that we are talking in our sleep. But we cannot talk as fast as we read, so our dream invents a reason for the slowness.' Or he speculated about noises in dreams: 'In sleep our senses are dormant, except the sense of hearing, which is always awake, since you can't close your ears. So any sound that comes to our ears during sleep is turned into a dream.' [78] Another companion, Myron Nutting, then very interested in psychoanalysis, used to tell his dreams to Joyce and was amazed at the shrewdness of the interpretations Joyce suggested. Mrs. Nutting preserved one of Joyce's own dreams and the interpretation he put upon it:

I had a curious dream after the Russian ballet. I dreamed that there was a Persian pavilion with sixteen rooms, four on each floor. Someone had committed a crime, and he entered the lowest floor. The door opened on a flower garden. He hoped to get through but when he arrived at the threshold a drop of blood fell on it. I could know how desperate he felt, for he went from the first floor all the way up to the fourth, his hope being that at each threshold his wound was not capable of letting fall another drop. But always it came, an official discovered it, and punctually at the sixteen rooms the drop fell. There were two officials in brocaded silk robes, and a man with a scimitar, who watched him.

Can you psychoanalyze it? I will. The rooms represented the twelve signs of the zodiac. Three doors are the Trinity. The man who had committed the crime is evidently myself. The drop of blood left on each threshold were five franc notes which I borrowed from Wyndham Lewis [with whom Joyce had spent the previous evening]. The man with the scimitar represents my wife next morning. The pavilion with light blue lattices was like a box. [79]

The interpretation is a heady mixture of Freud and the Arabian Nights. Another dream, which Joyce wrote out for Gorman, was more indigenous:

I saw Molly Bloom on a hillock under a sky full of moonlit clouds rushing overhead. She had just picked up from the grass a child's black coffin and flung it after the figure of a man passing down a side road by the field she was in. It struck his shoulders, and she said, 'I've done with you.' The man was Bloom seen from behind. There was a shout of laughter from some American journalists in the road opposite, led by Ezra Pound. I was very indignant and vaulted over a gate into the field and strode up to her and delivered the one speech of my life. It was very long, eloquent and full of passion, explaining all the last episode of *Ulysses* to her. She wore a black opera cloak, or *sortie de bal,* had become slightly grey and looked like *la Duse.* She smiled when I ended on an astronomical climax, and then, bending, picked up a tiny snuffbox, in the form of a little black coffin, and tossed it towards me, saying, 'And I have done with you, too, Mr. Joyce.' I had a snuffbox like the one she tossed to me when I was at Clongowes Wood College. It was given to me by my godfather, Philip McCann, together with a larger one to fill it from.* [80]

This dream resulted in a parody which suggests how Molly was fusing into the character of Anna Livia Plurabelle, heroine of *Finnegans Wake:*

(To the tune of 'Molly Brannigan')

Man dear, did you never hear of buxom Molly Bloom at all
As plump an Irish beauty, sir, as Annie Levy Blumenthal,
If she sat in the vice-regal box Tim Healy'd have no room at all,
    But curl up in a corner at a glance from her eye.
The tale of her ups and downs would aisy fill a handybook
That would cover the whole world across from Gib right on to Sandy Hook,
But now that tale is told, ahone, I've lost my daring dandy look
    Since Molly Bloom has gone and left me here for to die.

Man dear, I remember when my roving time was troubling me
We picnicked fine in storm or shine in France and Spain and Hungary,
And she said I'd be her first and last while the wine I poured went
    bubbling free.
Now every male she meets with has a finger in her pie.
Man dear, I remember how with all the heart and brain of me
I arrayed her for the bridal, but, oh, she proved the bane of me,
With more puppies sniffing round her than the wooers of Penelope
    She's left me on the doorstep like a dog for to die.

My left eye is awash and his neighbour full of water, man,
I cannot see the lass I limned for Ireland's gamest daughter, man,
When I hear her lovers tumbling in their thousands for to court her, man,
    If I were sure I'd not be seen I'd sit down and cry.
May you live, may you love like this gaily spinning earth of ours,
And every morn a gallous son awake you to fresh wealth of gold,
But if I cling like a child to the clouds that are your petticoats,
    O Molly, handsome Molly, sure you won't let me die? [81]

So the Biblical crime in the Garden became the crime in the garden in Joyce's dream and finally the crime in Phoenix Park which Ear-

---

* In a different version he told to John Sullivan, Joyce said, 'Molly Bloom came calling on me and said, "What are you meddling with my old business for?" She had a coffin in her hand and said, "If you don't change this is for you." ' [82]

wicker is alleged to have committed. Molly Bloom, once Marie Tallon, Amalia Popper, and Nora Joyce, became the river Liffey. In all his books Joyce makes his characters out of both real and mythical proto-types, but in *Finnegans Wake* he does this much more explicitly than elsewhere. So Earwicker's two sons, Shem and Shaun, were based in part upon two feeble-minded hangers-on, James and John Ford, who lived in Dublin on the North Strand. They were known as 'Shem and Shaun,' and were famous for their incomprehensible speech and their shuffling gait. Their only occupations were bringing the hurley sticks on to the field for the hurley teams, and carrying two of Hely's sandwich-signs. Of course, Joyce had for models also himself and his brother, *John* Stanislaus Joyce Jr. But as Adaline Glasheen indicates,[83] he had in mind also *Jim the Penman,* a play about a forger by Sir Charles Young, and Sean the Post, a character in Boucicault's *Arrah-na-Pogue.* From these Shem and Shaun easily are dilated into old Nick and Saint Mick (Michael), and into other forms of the miscreant and the censor, the artist and his often hypocritical critic. The accumu-lation of identities is intended. For Joyce no individual is so unusual and no situation so distinct as not to echo other individuals and situa-tions. Stephen Dedalus goes out to encounter reality for the *millionth* time. Ulysses, as Victor Bérard confirmed for Joyce, followed estab-lished trade routes in his legendary wanderings. Joyce not only binds fable to fact, but also fact to fable. He was forever trying to charm his life; his superstitions were attempts to impose sacramental impor-tance upon naturalistic details. So too, his books were not to be taken as mere books, but as acts of prophecy. Joyce was capable of mocking his own claims of prophetic power—he does so in one section of *Finnegans Wake* [84]—but he still made the claims. For Joyce life *was* charmed; nature was both stolid and magical, its ordinary details suffused with wonder, its wonderful manifestations permeated by the ordinary.

Joyce's fictional method does not presume that the artist has any supernatural power, but that he has an insight into the methods and motivations of the universe. Samuel Beckett has remarked that to Joyce reality was a paradigm, an illustration of a possibly unstatable rule.[85] Yet perhaps the rule can be surmised. It is not a perception of order or of love; more humble than either of these, it is the perception of coincidence. According to this rule, reality, no matter how much we try to manipulate it, can only assume certain forms; the roulette wheel brings up the same numbers again and again; every-one and everything shift about in continual movement, yet movement limited in its possibilities. Joyce was interested in variation and same-

ness in time: Bloom consoles himself with the thought that every
betrayal is only one of an infinite series; [86] if someone mentioned a
new atrocity to Joyce, he at once pointed out some equally horrible
old atrocity, such as an act of the Inquisition in Holland.[87] He was
interested also in variation and sameness in space, in the cubist method
of establishing differing relations among aspects of a single thing, and
he asked Beckett to do some research for him in the possible permu-
tations of an object. That the picture of Cork in his Paris flat should
have, as he emphasized to Frank O'Connor, a cork frame,[88] was a
deliberate, if half-humorous, indication of this notion of the world,
where unexpected simultaneities are the rule. The characters pass
through sequences of situations and thoughts bound by coincidence
with the situations and thoughts of other living and dead men and
of fictional, mythical men. Do Bloom and Stephen coincidentally think
the same thoughts at the same times? Do they wander and fly like
Ulysses and Daedalus? They are examples of a universal process.

In all his books up to *Finnegans Wake* Joyce sought to reveal the
coincidence of the present with the past. Only in *Finnegans Wake*
was he to carry his conviction to its furthest reaches, by implying that
there is no present and no past, that there are no dates, that time—
and language which is time's expression—is a series of coincidences
which are general all over humanity. Words move into words, people
into people, incidents into incidents like the ambiguities of a pun, or
a dream. We walk through darkness on familiar roads.

Joyce began to weave *Finnegans Wake* like a new integument.* On
March 11, 1923, he announced to Miss Weaver, 'Yesterday I wrote
two pages—the first I have written since the final *Yes* of *Ulysses*.
Having found a pen, with some difficulty I copied them out in a large
handwriting on a double sheet of foolscap so that I could read them.
Il lupo perde il pelo ma non il vizio, the Italians say. The wolf may
lose his skin but not his vice or the leopard cannot change his spots.' [89]
So he undertook the work that was to occupy the next sixteen years
of his life.

* For a table of composition of the book during the first ten years, see note 89,
pp. 801-3.

1923–1926

... look at this prepronominal *funferal,* engraved and retouched and
edgewiped and puddenpadded very like a whale's egg farced with
pemmican as were it sentenced to be nuzzled over a full trillion times
for ever and a night till his noddle sink or swim by that ideal reader
suffering from an ideal insomnia. ...

— *Finnegans Wake* (120)

THE Joyces, except for Giorgio, arrived in London in mid-June.
They had invited Nora's youngest sister Kathleen to visit them,
and the trip from Galway had been arranged by Mrs. Barnacle and
Michael Healy with great trepidation and many warnings. Kathleen
arrived at Euston Station at 5 o'clock in the morning, well frightened
by her experience, and when it seemed there was no one to greet her,
'cried like the rain.' Suddenly she caught sight of a man with bleary
glasses, and said to him, 'Are you Jim?' 'My goodness, Kathleen,' he
replied, 'what a description of you they gave me! Where did you
get your eyebrows?' 'On the vine,' she said, and evoked a slight smile,
Joyce's first of the day. Kathleen managed to get lost in the lift before
they had left the station, a mishap which made Joyce smile again.
When she had put on her best clothes and displayed unexpectedly
good manners at the table, he said to Nora approvingly, 'She'll do.' [1]
Kathleen went along with them to Bognor in Sussex, where they had
decided to spend the summer.

At Alexandra House on Clarence Road, the rococo boardinghouse
they stayed in at Bognor, Joyce was always pleased to leave his work
to walk and talk with his sister-in-law. In Galway she had not been
allowed to wear make-up, and he watched her discoveries of scented
soaps, creams, and powders with the rapt attention of an anthropologist.
He even took her to mass on Sunday, saying, 'You know what they'll
say at home if I don't.' When she went to Woolworth's to buy some

teacups as gifts for her Galway friends, and cried out in pleasure, 'Aren't they lovely, Jim?' he looked on with indulgence. Another purchase, of some suede shoes—then a rarity, proved less fortunate: one shoe split the next day, and Nora went back to the store with Kathleen to exchange them. When the manager was reluctant, Nora said, 'My husband is a writer and if you don't change them I'll have it published in the paper.' This was perhaps the only recorded occasion on which Nora spoke of her husband's occupation with approval, and the manager gave way at once. Her more habitual reaction was brought on by Joyce's purchase, at her insistence, of a pair of white trousers. They proved to be translucent and she had to tell him, 'For goodness' sake, take those off.' Later she confided to her sister, 'He's a weakling, Kathleen. I always have to be after his tail. I wish I was married to a man like my father. Being married to a writer is a very hard life.' Kathleen was astonished at the difference between them, 'Nora all go and Jim all stand-still.' ²

In Bognor Nora remarked to Kathleen, 'He's on another book again.' Joyce worked at *Finnegans Wake* with passion. The structural problems were much more perplexing than those of *Ulysses*, where, as he wrote Miss Weaver, the ports of call at least were known beforehand.³ To give form to his 'storiella as she is syung' (and not merely recorded), he restudied Giambattista Vico. He was particularly drawn to the 'roundheaded Neapolitan's' ⁴ use of etymology and mythology to uncover the significance of events, as if events were the most superficial manifestations of underlying energies. He admired also Vico's positive division of human history into recurring cycles, each set off by a thunderclap, of theocratic, aristocratic, and democratic ages, followed by a *ricorso* or return. Joyce did not share Vico's interest in these as literal chronological divisions of 'eternal ideal history,' but as psychological ones, ingredients which kept combining and recombining in ways which seemed always to be *déjà vus*. 'I use his cycles as a trellis,' ⁵ he told Padraic Colum later; he wrote Miss Weaver, 'I would not pay overmuch attention to these theories, beyond using them for all they are worth, but they have gradually forced themselves on me through circumstances of my own life. I wonder where Vico got his fear of thunderstorms. It is almost unknown to the male Italians I have met.' ⁶ To another friend he explained, 'I might easily have written this story in the traditional manner. Every novelist knows the recipe. It is not very difficult to follow a simple, chronological scheme which the critics will understand. But I, after all, am trying to tell the story of this Chapelizod family in a new way. Time and the river and the mountain are the real heroes of my book. Yet the elements are exactly what every novelist might use: man and woman, birth, childhood, night, sleep, marriage, prayer, death. There is nothing paradoxical about all this. Only I am trying to build many planes of narrative with a single esthetic purpose. Did you ever read Laurence Sterne?' [7]

In Bognor he rewrote the passage dealing with King Mark, Tristam and Iseult, a sketch of which he had read to Larbaud the previous March; this revived his favorite theme of cuckoldry, and the squawking of the sea gulls on the Bognor strand made him think of imitating their sounds to suggest the derision visited upon King Mark:

> —Three quarks for Muster Mark!
> Sure he hasn't got much of a bark
> And sure any he has it's all beside the mark. . . .
> Hohohoho, moulty Mark! [*]

Another passage he drafted dealt with St. Kevin,[†] who as founder embodied an aspect of his hero, and still another dealt with the philosopher Berkeley, whose incursions upon the phenomenal world were as violent as those of the Scandinavian invaders—Earwicker's ancestors—upon the Irish coast.

Before the end of the year most of the first part of the book—made up of eight chapters—was sketched out. It was an introduction of the *dramatis personae*: Earwicker, his wife Anna Livia Plurabelle, and their three children. Earwicker's original sin, never precisely described, occurred in the Phoenix Park and involved exhibitionism, or voyeurism, with two nursemaids as accomplices, and three soldiers (imported perhaps from the *Circe* episode of *Ulysses*) as witnesses, quite possibly themselves involved in the offense through promiscuity with the girls or homosexuality with each other. As chorus for the action Joyce evolved four old men, representing the four evangelists, whose names he coded as Mamalujo (Matthew, Mark, Luke, and John), the four masters who wrote a history of Ireland, [‡] and sometimes manifesting themselves as six rann singers or as twelve customers in Earwicker's pub. He drafted the Mamalujo episode [**] as 'a study of old age,' he told Miss Weaver, and finished its first version in October 1923. Since the earliest passages to be written were from different parts of the book,[††] it is clear that, in

---

[*] *Finnegans Wake* (383).
[†] Kevin (498?-618) founded a monastery at Glendalough. He was rescued from a temptress by falling propitiously into a bed of nettles or, according to another account, by kicking her out of his cave so that she fell in the lake and was drowned. Joyce knew both versions.
[‡] *The Annals of the Four Masters*, which they completed in 1636.
[**] *Finnegans Wake* (383-99).
[††] Ibid. (604-5, 611-12, 383-99, and then 3-218).

spite of his disclaimers, Joyce had a general notion of how to proceed in the later sections, but had not yet worked them out in detail. With mock disparagement he referred to the book as 'a mah jong puzzle.' [8]

Aside from a visit from T. S. Eliot, the sojourn at Bognor was uneventful. In August 1923, the Joyces returned to Paris, staying this time, thanks to an additional gift from Miss Weaver, at a better lodging, the Victoria Palace Hotel at 6 rue Blaise Desgoffes. On October 17, Joyce, now flat-hunting, wrote her that 'The wild hunt still continues in the Paris jungle, stampede of omnibuses and trumpets of taxi-elephants etc and in this caravanserei peopled by American loudspeakers I compose ridiculous prose writing on a green suitcase which I bought in Bognor.' [9] His children, though they rarely figure in his correspondence, were equally dislocated. Lucia was transferred from school to school, as later from career to career. Giorgio worked in the Banque Nationale du Crédit on the corner of the Rue Lafitte and the Grands Boulevards, but disliked the long tedious hours, and eventually, like his father before him, gave up banking as a career. (His father always sought Giorgio's financial advice, however, because of this brief experience.) He decided to embark seriously on a singing career instead, as friends who admired his bass voice had often suggested. He therefore entered the Schola Cantorum where he studied for several years. Joyce was pleased and suggested to Ezra Pound, whose opera *Villon* was soon to be performed, that Giorgio sing in it; but this plan fell through.

At the Schola Cantorum, Giorgio, or George (as he now preferred to be called) made friends with Arthur Laubenstein, a young American organist who at first annoyed him by not recognizing the name of Joyce. Laubenstein began to coach him and eventually was brought into the family circle. Joyce found the young man agreeable, and took to conversing with him about his favorite subjects, which at that moment were astronomy and the Jesuits, on neither of which Laubenstein had much information. Joyce would question him, too, about elements in the Episcopal liturgy, or note down some American expressions, such as 'Hell's bells,' 'Sufferin' bald-headed Moses,' or 'Adam and Eve on a raft' (for poached eggs on toast), which he declared he would make use of. They met as often as three evenings a week, and on subsequent nights Joyce would often begin a conversation at the point where it had stopped the night before, saying, 'And——.' Sometimes he was avuncular: 'If you have an ideal, young man, stick to it.' Or he might be whimsical, 'I see in the paper today that a man by the name of Icicle got married. That must make him a bicycle. It might even make him a tricycle.' Or, more pensive, he would ask, 'Which would you say was the greater power in holding people together, complete faith or doubt?' Laubenstein plumped for faith but Joyce was firm, 'No, doubt is the thing. Life is suspended in doubt like the world in the void. You might find this in some sense treated in *Exiles*.' (Stephen, in *Ulysses*, is of the same opinion.) He was bent upon Laubenstein's reading his book, and to this end presented him with a copy of *Ulysses*. 'How did you like it?' he inquired a few days later. 'I lost it,' said Laubenstein. Joyce laughed and gave him another copy, and asked him repeatedly how he was getting on with it. At last Laubenstein replied, 'Frankly, Mr. Joyce, I must tell you I don't understand it.' Joyce was not at all annoyed. He answered, 'Only a few writers and teachers understand it. The value of the book is its new style.' At other times he was less calm, and having drunk himself into abject melancholy, retailed his misfortunes at such a pace that Nora remonstrated, unheeded, 'Now Jim, now Jim, we've heard all that before,' or at an even later stage, exclaimed at his drunkenness and threatened, 'I'll be taking the children and going back to Ireland.' One such evening ended with Joyce alighting from the taxi at his door and suddenly plunging up the street shouting, 'I made them take it,' presumably an angry brag that he had foisted *Ulysses* upon the public. Nora looked at Laubenstein and said, 'Never mind, I'll handle him,' and soon deftly collected her fugitive.* [10]

Another musical friend was George Antheil, the 'bad boy of music,' who lived in a small flat directly over Sylvia Beach's bookshop, and was one of Ezra Pound's special enthusiasms.† Joyce attended a private performance of Antheil's *Ballet Méchanique*, a part of which he said was like Mozart,[11] and he was also present at the Ballets Suédois on October 4, 1923, when the composer played his *Sonata Sauvage, Airplane Sonata,* and *Mechanisms.* The music interested him somewhat, at least as a phenomenon, and he was even more interested in the emphatic responses to it of Erik Satie and Darius Milhaud, the eminent composers; the intrigue of music was almost as fascinating as that of literature,‡ and eventually he was to enter that too. Joyce discovered that on Sunday mornings a wealthy woman was holding private Henry Purcell concerts, and persuaded Antheil to enter with him uninvited. They had a carefully prepared scenario, devised by Joyce, of what each would say to the attendant at the door. But at the third concert, Antheil bragged later, the hostess noticed and encouraged

---

* Myron Nutting was with Joyce on a similar occasion when he threw up his arms suddenly and leaped into the street crying, 'No, I'm free, *free.*' [12]

† Pound wrote a small book, *George Antheil and the Treatise on Harmony,* in which, as the subject complained, he imposed his own musical theories on Antheil.

‡ When Antheil, in an equivalent burst of literary fervor, asked what French or English novelists he should read, Joyce advised him to begin with Stendhal's *Le Rouge et le Noir* and *La Chartreuse de Parme.*[13]

them to leave.

Antheil concocted a magnificent plan for an electric opera which would use the *Cyclops* episode of *Ulysses* as libretto. As Al Laney of the *New York Herald* of Paris describes it,[14] the opera was to have for orchestra twelve electric pianos hooked to a thirteenth which played the master roll; on this would be recorded also drums, steel xylophones, and various blare instruments. The score was to be run off at top speed, with crescendos and diminuendos achieved by switching pianos on and off. The singers, seated below the stage and out of sight, would sing into microphones attached to loud speakers on the stage, and a *corps de ballet* would present the action in pantomime. The idea fascinated Joyce, but Antheil disappointed him by turning to other work.

During October 1923, Joyce and John Quinn met for the first time. The encounter had been carefully arranged, with an eye to future patronage, by Ezra Pound, who had also issued an invitation to Ford Madox Ford. A few minutes before Quinn's arrival Natalie Barney dropped in for a visit, but was hastily put to flight.[15] When the four men were at last gathered, a photograph was taken which showed Quinn severe, Ford agape, Pound sinister, Joyce relaxed and opaque.* Joyce's attitude toward the New York lawyer was skeptical: he had never wholly accepted Quinn's practical methods in the *Little Review* case, feeling that a chance for a brilliant defense of his book had been muffed, and he now began to regret the price at which he had sold Quinn the *Ulysses* manuscript. These feelings were not allayed when Quinn announced he would dispose of his whole collection at auction the following winter. He offered to turn over to Joyce half the expected purchase price for his manuscript, which he estimated at $2000—a sum that seemed to the author far too low. Joyce maintained an 'unenthusiastic silence,'[16] but to indicate he had no ill will, offered to read Quinn parts of his new book. Quinn said he was pressed for time, but promised to return next summer to hear them.[17]

The Pounds had invited other guests for later in the day, Hemingway among them. While Hemingway shadowboxed in another room, Ford took Joyce aside and asked him to contribute something to the new *transatlantic review*, a monthly edited by Ford which was to appear for the first time in January 1924. Ford said that the review's backers had stipulated at first that no work by Joyce be published in it, but had given way when he refused to undertake the editorship with that condition.[18] Joyce said ironically that it was a pity Ford had not been in time to ask Proust for a contribution. 'I have been told,' he said, 'that a single sentence of Proust would fill a whole magazine. Not that I have read any of him to speak of. My eyes won't let me read any work of other

* Plate XV.

people; I can hardly see to correct my own proofs.'[19] He was reluctant at first to contribute, having tentatively decided that *Finnegans Wake* would not show to advantage if segmented like *Ulysses* in the *Little Review;* and he had just refused to give Eliot a piece of it for the *Criterion.* He agreed, however, to allow his name to be listed among the contributors, and eventually yielded to Ford's urgency and promised him the Rabelaisian chapter in which Earwicker is introduced, on condition that he be allowed two thoroughgoing revisions of the proofs.

A few days later Joyce had occasion to describe his meeting with Quinn to Wyndham Lewis, and he then read his friend a little lecture. 'If I may be allowed to make an observation,' he said, 'with a person like Quinn you should never hint at any imperfection in your work; he wouldn't understand it.'[20] Lewis had already perceived that Joyce kept a standard set of things to say to people, and had carefully arranged modes of behavior which in sum amounted to what Lewis called 'adequate duplicity.'[21] It was not adequate to dissuade Quinn from the sale of the *Ulysses* manuscript, which took place at auction at the Anderson Galleries on January 16, 1924. The purchaser, for a price of $1975, was the well-known American collector and dealer A. S. W. Rosenbach. Joyce was chagrined at the price but at first philosophical; in this mood he said to McAlmon, 'Probably they are right. Who can say what the next generation will think of me? What do we think of the great men of the past generation?'[22] But when he heard that Quinn, a few days after the sale, had bought back two Meredith poems in manuscript for $1400, he became indignant, refused to accept his share of the sale which Quinn offered to send him,[23] and instead asked Quinn to ascertain from Rosenbach at what price he would relinquish the manuscript. Rosenbach refused to sell, and countered by offering to buy the corrected page proofs of *Ulysses.* 'When he receives a reply from me,' Joyce wrote Miss Weaver on May 24, 1924, 'all the rosy brooks will have run dry,' and he composed a rhyme:

> Rosy Brook he bought a book
> Though he didn't know how to spell it.
> Such is the lure of literature
> To the lad who can buy it and sell it.* [24]

At the beginning of January, 1924, Joyce was able to help Ettore Schmitz, by rescuing him from oblivion as effectively as two years before he had rescued Édouard Dujardin. Schmitz had continued to

---

* But his irritation with Quinn left him when the lawyer died at the beginning of August 1924. Joyce cabled his 'grateful remembrance of his friendship and kindness,'[25] and spoke to Miss Weaver of his 'many good qualities.'[26]

write during and after the First World War, but in 1923 had gathered himself for his greatest effort in *La Coscienza di Zeno,* a novel about a man trying desperately to give up smoking, which he published at the beginning of 1924. He sent a copy to Joyce, who was impressed by the book's irony and languid power. When Schmitz wrote in January that he was discouraged by the book's reception and felt that he had again done a foolish thing, and at an age—sixty—when one hates to cut a foolish figure, Joyce reassured him: 'Why are you discouraged? You must know that it is by far your best work.' [27] The reading of it was affording him 'great pleasure,' he said, and went on: 'At present two things interest me. The theme: I would never have thought that smoking could dominate a person in such a way. Secondly: the treatment of time in the novel. There is no absence of wit in it and I notice that the last line of *Senilita:* "Yes, Angiolina thinks and weeps, etc." [*] has impressively developed in privacy.' [28] He made careful suggestions for bringing *Zeno* to world notice. Schmitz must send copies to Larbaud, Benjamin Crémieux, Eliot, Ford, and Gilbert Seldes (then editor of the *Dial*), mentioning Joyce's name. Joyce spoke to the first two, telling them that the only modern Italian writer who interested him was 'Italo Svevo.' By April 1, 1924, he could write Schmitz the good news that Larbaud was very pleased with the book; and Larbaud himself, after reading some of Schmitz's other books as well, sent him two effusive letters. Schmitz replied to Larbaud gratefully, 'If you only knew what an upheaval your two letters have caused in my life! I've reread *Senilità* and now see the book, which I had resigned myself to dismiss as null, in the light which your judgment throws upon it. I have also reread *Una Vita.* James Joyce always used to say that there is room in a man's heart for one novel only (He hadn't even begun *Ulysses* at the time) and that the others are always the same one artificially masked under other words. But if this is so then *Una Vita* is my only novel.' [29] Larbaud planned an article on Schmitz in the *Nouvelle Revue Française,* then in *Commerce,* but when these were not at once forthcoming Joyce wrote Larbaud on June 6, 1924, 'I had a letter from "Italo Svevo" this morning. He is in despair about his book. If you manage a short note on it somewhere or, as you suggested, give some pages of it in the second number of *Commerce* you would do much more for him than my mention of *Les Lauriers sont coupés* did for Dujardin.' [30]

The advocacy of Joyce, Larbaud, and Crémieux won for Schmitz the attention of Eugenio Montale, who wrote in 1925 the first respectful

---

[*] 'Yes, Angiolina thinks and sometimes cries, thinks as though the secret of the universe had been explained to her or the secret of her own existence, and is sad as though in all the whole wide world she could not find one solitary *deo gratias.*'

study of him outside of Trieste, where Silvio Benco had always been an admirer. Then in February 1926, Adrienne Monnier dedicated an issue of *Le Navire d'Argent* to him, and Larbaud published an article, with extended quotations from Svevo's works, in *Commerce*. When Schmitz published a second edition of *Senilità*, he thanked Joyce, as Dujardin had done, for resuscitating him like Lazarus. During these four years, 1924-1928, which were the last in Schmitz's life, the two men met frequently in Paris. The relationship was friendly but always had an element of formality; sometimes Nora Joyce broke into it by saying of her husband, to the astonishment of Schmitz, 'I've always told him he should give up writing and take up singing. To think he was once on the same platform with John McCormack!' [31] Schmitz amused them all by finding in his warm reception by Paris writers * a new reason for smoking, like his hero Zeno, *'la sua ultima sigaretta.'* †

Joyce and Schmitz were drawn together again when Joyce wrote on February 20, 1924, that he was making use of Signora Livia Schmitz's name and hair for the heroine (Anna Livia Plurabelle) of his new book. 'Ask her, however, not to take up arms, either of steel or fire, since the person involved is the Pyrrha of Ireland (or rather of Dublin) whose hair is the river beside which (her name is Anna Liffey) the seventh city of Christianity springs up, the other six being Basovizza, Clapham Junction, Rena Vecia, Limehouse, S. Odorico in the Vale of Tears and San Giacomo in Monte di Pietà.' ‡ [32] Signora Schmitz was a little disturbed, notwithstanding; she had to be assured again that he was not denigrating her. Later Schmitz sent her portrait (with her hair let down) by Veruda to Joyce as ceremonious thanks for 'the golden sunset' [33] Joyce had given him. As Joyce remarked to an Italian journalist, 'They say I have immortalized Svevo, but I've also immortalized the tresses of Signora Svevo. These were long and reddish-blond. My sister who used to see them let down told me about them. The river at Dublin passes dye-houses and so has reddish water. So I have playfully compared these two things in the book I'm writing. A lady in it will have the tresses which are really Signora Svevo's.' [34]

---

* In 1927 there was a dinner for Schmitz which was attended by Isaak Babel, Jules Romains, Ivan Goll, Jean Paulhan, and Benjamin Crémieux, as well as Joyce.
† When in 1928 Schmitz was fatally injured in an automobile accident, his distressed Christian wife asked him if he would not like to see a priest. Schmitz, Jewish by birth and infidel by temperament, smiled gently and replied, 'It's too late,' and asked for a cigarette instead. 'There's no doubt that this one will be the last,' he said. [35]
‡ Harry Levin points out that Basovizza and S. Odorico are two villages near Trieste; S. Giacomo and Rena Vecia are two ancient quarters of that city; Clapham Junction and Limehouse are a suburb and a district in London; 'in the Vale of Tears' and 'in Monte di Pietà' (pawnshop) are Joyce's additions.

In March 1924, Ludmila Savitsky's translation of *A Portrait of the Artist as a Young Man (Dedalus)* was published. The book was received with respect if not with enthusiasm by French reviewers. Joyce was now more concerned with the translation of *Ulysses* into French. At first he had thought, as he told Daniel Hummel, that the book could not be translated into another language, but might be translated into another medium, that of the film.[36] But the success of the translations read at Larbaud's séance persuaded him that the book should be put into French, and he was eager to have Larbaud undertake the task. Larbaud, having just finished *The Way of All Flesh,* thought it would be too much labor, but at the beginning of 1923 consented to translate sections of it. Joyce protested this would make Ulysses a *mutilé de guerre.*[37] Larbaud then agreed to fill in the interstices with summaries, 'to produce a skeleton of the whole book,' Joyce wrote Miss Weaver, or rather, 'a mariner's chart where some regions are fully done, others sketched, others indicated, and the whole representative.'[38] Larbaud did not make much headway, however, and Adrienne Monnier, who had contracted for the book, called in a young Breton, Auguste Morel, who had translated with great dexterity Thompson's 'The Hound of Heaven' and other English poems. Morel retreated to Belle-Isle-sur-Mer near Quiberon on the Breton coast to begin the work, making sporadic dashes to Paris for consultation with Adrienne Monnier, Larbaud, or Joyce. He was imaginative and gifted, but did not know English as well as Larbaud, not that even Larbaud's competence was equal to Joyce's local allusions. The first translated fragments were at last got ready with the help of Larbaud, Fargue,* and Sylvia Beach, for publication in the review *Commerce* prior to the appearance of the whole book; Joyce insisted they were insufficient, and a few more were added. At this point the Princess Caetani, who was backing *Commerce,* objected to some of the passages, but allowed Joyce to overrule her. Then the French printer replaced the accents on the words in Molly Bloom's monologue.[39] Joyce insisted they be removed, writing Adrienne Monnier in a pneumatique of July 5, 1924, '*Selon mon plus secret conseil je lui ai enlevé toutes les épines—les graves et les aiguës. Je ne lui ai laissé que la dernière—son accent irlandais. Il ne cédait pas.*' †
Mlle Monnier did not agree, so that finally Larbaud received in Italy a telegram asking him to resolve the controversy. He at once replied from Pisa on July 6, '*Joyce a raison Joyce ha ragione.*' ‡ [40] Joyce thanked

---

* Larbaud thought Fargue had made Molly too plebeian.[41]

† 'Following my most secret conception, I've taken all the thorns (the grave and acute) off her. I've only let her keep the last—her Irish accent. It wouldn't give way.'

‡ 'Joyce is right' (in French and Italian).

him for this decision about Molly's hairpins, 'I mean her accents,'[42] which he considered the last formality to be removed by a woman going to bed.

The first fragments comprised the *Telemachus* episode and parts of *Ithaca* and *Penelope,* and were published in *Commerce* for Summer, 1924, under the names of Larbaud and Morel. But difficulties developed later in the year when Larbaud's stock, usually high at the Maison des Amis des Livres, dropped sharply as the result of a quarrel between him and Princess Caetani, in which Adrienne Monnier and Sylvia Beach took the part of the princess. Joyce was much entertained and informed Miss Weaver, 'Larbaud has been warned not to walk, run or creep through the rue de l'Odéon.'[43] Then there was a quarrel between Larbaud and Léon-Paul Fargue, who was also to continue to have a hand in the translation. Joyce duly reported on December 30, 1924, 'There was a meeting of editors. V. L. offered his hand to L. P. F. In presence of all John Henry Fargue turned his back and walked away over the asphodel fields. The princess wept on L. P. F.'s new overcoat who then wrote to V. L. three times, *comme ça:* Odysseus, you have treated me badly. V. L. replied: My dear Achilles etc etc. So now they meet.'[44] There was also, perhaps, as Adrienne Monnier remembered, tension between Larbaud and Joyce: Larbaud was irritated because Joyce treated him too much as a literary agent, and scarcely acknowledged his coexistence as novelist and poet. Most of Joyce's literary friends had this feeling at one time or another, and Larbaud was too sensitive and high-strung not to have had it too. But his correspondence with Joyce indicates that the serious rifts, though always mended eventually, were with Adrienne Monnier and her friends, not with Joyce. At all events, the translation proceeded slowly.

Joyce did not allow his friends' tiffs over *Ulysses* to distract him from *Finnegans Wake.* In February 1924, the *transatlantic review* sent him proofs, but these were so botched,[45] no doubt because of Joyce's interlineations in the manuscript, that the fragment was not ready until the April number. Ford Madox Ford was suddenly squeamish over the possibility that some passages would cause the review to be suppressed; he called in Sisley Huddleston for an expert opinion. Huddleston could not find the obscenity, and assured Ford no British or American policeman would either.[46] In April, then, the fragment was included in a Literary Supplement of 'Work in Progress' which also contained some writing by Tristan Tzara, the surrealist, and Hemingway. Joyce liked Ford's term, and 'Work in Progress' remained the title until the book was published in 1939. He said playfully that Ford was its godfather by virtue of this suggestion,[47] and that he had reciprocated by acting as godfather * (though he did not like to stand at the font) to one of Ford's daughters.

The first faint signs of disaffection with his new work had begun to reach Joyce, and in February he wrote McAlmon of his concern over Miss Weaver's reaction: 'I don't think she likes the tone of my last effusion though Larbaud to whom I read it thinks they are the strongest pages I have written. The task I have set myself is dreadfully difficult but I believe it can be done. O dear me. What sins did I commit in my last incarnation to be in this hole?' [48] By March 7 he had sent her a draft of *Anna Livia Plurabelle,*† which he described to her as 'a chattering dialogue across the river by two washerwomen who as night falls become a tree and a stone. The river is named Anna Liffey. Some of the words at the beginning are hybrid Danish-English. Dublin is a city founded by Vikings. The Irish name is Baile atha Cliath. Ballyclee = Town of Ford of Hurdles. Her Pandora's box contains the ills flesh is heir to. The stream is quite brown, rich in salmon, very devious, shallow. The splitting up towards the end (seven dams) is the city abuilding. Izzy will be later Isolde (cf. Chapelizod).' [49] He hoped the piece would please her and noted, invitingly, that Larbaud was 'in a trance about it.' [50] His next obstacle would be Shaun the Post (Chapter VI, 126-68), which, when done, would mean that almost all of Chapters V-VIII were completed, at least for the moment. 'You did not say if you liked the piece,' he reminded her shortly in another letter,[51] and was relieved when she said she did. As for Shaun the Post, that would be a 'description of a postman travelling backwards in the night through the events already narrated. It is written in the form of a *via crucis* of 14 stations but in reality it is only a barrel rolling down the river Liffey.' [52] He urged her now to read Vico's *Scienza Nuova,* as with *Ulysses* he had urged her to read the Odyssey.

His rapid progress was slowed by Dr. Borsch, who in April observed that a secretion was forming in the conjunctiva of Joyce's left eye, and ordered him to curtail his work severely. An operation would be necessary later, he warned. In May, Joyce succeeded nonetheless in finishing Shaun the Post; then, aware that the only way to rest his eye was to pack up his manuscripts, he did so and stored them with Sylvia Beach. It was just at this time, about May 20, that he wrote his first poem in six years, and sent it to Larbaud on May 22:

* On April 18, 1928.
† The idea for the episode, he said once, came to him on a trip to Chartres,[53] where he saw women washing clothes on both banks of the Eure.

A Prayer

Again!
Come, give, yield all your strength to me!
From far a low word breathes on the breaking brain
Its cruel calm, submission's misery,
Gentling her awe as to a soul predestined.
Cease, silent love! My doom!

Blind me with your dark nearness, O have mercy, beloved enemy
           of my will!
I dare not withstand the cold touch that I dread.
Draw from me still
My slow life! Bend deeper on me, threatening head,
Proud by my downfall, remembering, pitying
Him who is, him who was!

Again!
Together, folded by the night, they lay on earth. I hear
From far her low word breathe on my breaking brain.
Come! I yield. Bend deeper upon me! I am here.
Subduer, do not leave me! Only joy, only anguish,
Take me, save me, soothe me, O spare me!

The poem, like his letters to his wife in 1909 and 1912, combines the
votary's prayer for mercy with the ecstatic self-surrender of the lover.
The speaker's attitude confuses desire and pain, the latter because his
mind associates his subjection to his beloved with other subjections—
to eye trouble and to death. For a moment he withholds complete submission and sees himself and her as 'they,' but then he yields utterly.*
As he exerted total control over his books, Joyce dreamed of agonizing
self-abandonment to female power.

In May, about the time he wrote his poem, Joyce was approached by
the Irish painter Patrick Tuohy, then a young man of twenty-eight, with
a request that he sit for a portrait.† 54 He was not pleased, and showed
some irritation too with the young woman, Phyllis Moss, who accom-

---

* The emotions aroused here are reminiscent of those Joyce attached, as a boy,
to sin, even though he had long since discarded the concept. The reality of the
emotions had stayed with him; in January 1924, when he was drinking with
McAlmon, Dr. William Carlos Williams, and Mrs. Williams, he ironically described
Nora and himself, as they went from bar to bar, as '*beati innocenti.*' 55 And when
McAlmon proposed a toast, 'Here's to sin,' Joyce looked up suddenly and declared,
'I won't drink to that.' 56

† He had not met Tuohy when he commissioned him to paint John Stanislaus Joyce
a year before. Arthur Power had suggested the painter Paul Henry, but when
Tuohy's name came up Joyce said, 'I'll have him do it. I knew his father.' (Tuohy's
father was a well-known Dublin doctor.) The portrait of John Stanislaus Joyce
(Plate XVI) admirably presented that witty, dapper old reprobate. Joyce wished
to hang it in his flat, for which it was too big, but eventually he found a flat large
enough for it.

panied Tuohy and discoursed at large upon various subjects. Joyce kept interrupting her to say 'For example?' or 'I hate generalities.'[57] He argued with Tuohy for a long time, 'having,' as he said, 'a very profound objection to my own image, needlessly repeated in a picture or bust.' He asked him, 'Do you wish to paint me or my name?'[58] Tuohy gave the right answer, and with an irresistible Dublin accent, so Joyce reluctantly consented. But when, at the innumerable sittings that proved necessary, Tuohy began to philosophize about the importance to an artist of capturing his subject's soul, Joyce replied, 'Never mind my soul. Just be sure you have my tie right.'[59] Eventually * he was pleased best by the tie and the folds of the jacket.[60] Tuohy, a small moustached man whose life was to end in suicide, amused Joyce at first and later bored him by urging him to write a best-seller.

Having rested his eyes during the sittings, Joyce submitted on June 10 to a fifth operation. This one, more unpleasant than the last, was his second iridectomy on his left eye.† Borsch intended it as a precaution against another attack of glaucoma, which seemed imminent. The most unpleasant part of the operation for Joyce was the aftermath, when, lying with face bandaged in a darkened room, he saw before his mind's eye a cinema of disagreeable events of the past.[61] This was varied by thoughts of *Finnegans Wake.* Myron Nutting went to the clinic, 'Madame de la Vallière's château, rue Cherche-Midi' (as Joyce derisively called it),[62] to visit his friend, and found him lying on his back in the dark, his eyes under dressings as big as small pillows. 'Hello, Joyce,' he said cheerily. Joyce remained silent and motionless for a few seconds, then reached under his pillow and drew out a composition book and a pencil. Slowly and carefully, by touch, he made an entry, put his book and pencil back under the pillow, then held out his hand to say, 'Hello, Nutting.' Aware of his friend's bafflement, he took up the notebook again and showed him the words, 'Carriage sponge,' which left Nutting no wiser.[63] On June 16 the gloom of the clinic was alleviated by the arrival of a bouquet of hydrangeas, white and dyed blue, which some friends sent him in honor of 'Bloomsday,' as the day of *Ulysses* was already called. In his notebook Joyce scrawled, 'Today 16 of June 1924 twenty years after. Will anybody remember this date.'[64]

Although he doubted the power of the iris to absorb the deposits in the eye, he found, when his bandages were removed, he had enough sight to go about with, so he determined to leave Paris for Brittany. Having concluded that the Paris climate, which he described to McAlmon as 'a Methodist minister's dream of purgatory,' was too harsh

---

* The portrait was not finished until January 1927.
† The first was in Zurich in 1917.

for him, he also took a flat at Nice for the following October, though
he was not destined to occupy it. Joyce arrived at Saint-Malo about
July 7, and stayed there at the Hôtel de France et Chateaubriand into
August. The weather was poor, and his spirits flagged in spite of a
cordial letter from Yeats which he had copied * and sent to Miss
Weaver and Stanislaus, and in spite of the colorful bustle of a Breton
fair that he attended.[65] But by late July he wrote Larbaud with some
animation about the differences between Breton and Irish, finding that
Breton had more Latin words while Irish was purer: 'And though
Breton (when costumed and visited by tourists and Blessed by Rome
and caliné [fawned upon] by S. Prendonymous & Co) is probably more
picturesque of course Irish as a language is FAR SUPERIOR.' [66] The
Breton language left its mark too upon his book.

During his holiday at Saint-Malo Joyce labored to bring together the
different parts of *Work in Progress.* With a patch on one eye, he wrote
Miss Weaver, 'my one bedazzled eye searched the sea like Cain—Shem
—Tristan—Patrick from his lighthouse in Boulogne. I hope the solution
will presently appear. At least I have never found anything in any other
way than sitting with my mouth open picturesquely.' [67] But he was a
good enough tourist to visit at Tréguier the birthplace of Renan, another
disbeliever fascinated by belief. He and Nora also made an excursion
with the American writer Lloyd Morris and Morris's mother, to see
the huge stones at Carnac. Before they reached them, Joyce drew
Morris aside for an embarrassed admonition. 'If the ladies of the party
were to remark the shape of the stones, nothing was to be said about
their significance; in Joyce's view,' as Morris wrote later, 'any discussion of a phallic symbol was taboo in the presence of ladies.' [68]

The Joyces went on to Quimpaire late in August, and returned to the
Victoria Palace Hotel early in September. Joyce found a flat at 8 avenue
Charles Floquet a few days afterwards. Then late in the month he
crossed to London for about three weeks, staying again at the Euston
Hotel. While he was there Miss Weaver was persuaded by Bryher
(Winifred Ellerman McAlmon), Robert McAlmon, and H. D., to go
over to Paris, and she left after arranging to meet the Joyces in Paris
on their return. She was greatly upset when in October, for the first
time, she saw Joyce drunk, but, difficult as it was to reconcile herself

---

* In August 1924, Yeats, in awarding Tailteann prizes in Dublin, said: 'We need
not consider Mr. Padraic Colum's *Castle Conquer,* nor Mr. James Joyce's *Ulysses,*
nor Mr. George Moore's *Conversations in Ebury Street,* as, like Mr. Bernard Shaw,
they have not been resident in Ireland. We feel, however, that it is our duty to say
that Mr. James Joyce's book, though as obscene as Rabelais, and therefore forbidden by law in England and the United States, is more indubitably a work of genius
than any prose written by an Irishman since the death of Synge.' [69]

to this aspect of his life, she did not alter in her attitude towards him.

In November Joyce heard from his brother Charles, who had visited him in Paris in early September, that his Aunt Josephine Murray was dying. Joyce regretted the severity of his recent letters to her; he cabled her [70] and then wrote her a message which was unusual for him, during this reticent period of his life, in its emotional intensity:

> 8 avenue Charles Floquet
> Paris VII

Dear Aunt Josephine: On receipt of a letter from Charlie last night I wired to you to tell you how shocked we all were to hear such sudden bad news of your health. I hope he has misled himself about you. I had even hoped to meet you in London a couple of weeks [ago]. I wrote to Alice and rang her up several times before we left but she was still in Dublin. They did not tell me at the hospital (S. George's) that your grave illness was the cause of her absence. I thought she was simply on holidays. I do not remember your ever having been ill and I sincerely hope your strength will carry you through this severe strain— whatever your illness is Charlie did not say. I go to England more frequently now and I was looking forward so much to meeting you either there or in Dublin in the near future. Only yesterday morning I was going to write to you—as usual about some point in my childhood as you are one of the two persons in Ireland who could give me information about it. Charlie sent me an extremely kind message from you. I am very deeply touched that you should have considered me worthy of remembrance at such a grave hour. You attached me to you in youth by so many acts of kindness, by so much help and advice and sympathy, especially after my mother's death, that it seems to me as if your thought of me now is one of reproach. Nothing would give me greater pleasure than to talk with you over many things. I cannot employ the usual language or invoke assistance but if I am estranged in that I am still attached to you by many bonds of gratitude and affection and of respect as well. I hope these hurried words may be acceptable to you. I shall feel glad and honoured always if they are.

Nora, Giorgio and Lucia send their best wishes for your recovery. I hope you will see them as I know you would like to.

I am going to wire to Charlie to let me know how you are.

Charlie's letter is so grave that he suggests that I should write to you a word * which I cannot bring myself to write. Forgive me if my reluctance to do so is wrong. But I send you this poor word of thanks and I will still hope in spite of the bad news.

> Very gratefully and affectionately
> Your nephew
> Jim [71]

2 November 1924

* Goodbye.

Mrs. Murray died, leaving from the old Dublin only John Joyce. The previous year Richard Sheehy, Joyce's schoolmate, had died, and in August 1924, Quinn's death took place. In December William Archer was to die, and Joyce noted to Miss Weaver, 'He was very kind to me at one time. I am afraid he forgot it and me.'[72] Archer had willingly accepted Ibsen, but had boggled at Joyce as Ibsen's successor.

As a result, perhaps, of Joyce's grief over his aunt's death, his eyesight began to dim once more. Borsch made good his warning that there would have to be additional operations. He performed his sixth operation on Joyce's left eye on November 29 to remove a secondary cataract which had formed. 'I saw splendid sights for a minute or so,' Joyce wrote Miss Weaver on December 23. 'Dr. Borsch says the sight cannot come back quickly but it will come. "The readiness is all." There is to be an electric cure when the broken window of my soul can stand more shocks. He is positive as to the result.' In January 1925, the sight had not much improved; and Joyce reported the conversation that took place with his doctor, ironically exaggerating his respect for Borsch's diplomacy:

Dr. Borsch.	How are you?
J.J.	Slightly inclined to pessimism.
Dr. Borsch.	You don't think etc.
J.J.	Well . . .
Dr. B.	What will you bet?
J.J.	Fixing a date.
Dr. B.	A month. How much will you bet?
J.J.	O well. . . .
	(later) *
J.J.	You removed the front wall of the capsule and the lens?
Dr. B.	Yes
J.J.	Can a cataract form on the back wall?
Dr. B.	Sure
J.J.	Is it likely in my case?
Dr. B.	No. If it did I'd win my bet quicker.
J.J.	(prolonged smile)

He beats me every time. He ought to have written *Ulysses*.[73]

Dr. Borsch greeted Joyce's forty-third birthday on Friday, February 2, with the unceremonious tidings that a slight subsidiary operation on the left eye was the next in order. He offered to perform it at once, but on Joyce's insistence that the day was inappropriate, postponed it. The operation was postponed further when conjunctivitis developed in

* The sixth operation was a capsulotomy to remove the front wall of the left eye's capsule and lens. The capsule is the posterior part of the sheath of the eyeball.

Joyce's right eye: it was severe enough to send him back to the eye clinic at 39 rue du Cherche-Midi from about February 15 to February 25. The conjunctivitis turned to episcleritis, a malady more painful than dangerous. Six leeches were applied to the eye, but at night the pain was especially bad. 'On Friday night I really thought I was as near unreason as my worst critics think me but they gave me some morphine which gave me relief.' [74] One small consoling glimmer was the production of *Exiles* at the Neighborhood Playhouse in New York on February 19; * Joyce noted the coincidence that the leading actress's first name was Joyce, [75] and was pleased that the play continued for forty-one performances, though it did not create the sensation for which he hoped.

After his release from the eye clinic, Joyce went home to 8 avenue Charles Floquet to rest for the next operation. He had to prolong his lease from March 15 to May 15, and reconcile himself to remaining in Paris for the spring. Borsch cautiously decided to have Joyce's mouth checked for possible new abscesses, and an X-ray revealed an imbedded fragment of tooth. This would have been removed by a dentist on March 24 had not fresh trouble broken out in the right eye. Borsch put his patient on a strict diet and advised him to walk eight or ten kilometers a day. 'If I can do this with one eye sightless and the other inflamed in today's thick damp fog through the traffic of Paris on an unfed stomach I shall apply for the legion of honor.' [76]

Early in April the fragment of tooth was removed, and in the interval between dentist and ophthalmologist Joyce had just enough sight to be able, with the aid of three magnifying glasses and his son, to revise Chapter V (104-25) for the *Criterion,* where it was published in July. He submitted to the seventh operation on his left eye in the middle of April and remained in the clinic for ten days. There were not many visitors. When Wyndham Lewis came one day, Nora complained that though Joyce was supposed to be surrounded by admirers, she and he had sat there together, the two of them like a couple of old hens, for hours on end without a visitor. Another day Mrs. Nutting came, and he asked her to read the footnotes and appendix of a book he had on the city of Dublin, while he listened attentively and seized quickly and eagerly on the points he wanted. He was much preoccupied with all aspects of the Danish invasions, such as the record that they had gone into the land 'as far as the salmon goes.' He and Mrs. Nutting talked then about the earwig, which he associated with his hero Earwicker; she recalled that a Yorkshire name for earwig is 'twitchbell.' 'Will you give me that?' said Joyce, much pleased. He remarked that

* This had been arranged by the sculptor Jo Davidson.

an old legend recounted that Cain got the idea of burial from watching an earwig beside his dead brother Abel.° They discussed also the white ant, which Joyce had read about for his fable of 'The Ondt and the Gracehoper'; it was wonderful, he said, that this ant could tell before the egg hatched what it would develop into, while the slow human brain had to wait for perhaps twenty years before knowing.[77]

Another visitor was Helen Kastor Fleischman, in whom George Joyce was now taking an interest. A wealthy, handsome, restless woman, she was soon to separate from her husband, Leon Fleischman, Paris agent for Boni and Liveright, whom she had married in 1916 at the age of twenty-one. She came bearing a gift of blackberry jam, Joyce's favorite, and in thanking her he said learnedly, 'They never eat them in France. Do you know why? Because Christ's crown was made of blackberry thorns.'[78] He also received a visit from Simone Téry, the French journalist who admired equally Russian communism and Irish mysticism. 'Do you think Irish self-government a good thing?' she asked him. 'I don't think anything about it,' Joyce replied unhelpfully. 'What is your attitude towards the national movement in Ireland?' she pressed him. 'To use an expression of your country, *j'en ai marre* [I'm fed up with it].' 'I think you were already fed up with it twenty years ago.' Joyce nodded, 'You could say forty.'[79] Most reporters failed to gain admission to Joyce at all during the 1920's and 1930's, but one broke through with the proposal that he write a magazine article on the subject, 'What do you feel and do when you are going blind?' Joyce used the episode afterwards to justify his cold-blooded rejection of all requests for interviews from this cold-blooded profession.

Whether or not the seventh operation had been successful was uncertain. Joyce noticed at least 'a very slight return of vision' in the left eye, but the right eye, still suffering from conjunctivitis, could read print only with the aid of a magnifying glass. As he wrote Miss Weaver on April 25, 1925:

> I am heartily tired of iodine, aspirin, and scopolamine.† In your letter you mentioned something called warm sunlight. What is it like? There are allusions to it in the works of the great writers. . . . I go to the clinic every morning and rue de la Paix [Borsch's office] every evening. You know the poem Little Jim 'The cottage was a thatched one.' I rhyme it,

---

° Joyce investigated the earwig carefully, even to the point of writing the entomological laboratory of the Museum National d'Histoire Naturelle for papers on *forficula*. He liked the French word for earwig, *perce-oreille*, and quickly associated it with Pierce O'Reilly, a famous player from West Meath in the All Ireland Polo Club in 1905. Then he wrote 'The Ballad of Persse O'Reilly' (*Finnegans Wake*, 44-6).

† Scopolamine is a drug taken orally to dilate the pupil and so prevent its adhesion.

The clinic was a patched one,
Its outside old as rust,
And every stick beneath that roof
Lay four feet thick in dust.[80]

He felt a little better on May 1, though to his dim sight the day seemed as dark as December 1. In early June 1925, he at last found a flat at 2 Square Robiac, a cul-de-sac running off 192 rue de Grenelle, where he remained longer than at any other of his Paris addresses, until April 30, 1931. As usual, the difficulties of moving threw him off:

There has been so much hammering and moving going on here that I could scarcely hear my thoughts and then I have just dodged an eye attack. In fact when I was last writing to you I felt pain and rushed off to the clinic where the nurse sent me on to Dr Borsch. He said I had incipient conjunctivitis from fatigue probably. Next day it was worse nevertheless he insisted I was not to put off a theatre engagement I had accepted (Chaliapine). I went but had to leave in mid-opera. He then told me it would be better if I went about and amused myself. It got better, but I had three or four very unpleasant days. We are settling down here slowly, but there is a dreadful lot to do.[81]

He and Nora bought some furniture, undistinguished but comfortable. On the walls he ranged as usual his family portraits, including the new one of his father by Tuohy, and also a photograph of the Dublin Custom House with the Liffey flowing past it, and, incongruous touch, a reproduction of Vermeer's *Head of a Girl.*

On July 8 his left eye was still not much better, and on July 21 Dr. Borsch, always eager to commit surgery, informed him the next operation would be necessary in September, but that he might holiday where he liked in the meantime. Accordingly the Joyces departed for Fécamp in Normandy, remaining there at the Grand Hôtel des Bains et de Londres, while Joyce worked out the form of the last watch of Shaun (555-90). Bad weather drove them on July 28 to the Hôtel de la Poste at Rouen.[82] When the weather there proved to be worse, they hurried down to the Regina Palace Hôtel at Arcachon, staying a night at Niort and another at Bordeaux *en route.* The imagery of *The Waste Land* (dampened by that of Blake's *The French Revolution*) suited Joyce's mood, and he sent Miss Weaver a parody:

Rouen is the rainiest place getting
Inside all impermeables, wetting
Damp marrow in drenched bones.
Midwinter soused us coming over Le Mans
Our inn at Niort was the Grape of Burgundy

> But the winepress of the Lord thundered over that
>   grape of Burgundy
> And we left it in a hurgundy.
>   (Hurry up, Joyce, it's time!)
>
> I heard mosquitoes swarm in old Bordeaux
> So many!
> I had not thought the earth contained so many
>   (Hurry up, Joyce, it's time)
>
> Mr Anthologos, the local gardener,
> Greycapped, with politeness full of cunning
> Has made wine these fifty years
> And told me in his southern French
> *Le petit vin* is the surest drink to buy
> For if 'tis bad
> *Vous ne l'avez pas payé*
>   (Hurry up, hurry up, now, now, now!)
>
> But we shall have great times,
> When we return to Clinic, that waste land
> O Esculapios!
>   (Shan't we? Shan't we? Shan't we?)[83]

At Arcachon Joyce tried to walk down the beach only to realize that his sight was too poor. He attended a play and found that even from the ninth row he could not see the actors' faces. A new eye attack seemed imminent, but he managed to stay out his term in Arcachon, returning to Paris on September 5. Borsch dosed him further with scopolamine. It became a symbol of all his medications, and Joyce wrote a limerick about it:

> There's a coughmixture scopolamine
> And its equal has never been seen
>   'Twould make staid Tutankamen
>   Laugh and leap like a salmon
> And his mummy hop Skotch on the green.[84]

By September 27 his eyes were better, and he put off his seventh operation so that he could finish the last watch of Shaun. This chapter was organized about roads as the *Anna Livia Plurabelle* chapter was organized about rivers. On October 10 he wrote Miss Weaver that he had 'produced about three foolscapes of hammer and tongs stratification lit up by a fervent prayer to the divinity which shapes our roads in favour of my ponderous protagonist and his minuscule escort.'[85] He also sent a cordial invitation to his brother Stanislaus, who had just become engaged to a former student, Nelly Lichtensteiger, to visit him 'before the Berlitz-Biarritz season begins. Surely to God it is not necessary for you to give barking lessons to fili-de-cani from dawn till gutter-dammerung!' [86] Stanislaus could not come at once, but promised to come later.

Borsch now set the date of the operation on the left eye for November 23, 1925, but the right eye had a 'suffusion' and the surgery did not take place until December 8 and the following Tuesday, being divided into two parts,[87] Joyce's eighth and ninth operations. When he returned home from the clinic about the middle of December, he was dizzy and in pain, the left eye quite blind. The Nuttings came to see him on Christmas night, and found him feeling almost hopeless. 'Twice a day they flash a light before my eyes and say, "You see nothing? Not anything?" I am tired of it all. This has gone on so long.' [88]

At the beginning of 1926 Joyce could write only in exaggeratedly large letters. He borrowed Myron Nutting's black pencil to see if that would work, and made a rude sketch of Bloom with the first line of Homer's Odyssey to accompany it.* There was no possibility of dictating; he must write and see what he was writing, he said. William Bird suggested a typewriter might be used, but Joyce, after a long silence at this impertinence, said he had no interest in such a device. (He later learned to type a little.) His pain persisted, and the eye was at first unable to absorb the exudations that followed the operation. He lay on the couch 'waiting,' as he said, 'for Ireland's eye † this day to do his duty.' [89] But by spring he felt a little better, and for a space of a few months he had no major difficulties with his eyes.

The whole of 1925 was taken up with the writing of the Shaun section (Part III, 403-590) in four chapters or watches and with the revision of Part I. The first two chapters of Shaun and some of the third were finished by January 27, and he sent copies to Miss Weaver and Larbaud. In February he reverted to the fifth chapter of Part I, to revise it for the *Criterion.* McAlmon published a few pages (30-34) in the *Contact Collection of Contemporary Writers,* and again there were printing difficulties. In June Joyce announced happily to Miss Weaver that he was putting a few more puzzles in this piece, and was working hard at two other chapters of Part I, the Shem chapter, which Ernest Walsh was to publish in *This Quarter* (Autumn-Winter, 1925-26) and the *Anna Livia Plurabelle* chapter, to be published in an English review called *The Calendar.* The English printers timidly refused to set *Anna Livia,*

* Plate X.
† The name of a small island off Howth.

however, and Joyce withdrew it, arranging to publish it in the *Navire d'Argent* (October 1, 1925) instead.

So, in spite of pain and sporadic blindness, Joyce moved irresistibly ahead with the grandest of all his conceptions. No ophthalmologists could seriously impede him. Through blear eyes he guessed at what he had written on paper, and with obstinate passion filled the margins and the space between lines with fresh thoughts. His genius was a trap from which he did not desire to extricate himself, and his life seemed to withdraw inside him so that Henri Michaux and others who met him then thought him the most *renfermé*, disconnected from humanity,[90] of men. Joyce, who knew he was writing about nothing but man, was in too great discomfort to attempt the correction of this impression.

◇◇

1926–1929

Hirp! Hirp! for their Missed Understandings! chirps
the Ballat of Perce-Oreille.

　　　　　　　　　　　—*Finnegans Wake* (175)

THE next three years were to provide another major trial of Joyce's
tenacity, but they began auspiciously enough with the production
of *Exiles* at the Regent Theatre in London. The Stage Society, which
had hesitated so infuriatingly over the play in 1917 and 1918, presented
it on February 14 and 15, with W. G. Fay directing. Joyce sent bouquets
to the principal actresses [1] and instructed his friends in London to
attend the performances. In Paris he urged Benoît-Méchin to read the
play and then asked him eagerly, 'Is it as good as Hauptmann?' to which
the unaccommodating young man retorted, 'I find some scenes even
worse.' [2] Joyce, still suffering from the effects of his most recent operation, could not go to London himself, but he received full reports from
Miss Weaver, Claud Sykes, and Ettore Schmitz. The house was nearly
full, and the audience was laudatory, especially for the first two acts,
the third puzzling them perhaps by its ambiguous ending. One woman,
sitting beside Miss Weaver, walked out during the conversation of
Richard and Bertha at the end of Act I, muttering, 'I call this collusion.' [3]
The leading actor, Rupert Harvey, and the leading lady, Gwaldys
Black-Roberts, were generally approved, though Wyndham Lewis, who
accompanied Miss Weaver, thought Miss Roberts too emotional in the
part. [4] Schmitz reported that after the play someone near him said,
'They want to force on us Italian ways,' a remark which he glossed by
saying, 'Italians, of course, are known for being jealous even when they
are not in love.' [5] Bernard Shaw attended the performance on the afternoon of February 15, and at the public debate held by the Stage Society
two days later spoke favorably of Joyce's play, which reviewers had

disparaged. His attitude toward Joyce had mellowed; he recognized his talent but distrusted his subjects and his language.*

At Easter time another exile, Joyce's brother Stanislaus, at last made his long expected visit. The relations of the brothers had been strained

---

* Shaw said to Archibald Henderson later, 'When they asked me to pay three guineas for *Ulysses* I said I would not go a penny beyond seven and sixpence. I read scraps of it in *The Little Review*, not knowing that they all belonged to the history of a single day in Dublin. I was attracted to it by the fact that I was once a young man in Dublin, and also by Joyce's literary power, which is of classic quality. I do not see why there should be any limit to frankness in sex revelation; but Joyce does not raise that question. The question he does raise is whether there should be any limit to the use in literature of blackguardly language. It depends on what people will stand. If Dickens or Thackeray had been told that a respectable author like myself would use the expletive "bloody" in a play, and that an unexceptionally fastidious actress of the first rank, associated exclusively with fine parts, would utter it on the stage without turning a hair, he could not have believed it. Yet I am so old-fashioned and squeamish that I was horrified when I first heard a lady describe a man as a rotter.

'I could not write the words Mr. Joyce uses: my prudish hand would refuse to form the letters; and I can find no interest in his infantile clinical incontinences, or in the flatulations which he thinks worth mentioning. But if they were worth mentioning I should not object to mentioning them, though, as you see, I should dress up his popular locutions in a little Latinity.... *Ulysses* is a document, the outcome of a passion for documentation that is as fundamental as the artistic passion—more so, in fact; for the document is the root and stem of which the artistic fancyworks are the flowers. Joyce is driven by his documentary demon to place on record the working of a young man's imagination for a single day in the environment of Dublin. The question is, is the document authentic? If I, having read some scraps of it, reply that I am afraid it is, then you may rise up and demand that Dublin be razed to the ground, and its foundations sown with salt. And I may say do so, by all means. But that does not invalidate the document.

'The Dublin "Jackeens" of my day, the medical students, the young bloods about town, were very like that. Their conversation was dirty; and it defiled their sexuality, which might just as surely have been presented to them as poetic and vital. I should like to organise the young men of Dublin into clubs for the purpose of reading *Ulysses;* so that they should debate the question "Are we like that?" and if the vote was in the affirmative, proceed to the further question: "Shall we remain like that?" which would, I hope, be answered in the negative. You cannot carry out moral sanitation any more than physical sanitation, without indecent exposures. Get rid of the ribaldry that Joyce describes and dramatises and you get rid of *Ulysses;* it will have no more interest on that side of it than a twelfth century map of the world has to-day. Suppress the book and have the ribaldry unexposed; and you are protecting dirt instead of protecting morals. If a man holds up a mirror to your nature and shows you that it needs washing—not whitewashing—it is no use breaking the mirror. Go for soap and water.' [6]

Shaw was later to demonstrate his goodwill towards Joyce more eloquently in a letter to the editor of *Picture Post*, June 3, 1939:

'In your issue of the 13th, Mr. Geoffrey Grigson, in an interesting article on Mr. James Joyce, states that I was "disgusted by the unsqueamish realism of *Ulysses*, and burnt my copy in the grate."

Somebody has humbugged Mr. Grigson. The story is not true. I picked up *Ulysses* in scraps from the American *Little Review*, and for years did not know that it was the history of a single day in Dublin. But having passed

since 1919, and Stanislaus's attitude towards *Ulysses* and *Finnegans Wake* was much too captious for Joyce's taste. On August 7, 1924, Stanislaus had written him:

I have received one instalment of your yet unnamed novel in the transatlantic review. I don't know whether the drivelling rigmarole about half a ball hat and ladies' modern toilet chambers (practically the only things I understand in this nightmare production) is written with the deliberate intention of pulling the reader's leg or not. You began this fooling in the Holles Street episode in *Ulysses* and I see that Wyndham Lewis (the designer of that other piece of impudent fooling 'The Portrait of an Englishwoman') imitates it with heavy-footed capering in the columns of the 'Daily Mail.' Or perhaps—a sadder supposition —it is the beginning of softening of the brain. The first instalment faintly suggests the Book of the Four Masters and a kind of Biddy in Blunderland and a satire on the supposed matriarchal system. It has certain characteristics of a beginning of something, is nebulous, chaotic but contains certain elements. That is absolutely all I can make of it. But! It is unspeakably wearisome. Gorman's book on you practically proclaims your work as the last word in modern literature. It may be the last word in another sense, the witless wandering of literature before its final extinction. Not that I imagine that literature will ever die so long as men speak and write. But they may cease to read or at least to read such things. I for one would not read more than a paragraph of it, if I did not know you.

What I say does not matter. I have no doubt that you have your plan, probably a big one again as in *Ulysses*. No doubt, too, many more competent people around you speak to you in quite a different tone. My only excuse for saying what I think is that it is what I think, and it is so little pleasure to me to say it that this is perhaps the chief reason why I cannot bring myself to write to you. Why are you still intelligible and sincere in verse? If literature is to develop along the lines of your latest work it will certainly become, as Shakespeare hinted centuries ago, much ado about nothing. Ford in an article you sent me suggests that the whole thing is to be taken as a nonsense rhythm and that the reader should abandon himself to the sway of it. I am sure, though the article seems to have your approval, that he is talking

---

between seven and eight thousand single days in Dublin I missed neither the realism of the book nor its poetry. I did not burn it; and I was not disgusted. If Mr. Joyce should ever desire a testimonial as the author of a literary masterpiece from me, it shall be given with all possible emphasis and with sincere enthusiasm.

                              G. Bernard Shaw,
                                   Ayot St. Lawrence, Welwyn, Herts'

The most amusing aspect of these pronouncements is that they confirm that Shaw, like Yeats, never finished the novel.

through his half a tall hat. In any case I refuse to allow myself to be whirled round in the mad dance by a literary dervish.

I wrote to you in much the same strain when you sent me *Ulysses,* and yet a good part, the greater part of it, I like. I have no humour for the episodes which are deliberately farcical: the Sirens, the Oxen of the Sun; and as the episodes grow longer and longer and you try to tell every damn thing you know about anybody that appears or anything that crops up, my patience oozes out. The talent however is so obvious that I almost take it for granted. Dublin lies stretched out before the reader, the minute living incidents start out of the pages. Anybody who reads can hear the people talk and feel himself among them. At every turn of this, the longest day on record, there are things to give him pause. There is many a laugh, but hardly one happy impression. Everything is undeniably as it is represented, yet the 'cumulative effect' as Grant Richards would say, makes him doubt truth to be a liar. You try to shift the burden of your melancholy to the reader's shoulders without being yourself relieved. To me you seem to have escaped from the toils of the priest and the king only to fall under the oppression of a monstrous vision of life itself. Where so much has been recorded, I object to what has been omitted. There is no serenity or happiness anywhere in the whole book. I suppose you will tell me ironically that this is my chance and my work; to set to and write up all the eucharistic moments of Dublin life. It is not my business. Yet in these same surroundings that you describe I have not rarely been penetrated by a keen sense of happiness. I cannot exploit these moments either in prose or verse, but the fact remains that they have been.

In the Tyrone Street episode, for instance, the relation or at least the analogy between the imagination in the intellect and the sexual instinct in the body (my fixed idea, by the bye, old chap, explained to you first in Dublin apropos of Yeats's phrase 'world troubling seamen,' which I corrected to 'world-troubling semen,' and later in Trieste to you and Francini when I pointed out the resemblance between the 'Bacchanals' of Euripides and Ibsen's *Ghosts*) is worked out with a fantastic horror of which I know no equal in literature, painting or music, but not more fantastically horrible than some of the manifestations of the instinct with which it deals. It is undoubtedly Catholic in temperament. This brooding on the lower order of natural facts, this re-evocation and exaggeration of detail by detail and the spiritual dejection which accompanies them are purely in the spirit of the confessional. Your temperament, like Catholic morality, is predominantly sexual. Baptism has left in you a strong inclination to believe evil. For of all the manifestations of Circe, the most benign, that which has inspired poets of all kinds for thousands of years (including the poet of *Chamber Music*) is represented by a couple of lines by Yeats, murmured by a student in drunken slumber. This is bias. The close, however, with dream figure of

Bloom's young son and the suggestion that children are the real lambs who take away just these sins of the world, is so unexpected and so unexpectedly tender, that one reader at least could not read it unmoved.

When he appeared in April 1926, Stanislaus was his usual unconciliatory self. Annoyed and alerted for annoyances, he found them at 2 Square Robiac. His brother was surrounded by admirers whose attitude seemed to Stanislaus sycophantic. James was too moneyed and pampered; he drank and played with words too much. Echoes of Stanislaus's attitude emerge in Shaun's comments on the 'illstarred punster' in *Finnegans Wake;* * 'could he quit doubling and stop tippling, he would be the unicorn of his kind.' † Stanislaus summed up his opinion of the new book by saying, 'You have done the longest day in literature, and now you are conjuring up the deepest night.' This was the first determined attack by an intimate upon *Finnegans Wake*, and Joyce duly reported it, but without comment, to Miss Weaver.[7] He could discount his brother's judgment the more readily, however, because of Stanislaus's objections to episodes of *Ulysses*.

After Stanislaus had returned to Trieste, the Joyces received visits from Eileen Schaurek, who was taking her two children from Trieste to Ireland for a visit, from Nora's uncle Michael Healy, and from old Dublin friends like Mrs. Sheehy-Skeffington and Harry Sinclair. Joyce always received Irish visitors cordially, and delighted in testing his memory, and theirs, by naming all the shops in order along O'Connell Street, or by questioning them about other people and places he had known. When a shop had changed hands he was a little disgruntled, as if a picture had been removed from his museum. Now that Mrs. Murray was dead, he several times sent friends to interview his father so as to rescue from oblivion some small fact about family history or Dublin gossip. John Joyce co-operated as well as his memory allowed,[8] but occasionally balked at some query about an unimportant person and asked his interviewer, 'Is Jim mad entirely?'

In May, Joyce found he had overworked on the third book of *Finnegans Wake*, the section dealing with Shaun; he nevertheless carried it to completion and sent it to Miss Weaver on June 7, 1926, with a rather urgent request for her opinion. Soon after he suffered an attack in his left eye so serious as to necessitate a tenth operation during this same month. After it he made slow progress, unable until July 15 to perceive objects with the operated eye, but he showed himself, with his now famous black patch, in company. By August 11 he went with Nora to another watering place, Ostend. The porter of the Hôtel de

* P. 467.
† P. 462.

l'Océan, where they stayed, entertained him by always answering the telephone with the words, '*Ici le portier de l'Océan,*' [9] a position Joyce envied. Ostend proved to his liking, especially the strand, and he went so far as to run six or seven kilometers along it, a burst of exercise out of keeping with his usual languor during these years. In another seizure of energy, he took sixty-four lessons in Flemish, and worked some Flemish words into his description of the man-servant Sockerson in *Finnegans Wake*.° [10]

At Ostend Joyce renewed acquaintance with Juda de Vries, his old Zurich friend, who had become a dentist and was now, as Joyce wrote Sykes, 'pulling all the teeth and legs he can' in Ostend. He spent four days with Georg Goyert, who had won a contest conducted by the Rhein-Verlag, Joyce's Swiss (German) publisher, to choose a translator for *Ulysses*. Goyert brought the whole typescript from Munich, and Joyce helped him to revise eighty-eight pages.[11] There were still many changes to be made, and they arranged for another meeting in Paris later. On August 26, James Lyons, a relative of Joyce on his mother's side, flew to Ostend, spent a few hours with Joyce, and flew out again. Joyce was appalled by his daring, and said he would have to be chloroformed before he would venture into a plane.[12]

While Joyce was on his holiday he received the disturbing news that *Ulysses* was being pirated by Samuel Roth. Roth had first written him in 1922 to regret that *Ulysses* was not available in America, and he had now set himself to repair the lack without authorization. Though Joyce had not met him, they had established a kind of relationship in September 1925, when Roth began reprinting in a magazine called *Two Worlds* the fragments of *Work in Progress* that were then available in Europe. To appease their author, Roth sent him $200 on account and promised more, which never came. Five fragments were published, the last in September 1926. This venture emboldened Roth to go on to *Ulysses,* and in a second (simultaneously issued) review, *Two Worlds Monthly*, he published in July 1927, the whole of the *Telemachiad* (the first three episodes) in slightly expurgated form.† He took advantage of the fact that the United States was not a signatory of the Bern copyright convention. Joyce asked Quinn's law partner to institute proceedings against Roth, but he declined to take the case. Pound, who knew Roth, was appealed to, and asked his father to start suit,

---

° P. 370.

† In *Finnegans Wake* (422), Joyce has Shaun say of his brother Shem, 'Obnoximost posthumust! With his unique hornbook [*Ulysses*] and his prince of the apauper's pride, blundering all over the two worlds!'

Joyce and his family in Paris, 1924. *Wide World Photos*

XIII

The tenor John Sullivan. (p. 632)
Courtesy of the late John Sullivan

César Abin's caricature of Joyce, 1932. (p. 658)

XIV

The Giant's Grave at St. Andrew's, Penrith. (p. 594)
Courtesy of Kenneth Smith, City Librarian, Carlisle

but the elder Pound found it would be too expensive. Joyce had to defer any new defensive action until his return to Paris.

He went on with his family to Antwerp, which he renamed Gnantwerp [13] because of the mosquitoes, to Ghent and Brussels, and made a side-trip to Waterloo * to secure details for the description of the battlefield and the Napoleon-Wellington struggle in the first chapter of his book. He returned to Paris in September to confront a series of incidents all of which put *Finnegans Wake* into question. To begin with, the *Dial* (New York), to which Joyce had offered the Shaun chapters, at first accepted them, then wanted to cut them, and finally refused them. Joyce was annoyed, but he was more disturbed by a growing resentment of his book. Most of his friends had withheld comment on its first sections, waiting until more of it was available;

---

* Thomas Wolfe was a fellow-passenger on the bus to Waterloo. Though he did not venture to speak to Joyce, he observed him carefully, and wrote Aline Bernstein on September 22, 1926: 'He was with a woman about forty, and a young man, and a girl.... He was wearing a blind over one eye. He was very simply—even shabbily—dressed.... The young man [George], who wore horn-rim spectacles, and a light sporty looking overcoat, looked very much like an American college boy.... The woman [Nora] had the appearance of a thousand middle class French women I've known—a vulgar, rather loose mouth; not very intelligent looking.... The girl [Lucia] was rather pretty—I thought at first she was a little American flapper.

'Joyce was very simple, very nice. He walked next to the old guide who showed us around, listening with apparent interest to his harangue delivered in broken English, and asking him questions. We came home to Brussels through a magnificent forest, miles in extent—Joyce sat with the driver on the front seat, asked a great many questions. I sat alone on the back seat—it was a huge coach; the woman sat in front of me, the girl in front of her, the young man to one side. Queer arrangement, eh?

'Joyce got a bit stagey on the way home, draping his overcoat poetically around his shoulders. But I liked Joyce's looks—not extraordinary at first sight, but growing. His face was highly colored, slightly concave—his mouth thin, not delicate, but extraordinarily humourous. He had a large powerful straight nose—redder than his face, somewhat pitted with scars and boils.' [14]

Wolfe met Joyce again at Frankfurt, on a bus tour of that city, in September 1928; they went to the Rathaus and Goethe's house, and exchanged a few words, but Wolfe was still too shy to strike up acquaintance.[15]

Another American writer, F. Scott Fitzgerald, met Joyce in 1928, and tried to exhibit his respect more flamboyantly by offering to jump out the window in tribute. Joyce said, 'That young man must be mad—I'm afraid he'll do himself some injury.' [16] A letter of July 11, 1928, to Fitzgerald seems to refer to the incident: 'Dear Mr Fitzgerald: Herewith is the book you gave me signed and I am adding a portrait of the artist as a once young man with the thanks of your much obliged but most pusillanimous guest. Sincerely yours, James Joyce.' [17]

Sherwood Anderson returned to Paris in 1927, but this time his meeting with Joyce did not go so well as in 1921. Joyce invited him to dinner and suggested he have oysters; Anderson was too embarrassed to refuse, though he detested them. He preferred to think it was the sight of Joyce cutting a figure, rather than the oysters, which made the evening a failure.[18]

but as they perceived that it was almost all to be written in *calembours,* they became puzzled, then irritated, and finally indignant, sad, or mocking. Even Miss Weaver's references to the book in her letters, while sympathetic, were guarded. Joyce did not wish to lose this adherent, and in various ways sought to make her not only a reader but an accomplice in the perpetration of *Finnegans Wake.* One of the most curious he introduced in a letter of September 24:

> A rather funny idea struck me that you might 'order' a piece and I would do it. The gentlemen of the brush and hammer seem to have worked that way: Dear Sir. I should like to have an oil painting of Mr Tristan carving a raw pork for Cornish countrymen or anicebust of Herr Ham contemplating his cold shoulder.[19]

The offer was less extravagant than it seemed, for scarcely anything could be altogether alien to *Finnegans Wake*'s universal history. The game amused Miss Weaver, and since she was staying then near Penrith, she picked on a bit of local legend as appropriate to his plan. On October 1 she replied:

> You have made a curious request indeed! Here then followeth my 'order': To Messrs Jacques le Joyeux, Giacomo Jakob, Skeumas Sheehy and whole Company:
> Sirs: Kindly supply the undersigned with one full length grave account of his esteemed Highness Rhaggrick O'Hoggnor's Hogg Tomb as per photos enclosed * and oblige
>
> Yours faithfully
Henriette Véavère
>
> It seems to me that that might come within the scope of your present book. There is a short monograph inside the church which says that the grave was reputed to be that of a hero king (of Scotland, or Northumbria) whose name I 'misremember' but it began with O—Ossian or something in that way, not quite that I think. Such is my 'order' for this book. But what I would really like is to place an order well in advance when another book is under contemplation! But that time is far away.

The wistful fall of the last sentences was not lost on Joyce, but he took no official notice of them as he began work on the giant's grave which, as the pamphlet by the Reverend James Cropper said, was probably not really a giant's grave at all. 'I know it is no more than a game,' he wrote her on October 16, 'but it is a game that I have learned to play in my own way. Children may just as well play as not. The ogre will come in any case.'[20]

* Plate XIV.

The configuration of the giant's grave, with vertical stones at head and toe and four horizontal stones between, suggested at once to Joyce the configuration of his hero Earwicker in his topographical aspect, his head at Howth, his toes at Castle Knock in the Phoenix Park, and also suggested the barrel of whiskey at the head and the barrel of Guinness at the feet of Finnegan, whose modern incarnation Earwicker was to be. He decided to put the passage in 'the place of honour' [21] at the beginning of the book to set the half-mythological, half-realistic scene. The first draft, composed alternately with readings in Anita Loos's *Gentlemen Prefer Blondes*,[22] was dated 15 November 1926, and began in the middle of a sentence just as the book was to end in the middle of the same sentence.

brings us back to Howth Castle & Environs. Sir Tristram, violer d'amores, had passencore rearrived on the scraggy isthmus from North Armorica to wielderfight his penisolate war; nor had stream rocks by the Oconee exaggerated themselse to Laurens County, Ga, doublin all the time; ° nor avoice from afire bellowsed mishe to tauftauf thuartpeatrick; not yet, though venisoon after, had a Kisdcad buttended a bland old isaac; not yet, though all's fair in vanessy, were sosie sesthers wroth with twone jonathan. Rot a peck of pa's malt had Shem or Shen brewed by arclight and rory end to the regginbrow was to be seen ringsome on the waterface.

With it he sent a key:

Howth (pron Hoaeth) = Dan Hoved (head)
Sir Amory Tristram 1st earl of Howth changed his name to Saint Lawrence,
    b in Brittany (North Armorica)
Tristan et Iseult, passim
viola in all moods and senses
Dublin, Laurens Co, Georgia, founded by a Dubliner, Peter Sawyer, on
    r. Oconee. Its motto: Doubling all the time.
The flame of Christianity kindled by S. Patrick on Holy Saturday in
    defiance of royal orders
Mishe = I am (Irish) i.e. Christian
Tauf = baptise (German)
Thou art Peter and upon this rock etc (a pun in the original aramaic)
Lat: Tu es Petrus et super hanc petram
Parnell ousted Isaac Butt from leadership
The venison purveyor Jacob got the blessing meant for Esau
Miss Vanhomrigh and Miss Johnson had the same christian name

° Joyce asked an American visitor, Julien Levy, to look up Dublin, Georgia, for him. Levy found there were three Dublins in the United States, one of them named from the custom of bundling or doubling in. Joyce was anxious to find out if it lay on a river.[23]

Sosie = double
Willy brewed a peck of maut
Noah planted the vine and was drunk
John Jameson is the greatest Dublin distiller
Arthur Guinness "   "   "   " brewer
rory = Irish = red
rory = Latin, roridus = dewy
At the rainbow's end are dew and the colour red: bloody end to the lie in
    Anglo-Irish = no lie
regginbrow = German regenbogen + rainbow
ringsome = German ringsum, around
When all vegetation is covered by the flood there are no eyebrows on the
    face of the Waterworld
exaggerare = to mound up
themselse = another dublin 5000 inhabitants
Isthmus of Sutton a neck of land between Howth head and the plain
Howth = an island for old geographers
passencore = pas encore and *ricorsi storici* of Vico
rearrived = idem
wilderfight = wiederfechten = refight
bellowed = the response of the peatfire of faith to the windy words of
    the apostle [24]

Miss Weaver replied gratefully, but took up for the first time the cause
of the common reader:

But, dear sir, (I always seem to have a 'but') the worst of it is that without comprehensive key and glossary, such as you very kindly made out for
me, the poor hapless reader loses a very great deal of your intention;
flounders, helplessly, is in imminent danger, in fact, of being as totally lost
to view as that illfated vegetation you mentioned. Perhaps you wish him,
her and them to disappear from the horizon in this way—and in particular
all officials—so that at least the book itself may float across safely to that
far shore of 'Doublin all the time.' Otherwise, would it be utterly against
the grain, your convictions and principles to publish (when the day comes),
along with an ordinary edition, also an annotated edition (at double or
treble price, say?) I throw this out as a mere suggestion.[25]

Her letter arrived only two or three days after one in which Ezra
Pound, to whom Joyce had also sent a typescript of the Shaun book
with a request for his opinion, threw up his hands in despair:

Nov. 15, 1926

Dear Jim:

Mss. arrived this a,m,; all I can do is to wish you every possible
success.

I will have another go at it, but up to present I make nothing of it whatever. Nothing so far as I make out, nothing short of divine vision or a new cure for the clapp can possibly be worth all that circumambient peripherization.

Doubtless there are patient souls, who will wade through anything for the sake of the possible joke. . . . . but . . . . having no inkling whether the purpose of the author is to amuse or to instruct . . . . in somma. . . .
Up to the present I have found diversion in the Tristan and Iseult paragraphs that you read years ago . . . mais apart ca. . . .
   and in any case I dont see what
which has to do with where . . . .

undsoweiter
Yrs ever
E P [26]

Miss Weaver's near miss and Pound's direct hit momentarily staggered Joyce. He lay down on the sofa in exhaustion. The next day, however, he began again, and offered one of his rare statements in his own defense: 'One great part of every human existence is passed in a state which cannot be rendered sensible by the use of wideawake language, cutanddry grammar and goahead plot.' [27] He made some effort to bring Pound around by discussion, but Pound said firmly, 'Nothing would be worth plowing through like this, except the Divine Vision—and I gather it's not that sort of thing.' [28] Joyce wrote him a letter which mentioned with indirect reproach 'a few halfpennies of encouragement' from others, and continued the play on Pound's name in a postscript:

I forgot to send a little epigram I made after our last conversation, I think, about my new book. So here it is . . .
   E. P. exults in the extra inch
   Wherever the ell it's found
   But wasn't J. J. a son of a binch
   To send him an extra pound?
The title I gave it (the epigram) was:
   Troppa Grossa, San Giacomone! [29]

Pound's receptivity to innovation had, as he now knew, its limits.

There was also news from Trieste, first good then bad. At the beginning of November 1926, Joyce heard from Stanislaus that he was to end his forty-two years of celibacy by marrying Nelly Lichtensteiger during the next year. James promptly sent a gift of money and wished them *'Buona fortuna.'* [30] Immediately thereafter he received a sudden sharp demand for money from his sister Eileen, who was again in Dublin; and then he heard from Stanislaus that Schaurek had died suddenly. Eileen passed through Paris, still unaware of her husband's death, and Joyce could not bring himself to tell her the ghastly news, which in fact she did not discover until she arrived in Trieste. There she refused to believe it, and had her husband's body dug up before she found it credible. After the exhumation she collapsed for three months,[31] and Stanislaus, with sporadic help from James, had again to take over the maintenance of a luckless family.

While worried by these family difficulties, Joyce applied himself to the task of stopping Roth, whose magazine *Two Worlds Monthly* was rumored, no doubt incorrectly, to be selling 50,000 copies an issue. He sought out Benjamin Conner, one of the foremost American lawyers in Paris, and Conner arranged to start legal action through the firm of Chadbourne, Stanchfield, and Levy in New York, with which he was associated. But legal action was bound to be slow, and in the meantime Joyce conceived the idea of an International Protest against Roth's piracy of his book. Ludwig Lewisohn and Archibald MacLeish, the only lawyer in the Joyce circle, drew up the protest, and then copies of it were sent with great dispatch to the principal writers all over the world for signature:

It is a matter of common knowledge that the *Ulysses* of Mr. James Joyce is being republished in the United States, in a magazine edited by Samuel Roth, and that this republication is being made without authorization by Mr. Joyce; without payment to Mr. Joyce and with alterations which seriously corrupt the text. This appropriation and mutilation of Mr. Joyce's property is made under colour of legal protection in that *Ulysses* which is published in France and which has been excluded from the mails in the United States is not protected by copyright in the United States. The question of justification of that exclusion is not now in issue; similar decisions have been made by government officials with reference to works of art before this. The question in issue is whether the public (including the editors and publishers to whom his advertisements are offered) will encourage Mr. Samuel Roth to take advantage of the resultant legal difficulty of the author to deprive him of his property and to mutilate the creation of his art. The undersigned protest against Mr. Roth's conduct in republishing *Ulysses* and appeal to the American public in the name of that security of works of the intellect and the imagination without which art cannot live, to oppose to Mr. Roth's enterprise the full power of honorable and fair opinion.

The 167 signers included such names as Robert Bridges, Croce, Duhamel, Einstein, Eliot, Havelock Ellis, E. M. Forster, Galsworthy, Giovanni Gentile, Gide, Ramon Gomez de la Serna, Lady Gregory, Hemingway, Hofmannsthal, D. H. Lawrence, Wyndham Lewis, Maeterlinck, Masefield, Merejkowsky, Sean O'Casey, Jean Paulhan, Pirandello, George Russell, James Stephens, Symons, Unamuno, Valéry, Hugh Walpole, H. G. Wells, Rebecca West, Thornton Wilder, Virginia Woolf, and Yeats. The signatures of Einstein, Croce, and Gentile gave Joyce special pleasure.[32] Bernard Shaw refused to sign, perhaps recalling a question of piracy of his own work in Zurich. Ezra Pound objected to signing, because he thought Joyce was putting personal advertisement ahead of the general evils of the copyright and pornography laws and using 'a mountain battery to shoot a gnat.' [33] The real quarrel was, he insisted, 'with the whole American people which sanction the state of the laws.' [34] He wrote Joyce on December 25, 'I consider it a missfire, that omits the essential part and drags in an irrelevancy.' [35] Joyce wrote a courtly reply to say he assumed Pound felt his signature to be one of those that were supererogatory, and no open quarrel took place. A few months later Pound agreed to give testimony against Roth by affidavit,[36] but continued to urge Joyce, as 'the leader of European prose,' to denounce, with Roth as pretext, everything American. Hemingway told Joyce this idea was 'moonshine,' [37] and of course Joyce did not follow it. The protest was dated and issued to the press on Joyce's birthday, February 2, 1927, a day for which each year his respect increased. That night a party of friends, including Larbaud, Sylvia Beach, Adrienne Monnier, the MacLeishes, Sisley Huddleston, and two visitors from Ireland met by Joyce's invitation at Langer's for a dinner celebration.[38]

The protest had no effect upon Roth, who continued to print *Ulysses* through October 1927, the last pirated passage being the fine blasphemy at the end of *Oxen of the Sun.* By that time the legal net of Joyce's attorneys had begun to close in on Roth, who suspended publication; but it was not until December 27, 1928, that he was finally enjoined by Justice Richard H. Mitchell of the Supreme Court of the State of New York from using Joyce's name in any way. A consent decree without damages was entered. Joyce at first was pleased but later became annoyed with his lawyers; * he paid only about a third of their fee, and an acrimonious correspondence ensued.

---

* To preclude the piracy of *Work in Progress,* Joyce decided to have sections of it printed in editions of a few copies solely for copyright purposes. The first of these was undertaken by Donald Friede in 1927, mostly at the suggestion of Elliot Paul. The copyright was issued in Friede's name instead of Joyce's. Joyce suspected a trick, and was with difficulty prevailed upon to receive Friede, who assured him the transfer of copyright was a mere formality. 'In that case,' said Joyce, 'would you mind making the subject of the conversation you have planned to have with me an accompanying letter to this transfer of copyright? I will be glad to read it carefully and write you my decision. In the meantime I must ask to be excused. I am a very busy man.' The copyright was transferred to Joyce on February 17,

At the end of 1926 the *dramatis personae* began to gather for the last period in Joyce's life. The first of these were Eugene Jolas and his wife Maria. Jolas, born in the United States of Lorraine parents, had spent his childhood in Lorraine, then returned to America at the age of fifteen. His tall, good-looking wife was from Kentucky. Jolas was fluent in English, French, and German, and, like Joyce, was fascinated by words. A sensitive man, he was searching for a theory of art which would also be a philosophy of life; he thought he had found it in a 'religion of the word,' the ritual of which he saturated with terms like 'phantastic,' 'mantic,' and his neologism, 'paramyth.' Art alone could be trusted, and trusted only if it abjured externality in the name of imagination. It was a time to be revolutionary, and Jolas centered his revolution in language. He wrote a little book called *Mots Déluge* (the deluge being his revolution), which Joyce, when he knew Jolas better, twitted him about in a limerick:

> There's a genial young poetriarch Euge
> Who hollers with heartiness huge:
> Let sick souls sob for solace
> So the *jeunes* joy with Jolas!
> Book your berths! *Après mot, le déluge.*[39]

Jolas eagerly devised a manifesto which most of his friends signed with him.* He and his wife decided they must have a review; they

---

1928, and Joyce then instructed his New York attorneys to copyright four additional fragments in 1928, 1929, and 1930. In all these the name of the printer, the date, and the name of the copyright holder were omitted, thus making the copyright invalid. Joyce contended that his instructions had not been carried out; the New York law firm pointed to its considerable outlay of money for printing, and to other services on his behalf.

* Jolas's document read as follows:

Manifesto: The Revolution of the Word

Tired of the spectacle of short stories, novels, poems and plays still under the hegemony of the banal word, monotonous syntax, static psychology, descriptive naturalism, and desirous of crystallizing a viewpoint...

we hereby declare that:

1. The revolution in the English language is an accomplished fact.
2. The imagination in search of a fabulous world is autonomous and unconfined.
   (Prudence is a rich, ugly old maid courted by Incapacity.... Blake)
3. Pure poetry is a lyrical absolute that seeks an a priori reality within ourselves alone.
   (Bring out number, weight and measure in a year of dearth.... Blake)
4. Narrative is not mere anecdote, but the projection of a metamorphosis of reality.
   (Enough! Or Too Much! ... Blake)

had once, while living in New Orleans, considered taking over the *Double Dealer,* but, back in Europe, they founded *transition,* an alto- gether new one. Subtitling it 'An International Quarterly for Creative Experiment,' they intended to publish, if they could get it (as they quickly did), the latest and most experimental work of Joyce, Stein, and younger writers.

Jolas was slightly acquainted with Joyce, but approached him through Sylvia Beach. As a result, on a Sunday afternoon, Decem- ber 21, Joyce invited the Jolases, Elliot Paul (*transition*'s associate editor), and of course Sylvia Beach and Adrienne Monnier to hear him read the first section of *Finnegans Wake.* A smile occasionally passed over his face as he read. 'What do you think of it? Did you like it?' he asked them eagerly when he had finished. It was not easy to reply. Soon afterwards Joyce lent Jolas the first hundred and twenty pages, which he said contained the outline of the whole book. 'I imagine I'll have about eleven readers,' he said, with a kind of self- protective humility. Jolas found in *Finnegans Wake* the principal text for his revolution of the word. The mixture of childish nonsense and ancient wisdom had been prepared for by the Dadaists and surrealists, while the overriding sense of form in Joyce's book distinguished it from their productions. It was decided that the Jolases would publish the book serially in *transition,* beginning with the beginning of the book, and including in revised form the fragments published at random during the last several years. They continued steadily from April 1927 through November 1927; then publication was a little more sporadic, and after November 1929, for reasons that will appear, there was a long interval. Joyce was highly content to have this outlet for his work,

---

5. The expression of these concepts can be achieved only through the rhythmic 'hallucination of the word.' (Rimbaud)

6. The literary creator has the right to disintegrate the primal matter of words imposed on him by textbooks and dictionaries.

   (The road of excess leads to the palace of Wisdom . . . Blake)

7. He has the right to use words of his own fashioning and to disregard existing grammatical and syntactical laws.

   (The tigers of wrath are wiser than the horses of instruction . . . Blake)

8. The 'litany of words' is admitted as an independent unit.

9. We are not concerned with the propagation of sociological ideas, except to emancipate the creative elements from the present ideology.

10. Time is a tyranny to be abolished.

11. The writer expresses. He does not communicate.

12. The plain reader be damned.

   (Damn braces! Bless relaxes! . . . Blake)

   (Signed) Kay Boyle, Whit Burnett, Hart Crane, Caresse Crosby, Harry Crosby, Martha Foley, Stuart Gilbert, A. L. Gillespie, Leigh Hoffman, Eugene Jolas, Elliot Paul, Douglas Rigby, Theo Rutra, Robert Sage, Harold J. Salemson, Laurence Vail.

and *transition* also published essays about him so that it was a continuing advocacy.

But now Miss Weaver's uneasiness about *Finnegans Wake* had grown to the point where she could no longer keep it to herself. During January 1927, she steeled herself to articulate her objections, and on January 29 began them a little timidly. Joyce had followed her advice to work a bit less hard, and she wished to take advantage of his amenability:

As the ceasework order was followed so promptly I feel encouraged to 'try my hand at it again' and give another and different order—but also for eyes and health's sake. As its subject matter is, however, not such as to present any very strong appeal to you (unless perhaps on the minus side of the line) and is indeed, as we read, an 'ungrateful' one, I shall await your express permission to mention it. . . . And perhaps when the present book is finished you will see fit to lend ear to several of your older friends (E. P. to be included in the number): but the time to talk of that matter is not yet.

Joyce was much disturbed. He answered by return mail on February 1:

Your letter gave me a nice little attack of brainache. I conclude you do not like the piece I did? I have been thinking over it. It is all right, I think —the best I could do. I will gladly do another but it must be for the second part or fourth and not till after the first week in March or so. . . . Do you not like anything I am writing. Either the end of Part I △ [*Anna Livia Plurabelle*] is something or I am an imbecile in my judgment of language. I am rather discouraged about this as in such a vast and difficult enterprise I need encouragement. It is possible Pound is right, but I cannot go back. I never listened to his objections to *Ulysses* as it was being sent him once I had made up my mind but dodged them as tactfully as I could. He understood certain aspects of that book very quickly and that was more than enough then. He makes brilliant discoveries and howling blunders. He misled me hopelessly as to the source of the first benefaction in Zurich [Miss Weaver] and since then I have not relied on his perspicacity. A minute after I had made his acquaintance in Desenzano, as we drove across the country by night, he asked me, 'Was it John Quinn then?' My high tenor shout of 'Who?' must have been heard in Milan.

Miss Weaver apologized for worrying him, but held to her position. She wrote on February 4, 1927:

Some of your work I like enormously—as I am sure you know—especially the more straightforward and character-analytical parts and the (to me) beautifully expressed ghost-parts (for instance the sentence in Shaun about the date and the ghostmark and the one about the waterworld's face before you, as I think, distorted it—though I confess it couldn't otherwise have been inserted where it was); but I am made in such a way that I do not care much for the output from your Wholesale Safety Pun Factory nor for the darknesses and unintelligibilities of your deliberately-entangled language system. It seems to me you are wasting your genius. But I daresay I am wrong and in any case you will go on with what you are doing, so why thus stupidly say anything to discourage you? I hope I shall not do so again.

Joyce was now so upset that he took to his bed. Nora was not sympathetic. 'Why don't you write sensible books that people can understand?' she asked. But she went to tell Eugene and Maria Jolas that her husband was too disturbed to prepare the manuscript for their next number.[40] After a day or two Joyce got up and went to consult McAlmon, a candid man. 'Do you think I may be on the wrong track with my *Work in Progress?*' he asked him. 'Miss Weaver says she finds me a madman. Tell me frankly, McAlmon. No man can say for himself.' McAlmon assured him he was not mad, 'just touched enough for genius in the James Jesus Joyce manner.' [*] [41] To William Bird Joyce said, more pensively, 'About my new work—do you know, Bird, I confess I can't understand some of my critics, like Pound and Miss Weaver, for instance. They say it's *obscure*. They compare it, of course, with *Ulysses*.[†] But the action of *Ulysses* was chiefly in the daytime, and the action of my new work takes place at night. It's natural things should not be so clear at night, isn't it now?' [42] To Claud Sykes he insisted, 'It is all so simple. If anyone doesn't understand a passage, all he need do is read it aloud.' [43] To another friend he declared, more loftily, 'Perhaps it is insanity. One will be able to judge in a century.' [44] Though he was beginning to take hold again, he was still disconcerted enough to address Harriet Weaver in his next letter to her as 'Dear Miss Marsden' instead of 'Dear Miss Weaver.' [45] She was rather frightened by his anguish, and urged him not to bother to defend himself.[46]

Joyce thought at first he could check Pound's criticism by showing him the manuscript of the thirteen poems he had written since *Chamber Music*, which at the suggestion of Mrs. Arthur Symons he was thinking of having published. But this overture did not work out well. Pound handed them back without a word. Joyce pressed him for an opinion, and Pound said, 'They belong in the Bible or in the family album with the portraits.' 'You don't think they are worth printing at any time?' Joyce asked. 'No, I don't,' said Pound, and began to extol the work of a young man he had just discovered named Ralph Cheever

[*] Shem is described in *Finnegans Wake* (421) as 'the pixillated doodler.'
[†] About this time he began to lose interest in *Ulysses*. When the book was mentioned in conversation, he turned to Maria Jolas to say, '*Ulysses!* Who wrote it? I've forgotten it.'

Dunning.[47] Joyce read Dunning and got Miss Weaver to read him. She agreed it was poor stuff.[48] Joyce then, at the beginning of March, asked Archibald MacLeish to read his new poems, and MacLeish sent him two letters so enthusiastic as to renew Joyce's self-esteem, confirm him in his opinion of Pound's caprice, and encourage him to have his poems published under the modest title of *Pomes Penyeach*.[49]

The criticism of *Finnegans Wake* continued, however, to weigh on his mind, especially since other friends and sometime adherents like Sidney Schiff were also making their opposition open. Perhaps to counter such hostility he accepted an invitation from the English P.E.N. Club to be guest of honor at their dinner on April 5, 1927, and, without feeling much better, he made a short trip to London from April 3-9 for the purpose. John Drinkwater presided and Galsworthy attended. Joyce disappointed the audience by not making the customary speech in reply. Afterwards he played again with the idea of going to Ireland but of course did not go. Back in Paris, he wrote Miss Weaver on May 12 that he would gladly turn over the book to somebody else to finish. 'But who is the person?'[50] One name came to him, and on May 20 he disclosed to her one of the strangest ideas in literary history:

As regards that book itself and its future completion I have asked Miss Beach to get into closer relations with James Stephens. I started reading one of his last books yesterday *Deirdre*. I thought he wrote *The Return of the Hero*, which I liked.* His *Charwoman's Daughter* is now out in French. He is a poet and Dublin born. Of course he would never take a fraction of the time or pains I take but so much the better for him and me and possibly for the book itself. If he consented to maintain three or four points which I consider essential and I showed him the threads he could finish the design. JJ and S (the colloquial Irish for John Jameson and Son's Dublin whisky)† would be a nice lettering under the title. It would be a great load off my mind. I shall think this over first and wait until the opposition becomes more general and pointed.[51]

He continued to fondle the idea during a holiday which he began the next day by going to Holland. He stayed at the Hague for a few days, chiefly lying on the beach at Scheveningen nearby. This idyll was interrupted by a dog, which attacked him repeatedly and broke

---

* Joyce did not like *The Crock of Gold*, and said of it to Elliot Paul, 'It's all right, but it isn't *written*. I don't see why anybody couldn't do that.'[52]

† This was Joyce's favorite Irish whisky: he explained why to Gilbert Seldes: 'All Irish whiskies use the water of the Liffey; all but one filter it, but John Jameson's uses it mud and all. That gives it its special quality.' And the next day, which happened to be Easter, a bottle of John Jameson's arrived with a card inscribed, 'James Joyce presents Anna Livia's fireheaded son.'[53]

his glasses, confirming his childhood fear. 'His master and I spent a chatty time afterwards groping on our knees in the sand for the debris of my glasses—now restored. It is a majestic beach indeed. A very restful country too, it seems.'[54] He and Nora went on then to a hotel in Amsterdam, but here, like another nightmare of the child, thunderstorms descended upon him, the church steeple opposite his hotel was struck by lightning, and Joyce fled before a month was out. He did not feel badly towards the Dutch, he even liked the way they laughed all the time, 'though perhaps my presence there explains their mirth.'[55] (He was feeling very conscious of himself as the butt of ridicule.) 'To see 600 of them in a square eating silvery raw herrings by moonlight is a sight for Rembrandt.'[56]

On May 31, Joyce remarked upon the coincidence that for several years he had been carrying in his pocket photographs of the portraits by Tuohy of his father, himself, and—James Stephens. Another coincidence however topped all the others: 'The combination of his name from that of mine and my hero in A.P.O.T.A.A.A.Y.M. [*A Portrait*] is strange enough. I discovered yesterday through enquiries made in Paris, that he was born in Dublin on the 2 February 1882.'[*][57] To Joyce this new fact was clinching, and he gathered himself, if not to surrender the book to Stephens, at least to talk to Stephens about surrendering it. His approach was none the less so circumspect that he did not broach it for seven months. Meanwhile, however, he arranged a meeting. Stephens had felt a moral distaste for *Ulysses*, but he was soon won over. As he has written,

One evening my concierge told me as I came in that a tall, beautiful, blind gentleman had called and had left a note for me. It was from Joyce, and it asked me to meet him the next day. After that we met several times a week for a long time. I discovered that he approved of me in the most astonishing fashion, but it took me a little time to find out why. Then as the Dublin newsboys used to yell at customers, the whole discovery was found out.

How Joyce had made this discovery, I don't know, but he revealed to me that his name was James and mine was James, that my name was Stephens, and the name he had taken for himself in his best book was Stephen: that he and I were born in the same country, in the same city, in the same year, in the same month, on the same day, at the same hour, six o'clock in the morning of the second of February. He held, with a certain contained passion, that the second of February, his day and my day, was the day of the bear, the badger and the boar. On the second of February the squirrel lifts his nose out of his tail and surmises lovingly of nuts, the bee blinks and

---

[*] Joyce also made it a point of resemblance that both he and Stephens had two children, a boy and a girl. This was less convincing, however, because Stephens's son was actually his wife's by a previous marriage.

thinks again of the Sleeping Beauty, his queen, the wasp rasps and rustles and thinks that he is Napoleon Bonaparte, the robin twitters and thinks of love and worms. I learned that on that day of days Joyce and I, Adam and Eve, Dublin and the Devil all shake a leg and come a-popping and a-hopping, yelling here we are again, we and the world and the moon are new, up the poets, up the rabbits and the spiders and the rats.

Well, I was astonished. I was admired at last. Joyce admired me. I was beloved at last: Joyce loved me. Or did he? Or did he only love his birthday, and was I merely coincident to that? When I spoke about my verse, which was every waking minute of my time, Joyce listened heartily and said 'Ah.' He approved of it as second of February verse, but I'm not certain that he really considered it to be better than the verse of Shakespeare and Racine and Dante. And yet he knew the verse of those three exhaustively!

Now, in order to bring this birthday to an end, let's do it in the proper way. If I were Joyce's twin, which he held, then I had to celebrate this astonishing fact in my own way. So upon our next birthday I sent him a small poem. . . . Joyce reported back to me that he was much obliged. He practically said 'Ah' to my poem ['Sarasvata'], and I could almost see him rubbing his chin at it.[58]

Paris, even with the ebullient Stephens as a companion, was hot and stuffy; Joyce talked of going to Torquay, but remained in the city all summer. On July 7, 1927, *Pomes Penyeach,* a tiny volume covered in the green of Joyce's favorite apple, the Calville, was published by Shakespeare and Company, selling, as the title suggested, for a shilling or twelve francs. The response to the book was weak; George Slocombe reviewed it in the *Daily Herald,* and was assured by Joyce that he had 'the melancholy distinction' [59] of being the only reviewer. There were a few other notices, but the book could not bear the burden Joyce tried to put upon it, of silencing the critics of *Finnegans Wake.* His *libromaccione* (*Finnegans Wake*) suffered obloquy and his *libricciatoluccio,* as he called it, fell seemingly into oblivion. Stanislaus sent another fraternal attack from Trieste. MacLeish, to whom Joyce had intrusted the proof copy of *Dubliners* (Maunsel edition) for sale to Rosenbach, reported that he was unable to dispose of it. Joyce was depressed, and berated Miss Weaver as one of the most depressing influences upon him. He wrote her on August 14, 1927, to berate everything:

My position is a farce. Picasso has not a higher name than I have, I suppose, and he can get 20,000 to 30,000 francs for a few hours' work. I am not worth a penny a line and it seems I cannot even sell such a rare book as *Dubliners* (Dublin). Of course I have turned down a number of lecture tours in America and refused interviews. I ought to hold on here till spring, I suppose, to see whether the German and French translations [of *Ulysses*] come out and how they go if they do. But it becomes more and more of a strain. I know if I go it will collapse. . . . I am more and more aware of the indignant hostility shown to my experiment in interpreting the 'dark night of the soul.' The personal rancours of disappointed artists who have wasted their talents or perhaps even their genius * while I with poorer gifts and a dreadful lot of physical and mental hardships have or seem to have done something would not apply in your case. I saw AE's review of P.P. [Pomes Penyeach] It is not unfriendly, though I doubt if he can like very much verse which is not about an idea. I don't think reviews mean much always. Not a single notice appeared in the English press. Yet a London bookseller ordered 850 copies a few days ago and Dublin took 250. I saw orders from Naples, The Hague, Budapest etc. I suppose on certain types it will make the same impression as its author at the suppertable. One lady who came to pray remained to scoff. 'He looked as if he were drowned,' she remarked. *Et ça m'est parfaitement égal.* . . . [60]

Miss Weaver again entreated him on September 17, 1927, to take no notice of her criticism, but during this same month another old friend severely attacked his work. In *Time and Western Man* Wyndham Lewis, with a fine indifference to their drinking sessions in Paris, even included in his onslaught a few thrusts at Joyce's personality. Lewis mocked him for his habit of calling people 'Mister,' and in general treated him as an Irish *parvenu.* Joyce, he said, is 'the poet of the shabby-genteel, impoverished intellectualism of Dublin. His world is the small middle-class one.' [61] Joyce was hit by this barb, and added to the livery of humiliation and destitution he wore, the remark, 'I'm only a simple middle-class man,' which Arthur Power and Louis Gillet heard from him. He did not break with Lewis, but his resentment was clear. Lewis said later, 'I feel I should have been more circumspect: I warmed to my subject.' [62] Like Virginia Woolf, he could not resist judgment by social class, which he confused with literary criticism. He tried to make amends by a letter to Joyce in which he signed himself, 'an everdevoted friend,' [63] but Joyce was unappeased.

At the end of his life Lewis spoke of *Ulysses* as a 'splendid book,' [64] but in *Time and Western Man*, while respectful, he was much less laudatory. It was, he said, a time-book, deriving from Bergson and Einstein who had substituted a flux for solid objects. *Ulysses* contained a 'suffocating, noetic expanse of objects, all of them lifeless,' [65] a remark which Joyce promptly echoed in *Finnegans Wake* (292) by calling that book 'a jetsam litterage of convolvuli of times lost or strayed, of lands derelict and of tongues laggin too.' † He went on

---

* An allusion to Miss Weaver's letter of February 4, 1927 (p. 603).

† Lewis's argument seemed to Joyce to be that of a man about to turn Catholic. 'He is preparing to make a clamorous conversion,' Joyce said to Padraic Colum.[66]

to denounce Stephen Dedalus as a cliché, Bloom as a theatrical Jew
through whose thin disguise one could easily make out the mature
Joyce. Another criticism that deeply annoyed Joyce was Lewis's attack upon the diction of *A Portrait of the Artist*. Lewis took up the
sentence, 'Every morning, therefore, uncle Charles repaired to his
outhouse, but not before he had greased and brushed scrupulously
his back hair,' and said, 'People *repair* to places in works of fiction
of the humblest order,' and *'brushed scrupulously* is a conjunction that
the fastidious eye would reject.' [67]

Joyce acknowledged to Miss Weaver a little later that Lewis's was
by far the best hostile criticism that had appeared, but he said to
Budgen, 'Allowing that the whole of what Lewis says about my book
is true, is it more than ten per cent of the truth?' [68] The installments
of *Finnegans Wake* in *transition* for February and March 1928 (there
being no contributions from Joyce in the previous December or January
numbers), suggest that he had drawn a long breath and begun a reply,
couched in the jocular language of the book, but serious nevertheless.
Shaun's lecture in the February issue was in part a parody of Lewis
'in his knowall profoundly impressive role.' * [69] But the main counter-
argument was contained in the fable of the 'Ondt and the Gracehoper,'
in the March issue. While Stanislaus, as the saving ant, and others
played a part in the 'ondt,' the description of him as 'chairman-looking'
suggests Lewis's Prussian aspect, and the ending of the fable, with the

---

* Joyce takes the occasion to refer to another attack upon him, a more refined one,
by Yeats in the first edition of *A Vision*, which (though dated 1925) appeared at
the beginning of 1926. Yeats treated Joyce, along with Eliot, Pound, and Pirandello,
as examples of the disintegration of the unified consciousness of earlier artists. In
them, he said, 'There is hatred of the abstract. . . . The intellect turns upon itself.'
He had in mind Joyce's hatred of generalizations, as expressed to him in 1902.
Then, he went on, they 'either eliminate from metaphor the poet's phantasy and
substitute a strangeness discovered by historical or contemporary research or . . .
break up the logical processes of thought by flooding them with associated ideas
or words that seem to drift into the mind by chance; or . . . set side by side as in
Henry IV, The Waste Land, Ulysses . . . a lunatic among his keepers, a man fishing
behind the gas works, the vulgarity of a single Dublin day prolonged through
700 pages—and . . . delirium, the Fisher King, Ulysses' wandering. It is as though
myth and fact, united until the exhaustion of the Renaissance, have now fallen so
far apart that man understands for the first time the rigidity of fact, and calls up,
by that very recognition, myth.' [70] It is curious that Joyce's comment on *A Vision*,
as recorded by Eugene Jolas, bears out part of Yeats's picture of him and recalls
their old argument. Jolas says, 'He was deeply absorbed by the colossal conception,
only regretting that "Yeats did not put all this into a creative work."' To Joyce,
Yeats was still a man of letters, theorizing when he should have been creating.
To Yeats, Joyce was too concerned with the commonplace, and unable to effect an
adequate union between new material and a heroic, mythical background.

As John V. Kelleher points out, the diagram Shaun uses in *Finnegans Wake*
(293) is one of the many places where Joyce is parodying Yeats's *A Vision*.

gracehoper mocking the ondt as a space-man, was the fine ironic question:

> Your genus its worldwide, your spacest sublime!
> But, Holy Saltmartin, why can't you beat time? [71]

Lewis might be a classicist and cling to space and sharp outlines, but he could not write a book which would live in its rhythm and conquer time, as Joyce had done.

The undeclared quarrel with Wyndham Lewis stirred Joyce's blood as that with Miss Weaver had not, but even with Miss Weaver his relations were not altogether without spirit. While in London for the P.E.N. Club meeting in April 1927, he had suggested that she try to guess the title of his book. It was another effort to bring her within *Finnegans Wake*'s binding circle. For the next several months their correspondence was full of rather misleading hints and good, but wrong, guesses. So on April 16, he wrote her, with at least the intention of enlightenment:

I am making an engine with only one wheel. No spokes of course. The wheel is a perfect square. You see what I am driving at, don't you? I am awfully solemn about it, mind you, so you must not think it is a silly story about the mookse and the grapes. No, it's a wheel, I tell the world. *And* it's all *square.** [72]

He meant that the book ended where it began, like a wheel, that it had four books or parts, like the four sides of a square, and that *Finnegans Wake* contained the *doubles entendres* of wake (funeral) and wake (awakening or resurrection), as well as of Fin (end) and again (recurrence). Miss Weaver, whom he did not allow to forsake the game, suggested 'a wheeling square' or 'squaring the wheel,' [73] and while these were wrong Joyce found them useful. On May 12, 1927, he wrote beguilingly:

The title is very simple and as commonplace as can be. It is not Kitty O'Shea as some wit suggested, though it is in two words. I want to think over it more as I propose to make some experiments with it also. My remarks about the engine were not meant as a hint at the title. I meant that I wanted to take up several other arts and crafts and teach everybody how to do everything properly so as to be in the fashion.[74]

Her next suggestion, on May 19, 1927, was 'One Squared.' Joyce liked this one too, but said, 'The title I have projected is much more commonplace and accords with JJ and S and AGS & Co., and ought to be fairly plain from the reading of ⊔. The sign in this form means

* 'Now by memory inspired, turn wheel again to the whole of the wall'; 'riding round Nunsbelly Square.' *Finnegans Wake* (69, 95)

HCE interned in the landscape.' (He was hinting at Finnegan's inter-
ment.) Her next try was 'Dublin Ale' on June 13, Dublin being a
play on 'doubling,' then on June 28, 'Ireland's Eye,' 'Phoenix Park,'
and others in a reckless heap. He said Phoenix Park was close. She
came closer yet with 'Finn MacCool,' and, abetted by more hints,
'Finn's Town' or 'Finn's City' on September 17. This was close enough
so that Joyce, who did not really want her to guess the title, but
only to guess around it, did not encourage her further. Finnegan went
unidentified.

As his best answer to his critics, Joyce was busy perfecting *Anna
Livia Plurabelle* for her third appearance, this time in *transition*. He
was prepared, he said, 'to stake everything' [75] on this section of his
book. With his unfailing appetite for computation, he told Valery
Larbaud it had cost him 1200 hours of work; and to Sisley Huddleston
he remarked, 'Critics who were most appreciative of *Ulysses* are complaining about my new work. They cannot understand it. Therefore
they say it is meaningless. Now if it were meaningless it could be
written quickly, without thought, without pains, without erudition; but
I assure you that these twenty pages now before us cost me twelve
hundred hours and an enormous expense of spirit.' [76] On October 27,
1927, the chapter was triumphantly finished, [77] with three hundred and
fifty river names incorporated in the text. A few days later he read
the piece to a group of about twenty-five friends, whose responses
elated him.[*] MacLeish's letter was among the most delighted:

Dear Mr. Joyce:

I had not yesterday—nor have I today for that matter—words to tell
you how the pages you read us moved and excited me. This pure creation that goes almost beyond the power of the words you use is something I cannot talk about. But neither can I keep silence. This I am
sure—that what you have done is something even you can be proud
to have written.

Faithfully yours
Archibald MacLeish † [78]

[*] Max Eastman attacked *Anna Livia Plurabelle* when it was published, but granted
it was often humorous. He met Joyce later, and Joyce told him he was glad Eastman had at least enjoyed his humor: 'It would be terrible to think that I had done
all that work and not given you any pleasure at all. . . . For certainly the motive of
an artist—of all artists, whether they are conscious of it or not—is to give pleasure
to others.' Eastman said, 'I am very much surprised to hear you say that.' 'But it is
true, isn't it?' said Joyce. He then remarked on his use of so many river names, and
said he liked to think how some day, way off in Tibet or Somaliland, some boy or
girl in reading that little book would be pleased to come upon the name of his or
her home river.[79]
† MacLeish has written of Joyce: 'But then I never found Joyce warm. I liked him.

The strain of this work had left him, Joyce said, 'literally doubled in two from fatigue and cramp.'[80] He was glad to receive a visit the following month from John Francis Byrne, whom he had not seen since 1909. Byrne's appearance was distinguished, and Joyce was pleased with his old friend. He was also excited to learn that Cosgrave, the prototype of Lynch, had been found drowned in the Thames,[81] a presumed fulfillment of Stephen Dedalus's prophecy in the Circe episode, 'Exit Judas. Et laqueo se suspendit.' Byrne, at a hint from Nora, interceded with Joyce to suggest he raise their marriage from common law to civil, and Joyce, who no longer much cared, was surprisingly unresisting. But Byrne left and nothing further was said about it.

In January 1928, Miss Weaver paid the Joyces a visit. She had come to feel that her intervention in his literary life was illadvised, and wished to mend matters as best she could, and to assure him that he would have her complete support. Right or wrong, he could do no other than continue with his book. Joyce spent long hours explaining the book to her, and she became much more sympathetic to it than she had thought possible.[82] On February 2 there was the usual gala birthday party at the Joyce flat, and Helen Nutting has left an account of it:

Miss Weaver sitting on the sofa with Bob MacAlmon beside her. . . . I know Joyce has been reading to her a great deal and talking over his work.

Adrienne Monnier filled a chair near her, whiter, more blue-eyed and golden than ever, immense and shapeless. She is a gourmet and looks it. Bright and talkative, trying to keep the conversation going.

Power came in, with a beautiful violet-red silk handkerchief peeping from his pocket, and a sumptuous English silk tie of violet and red checks, a fine subdued harmony. His rather awkward figure and . . . face keep him from elegance, but he has an air of solid, sober propriety.

Lucia, Mrs. Antheil, and Kitten ° sat on the sofa. Lucia's face is fine and thoughtful this winter, Kitten handsome and plump, and Mrs. Antheil small and dark, in a *robe de style,* elegant and discreet. Joyce stayed in the back-

---

The little beard. The thick lenses. Like a very professional doctor—not a practicing one but a man about a hospital, rarely seen. I liked his shyness and his stiffness and the sense of something vivid and maybe dangerous under it. I don't know what "greatness" in a man is though I think I know what it is in a man's work. But a great *man!* I've been close to some accounted so but it was always the deeds or the work I felt—not a greatness in the man himself. But in Joyce you felt a hard, strong actuality that, if not greatness, was at least something you were always conscious of.'[83]

° Kitten was Kitty Connell, a friend of the Nuttings.

ground, and Nora too, until Adrienne began to tell of table-tapping and a long story of messages she and her friends had received from the spirits. Joyce remarked that *'le seul esprit'* he believed in was *'l'esprit de l'escalier.'*°

Antheil was asked to play old English music, and Joyce and McAlmon danced quietly in the back parlor, improvising rhythmic movements, McAlmon on Negro themes and Joyce Greek, so that Adrienne exclaimed, *'Mais regardez donc ce Joyce; il est tout à fait Grecque. C'est le satyre sur un vase Grecque!'* And it was so, skipping, delicate, with a clean line.

Then McAlmon sang a negro blues on the sinking of the Titanic, saying, 'I will leave out the ribald verses.' He gave us several songs, then I asked Joyce if he would sing. After several ballads I was not familiar with I asked for, 'Oh, the brown and the yellow ale!' He sang more beautifully than I had ever heard him, his voice charged with feeling. There were pauses, long-held notes, rolled r's, melancholy, a rightness of pronunciation.

I said to Power, beside me, 'It is the most wonderful racial thing I have ever listened to,' and Power replied, 'You may hear a great deal of singing, but you will never hear anything so Irish as that. It is pure Irish.' Tenderness, melancholy, bitterness.

After three songs he stopped, and we had champagne, dancing and singing, and everything was gay, stiffness melted. Only Miss Weaver kept her calm and stillness. McAlmon got very gay, mixing champagne and Irish whisky. Joyce's silence comes, I think, from a profound weariness of spirit, but Miss Weaver's is like the stillness of a stone, a quality.

Miss Weaver's visit seems to have dispelled some clouds, and made JJ more at rest as to the cares of living. And now, as soon as she leaves, they are to go away, they think to Liége, for two weeks.[84]

The visit was reassuring to Joyce, who wrote Miss Weaver on February 15, after her return to London, 'At least I know where I stand,' and on April 8 said, 'There is a great difference in the state of my mind since your visit.' While he was still to feel twinges of uncertainty, he felt his position to be much stronger, and knew he could depend upon her to his death.

The translation of *Ulysses* into German was published during 1927, to Joyce's dissatisfaction, and a new edition was immediately planned to include revisions. Georg Goyert was in Paris in April for this work, and Joyce gave him as much time as he could. He was more interested, however, in the French translation. This received new impetus from another recruit to the Joyce circle, Stuart Gilbert. Gilbert was educated at Oxford, and had gone to Burma as a young man and served

---

° He also believed in 'doblingangers' (*Finnegans Wake,* 490).

in the civil service there as a judge for nineteen years.* Then, an opportunity being given to retire on pension, he enthusiastically took it and came to Paris with his French wife. Gilbert's temperament was at once conscientious and wittily skeptical.† After he arrived in Paris early in 1927, Gilbert soon found out Sylvia Beach's bookshop. She showed him a fragment of *Ulysses* in French, translated by Morel, and published in the review *900: Cahiers d'Italie et d'Europe* (Autumn, 1926). He called her attention to some significant errors, and at her request sent them to Joyce, whom he had not met, on May 9, 1927. 'If you would care,' he wrote, 'I am prepared to go through the French version and, tentatively, to make suggestions. I fully appreciate your translator's colossal task and his skill in execution and would assist without officiousness and, I hope, with tact.' He wished no remuneration or acknowledgement. This generous offer was entirely agreeable to Joyce, but less so to Morel. A series of complicated maneuvers followed. Gilbert said later that Joyce liked to think of himself as a diplomat negotiating among major powers, but that his translators actually got on well enough together. It is clear from correspondence, however, that Morel was not pleased to have even so pleasant a person as Gilbert sitting in judgment upon him, and the fact that Gilbert was in almost daily communication with Joyce,‡ as Morel, being on his island, was not, did not improve matters. Larbaud, who had agreed to oversee Gilbert, the overseer, was several times embroiled with Adrienne Monnier and Sylvia Beach; they seemed to wish to diminish his role. In 1928 Larbaud suggested to Joyce in despair that André Maurois take his place, but Joyce would have none of this, convened all of his translators and publishers at Les Trianons and got them to

---

* Joyce got some Burmese words from Gilbert's grammar of that language, which he borrowed and did not return.

† So in Burma he sternly sentenced a Burmese to death for murder plus robbery, but when the man, through friends, managed to get off, Gilbert chatted affably with him when they happened later to meet.

‡ Gilbert, through these meetings, came to know the book so well that he decided, with Joyce's encouragement, to write a study of it based upon his notes. Joyce had been determined to express his intentions in writing *Ulysses* through someone else's agency almost since the book appeared. Originally he had planned to help Larbaud in this way, and wrote Miss Weaver on December 22, 1922, 'It will allow me to send out to the world in those parts where he uses critical exegesis certain suggestions as to the scheme and technique which I shall then have the pleasure of rehearing and rereading when they have gone the rounds.' [85] Gilbert soon became a more obvious choice. Joyce sometimes steered him directly to points he wished to be stated, but more often he said, 'Have you read such-and-such a book?' and allowed Gilbert to formulate his own conclusions. These, unless Joyce disagreed completely, were allowed to stand. Gilbert's book is therefore not an exact formulation of Joyce's views, but a perceptive interpretation of them.

consent to what he afterwards described as the 'Trianons Treaty.'⁸⁶
This established Larbaud as final arbiter.*

When *Ulysse* was published by Adrienne Monnier in February 1929,
it bore on the title page an elaborate hierarchy: '*Traduit de l'anglais par
M. Auguste Morel assisté par M. Stuart Gilbert. Traduction entière-
ment revue par M. Valery Larbaud avec la collaboration de l'auteur.*'

While the translation was being finished, Joyce was able to take
several holidays from Paris though not from his work, on which he
continued to spend most of his time. In March 1928 he went to
Dieppe,⁸⁷ where he finished the fable of 'The Ondt and the Gracehoper'
for *transition*. Since the port city was damp,⁸⁸ he went on to Rouen
on March 27, and returned to Paris a few days later. After arbitrating
another quarrel of his translators, he accepted a suggestion of Ford

---

* Each of the translators had his virtues, Morel was imaginative, Gilbert precise and
clever, and Larbaud brilliantly sensitive to style. Larbaud on June 14, 1928, sent
Joyce examples of his revision of the Morel-Gilbert text:

> Two samples of what I am doing for the translation. These are extreme
> cases, though. (Not to be shown, would give useless pain.)
>
> V. L.

Text: ... *he liked grilled mutton kidneys/ which gave to his palate a fine
tang of scented urine.*

A. Morel: ... *il aimait..../ qui gratifiaient ses papilles gustatives d'un
fumet de chaix mâtiné d'un rien d'urine.*

This is pure journalese, something for 'Moeurs des Diurnales,' of the
'comme dit l'autre' style.
'Fumet de chaix' is a *cliché*, while 'a fine tang' is not. 'Mâtiné de,' another
cliché. 'd'un rien de' is both *recherché* and facile. The feeble strain of
humour in the French sentence is vulgar; of the commercial-traveller sort;
the way they talk when they try to talk 'well.'
I leave 'gratifiaient' because it is etymologically right; I accept 'papilles
gustatives,' though the expression is a little *pretentieuse,* more 'learned'
(cheap science) than the simple 'palate' of the text, because it gives equilibrium to the French sentence and arrests the reader's attention on that
aspect of Mr. Bloom's physical life.
The rest I reject, and translate more literally: 'd'une belle saveur' (= 'fine
tang') 'un léger parfum d'urine' (= 'of faintly scented urine.')

Thus in my interpretation the phrase stands as follows: ... il aimait..../
*qui gratifiaient ses papilles gustatives d'une belle saveur au léger parfum
d'urine.*

Text: *Kidneys were in his mind as he* ...

A. Morel: *Il songeait à des rognons tant en* ...

Of course, this is the meaning, but it is not a literary translation of a literary
sentence. The humourous side of the phrase in the text is lost. I translate:

Il avait des rognons en tête tandis qu'il ...⁸⁹

Madox Ford, to take his small house in Toulon.[90] The Joyces were in Toulon by April 26, and liked the city very much. Neither dogs nor thunderstorms marred the visit. Joyce was delighted to find that Clos S. Patrice, which has been renamed Châteauneuf-du-Pape, was the oldest wine in Provence; [91] he imposed it upon Irish friends and would have drunk it himself if only it had been white instead of red.°
'Saint Patrick is the only saint a man can get drunk in honor of,' he reminded Padraic Colum, and then added, 'But he waited too long to write his *Portrait of the Artist.*' † [92]

They returned to Paris about May 24, 1928, to find the proofs of *Anna Livia Plurabelle* and of the second and third watches of Shaun awaiting Joyce. ALP, as Joyce usually called his most melodic chapter, was to be published, with a preface by Padraic Colum, in a de luxe edition of 850 copies by Crosby Gaige in New York on October 29, 1928, the watches of Shaun in *transition* in 1928 and 1929. After reading the proofs Joyce received a visit from his sister, Eileen Schaurek, and her children. They found him kind and considerate; Bertha Schaurek, then twelve years old, refused to eat meat, but her uncle promised her a string of pearls if she did, and kept the promise. When his relatives had gone, Joyce thought of going to Denmark, since he had again been brushing up his Danish.‡ But in the end he went to Salzburg about July 8, 1928, with Stuart and Moune Gilbert. There he met Stanislaus and his new wife, who had been married on August 13 and took their wedding trip to meet him. When Stanislaus rebuked him for writing an incomprehensible night-book, James replied that there would be a sequel, a reawakening.°° Stanislaus urged him to get on with it. In Salzburg Joyce had also a pleasant meeting with John Drinkwater, and succeeded in enlisting Drinkwater as a sympathizer, a position which Stanislaus of course abjured. Joyce was a little less melancholy than usual about his book because two American publishers had offered him an $11,000 advance and 20% royalties on *Finnegans Wake.*[93] While at Salzburg he felt twinges of eye trouble, and consulted an ophthalmologist there, Dr. A. Toldt, before proceeding to Frankfurt, to Munich, and then, for another stay at the ocean, to Le Havre.

In September 1928, back in Paris, Joyce collapsed again with eye trouble, and could no longer see print. He had injections of arsenic and phosphorus from Borsch and his assistant, Collinson, who assured

---

° There was a white wine of this name, but he did not like it.
† *The Confessions.*
‡ With a young Dane ('Mr. Max') who now has an interior decorator's shop on Bredgade in Copenhagen. Joyce met him at the Danish Church in Paris.
°° This is one of the few hints of what Joyce might have written.

him that he was suffering this time from 'nerves' rather than anything organic. On September 20 he wrote, or rather dictated, a letter to Harriet Weaver which summarized all his activities:

Dear Miss Weaver, We got back here a few days ago. The [French] translation [of *Ulysses*] is now finished. V.L. [Valery Larbaud] sent me a list of difficulties which I solved for him and informed me that he would celebrate his birthday, twenty-ninth of August, by going off his diet of milk and rusks in favor of some wine of the country in my honour and to celebrate both events. His work is now at an end. A. Morel, the translator, had taken a great deal of license here and there, sometimes incorporating whole sentences of his own manufacture. These were struck out. The translation is really his and has been done with great care and devotion, but like many other people by dint of brooding on it he sees one aspect to the exclusion of another. In his case it is the coarseness which excludes the others, or perhaps I should say the violence. I said to A. Monnier, the publisher, about these bits, 'A little too much Madagascar here.' He is in fact a French colonial born. Perhaps this explains it. I hope the three patch up their differences when the work is out. S.G.'s [Stuart Gilbert's] work was very useful, but it was absolutely necessary to have V.L.'s final revision, as he is very accurate, slow, fastidious, and rather timid. I saw, or rather was shown, the Prospectus yesterday, which A.M. [Adrienne Monnier] brought me along with some other difficulties which I solved much to her delight. The Prospectus will be out this week, and the volume of nearly a thousand pages in December or January, which in France usually means June; but in this case will probably be speeded up to mean the second of February. She is having it printed by a very old established printer (1500 and something) at Chartres under the shadow of the cathedral almost. She brought me down there to see the place, which is a few miles from her place in the country and insisted on lighting a candle for me in the cathedral, all for good luck. She becomes more and more superstitious, thinks that V.L. is bewitched by L.P.F. [Fargue] and I wish she could find out who is bewizarding me, for I have at the present moment, and all for my own self, episcleritis, conjunctivitis, blepharitis and a large boil on my right shoulder. So much for candles. Besides which I am most uncommonly fatigued, and it is a physical impossibility for me to attempt revision of the piece for *t.* 14 [*transition* 14], which therefore will have to come out without me for they have been ringing me up ever since I got back.

The case against Roth is up for next month. At the last moment almost Conner's partners in N. Y. cabled me that I ought to withdraw the suit for damages, as there was no copyright case and get an injunction against use of name. There never was any case on copyright and I understood always that it was to be tried under the law of property but as it would have been folly for me to have opposed the opinion of

American lawyers on the spot and as, on the other hand, I considered that I held to a certain extent a position of trust I instructed them, if they had satisfactory means of knowing that Roth had so disposed of all the money which he had made in America by misuse of my name and mutilation of my text, that no considerable part of it could be recovered either under copyright or property laws, to press for some judgment, an injunction against further use of my name with nominal damages of one dollar or whatever is the American equivalent for the English farthing: a judgment, that is, which, when recorded, would establish a precedent in case law in favor of unprotected European writers whose cause in this matter was the same as my own. The bill of costs will now come rolling over the Atlantic. I think they were probably influenced by the number of offers which have been recently made me for publication of W in P [Work in Progress]. But I had these offers made to them and through them simply in order to substantiate the claim for damages which they were advancing when the case came into court. At all events, D.F. [Donald Friede] has transferred his copyright of my property (and most uncommon kind of him) to me, that is part one, and Conner's partners at my instruction and at my expense have printed and deposited at Washington printed copyright dummies in my name for the fragments in *t.* 10-12 and 13.

ALP has not arrived but I expect her every day. I promised Drinkwater that I would reserve a copy for him though it is not easy to do this with such an edition. Did Miss Beach send you photos he took of us and his letter in which he said that his wife, under the influence of reading me, had announced that she was terribly sick of bluggage. I think it not impossible that he may consent to do a preface for another fragment and I even thought of proposing to Gaige that he ask Edgar Wallace to do one, the tortoise and the hare.

I have received three offers to give a series of lectures in Switzerland, two most urgent letters in which that most extraordinary person Mr. Wilson of Willington announces his willingness to pay mine and my wife's expenses up there and back and hotel expenses and what he calls a royal welcome from the miners and for all I know a present of a few tons of coal also. He sent me some sort of gift, I am not sure whether it is a cartridge pouch or a case for cigars and cigarettes. It is rather embarrassing to reply. I also had a visit from a very high up person of the Russian Embassy here. Full of great admiration and proposing to bring me 'Là-bas.' But from all I can gather, the condition of that country is dubious enough without inflicting on it the blighting influence of my one-quartered personality.

I have also bad news. Poor Italo Svevo was killed on Thursday last in a motor accident. I have no details as yet, only a line from his brother and so I am waiting before I write to his widow. Somehow in the case of Jews I always suspect suicide though there was no reason in his case especially since he came into fame, unless his health had taken a very bad turn. I was very sorry to hear of it but I think his last five or six years were fairly happy.

About fifty pages of Rebecca West's book ° were read to me yesterday, but I cannot judge until I hear the whole essay. I think that P.P. [*Pomes Penyeach*] had in her case the intended effect of blowing up some bogus personality and that she is quite delighted with the explosion. It is a pity that W.L. [Wyndham Lewis] did not wait for its publication too, as it would probably have mollified his attack. By the way, have you not received any press cuttings lately about his book and can you tell me how many more books he has published since I left Paris a few months ago? There seems to be a mention of me every week in the New Statesman. The Irish Statesman, which you don't get, has an article about *t.* 13 and some correspondence. Buck Mulligan fell out of an aeroplane with or after or before a Lady Martin. One may joke a little about it because fortunately neither the airman nor the airmaid seems to be any the worse. In fact they fell into a very shallow sea and I suppose are now merman and mermaid. The story seems rather curious but there is a comic poem about it in a Galway paper and the information comes from an allusion in a letter from my mother-in-law whose method of writing is often as cryptic as my own. The plane must have been very low but I am glad that they are both uninjured.

I have probably forgotten several things I wanted to say. I had no iritis of the eyes but the thing I told you, proceeding from outward infection it seems but it is very bothering and troublesome and I have to go to the clinic every morning. Mrs Bécat [Adrienne Monnier's sister] is making a wonderful carpet for me representing the Liffey flowing through Dublin into the Irish Sea with the arms of Norway, Dublin, Ireland and my own woven into the scheme. There is a case pending in Germany and Switzerland between Rascher of Zurich (I wish somebody would make bacon of him . . .) and the Rheinverlag but I need not weary you about that nor with an account of my holidays.

What are your plans for the autumn and winter? If my eyes do not get better to allow me to work (and what joy there will be in some quarters if they do not) I thought it would be useless for me to stay in Paris doing nothing and that I would go to Torquay but I am always making imaginary journeys. The complete eclipse of my seeing faculties so kindly predicted by A.M.'s young friend from Oxford, the ghost of Banquo, I am warding off by dressing in the three colours of successive stages of cecity as the Germans divide them, namely: green Starr, that is, green blindness, or glaucoma; grey Starr, that is, cataract;

° *The Strange Necessity.* Miss West writes that her essay, which was in a personal and almost fictional framework, was intended 'to show the power of James Joyce breaking into a mind unprepared for it.' [94] But it was immediately taken in a different way. Joyce mocked the essay in *Finnegans Wake*.

and black Starr, that is dissolution of the retina. This therefore forms a nocturnal tri-color connected by one common colour, green, with Shaun's national flag of peas, rice, egg yolk, the grey of evening balancing the gold of morning and the black of something balancing the white of something else, the egg probably. So I had a jacket made in Munich of green stuff I bought in Salzburg and the moment I got back in Paris I bought a pair of black and grey shoes and a grey shirt; and I had a pair of grey trousers and I found a black tie and I advertised for a pair of green braces and Lucia gave me a grey silk handkerchief and the girl found a black sombrero and that completed the picture.

I will now close this letter, which I ought to have written long ago. It was rather amusing to dictate it because my mind has been a stupid blank for weeks and I have the vapours or the languors or something of that kind. So I hope it will amuse you, though I really am not in such good humour as you may suppose from the few damp squibs of humour contained herein.

Just one paragraph more. What about Miss Marsden's book? Is it coming out this year or any part of it? I am glad you have had good weather, but a more boring summer I never passed, with one heat wave after another in central Europe. Pound's book of Cantos is out, a most magnificent thing in gold and scarlet at prices ranging from 5 to 50 pounds. Antheil wrote to me he was coming to Salzburg to see Otto Kahn (who by the way must have most of his time taken up dodging people who want to see him for one purpose only) but he did not come. He writes that the Cologne Opera affair at which we are supposed to assist from the Royal Box is a sure thing and that he has some splendid proposals from one of the three greatest publishing combines in Europe.

> With kindest regards,
> Sincerely yours,
> James Joyce [95]

His worries soon multiplied. A review of *Anna Livia Plurabelle* by Sean O'Faolain in Eliot's *Criterion* bothered Joyce a good deal, perhaps in part because he wrongly suspected it might be a prelude to Eliot's turning against his new work as Pound and Lewis had done. He took to his bed, with his eyes inflamed again, and whiled away the hours during which he was forbidden to work by learning Spanish from a tutor. Then Nora, whose health had been excellent for many years, was suddenly suspected of having cancer, and the doctors recommended an operation. She went into the hospital, and Joyce, refusing to be separated from her, had a bed set up in her room so that he could stay there too. An exploratory operation on November 8, 1928, was followed by radium treatments; and when these were ineffective,

Nora returned to the hospital in February 1929, for a hysterectomy. Miss Weaver came to Paris to help, and Joyce again had a bed beside Nora's in the hospital during February and most of March, when she was pronounced well. He depended upon Nora to hold his life together by her loyalty and by her contempt for his weaknesses. There was no one else to whom he spoke without deliberation.

Between the two visits to the American Hospital, Joyce nursed his eyes and visited Dr. Borsch several times a week for pilocarpin treatment. He also pursued a new idea, formed as a result of a luncheon he had had with H. G. Wells just before going to the hospital with Nora. It was their first meeting and went unexpectedly well. He had impressed Wells, who expected to see 'a tall fierce aggressive man in a frieze overcoat carrying a heavy stick,' by being slender, frail, and rather supplicatory. Wells offered to do what he could to aid this helpless creature with the ailing wife, and from the hospital Joyce energetically instructed Sylvia Beach to send Wells all the issues of *transition* that contained *Work in Progress*. After an appropriate delay he asked Wells's help in persuading the public to accept the new book. Wells refused most eloquently:

> Lou Pidou, Saint Mathieu,
> Grasse, A.M.
> Nov 23, 1928

My dear Joyce,

I've been studying you and thinking over you a lot. The outcome is that I don't think I can do anything for the propaganda of your work. I've an enormous respect for your genius dating from your earliest books and I feel now a great personal liking for you but you and I are set upon absolutely different courses. Your training has been Catholic, Irish, insurrectionary; mine, such as it was, was scientific, constructive and, I suppose, English. The frame of my mind is a world wherein a big unifying and concentrating process is possible (increase of power and range by economy and concentration of effort), a *progress* not inevitable but interesting and possible. That game attracts and holds me. For it, I want language and statement as simple and clear as possible. You began Catholic, that is to say you began with a system of values in stark opposition to reality. Your mental existence is obsessed by a monstrous system of contradictions. You may believe in chastity, purity and the personal God and that is why you are always breaking out into cries of cunt, shit and hell. As I don't believe in these things except as quite personal values my mind has never been shocked to outcries by the existence of waterclosets and menstrual bandages— and undeserved misfortunes. And while you were brought up under the delusion of political suppression I was brought up under the delusion of political responsibility. It seems a fine thing for you to defy and break up. To me not in the least.

Now with regard to this literary experiment of yours. It's a considerable thing because you are a very considerable man and you have in your crowded composition a mighty genius for expression which has escaped discipline. But I don't think it gets anywhere. You have turned your back on common men, on their elementary needs and their restricted time and intelligence and you have elaborated. What is the result? Vast riddles. Your last two works have been more amusing and exciting to write than they will ever be to read. Take me as a typical common reader. Do I get much pleasure from this work? No. Do I feel I am getting something new and illuminating as I do when I read Anrep's dreadful translation of Pavlov's badly written book on Conditioned Reflexes? No. So I ask: Who the hell is this Joyce who demands so many waking hours of the few thousands I have still to live for a proper appreciation of his quirks and fancies and flashes of rendering?

All this from my point of view. Perhaps you are right and I am all wrong. Your work is an extraordinary experiment and I would go out of my way to save it from destructive or restrictive interruption. It has its believers and its following. Let them rejoice in it. To me it is a dead end.

My warmest good wishes to you Joyce. I cant follow your banner any more than you can follow mine. But the world is wide and there is room for both of us to be wrong.

Yours

H. G. Wells [96]

Joyce was not at all offended, and did not despair of converting Wells in subsequent conversations. After all, the language of *Finnegans Wake* was as scientific an attempt to represent the non-waking state as any of Wells's novels to represent the waking state. 'I doubt whether his attitude towards words and language is as scientific as he himself ought to wish it to be,' [97] Joyce wrote Miss Weaver. It was in fact absurd of Wells to pretend that language was fixed, or exclusively rational. Joyce denied, too, that the Irish Catholics were addicted to experimental literature and the English not. The contrary was true, he maintained, again with justice. 'To the rest of his remarks, however, I could wholeheartedly subscribe and the more I hear of the political, philosophical, ethical zeal and labours of the brilliant members of Pound's big brass band the more I wonder why I was ever let into it "with my magic flute"....' * [98] He was a musician surrounded by preachers and generalizers, and forced to plead for himself because they did not tolerate his kind of music. The controversy with Miss Weaver, Pound, Stanislaus, and other skeptics had put him in a position of defense from which he could never work free.

* He said to Arthur Power that the way to test a work of art is to copy out a page of it, and gave Wells as an instance of the disastrous revelations such an exercise would provide.[99]

◇◇

1929–1932

The house of Atreox is fallen indeedust (Ilyam, Ilyum! Maeromor Mournomates!) averging on blight like the mundibanks of Fennyana, but deeds bounds going arise again.

—*Finnegans Wake* (55)

THE depiction of the Earwickers' family life had left Joyce, during the past years, only a little time to think of his own role as son and father. In 1929, however, his pace began to slow a little, and he pondered his responsibilities. John Stanislaus Joyce had reached the age of eighty, and continued to plead with his son to pay him one visit before he died. But James contented himself with sending his father a little money, writing to him, and asking friends like McAlmon, Tuohy, and others to pay him visits. John Joyce, largely neglected by the other children who could still remember the mistreatment they had suffered from him, loved James more and more with the years, and made out a will leaving everything (if there was anything) to him as the only child who was faithful.* He continued to delight James with his caustic remarks, as relayed through friends. So, when asked about the new Irish government, he commented, 'That blackguard Lloyd George knew what he was doing when he gave them the Free State; he knew they'd make a mess of it.' [1] His god was still

---

* A characteristically patriarchal letter from him, of July 5, 1926, reads:

My dear Jim,

Very many thanks for your kind and welcome letter with enclosures. It is very gratifying to find at the finish of my life that I have at least one son, and he *the one* I so love, who does remember me on what, perhaps, is my last birthday. May God bless you and spare you to your children. Give them my fondest love. I am glad to learn your eyes are improving and I am anxiously looking forward to *seeing* you once before I die. With fondest love

I am still, your loving
Father

623

Parnell. As to his son's work, when told the new book would be about a night as *Ulysses* had been about a day, he said, 'I hope his night-thoughts are better than his day-thoughts.' Like Nora, he still felt James should have become a singer, 'But he has done well enough.' [2]

As a father, Joyce wished to interfere as little as possible with his children's lives, a principle which was better suited to his own insuperable personality than to theirs. Because he rarely ordered or forbade them anything, and always treated them kindly and generously, he assumed they had their freedom. But by delicate requests, by sighs, by suggestions, he bound them into his affairs. They were slow to make their own careers. George's voice, a fine bass, was now well-trained, and he made his public debut on April 25, 1929, [3] by singing two songs of Handel at a Concert of the Studio Scientifique de la Voix of Professor Georges Cunelli. But he was not disposed to push himself, and his love affair with Helen Kastor Fleischman made him still less occupied with audience and career. He was devoted to his father, but began to draw away towards a life that was almost his own. His sister Lucia, who was much attached to him, felt herself imperiled, and began to manifest the little oddities of behavior that later exploded into something worse. Some of Joyce's friends, such as Valery Larbaud, had always thought Lucia strange; others dismissed her somewhat unusual behavior as the effect of her extraordinary father. At parties she was gay and talkative, and sometimes did an impersonation of Charlie Chaplin with baggy trousers and cane. Chaplin alternated with Napoleon as her favorite hero, and was the subject of a brief article she wrote in 1924 for a Belgian review, *Le Disque Vert,* which Larbaud prefaced and slightly revised for her. The combination of heroes was reminiscent of her father's joining of Dedalus and Bloom, and was taken as an amusing foible.

In 1929 Lucia became more self-conscious about her appearance, which she felt was marred by a squint (strabismus) and a little scar on her chin. William Bird had suggested several years before that the squint might be corrected by an operation, but Joyce, after frowning, had said only, 'Some people think it attractive.' [4] But Lucia began now to talk of an operation herself, and finally had it performed, though not successfully. It was impossible to know, though Joyce worried about it, to what extent the increasing disarray of Lucia's mind was due to the strange nomadic life her father had provided for her. She had had two years of elementary education in Trieste, then moved to Zurich and lost a year while she learned German. After four and a half years at a Volksschule there, she returned to Trieste in 1919, at the age of twelve, and attended a Scuola Evangelica for a year. On

Joyce after an eye operation, during the 1920's. *Courtesy of the Yale University Library*

James and Nora Joyce on their way to be married in London, July 4, 1931. (p. 650)

XV

Ford Madox Ford, James Joyce, Ezra Pound, and John Quinn, in November 1923. (p. 569) *Courtesy of Harriet Shaw Weaver*

Four generations of Joyces. James with his son George and grandson Stephen beneath the portrait of Joyce's father by Tuohy. *Gisèle Freund from Monk-meyer*

Nora Joyce painted by Myron C. Nutting in Paris in the 1920's. *Courtesy of the artist*

Lucia Joyce. *Courtesy of the Yale University Library*

her arrival in Paris in 1920, she had again to learn a new language, this time at a private school where she spent six months before attending the Lycée Duruy for a year. Her activities outside of school were another history of false starts. In Zurich and Trieste she took piano lessons for three years, in Paris and again in Salzburg she took singing lessons. She took drawing lessons at the Académie Julian in Paris. But her main interest in Paris was in dancing; with a concentration that equalled her father's, she worked six hours a day from about 1926 to 1929, taking in rapid succession courses lasting from three months to a year. These included the Cours Jaques Dalcroze (Swiss), Cours Jean Borlin (Swedish), Cours Madika (Hungarian), Raymond Duncan (American), Egorova (Russian), Lois Hutton and Hélène Vanel (rhythm and colour), and Margaret Morris (modern). As a dancer Lucia, tall, slender, and graceful, attained a style of some individuality. She appeared several times in recitals: on November 20, 1926, in a Lois Hutton 'Ballet Faunesque' at the Comédie des Champs-Élysées, and again on February 19, 1927, in the role of one of *'les vignes sauvages.'* On April 9, 1928, she danced in the *'Prêtresse Primitive'* at the Théâtre du Vieux-Colombier, and on February 18, 1928, in another Lois Hutton recital at the Comédie des Champs-Élysées in *Le Pont d'Or,* an *operette-bouffe,* with music by Émile Fernandez, a young man with whom she was briefly in love. She danced once in Brussels with the same company. Her last performance was on May 28, 1929, at an international competition at the Bal Bullier; here she appeared in a shimmering silver fish costume she had designed herself, and though she did not win the prize, she won many of the audience, who shouted, *'Nous réclamons l'Irlandaise,'* to the great pleasure of her father.[5] But she now made another turnabout; she decided, with her father's approval, that she did not have the physical stamina to be a dancer, and in October and November gave up this career with 'a month's tears.'[6] It was about this time that Eugene and Maria Jolas, sitting one night at a restaurant with a woman doctor not far from where Lucia and her parents were eating, were surprised when the doctor remarked, 'If I were the mother of James Joyce's daughter and saw her staring off into space in that way, I'd be very concerned about it.'[7] Joyce did begin to pay more attention to her plight, and encouraged her to take up again her interest in drawing. But Lucia's thoughts jumbled during the next two years towards panic.

At the beginning of 1929 Joyce's eyes were still troubling him; it seemed likely an operation would be necessary, but until his sight diminished farther nothing was to be done. In spite of fatigue and intermittent pain, he struggled to finish a new version of the third watch of Shaun, a chapter that held him through the month of April. In May there appeared the first apologia for *Finnegans Wake,* entitled with mock-portentousness, at Joyce's suggestion, *Our Exagmination round His Factification for Incamination of Work in Progress.* The spelling of Exagmination was to claim its etymological derivation from *ex agmine,* a hint that his goats had been separated from the sheep. (As Joyce wrote Larbaud, 'I am now hopelessly with the goats and can only think and write capriciously. Depart from me ye bleaters, into everlasting sleep which was prepared for Academicians and their agues!') [8] The book had twelve writers, like the twelve customers of Earwicker's public house, or the twelve apostles of Christ: * Samuel Beckett, Marcel Brion, Frank Budgen, Stuart Gilbert, Eugene Jolas, Victor Llona, Robert McAlmon,† Thomas McGreevy, Elliot Paul, John Rodker, Robert Sage, and William Carlos Williams; these were followed by two 'letters of protest' by G. V. L. Slingsby and Vladimir Dixon, both hostile and humorously illiterate. Vladimir Dixon was Joyce himself. Most of the essays had already been published in *transition,* and Joyce admitted to Larbaud he had stood behind 'those twelve Marshals more or less directing them what lines of research to follow.' [9] Some of the essays were seriously intended, and among these the best was by Samuel Beckett, then fresh from Dublin and lecturing at the École Normale Supérieure. Joyce saw to it that one or another of the twelve answered the chief critics of the book, at that time Sean O'Faolain, Wyndham Lewis, and Rebecca West.

The book did not sell well, but Joyce planned to follow this work, which he designated by the symbol O, by X, a book of four long essays (for the *Wake*'s four old men) on the subjects of the treatment of night, mechanics and chemistry, humor, and one other which on May 28 he had not yet determined.[10] The first was to be written by Harry Crosby, the rich, sun-dazzled young man who, with his wife (née Polly, but rechristened Caresse), was publishing books. Their Black Sun Press, 'the foal of Necessity, out of Desire' (as Caresse Crosby called it), had been founded in Paris in 1927. From an uncle, Harry Crosby had received a huge illustrated copy of the Egyptian Book of the Dead, and Joyce took this into consideration, rather than Crosby's claim of being a sun-worshipper, in delegating to his American friend the difficulties of Finnegan's night. The Crosbys also threw

---

* Joyce mentioned the book on *Work in Progress* in *Work in Progress:* 'Imagine the twelve deaferended dumbbawls of the whowl abovebeugled to be the contonuation through regeneration of the urutteration of the word in pregross.' (*Finnegans Wake,* 284)

† McAlmon connected Joyce's style and method with glaucoma; Joyce said, 'You may be right, and do you think it has impaired my intellect?' [11]

themselves into the project which was now the aim of all private presses, to publish an excerpt from *Work in Progress*. They negotiated with Eugene and Maria Jolas to ask Joyce for a fragment; he was willing enough, and arranged with them for *Tales Told of Shem and Shaun*, to include 'The Mookse and the Gripes,' 'The Muddest Thick that Ever was Dumped,' and 'The Ondt and the Gracehoper.' They suggested to Joyce that someone write an introduction. He proposed Julian Huxley and J. W. N. Sullivan; when the scientist and the musicologist made excuses, he then proposed C. K. Ogden, rightly surmising that the co-author of *The Meaning of Meaning* and the inventor of Basic English would not resist an invitation to discuss this linguistic experiment. He wished also for Ogden to comment, as a mathematician, upon the structure of *Finnegans Wake*, which he insisted was mathematical.[12] If Ogden had refused, Ford Madox Ford was to have been asked, but Ogden accepted, and later was to translate *Anna Livia Plurabelle* into Basic, and to arrange for Joyce to record that fragment for the Orthological Institute.

Harry and Caresse Crosby wished also to print as a frontispiece to their book a portrait of Joyce. The first thought was for Picasso, who proved however entirely indifferent to Joyce, in part perhaps because Joyce did not belong to Gertrude Stein's company; at any rate, he said he never did portraits *sur commande*.[13] The next choice was Brancusi, who agreed and did several sketches of Joyce. The two men got on well together, both 'deploring,' Joyce wrote Miss Weaver, 'modern feminine fashions, the speed of modern trains etc etc.' [14] Mrs. Crosby thought the sketch, when completed, looked like Joyce but not like a Brancusi, and asked if he could not do something more abstract. He had, he said, a 'Symbol of Joyce' which might be what she wanted. It was a curleycue intended, as Brancusi said later,[15] to express the *'sens du pousser'* which he found in Joyce; the sense of enigmatic involution is also conveyed. Joyce was amused and wrote to Miss Weaver that the design would attract some customers, 'But I wish he or Antheil, say, could or would be as explicit as I try to be when people ask me: And what's this here, Guvnor?' [16] When Brancusi's sketch * was shown to John Joyce in Dublin, he remarked gravely, 'The boy seems to have changed a good deal.' [17]

Joyce kept the Crosbys in a state of controlled fury by endlessly revising the proofs, heaping more and more epithets upon the fabled mookse, ondt, and gracehoper. At last the book was completely set, when the printer came to Mrs. Crosby with the bad news that the last page now contained only two lines, and to look well should have at

* Frontispiece.

least ten. Would she not ask Joyce to add eight lines? She indignantly refused this preposterous suggestion, and the printer went sadly away. The next day he was buoyant again, and showed her the final page, now with ten lines on it. 'Where did you get these?' she asked accusingly. 'Madame will I hope forgive me,' said the printer, 'I went to see Mr. Joyce personally to tell him our troubles. He was very nice—he gave me the text right away. He told me he had been wanting to add more, but was too frightened of you, Madame, to do so.' [18] The book was published in August 1929.

During this year the Italian writer Nino Frank persuaded Joyce to do something unprecedented for him; he allowed his name to appear as one of the editorial committee of the review *Bifur,** which G. Ribemont-Dessaignes was about to launch. Joyce's suggestions for material were all, to Frank's mind, bizarre; he proposed translating Dunsany, the Irishman, Hamish Miles, the Scotsman, or various Australians and Afrikanders, but no English writers. When Frank mentioned Eliot, Joyce grimaced; when Frank remarked that D. H. Lawrence was in Paris, Joyce replied, '*Cet homme écrit vraiment très mal. Demandez plutôt quelque chose à son ami Aldous Huxley, qui s'habille au moins convenablement.*' [19] †

On June 27, Adrienne Monnier was hostess at one of the innumerable celebrations which Joyce's friends arranged to please him. This was a *Déjeuner Ulysse,* a luncheon held a little tardily to commemorate the publication of the French translation of the book in February 1929, and the twenty-fifth anniversary of Bloomsday on June 16. A chartered bus carried the guests from the rue de l'Odéon to Les Vaux-de-Cernay, a tiny village beyond Versailles, chosen because it contained the Hôtel *Léopold.* The guests included Dujardin, Paul Valéry, Soupault, Jules Romains, Fargue, Sylvia Beach, Samuel Beckett, Thomas McGreevy,

---

* Some translations by Auguste Morel of *Pomes Penyeach* appeared in the September 1929 issue of this review.

† 'That man really writes very badly. You might ask instead for something from his friend Aldous Huxley, who at least dresses decently.' When *Lady Chatterley's Lover* began to vie with *Ulysses* as a book for tourists in Paris to buy, Joyce asked Stuart Gilbert to read him some pages from it. He listened carefully, then pronounced only one word: 'Lush!' [20] On December 17, 1931, he wrote Miss Weaver of '*Lady Chatterbox's Lover*': 'I read the first 2 pages of the usual sloppy English, and S. G. read me a lyrical bit about nudism in the wood and the end which is a piece of propaganda in favor of something which, outside of D. H. L.'s country at any rate, makes all the propaganda for itself.' [21] Lawrence had reciprocal feelings about *Ulysses*; as he said to Frieda Lawrence, 'The last part of it is the dirtiest, most indecent, obscene thing ever written. Yes it is, Frieda. . . . It is filthy.' [22] The book's wealth of detail also annoyed him; he wrote in 'Surgery for the Novel—or a Bomb,' ' "Did I feel a twinge in my little toe, or didn't I?" asks every character of Mr. Joyce. . . .' [23]

George Joyce, and Helen Fleischman. After the luncheon, which began
with Paté Léopold, Valéry and Fargue called for speeches, but Joyce,
as usual, objected.[24] On the return journey Beckett kept imploring
Joyce to have the bus stopped so they might have a drink at some way-
side café; Joyce several times obliged him, rousing Paul Valéry and
Adrienne Monnier to anger. At last Beckett had to be, as Joyce said,
'ingloriously abandoned by the wagonette in one of those temporary
palaces which are inseparably associated with the memory of the
Emperor Vespasian.'[25]

The next month James and Nora Joyce went to Torquay, as they had
long wished to do, and Stuart and Moune Gilbert went with them.
They stayed at the Imperial Hotel for a month, and were joined there
by friends from time to time. Miss Weaver came for a week, August
7-14, and went with the Joyces to visit Kent's Cavern where Joyce
wished to see the prehistoric remains. In his usual deliberate, though
seemingly desultory way, Joyce read a series of strange newspapers
and magazines: *The Baker and Confectioner, Boy's Cinema, The
Furniture Record, Poppy's Paper, The Schoolgirls' Own, Woman,
Woman's Friend, Justice of the Peace, The Hairdressers' Weekly*. Most
of these were for use in the second book, that of the children. During
the afternoons he lay on the beach, as he loved to do, fingering the
pebbles for texture and weight. Occasionally he had a rush of energy,
and during one of these vaulted over a wall but fell, because his sight
was poor, on the other side, hurting his arm. In the evenings he went
with Gilbert to local pubs, sipping a little cider (which he did not like),
but mainly listening to several conversations at once and, to Gilbert's
wonder, following them all. He also helped Gilbert to finish his book,
James Joyce's Ulysses, which he listened to chapter by chapter, and
assisted in arranging for its publication in both serial and book form.

The stay in England was made doubly agreeable by the praise which
Joyce received from several of his visitors.* Eliot discussed with him
Faber and Faber's plan of bringing out Gilbert's book and, even more
gratifying, a two-shilling edition of *Anna Livia Plurabelle*.† John

---

* He was equally pleased and more surprised by the praise of Robert Bridges a few
months later. Bridges sent him a copy of *The Testament of Beauty*, inscribed, 'To
Mr. James Joyce from the author in hermeneutic sympathy, R.B. Oct. 1929.'[26]

† Joyce wrote rhymes for the 'blurb' on the dust jacket of *Anna Livia Plurabelle*
and of another booklet, *Haveth Childers Everywhere*. He advertised the first in this
way:

> Buy a book in brown paper
> From Faber & Faber
> To see Annie Liffey trip, tumble and caper.
> Sevensinns in her singthings,

Drinkwater praised the last pages of *Anna Livia* as 'one of the greatest things in English literature,'[27] and James Stephens, to whom Joyce had by now formally proposed that he continue the writing of *Finnegans Wake* if Joyce should lose his sight or heart for the job, promised full help but added, 'You will do it,' and said, '*Anna Livia Plurabelle* is the greatest prose ever written by a man.'[28]

In August the Joyces went to Bristol, perhaps because Henry II presented Dublin as a colony to the Bristolmen,* then went back to London. They paid Claud Sykes a visit at Letchworth, and Joyce was glad to hear of a local resident who was like Earwicker; he succeeded in obtaining a photograph of him. At Drinkwater's suggestion, he consulted a London ophthalmologist, Dr. Euston. He found time also to record the last pages of *Anna Livia* for Ogden at the Orthological Institute; the pages had been prepared for him in half-inch letters, but the light in the studio was so weak that Joyce still could not read them. He had therefore to be prompted in a whisper throughout, his achievement being, as Ogden said, all the more remarkable.

Joyce took the occasion also to meet George Moore, with whom he had one of those contests of politeness in which he took a curious pleasure. As Moore wrote John Eglinton, 'He [Joyce] was distinguished, courteous, respectful, and I was the same. He seemed anxious to accord me the first place. I demurred, and declared him first in Europe. We agreed that our careers were not altogether dissimilar....'[29] Moore said, 'I have been only a revolutionary, while you have been a *heroic* revolutionary, for *you* had no money.' Joyce said, 'Paris has played an equal part in our lives,'[30] and referred to their mutual friend Dujardin, who figures largely in Moore's *Confessions of a Young Man.* Moore asked how the action or the thought of *Ulysses* was advanced by associating the minor acts of Bloom with the acts of Ulysses, and Joyce

---

> Plurabelle on her prose,
> Seashell ebb music wayriver she flows.

and the second:

> Humptydump Dublin squeaks through his norse,
> Humptydump Dublin hath a horrible vorse
> And with all his kinks english
> Plus his irismanx brogues
> Humptydump Dublin's grandada of all rogues.

He was a little annoyed when the publicity department of Faber & Faber used them only on a mimeographed publicity release, to which they prefixed a note: 'The Sales department, puzzled as such departments are wont to be, have sought some light on the two James Joyce contributions to Criterion Miscellany. Below the explanations offered are passed on that you may be able to derive similar enlightenment.'

* *Finnegans Wake* (545).

answered, 'I see I am on my defense.' [31] Moore apologized, and then
Joyce said it would please him if Moore would accept a copy of the
French translation of *Ulysses*. Moore answered, 'I shall be delighted
to accept any book you choose to send me, but I hope you don't mind
my reminding you that I can read English.' Joyce smiled 'a hesitating
smile, reminding me,' said Moore to Louis Gillet, 'of La Gioconda,' [32]
but sent the book anyway. Moore wrote to thank him, but in French.
'I look forward to reading it all the winter.' [33] After having read a few
pages he commented to Janet Flanner, 'It cannot be a novel, for there
isn't a tree in it.' * [34]

From London the Joyces went to Dover, where they hesitated over
the crossing until Nora felt certain no storm was brewing, since light-

---

* Moore expressed this view more fully in a letter of August 20, 1931, to Louis
Gillet:

My dear Mr. Gillet,

It was kind indeed of you to send me the number of 'La Revue des Deux
Mondes,' containing your article on Joyce, and it is my pleasure to write to
congratulate you on having achieved an article on a literary subject as well
considered as an article by Sainte-Beuve. I am lost in admiration of the
thought that you have put into this article and it required thought and consideration and reading and re-reading to disentangle Joyce's metaphysics. I
say metaphysics for Joyce's book has nothing to do with art, nor yet science,
so I suppose it must be metaphysics. Art is concerned with what the eye sees
and not with the thinking mind. To the mind life is but the dreaming of a
shade, but our actions arise from the belief that it is a great deal more than
a shade and history will continue to be written notwithstanding Mr. Joyce's
protest. I am by temperament an artist, that is to say by temperament one
who is interested in appearance; a metaphysician only in the belief that the
appearance may be illuminated faintly by a moral conception, but oh so
faintly! With Joyce it is just the opposite. There are no appearances in Joyce;
it is all syllogism, but I hope it will serve my present purpose. Joyce was in
England some time ago. He had recovered his sight to some extent and lost
his speech. I always heard of him in Dublin as one of the most garrulous of
men. Now, he sits as silent as a mummy. He dined with me two nights and
I had to make conversation all the time, which was tedious. . . . And by the
next post I received a primer explaining all the mysteries of *Ulysses* and
learnt from it that when Bloom smokes a corpulent cigar the reader is
obliged to think of the Greek wanderer who blinds Polyphemus with a fire-
hardened stake. I wrote to Joyce telling him that up to the present I had
looked upon myself as a competent judge of a work of art and failing completely to discover the literary effect aimed at in the analogy of Bloom and his
cigar and the wanderer's fire-hardened stake, I concluded that one of us had
a blind patch in his mind somewhere. Which of us it is it would be an af-
fectation for me to decide. . . . [35]

Joyce and Moore maintained exaggeratedly courteous relations until Moore's
death, when Joyce sent a funeral wreath inscribed 'To George Moore from James
Joyce.' The newspapers made no mention of this tribute, to Joyce's great indignation, which he expressed in a flood of letters. Moore's executors apologized for
the omission.

ning on the Channel was more than her husband could stand. During
October Joyce completed in Paris the last watch of Shaun for the
November issue of *transition,* in which he was not to publish again until
February 1933. The review was suspended for two years for financial
reasons, and in the interval Joyce took to private presses. The first and
third books were now virtually drafted; he had left most of the second
book and all the fourth, which however was to be only a single chapter.
He felt for the moment unwilling to launch out upon the difficult problems of the second book. Instead he talked with Fargue about turning
Anna Livia Plurabelle into French; he encouraged Herbert Hughes
in his plan to compile *The Joyce Book,* a group of musical settings of
Joyce's poems, which was not published until early 1933; and he spent
a week in November explaining to James Stephens the whole plan of
Finnegans Wake. Stephens promised him 'if I found it was madness to
continue, in my condition, and saw no other way out, that he would
devote himself heart and soul to the completion of it, that is the second
part and the epilogue or fourth.'[36] Stephens had by now become so
much a part of Joyce's phantasmagoria that Joyce could freely beguile
himself with the fancy of transferring authorship.

During these November days, when the knowledge that he had no
more *transition* deadlines to meet made Joyce feel what he described
as 'a sudden kind of drop,'[37] he suddenly came upon an interest even
more engrossing than the English Players had been in Zurich. Stanislaus
wrote to tell him of an Irish tenor, John Sullivan,[*] who had sung in
Trieste and, when Stanislaus met him, was engaged in reading *A Portrait of the Artist as a Young Man.*[38] Stanislaus had urged Sullivan to
call on James when he returned to sing at the Paris Opera in late 1929;
James was greatly pleased with him. He felt an immediate burst of com-
patriotic tenderness for this Corkman, of a Kerry family, who at the age
of twelve had come to Rouen,[†] and now after many vicissitudes was a
leading tenor of the French opera company. But his attitude changed
from sympathy to violent partisanship when he heard Sullivan sing for
the first time. The opera was *Tannhäuser,* the plot ridiculous to Joyce
('What sort of a fellow is this Tannhäuser who, when he is with Saint
Elizabeth, longs for the bordello of Venusberg, and when he is at the
bordello longs to be with Saint Elizabeth?'),[39] but Sullivan's voice
thrilled him. He booked tickets for every opera, went next to hear
Samson, jubilant at seeing an Irishman from Dan O'Connell's county
singing the role of the Hebrew from the land of Dan. Next he saw *Les*

---

[*] He sometimes called himself John O'Sullivan, but Joyce asked him to drop the
O' 'for the love of music.'[40]
[†] Sullivan made his debut in Toulouse in 1911.

Huguenots, then Berlioz' *La Damnation de Faust,* of which Sullivan complained that he did not so much mind the damnation of Faust as the domination of Mephistopheles,[41] and finally in October Joyce attended the centenary performance of *Guillaume Tell,* in which Sullivan sang the role of Arnold with such address that Joyce was beside himself.* Sullivan could reach high C's with an ease no tenor of the time could match; Joyce followed the music counting ecstatically the number of his friend's high notes. 'I have been through the score of *Guillaume Tell,*' he reported, 'and I discover that Sullivan sings 456 G's, 93 A-flats, 54 B-flats, 15 B's, 19 C's and 2 C-sharps. Nobody else can do it.'[42] To Sullivan he wrote jokingly, '*La bénédiction des poignards n'est rien à côté de vous.*'[43] † and to Samuel Beckett he said soberly, 'Sullivan's voice has three dimensions.'[44] When Frank Budgen said Sullivan's voice reminded him of the Forth Bridge, Joyce pondered and then said, 'That's very good, Budgen, but it isn't right. That is not the voice of iron, it is the voice of stone. Stonehenge is the comparison, not the Forth Bridge.'[45]

He and Sullivan began to meet often; once they were photographed together with James Stephens, and Joyce suggested the picture be captioned, 'Three Irish Beauties.'[46] Sullivan had, as Joyce noted, the body of a member of the Dublin Metropolitan Police, and looked like someone who had 'escaped from a boarding-school at the age of forty-nine.'[47] His family life was deeply entangled between a wife and a mistress, he supported eleven people, and did not need much persuasion from Joyce to have a drink. His complicated personality seems to have aroused Joyce's comradely impulses; as he said to Miss Weaver in summary, 'In temperament he is intractable, quarrelsome, disconnected, contemptuous, inclined to bullying, undiplomatic; but on the other hand good humoured, sociable, unaffected, amusing and well informed.'[48] Sullivan explained to Joyce that he had been prevented by the 'Italian ring,'[49] which favored the tenors Caruso, Martinelli, and Lauri-Volpi, from singing at Covent Garden, the Metropolitan Opera, and the Chicago Opera. As Joyce's agile mind reconstructed a whole history of persecution of his fellow-artist, Sullivan became for him a cause as well as a friend. The charming tribute Joyce wrote to Sullivan a year later, 'From a Banned Writer to a Banned Singer,'[50] suggests his

---

* Thereafter Joyce always skipped the third act of this opera, because Arnold does not appear in it. But he admired Rossini's evocation of the theme of father and fatherland.[51]

† 'The blessing of the daggers is nothing beside you.' The blessing of the daggers is, as Sullivan said, 'a big noise in the fourth act of *Les Huguenots.*'[52]

insistence upon the resemblance of their situations. Those of his friends who did not understand Joyce's constant search for likenesses between himself and other people, wondered what he was about; Wyndham Lewis, refusing to wonder, wittily assured Augustus John that Sullivan was only an *idée fixe* of Joyce, a kind of 'Mrs. Harris,' who had no real existence. But Joyce saw Sullivan as an *alter ego* who had pursued the career he himself had rejected, and had then encountered the same opposition in music which Joyce had encountered in literature. Roused by the challenge of making another career, now vicariously in another art, Joyce extended to Sullivan an almost motherly solicitude.

His exertions for Sullivan began in November. At first there was a vague notion that Sullivan would help George, as in fact he was eager to do, but he was soon so busy receiving Joyce's help himself that this minor mission faded from sight. Joyce's method was simple: he bestirred all his friends to come to the opera, usually in seats he provided for them, to cheer for Sullivan (he himself cried 'Bravo Cork!'),⁵³ and then to meet the tenor afterwards at the Café de la Paix or, less formally, at the Café Versailles on the Place de Rennes. If any failed to come, he was vexed and even angry. These friends were then expected to write to patrons of the arts; in this way Aldington and Richard Le Gallienne were deputed to approach Otto Kahn, and Joyce reinforced them by sending Kahn a signed copy of *Ulysses*. Kahn came with Joyce to see *Tell* in November 1930, but did nothing. Joyce urged Antheil to take an interest, got John Pollock of the *Morning Post* to write two articles, brought Philippe Soupault, who knew some musical bigwigs, to hear him, and persuaded Gilbert, Jolas, Sylvia Beach, and Adrienne Monnier to join in the propaganda. He persuaded William Bird to write an article in the *New York Sun* ascribing a boycott of Sullivan by the Boston Opera House to a promise made to John McCormack, supposedly jealous of Sullivan, that no other Irish tenor would sing there. The Boston authorities vigorously denied that any such promise had been made, and Bird felt foolish, but Joyce assured him it was still good publicity for Sullivan.⁵⁴ By March 18, 1930, Joyce announced that he had got notices about Sullivan into the *Daily Telegraph, Daily News, Manchester Guardian, Irish Independent, Irish Statesman, Chicago Daily Tribune, New York World, New York Sun* (twice), *Daily Mail, New York Times* (with a photograph), *l'Intransigeant* and *La Rampe* of Paris. Then Sullivan had an engagement to sing in Algiers, to the great relief of Nora Joyce, and there was a respite.

Joyce's activities on Sullivan's behalf were made more difficult by his fading eyesight. He had lugubrious discussions about this time with

Aldous Huxley,* [55] also a victim of eye trouble, and with Thomas W. Pugh, a fellow-Dubliner who pleased him by knowing *Ulysses* and Dublin almost as intimately as he did himself. Pugh was blind in one eye, and Joyce eagerly asked his birth year, which was 1883; he then said with more friendliness than accuracy, 'We are much alike, both of us blind in one eye, and both born in the same year.' [56] He was excited to learn that Eamon De Valera had eye trouble and was born in 1882, and both Pugh and De Valera appear in *Finnegans Wake*, the latter as one of the models for Shaun. While mulling over such unities of fate, Joyce continued to see Dr. Borsch, until Borsch died. Joyce, always tender of eye specialists, went to the funeral. Later he went first to Collinson, Borsch's assistant, then to Dr. Edward Hartmann, who also tried to help Lucia's strabismus. Neither was able to give the instant relief he craved. Then in February 1930, as a result of an article about Joyce in the *Neue Zürcher Zeitung*, he had letters from two Swiss friends. Georges Borach wrote to urge Joyce to see Professor Alfred Vogt, [57] a brilliant Swiss surgeon in Zurich who took spectacular chances and often achieved spectacular results. The second letter was from a stranger source, Marthe Fleischmann; it was written with formality, recalling that they had once been 'neighbours' in Zurich, and told of several of Vogt's miraculous cures. She signed her letter, '*Mit den freundlichen Grüssen.*' [58] Joyce listened also to praise of Vogt by two new friends from Zurich, Sigfried Giedion, the author of *Space, Time and Architecture*, and his wife Carola Giedion-Welcker, the art critic. He now made arrangements through Borach to consult Vogt in April 1930. It seemed the moment also to change his way of life, which had been unduly stabilized for several years by his residence in Square Robiac. The flat had become too noisy, he complained; he might have to spend much time in Zurich, and he would be better off with a less permanent arrangement. He also considered establishing domicile in England, chiefly for testamentary purposes, so that his children could inherit his property under English law without complication. For this purpose it would be prudent to be legally married, and he concocted a fine tale about a putative marriage in Trieste which was not legally binding for various imaginative reasons. Miss Weaver came to Paris

---

* Joyce and Huxley exchanged a few visits. Huxley's account of one suggests why there were not more: 'I remember a dinner party at which we unfortunately served red wine, whereas he liked only white. At her end of the table my wife and another literary guest, the late Pierre Drieu la Rochelle, had the greatest difficulty in drawing him into conversation. Finally in despair my wife said something about the flowers on the table: to which he said laconically, "I hate flowers," and lapsed into silence.' [59]

to discuss his plans with him in early April, and immediately thereafter, quite properly putting eyesight before matrimony, he went to Zurich.

It was unexpectedly pleasant to see Zurich again. 'What a city!' Joyce exclaimed to the Giedions, 'A lake, a mountain, and two rivers!' [60] Vogt, when consulted, was surprisingly optimistic, and promised him the sight of at least one eye. Joyce wrote this news to George Moore, who replied dogmatically, 'One eye is quite sufficient; a man is as well off with one as with two.' [61] Joyce was a little frightened, even though he said Zurich had always brought him luck, and checked again with Dr. Collinson in Paris before consenting to his eleventh operation. On May 15, 1930, Vogt operated on the left eye for tertiary cataract; he cut through the cataract horizontally but could not complete the surgery because the vitreous body (the gelatinous substance which fills the eyeball behind the crystalline lens), much of it lost in the last two operations, seemed likely to collapse completely. Ten days later Joyce suffered an attack of mechanical iritis due to the presence of blood, but after ten hours this passed away. A week later leeches were applied which removed all the blood from the anterior chamber of the eye. Then on June 3 Vogt examined the eye microscopically and determined that the incision made had remained open and unclogged; blood had however entered into the vitreous body, and the eye, weakened by so many operations, would need some months to eliminate it. Vogt also predicted that he would have to perform a tenth operation, a capsulotomy, to remove the back wall of the capsule of the lens, which had gradually become over-clouded since Borsch's last operation and was now in a condition of almost secondary cataract, occluding practical sight. The right eye had a complicated cataract which would also have to be operated upon in an eleventh operation. In June Vogt offered some general observations:

It has been decided to defer the tenth operation till middle of September 1930. The operation just performed will probably produce a slight ameliora-tion of vision in the left eye, which before had a seeing power of 1/800 to 1/1000. On the other hand the seeing power of the right eye, estimated some months ago at 1/30, diminished constantly but slowly as the cataract de-veloped. The most favorable factor in the case is that, according to all medical opinions, in both eyes optic nerve and periphery of the retina func-tioned perfectly normally. It is Professor Vogt's belief that the macula also is normal and that, if the two operations still necessary are made with special instruments and when the eyes are in a non-glaucomatous condition, there is every hope of obtaining ultimately a fair measure of clear and practical vision.° [62]

° Vogt never allowed Joyce to pay for treatment. Eamon de Valera also became one of Vogt's patients, but did not receive the same favor.

The first thing Joyce saw with his operated eye was a red rose on Helen Fleischman's dress. By mid-June he could safely take a train, and he had Nora write Miss Weaver of his regret that he could not come to London to hear Sullivan sing, at long last, at Covent Garden on June 20, 1930. His eyes were better, but he expressly asked her not to mention them to anyone.[63] He returned to Paris and heard from Sullivan that Lauri-Volpi had just sung *William Tell* and had been applauded by the critics for a splendid performance. It is easy to see Joyce's hand behind the letter (in French) which Sullivan now sent to the press:

39 rue de Clichy, Paris

CHALLENGE

Justice above everything!

Since the music critic of the New York Herald of Paris, M. Louis Schneider, has described to his numerous readers the presentation of Rossini's *Guillaume Tell* with M. Lauri-Volpi in the role of Arnold as one worthy of a great artist, I permit myself, in my capacity as holder of this role for years at the Académie Nationale de Musique, to declare that M. Volpi has permitted himself to cut out a little over half of his part, suppressing the recitatives, diminishing the trio, and completely avoiding the perilous duel with the final chorus. Moreover I challenge M. Lauri-Volpi to sing this role in the way his compatriot Rossini wrote it and in the way I have myself sung it hundreds of times in the principal cities of France, Belgium, and even of Italy, where this opera, buried for want of a tenor who could sing it since the death of the celebrated Tamagno (who sang it last in 1889), was resuscitated by me in 1922 at the San Carlo theatre in Naples, under M. Tullio Serafin's direction. I therefore propose to M. Volpi to sing this role complete, without transpositions or cuts, in any concert hall in Paris where I can sing it too. I allow as arbiter of these two performances M. L. Schneider himself, to whom I will offer on the occasion a copy of the original publication of this opera in an elegant binding, convinced as I am that a musical amateur such as he seems to be can only be particularly pleased at making direct acquaintance again with a masterpiece which he seems to have largely forgotten.

(Signed)   John Sullivan [64]

Paris, June 18, 1930

Sullivan's engagement at Covent Garden was mysteriously canceled, however, and Joyce now put into effect the plan that had been in his mind since he discovered his sight was returning. On June 30, 1930, he attended a performance of *Guillaume Tell* by Sullivan in the Paris Opéra, and in the midst of it, as a newspaper notice said, 'the audience were witnesses of a dramatic scene which exceeded in intensity the drama being played on the stage. . . . A sudden hush fell . . . when a man in one of the boxes, whom many recognized as James Joyce, the Irish novelist and poet, dramatically leaned forward, raised a pair of heavy dark glasses from his eyes, and exclaimed: '*Merci, mon Dieu, pour ce miracle. Après vingt ans, je revois la lumière.*' * [65] This was the most spectacular bit of publicity Joyce had ever devised. In the newspaper articles he contrived to have Sullivan mentioned prominently, and Vogt also. His Paris doctors had given him permission to take off his dark glasses only during the opera, he said (and the journalists obediently reported). It was no wonder that at manifestations of such zeal Adrienne Monnier and Sylvia Beach asked him why he was doing so much for a little known tenor. But Joyce truculently replied, 'Since I came to Paris I have been introduced to a great number of recognized geniuses in literature, music, painting and sculpture; for me all these persons are quite sympathetic and friendly, but they are all, for me, perhapses; there is no perhaps about Sullivan's voice.' [66]

He rapidly followed this first fine maneuver in the boxes with another. After Sullivan sang the aria, '*Asile héréditaire,*' in the fourth act,† Joyce shouted in excitement, '*Bravo Sullivan! Merde pour Lauri-Volpi!*' There was laughter and applause, though someone in a nearby box commented, '*Il va un peu fort celui-là!*' [67] He next decided to put pressure upon Sir Thomas Beecham through Nancy Cunard, whom he had not met. Without hesitation he paid a call on her one day when she was in bed with throat trouble, groped his way to a chair, and said, 'I am James Joyce.' Nancy Cunard's description of the incident gives a fine impression of his tenacity:

Soon he came to the point: Sullivan, a very great Irish singer. Now, Sullivan was not getting the recognition he deserved and this must be set right at once. Well, Lady Cunard, my mother, was a very great friend of the orchestra leader, Sir Thomas Beecham, who should be made to realize that Sullivan must be engaged forthwith. Had Beecham ever heard of him? I could not say. Why was Beecham not interested? Well, what he, Joyce, wanted me to do was to use all my influence with Lady Cunard so that Beecham should hear, and engage, Sullivan. I presume Joyce thought this quite simple. What he probably did not know was that my relations with her were not of the friendliest; at any rate, I had no 'influence' with her whatsoever—as I now tried to make clear. Joyce would have none of that and brushed it aside. I assured him that I would, of course, tell her that he

---

* 'Thanks be to God for this miracle. After twenty years I see the light once more.'
† Joyce later proposed to the Giedions a new fourth act for *William Tell,* in which, to apotheosize Switzerland, countless hotel porters would gather and sing a final triumphant aria. [68]

had come to see me about the matter; more than that I could not possibly do. I thought he seemed annoyed and did not believe me. Sullivan *must* be engaged. And when I reminded him that he knew Lady Cunard himself and that she would be likely to listen to him, that too was brushed aside, and, somehow, I did not feel like recalling to him that she had been very instrumental, indeed, in 1917 or so, in obtaining public recognition for his great talent as a writer, recognition that could not have been more official, and on a financial plane, too. Joyce went on: Lady Cunard was in Paris now, Thomas Beecham as well, or soon coming, Sullivan was in Paris, and so they must be brought together. I must have said that this was more than I could do, but that he could accomplish it, if only he would get in touch with Lady Cunard; or why not directly with Sir Thomas? I fancy Joyce liked none of this. Obviously his mind had been made up: I, and I alone, must be the approach. 'How displeasing it is to be put in a false position—maybe he has taken offence,' I thought, as I sprang off the bed to try and guide him discreetly to the door after the half-hour's conversation. It was horrifying to see him grope, miraculous to see his adroit descent of the stairs, the tall, cathedral-spire of a man. As for Lady Cunard, would she even listen? She did not listen much.[69]

In two weeks Joyce was back again, this time at Nancy Cunard's Hours Press. Sullivan *must* be engaged. Could Miss Cunard not realize the urgency? He even dropped a hint that if Sullivan were engaged, a little piece of writing by a well-known author might find its way to the Hours Press for publication. She spoke to her mother again.[70]

Then Joyce and Nora left for London, where Joyce persisted in his Sullivanizing. Through Wyndham Lewis he got in touch with Lady Ottoline Morrell; he saw the Irish High Commissioner in London, John Dulanty, and several members of the Guinness family. Then he went on to Oxford for a few days and finally, in Llandudno (Wales), quelled his busy spirit momentarily on the strand. He listened, however, to Welsh, as several years before he had listened to Breton, trying to master the differences among the various Celtic languages. From Wales he and Nora came back to France, and in early September spent some days at Étretat. They returned to Paris in time to renew the Sullivan campaign with the opening of the fall opera season. A taxi accident in which Joyce was slightly injured did not impede his efforts.

Like many of Joyce's unreasonable plans, the one involving Sir Thomas Beecham worked. The much importuned Beecham consented to attend *Guillaume Tell* with Lady Cunard at the end of September, and Joyce, who accompanied them, listened with impatience for the conductor's verdict. 'It is certainly an amazing voice,' Beecham granted,[*][71] and

* In writing to Mrs. Herbert Gorman on October 5, 1930, Joyce slightly dilated Beecham's comment into, 'It is the most amazing tenor voice I have ever heard.'

promised to try to bring him to London. With this encouragement, Joyce broached to George Antheil the idea of writing an opera for Sullivan based upon Byron's *Cain*,[72] a drama in which Byron antici- pated Joyce's interpretation of Cain and Abel as light-bringing Shem and conforming Shaun. Joyce would be willing to suggest cuts in the libretto. But would he be willing to rewrite it? asked Antheil. 'I would never have the bad manners to rewrite the text of a great English poet,' Joyce replied.[73] 'Somebody must curtail the text of the first and third acts and if it is to the advantage of the scheme in general my name may be used. I am quite content to go down to posterity as a scissors and paste man for that seems to me a harsh but not unjust description. The second act is more difficult. In my opinion this will have to be done choreographically.' To Antheil's objection that he could scarcely dictate the choice of the tenor to an opera house, Joyce urged him to write the part in 'the pure tenor tradition,'[74] thus automatically excluding all tenors but Sullivan. But Antheil was in such great discomfort, that Joyce reluctantly allowed him to wrench free of the scheme, not with- out a last-minute hope of pulling him back.

It would be most unfair on my part to try to influence you in any way as to your future plans so please discount me altogether. I offered this suggestion to you because you asked me for one and because of certain parts of your music deemed by me to be akin to the voice which is causing all this unnecessary correspondence. If you feel that you cannot write this opera at once with enthusiasm and with spiritual profit to yourself and your art without any consideration for the veer- ing tastes of impresarios please say so without hesitation and allow me to offer poor Byron and poorer Sullivan elsewhere.

I enclose a notice, which please return to me with your reply, from a Genoese paper of last week about Sullivan's reappearance in the land of song after seven years in the musical wilderness. Quite a lot of Ligurian spray will dash the quays of La Superba before any sex- appealing hack from Covent Garden or the Metropolitan obtains from the only audience in the world which knows what singing is one tithe of that recognition.

I got up out of bed at three o'clock a.m. to type this and will now ring down the curtain for this night, sending you both in valediction my best wishes for the coming year and again asking you to let me hear from you by return of post.

One point more. You will be in error if you imagine that I have any real influence with the wealthy musicophiles in London and New York who control the destinies of opera in those cities. My experience of them so far is that they are uncommonly pleased to accept from me signed editions de luxe of my literary works and that when they are told what notes a singer is actually emitting at any given moment, their faces express the most sympathetic interest.

　　　　　　　　　　　　　　　　Sincerely yours
　　　　　　　　　　　　　　　　James Joyce

3/1/1931

Apart from cutting *Cain* and trying to win Antheil over, there was not much Joyce could do for Sullivan while the singer was away on tour from November 1930 until the following spring. In mid-November, between sitting for Augustus John * and having his eyes checked by Vogt in Zurich, he found time to turn at last to *Finnegans Wake,* to which he had added nothing for over a year, and he now wrote out the first section of the second part. It cost him much trouble, coming out, he said, 'like drops of blood,' yet it pleased him as 'the gayest and lightest thing I have done.' [75] He based this section, the games of the children, upon the game of 'Angels and Devils' or 'Colours' which he had played as a child, and saw beneath the surface a vigorous sexual combat of Shem and Shaun.

During 1930 Joyce had published only one fragment, *Haveth Childers Everywhere,* with Henry Babou and Jack Kahane; Faber and Faber's edition of it appeared the following year. The German translation of *Ulysses* went into second and third editions, and Dr. Daniel Brody, who owned and managed the Rhein-Verlag in Zurich, asked the psychologist Jung to write a preface for the third edition. Jung did so, but it was disparaging to Joyce, and Brody felt obliged to submit it to Joyce in late September for his approval. It was a useful expression of Jungian theory, but showed little comprehension of the text, and contained such gratuitous slurs as that the book could be read as easily backwards as forwards. Joyce's book was made an example of the schizophrenic mind. Joyce read the preface and sent Brody a curt wire, '*Niedrigerhängen,*' [76] meaning 'Ridicule it by making it public.' His friends Ivan Goll and Valery Larbaud wrote Brody privately, however, to urge him not to follow Joyce's instructions, and he decided to accept their advice. Joyce commented to Georg Goyert of Jung, 'He seems to have read *Ulysses* from first to last without one smile. The only thing to do in such a case is to change one's drink.' [77] When he met Brody he asked, 'Why is Jung so rude to me? He doesn't even know me.

---

* John said Joyce had 'a buttoned-up look,' and surprised Joyce, at the end of the sittings, by embracing him. Joyce did not, however, like John's drawings, which he thought failed to represent accurately the lower part of his face.

　　He sat for a series of artists including Ivan Opfer, Émile Bécat, Myron Nutting, Frank Budgen, Jo Davidson, Sean O'Sullivan, and Jacques Émile Blanche. To Blanche he remarked, 'I was fond of pictures, but now the nails on the walls are quite enough.'

People want to put me out of the church to which I don't belong. I have nothing to do with psychoanalysis.' Brody replied, 'There can be only one explanation. Translate your name into German.' * [78]

Jung greatly improved his article and published it separately in 1932. In its modified form it was not devoid of respect, and Jung sent Joyce a copy with a rather flattering letter:

Küsnacht-Zürich
Seestrasse 228

James Joyce esq.
  Hotel Elite
    Zurich

Dear Sir,

Your Ulysses has presented the world such an upsetting psychological problem, that repeatedly I have been called in as a supposed authority on psychological matters.

Ulysses proved to be an exceedingly hard nut and it has forced my mind not only to most unusual efforts, but also to rather extravagant peregrinations (speaking from the standpoint of a scientist). Your book as a whole has given me no end of trouble and I was brooding over it for about three years until I succeeded to put myself into it. But I must tell you that I'm profoundly grateful to yourself as well as to your gigantic opus, because I learned a great deal from it. I shall probably never be quite sure whether I did enjoy it, because it meant too much grinding of nerves and of grey matter. I also don't know whether you will enjoy what I have written about Ulysses because I couldn't help telling the world how much I was bored, how I grumbled, how I cursed and how I admired. The 40 pages of non stop run in the end is a string of veritable psychological peaches. I suppose the devil's grandmother knows so much about the real psychology of a woman, I didn't.

Well I just try to recommend my little essay to you, as an amusing attempt of a perfect stranger that went astray in the labyrinth of your Ulysses and happened to get out of it again by sheer good luck. At all events you may gather from my article what Ulysses has done to a supposedly balanced psychologist.

With the expression of my deepest appreciation, I remain, dear Sir,

Yours faithfully
C. G. Jung

Joyce proudly displayed this tribute to his psychological penetration, but Nora said of her husband, 'He knows nothing at all about women.' [79]

In his affairs during 1930 and almost to the end of his life Joyce

* Freud.

had the assistance of a new friend, Paul Léopold * Léon, a name
which, since it included Bloom's two names Leopold Paula, seemed
a talisman. Léon and his wife Lucie † had emigrated from Russia at
the end of 1918, going first to London, and then in 1921 to Paris.
Léon had been trained in law as well as in literature; he did editorial
work for a review of jurisprudence, and had published two books,
Lettres de Nicolas II et de sa mère (1928) and *Benjamin Constant*
(1930). In spite of these studious undertakings, Léon was personally
light and whimsical. He and Joyce met through George's friend Alex
Ponisovsky, Léon's brother-in-law, who was giving Joyce lessons in
Russian. The friendship suited both men. Léon's attitude towards Joyce
was respectful but bantering, and utterly devoted. When Joyce wrote
a note of thanks to him in April 1930, for help he had given, Léon
replied sincerely, 'One thing I do object to—it is your thanks to me
which I do feel I cannot ever thank you enough for having allowed
me to observe the formation of your thoughts which is, I confess, both
captivating and meaningful. I think that had I known Browning I
would have hardly enjoyed anything comparable to the joys of listening to you.' [80] Léon made a jest of the fact that he had never read
Ulysses and understood nothing of *Finnegans Wake;* he assumed unquestioningly, however, that both were masterpieces, and wrote his
brother on June 3, 1930:

Lately I've been spending a lot of time with literature. I have been working
with Joyce. The name probably means nothing to you, but it is that of the
great, the greatest writer of our time. And yet he is writing in a way that
nobody understands or can understand. It's a kind of 'petit nègre' which is
probably perfect. I've found it wonderfully amusing to translate simple ideas
into incomprehensible formulas and to feel it may be a masterpiece. [81]

Such irreverent reverence before the new evangel drew Joyce to him,
and as for Léon, he found his life surrounded by Joyce's. '*Il y a une
ambiance qui vous enveloppe,*' he said to his wife, trying to explain
it; '*c'est comme du coton.*' ‡ [82] Or, as he put it more formally in print,
'As one grew to know him [Joyce], one became as it were enveloped
by a fine network of half-expressed thoughts and feelings that created
an atmosphere of such suavity that it was difficult to resist, all the
more so since it contained no element of restraint.' [83] He sank into it
without regret. Philippe Soupault, observing them walking together,

---

* Actually the patronymic Leopoldovich.
† Madame Léon writes for the *New York Herald Tribune* of Paris under the name
of Lucie Noël.
‡ Helen Nutting said, 'He puts out feelers, like a sea anemone.' [84]

Joyce groping, Léon tall but stooped, called them 'l'aveugle et le paralytique.' [85]

The friendship was made firmer by the fact that the Léons were friendly with Helen Fleischman and George Joyce, and on December 10, 1930, when these two were married, the Léons were present at the ceremony. The marriage, though not unexpected, at first displeased Nora as well as Lucia, since George and his wife were ten years apart in age. Joyce also had his reservations, but made no attempt to change George's mind. After the marriage Helen and her mother-in-law became close friends, and Helen, who dressed remarkably well, taught Nora a great deal about clothes. As a result Nora began to buy her hats from Agnès, the fashionable milliner, and her dresses from Helen's skillful dressmaker. Joyce approved this new interest; as he grew older, women more and more seemed to him dolls, unfortunately not mindless, to be got up as prettily as possible. When Frank Budgen protested, in the midst of one of his now frequent diatribes against women, that in the old days he had at least thought their bodies desirable and provoking, Joyce retorted, 'Macchè! Perhaps I did. But now I don't care a damn about their bodies.* I am only interested in their clothes.' [86] The bills from Agnès and others that came in to gratify this interest did not dismay him.

Out of consideration for himself as well as posterity, Joyce had decided that a book about his life should follow Gilbert's book on *Ulysses.* In this way he could make sure that his image, mirrored in another man's eyes, might be given the world as little distorted as possible. While in Salzburg in 1927, he broached the matter to Gilbert, who declined, perhaps feeling that he would be called upon to interpret Joyce in Joyce's way rather than his own. He took pleasure in needling Joyce gently, at the height of some recitation of miseries, by saying, 'You're a very lucky man. You have money, fame, a family.' [87] Joyce smiled slightly, did not contradict him, and looked for another biographer. Fortunately there was one in Paris, Herbert Gorman, who had already written one book on Joyce and could easily write another. Gorman's work had been chiefly in the historical novel, but Joyce thought this training might help him. Without saying so to Gorman directly, he made clear that he was to be treated as a saint with an unusually protracted martyrdom.

Gorman began his work enthusiastically at the end of December

---

* He told Helen Nutting, when they spoke of beautiful women, 'I don't see any and I don't think there are any.' [88] When Arthur Power asked what Italian women were like, he replied, 'Cold like all women.' [89] Love he dismissed as 'a temptation of nature in one's youth,' [90] and even said to Jolas, 'When I hear the word "love" I feel like puking.' [91]

1930, talked with Joyce, submitted questionnaires to him and other friends, and wrote to Stanislaus Joyce for assistance. As he proceeded, he found his subject sometimes co-operative, at other times oddly reticent; Joyce furnished Gorman with much information about some incidents, about others suggested he go to ask people in other cities, a procedure which Gorman, pressed for money, was not able to follow. Gorman had difficulty also with some of Joyce's friends such as Ezra Pound, who refused to be bothered with the past, or with others who planned their own volumes of reminiscence. Even those who were disposed to co-operate, such as Harriet Weaver and Sylvia Beach, were not so immediately available for candid discussion as Gorman would have liked.[92] Joyce had let it be understood that the biography was to be an authorized one, but there were moments when he lost interest; so he said to Byrne, who protested the choice of Gorman as biographer, 'I don't care what they write.' [93] On the other hand, he prodded Stanislaus to send Gorman copies of his letters, and Stanislaus did so, reluctantly and slowly. The original plan had been for Gorman to finish his book in about a year, but to Joyce's irritation it was not ready then or for many years thereafter.*

In the month just before Gorman began work, and during the days of their early consultations in December 1930, Joyce, with his secondary passion for extending other languages as he had extended English, was hard at the French translation of *Anna Livia Plurabelle*. It had been begun by Samuel Beckett and a young French friend, Alfred Péron, who had spent a year at Trinity College in Dublin. The original plan was for Beckett to continue as the principal translator, but he had to return to Ireland. His work was thereupon revised by Paul Léon, Eugene Jolas, and Ivan Goll, under Joyce's supervision. It was decided that the French version must be revamped again, and at the end of November Philippe Soupault was enlisted to meet with Joyce and Léon every Thursday at 2:30 in Léon's flat on the rue Casimir Périer. They sat for three hours at a round table, which Léon threatened to sell if Joyce would inscribe his name upon it; [94] and while Joyce smoked in an armchair Léon read the English text, Sou-

---

* Joyce was always friendly with the Gormans, and on one occasion, when Mrs. (Jean) Gorman complained to him that John Holms, who came often with Peggy Guggenheim to see them, never wanted to leave, he wrote a poem:

To Mrs. Herbert Gorman who complains that her visitors kept late hours:
  Go ca'canny with the cognac and of the wine fight shy
  Keep a watch upon the hourglass but leave the beaker dry
  Guest friendliness to callers is your surest thief of time
  They're so much at Holms when with you, they can't dream of
                                      Guggenheim.[95]

pault read the French, and Joyce or one of the others would break into the antiphony to ask that a phrase be reconsidered. Joyce then explained the ambiguities he had intended, and he or one of his collaborators dug up an equivalent. Joyce's great emphasis was upon the flow of the line, and he sometimes astonished them (as later, when he was helping Nino Frank with the Italian translation, he astonished him), by caring more for sound and rhythm than sense. But one or the other would insist upon rigor of this kind, too. The final draft, arrived at in March after fifteen meetings, was sent to Jolas and Adrienne Monnier, both of whom made important suggestions which were then considered at two further meetings. The completed version, published on May 1, 1931, in the *Nouvelle Revue Française,* is even more than the French translation of *Ulysses* a triumph over seemingly impossible obstacles.*

At the end of 1930 Joyce received a stern suggestion from Monro Saw & Co., Miss Weaver's solicitors and now his, that he make an effort to live on his income.[96] While his repeated incursions upon the principal had reduced this, the income was still substantial, perhaps 9,000 francs ($350, £70) a month, besides 12,000 francs ($470, £94) a month from the royalties of *Ulysses.* But Joyce was more reckless with his money than ever, and made himself sporadically poor. So on February 2, 1931, he forewent his usual birthday party, and was only rescued from the ignominy of spending the evening at home by the arrival of George and Helen, just back from a honeymoon in Germany, who took him to Les Trianons for dinner. In more than his usual

---

* The closing lines may serve as an example:

English: Can't hear with the waters of. The chittering waters of. Flittering bats, fieldmice bawk talk. Ho! Are you not gone ahome? What Thom Malone? Can't hear with bawk of bats, all thim liffeying waters of. Ho, talk save us! My foos won't moos. I feel as old as yonder elm. A tale told of Shaun or Shem? All Livia's daughtersons. Dark hawks hear us. Night! Night! My ho head halls. I feel as heavy as yonder stone. Tell me of John or Shaun? Who were Shem and Shaun the living sons or daughters of? Night now! Tell me, tell me, tell me, elm! Night night! Telmetale of stem or stone. Beside the rivering waters of, hitherandthithering waters of. Night!

French: N'entend pas cause les ondes de. Le bébé babil des ondes de. Souris chance, trottinete cause pause. Hein! Tu n'est pas rentré? Quel père André? N'entend pas cause les fuisouris, les liffeyantes ondes de. Eh! Bruit nous aide! Mon pied à pied se lie lierré. Je me sense vieille comme mon orme même. Un conte conté de Shaun ou Shem? De Livie tous les fillefils. Sombre faucons écoutent l'ombre. Nuit. Nuit. Ma taute tête tombe. Je me sens lourde comme ma pierrestone. Conte moi de John ou Shaun. Qui furent Shem et Shaun en vie les fils ou filles de. Là-dessus nuit. Dis-mor, dis-mor, dis-mor, orme. Nuit, Nuit! Contemoiconte soit tronc ou pierre. Tant riviérantes ondes de, couretcourantes ondes de. Nuit.

dejection, he broke up his Square Robiac flat, giving away what it was impractical to store, wondering out loud where he would find the money to pay the movers.

There was no real reason for dejection, however. He made, at the beginning of January 1931, a new convert of great importance, Louis Gillet. Sylvia Beach had persuaded Joyce to come to hear Edith Sitwell give a reading; afterwards Miss Beach presented Gillet to him, and Gillet apologized for an unpleasant article * of 1924 on Joyce's work, which he said he had now reconsidered. Joyce made clear he bore him no ill-will, Gillet wrote him an adulatory letter,[97] and they were soon exchanging dinner invitations, Gillet evincing a disposition to praise not only *Ulysses* but also *Finnegans Wake*. When Joyce reported this success to Adrienne Monnier, she voiced a flood of 'Extraordinaires!' [98] That the *Revue des Deux Mondes* should consent to admit either of Joyce's recent works into its canon of great literature was something she had thought impossible.

Among Joyce's other visitors of the time were Padraic and Mary Colum. With them Joyce felt friendlier than ever before, although Mary Colum occasionally annoyed him. So one afternoon, after they had gone together to hear an experimenter in linguistic theory, Père Marcel Jousse, Joyce happened to lecture a young American about the technique of the *monologue intérieur* and its origin in Dujardin's *Les Lauriers sont coupés*. Mary Colum waited until the young man left before rebuking Joyce in her forceful way, 'Haven't you had enough fun with this? Haven't you pulled enough people's legs? And anyway, why deny your indebtedness to Freud and Jung? Isn't it better to be indebted to great originators like that than to——?' No one had spoken to Joyce in this way for many years, and he did not like it. His lips tightened, he moved in his chair with annoyance and said, 'I hate women who know anything.' But Mary Colum, not to be put down, said, 'No, Joyce, you don't. You like them, and I am going to contradict you about this in print when I get the chance.' He fumed silently for a few moments, then abruptly detached himself from his anger and let a half-smile show on his face. Mrs. Colum thought she had converted

* Even at the time Joyce had not minded Gillet's attack. He wrote Miss Weaver on August 29, 1925: 'As regards the article in the *R. de D. M.* I have been planning that for three years. I tried first the *Revue de Paris,* then the *Revue de France.* It does not matter as the *R. de D. M.* is even better. The tone of the article does not matter much. M Gillet is a son-in-law of M René Doumic [the editor]. He suppresses the fact of my having resurrected M Dujardin which is unfair but everyone knows it. I think it remarkable that attacks have not been more frequent and bitter.' [99]

him, but the poem he recited to her a few days later about his women friends * was scarcely corroborative evidence:

> As I was going to Joyce Saint James'
> I met with seven extravagant dames;
> Every dame had a bee in her bonnet,
> With bats from the belfry roosting upon it.
> And Ah, I said, poor Joyce Saint James,
> What can he do with these terrible dames?
> Poor Saint James Joyce.[100]

On another occasion he read from *Work in Progress* to a small group which included Mrs. Colum, and at the end asked her, 'What did you think of it?' She replied with her accustomed forthrightness, 'Joyce, I think it is outside literature.' He did not make any comment then, but later he took Padraic Colum aside to remark, 'Your wife said that what I read was outside literature. Tell her it may be outside literature now, but its future is inside literature.'[101]

His relations with Padraic Colum were easier. Colum was asked to help with *Work in Progress*, by typing and by making suggestions. In *Haveth Childers Everywhere* he afterwards discovered two small contributions he had accidentally made to the text. Joyce asked him the Irish for mother, and he replied, '*Mauher*. But you ought to know, Joyce, because John MacCormack sings something with *maureen machree* in it.' 'I'll use that,' said Joyce, and evolved a phrase about 'the Maugher machrees.' Then Joyce asked him, 'The carriage driven by one person seated on a high box behind—what is it called?' Colum didn't know, but he said that the driver looked 'very lawdy-daw.' 'I'll put that in,' said Joyce, and ended a passage with 'my damsells soft-sidesaddled, covertly, covertly, and Lawdy Dawe.' As a small compensation for these and like hints, Joyce worked Colum's first name into the book in the phrase, 'The S. S. Paudric's in the harbour.'[102]

In March, Joyce had to cope with a claim upon him from an old friend. Livia Schmitz asked him to write a preface to the English translation of *Senilità*,† which Putnam's was about to publish in England.

---

* Joyce objected to Budgen that the female was attempting to usurp all the functions of the male except that which is biologically preempted, and even on that, he said, she was casting jealous, threatening eyes. 'Women write books and paint pictures and compose and perform music. And there are some who have attained eminence in the field of scientific research. . . . But you have never heard of a woman who was the author of a complete philosophic system, and I don't think you ever will.'[103] But he acknowledged later to Carola Giedion-Welcker, 'Throughout my life women have been my most active helpers.'[104]

† Joyce told Signora Schmitz the English word *senility* had a different meaning, and suggested *As a Man Grows Older* as the English title.[105]

Joyce had written her after Schmitz's death that she should remember him 'if at any time my help can serve to keep alive the memory of my old friend for whom I had always affection and esteem.'[106] In 1931, when a monument to Schmitz was unveiled in Trieste, he had sent her a congratulatory telegram. But when it came to writing a preface, he was unexpectedly retiring. He had made a point of refusing to comment formally on the work of other writers, and did not wish to change. He suggested an introduction by Ford Madox Ford,* [107] but the publisher rejected this. Then Signora Schmitz wrote Larbaud asking his intercession, and Larbaud prodded Joyce,[108] but also with no effect. To Stanislaus, Joyce wrote saying he had never promised to write a preface, a fact which was at least literally true, and remarking that his relations with Schmitz had always been quite formal. He had visited only as a teacher, never as a guest; Nora thought that Signora Schmitz had snubbed her; and Schmitz had always been careful of his money.[109] A compromise was finally worked out by which Stanislaus Joyce wrote the introduction to detail his brother's reaction to Schmitz's books. This introduction was sent by Putnam's to Joyce in a last hope of eliciting some comment from him, and he replied in high spirits:

> 2 avenue Saint Philibert
> Passy, Paris.

Dear Mr Huntington,

I do not think I can usefully add anything to what my learned friend, the professor of English at the University of Trieste (see title-page) has written in his preface to *Senilità*, (As) *A Man Grows Older*.

With regard to the other book by the author of *Senilità* the only thing I can suggest as likely to attract the British reading public are a preface by Sir James M. Barrie, author of *My Lady Nicotine*, opinions of the book (to be printed on the back of its jacket) from two deservedly popular personalities of the present day, such as, the rector

---

* Ford had recently appeared in Paris with a new wife, 'an eighth or eighteenth,' as Joyce wrote Miss Weaver on February 16, 1931; he advised Joyce as usual to shift from white wine to a more healthful red.[110] Joyce, also as usual, made no comment, but afterwards wrote Miss Weaver two verses to the tune of 'Father O'Flynn':

> O Father O'Ford, you've a masterful way with you,
> Maid, wife and widow are wild to make hay with you,
> Blonde and brunette turn-about run away with you,
> You've such a way with you, Father O'Ford.

> That instant they see the sun shine from your eye
> Their hearts flitter flutter, they think and they sigh:
> We kiss ground before thee, we madly adore thee,
> And crave and implore thee to take us, O Lord.[111]

He remarked also that Ford's six wives were one less than Earwicker's.[112]

of Stiffkey and the Princess of Wales and (on the front of the jacket)
a coloured picture by a Royal Academician representing two young
ladies, one fair and the other dark but both distinctly nicelooking,
seated in a graceful though of course not unbecoming posture at a table
on which the book stands upright, with title visible and underneath
the picture three lines of simple dialogue, for example:
Ethel: Does Cyril spend too much on cigarettes?
Doris: Far too much.
Ethel: So did Percy (points)—till I gave him ZENO.

Sincerely yours
James Joyce

22—V—1932.

While plans for Schmitz's publicity were in dispute, Adrienne Monnier arranged to renew interest in *Work in Progress*. There was to be
on March 26, 1931, a séance for the reading of *Anna Livia Plurabelle*
in its French version. Joyce wrote Miss Weaver, who decided to come
over for it, that the séance 'may celebrate the close of my Paris career
just as that of the 7th of December, 1921, opened it.'[113] Adrienne Monnier began the evening by recalling her first encounter with Joyce at
André Spire's in 1920, and by tracing briefly his influence in France.
Soupault described the labor of translating *Anna Livia*.[114] The record
of Joyce reading it in English was then played, and after it Adrienne
Monnier read the French translation. Joyce sat dignified and inert
throughout, but Robert McAlmon, who reluctantly escorted a friend
to the séance, was bored and irritated by the general tone of hushed
veneration. He lifted his hands for a second in a gesture of prayer, and
an old man rushed across the room and slapped him in the face. It was
Dujardin, who had misinterpreted McAlmon's gesture; Madame Dujardin had large ankles, and her husband thought McAlmon had looked
at them and then put up his hands in mock horror.[115] Joyce did not
mind the comic interposition, and Dujardin was eventually mollified.

Joyce felt free now to go to England for the next six months. Nora
was uneasy, knowing that he throve neither on the English climate nor
his London acquaintanceship, but on April 11 they gave up their flat
on Square Robiac, moved briefly to the Hotel Powers, 52 rue François
Premier, and a few days later began what he called their 'fifth Hegira.'[116]
In London they stayed for a little over a month in the Hotel Belgravia
in Grosvenor Gardens, S.W.1, then moved at the beginning of May to
a flat at 28b Campden Grove, Kensington, where they planned to stay
indefinitely. Joyce now completed his arrangements to establish permanent domicile in England, and also consulted with Monro Saw & Co.
to legalize his marriage. He chose his father's birthday, July 4, as the

wedding day, perhaps remembering that John Joyce had been grieved by his elopement. At the registry office the Joyces hoped to avoid reporters, but there was some delay when Joyce announced that he and Nora had already been married, but that she had given another name at the ceremony. The clerk objected that they should be divorced before he could marry them a second time, but Joyce's solicitor showed him in the statutes that a ceremony of this kind was legal.[117] No official notice was taken of the 'prior' marriage in the entry in the Registry Office:

James Augustine Aloysius Joyce, aged 49, Bachelor, Independent means married Nora Joseph Barnacle, Spinster, aged 47, each then residing at 28B Campden Grove, London, W.8, on 4th July 1931. Father of man, John Stanislaus Joyce, Government Clerk (Pensioned). Father of woman, Thomas Barnacle, decd. Baker.

'When I was signing the roll,' Joyce wrote to the Colums, 'the King was signing the new law the English call the Marry-Your-Aunt Bill. He should have signed a Marry-Your-Wife Bill.'[118] But as they left the office reporters and photographers rushed at them. Nora remarked, 'All London knows you're here,' and the next day the *Evening Standard* carried on the front page a headline and a photograph of the newlyweds. Joyce was angry at being made ridiculous; when Arthur Power came up to him after the ceremony and jokingly alluded to it, Joyce said curtly, 'If you want information about this, see my solicitors,' and turned away. They were never quite so friendly again.[119] Only to Stanislaus, in a letter of July 18, did he reveal his secret amusement about the affair:

Having eloped with my present wife in 1904 she with my full connivance gave the name of Miss Gretta Greene which was quite good enough for il cav. Fabbri who married us and the last gentleman in Europe il conte Dandini who issued the legitimate certificates for the offspring but this full connivance voided the marriage in the eyes of English law see Hargrave's Laws of England page 471-2 and the second ceremony was thought advisable to secure the inheritance under will.* I have a slight cough this morning so please forgive me if I desist.

* Among Joyce's papers was a note on *jactitation,* the false and malicious claim to be married to another person. In *Finnegans Wake* (243) he uses the word to refer to the marital state of Earwicker and Anna Livia: 'Yet jackticktating all around her about his poorliness due to pannellism and grime for that he harboured her when feme sole [single woman], her zoravarn lhorde and givnergeneral, and led her in antient consort ruhm and bound her durant coverture so as if ever she's beleaved by chechbrooth death since both was parties to the feed it's Hetman MacCumhal foots the funeral.'

With best wishes to Mr and Mrs Joyce from Mr and Mrs Ditto Mac-
Anaspey and here's jumping that bucket as Tinker said to his gipsy

I remain, dear professor,
matrimonially yours
Monico Colesser *

Shortly after their marriage, the Joyces received another visit from
Nora's sister Kathleen. Joyce observed that the handsome young woman,
now literally his sister-in-law, was not carrying the watch he had given
her in Bognor, and said in surprise, 'Have you no watch, Kathleen?'
'I pawned it,' she said, abashed. Joyce howled with laughter and said,
'That's just what I'd do.' [120] He was pleased to have her for company
on a trip to Stonehenge, where Nora did not wish to go, and they also
made trips to the Tower of London, Windsor Forest, and to places
associated with Shakespeare. As they walked along he would ask her
to name the trees, which he found it difficult to see. They even visited
Madame Tussaud's Waxworks; when Kathleen said, 'I want to see you
there,' Joyce replied dourly, 'You never will.' Then, as if unwilling to
let his immortality go so easily, he said, 'I'm going to buy you a record.
It's about the Liffey.'

Nora complained vigorously to Kathleen about her life in Paris.
'There's one thing I hate—going out to dinner and sitting with artists
till 1:00 in the morning. They'd bore you stiff, Kathleen.' Bound as she
was to her husband by their life together and by sympathy for his eye
troubles, she also felt, as the line in *Finnegans Wake* expresses it, 'win
me, woo me, wed me, ah weary me!' [121] The physical side of marriage
had become less attractive to her, perhaps also to him.† And Joyce's
extravagance was a subject of daily dismay. Kathleen noticed at a
restaurant that he was giving the waiter two five-pound notes instead
of one. Nora said with resignation, 'Oh, he's always doing that sort of
thing.' Joyce turned the second five-pound note over to Kathleen instead. But the next day they went to the theater, and Nora exhorted
him, 'Now don't tip the usher when we go in here.' Her husband slipped
a 10-shilling note into the usher's hand nonetheless. Nora was angry
and walked out; Joyce came back to the flat looking woebegone.[122]

The stay at Campden Grove was enlivened by one of those possibilities of litigation which always roused Joyce. It began on July 19, 1931,

---

* A reference to the ludicrous German teacher at the Berlitz School in Trieste.
See p. 194.
† See p. 548. Edmund Wilson points out that the end of *Finnegans Wake* marks
the ending of the sexual relations of Earwicker and his wife.

when the *Frankfurter Zeitung* * published a story entitled 'Vielleicht *ein Traum*,' with the name of James Joyce as author. Daniel Brody of the Rhein-Verlag, Joyce's Swiss publisher, heard of it first, and immediately informed Joyce that his name had been 'forged.'[123] Joyce responded, ' "*Vielleicht ein Traum" aber gewiss eine Schweinerei.*' †[124] In no time he was in touch with Miss Beach, Miss Weaver, Professor Curtius, Harold Nicolson, T. S. Eliot, Georg Goyert, his brother Stanislaus, his son George, and his London solicitors, hoping to institute legal proceedings. Nicolson urged him to demand a strong apology on threat of suit,[125] but in the meantime the *Frankfurter Zeitung* printed a retraction headed, '*Michael und James,*' which passed off the matter lightly as an *Irrtum* of Irene Kafka, the translator, who had accidentally changed the names. Joyce at once decided that Michael Joyce was an invention of the newspaper staff,[126] but he was soon proved to exist, and even wrote Joyce a letter regretting that the error had been made.[127] Irene Kafka, also approached, insisted the fault was her secretary's, and sent regrets, too.

At Joyce's prodding Monro wrote to the editors of the *Frankfurter Zeitung* to demand a more elaborate apology, which, however, they declined to give, on the ground that they had made amends enough.[128] Monro then wrote to Willi Rothschild, a German lawyer in Frankfurt, who replied sensibly on September 19 that there was no point in suing for damages, since the maximum amount to be gained would be only twenty-five pounds. Moreover, he warned that public opinion in Frankfurt would regard the slip as a trifling one, and would consider Joyce's position 'vindictive and exacting and unworthy of a writer of standing and repute—*infra dig.*'[129] On the basis of this letter, Monro on October 6 cautioned Joyce to consider the case closed:[130] Joyce reluctantly gave up hope of a fine international set-to, and paid the legal fees which were already of some dimension.

When he was not diverted by the *Frankfurter Zeitung*, Joyce was again proposing that Sullivan be brought to Covent Garden. He had Miss Weaver write his friend on July 19:

Mr. Joyce has asked me to write to you once again for him, to give you his address—28b Campden Grove, Kensington, London, W.8—and to say that he has had so much worry and business the last two months that he prefers not

---

* '. . . swobbing broguen eeriesh myth brockendootsch, making his reporterage on Der Fall Adams for the Frankofurto Siding, a Fastland payrodicule . . . he would, with tosend and obertosend tonnowatters, one monkey's damages become.' *Finnegans Wake* (70).
† ' "Perhaps a Dream" but certainly a filthy outrage.'

to write to you himself just now or his family would imagine he was launch-
ing another crusade on your behalf which would wear him to a shred several
degrees more threadlike than even his present appearance makes.[131]

Covent Garden, it seemed, was impossible; but Joyce did not give it up
without first informing the management, according to one witness, 'Do
you call this an opera house? It's a W.C.' [132] A group of Sullivan's Irish
and French supporters, led by John Dulanty, the Irish High Commissioner in London, thought of engaging a London hall and persuading
Beecham to conduct the orchestra while Sullivan sang *William Tell*.
Joyce quickly secured a promise from two music critics to write notices.
The plan fell through, however, and it was probably at this time that
Joyce, happening to be in a lavatory, after having carefully made sure
he was alone there except for one Irish friend, put his hands to his face
and burst into a high-pitched, bloodcurdling scream. After almost
thirty seconds of it, the friend said, 'Look, that'll be enough now, do
you mind?' [133] Joyce's feelings were sufficiently relieved, he stopped
abruptly and resumed his formal manner without comment.

His English sojourn was coming to an end. He and Nora disliked
Campden Grove, which Joyce said was inhabited by mummies and was
properly Campden Grave.[134] They decided to go back to Paris for the
winter, and return to England the following spring. Late in July,
accordingly, Joyce, Nora, and Lucia went to Dover and stayed at the
Lord Warden Hotel, where the proprietors were Irish and friendly.
In August, Lucia was acting strangely; she had been much put out by
her parents' marriage and by their warm reception of Kathleen, of
whom she was illogically jealous, and now she grew tired of their delay
in Dover and crossed the Channel without them to stay with George
and Helen. Her indulgent parents accepted this behavior as girlish,
and did not follow her until the end of September. They stayed first at
the fashionable *La Résidence,* 4 avenue Pierre Premier de Serbie, then
in December took a furnished flat at 2 avenue St. Philibert. They stored
their furniture. Joyce tried to improve his daughter's spirits by encouraging her to do designs for materials, and next to design large initial
letters (*lettrines*) for the poems to be included in Herbert Hughes's
The Joyce Book, which the Oxford University Press was to publish. She
made these in November 1931, but Hughes said the book was already
printed.[135] Joyce decided to find some other way of using them, at his
own expense if necessary, but had to proceed by ruse to avoid Lucia's
discovering a paternal subsidy.

During the last several months he had been receiving offers steadily
for both *Finnegans Wake* and *Ulysses.* To some extent both books were
committed to Sylvia Beach, to whom Joyce had ample reason for grati-

tude, and at first she opposed an American publication of *Ulysses* in particular, feeling that it would reduce her sales to nothing. Eventually, however, she was persuaded, in exchange for some of Joyce's manuscripts, to give up her rights, and Joyce was free to consider various publishers' offers. There would have to be a court test of the book, but the legal climate had changed so much in America during the last ten years that a victory seemed likely. The successful bid for *Ulysses* was brought from New York by Helen Joyce's brother, Robert Kastor, in February 1932; it was from Bennett Cerf at Random House, and Joyce signed a contract in March. Meanwhile B. W. Huebsch, having published all Joyce's earlier work, was eager to secure the rights for *Finnegans Wake,* and in 1931 Joyce signed a contract in which he testified to his appreciation of Huebsch's efforts by inserting a special clause: 'If at any time during the continuance of this agreement, Mr. B. W. Huebsch should sever his connection with the said Viking Press and either set up publishing on his own account or acquire interest in another firm of publishers than the Viking Press, then the said Author shall have the option of transferring the benefits of this contract to such new firm.' [136]

It would be wrong, however, to suppose that Joyce could now rely upon adulation in any country. Harold Nicolson in November 1931, was to speak for the British Broadcasting Company on Joyce, but at the last moment the talk was cancelled, and Nicolson had to fight very hard to give it finally on December 6. In America the *Catholic World* carried an attack on Joyce by a Dublin judge, Michael Lennon, with whom he had been friendly for several years; it cast slurs upon his family as well as upon the author,[137] and seemed to Joyce another inexplicable betrayal. He followed again the method he had suggested for exposing Jung, *'Niedrigerhängen';* when Eugene Jolas announced he wished to devote an issue of *transition* to Joyce in homage, with Goethe as whippingboy (because, the year being the centenary of Goethe's death, everyone was overpraising him), Joyce agreed on condition that quotations be included from Lennon's article, from a vicious article by Oliver Gogarty, and from an anonymous attack by 'one who knows him' which appeared in the English press.[138] While Joyce wished to promote controversy about himself, he exhibited also a certain abandon about its outcome.

At the end of December 1931, Joyce was recalled once more to his family affairs when word reached him that his father was fatally ill. All his remorse at having eloped from Ireland in 1904 against his father's wishes, and at having failed to visit the old man during the last eleven years, welled up in him. He telegraphed a friend, Dr. Kerry Reddin, on December 27:

My father dangerously ill Drumcondra Hospital diagnosis uncertain will you please arrange he gets best medical specialists all expenses my charge my thanks advance James Joyce 2 avenue St. Philibert Paris.[139]

He telephoned and telegraphed the hospital every day, but John Joyce was past saving. The old man retained his gusto to the end; he said to his daughter May, 'I've got more out of life than any white man.' [140] On his deathbed he gasped, 'Tell Jim he was born at six in the morning.' [141] It was thought he was delirious, but James had written some time before to ask his birth hour because an astrologer was doing his horoscope. On December 29, 1931, his father was dead.

Joyce was grief-stricken. He asked Curran and Michael Healy, who attended the funeral, to find out anything the old man might have said of him before he died, and both assured him that his father always said, 'Jim never forgets me.' [142] What Joyce hoped for was some word of praise for his writing; but his father, not understanding or not approving, never uttered it. To Ezra Pound, Joyce wrote on January 1, 1932, 'He loved me deeply, more and more as he grew older, but in spite of my own deep feeling for him I never dared to trust myself into the power of my enemies.' The same day he wrote T. S. Eliot:

He had an intense love for me and it adds anew to my grief and remorse that I did not go to Dublin to see him for so many years. I kept him constantly under the illusion that I would come and was always in correspondence with him but an instinct which I believed in held me back from going, much as I longed to. *Dubliners* was banned there in 1912 on the advice of a person who was assuring me at the time of his great friendship.* When my wife and children went there in 1922, against my wish, they had to flee for their lives, lying flat on the floor of a railway carriage while rival parties shot at each other across their heads and quite lately I have had experience of malignancy and treachery on the part of people to whom I had done nothing but friendly acts.† I did not feel myself safe and my wife and son opposed my going.[143]

On January 17 he informed Miss Weaver that since his father's death he had been plunged into such 'prostration of mind' that he was considering once again abandoning *Work in Progress*. With more self-knowledge, he suggested that his talent sprang from a trait of character which he shared with John Joyce:

Why go on writing about a place I did not dare to go to at such a moment? Where not three persons know me or understand me (in the obituary notice the editor of the Independent raised objection to the allusion to me)? My

* Kettle.
† Lennon.

father had an extraordinary affection for me. He was the silliest man I ever knew and yet cruelly shrewd. He thought and talked of me up to his last breath. I was very fond of him always, being a sinner myself, and even liked his faults. Hundreds of pages and scores of characters in my books came from him. His dry (or rather wet) wit and his expression of face convulsed me often with laughter. . . . I got from him his portraits, a waistcoat, a good tenor voice, and an extravagant licentious disposition (out of which, however, the greater part of any talent I may have springs) but, apart from these, something else I cannot define. But if an observer thought of my father and myself and my son too physically, though we are all very different, he could perhaps define it. It is a great consolation to me to have such a good son. His grandfather was very fond of him and kept his photograph beside mine on the mantelpiece. I knew he was old, but I thought he would live longer. It is not his death that crushed me so much as self-accusation.[144]

The 'extravagant licentious disposition' was something James always cherished, and much of his seemingly irrational spending and drinking justified itself to him as a way of holding the source of his talent inviolate.

Joyce asked Alfred Bergan, his father's oldest friend, to take charge of setting up a monument; Bergan informed him that John Joyce had expressed the wish ('in the curious roundabout delicate and allusive way he had in spite of all his loud elaborate curses,' Joyce commented) [145] that his wife's name as well as his own should be engraved on his tombstone, so their son wrote the simple inscription:

IN

LOVING MEMORY

OF

JOHN STANISLAUS JOYCE

OF CORK,

BORN 4TH JULY 1849

DIED 29TH DEC. 1931

AND OF HIS WIFE

MARY JANE

OF DUBLIN

BORN 15TH MAY 1859

DIED 13TH AUGUST 1903 °

° In searching for another form of memorial, Joyce thought he had hit on a good one in the form of a public bench at the end of Claude Road on the Whitworth Road. He wrote his brother on January 22, 1934, that he intended having this erected anonymously. Only Paris seems to understand that John Citizen wants to sit down at times without paying for his seat in the open street.' It was also a tribute to his father's many years of sitting around. Nothing came of the idea.

John Joyce kept his word and made James his sole heir. Surprisingly enough there was a little property,* and in any case the gesture was not empty.

'Poor foolish man!' Joyce wrote Miss Weaver. 'It seems to me his voice has somehow got into my body or throat. Lately, more than ever —especially when I sigh.' [146] Appalled by his own dolorousness, he offered Louis Gillet a new calendar of weekdays: 'Moansday, Tearsday, Wailsday, Thumpsday, Frightday, Shatterday.' [147] All his friends tried to comfort him. His behavior was almost maudlin; he said to Eugene Jolas suddenly, 'I hear my father talking to me. I wonder where he is.' [148] Maria Jolas came in one day and found him reading Maeterlinck on life after death. She asked if she could do anything, and he gave her a hundred francs and asked her to give it to some needy old man in memory of his father. She had trouble finding one, but at last approached an old derelict and said, *'J'ai un ami qui en mémoire de son père veut vous donner cet argent.'* The man looked up and said, *'Sans blague!'* [149] Sylvia Beach, though somewhat estranged, telephoned to remind Joyce that February 2 would be his fiftieth birthday, and called for a jubilee. Joyce was too dejected to agree, but he did not oppose it. As he remarked to Louis Gillet, 'Life is so tragic—birth, death, departure (separation), sickness, death, that we are permitted to distract ourselves and forget a little.' [150]

The Jolases wished to print in *transition* a portrait of Joyce to honor his birthday, and Joyce agreed to allow the Spanish artist César Abin to draw him. But when the portrait turned out to be the classical figure of the artist in a dressing-gown surrounded by his books, Joyce was dissatisfied and during fifteen days suggested one change after another. 'Paul Léon tells me that when I stand bent over at a street corner, I look like a questionmark,' he said. Someone had called him 'a blue-nosed comedian,' so he insisted that a star be put at the end of his nose to illuminate it. To suggest his mourning for his father, and his chronic dejection, he wished to be wearing a black derby, with the number 13 marked on it, and cobwebs surrounding it. Sticking out of his trouser pocket should be a roll of paper bearing the song, 'Let me like a soldier fall.' His poverty should be suggested by patches on the trouser knees. The point of the questionmark must be shaped like a world, with Ireland as the only country visible on the world's face, and Dublin shown in black. So it was done.† [151]

February 2 did not prove a lucky day this year. During the afternoon

* John Joyce's effects amounted to £665/9/0, as his will at the Public Record Office in Dublin reveals.
† See Plate XIV.

Lucia, in whom signs of mental derangement were becoming increasingly apparent, turned in a fury upon her mother and threw a chair at her. Nora was terrified, but George, who still had some ascendancy over his sister, called a taxi and took her to a *maison de santé*, where after a few days she seemed partly recovered. Joyce was greatly disheartened when he arrived at the Jolas flat at 40 bis rue de Sevigné for the jubilee party the night of the 2nd, and even the sight of a cake with fifty candles, and upon it a replica in sugar of *Ulysses* with ten candles, did not revive his spirits.

His melancholy was, however, suddenly relieved on February 15. Helen Joyce, after a difficult pregnancy, gave birth to a son, who was named in his grandfather's honor Stephen James Joyce. In some sense the birth seemed to countervail John Joyce's death, and James wrote the same day his most moving poem: [152]

Ecce Puer

Of the dark past
A boy is born.
With joy and grief
My heart is torn.

Calm in his cradle
The living lies.
May love and mercy
Unclose his eyes!

Young life is breathed
Upon the glass,
The world that was not
Comes to pass.

A child is sleeping;
An old man gone.
O, father forsaken,
Forgive your son!

1932–1935

. . . but we grisly old Sykos who have done our unsmiling bit on 'alices, when they were yung and easily freudened, in the penumbra of the procuring room and what oracular comepression we have had apply to them! could (did we care to sell our feebought silence *in camera*) tell our very moistnostrilled one that *father* in such virgated contexts is not always that undemonstrative relative (often held up to our contumacy) who settles our hashbill for us and what an innocent all-abroad's adverb such as Michaelly looks like can be suggestive of under the pudenda-scope and, finally, what a neurasthene nympholept, endocrine-pineal typus, of inverted parentage with a prepossessing drauma present in her past and a priapic urge for congress with agnates before cognates fundamentally is feeling for under her lubricitous meiosis when she refers with liking to some feeler she fancie's face. And Mm. We could. Yes what need to say? 'Tis as human a little story as paper could well carry. . . .

—*Finnegans Wake* (115)

JOYCE was not allowed to practice the art of being a grandfather, as Mr. Best and Victor Hugo call it,[1] undisturbed. The question of Stephen's baptism arose, and Joyce made his unalterable opposition clear.* George and Helen pretended to agree, but secretly carried the baby to a church, with the connivance of Padraic and Mary Colum and Eugene Jolas, who stood for him at the font. When J. F. Byrne came to Paris some time after, Joyce, who had drunk a good deal of wine, remarked, 'Well you know, Byrne, when my grandson was born they couldn't make up their minds whether to baptize him or circumcise

---

* He remarked to Budgen that he had been reproached for not having his children brought up religiously. 'But what do they expect me to do? There are a hundred and twenty religions in the world. They can take their choice. I should never try to hinder or dissuade them.'[2] But the imminent possibility of having one of his family baptized made him less tolerant.

him.' 'And so they baptized him,' laughed Jolas, carried away by the convivial talk. Joyce started. 'They baptized him?' he demanded. Jolas had presence of mind enough to say he was only joking,[3] and it was some years before Joyce found out the truth. By that time he was so involved in the problem of Lucia that he could not spare indignation for his grandson.

Lucia's recent crisis had been brought to a head by her difficulties in love. For two or three years she had been interested in Samuel Beckett, the eccentric, likable young man who visited the Joyces frequently whenever he was in Paris. Peggy Guggenheim in her memoirs compared Beckett later to Goncharov's hero Oblomov,[4] who can scarcely bring himself to leave his bed, and even in these younger days Beckett rose in mid-afternoon, struggling with the apathy he was to render in such precise Parisian dialect in *En attendant Godot*. Beckett was addicted to silences, and so was Joyce; they engaged in conversations which consisted often of silences directed towards each other, both suffused with sadness, Beckett mostly for the world, Joyce mostly for himself. Joyce sat in his habitual posture, legs crossed, toe of the upper leg under the instep of the lower; Beckett, also tall and slender, fell into the same gesture. Joyce suddenly asked some such question as, 'How could the idealist Hume write a history?' Beckett replied, 'A history of representations.'[5] Joyce said nothing, but some time afterwards he informed the young man, 'The only amateur philosopher of any value I know is Carducci.'[°] Later, 'For me,' he said, 'there is only one alternative to scholasticism,[†] scepticism.'[‡][6]

Though he liked having Beckett with him, Joyce at the same time kept him at a distance. Once he said directly, 'I don't love anyone except my family,'[7] in a tone which suggested, 'I don't like anyone except my family either.' But Beckett's mind had a subtlety and strangeness that attracted Joyce as it attracted, in another way, his daughter. So he would ask the young man to read to him passages from Mauthner's *Beiträge zu einer Kritik der Sprache*, in which the nominalistic view

---

[°] Edgardo Carducci, nephew of the poet, who set Joyce's poem, 'Alone,' to music.

[†] He often marvelled at the Catholic Church. 'Look, Budgen,' he said once, 'in the nineteenth century, in the full tide of rationalistic positivism and equal democratic rights for everybody, it proclaims the dogma of the infallibility of the head of the Church and also that of the Immaculate Conception.'[8]

[‡] Joyce attended a party in Zurich where the guests were brought out on the balcony to look at the stars, and a priest who was present embarked upon a cosmological proof of the existence of God, adduced from the intricate order of the starry heavens. Joyce interjected, '*Schade dass alles von der gegenseitigen Zerstörung abhängt.*'[9] ('What a pity that the whole thing depends upon reciprocal destruction.') To a friend who asked him, 'What do you think of the next life?' he answered, 'I don't think much of this one.'

of language seemed something Joyce was looking for. Once or twice he dictated a bit of *Finnegans Wake* to Beckett, though dictation did not work very well for him; in the middle of one such session there was a knock at the door which Beckett didn't hear. Joyce said, 'Come in,' and Beckett wrote it down. Afterwards he read back what he had written and Joyce said, 'What's that "Come in"?' 'Yes, you said that,' said Beckett. Joyce thought for a moment, then said, 'Let it stand.' [10] He was quite willing to accept coincidence as his collaborator. Beckett was fascinated and thwarted by Joyce's singular method.

Sometimes Beckett took Lucia with him to restaurants or theaters, and sometimes felt he should have more than a casual interest in this tortured and blocked replica of genius. As her self-control began to leave her, she made less effort to conceal the passion she felt for him, and at last her feelings became so overt that Beckett told her bluntly he came to the Joyce flat primarily to see her father. [11] He felt he had been cruel, and later told Peggy Guggenheim that he was dead and had no feelings that were human; hence he had not been able to fall in love with Lucia.

Lucia was deeply hurt. She irrationally blamed her mother for the break-up, but Nora was sympathetic and tried to help her. She remarked, 'What Lucia needs is a nice young husband.' [12] Lucia herself put the matter more baldly to William Bird, 'Mr. Bird, the trouble with me is that I'm sex-starved.' 'That's rot, Lucia. What have you been reading?' he replied, and Nora broke up the conversation. [13] Mary Colum urged Joyce to provide a dowry for his daughter and arrange a marriage after the French style, and Joyce took some steps in that direction. [14]

Paul and Lucie Léon, who saw the Joyces more often than anyone else, were full of sympathy for Lucia, and Léon persuaded his young brother-in-law, Alex Ponisovsky, to take an interest in her. Ponisovsky, just recovering from another affair and at loose ends, was willing enough; but after he had seen Lucia a number of times, Léon said to him, 'You can't treat this girl like an American. She has been brought up properly and your frequent meetings with her can have only one meaning for her family.' Ponisovsky, with some reluctance, and almost more to oblige the importunate Léon than Lucia, proposed marriage to Lucia at the beginning of March 1932, and was accepted. [15]

Joyce sent a telegram to George and Helen, then in the south of France, to announce the engagement. George read it with amazement, and when Helen proposed that they wire congratulations, he refused. They hastily returned to Paris. 'What do you mean by sending me that wire?' George asked his father. Joyce replied hesitatingly, 'Well, if they want to get engaged—.' 'You can't talk about engagement with a girl in Lucia's condition,' said George.[16]

Léon exerted the opposite kind of pressure upon Ponisovsky. He often called up at noon to say, 'By the way, I think you should send your fiancée some flowers today. I don't think you've remembered to do so.'[17] Ponisovsky could not see how to extricate himself. As for Lucia, she thought more about Beckett than about her future bridegroom. Her behavior however was strangely tranquil.[18]

After some days of bouquets and visits, Joyce insisted upon a formal engagement party at the Restaurant Drouand in Place Gaillon. The scene was more funerary than romantic. Following it Lucia went to the Léons' flat and lay down on the sofa. To their horror she remained there, inert, catatonic.[19] The engagement was forgotten (though Nora maternally spoke of a suit for breach of promise, and was somewhat estranged from Léon), as the girl lingered out of consciousness. The sources of schizophrenia are not known, but the possibility that a more regular family life might have prevented her illness invaded and occupied Joyce's mind. He did not disavow guilt; he embraced it eagerly. 'Whatever spark of gift I possess has been transmitted to Lucia,' he said bitterly, 'and has kindled a fire in her brain.'[20] He identified himself closely with her. Now began the consultations with doctors, the long periods of time in clinics, the injections and operations that were to engross him and dismay his friends for the rest of his life. The gloom that settled upon him now was of almost tragic dimensions.

The first doctors consulted warned Joyce that apathy was his daughter's greatest danger, and attempted various kinds of injections. Lucia came to herself but acted wildly. Joyce wrote Miss Weaver on April 20, 1932, 'I shall try to put up a home for her here, though she [is] terribly difficult; but she is really a child, and I think the lettrines she did are excellent.' Lucia was at this time twenty-five. Joyce had a remarkable capacity to follow her swift jumps of thought which baffled other people completely. Where they should live remained a perplexing problem; Lucia spoke of wanting to go to England, while Joyce had given up the idea of living there and wished to find another flat in Paris, their lease at 2 avenue St. Philibert having expired.

They decided to make a visit to London, however, and on April 17 went to the Gare du Nord, had their baggage put on the train, and were about to take their seats when Lucia suffered a *crise des nerfs* and, screaming that she hated England, refused to go. After forty-five minutes, during which only Joyce remained calm, there was nothing to do but remove the baggage from the train.[21] Lucia asked to go to the Léons, and they kindly put her to bed, where she remained for nine days, then as suddenly demanded to go to Padraic and Mary Colum, who were living in Paris at the time. Mary Colum was about to undergo an operation, but kept Lucia for a week. Joyce wished to send his daughter to a psychiatrist, but when she absolutely refused, he asked a doctor to call every morning at the Colums' flat. Lucia was deceived into thinking it was Mrs. Colum's doctor, and the psychiatrist listened politely to the two women as they explained to him each other's illnesses. At intervals Mary Colum left Lucia and the doctor alone on some pretext; but he could do little except to conclude that Lucia was more deranged than anyone had admitted.²² On May 29 George Joyce came and with Mrs. Colum escorted his sister to Dr. G. Maillard's clinic at l'Hay-les-Roses, having misled her about their destination. Maillard diagnosed her condition as 'hebephrenic * psychosis with serious prognosis.' ²³ There she remained for several weeks while her father thought what to do.

The early months of 1932 had been marked also by some tension between Joyce and Miss Weaver and between Joyce and Miss Beach. Miss Weaver had ventured to relay another comment by Monro that Joyce was spending his capital and should try to live on his income. Joyce responded as usual with a great display of annoyance, a convincing list of indispensable expenditures, and a reproach that she was spoiling his fiftieth anniversary. Miss Weaver was humble and apologetic, and even came to Paris to reassure him. As for Sylvia Beach, Joyce's relations with her had been worsening, in spite of sporadic attempts to renew old comradeship, during 1929 and 1930. The main blow, however, was struck not by Sylvia Beach herself, but by Adrienne Monnier on her behalf. She had meditated a letter to him for a long time, and now, on May 19, 1931, wrote it. She spoke openly of the way that she and Miss Beach had, as they felt, been put upon. Though André Gide might suppose that Joyce was indifferent to fame and fortune, their own experience had supported a contrary opinion. Joyce had importuned her and Miss Beach to sell the limited editions of sections of *Work in Progress;* he had made repeated inquiries about royalties on *Ulysses.* Mlle Monnier made clear, without trying to be tactful, that she and her friend could do no more than they were already doing. Joyce must understand that their lives were very hard compared to his. The letter ended in courteous phrases.

Joyce treated this attack with studied indifference. He was grateful to Miss Beach and Mlle Monnier; he might have argued, if he had wished, that the causes for gratitude were distributed less unequally than the letter had indicated. But he chose to keep amicable relations.

---

* Hebephrenia is a form of schizophrenia characterized by hallucinations, absurd delusions, silly mannerisms, and other kinds of deterioration.

Miss Beach he knew to be in distress; the depression had cut her sales, her health was impaired, and she had other troubles as well. In her behavior towards Joyce she varied between affection and recrimination. There was one occasion when she accidentally knocked some of Joyce's reviews to the floor and, knowing his passion for them, seemed (or so he imagined) to challenge him to kneel down and pick them up. He, of course, proudly disregarded them.[24]

It was hard to know what arrangement to make with Miss Beach now that the publication of *Ulysses* in the United States and England impended. She had almost sold out the eleventh printing of the book, and did not seem to want to print a twelfth. Since Joyce had recently signed an agreement with her which granted her world rights, she was a party to the negotiations for the book, and at first demanded a large payment from Random House. Eventually, however, she withdrew this claim, in view of Joyce's gift of manuscripts. It seemed reasonable that she should receive a share of the royalties for the European edition if another publisher were to bring it out. Joyce offered also to let her publish *Finnegans Wake,* but she did not feel she could undertake such a task. J. Holroyd-Reece and M. C. Wegner, the Paris representatives of the Albatross Press, with headquarters in Hamburg, offered to take over the publication of *Ulysses,* and Joyce signed with them a contract that allocated 25% of the royalties to Sylvia Beach. Their edition, issued under the imprint of the Odyssey Press, in December 1932, had the advantage of being corrected by Stuart Gilbert, and, in its fourth printing, became the most accurate text of *Ulysses.*[25]

Joyce wanted to arrange for publication of *Ulysses* in England, if possible with Faber & Faber, but while T. S. Eliot (the director of the firm with whom Joyce customarily dealt) was eager to publish a series of episodes in the *Criterion Miscellany,* he thought publication of the whole book was sure to bring prosecution.[26] Joyce was averse to publication in part; 'it implies,' he wrote Eliot, 'that I have recognised the right of any authorities in either of Bull's islands to dictate to me what and how I am to write. I never did and never will.' [27] On April 20, 1932, Eliot therefore had to withdraw. Joyce was averse also to a plan for an expurgated edition. 'There is no expurgated edition of *Ulysses,*' he told Alfred Kerr, 'and there won't be any.' [28] To an advocate of expurgation, he retorted, 'My book has a beginning, a middle, and an end. Which would you like to cut off?' [29] To another, Gerald Griffin, he said, 'Griffin, I'm like Pilate. *Quod scripsi, scripsi.*' [30] He explained to Sisley Huddleston, 'To consent would be an admission that the expurgated parts are not indispensable. The whole point about them is that they cannot be omitted. Either they are put in gratuitously without reference to my general purpose; or they are an integral part of my book. If they are mere interpolations, my book is inartistic; and if they are strictly in their place, they cannot be left out.' It was true that he was publishing sections of *Work in Progress:* 'These sections serve to indicate what I am doing, but what I am doing should not be judged until it is completed. They are, if you like, serial contributions, which will eventually take their place in the whole. They have also a certain independent life of their own.'[31] Paul Léon, hearing from Harold Laski that Sir Frederick Pollock, the legal expert, had read the book, sought to obtain an informal opinion from him, apparently without success. But in November 1932, Joyce learned that the prime minister and the attorney general had spoken of the book and decided not to prosecute it. Now Paul Léon negotiated delicately and skillfully to find a publisher. After Jonathan Cape and Werner Laurie resisted his overtures, Léon eventually, in January 1934, persuaded John Lane to undertake to publish the book. It was hoped that Joyce would write a preface, but he refused. In July 1934 the printers protested against certain passages, and the book did not appear until 1936.

Another possibility was to turn *Ulysses* into a film. Warner Brothers wrote to Joyce about the movie rights. Officially he discountenanced the idea (though he had once endorsed it), on the ground that the book could not be made into a film with artistic propriety. But he allowed Paul Léon to keep the matter going, talked with Eisenstein about it,[*] and did not discourage Stuart Gilbert from trying his hand at scenarios for *Ulysses* and *Anna Livia Plurabelle.*[†] Someone suggested Charles Laughton for Bloom, but Joyce thought him 'too Aryan' and preferred George Arliss, who had played Disraeli.[32]

The translation of *Ulysses* into foreign languages was more certainly to his taste, but in February 1932, he received word that the Japanese had translated the book and published a pirated edition. He had the indefatigable Léon write the British consul in Tokyo to ask for a lawyer to take the case, but again Joyce was thwarted in his desire to litigate when it was discovered that European copyright was applicable in Japan for only ten years, and had therefore expired in February. A small sum was eventually paid over to Joyce, who however promptly returned it with continuing indignation.

---

[*] Eisenstein described a visit to Joyce as 'a ghost experience,' because the room in which they met was so dark that both seemed shadows. They stood and talked about *Ulysses,* and afterwards Eisenstein remarked to a friend, 'A great man! This fellow really *does* what all of you *wanted* to do, because you feel it but he knows it.'[33]

[†] Louis Zukofsky also attempted a scenario of *Ulysses.*[34]

Joyce made merry of most of these events in a poem which he wrote during this year:

A Portrait of the Artist as an Ancient Mariner

1) I met with an ancient scribelleer
    As I scoured the pirates' sea
    His sailes were alullt at nought comma null
    Not raise the wind could he.

2) The bann of Bull, the sign of Sam *
    Burned crimson on his brow.
    And I rocked at the rig of his bricabrac brig
    With K.O.11 on his prow.†

3) Shakefears & Coy danced poor old joy
    And some of their steps were corkers
    As they shook the last shekels like phantom freckels
    His pearls that had poisoned porkers.

4) The gnome Norbert read rich bills of fare
    The ghosts of his deep debauches
    But there was no bibber to slip that scribber
    The price of a box of matches

5) For all cried, Schuft! ‡ He has lost the Luft
    That made his U boat ** go
    And what a weird leer wore that scribeleer
    As his wan eye winked with woe.

6) He dreamed of the goldest sands uprolled
    By the silviest Beach of Beaches
    And to watch it dwindle gave him Kugelkopfschwindel ††
    Till his eyeboules bust their stitches.

7) His hold shipped seas with a drunkard's ease
    And its deadweight grew and grew
    While the witless wag still waived his flag
    Jemmyrend's white and partir's blue.‡‡

* That is, John Bull and Uncle Sam.
† Knockout in the eleventh round, that is, the eleventh year since *Ulysses* was published.
‡ Blackguard.
** *Ulysses.*
†† Round-head-vertigo; possibly a reference to the Nazi theory that brachycephalic peoples (including the Celts) were inferior to dolichocephalic ones, though it could also be dizziness from eating too many cupcakes.
‡‡ The Greek colors, and colors of *Ulysses.*

8) His tongue stuck out with a dragon's drouth
   For a sluice of schweppes and brandy
   And but for the glows on his roseate nose
   You'd have staked your goat he was Gandhi.

9) For the Yanks and Japs had made off with his traps; *
   So that stripped to the stern he clung
   While increase of a cross, an Albatross †
   Abaft his neck was hung.

J.J.

In the same vein he found time in May 1932, to finish translating a poem of James Stephens, 'Stephen's Green,' into French, German, Latin, Norwegian, and Italian, to celebrate their jointly held jubilee year (about which he was bestirring himself at last). He hoped to have Stephens translate it into Irish, but Stephens did not know the language well enough.‡

* *Ulysses* had been pirated by the Japanese and Americans.
† The press that took over publication of *Ulysses* in Europe from Sylvia Beach.
‡ Stephens's modest poem scarcely demanded such linguistic virtuosity:

> The wind stood up and gave a shout.
> He whistled on his fingers and
>
> Kicked the withered leaves about
> And thumped the branches with his hand
>
> And said he'd kill and kill and kill,
> And so he will and so he will.

Joyce's French, German, Latin, Norwegian, and Italian versions read:

> Les Verts de Jacques
> Le vent d'un saut lance son cri,
> Se siffle sur les doigts et puis
>
> Trépigne les feuilles d'automne,
> Craque les branches qu'il assomme.
>
> Je tuerai, crie-t-il, holà!
> Et vous verrez s'il le fera!

(Of this version Joyce wrote to Stephens on December 19, 1931: 'It is only a pleasantry but I hope it may amuse you. Strictly speaking, *craquer* is a neuter verb but in popular usage it is employed transitively like *croquer* as being more expressive. I could not resist the obvious pun on your title.')

> Jakobsgrässlicher
> Der Wind stand auf, liess los einen Schrei,
> Pfiff mit den Fingern schrill dabei.
>
> Wirbelte duerres Laub durch den Wald
> Und haemmerte Aeste mit Riesengewalt.
>
> Zum tod, heult, zum Tod und Mord!
> Und meint es ernst: ein Wind, ein Wort.

———

From such diversions, palliative to his sense of the oppression of circumstances, Joyce turned to consider his daughter's future. It was apparent that her relations with both him and Nora were intricately enwound in her condition; she exhibited the familiar pattern of hostility towards the mother and excessive preoccupation with the father. The doctors were beginning to advise that she be kept strictly away from both parents. Dr. Maillard urged them to leave the young woman at l'Hay-les-Roses, but when the immediate cure for which Joyce continued to hope was not forthcoming, he determined upon a treatment of his own, by which he might avoid the impersonality of mental homes. He was obliged to go to Zurich to consult Vogt about his right eye, which was developing a cataract; the Jolas family was to be close by at Feldkirch, and Joyce decided to take Lucia, with a nurse from the clinic, to Feldkirch, where Maria Jolas had agreed to look after her.

Léon urged him to consult a neurologist rather than take Lucia's cure upon himself, but Joyce's mind was fixed. The night before the trip to Zurich, Joyce and Nora were joined at the Trianons by William Bird, who urged them to come for a ride in his car through the Bois de Boulogne. When they reached the Bois Joyce began guiding him, right here and left there, and soon they pulled up at a restaurant under the same management as the Trianons. Nora protested but Joyce said they would have just one bottle. Nora kept insisting they leave, but her

---

Surgit Boreas digitorum
Fistulam, faciens et clamorem.

Pes pugno certat par (oremus!)
Foliis quatit omne nemus.

Caedam, ait, caedam, caedam!
Nos ne habeat ille praedam.

Vinden staar op med en vild Huru,
Han piber paa fingerne og nu

Sparker bladenes flyvende flok.
Traeerne troer han er Ragnarok.

Skovens liv og blod vil han draebe og drikke.
Hvad der bliver at goere, det ved jeg ikke.

Balza in piè Fra Vento e grida.
Tre dita in bocca fischia la sfida.

Tira calci, pesta botte:
Ridda di foglie e frasche rotte.

Ammazzerò, ei urla, O gente!
E domeneddio costui non mente.[35]

husband delayed. Then Joyce asked Bird to see him to the men's lavatory, because he was afraid of stumbling in the dark. As soon as they
were out of Nora's sight he whirled on Bird and said, 'Bird, I may
never see you again. Will you do me a great favor?' 'Anything in my
power,' said Bird, 'but surely we shall have many more occasions to
meet.' 'To meet, yes. But I go to Zurich tomorrow for another operation,
and this time I feel sure it will leave me sightless. So I say, I may never
see you again.' Bird tried clumsily to reassure him, and asked what
favor he wanted. Joyce grasped him by the arm and said gleefully,
'Come back and have another bottle.' Nora, however, refused to stay
if more champagne was ordered, and when her husband nevertheless
persisted, she summoned a taxi and left. Bird saw her into it and
promised to have Joyce home in half an hour. It was somewhat longer.[36]

The next day, July 3, 1932, Joyce 'smuggled' Lucia and her nurse out
of the clinic and by train to Feldkirch.[37] He left them there under the
surveillance of the Jolases, having first urged Lucia to continue work
on her lettrines. Then with Nora he traveled to Zurich for his much
postponed consultation with Dr. Vogt. This went badly; Vogt was
annoyed with Joyce for having stayed away for two years instead of
reporting at frequent intervals; Joyce replied, 'I have had one damned
thing after another.'[38] As the result of neglect, Vogt said, the right eye
had deteriorated to the point where blindness in it was almost inevitable. His preliminary recommendation was that he perform two operations on it, though the prognosis was doubtful, and if they succeeded,
he would then operate on the left eye.[39] He warned Joyce that both
eyes would profit from 'psychische Ruhe,' but this was not easy for
a man with an insane daughter to come by. Vogt's proposed treatment
was so radical that Joyce wrote Drs. Hartmann and Collinson in Paris,
who disagreed with Vogt and thought the eye not fit for an operation.[40]
George Joyce and even Lucia warned their father against it by letter.

Five weeks in Zurich left Joyce indignant that the 'best eye doctor
in the world' should live in 'the world's worst climate.'[41] The reports
from the Jolases about Lucia were reassuring, but Joyce feared they
were 'rigged.' Lucia's own letters worried him by their 'lack of even
casual connections,' though he found some of her phrases 'very fine.'[42]
She kept suggesting that she come to Zurich, and in part to forestall
more scenes at railroad stations Joyce and Nora went to the Hotel
Löwen at Feldkirch and stayed there from August 10 to September 6.
For a time Lucia was quiet and worked on her decorative alphabet,
reaching the letter O, and her father wrote everyone, and had Léon
and Pinker write also, to arrange for the use of the initial letters in
some book of children's poems grouped in alphabetical order. At last

he hit upon the notion of using her letters in *A Chaucer A B C,* which was published with a preface by Louis Gillet in 1936. A few of Lucia's designs were used in October 1932 in Desmond Harmsworth's edition of the facsimile manuscript of *Pomes Penyeach,*[43] deposited at Joyce's request in the Bibliothèque Nationale and the British Museum, then in June 1934, in the *Mime of Mick, Nick and the Maggies,* and in October 1937, in *Storiella as She Is Syung.*

While his daughter worked at her lettrines Joyce felt able to write a little more of the beginning of the second part of *Finnegans Wake.* On September 7 he returned to Vogt for another examination. He fully expected to submit to an operation, and had friends leak the news to the press that he had been operated upon; but in fact Vogt, after testing his right eye for tension, decided the operation was too dangerous and had better be put off. There was no room in the interior chamber of the right eye, so that he would have to cut through the lens to work; this surgery might produce a traumatic iritis, which could pass over to the good eye (as the much-operated left eye was now considered) and perhaps damage it. In a year or two the capsule would shrink, he said, and leave him some space.[44] He changed Joyce's glasses and solemnly charged him to return every three months for examination.

Joyce felt some relief at this respite from surgery. He took long walks with Jolas along the mountain river Ill near Feldkirch, and climbed the hills. Of the mountains and rivers he said solemnly, 'They are the phenomena that will remain when all the peoples and their governments will have vanished.' [45] In the afternoon, after a nap, he would go walking again. Since his hour for taking his first drink was eight o'clock, he had a curious ritual just before that time. 'At half-past seven he would race suddenly for the railroad station,' Jolas says, 'where the Paris-Vienna express was due to stop for ten minutes each day. He would walk quietly up and down the platform. "Over on those tracks there," he said one evening, "the fate of *Ulysses* was decided in 1915." ' His journey into Switzerland had been delayed at that point. 'When the train finally came in, he rushed to the nearest car to examine the French, German, and Yugoslav inscriptions, and palped the letters with the sensitive fingers of defective vision.' Then he asked Jolas questions about the people getting off the train, and tried to listen to their conversations. 'When the train continued on its way, he stood on the platform waving his hat, as if bidding farewell to a dear friend. . . . Eight o'clock was approaching, and he hastened back to the hotel for his first glass of Tischwein—or as Mrs. Joyce used to call it disparagingly, "Dishwine." ' [46]

At Feldkirch Joyce discussed with Maria Jolas the best plan for Lucia. She was of the opinion that Lucia's mental condition was serious and that Dr. Jung, being nearby, should be consulted. Joyce did not like Jung and was still unwilling to acknowledge that his daughter was mad. He thereupon sent Lucia and her nurse on to Vence, and made plans to stay at Nice nearby, close enough to help out in emergencies and distant enough to make her free of family pressure. Before his own departure late in September he received a letter from Yeats:

> Riversdale,
> Willbrook,
> Rathfarnham,
> Dublin.
>
> September 2 1932
>
> My dear Joyce
>
> Bernard Shaw and I are busy founding an Academy of Irish Letters, we are nominating the first members, twenty five, who have done creative work with Ireland as the subject matter, and ten who have given adequate grounds for their election but do not fall within this definition. The creators Academicians, the others Associates. When we began talking over members we found we had to make this division or we should have been overrun with people from England or Scotland with a little Irish blood and a great desire to acquire a national character.
>
> Of course the first name that seemed essential both to Shaw and myself was your own, indeed you might say of yourself as Dante said 'If I stay who goes, if I go who stays?' Which means that if you go out of our list it is an empty sack indeed. By the end of next week I shall have the signed form of nomination and I will send it to you with a copy of the rules. I would however think it a great thing if you would trust us so far as to give your assent when this letter reaches you. It will have to be sent on from your London solicitor's and I am alarmed lest your name does not reach me in time. There will be no subscription, the little money wanted apart from fifty pounds Shaw has given us will be raised by lectures. The Academy will be a vigorous body capable of defending our interests, negotiating with Government, and I hope preventing the worst forms of censorship. All the writers here who are likely to form our Council are students of your work.
>
> Yours sincerely
> W B Yeats

Joyce was urged by the Colums, by James Stephens, and by others to accept, but on October 5 he firmly answered the symbolic overture by an equally symbolic refusal:

Hotel Metropole, Nice

Dear Yeats,

Many thanks for your letter and the kind words you use. It is now thirty years since you first held out to me your helping hand.* Please convey my thanks also to Mr. Shaw whom I have never met.

I hope that the Academy of Irish Letters (if that is its title) which you are both founding, will have the success it aims at. My case, however, being as it was and probably will be, I see no reason why my name should have arisen at all in connection with such an academy: and I feel quite clearly that I have no right whatsoever to nominate myself as a member of it.

I am returning under separate cover the rules you were good enough to send me.

I hope your health keeps good. For myself I have to go back to Zurich every three months about my eyes. Still, I work as best I can.[47]

He responded with more alacrity to a request from Ford Madox Ford for a few words of testimonial about Ezra Pound, to help advertise an American edition of the *Cantos*. Joyce had no interest in Pound's later work, which he had probably not read. His reply, dated September 15, 1932, artfully succeeds in praising Pound without praising his work:

. . . I am very glad to hear that Pound is at last to be published in a befitting form in his own country. Last year I tried to arrange in London a publication by subscription of his collected prose writings. For some reason the scheme fell through. But evidently what you write about is far better.

Nothing could be more true than to say that we all owe a great deal to him. But I most of all surely. It is nearly twenty years since he first began his vigorous campaign on my behalf and it is probable that but for him I should still be the unknown drudge that he discovered—if it was a discovery.

Joyce remained at Nice only until October 20, 1932, when dental trouble combined with anxiety about Lucia to bring him back to Paris.

---

* When Yeats died on January 28, 1939, Joyce was much moved. He sent a wreath to the funeral, and conceded to a friend that Yeats was a greater writer than he, a tribute he paid to no other contemporary. It was Yeats's imagination which always dazzled him: 'No surrealist poet can equal it,' he said. One day he was reading *Wuthering Heights* when Eugene Jolas came in, and Joyce said to him, 'This woman had pure imagination; Kipling had it too, and certainly Yeats.' [48]

Of Kipling's imagination he remarked to David Fleischman (Helen Joyce's son by her first marriage): '*Plain Tales from the Hills* shows more promise, I believe, than any other contemporary writer's youthful work. But he did not fulfill that promise. I believe the three writers of the nineteenth century who had the greatest natural talents were D'Annunzio, Kipling, and Tolstoy—it's strange that all three had semi-fanatic ideas about religion or about patriotism.' [49]

Joyce often recited Yeats's poems from memory, and seemed to wonder if his own work was imaginative enough.

He, Nora, and Lucia stayed briefly at a disagreeable hotel on the Champs-Élysées, Nora looking after Lucia with the aid during the mornings of a young woman, and when this proved insufficient, with the aid of another young woman in the afternoons. As often before in impossible circumstances, Joyce went ahead with his work. He was still engaged during early November with the ninth chapter, the games of the children. Léon conducted almost all his correspondence for him, and Joyce straddled chaos with forced calm. His attitude in talking to Lucia was deliberately light and breezy, and remained so, and while he said he was only pretending, his letters indicate that he could still hopefully minimize her disorder. So he wrote Miss Weaver, 'In fact I am sure she tells a good few lies and does a fair amount of comedy but so do most girls in one way or another.' [50] His newest therapy was to give her 4,000 francs to buy a fur coat 'as I think that will do her inferiority complex more good than a visit to a psycho-analyst.' [51] For the time being, instead of consulting doctors, he placed a foolish trust in such improbable solutions.

The fur coat was not a great success. In the middle of November Lucia abruptly stopped her drawing, on the ground that she had not been paid for her designs in *Pomes Penyeach*. Joyce sent 1,000 francs to the publisher instructing him to pay the money to Lucia without mentioning whose money it was. Lucia shifted to bookbinding and painting anyway. Joyce took a furnished flat at 42 rue Galilée, in the eighth arrondissement, and, while conceding that Lucia alarmed him when she wept or boxed her attendant's ears, he announced to Miss Weaver, 'I will take a sporting chance.' [52] A new doctor subjected her to a 'cure' of drinking sea water by mouth, and for a month she seemed better, then relapsed. If Lucia's malady had been curable, Joyce's jumpy supervision would have been reprehensible; since it was incurable, his obstinate moving from doctor to doctor was at least proof of his affection. There was another reason which Paul Léon shrewdly perceived; Joyce had had difficulty since 1931 in working out the final aspects of *Finnegans Wake,* and saw Lucia's turmoil during the same period as parallel to his own. Léon was also to reprove him at times for taking his daughter's tragedy too much to heart, and at times for 'cerebralizing' it; [53] Joyce remained capable of these moments of detachment, but rarely achieved them now. He had always before put his writing beyond all other considerations; now, as an expression of guilt, he put his daughter's health beyond his art, and punished himself for past obtuseness by writing hardly at all and by devoting his thoughts frantically and impotently to his daughter.

As her schizophrenia became more and more manifest, he became more and more partial to her. 'Unfortunately,' he wrote Miss Weaver, 'she seems to have antagonised a great number of people including her immediate relatives and as usual I am the fellow in the middle of the rain holding out both hands though whether she is right in her blunt outspokenness or not is a question my head is too addled to answer.' [54] He relayed with exclamation-points Lucia's newest idea, to go over and stay with Miss Weaver; [55] this was the beginning of a new messianic phase in which Lucia hoped to restore her father and his patron to their former close understanding.

It was inevitable that the fellow in the rain, holding out both hands, should soon be diverted by his own sense of discomfort. Joyce acknowledged this new concern in mid-January 1933, when he went to hear Sullivan in Rouen with the Jolases and a young Indo-Chinese prince, a nephew of the king of Cambodia who had ten years before changed his name to René-Ulysse. Rouen was full of grippe, and the opera-goers were also afflicted; only Sullivan, shining in the golden armor of Reyer's *Sigurd*, seemed invulnerable. Joyce fancied himself sick, got home with difficulty, began to feel worse, and finally wandered over to Léon's house in the early morning to ask for help. The doctors found his liver and stomach healthy, and nothing wrong except some minor eye trouble; they therefore diagnosed his complaint as nervous. He himself suspected meningitis and alcoholic poisoning. He was pleased at the solicitude his condition aroused in 'that subtile et barbare person—my daughter.' [56] Miss Weaver too was sympathetic, and came to Paris to pay him a visit; but it did not go so well as usual, in part because of her concern over his drinking, and in part because of Joyce's unwillingness to defend himself in any way. Paul Léon wrote her to say that the patient 'varies from states of great irritation and impotent fury to sudden lachrymose fits.' [57] He urged her to write to Joyce and suggest he go to see Vogt in Zurich. In April, Joyce thought he was suffering from colitis, premonitory of his later stomach trouble, and knew he had insomnia. Léon's letters about his friend were almost unrelieved in their melancholy. As to *Work in Progress*, he reported, Joyce 'merely waves his hand in despair and resignation.' [58]

The Giedions came to Paris for a visit, and helped persuade Joyce to return to Zurich with them; they left together on May 22, 1933, with the hapless Lucia in tow. Frau Giedion-Welcker brought young architects to meet the girl, but there were no marriage proposals. Joyce was examined twice by Vogt on his arrival. His left eye was slightly better, his right eye slightly worse, or, as Vogt put it delicately in his report, 'disimproved.' Its cataract was almost completely calcified, so that the eye showed almost no sensitivity to light. The retina was at least in part atrophied. If total blindness in the right eye was to be avoided, an operation was necessary; Vogt again admitted this might have unfortunate results. 'He "refused to advise," ' Joyce wrote Stanislaus, 'but said if in my place and could be sure of operator like himself would run risk.' [59] The operation might take place now or in September. For the moment Joyce did not decide, but he said to Louis Gillet of possible blindness, *'Ce qu'apportent les yeux n'est rien. J'ai cent mondes à créer, je n'en perds qu'un.'* [*][60]

He now applied himself to the tenth chapter, the children's home-work lesson, which makes the history of Dublin a universal one. In July he asked Paul Léon to find a passage in the notebooks left behind in Paris; it was Edgar Quinet's beautiful sentence, which he had once astounded John Sullivan by reciting as they walked by the cemetery on the Boulevard Edgar Quinet,[61] and it recapitulated Joyce's view of history without Viconian apparatus:

Aujourd'hui comme aux temps de Pline et de Columelle la jacinthe se plaît dans les Gaules, la pervenche en Illyrie, la marguérite sur les ruines de Numance et pendant qu'autour d'elles les villes ont changé de maîtres et de noms, que plusieurs sont entrées dans le néant, que les civilisations se sont choquées et brisées, leurs paisibles generations ont traversé les âges et sont arrivées jusqu'à nous, fraîches et riantes comme aux jours des batailles.†

This was one of the very few passages from other authors which Joyce honored by quoting in *Finnegans Wake* in its original as well as in appropriately distorted form.

In July the Joyces sojourned briefly at Évian-les-Bains; they returned on July 17 for a month in Zurich. There a new scene of hysteria

---

* 'What the eyes bring is nothing. I have a hundred worlds to create, I am losing only one of them.'

† 'Today as in the time of Pliny and Columella the hyacinth disports in Wales, the periwinkle in Illyria, the daisy on the ruins in Numantia and while around them the cities have changed masters and names, while some have ceased to exist, while the civilizations have collided with each other and smashed, their peaceful genera-tions have passed through the ages and have come up to us, fresh and laughing as on the days of battles.'

Made Irish in *Finnegans Wake* (14-15), this passage becomes:
'Since the bouts of Hebear and Hairyman the cornflowers have been staying at Ballymun, the duskrose has choosed out Goatstown's hedges, twolips have pressed togatherthem by sweet Rush, townland of twinedlights, the white-thorn and the redthorn have fairygeyed the mayvalleys of Knockmaroon, and, though for rings round them, during a chiliad of perihelygangs, the Formoreans have brittled the tooath of the Danes and the Oxman has been pestered by the Firebugs and the Joynts have thrown up jerrybuilding to the Kevanses and Little on the Green is childsfather to the City (Year! Year! And laughtears!), these paxsealing buttonholes have quadrilled across the centuries and whiff now whafft to us, fresh and made-of-all-smiles as, on the eve of Killallwho.'

occurred at the railroad station, and Joyce was again constrained to consult specialists about his daughter. Professor Hans W. Maier, who held the chair of psychiatry at the University of Zurich and was also Chief Physician of the Mental Asylum of Burghölzli in Zurich, examined Lucia. He said that she was not lunatic but markedly neurotic, and advised that she be placed in 'Les Rives de Prangins' at Nyon, a sanatorium under the direction of Dr. Oscar Forel. Lucia arrived there on July 30, no longer violent, but in a dreamlike state; for the moment she was obsessed with fear about the supposed conflicts between her parents, although in their presence she was expansive and loquacious. Six days later she appeared so panic-stricken that Joyce hastily withdrew her on August 4, in spite of the diagnosis of schizophrenia with pithiatric° elements which Forel's staff had made.† [62]

Nora's position was more difficult than her husband's, because so much of Lucia's animosity was directed towards her, while at the same time so much of their daughter's care remained in her hands. With fortitude, she accepted the role of keeper, and, when Joyce was not too preoccupied to notice, he was full of admiration for her calm and ingenuity. She does not seem to have questioned her husband's right to act as his daughter's psychiatric director.

The family returned to Paris in early September 1933, and again stayed in the furnished flat on the rue Galilée. Lucia, with a companion, lived at home. When they first arrived Joyce took to his bed for a week with stomach pains, which were relieved by laudanum and were again attributed to nerves. He recovered himself to read with keen interest the proofs of Frank Budgen's new book, *James Joyce and the Making of 'Ulysses.'* He had Budgen and Stuart Gilbert to help him; as the long galley proofs kept slipping off their knees, he remarked, 'Galley proofs remind me of the persons of the Trinity. Get firm hold of one and you lose grip on the others.' [63] Budgen's book, for which he had furnished some of the details, pleased him. 'I never knew you could write so well. It must be due to your association with me,' he told his friend.[64] He also helped Gilbert translate Dujardin's *Les Lauriers sont coupés.* Only Herbert Gorman of the retinue seemed to have failed him; for months he had done nothing with his biography, and on October 27 Joyce, in irritation, withdrew authorization for the book.‡

The tenor of Joyce's days remained melancholy, but occasionally

---

° Capable of being cured by persuasion and suggestion.

† He may also have been annoyed by Forel's advice that he himself give up drinking completely.

‡ But he eventually gave it back. The delay was caused by Gorman's divorce and remarriage.

he was enlivened. During the autumn he awaited anxiously the result of the trial of *Ulysses* for obscenity in the United States District Court in New York. The case was ably prepared and argued by Morris L. Ernst, who with his assistant Alexander Lindley collected letters and opinions from hundreds of educators, writers, clergymen, businessmen, and librarians.[65] Ernst's brief quoted Stuart Gilbert, Rebecca West, Shane Leslie, Arnold Bennett, Ernest Boyd, Gilbert Seldes, and Edmund Wilson. The argument contended that standards of obscenity change, and that *Ulysses* was not obscene by the standards of 1933. It was, instead, a classic, far too complicated to challenge the curiosity of the lascivious, and written on the whole for 'edification and delight.'[66] The intelligent judge, John M. Woolsey, listened carefully to the arguments on November 25. He had devoted most of the summer to reading the book. On December 6 he announced his decision so eloquently and emphatically that Joyce at last achieved his old ambition of obtaining a famous verdict. Woolsey's decision said much more than it had to; it suggested that Joyce was seeking to represent the screen of consciousness, by means of a clear foreground and a background visible but somewhat blurred and out of focus in varying degrees. The intention and method required frankness, and without it would have been dishonest. He nowhere found 'the leer of the sensualist,' but an 'honest,' 'sincere,' 'somewhat tragic but very powerful commentary on the inner lives of men and women.' His final words put his view neatly and pungently:

I am quite aware that owing to some of its scenes 'Ulysses' is a rather strong draught to ask some sensitive, though normal, persons to take. But my considered opinion, after long reflection, is that whilst in many places the effect of 'Ulysses' on the reader undoubtedly is somewhat emetic, nowhere does it tend to be an aphrodisiac.

'Ulysses' may, therefore, be admitted into the United States.[67]

The verdict was at once telephoned to Bennett Cerf at Random House, and within ten minutes he had the typesetters at work on the book.[68] There was some fear of another piracy,[69] so the first one hundred copies were published to secure copyright in January 1934, and the rest followed in February, Joyce's pet month. By coincidence, as Morris L. Ernst noted,[70] the prohibition law was repealed during the same week that the *Ulysses* decision was announced, and a general shift in moral standards seemed confirmed by the two events.

News of Woolsey's decision reached Joyce by cable, and was soon spread over Paris. The telephone kept ringing as friends called to congratulate Joyce. Lucia, exasperated by the noise of her father's fame, abruptly cut the telephone wires. They were repaired and she cut them again. Reporters tried to obtain a statement from Joyce, and he authorized Paul Léon to say simply, 'Mr. Joyce finds the judge to be not devoid of a sense of humour.' But on 20 December he sent his friend Curran twelve bottles of Clos S. Patrice, 1920, rouge, and then commented triumphantly on the Woolsey decision: 'Thus one half of the English speaking world surrenders. The other half will follow.' * [71]

Lucia was now receiving psychiatric treatment, but without success. She continued to upset family and friends by her disconcerting bluntness, which sometimes struck home with mad insight. Her father listened to her always with respect, and when she concocted a story of having been seduced by all the young men who visited him, he sent them all away, even a Dublin bachelor of exemplary piety and almost notorious chastity, who was deeply offended. This display of paternal gullibility did not appease Lucia, who ran away from home in January 1934, and was persuaded to return only by threats of police intervention. Incidents of this kind had become numerous; yet Joyce maintained his insulation against what they implied, and continued desperately to treat his daughter as a slightly confused but on the whole typical young woman. Clinging to a conviction that a change of surroundings might cure her, he wrote to Stanislaus to ask if she might visit Trieste. But before his brother could reply, Lucia upset the birthday party on February 2, 1934, by striking Nora, and her internment in a sanatorium could no longer be deferred.

Joyce sent her, accompanied by a nurse, back to Forel's sanatorium at Nyon. On her arrival she was apathetic, incapable of concentration, full of ambivalent wishes, but a few days later she seemed oddly content with her surroundings. Then in March, Joyce's unquenchable expectation of a miraculous cure was momentarily dashed by her 'pseudo-hallucinative dissociation' of mind, and by her several attempts to run away to Paris. During one of these she tried to seek refuge in a peasant hut, intending to cross the border next day, but was found and brought back. Her condition was to grow worse instead of better. Joyce continued to hope; he wrote Frank Budgen on April 25, 'She'll get all right they say. One needs all Solomon's wisdom and the Queen of Sheba's pin money thrown in.' [72]

With Lucia away, it became possible for him to live at least a semblance of ordinary life in Paris. Léon protected him from intrusion, though Joyce was not unwilling to be intruded upon. So he was

---

* In anticipation of the decision, Joyce had written to Harriet Weaver two years before, 'I suppose England will follow suit a few years later, and Ireland 1000 years hence.' [73]

unexpectedly receptive when the Honorable Mrs. Reginald (Daisy) Fellowes, a well-known figure in society with literary pretensions, announced that she wished her group, *Les Amis de 1914,* to hold a celebration in Joyce's honor. She made the usual roundabout approach through Léon, then cut through this folderol by suddenly appearing at Joyce's door and pushing in with a photographer at her heels. Her intention was to be photographed alone with Joyce, but Joyce insisted that Léon, who was present, join the group, added Eugene Jolas who appeared during the preparations, and even drew the buxom concierge into the picture in spite of Mrs. Fellowes's protests. 'This is wonderful; we can have a family group,' he said.[74] But when the picture appeared only Joyce and Mrs. Fellowes could be seen, the others having been cut off. Nora was indignant.

The meeting was arranged for February 23, 1934. Joyce thought it might help to revive the interest in *Finnegans Wake* which was flagging as publication was delayed. The Honorable Mrs. Fellowes presided, testifying to her enthusiasm for Joyce's work. When she sailed her yacht in the Aegean, she said, 'I never lie in my deck chair without a copy of *Ulysses* by my side.' Then Dujardin was called upon, to salute Joyce's development of the *monologue intérieur;* Louis Gillet and Léon-Paul Fargue also made speeches, and the actress Rachel Behrendt, who knew English and was coached by Joyce, read fragments from *Work in Progress.* Throughout the meeting Joyce sat languid in his chair, his long, fine hands clasped on his knees, his eyes cast down like a bashful boy's, and of course altogether silent, having refused the Honorable Mrs. Fellowes' invitation to reply on the grounds that, 'It's not polite to speak about oneself.'[75] Afterwards, however, he sought to have Rachel Behrendt's reading recorded by the British Broadcasting Corporation, and Maria Jolas talked at his request to Harley Granville-Barker about it.[76] But the B.B.C. was not interested.

Miss Weaver had come to feel that Joyce's life must somehow be put in better order. He had failed to return to Vogt for his consultation, thus further endangering his eye; his furnished flat was inadequate for his needs; his book was not getting finished. She visited him briefly in early March and tactfully suggested he pull his affairs together, at the same time making clear that he could depend on her financial help as well as her loyalty. He should begin by having his eyes looked after. Joyce was in a mood to pay attention, and when, at the beginning of April 1934, his friend René Bailly, a French industrialist married to a woman from Galway who had become friendly with Nora, invited the Joyces to motor with them to Zurich by way of Monte Carlo and Neuchâtel, he decided to accept. His departure was made melancholy by the news that his old friend Georges Borach had been killed in an automobile accident along the same route. Joyce avoided telling Nora of the death until they arrived in Zurich, but she too felt keenly the loss of this friend. They visited his mother and found her, 'a *Pietà*,' in tears before her son's photograph.[77] 'Why should Borach have gone off on such a wild trip?' Joyce asked Carola Giedion-Welcker afterwards. Then he answered himself, 'It was to compensate for his physical disabilities. But why on a Good Friday and on the thirteenth?' [78]

Professor Vogt informed Joyce that he still needed the two operations on his right eye and would gain more sight by them.[79] These two operations ('world's amateur championship,' as Joyce wrote Budgen) [80] might however be again postponed until September. Joyce remained in Zurich a few more days. Bernhard Fehr, professor of English at the University of Zurich, brought him to a concert where they heard Othmar Schoeck's Lied-Zyklus *Lebendig-Begraben* (opus 40), a suite of fourteen songs by Gottfried Keller for male voice and orchestra. Joyce was amazed by them and later translated them.[81] He made a point of meeting Schoeck, the only modern composer besides Antheil for whom he had any taste. He congratulated Schoeck on composing for the singing voice, unlike Stravinsky, whose works, he said, 'not even a canary could sing.' [82] With his usual pertinacity, he sought to persuade Schoeck to write the opera based on Byron's *Cain* which Antheil had abandoned, and searched second-hand bookstores in Zurich until he found it in German translation. But Schoeck was not attracted.[83]

The Joyces returned to Paris by train, and on the way Joyce, recalling a performance of *Ghosts* he had seen the month before at the Théâtre des Champs-Élysées, with Ginette Faccone in the leading role, and perhaps also with his friend Borach's twisted body in mind, wrote a half-comic, half-serious poem, 'An Epilogue to Ibsen's "Ghosts".' [84] He was worried later that it might be considered autobiographical, and cautioned Gorman to print it near the beginning rather than the end of his biography.* Captain Alving, the speaker in the poem, points

---

* Since the poem parodies Ibsen's familiar devices of Spreading the Guilt and the Horrible Hint, Joyce carefully emphasized that he had not lost his respect for his Norwegian precursor. He dictated for Gorman the remark: 'This (which is in fact a grotesque amplification of Osvalt's own attempted defense of his father in the play) is not to be interpreted, however, in the sense that he does not consider Ibsen to be the supreme dramatic poet, basing his belief, however, on the later plays from the *Wild Duck* onwards, and of course does not mean that he considers *Ghosts* as anything but a great tragedy.' [85]

out that he is assumed to have fathered two children, one out of wedlock and one in, the first (Regina) healthy, the second (Oswald) congenitally sick. Pursuing the trail of guilt with the zeal of the ghost in *Hamlet,* and profiting from suggestions in *Ghosts* that Parson Manders and Mrs. Alving were once in love, the captain suggests that Manders was Oswald's begetter. Joyce's interest in the profligate father suggests both his own father and himself. The parallel could be pressed a little farther; however much he might deny Lucia's malady, he too had one sick and one healthy child. But only in the otherness of composition, in the dramatic stance of his poem, would he have allowed himself to think of his children in these terms. While Joyce is immanent in Captain Alving, Captain Alving was someone else:

Epilogue to Ibsen's 'Ghosts'

Dear quick, whose conscience buried deep
The grim old grouser has been salving,
Permit one spectre more to peep.
I am the ghost of Captain Alving.

Silenced and smothered by my past
Like the lewd knight in dirty linen
I struggle forth to swell the cast
And air a long-suppressed opinion.

For muddling weddings into wakes
No fool could vie with Parson Manders.
I, though a dab at ducks and drakes,
Let gooseys serve or sauce their ganders.

My spouse bore me a blighted boy,
Our slavey pupped a bouncing bitch.
Paternity, thy name is joy
When the wise sire knows which is which.

Both swear I am that self-same man
By whom their infants were begotten.
Explain, fate, if you care and can
Why one is sound and one is rotten.

Olaf may plod his stony path
And live as chastely as Susanna
Yet pick up in some Turkish bath
His *quantum est* of *Pox Romana.*

While Haakon hikes up primrose way,
Spreeing and gleeing while he goes,

To smirk upon his latter day
Without a pimple on his nose.

I gave it up I am afraid
But if I loafed and found it fun
Remember how a coyclad maid
Knows how to take it out of one.

The more I dither on and drink
My midnight bowl of spirit punch
The firmlier I feel and think
Friend Manders came too oft to lunch.

Since scuttling ship Vikings like me
Reck not to whom the blame is laid,
Y.M.C.A., V.D., T.B.
Or Harbourmaster of Port-Said.

Blame all and none and take to task
The harlot's lure, the swain's desire.
Heal by all means but hardly ask
Did this man sin or did his sire.

The shack's ablaze. That canting scamp,
The carpenter, has dished the parson.
Now had they kept their powder damp
Like me there would have been no arson.

Nay, more, were I not all I was,
Weak, wanton, waster out and out,
There would have been no world's applause
And damn all to write home about.

Back in Paris Joyce prepared *The Mime of Mick Nick and the Maggies* (Chapter IX) for publication by the Servire Press in the Hague in June 1934. It ended with the prayer which finely summed up its author's view of life: 'Loud, heap miseries upon us yet entwine our arts with laughters low!' [86] To assist him in completing it he had the help of Madame France Raphael, an intelligent woman whose duty it was to copy in large letters his almost illegible notations. Confused by idioms in different languages, she said to him, 'I hope that what I have been doing makes sense, but sometimes I feel as if I were floundering in a bog.' Joyce replied handsomely, 'Oh well, you have understood better than most people will after it is finished.' * [87] Soon after

---

* He paid a similar compliment to Armand Petitjean, who translated some of the book into French. 'Why,' said Joyce with a strange look, 'you've nearly understood me.' And in acknowledgment he recited the whole of *Anna Livia Plurabelle.* As Petitjean commented in remembering the scene, 'He was Orpheus.' [88]

his return to Paris she was thrown from an automobile and suffered a skull fracture. Joyce was astounded, remarking that she was the third secretary to be seriously injured while working for him. His letter to her of April 24, 1934, suggests the solicitous courtesy he extended in his friends' misfortunes:

> Dear Mrs Raphael
>
> I am very sorry to hear of the dreadful accident. Your niece says you are now out of danger, but what a frightful shock! It is well you are not disfigured, and I understand that it is not likely to leave any serious trace.
>
> I do hope you will get some compensation in spite of the lack of witnesses and that your suffering is not too great.
>
> Let me thank you once again for your quick and excellent transcriptions. You have rendered me a very great service.
>
> With my very best wishes for your speedy and complete recovery
>
> > Sincerely yours
> > James Joyce [89]

He followed the letter by a visit, during which he placed a hand on her shoulder and said, 'Well, now you can be sure nothing else will ever happen to you.' [90]

Robert McAlmon invaded Paris again with the news, not wholly welcome, that he had finished the manuscript of his autobiographical book, *Being Geniuses Together*. Joyce asked him to read the manuscript to him, and McAlmon did so during several afternoons. The tone was quite different from that of Frank Budgen's book, which was to appear a few months later in 1934. While Budgen never lost sight of Joyce as a writer, McAlmon was more concerned with him as a member of the heavy-drinking Bohemian set. The result was a less amiable portrait than McAlmon intended. Joyce confided to Miss Weaver that the book made him feel 'actionable,' [91] but to McAlmon he only laughed and said, 'You should call it *Advocatus Diaboli*.' McAlmon answered forthrightly, 'What in hell do you think the title means, that I take genius without salt?' [92] But when it was reported to McAlmon later that Joyce had referred to the book as 'the office boy's revenge,' he was in turn displeased. Joyce speculated to Miss Weaver on the source of McAlmon's 'malice,' which he thought he detected in passages referring to her as well; but McAlmon had not intended malice, only candor. Joyce did not break with him, but their friendship, which had lost in warmth over the last few years, became perfunctory.

Another dislocation of the family was now to take place. Helen had been urging George Joyce to come to the United States, both to meet her family and to see if his singing career might be advanced there. Nora vigorously opposed their going, suspecting they might well remain away permanently, but her husband did not try to dissuade them. They sailed on May 19, and did not come back for over a year. Joyce kept up a steady correspondence, writing to them, as he spoke to Lucia, with a deliberate lightness. So on June 1 he told them:

I work every day alone at one big long wide high deep dense prose-work. We went to hear Gigli (who sang in a gymnasium, *Palais des Sports,* but has a beautiful voice. He imitates MacCormack but has an ampler organ—not so true.) S. [Sullivan] in *La Favorite* (this time he surprised us all by his acting). *La Machine Infernale,* very well given. Mrs J. J. and Mrs Maria J. went to the *Folies Bergeres* while E. J. [Jolas] and I went to see a Palestine company playing *Jacob and Rachel* in . . . Hebrew, not Yiddish. It was very remarkable and barbarian. . . .

They called in a German specialist at Nyon and he advised them to treat Lucia as if she had something or other, though there is no trace of it. And this apparently is doing her good. . . .

Our best wishes to you both and regards to you both, and trilingual greetings to your lively charge. I shake all your amalgamated hands several times over in rapid succession with that charming grace for which I have always been noted and blow to you in valediction my parental and parento-legal blessings from this little old log cabin down the Seine.

Babbo [93]

And a month later, on July 1, after retailing his flat-hunting troubles, he went on:

We dine in Fouquet's very frequently, in fact almost always. It has become a chic prize-ring. The other night an advanced lady slapped a perfect gentleman's face on account of another perfect lady's being with him. The well bred diners jumped up on benches and chairs. And the row went on. I refused to have my attention distracted from the business in hand, to wit, a carafe of champagne nature but I could hear a great deal. Again a few nights ago there was a sudden scuffle, blows, fall of plates, shrieks of women etc. Léon was with us. My wife became a little alarmed but I did as before and she is getting used to it. Some people are so playful. . . .

I am sorry to note that as a result of the sea voyage Giorgio is over a half-foot shorter than when he left since the reporter found him to be of medium height. But shure plaise the Lord he'll be shootin' up again on the way back and be his owld sex foot wan be the time yiz are landed in the Frinch metrollops.[94]

Nora also, when she could bring herself to write, gave an amusing picture of the old folks at home. She had bought a new evening dress for a party:

Jim thought the back was a bit too decolleté so he decided he would have to stitch up the back of the dress can you imagine the result? Of course he stiched it all crooked. So I had to undo the stiches again. I decided it was better [to] have a bare back. I wish you could have seen him stiching my skin [and] back bone altogether.[95]

His letters to Lucia were softer in tone, written in Italian:

42, rue Galilée, Paris

Dear Lucia:

Mamma has dispatched to you today some articles of clothing. As soon as the list of what you want comes we will send off the things immediately. There was no list in the letter of the 29 ult. As to the typewriter, it would be a huge expense, about 4000 francs. There is one here in the house and I gather from Dr. Forel's last letter, which gave me great joy, that your sojourn on the pleasant shores of the lake of Geneva will not be too much prolonged now. (The devil take the summer! The heat clouds my spectacles and I see with difficulty what I write!) But you could hire a machine. At Geneva certainly you would find one.

Something is always lacking in my royal palace. Today is the turn of ink. I send you the programme of the Indian dancer Uday Shankar. If he ever performs at Geneva don't miss going there. He leaves the best of the Russians far behind. I have never seen anything like it. He moves on the stage floor like a semi-divine being. Altogether, believe me, there are still some beautiful things in this poor old world.

I am glad that you are on good terms with that Dutch doctor but does it not seem to you that it would be rude on my part to write to him when I am in correspondence with doctors Forel and Humbert? But if he writes to me first then I could reply to him. (Saint Francis de Sales, protector of writers, pour a little ink into this inkstand!)

Mamma is chattering on the telephone with the lady above who dances the one-step so well and fished my note of a thousand lire out of the lift. The subject of the conversation between them is the lady on the fifth floor who breeds dogs. These 'friends of man' hinder the lady on the fourth floor from meditating like the Buddha. Now they have finished with gods and are speaking of me.

I see great progress in your last letter but at the same time there is a sad note which we do not like. Why do you always sit at the window? No doubt it makes a pretty picture but a girl walking in the fields also makes a pretty picture.

Write to us oftener. And let's forget money troubles and black
thoughts.

Ti abraccio,
Babbo [96]

15 June 1934

After much hunting and several disappointments Joyce found a flat
on the fifth floor at 7 rue Edmond Valentin, close to the river and
not far from the Eiffel Tower. 'My forty months of wandering in the
wilderness must come to an end,' he agreed with Miss Weaver.[97] It
had five rooms, a telephone, and heat, and it could be reached by
elevator.[98] When Joyce signed a lease on July 12, 1934, it was not
ready for occupancy; he commissioned Paul Léon to supervise the
necessary arrangements for decorating and seized the occasion to take
Nora off to the Hôtel Britannique at Spa, Belgium. As usual during
his holidays, the weather was bad; since it was the time of the
Nazi *Putsch* in Austria, the news was another source of disquiet. Joyce
had surveyed the rise of German nationalism without sympathy; the
world of discipline, anti-Semitism, and national frenzy was not his. He
wrote now to Miss Weaver, 'I am afraid poor Mr Hitler-Missler will
soon have few friends in Europe apart from your nieces and my
nephews, Masters W. Lewis and E. Pound.' [99]

Other cares he brought with him. Holroyd-Reece of the Albatross
Press had lost Lucia's *lettrines,* and after some months of equivocation
confessed as much. Joyce thought the loss 'sinister,' and threatened to
sue him; they were at last recovered. He also wished to make sure
that Henri Matisse, who had agreed to illustrate *Ulysses* for a special
American edition by the Limited Editions Club, would have his Irish
details right. So he wrote to T. W. Pugh, that knowledgeable Dubliner,
asking him to find some illustrated weekly published in Dublin about
1904. Matisse, he told Pugh, 'knows the French translation very well
but has never been in Ireland.' [100] But Pugh's researches were in vain;
Matisse, after consulting briefly with Eugene Jolas, went his own way,
in the late summer and early fall of 1934; when asked why his drawings bore so little relation to the book, he said frankly, '*Je ne l'ai pas
lu.*' [101] He had based them on the Odyssey.

After resting in Belgium until the middle of August, Joyce and
Nora went on to Luxembourg, Metz, and Nancy, making their way
slowly towards Lucia. On August 28, 1934, they had reached Montreux, and with grim forebodings went to see Dr. Forel at Les Rives
de Prangins. As they feared, he had bad news for them: Lucia was
worse, and the several treatments attempted had all failed. Besides

her mental trouble, she suffered from leucocytosis,[102] an excess of white blood corpuscles. They went to see her, and their presence excited her to new bursts of causeless fear and scenes of violence with doctors and nurses, shot through by flashes of lucidity. In some of these Joyce found clairvoyant power: she insisted he take up pipe-smoking, and the next day, when he was sitting on a bench in Geneva, he felt a hard object beside him and discovered it was a pipe, or as he preferred to believe, *the* pipe. 'She has sometimes,' he reported to George, 'the wisdom of the serpent and the innocence of the dove.' [103]

Joyce had not intended to move Lucia again, but decided that he must try something else. Forel agreed that Lucia might be put under the *'cure libre'* of a Dr. Loy in Geneva; but on September 15, the day before her proposed transfer, she started a fire in her room in four places, and nearly succeeded in burning it up. Forel now felt that permanent clinical observation was essential, and Joyce decided to have her transferred to Burghölzli, the mental asylum in Zurich, so that Professor Naegeli, a famous blood expert, might treat her blood condition and perhaps effect a physical cure of her mental condition. She arrived there on September 20 and seemed momentarily in command of herself, but Professor Maier, who examined her, found it impossible to establish a meaningful relation with her and described her condition as catatonic. He pressed her as to why she had tried to set fire to her room at Prangins, but she would not answer him. She remarked later to a nurse, however, that her father's complexion was very red and so was fire.[104]

Lucia had heard tales of Burghölzli during her childhood, and stayed there a week in gathering alarm, her father's sympathy swelling in concert. He and Nora came every day at teatime to take her for a walk in the city. 'The poor child is not a raving lunatic,' he wrote Miss Weaver, in defiance of the doctors' verdict, 'just a poor child who tried to do too much, to understand too much. Her dependence on me is now absolute, and all the affection she repressed for years pours itself out on both of us. Minerva direct me.' [105] He had to decide where to send her next, and remembered the suggestion of Mrs. Jolas that he put her under the care of Jung, who, for all his shortcomings as a critic of *Ulysses*, might perform a psychiatric miracle. 'My daughter is not myself,' he said to the Giedions, 'I wouldn't go to him, but maybe he can help her.' [106] Accordingly, on September 28, Joyce had Lucia transferred to the private sanatorium of Dr. Brunner at Küsnacht, where Jung, the twentieth doctor to be consulted for Lucia, was on the staff.

Lucia spoke freely to Jung instead of being mute as she usually was with doctors. She seemed happier and gained weight.[107] Jung did not at first give her up completely, and the few words of hope he expressed had an extraordinary effect upon Joyce, who, though he was absolutely resolved to regard her as curable, desperately wanted reassurance. In October 1934, Lucia wrote her father a letter in Italian which Jung, who did not know the language, asked Joyce to translate. It said:

Father dear,

I am very fond of you. Thanks for the pretty pen. Zurich is not the worst place in the world is it? Maybe one day, you can come with me to the museum, father. I think that you are spending a lot of money on me. Father, if you want to go back to Paris you would do well to do so. Father dear, I have had too nice a life. I am spoiled. You must both forgive me. I hope that you will come again here. Father, if ever I take a fancy to anybody I swear to you on the head of Jesus that it will not be because I am not fond of you. Do not forget that. I don't really know what I am writing Father. At Prangins I saw a number of artists, especially women who seemed to me all very hysterical. Am I to turn out like them? No, it would be better to sell shoes if that can be done with simplicity and truth. And besides, I don't know whether all this I am writing means anything to you.

I should like to have a life as quiet as I have now with a garden and perhaps a dog, but nobody is ever contented, isn't that so? So many people were envious of me and of Mama because you are too good. It is a pity that you don't like Ireland for after all, it is a lovely country if I may judge by the pictures I have seen, and the stories I have heard. Who knows what fate has in store for us? At any rate, in spite of the fact that life seems full of light this evening, here, if ever I should go away, it would be to a country which belongs in a way to you,* isn't that true father? I am still writing silly things you see.

I send you both affectionate greetings, and I hope you did not miss your train the other day.

Lucia

P.S. Why don't you go and have dinner in that little restaurant near the Hotel Habis Royal where we went years ago?

The seemingly innocent suggestion in the postscript referred to the hotel (under a new name) in which her father and mother had spent their honeymoon.[108] Lucia's world turned, as much as her father's, about a family axis.

As her madness increased, his belief in her clairvoyance increased

---

* A paraphrase of remarks by Joyce and by his Stephen Dedalus.

too.* On October 21, 1934, still smarting perhaps from the implication that her incendiary attack was directed against himself, he wrote Miss Weaver:

It seems to me that the attempts made by more than one person to poison her mind against me have failed and that I am in such a position that whether I go or stay I shall be blamed as the culprit. Maybe I am an idiot but I attach the greatest importance to what Lucia says when she is talking about herself. Her intuitions are amazing. The people who have warped her kind and gentle nature are themselves failures and if they smile at her remarks as those of a spoilt bourgeoise child it is because they are stupid failures into the bargain. My wife and I have seen hundreds of examples of her clairvoyance. Of course I don't mean the juggling variety.[109]

The proofs he adduced of Lucia's clairvoyance were touching. He pointed out that Lucia was suddenly aware that her Aunt Eileen Schaurek had moved to Bray, though she had not seen the letter in which the fact was reported.[110] He did not bother to investigate the possibility that her doctor had informed her. Again, Lucia remarked on October 25 that she had been thinking all day of John McCormack, and was jealous of his success. 'I thought of writing to the Pope,' she told her father. 'Be careful of your grammar,' replied her father banteringly, 'he is a learned man.' 'He's an old dotard,' said Lucia, 'but it is unjust. How long will your country refuse to recognize what you have done?' 'How long indeed?' said her father. Lucia went on, 'I want to reconcile you. It is time for some great person of your country to come forward and hold out a hand to you and to us.' To which Joyce replied, 'Hear, hear.' [111] But the next morning he received a cable from McCormack promising to help George,[112] and the day following, the *Irish Times* carried a long and not unfriendly article on *Work in Progress.*† [113] Her father wrote Curran, 'It is terrible to think of a vessel of election as the prey of impulses beyond its control and of natures beneath its comprehension and, fervently as I desire her cure, I ask myself what will happen when and if she finally withdraws her regard from the lightning-lit revery of her clairvoyance and turns it upon that battered cabman's face, the world.' [114]

* He had sometimes found instances of clairvoyance in his own work. As he said long before to Oscar Schwarz in Trieste, echoing Wilde, 'My art is not a mirror held up to nature. Nature mirrors my art.' [115] And he had many examples, such as Cosgrave's suicide in the Thames in accordance with Stephen's prediction about 'Lynch' in *Ulysses*.
† Joyce's friends had other instances to prove Lucia was a Cassandra. So when, a little later, Lucia showed Lucie Léon a picture of a coffin with the rubric, 'This is Jim,' Mme Léon assumed the reference was to her brother James, who died not long afterwards.[116] But Lucia must have had another Jim in mind.

The news from George was for a time fairly good. McCormack did give him a little help, and he had several engagements. In November and December he sang on National Broadcasting Company programs, the selections being Irish songs and arias by Mozart and Tchaikowsky. One of the songs was his father's favorite, 'The Brown and the Yellow Ale,' the other was 'The Salley Gardens.' George's difficulty with such material came from the fact that his accent was European rather than Irish. He was nervous but for the moment elated.[117] Before each performance his father sent a cable of encouragement, and after the second Joyce wrote from Paris to remark on two coincidences: he also had sung 'The Salley Gardens' at his first public concert and received two guineas, the same as George's ten-dollar fee.[118] For good measure he reminded his son that to change from the Banque Nationale de Crédit (where George had once worked) to the National Broadcasting Company was merely to alter the order of the initial letters.[119] The *New Yorker* carried an interview with George on January 12, 1935, but devoted it chiefly to small talk about his father.

Although Joyce wrote to his son frequently, he said little about Lucia's condition, not wishing to burden him and knowing that George was convinced she could not be cured. Jung was still trying to help her, and, to give the doctor free play, Joyce informed his daughter he was leaving Zurich for a month, an announcement she did not take calmly. Actually he remained, at considerable expense, in the Carlton Élite Hotel in Zurich. He was bothered again by 'colitis' (as he diagnosed it) and, in spite of news from the United States that the Attorney General's appeal from Woolsey's decision about *Ulysses* had been lost,* he fell into black melancholy. Paul Léon, steadfast through these troubles, wrote and even telephoned him from Paris to get a grip on himself,[120] but Joyce, except for occasional work on his book, sank deeper into his depression. As he wrote Budgen on December 18, 1934, 'If anything is ahead of us except ruin I wish someone would point it out.'

Jung, after his initial success, could not keep his hold over Lucia. 'To think that such a big fat materialistic Swiss man should try to get hold of my soul!' she commented later.[121] Her only trust was in her father, and his supposed absence upset rather than quieted her. Her mind veered from one whim to another. She announced she wished to have plastic surgery for removal of the scar on her chin, and a

---

* The United States Circuit Court of Appeals ruled on August 8, 1934, that *Ulysses* was not lewd or immoral. Justices Learned Hand and Augustus N. Hand in the majority opinion held that 'Art certainly cannot advance under compulsion to traditional forms.' Justice Martin T. Manton (later imprisoned for corruption in office) dissented. The government decided not to press the case any further.

surgeon was sent for, but at the last moment she objected to his face and jumped out of her chair.[122] On Christmas day, Joyce having told Lucia he was back in the city, she came in for lunch, and again on Boxing Day. She was not hysterical on these occasions, but was far from well. Her father had several discussions with Jung. When the psychologist pointed out schizoid elements in poems Lucia had written, Joyce, remembering Jung's comments on *Ulysses,* insisted they were anticipations of a new literature, and said his daughter was an innovator not yet understood.[123] Jung granted that some of her portmanteau words and neologisms were remarkable, but said they were random; she and her father, he commented later, were like two people going to the bottom of a river, one falling and the other diving.* [124] It is true that in an uncontrolled way she imitated ideas, fixations, and language that her father controlled. The relationship of father and daughter Jung thought to be a kind of mystical identity or participation; he called Lucia her father's *anima inspiratrix.*† But Jung was reading Joyce, as he once said he had read *Ulysses,*‡ backwards. It was not Lucia who, going out of her mind, invented portmanteau words; it was her father, after a quarter-century of study of the possibilities of language. Joyce did, it is true, push Lucia as he had pushed

---

* Early in 1935 Lucia wrote a letter to the King of England which, like Anna Livia Plurabelle's letter in *Finnegans Wake,* began with the salutation: 'Majesty.' About ten years before Lucia had met the King of Spain at a summer resort, and her father said jokingly at the time that the encounter had turned her head.

† In a letter to Patricia Hutchins Jung summarized his interpretation in this way:

    If you know anything of my Anima theory, Joyce and his daughter are a classical example of it. She was definitely his 'femme inspiratrice,' which explains his obstinate reluctance to have her certified. His own Anima, i.e., unconscious psyche, was so solidly identified with her, that to have her certified would have been as much as an admission that he himself had a latent psychosis. It is therefore understandable that he could not give in. His 'psychological' style is definitely schizophrenic, with the difference, however, that the ordinary patient cannot help himself talking and thinking in such a way, while Joyce willed it and moreover developed it with all his creative forces, which incidentally explains why he himself did not go over the border. But his daughter did, because she was no genius like her father, but merely a victim of her disease. In any other time of the past Joyce's work would never have reached the printer, but in our blessed XXth century it is a message, though not yet understood.[125]

‡ Joyce alludes to Jung's comment that *Ulysses* could be read backwards or forwards in *Finnegans Wake* (121), 'The words which follow may be taken in any order desired . . .' He included among the titles of schoolboy essays, 'Is the Co-Education of Animus and Anima Wholly Desirable?' (307), one which indicates that he understood fully what Jung was driving at. Elsewhere he makes merry at Jung's expense: 'we grisly old Sykos who have done our unsmiling bit on 'alices, when they were yung and easily freudened' (115); 'anama anamaba anamabapa' (267), 'The law of the jungerl' (268).

Nora into a superior role; he punished his imaginary guilt for her
illness by a subservience to her wishes, however capricious. But she
was his daughter, not his muse.

Jung was equally mistaken in insisting that Joyce was a latent
schizoid who used drinking to control his schizoidal tendencies. It was
not easy for Jung, who had been brought up in a 'fanatical anti-alcoholic
tradition,' [126] to understand the attitude of Joyce, whose rearing was
diametrically opposite. Joyce was abstemious during the day, and drank
only at night.* He drank with a nice combination of purpose and
relaxation: during his convivial evenings he filled his mind with the
way people talked and behaved, storing up what he needed for his
writing; he also confided to intimate friends the latest anxieties of his
life; and as the hour grew later he sang and cavorted to forget his
troubles and circumvent his reticences. He engaged in excess with
considerable prudence.

As Jung made his pronouncements about Lucia, Joyce listened in
silence; he seemed so unswayed by them that Jung took his manner
to indicate he had no emotional *rapport* with others, when in fact he
had no emotional rapport with 'the Reverend Doctor Jung' (as he
later referred to him). A man who had so misconstrued *Ulysses* could
scarcely be expected by Joyce to construe Lucia correctly.

Joyce decided there was no purpose in keeping Lucia at Küsnacht
any longer. Dr. Brunner tried to dissuade him from a new plan of
placing her in a private pension in Zurich with a nurse; but Jung
pleased Joyce this time by approving. According to a letter of Joyce,
he 'told me nobody could make any head of her but myself as she
was a very exceptional case and certainly not one for psychoanalytic
treatment which he said might provoke a catastrophe from which she
would never recover.' [128] Joyce installed her on January 14, 1935, in
his Zurich hotel's annex, the Villa Élite, with a nurse-companion. Lucia
asked her indulgent father to send for Eileen Schaurek to take care
of her, and Joyce did so.

With Eileen at hand and on good terms with Lucia, Joyce led his
entourage back to Paris at the end of January. Miss Weaver then invited Lucia to visit her in London, and Lucia took up the idea with
unforeseen zest. Paris was full of unpleasant memories for her, Joyce
said, and besides Beckett was in London and she wished to see him. [129]

---

* Joyce said once to Padraic Colum, 'What is better than to sit at the end of the
day and drink wine with friends, or with substitutes for friends? I say at the end
of the day, for I would not drink wine until the sun goes down. Wine is sunshine;
under the figure of wine the Creator of the Universe could manifest himself. Can
you imagine a manifestation under another figure?' [130]

She had also a motive which she told only to her father, 'to establish a final link,' as Joyce wrote Miss Weaver several months later, 'between the dissolute being who is writing these lines and your honourable self.' [131] Then she would go on to Dublin to mend the relations of Joyce and Ireland.

Since Mrs. Schaurek felt she must return to Ireland, she took Lucia to London about February 15 and remained for a few days to make sure all went well. Miss Weaver's first response to Lucia was altogether favorable. 'She is very depressed of course though by no means all the time, and as she herself says, lacks concentration, but that anyone could call her insane seems to me (so far) absurd.' [132] Yet her next sentence contained a muted warning: 'To her aunt she has spoken of buying a pistol but when the former suggested her buying two in case one should not work she laughed and slapped her on the back.' [133] Joyce, heartened again, sent Lucia Dante's *Vita Nuova* as a meaningful gift. For a week she was sufficiently docile so that Eileen felt safe in returning briefly to Dublin, but the news that her aunt was leaving disturbed Lucia. She saw Eileen off on February 24, 1935, then began a series of mad maneuvers which left Miss Weaver, brave and conscientious as she was, beside herself. One night Lucia failed to appear, having taken a room somewhere else. Then she decided to have her chin operated upon, and demanded consultations with doctors.[134] Eileen was hastily recalled early in March, but Lucia was increasingly unmanageable. There was a pathetic and yet comic *contretemps:* Lucia had spoken of going to Windsor, and suddenly jumped into a bus with that marking. Eileen with presence of mind jumped in after her, then telephoned Miss Weaver from a hotel in Windsor to ask that she bring some clothes. Now Lucia telegraphed Miss Weaver she was returning to London, but instead of doing so she went back to the hotel. Then she disappeared again.[135] Joyce pooh-poohed these goings-on, saying they were nothing compared with what Nora had put up with for four years. He decided to send Lucia to Bray with Eileen, and she left on March 16.

It was impossible for Miss Weaver now to say anything that would please Joyce. When she spoke of being sorry for Eileen, he replied impatiently on April 7,

Your letter expresses great sympathy for my sister. Possibly Lucia, not having been brought up as a slave and having neither Bolshevik nor Hitlerite tendencies, made a very bad impression on you and she certainly does not flatter, but in my opinion the difference between my daughter and my sister is the difference between a knife and a corkscrew which any intelligent person can see by a glance at their faces.[136]

He forced her to discuss his daughter as if she was sane. 'What I would like to know if you are writing to me is whether you liked Lucia or not. . . . I do not like you to mention her in the same breath with my cousin or sister or anybody else. If she should be so mentioned then it is I who am mad.' [137] It was true that 'She behaves like a fool very often but her mind is as clear and as unsparing as the lightning.' [138] Paul Léon wrote Miss Weaver on April 4 to explain,

Mr. Joyce has an inner conviction that he has saved his daughter from schizophrenia and though he is naturally unable to say that she is absolutely normal and cured, the symptoms of her mental state appear to corroborate his view since there is no apathy to be noted. On the other hand the letters received here from Lucia sound very lucid, not devoid of a sense of humour, so that I am beginning to give up my all too pessimistic outlook. However this has developed a peculiar atmosphere here. Mr. Joyce trusts one person alone, and this person is Lucia. Anything she says or writes is the thing by which he is guided. And though of course he is apt to substitute his own logic for hers, and to put her thoughts and sentences in his own way, I do not think that from a medical point of view it can do any harm. But it leads us to an attitude of great patience, to which we must cling constantly, especially as no one not even the greatest physicians has been able to do anything with the case. On the other hand naturally his attitude merely covers up a constant strain and anxiety. . . .

Joyce insisted again that Lucia's initial letters were beautiful, far better than what Matisse had done for the limited edition of *Ulysses.* He was able to be irritated with her when she sent no congratulations to Nora on her fifty-first birthday on March 25, but grew very distressed when she wrote that the next money he sent would be for the funeral after her suicide. Her cause was linked in his mind with that of other victims of popular disapproval, himself, Sullivan, and even in one way Cardinal Newman:

As usual I am in a minority of one. If I tell people that no tenor voice like Sullivan's has been heard in the world for 50 years or that Zaporoyetz, the Russian basso, makes Chaliapin sound like a cheap whistle or that nobody has ever written English prose that can be compared with that of a tiresome footling little Anglican parson who afterwards became a prince of the only true church they listen in silence. These names mean nothing to them. And when I have stumbled out of the room no doubt they tap their foreheads and sigh.[139]

Joyce could hardly contain his sense of exasperation. He warned Lucia that in London every second person was a scoundrel; yet he feared with what eyes she would be regarded in Ireland when she went there. Nothing was going well anywhere. John Lane, his Eng-

lish publisher for *Ulysses*, was proceeding much too slowly; Sylvia
Beach was about to sell the manuscript of *Stephen Hero* which he had
given her, and though she secured his permission first, he did not like
the sale, feeling that the writing was bad. George and Helen were
disheartened on their own account, George having failed to secure
the engagements he hoped for and having suffered badly in health.
At the same time he considered staying in the United States, appalling
news for his father. Joyce, who disliked America, wrote Lucia acidly,
'I didn't know my son had such a strong stomach.' [140] Though outraged,
he did not try directly to dissuade George; on June 17, 1935, he wrote
him:

Dear Giorgio: Your letter seems to me perfectly fair and reasonable. Keep
your independence of spirit. You must not let yourself be influencd by the
fact that I, for example, have little or no desire to go there or to stay there.
I know nothing of the country which may seem very beautiful to many. I feel
that way because I feel that way. But there are 20 million of our compatriots
who feel the opposite. Each for himself and God for all.* [141]

The matter was not ended, howe. er. During the summer Philippe
Soupault was in the United States and went to see George and Helen
with what he said was a very important message. Joyce was quite
ill with stomach pains, and showed no interest in anything; Nora was
worried about him, and so were all his friends. If Helen and George
did not return, Soupault said, Joyce would become seriously ill. [142]
They were skeptical, but the Jolases and Thomas McGreevy wrote
them to the same purpose. They succumbed to this campaign and
agreed, to Joyce's relief, to return at the end of September. Other
letters of the spring of 1934 to Miss Weaver show signs of great strain:
'Perhaps I shall survive and perhaps the raving madness I write will
survive and perhaps it is very funny. One thing is sure, however. *Je
suis bien triste.*' [143] And again he writes: 'I feel like an animal which
has received four thunderous mallet strokes on the top of his skull.
Yet in my letters to both my children and my daughter-in-law I keep
up a tone of almost gay irresponsibility.' [144] Lucia's absence was harder
on him than her presence, for when she was near he felt, he said, he
could control her and himself.

But now though I have the faithful support of my wife and Léon's loyal
friendship and that of some others here to say nothing of your own patience
and sympathy there are moments and hours when I have nothing in my heart
but rage and despair, a blind man's rage and despair.
    I cannot be such an utter fool as to be inventing all this. But I can no

* *'Chacun pour soi et Dieu pour tous,'* as Sullivan sang in an aria in *Les Huguenots.*

longer control matters. On many sides I hear that I am and have been an evil influence on my children. But what are they doing away from that evil influence? On the other hand what can I honestly ask them to come back to? Paris is like myself a haughty ruin or if you like a decayed reveller. And any time I turn on the radio I hear some British politician mumbling inanities or his German cousin shouting and yelling like a madman. Perhaps Ireland and the U.S. are the safe places. And perhaps this is where the gas is really going to be turned on. Well, so be it. The motto under my coat of arms, however, is *Mors aut honorabilis vita.* . . . [145]

Joyce had not wept in a letter since he suspected Nora of infidelity in 1909. Though not so blind as Homer, nor so exiled as Dante, he had reached his life's nadir. 'People talk of my influence on my daughter,' he said to Mrs. Jolas, 'but what about her influence on me?' [146] His exasperation and despair exfoliated like a black flower.

There were occasional lightenings. When two prowlers invaded his sister's bungalow in Bray without, however, finding anything of value, he wrote Eileen to ask what any burglar could hope to get by entering the house of any member of the Joyce family. [147] He wrote to his daughter, gleefully speculating that the marauders must have been after 'the art treasures, cases with gold coins and precious stuffs which doubtless it [the bungalow] contained. There are still idealists, apparently. . . .' [148] Lucia got on well enough with Eileen's daughters, her cousins Boschenka and Nora, but they were not intended to be nurses and had great trouble saving her from serious harm. Once she overdosed herself with aspirin, another time she built a turf fire on the bungalow floor and explained that she wanted to smell burning turf. [149] Lucia's obsession with her father was all too clear; she sent him a telegram to say, 'You look like Bray Head,' [150] which he chose to interpret lightly and rejoined, 'You think you're in Ireland but you're also in Norway. The Norwegians founded the city of Wicklow which means Wick, an inlet of the sea, and low, lighthouse.' [151] Lucia appealed to him over Eileen's head for money and found fault with the care she received. Joyce requested his friend Madame Bailly, who was visiting her native Ireland too, to find out what was happening, and also asked C. P. Curran and Michael Healy to check on Lucia. Their letters alarmed him: it appeared that Lucia decided on her own to leave Bray and stay with Kathleen Barnacle in Galway; she came to Dublin and by coincidence met Kathleen, who was in Dublin for an operation, at the Post Office. [152] They greeted each other warmly, but Kathleen had to go to the hospital. Lucia then led Healy (a very old man with only a few months to live) * a chase for six days around

* Healy died November 7, 1935.

Dublin, which ended in a police station where the guards mercifully detained her. Her aunts Eva and Florence went to rescue her and were staggered by her disheveled appearance. Lucia asked to be put into a nursing home, and Joyce telephoned to Curran to arrange it.[153] On July 13 she was installed in a home in Finglas.

Lucia's new troubles affected her father intensely. He could not sleep for six or seven nights except for brief spells of nightmare; he felt as if he were wound up and then suddenly shooting out of water like a fish. During the day he was troubled by auditory hallucinations, and went to see a Doctor Debray, who decided as usual the trouble was nerves and ordered him to work on his book. Joyce turned to say to Léon, 'There are not ten centimes of money in my work. I can see nothing but a dark wall in front of me, a dark wall or a precipice if you prefer, physically, morally, materially.' [154] He discussed Lucia's situation with Maria Jolas, and said that the worst of it was that he could not assess the reports he had of her condition. Would she be willing to go to Ireland for him and see what should be done? She agreed and left at once.

In Dublin Mrs. Jolas saw that Lucia's condition was perilous. Joyce agreed his daughter should leave Ireland, and Curran and his wife kindly took her to London,[155] where Miss Weaver was once again willing to take care of her. Joyce's new plan was to have Dr. W. G. Macdonald, a London surgeon associated with St. Andrew's Hospital, Northampton, give her a glandular cure which he had used with success on some of his mental patients. The treatment, which presumed that Lucia's difficulties were of physical origin, was in accord with Joyce's own theory of her malady. She received the injections over a period of five weeks at Miss Weaver's flat in London; then Macdonald suggested convalescence in quieter surroundings, so Miss Weaver took a bungalow in Kingswood near Reigate, Surrey, twenty-three miles from London, and, with a trained nurse to help, brought Lucia there. She remained until mid-December, while her father and mother, badly in need of some respite, spent part of August and September with Herbert Gorman and his second wife, Claire, at Fontainebleau, then returned to Paris to greet George and Helen.

Miss Weaver's reports were optimistic, and at first Lucia seemed better and wrote her father a letter which renewed his hopes. He at once suggested that she buy a new fur coat * [156]—his old panacea for feminine woes—but Miss Weaver advised him to wait because Lucia's desires changed daily.[157] Joyce exacted detailed accounts of his daughter's

---

* Her two trunks in Dublin, which contained a fur cloak and all her best clothes, were lost.

condition and behavior, and was annoyed if anything was left out; on the other hand, he could not bear the suggestion that Lucia was incurable, and none of his friends dared make it. Only George said so, but without swaying him.

In November 1935, Joyce asked Maria Jolas to cross the Channel again and give him an independent report; he suspected Miss Weaver of blurring the facts out of concern for him. As a matter of fact, Miss Weaver and the nurse were in constant fear of new bursts of hysteria, and only by the utmost vigilance kept their charge within bounds. It was evident that the stay in the country was not working well, and in the middle of December, at the instigation of Dr. Macdonald, Lucia was transferred to Northampton for more glandular treatments. The next month Macdonald informed Joyce that Lucia wished to leave Northampton and could not be kept there without being certified by her parents as of unsound mind. Joyce refused to certify her and said he would not give authority over his daughter to an Englishman (or Scot); so Mrs. Jolas consented to go to England at the end of February and bring her to Paris. She offered to keep her in her own large house in Neuilly, but soon discovered that Lucia's improvement in England had been more apparent than real. In March 1936, after three weeks in Paris, Lucia had to be carried out of the house in a straitjacket. She was installed in a clinic in Le Vésinet, where the doctor insisted that she was dangerous and must be withdrawn to a special institution. Joyce was able to transfer her in April to Dr. Achille Delmas's comfortable *maison de santé* in Ivry. There the doctors thought for a time she had cyclothymia, which they might cure, rather than dementia praecox. Joyce continued to visit her, write to her, and insist that she would some day get well. His defiant attitude was that she was no madder than her father. But he was bitterly sane, and foolish fond like Lear.

1936-1939

No, so help me Petault, it is not a miseffectual whyacinthinous riot of
blots and blurs and bars and balls and hoops and wriggles and juxtaposed jottings linked by spurts of speed: it only looks as like it as
damn it. . . .

—*Finnegans Wake* (118)

J OYCE'S expenses had mounted with staggering rapidity during the
last two years. His daughter's needs and whims accounted, Léon
said, for three-fourths of his income, including the considerable American royalties on *Ulysses*. To the distress of his solicitors, he sold much
of his stock, and at a time when the price was low. He remarked to
Léon, 'I will go on selling; it's not my fault that the stock has fallen
in price. When it is exhausted I will give lessons.' [1]

Goaded by worry over his daughter into drinking more heavily than
before, he alarmed and then infuriated Nora, who threatened to leave
him and on two or three occasions swept off briefly to a hotel. The next
day a deputation, consisting of Léon or Jolas or both, waited upon her
to beg her to return to her penitent husband. 'I wish I had never met
anyone of the name of James Joyce,' she said. Mollified by absence and
promises, she consented to go back at last, and for a few days her
husband drank a little less. Soon, however, he thought up a subterfuge
to circumvent her vigilance. Yet he matched his irresponsibility by
night with a tremendous concentration upon his work by day.

The return of George and Helen had been consolatory, but George
had developed in America a throat condition which required an operation,[2] and Helen was not well either. Joyce sat languid beneath these
heaping misfortunes, now plaintive like Job, now detached from them
like Stephen Dedalus. Those who expected to find him melancholy
were sometimes surprised to find him gay and full of banter, though for
the most part he reserved this lighter mood for his work.

The German critic Alfred Kerr, who had been an early European adherent of Ibsen, came to see Joyce at the beginning of 1936. Joyce's conversation moved in sudden rushes of indignation followed by renewals of a composure that was not quite serene. In a reminiscent mood, he talked of mistreatment in the stylized way that had become habitual to him. '*Ulysses*, when it first came out, had a strangely hostile reception,' he said. Kerr interpolated, 'I know, but also so much admiration....' Joyce pursued his thought as if Kerr had not spoken, 'This hostility—I didn't begin to understand it. The most natural thing for a writer to do is to call a spade a spade. The mistake which some moralists make, even today, is that they hate unpleasant phenomena less than they do those who record them. It's always the same. People go on judging an author immoral who refuses to be silent about what in any case exists. Immoral! Why, it's a mark of morality not only to say what one thinks is true—but to create a work of art with the utmost sacrifice; that's moral, too. I admire Ibsen precisely for these two reasons: his morality consisted not only in the proclamation of his ethical ideals, but in the fierce struggle for the perfection of his work.' He meditated for a moment, then continued, 'I am thinking particularly of *The Wild Duck*, which was recently revived in Paris. By the way, you went to Oslo for Ibsen's funeral, that interests me; you told me you saw him as a corpse in the best room in his flat. I'd like so much to know what his flat looked like, what his street was like. You know, I was hardly eighteen when I sent off my first article—it was on Ibsen—to the *Fortnightly Review*. I was almost astonished when the editor published it. Ibsen sent me a letter of thanks; imagine how happy I was—at that age!'

Kerr asked him if the Irish had not treated him as the Norwegians had treated Ibsen, a comparison Joyce was glad to accept. 'I described the people and the conditions in my country; I reproduced certain city types of a certain social level. They didn't forgive me for it. Some grudged my not concealing what I had seen, others were annoyed because of my way of expressing myself, which they didn't understand at all. In short, some were enraged by the realistic picture, others by the style. They all took revenge.' * [3]

With Lucia at Ivry, Joyce had time for a new misfortune, and one came his way in a letter from Stanislaus of April 12, 1936:

Trieste   Via Cesare Battisti 6
12th April 1936

Dear Jim,

The latest is that an order has been issued for my expulsion from Italy. It was communicated to me yesterday by the Vice Questore here,

---

* Kerr confirmed Joyce's low view of journalists by publishing his interview against Joyce's wishes.

without notice, without warning, without explanation. I cannot understand it. At my lessons at the University and elsewhere I am very careful not to say anything that might be interpreted as a political allusion.
I go nowhere, to no cafe, bar, or restaurant. I live a more retired life
than you did here before the war. I see only my private pupils, who all
come here—so the root of the evil must be there. I have a rather nicely
furnished flat—the result of thirty years of incessant work—and, though
still in debt owing to . . . Schaurek's end, have lived fairly comfortably, sometimes even taking a holiday. Now I feel my feet cut from
under me. I am doing what I can to have the order rescinded. I have
written to Suvich, who was my pupil, and some of the political authorities here have promised to do the same. The Rector of the University,
who was greatly surprised and displeased, especially as the authorities
did not ask his opinion regarding me, has telegraphed to the Ministero
dell' Educazione Nationale. I shall try to bring other influences to bear
chiefly on Suvich, whose brother was a friend of mine before the war
(he was killed) but of course I cannot know with what success. If all
fails I shall be accompanied to the French frontier on Saturday next.

Joyce's first thought was that Stanislaus was unduly alarmed, and
he did not respond with much sympathy. Stanislaus went on to Rome
to plead his case,[4] only to learn there that the British had just expelled
an Italian professor from Malta. He was nevertheless able, through the
influence of a friend,[*] to have the expulsion order stayed indefinitely.
He could remain in Italy, a useless concession since he could not teach.
'I must study the political conjuncture every day,' he wrote James, 'like
a speculator on the Exchange, to see whether I am a sheep or a goat.'[5]
Suspecting that his brother might feel he was seeking martyrdom, he
said forcefully, 'I have no ambitions at all to play the part of Public
Enemy No. 1. To tell the truth, I am pretty sick of this conclusion to
thirty odd years of drudgery in this part of the world, four of them
spent behind barbed wire because of my sympathy with the Italian
cause.'[6] At the beginning of June, he decided to come to Paris,[7] but this
visit was deferred.

Joyce turned back to his daughter. Although Miss Weaver never
articulated her conviction that Lucia was incurable, Joyce felt it in her
correspondence, and because of it he scarcely wrote to her now at all.[†]
When he did, it was with some defiance. He had decided to publish
Lucia's designs for *A Chaucer A B C* for her birthday, July 26; for the
purpose he bought a moneybox to save in, and entrusted Léon with

[*] Fulvio Suvich.
[†] But he designated her his literary executor in his will. She continues to perform
in that capacity what T. S. Eliot called, in his dedication to *Selected Essays,* 'her
great service to English literature.'

the key. In defending this paternal but extravagant project he spoke
with an eloquence that he usually reserved for his books:

> I believe I can cover most of the expenses of publication of my daughter's
> alphabet. My idea is not to persuade her that she is a Cezanne but that on
> her 29th birthday . . . she may see something to persuade her that her whole
> past has not been a failure. The reason I keep on trying by every means to
> find a solution for her case (which may come at any time as it did with my
> eyes) is that she may not think that she is left with a blank future as well.
> I am aware that I am blamed by everybody for sacrificing that precious
> metal money to such an extent for such a purpose when it could be done so
> cheaply and quietly by locking her up in an economical mental prison for
> the rest of her life.
>
> I will not do so as long as I see a single chance of hope for her recovery,
> nor blame her or punish her for the great crime she has committed in being
> a victim to one of the most elusive diseases known to men and unknown to
> medicine. And I imagine that if you were where she is and felt as she must
> you would perhaps feel some hope if you felt that you were neither aban-
> doned nor forgotten.[8]

Miss Weaver promptly offered to share the cost of the book with him.
Joyce drew up a list of possible subscribers, and decided that no one
who failed to subscribe could remain his friend. Several of his acquaintances did not avail themselves of this opportunity, and so were dropped.

When Lucia's book, *A Chaucer A B C*, appeared in July 1936, Joyce
felt he had done all that for the moment he could. He decided to go
somewhere without allowing Lucia, who would react violently, to know.
His thoughts had been running throughout the year on Ibsen and
Scandinavia, and he decided, before all his money was gone, to make
a trip to Copenhagen. The fact that Earwicker was of Scandinavian
extraction made it likely that he could pick up some useful bits and
pieces; he also felt that, since only the Swedes had begun to translate
his books, he might come to terms with the Danish firm of Martins
Forlag which had expressed interest in putting *Ulysses* into Danish.
Accordingly, after spending a few days with the Baillys at Villers-sur-
Mer in Calvados,* the Joyces traveled to Copenhagen on August 18,

---

* Here Joyce took time to write a story to his grandson Stephen:

Villers s/Mer

> My dear Stevie: I sent you a little cat filled with sweets a few days ago but
> perhaps you do not know the story about the cat of Beaugency.
>
> Beaugency is a tiny old town on a bank of the Loire, France's longest river.
> It is also a very wide river, for France, at least. At Beaugency it is so wide
> that if you wanted to cross it from one bank to the other you would have to
> take at least one thousand steps.
>
> Long ago the people of Beaugency, when they wanted to cross it, had to go

stopping en route at Liége and Hamburg. They installed themselves modestly at the Turist Hotel (now the Alexandra Hotel) and Joyce began to practice his Danish.

It was impossible to remain unknown for long. Joyce went into a bookshop in the *Politiken* building, and ordered a book to be sent to his hotel. The bookseller at once recognized his name, and showed him that *Ulysses* was on sale there, news which pleased Joyce as much as

in a boat for there was no bridge. And they could not make one for themselves or pay anybody else to make one. So what were they to do?

The Devil, who is always reading the newspapers, heard about this sad state of theirs so he dressed himself and came to call on the lord mayor of Beaugency, who was named Monsieur Alfred Byrne. This lord mayor was very fond of dressing himself too. He wore a scarlet robe and always had a great golden chain round his neck even when he was fast asleep in bed with his knees in his mouth.

The devil told the lord mayor what he had read in the newspaper and said he could make as good a bridge as was ever made, and make it in one single night. The lord mayor asked him how much money he wanted for making such a bridge. No money at all, said the Devil, all I ask is that the first person who crosses the bridge shall belong to me. Good, said the lord mayor.

The night came down, all the people in Beaugency went to bed and slept. The morning came. And when they put their heads out of their windows they cried: O Loire, what a fine bridge! For they saw a fine strong stone bridge thrown across the wide river.

All the people ran down to the head of the bridge and looked across it. There was the devil, standing at the other side of the bridge, waiting for the first person who should cross it. But nobody dared to cross it for fear of the devil.

Then there was a sound of bugles—that was a sign for the people to be silent—and the lord mayor M Alfred Byrne appeared in his great scarlet robe and wearing his heavy golden chain round his neck. He had a bucket of water in one hand and under his arm—the other arm—he carried a cat.

The devil stopped dancing when he saw him from the other side of the bridge and put up his long spyglass. All the people whispered to one another and the cat looked up at the lord mayor because in the town of Beaugency it was allowed that a cat should look at a lord mayor. When he was tired of looking at the lord mayor (because even a cat grows tired of looking at a lord mayor) he began to play with the lord mayor's heavy golden chain.

When the lord mayor came to the head of the bridge every man held his breath and every woman held her tongue. The lord mayor put the cat down on the bridge and, quick as a thought, splash! he emptied the whole bucket of water over it. The cat who was now between the devil and the bucket of water made up his mind quite as quickly and ran with his ears back across the bridge and into the devil's arms.

The devil was as angry as the devil himself.

Messieurs les Balgentiens, he shouted across the bridge, vous n'êtes pas de belles gens du tout! Vous n'êtes que des chats! And he said to the cat: Viens ici, mon petit chat! Tu as peur, mon petit chou-chat? Tu as froid, mon pau petit chou-chat? Viens ici, le diable t'emporte! On va se chauffer tous les deux.

And off he went with the cat.

And since that time the people of that town are called 'les chats de Beaugency.'

the information that *Lady Chatterley's Lover* had sold more copies displeased him. By chance the distinguished Danish writer Tom Kristensen
was also in the shop, and the bookseller introduced him to Joyce, who
remembered seeing two articles by Kristensen on *Ulysses* that had
appeared in 1931. He invited Kristensen for a drink, and even made
a play on the Danish words 'to work' and 'to order a glass of wine'
(*at bestille noget* and *at bestille en flaske vin*), saying he was in Copenhagen to do both. The language, which he spoke fluently for a foreigner,
interested him very much; he told Kristensen he had studied with eight
teachers, but that the first seven, who were Norwegians, had misled
him; he had not apprehended that Danish was a weeping language and
the Danes a nation of weepers, of wild men with soft voices. Only the
eighth teacher, who was a Dane, had appropriately sobbed.[10] (Joyce's
own intonation, perhaps influenced by Triestino, veered in this direction.) It was agreed that he and Kristensen should meet the following
day, and next he went over to Martins Forlag. There it was suggested
that Mrs. Kastor Hansen translate *Ulysses*, and Joyce called upon her
without notice, saying, 'I am James Joyce. I understand that you are to
translate *Ulysses*, and I have come from Paris to tell you not to alter
a single word.' °[11]

Next day Joyce met Kristensen and Kai Friis-Møller, the Danish poet
and critic who translated Eliot's verse into Danish. He asked Kristensen
if he would translate *Ulysses*, and Kristensen replied, 'Yes, but give me
ten years.' Joyce laughed and remarked that Martins Forlag thought
an hour would be enough. He next suggested that Kristensen and
Friis-Møller collaborate, but nothing was to come of this plan either.

In Copenhagen Joyce was reading proofs for the English edition
which John Lane had scheduled at last for October 3, 1936,† and he
told Friis-Møller, 'I have been fighting for this for twenty years.'[12] To
Kristensen he remarked, even more grandly, 'Now the war between
England and me is over, and I am the conqueror.'[13] He was still annoyed

---

But the bridge is there still and there are boys walking and riding and
playing upon it.

I hope you will like this story.

Nonno.

P.S. The devil mostly speaks a language of his own called Bellysbabble
which he makes up himself as he goes along but when he is very angry he
can speak quite bad French very well though some who have heard him say
that he has a strong Dublin accent.[9]

° Mrs. Kastor Hansen proved to be too occupied with other work to undertake so
formidable a task. The translation, an excellent one, was made by Colonel Mogens
Boisen after Joyce's death.

† The first edition was only 1,000 copies; it was followed a year later by the ordinary trade edition.

with his own countrymen and said, 'We'll see how the Irish will take it now.' Friis-Møller had talked of Joyce to Yeats in 1924, on the occasion of Yeats's receiving the Nobel prize, and quoted Yeats's reflection: 'Isn't it remarkable that Joyce, who hasn't been in Dublin since he was a young man, writes only about Dublin?' ° Joyce, hearing this story, laughed and said, 'I will not go back to Dublin.'

He was amused to hear from Kristensen how the latter had read *Ulysses* and Stuart Gilbert's study of it in Riga, where he had gone to escape a love affair in Copenhagen. 'You have to be in exile to understand me,' said Joyce; 'Stuart Gilbert was living in Burma when he read my book.' When Kristensen asked if his review had been right in saying that Bloom was God, Stephen Jesus, and Molly Earth, Joyce would not confirm or deny, said only 'Perhaps.' It was evident that he preferred not to explain himself. Kristensen asked him for help on *Work in Progress*, and Joyce referred him to Vico. 'But do you believe in the *Scienza Nuova*?' asked Kristensen. 'I don't believe in any science,' Joyce answered, 'but my imagination grows when I read Vico as it doesn't when I read Freud or Jung.' Kristensen had been trying to read the fragments of Joyce's new work by making out the multi-lingual puns; 'Is this the way to proceed?' he asked. Joyce said, 'Perhaps it would help,' but smiled doubtfully. He remarked with boyish pride that he had put some Danish words into the book, then volunteered the story of the tailor and the Norwegian captain, which he recounted with great amusement. He emphasized his book's humor and said, 'Now they're bombing Spain. Isn't it better to make a great joke instead, as I have done?' He showed considerable interest in the books of his new friends, and asked Kristensen particularly for a copy of his novel *Haermerk*, which was influenced by *A Portrait* in its description of childhood and youth in Copenhagen. Friis-Møller sent him a copy of his translations of French love poems written before 1800, and Joyce read them at once and commented, 'You should have included Maurice Scève's poems to Délie.'14

Joyce had requested that no interviewers be sent to him, and partly because his manner of making the request was so gentle, it was complied with. One journalist, however, Ole Vinding, was able to break through Joyce's guard by posing as an artist. As a result he spent more time with Joyce than anyone else, and wrote a long interview which he sent to him later, only to be checked by Joyce's absolute refusal to

° Yeats wrote of Joyce in 1923, 'James Joyce, the son of a small Parnellite organiser, had begun to write [in 1902] though not yet to publish; he was an exile, at first in Zurich, then in Paris, in flight from the objects of his hatred, bearing in mind always in minute detail, even to the names over the shops, the Dublin that he hated but would not forget.'

allow its publication. It appeared, however, after Joyce's death, and gives an unusually detailed account of their conversation. Vinding was astonished when Joyce addressed him in good Danish, but when he exclaimed over it Joyce pointed out that the Danes had occupied Dublin, so that undoubtedly some of the blood in his own veins was Danish. He was interested in the ancient Irish distinction between the dark and light Scandinavians, the *dubhghalls* and *fionnghalls,* and kept looking to see which type the people they passed belonged to. He had read Gunnar Heiberg as well as Ibsen. Vinding asked the predictable question, 'Do you rank Ibsen high?' 'He's the greatest playwright I know. No one can construct a piece as he can. There's not a superfluous word in his plays. It was wonderful to see what Lugné-Poë achieved as old Ekdal in *The Wild Duck.* I'm sorry never to have seen *Little Eyolf;* the first act is a pure wonder.' 'Do you then place Ibsen higher than Shakespeare?' asked Vinding. 'He towers head and shoulders above him when it comes to drama. No one approaches him there. It's very difficult to believe that Ibsen will grow stale; he will renew himself for every generation. His problems will be seen from a new angle as time goes on. There are some who think he was a feminist in *Hedda Gabler,* but he was no more a feminist than I am an archbishop.'

With Vinding as guide and companion Joyce and his wife visited various places around Copenhagen, including, of course, Hamlet's castle at Elsinore.* At Fredericksburg, as they walked through the grounds, Vinding asked, 'Do you like flowers, Mr. Joyce?' 'No. I love plants, green growing things, trees and grass. Flowers annoy me.' Molly Bloom's affection for flowers was evidently a feminine trait. It began to rain and Joyce turned reproachfully to his wife, 'Why didn't you bring an umbrella, Nora?' 'I hate umbrellas,' she said, as Molly had said before her.† Vinding sided with her by saying the umbrella was comical, but Joyce smiled and replied, 'I don't think so. I think the umbrella is a royal instrument. I know a young lord of Cambodia who lives in Paris; because of his high rank his father has the right to carry seven umbrellas, and my noble friend himself walks with six umbrellas, suspended one over the other. Yes, the umbrella is a mark of distinction.'

Vinding pressed him for his opinion of various writers. 'Do you like D'Annunzio?' he asked. 'He was at one time a magnificent poet,' Joyce replied. 'Do you like Italy now that Mussolini is there?' 'Naturally. Now as always. Italy is Italy. Not to like it because of Mussolini would be

---

* From here Joyce sent John Sullivan a card on August 26, saying, 'Greetings from the place which inspired Ambroise Thomas,' [15] a reference to their standing joke that the opera *Hamlet* had preceded the Shakespearean play.
† Earwicker carries one, however.

just as absurd as to hate England because of Henry the Eighth.' The conversation moved on to Hemingway, and Joyce said, 'We were with him just before he went to Africa. He promised us a living lion. Fortunately we escaped that. But we would like to have the book he has written. He's a good writer, Hemingway. He writes as he is. We like him. He's a big, powerful peasant, as strong as a buffalo. A sportsman. And ready to live the life he writes about. He would never have written it if his body had not allowed him to live it. But giants of his sort are truly modest; there is much more behind Hemingway's form than people know.' ° On O'Neill he would not comment, except to say that the playwright was thoroughly Irish. He was more indulgent towards André Gide, saying, 'I like two of Gide's books very well, *La Symphonie Pastorale,* and *Les Caves du Vatican,* which is certainly delightful.' Then he burst into anecdote: 'Gide is of course a Communist as you know. Some time ago a young man named Armand Petitjean looked him up. When Petitjean was sixteen he began to write a giant work on my *Work in Progress* which he finished long before *my* work was ended. He is now twenty. His book and his interests made him a serious admirer of mine, and he went to Gide with this question: "Maître, when we have communism in France, whatever will we do with Joyce?" Gide thought for a long time before he answered, and finally said, "We'll leave him be." '

The talk came round once more to *Finnegans Wake.* Joyce talked of what it had meant to him to write it. 'It is a wonderful experience to live with a book,' he said. 'Since 1922, when I began *Work in Progress,* I haven't really lived a normal life. It has required an enormous expenditure of energy. Having written *Ulysses* about the day, I wanted to write this book about the night. Otherwise it has no connection with *Ulysses,* and *Ulysses* didn't demand the same expenditure of energy. Since 1922 my book has been a greater reality for me than reality. Everything gives way to it. Everything outside the book has been an insuperable difficulty: the least realities, such as shaving myself in the morning, for example.' His remarks gave a sudden insight into his true measure of things; all his gloomy sense of others' criticism of the book and of his own thwarted efforts to defend it was incidental, even irrelevant, to the experience of writing it.

° Hemingway has said of Joyce, 'Once in one of those casual conversations you have when you're drinking, Joyce said to me he was afraid his writing was too suburban and that maybe he should get around a bit and see the world. He was afraid of some things—lightning and things, but a wonderful man. He was under great discipline—his wife, his work, and his bad eyes. His wife was there and she said, yes, his work was too suburban—"Jim could do with a spot of that lion-hunting." We would go out to drink and Joyce would fall into a fight. He couldn't even see the man so he'd say: "Deal with him, Hemingway! Deal with him!" ' ¹⁶

'There is,' he went on, 'no connection between the people in *Ulysses* and the people in *Work in Progress*. There are in a way no characters. It's like a dream. The style is also changing, and unrealistic, like the dream world. If one had to name a character, it would be just an old man.* But his own connection with reality is doubtful.' 'How much have you left to write?' asked Vinding. 'Not very much. I'm near the end of the work now. I should say that three-quarters is written. The work will go more quickly from now on.'

Joyce's stay in Copenhagen contented him. He liked the postmen with their red coats, the pillarboxes, the fur-helmeted guards. The Hermitage Villa failed to interest him, but a Danish farm did. He and Nora were delighted with a performance of Délibes' *Coppélia* at the opera, and thought it as a spectacle the best they had ever seen. Joyce had the pleasure of meeting the philosopher Lucien Lévy-Bruhl, also a visitor to the city and, as it turned out, an admirer of *Ulysses*. So after a crowded three weeks Joyce left with the intention, not to be realized, of renting a house in Copenhagen the following spring. On the return journey he stopped at Bonn to talk with Professor Curtius about *Work in Progress*. 'I want to prove to you,' he told him, 'that I am not suffering from softening of the brain.' [17]

Back in Paris by September 13, Joyce was still full of thoughts of Ibsen. On September 18 he asked James Stephens to read *Little Eyolf*, a copy of which he lent him. 'I should like to hear what you think of it. If you read it you should not interrupt any act of it.' [18] But Stephens could not be won, and replied two days later:

Campagne 1re 11. Paris.
Sept 20th. 1936

My dear Joyce—There are two things about you which are unchange-able: you are the most subtil man, and the most continuously kind male creature I have ever known. All that merely apropos des bottes. I got the Ibsen book you left with my concierge—to think of you, with your poor sight, navigating the wildernesses of Paris merely to give me a book, scandalises me, and makes me proud. I send you my love in return, but that is so easy to send by a postman, that it is not worth signing a receipt for at the other end.

I take it that you sent me this book because of the remarks I made to you upon Ibsen. I will agree, with any man who cares to be agreed with, that Ibsen is a more than competent stage-manager. If a character of his sneezes in the first-act, he will have a cold in the second-act, and will die of pneumonia in the third. My criticism (fault-finding) goes deeper than his handling of a selected matter in a first, a second and

* Finn MacCumhal, Earwicker or some androgynous ancestor.

a third act. It is this: that of all those who have come to (deserved) eminence in drama, or, generally, in literature, Ibsen is the most thorough-going liar, or falsifier of the truth, that ever attained such eminence. His idealist in (was it?) The Wild Duck was no idealist, he was a mere, uncomplicated, commonplace swindler. His Master-Builder man was, similarly, an ordinary and exceedingly-mere ass.

Now I have read, at your behest, his Little Eyolf—and again, I take off all my hats to that exceedingly skilful presentation, and withdraw every demi-semi-quaver of my soul from his tale, and the truth of it. The catastrophe he so cogently engineers is everywhere unmerited: has not, by a single one of his characters, been worked for, or earned, or deserved. The man is a pestilent dramatist, and all his works are framed with the desire to make those pay who do not owe, and to make them suffer who have not merited it. If ever there was in literature a sadist such an one was Ibsen, and that anyone could ever have been taken in by him, critically or morally, remains for me as an inexplicable enigma. This play is, for me, an effect without a cause—which is ridiculous: and equally ill-founded, and as equally ridiculous are all his other triumphs. To hell with that dark man of the black north, for that is where he came from, and his literature is as nigh to hellish as the complete-bourgeois can possibly manage.

Mise agat-sa do chara go deó
James Stephens [19]

To this Joyce replied, on September 25, 1936, sounding more weary than persuasive, 'What you say is true but it is by no means all, in my opinion,' [20] and invited Stephens to dinner. It was hard for him to accept the fact that his spiritual twin should not agree with him about his spiritual father.

Joyce went to Zurich for a few days to meet Stanislaus. His brother still had no job, and thought of taking one in Switzerland. Joyce enlisted the help of Professor Bernhard Fehr and others, and a position was found at a school on top of the Zugerberg. The position was well-paid, but, as Joyce, Paul Ruggiero, and Stanislaus discovered when they reached it, the top of the mountain was extremely isolated. The town of Zug nearby looked as dull as it sounded. [21] Stanislaus decided not to risk it, and James concurred. The younger brother wanted to talk about the political situation in Italy and in Trieste, but James was impatient, 'For God's sake don't talk politics. I'm not interested in politics. The only thing that interests me is style.' [22] In spite of this rebuff, the brothers parted amicably. Stanislaus returned to Trieste, where after many delays he was restored to his position at the University. He remained there until war broke out.

In Paris Joyce's social life had shrunk perceptibly during the last few years. Although he regularly sent Sylvia Beach a plant on the anniversary of her publication of *Ulysses,* he saw her rarely, and then only when flanked by other friends. Her bookstore was no longer the means of access to him. For a time Joyce had made new acquaintances on his own by exertions on behalf of John Sullivan; but by 1936 these were over even though Joyce never said so. Sullivan himself knew what Joyce refused to admit, that they had met too late, at a time when Sullivan's voice was losing its timbre.[23] Although Joyce was too restless not to seek out new acquaintances from time to time, he relied heavily on a small group of friends, most of whom he had known since the 'twenties.

Among them Paul Léon remained the principal helper. He abjured the title of secretary, and refused to be paid for his endless letter-writing. Sometimes he wrote for Joyce directly, at other times he wrote at Joyce's indirect suggestion to see how the wind blew, and sometimes he originated plans of his own with which he hoped Joyce might eventually be persuaded to agree. Léon adopted towards Joyce a tone of bantering affection, which Joyce reciprocated. So, when one day Joyce had, without being asked, joined Léon and a handsome woman guest at a restaurant, he presented Léon shortly afterwards with Byron's *Don Juan,* inscribed, by way of Mozart's *Don Giovanni,* to

> Don Leone, a pranzar teco
> non m'invitasti, ma son venuto
> Il Commendatore
> April 21st Chez Chauland

A basket of fruit was delivered to Léon during a spell of asthma with the message, 'Hope this fruit is acceptable to your invalidship. J.J.' Joyce presented him with a copy of *Finnegans Wake* when it appeared with the inscription,

> To that Eurasian Knight, Paul Léon,
> with the Thousand and one thanks
> of that most distressful writer,
> James Joyce.
> Paris, May 4th, 1939 [24]

And in a serious mood, he dictated for Gorman's biography a few sentences of tribute: 'For the last dozen years, in sickness or health, night and day, he [Léon] has been an absolutely disinterested and devoted friend and I could never have done what I did without his help.' [25]

Besides Léon and Sullivan, Joyce was in touch quite steadily with

the Gilberts, the Jolases, and Samuel Beckett, and more sporadically
with René Bailly and his Irish wife, with Soupault, and Nino Frank,*
besides other flurries of friendship. All except Jolas, who was supremely impractical, were called upon for their help as well as their
friendship. Joyce approached them with great politeness and consideration, 'Would you have time to. . . .' 'For all that,' as Soupault remarked,
'he is *formidable*. You go to see him; he asks which way you will be
going when you leave. You say, "To the Étoile," and before you know it
he has you doing an errand for him at the Bastille.' [26] His friends were
always finding him a book, or telephoning to someone, or reading
proof, or looking up something. As Nora said, 'If God Almighty came
down to earth, you'd have a job for him.' † [27] Yet he was, as if to make
up, punctiliously thoughtful. He remembered his friends' birthdays and
anniversaries as faithfully as he required they remember his. When
they were sick, he was invariably solicitous, calling up daily to find out
how they felt, what their temperature was. When little Tina Jolas was
ill in Switzerland, Joyce learned that her mother would have to take

---

* The course of these friendships, even the closest, was never smooth; there were
occasional periods of estrangement, usually over something trivial, and sometimes
brought about by Nora.

† A good example of Joyce's commissions is a letter of August 8, 1937, to David
Fleischman, the son of Helen Joyce by her first marriage. Joyce sent Fleischman,
who was then eighteen, a copy of *Huckleberry Finn,* and wrote:

7 rue Edmond Valentin
Paris 7e

Dear David: If your mother has had more quieting news from New York
and if you can find an evening hour in this blistering heat cooled off by
imber serotium I should be much obliged if you could do me a favour.

   I have sent you registered a book you certainly will have read as a young
boy, probably more than once. I need to know something about it. I never
read it and have nobody to read it to me and it takes too much time with
all I am doing. Could you perhaps refresh your memory by a hasty glance
through and then dictate to your mother (who, I hope, will buy me a bunch
of new ribbons to spry up—her typewriter) an account of the plot in general
as if it were a new book the tale of which you had to narrate in a book
review. After that I should like you to mark with blue pencil in the margin
the most important passages of the plot itself and in red pencil here and
there wherever the words or dialogue seem to call for the special attention of
a European. Don't care about spoiling the book. It is a cheap edition. If you
can then return it to me soon I shall try to use whatever bears upon what I
am doing.

   Many thanks in advance but if for any reason you cannot do this it will
be no great loss.

   The heat is abominable. I hope you all, especially Stevie [Stephen Joyce],
keep out of the sight of that monotonous old gasometer, the sun.

Sincerely yours
James Joyce [29]

8.8:'37

a train next day; and he and Léon paid her a visit, Joyce bringing her a doll to take to the child. When the Jolases' third child was, as it later proved, mortally ill, Joyce, as sympathetic as Mr Bloom, telephoned twice a day.[28]

He relied upon Soupault and Gilbert, especially, to accompany him to the theater. He had lost his taste for serious dramas, and preferred to go to *pièces du Palais-Royal,* light comedies at which, sitting in the first row so he could see, he would unleash peals of laughter.[*] Occasionally he went to a movie with Nino Frank, or to operas and operettas, a favorite being Mascagni's *L'Ami Fritz,* which he had once seen in Dublin. A song of Maurice Chevalier, '*Quand un vicom-te rencontre un autre vicom-te,*' pleased him by its play with words; yet he could be pleased also by a quite simple lyric such as Yvonne Printemps' '*Je ne suis pas ce que l'on pense.*'

The simplicity of his tastes surprised friends who had not known him long. Frau Giedion brought him together with the architect Le Corbusier, who had spoken of *Ulysses* as '*une grande découverte de la vie.*' To her dismay the conversation turned entirely on two parakeets, Pierre and Pipi, which Joyce had recently acquired.[†] After the meeting Le Corbusier said that Joyce was wonderful. 'But you talked about nothing at all,' said Frau Giedion. '*C'est admirable comme il parle d'oiseaux,*' said Le Corbusier, still dazzled.[30]

Nino Frank was often with Joyce in 1937 because Joyce proposed to him that they translate *Anna Livia Plurabelle* into Italian. 'We must do the job now before it is too late,' he said; 'for the moment there is at least one person, myself, who can understand what I am writing. I don't however guarantee that in two or three years I'll still be able to.' Frank protested, too late, that the genius of Italian was not suited to puns, and that the chapter could not be translated. The two met twice a week for three months. Joyce's whole emphasis was again on sonority, rhythm, and verbal play; to the sense he seemed indifferent and unfaithful, and Frank had often to recall him to it. With a fine carelessness Joyce threw in the names of more rivers. Frank told him of a *Sonetto* of Petrarch, '*Non Tesin, Po, Varo, Adige e Tebro,*' which gathered many river names, and Joyce had to see it immediately. Once, curbing the master's recklessness, Frank protested a phrase Joyce liked,

---

[*] He told Beckett of a play opening in the dining room of a hotel, with a man beginning his soup. The shabby waiter looks out the window and says, 'Looks like rain, sir.' The diner replies, 'Tastes like it, too.'

[†] This collection began accidentally when a bird came to a window of Joyce's flat and allowed itself to be captured. It was just after Joyce had received from Sean O'Faolain a copy of the latter's novel, *Bird Alone,* and the coincidence impressed him.

'*con un fare da gradasso da Gran Sasso,*' because it sacrificed the original rhythm. Joyce merely replied, 'I like the new rhythm.' [31]

Another translating job was undertaken by a new friend, George Pelorson, whom Jean Paulhan asked to put *Pomes Penyeach* into French for *Mesures.* Pelorson was a teacher at Mrs. Jolas's École Bilingue at Neuilly, and had come to know Joyce because of a similar taste for obscure operatic music. He entered into the translation with enthusiasm, which Joyce soon dampened by coaxing him (unlike Frank) to retain the identical rhythms in French as in English; in French, it seemed to Pelorson, they sounded banal. When Pelorson objected Joyce sighed; he left upon Pelorson the impression of being 'a great sigher.' Sometimes, when sighing and translating were equally repugnant, Joyce suggested they go for a walk, and once, during Lent, he proposed they listen to Father Pinard de la Boulaye who was preaching at Notre-Dame. But his main interest was in the priest's name, Pinard, which he knew was slang for wine during World War I. He began joking about it, made a limerick in French, a mixture of *argot* and old French four or five stanzas long with a rollicking tune, and sang it with great hilarity. They ended up with Pinard at a bistro, not a cathedral.

Joyce sometimes went out with Samuel Beckett, of whom he wrote to his son, 'I think he has talent,' a compliment in which he rarely indulged. When Beckett presented him with a copy of *Murphy,* Joyce replied only by a bad limerick beginning, 'There was a young man named Murphy.' But later he pleased Beckett by quoting from memory the description of the disposal of Murphy's body.[33] Beckett reciprocated with an acrostic, 'Home Olga,' * which was a joke but an acute one:

> J might be made sit up for a jade of hope (and exile, don't you know)
> And Jesus and Jesuits juggernauted in the haemorrhoidal isle,
> Modo et forma anal maiden, giggling to death in stomacho.
> E for the erythrite of love and silence and the sweet noo style,
> Swoops and loops of love and silence in the eye of the sun and view
> > of the mew,
> Juvante Jah and a Jain or two and the tip of a friendly yiddophile.
> O for an opal of faith and cunning winking adieu, adieu, adieu;
> Yesterday shall be tomorrow, riddle me that my rapparee;
> Che sarà sarà che fu, there's more than Homer knows how to spew,
> Exempli gratia: ecce himself and the pickthank agnus—e.o.o.e.† [34]

Joyce commented only that 'giggling' should be changed to 'tickled.'

---

* That is, 'Homo Logos,' word-man.

† The sense of the poem is perhaps this: 'If Joyce had any hope in his exile that the Irish would renounce Catholicism, the national malady, he, untouched by it, might be able to yield to his comic spirit. His books are full of natural love and

He made clear to Beckett his dislike of literary talk. Once when they had listened silently to a group of intellectuals at a party, he commented, 'If only they'd talk about turnips!' ° Occasionally, however, his own point of view emerged in a casual word or two. He liked Valéry's *Ébanches d'un serpent,* and particularly admired the initial phrase, '*Parmi l'arbre,*' in which the tree is considered as a multiplicity. But when Valéry had at his request read the passage aloud, Joyce thought the rendition poor. Another line by a contemporary that interested him was Soupault's, '*La dame a perdu son sourire dans le bois.*' [35] But of modern writers in general he remarked, 'If you took a characteristic obscure passage of one of these people and asked him what it meant, he couldn't tell you; whereas I can justify every line of my book.' And another day he remarked, 'I have discovered I can do anything with language I want.' But it was like him to counter these statements by saying to Beckett with impressive modesty, 'I may have oversystematized *Ulysses.*' [37]

In general he had lost interest in his earlier book, *Finnegans Wake* having pre-empted its position, but he allowed himself one day to ask Beckett, 'Does anyone in Dublin read *Ulysses?*' 'Yes,' said Beckett. 'Who?' Beckett named some names. 'But they're all Jews,' Joyce said. Beckett mentioned then that many intellectuals were turning now to Kafka. The name was known to Joyce only as that of the sinister translator of the *Frankfurter Zeitung,* Irene Kafka, and he was perplexed and bothered by this new aspirant to literary pre-eminence. Then his thoughts veered back to *Finnegans Wake.* He had obviously in mind a full defense of it, and fragments of this defense fell into his talk. One day a visiting Englishwoman listened to him reading a passage from the book and sternly remarked, 'That isn't literature.' 'It was,' Joyce replied, meaning that it was while she was listening to it.[38] The musical aspect of the book was one of its justifications. 'Heaven knows what my prose means,' he wrote his daughter. 'But it's pleasing to the ear. And your designs are pleasing to the eye. That's enough, it seems to me.' [39] Another visitor, Terence White Gervais, asked him if the book were a blending of literature and music, and Joyce replied flatly, 'No, it's pure music.' 'But are there not levels of meaning to be explored?'

---

silence, in man and woman, and in their portrayer (Joyce), expressed in a *dolce stil nuovo,* and also full of faith and cunning. When he says goodbye he winks because what was shall be again, a point unknown to Homer, but demonstrated by Joyce because he himself is a kind of Christ (another word-man) returned to life: hail and alas!' There is a covert reference to Stephen's 'silence, exile, and cunning.'

° To an art critic, who began to expatiate on the merits of a painting by Jack Yeats which Joyce had bought, he said curtly, 'There are great silences in that picture, Mr. M——.' But he added, 'Jack Yeats and I have the same method.' [36]

'No, no,' said Joyce, 'it's meant to make you laugh.' [40] Of course, laughter and levels of meaning were not mutually exclusive, and to someone else, a drinking companion, Joyce corrected '*In vino veritas*' to '*In risu veritas.*' 'Why have you written the book this way?' somebody questioned. 'To keep the critics busy for three hundred years.' [41] 'The demand that I make of my reader,' he said with a disarming smile to Max Eastman, 'is that he should devote his whole life to reading my works.' [42] In *Finnegans Wake* he gave his humorous approval to 'that ideal reader suffering from an ideal insomnia.' [43]

These and other remarks of Joyce were mostly directed towards the defense of his book in terms which were not new to criticism. He justified its content as a third of human life—the night third. Those who objected to his method must consider what better way there might be to represent the shiftings of dream life. He defended its theme, its view of life as a recurrence of stock characters and stock situations, another aspect in which the psychology and anthropology of his time did not controvert him. He defended the complexity of the book as necessary to the theme, a claim which has come to be accepted for modern poetry. He defended its technique or form in terms of music, insisting not on the union of the arts—although that seems to be implied—but on the importance of sound and rhythm, and the indivisibility of meaning from form, an idea which has become a commonplace in the critical assessment of Eliot's later verse. Finally, he defended his language both in terms of linguistic theory, as a largely emotional medium built up by sifting and agglutination, and in terms of the appropriateness of linguistic distortion to a book which traced the distortion of dreams and suggested that history was also paronomastic, a jollying duplication of events with slight variations.

Joyce lived more and more quietly as he worked to finish his book. He paid his weekly visits to Lucia, and on June 30, 1937, wrote Myron Nutting that 'it seems that she is at last on the road to recovery.' [44] But again the signs of improvement passed away. He allowed himself only one public appearance, at a meeting of the P.E.N. Club in Paris that same month. He had always insisted that the piracy of *Ulysses* was a matter of international literary concern, and he brought along a short speech to announce the important American judicial decision that, quite apart from the Bern copyright convention, an author could not be deprived of his rights in his own property. The speech was respectfully heard, the chairman politely ordered Joyce's remarks included in the minutes, but there, to Joyce's annoyance, the matter was dropped.

He was still resentful at dinner afterwards with Huebsch and Franz

Werfel, but forgot his injury when he discovered that Werfel had translated the libretti of some of Verdi's operas. A few days later Nancy Cunard sent him a questionnaire about his views on the Spanish War, and this renewed his indignation. He telephoned to say, 'I am James Joyce. I have received your questionnaire.' 'Are you going to answer it?' she asked. 'No! I won't answer it because it is politics. Now politics are getting into everything. The other night I agreed to let myself be taken to one of the dinners of the P.E.N. Club. The charter of the P.E.N. states that politics shall never be discussed there. But what happened? One person made a speech, referring to one angle of politics, someone else brought up a conflicting argument, a third read a paper on more politics. I wanted the P.E.N. to take an interest in the pirating of *Ulysses* in the United States, but this was brushed aside. It was politics all the way.' He concluded by saying he was sending her the script of his remarks at the P.E.N. meeting and commanded, 'Print that, Miss Cunard!' [45]

The possibility of that old impossibility, a trip to Ireland, arose once more. Nora at least seriously considered it,* and Constantine Curran urged Joyce to come over. He contemplated approaching as close to Ireland as the Isle of Man, but no farther:

I am trying to finish my wip [Work in Progress] (I work about 16 hours a day, it seems to me) and I am not taking any chances with my fellow-countrymen if I can possibly help it until that is done, at least. And on the map of their island there is marked very legibly for the moment Hic sunt Lennones.† But every day in every way I am walking along the streets of Dublin and along the strand. And 'hearing voices.' *Non dico giammai ma non ancora.*[47]

When Mrs. Sheehy-Skeffington asked him why he did not return there, he replied, 'Have I ever left it?' Old thoughts of the city had infiltrated his mind since he had heard from Alfred Bergan in May of the death of Tom Devin. He wrote Bergan on May 25,

> 7 rue Edmond Valentin
> Paris 7e

Dear Mr Bergan: I am so sorry to hear your bad news that our old friend Mr Devin is gone. Only on Wednesday last I gave his name to a young American writer who is doing my biography and has gone to Dublin, Mr Herbert Gorman. I told him to see you and Mr Devan

---

* Her sister Kathleen had just married John Griffin, and had sent them in lieu of an announcement 'a parcel containing a chunk of old but still combative wedding cake for my wife,' Joyce wrote, 'and a silver shoe for me.' [46]
† Judge Michael Lennon. See p. 655.

as you were the only people still left (as I thought) who could remember all the pleasant nights we used to have singing. Mr Devin's song was 'O boys, keep away from the girls I say.' The moral of it fell on deaf ears in my case and I don't think it meant very much to him either. He used to play the *intermezzo* from *Cavalleria Rusticana*—a version of his own and would have been a fine pianist if he had studied as he had a very agreeable touch on the keys. He used to collapse with laughter after a preliminary scream in a high tone at certain sallies of my father's. He must have been a fine looking fellow when he was young, and he had charming manners. He comes into *Ulysses* under the name of 'Mr Power' and also into 'Dubliners.' I regret that my friend (who, by the way, is staying quite close to you at the Royal Hibernian Hotel) did not meet him and talk with him. He has letters to and from a number of literary people in Dublin. Many of them are very fair written too and one or two more than that but they never meant much to me personally and mean less now.

The Lord knows whether you will be able to pick the Kersse-McCann story out of my crazy tale. It was a great story of my father's and I'm sure if they get a copy of *transition* in the shades his comment will be 'Well, he can't tell that story as I used to and that's one sure five!'

I hope you are well and send you all good and friendly greetings

Sincerely yours
James Joyce

23.5.'37

The caution he displayed to Curran easily controlled his nostalgia, and Joyce went with Nora about August 12 not to Ireland but to Switzerland. On the way to Zurich he stopped at Rheinfelden, which he rechristened, 'Erin on the Rhine,' the Rhine being 'Anna Rhenana.' [48] Then in September he came back to France, and in the middle of the month stayed for a few days at the Grand Hôtel in Dieppe. He was much excited over a throwaway someone had sent him which advertised a three-hour coastal cruise on board the pleasure steamer *John Joyce*, sailing from Dun Laoghaire. When Lloyd's Register did not list it, he called upon Budgen, as a former sailor, to ascertain if John Joyce was really 'employing his postvital hours transporting Dubliners round the bay.' [49] But no trace of the 'phantom ship' could be found.* [50]

Joyce still hoped to publish his book on February 2, 1938, and often worked late at night upon it.† He asked Herbert Gorman, who had

---

* John V. Kelleher informs me that the *John Joyce* is the tender that meets the liners at Cobh harbor. It was originally a River Mersey ferry boat.
† He took time, however, to write one bit of light verse for a Thanksgiving party at the Jolases in November. The fact that the turkey had been dropped on its way

also suddenly become eager to finish his biography, to defer publication until March 1938. Gorman agreed with reluctance, and to his publisher (Farrar and Rinehart), complained 'I will never write another biography of a living man. It is too difficult and thankless a task.' [51] But both books were postponed further.

---

from the market, and had somehow lost its liver in the process, so diverted Joyce that he wrote a 'Come-all-ye' about it:

> Come all you lairds and ladies and listen to my lay!
> I'll tell of my adventures upon last Thanksgiving Day
> I was picked by Madame Jolas to adorn the barbecue
> So the chickenchoker patched me till I looked as good as new.
>
> I drove out, all tarred and feathered, from the Grand Palais Potin
> But I met with foul disaster in the Place Saint Augustin.
> My charioteer collided—with the shock I did explode
> And the force of my emotions shot my liver on the road.
>
> Up steps a dapper sergeant with his pencil and his book.
> Our names and our convictions down in Leber's code he took.
> Then I hailed another driver and resumed my swanee way.
> They couldn't find my liver but I hadn't time to stay.
>
> When we reached the gates of Paris cries the boss at the Octroi:
> Holy Poule, what's this I'm seeing. Can it be Grandmother Loye?
> When Caesar got the bird she was the dindy of the flock
> But she must have boxed a round or two with some old turkey cock.
>
> I ruffled up my plumage and proclaimed with eagle's pride:
> You jackdaw, these are truffles and not blues on my backside.
> Mind, said he, that one's a chestnut. There's my bill and here's my thanks
> And now please search through your stuffing and fork out that fifty francs.
>
> At last I reached the banquet-hall—and what a sight to see!
> I felt myself transported back among the Osmanli
> I poured myself a bubbly flask and raised the golden horn
> With three cheers for good old Turkey and the roost where I was born.
>
> I shook claws with all the hammers and bowed to blonde and brune
> The mistress made a signal and the mujik called the tune.
> Madamina read a message from the Big Noise of her State
> After which we crowed in unison: That Turco's talking straight!
>
> We settled down to feed and, if you want to know my mind,
> I thought that I could gobble but they left me picked behind,
> They crammed their crops till cockshout when like ostriches they ran
> To hunt my missing liver round the Place Saint Augustin.
>
>   J.J.[52]

Thanksgiving Day, 1937
Neuilly, Paris

> Still I'll lift my glass to Gallia and augur that we may
> Untroubled in her dovecot dwell till next Thanksgiving Day
> So let every Gallic gander pass the sauceboat to his goose—
> And let's all play happy homing though our liver's on the loose.

(In the first stanza, Joyce writes 'lairds' in tribute to Maria McDonald Jolas's Scottish descent. In the second stanza, the Grand Palais Potin refers to Félix Potin,

Joyce's comfortable circle was again disrupted in December 1937, when George and Helen had to go to the United States because of sickness in her family. He pressed his son to find out when he would return, and, on hearing that the *Queen Mary* would bring George and Helen to Cherbourg on April 26, he proposed to meet them there. They dissuaded him, but he jokingly threatened to fly to the Azores to escort them back to France.[53] He used the interval to pay a quick trip to Dr. Vogt in Zurich (as he had done also the previous March), to consult him about retinal congestion in his left eye. Vogt reassured him that while he would see badly, he would continue to see.

Joyce now hoped to make July 4, his father's birthday, the date of publication of *Finnegans Wake*. The publisher objected that summer publication would find everyone on holiday and defeat sales. Joyce retorted that his name would be enough. But this deadline also passed with the work still in progress. When the publisher begged for the book's title, still undivulged, Joyce said he would give it to him just before the book went to the binder, and no sooner.

During the early summer he had help from James Johnson Sweeney, the museum director and art critic, who read the manuscript aloud and inserted phrases which Joyce dictated to him. They came to a passage, 'Clontarf one love one fear' (*Finnegans Wake* [324]), and Joyce asked, 'Do you understand that, Sweeney?' 'Oh yes,' he said, 'the last two numbers of the date of the Battle of Clontarf [1014].' Joyce seemed to agree. Later Sweeney realized that 'one love' would in tennis represent the first two numbers of the date and the next afternoon he said, 'Mr. Joyce, I pretended to understand more of that Clontarf reference than I did.' Joyce replied, 'Oh yes, the telephone number of that public house.' And Sweeney realized he had still understood only part of the phrase, that Joyce was referring also to Clontarf as the telephone exchange in Chapelizod. They came to the catchphrase, 'Knock knock who's there?' Joyce had altered it [330] to 'Knock knock. War's where!' and given for answer, 'The Twwinns.' He explained to Sweeney that Cain and Abel were the origin of war; the second 'w' in 'Twwinns,' Joyce said laughing, was for Eve, and meant, as the next phrases indicated, 'without an apple,' for she had been born without an Adam's apple.[54]

Joyce was quite ready to clarify phrases and even pages for people

---

a pre-war grocery chain. The 'Mujik' in the sixth stanza was a faithful Russian servant who served at table; 'Madamina' is the first word of an aria in *Don Giovanni* as well as a combination of 'Madame' (Jolas) and 'Balamina' (a Southern song she used to sing); the 'message from the Big Noise' was Franklin D. Roosevelt's Thanksgiving Day message.)

he knew. One day he was explaining the plan of a section to the Swiss writer Jacques Mercanton when he suddenly paused to ask the rhetorical question, '*N'est-ce pas? C'est bien ainsi que doit pratiquer le démiurge pour fabriquer notre beau monde?*' * Mercanton hesitated before agreeing with what seemed obvious. Joyce puffed on his cigarette, passed his hand over his forehead, and then said ruminatively, '*Peut-être, en somme, qu'il réfléchit moins que nous.*' † ⁵⁵

That summer Joyce had to give up to some of his Paris friends, though still not to Faber & Faber or the Viking Press, the one secret about his book which he wished to keep a little longer, its title. He had often issued a challenge to his intimates to guess what it might be, and offered a thousand francs to anyone who succeeded. Gilbert, Gorman, Beckett, Léon, and Jolas had all tried and failed, like Miss Weaver before them. One July night on the terrace of Fouquet's Joyce repeated his offer over several bottles of Riesling. Mrs. Joyce spoke cheerily about 'that chop suey he's writing,' ⁵⁶ and began to sing an Irish song about Mr. Flannigan and Mr. Shannigan. Joyce, startled, asked her to stop. When he saw no harm had been done, he very distinctly, as a singer does it, made the lip motions which seemed to indicate *F* and *W*. Maria Jolas guessed, 'Fairy's Wake.' Joyce looked astonished and said, 'Brava! But something is missing.' The Jolases thought about it for some days, and suddenly on the morning of August 2 Eugene Jolas saw that the title must be *Finnegans Wake*. At dinner that evening he threw the words in the air, and Joyce blanched. Slowly he set down the wineglass he held. 'Ah Jolas, you've taken something out of me,' he said almost sadly, then became quite gay. When they parted that night, Jolas wrote later, 'He embraced me, danced a few of his intricate steps, and asked: "How would you like to have the money?"' Jolas replied, 'In sous,' and the following morning Joyce arrived with a bag filled with ten-franc pieces, which he instructed Jolas's daughters to serve their father at lunch.⁵⁷ But he swore the Jolases to secrecy until he had written 'the final full stop, though there is none.'

By this time Book I was in page proof, Book II in galley proof except for thirty or forty pages, of which more than half was in typescript; Book III was in galley proof; half of Part IV was typewritten and ready for the printer. In spite of his desire to think of nothing but completing his book, politics sought Joyce out. The German and Italian translations of *Anna Livia Plurabelle* were postponed because of 'influential pressure,' and the Russians also regarded Joyce with

---

* 'Isn't this the way the demiurge must calculate in making our fine world?'
† 'Perhaps, after all, he reflects less than we.'

suspicion. He refused to commit himself publicly in any way. For some years he had referred to Germany derisively as 'Hitlerland,' and no one could have been less attracted than he to the frenzied personality of the Fuehrer. But he cultivated disengagement, and remarked one night at dinner at Paul Léon's, 'Isn't this Hitler a phenomenon? Think of getting a whole people behind you.' Nora picked up a knife and said, 'You stop that, Jim.' [58] He spoke highly of German precision to friends whom he knew to be hostile to any favorable mention of Germany. Samuel Beckett spoke to Joyce of the Nazis' persecution of the Jews, but Joyce pointed out there had been similar persecutions before.[59] It was not that he condoned them, but that he wished to withdraw to another perspective. When Jacques Mercanton asked him to contribute something to *Mass und Werk*, Joyce at first agreed, then remembered that Thomas Mann had stated his anti-Nazi position there in 1937, and said, 'No, the review is politically oriented.' [60] He did not wish *Finnegans Wake* to be banned by any country because of its author's supposed political bias.

On the other hand, Joyce did not blind himself to what was going on. He remarked to Maria Jolas of anti-Semitism, 'It's one of the easiest and oldest prejudices to "prove".' [61] When a young Harvard student wrote to him to praise *Ulysses* but complain of Joyce's attitude towards his race, Joyce remarked, 'I have written with the greatest sympathy about the Jews.' [62] *Ulysses* was, in fact, if anyone cared to examine it, so anti-totalitarian a book that there was no more to be said. Joyce's views were reaffirmed by his actions; in 1938 he began to help people to escape from Nazi territory to Ireland and America. The first of these was Hermann Broch, whom Joyce knew through an essay, '*James Joyce und die Gegenwart*'; Broch was obliged by the *Anschluss* of March 1938 to leave Vienna, and Joyce helped him reach England. Two others were relatives of old friends: one was the son of Charlotte Sauermann,° the second a nephew of Edmund Brauchbar. Joyce had friends in the French Foreign Office and elsewhere whose help he enlisted, with his usual energy, in behalf of about seven refugees in various stages of flight or resettlement.

Joyce had put off leaving the Paris summer heat as long as he could. Nora was impatient with him. As she remarked to David Fleischman one night at dinner, 'I don't bother with him any more, he can do what he pleases. But it's terrible in the summer. He doesn't want to go away at all. It'll be like last year. I'll drag him away somewhere and he'll get terrible nervous pains in his stomach. I never get but three words out of him all day these days: in the morning,

° She had married Richard Ofner and was now dead.

"The papers!", at lunch, "What's that?", and the third—Jim, what is
the third, I can't remember it? Ah yes, about his bottle of water on
the floor: "Don't touch that!" Don't touch that! Goodness!' [63] She got
him away at last on August 19, 1938, and Paul Léon traveled with
them to Lausanne. There was a fine dinner in that city with Léon
and a Russian friend, Alexander Troubnikoff, when, not being sure
which wine to choose, they ordered 3 decima of each of 20-odd
crus represented on the walls of the restaurant.[64] In soberer moments
Joyce took pleasure in mocking Léon's esthetic passion for the liturgy
of the Orthodox church, which to his mind was unformed and sopho-
moric. He also sent Madame Léon a playful card that said, 'Léon is
at his fourth bath and turning a delicious Nubian.' [65] At Lausanne
Joyce also sought out his young admirer, Jacques Mercanton, whom
he wanted to encourage to continue his work on *Finnegans Wake*.
There were hints that Mercanton would be chosen ultimately as its
principal expositor. When he asked Joyce to inscribe his *Ulysses*, Joyce
did so with a blasphemous flourish that perturbed Nora:

> A Jacques Mercanton
> James Joyce
> Lausanne
> Veille de la Fête de Madone Bloom *1938* [66]

It was September 7, the eve not only of Molly Bloom's nativity but
also of the Virgin Mary's.

Jocular as he seemed, Joyce was troubled by a new problem, the
worsening relations of his son and daughter-in-law. Helen Joyce had
suffered a mental breakdown shortly before, and was obliged to go
to a private sanitorium in Montreux, where Joyce and Nora visited
her. They were encouraged to find her apparently better, and went
on to Zurich for a short stay. There Joyce was overcome by severe
stomach cramps, as his wife had predicted, and consulted a specialist,
who advised him to have immediate X rays. Disregarding this good
counsel, as well as the crisis in the Sudetenland of Czechoslovakia,
Joyce returned to Paris, then went on to Dieppe, where he lay con-
tentedly on the pebbles listening to the sounds of the sea.[67] As war
drew nearer, he and Nora hurried back to Paris to see about Lucia.
Dr. Delmas informed Joyce that plans had already been made for
evacuating the *maison de santé*, in case of war, to La Baule. Joyce
and Nora went there so as to meet the evacuees, and were there when
the Munich pact was signed on September 30. After the pact, they
went back to Paris, Joyce a little scornful about Chamberlain and
his English diplomacy with Hitler ('Give him Europe!' he said to

Colum), but mainly relieved to be able to finish his book with the tension at least momentarily lessened.[68]

He had left only the last pages of Book IV of *Finnegans Wake*, the monologue of Anna Livia Plurabelle which begins, 'Soft morning, city! Lsp! I am leafy speafing.' * The ending was in a way a recapitulation of all the endings of his previous books. As Frank Budgen points out, it is a contemplation of death like that of Gabriel at the end of *Dubliners*.[69] But it is also like *A Portrait of the Artist* in that a woman is setting a man's clothes in order and a journey into the Irish Sea is about to take place. Stephen calls upon his spiritual father with as much feeling as Anna Livia upon her husband-father. At the end of *Exiles* Bertha cries, 'Forget me and love me again as you did the first time. I want my lover. To meet him, to go to him, to give myself to him. You, Dick. O, my strange wild lover, come back to me again.' At the end of *Ulysses*, in another female monologue Molly Bloom returns in memory and imagination to the moment of passionate consent, echoed here by Anna Livia with her punning plea, 'Finn, again!' The last page was a wonderful absorption of old recollections in new purposes:

I done me best when I was let. Thinking always if I go all goes. A hundred cares, a tithe of troubles and is there one who understands me? One in a thousand of years of the nights? All me life I have been lived among them but now they are becoming loathed to me. And I am lothing their little warm tricks. And lothing their mean cosy turns. And all the greedy gushes out through their small souls. And all the lazy leaks down over their brash bodies. How small it's all! And me letting on to meself always. And jilting on all the time. I thought you were all glittering with the noblest of carriage. You're only a bumpkin. I thought you the great in all things, in guilt and in glory. You're but a puny. Home! My people were not their sort out beyond there so far as I can. For all the bold and bad and bleary they are blamed, the seahags. No! Nor for all our wild dances in all their wild din. I can seen meself among them, allaniuvia pulchrabelled. How she was handsome, the wild Amazia, when she would seize to my other breast! And what is she weird, haughty Niluna, that she will snatch from my ownest hair! For 'tis they are the stormies. Ho hang! Hang ho! And the clash of our cries till we spring to be free. Auravoles, they says, never heed of your name! But I'm loothing them that's here and all I lothe. Loonely in me loneness. For all their faults. I am passing out. O bitter ending! I'll slip away before they're up. They'll never see. Nor know. Nor miss me. And it's old and old it's sad and old it's sad and weary I go back to you, my cold father, my cold mad father, my cold mad feary father, till the near sight of the mere size of him, the moyles and moyles of it, moananoaning, makes me seasilt saltsick and I rush,

---

* *Finnegans Wake* (619).

my only, into your arms. I see them rising! Save me from those therrble
prongs! Two more. Onetwo moremens more. So. Avelaval. My leaves have
drifted from me. All. But one clings still. I'll bear it on me. To remind me of.
Lff! So soft this morning, ours. Yes. Carry me along, taddy, like you done
through the toy fair! If I seen him bearing down on me now under white-
spread wings like he'd come from Arkangels, I sink I'd die down over his
feet, humbly dumbly, only to washup. Yes, tid. There's where. First. We pass
through grass behush the bush to. Whish! A gull. Gulls. Far calls. Coming,
far! End here. Us then. Finn, again! Take. Bussoftlhee, mememormee! Till
thousendsthee. Lps. The keys to. Given! A way a lone a last a loved a
long the

Anna's question, 'Is there one who understands me?', was Joyce's
own question to Nora thirty-four years before in Dublin. The phrase,
'Carry me along, taddy, like done through the toy fair,' was inspired by a memory of carrying his son George through a toy fair
in Trieste to make up for not giving him a rocking horse. But
Anna Livia is the Liffey as well as the human heroine, and Joyce, as
John Kelleher points out, bore in mind the topography of Dublin Bay;
as she passes towards the bitter salt sea she must first go between
those 'terrible prongs,' the North and South Walls of Dublin. As for
the last word of the passage, Joyce pondered it a good deal. He said
to Gillet in announcing what he had found, '*Dans Ulysse, pour peindre
le balbutiement d'une femme qui s'endort, j'avais cherché à finir par
le mot le moins fort qu'il m'était possible de découvrir. J'avais trouvé
le mot "yes," qui se prononce à peine, qui signifie l'acquiescement,
l'abandon, la détente, la fin de toute résistance. Dans le* Work in
Progress, *j'ai cherché mieux, si je pouvais. Cette fois, j'ai trouvé le
mot le plus glissant, le moins accentué, le plus faible de la langue
anglaise, un mot qui n'est même pas un mot, qui sonne à peine entre
les dents, un souffle, un rien, l'article* the.' * [70]
The character of Anna Livia was like that of Molly Bloom, but put
more emphasis on ultimate attachment if not on fidelity. The words
which Joyce had applied earlier to woman, 'untrustworthy' and 'indifferent,' were scarcely adequate to convey the total female temperament, as he had observed it in Nora during thirty-four years. Anna
has seen through her husband, yet she is full of submission, if not

---

* 'In *Ulysses*, to depict the babbling of a woman going to sleep, I had sought to
end with the least forceful word I could possibly find. I had found the word 'yes,'
which is barely pronounced, which denotes acquiescence, self-abandon, relaxation,
the end of all resistance. In *Work in Progress*, I've tried to do better if I could.
This time, I found the word which is the most slippery, the least accented, the
weakest word in English, a word which is not even a word, which is scarcely
sounded between the teeth, a breath, a nothing, the article *the*.'

precisely to him, at least to the male principle. Whether the man coming down on her from Archangel is her husband or her father or both doesn't greatly matter,* nor does her grammar. She dissolves into a force of nature, eternally constant in spite of inconstancies, tied indissolubly to her image of man.

This final passage, in which the Liffey's fresh water mixed with the salt water of the Irish Sea in Dublin Bay, was sketched out in one afternoon, and in its first stage was only two and a half pages long.† After finishing it, Joyce told Jolas, 'I felt so completely exhausted, as if all the blood had run out of my brain. I sat for a long while on a street bench, unable to move.' [71] He brought it first to Madame Lapeyre's bistro, at the corner of the rue de Grenelle and the rue de Bourgogne, where he and Léon usually met before dinner, and then to dinner at Fouquet's. There he asked Helen Joyce to read the fragment aloud, and listened with evident and intense pleasure to what he had created. Léon, full of affection, watched him and saw that for one of the rare times in their friendship Joyce looked satisfied and proud of himself.[72] In the next few days Joyce expanded the two and a half pages to ten, and lent them to Beckett, who read them on the way to the railroad station and called him up to say how much they moved him.[73] Joyce was very pleased. He read it

---

* Molly similarly confuses her husband and an old lover, but also recognizes Bloom's distinctness.

† This earlier version read:

'Soft morning, city! I am leafy speaking. Folty and folty all the nights have been falling on to long my hair. Not a sound falling. The woods are so fond always. It is for my golden wedding. Rise up, man of the hooths, you have slept so long! I am leafy, your golden, so you called me, exaggerator! Here is your shirt, the day one, come back. The stock, your collar. Also your double brogues. I want to see you looking fine for me. The children are still fast. There is no school today. It's Phoenix, dear. It is the softest morning that I can ever remember me. The trout will be so nice at breakfast. Are my not truly? Only you must buy me a new girdle too. Come. Give me your great big hand for miny tiny. We will take our walk before they ring the bells. Not such big steps. It is hardly seven mile. It is very good for health in the morning. It seems so long since. As if you had been long far away. You will tell me some time if I can belive its all. You know where I am bringing you? You remember? Not a soul but ourselves. We might call on the Old Lord, what do you say? He is a fine sport. Remember to take off your white hat, eh? I am so exquisitely pleased about the lovely dress I have. You will always call me leafy, won't you? Queer grand old Finn, If I knew who you are! I will tell you all sorts of stories, strange one. About every place we pass. It is all so often and still the same to me. Look! Your blackbirds! That's for your good luck. How glad you'll be I waked you. My! How well you'll feel. For ever after. First we turn a little here and then it's easy. I only hope the heavens sees us. A bit beside the bush and then a walk along the'

also to George Pelorson, and said, 'Do you like it?' 'Yes, when you recite it.' Joyce laughed, then explained it. 'There are people who say it's crazy,' he said, 'I wonder. . . .' And he hesitated. Pelorson said, 'You put your bitter message at the end,' but Joyce denied that this was what he meant.[74] Anna Livia recriminates and laments and expresses disgust, but she accepts too.

By November 13 the '*maledetto*' book, as Joyce wrote his Zurich friend Paul Ruggiero,[75] was finished. The following week Maria Jolas had another Thanksgiving dinner, and Joyce wrote Ruggiero in Zurich to ask for the words of a modern Greek lovesong which he remembered hearing long before. Its plaint for lost love harmonized with the mood of Anna Livia Plurabelle, but in other ways suggested Joyce's curious taste for the most predictable poetry, which was somehow compatible with his desire for the most extraordinary prose:

> I walked out all alone on the strand
> To remember how we had wept together
> When I kiss you, you remember it too.
> When I kiss you, you remember it too.
> Now I love another, a blonde
> Much prettier than you.
> But at the bottom of the heart
> First love keeps its deep roots.

The next month and a half passed in a frenzy of proofreading. It was understood that the printer must deliver a book to Joyce by his birthday at all costs. Mrs. Jolas at Neuilly, with the aid of some professional proofreaders, Stuart Gilbert on the rue Jean-du-Bellay, and Léon on the rue Casimir-Périer were working full time; Joyce scarcely slept and collapsed once during a walk in the Bois de Boulogne. Léon supplied a last drama by forgetting a section of the revised proofs in a taxi. He rushed back to stop the driver, but the taxi was gone. Bitterly ashamed, he hurried to Joyce's flat to inform him; Joyce did not reproach him, seemed rather to take it as the usual sort of bad luck.* Léon telephoned to London to send more proofs, but the taxi driver, after two hours, miraculously appeared with the missing package.[76] On New Year's Day, except for a few last-minute telegrams, the work was done, and Joyce informed Livia Schmitz:

> Dear Signora: I have at last finished my book. For three lustra I have been combing and recombing the hair of Anna Livia. It is now time that she appear on the stage. I hope that Berenice will intercede for

---

* He had the precedents to recall of the burning of some of the *Ulysses* manuscript by a typist's husband in 1921, and the guillotining of the *Dubliners* sheets in 1912.

her little sister so that she may find in this great world, thanks to the gods, 'at least some small Deo Gratias.' *

Merry Christmas and Happy New Year to you and your family.

James Joyce

A copy of the book arrived on January 30, and Joyce telegraphed to Faber & Faber, 'MY WARM THANKS TO ALL CONCERNED FOR PATIENCE PROMPTITUDE WHICH I GREATLY APPRECIATE.' 77 He had Léon bring the copy to Gillet to look at, and the Frenchman exclaimed that 'It was like the arrival of Desaix at Marengo.' 78 Frank Budgen came over from London to help Joyce celebrate: when he left after a happy reunion Joyce called out to him, 'Lots of fun,' and Budgen, alive to the new pass-word, called back, 'At Finnegans Wake.' 79

For the birthday party on February 2, Helen Joyce, who had been away with George and Stephen for the Christmas holidays,† decided to do something special to make up for their absence. She went to the best caterer in Paris with Joyce's seven books under her arm, and instructed him to bake a cake with a replica of the seven books be-tween bookends on the top. He should begin with the smallest and be sure to ice all the books in the color of their bindings, with *Finnegans Wake* as the largest and latest at the end.‡ The table was prepared with a round mirror tray as centerpiece, to represent the English Channel, with Dublin at one end and Paris at the other. A glass decanter shaped like the Eiffel tower, and a night lamp shaped like a windmill stood on the French side; another night lamp, shaped like a church, and a glass bottle in the form of Nelson's Pillar, stood on the Irish side. The rivers Liffey and Seine were represented in silver paper, complete with boats and, for the Liffey, with swans.

At the celebration Nora wore for the first time a ring set with an aquamarine which her husband had given her to symbolize the Liffey (her counterpart in the landscape). Stuart and Moune Gilbert, Paul and Lucie Léon, Eugene and Maria Jolas, Philippe Soupault, and Dr. Daniel P. O'Brien, a new member of the circle,** all attended. Joyce was more open than usual; he told how the idea of the book had come to him in 1922 when he was at Nice. After dinner Maria Jolas played the piano, George Joyce and his father sang a duet; then

---

* See p. 571.

† They were visiting Laurence Vail and his wife, Kay Boyle, in Megève.

‡ She also ordered at a jeweller's a tiny golden book with the words, '*Finnegans Wake* by James Joyce,' engraved on the cover, and inside a birthday message and 'Love from Giorgio, Stephen, and Helen.' This was to be attached to a fountain pen.

** Dr. O'Brien, of the Rockefeller Foundation, met Joyce through William Bird.

Helen read the last pages of *Finnegans Wake*. Joyce drank Swiss wine, and all was as it had been at those many festive dinners in Paris during the past twenty years. Or almost so.

In retrospect, it seems clear that the 'monster,' as Joyce several times called *Finnegans Wake* in these days, had to be written, and that he had to write it. Readers may still sigh because he did not approach them more directly, but it does not appear that this alternative was open to him. In *Dubliners* he had explored the waking consciousness from outside, in *A Portrait* and *Ulysses* from inside. He had begun to impinge, but gingerly, upon the mind asleep. There lay before him, as in 1922 he well knew, this almost totally unexplored expanse. That the great psychological discovery of his century was the night world he was, of course, aware, but he frowned on using that world as a means of therapy. Joyce's purpose was not so didactic; he wished, unassumingly enough, to amuse men with it.

The night attracted him also for another reason.* He had begun his writing by asserting his difference from other men, and now increasingly he recognized his similarity to them. This point of view was more easily demonstrable in sleeping than in waking life. Sleep is the great democratizer: in their dreams people become one, and everything about them becomes one. Nationalities lose their borders, levels of discourse and society are no longer separable, time and space surrender their demarcations. All human activities begin to fuse into all other human activities, printing a book into bearing a baby, fighting a war into courting a woman. By day we attempt originality; by night plagiarism is forced upon us. In *A Portrait of the Artist as a Young Man* Joyce had demonstrated the repetition of traits in the first twenty years of one person's life; in *Ulysses* he had displayed this repetition in the day of two persons; in *Finnegans Wake* he displayed it in the lives of everyone.

The language of the new book was as necessary to it as the verbal arrangements of his previous works to them. He had already succeeded in adapting English to suit states of mind and even times of day, but chiefly by special arrangements and special kinds of words in different chapters. Now, for *Finnegans Wake,* a polyglot language had to be brought, even more daringly, to its own making-house. To imitate the sophistication of word- and image-formation in the uncon-

---

* The theory that Joyce wrote his book for the ear because he could not see is not only an insult to the creative imagination, but an error of fact. Joyce could see; to be for periods half-blind is not at all the same thing as to be permanently blind. The eyes are closed in *Finnegans Wake* because to open them would change the book's postulate.

scious mind (for Joyce discarded the notion that the mind's basic movements were primitive), he took settled words and images, then dismembered and reconstituted them.

In his earlier books Joyce forced modern literature to accept new styles, new subject matter, new kinds of plot and characterization. In his last book he forced it to accept a new area of being and a new language. What is ultimately most impressive is the sureness with which, in the midst of such technical accomplishments, he achieved his special mixture of attachment and detachment, of gaiety and lugubriousness. He was no saturnine artificer contriving devices, but one of life's celebrants, in bad circumstances cracking good jokes, foisting upon ennuis and miseries his comic vision.

PART V:

RETURN TO ZURICH

✧✧

1939–1941

Quiet takes back her folded fields. Tranquille thanks. Adew.

—Finnegans Wake (244)

ANNA Livia's thoughts of death in her final soliloquy prefigured the mood of the last two years of Joyce's life. He was the prey of events outside him, and of occurrences within his body which he could not control. He did not have the composition of *Finnegans Wake* to make him laugh. Unable to bring himself to begin a new book, he sorted old worries. To a friend he said, 'I've tried everything,' [1] in a tone that suggested he saw no more to experience or to discover. Sick fatigue was to deprive his actions and choices of meaning.

In spite of the festivities for *Finnegans Wake*, the book was not yet published. Between February 2 and the official date of publication, May 4, Joyce grew exceedingly impatient. Huebsch still hoped to delay the American edition until fall, but Joyce made his opposition so peremptory that Huebsch gave way. Joyce said, 'They had better hurry. War is going to break out, and nobody will be reading my book any more.' [2] On March 15 Hitler took over what remained of Czechoslovakia, and soon after seized Memel from Lithuania, extorted concessions from Rumania, and demanded from Poland Danzig and a way through the Polish Corridor. Joyce decided to move again, from the flat at 7 rue Edmond Valentin which, without Lucia, was too large, to another at 34 rue des Vignes. He wrote Mary Colum on March 28, 1939, 'It is a great bore having to move but we are lucky if we have not to move much farther and more hastily.' The sense of impending disaster caused Nora Joyce, shortly before their arrival in the flat on the rue des Vignes on April 15, to put some of her papers in order. She remarked to Maria Jolas, 'I've just spent the most awful day— tearing up Jim's letters to me.' 'Why did you do that?' asked Mrs. Jolas. 'Oh, they were nobody's business. There weren't many, anyway— we've never been separated.' Joyce was silent. [3]

On May 4 *Finnegans Wake* appeared simultaneously in London and New York. The Joyces and Jolases had a small party, and Nora said, 'Well, Jim, I haven't read any of your books but I'll have to some day because they must be good considering how well they sell.' [4] Joyce complained that the price was too high this time, and wrote grimly to Georg Goyert, 'Perhaps I still have a future as a streetsinger— behind me.' [5] He complained to Beckett about his financial situation, which would make it necessary for him to teach again. Beckett found out there was a position open as lecturer in Italian at the University of Capetown. Joyce thought it over for a few days, then, having heard thunderstorms were frequent there, gave it up. [6]

He devoured the reviews of *Finnegans Wake*, but quickly grew disappointed and even morose. As each one was read he listened intently, then sighed. Some were tentative, saying this presumably great book would require study; others were cavalier, dismissing it as madness; and others impudent, assuming it was an interminably protracted bad joke. Joyce was infuriated by the *Irish Times*, which listed the work among books received as by Sean O'Casey, and O'Casey, as indignant with Ireland as Joyce, wrote him: 'I know many of Dublin's Literary Clique dislike me, and they hate you (why, God only knows), so that "misprint" was a bit of a joke.' [7] He wished he had the power to write such an 'amazing book,' he said, and his autobiography demonstrates by its strong Joycean influence that he meant it. One review that unexpectedly pleased Joyce was that by Oliver Gogarty in the *Observer* for May 7, 1939. Gogarty called it 'the most colossal leg pull in literature since Macpherson's *Ossian*,' but acknowledged Joyce's 'indomitable spirit' and his book's 'magnitude.' Joyce said to Budgen that Gogarty, being an athlete, knew the value of being a 'stayer.' [8]

There were a few reviews that dealt with the book usefully,* Harry Levin's being the one Joyce liked best. He thought Edmund Wilson's review in the *New Republic* had flashes of insight but made a few mistakes, such as the assumption that Johnny MacDougal was Ulster (instead of Connaught). Joyce was anxious for French criticism too. George Pelorson was doing an article, and Jacques Mercanton another. Mercanton ran into Jean Paulhan on the street in Paris, and Paulhan, observing a copy of *Finnegans Wake* under his arm, said to him, with the tone of someone inquiring about a new and unknown writer, '*Qu'est-ce que ça vaut?*' ('Any good?'), a question which delighted Joyce when he heard it from Mercanton later. [9] Louis Gillet, always to be depended upon now for a favorable notice, had been in the United States, but wrote Joyce on June 18, 1939, 'I am in a

* Joyce wrote the authors of some of these to thank them warmly.

hurry to return to Chalais and take some days' vacation with *Finnegans Wake*. Is the monster causing a big racket? You will tell me all about it. I still have a paper of yours on some subject or other of Scandinavian mythology. I shall give it back to you after my return.' Joyce's answer implied a reproach for Gillet's casual mention of the paper on Scandinavian mythology: 'The paper about which you tell me is a summary of the theories of Heinrich Zimmer, made for me by his son, on the Scandinavian origin of the legend of Finn MacCool, Arthur and King Mark of the first Irish epic. . . .'[10] It was, in fact, a confirmation of Joyce's book, which gave Finn and his modern avatar, Earwicker, a Scandinavian origin. As to the reviews, Joyce admitted that there were a great many: 'Yes, I have already received some hundred criticisms of my book from England and the United States. The only English article perhaps that seems to rise above the stupor with a certain critical ease, is the leading article of the *Times.** Among the American articles, there are some glimmers in about ten and even some light. . . . I could take a leap to your house and bring you the whole dustbin. I'll have Giorgio's car, naturally, for criticism is heavy to bear.'[11] He was pleased to announce that Alfred Péron was to speak on the Paris radio in late June on *Finnegans Wake*. 'This will be the first voice to break the silence in these parts.[12]

In June, too, Herbert Gorman wrote Joyce that his book was now ready, and that the publishers, Farrar and Rinehart, hoped to publish it in July. Joyce had no intention of authorizing so important a work without carefully reviewing its contents, and dictated a strong letter to Paul Léon for transmission to his biographer:

Paris, June the 6th. 1939

Dear Mr. Gorman,

Mr. Joyce asks me to confirm his personal cable to you in which he stated that he could not authorise the publication of your biography of him without having in his possession for perusal and comparison the entire set of the typescript and of course the subsequent proofs and requesting the immediate dispatch of the other chapters namely those which he has heard in non-consecutive order at intervals during the last several years and those which he has not heard yet. His reason for cabling you was, as he stated, that the exposition of two points in chapters II and IV was incorrect and misleading on two vital points. In fact as he expresses it the latter chapter read almost as if it had been inspired by Mr. Michael Lennon's article in the 'Catholic World' of some years ago. Mr. Joyce is definitely of opinion that his friends did him a singular disservice in not drawing his attention to this article at the

* By Thomas McGreevy.

time; it was highly libellous and defamatory both to his father and to himself and in fact there is little doubt that the fact of its publication having gone without legal challenge had an extremely harmful effect on the artistic career of his son in the U.S.A.

The two points in question are the relations of Mr. Joyce and his late father and the question of his marriage in 1904 which subsequently and for testamentary reasons was supplemented by retroactive civil marriage according to English law in 1931. The accounts you give to the public are, as above stated, incorrect and misleading. On the first point your account is so hopelessly wide of the mark that he despairs of even attempting to rectify it by this extremely tardy correspondence and consequently suggests that you cancel completely the pages dealing with his father in these chapters. The second point is a very complicated legal problem which has already caused Mr. Joyce heavy expenditure in the matter of legal opinions involving as it did the marriage laws of three different countries. It would be necessary to devote an entire chapter of your book to its elucidation and I doubt whether his solicitors in London would advise him to place the dossier concerning it at your disposal. For the purpose of your book the only way now is to obliterate this passage and any subsequent reference of the same tenor confining yourself to a formal statement.

It is, he finds, incomprehensible that it should be necessary to write this letter now in response to a summary communication of yours after you had been engaged on the book for ten years, had resided in Paris for several years and after a silence on your part of some 8 or 9 months, on the eve of what you announce as a publication of a limited edition de luxe the sense of which completely mystifies him. In this connection I am enclosing a very emphatic denial by G.B.S. of another piece of gossip which is retailed in your pages. There is so much conscientious work and artistic understanding in the rest of your work that it would be lamentable from every point of view that it should be disfigured by passages such as these.

Mr. Joyce who has always been willing to give you all assistance in his power has made a number of rectifications on many pages of the typescript in his possession and these will be returned to you promptly on receipt of the rest. Incidentally may I ask you to number your pages so as to facilitate this work. Mr. Joyce would also do what he can to help you out with your publishers in the matter of additional photographs, but in his opinion the idea of printing on the cover the arms of Dublin or those of the Joyce family had better be abandoned at once. As to the colour of the binding he is more or less indifferent.

With kind regards to Mrs. Gorman and yourself

Sincerely yours
Paul Léon

In general, when Gorman's biography duly reached him in proofs during the summer, it proved to be what he expected, but Joyce could not resist the opportunity to ventriloquize a little. Some of the changes he put in Gorman's mouth were corrections or additions of detail: when Gorman said Nora was blond, Joyce wrote in, 'rousse auburn.' When Gorman said he received about ten pence a lesson in Trieste, Joyce punctiliously noted that his salary actually rose to two shillings, two shillings and six pence, and in the case of some classes to four shillings and five pence. He added bits about his father's friends, about old singers, about his own repertory of songs. But as Léon's letter declares, he had no intention of allowing Gorman to contradict his claim in 1931 that he was being married to Nora for the second time. In the same temper, a passage about the impossibility of living in sin in Dublin in 1904 had to be removed. As Léon's letter also makes clear, Gorman's picture of John Stanislaus Joyce was not sufficiently filial to suit his son. So when Gorman wrote, in explanation of the Joyce family's frequent removals in Dublin, 'Either John Stanislaus was restless or he neglected to find out why rent bills were sent,' Joyce altered the sentence to read innocuously, 'Either John Stanislaus was restless or his growing family required larger quarters.' He also wrote in several sentences to affirm that he had listened to John Joyce's advice. One was: 'Mr. Joyce's father (this should be inserted somewhere) was coming to the conclusion that his son's literary intransigence was up against an insurmountable barrier in reactionary Dublin and in fact later advised him to seek a freer atmosphere in which to live and work according to his own ideas.' When Gorman wrote a rhetorical question, 'Of whom was he the spiritual son and where would he find the Mystical Father?' Joyce inserted with evident impatience, 'His spiritual father is Europe, to which his natural father constantly urged him to go.' And, in the discussion of his reasons for leaving Trieste, he wrote into Gorman's text, 'His father had never ceased to tell him that he should leave Trieste.'

Joyce also used Gorman's book to pay off old scores. There were veiled reproaches of some friends for failing him. More openly, Joyce reminded Stanislaus in Gorman's text of the coolness in their relations since 1920, castigated Francini Bruni for his lecture *Joyce Intimo Spogliato in Piazza*, and pointed out that Michael Lennon, the author of the peculiar attack on Joyce in the *Catholic World*, had accepted favors from him and his family.* He instructed Gorman to leave out

---

* Joyce dictated on this topic of Lennon's article: 'You could collect much more information from Mr. Ernst if he feels inclined to sanction its publication by you,

one of his limericks against Consul-General Bennett in Zurich, however, on the grounds that enough had already been said on this
subject. The effect of these changes was to curb a sporadic cheeriness
in Gorman's book, and to render more solemn and sardonic its picture
of the persecuted artist. Joyce's life after 1922 Gorman scarcely dared
touch upon; George and Helen did not like his references to them,
which had to be removed; he could say nothing of Lucia's illness, and
was in general as distracted by Joyce's curbs and prods as Joyce was
by Gorman's delays and revelations.

After reading some of Gorman's proofs, Joyce, with Nora, left Paris
about July 21 to see Stephen, who was at summer camp at Étretat,
then returned to Paris in George's automobile on July 26 so as to be
with Lucia on her birthday. In August they went on to Montreux,
where Helen, after several nervous collapses, was again convalescing.
George, much upset by his wife's illness, remained in Paris. From
Montreux Joyce and Nora proceeded to Lausanne, spending a few
days there in the second week of August, chiefly to enable Joyce to
talk with Mercanton about his forthcoming article on *Finnegans
Wake.**° They went on then to Bern and Zurich, but when, during
the latter part of August, the threat of war became again unmistakable, they returned to Paris.

Joyce's main concern was for Lucia. Having ascertained again from
Dr. Delmas that the *maison de santé* was to be moved to the Hotel
Edelweiss in La Baule, he and Nora went on Monday, August 28, to
Brittany to await Lucia's arrival there. Delmas had been there the
day before arranging with governmental authorities to requisition
the hotel. During the next few days Joyce walked repeatedly to consult with Mme Delmas, whose villa was two miles outside the town.
He was assured that all was in readiness. But on September 2, seeing
signs of activity in the closed hotel, he asked the caretaker when
Delmas's party was expected, only to be told that no such arrangements had been made. He wrote hastily to Paul Léon begging him

---

about the extent of campaign which was organised by the Irish and Catholic elements in America against the proposed repeal of the ban. There can be little doubt
that the defamatory article already alluded to in my letter by such a widely circulated review as the Catholic World written by Mr. Michael Lennon of Dublin
(at present a Dublin police magistrate) alleging that the author of Ulysses had
amassed 'ample means' by breaking his parole to the Austrian government which
had released him and his family and entering the British government propaganda
service in Italy at a time when the British government was carrying on a war of its
own against the nationalist forces in Ireland which culminated in the Easter Week
rebellion had no small effect in forming the virulence of this campaign.'
° This did not appear.

to find out whether the hotel was in fact reserved. 'You have troubles enough of your own,' he said apologetically, 'but if you can find this out by telephone so much the better. Nothing else is of much importance for the moment. I suppose your idea of staying in Paris is to show your zeal and readiness. Perhaps you are not there now.' [13] The next day, having checked again at the hotel, he wired his son George in Paris: '*Absolument aucune provision faite ici pour recevoir maison de sante stop Delmas pense pouvoir arranger eventuellement d'ici huit a quinze jours stop en attendant Lucia abandonnee seule Ivry malgre tous mes preparatifs stop essaye te mettre en rapport avec personnel maison nous sommes Hotel Saint Cristophe ici telephone 21-30 courage bonne chance Babbo.*' * [14]

Delmas explained that his contract for the hotel had been broken, but that he would soon find another place. Without waiting Joyce telephoned a doctor who had a sanitorium between La Baule and Le Croisic to ask if he would take Lucia; the doctor agreed, subject to Delmas's consent, but Delmas pointed out that the other sanitorium had no facilities to handle patients of Lucia's violent type. On September 3 Joyce proposed to bring Lucia down himself by automobile with the aid of two attendants, but Delmas said that no automobiles could be had and that, since war had been declared that day, the roads would be blocked by military and other traffic. Joyce went home to write George and Helen the despairing words, 'Lucia is therefore left alone in a Paris about to be bombed until Delmas arranges something.' [15] He was relieved to hear that they and Stephen at least were safe in their villa outside Paris, but wrote importunately again on September 5: 'There are two points about Lucia. She must not be left alone in terror, believing she is abandoned by everybody in case of a bombardment in Paris. Somebody must either speak to her on the phone or visit her and if she is in danger she should be removed.' [16]

During these shattering days, when La Baule was filling up, as during the first World War, with refugees, Joyce renewed his friendship with Dr. Daniel O'Brien, who was stopping there for a time too. O'Brien, having been trained in psychiatry, gave Joyce what help he could with Lucia, but mostly he companioned him in his misery. One night they went together to a large restaurant with dancing at La Baule. It was close to where the French and British soldiers were encamped, and two or three hundred of them having crowded into

---

* 'Absolutely no provision made here for receiving *maison de santé*. Delmas thinks he can arrange matters within one to two weeks. Meanwhile Lucia is abandoned alone at Ivry in spite of all my arrangements. Try to contact the staff there. We are at Hotel Saint Christophe here telephone number 21-30. Courage. Good luck. Babbo.'

the place, they began to sing the 'Marseillaise.' Joyce joined in the singing, and gradually his voice caught the soldiers' attention. They turned and stared at him, and then a group hoisted him onto a table so he might sing it all over again. As O'Brien recalled later, 'You never saw such an exhibition of one man dominating and thrilling a whole audience. He stood there and sang the "Marseillaise" and they sang it again afterwards with him and if a whole German regiment had attacked at that moment, they would never have got through. That was the feeling. Oh, Joyce and his voice dominated them all!' [17]

Lucia arrived at last in the middle of September, and with the other patients was settled at Pornichet, adjoining La Baule to the south. Joyce and Nora stayed on to try to assuage the terror of bombardment which Lucia felt acutely. They were still there on October 8, their 'wedding' anniversary; O'Brien arranged a surprise party at a restaurant on top of a hill. It was a stormy night, and on the way Joyce became nervous and almost got out of the taxi. But he was coaxed into riding along, and when he arrived at the restaurant to discover a party was in the offing, he laughed like a child and joked and cavorted all evening.[18]

In Paris, Helen Joyce was heading towards another breakdown. George, unable to cope with her increasingly erratic behavior, was now living apart from her. Helen's close friends, who included the Léons, were convinced that the fault lay with George's want of affection, and kept trying to mend the marriage. On October 11 Léon wrote Joyce that he had just had a visit from George, whose attitude was 'incomprehensible.' George wished to have Helen sent to New York and asked Léon to write her brother, Robert Kastor, to make the necessary arrangements. Lucie Léon opposed her husband's writing such a letter, but Paul Léon said he would do so if Joyce agreed, at the same time insisting that Helen was not sick, only hysterical. Joyce had exhausted his reserves of sympathy for mental illness. He telephoned from La Baule to say that Helen and George should be kept apart and that he was himself writing to Kastor. His own letters to Helen, according to a woman doctor who knew both,[19] were not calculated to calm her. Under the stress of the new crisis Joyce and Nora returned on October 15, 1939, to Paris.

Paris was no longer bearable. The alerts made it difficult for Joyce to move about at night with his bad sight. Friends were gone or going. Eugene Jolas was in New York temporarily, Maria was in Paris preparing to transfer her École Bilingue to the village of Saint-Gérand-le-Puy near Vichy. Nora decided that the flat in the rue des Vignes would no longer do; in the emergency housekeeping seemed an additional

burden. So the Joyces established themselves in the Hôtel Lutétia.
Joyce went with Samuel Beckett to get some books from the flat and,
extremely nervous, jumped to the piano and sang at the top of his
voice for half an hour. 'What is the use of this war?' he demanded
of Beckett, who thought it had a use and a reason; Joyce was convinced it had none.[20] What was worse, it was distracting the world
from reading *Finnegans Wake,* in which the unimportance of wars in
the total cycle of human activity was made perfectly clear.

The stay in Paris was rendered more lugubrious by the strain in
Joyce's friendship with Paul Léon; Léon was as stubborn in Helen's
defense as Joyce was in his son's. When he had to choose, Joyce was
a father and not a father-in-law. A rift with Léon developed, which
culminated in Joyce's asking Léon's brother-in-law, Ponisovsky, to
request that Léon return him his publishing contracts. Léon telephoned on November 19 to find out if Joyce meant this, and when
Joyce said he did, Léon wrote him a cold letter saying he would leave
the contracts with Ponisovsky and asking Joyce to acknowledge their
receipt. A friendship of ten years was apparently broken.

Helen's condition grew worse, and she had to be hospitalized at
Suresnes. Stephen was taken by his grandparents to the Hôtel Lutétia.
In November Joyce telephoned Maria Jolas to say he was sending
Stephen down to her at Saint-Gérand-le-Puy. Mrs. Jolas suggested
that Joyce, George, and Nora come later to spend Christmas with her.
Joyce hesitated, then accepted. He was drinking and spending heavily;
to Beckett, who saw him before he left, he said, with something like
satisfaction in his voice, 'We're going downhill fast.'[21] He kept traces
of the self-abandonment which had characterized his father.

On December 24 the Joyces arrived at the nearest railway station,
Saint-Germain-des-Fossés, and Mrs. Jolas brought them, in the only
taxi to be had in the area, to their rooms at the Hôtel de la Paix in
Saint-Gérand. Scarcely had Joyce arrived when he was seized by
stomach pains so violent as to send him to bed. Everyone assumed
that his trouble was 'nerves' again, as his doctor in Paris had long
ago suggested, and Joyce was glad to accept this diagnosis. Dr. O'Brien
at La Baule had suggested liver trouble, an idea which Joyce apparently kept in his mind but did not mention to anyone. Whatever the
cause of the pain had been in the past, it was now connected with
the duodenal ulcer which was to prove fatal. Joyce did not consult
a doctor again.

Christmas dinner began sadly enough; Joyce scarcely ate anything,
only drank white wine, bending before his glass as if overwhelmed,
Maria Jolas thought, by physical and mental anguish. His pain, his

daughter at Pornichet, his daughter-in-law at Suresnes, and the war were pressing him down. If spoken to directly, he gave the shortest possible answer and lapsed back into silence, staring blankly ahead. After dinner Mrs. Jolas played the piano and in solo or chorus everyone sang carols in English, French, and German. Suddenly Joyce rose to his feet. Mrs. Jolas left the piano at once and asked, 'Are you going to play for us?' Joyce joined her in singing 'Ye Banks and Braes,' then launched into Irish and English songs, encouraging the others to sing too. At the evening's end he had a sudden explosion of gaiety, and began to dance on the narrow stairs to the tune of an old waltz. He approached Maria Jolas and said, 'Come on, let's dance a little.' There was so little room, and his sight was so bad, that she hesitated. 'Come on then,' he said, putting his arm around her, 'you know very well that it's the last Christmas.' After the dance he had to be quieted down to permit the guests to leave. Next day, still pleased with the party, he wrote Eugene Jolas in New York an eight-page account of the festivities that Jolas had had to miss.[22]

George Joyce had no desire to remain at Saint-Gérand, and returned to Paris. Nora persuaded her husband to remain in spite of the dislike of village life which he shared with his son. He was still preoccupied with his book, with thoughts of its poor reception which made him gloomy, and with thoughts of its prophetic implications, which made him occasionally happy again. The invasion of Finland by the Russians in November 1939 seemed to bear out his interpretation of the Finn MacCumhal myth, for in the manful resistance of the Finns it seemed that 'the Finn again wakes.'[23] As he wrote Fritz Vanderpyl,

Et à ce propos il est bien singulier comment après la publication de mon livre dont le titre signifie à la fois la veillée mortuaire et le reveil du Finn, c-à-d, notre héros légendaire celto-nordique, la Finlande, jusqu'à alors terra incognita occupe tout-à-coup le centre de la scène d'abord par le fait que le prix Nobel de littérature a été donne à un écrivain finnois et après à la suite du conflit russo-finnois. J'ai reçu juste avant l'ouverture des hostilités un commentaire bizarre de Helsinki, à ce sujet.* [24]

He made the same observation to all his friends, in conversation or by letter, solacing himself with the conviction that it was a quasi-mystical coincidence. He was also encouraged momentarily by the appearance

---

* 'And in this connection it is certainly odd that after the publication of my book, the title of which means at once the wake and the awakening of Finn (that is, of our legendary Celto-Nordic hero), Finland, until now *terra incognita,* suddenly holds the center of the stage, first by the award of the Nobel Prize for Literature to a Finnish writer and next by the Russo-Finnish conflict. Just before the opening of hostilities I received a strange commentary about this from Helsinki.'

in *Prospettiva* of the Italian translation of *Anna Livia Plurabelle,* signed
by Ettore Settani but chiefly the work of Nino Frank and himself.
Yet it was clear that even the name of Joyce counted for little in
time of war, and he said bitterly to Maria Jolas, 'Why should I write
anything else? Nobody reads this book.' [25]

The days passed tediously enough in the village. Joyce rose late—
'What is there to get up for?'—and walked slowly down the village
street, feeling his way with the cane he always carried. His long dark
overcoat and large dark glasses made him a conspicuous figure, and
the villagers referred to him as 'that poor old man' and could hardly
be brought to believe in his international fame. Life in Saint-Gérand
was less peaceful for Joyce than for others because of the abundance
of dogs, which kept him at private war, his cane poised in defense
and his pockets filled with stones—'My ammunition,' as he said.[26]
When asked why he disliked them, he replied, 'Because they have
no souls.' Most of the time he was sepulchrally silent. One day he
and Nora came to tea at the tiny flat of Mrs. Muriel Elliott, another
refugee whose child was at Mrs. Jolas's school, and Nora said as they
sat down, 'There sits a man who has not spoken one word to me all
day.' 'What is there to talk about when you have been married thirty
years?' Joyce retorted. 'You can at least say "Good morning," ' said
Mrs. Elliott helpfully, at which he grunted. Another desperate afternoon Nora came to Mrs. Elliott and said, 'For goodness sake do come
and have dinner with us. I can't stand that man a minute longer. He
likes you and if you come over for dinner he will surely talk and I
can relax.' Mrs. Elliott came and engaged him in conversation about
opera, and Joyce at once livened up and sat talking until late.[27]

Sometimes he talked with Maria Jolas about education, and attacked
Catholic methods with such vehemence that she said to him, 'You
make me sad, since I'm bringing up my children as Catholics.' Joyce
replied, 'Ah, it's different in France. In Ireland Catholicism is black
magic.' [28] Once in a long while they allowed themselves to speak of
the war, and Joyce was already saying, before most people, that it
was for the moment *'un drôle de guerre.'* But mostly he said nothing;
he read Goethe's *Conversations with Eckermann.* On Sundays Stephen
Joyce came in from his school, sat on his grandfather's bed, and listened
to Joyce, clad in a dressing gown and smoking a Parisienne, tell stories
of Ulysses until it was time for lunch. He remembered each week
where he had stopped the week before.[29]

In April Mrs. Jolas invited the Joyces to stay with her in the château,
La Chapelle, which was serving as a school, while the school children
were away for the Easter holidays. It seemed to her that Joyce was

gathering himself again for another book, though he said nothing about it. The news from Paris was, however, no better: Helen's condition had not improved, and George was oddly uncommunicative. A few other visitors came to liven up the snowy spring. Beckett arrived, and Joyce spoke of going to Moulins with him for Easter services, but they did not get there. On April 14 George Pelorson stopped by on his way to join his regiment. There was a late dinner party, and afterwards Joyce and Pelorson remained talking after everyone else had gone to bed. Joyce was interested in the Gracchi, about whom Pelorson had written a long poem; then he shifted the conversation to Easter, praising the liturgy. He made jokes about the Dominicans, as had his masters at Belvedere. Finally Pelorson asked him, 'What are you going to do? Are you writing?' 'No,' said Joyce, 'I'm rereading and revising *Finnegans Wake*.' 'Why?' 'Well, I'm adding commas.' 'Have you plans for a new book?' Joyce said, 'Well, no,' then turned in his chair and added, 'Yes, I think I'll write something very simple and very short.' [30]

When classes at the school began again in mid-April, the Joyces decided to go to Vichy, where they stayed at the Hôtel Beaujolais.° Maria Jolas wrote her husband of the difficulties they were experiencing:

The Joyces are staying for 15 days in Vichy on account of the heating problem and they plan to return here around May 1, when they have taken a little flat. Their situation is rather desperate from many standpoints. First of all, the break with Léon, which has never been patched up, has deprived him of all help in his business matters. Giorgio's life is now shrouded in mystery, he gives no news of himself, lets weeks go by without writing, and, even when he was here, gave literally no inkling as to the life he is living in Paris. . . . This, as you can guess, is a source of preoccupation to both his parents. Then comes the financial problem which is really acute. . . . They cling to me considerably and I must say that there seems to be no one else about for the moment.

Joyce was tormented always by the thought of Lucia at Pornichet. He kept turning over in his mind possible ways of bringing his daughter closer to Saint-Gérand; having heard of an asylum at Moulins he went to see the director. The doctor was sympathetic and arrangements were being made when suddenly the tempo of the war changed. Germany invaded Denmark and Norway on April 9, then invaded Belgium, the Netherlands, and France in May. By May 28 Belgium had sur-

° While there Joyce paid a sad visit to Valery Larbaud, who since 1935 had been paralyzed and unable to speak. He insisted, out of sympathy and gratitude, that Herbert Gorman include a full-page photograph of Larbaud in his biography.

rendered, and on June 10 Italy entered the war. The next day Maria Jolas called Joyce, who had stayed at Vichy longer than he expected because he preferred the city to Saint-Gérand; she urged him to move back for safety's sake to a small flat near her. Joyce refused, and reminded her she had promised to send to the Gotham Book Mart for Conrad Aiken's book, *The Coming Forth by Day of Osiris Jones*. She had not done so. 'Well,' said Joyce, 'it wouldn't hurt to drop a postal card into the box.' The title of Aiken's book sounded so close in theme to *Finnegans Wake* that it seemed more urgent for him to read the book than for him to move. Two days later Mrs. Jolas called to tell him that the Gare de Lyon in Paris was closed. Joyce said that couldn't possibly be true, because Samuel Beckett had just come from Paris, and added inexorably, 'Have you heard anything about the book I asked you to get me from the Gotham Book Mart?' [31]

Beckett was penniless and could not cash a check on an Irish bank; Joyce wrote a letter for him to Larbaud, heading it, '*Samedi soir après le turbin* [grind]' from a French song then in vogue. Larbaud kindly cashed Beckett's check. The mounting crisis slowly intruded upon the Joyces. When Paris fell on June 14, the Hôtel Beaujolais was requisitioned by the government; and so, on the morning of Bloomsday, June 16, Joyce arrived at La Chapelle with Lucie Léon, her father, and her sister-in-law, who had come from Beaugency. George appeared at almost the same moment, having fled Paris barely in time.* His presence was a comfort, but also a cause of anxiety, because he was of military age, and therefore liable to conscription by the French or internment by the Germans. From his home in Saint-Gérand Joyce sent Maria Jolas at the château a note bearing the ominous date, '18 June, Waterloo, 1940,' which he asked her to destroy; she was to say to the Germans, who might arrive at any moment, that George was attached to her school as a teacher of Italian or singing or any other subject she regarded as plausible.

The same day Paul Léon arrived too, sitting exhausted and dusty in a cart drawn by a small donkey. In mock self-justification he said, 'The Lord Jesus Christ rode into Jerusalem on a donkey.' [32] Joyce could hardly be icy in these circumstances. Some hours later Maria Jolas came across the two men walking together, just as Léon was saying, '*Expliquons-nous entre soldats*,' to which Joyce replied, with the same irony, '*Et dans l'honneur*.' [33] They returned from the walk reconciled insofar as reconciliation was possible for Joyce.

---

* His wife had been taken back to the United States by her brother Robert Kastor on May 2.[34] Helen Joyce recovered her health in America and did not return to Europe. She died 9 January 1963.

The Germans occupied Saint-Gérand-le-Puy for six days before retiring to the line of demarcation a few miles farther north. For the first two days of this temporary occupation George stayed indoors, then announced he was going out. 'Better not,' said his father, 'no use looking for trouble.' [35] He went anyway and stared back moodily at the German soldiers who stared at him. But he was not molested, and his foresight in failing to register at the Mairie enabled the local authorities to be officially unaware of his presence.

His parents stayed briefly in the flat of a woman who was in a hospital; then, when she returned, mortally ill, they moved back to an uncomfortable room in the Hôtel du Commerce, which had served Mrs. Jolas for some time as a school. The Léons also had a room in this hotel, most of the pupils having left. It was Mrs. Jolas who kept her head, watching over children and friends alike, and nursing the sick woman from the hospital as well. One day, July 10, Joyce volunteered to watch in her place at the woman's bedside. The woman grew worse during his vigil, and he tried hard to help her. She died as he watched her.[36]

During July and August the search for news was almost as avid as the search for provisions. Everyone listened to the radio, hoping for a decisive Allied victory which would enable them to return to Paris life. Joyce indomitably reserved a few hours each day to correct misprints in *Finnegans Wake*, with the help now of Paul Léon. They met at 3 o'clock in the afternoon, taking pleasure in this gratuitous precision of their working hours.[37] Before dinner they separated, and Joyce, without informing his friends, entered the local café by a back door and drank two or three Pernods. Then he turned up at dinner with a haggard air, unable to eat or drink any more. Nora, who was taken in by his stratagem, would say, 'Look at the man; he can't stand a glass of wine.' [38] His physical condition was steadily deteriorating, and he began to feel quite unwell.

To stay at Saint-Gérand-le-Puy indefinitely seemed out of the question to people accustomed to the city. Lucie Léon was the first to leave; she still had her job on the *New York Herald-Tribune* of Paris, and wanted to see to her flat there. Joyce went with her to the bus stop, and unexpectedly kissed her goodbye. 'Mr. Joyce, do you think this is ever going to end?' she asked, and he replied, in distraction, 'Och, Mrs. Léon, I don't know.' [39] Léon's position was much more hazardous; Joyce urged him not to put himself into the Nazis' hands. But Léon decided to risk it for a while at least, and he left in September.°

° Léon persisted in remaining in Paris during the Nazi occupation; he rescued some of Joyce's books and papers from the flat on the rue des Vignes, and bought

In the meantime Maria Jolas, who had remained in France much longer than was prudent, received an urgent cable from her husband, and in early August went to Marseilles to put her passport and that of her two daughters in order for passage to the United States. Joyce asked her to try to find out from the Greek consul in Marseilles what had happened to Nicolas Santos and his wife, Greek friends from the Trieste days who were supposed to have settled in Marseilles. On her return he consulted with her about what to do. She urged him to come to the United States, and the American chargé-d'affaires at Vichy, Robert Murphy, thought it possible to arrange for the family, including Lucia, to go, provided they would take a plane. But America and airplanes were equally alien to Joyce's mind, and he mulled instead over the chance of reaching Switzerland as he had done during the first World War. The Giedions were urging him to come to Zurich. The difficulty was that George, because of his age, would probably be stopped at the border. Joyce was nonplused. Mrs. Jolas wrote to her husband, 'He [Joyce] has never seemed so helpless, so tragic, as he does to me now and I assure you I feel very sad about leaving them all. They're very stubborn and undecided with each other on every point and goodness knows what they eventually will do.' Her own reservations made, she left on August 28. Joyce entrusted to her his corrections of misprints in *Finnegans Wake*, which were later added to the book, and reminded her again to send him Aiken's *Osiris Jones*. At the station he insisted upon helping with the bags, and waved goodbye with his blind man's stick. He sent her a telegram to Banyuls saying he had '*soupé de Saint-Tempion-le-Machin*' (his fill of Saint-Gérand-le-Puy *) and wishing her well, and on September 7 wrote her a letter which suggested the reserves of energy and wit still in his discouragement:

Saint-Gérand-le-Puy

Dear Mrs. Jolas: Thanks for your letter of 4th just received though by your wire of 6th you are still in France. I hope you got my wire to Banyuls. It seemed useless to write to you as we never knew where

---

others back at an auction sale held illegally by the landlord. Then, wanting to preserve his friend's secrets as well as his properties, he deposited the papers with Count O'Kelly, the Irish Ambassador to occupied France, with instructions that they should be turned over to the National Library of Ireland, there to be kept sealed for fifty years. Léon lived furtively in Paris into 1941. One day Samuel Beckett saw him and said in alarm, 'You must leave at once.' 'I have to wait till tomorrow when my son takes his *bachot*,' [40] said Léon, as good a father as Joyce. The next day he was arrested by the Germans and interned near Paris. In 1942 he was killed as a Jew by the Nazis.[41]

* Joyce was sparing the feelings of the postmistress. 'Saint-Tempion-le-Machin' means 'St. What-you-may-call-'em Thingumajig.'

you might be. I hope this finds you all safe and sound in Lisbon and about to sail. Léon and his son have gone to Paris. I hear we have all to clear out by the 20th as the landlord wants to overhaul the place. No reply from Dublin. None from Cerf or Huebsch. We got our dole on the passports, partly that is, and I paid Mme Astafiew * for August. A remittance Kastor wrote he had cabled you for Giorgio has also not come. You ought to feel glad when the good ship moves off. The family is not keen on Helvetia on account of the air alarms etc. Nevertheless I wrote to the clinique near Vallorbe. Thanks for the kind offer in your letter. At the station I literally had no breath to say what I wanted as I was doubled up by my efforts with a trunk or case. You seemed to me to be downcast. Well, if you never did anything else you made scores of children happy for many years. When they turn out to be jacobins, countesses, saints and explorers they will always remember it —'in their soberer moments.' But the Lord knows you did a lot more. I wish you all a smooth sea and a following wind! And remember me to Jolas and any others who may remember me.

Mr Huber is still at work on his trunk in the lobby (it is exactly 148° in the shade today) and the day you left Mrs Huber asked me to lend her *Finnegans Wake* which I did. More anon. If you see Prince Makinsky the name of the book is *Life and Works of G. B. Vico*, on sale at 12 or 14 Troy Street, W.1 price 5/-. Osiris Jones has not yet come forth by day or by night and I am waiting for a copy of that biography to be sent me by Gorman or his publisher. The Irish Legation wired again to Dublin but had no reply. If you are pressed for quarters in Lisbon probably Makinsky will be able to find you something. My friend Byrne's daughter, Phyllis, at the C.G. may also be able to help. She has been there about a year.

Dialogue. 1980. Lilac Doorway U.S.A. Time: Spring. She: (laying aside a copy of How to Get Rid of Parasites) I have been thinking. What *was* the name of that family that was always in trouble over there in Europia?

He: (seizes jug) You're asking me.

She: The man had a wall eye, I think. Was it Wallenstein?

He: (replaces jug) Jucious!

She: Jucious! That was the name. I knew it had something to do with Scotland.

Fait rien. Bon voyage! Merci! Au revoir! Vous avez oublié le pourboire, Madame. Pour le porteur. Fait rien! ...

Cordially yours,
James Joyce

7 September 1940

* Secretary of the school.

In considering Zurich, Joyce's special concern was for Lucia, and he had first to determine whether the Swiss authorities would permit her to cross the border. He asked the Giedions to find out about Kilchberg, a *maison de santé* near Zurich which he had once visited, and then on August 4 wrote the Swiss Legation in Vichy for permits for his family, including Lucia. Crossing to Switzerland was not so easy in this war as it had been in the last, and Joyce had to marshal all kinds of heavy and light artillery in his support. Early in August he mobilized his old friend Paul Ruggiero, who could help with the financial details because of his position in a Zurich bank. Joyce had already written a general statement of his plight to his old friend Edmund Brauchbar, an exporter now in the United States but in control of branch offices in Zurich and Lyons, and Brauchbar instructed his son Rudolph and his son's business associate, Gustav Zumsteg, in Zurich, to give all possible support.[42] 'I thank you very much for having remembered me, whom so many seem to have forgotten,'[43] Joyce wrote Brauchbar.

Zumsteg suggested that a lawyer in Geneva would be able to secure entry permits for the Joyce family in a very short time, provided they went to Berń instead of Zurich. Joyce agreed, wrote the lawyer, and made plans to install Lucia at Corcelles, near Chavorny. Delmas was able to provide an escort for part of the journey, and the Swiss Maison de Santé Pré Carré arranged for the rest. On August 4 the German authorities granted without ado a *permis de sortie* for Lucia, and now the main difficulties were with the Vichy and Swiss authorities.

The plan for Bern came to nothing. Some place in Switzerland, however, became for certain the goal of the family, and Joyce thought they had a favorable omen when one evening he turned on the radio in a café and suddenly heard his friend Schoeck's *Lebendig Begraben* sung by Felix Lifford on a Swiss program. On September 13, 1940, Joyce returned to his original idea of going to Zurich, and applied to the Swiss consulate in Lyons for visas and for permission to stay in Zurich for the duration of the war. His application was sent to the office of the Eidgenössische Fremdenpolizei (Federal Aliens' Police), which sent it on to the Kantonal Fremdenpolizei of Zurich on September 23.[44] These authorities had an opportunity to display the same respect for genius that the British had shown in admitting Sigmund Freud, but they did not recognize Joyce's name and merely advised on September 30 the rejection of his application. One of Joyce's friends went to the office to ask the reason, and was told it was because Joyce was a Jew. '*C'est le bouquet, vraiment,*'[45] Joyce exclaimed on being informed of this.

In the meantime further documents had arrived, and the Federal Aliens' Police sent the application back to Zurich on October 18 for reconsideration. An imposing group of Swiss citizens now ranged themselves on Joyce's side: in Lausanne Jacques Mercanton deposed that Joyce was not a Jew, or, in Joyce's own words to Armand Petitjean and Louis Gillet, *'que je ne suis pas juif de Judée mais aryen d'Erin.'*[46] In Zurich Giedion, Vogt, Othmar Schoeck, Robert Faesi, Theodor Spörri, Dr. Emil Klöti, the mayor of the city, Professor Löffler (director of the University Clinic), and Ernst Howald, then rector of the University of Zurich, lent their names to his cause. Professor Heinrich Straumann of the University certified that the works of Joyce were without question the best published writings of the English-speaking world, and the Swiss Society of Authors also endorsed him. Before this assault the cantonal authorities ponderously relented, but demanded financial guarantees, at first for the unreasonable amount of 50,000 Swiss francs, reduced after persuasion to 20,000.

Joyce had hopes of financial aid from America, but this was not immediately forthcoming, and in the meantime Sigfried Giedion and Edmund Brauchbar (through his son Rudolph) generously deposited the amount in Ruggiero's bank.[47] But the insatiable Fremdenpolizei now added another condition, that he write out a declaration of his fortune and goods, with suitable evidence attached, and have it legalized. Joyce had no records with him, composed one declaration which was not accepted, then another which at last the authorities took. On November 28 the Cantonal Aliens' Police suggested to the Federal Aliens' Police that the application of the Joyce family be granted, and on November 29 the Swiss Embassy at Vichy was instructed to issue visas accordingly.

Meanwhile it had been necessary to secure permission from the French to leave unoccupied France. Joyce enlisted the help of Armand Petitjean, now an official in the Vichy government, and of Jean Giraudoux; in October Louis Gillet also came to lend his influence to Joyce's request. The villagers in Saint-Gérand-le-Puy were dazzled by the arrival of a member of the French Academy to see Joyce, and Joyce was pleased by this visit and by the article, *'À Propos de Finnegans Wake'* (published in the English review *Babel*), which Gillet brought him; it was soon to be published in the *Revue des Deux Mondes*. But everything was subordinated to departure; Joyce could think of little but his impending journey.

Thanks to Petitjean, Gillet, and others, Joyce obtained permission for the departure of himself, Nora, and Lucia; but he could not obtain similar permission for George. As the Swiss boggled at accepting him, the time limit for all their permissions began to run out. Twice gendarmes came to their lodgings to list them in a census of British residents in

France, and the second time they expressed polite surprise that 'we who had been so insistent on our desire to leave and had obtained ministerial permission to do so were still here.'[48] A new law forbade British and other foreigners to leave the village in which they were resident for any purpose without a special permit, so that even to go to Vichy might result in arrest. Joyce's exasperated feelings reached a sudden climax when news reached him and Nora that Mrs. Barnacle had died in Galway, and he wept like a child.[49]

George meanwhile disregarded regulations by repeatedly bicycling from Saint-Gérand to Vichy. Being unable to obtain a *permis de sortie*, he went at a friend's suggestion to the Irish Minister, who suggested he ask for an Irish passport and so depart from France easily as a neutral. He went home and told his father, who asked, 'What do you think of it?' 'Not much,' said George. 'Neither do I,' said his father, who had resisted the same temptation himself on the grounds that he should not accept in wartime something he did not desire in peacetime. 'What are you going to do?' he asked his son, and George replied, 'I am not going to do anything.' 'Good!' said Joyce, 'in that case we'll all stay here.'[50] But he pulled some more strings and learned that, subject to consent of the sous-préfet of Allier at Lapalisse, George might leave too. Accordingly George cycled to Lapalisse and in considerable trepidation presented to an official there four passports and three *permis de sortie*. The official counted them up carefully, looked at George, and winked; he took the passports alone to the sous-préfet, who stamped all four. 'Well, we're getting out,' George surprised his father by announcing on his return.[51] But there was a new obstacle. The passports of Joyce and his wife had expired, and the only official at Vichy who could possibly help was the American chargé-d'affaires. George hopped on the bicycle again and went to him. 'But I can't extend British passports,' said the American. 'If you can't, who else can?' George demanded, and to this logic the chargé-d'affaires capitulated. As a last fillip, the Swiss visas were good only until December 15, and these had to be extended too. That Lucia's *permis de sortie* had also expired was at this point of less consequence, because Joyce had decided he could arrange more easily from Switzerland for her transfer.

The best train was one that left Saint-Germain-des-Fossés at three o'clock in the morning. The Joyces made arrangements to take it on December 14, but to do so needed an automobile to carry them and their baggage from Saint-Gérand-le-Puy to the station. George was able to find a car and a chauffeur, but no gasoline. He borrowed the bicycle again and went to Vichy to ask the American Embassy, which had none. At last, after several hours of cajolery in Vichy, he succeeded in buying a single gallon from a bank clerk at a preposterous price, and carried it back on his bicycle.[52] The train was met on schedule, and brought them to Aix-les-Bains and, five hours late, to the border. Stephen kept talking excitedly in English, and would not be silenced by his family's fear of incrimination. At the border the Swiss demanded duty on Stephen's bicycle, but there was no money for the purpose and it had to be left behind. George promised the boy a new one.[53] They arrived in Geneva at ten o'clock in the evening, and spent the night at the Hotel Richmond.

The next day, December 15, they went on to Lausanne, where they unpacked their bags for the first time at the Hôtel de la Paix. Nora suddenly cried out, 'Jim, look at this mess. There's green ink over everything.' He had forgotten to fasten the top of the bottle properly. But now he lay on the bed in a dressing gown, oblivious to her complaints, puffing at a cigarette and gazing at the ceiling. He roused to go out with Stephen and buy the boy some marzipan and Swiss chocolate to make up for their dearth in France.[54] Then in the afternoon he went to the *maison de santé* near Chavornet to see about Lucia, and returned at dinner time to the station where by arrangement Jacques Mercanton met him. Joyce looked sick and discomposed. He had no plans for the future, he didn't want to discuss it even. He was a little cheered by his friend, and also by Edmond Jaloux, whom he saw for a few minutes. Then too, there had been a review of *Finnegans Wake* in *Osservatore Romano,* which shrewdly insisted that the book was spiritual and so countered the realistic spirit of the nineteenth century; this judgment, read to him by Mercanton, enchanted Joyce.[55]

On December 17 the Joyce family left for Zurich and arrived at the Hauptbahnhof at eight o'clock in the evening. Ruggiero and the Giedions were there to meet them. Joyce thanked the Giedions effusively, and told Ruggiero, who had managed most of the arrangements with the authorities, that what he had done for him was '*impayable.*' [56] They all dined together in the station restaurant, then went to the Hotel Pension Delphin. The Joyces installed themselves in two rooms there, intending later to seek a flat.

Joyce was back now in the city where he and Nora had come thirty-six years before, full of energy and hope, and where he had spent the years of the first World War, arrogant in the flush of his own genius. Now he knew too much for arrogance; he arrived broken and sick, prematurely aged, among the scenes of his past strength.

For some days he lived peaceably, struggling to find his bearings. He wrote a letter in his most elaborate German to the Mayor of Zurich to thank him for interceding on his behalf, and said, 'The connection

between me and your hospitable city extends over a period of nearly
forty years and in these painful times I feel highly honoured that I should
owe my presence here in large part to the personal guaranty of Zurich's
first citizen.'[57] He saw a few old friends, and cordially received a few
new ones, like Professor Heinrich Straumann, but seemed to prefer
after his hardships in France a contracted life.[58] He had promised
George to tell him when they got to Switzerland what symptoms of illness he had been experiencing, but now such matters appeared to have
left his mind. Most of his afternoons he spent with Stephen, walking in
the snow with the boy along the Zürichsee or to the confluence of the
Sihl and Limmat.[59] He walked in silence, seeming absorbed in thought,
but occasionally jotting down some new wartime expression he over-
heard in a tiny address book. He bought his grandson three books of
Greek mythology at a Zurich shop, and, with a characteristic mental
leap, followed closely the resistance of the modern Greeks to the Italian
armies. He did not live to see Greece overthrown by German arms.

Christmas approached, and he bought Stephen a small artificial
Christmas tree in a little pot with artificial snow on its branches.[60] He
was grateful to James Johnson Sweeney in New York for help during
his recent troubles, and sent him all his correspondence about going to
Switzerland in two bundles, the first labeled 'A packet for the Christmas fire,' the second 'For your New Year's blaze.'[61] The Joyce family
spent Christmas day with the Giedions at their house at 7 Doldertal.
The food and security pleased Joyce. 'Here you know where you stand,
life is settled,' he said. When they talked vaguely of moving some day
out of their old house into one of the new ones designed by Marcel
Breuer nearby, Joyce was much opposed. 'Look at these fine walls and
windows,' he said, admiring the walls' thickness and windows' small-
ness; in comparison with this solidity the Breuer houses seemed to
him sterile and commonplace. But he also mocked Swiss cleanliness and
order: 'You don't know how wonderful dirt is.' The pleasant dinner
ended late; after it Joyce and his son sang songs in Irish and Latin, and
played a record of McCormack singing 'O moon of my delight.' Giedion
encouraged his guests to stay for the night, but Joyce refused because
the house, for all its thick walls, stood on a 'mountain,' and therefore
was in especial peril from electrical storms. 'Besides,' he said softly, 'the
Pope does not leave the Vatican . . .'[62]

On January 7, 1941, having learned that Stanislaus had been compelled by the Italians to move from Trieste to Florence the month
before, he sent his brother a post card, listing a group of people who
might be useful in case of need.[63] It was his last post card. That evening
he had dinner, as often, at the Kronenhalle, where the Zumstegs had

often been kind to him, and afterwards he remarked casually to Frau Zumsteg over a bottle of Mont Benet, 'Perhaps I won't be here much longer.' [64] At the moment the remark was inexplicable. Two days later, on Thursday, January 9, he came again to the restaurant after visiting an exhibition of nineteenth-century French painting; this time he was celebrating Paul Ruggiero's birthday.[65] At home afterwards, Joyce was suddenly overcome by stomach cramps. These grew worse, and at two o'clock in the morning George called a local doctor, who administered morphine to alleviate the pain for the night. The morphine did not work, however, and early the next morning Joyce had to be moved by ambulance to the Schwesterhaus vom Roten Kreuz. Stephen watched his grandfather being carried out on a stretcher, his eyes wide open and sunken, his body, in spite of the binding straps, 'writhing like a fish.' [66]

An X ray showed Joyce had a perforated duodenal ulcer. After a consultation of doctors it was decided to operate at once. At first Joyce, who wanted desperately to live and had his old fear of losing consciousness, refused; George had to be sent in to persuade him there was no other course. 'Is it cancer?' his father asked. 'No.' Joyce was skeptical: 'You've never lied to me. Tell me the truth now,' he begged. George said, 'It is not cancer.' His father said, 'All right, then,' but suddenly bethought himself, 'How are you going to pay for this?' 'Never mind,' said George, 'we'll manage somehow or other.' [67] Dr. H. Freysz, a specialist whom Frau Giedion-Welcker had suggested, operated the same morning at ten o'clock, and in the afternoon, when Joyce recovered consciousness, the surgery seemed to have been successful. 'I thought I wouldn't get through it,' he told Nora, then spoke again of the cost. For a time he seemed to regain strength, then on Sunday morning he weakened. Transfusions became necessary, and two Swiss soldiers from Neuchâtel contributed their blood. Nora said hopefully, 'Jim is tough,' but there was not much toughness left. Sunday afternoon he passed into coma, from which he emerged momentarily to ask that Nora's bed be placed close to his. The doctors, however, urged her and George to go home, and promised to telephone if there was the slightest change. At one o'clock in the morning Joyce awoke and asked the nurse to call his wife and son, then relapsed into coma. Nora and George were summoned at two o'clock to the hospital. But at 2:15 on January 13, before they arrived, Joyce died.

George and Nora returned to the Pension Delphin at 3:30, just as an air raid alert was sounded. They woke up Stephen and went with him to sit on the cellar steps. To the boy's questions about Nonno they answered only that he was fine. In the morning they sent him to stay with a relative of his mother, and made preparations for the funeral.

On Joyce's desk they found two books, a Greek Lexicon and Oliver Gogarty's *I Follow Saint Patrick*. Frau Giedion-Welcker arranged, with Nora's consent, for a death mask of Joyce by the sculptor Paul Speck. A Catholic priest approached Nora and George to offer a religious service, but Nora said, 'I couldn't do that to him.' [68]

The body was carried on January 15, a cold snowy day, to the Fluntern cemetery on the hill, and in the Friedhofkapelle there the burial speeches were given. Lord Derwent, British Minister to Bern, spoke in English; he was followed by the poet Max Geilinger, representing the Swiss Society of Authors, and then by Professor Heinrich Straumann. The tenor Max Meili sang Monteverdi's '*Addio terra, addio cielo.*' As the wooden coffin was lowered into the grave Nora Joyce stretched out her arm, half in farewell and half as if to hold it back. A tiny, deaf old man, who was also a boarder at the Pension Delphin, asked one of the undertaker's men, who was holding the rope which went under the coffin, 'Who is buried here?' The undertaker said, 'Herr Joyce.' The old man did not understand, and asked again, 'Who is it?' 'Herr Joyce,' the undertaker shouted, and at that moment the coffin came to rest at the bottom of the pit.[69] The grave was left simple and middle class. Because Joyce disliked flowers, there was a green plant. A green wreath at the funeral had a lyre woven in it as emblem of Ireland. Otherwise Ireland had no part in the funeral.

Lucia was notified of her father's death, but could not believe it, and said to Nino Frank when he visited her, 'What is he doing under the ground, that idiot? When will he decide to come out? He's watching us all the time.' [70] Nora Joyce lived on in Zurich, often complaining, 'Things are very dull now. There was always something doing when he was about.' Someone asked her if she was Molly Bloom, and she replied, 'I'm not—she was much fatter.' [71] The disregard of Joyce's last book distressed her at last: 'What's all this talk about *Ulysses*?' she asked Maria Jolas, '*Finnegans Wake* is the important book. When are you and Eugene going to write about *it*?' [72] Sometimes interviewers questioned her about great writers she had known, but she had never observed other writers very much, and now remembered even less. But loyalty covered these omissions. So, when asked about André Gide, she remarked, 'Sure, if you've been married to the greatest writer in the world, you don't remember all the little fellows.' To a sister she wrote, 'My poor Jim— he was such a great man.' The turbulence of her husband, and his keen pleasure in sounds, were her dominant recollections of him. She took visitors to the cemetery, which adjoins the zoological garden that he had compared to the one in the Phoenix Park, and said, 'My husband is buried there. He was awfully fond of the lions—I like to think of him lying there and listening to them roar.' [73]

Nora Joyce died of uremic poisoning on April 10, 1951. She had not renounced Catholicism as thoroughly as her husband, and in her last years she occasionally went to church and prayer. When she was dying at the convent hospital she allowed a priest to be brought, and received the last rites. At her funeral a priest delivered, after the Swiss custom, a funeral speech at the grave, and described her as *'eine grosse Sünderin'* (a great sinner).[74] Few epithets could have been less apt. She was buried in the same cemetery as Joyce but not next to him, for the space was already filled. The casualness of their lodgings in life was kept after death.

There are not many left of the family of Joyce. His brother Charles died in London five days after James on January 18; his brother Stanislaus died in Trieste on June 16 (Bloomsday), 1955.* Eva Joyce died on November 25, 1957, Mrs. Eileen Schaurek on January 27, 1963, and Margaret Joyce, who had been a nun in a Convent of Mercy in New Zealand, in March 1964. Two other sisters, Florence Joyce and Mrs. May Monaghan, live in Dublin. As for Joyce's immediate family, George Joyce was divorced, and married on May 24, 1954, Dr. Asta Jahnke-Osterwalder, with whom he lives in Munich. Lucia Joyce is at St. Andrew's Hospital, Northampton. Stephen Joyce married Solange Raytchine on April 15, 1955, and lives in Paris.

The surface of the life Joyce lived seemed always erratic and provisional. But its central meaning was directed as consciously as his work. The ingenuity with which he wrote his books was the same with which he forced the world to read them; the smiling affection he extended to Bloom and his other principal characters was the same that he gave to the members of his family; his disregard for bourgeois thrift and convention was the splendid extravagance which enabled him in literature to make an intractable wilderness into a new state. In whatever he did, his two profound interests—his family and his writings—kept their place. These passions never dwindled. The intensity of the first gave his work its sympathy and humanity; the intensity of the second raised his life to dignity and high dedication.

* He left his wife, Nelly, and their son, James, born February 14, 1943.

James Joyce in Paris in the early 1930's.
Gisèle Freund from Monkmeyer

XVII

NOTES

The following abbreviations and short titles are used in the Notes:

Critical Writings   *The Critical Writings of James Joyce,* ed. Ellsworth Mason and Richard Ellmann (New York, The Viking Press, and London, Faber & Faber, 1959)

Gorman   Herbert Gorman, *James Joyce* (New York, Farrar & Rinehart, 1939, now Rinehart & Co.)

Letters   *Letters of James Joyce,* ed. Stuart Gilbert (New York, The Viking Press, and London, Faber & Faber, 1957)

My Brother's Keeper   Stanislaus Joyce, *My Brother's Keeper,* ed. Richard Ellmann (New York, The Viking Press, and London, Faber & Faber, 1958)

S. Joyce   Stanislaus Joyce

Except where confusion might result, Joyce's name is omitted before books and letters written by him. The editions of his works to which reference is made are listed in the Preface, p. xi. Page numbers are given first for the American edition and then following for the English.

The locations of the principal collections of Joyce material are as follows:

MANUSCRIPTS OF BOOKS:
    Stephen Hero, Houghton Library of Harvard University
    Ulysses, Rosenbach Foundation, Lockwood Memorial Library of the University of Buffalo, Joyce Collection at Cornell University
    Finnegans Wake, British Museum.

LETTERS: The letters from Joyce to his wife and to his brother Stanislaus are in the Joyce Collection at Cornell University; the letters to Frank Budgen, Claud W. Sykes, and others, are in the Slocum Collection in the Yale University Library; other letters from Joyce are in the Houghton Library of Harvard University, the T. E. Hanley Collection in the University of Texas Library, the Berg Collection of the New York Public Library, the Croessmann Collection at the Southern Illinois University Library, the British Museum, the National Library of Ireland, and private collections such as those of John H. Thompson, Professor Heinrich Straumann, and Professor Norman Pearson. The letters to Harriet Shaw Weaver are in the British Museum, those to Valery Larbaud in the Bibliothèque Municipale at Vichy.

    The letters to Joyce are, for the period of his life up to 1920, chiefly in the Joyce Collection of the Cornell University Library and in the Slocum Collection at the Yale University Library; for the later period of his life, the letters to him are mostly at the Lockwood Memorial Library of the University of Buffalo and, under seal, at the National Library of Ireland.

    The papers of Herbert Gorman are in the Croessmann Collection in the Southern Illinois University Library; the Grant Richards papers are chiefly in the Houghton Library of Harvard University and the University of Illinois Library. Other libraries which have material include the University of Kansas Library, the Princeton University Library, the Stanford University Library, and the Northwestern University Library.

Other information about Joyce's published and unpublished work will be found in John J. Slocum and Herbert Cahoon, *A Bibliography of James Joyce (1882–1941)* (New Haven, 1953).

CHAPTER I

1. J. M. Cohen, 'Introduction,' in François Rabelais, *Gargantua and Pantagruel* (London, Penguin Edition, 1955), pp. 17-19.
2. This was T. S. Eliot, in conversation. See p. 542.
3. Interview with Mrs. Maria Jolas, 1954.
4. Interview with Signora Livia Svevo, 1953.
5. Lucia Joyce medical papers.
6. Sylvia Beach, *Ulysses in Paris* (New York, Harcourt, Brace, 1956), p. 16.
7. Eugene Jolas, 'Homage to the Mythmaker,' *transition* 27 (1938), p. 174.
8. In 'James Clarence Mangan,' *Critical Writings*, p. 76.
9. *Finnegans Wake*, p. 55.

CHAPTER II

1. *Stephen Hero*, p. 110 (115). This book, like *A Portrait of the Artist as a Young Man*, is both autobiographical and fictional. While some details of Joyce's life are stylized or otherwise changed, many are kept intact. For confirmation of this detail about his father's attitude toward his mother's family, compare Stanislaus Joyce, *My Brother's Keeper*, p. 35 (55).
2. *Ulysses*, p. 557 (540).
3. *A Portrait*, p. 466 (230).
4. *Ulysses*, p. 32 (29).
5. Stanislaus Joyce thought the paintings were by Roe, but, according to Arthur Power, James Joyce used to say they were by John Comerford. Interview with Power, 1953.
6. 'James Clarence Mangan,' *Critical Writings*, p. 83.
7. *A Portrait*, p. 307 (69).
8. Interview with Mrs. Eileen Joyce Schaurek, 1953.
9. *A Portrait*, pp. 305-6 (67).
10. Some of this information came to me from Eoin O'Mahony, K.M., whose knowledge in such matters is prodigious, and some from another person who wished not to be identified.
11. *My Brother's Keeper*, p. 21 (43).
12. The marriage settlement specified that John O'Connell had given £1000 as a portion with his daughter. James Augustine Joyce was also assigned 'a moiety of a plot of ground at Skahard formerly in the South Liberties of Cork (demised by lease of 1 April 1817) and one field part of Skahard, parish St. Finn Barry and a plot of ground used as a quarry, part of the lands of Ballintemple in sd. parish, and of the Island called Goat Island, part of the lands of Ronans Court to hold to sd. Jas. A. Joyce for the estates under sd. leases. Sd. Jas. Joyce assigned to the trustees, premises at White St., at the rere of the South Terrace, on the west side of Anglesea St. & in Stable Lane & on Anglesea Road, all in St. Nicholas parish.'
13. Gorman notes. See also Herbert Gorman, *James Joyce*, p. 41. Gorman's book was based in many parts on information given him by Joyce, and was corrected by Joyce in proof. Its testimony cannot therefore be lightly dismissed. For an account of Joyce's changes in the book, see above, pp. 735-8.

14. *My Brother's Keeper*, p. 23 (45).

15. This is the occupation listed on his death certificate.

16. Gorman, p. 9.

17. These records were kindly sent to me by the Reverend D. F. Duggan, President of St. Colman's College.

18. That the family had financial difficulties at this time is suggested by a mortgage of March 30, 1861, taken by James A. Joyce on some of the property he had received by his marriage settlement; he had to make over an insurance policy at the same time.

19. 'Interview with Mr. John Stanislaus Joyce,' *A Joyce Yearbook*, ed. Maria Jolas (Paris, 1949), p. 169. The authenticity of this interview, which is unsigned, has been questioned; a Dublin writer is said to claim he invented it. It is, however, one of several transcripts of his father's conversation which James Joyce had friends make during the 1920's; he supplied the questions which they put to John Joyce.

20. *My Brother's Keeper*, p. 23 (45).

21. 'He knew I wanted to go to the theatre to hear *Carmen*. He told my mother to give me a shilling. I kissed him and went. When I came home he was dead.' *Exiles*, p. 538.

22. 'Interview with Mr. John Stanislaus Joyce,' *A Joyce Yearbook*, p. 169.

23. *My Brother's Keeper*, p. 24 (45).

24. 'Queen's College Dramatic Society,' *Constitution or Cork Advertiser*, March 12, 1869; 'Theatre Royal,' ibid. April 17, 1869.

25. These bare outlines of John Joyce's academic career are in the records of University College, Cork, and were transcribed by J. Hurley, Secretary.

26. *My Brother's Keeper*, p. 27 (48).

27. Ibid. p. 26 (47).

28. 'Interview with Mr. John Stanislaus Joyce,' *A Joyce Yearbook*, pp. 164-5.

29. Ibid. pp. 159-60.

30. *Freeman's Journal*, April 7, 1880.

31. 'Interview with Mr. John Stanislaus Joyce,' *A Joyce Yearbook*, pp. 166-8.

32. Interview with Eva Joyce, 1953.

33. *My Brother's Keeper*, p. 31 (51).

34. This address is given on the marriage certificate.

35. The marriage certificate lists John Joyce's occupation simply as 'gentleman.' He did not yet have his position in the office of the Collector of Rates. The priest who performed the ceremony was Patrick Gorman; the witnesses were John George Lee and a relative of Mrs. Joyce, Margaretta Lyons.

36. *Ulysses*, p. 39 (35). Joyce's sisters confirm that their father used these phrases.

37. *My Brother's Keeper*, p. 31 (51).

38. *Ulysses*, p. 39 (35).

39. *My Brother's Keeper*, p. 37 (56-7).

40. S. Joyce, Diary.

41. Padraic Colum, *The Road Round Ireland* (New York, 1926), p. 327.

42. Interview with Mrs. May Joyce Monaghan, 1953.

43. S. Joyce, Diary.

44. Undated letter from John Stanislaus Joyce to James Joyce.

45. Interview with Stanislaus Joyce, 1953.

46. Interview with Judge Eugene Sheehy, 1953.

47. Interview with Eva Joyce, 1953.

48. These properties were at Cotter Street, White Street, Stable Lane, Joyce Court, Anglesea Street, and the rere of the South Terrace. A schedule of the property, in a mortgage of 1893, records that the annual rents then amounted to £315.14. After having executed a series of mortgages on this property between 1881 and 1893, John Joyce in 1894 sold the White Street premises for an unrecorded price, and at the same time sold Nos. 7-8 Anglesea Street for £475, and the premises at the rere of the South Terrace and at Stable Lane for £1400.

49. This address is given in James Joyce's birth certificate.
50. Margaret was apparently the first Joyce baby to be delivered by the midwife Mrs. Thornton of 19A Denzille Street, whom Bloom in *Ulysses* remembers having summoned to deliver his daughter Milly. Mrs. Thornton also delivered Charles, Eileen, and Florence Joyce.
51. *A Portrait*, p. 511 (357).
52. Unpublished notes of Gillet.
53. *Finnegans Wake*, p. 173.
54. Unpublished notes of Gillet.

CHAPTER III

1. From the baptismal record at the Church of St. Joseph, Terenure.
2. The General Register Office records Philip McCann's death on January 12, 1898, at the age of fifty-two, from tuberculosis.
3. Letter to Alfred Bergan, May 25, 1937.
4. The family was living at this address on December 17, 1884, when John Stanislaus Joyce, Jr. was born.
5. A mortgage dated April 21, 1887, gives John Joyce's address as Castlewood Avenue, while a mortgage of May 6, 1887, gives the new address of 1 Martello Terrace, Bray.
6. *My Brother's Keeper*, p. 35 (55).
7. Letter to Bergan, Dec. 20, 1934.
8. Interview with Eva Joyce by Niall Sheridan, March 20, 1949.
9. *My Brother's Keeper*, p. 13 (36).
10. Ibid. p. 12 (35).
11. The story is told in *A Portrait*, p. 278 (199), and *My Brother's Keeper*, pp. 8-9 (31-2).
12. Even Molly Bloom acknowledges this quality in 'Mrs Riordan' (that is, Mrs. Conway) in *Ulysses*, p. 723 (698), but supposes none the less that her husband 'was glad to get shut of her.'
13. *My Brother's Keeper*, p. 18 (40).
14. Ibid. p. 135 (144).
15. Interview with Mrs. Eileen Vance Harris by Professor Carlyle King, Dec. 28, 1953. See also *A Portrait*, p. 246 (177).
16. Interview with Mrs. Harris by Professor Carlyle King, 1953.
17. *My Brother's Keeper*, p. 3 (27).
18. Interview with Mrs. Harris by Professor King.
19. *My Brother's Keeper*, p. 14 (36).
20. Gorman, p. 27; *My Brother's Keeper*, p. 40 (60).
21. Interview with Mrs. Eileen Joyce Schaurek, 1953.
22. Kevin Sullivan, *Joyce among the Jesuits* (New York, 1958), p. 29.
23. *A Portrait*, p. 267 (191).
24. Interview with Philipp Jarnach by Dr. Alfred Dutli, 1954, and by Dr. Hans Joachim-Lang, 1957.
25. Interview with Frank Budgen, 1954.
26. Interview with August Suter, 1956. Frank Budgen, 'Further Recollections of James Joyce,' Partisan Review, XXIII (Fall, 1956), p. 533.
27. *A Portrait*, p. 247 (178); *Ulysses*, p. 40 (36).
28. Gorman, pp. 33-4.
29. Gorman papers.
30. This letter is in the Slocum Collection at Yale.
31. Letter to C. P. Curran, July 14, 1937, in *Letters*, p. 393.
32. Interview with Mrs. Eileen Schaurek, 1953.
33. Letter from Joyce to Budgen, May 2, 1934.

34. Gorman papers.
35. Interview with S. Joyce, 1953.
36. *My Brother's Keeper*, p. 41 (61).
37. *A Portrait*, p. 512 (358).
38. Letter to me from Lt.-Col. P. R. Butler, D.S.O.
39. Letter from Mrs. Eileen Vance Harris to Joyce, Feb. 7, 1935, and interview with her by Professor Carlyle King, Dec. 28, 1953.
40. Interview with Arthur Power, 1953.
41. See T. P. O'Connor, *Memoirs of an Old Parliamentarian* (London, 1929), vol. I, pp. 377-8.
42. Information from Eoin O'Mahony, K.M.
43. Conor Cruise O'Brien, *Parnell and His Party* (Oxford, 1957), p. 290.
44. Yeats, 'Parnell's Funeral.'
45. R. Barry O'Brien, *The Life of Charles Stewart Parnell* (London, 1910), gives the title, 'At Bay,' to one of his last chapters.
46. *A Portrait*, p. 275 (197).
47. Miscellaneous biographical notes by Niall Sheridan.
48. Joyce confirms in a biographical note sent to B. W. Huebsch by way of Harriet Weaver on Nov. 8, 1916, that it was written in 1891 and during his ninth year.
49. *My Brother's Keeper*, p. 46 (65).
50. Interview with Mrs. Eileen Vance Harris by Professor Carlyle King, Dec. 28, 1953.
51. Information from Jacob Schwartz.
52. Letter to me from John Garvin, Secretary of the Department of Local Government of Ireland. While some governmental offices were taken over by the Dublin Corporation in 1898, the Rates office was shifted earlier. Mrs. Eileen Joyce Schaurek also confirms that her father was forty-two when he was retired on pension.
53. *Finnegans Wake*, pp. 35-47.
54. *My Brother's Keeper*, pp. 49-50 (68).
55. John Garvin (see note 52 above), confirms the amount of this pension.
56. Most of these jobs were election duties handed to him by his friend Henry Campbell, town clerk, who is mentioned in *Ulysses*.
57. He was still at 1 Martello Terrace, Bray, when his daughter Eva was born on Oct. 26, 1891.
58. The birth certificate of Florence Joyce, born Nov. 8, 1892, gives the family's address as 23 Carysfort Avenue, Blackrock.
59. John Joyce continued to use the address of 23 Carysfort Avenue, Blackrock, in a mortgage dated Jan. 13, 1893, as well as in one dated Feb. 8, 1894. He was probably in lodgings during this period. The address 14 Fitzgibbon Street first appears on a conveyance of property dated Feb. 16, 1894.
60. Interview with S. Joyce, 1954, and *My Brother's Keeper*, p. 52 (70). The Christian Brothers' own records for these years are missing.
61. Information from the rector of Belvedere.
62. Late in 1921 Joyce checked on the connection of Belvedere House with the first Earl of Belvedere by writing to Father Charles Doyle, S.J. Doyle made clear that the countess had never lived in Belvedere House. Letter from Doyle to Joyce, Oct. 3, 1921, now at the University of Buffalo. For the story of the first Earl, see James Woods, *Annals of Westmeath* (Dublin, 1907).
63. Letter to me from Mervyn Wall, Sept. 16, 1953.
64. *My Brother's Keeper*, p. 58 (76).
65. *Critical Writings*, pp. 15-16.
66. *A Portrait*, p. 346 (245).
67. *My Brother's Keeper*, p. 60 (77).
68. Information from Mrs. Eileen O'Faolain and Nancy MacCarthy.
69. *A Portrait*, p. 339 (241).
70. Interview with Alessandro Francini Bruni, 1954.

71. *A Portrait*, p. 522 (365).
72. Interview with Reuben J. Dodd, Jr., 1956.
73. Idem.
74. *My Brother's Keeper*, p. 63 (80).
75. Ibid. p. 54 (72).
76. *A Portrait*, p. 327 (233). It is possible that Joyce has altered details, but the substance of this incident is confirmed by *My Brother's Keeper*, p. 55 (73-4).
77. Albrecht Connolly was the fop of Belvedere College. He wore a Norfolk jacket with flapless sidepockets and, as Joyce says, he carried a cane. But in *A Portrait* Joyce combines Albrecht's attire and his brother Vincent Connolly's face to compose the fictional personage Heron. Interviews with Connie Connolly, sister of Albrecht and Vincent, and with Judge Eugene Sheehy, 1953.
78. 'Araby' in *Dubliners*.
79. S. Joyce, Diary.
80. *My Brother's Keeper*, p. 60 (78).
81. Ibid. p. 56 (74).

CHAPTER IV

1. *A Portrait*, p. 430 (302).
2. 'Oscar Wilde: The Poet of "Salomé"' in *Critical Writings*, p. 205.
3. Interview with T. W. Pugh, 1953.
4. *Ulysses*, p. 343 (333).
5. Interview with Mrs. May Joyce Monaghan, 1953.
6. Interview with Stanislaus Joyce, 1954.
7. Interview with Mrs. Monaghan, 1953. Eveline Thornton's mother actually out-lived Eveline.
8. Interview with David H. Charles, 1953.
9. Interviews with S. Joyce, 1953, Mrs. Eileen Joyce Schaurek, 1953, and Brendan Gallaher, 1956.
10. Eugene Sheehy, *May It Please the Court* (Dublin, 1951), p. 24.
11. *Ulysses*, p. 295 (286).
12. Interview with Eva Joyce, 1953.
13. *My Brother's Keeper*, p. 61 (78).
14. Letter to me from Philip Sayers, 1953. Sayers recalled that James Joyce was employed for a time as an office boy. One morning his employer was busy and, handing him a half-crown, said, 'Go and get some lunch.' Joyce went round the corner to Hynes' Restaurant, ordered lunch, and bought a pack of cigarettes with the change. When he got back to the office he found his employer in a rage. 'Where in the name of God is my lunch?' 'I've just eaten it,' said Joyce. The old solicitor, if the story is true, made him pay sixpence a week until the debt was paid off.
15. Interview with Mr. McGinty, 1953.
16. Interview with Alfred Bergan by Niall Sheridan.
17. Idem.
18. It so appears in *Ulysses*, p. 87 (80).
19. Interview with Brendan Gallaher, 1956.
20. Gorman papers.
21. Gorman, p. 45.
22. Interview with Alfred Bergan by Niall Sheridan.

23. Numbers in parentheses indicate the possible maxima:

	1894		1895	
Latin	700	(1200)	636	(1200)
English	455	(1200)	540	(1200)
French	400	(700)	410	(700)
Italian	211	(500)	223	(500)
Arithmetic	430	(600)	250	(500)
Euclid	230	(600)	175	(600)
Algebra	130	(600)	175	(600)
Natural Philosophy	—		190	(500)
Chemistry	—		100	(500)
	2556		2699	

24. *My Brother's Keeper*, p. 66 (83), and p. 62 (79).
25. Information from the rector of Belvedere.
26. S. Joyce, Diary.
27. *My Brother's Keeper*, p. 69 (85).
28. S. Joyce, Diary.
29. Interview with Brendan Gallaher, 1956.
30. *My Brother's Keeper*, p. 70 (86).
31. *A Portrait*, p. 356 (252).
32. Ibid. p. 405 (285).
33. Interview with Mrs. Eileen Joyce Schaurek, 1953.
34. *My Brother's Keeper*, p. 91 (106).
35. Ibid. p. 90 (104).
36. Gorman, pp. 45-6.
37. Kevin Sullivan, *Joyce among the Jesuits*, p. 100.
38. Interviews with Judge Eugene Sheehy, 1953, and with Mrs. Mary Sheehy Kettle, 1953.
39. Connie Connolly, sister of Albrecht and Vincent Connolly, had heard of this paper from her brothers, but was unable to find any trace of it.
40. *My Brother's Keeper*, p. 58 (76).
41. Interview with Mrs. Mary Sheehy Kettle, 1953.
42. Idem.
43. Idem.
44. Idem.
45. Mary and Padraic Colum, *Our Friend James Joyce* (New York, 1958), pp. 12-13.
46. Interview with Judge Eugene Sheehy, 1953.
47. Interview with Mrs. Kettle, 1953.
48. Patricia Hutchins, *James Joyce's World* (London, 1957), p. 49.
49. *My Brother's Keeper*, p. 74 (90).
50. Sisley Huddleston, *Paris Salons, Cafés, Studios* (Philadelphia, 1928), p. 217.
51. See *Critical Writings*, p. 255, for a later view of Hardy.
52. *A Portrait*, p. 436 (306).
53. Yeats, *A Vision* (New York, 1938), p. 35.
54. *Stephen Hero*, p. 93 (98).
55. *My Brother's Keeper*, p. 87 (102).
56. Interview with Judge Eugene Sheehy, 1954.
57. Idem.
58. Idem.
59. S. Joyce, 'Open Letter to Dr. Oliver Gogarty,' *Interim*, IV (1954), Nos. 1 & 2, p. 51; Gorman, p. 47.

60. That the incident occurred is confirmed by an unpublished letter to Marthe Fleischmann of 1918, in the possession of Professor Heinrich Straumann.

61. Yeats, 'Under Ben Bulben.'

62. *A Portrait*, p. 432 (304).

63. Sheehy, *May It Please the Court*, p. 8.

64. Interview with Judge Eugene Sheehy, 1954.

65. Idem. Connie Connolly also confirmed that this act of insubordination had occurred, in an interview of 1953.

66. The numbers in parenthesis indicate the possible maxima:

	1897		1898	
Latin	642	(1200)	560	(1200)
English	457	(1200)	650	(1200)
French	528	(700)	345	(700)
Commercial French	33	(200)	102	(200)
Italian	342	(500)	205	(500)
Arithmetic	340	(500)		
Algebra & Arithmetic			145	(900)
Euclid	180	(600)	40	(600)
Algebra	230	(600)		
Plane Trigonometry			20	(700)
Natural Philosophy	175	(500)	10	(500)
	2927		2077	

67. Interview with Professor Felix Hackett, 1953.

CHAPTER V

1. *A Page of Irish History, 1883-1909*, compiled by the Fathers of the Society of Jesus (Dublin and Cork, 1930), pp. 29-44.

2. Michael Tierney, ed., *Struggle with Fortune* (Dublin, 1954), pp. 1-50.

3. *A Page of University History*, pp. 88-95.

4. *My Brother's Keeper*, p. 100 (113).

5. C. P. Curran, 'Memories of University College,' in Tierney, *Struggle with Fortune*, pp. 227-8.

6. Gerald Griffin, *The Wild Geese* (London, 1938), p. 24.

7. Eugene Sheehy in James Meenan, ed., *Centenary History of the Literary and Historical Society of University College Dublin 1855-1955* (Tralee, 1955), p. 86.

8. Sheehy, *May It Please the Court*, pp. 13-14.

9. A kind letter from Ghezzi, Nov. 15, [1902], congratulating Joyce on being graduated from University College, is in the Slocum Collection at Yale.

10. See 'The Day of the Rabblement,' in *Critical Writings*, p. 71. Compare *My Brother's Keeper*, p. 147 (154).

11. C. P. Curran in *Struggle with Fortune*, p. 226; and Ghezzi correspondence at Cornell.

12. Louis Gillet, Notes.

13. *A Portrait*, p. 520 (364).

14. Constantine P. Curran, 'When James Joyce Lived in Dublin,' *Vogue* (May 1, 1947), p. 199.

15. Interview with Mrs. Mary Sheehy Kettle, 1953.

16. Sheehy, *May It Please the Court*, p. 15.

17. Idem.

18. Frank Budgen, *Further Recollections of James Joyce* (London, privately printed, 1955), p. 10.

19. Judge Eugene Sheehy confirms this one weakness. Interview, 1953.
20. *My Brother's Keeper*, pp. 148-9 (155).
21. Sheehy, *May It Please the Court*, p. 26.
22. Interview with S. Joyce, 1954.
23. Interview with Samuel Beckett, 1954.
24. Stanislaus Joyce thought this name came from a nurse whom the Joyces employed at Bray. The name 'Mary Cranley' does appear as informant on the birth certificate of Eva Joyce, born at Bray Oct. 26, 1891. But J. F. Byrne, in a detailed account, says it came from Archbishop Cranly. Byrne, *Silent Years*, pp. 43-4.
25. *Stephen Hero*, p. 124 (129).
26. Alphabetical notebook at Cornell.
27. Interview with William Fallon, 1953.
28. Interview with Judge Eugene Sheehy, 1954.
29. S. Joyce, Diary.
30. Kevin Sullivan, *Joyce among the Jesuits*, p. 168.
31. Morris L. Ernst, *The Best Is Yet* (New York, 1945), p. 118.
32. *Critical Writings*, p. 37.
33. Interview with S. Joyce, 1954.
34. Seumas O'Sullivan, *The Rose and Bottle* (Dublin, 1946), pp. 119-120. O'Sullivan was sitting close to Joyce at the performance.
35. Henry James's description of Fleda Vetch's behavior in *The Spoils of Poynton*.
36. The letter, dated May 8, 1899, said in part:

'Sir—Mr William Butler Yeats, as the most prominent among the founders of the Irish Literary Theatre, has at length fulfilled to his own satisfaction the contract concluded with the Irish public some months ago. By the terms of that contract, Mr Yeats promised, if sufficiently supported, to "put on the stage plays dealing with Irish subjects or reflecting Irish ideas and sentiments." The drama in which Mr Yeats claims to have satisfied at least one of these alternatives, "The Countess Cathleen," has by this time acquired some notoriety. Two criticisms of the work, supported by extracts, have been generally circulated, that of Mr O'Donnell and that of the "Irish Daily Nation." In replying to these criticisms on Saturday Mr Yeats wisely confined himself to abstract platitudes, and sheltered himself behind an objection, which is in general valid, that a work cannot be fairly judged from mere quotations of words used by personages who figure in that work. . . .
Let us sum briefly the results of our examination. The subject is not Irish. It has been shown that the plot is founded on a German legend. The characters are ludicrous travesties of the Irish Catholic Celt. The purpose of Mr Yeats's drama is apparently to show the sublimity of self-sacrifice. The questionable nature of that self-sacrifice forced Mr Yeats to adopt still more questionable means to produce an occasion for it. He represents the Irish peasant as a crooning barbarian, crazed with morbid superstition, who, having added the Catholic faith to his store of superstition, sells that faith for gold or bread in the proving of famine.
Is Mr Yeats prepared to justify this view of our national character . . . ? Has Mr Yeats thoroughly considered the probable effect of presenting this slanderous caricature of the Irish peasant . . . ?
We have no personal quarrel with Mr Yeats, we know him only from his books. We recognise him as a fine literary artist. We recognise him, further, as one endowed with the rare gift of extending an infinitesimal quantity of the gold of thought in a seemingly infinite area of the tinsel of melodiously meaningless verse. . . . we feel it our duty, in the name and for the honour of Dublin Catholic students of the Royal University to protest against an art, even a dispassionate art, which offers as a type of our people a loathsome brood of apostate.' *Freeman's Journal*, May 10, 1899.

37. Gorman, p. 135.
38. *Critical Writings*, pp. 17-24.
39. *My Brother's Keeper*, p. 89 (104).
40. Joyce rewarded Fallon for this question by referring to him under his own name as a boy 'with a silly laugh' in *A Portrait*, p. 422 (297).
41. *My Brother's Keeper*, p. 122 (132).
42. Idem.
43. Interview with Alfred Bergan by Niall Sheridan.
44. Interview with Eva Joyce, March 20, 1949, by Niall Sheridan.
45. Interview with Judge Eugene Sheehy, 1953.
46. Minute book of the society, in the Library of University College, Dublin.
47. *Centenary History of the Literary and Historical Society*, p. 47.
48. S. Joyce, Diary.
49. *My Brother's Keeper*, p. 113 (124).
50. *Ulysses*, p. 417 (406).
51. It is printed in Clery's *Dublin Essays*.
52. *Stephen Hero*, pp. 86-8 (91-3).
53. *Stephen Hero*, pp. 88-98 (93-103), and *My Brother's Keeper*, p. 144 (151-2).
54. Courtney's letters are in the Joyce Collection at Cornell.
55. *Stephen Hero*, pp. 100-101 (105).
56. *Critical Writings*, pp. 45-6.
57. Ellsworth Mason, 'Joyce's Categories,' *Sewanee Review*, LXI (Summer, 1953), 427-32.
58. *Stephen Hero*, p. 103 (107).
59. Eugene Sheehy, in *Centenary History of the Literary and Historical Society*, p. 85.
60. Ibid. pp. 61, 327.
61. Letter from Ibsen to Archer, April 16, 1900, in the British Museum.
62. Letter from Archer to Joyce, now in the Slocum Collection at Yale.
63. Gorman, p. 69.
64. This letter is in the British Museum.

CHAPTER VI

1. Interview with S. Joyce, 1954.
2. S. Joyce, Diary.
3. 'A French Religious Novel,' in *Critical Writings*, p. 123.
4. Padraic Colum in *Our Friend James Joyce*, p. 47; see also note following.
5. Curran, 'When James Joyce Lived in Dublin,' *Vogue* (May 1, 1947), p. 199.
6. Gorman, p. 59.
7. Interview with S. Joyce, 1954.
8. Interview with Alfred Bergan by Niall Sheridan.
9. Interview with Alfred Bergan by Niall Sheridan.
10. *My Brother's Keeper*, pp. 186-7 (188-9).
11. Interview with Bergan by Niall Sheridan.
12. Archer's letters to Joyce are at Yale and at Cornell.
13. *My Brother's Keeper*, p. 186 (188).
14. Interview with Bergan by Niall Sheridan.
15. Gorman, p. 137, and *My Brother's Keeper*, 96 (110).
16. One letter from Lerouin, begging Joyce to write him a little in English, is in the Joyce Collection at Cornell.
17. Interview with S. Joyce, 1954.
18. *Stephen Hero*, p. 246 (249).
19. On the back of Joyce's letter to Archer of August 30, 1900, now at the British Museum, Archer copied out Joyce's extraordinary dedication.
20. Interview with S. Joyce, 1954.

21. Letter at the British Museum.

22. *My Brother's Keeper*, pp. 115-16 (126-7), and Archer's letter to Joyce, Sept. 15, 1900, in the Slocum Collection at Yale.

23. *Finnegans Wake*, p. 535.

24. In a notebook in the Joyce Collection at Cornell.

25. S. Joyce says that his brother destroyed much of his early work in that year.

26. S. Joyce's Diary was written in part on the back of discarded sheets of James Joyce's compositions.

27. Yeats, 'To Some I Have Talked with by the Fire.'

28. *Stephen Hero*, p. 178 (183-4); compare S. Joyce, *Recollections of James Joyce*, tr. by Ellsworth Mason (New York, 1950), p. 9.

29. *My Brother's Keeper*, pp. 85-6 (100).

30. Now in the Joyce Collection at Cornell.

31. All except one of these titles are mentioned in a letter from William Archer to Joyce, no date, quoted in *My Brother's Keeper*, p. 142 (150).

32. Idem.

33. *Stephen Hero*, pp. 211-13 (216-18).

34. A copy of this epiphany, in S. Joyce's hand, is at Cornell. See also James Joyce, *Epiphanies*, ed. O. A. Silverman (U. of Buffalo, 1956).

35. Joyce's English version of this letter is at Cornell.

36. Joyce's copy of this play is dated July 23, 1901, and is also inscribed 'Mullingar Westmeath.'

37. *A Portrait*, p. 442 (310).

38. *A Page of Irish History*, p. 586.

39. In *Centenary History of the Literary and Historical Society*, Professor Felix Hackett says Joyce and Skeffington were charged 10 guineas by Gerrard Brothers, and paid it. The price seems improbably high.

40. *Critical Writings*, pp. 68-72.

41. Gorman papers.

42. Interview with Professor Felix Hackett, 1953.

43. *My Brother's Keeper*, p. 146 (153).

44. Joyce, *Epiphanies*, ed. O. A. Silverman, p. 11.

45. *St. Stephen's* (Dec. 1901).

46. *St. Stephen's* (Feb. 1902).

47. The *Evening Telegraph* account of the trial (October 21, 1899), does not report these phrases, but shows that Bushe did speak on the law of evidence: 'I ask you as sensible and honorable gentlemen, men of common sense and knowledge of the affairs of the world, if your brother or mine stood in that dock and a jury convicted him on such evidence as that, what would be your judgment? Is it not the very sort of evidence which has been a weapon of wrong, which there have been so many occasions to deplore at all times?' The evidence that Samuel Childs had murdered his brother Thomas rested chiefly on the fact that only Samuel had a key to the house, and that there was no evidence for the murderer's having entered by force. It was Samuel Childs who discovered the body, but Bushe maintained that he could scarcely have premeditated so dreadful a crime, committed it, and then cold-bloodedly returned to play the innocent with the police. The jury agreed.

A good account of the Childs murder case is given in the *Evening Herald* (Dublin), Nov. 12, 1957, p. 6.

48. ' "The Irish Revival," ' *Freeman's Journal* (Oct. 25, 1901). I am grateful to Judge Michael Lennon for tracing this article. Joyce's phonograph recording of his version of Taylor's speech, made in 1924, was never circulated.

49. A copy of the pamphlet is in the Berg Collection of the New York Public Library. Though undated, it refers to 'the late John F. Taylor,' who died in 1902.

50. Interview with Judge Sheehy, 1954.

51. Eugene Sheehy, in *Centenary History of Literary and Historical Society*, p. 89.

52. Interview with Judge Sheehy, 1953.
53. Sheehy, *May It Please the Court*, p. 25.
54. Interview with Mrs. Mary Sheehy Kettle, 1953.
55. Sheehy, *May It Please the Court*, p. 24.
56. This agreement was printed in an undated catalogue of the Ulysses Bookshop in London, of which Jacob Schwartz was proprietor.
57. Interview with Mrs. Mary Sheehy Kettle, 1953.
58. Joseph Holloway's Diary for January 8, 1901, in the National Library of Ireland, gives this information.
59. Patricia Hutchins, *James Joyce's World*, p. 50.
60. Though unsigned, the article, which was published in the *Freeman's Journal* (Jan. 9, 1901), was apparently written by Hall.
61. Interview with Judge Sheehy, 1953.
62. *My Brother's Keeper*, p. 135 (143).
63. Joyce, *Epiphanies*, ed. Silverman, p. 17.
64. Interview with Mrs. May Joyce Monaghan, 1953.
65. Joyce's grades at the University varied a good deal from year to year and course to course:

| | 1898-1899 | | 1899-1900 | | 1900-1901 | | 1901-1902 | |
	Grade	Maximum	Grade	Maximum	Grade	Maximum	Grade	Maximum
Latin	725	1200	756	1200	353	1200	—	
French	416	800	—		489	900	465	800
English	490	800	358	800	313	900	344	800
Mathematics	220	1000	715	1200	—		—	
Natural Philosophy	183	500	373	800	—		—	
Italian	—		373	800	295	900	417	800
Logic	—		—		240	900	—	

(*From records of the National University of Ireland.*)

66. *Critical Writings*, pp. 73-83.
67. Professor Felix Hackett and Judge Eugene Sheehy are both of the opinion that the 'boy orator' was Walsh.
68. John Kennedy, brother of Hugh Kennedy, attacked the talk as 'too flowery,' according to Professor Hackett.
69. Felix E. Hackett in *Centenary History of the Literary and Historical Society*, p. 66.
70. *Freeman's Journal*, Feb. 3, 1902.

CHAPTER VII

1. Based on a typescript by George Russell, 'Some Characters of the Irish Literary Movement.'
2. Interview with Monk Gibbon, 1953.
3. S. Joyce, Diary.
4. *Ulysses*, p. 189 (180).
5. This letter is to be included in Alan Denson's edition of George Russell's letters.
6. This letter, also kindly sent me by Alan Denson, is dated 'March 1903.'
7. Undated letter, quoted in R. Ellmann, 'Joyce and Yeats,' *Kenyon Review*, XII (Autumn, 1950), pp. 622-3.
8. Russell, 'Some Characters of the Irish Literary Movement.'

9. Russell's letter to Joyce is in the Slocum Collection at Yale.
10. *Finnegans Wake*, p. 211.
11. Letter to his mother, March 20, 1903.
12. Interview with S. Joyce, 1954. Compare *My Brother's Keeper*, p. 195 (196).
13. Gorman papers.
14. Alan Denson has kindly given me this information.
15. Information from Padraic Colum.
16. Gorman, pp. 95, 138.
17. Quoted in R. Ellmann, *The Identity of Yeats* (New York and London, 1954), pp. 86-9.
18. The letter as given in *My Brother's Keeper*, pp. 208-9 (207-9), is perhaps a combination of two letters, each incomplete. These are now in the Slocum Collection at Yale.
19. Yeats's note to Joyce relaying this invitation, dated Nov. 3, 1902, is in the Slocum Collection at Yale.
20. J. F. Byrne recalls in *Silent Years*, p. 76, that he brought Joyce, Cosgrave, and another friend to the registrar of the Medical School in April 1902, and that Joyce and Cosgrave applied at once for admission. The Medical Registration Office officially entered Joyce on the Register of the Medical School on Oct. 2, 1902.
21. Patricia Hutchins, *James Joyce's World*, pp. 44-5.
22. Interview with Alfred Bergan by Niall Sheridan.
23. *Ulysses*, p. 43 (39).
24. The reply, dated Nov. 20, 1902, is in the Joyce Collection at Cornell.
25. Oliver St. John Gogarty, *Mourning Became Mrs. Spendlove* (New York, 1948), p. 50.
26. The letter read:

Mansion House
Dublin.

    I know the bearer Mr. Joyce since his childhood, and I am also well acquainted with his family. He is a young man of excellent character and whose career as a student has been distinguished by industry and talent.

    He goes abroad to have an opportunity of further pursuing his studies and I look forward with very great hopes to his having the same brilliant success that he has had at home.

T. C. Harrington
Lord Mayor.

29th Nov. 1902.

27. Archer's letter, dated Nov. 25, 1902, is given complete in *My Brother's Keeper*, pp. 192-3 (194).
28. Letter to S. Joyce, Feb. 8, 1903.
29. Letter of Dec. 22, 1902.
30. Interview with S. Joyce, 1954; compare *Ulysses*, p. 41 (37).
31. Frank Budgen, *James Joyce and the Making of 'Ulysses'* (London, 1937), p. 155.
32. *Ulysses*, p. 676 (653).
33. Interview with Claud W. Sykes, 1954.
34. Interview with Carola Giedion-Welcker, 1956.
35. S. Joyce, Diary.

CHAPTER VIII

1. *The Letters of W. B. Yeats*, ed. Allan Wade (London and New York, 1954), p. 386. The letter is dated Dec. 4, 1902.
2. *My Brother's Keeper*, p. 197 (198), and Gorman, p. 85.
3. *The Joyce Book*, ed. Herbert Hughes (London, 1932), p. 79.
4. *My Brother's Keeper*, p. 197 (198).

5. In 1926 Joyce and Rivière renewed acquaintance, as a letter from the latter, May 4, 1926 (now at Cornell), reveals.

6. Letter card from Joyce to his father, Dec. 3, 1902.

7. Gorman, pp. 88-9.

8. The letter is given in *My Brother's Keeper*, pp. 198-9 (199).

9. All these reviews have been republished in *Critical Writings*.

10. Richard M. Kain cleverly identified Joyce's unsigned review on the basis of this sentence.

11. Letter addressed to 'Dear Everybody,' Dec. 6, 1902.

12. Letter to 'Dear Everybody,' Dec. 6, 1902.

13. Letter to mother, Dec. 15, 1902.

14. Gorman, p. 90.

15. Letter to mother, Dec. 15, 1902.

16. Idem.

17. Quoted in *My Brother's Keeper*, p. 208 (207-8).

18. Letter to mother, Dec. 15, 1902.

19. Undated letter from Mrs. John Stanislaus Joyce, at Cornell.

20. Another letter from her, also at Cornell.

21. Letter card to his mother, Dec. 1902.

22. This letter card is in the Slocum Collection at Yale.

23. At Cornell.

24. *My Brother's Keeper*, pp. 211-12 (210-11). A letter from S. Joyce to John J. Slocum, Sept. 4, 1950, tells the incident in much the same words. Byrne, now living in New York, denies he gave the card to Cosgrave.

25. *My Brother's Keeper*, p. 212 (211).

26. *Letters*, p. 54, and Gorman, p. 137.

27. *Stephen Hero*, p. 145 (150).

28. Ibid. p. 209 (214).

29. *Ulysses*, p. 29 (46).

30. Ibid. p. 15 (12).

31. *My Brother's Keeper*, p. 213 (212).

32. Ibid. p. 205 (205).

33. John Eglinton, on the B.B.C. 'Portrait of James Joyce.'

34. Eglinton, 'The Beginnings of Joyce,' in *Irish Literary Portraits* (London, 1935), p. 132.

35. Letter to mother, March 20, 1903.

36. Letter card to mother, March 17, 1903.

37. Sheehy, *May It Please the Court*, pp. 25-6. S. Joyce says in *My Brother's Keeper*, p. 195 (196), that James did not make this reply, only thought of making it. In either event Joyce's conduct was insolent enough to cause Yeats to admonish him for it.

38. Joseph Hone remembered hearing this from Eglinton. Interview with Hone, 1953.

39. An undated letter from Yeats promising to bring him to Dunlop is in the Slocum Collection at Yale. Joyce's letters to his family, Jan. 21 and 25, 1903, also deal with this new review.

40. Letter to mother, Jan. 25, 1903.

41. Professor David Greene has kindly given me a copy of this letter of Synge's.

42. In my possession.

43. *Ulysses*, p. 26 (23).

44. Ibid. p. 184 (174).

45. Notes on esthetics, dated Feb. 13, 1903, now in the Slocum Collection at Yale. For complete text see *Critical Writings*, pp. 141-6.

46. Letter to S. Joyce, Feb. 8, 1903.

47. Letter to mother, March 20, 1903.

48. In Joyce Collection at Cornell.

49. Interview with Mrs. Eileen Joyce Schaurek, 1953.
50. Letter to father, Feb. 26, 1903.
51. Gorman, p. 100.
52. *My Brother's Keeper*, p. 200 (200).
53. Letter card to mother, March 17, 1903.
54. Gorman notes; Djuna Barnes, 'Vagaries Malicieux,' *Double Dealer*, III (May, 1922).
55. Interview with Arthur Power, 1953.
56. Jarnach's reply is at Cornell.
57. Letter to S. Joyce, March 9, 1903.
58. Gorman notes.
59. Letter to mother, March 20, 1903.
60. Gorman, pp. 101-2.
61. Synge's notes to Joyce are at Cornell.
62. *Devoy's Post Bag*, ed. William O'Brien and Desmond Ryan (Dublin, 1953), vol. II, p. 161.
63. In unpublished notes.
64. *Ulysses*, p. 44 (40).
65. Ibid. p. 45 (41).
66. Gorman, p. 138.
67. Samuel Beckett told Joyce of Esposito's remark. Interview with Beckett, 1953.
68. Joyce recounted this incident later to James Laughlin, who published Stuart Gilbert's translation of Dujardin's book. Interview with Laughlin, 1955.
69. Gorman, p. 326.
70. Letter to mother, Feb. 8, 1903.
71. Letter card to father, March 4, 1903.
72. Letter to mother, March 20, 1903.
73. Letter card to mother, March 17, 1903.
74. Gorman, p. 108; *Ulysses*, p. 43 (39).
75. Gorman, p. 108; *My Brother's Keeper*, p. 229 (226).
76. *Ulysses*, p. 43 (39); *My Brother's Keeper*, p. 230 (227).

Chapter IX

1. *A Portrait*, p. 514 (359).
2. Patricia Hutchins, *James Joyce's World*, p. 68.
3. Yeats, letter to Lady Gregory, late April 1903, *The Letters of W. B. Yeats*, p. 398.
4. S. Joyce, Diary.
5. Byrne, *Silent Years*, p. 84.
6. Ibid. pp. 86-7; S. Joyce, *Recollections of James Joyce*, p. 10; *A Portrait*, pp. 508-12; *Stephen Hero*, pp. 138-43 (143-8). See also *Exiles*, with introduction by Padraic Colum (New York, 1951), p. 118.
7. Gogarty so explained the nickname to Sean O'Faolain.
8. *My Brother's Keeper*, pp. 174-5 (178).
9. Ibid. pp. 245-6 (240-41), and S. Joyce, 'Open Letter to Dr. Oliver Gogarty,' *Interim*, IV (1954), pp. 49-56.
10. Idem.
11. *Ulysses*, p. 290 (280).
12. Epiphany quoted in *My Brother's Keeper*, p. 253 (247).
13. *Ulysses*, p. 417 (405); *My Brother's Keeper*, p. 249 (244).
14. *My Brother's Keeper*, p. 248 (243).
15. *Ulysses*, p. 208 (199).
16. S. Joyce, Diary, and *My Brother's Keeper*, p. 139 (147).
17. *My Brother's Keeper*, pp. 138 (146), 104 (117).
18. Ibid. pp. 177-8 (181).

19. Letter from Russell to Thomas Bird Mosher, Nov. 3, 1903, to be included in Alan Denson's edition of Russell's letters.
20. Mary and Padraic Colum, *Our Friend James Joyce,* pp. 39, 80.
21. John Eglinton, *Irish Literary Portraits,* p. 138.
22. Interview with Dr. Richard Best, 1953.
23. *My Brother's Keeper,* p. 233 (229), and *Ulysses,* p. 6 (10).
24. *My Brother's Keeper,* p. 233 (229).
25. Interview with Eva Joyce by Niall Sheridan, 1949.
26. Her death certificate records the cause of death as 'Cirrhosis of liver 4 months 5 days with persistent bilious vomiting.' Mrs. Josephine Murray is named as having been present at the time of death.
27. Interview with Mrs. May Joyce Monaghan, 1953; *My Brother's Keeper,* p. 233 (231).
28. *Ulysses,* p. 103 (97); his daughters confirm that he spoke in this way.
29. *My Brother's Keeper,* p. 236 (232).
30. Ibid. p. 237 (233).
31. Ibid. p. 239 (235).
32. *Ulysses,* p. 11 (7-8).
33. S. Joyce, Diary, quoted in Introduction, *My Brother's Keeper,* pp. xiii-xiv (18-19).
34. S. Joyce, Diary.
35. Oliver Gogarty, *Mourning Became Mrs. Spendlove,* p. 48.
36. 'Mr. Arnold Graves' New Work,' *Critical Writings,* p. 127.
37. 'A French Religious Novel,' ibid. p. 122.
38. Ibid. pp. 113-15.
39. 'A French Religious Novel,' ibid. p. 122.
40. Miscellaneous notes of Niall Sheridan.
41. Information from John Eglinton.
42. Skeffington's note, dated Sept. 29, 1903, is now at Cornell; in it he asks Joyce to take a few French classes for three or four days. Joyce's reaction is described in *My Brother's Keeper,* pp. 187-8 (190).
43. *My Brother's Keeper,* p. 188 (190).
44. Letter to Harriet Weaver, Feb. 25, 1920, in *Letters,* p. 137.
45. S. Joyce, Diary.
46. Idem.
47. Gorman, p. 114, says the title was registered, but the British Post Office and the Registrar of Companies at the British Board of Trade report they have no record of it. See also Padraic Colum, *The Road Round Ireland* (New York, 1926), pp. 317-18.
48. Joseph Holloway's Diary, in National Library of Ireland.
49. Kelly's letter and telegram are in the Joyce Collection at Cornell.
50. Interview with S. Joyce, 1954.
51. Gorman, p. 114.
52. Padraic Colum, *The Road Round Ireland,* pp. 318-19.
53. Yeats's phrase in a letter to Lady Gregory of August 1902, quoted in R. Ellmann, *The Identity of Yeats,* p. 92.
54. S. Joyce, Diary.
55. Interview with Kathleen Murray, 1953.

CHAPTER X

1. S. Joyce, Diary.
2. Gogarty, on B.B.C. broadcast, 'Portrait of James Joyce.'
3. S. Joyce, Diary.
4. *Ulysses,* p. 235 (225).

5. A copy of this essay is at Cornell.
6. Eglinton, *Irish Literary Portraits*, p. 136.
7. S. Joyce, Diary.
8. Louis Gillet, *Claybook for James Joyce*, translated with introduction by Georges Markow-Totevy (London and New York, 1958), p. 133.
9. Yeats's description of the writer's profession.
10. See Gilbert's note in *Letters*, p. 54.
11. Gorman papers.
12. Interview with S. Joyce, 1953; *My Brother's Keeper*, p. 150 (157).
13. The manuscript of this poem is in John H. Thompson's possession.
14. Gorman papers.
15. S. Joyce, Diary.
16. *Letters*, p. 55.
17. Oliver St. John Gogarty, *Intimations* (New York, 1950), pp. 58-9.
18. S. Joyce, Diary.
19. Judge Eugene Sheehy tells me he remembers seeing the three young men on the steps of the National Library that night, engaged in denouncing the judges.
20. The *Irish Daily Independent* reported on May 11, 1904, 'Mr. Joyce showed himself possessed of the finest quality voice of any of those competing, but lost considerably in marks owing to not attempting the piece at sight.'
21. Letter to me from E. P. Porter, 1953. Cecil Wright does not remember Joyce.
22. This poem is in the Berg Collection of the New York Public Library. See also Gogarty, *Intimations*, p. 61.
23. Gogarty's letters are at Cornell.
24. *Letters*, p. 54.
25. Interview with S. Joyce, 1953.
26. Joseph Holloway's Diary at the National Library of Ireland.
27. This letter is at Cornell.
28. Idem.
29. *Ulysses*, p. 611 (589).
30. A letter of Joyce to Karl Bleibtreu, written during the first World War, asked urgently whether Bleibtreu had evolved his theory of the authorship of Shakespeare's plays by June 1904.
31. S. Joyce, Diary.
32. James H. Cousins and his wife Margaret mention Joyce in their autobiography, *We Two Together* (Madras, 1950), pp. 61, 106, 216.
33. Diary of Mrs. Vera Esposito Dockrell, in her possession.
34. S. Joyce, Diary.
35. Letter to Nora Joyce, August 1909.
36. Interview with Mrs. Kathleen Barnacle Griffin, 1953.
37. Interview with Eva Joyce, 1953.
38. At Cornell.
39. Letter to me from Mrs. Mary Barnacle Blackmore, 1953.
40. She was fourteen when she went to work in the convent. Letter to me from Mother M. Magdalen of the Presentation Convent, 1955.
41. Mentioned in Joyce's letter to S. Joyce, Dec. 3, 1904.
42. Interview with Mrs. Maria Jolas, 1956.
43. *Exiles* (New York, 1951), p. 118.
44. *Exiles* (Viking Portable and Essential James Joyce), p. 548 (384).
45. Joseph Holloway's Diary in National Library of Ireland.
46. Correspondence with Mrs. Vera Esposito Dockrell, 1955.
47. W. G. Fay and Catherine Carswell in *The Fays of the Abbey Theatre* (London, 1935), p. 148, do not mention this episode, but say that Joyce 'was so very shy that it was a long time before he could be persuaded to come' to George Russell's house.

Joyce's limericks are in the Slocum Collection at Yale.

48. S. Joyce, Diary.
49. Letter to C. P. Curran, June 23, 1904, *Letters*, p. 55.
50. B.B.C. broadcast, 'Portrait of James Joyce.'
51. *Letters*, p. 55.
52. Interview with Dr. Richard Best, 1953.
53. *Letters*, p. 55.
54. This letter is in the Slocum Collection at Yale.
55. Letter at Cornell.
56. Letter to Curran [July 1904], *Letters*, p. 55.
57. *My Brother's Keeper*, pp. 103-4 (116).
58. S. Joyce, Diary.
59. Letter at Cornell.
60. *Ulysses*, p. 190 (181).
61. B.B.C. broadcast, 'Portrait of James Joyce' (uncut version).
62. The letters from Baillie are at Cornell.
63. Curran's letter is at Cornell.
64. Gorman notes.
65. In a letter of Aug. 14, 1904, now at Cornell, the Dublin Printing Co., which had printed the pamphlet, asked Joyce to correct and return the proofs.
66. On Nov. 19, 1904, Joyce still hoped to be able to pay the Dublin printer the ten shillings and sixpence still owed, but he failed to do so, and the copies were apparently discarded. Letters from Joyce to S. Joyce, Nov. 19, 1904, and Dec. 3, 1904.
67. At Cornell.
68. S. Joyce, Diary.
69. Interview with Eileen Reidy, 1953.
70. Joseph Holloway's Diary.
71. *Freeman's Journal*, Aug. 29, 1904.
72. *Exiles*, p. 584 (409).
73. S. Joyce, Diary.
74. Idem.
75. *A Portrait*, p. 280 (201).
76. Interview with S. Joyce, 1954.
77. Interview with Joseph Hone, 1953.
78. Oliver St. John Gogarty, *It Isn't This Time of Year at All* (London, 1954), pp. 69-70.
79. *Ulysses*, p. 189 (180).
80. William Bulfin, *Rambles in Eirinn* (Dublin, 1907), pp. 322-4.
81. *My Brother's Keeper*, p. 255 (249); Gogarty, *Mourning Became Mrs. Spendlove*, p. 54.
82. S. Joyce, Diary.
83. Gogarty, *Mourning Became Mrs. Spendlove*, pp. 56-7.
84. Date is given in S. Joyce, Diary.
85. *Ulysses*, p. 87 (81).
86. S. Joyce, Diary.
87. Byrne, *Silent Years*, p. 148.
88. Interview with Mrs. Kathleen Barnacle Griffin, 1953.
89. Most of the correspondence from E. Gilford is in the Slocum Collection at Yale.
90. *Exiles*, p. 545 (381).
91. *Ulysses*, p. 64 (57).
92. In Slocum Collection at Yale.
93. Lady Gregory seems to be quoting this remark of Joyce in her reply.
94. Letter of Oct. 4, 1904, *Letters*, p. 56. See also p. 57. Roberts must have been slow to disgorge the ten shillings.
95. At Cornell.
96. Letter at Southern Illinois University (Feinberg).

97. Letter to S. Joyce, Oct. 11, 1904.
98. Interview with Eva Joyce, 1953.

CHAPTER XI

1. Letter to S. Joyce [October, 1905].
2. Idem.
3. Letter to S. Joyce, Oct. 11, 1904.
4. Made clear by letters to Nora Joyce in 1909.
5. Letter to S. Joyce, Oct. 12, 1904.
6. Letter to S. Joyce, Nov. 19, 1904.
7. Letter to S. Joyce, Oct. 12, 1904.
8. Letter to S. Joyce, Nov. 10, 1904.
9. Letter to S. Joyce, Nov. 3, 1904.
10. A fragment of this uncompleted story is in the Slocum Collection at Yale.
11. Letter to S. Joyce, Nov. 3, 1904.
12. Alessandro Francini Bruni, *Joyce Intimo Spogliato in Piazza* (Trieste, 1922).
13. Interview with A. Francini Bruni, 1954.
14. Letter to Mrs. William Murray, New Year's Eve, 1904, *Letters*, p. 57.
15. Interview with S. Joyce, 1953.
16. Interview with A. Francini Bruni, 1954.
17. Francini Bruni, *Joyce Intimo Spogliato in Piazza*.
18. Idem.
19. Interview with A. Francini Bruni, 1954.
20. Idem.
21. A. Francini Bruni, 'Ricordi personali su James Joyce,' *Nuova Antologia*, LXXXII (Sept. 1947), 71-9.
22. Letter to S. Joyce, Dec. 15, 1904.
23. Interview with Amalija Globocnik by Stanislav Šimić.
24. Letter to S. Joyce, Dec. 3, 1904.
25. Interview with A. Francini Bruni, 1954.
26. Idem.
27. Letter to S. Joyce, Dec. 15, 1904.
28. Letter to S. Joyce, Jan. 19, 1905.
29. *Critical Writings*, p. 217.
30. *Exiles*, pp. 576, 581 (404, 407).
31. Letter to S. Joyce, Dec. 28, 1904.
32. *Letters*, pp. 57-8.
33. Letter to S. Joyce, Dec. 3, 1904.
34. Letter to S. Joyce, Nov. 19, 1904.
35. He sent this story to S. Joyce on Jan. 19, 1905.
36. S. Joyce, 'Early Memories of James Joyce,' *Listener*, XLI (May 26, 1949), p. 896.
37. *Critical Writings*, pp. 146-8; letter to S. Joyce, Nov. 19, 1904.
38. Letter to S. Joyce, Dec. 12, 1904.
39. Letter to S. Joyce, Feb. 28, 1905.
40. Idem.
41. Letter to S. Joyce, Nov. 19, 1904.
42. Letter to S. Joyce, Dec. 3, 1904.
43. Letter to S. Joyce, Feb. 28, 1905.
44. Letters to S. Joyce, Nov. 19, 1904, and Dec. 3, 1904.
45. Idem.
46. Letter to S. Joyce, Jan. 13, 1905.
47. Letter to S. Joyce, Nov. 19, 1904.
48. Quoted in R. Ellmann, *Yeats: The Man and the Masks* (New York, 1948), p. 179.

49. Letter to S. Joyce, Jan. 19, 1905.
50. Letter to S. Joyce, Feb. 28, 1905.
51. Letter to S. Joyce, Dec. 15, 1904.
52. Interview with A. Francini Bruni, 1954.

CHAPTER XII

1. Letter to S. Joyce, April 4, 1905.
2. Halvdan Koht, *The Life of Ibsen* (New York, 1931), vol. I, p. 247.
3. Interview with A. Francini Bruni, 1954.
4. Letter to S. Joyce, ?Aug. 3, 1906.
5. Letter to S. Joyce, written between May 8 and June 3, 1905.
6. A. Francini Bruni, *Joyce Intimo Spogliato in Piazza*.
7. Interview with Mrs. Kathleen Barnacle Griffin, 1953.
8. Letter to S. Joyce, April 4, 1905.
9. Letter to S. Joyce, June 6?, 1905.
10. Letter to S. Joyce, written between May 8 and June 3, 1905.
11. Letter to S. Joyce, written after Sept. 23, 1905.
12. A letter from McGinty to Joyce is in the Joyce Collection at Cornell.
13. Letter to S. Joyce, July 12, 1905.
14. Idem.
15. Letter to S. Joyce, March 15, 1905.
16. Letter to S. Joyce, July 12, 1905.
17. Post card to S. Joyce, July 8, 1905.
18. Letter to S. Joyce, July 12, 1905.
19. Idem.
20. Letter to S. Joyce, July 19, 1905.
21. Letter to S. Joyce, July 29, 1905.
22. Alphabetical notebook kept by Joyce in Trieste, now at Cornell.
23. Telegram in Joyce Collection at Cornell.
24. *Exiles*, p. 538 (377).
25. Letter to S. Joyce, July 29, 1905.
26. Letter to S. Joyce, October 1905.
27. Letter to S. Joyce, Sept. 18, 1905.
28. Interview with Eva Joyce, 1953.
29. Letter to S. Joyce, written between May 8 and June 3, 1905.
30. Letter card to S. Joyce, June 6, 1905.
31. At Cornell.
32. Letter from Charles Joyce to S. Joyce, April 12, 1906.
33. Letter to S. Joyce, written after Sept. 23, 1905.
34. Joyce wrote S. Joyce on Oct. 3, 1905, of Kettle, 'He is too polite to suspect treachery.'
35. Letter to S. Joyce, July 12, 1905.
36. M. Lermontov, *A Hero of Our Time,* tr. Martin Parker (Moscow, 1947), p. 9.
37. Letter to S. Joyce, July 12, 1905.
38. Letter to Grant Richards, May 5, 1906, in Gorman, p. 150.
39. Letter to S. Joyce, written after Sept. 23, 1905.
40. Letter to Grant Richards, May 5, 1906, in Gorman, p. 150.
41. Idem.
42. *Critical Writings*, p. 168.
43. Letter to S. Joyce, July 12, 1905.
44. Alphabetical notebook, at Cornell.
45. Letter to S. Joyce, end of September 1905.
46. Letter from S. Joyce to his father, 1910, never sent.

Chapter XIII

1. A letter from Mrs. Josephine Murray to S. Joyce, Jan. 22, 1906, refers to this remark.
2. *Finnegans Wake*, p. 175.
3. Interview with A. Francini Bruni, 1954.
4. He first mentioned this possibility in a post card to S. Joyce, ?June 6, 1905.
5. Letter to S. Joyce, Sept. 18, 1905.
6. Letter card from S. Joyce to Kathleen Murray, April 11, 1906, in Slocum Collection at Yale.
7. Letter to Budgen, Aug. 16, 1921, *Letters*, p. 170.
8. Interview with A. Francini Bruni, 1954.
9. Idem.
10. A. Francini Bruni, *Joyce Intimo Spogliato in Piazza*. I am grateful to Mrs. Vera Esposito Dockrell and to Professor Louis Rossi for help on the translation of Francini's extraordinarily colloquial Tuscan. I had some assistance also from Constance Barbentini.
11. Gorman, p. 159.
12. Interview with A. Francini Bruni, 1954.
13. Letter to Grant Richards, Sept. 23, 1905. Joyce says he has no money: 'My music must therefore justify its name strictly.'
14. Letter to Grant Richards, Feb. 28, 1906, in Gorman, p. 147.
15. Letter of this date from Richards to Joyce, copy in University of Illinois Library.
16. Letter to Grant Richards, June 16, 1906, in Gorman, p. 156. Joyce wrote Richards on April 26, 1906, 'I have written my book with considerable care, in spite of a hundred difficulties and in accordance with what I understand to be the classical tradition of my art.' *Letters*, p. 60.
17. Letter to Grant Richards, May 5, 1906, in Gorman, p. 149.
18. Idem.
19. Idem.
20. Gorman, p. 152.
21. Letter to Grant Richards, May 20, 1906, *Letters*, p. 63.
22. *Letters*, pp. 63-4.
23. Letter to Grant Richards, July 9, 1906, in Gorman, p. 157.
24. The correspondence from the Roman bank is in the Joyce Collection at Cornell.

Chapter XIV

1. Halvdan Koht, *The Life of Ibsen*, vol. I, p. 258.
2. Post card to S. Joyce, July 31, 1906.
3. Letter to S. Joyce, Aug. 7, 1906.
4. *Finnegans Wake*, p. 298.
5. Letter to S. Joyce, Aug. 2, 1906.
6. Letter to S. Joyce, Aug. 7, 1906.
7. Letter to S. Joyce, Oct. 4, 1906.
8. Letter to S. Joyce, Aug. 19, 1906.
9. Letter to S. Joyce, Dec. 7, 1906.
10. Letter to S. Joyce, Aug. 7, 1906.
11. Letter to S. Joyce, Dec. 7, 1906.
12. Letter to S. Joyce, Dec. 3, 1906.
13. Idem.
14. Letter to S. Joyce, Aug. 19, 1906.
15. Letter to S. Joyce, Sept. 15, 1906.
16. Letter to S. Joyce, Sept. 6. 1906.

17. Letter to S. Joyce, ?Oct. 9, 1906.
18. Letter to S. Joyce, Aug. 7, 1906. Another letter, Sept. 15, 1906, instructs Stanislaus to pay no more of James's debts.
19. Letter to S. Joyce, ?Oct. 9, 1906.
20. Letter to S. Joyce, Nov. 20, 1906.
21. Letter to S. Joyce, Sept. 18, 1906.
22. Letter to S. Joyce, Dec. 7, 1906.
23. Idem.
24. Idem.
25. Letter to S. Joyce, Dec. 7, 1906, part of it written later.
26. Letter to S. Joyce, Jan. 1907.
27. Letter to S. Joyce, Sept. 22, 1906.
28. Letter to S. Joyce, Dec. 3, 1906.
29. Letter to S. Joyce, Dec. 7, 1906.
30. Idem.
31. Interview with Ottocaro Weiss, 1954.
32. *Ulysses,* p. 606 (584).
33. Letter to S. Joyce, Dec. 7, 1906.
34. Letter to S. Joyce, Nov. 13, 1906.
35. S. Joyce, 'The Background to "Dubliners," ' *Listener,* LI (March 25, 1954), p. 526.
36. Gorman, p. 176; letter to S. Joyce, Feb. 6, 1907.
37. Interview with S. Joyce, 1954.
38. Idem.
39. Letter to S. Joyce, Nov. 13, 1906.
40. Idem.
41. Letter to S. Joyce, Sept. 25, 1906.
42. A copy of Richards's letter is at the University of Illinois Library.
43. Letter to S. Joyce, Oct. 4, 1906.
44. The letter is quoted in the *Dublin Magazine,* I (April, 1924).
45. Letter to Elkin Mathews, Oct. 17, 1906, in Slocum Collection at Yale.
46. Letter to S. Joyce, Oct. 18, 1906.
47. Letter to S. Joyce, Feb. 6, 1907.
48. Letter to S. Joyce, Aug. 19, 1906.
49. Letter to S. Joyce, Dec. 3, 1906.
50. Letter to S. Joyce, Nov. 6, 1906.
51. Letter to S. Joyce, Sept. 13, 1906.
52. Idem.
53. Letter to S. Joyce, Sept. 18, 1906.
54. Letter to S. Joyce, Nov. 20, 1906.
55. Letter to S. Joyce, Dec. 1906.
56. Letter to S. Joyce, Oct. 18, 1906.
57. S. Joyce, Diary.
58. Letter from Charles Joyce to S. Joyce, April 12, 1906.
59. Letter to S. Joyce, Oct. 18, 1906.
60. Letter from Gogarty to Joyce, June 14, 1906; letter to S. Joyce, Oct. 4, 1906.
61. Letter to S. Joyce, Sept. 6, 1906.
62. Idem.
63. Idem.
64. Letter to S. Joyce, Nov. 6, 1906.
65. Letter to S. Joyce, Nov. 13, 1906.
66. Letter to S. Joyce, Oct. 9, 1906.
67. Letter to S. Joyce, Nov. 6, 1906.
68. Idem.
69. Letter to S. Joyce, Feb. 11, 1907.
70. Letter to S. Joyce, Feb. 6, 1907.

71. Idem.
72. Letter to S. Joyce, Feb. 11, 1907.
73. R. Ellmann, *Yeats: The Man and the Masks*, p. 176.
74. Letter to S. Joyce, Feb. 11, 1907.
75. Idem.
76. Letter to S. Joyce, Feb. 1907.
77. Idem.
78. Letter to S. Joyce, Jan. 1907.
79. Letter to S. Joyce, Feb. 16, 1907.
80. Letter to S. Joyce, Feb. 15, 1907.
81. Letter card to S. Joyce, Feb. 20, 1907.
82. Letter to S. Joyce, Nov. 13, 1906.
83. Letter to S. Joyce, Feb. 16, 1907.
84. A. Francini Bruni heard the story later from Nora Joyce, though her husband never mentioned it. Joyce's last-minute telegram to Stanislaus, March 6, 1907, asking for 40 crowns, is at Cornell.

CHAPTER XV

1. Letter to me from Mrs. Kathleen Barnacle Griffin.
2. See p. 222.
3. S. Joyce, 'The Background to "Dubliners,"' *Listener*, LI (March 25, 1954), 526-7.
4. *Ulysses*, p. 12 (8).
5. Ibid. p. 48 (44).
6. Interview with Mrs. May Joyce Monaghan, 1953.
7. Idem.
8. Birkin in *Women in Love*.
9. Information from Professor Joseph Prescott.
10. At Cornell.
11. See p. 316.
12. Interview with Mrs. Mary Sheehy Kettle, 1953.
13. *My Brother's Keeper*, p. 38 (58).
14. See p. 17.
15. Interview with S. Joyce, 1953.
16. Suggested to me by Professor Vivian Mercier.
17. Gerhard Friedrich, 'Bret Harte as a Source for James Joyce's "The Dead,"' *Philological Quarterly*, XXXIII (Oct. 1954), pp. 442-4.
18. Letter to S. Joyce, Feb. 1907.
19. W. Y. Tindall, *The Literary Symbol* (New York, 1955), p. 227.
20. I am indebted to Mrs. Glasheen for pointing this out to me.
21. *Critical Writings*, p. 71.
22. Professor Walter B. Rideout kindly called my attention to the similarity of these passages.
23. *Critical Writings*, p. 83.
24. Letter to S. Joyce, Feb. 11, 1907.
25. Letter to S. Joyce, Sept. 25, 1906.

CHAPTER XVI

1. At Cornell.
2. Letter from S. Joyce to his father, 1910, not sent.
3. *Finnegans Wake*, p. 172.
4. Letter from S. Joyce to father, 1910, not sent.
5. Idem.
6. Interview with A. Francini Bruni, 1954.

7. Idem.
8. Silvio Benco, 'James Joyce in Trieste,' *Bookman* (New York), LXXII (Dec. 1930), 375-80.
9. S. Joyce, Diary.
10. These articles, translated by Ellsworth Mason, are in *Critical Writings*.
11. *Ulysses*, p. 22 (18).
12. Yeats, 'September 1913.'
13. *Critical Writings*, p. 189.
14. Ibid. p. 190.
15. Ibid. p. 192.
16. Ibid. p. 196.
17. A. Francini Bruni, *Joyce Intimo Spogliato in Piazza*.
18. *Critical Writings*, p. 190.
19. Ibid. p. 191.
20. Ibid. pp. 198-9.
21. Ibid. p. 198.
22. A phrase used several times in *Ulysses*.
23. His letter card to Elkin Mathews, March 21, 1907, says the lectures are to be on 'The Celtic Revival.' Croessmann Collection at Southern Illinois University.
24. Interview with A. Francini Bruni, 1954.
25. *Critical Writings*, p. 171.
26. Ibid. p. 169.
27. Ibid. p. 185.
28. Letter to S. Joyce, Dec. 1906.
29. Quoted in letter to Joyce from John Joyce, April 24, 1907.
30. Idem.
31. The reply from the *Corriere* is at Cornell.
32. S. Joyce, *Recollections of James Joyce*, p. 26.
33. Arthur Symons in the *Nation* (London), LXXIII (Oct. 15, 1907).
34. 'Mananan' wrote in the review *Hermes*.
35. Clery's review appeared long after the publication of *Chamber Music*, probably in 1909.
36. Gorman notes.
37. *Freeman's Journal*, June 1, 1907.
38. *Exiles*, p. 613 (430).
39. These royalty statements are in the Joyce Collection at Cornell.
40. *Letters*, p. 67.
41. The reply is at Cornell.
42. He told an ophthalmologist in Paris that it was an aftermath of a night on the ground after a drinking bout.
43. S. Joyce, letter to father, 1910, not sent.
44. Idem.
45. Interview with A. Francini Bruni, 1954.
46. Interview with George Joyce, 1953.
47. S. Joyce, letter to father, 1910, not sent.
48. Idem.
49. Interview with S. Joyce, 1954.
50. There is correspondence about this at Cornell.
51. Letter at Cornell.
52. S. Joyce, 'Open Letter to Dr. Oliver Gogarty,' *Interim*, IV (1954), p. 55.
53. At Cornell.
54. S. Joyce, Diary, Feb. 21, 1908.
55. Ibid. March 12, 1908.
56. A. Francini Bruni, *Joyce Intimo Spogliato in Piazza*.
57. S. Joyce, Diary.
58. Interview with A. Francini Bruni, 1954.

59. Idem.
60. Idem.
61. Correspondence relating to this translation is in the Joyce Collection at Cornell; Gorman, p. 196.
62. Hone's letter is at Cornell.
63. Interview with S. Joyce, 1954.
64. S. Joyce, Diary, Feb. 6, 1908.
65. Ibid. Feb. 12, 1908.
66. Interview with A. Francini Bruni, 1954.
67. S. Joyce, Diary, May 29, 1908.
68. S. Joyce, Diary.
69. Ibid. Aug. 4, 1909.
70. S. Joyce, Diary.
71. Ibid., Aug. 25, 1908.
72. Ibid. Oct. 5, 1908.
73. Interview with S. Joyce, 1954.
74. In the Joyce Collection at Cornell.
75. S. Joyce, letter to father, 1910, not sent.
76. Interview with Signora Svevo, 1956.
77. Idem.
78. S. Joyce, Introduction to Italo Svevo, *As a Man Grows Older* (New York, no date).
79. Interview with S. Joyce, 1953.
80. Interview with Signora Livia Svevo, 1953.
81. S. Joyce, unpublished B.B.C. talk, 'The Younger Generation Knocks at the Door.'
82. S. Joyce, letter to James Joyce, May 5, 1931, and Introduction to *As a Man Grows Older.*
83. S. Joyce, Introduction to *As A Man Grows Older.*
84. Idem.
85. Interview with Ottocaro Weiss, a relative of Schmitz by marriage.
86. S. Joyce, Introduction to *As a Man Grows Older.*
87. In Joyce Collection at Cornell.
88. Also at Cornell.
89. Letter from John S. Joyce to James Joyce, March 27, 1909, is partial answer to this inquiry.
90. Some canceled pages of *A Portrait,* in Miss Weaver's possession, indicate that this was Joyce's intention. See also Walton Litz, 'Early Vestiges of Joyce's *Ulysses,*' *PMLA,* LXXI (March 1956), pp. 51-60.
91. Letter from S. Joyce to Ellsworth Mason.
92. Ross's reply is in the Joyce Collection at Cornell.
93. 'Oscar Wilde...,' *Critical Writings,* pp. 201-5.

CHAPTER XVII

1. Letter card to S. Joyce, postmarked July 29, 1909.
2. Letter from S. Joyce to father, 1910, not sent.
3. Interview with Mrs. Eileen Joyce Schaurek, 1953.
4. Louis Gillet, *Claybook for James Joyce,* tr. Georges Markow-Totevy, p. 103.
5. Letter to S. Joyce, Aug. 4, 1909.
6. In the Joyce Collection at Cornell.
7. Letter to S. Joyce, Aug. 4, 1909.
8. Idem.
9. Gogarty, 'They Think They Know Joyce,' *Saturday Review* (March 18, 1950), p. 9.
10. Letter to S. Joyce, Aug. 4, 1909.

11. Alphabetical notebook kept at Trieste, now in Joyce Collection at Cornell.
12. Joyce uses this word frequently in *Ulysses*.
13. Letter to S. Joyce, Aug. 4, 1909.
14. Idem.
15. Byrne, *Silent Years*, pp. 156-60.
16. Letter to S. Joyce, Aug. 4, 1909.
17. The date of a letter to Nora Joyce written a few hours after the talk with Cosgrave.
18. Letter to Nora Joyce, Aug. 6, 1909.
19. *Exiles*, pp. 583-4 (409).
20. Byrne, *Silent Years*, p. 156.
21. Letter to Nora Joyce, Aug. 19, 1909.
22. Interview with S. Joyce, 1953.
23. It was stamped at the Stamp Office on Aug. 20, 1909. Letter to S. Joyce, Aug. 21, 1909.
24. Letter to Nora Joyce, Aug. 31, 1909.
25. Alphabetical notebook kept in Trieste, now at Cornell.
26. Letter card to S. Joyce, Aug. 16, 1909.
27. *Exiles*, p. 626 (439).
28. A letter from Joyce to Nora Joyce, Aug. 19, 1909, says his sister will leave the next day.
29. Letter to S. Joyce, Sept. 7, 1909.
30. Interview with Mrs. Eileen Joyce Schaurek, 1953.
31. Letter to S. Joyce, Sept. 4, 1909.
32. Letter card to S. Joyce, Aug. 25, 1909.
33. 'Bernard Shaw's Battle with the Censor,' *Critical Writings*, pp. 206-8.
34. Interview with Judge Eugene Sheehy, 1954.
35. Sheehy, *May It Please the Court*, p. 28.
36. Interview with Mrs. Kathleen Barnacle Griffin, 1953.
37. Interview with George Joyce, 1954.
38. Interview with Mrs. Griffin, 1953.
39. Letter to Nora Joyce, Sept. 1909.
40. Letter to Nora Joyce, Sept. 2, 1909.
41. Letter to Nora Joyce, Sept. 5, 1909.
42. Idem.
43. For most of the details about the *Evening Telegraph* I am indebted to Piaras Béaslai.
44. Interview with Kathleen Murray, 1953.
45. Letter to Nora Joyce, Sept. 5, 1909.
46. Joseph Holloway's Diary at the National Library of Ireland.
47. Byrne, *Silent Years*, p. 157.
48. Letter card to S. Joyce, Sept. 9, 1909.
49. Interview with Eva Joyce, 1953.
50. Italo Svevo, *James Joyce*, tr. by S. Joyce (Norfolk, Conn., New Directions, 1950).

CHAPTER XVIII

1. Interview with Mrs. Maria Jolas, 1953.
2. Joyce, *Exiles* (New York, 1951), p. 118 (Joyce's notes for the play). The expression is also used by Bertha in the play itself (Viking Portable), p. 617 (432).
3. Letter to Georg Goyert, Oct. 19, 1927, in the Croessmann Collection at Southern Illinois University.
4. *A Portrait*, p. 481 (336-7).
5. Interview with William Faulkner, 1958.
6. Byrne, *Silent Years*, pp. 33-5.
7. *A Portrait*, p. 349 (248).

CHAPTER XIX

1. Letter from S. Joyce to his father, 1910, not sent.
2. Idem.
3. Interview with Eva Joyce, 1953.
4. Interview with S. Joyce, 1954.
5. Letter card to S. Joyce, Oct. 21, 1909.
6. Letter card to S. Joyce, Oct. 28, 1909.
7. Letter card to S. Joyce, Nov. 4, 1909.
8. Letter card to S. Joyce, Nov. 17, 1909.
9. Idem.
10. Interview with Kathleen Murray, 1953.
11. Letter card to Nora Joyce, Nov. 27, 1909.
12. Y.Y., 'On Meeting Authors,' *New Statesman*, xxi (Jan. 25, 1941), pp. 80-81.
13. Letter to S. Joyce, Dec. 15, 1909.
14. Charles Duff, *Ireland and the Irish* (New York, 1953), pp. 169-70.
15. Letter to S. Joyce, Dec. 15, 1909.
16. *Evening Telegraph*, Dec. 21, 1909.
17. Letter card to S. Joyce, Dec. 22, 1909.
18. Letter card to S. Joyce, Nov. 8, 1909.
19. Joyce corrected in Gorman's proofs a remark that nothing had come of his agency for Irish tweeds in Trieste; and he wrote the footnote in Gorman, p. 200.
20. Interview with Dr. Richard Best, 1953; preliminary version of B.B.C. program, 'Portrait of James Joyce.'
21. Charles Duff, *Ireland and the Irish*, pp. 169-70.
22. Letter to Nora Joyce, late October 1909.
23. Idem.
24. Letter to Nora Joyce, Nov. 1, 1909.
25. Letter to S. Joyce, Dec. 15, 1909.
26. Idem.
27. Letter to Nora Joyce, Nov. 18, 1909.
28. *A Portrait*, pp. 484-5 (339).
29. *Exiles*, p. 546 (382).
30. *Ulysses*, p. 767 (741).
31. Letter to Nora Joyce, Dec. 6, 1909.
32. Letter to Nora Joyce, Dec. 11, 1909.
33. Idem.
34. Letter to Nora Joyce, Dec. 22, 1909.
35. Interview with Eva Joyce, 1953.
36. The Excise Licenses Book for the City of Dublin reports the grant of the license on Jan. 19, 1910, to James Joyce, 'Cinematograph Manager,' for 'music only [without dancing] and not at all on Sunday.' His solicitor was C. J. Murray.
37. Letter to S. Joyce, Dec. 23, 1909.
38. Interview with Mrs. Eileen Joyce Schaurek, 1954; letter to S. Joyce, Nov. 17, 1909.
39. Budgen, *James Joyce and the Making of 'Ulysses,'* p. 109.
40. Interview with Mrs. Eileen Joyce Schaurek, 1953.
41. Idem.
42. Idem.
43. Gorman, p. 191.
44. Interview with Mrs. Eileen Joyce Schaurek, 1953.
45. Interview with Eva Joyce, 1953.
46. Idem. Eva Joyce remarked to me that there was no quarrel over this point.
47. Letter to S. Joyce, April 4, 1905.
48. A letter from May Joyce to S. Joyce, July 25, 1911, says, 'Pappie had a very

nice letter from Jim of course rather strange and bitter but still it showed that he felt her death very much.'

49. Letter card to S. Joyce, June 15, 1910.
50. Letter from Schmitz to Joyce, June 15, 1910.
51. Interview with Mrs. Eileen Joyce Schaurek, 1953.
52. S. Joyce, letter to father, 1910, not sent.
53. Idem.
54. Idem.
55. Interview with Mrs. Eileen Joyce Schaurek, 1953.
56. Interview with Eva Joyce, 1953.
57. Letter from S. Joyce to father, 1910, not sent.
58. Letter from S. Joyce to James Joyce, 1933?.
59. In Joyce Collection at Cornell.
60. Letter to George Roberts, Jan. 3, 1911, in National Library of Ireland.
61. At Cornell.
62. Interview with Mrs. Eileen Joyce Schaurek, 1953; B.B.C. program, 'Portrait of James Joyce.'
63. Letter to Harriet Weaver, Jan. 6, 1920, in *Letters*, p. 136.
64. Gorman, p. 255; Budgen, *James Joyce and the Making of 'Ulysses,'* p. 202.
65. Copy of this letter at the University of Illinois Library.
66. Interview with A. Francini Bruni, 1953.
67. Interview with Mrs. Eileen Joyce Schaurek, 1953.
68. Interview with Tullio Silvestri, 1953.
69. Interview with Amalija Globocnik by Stanislav Šimić.
70. *Ulysses*, p. 767 (741).
71. Interview with Silvestri, 1953.

CHAPTER XX

1. Letter to S. Joyce, Aug. 1912.
2. From partial typescript, now at Cornell.
3. Interview with Oscar Schwarz, 1956; Schwarz attended the lecture.
4. *Critical Writings*, pp. 221-2.
5. Ibid. p. 218.
6. Ibid. p. 220.
7. Ibid. p. 221.
8. 'The Shade of Parnell,' ibid. p. 227. Compare Yeats, *Autobiography* (New York, 1958), p. 211: 'During the quarrel over Parnell's grave a quotation from Goethe ran through the papers, describing our Irish jealousy: "The Irish seem to me like a pack of hounds, always dragging down some noble stag." '
9. Ibid. p. 228.
10. Djuna Barnes, 'James Joyce,' *Vanity Fair*, XVIII (April 1922), pp. 65, 104.
11. Records of the University of Padua.
12. This correspondence is in the Joyce Collection at Cornell.
13. Letter to S. Joyce, late 1912.
14. Interview with Mrs. Eileen Joyce Schaurek, 1953.
15. Interview with Signora Livia Svevo, 1954.
16. Idem.
17. Letter from Nora Joyce to James Joyce, July 17, 1912.
18. Idem.
19. Idem.
20. Letter card to S. Joyce, July 17, 1912.
21. Joseph Hone, 'A Recollection of James Joyce,' *Envoy*, v (April 1951), p. 45.
22. Letter from Charles Joyce to S. Joyce, 1912.
23. Letter card to S. Joyce, July 17, 1912.
24. Idem.

25. Letter to S. Joyce, Aug. 1912.
26. *Exiles* (New York, 1951), p. 118.
27. Letter to S. Joyce, Aug. 1912.
28. 'The Mirage of the Fisherman of Aran,' *Critical Writings*, p. 234.
29. Letter to Joyce from Henry N. Blackwood Price, quoted in letter from James Joyce to S. Joyce, Aug. 1912.
30. *Evening Telegraph*, Aug. 19, 1912.
31. 'Politics and Cattle Disease,' *Critical Writings*, pp. 238-41.
32. Letter to S. Joyce, Aug. 1912.
33. 'The Mirage of the Fisherman of Aran,' *Critical Writings*, p. 235.
34. Letter to S. Joyce, Aug. 1912.
35. Letter from S. Joyce to Gorman, about 1933.
36. Idem.
37. Correspondence at Cornell.
38. Joseph Hone, 'A Recollection of James Joyce,' *Envoy*, v (April, 1951), p. 44; interview with George Roberts, 1953.
39. Interview with A. J. Leventhal, 1953.
40. Letter card to S. Joyce, Aug. 18, 1912.
41. Idem.
42. Idem.
43. *My Brother's Keeper*, p. 63 (80).
44. Idem.
45. Joseph Holloway's Diary at the National Library of Ireland.
46. A copy of this undated letter is in the Joyce Collection at Cornell.
47. Letter to Nora Joyce, Aug. 23, 1912.
48. Idem.
49. Idem.
50. Letter to S. Joyce, Aug. 23, 1912.
51. Idem.
52. Letter from Charles Joyce to S. Joyce, Sept. 5, 1912.
53. Letter to Nora Joyce, late Aug. 1912.
54. *A Portrait*, p. 525 (367).
55. James Stephens, 'The James Joyce I Knew,' *Listener*, xxxvi (Oct. 24, 1946), p. 565.
56. Roger McHugh, 'James Joyce's Synge-Song,' *Envoy*, iii (Nov. 1950), pp. 12-16.
57. Joyce wrote out the song in this way for his son in 1935.
58. Interview with Mrs. Ada MacLeish, 1958.
59. Letter card to S. Joyce, Aug. 30, 1912.
60. Letter to W. B. Yeats, Sept. 19, 1912, *Letters*, pp. 71-2; Gorman, p. 216.
61. Patricia Hutchins, *James Joyce's World*, p. 88.
62. Letter from Charles Joyce to S. Joyce, Sept. 11, 1912, with note by James Joyce appended to it.
63. Interview with George Roberts, 1953.
64. Letter from Charles Joyce to S. Joyce, late 1912.
65. Letter to Grant Richards, March 4, 1914, *Letters*, p. 75.
66. Gorman papers, and Gorman, pp. 216-17.
67. Italo Svevo, *James Joyce* (Norfolk, Conn., New Directions, 1950).

CHAPTER XXI

1. This is clear from Charles Joyce's reply, late 1912.
2. Interview with Paolo Cuzzi, 1953.
3. Letters to me from Signora Emma Cuzzi Brocchi and from Signora Olivia Ferreri.
4. He borrowed the book from Dario de Tuoni, as the latter informed me in 1953.

5. Letters to me from Dr. Boris Furlan.
6. Unpublished notebook.
7. *Ulysses*, p. 100 (93).
8. 'Giacomo Joyce' notebook.
9. Interview with S. Joyce, 1953.
10. Letter to S. Joyce, Sept. 9, 1912.
11. A letter from her, dated Feb. 19, 1933, was among Joyce's papers.
12. Letter to G. Molyneux Palmer, July 19, 1909, *Letters*, p. 67.
13. Letter to W. B. Yeats, late 1912.
14. Letter to Elkin Mathews, March 25?, 1913.
15. Letter to Palmer, October 6, 1913, *Letters*, p. 74.
16. A copy of the letter from the firm is in the University of Illinois Library.
17. That his conscience troubled Richards is clear in a letter from him to James H. Cousins, Aug. 19, 1914, in which he admits that Joyce may have been right in holding a grudge against him. Copy of this letter in University of Illinois Library.
18. Interview with Robert Frost, 1947.
19. *Letters of Ezra Pound* (New York and London, 1950), p. 40.
20. *New Freewoman*, 1 (Dec. 1913).
21. Ibid. p. 245.
22. Interview with Harriet Weaver, 1956.
23. Letter from Harriet Weaver to Joyce, about 1920.
24. *New Freewoman*, 1 (Dec. 15, 1913), p. 245.
25. Letter to Harriet Weaver, July 12, 1915.
26. Ezra Pound, *Literary Essays* (London, 1954), pp. 399-402.
27. June 27, 1914.
28. Copy of a letter, dated April 12, 1915, at University of Illinois Library.
29. At Cornell.
30. Stuart Gilbert kindly brought this passage to my attention.
31. At Cornell.
32. *Exiles* (New York, 1951), p. 115.
33. Ibid. p. 123.

Chapter XXII

1. *Exiles* (New York, 1951), p. 119.
2. In a letter to me, 1958.
3. *Exiles* (1951), p. 115.
4. Ibid. p. 124.
5. Interview with Arthur Power, 1953.
6. Letter to me from Aldous Huxley, 1957. Stuart Gilbert informs me he also heard this etymology from Joyce; see Gilbert, *James Joyce's Ulysses* (New York, 1952), p. 263.
7. *Ulysses*, p. 231 (222).
8. Letter to me, 1958.
9. Ibid. p. 57 (50).
10. Ibid. p. 58 (51).
11. *Ulysses*, p. 59 (52).
12. Ibid. p. 61 (54).
13. Ibid. p. 216 (206).
14. Ibid. p. 247 (238).
15. Interview with John Garvin, 1953. Dr. Best tells me the quotation is not quite accurate, but adds that 'it doesn't matter.'
16. *Finnegans Wake*, p. 107.
17. Ibid. pp. 185-6.
18. See *Ulysses*, p. 25 (21).
19. I am indebted for much of this information about Dublin to T. W. Pugh.

20. Mrs. Adaline Glasheen kindly called this reference to May Oblong to my attention.
21. *Ulysses*, p. 573 (555).
22. Ibid. p. 327 (317).
23. Ibid. p. 458 (444).
24. Ibid. p. 460 (446).
25. Ibid. p. 460 (446).
26. Ibid. p. 533 (517).
27. Ibid. p. 574 (556).
28. Ibid. p. 593 (574).
29. Ibid. p. 708 (684).
30. Ibid. p. 597 (575).
31. Ibid. p. 650 (627).
32. Frank Budgen, 'James Joyce,' *Horizon*, III (Feb. 1941), p. 107.
33. Marvin Magalaner, 'The Anti-Semitic Limerick Incidents and Joyce's "Bloomsday," ' *PMLA*, LXVIII (1953), pp. 1219-23.
34. Interview with S. Joyce, 1954.
35. Interview with Frank Budgen, 1953.
36. *Finnegans Wake*, p. 463.
37. Interview with Dr. Daniel Brody, 1954.
38. Interview with S. Joyce, 1953; compare S. Joyce's Introduction to Svevo, *As a Man Grows Older*, p. viii.
39. Interview with Signora Livia Svevo, 1954.
40. Marvin Magalaner, solely on the basis of internal evidence, made this shrewd guess in his article, 'Leopold Bloom before "Ulysses," ' *Modern Language Notes*, LXVIII (Feb. 1953), pp. 110-12. External evidence confirms it.
41. *Finnegans Wake*, p. 65.
42. Letter to me from Mrs. Vera Esposito Dockrell.
43. *Thom's Directory* for 1903.
44. Interview with Brinsley Macnamara, 1954.
45. Interview with T. W. Pugh, 1953.
46. Interview with Mrs. Maria Jolas, 1953.
47. Letter to Mrs. Josephine Murray, Oct. 12 (not 14), 1921, *Letters*, p. 174.
48. Interview with Dr. Carola Giedion-Welcker, 1956.
49. Letter to Frank Budgen, Aug. 16, 1921, *Letters*, p. 170.
50. A phrase used in *Finnegans Wake*.
51. Interview with Ted Keogh, 1954.
52. *Ulysses*, p. 327 (317).
53. These notes, about which Walton Litz has written, are in Harriet Weaver's possession.

CHAPTER XXIII

1. Letter to me from Dr. Boris Furlan, 1955.
2. Interview with S. Joyce, 1953.
3. Letter to me from Oscar Schwarz, 1955, and interview with him, 1956.
4. Idem.
5. Idem.
6. Tullio Silvestri wrote an account of his friendship with Joyce, and a copy of it is in my possession.
7. Interview with Signora Livia Svevo, 1954.
8. Interview with Ottocaro Weiss, 1956.
9. Silvestri's account of his friendship with Joyce.
10. Interview with Oscar Schwarz, 1956, and Gorman papers.
11. A. Francini Bruni, *Joyce Intimo Spogliato in Piazza*.
12. Silvio Benco, 'James Joyce in Trieste,' *Bookman* (New York), LXXII (Dec. 1930), pp. 375-80.

13. Gorman, p. 230.
14. Gorman, p. 229, and interview with Ottocaro Weiss, 1956.
15. Pinker's letter is in the Joyce Collection at Cornell.
16. Quoted by Joyce in letter to Grant Richards, April 5, 1915.
17. H. G. Wells, 'James Joyce,' *Nation* (London), xx (Feb. 24, 1917), pp. 710-11.
18. Copy of letter in University of Illinois Library.
19. Interview with Mrs. Eileen Joyce Schaurek, 1953.
20. Idem.
21. Idem.
22. John V. Kelleher has kindly given me this information.
23. Gorman, p. 234.
24. Gorman, p. 229.
25. Joyce had continued to buy books up to the last. A typical bill from the book-seller, F. H. Schimpff, indicates that between October 1, 1913, and May 9, 1914, Joyce bought the following:

Oriani, Gelosia	*The Egoist,* Feb. 16, 1914
Ibsen, *Collected Works* (vol. vii)	Sauer, *Engl. Grammatik*
Lecky, *History of European Morals*	Schlüssel, *Engl. Grammatik*
Rickeby, *Of God and His Creatures*	Dostoevsky, *The Idiot*
Berlitz, *I*	Bergson, *L'évolution créatrice*
Ibsen, *Peer Gynt* (vol. iv)	Flaubert, *Premières Œuvres,* 2 vols.
Chennevière, *Claude Debussy*	Turgenev, *Smoke*
Shaw, *Major Barbara*	Shaw, *The Devil's Disciple*
Flaubert, *Saint Antoine*	Byington, *Anarchism*
Mérimée, *Carmen*	Collodi, *Pinocchio*

The books cost a total of 222 crowns 90, of which Joyce had paid 172 crowns 90.
26. Gorman notes.
27. Interview with Signora Vela Bliznakoff Pulitzer.

Chapter XXIV

1. Interview with Nino Frank, 1953.
2. Mary Colum, *Life and the Dream* (New York, 1947), p. 383.
3. Elliot Paul, 'Farthest North,' *Bookman* (New York), lxxv (May 1932), p. 158.
4. *Letters,* p. 82.
5. Interview with Claud W. Sykes, 1954.
6. Interview with Signora Vela Bliznakoff Pulitzer, 1956.
7. Letter from Yeats to Gosse, July 6, 1915, *Letters of W. B. Yeats,* p. 596.
8. Letter from Yeats to Gosse, Aug. 28, 1915, ibid. pp. 600-601.
9. Archives of the Royal Literary Fund. I am grateful to John Broadbent for permitting me to examine the correspondence relating to Joyce.
10. Idem.
11. *Ulysses,* p. 485 (471).
12. Interview with Rudolf Goldschmidt, 1954.
13. This book is in Rudolf Goldschmidt's possession.
14. Interview with Victor A. Sax. The limericks are in his possession.
15. Interview with Ottocaro Weiss, 1956.
16. *Ulysses,* p. 300 (290).
17. Interview with Signora Vela Bliznakoff Pulitzer, 1954.
18. Idem.
19. Stefan Zweig, *The World of Yesterday* (New York, 1943), p. 275.
20. Interview with Beran's widow, Frau Lisa Beran, by Dr. Alfred Dutli, 1956.
21. Yeats afterwards changed the line to read more mildly, 'A poet's mouth be silent.'
22. Joyce told Gorman of this remark he had made. Gorman papers and Gorman, p. 234.

23. Joyce used the remark about Ireland in *Ulysses*, p. 576 (558); letter to F. Guillermet, Aug. 5, 1918, *Letters*, p. 118.
24. *Letters*, p. 96.
25. Letter to Harriet Weaver, in her possession.
26. *Letters*, p. 88.
27. Letter to J. B. Pinker, in the possession of Charles A. Feinberg.
28. Letter from Pound to Pinker, Oct. 5, 1915, in the possession of Provost Gordon N. Ray of the University of Illinois.
29. Unpublished letter, at Cornell.
30. *Letters*, pp. 84-6.
31. A copy of this report is in the Slocum Collection at Yale, with a letter from Duckworth & Co. dated Jan. 26, 1916.
32. Letter dated Jan. 30, 1916, at Yale.
33. *Letters of Ezra Pound* (New York and London, 1950), pp. 74-5.
34. Letter to J. B. Pinker, March 31, 1916 (Feinberg Collection).
35. Letter card to Pinker, May 17, 1916.
36. *Letters*, p. 92.
37. B. W. Huebsch's letter to Harriet Weaver of June 16, 1916, expressed his desire to publish *A Portrait*, 'though I am inclined to believe that such success as it may attain will be artistic rather than popular.'
38. Letter to me from Nancy Cunard, 1958.
39. Letter from George Moore to Edward Marsh, Aug. 3, 1917. I am indebted to Bertram Rota for sending me, with the permission of the owner, Christopher Hassall, a copy of this letter.
40. At Yale.
41. Joyce says in a letter to Harriet Weaver, Oct. 30, 1916, that he has had three or four collapses, which his doctor attributed to nervous breakdowns.
42. Letters from Grant Richards to Huebsch, Nov. 6, 1914; Jan. 28, 1915; April 12, 1915. Copies of letters in University of Illinois Library.

CHAPTER XXV

1. Interview with Paul Ruggiero, 1953.
2. Frank Budgen, *Further Recollections of James Joyce*, p. 10.
3. Interview with Paul Ruggiero, 1953.
4. Idem.
5. Interview with Philipp Jarnach by Dr. Alfred Dutli, 1953, and by Dr. Hans Joachim Lang, 1956.
6. This letter is in the Joyce Collection at Cornell.
7. Interview with Philipp Jarnach by Dr. Dutli, 1953.
8. Idem.
9. Interview with Philipp Jarnach by Dr. Lang, 1956. There is a letter from Busoni to Joyce, dated July 5, 1917, in the Joyce Collection at Cornell.
10. Interview with Signora Vela Pulitzer, 1954, by Lucy von Hibler.
11. A letter written on this stationery is in the Joyce Collection at Cornell.
12. Gorman, pp. 243-4.
13. Interview with Paul Ruggiero, 1953.
14. Interview with Claud W. Sykes and Mrs. Sykes, 1954.
15. Idem.
16. *Ulysses*, p. 211 (202).
17. Letter from Bleibtreu to Joyce, Nov. 28, 1918, at Cornell.
18. Interview with Claud W. Sykes, 1954.
19. Djuna Barnes, 'James Joyce,' *Vanity Fair*, XVIII (April 1922), pp. 65, 104.
20. Interview with Claud W. Sykes, 1954.
21. Interview with Ottocaro Weiss, 1954.
22. Interview with Claud W. Sykes, 1954.

23. Joyce wrote this description of himself on a clipping from the *Irish Statesman* about a novel on Clongowes, which he sent Harriet Weaver.
24. Letter to Harriet Weaver, April 22, 1917, *Letters,* p. 102.
25. Letter to Harriet Weaver, June 13, 1917.
26. Felix Beran's account of his friendship with Joyce is in the Gorman papers, now in the Croessmann Collection at Southern Illinois University.
27. Sylvia Beach, *Ulysses in Paris* (New York, Harcourt, Brace, 1956), p. 14.
28. Frank Budgen, *James Joyce and the Making of 'Ulysses,'* p. 108.
29. 'Wild Youth,' *Times Literary Supplement,* xvi (March 1, 1917), pp. 103-4. Clutton-Brock and Joyce later became acquainted.
30. Frank Budgen, *James Joyce and the Making of 'Ulysses,'* p. 76.
31. Letter to Pound, April 9, 1917, *Letters,* p. 102.
32. Ibid. p. 101.
33. The contract, at Yale, is dated Aug. 31, 1917.
34. Interview with Claud W. Sykes, 1954.
35. Letter card to J. B. Pinker, July 2, 1917, in Feinberg Collection.
36. Georges Borach, 'Conversations with Joyce,' tr. by Joseph Prescott, *College English,* xv (March 1954), pp. 325-7.
37. Telegram from Nora Joyce to Joyce, at Cornell.
38. Letter card from Nora Joyce to Ezra Pound, Aug. 28, 1917, in Harriet Weaver's possession.
39. Interview with Paul Ruggiero, 1953.
40. Gorman, p. 245.
41. Idem.
42. Gorman, pp. 248-9.
43. Letter card to Sykes, Nov. 24, 1917, in the Slocum Collection at Yale.
44. Undated letter card to Sykes.
45. Undated letter card to Sykes, Oct. 1917.
46. Undated letter card to Sykes, Dec. 1917.
47. Letter card to Sykes, Dec. 1917.
48. Idem.
49. Interview with Claud W. Sykes and Mrs. Sykes, 1954.
50. Letter from Pound to Joyce, Dec. 18, 1917, in Patricia Hutchins, *James Joyce's World,* p. 118.
51. In a letter to Joyce, undated but written in the early 1920's.
52. Margaret Anderson, *My Thirty Years' War* (New York, 1930), pp. 174-5.
53. *Letters of Ezra Pound,* p. 133.
54. Interview with Claud W. Sykes and Mrs. Sykes, 1954.
55. Joyce gave this version of the incident to Dr. Daniel Brody, who related it to me in 1954.
56. Interview with Paul Ruggiero, 1953.
57. Interview with Cecil Palmer, 1954.
58. Interview with Claud W. Sykes, 1954.
59. Idem.
60. *Critical Writings,* pp. 246-8.
61. Interview with Claud W. Sykes, 1954.
62. Idem.
63. Interview with Tristan Rawson, 1954.
64. Joyce so reported what he had said in various formal accounts of the incident.
65. Interview with Cecil Palmer, 1954.

CHAPTER XXVI

1. Frank Budgen, *James Joyce and the Making of 'Ulysses,'* p. 15.
2. Interview with August Suter, 1956, and with Paul Suter, 1956.

3. Interview with August Suter, 1956, who informs me that Joyce was mistaken: Bach did not mix the two gospels, though he did intercalate some chorals.

4. Frank Budgen, *James Joyce and the Making of 'Ulysses,'* p. 156.

5. Interview with Daniel Hummel, 1956.

6. Interview with Paul Suter by Dr. Alfred Dutli, 1956.

7. Interview with Daniel Hummel, 1956.

8. Frank Budgen, *James Joyce and the Making of 'Ulysses,'* p. 188.

9. Ibid. p. 181.

10. Ibid. p. 13.

11. From the copy in possession of Frau Lisa Beran.

12. Interview with Paul Suter by Dr. Dutli, 1956.

13. Idem.

14. Idem.

15. This poem is in the Slocum Collection at Yale.

16. Interview with Paul Suter by Dr. Dutli, 1956.

17. Frank Budgen, *James Joyce and the Making of 'Ulysses,'* p. 38; Joyce told the same story to Sisley Huddleston in Paris.

18. Interview with Frank Budgen, 1953.

19. Interview with Claud W. Sykes, 1954.

20. Idem.

21. Ackermann mentions the incident in his autobiography. Among Joyce's books at the time of his death was Ackermann's *Bordbuch eines Verkehrsfliegers,* inscribed to Joyce by the author. Thomas E. Connolly, *The Personal Library of James Joyce,* in University of Buffalo Studies, xx, No. 1 (April, 1955), p. 7.

22. Frank Budgen, *James Joyce and the Making of 'Ulysses,'* pp. 15-17, 191.

23. *Ulysses,* p. 538 (521).

24. Letter to me from Dr. Hans Kraus, now of New York, 1958; Dr. Kraus was a pupil of Joyce's in Zurich.

25. Frank Budgen, *James Joyce and the Making of 'Ulysses,'* p. 21.

26. Ibid. p. 8, and interview with Frank Budgen, 1956.

27. Interview with Daniel Hummel, 1956.

28. Frank Budgen, *James Joyce and the Making of 'Ulysses,'* p. 138.

29. Frank Budgen, *Further Recollections of James Joyce,* p. 8.

30. Interview with Philipp Jarnach by Dr. Dutli, 1953.

31. Frank Budgen, *Further Recollections of James Joyce,* p. 14.

32. Frank Budgen, *James Joyce and the Making of 'Ulysses,'* p. 194, and interview with Paul Suter by Dr. Dutli, 1956.

33. Interview with Claud W. Sykes, 1954.

34. In a private collection.

35. Gorman, p. 254.

36. Letter to Sir Horace Rumbold, Nov. 30, 1918, copy in Joyce Collection at Cornell.

37. Interview with Claud W. Sykes, 1954.

38. For these program notes, see *Critical Writings,* pp. 249-52.

39. Gorman, p. 230.

40. Virginia Woolf, *A Writer's Diary* (London, 1954), p. 363. In *The Letters of Katherine Mansfield,* ed. J. Middleton Murry (London, 1928), vol. II, p. 173, she writes to Sydney Schiff on Jan. 15, 1922, 'About Joyce, and my endeavour to be doubly fair to him because I have been perhaps unfair and captious. Oh, I can't get over a great great deal. I can't get over the feeling of wet linoleum and unemptied pails and far worse horrors in the house of his mind—He's so terribly *unfein;* that's what it amounts to. There is a tremendously strong impulse in me to beg him not to shock me!'

41. Letter to John Quinn, March 11, 1920, says that *Exiles* was rejected 'owing to a veto of Mr Shaw's, as I am informed.'

42. Interview with Claud W. Sykes, 1954.

43. Interview with Paul Suter by Dr. Dutli, 1956.
44. Records of the Bezirksgericht, signed by Judge Billeter, Nov. 16, 1918.
45. Borach, 'Conversations with Joyce,' tr. by Joseph Prescott, *College English*, xv (March 1954), 325-7.
46. Interview with Paul Ruggiero, 1953.
47. A typed copy of this letter is in the Joyce Collection at Cornell.
48. Court records in Zurich.

CHAPTER XXVII

1. Interview with Professor Heinrich Straumann, 1953.
2. The letters referred to here are in the possession of Professor Straumann, who has kindly shown them to me.
3. Interview with Frau Walter Bollmann, Marthe Fleischmann's niece, 1954.
4. Idem.
5. Now in the Municipal Library in Zurich.
6. Interview with Ottocaro Weiss, 1956.
7. Court records in Zurich.
8. Interview with Claud W. Sykes, 1954.
9. Interview with Frank Budgen, 1953.
10. Desmond Harmsworth in *Harper's Bazaar*, LXXXIII (April, 1949).
11. This is clear from Joyce's letter to J. B. Pinker, May 17, 1919, in Feinberg Collection.
12. Djuna Barnes, 'Vagaries Malicieux,' *Double Dealer*, III (May 1922); some of the details are from interviews with Frank Budgen, Paul Suter, and August Suter; see also Frank Budgen, *James Joyce and the Making of 'Ulysses,'* pp. 247-8.
13. Frank Budgen, *James Joyce and the Making of 'Ulysses,'* p. 204.
14. Letter to Frank Budgen, July 11, 1919, *Letters*, p. 128; see also Mary Colum, *Life and the Dream*, pp. 383-4.
15. Mary M. Colum, *Our Friend James Joyce*, p. 114.
16. Letter to Frank Budgen, July 11, 1919, at Yale.
17. Letter card to Claud W. Sykes, 1920.
18. Letter to Frank Budgen, June 19, 1919, *Letters*, p. 126.
19. Idem.
20. Frank Budgen, *James Joyce and the Making of 'Ulysses,'* p. 107.
21. Borach, 'Conversations with Joyce,' *College English*, xv (March 1954), pp. 325-7.
22. Interview with Ottocaro Weiss, 1954.
23. *Ulysses*, p. 547 (530).
24. Interview with Ottocaro Weiss, 1954.
25. Letter to Herbert Palmer, July 7, 1919, *Letters*, p. 127, indicates this plan was under way.
26. Letter to Harriet Weaver, July 20, 1919, *Letters*, pp. 128-9.
27. *Letters*, p. 129.
28. Interview with Ottocaro Weiss, 1954.
29. Letter to Harriet Weaver, Aug. 26, 1919.
30. *Ulysses*, p. 325 (315).
31. Ibid. p. 483 (469).
32. Interviews with Mrs. Eileen Joyce Schaurek, 1953, and with Frank Budgen, 1956.
33. *Ulysses*, pp. 692-3 (669).
34. Interview with Ottocaro Weiss, 1954.
35. This letter is in the Hanley Collection at the University of Texas.
36. Interviews with Ottocaro Weiss, 1954, and with Frank Budgen, 1956.
37. Interview with Paul Ruggiero, 1953.
38. Gorman papers; compare Gorman, p. 265.

39. The letter from Mrs. McCormick is in the Lockwood Memorial Library of the University of Buffalo.
40. Idem.
41. Interview with Dr. Carl G. Jung, 1953.
42. Letter to Dr. Daniel Brody, Aug. 29, 1932, *Letters,* p. 324.

Chapter XXVIII

1. Letter to Frank Budgen, Dec. 10, 1920, *Letters,* p. 152.
2. Letter to Harriet Weaver, Oct. 28, 1919.
3. Interview with S. Joyce, 1954.
4. Interview with Mrs. Eileen Joyce Schaurek, 1953.
5. Letter card to Frank Budgen, Nov. 7, 1919, *Letters,* p. 130.
6. Letter to Frank Budgen, Jan. 3, 1920, *Letters,* p. 134.
7. Letter from S. Joyce to Gorman, about 1933.
8. Interview with A. Francini Bruni, 1954.
9. A. Francini Bruni, *Joyce Intimo Spogliato in Piazza.*
10. Interview with Oscar Schwarz, 1956.
11. Italo Svevo, *James Joyce* (Norfolk, Conn., New Directions, 1950).
12. Interview with Oscar Schwarz, 1956.
13. Tullio Silvestri, 'Recollections of James Joyce.'
14. Letter to S. Joyce, July 25, 1920, in Gorman papers.
15. Letter to Frank Budgen, Jan. 3, 1920, *Letters,* p. 134.
16. Interview with Lojce Berce, 1954.
17. *Letters,* p. 134.
18. Letter card to Mrs. Josephine Murray, Jan. 5, 1920, *Letters,* p. 135. He had asked for the same information in another card a month or two earlier.
19. *Letters,* p. 34, with some additions from original at Yale.
20. Letter from Harriet Weaver to Joyce, March 16, 1920.
21. Letter to Harriet Weaver, Feb. 25, 1920, *Letters,* p. 137.
22. Idem.
23. This diagram is in the Joyce Collection at Cornell.
24. Interview with S. Joyce, 1954.
25. *Letters,* pp. 138-9. The date is apparently March 20, 1920.
26. Interview with Frank Budgen, 1954.
27. Virginia Woolf, *A Writer's Diary,* ed. Leonard Woolf (London, 1954), p. 50, entry for Sept. 26, 1922.
28. Letter to Frank Budgen, May 18, 1920, in Slocum Collection at Yale.
29. Letter from Harriet Weaver to Joyce, June 30, 1920.
30. Letter to Harriet Weaver, Aug. 16, 1920.
31. Letter from Harriet Weaver to Joyce, Aug. 25, 1920.
32. *Letters,* p. 140. Date appears to be March 15, 1920.
33. Frank Budgen's letter to Joyce of May 30, 1920, indicates that Joyce even considered going to Cornwall.
34. Letter from a friend of John Joyce to Joyce, July 1, 1920.
35. Letter in Pound Collection at Yale.
36. Letter at Cornell.
37. Letter to Harriet Weaver, July 12, 1920, *Letters,* p. 142.
38. Letter from Pound to Carlo Linati, June 9, 1920, says Joyce had arrived the night before.
39. Letter to Harriet Weaver, Feb. 1, 1927.
40. On the back of a letter to Pound.
41. Pound, *Letters,* p. 153.
42. Letter card to Mrs. Josephine Murray, 1920.
43. Joyce made an inventory of his books before leaving his flat in Trieste. A part of it has survived:

Shelf 3, Front:

1. Tolstoi, *Pensieri di saggi per ogni giorno* (1908)
2. Tolstoi, *Scritti*
3-13. Turgenev, *Novels* (11 vols.)
14. Paul de Kock, *Le Cocu*
15. Jacob Behmen, *The Signature of All Things*
16. Lennox Robinson, *Two Plays: Harvest; The Clancy Name* (1911)
17. Yeats, *The Land of Heart's Desire*
18. St. John Ervine, *Mixed Marriage*
19. Lennox Robinson, *Patriots* (a play in three acts)
20. T. C. Murray, *Maurice Harte* (a play in two acts)
21. Oliver Wendell Holmes, *Ralph Waldo Emerson*
22. Molière, *Works* (2 vols.)
23. Joseph Campbell, *Judgment* (a play in two acts)
24. Mikhail Bakunin, *God and the State*
25. Balzac, *Petites Misères de la vie conjugale.*
26. Luigi Molinari, *Il Tramonto del Diritto Penale*
27. John Eglinton, *Bards and Saints* (1906)
28. Ugo Foscolo, *Ultime Lettere di Jacopo Ortis*
29-30. Pierre Kropotkin, *La Grande Rivoluzione*
31. Jonas Lie, *Østenfor sol*
32. Tolstoi, *Der Roman der Ehr* (Berlin, 1891)
33. Silvio Benco, *La Fiamma Fredda*
34. Marco Praga, *La Biondina* (novel)
35. Praga, *Le Vergini* (play in four acts)
36. Praga, *Alleluja* (play in three acts)
37. Praga, *La Moglie ideale* (play in three acts)
38. Frank Wedekind, *Die Zensur*
39. *Lustful Acts*
40. Comte de Mirabeau, *The Curtain Drawn Up*
41. Leopold von Sacher-Masoch, *Catherine II*
42. Sacher-Masoch, *Liebesgeschichten*
43-46. Sacher-Masoch, *Grausame Frauen* (4 vols.)
47. Sacher-Masoch, *Scene del Ghetto*
48. Knut Hamsun, *Aftenröde*
49. Hamsun, *Ved rikets port*
50. Hamsun, *Livets Spil*
51. Ricard, *Der Zorn*

Shelf 3, Back:

1. Ferdinando Bracciforti, *Grammatica della lingua inglese*
2. Bracciforti, *Chiave dei temi sceneggiati*
3. *The Tabernacle and the Church,* catechetically explained (London, 1859)
4. John Lingard, *School History of England*
5. William Ballantyne Hodgson, *Errors in the Use of English*
6. William Andrews Holdsworth, *The Law of Wills*
7-8. Melani, *Lettera Italiana* (2 vols.)
9. George Eliot, *The Mill on the Floss*
10. *Nouveau Scandale de Londres*
11. Thomas Robert Macquoid, *Pictures and Legends from Normandy and Brittany*
12. *History of Excess*
13. Aldo Palazzeschi, *Il Codice di Perelà*
14. Mercredy, Map of Ireland
15. Guglielmo Ferrero, *L'Europa giovane*
16. Giovanni Boine, *Il Peccato*

17. George Payne Rainsford James, *The Smuggler*
18-21. Alain René Lesage, *Gil Blas* (4 vols.)
22. Samuel Johnson, *Rasselas*
23. Francis Hueffer, *The Troubadours*
24. *Guide to Troubadours*
26 [sic]. Lady Gregory, *The White Cockade* (play in three acts)
27. Colette, *Claudine à l'École*
28. *Dana* (Dublin)
29. Giorgio Ohnet, *Eva*
30. Ohnet, *La Via della gloria*
31. Brunetto Latini, *Il Libro delle bestie*
32. Shakespeare, *Hamlet*

44. Letter from S. Joyce to Joyce, July 6, 1920.
45. Letter to S. Joyce, July 25, 1920, in Gorman papers.
46. Letter to S. Joyce, July 12, 1920, in Gorman papers.
47. Interview with Philippe Soupault, 1954.

CHAPTER XXIX

1. Interview with August Suter, 1956.
2. Sylvia Beach, *Ulysses in Paris,* p. 17.
3. Interview with Samuel Beckett, 1954.
4. Interview with Mme Jenny Serruys Bradley, 1953.
5. Ludmila Savitsky, 'Dedalus in France,' in Joyce, *Dedalus* (Paris, 1943), p. 7.
6. Letter from Mme Ludmila Bloch-Savitsky to Joyce, Aug. 29, 1920.
7. Interview with Mme Ludmila Bloch-Savitsky, 1953; letter from her to Joyce, Dec. 21, 1921; see also Joyce, *Dedalus,* p. 11.
8. Gorman papers.
9. Letter from M. Bloch to Joyce, July 9, 1920.
10. Interview with Mme Jenny Bradley, 1953.
11. Letter from Jenny Serruys to Joyce, Aug. 3, 1920. A letter from Joyce to her, Nov. 5, 1920, says he is returning the bed.
12. Letter to Jenny Serruys, July 22, 1920.
13. Interview with Mme Jenny Bradley, 1953.
14. Letter from W. A. Bradley to Joyce, Sept. 16, 1920, agrees with Joyce's position and repeats it.
15. Letter to Frank Budgen, Oct. 24, 1920, *Letters,* p. 148.
16. Interview with Mme Jenny Bradley, 1953.
17. Letter to Carlo Linati, Dec. 10, 1919.
18. Interview with Natalie Clifford Barney, 1954.
19. William Carlos Williams, *Autobiography* (New York, 1951), p. 193.
20. Sylvia Beach, *Ulysses in Paris,* pp. 7-15, and ' "Ulysses" à Paris,' *Mercure de France,* CCCIX (May 1950), pp. 11-18.
21. Interview with Jean Paulhan, 1954.
22. Sylvia Beach, *Ulysses in Paris,* p. 16.
23. Letter to S. Joyce, July 25, 1920, in Gorman papers.
24. Idem.
25. Interview with Fritz Vanderpyl, 1954.
26. Letter to Ezra Pound, July 31, 1920, at Yale.
27. Interview with John Rodker and Mrs. Rodker, 1954.
28. Letter to Ezra Pound, July 31, 1920, at Yale.
29. Letter from Harriet Weaver to Joyce, Aug. 25, 1920.
30. Interview with Mrs. Claud W. Sykes, 1954.
31. Interview with Mme Yasushi Tanaka, 1954.
32. Interview with Philippe Soupault, 1954.

33. Letter to Harriet Weaver, Nov. 6, 1921, *Letters*, p. 176.
34. Letter to Frank Budgen, Oct. 24, 1920, *Letters*, pp. 148-9.
35. Letter to Ezra Pound, July 31, 1920, at Yale.
36. Interview with Fritz Vanderpyl, 1954.
37. Letter from T. S. Eliot to Joyce, Aug. 11, 1920, at University of Buffalo.
38. Wyndham Lewis, *Blasting and Bombardiering* (London, 1937), p. 272.
39. Ibid. pp. 274-6.
40. Ibid. p. 289.
41. Ibid. p. 287.
42. Idem.
43. Ibid. p. 291.
44. Ibid. pp. 293-4.
45. Interview with T. S. Eliot, 1954: 'T. S. Eliot Talks about His Poetry,' *Columbia University Forum*, II (Fall, 1958), p. 14.
46. Diary of Helen (Mrs. Myron) Nutting.
47. Notebook in Lockwood Memorial Library of the University of Buffalo.
48. Letter to Frank Budgen, July 27, 1920, *Letters*, p. 144.
49. Letter to Frank Budgen, Michaelmas 1920, *Letters*, p. 147.
50. Max Eastman, *The Literary Mind* (New York, 1931), pp. 103-4.
51. Diary of Helen (Mrs. Myron) Nutting.
52. Letter to Frank Budgen, Oct. 24, 1920, *Letters*, p. 149.
53. Letter from Baroness St. Leger to Joyce, 1920.
54. Letter to Frank Budgen, Oct. 24, 1920, *Letters*, p. 149, and a notebook at the University of Buffalo.
55. Letter to Frank Budgen, Michaelmas 1920, *Letters*, pp. 147-8.
56. Card to Frank Budgen, Dec. 20?, 1920.
57. Letter to A. Francini Bruni, 1920.
58. Walton Litz, 'Joyce's Notes for the Last Episodes of "Ulysses," ' *Modern Fiction Studies*, IV (Spring 1958), pp. 19-20.
59. Fleischman was first interested in the book by Ezra Pound, as a letter from Fleischman to Pound, Oct. 11, 1919 (in the possession of Gordon N. Ray), indicates.
60. Letter to Jenny Serruys, Oct. 20, 1920. A letter to her from Jacques Natanson, Feb. 2, 1921, says *Exiles* will be produced before the end of the season.
61. Frank Budgen, *Further Recollections of James Joyce*, p. 4.
62. Letter to Harriet Weaver, June 24, 1921, *Letters*, p. 166.
63. Letter to Andre Suarès, Oct. 20, 1920, quoted in part in International Autographs (285 Riverside Drive, New York), Catalogue No. 7 of Autograph Letters, no date.
64. Letter to John Quinn, 1920.
65. *Letters*, p. 151.
66. *Letters*, p. 150.
67. Letter to Michael Healy, Dec. 30, 1920, *Letters*, p. 153.

Chapter XXX

1. Sylvia Beach, ' "Ulysses" à Paris,' *Mercure de France*, CCCIX (May 1950), p. 19.
2. Quoted by Joyce in letter to Harriet Weaver, March 1, 1921.
3. Interview with Jacques Benoît-Méchin, 1954.
4. Letter to Frank Budgen, Feb. 28?, 1921, *Letters*, p. 159.
5. Letter to Harriet Weaver, April 10, 1921, *Letters*, p. 163.
6. Letter to Ettore Schmitz, Jan. 5, 1921, *Letters*, p. 154.
7. Letter to Robert McAlmon, Nov. 2, 1921, *Letters*, p. 176.
8. Letter to Claud W. Sykes, 1921, *Letters*, p. 164.
9. Letter to Frank Budgen, Feb. 28?, 1921, *Letters*, pp. 159-60.
10. Letter to Frank Budgen, Aug. 16, 1921, *Letters*, p. 170.

11. Margaret Anderson, *My Thirty Years' War*, p. 157.
12. *Letters*, p. 137.
13. Letter to Frank Budgen, Nov. 1920.
14. Margaret Anderson, *My Thirty Years' War*, p. 217.
15. Ibid. pp. 220-21.
16. Letter from John Quinn to Joyce, October 1920.
17. Margaret Anderson, *My Thirty Years' War*, p. 222.
18. Ibid. p. 226.
19. Letter from John Quinn to Joyce, October 1920.
20. Sisley Huddleston, *Paris Salons, Cafés, Studios* (Philadelphia, 1928), p. 210.
21. Sylvia Beach, *Ulysses in Paris*, p. 24.
22. *New York Tribune*, Feb. 28, 1921.
23. Interview with Arthur Power, 1953.
24. Arthur Power, *From an Old Waterford House* (London, no date), pp. 63-4.
25. Interview with Arthur Power, 1953, and Arthur Power, 'James Joyce—The Man,' *Irish Times*, Dec. 30, 1944.
26. Arthur Power, *From an Old Waterford House*, pp. 65-6.
27. Desmond Harmsworth, 'James Joyce: A Sketch,' *Harper's Bazaar* (April 1949), p. 198.
28. Letter from Harriet Weaver to Joyce, April 13, 1921; his reply, April 17, 1921, is in *Letters*, p. 163.
29. Letter to A. Francini Bruni, June 7, 1921.
30. Interview with John Rodker, 1954.
31. Letter to A. Francini Bruni, Dec. 30, 1921.
32. Letter to Robert McAlmon, Oct. 10, 1921, *Letters*, p. 173; letter to Harriet Weaver, Oct. 13, 1921.
33. Quoted by Joyce in letter to Harriet Weaver, April 10, 1922, *Letters*, p. 184.
34. Letter to Claud W. Sykes, Feb. 1921, in Slocum Collection at Yale.
35. Letter to Harriet Weaver, April 9, 1921; see letter to her of April 10, 1921, *Letters*, p. 161.
36. See Pound, *Letters*, p. 166.
37. Interview with Wyndham Lewis, 1953.
38. Letter to Harriet Weaver, Nov. 25, 1922, establishes that Joyce had met Proust in May.
39. Padraic Colum, *Our Friend James Joyce*, p. 151.
40. William Carlos Williams, *Autobiography* (New York, 1951), p. 218.
41. Margaret Anderson, *My Thirty Years' War*, p. 245.
42. Arthur Power, 'James Joyce—The Man,' *Irish Times*, Dec. 30, 1944, and interview with Power, 1953.
43. Frank Budgen, *Further Recollections of James Joyce*, pp. 10-11. John H. Thompson called my attention to the variety of accounts of this episode.
44. Letter to me from Mrs. Violet Schiff, 1957.
45. Interview with Samuel Beckett, 1954.
46. Diary of Helen (Mrs. Myron) Nutting.
47. Notebook at the University of Buffalo.
48. Diary of Helen (Mrs. Myron) Nutting.
49. Interview with Arthur Power, 1953. See also letter to Harriet Weaver, Nov. 25, 1922, where Joyce says that Proust's name 'has often been coupled with mine.'
50. Letter to S. Joyce, Sept. 14, 1920.
51. *Letters*, pp. 165-7.
52. Interview with Jacques Benoist-Méchin, 1954.
53. Letter to Valery Larbaud, June 5, 1921, in Bibliothèque Municipale at Vichy.
54. Letter to A. Francini Bruni, June 7, 1921.
55. Interview with A. J. Leventhal, 1953.
56. Arthur Power, *From an Old Waterford House*, p. 67, and interview with Power, 1953.

57. Interview with Arthur Power, 1953.
58. Idem.
59. Arthur Power, *From an Old Waterford House*, p. 71.
60. Joyce's letters to McAlmon are in the possession of Professor Norman Holmes Pearson.
61. Letter to me from Robert McAlmon, 1954.
62. Interview with Samuel Beckett, 1954.
63. Robert McAlmon, *Being Geniuses Together* (London, 1938), p. 21.
64. Letter to me from Robert McAlmon, 1954.
65. Idem, and McAlmon, *Being Geniuses Together*, pp. 90-91.
66. *Letters*, p. 228.
67. Letter to me from Robert McAlmon, 1954.
68. Sisley Huddleston, *Paris Salons, Cafés, Studios* (Philadelphia, 1928), p. 217.
69. Wyndham Lewis, *Rude Assignment* (London, 1950), p. 56.
70. Interview with Wyndham Lewis, 1953.
71. Idem.
72. Idem.
73. Idem.
74. Letter to me from Myron Nutting, 1957.
75. Idem; *Ulysses*, p. 756 (730).
76. See Gorman, p. 11.
77. Letter to Valery Larbaud, Summer, 1921, *Letters*, p. 169.
78. Letter to Harriet Weaver, April 3, 1921, *Letters*, p. 161.
79. Robert McAlmon, *Being Geniuses Together*, p. 23.
80. Letter to Harriet Weaver, Aug. 7, 1921, *Letters*, p. 168.
81. Interview with Arthur Power, 1953.
82. *Letters*, p. 168.
83. Letter to Robert McAlmon, Aug. 27, 1921, *Letters*, p. 170.
84. Letters to Harriet Weaver, Aug. 30, 1921, and to Frank Budgen, Sept. 6, 1921, *Letters*, p. 171.
85. *Letters*, p. 171.
86. Interview with Wyndham Lewis, 1953.
87. Interview with Jacques Benoîst-Méchin, 1956.
88. Letter to Harriet Weaver, Oct. 7, 1921.
89. *Letters*, p. 174. The date is probably Oct. 12, 1921.
90. *Letters*, p. 175.
91. Letter to me from Myron Nutting, 1957.
92. Letter to Valery Larbaud, Oct. 20, 1921.
93. Letters to Robert McAlmon, Oct. 29, 1921, and to Valery Larbaud, same date.
94. Valery Larbaud, 'Préface,' in Édouard Dujardin, *Les Lauriers sont coupés* (Paris, 1924), p. 7.
95. Stuart Gilbert, *Contempo* (Chapel Hill, N.C.), III (Feb. 15, 1934), p. 6.
96. Letter to Harriet Weaver, Nov. 22, 1929, *Letters*, p. 287.
97. Letter to Édouard Dujardin, Dec. 5, 1938, quoted in Parke-Bernet Auction Catalogue, April 1 and 2, 1958.
98. Letter to Harriet Weaver, Nov. 22, 1929, *Letters*, p. 287.
99. Édouard Dujardin, *Le Monologue intérieur* (Paris, 1931), p. 24.
100. Adrienne Monnier, 'La Traduction d' "Ulysse,"' *Mercure de France*, CCCIX (May 1, 1950), pp. 30-32.
101. Interview with Jacques Benoîst-Méchin, 1956.
102. Idem.
103. Idem.
104. Sylvia Beach, '"Ulysses" à Paris,' *Mercure de France*, CCCIX (May 1, 1950), p. 27.
105. Letter to Harriet Weaver, Dec. 10, 1921, *Letters*, p. 178.
106. Letter to Carlo Linati, Sept. 21, 1920, *Letters*, pp. 146-7.

107. Letter to Harriet Weaver, Dec. 10, 1921, *Letters*, p. 178.
108. Idem.
109. 'Ulysses,' a report of Larbaud's conférence, in *Observer* (London), Dec. 11, 1921, p. 9.
110. Letter to Harriet Weaver, Dec. 10, 1921, *Letters*, p. 178.
111. Sisley Huddleston, *Paris Salons, Cafés, Studios*, p. 203.
112. Letter to Harriet Weaver, Dec. 10, 1921, *Letters*, p. 178.
113. Letter to Harriet Weaver, Nov. 1, 1921.
114. Djuna Barnes, 'James Joyce,' *Vanity Fair*, XVIII (April 1922), p. 65.
115. Idem.
116. Burton Rascoe, *A Bookman's Daybook* (New York, 1929), p. 27.
117. Letter to Harriet Weaver, 1922.
118. Sylvia Beach, ' "Ulysses" à Paris,' *Mercure de France*, CCCIX (May 1, 1950), p. 29.
119. Diary of Helen (Mrs. Myron) Nutting.
120. Idem.
121. Idem.
122. Letter to Harriet Weaver, March 20, 1922.
123. Interview with Arthur Power, 1953.
124. Interview with Gilbert Seldes, 1958.
125. Undated letter.
126. Interview with August Suter, 1956.
127. Interview with Gilbert Seldes, 1958.

CHAPTER XXXI

1. Letter to Harriet Weaver, Feb. 6, 1923, *Letters*, p. 200.
2. T. S. Eliot, 'Ulysses, Order and Myth,' *Dial* (Nov. 1923); reprinted in Seon Givens, *James Joyce: Two Decades of Criticism* (New York, 1948), p. 201.
3. Letter to Harriet Weaver, Nov. 19, 1923.
4. Virginia Woolf, *A Writer's Diary*, p. 363.
5. Ibid. p. 49.
6. Ibid. p. 47.
7. Ibid. pp. 50-51.
8. Stuart Gilbert, *James Joyce's Ulysses* (1952), p. 28.
9. Samuel Putnam, *Paris Was Our Mistress* (New York, 1947), p. 153.
10. Letter in the Newberry Library, Chicago.
11. Interview with Alice B. Toklas, 1954.
12. Barrett H. Clark, 'George Moore,' in *Intimate Portraits* (New York, 1951), p. 110.
13. Interview with Jean Paulhan, 1954.
14. Letter from Gide to Joyce, April 30, 1931.
15. Interview with Jean Paulhan, 1954.
16. Reprinted in Louis Gillet, *Claybook for James Joyce*, pp. 123-7.
17. Dr. W. R. F. Collis, for example, informed me of his father's anxiety that the law firm of Collis & Ward, mentioned in the book, might have been made sport of.
18. Interview with L. A. G. Strong, 1947.
19. Yeats, letter to John Quinn, July 23, 1918, *The Letters of W. B. Yeats*, p. 651.
20. Letter from Thomas McGreevy to the editor of the *Times Literary Supplement* (Jan. 25, 1941), pp. 43, 45.
21. Letter from Yeats to Olivia Shakespeare, March 8, 1922, *The Letters of W. B. Yeats*, p. 679.
22. Letter from Yeats to Olivia Shakespeare, June 28, 1923, ibid. p. 698.
23. Letter to Yeats, June 1923. Joyce wrote to decline another invitation on July 12, 1924.

24. Letter from S. Joyce to Joyce, Feb. 26, 1922.
25. Letter to Harriet Weaver, April 30, 1922.
26. Letter to Robert McAlmon, March 17, 1922.
27. Letter to McAlmon, March 1922, *Letters*, p. 182.
28. Letters to McAlmon, Feb. 11, 1922, *Letters*, p. 181, and to S. Joyce, March 20, 1922, in Gorman papers.
29. Letter to Harriet Weaver, March 20, 1922.
30. Middleton Murry, 'Mr. Joyce's "Ulysses,"' *Nation* (London), XXXI (1922), p. 124.
31. Arnold Bennett, 'Concerning James Joyce's "Ulysses,"' *Bookman*, LV (August 1922), p. 567.
32. Letter to Harriet Weaver, May 16, 1922, *Letters*, p. 184.
33. Letter from Harriet Weaver to Joyce, Nov. 20, 1922.
34. Letter to Harriet Weaver, Oct. 22, 1922, *Letters*, p. 189.
35. Letter to Robert McAlmon, March 1, 1922, *Letters*, pp. 182-3.
36. Letter to McAlmon, March 1922, *Letters*, p. 182.
37. Interview with Samuel Beckett, 1954.
38. *Finnegans Wake*, p. 214.
39. Letter to S. Joyce, March 20, 1922, in Gorman papers.
40. Robert McAlmon, *Being Geniuses Together*, p. 219.
41. Interview with Mrs. Kathleen Barnacle Griffin, 1953.
42. Interview with George Joyce, 1953.
43. Letter to Mrs. Josephine Murray, Nov. 10, 1922, *Letters*, p. 194.
44. Interview with Dr. Morax's son, also an ophthalmologist, 1953.
45. Letter to me from Dr. Pierre Mérigot de Treigny, 1954.
46. Letter to Gorman, in Gorman papers.
47. Gerald Griffin, *Wild Geese: Pen Portraits of Famous Irish Exiles* (London, 1938), pp. 22-45.
48. Letter to Harriet Weaver, Jan. 20, 1926, *Letters*, p. 239.
49. Interview with Harriet Weaver, 1956.
50. Patricia Hutchins, *James Joyce's World*, p. 139.
51. Patricia Hutchins, *James Joyce's World*, p. 139, and interview with Kathleen Murray, 1953.
52. Letter to Harriet Weaver, Oct. 4, 1922.
53. Letter to Harriet Weaver, Sept. 20, 1922, *Letters*, p. 185.
54. Interview with Philippe Soupault, 1954.
55. Letter to Harriet Weaver, March 11, 1923, *Letters*, p. 201; and letter to her, Oct. 4, 1922.
56. Letter to Harriet Weaver, Oct. 27, 1922.
57. *Letters*, pp. 189-91.
58. Letter to Harriet Weaver, Nov. 17, 1922, *Letters*, pp. 195-6.
59. Idem.
60. Idem.
61. Idem.
62. Interview with August Suter, 1956.
63. Letters from Harriet Weaver to Joyce, March 27, April 6, and April 7, 1923.
64. Interview with George Joyce, 1954.
65. Letter to Harriet Weaver, June 10, 1923.
66. Interview with August Suter, 1956. See also Frank Budgen, 'James Joyce,' *Horizon*, III (Feb. 1941), p. 105.
67. *Finnegans Wake*, p. 135.
68. Letter to Frank Budgen, Oct. 24, 1920, *Letters*, p. 149.
69. Letter to me from Myron Nutting, 1957.
70. Arthur Power, *From an Old Waterford House*, p. 67, and interview with Power, 1953.
71. *Letters*, p. 198.

72. Interview with August Suter, 1956.
73. Interview with Samuel Beckett, 1954.
74. Max Eastman, *The Literary Mind* (New York, 1931), p. 101.
75. Frank Budgen, 'James Joyce,' in Givens, *James Joyce: Two Decades of Criticism*, p. 24.
76. Edmond Jaloux, 'James Joyce,' *Le Temps* (Paris), Jan. 30, 1941.
77. John Eglinton, *Irish Literary Portraits* (London, 1935), p. 154.
78. Letter to me from William Bird, 1955.
79. Diary of Helen (Mrs. Myron) Nutting.
80. Gorman, p. 283.
81. Gorman, pp. 282-3.
82. Interview with John Sullivan, 1953.
83. Adaline Glasheen, *A Census of Finnegans Wake* (Evanston, 1956), p. 119.
84. *Finnegans Wake*, pp. 189-90.
85. Interview with Samuel Beckett, 1953.
86. *Ulysses*, p. 716 (692).
87. Interview with Samuel Beckett, 1953.
88. Interview with Frank O'Connor, 1947.
89. *Letters*, p. 202.
90. The following chart, compiled by Walton Litz, describes the composition of *Finnegans Wake* during the first ten years.

COMPOSITION	PUBLICATION
1923	
March 10: Joyce begins *Finnegans Wake* by writing the King Roderick O'Connor fragment (now pp. 380-82).	
July-August: Joyce drafts Tristram and Isolde (now pp. 384-386), St. Kevin (pp. 604-605), and 'pidgin fella Berkley' (pp. 611-12) fragments.	
By middle September Joyce had finished a draft of 'Mamalujo' II.iv (pp. 383-399).	
By end of 1923 notebook containing rough drafts of all the episodes in Part I except i and vi (pp. 30-125, 169-216) was probably filled.	
1924	
January-March: Joyce was working on I.v (pp. 104-125), I.vii (pp. 169-195), and I.viii (pp. 196-210).	'From Work in Progress,' *transatlantic review*, I, April (FW II.iv, pp. 383-399).
March: Joyce began Shaun the Post section, III.i,ii,iii,iv (pp. 403-590).	
During the remainder of 1924 Joyce continued to revise the episodes in Part I already written, and to compose the four watches of Shaun.	

1925

Composition of Shaun section continued through 1925, interrupted from time to time by the need for revising other episodes, from Part I, for their initial publication.

'From Work in Progress,' *Contact Collection of Contemporary Writers* (Paris, May) (now FW pp. 30-34).

In early April Joyce was correcting copy for the *Criterion,* and late in the month was faced with the proofs for the *Contact Collection.*

'Fragment of an Unpublished Work,' *Criterion* III, July (FW I.v, pp. 104-125).

By the end of August Joyce had begun the last watch of Shaun III.iv (pp. 555-90), and on November 5 had almost completed a draft of it.

'From Work in Progress,' *Navire d'Argent,* I, October (FW I.viii, pp. 196-216).

'Extract from Work in Progress,' *This Quarter,* I, Autumn-Winter, 1925-26 (FW, I.vii, pp. 169-195).

1926

In April Shaun abcd, Part II (pp. 219-590) was put aside as 'finished,' after several months of intensive revision.

In the summer Joyce wrote 'a piece of the studies' called 'The Triangle,' later 'The Muddest Thick That Was Ever Heard Dump.' This eventually became the middle part of II.ii (pp. 282-304).

In the autumn Joyce drafted the opening episode, I.i (pp. 3-29).

1927

In 1927 Joyce was revising Part I (pp. 3-216) for publication in *transition.*

'Opening Pages of a Work in Progress,' *transition,* No. 1, April, pp. 9-30 (FW I.i).

In the summer he composed I.vi (pp. 126-168) as a connective episode between 'The Hen' and 'Shem the Penman.'

'Continuation of a Work in Progress,' *transition,* No. 2, May, pp. 94-107 (FW I.ii).

transition, No. 3, June, pp. 32-50 (FW I.iii).

transition, No. 4, July, pp. 46-65 (FW I.iv).

transition, No. 5, August, pp. 15-31 (FW I.v).

transition, No. 6, September, pp. 87-106 f. (FW I.vi).

COMPOSITION	PUBLICATION
	transition, No. 7, October, pp. 34-56 (FW I.vii).
	transition, No. 8, November, pp. 17-35 (FW I.viii).

1928

COMPOSITION	PUBLICATION
In the early months Joyce revised Shaun abc (pp. 403-455) for publication in *transition*.	*transition*, No. 11, February, pp. 7-18 (FW 282-304).
In the spring he re-worked *Anna Livia* for publication in book form.	*transition*, No. 12, March, pp. 7-27 (FW III.i, pp. 196-216).
Trouble with his eyes prevented Joyce from writing during most of the latter half of 1928.	*transition*, No. 13, Summer, pp. 5-32 (FW III.ii).
	Anna Livia Plurabelle (New York, Crosby Gaige, October) (FW I.viii, pp. 196-216).

1929

COMPOSITION	PUBLICATION
Joyce began to revise his 'fables,' 'The Mookse and the Gripes' (pp. 152-59), 'The Muddest Thick That Was Ever Heard Dump' (pp. 282-304), 'The Ondt and the Gracehoper' (pp. 414-19), in late 1928 and continued the process through the spring of 1929.	*transition*, No. 15, February, pp. 195-238 (FW III.iii).
	Tales Told of Shem and Shaun (Paris, Black Sun Press, August) (FW 152-59, 282-304, 414-19).
	transition, No. 18, November, pp. 211-236 (FW III.iv).

1930

COMPOSITION	PUBLICATION
Joyce began working on II.i (pp. 219-259) in September.	*Haveth Childers Everywhere* (Paris and New York, June) (FW 532-54).
	Anna Livia Plurabelle (London, Faber & Faber, June) (FW I.viii).

1931

COMPOSITION	PUBLICATION
Joyce was virtually idle in 1931, due to personal difficulties.	*Haveth Childers Everywhere* (London, Faber & Faber, May) (FW 532-554).

1932

COMPOSITION	PUBLICATION
Finnegans Wake II.i (pp. 219-259) was completed in 1932, in spite of great difficulties.	*Two Tales of Shem and Shaun* (London, Faber & Faber, December) (FW 152-159 and 414-419).

Chapter XXXII

1. Interview with Mrs. Kathleen Barnacle Griffin, 1953.
2. Idem.
3. Letter to Harriet Weaver, Oct. 9, 1923, *Letters*, p. 204.

4. Padraic Colum, *Our Friend James Joyce*, p. 122.
5. Ibid. p. 123.
6. Letter to Harriet Weaver, May 21, 1926, *Letters*, p. 241.
7. Eugene Jolas, 'My Friend James Joyce,' in Givens, ed., *James Joyce: Two Decades of Criticism*, pp. 11-12.
8. Letter to Harriet Weaver, Nov. 2, 1923.
9. Letter to Harriet Weaver, Oct. 17, 1923, *Letters*, p. 205.
10. Interview with Arthur Laubenstein, 1956.
11. Bravig Imbs, *Confessions of Another Young Man* (New York, 1936), p. 57.
12. Letter to me from Myron Nutting, 1958.
13. George Antheil, *Bad Boy of Music* (London, no date), pp. 124-5.
14. Al Laney, *Paris Herald: The Incredible Newspaper* (New York, 1947).
15. Interview with Natalie Clifford Barney, 1954.
16. Letter to Harriet Weaver, Aug. 16, 1924, *Letters*, p. 219.
17. Ibid. p. 220.
18. Letter to Harriet Weaver, Oct. 9, 1923, *Letters*, p. 204.
19. Ford Madox Ford, *It Was the Nightingale* (London, 1934), pp. 269-70.
20. Interview with Wyndham Lewis, 1953.
21. Idem.
22. Letter to me from Robert McAlmon, 1955.
23. Letter to Robert McAlmon, Feb. 1924.
24. *Letters*, p. 214.
25. Cablegram, Aug. 5, 1924, *Letters*, p. 219.
26. Letter to Harriet Weaver, Aug. 16, 1924, *Letters*, p. 220.
27. Letter to Ettore Schmitz, Jan. 30, 1924, in 'Carteggio Inedito, Italo Svevo—James Joyce,' with an introduction by Harry Levin, *Inventario*, II (Spring 1949), p. 120.
28. Idem.
29. Italo Svevo, *Corrispondenza con Valery Larbaud, Benjamin Crémieux e Marie Anne Comnène* (Milan, 1953), p. 12.
30. Letter in Bibliothèque Municipale at Vichy.
31. Interview with Signora Livia Svevo, 1953.
32. *Letters*, p. 212.
33. S. Joyce, 'The Younger Generation Knocks at the Door,' unpublished B.B.C. talk.
34. A clipping in Signora Livia Svevo's papers.
35. Interview with Signora Livia Svevo, 1956.
36. Interview with Daniel Hummel, 1956.
37. Letter to Harriet Weaver, Dec. 22, 1922, *Letters*, p. 199.
38. Idem.
39. Letter to Harriet Weaver, July 11, 1924.
40. Adrienne Monnier, 'La Traduction d' "Ulysses," ' *Mercure de France*, CCCIX (May 1, 1950), p. 37.
41. Interview with Adrienne Monnier, 1954.
42. Letter to Valery Larbaud, July 28, 1924, *Letters*, p. 218.
43. Letter to Harriet Weaver, Nov. 9, 1924.
44. Letter to Harriet Weaver, Dec. 30, 1924.
45. Letter to Robert McAlmon, Feb. 29, 1924, *Letters*, p. 212.
46. Sisley Huddleston, *Paris Salons, Cafés, Studios*, p. 219.
47. Letter to Harriet Weaver, April 8, 1928.
48. Letter to Robert McAlmon, Feb. 1924.
49. Letter to Harriet Weaver, March 7, 1924, *Letters*, p. 213.
50. Letter to Harriet Weaver, March 24, 1924, *Letters*, p. 213.
51. Letter to Harriet Weaver, March 15, 1924.
52. Letter to Harriet Weaver, May 24, 1924, *Letters*, p. 214.
53. Interview with Arthur Power, 1953.

54. Account by Mrs. Phyllis Moss Stein in Patricia Hutchins, *James Joyce's World,* p. 149.
55. William Carlos Williams, *Autobiography,* p. 189.
56. Ibid. p. 190.
57. Idem.
58. Letter to Harriet Weaver, May 24, 1924, *Letters,* pp. 214-15.
59. Interview with Frank Budgen, 1956; Budgen, *Further Recollections of James Joyce,* p. 13.
60. Letter to Harriet Weaver, June 27, 1924.
61. Idem.
62. Letter to Harriet Weaver, Sept. 27, 1925, *Letters,* p. 234.
63. Letter to me from Myron Nutting, 1955.
64. Notebook in the Lockwood Memorial Library of the University of Buffalo.
65. Letter to Harriet Weaver, July 11, 1924.
66. Letter to Larbaud, July 29, 1924, *Letters,* p. 218.
67. Letter to Harriet Weaver, Aug. 16, 1924, *Letters,* p. 220.
68. Lloyd Morris, *A Threshold in the Sun* (New York, 1943), p. 243.
69. See letter to Harriet Weaver, Aug. 16, 1924, *Letters,* p. 220.
70. Cablegram to Mrs. Murray, Nov. 1, 1924, in National Library of Ireland.
71. *Letters,* pp. 221-2.
72. Letter to Harriet Weaver, Dec. 30, 1924.
73. Letter to Harriet Weaver, Jan. 13, 1925, *Letters,* pp. 225-6.
74. Letter to Harriet Weaver, Feb. 26, 1925.
75. This is clear from Harriet Weaver's letter to Joyce, Feb. 24, 1925.
76. Letter to Harriet Weaver, March 25, 1925.
77. Diary of Helen (Mrs. Myron) Nutting.
78. Reminiscences of Mrs. Helen Joyce.
79. Simone Téry, *L'Ile des Bardes* (Paris, 1925), quoted in Maria Jolas, ed., *A James Joyce Yearbook* (Paris, 1949), p. 189.
80. *Letters,* p. 227.
81. Letter to Harriet Weaver, June 13, 1925, *Letters,* pp. 227-8.
82. Letter to Harriet Weaver, July 27, 1925, *Letters,* p. 230.
83. Letter to Harriet Weaver, Aug. 15, 1925, *Letters,* pp. 231-2.
84. Letter to Harriet Weaver, Jan. 20, 1926, *Letters,* p. 239.
85. *Letters,* p. 234.
86. Letter to S. Joyce, Sept. 28, 1925.
87. Letter to Robert McAlmon, Dec. 8, 1925.
88. Diary of Helen (Mrs. Myron) Nutting.
89. Letter to Harriet Weaver, Jan. 20, 1926.
90. Interview with Henri Michaux, 1954.

Chapter XXXIII

1. Letter to Harriet Weaver, Jan. 20, 1926, *Letters,* p. 239.
2. Interview with Jacques Benoîst-Méchin, 1954.
3. Letter from Harriet Weaver to Joyce, Feb. 15, 1926.
4. Idem.
5. Letter from Ettore Schmitz to Joyce, Feb. 15, 1926, in *Inventario,* ii (Spring, 1949), pp. 126-8.
6. Archibald Henderson, 'Literature and Science,' *Fortnightly Review,* cxxii (Oct. 1924), pp. 519-21.
7. Letter to Harriet Weaver, April 17, 1926.
8. Patrick Tuohy twice sent a solicitor's clerk to him in July 1926, but John Joyce delayed answering the questions until Tuohy himself appeared to take notes.
9. Interview with Stuart Gilbert, 1954.

10. Letter to Harriet Weaver, Sept. 24, 1926, *Letters*, p. 245.
11. Letter to S. Joyce, Nov. 5, 1926, Gorman papers.
12. 'Bro. James Lyons Writes' (article), *Columbus Blade*, Nov. 26, 1926, p. 12.
13. Letter to Harriet Weaver, Sept. 24, 1926, *Letters*, p. 245.
14. *The Letters of Thomas Wolfe*, ed. Elizabeth Nowell (New York, 1956), pp. 114-15.
15. Letter to Aline Bernstein, Sept. 7?, 1928, ibid. pp. 138-9.
16. Arthur Mizener, *The Far Side of Paradise* (Boston, 1951), p. 133.
17. Letter in the Princeton University Library. See also Fitzgerald's caricature of Joyce in *Les Années vingt* (exhibition catalogue, Paris, 1959), p. 80.
18. Elliot Paul, 'Farthest North,' *Bookman* (New York), LXXV (May 1932), pp. 156-63. See also *Letters of Sherwood Anderson*, ed. Howard Mumford Jones and Walter B. Rideout (Boston, 1953), p. 169.
19. *Letters*, p. 245.
20. Letter to Harriet Weaver, Oct. 16, 1925.
21. Letter to Harriet Weaver, Nov. 8, 1926, *Letters*, p. 246.
22. Idem.
23. Letter to me from Julien Levy, 1955.
24. *Letters*, pp. 247-8.
25. Letter from Harriet Weaver to Joyce, Nov. 20, 1926.
26. *Letters of Ezra Pound*, p. 202.
27. Letter to Harriet Weaver, Dec. 21, 1926.
28. Letter to Ezra Pound, Nov. 1927.
29. Idem.
30. Letter to S. Joyce, Nov. 5, 1926, in Gorman papers.
31. Interview with Mrs. Boezema Delimata, 1953.
32. Letter to Harriet Weaver, Jan. 16, 1927; see also letter to her, Feb. 1, 1927, *Letters*, p. 249.
33. Undated letter from Pound.
34. *Letters of Ezra Pound*, p. 206.
35. Idem.
36. Letter to Ezra Pound, March 2, 1927.
37. Letter to Harriet Weaver, May 28, 1929.
38. Letter to Valery Larbaud, Jan. 26, 1926.
39. Joyce wrote this limerick at Versailles in 1933.
40. Interview with Mrs. Maria Jolas, 1954.
41. Robert McAlmon, *Being Geniuses Together*, p. 251.
42. Letter to me from William Bird, 1954.
43. Interview with Claud W. Sykes, 1954.
44. Gillet, *Claybook for James Joyce*, p. 59.
45. Letter to Harriet Weaver, Feb. 18, 1927.
46. Letters from Harriet Weaver to Joyce, Feb. 11, Feb. 19, and Sept. 17, 1927.
47. Letter to Harriet Weaver, Feb. 18, 1927.
48. Idem.
49. Letter to Harriet Weaver, March 16, 1927.
50. *Letters*, p. 252.
51. Letter to Harriet Weaver, May 20, 1927, *Letters*, pp. 253-4.
52. Elliot Paul, 'Farthest North,' *Bookman*, LXXV (May 1932), pp. 156-63.
53. Interview with Gilbert Seldes, 1958.
54. Letter to Harriet Weaver, May 31, 1927, *Letters*, p. 256.
55. Letter to Michael Healy, July 1, 1927, *Letters*, p. 256.
56. Idem.
57. Letter to Harriet Weaver, May 31, 1927, *Letters*, p. 254.
58. James Stephens, 'The James Joyce I Knew,' *Listener*, XXXVI (Oct. 24, 1940), p. 566.
59. George Slocombe, *The Tumult and the Shouting* (New York, 1936), p. 221.

60. *Letters*, p. 258.
61. Wyndham Lewis, *Time and Western Man* (London, 1927), p. 93.
62. Wyndham Lewis, *Rude Assignment* (London, 1950), p. 55.
63. This is clear from Harriet Weaver's letter to Joyce, Sept. 2, 1927.
64. Interview with Wyndham Lewis, 1953.
65. Wyndham Lewis, *Time and Western Man*, p. 108.
66. Padraic Colum, *Our Friend James Joyce*, p. 145.
67. Wyndham Lewis, *Time and Western Man*, p. 126.
68. Frank Budgen, *Further Recollections of James Joyce*, p. 10, and interview with Budgen, 1956.
69. Quoted in Harriet Weaver's answering letter, Sept. 2, 1927.
70. Yeats, *A Vision* (London, 1925 [1926]), pp. 211-12.
71. *Finnegans Wake*, p. 419. See Geoffrey Wagner, *Wyndham Lewis* (New Haven, 1957), pp. 181-8.
72. *Letters*, p. 251.
73. Letter from Harriet Weaver to Joyce, April 26, 1927.
74. *Letters*, p. 252.
75. Letter to Harriet Weaver, Oct. 8, 1927.
76. Sisley Huddleston, *Paris Salons, Cafés, Studios*, p. 214.
77. Letter to Harriet Weaver, Oct. 28, 1927, *Letters*, p. 259.
78. Undated letter from Archibald MacLeish to Joyce.
79. Max Eastman, *The Literary Mind* (New York, 1931), pp. 99-100.
80. Letter to Harriet Weaver, Nov. 4, 1927, *Letters*, p. 260.
81. Letter to Harriet Weaver, Nov. 9, 1927, *Letters*, p. 261.
82. In a letter from Harriet Weaver to Joyce of March 30, 1928, she says she may be becoming a 'Jacobite' or even a 'Joycean.'
83. Letter to me from Archibald MacLeish, 1954.
84. Diary of Helen (Mrs. Myron) Nutting.
85. *Letters*, p. 199.
86. Letter to Valery Larbaud, March 28, 1928.
87. Letter to Valery Larbaud, March 28, 1928.
88. Letter to Harriet Weaver, April 8, 1928.
89. Letter from Larbaud to Joyce, June 14, 1928.
90. Letter to Harriet Weaver, April 16, 1928.
91. Letter to Frank Budgen, May 27, 1928.
92. Padraic Colum, *Our Friend James Joyce*, p. 183.
93. Letter to Harriet Weaver, June 3, 1928.
94. Letter to me from Rebecca West, 1958.
95. *Letters*, pp. 266-9, with some additions.
96. In Joyce's *Letters*, pp. 274-5.
97. Letter to Harriet Weaver, Dec. 2, 1928, *Letters*, p. 277.
98. Idem.
99. Interview with Arthur Power, 1953.

Chapter XXXIV

1. Interview with John Sullivan, 1953. Sullivan had called on John Joyce at James Joyce's request.
2. Interview with Niall Sheridan, 1953; compare 'Interview with Mr. John Stanislaus Joyce,' *A James Joyce Yearbook*, ed. Maria Jolas (Paris, 1949), p. 169.
3. Letter card to Harriet Weaver, April 26, 1929.
4. Letter to me from William Bird, 1954.
5. Interview with Samuel Beckett, 1953; see also letter to Harriet Weaver, May 28, 1929, *Letters*, p. 280.
6. Letter to Harriet Weaver, Oct. 19, 1929, *Letters*, p. 285.

7. Interview with Mrs. Maria Jolas, 1953.

8. Letter to Valery Larbaud, July 30, 1929, *Letters*, p. 284.

9. Letter to Valery Larbaud, July 30, 1929, *Letters*, p. 283.

10. Letter to Harriet Weaver, May 28, 1929, p. 281.

11. Letter to me from Robert McAlmon, 1955.

12. Letter to me from Caresse Crosby, 1957.

13. Caresse Crosby, *The Passionate Years* (New York, 1953), p. 184.

14. Letter to Harriet Weaver, May 27, 1929, *Letters*, p. 279.

15. Interview with C. Brancusi, 1954.

16. Letter to Harriet Weaver, May 27, 1929, *Letters*, p. 279.

17. Information from James F. Spoerri. Compare letter to Harriet Weaver, Jan. 17, 1932, *Letters*, p. 312.

18. Caresse Crosby, *The Passionate Years*, p. 187.

19. Interview with Nino Frank, 1954.

20. Interview with Stuart Gilbert, 1954; letter to Harriet Weaver, Sept. 27, 1930, *Letters*, p. 294.

21. *Letters*, p. 309.

22. Dorothy Brett, *Lawrence and Brett* (Philadelphia, 1933), p. 81.

23. D. H. Lawrence, *Phoenix*, ed. Edward D. McDonald (London, 1936), p. 517; see also pp. 250 and 270.

24. Letter to Valery Larbaud, July 30, 1929, p. 283.

25. Idem.

26. Thomas E. Connolly, *The Personal Library of James Joyce*, p. 9.

27. Letter to Harriet Weaver, July 16, 1929, *Letters*, p. 282.

28. Letter to Harriet Weaver, July 16, 1929, *Letters*, p. 282.

29. Letter from George Moore to John Eglinton.

30. Idem.

31. Quoted in letter from George Moore to Louis Gillet, Aug. 20, 1931, in Gillet, *Claybook for James Joyce*, p. 33.

32. Ibid. p. 33.

33. Letter from George Moore to Joyce, Sept. 11, 1929.

34. Quoted in Nancy Cunard, *GM, Memories of George Moore* (London, 1956), p. 162.

35. Gillet, *Claybook for James Joyce*, pp. 32-3.

36. Letter to Harriet Weaver, Nov. 22, 1929, *Letters*, p. 288.

37. Letter to Harriet Weaver, March 18, 1930, *Letters*, p. 290.

38. Interview with John Sullivan, 1953.

39. Idem.

40. Letter to John Sullivan, May 20, 1932.

41. Frank Budgen, *James Joyce and the Making of 'Ulysses,'* p. 16.

42. Gorman, p. 346.

43. Undated note, about 1932.

44. Interview with Samuel Beckett, 1953.

45. Frank Budgen, 'James Joyce,' in Givens, ed., *James Joyce: Two Decades of Criticism*, pp. 24-5.

46. Interview with John Sullivan, 1953.

47. Letter to Harriet Weaver, March 18, 1930, *Letters*, p. 291.

48. Ibid. p. 290.

49. Idem.

50. *Critical Writings*, pp. 258-68.

51. Padraic Colum, *Our Friend James Joyce*, p. 173.

52. Interview with John Sullivan, 1953.

53. Interview with Stuart Gilbert, 1954.

54. Letter to me from William Bird, 1955.

55. Letter to me from Aldous Huxley, 1957.

56. Interview with T. W. Pugh, 1953.

57. Borach's letter is dated Feb. 11, 1930.
58. Letter dated Feb. 14, 1930.
59. Letter to me from Aldous Huxley, 1957.
60. Carola Giedion-Welcker, 'James Joyce in Zürich,' *Horizon,* xviii (Sept. 1948), p. 210.
61. Letter from George Moore to Joyce, May 10, 1930.
62. Report of Dr. Vogt, on Georges Borach's stationery, dated June 1930.
63. Letter from Nora Joyce to Harriet Weaver, June 15, 1930.
64. Translated from the French.
65. This account is based upon articles in *L'Intermédiaire,* July 5, 1930, and in the *London Daily Express,* July 1, 1930.
66. Letter to Harriet Weaver, March 18, 1930, *Letters,* p. 291.
67. Letter from Paul Léon to Frank Budgen, 1933, quoted in Budgen, *Further Recollections of James Joyce,* pp. 13-14.
68. Interview with Sigfried Giedion and Carola Giedion-Welcker, 1956.
69. Letter to me from Nancy Cunard, 1957.
70. Idem.
71. Letter from Sir Thomas Beecham to Joyce, Sept. 22, 1930.
72. Letter to George Antheil, Sept. 7, 1930, *Letters,* p. 292.
73. Letter to George Antheil, Jan. 3, 1931, *Letters,* pp. 297-8.
74. Ibid. p. 297.
75. Letter to Harriet Weaver, Nov. 22, 1930, *Letters,* p. 295.
76. Interview with Dr. Daniel Brody, 1954.
77. Letter to Georg Goyert, Oct. 22, 1932, in Croessmann Collection at Southern Illinois University.
78. Interview with Dr. Daniel Brody, 1954.
79. Interview with Samuel Beckett, 1953.
80. Letter from Paul Léon to Joyce, April 25, 1930.
81. Letter (in French) from Paul Léon to Alexander Léon, in Mme Lucie Léon's possession.
82. Interview with Mme Lucie Léon, 1954.
83. Paul Léon, 'In Memory of Joyce,' *A James Joyce Yearbook,* p. 119.
84. Diary of Helen (Mrs. Myron) Nutting.
85. Paul Léon, 'In Memory of Joyce,' *A James Joyce Yearbook,* p. 120.
86. Frank Budgen, *Further Recollections of James Joyce,* p. 7.
87. Interview with Stuart Gilbert, 1954.
88. Diary of Helen (Mrs. Myron) Nutting, who was herself good-looking.
89. Interview with Arthur Power, 1953.
90. Mary Colum, *Life and the Dream* (New York, 1947), p. 398.
91. Interview with Mrs. Maria Jolas, 1953.
92. A letter from Herbert Gorman to Joyce, Jan. 3, 1931, complains of the delaying tactics he has encountered from some people.
93. J. F. Byrne, *Silent Years,* p. 145.
94. Letter from Paul Léon to Joyce, May 13, 1931; compare Philippe Soupault, *Souvenirs de James Joyce* (Algiers, 1943), pp. 73-8.
95. Peggy Guggenheim, *Out of This Century* (New York, 1946), p. 130.
96. Letter relayed by Harriet Weaver to Joyce, Dec. 30, 1930.
97. Letter from Louis Gillet to Joyce, Jan. 7, 1931; see also letter from Joyce to Harriet Weaver, Feb. 18, 1931, *Letters,* pp. 300-301.
98. Letter to Harriet Weaver, Feb. 18, 1931, *Letters,* pp. 300-301.
99. *Letters,* p. 232.
100. Mary Colum, *Life and the Dream,* pp. 394-5.
101. Mary Colum, *Our Friend James Joyce,* p. 130.
102. Padraic Colum, ibid. pp. 154, 160; *Finnegans Wake,* pp. 554, 550.
103. Frank Budgen, *Further Recollections of James Joyce,* p. 6, and interview with Budgen, 1956.

104. Interview with Dr. Carola Giedion-Welcker, 1954.

105. Interview with Signora Livia Svevo, 1954.

106. Letter to Signora Livia Schmitz (Svevo), Sept. 24, 1928, 'Carteggio Inedito, Italo Svevo—James Joyce,' *Inventario*, II (Spring 1949), p. 132.

107. Letter from Lucia Joyce to Signora Livia Schmitz (Svevo), Jan. 25, 1931.

108. Letter from Valery Larbaud to Joyce, March 15, 1931.

109. Letter to S. Joyce, March 29, 1932.

110. Letter from Ford Madox Ford to Joyce, March 9, 1931.

111. Letter to Harriet Weaver, Feb. 16, 1931.

112. Letter to me from Harriet Weaver, 1957.

113. Letter to Harriet Weaver, March 11, 1931, *Letters*, p. 302.

114. Leon Edel, 'A Paris Letter,' *Canadian Forum* (April 1931), p. 460; 'Une Soirée James Joyce,' *Les Nouvelles Littéraires*, April 4, 1931.

115. Robert McAlmon, *Being Geniuses Together*, pp. 285-6.

116. Letter to Harriet Weaver, April 17, 1931.

117. Letter to Padraic and Mary Colum, July 18, 1931.

118. Idem.

119. Interview with Arthur Power, 1953.

120. Interview with Mrs. Kathleen Barnacle Griffin, 1953.

121. *Finnegans Wake*, p. 556.

122. Interview with Mrs. Griffin, 1953.

123. Letter from Harriet Weaver to Joyce, July 17, 1931.

124. Letter to Dr. Daniel Brody, July 30, 1931, *Letters*, p. 305.

125. Letter from Harold Nicolson to Joyce, Aug. 13, 1931.

126. Letter from Harriet Weaver to Joyce, July 17, 1931.

127. Among Joyce's papers regarding the affair.

128. Letter from editors of *Frankfurter Zeitung* to Ernst Hitchmann, Aug. 13, 1931.

129. Letter from Willi Rothschild to Monro Saw & Co., Sept. 19, 1931.

130. Letter from F. R. D'O. Monro to Joyce, Oct. 6, 1931.

131. Letter from Harriet Weaver to John Sullivan, July 19, 1931.

132. Oliver Gogarty says he heard this from the singer Margaret Bourke-Sheridan. Gogarty, *Intimations*, pp. 62-7.

133. T. J. Kiernan, quoted on B.B.C. broadcast, 'Portrait of James Joyce.'

134. Letter to Harriet Weaver, April 20, 1932, *Letters*, p. 317.

135. Letter to Harriet Weaver, Nov. 21, 1931.

136. Stuart Gilbert, 'Introduction,' *Letters*, p. 38.

137. Michael J. Lennon, 'James Joyce,' *Catholic World*, CXXXII (March 1931), pp. 641-52.

138. Letter to Harriet Weaver, Jan. 28, 1932, *Letters*, p. 313.

139. *Letters*, p. 310. This telegram is in the Croessmann Collection at Southern Illinois University.

140. Interview with Mrs. May Monaghan, 1953.

141. Interview with Eva Joyce, 1953.

142. Letter from Michael Healy to Joyce, Jan. 1, 1932.

143. *Letters*, p. 311.

144. Ibid. p. 312.

145. Letter to Harriet Weaver, July 22, 1932.

146. Idem.

147. Louis Gillet, *Claybook for James Joyce*, p. 113.

148. Eugene Jolas, 'My Friend James Joyce,' in Givens, ed., *James Joyce: Two Decades of Criticism*, p. 9.

149. Interview with Mrs. Maria Jolas, 1953.

150. Louis Gillet, *Claybook for James Joyce*, p. 132.

151. Interview with Mrs. Maria Jolas, 1953, and newspaper clippings.

152. Original manuscript with this date is in possession of Robert N. Kastor. Joyce

was modest about its quality, and wrote to Louis Gillet, '*Je suis papa mais pas poète.*' Gillet, *Claybook for James Joyce*, p. 17.

CHAPTER XXXV

1. *Ulysses*, p. 193 (184).
2. Interview with Frank Budgen, 1953.
3. Interview with Mrs. Maria Jolas, 1953.
4. Peggy Guggenheim, *Out of This Century*, p. 197.
5. Interview with Samuel Beckett, 1953.
6. Idem.
7. Interview with Samuel Beckett, 1954.
8. Frank Budgen, 'Further Recollections of James Joyce,' *Partisan Review*, XXXIII (Fall, 1956), p. 532.
9. Interview with Samuel Beckett, 1954.
10. Idem.
11. Idem, and interviews with Mrs. Maria Jolas and Mme Lucie Léon, 1953.
12. Letter to me from William Bird, 1955.
13. Idem.
14. Mary Colum, *Life and the Dream*, p. 396.
15. Interview with Mme Lucie Léon, 1954.
16. Interview with George Joyce, 1954.
17. Interview with Mme Lucie Léon, 1954.
18. Nino Frank observed her in this state, walking on the Champs-Élysées. Interview with Frank, 1953.
19. Interview with Mme Lucie Léon, 1954.
20. Letter from Paul Léon to Harriet Weaver, quoting Joyce, July 19, 1935.
21. Letter to Valery Larbaud, May 13, 1932.
22. Mary Colum, *Life and the Dream*, pp. 396-7.
23. Lucia Joyce papers.
24. Letter to Harriet Weaver, 1932.
25. James F. Spoerri, 'The Odyssey Press Edition of James Joyce's "Ulysses,"' *Papers* of the Bibliographical Society of America, L (Second Quarter, 1956); see also R. F. Roberts, 'Bibliographical Notes on James Joyce's "Ulysses,"' *Colophon* (New York), New Series 1 (Spring, 1936), pp. 565-79.
26. Letter from Harriet Weaver to Joyce, May 13, 1932.
27. Letter to T. S. Eliot, Feb. 22, 1932, *Letters*, p. 315.
28. Alfred Kerr, 'Joyce in England,' tr. by Joseph Prescott, Marvin Magalaner, ed., *A James Joyce Miscellany* (New York, 1957), 37-43.
29. Louis Gillet, *Claybook for James Joyce*, p. 110.
30. Gerald Griffin, *The Wild Geese* (London, 1938), p. 28.
31. Sisley Huddleston, *Back to Montparnasse* (Philadelphia, 1931), pp. 195-6.
32. Letter to George Joyce, Aug. 28, 1935.
33. Letter to me from Professor Hans Richter, 1958.
34. Letter to me from Louis Zukofsky, 1954.
35. See letter to James Stephens, May 7, 1932, *Letters*, pp. 316-19.
36. Letter to me from William Bird, 1955.
37. Letter to Harriet Weaver, July 10, 1932, *Letters*, p. 321.
38. Letter to John Sullivan, Aug. 25, 1932.
39. Letter to Frank Budgen, dated 'Bundesfeier, 1932.'
40. Interview with Dr. Arthur Collinson by Professor Robert Mayo, 1955.
41. Letter to Harriet Weaver, July 10, 1932, *Letters*, p. 321.
42. Letter to Harriet Weaver, Aug. 6, 1932.
43. See letter to Harriet Weaver, Dec. 7, 1931, *Letters*, p. 308.
44. Letters to Harriet Weaver, Sept. 22, 1932, and to Frank Budgen, Oct. 9, 1932.
45. Eugene Jolas, 'My Friend James Joyce,' in Givens, ed., *James Joyce: Two*

Decades of Criticism, p. 10. Compare the article as it appeared in *Partisan Review,* VIII (March-April, 1941), pp. 82-93.
46. Idem.
47. *Letters,* p. 325.
48. Eugene Jolas, 'My Friend James Joyce,' in Givens, ed., *James Joyce: Two Decades of Criticism,* p. 14.
49. Diary of David Fleischman, July 21, 1938.
50. Letter to Harriet Weaver, Nov. 11, 1932, *Letters,* p. 327.
51. Idem.
52. Letter to Harriet Weaver, Oct. 21, 1932.
53. Interview with Mme Lucie Léon, 1953.
54. Letter to Harriet Weaver, Nov. 25, 1932, *Letters,* p. 328.
55. Idem.
56. Letter to Harriet Weaver, Jan. 18, 1933, *Letters,* pp. 331-3.
57. Letter from Paul Léon to Harriet Weaver, March 23, 1933.
58. Letter from Paul Léon to Harriet Weaver, April 25, 1953.
59. Letter to S. Joyce, May 30, 1933.
60. Notes by Louis Gillet, in Mme Gillet's possession.
61. Interview with John Sullivan, 1953.
62. Lucia Joyce papers.
63. Frank Budgen, *Further Recollections of James Joyce,* p. 4.
64. Ibid. p. 5.
65. Morris L. Ernst, *The Censor Marches On* (New York, 1940).
66. Idem.
67. Decision by Judge John M. Woolsey, reprinted in *Ulysses* (New York, 1934), p. xiv.
68. Ernst Reichl, the book's designer, gives these details in *Linotype News,* Feb. 1934.
69. Idem.
70. Morris L. Ernst, 'Foreword,' *Ulysses* (New York, 1934), p. viii.
71. *Letters,* p. 338.
72. Letter to Frank Budgen, April 25, 1934, in Slocum Collection at Yale.
73. Letter to Harriet Weaver, Oct. 27, 1931.
74. Lucie Noel [Léon], *James Joyce and Paul L. Léon: The Story of a Friendship* (New York, Gotham Book Mart, 1950), pp. 24-5.
75. 'James Joyce à la Coupole,' *Nouvelles Littéraires,* March 3, 1934, p. 6.
76. Interview with Mrs. Maria Jolas, 1954.
77. Interview with Dr. Carola Giedion-Welcker, 1954.
78. Idem.
79. Letter to Harriet Weaver, April 24, 1934, *Letters,* p. 339.
80. Letter to Frank Budgen, May 6, 1934, *Letters,* p. 340.
81. See Gorman, p. 345.
82. Interview with Othmar Schoeck by Dr. Alfred Dutli, 1955.
83. Idem.
84. *Critical Writings,* pp. 271-3.
85. Gorman papers.
86. *Finnegans Wake,* p. 259.
87. Letter to me from Mme France Raphael, 1955.
88. Letter to me from Armand Petitjean, 1958.
89. Letter to Mme France Raphael, in her possession.
90. Letter to me from Mme France Raphael, 1958.
91. Letter from Harriet Weaver to Joyce, May 10, 1934, makes clear that Joyce had complained to her about McAlmon's book.
92. Letter to me from Robert McAlmon, 1956.
93. Letter in possession of Robert Kastor.
94. *Letters,* p. 343.

95. Letter from Nora Joyce to George and Helen Joyce, about July 12, 1934.
96. *Letters*, pp. 341-2.
97. Letter to Harriet Weaver, July 10, 1934.
98. Letter to George and Helen Joyce, July 13, 1934.
99. Letter to Harriet Weaver, July 28, 1934.
100. Letter to T. W. Pugh, Aug. 6, 1934, in his possession.
101. Interview with Mme Lucie Léon, 1953, and letter to me from Mrs. Maria Jolas, 1959.
102. Letters to Frank Budgen, Sept. 5, 1934, and to George and Helen Joyce, Sept. 9, 1934.
103. Letter to George and Helen Joyce, Dec. 17, 1934.
104. Lucia Joyce papers.
105. Letter to Harriet Weaver, Sept. 22, 1934. Compare *Letters*, p. 346.
106. Interview with Professor Sigfried Giedion and Dr. Carola Giedion-Welcker, 1953.
107. Letter to George and Helen Joyce, Oct. 16, 1934.
108. Letter to Harriet Weaver, Oct. 21, 1934, *Letters*, p. 350.
109. *Letters*, pp. 349-50.
110. Ibid. p. 350-51.
111. Letter to Harriet Weaver, Dec. 17, 1934, *Letters*, pp. 353-4.
112. Cable dated Oct. 26, 1934.
113. Letter to Harriet Weaver, Dec. 17, 1934, *Letters*, pp. 353-4.
114. Letter to C. P. Curran, Aug. 10, 1935, *Letters*, p. 379.
115. Interview with Oscar Schwarz, 1956.
116. Interview with Mme Lucie Léon, 1954.
117. Letter to George Joyce, Nov. 21, 1934; also letter to him of Feb. 19, 1935.
118. Letter to George Joyce, Dec. 27, 1934.
119. Idem.
120. Letter from Paul Léon to Joyce, Dec. 14, 1934.
121. Interview with Dr. Carl G. Jung, 1953.
122. Letter from Harriet Weaver to Joyce, Feb. 25, 1935.
123. Interview with Dr. Carl G. Jung, 1953.
124. Idem.
125. Patricia Hutchins, *James Joyce's World*, pp. 184-5.
126. Ernest Jones, *Sigmund Freud* (London, 1955), vol. II, p. 165.
128. Letter to George and Helen Joyce, Feb. 5, 1935.
129. Letter to George and Helen Joyce, Feb. 19, 1935.
130. Padraic Colum, 'Portrait of James Joyce,' *Dublin Magazine*, VII (April-June 1932), p. 48.
131. Letter to Harriet Weaver, May 1, 1935, *Letters*, p. 366; and letter to her, April 7, 1935.
132. Letter from Harriet Weaver to Joyce, Feb. 17, 1935.
133. Idem.
134. Letter from Harriet Weaver to Joyce, Feb. 28, 1935.
135. Letter from Harriet Weaver to Joyce, March 17, 1935.
136. Letter to Harriet Weaver, April 7, 1935, partly in *Letters*, p. 361.
137. Letter to Harriet Weaver, May 1, 1935, *Letters*, p. 367.
138. Ibid. p. 366.
139. Ibid. pp. 365-6.
140. Letter to Lucia Joyce, May 29, 1935.
141. *Letters*, p. 370.
142. Interview with Mrs. Helen Joyce, 1954, and letter to me from Philippe Soupault, 1958.
143. Letter to Harriet Weaver, April 7, 1935, *Letters*, p. 362.
144. Letter to Harriet Weaver, May 1, 1935, *Letters*, p. 367.
145. Ibid. p. 366.

146. Interview with Mrs. Maria Jolas, 1953.
147. Letter to Mrs. Eileen Joyce Schaurek, April 27?, 1935.
148. Letter to Lucia Joyce, April 27, 1935, *Letters*, p. 364.
149. Interview with Mrs. Bertha Schaurek Delimata, 1953.
150. Idem.
151. Letter to Lucia Joyce, May 29, 1935.
152. Interview with Mrs. Kathleen Barnacle Griffin, 1953; letter to George and Helen Joyce, July 1935, *Letters*, p. 374.
153. Letter to Michael Healy, July 1935; see also letter to Healy, June 28, 1935, *Letters*, pp. 372-3.
154. Letter from Paul Léon to Harriet Weaver, July 19, 1935.
155. Letter to George and Helen Joyce, July 16, 1935.
156. Letter to Harriet Weaver, Oct. 11, 1935, *Letters*, p. 385.
157. Letter from Harriet Weaver to Joyce, Oct. 19, 1935.

Chapter XXXVI

1. Letter from Paul Léon to Harriet Weaver, July 19, 1935.
2. This took place at the end of May 1936, and was successful.
3. Alfred Kerr, 'Joyce in England,' tr. by Joseph Prescott, Marvin Magalaner, ed., *A James Joyce Miscellany*, pp. 37-43.
4. Letters from S. Joyce to Joyce, April 24 and May 11, 1936.
5. Letter from S. Joyce to Joyce, May 20, 1936.
6. Idem.
7. Letter from S. Joyce to Joyce, June 1, 1936.
8. Letter to Harriet Weaver, June 9, 1936.
9. *Letters*, pp. 387-8.
10. Interview with Tom Kristensen, 1956.
11. Interview with Mrs. Kastor Hansen, 1956.
12. Interview with Kai Friis-Møller, 1956.
13. Interview with Tom Kristensen, 1956.
14. Interview with Kai Friis-Møller, 1956.
15. This card was in Sullivan's possession in 1953.
16. Article on Hemingway, 'An American Storyteller,' *Time* (Dec. 13, 1954), p. 75.
17. Letter to me from Ernst Robert Curtius, 1954.
18. Letter to James Stephens, Sept. 18, 1936.
19. At the Lockwood Memorial Library of the University of Buffalo.
20. Letter to James Stephens, in Mrs. Stephens's possession.
21. Interview with Paul Ruggiero, 1953.
22. Interview with S. Joyce, 1954.
23. Interview with John Sullivan, 1953.
24. These inscriptions are in Mme Léon's possession. See her book, *James Joyce and Paul L. Léon*, p. 23.
25. Gorman papers; compare Gorman, p. 346.
26. Interview with Mrs. Maria Jolas, 1953.
27. Interview with Samuel Beckett, 1953.
28. Interview with Mrs. Maria Jolas, 1956.
29. This letter is in the possession of David Fleischman.
30. Interview with Dr. Carola Giedion-Welcker, 1956.
31. Interview with Nino Frank, 1953.
32. Interview with George Pelorson, 1953.
33. Interview with Samuel Beckett, 1954.
34. In *Contempo* (Chapel Hill, N.C.), III (Feb. 15, 1934), p. 3.
35. Interview with Samuel Beckett, 1953.

36. Interview with Frank O'Connor, 1952; see W. B. Yeats's letter to Lady Gregory, May 19, 1929, *The Letters of W. B. Yeats,* ed. Allan Wade, p. 764.
37. Interview with Samuel Beckett, 1954.
38. Idem.
39. Letter to Lucia Joyce, June 1, 1934.
40. Letter to me from Terence White Gervais, 1954.
41. Interview with Jacob Schwartz, 1956.
42. Max Eastman, *The Literary Mind,* p. 100.
43. *Finnegans Wake,* p. 120.
44. Letter to Myron Nutting, in his possession.
45. Letter to me from Nancy Cunard, 1957. His remarks are printed in *Critical Writings,* pp. 274-5.
46. Letter to C. P. Curran, June 8, 1937, *Letters,* p. 392.
47. Letter to C. P. Curran, Aug. 6, 1937, *Letters,* p. 395.
48. Letter to C. P. Curran, Aug. 19, 1937, *Letters,* p. 396.
49. Letter to Frank Budgen, Sept. 20, 1937, *Letters,* p. 397.
50. Letters to Frank Budgen, Aug. 28 and Sept. 9, 1937.
51. Letter from Gorman to John Farrar, Sept. 14, 1937.
52. *Pastimes of James Joyce* (New York, published by the Joyce Memorial Fund Committee, 1941), unpaged.
53. Letter to Helen Joyce, April 6, 1938.
54. Interview with James Johnson Sweeney, 1956.
55. Jacques Mercanton in *Labyrinthe* (Geneva), No. 1 (Oct. 14, 1944), p. 2.
56. Diary of David Fleischman, Aug. 2, 1938.
57. Eugene Jolas, 'My Friend James Joyce,' in Givens, ed., *James Joyce: Two Decades of Criticism,* pp. 16-17.
58. Interview with Dr. Carola Giedion-Welcker, 1954.
59. Interview with Samuel Beckett, 1954.
60. Interview with Jacques Mercanton, 1956.
61. Interview with Mrs. Maria Jolas, 1954.
62. Idem.
63. Diary of David Fleischman, Aug. 2, 1938.
64. Interview with Mme Lucie Léon, 1954.
65. Lucie Noel [Léon], *James Joyce and Paul L. Léon,* p. 10.
66. Interview with Jacques Mercanton, 1956.
67. Lucie Noel [Léon], *James Joyce and Paul L. Léon,* p. 30.
68. Padraic Colum, *Our Friend James Joyce,* p. 230; interview with Samuel Beckett, 1954. Stuart Gilbert remembers Joyce's feeling of relief that war had been averted.
69. Frank Budgen, 'Joyce's Chapters of Going Forth by Day,' in Givens, ed., *James Joyce: Two Decades of Criticism,* p. 367.
70. Louis Gillet, *Stèle pour James Joyce* (Marseilles, 1941), pp. 164-5.
71. Eugene Jolas, 'My Friend James Joyce,' in Givens, ed., *James Joyce: Two Decades of Criticism,* p. 18.
72. Paul Léon, 'In Memory of Joyce,' *A James Joyce Yearbook,* p. 123.
73. Interview with Samuel Beckett, 1954.
74. Interview with George Pelorson, 1954.
75. Letter to Paul Ruggiero, Nov. 18, 1938, *Letters,* p. 403.
76. Paul Léon, 'In Memory of Joyce,' *A James Joyce Yearbook,* pp. 123-4; Lucie Noel [Léon], *James Joyce and Paul L. Léon,* p. 17.
77. Patricia Hutchins, *James Joyce's World,* p. 189.
78. Louis Gillet, *Claybook for James Joyce,* p. 94.
79. Frank Budgen, 'James Joyce,' in Givens, ed., *James Joyce: Two Decades of Criticism,* p. 26.

CHAPTER XXXVII

1. Interview with Dr. Carola Giedion-Welcker, 1956.
2. Interview with Mrs. Maria Jolas, 1956.
3. Idem.
4. Idem.
5. Letter to Georg Goyert, 1939, in Croessmann Collection at Southern Illinois University Library.
6. Interview with Samuel Beckett, 1956.
7. Letter from Sean O'Casey to Joyce, May 30, 1939.
8. Frank Budgen, 'James Joyce,' in Givens, ed., *James Joyce: Two Decades of Criticism,* p. 26.
9. Interview with Jacques Mercanton, 1956.
10. Louis Gillet, *Claybook for James Joyce,* p. 21.
11. Idem.
12. Idem.
13. Letter to Paul Léon, Sept. 2, 1939.
14. Telegram to George Joyce, Sept. 3, 1939.
15. Letter to George and Helen Joyce, Sept. 3, 1939.
16. Letter to George and Helen Joyce, Sept. 5, 1939.
17. Interview with Dr. Daniel P. O'Brien by Mrs. Adaline Glasheen, 1958.
18. Idem.
19. Interview with Dr. T. Bertrand-Fontaine, 1956.
20. Interview with Samuel Beckett, 1954.
21. Idem.
22. For many details in the account of Joyce at Saint-Gérand-le-Puy I am indebted to Maria Jolas's essay, 'Joyce en 1939-1940,' *Mercure de France,* CCCIX (May 1, 1950), pp. 45-58, and to interviews with Mrs. Jolas in 1953, 1954, and 1956.
23. Letter card to Daniel Brody, Feb. 14, 1940, and letter card to James Laughlin, Feb. 21, 1940.
24. Letter to Fritz Vanderpyl, March 14, 1940.
25. Interview with Mrs. Maria Jolas, 1956.
26. Letter to me from Mrs. Muriel Elliott, 1954.
27. Interview with Stuart Gilbert, 1956.
28. Interview with Mrs. Maria Jolas, 1954.
29. Interview with Stephen Joyce, 1954.
30. Interview with George Pelorson, 1954.
31. 'Silence, Exile & Death,' *Time,* XXXVII (Feb. 10, 1941), pp. 72, 74.
32. Lucie Noel [Léon], *James Joyce and Paul L. Léon,* p. 33.
33. Interview with Mrs. Maria Jolas, 1954.
34. Interview with Robert Kastor, 1955.
35. Interview with George Joyce, 1953.
36. Interview with Mrs. Maria Jolas, 1954.
37. Maria Jolas, 'Joyce en 1939-1940,' *Mercure de France,* CCCIX (May 1, 1950), p. 56.
38. Letter to me from Mrs. Muriel Elliott, 1954.
39. Lucie Noel [Léon], *James Joyce and Paul L. Léon,* p. 36.
40. Interview with Samuel Beckett, 1954.
41. A moving account of Léon's last months of life is in Lucie Noel [Léon], *James Joyce and Paul L. Léon,* pp. 36-43.
42. Letter to me from Mrs. Olga Brauchbar, 1955, and interview with Gustav Zumsteg, 1956.
43. Letter to Edmund Brauchbar, Sept. 11, 1940.
44. I take these dates from correspondence in the possession of Paul Ruggiero.
45. Letter to Armand Petitjean, 1940.

46. Idem, and letter to Louis Gillet, Nov. 23, 1940, *Letters,* p. 424.
47. Interview with Paul Ruggiero, 1953.
48. Letter to Edmund Brauchbar, Nov. 3, 1940.
49. Interview with Stephen Joyce, 1954.
50. Interview with George Joyce, 1953.
51. Idem.
52. Idem.
53. Interview with Stephen Joyce, 1954.
54. Idem.
55. Interview with Jacques Mercanton, 1956.
56. Interview with Paul Ruggiero, 1953.
57. Letter to the Mayor of Zurich, Dec. 20, 1940, *Letters,* p. 427.
58. Heinrich Straumann, 'Last Meeting with Joyce,' *A James Joyce Yearbook,* pp. 109-115.
59. Interview with Stephen Joyce, 1956.
60. Idem.
61. Interview with James Johnson Sweeney, 1957.
62. I have drawn a good deal in these pages on Carola Giedion-Welcker's admirable 'Nachtrag' to the German translation of Gorman's biography of Joyce, 1957.
63. In the Joyce Collection at Cornell.
64. Interview with Gustav Zumsteg and his mother, 1956.
65. Interview with Paul Ruggiero, 1953.
66. Interview with Stephen Joyce, 1954.
67. Interview with George Joyce, 1953.
68. Interview with George Joyce, 1953.
69. B.B.C. program, 'Portrait of James Joyce.'
70. Interview with Nino Frank, 1953.
71. Sandy Campbell, 'Mrs. Joyce of Zurich,' *Harper's Bazaar* (Oct. 1952), p. 171.
72. Interview with Mrs. Maria Jolas, 1954.
73. Interview with John Prudhoe, 1953; he talked with Nora Joyce in Zurich.
74. Interview with George Joyce, 1954.

FURTHER ACKNOWLEDGMENTS

Apart from particular debts which are acknowledged in the preface or in the notes, I am happy to name the persons who, besides those I have mentioned, made it possible for me to assemble this record of Joyce's life:

In Denmark I am indebted to: Jørgen Budtz-Jørgenson, Lt. Col. Mogens Boisen, J. Max, Kai Friis-Møller, Frue Johana Kastor Hansen, Tom Kristensen, Frue Ingeborg Martin, and Ole Vinding.

In England I am indebted to: Lt. Col. P. R. Butler, Alan Denson, John Broadbent and the Royal Literary Fund, Jonathan Cape, Carl Dolmetsch, Gerald Duckworth & Co., T. S. Eliot, C. M. Fone and the Library of the British Foreign Office, Mary Garnham, Librarian of the British Drama League, Terence White Gervais, Patricia Hutchins, the late Wyndham Lewis and Mrs. Lewis, W. K. Magee ('John Eglinton'), the Honorable Harold Nicolson, John Prudhoe, Tristan Rawson, the late George Roberts and Mrs. Roberts, W. R. Rodgers, the late John Rodker, Bertram Rota, Peter du Sautoy, Philip Sayers, Mrs. Violet Schiff, Jacob Schwartz, O. D. Schwarz, Kenneth Smith and the City Library of Carlisle, Mrs. James Stephens, Claud W. Sykes and Mrs. Sykes, the late Allan Wade, and Rebecca West.

In France I must thank the following: Natalie Clifford Barney, Sylvia Beach, Mme Marie Monnier Bécat, Jacques Benoîst-Méchin, Dr. T. Bertrand-Fontaine, André du Bouchet, Mme W. A. Bradley, the late C. Brancusi, Ambassador C. Cremin, Nancy Cunard, Hélène Finsler, Janet Flanner, Jacques Fourcade, Nino Frank, Brendan Gallaher, Gaston Gallimard, Bernard Gheerbrandt, Mme Louis Gillet, Dr. Edward Hartmann, Edme Jeanson and Mme Jeanson, the late Valery Larbaud, Dr. Mérigot de Treigny, Henri Michaux, the late Adrienne Monnier, Dr. P. Morax, Jean Paulhan, George Pelorson, Armand Petitjean, Mme France Raphael, Robert Sage, Mme Ludmila Savitsky, Philippe Soupault, the late John Sullivan and Mrs. Sullivan, August Suter, Mrs. Yasushi Tanaka (Louise Gebhart Cann), Alice B.

Toklas, Fritz Vanderpyl, Mme Élise Vigneron and the Bibliothèque Municipale at Vichy.

In Ireland I am indebted to: Píaras Beaslai, Dr. Richard Best, Desmond J. Clarke, Dr. W. R. F. Collis, Connie Connolly, the late Reuben J. Dodd, Jr., the Reverend D. F. Duggan (President of St. Colman's College), Professor Felix Hackett, the late Joseph Hone, Dr. Sarsfield Kerrigan, Mrs. Mary S. Kettle, Justice Michael Lennon, A. J. Leventhal, Nancy MacCarthy, Brinsley Macnamara, N. McGuirch, Sean McKernan, Reverend Mother M. Magdalen and the Presentation Convent in Galway, Niall Montgomery, Kathleen Murray, Conor Cruise O'Brien, Ulick O'Connor, Mrs. Julie O'Faolain Martines, Gerard O'Flaherty, Mary O'Holleran, Eoin O'Mahony, K.M., Patrick O'Connor, Arthur Power, the rectors of Clongowes Wood College and Belvedere College, Justice Terry Reddin, Eileen Reidy, Patrick Schaurek, Professor P. Semple, the late Judge Eugene Sheehy, Owen Sheehy-Skeffington, Gerard Slevin, Kees Van Hoek, Professor H. O. White, and Sean Wilmot (Registrar of National University).

In Italy I wish to thank: Dr. Alyse Barison and the United States Information Library in Trieste, Dr. Angelo Bianchi, Rector of the University of Padua, Lojce Berce, Signora Emma Brocchi, Dr. S. Crise (Librarian of the University of Trieste), Paolo Cuzzi, Mrs. Vera Dockrell, Signora Olivia Ferreri, Dr. Aurelia Gruber-Benco, Peggy Guggenheim, Lucy von Hibler, Dr. Sauro Pesante, Luciana Pilleri, Signora Vela Pulitzer, Tullio Silvestri, the late Signora Livia Svevo (Schmitz), Fulvio Suvich, Francesco Toncic, and Dario de Tuoni.

In Switzerland I am indebted to: Frau Felix Beran, Frau Walter Bollman, Dr. Daniel Brody, Evelyn Cotton, Frau F. Fleiner, Professor Sigfried Giedion and Dr. Carola Giedion-Welcker, Frau Hotz, Daniel Hummel, Mme Edmond Jaloux, Dr. C. G. Jung, Siegfried Lang, Jacques Mercanton, Cecil Palmer, Paul Ruggiero, Othmar Schoeck, Dr. S. D. Steinberg, Paul Suter, Frau Louisa Wirth, and Gustav Zumsteg.

In the United States and Canada I am indebted to: Mrs. Janice Biala, Kay Boyle, Mrs. Olga Brauchbar, John Coddington, Dr. Arthur W. Collinson, Mrs. Sue Davies Colombo, Padraic Colum, Mrs. Leonard Crooke, Caresse Crosby, S. Foster Damon, George Dorris, John Edwards, James I. and Jeanette B. Ellmann, Achilles Fang, William Faulkner, Charles N. Feidelson, Jr., Robert Frank, Northrop Frye, Mrs. Adaline Glasheen, Rudolph Goldschmidt, David H. Greene, Jean Hagstrum, Bruce Harkness, Mrs. Eileen Vance Harris, Harrison Hayford, Mrs. Frances Herskovits, Edwin Honig, B. W. Huebsch, Aldous Huxley, Mrs. Charmaine Jeschke, Dr. Hans Kraus, Arthur Laubenstein, James Laughlin, Father J. C. Lehane, Stephen Lendt, Laurence

Lieberfeld, Walton Litz, Harold Loeb, the late Robert McAlmon, Archibald MacLeish and Mrs. Ada MacLeish, John Marshall, Linton Massey, Robert Mayo, Vivian Mercier, Theodore Miller, Ralph J. Mills, Harry T. Moore, Marianne Moore, Robert Murphy, Father William T. Noon, the late Dr. Daniel P. O'Brien, Robert O'Clair, Michael J. O'Neill, Ivan Opffer, Count von Ostheim, Mary Otis, Dr. Felix Pollak, Moody E. Prior, Joseph Prescott, Gordon N. Ray, Horace Reynolds, Walter B. Rideout, Robert W. Rogers, Sean T. Ronan (Irish Foreign Office), Louis Rossi, Victor A. Sax, Robert Scholes, Richard Scowcroft, W. B. Scott, Jr., William Sladen and Rinehart & Co., Inc., Stuart Small, Meno Spann, Norman B. Spector, Heinrich Stammler, Hugh B. Staples, E. R. Steinberg, James Johnson Sweeney, John L. Sweeney, John J. Thirlwall, John Train, Howard Vincent, William Wasserstrom, and Louis Zukofsky.

In Yugoslavia I am indebted to: Dr. Lavo Cermelj, the late Dr. Boris Furlan, A. Globocnik, Professor Mijo Mirnović, and Stanislav Šimić.

In Germany I must thank Mrs. Mabel Elliott, Dr. Georg Goyert, Hans Hennecke, Philipp Jarnach, and Dr. Hans Joachim-Lang. In Austria I am indebted to the late Professor Leo von Hibler. In Tangier I must thank William S. Bird, in India the late Professor James H. Cousins.

INDEX